EGYPTIAN GRAMMAR

PLATE I

ELABORATE PAINTED HIEROGLYPHS FROM A THEBAN TOMB

HIEROGLYPHS INCISED UPON A LIMESTONE STELA

CURSIVE HIEROGLYPHS WRITTEN WITH A REED ON PAPYRUS

DIFFERENT STYLES OF HIEROGLYPHIC WRITING (DYN. XVIII)

EGYPTIAN GRAMMAR

BEING AN INTRODUCTION TO THE STUDY OF HIEROGLYPHS

BY SIR ALAN GARDINER

THIRD EDITION, REVISED

GRIFFITH INSTITUTE
ASHMOLEAN MUSEUM, OXFORD

ISBN 0 900416 35 1

First published 1927
Second edition 1950
Third edition 1957, 1964, 1966, 1969, 1973, 1976, 1978, 1979, 1982, 1988, 1994

Printed in Great Britain
at the University Press, Cambridge

To the memory of

FRANCIS LLEWELLYN GRIFFITH

IN GRATEFUL REMEMBRANCE OF MY EARLIEST LESSONS IN HIEROGLYPHICS

PREFACE
TO THE THIRD EDITION

THE second edition of this work having sold out unexpectedly quickly, it became apparent that there was still a demand which would have to be met. The problem then arose as to how a third edition could be produced without jettisoning what seemed among the main advantages of its predecessor, namely its relative cheapness. In the meantime the cost of printing had gone up by leaps and bounds, and the sole practical course therefore appeared to be to dispense with the setting up of new pages so far as possible, and to leave most of the changes to be recorded in an extended *Additions and Corrections.* Considerable saving has been achieved by abandoning any attempt to bring up to date the bibliographical references in the footnotes to the Introduction, pp. 18–24c. An inevitable defect of the marginal notes which form so large a part of the work has been the impossibility, except at enormous expense, of replacing the original citations by others more correct or more easily accessible; for instance, I should have liked to use Anthes's edition of the Hat-nub texts with greater frequency. More serious has been my inability (in general) to reconsider my opinions in the light of E. Edel's great *Altägyptische Grammatik, I*, 1955; of Lefebvre's second edition, Cairo, 1955; of Sander-Hansen's *Studien zur Grammatik der Pyramidentexte*, Copenhagen, 1956; of Thacker's *Semitic and Egyptian Verbal Systems*, Oxford, 1954; of Vergote's essay on a kindred subject published in *Chronique d'Égypte* for January, 1956; and of Westendorf's *Der Gebrauch des Passivs in der klassichen Literatur der Ägypter*, Berlin, 1952. In fact, I admit having left my critics plenty of scope for their animadversions. In conclusion I must express my great indebtedness to several colleagues; above all, to Dr. T. G. Allen, not only for his able review in *JNES* x. 287–90, but also for a long list of minor corrections. Among others to whom I owe valuable comments are A. de Buck, J. Černý, E. Edel, and H. James. To the Oxford University Press my debt is immense; also to the Griffith Institute, which has again sponsored my task with its usual generosity.

PREFACE
TO THE SECOND EDITION

THE revision that has here been undertaken is more extensive than will appear at first sight. This fact is disguised by the retention of the same pagination as in the first edition throughout the whole of the grammar proper (pp. 25–421). That retention was desirable for many reasons, not the least being the need for economy. It was clear from the start that photographic reproduction would have to be the basis of the new edition, and that the bulk of the alterations must consist of fresh words and sentences pasted in over the original text. This has involved much time-robbing compression and counting of letters, but the plan proved feasible, and it has been necessary to append only six additional pages (pp. 422–7) to contain longer passages and new paragraphs which could not be inserted in the way just mentioned. From p. 428 onwards the pagination of the first edition has had to be altered, and in the Sign-list and the Vocabularies which follow it the lay-out has needed considerable change in order to introduce fresh matter, though photography continued to be used as the technical procedure. Not a few new words have been added to the Egyptian-English Vocabulary in the hope that, in the absence of any trustworthy and at present obtainable hieroglyphic dictionary, that Vocabulary may prove of greater assistance to the beginner. I have, however, disregarded the Book of the Dead, as well as the medical and mathematical texts, partly because these belong to later stages of the student's reading, and partly because here provisionally adequate indexes already exist; also catalogue-like writings such as the Longer List of Offerings and the Ramesseum Onomasticon have been ignored; more names of places and deities have been introduced, I am afraid rather capriciously, but no names of private persons or royalties have been admitted. The expansion of the Egyptian-English Vocabulary has increased the bulk of the book and consequently the cost of production; in order to avoid further extravagance I have regretfully refrained from serious additions to the English-Egyptian Vocabulary, which thus remains what it was intended to be at the outset, a help towards the satisfactory accomplishment of the Exercises. The 'preliminaries' have required to be reprinted almost in their entirety. Having discovered that neither pupils nor teachers make use of my elaborate 'Contents' (pp. xi–xviii of the 1st ed.) I have cut those pages to the bare minimum, substituting detailed subject-indexes at the end of the volume. And, needless to say, the List of Abbreviations has had to be completely reset.

To turn now to the alterations in the grammatical section, it must be admitted that but few newly published texts have been laid under contribution. In this abstention there is, however, the compensating advantage that those new texts will serve as touchstones to test the validity and comprehensiveness of my grammatical rules. A certain number of new examples have been added, but not enough to render seriously incomplete the admirable index of passages utilized, contained in Mme Gauthier-Laurent's *Supplement to Gardiner's Egyptian Grammar*, Neuilly-sur-Seine, 1935; although the grammatical notes there prefixed to the index by myself have now become superfluous through incorporation in the present new edition, the index retains all its utility and will, I trust, continue to be widely used. No small part of the corrections in my text consists of better formulation or necessary qualification of statements there made, and it is here, though by no means solely here, that the acute criticisms of my old friend Battiscombe Gunn have proved specially valuable. There is a certain irony in the fact that a reform for which I am personally responsible has imposed upon me the arduous duty of modifying throughout the book the form in which examples taken from hieratic texts are quoted, see below, p. 422, § 63 A. As regards grammatical doctrine, although I have taken scrupulous pains to read and weigh all dissentient criticisms that have appeared since 1927, I have been unable to persuade myself of the necessity of abandoning any of my main positions, particularly in respect of the theory of the verb; I have replied in a recent review (*JEA*. 33, 95 ff.) to Polotsky's able assault on my account of the nature of the Imperfective *śḏm·f* form. A bone of contention between Gunn and myself has long been the status and the formal aspects of the so-called Prospective Relative Form; an important new discovery by Clère seems to me to have greatly strengthened my own case, so much so that what in the first edition was described in that way now receives the appellation Perfective Relative Form, a name previously accorded to the relative form here given the title 'the *śḏmw·n·f* Relative Form'—a change very satisfactorily marking the relationship of the latter form to the narrative *śḏm·n·f* form; see on this subject below §§ 380. 387. 411 and the addition to p. 303 on p. 426. The only other terminological change in the book has been that from 'the *m* of equivalence' to 'the *m* of predication', an obviously more exact description, which may, moreover, become an absolute necessity if Černý's conjecture recorded in § 38, Obs. proves, on further investigation, to be justified by the evidence. On minor points of detail I owe much, not only to the reviews by Griffith and Allen already utilized by me in Mme Gauthier-Laurent's book, but also to a list of suggestions from Lefebvre, himself the author of an admirable *Grammaire de l'Egyptien classique* (Cairo,

1940), and to further suggestions from Clère, Allen, and several others. In the Sign-list the greatest improvements have been due to that learned and judicious scholar L. Keimer, though in this respect he has been almost rivalled through the acute powers of observation of Nina M. Davies, my close associate in Egyptological enterprise over a long series of years. My cordial thanks are due to all the above-mentioned, but my greatest debt is to Gunn, who, as a teacher, has used my manual ever since its first appearance and without whose invaluable aid this second edition could hardly have been undertaken with success. Gunn has read and discussed every page with me. It would have spoken ill for the independence of mind of each of us if we had always found ourselves in agreement, but I have accepted a high percentage of his criticisms, and for the infinite pains he has taken in seeking to improve my book, no words can express the gratitude that I feel.

I return to my opening statement that this second edition has involved more extensive revision than may appear at first sight. In point of fact there is hardly a page that has not been plastered with pasted-on corrections the safety of which has been the source of constant anxiety alike to the printers and to myself. As the result of this and of the vastly increased cost of production, the expenditure on the book in its republished form will not be far short of that on the original edition. It is with equal relief and gratitude, therefore, that I acknowledge the signal generosity of the Committee of Management of the Griffith Institute in consenting to finance the work as one of the Institute's own publications. It is in my eyes of the highest importance that they have also consented to sell the book at a price which, though necessarily higher than that of the first edition, will not place it beyond the reach of any but the poorest students. The tale of my indebtedness would be incomplete without reference to the enthusiastic and unflagging assistance rendered by my friends at the Oxford University Press, as well as by my personal secretary Miss N. M. Myers, who very rapidly acquired the necessary skill in preparing for the printers the preliminary pasted-up models required by them.

In conclusion, I would beg students and teachers alike to read once again the first page of my Preface to the First Edition. It contains my answer to certain critics who have complained of the formlessness of my work. Since the whole exposition centres round a series of thirty-three progressive Exercises it could hardly have assumed a very different shape, and I reiterate with all possible emphasis my conviction that no student will ever obtain a mastery of Egyptian or of any other foreign language unless he has schooled himself to translate *into* it with a high degree of accuracy.

June, 1949.

PREFACE
TO THE FIRST EDITION

WHEN the plan of the present work was first conceived, little more was intended than to provide English-speaking students with a simple introduction to the Egyptian hieroglyphs, and it was with this object in view that the first few lessons were drafted. It soon became apparent, however, that the book was destined to obtain a wider scope, both as the result of my own predilections and also through the necessities of the case. And so what has remained in form a book for beginners has become in substance an elaborate treatise on Egyptian syntax. I have tried to mitigate this discrepancy by a fullness of statement that would have been unnecessary for advanced scholars, and have not shrunk from repetition whenever repetition appeared to serve a useful purpose. Much thought has been devoted to the order in which the different topics are presented. I had long held that the learner ought to become thoroughly familiar with the forms of the non-verbal sentence, and also with the little words of the language (prepositions, particles, &c.), before tackling the complicated and difficult problems connected with the verb. At the same time I have always believed that reading of actual hieroglyphic texts, as well as translation from English into Egyptian, should begin at the earliest possible moment, and for those purposes some elementary knowledge of the verb is indispensable. It has been attempted to reconcile these conflicting principles by making shift with the *śḏm·f* and *śḏm·n·f* forms throughout the first twenty Exercises. To the Exercises I attach the greatest possible importance. Without them the beginner might well be bewildered by the mass of information imparted. Since, however, the sentences given for translation have been so chosen as to illustrate the more vital syntactic rules, the pupil who will take trouble with this side of his task ought to find himself rewarded by a firm grasp of the most essential facts. Like everything else in the book, the Sign-list at the end has assumed proportions which were not originally intended. The Egyptian-English Vocabulary in no sense constitutes a dictionary of Middle Egyptian, but will, it is hoped, enable students to translate easy pieces like many of those given in Professor Sethe's handy reading-book.

After these preliminary explanations I turn to the real business of this Preface, namely the statement of my manifold obligations to others. Were I to expatiate on my indebtedness to published works I should have a still longer tale to tell. The marginal notes relieve me of this necessity. Nevertheless, special mention must be made of Professor Adolf Erman's

Aegyptische Grammatik, for many years past the indispensable guide of every aspirant to a knowledge of hieroglyphics, as well as of Professor Kurt Sethe's fundamental and epoch-making treatise on the Egyptian verb. Although I have borrowed from these classics as much as seemed relevant to my purpose, their utility is very far from having been exhausted. In particular, Professor Sethe's work should be consulted on all questions connected with phonetic changes and the relation of Old and Late Egyptian to Coptic, aspects of the subject left almost entirely untouched in the present volume. But also on matters where our books overlap, I would earnestly recommend constant reference to these two earlier treatises by scholars whom I am proud to acknowledge as my teachers, and to whose personal influence and friendship my debt is enormous.

To Professor Kurt Sethe I am also directly indebted for many acute suggestions and criticisms on the first half of the book, which I was permitted to read through with him in manuscript during two visits to Göttingen in 1921 and 1922 respectively. At an earlier stage I had ample opportunities of discussing Egyptian syntax in all its aspects with Mr. Battiscombe Gunn, and his contributions to my book are very considerable. Some of Gunn's remarkable discoveries have been published in his *Studies in Egyptian Syntax* (Paris, 1924), but there are other important observations due to him which have not hitherto found their way into print. Points on which I am definitely conscious of having received new ideas from Gunn are as follows: the unequal range of meaning displayed by *iw* when its subject is nominal or pronominal (§§ 29. 117); the signification of *iḫ* (§§ 40, 3; 228); the inversions quoted in § 130; the distinction between *ir m-ḫt* and *ḥr m-ḫt* (p. 133, bottom); the function of *ink pw* to introduce narratives or answer questions (§ 190, 1); the rule as to the position of a nominal subject after the negatival complement (§ 343); lastly, the preference given to *iw sḏm·tw* over *iw·tw sḏm·tw* (§ 463). Some of these points are of great interest, and I can only regret that their discoverer is not the first to announce them. As it is, I am grateful that the privilege has been accorded to me. Furthermore, Gunn read not once only, but many times over, my manuscript of the first six Lessons, and here I often had occasion to avail myself of his advice.

Three visits to Berlin enabled me to supplement my own extensive collections with references from the Berlin dictionary; the Sign-list and the sections on the prepositions and particles are those parts of the book that have derived the most benefit from this source. Latterly, Professor Grapow and Dr. Erichsen have been most kind in answering from the Berlin *Zettelkasten* inquiries put to them by letter. Dr. Blackman has favoured me with notes on the expression *prt-ḫrw* (p. 172). Professor Griffith has provided the hieroglyphic transcript of the sample of demotic in Plate II.

Mr. P. W. Pycraft of the Natural History Museum has given valuable help as regards the signs representing birds, beasts, and fishes. Professor Breasted has permitted me to quote from the still unpublished Edwin Smith papyrus. My assistant, Mr. R. O. Faulkner, has been of much service in connection with the Sign-list, Vocabularies, and preliminary matter. I also owe a few valuable hints to Dr. A. de Buck.

The printing of the Grammar has brought in its train a whole host of further obligations, particularly in connection with the new hieroglyphic fount here employed for the first time. I should be the last to minimize the magnificent services rendered to Egyptology for more than fifty years by the Theinhardt fount. Nevertheless that fount, for which Richard Lepsius was mainly responsible, labours under two serious disadvantages. In the first place, the three-line nonpareil size is too large for convenient combination with ordinary romans, and in the second place, many of the forms, being derived from originals of the Saite period, are not palaeographically suitable for the printing of Middle Egyptian. These two considerations prompted me to undertake the production of a new fount based on Eighteenth Dynasty forms. After much unsuccessful experimenting, I was fortunate enough to obtain the co-operation of Mr. and Mrs. de Garis Davies, whose many years of work in the Theban necropolis have given them an unequalled familiarity with the Tuthmoside hieroglyphs. The admirable drawings which they provided would, however, have availed me little but for the skill of the technical craftsmen into whose hands they fell. The firm of Messrs. R. P. Bannerman and Son, Ltd., to whom the making of the matrices was entrusted on the advice of the late Mr. Frederick Hall, Controller of the Oxford University Press, has executed them in a manner for which I can barely find adequate words of praise. The unflagging enthusiasm and exceptional ability of the actual cutter of the matrices, Mr. W. J. Bilton, ensured the success of an enterprise which in less capable hands might easily have proved a failure.

The printed book itself is the best testimony to the extraordinary care that has been devoted to it at the Oxford University Press. No trouble could be too great for the late Mr. Frederick Hall, whose personal interest in the book I shall always remember with gratitude. It was thanks to the present Printer, whose connection with Egypt is of long standing, that I entrusted the work to Mr. Hall in the first instance; he too has shown an untiring interest in the task from start to finish, and has met my exacting demands in every conceivable way. I regret that I am unable to name personally all those members of the Oxford staff whose admirable efforts have contributed to the final result. The author's proof-reading has been an arduous affair, but I have been admirably seconded in it by Mr. G. E. Hay.

His vigilance has eliminated many an error, just as his experience of hieroglyphic printing proved an invaluable help at the time when the new fount was being designed. Professor Peet has likewise read a proof and furnished me with many useful comments.

In conclusion, I cannot leave unacknowledged a debt of a less direct kind, but one which is surely the greatest. It is to my Father that I owe all my leisure and opportunities for research. It was he who encouraged me and made my way easy, when as a boy I first began to take an interest in Egyptology. And it is he who now, more than thirty years later, has defrayed the cost of my new hieroglyphic fount. To him, therefore, as to all those who have aided me in a long and exacting piece of work, I tender my heartfelt thanks.

November, 1926.

CONTENTS

CONTENTS

LIST OF ABBREVIATIONS

abbrev. abbreviation.

ABUBAKR A. J. ABUBAKR, *Untersuchungen über die ägyptischen Kronen.* Glückstadt, 1937.

Ächt. K. SETHE, *Die Ächtung feindlicher Fürsten, Völker und Dinge auf altägyptischen Tongefässscherben des Mittleren Reiches.* Extracted from *Abhandlungen der Preuss. Akademie der Wissenschaften.* Berlin, 1926.

Add. the new Paragraphs and other Additions inserted below, pp. 422 foll.

adj. adjective.

Adm. A. H. GARDINER, *The Admonitions of an Egyptian Sage*, Leipzig, 1909. *Adm.* 5, 1 means page 5, line 1 of *Papyrus Leiden* 344, *recto.* The writing-board, British Museum 5645, occupies pp. 95–108, and is quoted as (*e.g.*) *Adm.* p. 105.

adv. adverb, adverbial.

AEO. A. H. GARDINER, *Ancient Egyptian Onomastica*, 3 vols. Oxford University Press, 1947.

AJSL. *American Journal of Semitic Languages*, 58 vols. Chicago, 1884–1941.

Amada The stela of Amenophis II at Amada, published by CH. KUENTZ, *Deux stèles d'Aménophis II*, in *Bibliothèque d'étude de l'Institut Français d'Archéologie Orientale.* Cairo, 1925.

Amarn. N. DE G. DAVIES, *The Rock Tombs of El Amarna*, in *Archaeological Survey of Egypt*, 6 vols. London (Egypt Exploration Fund), 1903–8.

Amrah D. RANDALL-MACIVER and A. C. MACE, *El Amrah and Abydos.* London (Egypt Exploration Fund), 1902.

Ann. *Annales du Service des Antiquités de l'Égypte*, 48 vols. Cairo, 1900–48.

ANTHES R. ANTHES, *Die Felseninschriften von Hatnub*, in K. SETHE, *Untersuchungen zur Geschichte und Altertumskunde Ägyptens*, vol. ix. Leipzig, 1928. See too under *Hat-Nub.*

Arch. äg. Arch. *Archiv für Ägypt. Archäologie*, 1 vol. Vienna, [1937–8].

Arch. Or. *Archiv Orientální*, Journal of the Oriental Institute, Prague, 11 vols. Prague, 1929–39.

Arm. SIR ROBERT MOND and O. H. MYERS, *Temples of Armant*, 2 vols. London (Egypt Exploration Society), 1940.

aux. vb. auxiliary verb.

ÄZ. *Zeitschrift für ägyptische Sprache und Altertumskunde*, 78 vols. Leipzig, 1863–1943.

B. of D. Book of the Dead.

BH. P. E. NEWBERRY [and F. Ll. GRIFFITH], *Beni Hasan*, in *Archaeological Survey of Egypt*, 4 vols. London (Egypt Exploration Fund), 1893–1900.

Berl. *ÄI.* *Ägyptische Inschriften aus den königlichen Museen zu Berlin*, 2 vols. Leipzig, 1913–24.

Berl. *Hi. Pap.* *Hieratische Papyrus aus den königlichen Museen zu Berlin*, 5 vols. Berlin, 1901–11.

Berl. leather A. DE BUCK, *The Building Inscription of the Berlin Leather Roll*, in *Studia Aegyptiaca I*, 48. Rome (Pontificium Institutum Biblicum), 1938.

Bersh. P. E. NEWBERRY, *El Bersheh*, in *Archaeological Survey of Egypt*, 2 vols. London (Egypt Exploration Fund), [1893–4].

Bibl. Or. *Bibliotheca Orientalis*, 6 vols. Leyden (Nederlandsch Instituut voor het nabije Oosten), 1944–9.

Brit. Mus. Stelae, statues, &c., quoted by their old registration nos., not by the new exhibition nos. Mostly published in *Hieroglyphic Texts from Egyptian Stelae, &c., in the British Museum*, 8 parts. London, 1911–39. A good photograph of the often quoted Brit. Mus. 614 in A. M. BLACKMAN, *The Stele of Thethi*, in *Journal of Egyptian Archaeology*, 17, 55.

BR. *Thes.* H. BRUGSCH, *Thesaurus Inscriptionum Aegyptiacarum*, 6 vols. Leipzig, 1883–91.

DE BUCK A. DE BUCK, *The Egyptian Coffin Texts*, 3 vols. Chicago (Oriental Institute Publications), 1935–47.

BUDGE E. A. WALLIS BUDGE, *The Book of the Dead: the chapters of coming forth by day*, 3 vols. London, 1898. The black-bound edition, quoted by author's name only with number of page and line in page.

BURCHARDT M. BURCHARDT, *Die altkanaanäischen Fremdworte und Eigennamen im Ägyptischen*. Leipzig, 1909–10.

Buhen D. RANDALL-MACIVER and C. LEONARD WOOLLEY, *Buhen*, 2 vols., in *University of Pennsylvania, Eckley B. Coxe Junior Expedition to Nubia*. Philadelphia, 1911.

Bull. *Bulletin de l'Institut Français d'Archéologie Orientale*, 47 vols. Cairo, 1901–48.

c. common gender.

Cairo Inscriptions in the Cairo Museum published in the *Catalogue général des antiquités égyptiennes du musée du Caire*. Numbers between 1 and 653 are to be sought in L. BORCHARDT, *Statuen und Statuetten von Königen und Privatleuten*, 2 vols., Berlin, 1911–25; between 20001 and 20780 in H. O. LANGE and H. SCHÄFER, *Grab- und Denksteine des Mittleren Reichs*, 4 vols., Cairo, 1902–25; between 28001 and 28086 in P. LACAU, *Sarcophages antérieurs au nouvel empire*, 2 vols., Cairo, 1904–6; between 34001 and 34186 in P. LACAU, *Stèles du nouvel empire*, 2 parts, Cairo, 1909–26.

CAPART, *Rue* J. CAPART, *Une rue de tombeaux à Saqqarah*. Brussels, 1907.

CART.–NEWB. *Th. IV.* HOWARD CARTER and P. E. NEWBERRY, *The Tomb of Thoutmôsis IV* (*Mr. Theodore M. Davis' Excavations*). London, 1904.

Cat. d. Mon. I. J. DE MORGAN, U. BOURIANT, and others, *Catalogue des Monuments et Inscriptions de l'Égypte Antique. Tome Premier, De la Frontière de Nubie à Kom Ombos*. Vienna, 1894.

CAULFEILD A. ST. G. CAULFEILD, *The Temple of the Kings at Abydos*. London, 1902.

caus. causative.

Cem. of Abyd. *Cemeteries of Abydos*, vol. i by É. NAVILLE, vols. ii, iii by T. E. PEET. London (Egypt Exploration Fund), 1913–14.

Cen. H. FRANKFORT, *The Cenotaph of Seti I at Abydos*, 2 vols. London (Egypt Exploration Society), 1933.

cf. *confer* = compare.

CHAMP. *ND.* CHAMPOLLION LE JEUNE, *Monuments de l'Égypte et de la Nubie. Notices Descriptives*, 2 vols. Paris, 1844–79.

CHASS. *Ass.* E. CHASSINAT and CH. PALANQUE, *Une Campagne de Fouilles dans la Nécropole d'Assiout*, in *Mémoires . . . de l'Institut Français d'Archéologie Orientale du Caire*. Cairo, 1911.

cl., cls. clause, clauses.

CL-VAND. J. J. CLÈRE and J. VANDIER, *Textes de la première période intermédiaire et de la XIème Dynastie*, 1st fascicle. Brussels, 1948.

Coffins Middle Kingdom coffins, quoted from unpublished copies. See too below under DE BUCK.

conj. conjunction.

D. el B. E. NAVILLE, *The Temple of Deir el Bahari*, 6 vols. London (Egypt Exploration Fund), [1895]–1908. Quoted by plate-numbers only, these running consecutively through the volumes.

D. el B. (*XI*). E. NAVILLE, *The XIth Dynasty Temple at Deir el-Bahari*, 3 vols. London (Egypt Exploration Fund), 1907–13.

DAR. *Ostr.* G. DARESSY, *Ostraca*, 2 vols., in *Catalogue Général des Antiquités Égyptiennes du Musée du Caire*. Cairo, 1901.

DAV. *Ḳen.* N. DE G. DAVIES, *The Tomb of Ḳen-Amūn at Thebes*, 2 vols. New York (Metropolitan Museum of Art), 1930.

DAV. *Ptah.* N. DE G. DAVIES, *The Mastaba of Ptahhetep and Akhethetep at Saqqareh*, Parts i, ii, in *Archaeological Survey of Egypt*. London (Egypt Exploration Fund), 1900–1.

DAV. *Rekh.* N. DE G. DAVIES, *The Tomb of Rekh-mi-rēʿ at Thebes*, 2 vols. New York (Metropolitan Museum of Art), 1943.

Dend. W. M. F. PETRIE, *Dendereh*. London (Egypt Exploration Fund), 1900.

Denkm. See under Leyd.

dep. pron. dependent pronoun.

LIST OF ABBREVIATIONS

Destr. — É. NAVILLE, *La Destruction des Hommes par les Dieux*, in *Transactions of the Society of Biblical Archaeology*, iv. (1876), 1–19; viii. (1885), 412–20. New edition by CH. MAYSTRE, *Bull.* 40, 53–115.

det. — determinative(s).

DÉV. *Graph.* — E. DÉVAUD, *L'Âge des Papyrus Égyptiens Hiératiques d'après les Graphies de Certains Mots.* Paris, 1924.

do. — ditto.

DÜM. *H.I.* — J. DÜMICHEN, *Historische Inschriften altägyptischer Denkmäler*, 2 vols. Leipzig, 1867–9.

DUNH. — Dows DUNHAM, *Naga-ed-Dêr Stelae of the First Intermediate Period.* Published for the Museum of Fine Arts, Boston, U.S.A. London, 1937.

Eb. — G. EBERS, *Papyros Ebers, das hermetische Buch über die Arzeneimittel der alten Ägypter*, 2 vols. Leipzig, 1875. Conveniently transcribed in W. WRESZINSKI, *Der Papyrus Ebers.* Leipzig, 1913.

Eleph. — Stela of Amenophis II from Elephantine, published by CH. KUENTZ, *Deux stèles d'Aménophis II*, in *Bibliothèque d'étude de l'Institut Français d'Archéologie Orientale.* Cairo, 1925.

encl. part. — enclitic particle.

ERM. *Gramm.*[4] — A. ERMAN, *Ägyptische Grammatik*, 4th edition, in the series *Porta linguarum orientalium.* Berlin, 1928.

ERM. *Hymn.* — A. ERMAN, *Hymnen an das Diadem der Pharaonen.* Extracted from *Abhandlungen der königl. Preuss. Akademie der Wissenschaften.* Berlin, 1911.

ERM. *Neuäg. Gramm.*[2] — A. ERMAN, *Neuägyptische Grammatik*, 2nd edition. Leipzig, 1933.

ERM. *Spr. d. Westc.* — A. ERMAN, *Die Sprache des Papyrus Westcar.* Göttingen, 1889.

ex., exx. — example, examples.

Exerc. — Exercise.

f. — feminine.

Five Th. T. — N. DE G. DAVIES, *Five Theban Tombs*, in *Archaeological Survey of Egypt.* London (Egypt Exploration Fund), 1913.

Florence — The numbers are those given in E. SCHIAPARELLI, *Museo Archeologico di Firenze. Antichità Egizie.* Rome, 1887.

foll. by — followed by.

FRASER, *Scar.* — G. FRASER, *A Catalogue of the Scarabs belonging to G. Fraser.* London, 1900.

GAILLARD — C. GAILLARD, *Les Poissons Représentés dans Quelques Tombeaux Égyptiens de l'Ancien Empire*, in *Mémoires . . . de l'Institut Français d'Archéologie Orientale du Caire.* Cairo, 1923.

GARD. *Sin.* — A. H. GARDINER, *Notes on the Story of Sinuhe.* Paris, 1916.

Gebr. — N. DE G. DAVIES, *The Rock Tombs of Deir el Gebrâwi*, Parts i, ii, in *Archaeological Survey of Egypt.* London (Egypt Exploration Fund), 1902.

Gemn. — F. W. VON BISSING, *Die Mastaba des Gem-ni-kai*, 2 vols. Leipzig, 1905, 1911.

Gîza — H. JUNKER, *Gîza I*, &c., 8 vols. Vienna (Akademie der Wissenschaften), 1929–47.

GOL. *Naufragé* — W. GOLÉNISCHEFF, *Le Conte du Naufragé*, in *Bibliothèque d'Étude de l'Institut Français d'Archéologie Orientale.* Cairo, 1912. See too under *Sh. S.*

Griff. Stud. — *Studies presented to F. Ll. Griffith.* London (Egypt Exploration Society), 1932.

GUNN, *Stud.* — B. GUNN, *Studies in Egyptian Syntax.* Paris, 1924.

GUNN, *Teti* — C. M. FIRTH and B. GUNN, *Teti Pyramid Cemeteries*, 2 vols.; vol. i, Text. Cairo, 1926.

Hamm. — J. COUYAT and P. MONTET, *Les Inscriptions Hiéroglyphiques et Hiératiques du Ouâdi Hammâmât*, in *Mémoires . . . de l'Institut Français d'Archéologie Orientale du Caire*, 2 vols. Cairo, 1912–13

Ḥaremḥab — Stela published in W. MAX MÜLLER, *Egyptological Researches*, i. 90–104, in *Publications of the Carnegie Institution.* Washington, 1906.

Ḥarḥ. — Tomb and sarcophagus of Ḥarḥotpe published in G. MASPERO, *Trois Années de Fouilles*, pp. 133–80, in *Mémoires . . . de la Mission Archéologique Française au Caire.* Paris, 1885.

Harris — *Facsimile of an Egyptian hieratic Papyrus of the Reign of Rameses III, now in the British Museum.* London, 1876.

Hat-Nub Hieratic inscriptions from the quarry of Hat-Nub, transcribed in *El Bersheh* (see above, *Bersh.*), ii. pls. 22–3. Quoted mainly from here, but for improved editions see above under ANTHES.

HAYES W. C. HAYES, *Ostraka and Name Stones from the Tomb of Sen-Mūt (No. 71) at Thebes.* New York (Metropolitan Museum of Art), 1942.

Hearst G. A. REISNER, *The Hearst medical Papyrus*, in *University of California publications, Egyptian Archaeology*, vol. i. Leipzig, 1905. Conveniently transcribed in W. WRESZINSKI, *Der Londoner medizinische Papyrus und der Papyrus Hearst.* Leipzig, 1912.

Herdsm. The fragmentary story of the Herdsman, published in A. H. GARDINER, *Die Erzählung des Sinuhe und die Hirtengeschichte*, in A. ERMAN, *Literarische Texte des mittleren Reiches* (*Hieratische Papyrus aus den königlichen Museen zu Berlin*, Bd. v.). Leipzig, 1909.

Hier. F. LL. GRIFFITH, *A Collection of Hieroglyphs*, in *Archaeological Survey of Egypt.* London (Egypt Exploration Fund), 1898.

ib., *ibidem* = in the same place or in the same book.

ideo. ideogram.

Ikhern. Stela of Ikhernofret, published by H. SCHÄFER, *Die Mysterien des Osiris in Abydos*, in K. SETHE, *Untersuchungen zur Geschichte und Altertumskunde Äegyptens*, vol. iv, part 2. Leipzig, 1904.

imper. imperative.

imperf. imperfective.

indep. pron. independent pronoun.

infin. infinitive.

Inscr. dédic. H. GAUTHIER, *La Grande Inscription Dédicatoire d'Abydos*, in *Bibliothèque d'Étude de l'Institut Français d'Archéologie Orientale.* Cairo, 1912.

interrog. interrogative

Iouiya É. NAVILLE, *The Funeral Papyrus of Iouiya*, in *Theodore M. Davis' Excavations.* London, 1908.

JAOS *Journal of the American Oriental Society*, 68 vols., Boston, &c., 1849–1948.

JEA *Journal of Egyptian Archaeology*, 12 vols. London (Egypt Exploration Society), 1914–26.

JÉQ. G. JÉQUIER *Les Frises d'Objets des Sarcophages du Moyen Empire*, in *Mémoires . . . de l'Institut Français d'Archéologie Orientale du Caire.* Cairo, 1921.

JNES *Journal of Near Eastern Studies*, 7 vols., Chicago, 1942–8.

JUNKER, *P.L.* H. JUNKER, *Die Politische Lehre von Memphis*, in *Abhandlungen der Preussischen Akademie der Wissenschaften*, Berlin, 1941.

Kopt. W. M. F. PETRIE, *Koptos.* London (Egyptian Research Account), 1896.

Kuban P. TRESSON, *La Stèle de Koubân*, in *Bibliothèque d'étude de l'Institut Français d'Archéologie Orientale.* Cairo, 1922.

L. *D.* R. LEPSIUS, *Denkmäler aus Ägypten und Äthiopien*, 6 vols. Berlin, 1849–58.

L.E. Late Egyptian.

L. to D. A. H. GARDINER and K. SETHE, *Egyptian Letters to the Dead.* London (Egypt Exploration Society), 1928.

LAC. *Sarc.* P. LACAU, *Sarcophages Antérieurs au Nouvel Empire*, 2 vols. in *Catalogue Général des Antiquités Égyptiennes du Musée du Caire.* Cairo, 1904–6.

LAC. *TR.* P. LACAU, *Textes Religieux Égyptiens*, Première Partie. Paris, 1910. Quoted by chapter and line. Chs. 85–7 will be found in *Recueil de Travaux* (see below, *Rec.*), vols. 32–4.

Leb. A. ERMAN, *Gespräch eines Lebensmüden mit seiner Seele*, extracted from *Abhandlungen der königl. Preuss. Akademie der Wissenschaften.* Berlin, 1896.

LEDR. E. LEDRAIN, *Les Monuments Égyptiens de la Bibliothèque Nationale.* Paris, 1879–81.

LEF. *Gr.* G. LEFEBVRE, *Grammaire de l'Égyptien Classique.* Cairo, 1940.

LEF. *Sethos.* E. LEFÉBURE, *Les Hypogées Royaux de Thèbes*, in *Annales du Musée Guimet.* Première division, *Le Tombeau de Séti I*er. Paris, 1886.

Leyd. Objects in Leyden, published in P. A. BOESER, *Beschreibung der ägyptischen Sammlung . . . in Leiden*, 12 vols., The Hague, 1908–25. The vols. here used (qu. as *Denkm.* i. ii. iv) are: vol. i, *Die Denkmäler des alten Reiches*; vol. ii, *Die Denkmäler der Zeit zwischen dem alten und mittleren Reich und des mittleren Reiches: erste Abteilung, Stelen* [the stelae are here, however, mostly quoted as Leyd. V 3, &c., the old museum designations]; vol. iv, *Die Denkmäler des neuen Reiches: erste Abteilung, Gräber.*

Lisht J.-E. GAUTIER and G. JÉQUIER, *Mémoire sur les Fouilles de Licht*, in *Mémoires . . . de l'Institut Français d'Archéologie Orientale.* Cairo, 1902.

lit. literally.

Louvre Stelae quoted by registration nos., *e.g.* Louvre C 11. Chief publications: P. PIERRET, *Recueil d'Inscriptions Inédites du Musée Égyptien du Louvre*, 2 parts. Paris, 1874–8; A. GAYET, *Musée du Louvre: Stèles de la XIIe dynastie*, Paris, 1889, in *Bibliothèque de l'École des Hautes Études.*

LUTZ H. F. LUTZ, *Egyptian Tomb Steles and Offering Stones of the Museum of Anthropology and Ethnology of the University of California.* Leipzig, 1927.

Lyons Stelae quoted from *Notice sur les Antiquités Égyptiennes du Musée de Lyon*, in TH. DÉVÉRIA, *Mémoires et Fragments* (*Bibliothèque Égyptologique*), i. 55–112. Paris, 1896.

m. masculine.

M.E. Middle Egyptian.

M.K. Middle Kingdom.

M.u.K. A. ERMAN, *Zaubersprüche für Mutter und Kind*, extracted from *Abhandlungen der königl. Preuss. Akademie der Wissenschaften.* Berlin, 1901.

MAR. *Abyd.* A. MARIETTE, *Abydos*, 2 vols. Paris, 1869–80.

MAR. *Karn.* A. MARIETTE, *Karnak.* Leipzig, 1875.

MAR. *Mast.* A. MARIETTE, *Les Mastabas de l'Ancien Empire.* Paris, 1889.

Medum W. M. FLINDERS PETRIE, *Medum.* London, 1892.

Meir A. M. BLACKMAN, *The Rock Tombs of Meir*, 4 vols., in *Archaeological Survey of Egypt*: London (Egypt Exploration Fund), 1914–24.

Mél. Masp. *Mélanges Maspero*, I. *Orient Ancien.* Cairo, 1935–8.

Menthuw. C. L. RANSOM, *The Stela of Menthu-weser*, publication of the Metropolitan Museum of Art. New York, 1913.

Mett. W. GOLÉNISCHEFF, *Die Metternichstele.* Leipzig, 1877.

Mill. A convenient transcription of the Millingen papyrus in *ÄZ.* 34, 38–49. See also G. MASPERO, *Les Enseignements d'Amenemhâit Ier à son Fils Sanouasrît Ier*, in *Bibliothèque d'Étude de l'Institut Français d'Archéologie Orientale.* Cairo, 1914.

Misc. Greg. *Miscellanea Gregoriana: Raccolta di scritti pubblicati nel I centenario della fondazione del Museo Egizio.* Rome, Vatican, 1941.

Mitt. viii. ix. *Mittheilungen aus den orientalischen Sammlungen.* G. STEINDORFF, *Grabfunde des mittleren Reiches in den königlichen Museen zu Berlin.* Heft VIII, *Das Grab des Mentuhotep.* Heft IX, *Der Sarg des Sebk-o — Ein Grabfund aus Gebelên.* Berlin, 1896, 1901.

Mitt. Kairo *Mitteilungen des deutschen Instituts für ägyptische Altertumskunde in Kairo*, 13 vols. Cairo, 1930–44.

MÖLL. *HL.* G. MÖLLER, *Hieratische Lesestücke*, 3 vols. Leipzig, 1909–10.

MÖLL. *Pal.* G. MÖLLER, *Hieratische Paläographie*, 3 vols. Leipzig, 1909–12.

MÖLL. *Rhind* G. MÖLLER, *Die beiden Totenpapyrus Rhind des Museums zu Edinburg*, 2 vols. Leipzig, 1913.

MONTET P. MONTET, *Les Scènes de la Vie Privée dans les Tombeaux Égyptiens de l'Ancien Empire*, in *Publications de la Faculté des Lettres de l'Université de Strasbourg.* Strassburg, 1925.

Munich Stelae published in W. SPIEGELBERG, *Ägyptische Grabsteine und Denksteine aus süd-deutschen Sammlungen*: II, *München*, von K. DYROFF and B. PÖRTNER. Strassburg, 1904. Quoted by the numbers of the stelae indicated in the plates.

Mus. ég. E. GRÉBAUT (later G. MASPERO and P. LACAU), *Le Musée Égyptien*, 3 vols. Cairo, 1890–1924.

n. noun.

n., nn. note, notes.

Nauri F. LL. GRIFFITH, *The Abydos Decree of Seti I*, in *Journal of Egyptian Archaeology*, 13, 193–208.

NAV. É. NAVILLE, *Das ägyptische Todtenbuch der XVIII. bis XX. Dynastie*, 3 vols. Berlin, 1886. Quoted by chapter and line.

Nebesh. W. M. F. PETRIE, *Nebesheh* (*Am*) *and Defenneh* (*Tahpanhes*). Bound up with W. M. F. PETRIE, *Tanis II.* London (Egypt Exploration Fund), 1888.

Nominals. K. SETHE, *Der Nominalsatz im Ägyptischen und Koptischen*, extracted from *Abhandlungen der philologisch-historischen Klasse der königl. Sächsischen Gesellschaft der Wissenschaften*, xxxiii. 3. Leipzig, 1916.

non-encl. part. non-enclitic particle.

NORTHAMPT. MARQUIS OF NORTHAMPTON, W. SPIEGELBERG, and P. E. NEWBERRY, *Report on some Excavations in the Theban Necropolis.* London, 1908.

Nu The papyrus of *Nu*, containing an XVIIIth Dyn. version of the Book of the Dead. Published in E. A. W. BUDGE, *The Book of the Dead. Facsimiles of the Papyri of Hunefer, Ānhai, Kerāsher and Netchemet, with supplementary text from the papyrus of Nu.* London, 1899.

obj. Object.

Obs. Observation.

O.E. Old Egyptian.

O.K. Old Kingdom.

OLZ. *Orientalistische Litteratur-Zeitung*, 29 vols. Berlin, then Leipzig, 1898–1926.

p., pp. page, pages.

P. papyrus, papyri.

P. Boul. xviii. *Papyrus de Boulaq*, xviii, published in facsimile by A. MARIETTE, *Les Papyrus Égyptiens du Musée de Boulaq*, Cairo, 1871–2, vol. ii, Pls. 14–55. Quoted by the section numbers given in the transcription by A. SCHARFF published in *Zeitschrift für ägyptische Sprache und Altertumskunde*, vol. 57, 1**–24**.

P. Kah. F. LL. GRIFFITH, *Hieratic Papyri from Kahun and Gurob*, 2 vols. London, 1898.

P. Leyd. F. CHABAS (C. LEEMANS), *Aegyptische Hiëratische Papyrussen I 343–71 van het Nederlandsche Museum van Oudheden te Leiden.* Leyden, 1853–62.

P. Louvre 3226. Papyrus of accounts published by H. BRUGSCH, *Thesaurus Inscriptionum Aegyptiacarum*, Part 5 (Leipzig, 1891), 1079–1106.

P. math. Mosc. W. W. STRUVE, *Mathematischer Papyrus des Staatlichen Museums der schönen Künste in Moskau.* Berlin, 1930.

P. med. Berl. W. WRESZINSKI, *Der grosse medizinische Papyrus des Berliner Museums.* Leipzig, 1909.

P. med. Lond. W. WRESZINSKI, *Der Londoner medizinische Papyrus und der Papyrus Hearst.* Leipzig, 1912.

P. Mook W. SPIEGELBERG, *Ein Gerichtsprotokoll aus der Zeit Thutmosis IV*, in *Zeitschrift für ägyptische Sprache*, 63, 105–15.

P. Pet. [W. GOLÉNISCHEFF], *Les Papyrus Hiératiques Nos. 1115, 1116 A et 1116 B de l'Ermitage Impérial à St.-Pétersbourg.* [St. Petersburg], 1913.

P. Ram. Papyri from a tomb below the Ramesseum, mostly unpublished. See, however, under *Semnah Disp.*

P. Turin F. ROSSI and W. PLEYTE, *Papyrus de Turin*, 2 vols. Leyden, 1869–76.

Paheri J. J. TYLOR and F. LL. GRIFFITH, *The Tomb of Paheri at El Kab*, bound up with E. NAVILLE, *Ahnas el Medineh.* London (Egypt Exploration Fund), 1894.

part. participle. Or sometimes particle, especially in encl. part., non-encl. part.

Peas. The story of the Eloquent Peasant, published by F. VOGELSANG and A. H. GARDINER, *Die Klagen des Bauern*, in A. ERMAN, *Literarische Texte des mittleren Reiches* (*Hieratische Papyrus aus den königlichen Museen zu Berlin*, Bd. iv). Berlin, 1908. The individual papyri are quoted as R (Ramesseum), Bt (Butler), B 1 (Berlin 3023), and B 2 (Berlin 3025). See too below, VOG. *Bauer.*

perf. perfect *or* perfective.

pers. person.

PETR. *Abyd.* W. M. F. PETRIE, *Abydos*, 3 vols. London (Egypt Exploration Fund), 1902–4.

LIST OF ABBREVIATIONS

PETR. *Court.* W. M. F. PETRIE, *Tombs of the Courtiers and Oxyrhynkhos.* London, 1925.

PETR. *Eg. Hier.* H. PETRIE, *Egyptian Hieroglyphs of the First and Second Dynasties.* London, 1927.

PETR. *Qurn.* W. M. F. PETRIE, *Qurneh.* London (School of Archaeology in Egypt), 1909.

PETR. *RT.* W. M. F. PETRIE, *The Royal Tombs of the Earliest Dynasties*, 2 vols. London (Egypt Exploration Fund) 1900–1.

phon. phonetic.

phon. det. phonetic determinative.

PIEHL, *IH.* K. PIEHL, *Inscriptions Hiéroglyphiques Recueillies en Europe et en Égypte*, 3 vols. Stockholm–Leipzig, 1886–95.

PIERRET P. PIERRET, *Recueil d'Inscriptions Inédites du Musée Égyptien du Louvre*, 2 vols., in *Études Égyptologiques*, livraisons 2 and 8. Paris, 1874–8.

pl., plur. plural.

POL. J. POLOTSKY, *Zu den Inschriften der 11. Dynastie*, in K. SETHE, *Untersuchungen zur Geschichte und Altertumskunde Ägyptens*, vol. xi. Leipzig, 1929.

POL. *Ét.* H. J. POLOTSKY, *Études de syntaxe Copte.* Cairo (Société d'archéologie Copte), 1944.

Pr. G. JÉQUIER, *Le Papyrus Prisse et ses variantes.* Paris, 1911. This abbreviation is used almost only for the maxims addressed to Kagemni, *Pap. Prisse*, pp. 1–2, see too *Journal of Egyptian Archaeology*, 32, 71–4. For the maxims of Ptaḥḥotpe, see below, *Pt.*

pred. predicate, predicatival.

prep. preposition.

pron. pronoun.

PSBA. *Proceedings of the Society of Biblical Archaeology*, 40 vols. London, 1879–1918.

Pt. E. DÉVAUD, *Les Maximes de Ptahhotep, texte.* Fribourg (Suisse), 1916. Quoted by the numbers in the right-hand margin of Dévaud's transcription.

Ptah. (*E.R.A.*) R. F. E. PAGET and A. A. PIRIE, *The Tomb of Ptah-hetep*, second part of the volume entitled J. E. QUIBELL, *The Ramesseum.* London (Egyptian Research Account), 1898.

Puy. N. DE G. DAVIES, *The Tomb of Puyemrê at Thebes*, in *Publications of the Metropolitan Museum of Art, Egyptian Expedition: Robb de Peyster Tytus Memorial Series*, 2 vols. New York, 1922–3.

Pyr. The religious texts found in the tombs of five kings of Dyn. V–VI at Saḳḳârah. See below, p. 18.

Pyr. K. SETHE, *Die altägyptischen Pyramidentexte*, 4 vols. Leipzig, 1908–22. Also posthumously, *Übersetzung und Kommentar zu den altägyptischen Pyramidentexten.* Glückstadt–Hamburg, no date.

qu. quoted (in full).

QUIB. *Saqq.* J. E. QUIBELL, *Excavations at Saqqara*, 6 vols. Cairo, 1907–23.

R. *IH.* E. DE ROUGÉ, *Inscriptions Hiéroglyphiques Copiées en Égypte*, 3 vols., in *Études Égyptologiques*, livraisons 9–11. Paris, 1877–8. The plates run consecutively, so that no volume number is quoted.

Rec. *Recueil de Travaux Relatifs à la Philologie et à l'Archéologie Égyptiennes et Assyriennes*, 40 vols. Paris, 1870–1923.

Rekh. P. E. NEWBERRY, *The Life of Rekhmara.* London, 1900. See too DAV. *Rekh.* above.

rel. relative.

Renni J. J. TYLOR, *The Tomb of Renni*, in *Wall Drawings and Monuments of El Kab.* London, 1900.

Rev. d'Ég. *Revue d'Égyptologie*, 5 vols. Paris (Société française d'Égyptologie), 1933–46.

Rev. ég. *Revue égyptologique*, 1st series, 14 vols., 2nd series, 3 vols. Paris, 1880–1924.

Rhind T. E. PEET, *The Rhind Mathematical Papyrus.* London, 1923.

Rifeh Tombs of Rîfah, quoted by tomb-number and line, as published in F. LL. GRIFFITH, *The Inscriptions of Siût and Dêr Rîfeh.* London, 1889.

Sah. L. BORCHARDT, *Das Grabdenkmal des Königs Śaȝḥu-reʿ* (in *Ausgrabungen der deutschen Orient-gesellschaft*), vol. 2 (in two parts, text and plates). Leipzig, 1913.

Saqq. Mast. i. M. A. MURRAY, *Saqqara Mastabas*, Part I. London (Egyptian Research Account), 1905.

SÄVE-SÖDERBERGH, *Äg. Denkm.* T. SÄVE-SÖDERBERGH, *Einige ägyptische Denkmäler in Schweden*. Uppsala, 1945.

SCHARFF A. SCHARFF, *Archäologische Beiträge zur Frage der Entstehung der Hieroglyphenschrift*, in *Sitzungsberichte der Bayerischen Akademie der Wissenschaften*, Munich, 1942.

Seas. W. M. F. PETRIE, *A Season in Egypt, 1887*. London, 1888.

Sebekkhu T. E. PEET, *The Stela of Sebek-khu*, in *The Manchester Museum Handbooks*. Manchester, 1914.

Sebekn. J. J. TYLOR, *The Tomb of Sebeknekht*, in *Wall Drawings and Monuments of El Kab*. London, 1896.

Semnah Disp. P. C. SMITHER, *The Semnah Dispatches*, in *Journal of Egyptian Archaeology*, 31, 3–10. See too under *P. Ram.*

sent., sents. sentence, sentences.

SETHE, *Ächtungstexte.* K. SETHE, *Die Ächtung feindlicher Fürsten, Völker und Dinge auf altägyptischen Tongefässscherben des Mittleren Reiches*, in *Abhandlungen der Preussischen Akademie der Wissenschaften*. Berlin, 1926.

SETHE, *Alphabet* K. SETHE, *Der Ursprung des Alphabets*, in *Nachrichten von der K. Gesellschaft der Wissenschaften zu Göttingen. Geschäftliche Mitteilungen, 1916, Heft 2.*

SETHE, *Lesestücke* K. SETHE, *Ägyptische Lesestücke.* Leipzig, 1924.

SETHE, *Rechts* K. SETHE, *Die Ägyptischen Ausdrücke für rechts und links und die Hieroglyphenzeichen für Westen und Osten*, in *Nachrichten der K. Gesellschaft der Wissenschaften zu Göttingen. Philologisch-historische Klasse, 1922.*

SETHE, *Zeitrechnung.* K. SETHE, *Die Zeitrechnung der alten Ägypter im Verhältnis zu der der andern Völker*, in *Nachrichten von der K. Gesellschaft der Wissenschaften zu Göttingen. Philologisch-historische Klasse, 1919–20.*

Sh. S. The story of the Shipwrecked Sailor, *Papyrus Leningrad 1115*, published as above, see *P. Pet.* Convenient transcription of the text in A. M. BLACKMAN, *Middle-Egyptian Stories*, Part I, pp. 41–8, being *Bibliotheca Aegyptiaca, II*, Brussels, 1932. See too above, GOL. *Naufragé.*

Sign Pap. F. LL. GRIFFITH, *The Sign Papyrus*, in *Two Hieroglyphic Papyri from Tanis*. London (Egypt Exploration Fund), 1889.

sim. similarly.

Sin. The story of Sinuhe, published by A. H. GARDINER, *Die Erzählung des Sinuhe und die Hirtengeschichte*, in A. ERMAN, *Literarische Texte des mittleren Reiches* (*Hieratische Papyrus aus den königlichen Museen zu Berlin*, Bd. v). Leipzig, 1909. The principal manuscripts are quoted as R (Ramesseum papyrus) and B (Pap. Berlin 3022). Convenient transcription in A. M. BLACKMAN, *Middle-Egyptian Stories*, Part I, pp. 1–41, being *Bibliotheca Aegyptiaca, II*, Brussels, 1932. See too above, GARD. *Sin.*

Sinai A. H. GARDINER and T. E. PEET, *The Inscriptions of Sinai, part I.* London (Egypt Exploration Fund), 1917. Second edition, by J. ČERNÝ, in preparation.

sing. singular.

Sitz. Bay. Ak. *Sitzungsberichte der Bayerischen Akademie der Wissenschaften.*

Sitz. Berl. Ak. *Sitzungsberichte der königlich Preussischen Akademie der Wissenschaften.*

Siut Tombs of Asyûṭ, quoted by tomb-number and line, as published in F. LL. GRIFFITH, *The Inscription of Siûṭ and Dêr Rîfeh.* London, 1889.

Sm. J. H. BREASTED, *The Edwin Smith Surgical Papyrus*, 2 vols., being *Oriental Institute Publications*, vol. iii. Chicago (University of Chicago Press), 1930.

Some Aspects A. H. GARDINER, *Some Aspects of the Egyptian Language*, in *Proceedings of the British Academy*, vol. xxiii. London, 1937.

Sphinx *Sphinx, Revue Critique embrassant le Domaine Entier de l'Égyptologie*, 22 vols. Uppsala, 1897–1925.

SPIEG.-PÖRTN. I. W. SPIEGELBERG and B. PÖRTNER, *Ägyptische Grabsteine und Denksteine aus süd-deutschen Sammlungen*, I *Karlsruhe, Mülhausen, Strassburg, Stuttgart.* Strassburg, 1902.

Stud. Aeg. I *Studia Aegyptiaca I*, in *Analecta Orientalia*, 17. Rome, 1938.

subj. subject.

Suppl. A. H. GARDINER and M. GAUTHIER-LAURENT, *Supplement to Gardiner's Egyptian Grammar.* Neuilly-sur-Seine, 1935.

T. Carn. The Carnarvon tablet, published by A. H. GARDINER, *The Defeat of the Hyksos by Kamōse*, in *Journal of Egyptian Archaeology*, iii. 95–110.

Tarkhan I W. M. F. PETRIE and others, *Tarkhan I and Memphis V.* London, 1913.

Th. T. S. *Theban Tombs Series*, edited by NORMAN DE G. DAVIES and ALAN H. GARDINER. London (Egypt Exploration Fund [Society]), 1915–33. Vol. I, *The Tomb of Amenemhēt*, by NINA DE G. DAVIES and ALAN H. GARDINER.
Vol. II, *The Tomb of Antefoḳer and of his wife Senet*, by NORMAN and NINA DE GARIS DAVIES.
Vol. III, *The Tombs of Two Officials of Tuthmosis IV*, by NORMAN and NINA DE GARIS DAVIES.
Vol. IV, *The Tomb of Ḥuy*, by NINA DE GARIS DAVIES and ALAN H. GARDINER.
Vol. V, *The Tombs of Menkheperrasonb, Amenmosě, and Another*, by NINA and NORMAN DE GARIS DAVIES.

Ti G. STEINDORFF, *Das Grab des Ti*, in *Veröffentlichungen der Ernst von Sieglin Expedition in Ägypten.* Leipzig, 1913.

Tôd F. B(ISSON DE LA) R(OQUE), *Tôd (1934 à 1936).* Cairo (Institut Français d'Archéologie Orientale), 1937.

trans. transitive.

Turin Stelae quoted by the numbers given in A. FABRETTI, F. ROSSI, and R. V. LANZONE, *Regio Museo di Torino*, 2 vols. Turin, 1882–8.

Two Sculptors N. DE G. DAVIES, *The Tomb of Two Sculptors at Thebes*, in *Publications of the Metropolitan Museum of Art, Egyptian Expedition: Robb de Peyster Tytus Memorial Series.* New York, 1925.

Unt. K. SETHE, *Untersuchungen zur Geschichte und Altertumskunde Ägyptens*, 7 vols. Leipzig, 1896–1915.

Urk. G. STEINDORFF, *Urkunden des ägyptischen Altertums.*
Section I, K. SETHE, *Urkunden des alten Reichs.* Leipzig, 1903.
Section IV, K. SETHE, *Urkunden der 18. Dynastie, historisch-biographische Urkunden*, 4 vols. Leipzig, 1906–9; vol. i, second edition, 1927–30.
Section V, H. GRAPOW, *Religiöse Urkunden*, 3 parts. Leipzig, 1915–17.

VAND. *Mo.* J. VANDIER, [Tomb of Ankhtifi-Nakht at Moʿalla]. Publication in preparation.

var. variant.

VARILLE, *Karnak I.* A. VARILLE, *Karnak I.* Cairo (Institut Français d'Archéologie Orientale), 1943.

vb. verb.

Verbum K. SETHE, *Das ägyptische Verbum im altägyptischen, neuägyptischen, und koptischen*, 3 vols. Leipzig, 1899–1902.

virt. virtual.

VOG. *Bauer* F. VOGELSANG, *Kommentar zu den Klagen des Bauern*, in K. SETHE, *Untersuchungen zur Geschichte und Altertumskunde Ägyptens*, vol. vi. Leipzig, 1913.

vs. verso, *i.e.* on the reverse of a papyrus.

Wb. A. ERMAN and H. GRAPOW, *Wörterbuch der ägyptischen Sprache*, 5 vols. Leipzig, 1926–31.

WEILL, *Décr.* R. WEILL, *Les Décrets Royaux de l'Ancien Empire Égyptien.* Paris, 1912.

Westc. A. ERMAN, *Die Märchen des Papyrus Westcar*, in *Mittheilungen aus den Orientalischen Sammlungen*, Heft v. vi. Berlin, 1890.

Wilb. Comm. A. H. GARDINER, *The Wilbour Papyrus*, 3 vols. Vol. II, Commentary. Brooklyn and Oxford, 1948.

WOLF, *Bewaffnung.* W. WOLF, *Die Bewaffnung des altägyptischen Heeres.* Leipzig, 1926.

WZKM *Wiener Zeitschrift für die Kunde des Morgenlandes*, 51 vols. Vienna, 1886–1948.

Zahlworte. K. SETHE, *Von Zahlen und Zahlworten bei den alten Ägyptern*, in *Schriften der Wissenschaftlichen Gesellschaft Strassburg*, part 25. Strassburg, 1916.

ADDITIONS AND CORRECTIONS

THROUGH the skill of the Oxford University Press minor errors, mostly pointed out by Dr. T. G. Allen and often consisting of no more than a single sign, letter or numeral, have been corrected on thirty-four pages without necessitating new negatives. On thirty-four other pages, however, the details to be rectified seemed important enough to call for photographic replacement. The pages in question are *51*, 65, *67*, *69*, *72*, *73*, *74*, *81*, 88, 99, *135*, *137*, 138, 139, *144*, *145*, 156, 189, 195, *197*, *205*, *206*, *258*, *358*, 363, 402, 405, 408, *427*, 445, *452*, 515, *557*, 585, and attention is invited especially to those pages the numbers of which have been printed in italics. For the rest, what now follows is necessitated by the reason stated in my Preface to the present edition; here, it will be observed, have been incorporated all the Additions and Corrections on p. xxviii of the Second edition.

pp. xix–xxviii. Additional abbreviations used in the marginal notes:

BARNS	J. W. B. BARNS, *The Ashmolean Ostracon of Sinuhe*, Oxford, 1952.
EDEL	E. EDEL, *Altägyptische Grammatik, I*, in *Analecta Orientalia 34*, Rome, 1955.
FIRCH.	O. FIRCHOW, *Ägyptologische Studien*, Berlin, 1955.
Kamose	Stela of king Kamose found at Karnak and to be published by LABIB HABACHI.
LAC. *Stèle jur.*	P. LACAU, *Une stèle juridique de Karnak, Supplément aux Annales du Service des Antiquités de l'Égypte, Cahier No. 13*, Cairo, 1949.
Lit. Fr.	R. CAMINOS, *Literary Fragments in the Hieratic Script*, Oxford, 1956.
Mo'alla	J. VANDIER, *Mo'alla, la tombe d'Ankhtifi et la tombe de Sébekhotep*, Cairo, 1950.
Oudh. Med.	Leiden, Rijks-Museum van Oudheden, *Oudheidkundige Mededeelingen.* Leyden, second series, 1920, foll.
P. Ḥeḳ.	T. G. H. JAMES, *The Ḥeḳanakhte Papyri.* In preparation.
P. Ram.	See now SIR ALAN GARDINER, *The Ramesseum Papyri*, Oxford, 1955; also for Nos. 1–5, J. W. B. BARNS, *Five Ramesseum Papyri*, Oxford, 1956.
WINLOCK	H. WINLOCK, *The Rise and Fall of the Middle Kingdom in Thebes*, New York, 1947.

p. 1, § 1, l. 3. It must be mentioned, however, that A. Scharff placed the accession of Menes in 2850 B.C.

p. 6, § 4, end. The date and localization of the Boḥairic dialect are discussed anew in P. E. Kahle, Bala'izah, Oxford, 1954, i. 248–52.

p. 12, n. 1. Griffith's admirable article has now been reprinted, *JEA* 37, 38 foll

p. 15, ll. 15 foll. from bottom. Champollion, however, mistakenly took [hieroglyph] to read *m*, not *ms*, see *JEA* 38, 127.

p. 23, n. 7. *Add*: Now published in full Lac. *Stèle jur.* [for this abbreviation see above].

p. 24 *b*, l. 3 from end. *For* Neferroḥu *read* Neferty, see G. Posener in *Rev. d'Ég.* 8, 174.

p. 27, n. 3. [hieroglyph] for *m* already under Kamose, *Ann.* 39, 252.

p. 78, n. 18. *Add*: Sim. *ky·s mnd* 'her other breast', *P. Ram. IV*, D 2, 2.

p. 94, ll. 6, 5 from end. Some modification is needed in the statement 'The other form of *wnn*, namely [hieroglyphs] (§ 107), is probably never used in simple affirmative statements with adverbial predicate.' For an exception see: [hieroglyphs] *ỉr m wn·ỉ m ẖrd, wn·ỉ m smr* when I was a child, I was a Friend, Anthes 22, 2–3. Here and in other cases the verb-form *wn·f* (§ 448; p. 373, l. 7) appears to carry an implication of past time as in later stages of the language.

p. 110, § 140. To the second ex. add the affirmative one: [hieroglyphs] *ẖsy pw grt ḥḏt* 'base it is to destroy', varr. of M and C to *P. Pet. 1116 A*, 121.

p. 120. In n. 2 delete *Amrah* 29, 2 and in n. 4, l. 7 for *ib.* 390, 7 read *Urk.* iv. 390, 7.

p. 130, n. 11. *For* 110, 3 *read* 110, 4. To n. 16 *add*: Sim. *Ann.* 4, 130, 10.

p. 135, n. 18. This supposed use must be cancelled, see Barns, 24, 33.

p. 152, § 202. For exx. of the negative relative adjective written [hieroglyphs] see *Mo'alla*, Index, p. 293. See too my article *JEA* 34, 23.

p. 156, § 205, 4, l. 5. Delete [hieroglyphs] *dwỉ* 'evilly' together with n. 36a. Edel has shown me that this writing, taken as an adverb p. 81, l. 3 from end in the 2nd edition, but now corrected, is merely an unusual writing of the adjective [hieroglyphs]; he points out that the status of this stem as a triliteral is proved by the masculine infinitive in *sḏw(ỉ·ỉ)* 'calumniating me' *Urk.* i. 223, 16; a further proof is the writing of the adjective in [hieroglyphs] *bw ḏwy* 'evil' (n.) quoted below, p. 417, l. 8.

p. 165, n. 10. Delete the reference *Sin.* B 255–6, see Barns, 28, 46.

p. 176, last line but one. *For* hands *read* fingers.

p. 198, n. 15. For *Sinai* 139, 8 substitute now *Sinai*², 141 w, 8.

p. 180, § 239. James quotes an example where *ḫr śḏm·f* refers to past time: [hieroglyphs] *ḫr wn Ḥr ḥr mrt grg·(ỉ) s(y)* now Horus wished that I should restore it, *Mo'alla* Ia 2.

p. 202. In the heading Expenditure out of this amount it would be preferable to substitute for the first word Apportionment or Specification; for this use of *sšmw*, not in my Vocabulary, see *Wb.* iv. 290, 13; for the following *ḫnt* see § 174, 2.

p. 204, n. 4. For my reply to Edel see *JNES* 8, 165 foll.

p. 210, n. 7. Another ex. of the rare transitive use of *špss*, see *JEA* 38, Pl. 8, 97.

p. 223, § 298, end. For forms like [hieroglyphs] *mswt* showing the plural strokes see the Sign-list, Z 2 (p. 536) with n. 19.

p. 225, § 300. In the ex. marked (*b*) *for* [hieroglyph] *read* [hieroglyph].

p. 226, § 301, l. 9. For *Nb-ḫrw-Rᶜ* read *Nb-ḥpt-Rᶜ*; hence also 'Nebḥepetrēᶜ' in l. 10 and see below on p. 499, P 8.

p. 228, § 304, 1. Much rarer is the use of *ḥr* + infinitive after *rdi*, ex. [hieroglyphs] *di·w st ḥr sḏm iꜣ(ᶜ)š n ᶜꜣmw* they placed themselves at the service (lit. at hearing the call) of the Asiatics, *Kamose* 18; somewhat similarly *Amarn.* 6, 15, 6.

p. 240, n. 8d, l. 5. *Before* 49, *insert JAOS.*

pp. 248 foll. Vergote in his article *La fonction du pseudoparticipe* in Firch. 338 foll. classifies the uses of the Old Perfective somewhat differently. It is unfortunate that he, like Lefebvre and Edel, retains the *lucus a non lucendo* nomenclature 'pseudo-participle'.

p. 246, § 322, first ex., *for* [hieroglyphs] *read* [hieroglyphs].

p. 250, l. 7 from end, for *Ḫrp-* read *Sḫm-*, see Gunn's note *JEA* 31, 6, n. 7, and in l. 5 from end *read* -powerful *for* -leader.

p. 255, l. 6. As an alternative to the negation of the construction with *r* + infinitive by *nn šḏm·f* James quotes [hieroglyphs] *nn sw r ḫpr* he shall not come into existence, *Moᶜalla* II*a* 2.

p. 256. At the end of sentence (4) in the Egyptian-English exercise *for* [hieroglyph] *read* [hieroglyph][2]. Three lines lower down *add* the note: [2] See § 76, 2.

p. 261, n. 34. After *Pt.* omit: 65, qu. § 349.

p. 262, § 342, l. 1 of third paragraph. *For* [hieroglyphs] *read* [hieroglyphs].

p. 267, § 352A. For the negative *w*, extremely rare in M.E., *add*: [hieroglyphs] *šsp w Ḥmn išwt·f nb, iwᶜ w sw iwᶜ·f* Ḥemen will not receive any things of his, and his heir shall not inherit from him, *Moᶜalla* III, 6–7 (p. 206); sim. *ib.* III, 5. 11.

p. 278, top line. *For* p. 303, n. 19 *read* p. 304, note [0a], to which add: *ḏdy·f*, Anthes, 20, 6.

p. 294, n. 1. To *Hamm.* 47, 10–1; *add* 191, 5;

p. 304, § 387, 3. **The *šḏmw·n·f* form.** Edel, §§ 665–7 has convincingly shown that all the O.E. writings with ending *-w* are either plurals or duals, and he therefore argues that the form should be called the *sḏmnf*, not the *sḏmwnf*, relative form (his spellings). He may be right, though his attempt to explain away the three M.E. exceptions quoted by me can hardly be regarded as satisfactory.

p. 314, delete n. 4a of the 2nd edition; I revert to my former reading *wnn*, see my arguments quoted Barns, p. 23, top left.

p. 321, § 407, 2. A clear ex. of *śḏmt·f* after *m* is [hieroglyphs] *m wnt ḫryt ḥnꜥ Tꜣ-wr* when there was war with the nome of Abydos, Cairo 46048.

p. 325. The omitted n. 6 should read: [6] Berl. *ÄI.* i. p. 258, 20.

p. 347, § 434. Add to the last line: But the negative verb *tm* can also be used, ex. [hieroglyphs] *tm·kꜣ ꜥḳ stpwt r nmt-nṯr* choice pieces of meat shall not enter into the god's slaughter-house, DE BUCK, ii. 174, *i*.

p. 348, n. 10*d*. *Add* a second ex.: *ḫr(y)·fy·i st* 'so say I it', LAC. *Stèle jur.* 18.

p. 359, § 446. R. A. Parker, in his article *The Function of the Imperfective* śḏm·f *in Middle Egyptian* (*Rev. d'Ég.* 10, 49 foll.) produces demotic evidence in favour of Polotsky's theory of this verb-form, but I see no reason for modifying my own statement on the subject.

p. 363, § 447. This paragraph has been left unaltered save for a short precautionary addition to n. 1, partly because I do not fully understand Edel's objections raised in correspondence with me, and partly because I have seen no means, in the limited space at my disposal, of bettering my general argument. I take it that Edel has no fault to find with my sub-sections (1) and (2). The forms ending in *-w* quoted under (3) have certainly become less mysterious through his fine discovery of a distinct *śḏmw·f* form with infixed formative *-w*, see his §§ 511–30; most, if not all, of my M.E. exx. are accepted by him; some of them, especially the *sḏdw·ṯn* of p. 365, n. 18, clearly have prospective or future meaning. My sub-section (4) requires further consideration, but I do not agree with Edel's attempted refutation of Sethe's view as stated at the bottom of my p. 363; the *ḥꜥy·f* and *iḥꜥ·f* of *Pyr.* 923*a* stand as direct variants of one another, and the writing *iḫnw* in *Pyr.* 1346*a* is not disposed of by his § 514. On the other hand I have no great confidence in my argument at the top of p. 364. As regards the following paragraph Clère's doubts printed on p. 427 of my 2nd edition still appear to me valid, but have been omitted in the present edition because no advantage is to be gained by prolonging discussion on so hypothetic a matter.

p. 377, § 456, first paragraph. Clère has shown (FIRCH. 38 foll.) that in *both* the *clichés* here discussed *im·(i)* should be read and that the general sense is 'Nothing (bad *or* reprehensible) came about from (*or* through) me'.

p. 389, § 468, end, *add* as a second OBS.: For *iw* followed by a noun other than the subject see below the addition to p. 412, § 507, 1.

p. 392. At the end of § 477 *add*: 5. For a unique case of *ꜥḥꜥ* followed by an adverbial predicate James quotes [hieroglyphs] *ꜥḥꜥ rs mḥt tꜣ pn r ḏr·f ḫr sdꜣw* 'and so South and North, the entire land is a-tremble' (lit. 'under trembling'), *Moꜥalla* IIβ 2. The ex. in 4 above is quite consistent with this, since the old perfective is in use the equivalent of an adverb or adverbial phrase (§ 311). See, moreover, the ex. with *ꜥḥꜥ·n* here immediately following.

p. 393, § 482, 1. At end *add*: A case closely similar to that quoted as an addition to p. 392 is once found: *ʿḥʿ·n tꜣ pn r ḏr·f ḥr sḫr nb ḏdy·f* then was this entire land subject to every counsel spoken by him, ANTHES, 20, 5.

p. 407, § 498. An exceptional use of *pw* is found in the context 'to make transformations into a phœnix, a swallow, a falcon or a heron, *pw mr·k* whichever you will', *Urk.* iv. 113, 14. A somewhat similar employment of *išst* is quoted in § 500, 5.

p. 410, l. 1. *For* *read* .

p. 412. To § 507, 1 *add*: DE BUCK quotes cases where *iw* introduces a noun other than the subject, exx. *iw Ḥr rdiw* (§ 465) *n·f irt·f* to Horus has been given his eye, BUDGE, 139, 5 (corrected); sim. NAV. ch. 1 B, 13 (*Ia*); had *iw rdiw irt nt Ḥr n·f* been written, this would have conformed to the rule of § 507, 1, but would have offended against the rule of word-order § 66. A somewhat similar case quoted by the same scholar is *iw Nwt tn srwḏ N pn sšp·s* this Nut, this N makes to flourish her light, DE BUCK, vi. 154, *k*.

p. 415, l. 8. *For* plan *read* foresee.

p. 417, ll. 11–13. Allen makes the plausible suggestion that we should render 'I have said this and what I have said is truth'. In that case the exceptional use postulated by me would be disposed of.

p. 442, A 1, n. 0. Allen, quoting DE BUCK iii, p. ix, n. 2, points out that the Coffin Text exx. where the of is replaced by are doubtful evidence of the reading *si*.

p. 462, under F 5, l. 3. *After* 'prescription' *read*: also det. in *bḫnt* 'pylon' *Urk.* iv. 167, 15.—Under F 14, to n. 2 *add*: Sim. *ib.* 109, 17.

p. 466, F 46, n. 1, l. 5. Delete the reference *Saqq. Mast.* i. 2. Černý notes that *dbn* here means, not the weight, but a basket or box, see *Wb.* v. 437, 16.

p. 470, G 26, l. 1. *For* Det. *read* Ideo.

p. 470, G 27, n. 2. A damaged, but certain, ex. of [*dš*]*r* 'flamingo' in the Ramesseum Onomasticon, see *AEO.* i. 9.

p. 470, G 29. The Latin name of the jabiru should have been given as *Mycteria ephippiorhyncus seu senegalensis*, SHAW; and in n. 1 *for* 30, 1. *read* 30, 12.

p. 481, M 19, The sign is more completely explained by M. A. MURRAY, *Ancient Egypt* 1929, 43; here is a later perversion of one of the half-loaves (*gsw*, X 7) seen on the earliest offering-tables, exx. *Saqq. Mast.* i. 1. 2. 23; depicts a vase of the type shown *ib.* 22, cf. also DAV. *Sheikh Said*, Pl. 9. In hieratic a sign like M 43 is substituted for , see MÖLL. *Pal.* i, No. 286.

p. 489, N 28. For the reading see DE BUCK i. 46, *a*.

p. 495, O 21. [hieroglyph] is used also as a more general word for 'temple', 'chapel', *Wb.* iii. 465, 6, masc. in *Urk.* iv. 734, 15; 743, 7.

p. 498, O 48. *After* Use as last *insert*: Phon. *mḫn* in [hieroglyph] *mḫnt* 'carnelian', see *JEA* 38, 13.

p. 499, P 8. The existence of variants of the prenomen [hieroglyph] giving [hieroglyph] (see n. 4 and WINLOCK, Pl. 40, 5; 41, 9. 17; 42, 19) shows that [hieroglyph] there represents a feminine word which, in spite of Sethe's view *ÄZ.* 62, 3 foll., can only be [hieroglyph] *ḥpt* 'oar', see below Aa 5, n. 5 and *Wb.* iii. 68, 4. The reading *Nb-ḥpt-Rꜥ* (so in my 1st edition, but changed to *Nb-ḫrw (?)-Rꜥ* in the 2nd) is further indicated by arguments showing that the king Menthotpe whose name was written with the oar was identical with him whose prenomen is written [hieroglyph]; see my article to appear in vol. i of the resuscitated *Mitt. Kairo.* At all events the word *ḫrwt* 'oar' listed in *Wb.* iii. 324, 6 lacks any foundation and should be deleted; the origin of the phonetic value *ḫr(w)* of [hieroglyph] remains unknown.

p. 508, S 34. For the reading of [hieroglyph] with initial ꜥ Allen quotes DE BUCK iii. 399, *e*, B5C; see too *Bersh.* ii. 6, 5.

p. 513, T 14, l. 4 from end: for (*e*) read (*f*) and before it *insert*: (*e*) of [hieroglyph] S 38 and [hieroglyph] S 39 in [hieroglyph] *ꜥwt* 'animals.'[13a] Also *add as note*: [13a] *Hamm.* 110, 2.

p. 520, U 36. *Add to n. 4*: also *Rev. d'ég.* i. 104.

p. 524, [hieroglyph] V 19; at end of n. 1 *read*: MONTET 95; according to KEIMER, *Bull. de l'Inst. d'Ég.* 32, 10 the horizontal stroke merely represents the ground-level. To n. 12 *add*: In *Westc.* 11, 7 'Gepäck' is suggested *Wb.* v. 51, 12; so too FAULKNER in *JEA* 37, 114.

p. 524, V 20, left, l. 2, *for* cross-bar *read* horizontal stroke.

p. 539 Aa 2 [hieroglyph], l. 8, *after* 'embalmer' *add*: hence also phon. det. in [hieroglyph] *mrwt* 'love'.[11a] At end add as note 11a: *Hamm.* 110, 8; 191, 7, further perverted to [hieroglyph] in [hieroglyph] ANTHES, 20, 4. 16; 30, 1.

p. 553, left-hand column, l. 8 from end, *instead of* estate, property *read* transfer of property.

p. 557, left. [hieroglyph] *ꜥwt* comprises sheep and goats, but excludes oxen and the like; it is used also of wild animals generally. The sense 'flock' 'herd' given by me is not entirely satisfactory.

p. 584, left-hand column, after l. 11 *insert*: [hieroglyph] *ḥy* 'what a . . . . !', § 258A, p. 427.

p. 591, left-hand column, l. 7 from bottom, *after* shrine of Anubis *add*: temple, chapel.

p. 593, right-hand column, l 13, *instead of* (probably caus.) *read*: (caus., infin. *sdꜣt*).

p. 594, right-hand column, ll. 13–11 from bottom, delete from *Tp* ([hieroglyph]) -*Šmꜥw* . . . *to* Elephantine. I hope to show elsewhere that the true reading is *Tp-rs*, and that the expression means no more than 'the extreme South'.

p. 603, right-hand column, l. 4, *after* same sense *insert*: also trans., amuse someone.

INTRODUCTION

A. THE EGYPTIAN LANGUAGE

§ **1.** THE subject of this manual is the **Language** of the ancient Egyptians as revealed in their **Hieroglyphic Writings**. The earliest inscriptions go back as far as the First Dynasty, which can in no case be placed later than 3000 B.C., while some authorities favour a date many hundreds of years earlier. The same script lived on far into the Christian era; the latest hieroglyphs known are at Philae and dated to A.D. 394; the next latest show the names of the Roman emperors Diocletian (yr. 12, A.D. 295) and Traianus Decius (A.D. 249–251). Thus the use of the earliest form of Egyptian writing, though at the last confined to a narrow circle of learned priests, covers a period of three or even four thousand years. In the course of so many centuries, grammar and vocabulary were bound to change very considerably, and in point of fact the Egyptian spoken under the Roman occupation bore but little resemblance to that which was current under the oldest Pharaohs. It is true that the new modes of parlance which came into existence from time to time were by no means adequately reflected in the contemporary hieroglyphic inscriptions; for in Egypt the art of writing was always reserved to a conservative and tradition-loving caste of scribes, upon whose interests and caprice it depended how far the common speech of the people should be allowed to contaminate the *mdw nṯr*, 'the god's words'. None the less, the idiom in which the public records of the Twentieth Dynasty (about 1200–1085 B.C.) are couched differs widely from that found, for example, in the royal decrees of the Sixth Dynasty (about 2420–2294 B.C.). To avoid confusing the beginner's notions, it is obviously desirable that he should confine his attention to some special phase of the language; and there are many reasons which render Middle Egyptian more suitable for that purpose than any other phase.

§ **2.** It is with **Middle Egyptian**, therefore, that this book will be exclusively concerned. Middle Egyptian, as here understood, is the idiom employed in the stories and other literary compositions of the Middle Kingdom (Dynasties IX–XIII, roughly from 2240 to 1740 B.C.), as well as in the public and private monumental inscriptions of that period and also far down into the Eighteenth Dynasty (1573–1314 B.C.). Much later, when the scribes of the Ethiopian and Saite Dynasties (715–525 B.C.) adopted a deliberately archaistic style of writing, it was to Middle Egyptian that they reverted. There is evidence to show that the renaissance which, after a certain interval of disruption, followed the end of the Old Kingdom, was marked by a great development of literary activity; a florid, metaphorical style now came into vogue, and a number of tales and semi-didactic treatises were written which obtained a wide celebrity, and were copied and recopied in the schools. For this reason, the period covered by Middle Egyptian may be considered the classical age of Egyptian literature. Another reason which makes the language of the Twelfth Dynasty particularly suited to the purposes of the novice is that linguistically the business documents belonging to that time differ less from the contemporary literary works than those of any other period. Middle Egyptian has further the advantage of being more consistently spelt than other phases of the language, and it is in this phase that the inflexions of the verb are best displayed in the writing. Lastly, the number of Middle Egyptian texts which have been preserved is very great, and comprises religious, magical, medical, mathematical, historical, and legal compositions, besides the literary works and business documents already mentioned.

§ 3. **Affinities and characteristics of Egyptian.**[1] The Egyptian language is related, not only to the Semitic tongues (Hebrew, Arabic, Aramaic, Babylonian, &c.), but also to the East African languages (Galla, Somali, &c.) and the Berber idioms of North Africa. Its connexion with the latter groups, together known as the Hamitic family, is a very thorny subject, but the relationship to the Semitic tongues can be fairly accurately defined. In general structure the similarity is very great; Egyptian shares the principal peculiarity of Semitic in that its word-stems consist of combinations of consonants, as a rule three in number, which are theoretically at least unchangeable. Grammatical inflexion and minor variations of meaning are contrived mainly by ringing the changes on the internal vowels, though affixed endings also are used for the same purpose; more important differences of meaning are created by reduplication, whole or partial (exx. *śn* 'brother', *śnśn* 'be brotherly towards'; *śmśw* 'elder', later form *śmśm*[2]), or, in one or two special cases, by prefixed consonants (causatives in *ś*, like *śꜥnḫ* 'cause to live'; nouns with the formative consonant *m*, like *mẖnt* 'ferry-boat' from *ẖnỉ* 'row'; *n*-formations, like *nftft* 'leap away', beside *ftft* 'leap'). There are, moreover, many points of contact in the vocabulary (exx. Eg. *ḥśb* 'count', Arab. *ḥasaba*; Eg. *ỉnk* 'I', Hebr. *'ānōkī*; Eg.

[1] The present state of the question is well summarized in G. Lefebvre, 'Sur l'origine de la langue égyptienne' in *Chronique d'Égypte*, July, 1936, with full bibliography; see too the same scholar's *Grammaire de l'Égyptien classique*, §§ 1–7. The relationship to both families is certain, but comparisons of vocabulary become the more hazardous the further they are pushed. For the Semitic affinities see especially A. Ember, *Egypto-Semitic Studies*, Leipzig, 1930; Fr. Calice, *Grundlagen der ägyptisch-semitischen Wortvergleichung*, Vienna, 1936; for the Hamitic, E. Zyhlarz, *Ursprung und Sprachcharakter des Altägyptischen*, Berlin, 1933. The comparison with Hamitic labours under the difficulty that hardly any ancient written records exist, while that with Semitic has rendered much good service, particularly in the realms of morphology and syntax.

[2] Egyptian writing omits the vowels, so that our transliterations of the hieroglyphs display only the consonantal skeleton; see below, § 7.

ḫmnw 'eight', Hebr. *shemōneh*), though these are very frequently obscured by metathesis and by unobvious consonantal changes (exx. Eg. *śḏm* 'hear', Arab. *samiʿa*; Eg. *ib* 'heart', Arab. *lubbu*; Eg. *śnb* 'be healthy', Arab. *salima*). In spite of these resemblances, Egyptian differs from all the Semitic tongues a good deal more than any one of them differs from any other, and at least until its relationship to the African languages is more closely defined, Egyptian must certainly be classified as standing outside the Semitic group. There are grounds for thinking that it is a language which, possibly owing to a fusion of races, had, like English as compared with the other Teutonic dialects, disintegrated and developed at an abnormally rapid pace. This may be well illustrated in the case of the verb: no trace of the old Semitic imperfect has survived in Egyptian, where, moreover, the old Semitic perfect is already much restricted in its use; and it is exceedingly interesting to note that the participial formations by which these tenses have been or are being replaced (*śḏm·f* 'heard of him' = 'he hears'; *śḏm·n·f* 'heard to him' = 'he has heard') find analogies in certain of the most recent offshoots of the Semitic family, namely the Neo-Syriac dialects.[1] The state of affairs just described is exhibited even in the oldest known stages of Egyptian. The evidence from the noun is less illuminating, but the oldest forms which can be deductively reconstructed (exx. *ḥăr* 'face'; *nắtᵉr* 'god') show by the quantity of their vowels that the case-endings of early Semitic had already vanished. The entire vocalic system of Old Egyptian may indeed be proved to have reached a stage resembling that of Hebrew or modern Arabic as compared with classical Arabic; the free and open vocalization of the earlier times (cf. in classical Arabic *ragŭlun*) has given place under the influence of a strong tonic accent to a system in which all the secondary syllables are shortened down and subordinated to the one accented vowel in the ultimate or penultimate syllable; a theoretic, prehistoric *natárata* 'goddess' has in historic Egyptian become *ᵉntắrᵉt*, which we may infer to have been the pronunciation about the time of the Pyramids.[2]

Towards the end of the Old Kingdom new grammatical tendencies manifest themselves. The 'synthetic' tenses *śḏm·f* and *śḏm·n·f* mentioned above are first supplemented and then gradually replaced by 'analytic' forms. Thus *iw·f ḥr śḏm* 'he is upon hearing' (cf. French *il est à lire*) appears in Old Egyptian side by side with *śḏm·f* 'he hears', though it does not wholly replace the latter until the Coptic period (below, § 4). In Late Egyptian, i. e. the vernacular of the Eighteenth Dynasty and after, such analytic forms already predominate. In various respects the relationship of Late Egyptian to Middle Egyptian is closely parallel to the relationship of French and the other Romance languages to their common parent Latin: in the already mentioned substitution of analytic for synthetic verb-forms, cf. *je vais faire*,

[1] See BROCKELMANN, *Grundriss der vergleichenden Grammatik der semitischen Sprachen*, i, § 264 *e*.

[2] See Appendix A and the literature there quoted.

'I am going to do', as against Latin *faciam*; in the possession of an indefinite article derived from the word for 'one' (Late Eg. *wꜥ*, French *un*) and a definite article derived from a demonstrative adjective (Late Eg. *pꜣ*, French *le* = Latin *ille*); in the substitution of new words for many old words signifying quite common things (ex. 'head', Middle Eg. *tp*, Late Eg. *ḏꜣḏꜣ*; Latin *caput*, French *tête*, from Latin *testa*); and, lastly, in the fact that Middle Egyptian, like Latin, survived as the monumental and learned language long after it had perished as the language of everyday life.

The most striking feature of Egyptian in all its stages is its concrete **realism**, its preoccupation with exterior objects and occurrences to the neglect of those more subjective distinctions which play so prominent a part in modern, and even in the classical, languages. Subtleties of thought such as are implied in 'might', 'should', 'can', 'hardly', as well as such abstractions as 'cause', 'motive', 'duty', belong to a later stage of linguistic development; possibly they would have been repugnant to the Egyptian temperament. Despite the reputation for philosophic wisdom attributed to the Egyptians by the Greeks, no people has ever shown itself more averse from speculation[1] or more wholeheartedly devoted to material interests; and if they paid an exaggerated attention to funerary observances, it was because the continuance of earthly pursuits and pleasures was felt to be at stake, assuredly not out of any curiosity as to the why and whither of human life. The place taken elsewhere by meditation and a philosophic bent seems with the Egyptians to have been occupied by exceptional powers of observation and keenness of vision. Intellectual and emotional qualities were ordinarily described by reference to the physical gestures or expressions by which they were accompanied, thus 'liberality' is 'extension of hand' (*ꜣwt-ꜥ*), 'cleverness' is 'sharpness of face (sight)' (*śpd-ḥr*). Another feature of Egyptian is its marked preference for **static** over dynamic expression; apart from the rare survivals of the active Old Perfective, there is no genuine active tense, all others being derived from passive or neuter participles.[2] No less salient a characteristic of the language is its **concision**; the phrases and sentences are brief and to the point. Involved constructions and lengthy periods are rare, though such are found in some legal documents. The **vocabulary** was very rich, though, as may be inferred from our previous statements, not equally well developed in every direction. The clarity of Egyptian is much aided by a **strict word-order,** probably due in part to the absence of case-endings in the nouns. There remains to be mentioned a certain **formality** that is conspicuous in Egyptian writings—a rigidity and conventionality which find their counterpart in Egyptian Art. The force of

[1] This general verdict is not vitiated by the sporadic occurrence of texts showing a real speculative or scientific interest, such as the exegetic text published by BREASTED under the title 'The Philosophy of a Memphite Priest' (*ÄZ.* 39, 39), or the Edwin Smith medical papyrus edited by the same scholar. These were doubtless the creations of individuals far above the average intellectual standard.

[2] GARDINER, 'Some Aspects of the Egyptian Language', in *Proc. Brit. Acad.* XXIII, 1937.

tradition discouraged originality alike in subject-matter and in expression, but there are some notable exceptions. For a brief estimate of the value of Egyptian literature see below, p. 24c.

§ 4. **Different stages of the language.**[1] Bearing in mind the fact that the written language reflects the spoken language of the different periods only to a limited extent, and that monumental records on stone are always more conservative than business documents and letters on potsherds and papyrus, we may roughly distinguish the following linguistic stages:

Old Egyptian: the language of Dynasties I–VIII, about 3180 to 2240 B.C.[2] This may be taken to include the language of the Pyramid Texts (below, § 13), which, however, displays certain peculiarities of its own and is written in a special orthography. Otherwise the surviving documents of this stage are mainly official or otherwise formal—funerary formulae and tomb-inscriptions, including some biographical texts. Old Egyptian passes with but little modification into

Middle Egyptian, possibly the vernacular of Dynasties IX–XI, about 2240–1990 B.C., later contaminated with new popular elements. In the later form it survived for some monumental and literary purposes right down to Graeco-Roman times, while the earlier form was retained as the religious language.

Late Egyptian: the vernacular of Dynasties XVIII–XXIV, about 1573 to 715 B.C., exhibited chiefly in business documents and letters, but also in stories and other literary compositions, and to some extent also in the official monuments from Dyn. XIX onwards. There are but few texts, however, wherein the vernacular shows itself unmixed with the 'classical' idiom of Middle Egyptian. Various foreign words make their appearance. For some other characteristics, see above, pp. 3–4.

Demotic: this term is loosely applied to the language used in the books and documents written in the script known as Demotic (see below, § 8), from Dyn. XXV to late Roman times (715 B.C. to A.D. 470). Here again the old 'classical' idiom is blended with later, vernacular elements, often inextricably.

Coptic: the old Egyptian language in its latest developments, as written in the Coptic script, from about the third century A.D. onwards; so called because it was spoken by the Copts,[3] the Christian descendants of the ancient Egyptians, in whose churches it is read, though not understood, even at the present day. After the Arab conquest (A.D. 640) Coptic was gradually superseded by Arabic, and became extinct as a spoken tongue in the sixteenth century. Coptic is written in the Greek alphabet supplemented by seven special characters derived ultimately from the hieroglyphs,

[1] B. H. Stricker, 'De Indeeling der Egyptische Taalgeschiedenis', in *Oudheidkundige Mededeelingen*, XXV, Leyden, 1944.

[2] The dates adopted are approximately those given by Sewell in *The Legacy of Egypt*, Oxford, 1942; those prior to Dyn. XII are much disputed.

[3] The name Copt is doubtless a corruption of the Greek 'Aiguptos', i.e. Egypt.

namely: ϣ = *sh* = hieroglyphic 𓈙 *š*(*ꜣ*)
ϥ = *f* = " 𓆑 *f*
ϧ = *kh* = " 𓐍 *ḫ*(*ꜣ*), only in the Boḥairic dialect;

the Akhmîmic ⳉ, a differentiation from ϩ, answers the same purpose.

ϩ = *h* = hieroglyphic 𓉔 *ḥ*
ϫ = *dj* = " 𓆓 *ḏ*(*ꜣ*)
ϭ = *g* = " 𓎡 *k*
ϯ = *ti* = " 𓂞 *dit*

The importance of Coptic philologically is due to its being the only form of Egyptian in which the vowels are regularly written.[1] It must not be forgotten, however, that Coptic represents a far later stage of the language than even the most vulgar examples of late Egyptian. The vocabulary is very different from that of the older periods and includes many Greek loan-words, even such grammatical particles as *μέν* and δέ. The word-order is more Greek than Egyptian. To a certain extent, at least, Coptic is a semi-artificial literary language elaborated by the native Christian monks; at all events it is extensively influenced by Greek biblical literature. The first tentative efforts to transcribe the old Egyptian language into Greek letters belong to the second century A.D., and are of a pagan character (horoscopes, magical texts, and the like). Several dialects of Coptic are distinguished, of which the following are the most important:

1. **Akhmîmic**: the old dialect of Upper Egypt, which early gave place to Ṣaʿîdic.
2. **Ṣaʿîdic** (less correctly written Sahidic): the dialect of Thebes, later used for literary purposes throughout the whole of Upper Egypt.
3. **Boḥairic**: doubtless originally the dialect of the Western Delta only,[2] but later, after the removal of the Patriarchate to Cairo in the eleventh century, the literary idiom of the whole of Egypt.

B. THE EGYPTIAN WRITING

§ 5. The **hieroglyphic writing**[3] is an offshoot of **pictorial art,** a very early and important function of which was to provide a visible record of facts and occurrences, accessible to those who for one reason or another were beyond the range of the spoken word. The limitations of pictorial art as a medium for conveying or storing information are, of course, obvious; and recorded history may be considered to have been non-existent until, shortly before the end of the Pre-dynastic period, the Egyptians discovered the principle of the **rebus** or **charade.** The new departure consisted in using the pictures of things, not to denote those things themselves or any

[1] See Appendix A at the end of the book. [2] See CRUM's remarks, *JEA.* 27, 180.

[3] For the general theory see SETHE, *Das hieroglyphische Schriftsystem*, Leipzig, 1935; also in wider perspective, ID., *Vom Bilde zum Buchstaben*, Leipzig, 1939. A popular account by the present writer, *JEA.* 2, 61.

cognate notions, but to indicate certain other entirely different things not easily susceptible of pictorial representation, *the names of which chanced to have a similar sound.* Obviously proper names could only be communicated in this way, and it is perhaps

Verso OF THE SLATE PALETTE OF NARMER (DYN. I).

This is one of the oldest specimens of Egyptian writing known. The name of the king, written with the *nꜥr*-fish and the *mr*-chisel, occupies the rectangle (below, p. 72) between the Hathor-heads. The other small hieroglyphs give the names or titles of the persons over whose heads they are written; the captured chieftain may have been named Washi (harpoon *wꜥ*, pool *š*). The group at top on right was probably intended as explanation of the picture in the centre; at this early date the gist of complete sentences could apparently be conveyed only by symbolical groups of which the elements suggested separate words. The conjectural meaning is: The falcon-god Horus (i.e. the king) leads captive the inhabitants of the papyrus-land (*Tꜣ-mḥw* 'the Delta').[1]

with them that hieroglyphic writing began (see the annexed cut). The method was that by which Prior Burton, in the Middle Ages, playfully symbolized his name by a thistle or *burr* placed upon a barrel or *tun*. In similar manner, the notion of high

[1] See RANKE in *Studia Orientalia* (Helsingfors, 1925), 167 ff.; KEIMER in *Aegyptus*, 7, 169 ff.

numbers such as 'thousand' or 'ten thousand' could only have been conveyed pictorially by the thousandfold or ten-thousandfold repetition of a stroke or of the object to which the number referred; and even if the draughtsman had accomplished this laborious task, the spectator desirous of grasping the meaning would have been condemned to the hardly less laborious task of counting the strokes or objects so depicted. The Egyptians adopted a simple way of avoiding this difficulty. The word for 'thousand' in Egyptian was *kha*, and that for 'ten thousand' was *djēbaʿ*; but *kha* in Egyptian also meant 'lotus' and *djēbaʿ* meant 'finger'. In order, therefore, to write '32,000 cattle' in hieroglyphs all that was necessary was to depict three fingers and two lotus-plants in close proximity to the image of an ox, thus :—𓃒𓂭𓂭𓂭𓆼𓆼. As is hinted by the example just quoted, Egyptian hieroglyphic writing did not attempt completely to replace pictorial elements by sound-elements; throughout the entire course of its history that script remained *a picture-writing eked out by phonetic elements*. Hieroglyphic writing may be said to have come into existence as a properly differentiated entity at the moment when, in a given pictorial representation, one portion of the objects figured was shown in miniature and was clearly intended to be interpreted in terms of language, while the other portion, of larger size, was no less clearly intended to be construed purely visually without reference to language. The development of Egyptian writing is well epitomized in those sculptured scenes on the walls of tombs or temples where what cannot easily be represented pictorially is conveyed by sequences of hieroglyphic signs graven above the figures to which they refer. By this means we may not merely watch the ancient craftsmen at their work, but even overhear their banter and listen to the songs they sang.

§ **6.** Even in the fully developed form of hieroglyphic writing only two classes of signs need be clearly distinguished. These are: (1) **sense-signs** or **ideograms** (Greek *idea* 'form' and *gramma* 'writing'); (2) **sound-signs** or **phonograms** (Greek *phonē* 'sound' and *gramma* 'writing').

1. **Ideograms** or **sense-signs** signify either the actual object depicted, as 𓇳 'sun', 𓈉 'hill-country', or else some closely connected notion, as 𓇳 the sun in the sense of 'day', 𓏞 a scribe's palette, water-bowl, and reed-holder in the sense of 'scribe', 'write', or 'paint'.[1]

2. **Phonograms** or **sound-signs** are signs used for spelling, which, although originally ideograms and in many cases still also employed elsewhere as such, have secondarily acquired sound-values on the principle explained in § 5. Examples are 𓂋 *r*, from original 𓂋 'mouth', in Egyptian *ra*; 𓉐 *p* + *r*, from original 𓉐 'house', Egyptian *pāru*.[2]

[1] In strictness ideograms represent words rather than objects or notions connected therewith. Nevertheless, substitution of the term 'word-sign' could only obscure the clear distinction above made.

[2] The pronunciations here given are reconstructions from Coptic ⲣⲟ 'mouth' and -ⲡⲱⲣ in ϫⲉⲛⲉⲡⲱⲣ 'roof'.

§ 7. Vowels not written.[1] In reading the last section, the student has doubtless noted that the sound-values derived from 𓂋, the ideogram of the 'mouth' (*ra*), and from 𓉐, the ideogram of the 'house' (*pāru*), were said to be, not *ra* and *pāru*, but simply the consonantal elements entering into those two words, namely *r* and *p* + *r*. To put it differently, the Egyptian scribes ignored the vowels in writing. It thus came about that both these signs could be used in a far greater number of different words than would otherwise have been the case: 𓂋 might virtually represent *ră*, *rā*, *rĕ*, *rē*, *ăr*, *ār*, *ĕr*, *ēr*, or any other combination of vowel and *r* that the Egyptian language might contain; similarly 𓉐 might stand, not only for *pāru*, but also for *pĕr*, *āpr*, *epr*, *epra*, and so forth. A like neglect of the vowels is seen in Phoenician, Hebrew, and Arabic, though in certain other Semitic scripts (Babylonian, Ethiopic) the vocalization is always indicated. The reason for the Egyptian omission of the vowels is not far to seek. It is characteristic of the family of languages to which Egyptian belongs that one and the same word presents different vocalizations according to the forms that it assumes and the contexts in which it appears; thus the ideogram for 'house' 𓉐, pronounced *pār* (from *pāru*) in isolation, may well have represented **pĕr*[2] when followed by a genitive and **pră(yyu)* in the plural. Such a variability of the vowels could not fail to engender the feeling that the consonants were all that mattered, whereby it became easier to utilize the sign 𓉐 for writing other words pronounced with *p*+*r* in that order, whatever vowels they may have possessed. In actual fact 𓉐 is found in the writing of words which we have reason to believe may have been spoken as **prāref* or **perrāref*, 'he habitually goes up', and **prāyet* 'spring'.

§ 8. Hieroglyphic writing is only one of three kinds of script which in course of time were evolved in Ancient Egypt. Out of hieroglyphic sprang a more cursive writing known to us as **hieratic,** and out of hieratic again there emerged, towards 700 B.C., a very rapid script formerly sometimes called **enchorial** but now always known as **demotic.** None of these styles of writing utterly banished the others, but each as it arose restricted the domain of its progenitor. In the Graeco-Roman period all three were in use contemporaneously.

Hieroglyphic owes its name to the fact that in the latest times it was employed almost exclusively for 'sacred' (Greek *hīeros*) inscriptions 'sculptured' (Greek *glūpho*) on temple-walls or on public monuments. At the outset hieroglyphic was used for all purposes; on stelae of stone and the like the signs are incised, or more rarely in raised relief, without interior markings; in temples and tombs where their decorative effect was of account the hieroglyphs were often executed with the most elaborate detail and beautifully coloured; upon papyrus the outlines were, on the other hand, abbreviated to a very considerable extent. For specimens of these different types of

[1] Sethe's convincing views on this topic are vindicated by De Buck in *Bibl. Or.* 1, 11 against Scharff in *Sitz. Bay. Ak.* 1942, 72, n. 311.

[2] The asterisk * indicates that the reconstruction so marked is purely hypothetical.

hieroglyphic writing see the Frontispiece, Plate I. As time went on, hieroglyphic became restricted more and more to monumental purposes, though for religious texts it was in general employment even on papyrus down to the end of Dyn. XX; as an occasional medium for writing texts on potsherds or papyrus it survives right down to Christian times.

Hieratic,[1] so called because in the Graeco-Roman age it was the usual script employed by the priests (Greek *hīeratikos* 'priestly'), is the name now given to all the earlier styles of writing cursive enough for the original pictorial forms of the signs to be no longer clearly recognizable. Hieratic was nothing more, in the beginning, than hieroglyphic in the summary and rounded forms resulting from the rapid manipulation of a reed-pen as contrasted with the angular and precise shapes arising from the use of the chisel. Under the Old Kingdom, hieratic is hardly differentiated from hieroglyphic. Under the Middle Kingdom and in the Eighteenth Dynasty hieratic is invariably used on papyrus, except for religious texts; it is developing a relatively consistent orthography of its own and distinguishes both more and less cursive varieties. Religious texts on papyrus begin to be written regularly in hieratic about Dyn. XXI, and from that time onward sporadic inscriptions on stone in the same script are found. In the latest period, as already said, hieratic was generally employed by the priests when writing religious texts on papyrus.

Demotic[2] (Greek *dēmōtikos* 'popular'), or **enchorial** (Greek *enkhōrios* 'native') as some of the earliest decipherers called it, is a very rapid form of hieratic that made its first appearance about the time of the Ethiopian Dynasty. Throughout the Ptolemaic and Roman ages it was the ordinary writing of daily life, and is occasionally found even upon stelae of stone.

For specimens of hieratic and demotic see Plate II. With demotic we are not concerned at all in this work, and with hieratic we deal only in so far as it has been converted or, to employ the usual term, 'transcribed', into hieroglyphic. Individual hieratic hands differ as all handwriting is apt to differ; for this reason Egyptologists, before translating a hieratic text, habitually transcribe it into hieroglyphs, just as the modern printer sets up a modern author's manuscript in type.

C. BRIEF HISTORY OF EGYPTIAN PHILOLOGY

§ 9. The tradition and its interpreters.[3] As Christianity spread throughout Egypt, the knowledge of the old native scripts and lore, long since the jealously

[1] See MÖLLER, *Hieratische Paläographie*, 3 vols., Leipzig, 1909–12; *Ergänzungsheft*, 1936; also ID., *Hieratische Lesestücke*, 3 vols., Leipzig, 1909–10. On the transcription of hieratic see Add. § 63 A.

[2] See W. SPIEGELBERG, *Demotische Grammatik*, Heidelberg, 1925; W. ERICHSEN, *Demotische Lesestücke*, 2 vols., Leipzig, 1937–9; FR. LEXA, *Grammaire démotique égyptienne*, I, II, Prague, 1939–40.

[3] See P. MARESTAING, *Les écritures égyptiennes et l'antiquité classique*, Paris, 1913; H. SOTTAS and E. DRIOTON, *Introduction à l'étude des hiéroglyphes*, Paris, 1922.

LITERARY HIERATIC OF THE TWELFTH DYNASTY (*Pr.* 4, 2–4), WITH TRANSCRIPTION

OFFICIAL HIERATIC OF THE TWENTIETH DYNASTY (*Abbott* 5, 1–3), WITH TRANSCRIPTION

LITERARY DEMOTIC OF THE THIRD CENTURY B.C. (*Dem. Chron.* 6, 1–3), WITH TRANSCRIPTION

SPECIMENS OF HIERATIC AND DEMOTIC

with hieroglyphic transcriptions in a modern Egyptological hand.

guarded secret of a dwindling priestly caste, fell into oblivion. In the second century candidates for the priesthood had still to show a knowledge of demotic and hieratic. In the third century demotic is no longer used for documents, though there are demotic inscriptions at Philae dating as late as A. D. 452,[1] i. e. some sixty years after the final disappearance of the hieroglyphs. After this, there remains only the tradition of the classical writers and the early Fathers, whose confused and mutually contradictory statements, if they point anywhere, point in a direction diametrically opposed to the truth. Scattered remarks in Herodotus, Diodorus, and Tacitus, to mention only the better known authors, do indeed imply that plain narratives of historical events formed part, at least, of the substance of the hieroglyphic inscriptions, and Josephus expressly states that the celebrated work of the historian Manetho was compiled from such sources. An obscure passage in the *Stromateis* of Clement of Alexandria (*flor.* A. D. 200) may also be interpreted as affirming that the hieroglyphs comprised phonetic signs. But the sane testimony just mentioned was altogether outweighed by the assertions of those whose beliefs and predilections were of a mystical kind. In the treatise *On Isis and Osiris* Plutarch compares the content of the hieroglyphic writings to the maxims of the Pythagoreans. The climax was, however, reached by Horapollo, a native of Upper Egypt who flourished in the second half of the fifth century. His treatise *Hieroglyphica*, written probably in Coptic but surviving only in a Greek translation, combines correct notions of the meanings of many hieroglyphic signs with the most grotesque allegorical reasons for those meanings. Thus, the goose 𓅬 symbolizes 'son' because of that bird's intense love of its offspring, the hare 𓃹 serves to write the word for 'open' because the hare's eyes always remain open, and so forth. Fantastic explanations of this type appealed all too readily to the medieval mind, and until the beginning of the nineteenth century the opinion persisted almost as an article of faith that the Egyptian hieroglyphs gave symbolic expression to recondite philosophical and religious doctrines. That erroneous opinion derived a new impetus from the learned speculations of the very man to whom the western world owes the revival of its interest in the Coptic language and literature. This was the Jesuit Athanasius Kircher, an accomplished Orientalist to whom was entrusted the translation of a Coptic-Arabic vocabulary brought home from Egypt by Pietro della Valle. Kircher's *Prodromus Coptus sive Aegyptiacus*, published in 1636, marks the beginning of a long sequence of books upon Coptic, a subject upon which no inconsiderable volume of information was available when at last scholars obtained the key to the decipherment of the hieroglyphs.[2] For this, however, the time was not yet ripe; and the theories of Kircher as to the content of the hieroglyphic inscriptions exceed all bounds in their

[1] F. Ll. Griffith, *Demotic Graffiti of the Dodecaschoenus*, p. 11.

[2] See the admirable account given by Ét. Quatremère, *Recherches sur la langue et la littérature de l'Égypte*, Paris, 1808.

imaginative folly. The cartouche of the Pharaoh Apries, encountered on a Roman obelisk, signifies to Kircher that 'the benefits of the divine Osiris are to be procured by means of sacred ceremonies and of the chain of the Genii, in order that the benefits of the Nile may be obtained'.

§ 10. The decipherment of the hieroglyphs.[1] Against such fruitless speculations the occasional acute observations of exceptional men like de Guignes, Warburton, and Carsten Niebuhr could avail but little in the absence of some definite clue to the decipherment of the ancient scripts. Such a clue was at last provided when some French soldiers, working on the foundations of a fortress at Rosetta, came across a trilingual inscription in Greek, demotic, and hieroglyphic (1799). This inscription, ever since famous under the name of the Rosetta stone, proved from its Greek portion to be a decree in honour of the young king Ptolemy Epiphanes, which the priests of Egypt caused to be erected in all the temples of the land (196 B.C.). Unhappily only a relatively small portion of the hieroglyphic text is preserved, and doubtless it was for this reason, though partly also on account of the symbolic nature then attributed to the hieroglyphs, that scholars first directed their attention towards the demotic section. The stone itself had passed into the hands of the English, but a copy remained with the celebrated French orientalist Silvestre de Sacy. After an abortive attempt of his own, de Sacy handed the copy on to the Swedish diplomatist Åkerblad, a man of considerable attainments at that time devoting himself to oriental researches in Paris. Within the short space of two months Åkerblad succeeded, by a comparison of the Greek and the demotic texts, in identifying in the latter all the proper names occurring in the former, besides recognizing, alphabetically written in their correct Coptic forms, the words for 'temples' and for 'Greeks', together with the pronominal suffix for 'him' and 'his'. In the *Lettre à Mr. de Sacy*, published in 1802, a first and most important step is taken towards the goal reached by Champollion just twenty years after. That Akerblad failed to make any further progress along the road where he had proved so admirable a pioneer was due to a prepossession from which he was unable to free himself; the words deciphered by him had been alphabetically written, and he therefore believed that the demotic writing was exclusively alphabetic.

The next great advance was due to an Englishman, no less a personage than the celebrated Thomas Young, the author of the undulatory theory of light. A man of deep learning and wide interests, Young was ever ready to try a new puzzle; so when in 1814 a copy of the Rosetta stone fell into his hands he attacked the problem with zest. While approving of Åkerblad's results so far as they went, he quickly realized that demotic teemed with signs that could not possibly be explained as

[1] See particularly A. ERMAN, *Die Entzifferung der Hieroglyphen* in *Sitzungsberichte der preussischen Akademie der Wissenschaften*, 1922; and an excellent article [by F. Ll. Griffith] in *The Times Literary Supplement*, 2 February 1922.

alphabetic. Further, he grasped the fact that the demotic and hieroglyphic systems of writing were intimately related. Noticing that the Greek section was full of words which repeated themselves, he used these as a basis for dividing up all three sections into their component words, and it was not long before his Greek-demotic vocabulary amounted to eighty-six groups, most of them correct, though his attempts to indicate the sounds of which they were composed and to adduce Coptic equivalents were as a rule mistaken. In 1816 he announced further discoveries obtained from material other than the Rosetta stone. He had now identified long passages on papyri (belonging to the 'Book of the Dead') written in hieroglyphic and in hieratic, and had so established the equivalence of the pictorial and cursive forms of the signs. He was certain that both demotic and hieroglyphic consisted largely of phonetic elements; and having demonstrated the fact, guessed long before by de Guignes and Zoega, that the 'cartouches' or 'royal rings' seen in the hieroglyphs contained the names of kings and queens, 'very ingeniously but rather luckily identified the cartouche of Berenice in addition to the known one of Ptolemy, and correctly suggested that another cartouche must be that of Manetho's Thuthmosis of the XVIIIth Dynasty. He also pointed out in hieroglyphic the alphabetic characters for *f* and *t*, and the "determinative" used in late texts for feminine names, and recognized from variants in the papyri that different characters could have the same powers—in short, the principle of homophony. All this was mixed up with many false conclusions, but the method pursued was infallibly leading to definite decipherment'.[1]

Meanwhile Jean François Champollion, the young French scholar who was destined to win immortal fame as the decipherer of the hieroglyphs, had as yet but few positive results to record. Born at Figeac in the Département du Lot on the 23rd December 1790, Champollion's interest in Egypt had awakened at a very early age. In his twelfth year he was already conversant with the rudiments of Hebrew and Arabic, and from that time onward his enthusiasm for things oriental, warmly encouraged by his elder brother Jacques Joseph Champollion-Figeac, never flagged. As a student at Grenoble he applied himself to the study of ancient history, together with Coptic and all alphabets and systems of writing which might lead him to his then already clearly perceived goal, the decipherment of the Rosetta stone. At the age of eighteen he became professor at the same university. A few years later his republican sympathies brought him into serious trouble. Banished from Grenoble, he returned in 1816 as a schoolmaster to his native town of Figeac. In 1817 he is back at Grenoble, conducting a school and serving as librarian of the local Academy of Sciences. These posts he lost in 1820, and sought refuge with his brother in Paris. Throughout this agitated period of his life, despite keen interests in other directions, Jean François was constantly adding to his store of Egyptian and Coptic

[1] Professor Griffith's verdict, in the article quoted above, p. 12, n. 1.

knowledge, ever and again trying new solutions of the problem; when at last the truth was borne in upon him with all the vividness of a revelation, his complete mastery of the available materials enabled him to extend his discoveries with a speed and a sureness far beyond the scope of any of his contemporaries.

Passing over Champollion's early writings, the first and most ambitious of which was the geographic portion, in two volumes, of a projected encyclopaedic work to be called *L'Égypte sous les Pharaons* (1814), we now turn our attention to the actual decipherment. Close study had brought him the conviction that the three kinds of Egyptian writing were mere modifications of one another, and when, in the summer of 1821, he printed his brochure on the hieratic script, he had no difficulty in converting the demotic groups known to him into hieratic, and thence into hieroglyphic. With the name of Ptolemy both in hieroglyphic and in demotic he was long since familiar from the Rosetta stone, and about this time he became acquainted with the demotic papyrus *Casati*, where he found and, as his biographer assures us, at once transcribed into hieroglyphs a name which he rightly conjectured to be that of Cleopatra. Confirmation of this conjecture was, however, for the moment missing. But only for the moment. In 1815 W. J. Bankes, exploring the temple of Philae, had discovered a base block covered with Greek inscriptions in honour of Ptolemy Physcon and the two Cleopatras, near to a fallen obelisk which appeared to have stood upon it. Both the base and the obelisk were transported to England in 1819 to adorn Mr. Bankes's park at Kingston Lacy. A lithograph of the Greek and hieroglyphic inscriptions was made for Bankes in 1821, and in the following January Letronne forwarded to Champollion a copy with Young's suggestion of Cleopatra scribbled by Bankes against the cartouche. It seems highly improbable that either on this occasion or previously Young's ingenious but unproven conjectures can have materially helped Champollion, or even have influenced him in any way; but his failure to state exactly what he knew of the Englishman's work has done untold harm, however unmerited, to Champollion's reputation.

Åkerblad had read the demotic name of Ptolemy alphabetically, and Champollion, though always inclined to hark back to his incompatible theory of the purely symbolic character of the hieroglyphs, had proved, by his identification of the demotic signs with those contained in the cartouche of Ptolemy [hieroglyphic cartouche], that the hieroglyphs also could, at least on occasion, be alphabetic. The values attached by him to the individual hieroglyphs were now confirmed by the cartouche of Cleopatra [hieroglyphic cartouche], for in both cartouches the signs [hieroglyph] for *p*, [hieroglyph] for *o*[1] and [hieroglyph] for *l*,

[1] The earlier stages of Egyptian, as we have seen (§ 7), do not indicate the vowels. Just as in the Hebrew writing of German employed by the German-Polish Jew the old semi-consonants *wāw* and *yōdh* are employed for *o* and *i* respectively, so too here the loop, originally *wꜣ* (see § 19 for this mode of transliteration), is secondarily employed for *o*. See *ÄZ.* 34, 54; also *Zeitschr. d. deutsch. Morgenl. Ges.* 77, 145–7.

were found standing in exactly the positions where they were to be expected. The sign ⌓ for *t* in 'Ptolemaios' differed, indeed, from the sign ⌓ which represented *t* in 'Cleopatra', but the discrepancy could be easily explained by the principle of homophony (the representation of the same sound by different signs), of which Champollion was well aware. For the rest, the two cartouches provided him with a number of other equivalences which could not fail to assist him in his search for further identifications. These the following months brought in unexpected abundance; among the cartouches successively transliterated and identified were those of Alexander, Berenice, Tiberius, Domitian, and Trajan, besides others containing such imperial titles as *Autocrator*, *Caesar*, and *Sebastos*.

The problem was thus solved so far as the cartouches of the Graeco-Roman period were concerned. But what of those belonging to the older times? Were the hieroglyphs of an earlier age also in part alphabetic, or were they wholly figurative, as Champollion had so often suspected? It must be remembered that he was far less well equipped with material for answering this question than many of his English contemporaries. It was on the 14th September 1822 that he received from the architect Huyot copies of bas-reliefs in Egyptian temples which finally dispelled his doubts. The first cartouche which he noticed was from a rock-temple at Abu Simbel between the first and second cataracts. In this cartouche (hieroglyphic cartouche) he at once recognized the two-fold ‖ familiar to him from his alphabet. Separated from this by a problematical sign was the circle of the 'sun', in Coptic *re*. The royal name Ramesses or Rameses flashed across his mind, as he read *re-?-s-s*. The possibility thus envisaged became a certainty a few minutes later, when on another sheet he observed the cartouche (hieroglyphic cartouche) with the ibis Thoth at its head and, following the ibis, the signs which he assumed to read *mes*. Surely this could be none other than the king Tuthmosis[1] of Manetho's Eighteenth Dynasty. Confirmation of the value of (hieroglyph) was soon found by him in the Rosetta stone, where this hieroglyph formed part of the group corresponding to the Greek *γενέθλια*, a word which at once suggested the Coptic *misi*, *mose* 'give birth'.

From that moment onward each day brought its new harvest. Champollion realized that there was no longer any reason for holding back his discoveries, and on the 29th September he read at the Academy his memorable *Lettre à M. Dacier relative à l'alphabet des hiéroglyphes phonétiques*. In this letter he characteristically makes no mention of his decipherment of the names Ramesses and Tuthmosis. Those discoveries, together with numberless others, were reserved for the marvellous *Précis du système hiéroglyphique*, which appeared in 1824. Prolonged visits to Turin and to Egypt filled no small part of the remainder of Champollion's short life. On the 4th March 1832 he died, at the early age of forty-one.

§ 11. The successors of Champollion. The collection of new materials and the

[1] More familiar to the general reader under the erroneous modern form Thothmes.

investigation of these left Champollion no time for setting forth a reasoned account of his conclusions, nor yet for forming pupils. Long before his death he had acquired a deep instinctive knowledge of the old Egyptian language; he could elicit with ease the meaning of most simple inscriptions and texts on papyri, and the whole perspective of Egyptian history lay clear before him. The posthumous grammar and dictionary appeared between 1836 and 1844, and though edited by Champollion-Figeac with the devotion of which the elder brother had shown himself so splendidly capable, sadly betrayed the lack of the master's revising hand. An unworthy scepticism as to the value of Champollion's achievement signalizes the years following his death. A new impetus was, however, given to the study of hieroglyphs by Richard Lepsius's *Lettre à M. le professeur H. Rosellini*, published at Rome in 1837. Here the eminent German scholar, whose colossal *Denkmäler aus Ägypten und Nubien* later supplemented the great publications of monuments by Champollion and Rosellini, submitted the decipherment to a penetrating and judicious re-examination and pronounced the foundations to be sound. Samuel Birch, whose first publications date from 1838, was an indefatigable translator and editor of hieroglyphic texts. His short but admirable *Dictionary of Hieroglyphics* (1867), printed in the fifth volume of Bunsen's work entitled *Egypt's Place in Universal History*, was at length succeeded by Heinrich Brugsch's far larger *Hieroglyphisch-Demotisches Wörterbuch* (vols. i–iv, 1867–8; supplement, vols. v–vii, 1880–2), which, even at the present time, retains a considerable value. Brugsch's philological work embraced all corners of the field, but his principal discoveries were in demotic, of which he may be considered the real pioneer (*Grammaire démotique*, 1855). In hieratic the greatest advances were made by Goodwin in England (1817–1878) and Chabas in France (1817–1882). In the latter country Emanuel de Rougé (1811–1872) was a brilliant translator of hieroglyphic texts and author of an important grammatical work. The late Sir Gaston Maspero, whose published work covers the years 1871–1916, had an admirable feeling for the civilization of Ancient Egypt, and his vast activities, extending over the entire range of the subject, make him the outstanding figure among the Egyptologists of two generations ago. The present survey deals with philology alone, but it would be wrong to omit all reference to the excavations which have added so greatly to the linguistic student's materials. Here the chief name is that of Mariette (1821–1881), whose excavations began in 1850; from 1884 onwards the late Sir Flinders Petrie brought new and stricter archaeological methods to bear; subsequently the Americans Reisner and Winlock improved even upon these.

It is, however, only during the last sixty years that our knowledge of the Egyptian language has come to rest upon a really scientific basis. The year 1880 saw the appearance of two grammars of the highest importance, the *Koptische Grammatik* of Ludwig Stern and the *Neuägyptische Grammatik* of Adolf Erman. The latter, which dealt with the vulgar dialect of the New Kingdom, was supplemented in 1889 by an elaborate study of the language of a papyrus containing stories written in Middle

Egyptian (*Die Sprache des Papyrus Westcar*). In 1894 appeared a little manual of Egyptian Grammar by Erman which long formed the indispensable guide for every beginner (English translation of the first edition, by J. H. Breasted, 1894; fourth German edition, 1928). The study of Coptic was greatly advanced by G. Steindorff's short grammar of the Ṣaʿîdic dialect (first edition, 1894; second edition, 1904). A yet more important contribution to Egyptian philology was Kurt Sethe's extensive and laborious treatise *Das ägyptische Verbum* (1899–1902), still a fundamental authority for verb-forms and for the general relationship of Egyptian to Coptic. The *Zeitschrift für ägyptische Sprache* served as a focus for new light thrown by Erman's pupils on the structure and details of the Egyptian language, but now, after the second world war, has come to a temporary standstill. In close sympathy with, though independent of, the work of the German school and its adherents in other lands were F. Ll. Griffith's remarkable successes in the palaeographical field; his decipherment of the cursive hieratic texts belonging to the Middle Kingdom and of the early demotic papyri opened up tracts thitherto unexplored. In the domain of demotic W. Spiegelberg proved the most prolific and serviceable editor of texts; in England Sir Herbert Thompson collaborated closely with F. Ll. Griffith in the publication of certain important papyri. Egyptian grammar made a brilliant advance with Battiscombe Gunn's *Studies in Egyptian Syntax*, Paris, 1924. As regards lexicography, Erman and his colleagues inaugurated in 1897 a vast enterprise of which a more extended account is called for. The *Wörterbuch der ägyptischen Sprache* promoted by the German Academies was to be based upon a collection of all words in all known inscriptions and manuscripts. The collection of the material, in the end amounting to more than a million and a half slips, was a task in which scholars from many different lands participated. Their part, however, necessarily terminated when the working out of results demanded the concentration of effort exclusively in Berlin. Erman, Sethe, and H. Grapow now remained as sole editors, and when the first-named became crippled with old age and failing eyesight and the second was claimed by other tasks, practically the whole responsibility came to rest on Grapow's shoulders. The last-named was fortunate in having the help of the Danish scholar Dr. (now Professor) Erichsen, to whose admirable handwriting we owe the five volumes of the *Wörterbuch* proper (1926–31). By a less fortunate decision, however, the publication of the all-important references to texts, later expanded into actual citations, was deferred until the skeleton of the whole should be complete. Down to 1940, when the last part appeared, these references (*Belegstellen*) had reached only to the end of the letter 𓉔 *h*, and the publication of the remainder is unpredictable. Lexicography thus constitutes our principal desideratum,[1] though for the final stage of the language an immense stride forward was made by W. E. Crum's great *Coptic Dictionary*, the title-page of which bears the date 1939.

[1] For further observations on this matter see A. H. GARDINER, *Ancient Egyptian Onomastica*, Oxford, 1947, vol. i, pp. xiii–xxi; also the article in *JEA*. vol. 34, pp. 12–18.

Until quite recently another urgent need was a handy selection of passages for study, since K. Sethe's widely used *Ägyptische Lesestücke* (*Texte des Mittleren Reiches*, 1924) is no longer available and is likely to have been a war-casualty, The place of this work has, however, now been taken by A. de Buck's *Egyptian Readingbook*, vol. I (Leyden, 1940).

In general, Egyptian philology has shown some progress since the first edition of the present work appeared, but not in the same degree or at the same speed as in the generation immediately preceding. In any case, we stand too close to the contributions which would have had to be recorded to make it desirable to bring this sketch further up to date.

D. BRIEF SURVEY OF EGYPTIAN LITERATURE

§ **12.** Throughout the entire course of history no people has been more afflicted with the *scribendi cacoethes* than the Egyptians. The decorative character of the hieroglyphic script and its close connexion with pictorial art made it a natural and handy medium of ornamentation. Hence in temple and tomb there is hardly a wall but bears hieroglyphic inscriptions, and even the common objects of daily life, such as toilet utensils, boxes, jewels, and weapons, often display the names and titles of their owners, or the cartouche of the Pharaoh under whom they were made. It would be tedious to enumerate all the types of inscription that have come down to us; but this Introduction may fitly include some account of those texts from which our knowledge of Egyptian grammar and literary style is derived. We shall confine our attention to the earlier periods and only the more important documents will be mentioned.[1]

§ **13. The religious literature.**[2] The oldest body of religious texts is the large collection of spells known as the **Pyramid Texts,**[3] since the most ancient and complete versions were discovered on the walls of chambers inside the pyramids of five kings of the Fifth and Sixth Dynasties. These texts, for the most part of very great antiquity, are exclusively concerned with the welfare of the dead king; they consist of incantations whereby his place in the sky and the other prerogatives of a dead king are assured to him; and they also incorporate the ritual which was recited in connexion

[1] The bibliographical references in the footnotes give only the best or the most easily accessible editions. Invaluable for inscriptions still *in situ* in Egypt is the *Topographical Bibliography of Ancient Egyptian Hieroglyphic Texts, Reliefs, and Paintings* by B. PORTER and R. L. B. MOSS, 6 vols., Oxford, 1927–39. A comprehensive guide to Egyptological books and articles down to 1941 is provided by IDA A. PRATT, *Ancient Egypt: Sources of Information in the New York Public Library*, 2 vols., New York, 1925 & 1942.

[2] A considerable collection of translations into German will be found in G. ROEDER, *Urkunden zur Religion des alten Ägypten*, in *Religiöse Stimmen der Völker, herausgegeben von Walter Otto*, Jena, 1915.

[3] KURT SETHE, *Die altägyptischen Pyramidentexte*, 4 vols., Leipzig, 1908–22; ID. (posthumously), *Übersetzung und Kommentar zu den Altägyptischen Pyramidentexten*, 4 vols., Glückstadt–Hamburg, no date. A handy, though not wholly reliable, vocabulary in L. SPELEERS, *Les textes des pyramides égyptiennes*, vol. ii., Brussels, 1924.

with the daily offerings made in the pyramid-temples. At a later date these texts were usurped for their own benefit by the nobles, and many excerpts are found written in the interiors of the large wooden coffins of Dyn. IX–XI.

The coffins just mentioned also contain an important collection of spells which are known specifically as the **Coffin Texts.**[1] These were composed on behalf of non-royal personages, and comprise incantations affording protection against hunger, thirst, and the manifold dangers of the netherworld, incantations for enabling the deceased to assume whatever forms he pleased, and incantations by virtue of which he could remain in the enjoyment of his former pastimes and partake of the society of his relatives and friends. The name of 'Coffin Texts' is reserved for those spells which are peculiar to the early coffins and do not recur later—not at least until the Saite period, when some of them were sporadically revived.

Other texts from the same source and of precisely the same nature constitute the nucleus and the earliest recension of a collection of texts to which Egyptologists have given the misleading name of the **Book of the Dead.** This is not really a book at all, but a heterogeneous assemblage of funerary spells of various dates, including also a few hymns to Rēʿ and Osiris, selections from which were written on papyrus and deposited in the tombs of most well-to-do Egyptians right down to the Roman period. The number of spells (wrongly called 'chapters') contained in individual copies, and the order in which they occur, vary greatly. The most complete 'Books of the Dead' belong to the Ptolemaic period, and count upwards of 150 spells, often embellished with vignettes. Fine specimens of rather less extent emanate from the tombs of the dignitaries of Dyns. XVIII–XIX; these are often admirably written and sumptuously illustrated in colour. It is thus convenient to distinguish three versions of the Book of the Dead: (1) the Middle Kingdom version, principally found on the early coffins;[2] (2) the New Kingdom version, consisting of papyri dating from the Eighteenth to the Twentieth Dynasties;[3] (3) the versions of the late period, from Dyn. XXI onwards.[4]

Other religious books, many of them very ancient, have survived only in copies

[1] Standard edition, still incomplete, A. de Buck, *The Egyptian Coffin Texts*, in *University of Chicago, Oriental Institute Publications*, 3 vols., Chicago, 1935–47. See too P. Lacau, *Sarcophages antérieurs au nouvel empire*, 2 vols., Cairo, 1904–6, in *Catalogue général des antiquités égyptiennes du musée du Caire*; P. Lacau, *Textes religieux égyptiens*, in *Recueil de Travaux*, vols. 26–34, also separately, Paris, 1910; besides other publications of less importance. The kind of writing employed for these texts may be seen in S. Birch, *Egyptian Texts of the Earliest Period from the Coffin of Amamu in the British Museum*, London, 1886.

[2] Being gradually incorporated into the work by de Buck cited in n. 1.

[3] The chief works, mostly in need of completion and revision, are: É. Naville, *Das ägyptische Todtenbuch der XVIII. bis XX. Dynastie*, 3 vols., Berlin, 1886; E. A. Wallis Budge, *The Book of the Dead: The Chapters of coming forth by Day*, 3 vols., London, 1898 (a later, rather fuller, re-edition, 1910); Id., *The Book of the Dead, Facsimiles*, &c., including complete text of the important papyrus of Nu, London, British Museum, 1899; É. Naville, *The Funeral Papyrus of Iouiya*, London, 1908; [E. Schiaparelli], *Relazione sui lavori della Missione . . . in Egitto*, Turin, [1927,] vol. ii, pp. 33–63 (the papyrus of Khaʿ); *Catalogue of Egyptian Religious Papyri in the British Museum*, [Part] I, by A. W. Shorter, London, 1938.

[4] The most famous of all is R. Lepsius, *Das Todtenbuch der Ägypter*, Leipzig, 1842.

of Dyn. XIX and even later. Such are the **Ritual of the Divine Cult,**[1] the spells accompanying the daily service performed in the temples of the gods, the most complete copies of which are found in the temple of Sethos I at Abydus. Of rather more limited extent is the **Ritual of the Funerary Cult,** the vignettes and texts of which are found in the tombs of many Theban nobles.[2] The tombs of the kings at Thebes bring to our knowledge four theological works of high importance: the **Book of what is in the Netherworld,**[3] often called the Am Duat, describing the strange regions and inhabitants visited by the sun-god during his nocturnal journey underground from west to east; the **Book of Gates**[4] and the **Book of Caverns,**[5] two other treatises dealing with the topography of the netherworld; and the so-called **Litany of the Sun.**[6] Of exceptional interest, though very corrupt, is an old magical text of which the most complete copies are found in the tombs of Sethos I and Ramesses III, recounting the **Destruction of Mankind**[7] by Rēʿ, the sun-god, and the establishment in the heavens of the celestial cow-goddess.

Hymns to the gods are found, not only in the Book of the Dead and on sepulchral stelae or grave-stones,[8] but also elsewhere. Some curious hymns to the snake-goddesses who were identified with the crowns of Pharaoh have been published by Erman from a papyrus of Dyn. XVII–XVIII formerly in the possession of M. Golénischeff.[9] Still earlier is a hymn to the crocodile-god Sobk (Greek Suchos) discovered in a tomb beneath the Ramesseum.[10] A hymn to the Nile is ancient, but very corrupt.[11] The hymns to Amen-Rēʿ on papyri in Cairo[12] and Leyden[13] are of

[1] Definitive copies of the scenes and texts in A. M. CALVERLEY and M. F. BROOME, *The Temple of King Sethos I at Abydos*, vols. i, ii, London, Egypt Exploration Society and Chicago, University of Chicago Press, 1933–5. See too A. MORET, *Le Rituel du culte divin journalier en Égypte*, Paris, 1902.

[2] N. DE G. DAVIES, *The Tomb of Rekh-mi-Rēʿ at Thebes*, New York, Metropolitan Museum of Art, 1943, vol. ii, Pls. 96–110. Other versions, E. SCHIAPARELLI, *Il libro dei funerali degli antichi Egiziani*, 3 vols., Turin, 1881–90.

[3] Earliest examples, P. BUCHER, *Les Textes des tombes de Thoutmosis III et d'Aménophis II*, vol. i, in *Mémoires de l'Institut Français d'Archéologie Orientale*, Cairo, 1932. Versions from later tombs, E. LEFÉBURE, *Les Hypogées royaux de Thèbes*, 3 parts, Paris, 1886–9, being *Annales du Musée Guimet*, vols. 9 and 16.

[4] CH. MAYSTRE and A. PIANKOFF, *Le Livre des Portes*, vol. i, in *Mémoires de l'Institut Français d'Archéologie Orientale*, Cairo, 1939–46.

[5] A. PIANKOFF, *Le Livre des Quererts*, extracted from *Bulletin de l'Institut Français d'Archéologie Orientale*, vols. 41–5, Cairo, 1946.

[6] É. NAVILLE, *La Litanie du Soleil*, Leipzig, 1875.

[7] CH. MAYSTRE, *Le Livre de la Vache du Ciel*, in *Bulletin de l'Institut Français d'Archéologie Orientale*, 40, 53–115; for the accompanying picture in the tomb of Sethos I see *JEA*. 28, Pl. 4.

[8] Those on stelae are collected in SÉLIM HASSAN, *Hymnes religieux du Moyen Empire*, Cairo, 1928.

[9] A. ERMAN, *Hymnen an das Diadem der Pharaonen*, Berlin, 1911, in *Abhandlungen der königl. Preuss. Akademie der Wissenschaften.*

[10] Still unpublished.

[11] G. MASPERO, *Hymne au Nil*, Cairo, 1912, in *Bibliothèque d'étude de l'Institut Français d'Archéologie Orientale*. A damaged duplicate text with numerous divergences in *P. Chester Beatty V*, rt. 1, 12–5, 5, published in A. H. GARDINER, *Hieratic Papyri in the British Museum*, Third Series, Pls. 23–4, London, 1935. An early Dyn. XVIII copy of the opening lines is on an unpublished writing-board now in the Ashmolean Museum, Oxford.

[Notes 12, 13, see p. 21.

later date; the latter indeed belongs to the border-line of the period covered by this book, as do also the wonderful hymns to the Aten[1] or Solar Disk inscribed in the tombs of El-Amarna and inspired by the heretic king Akhenaten (about 1373–1357 B.C.).

The **stelae** which all the larger collections of Egyptian antiquities possess in hundreds must here be mentioned.[2] Some record merely the names and titles of their dead owner and his relatives; but more frequently a stereotyped formula gives expression to his desire for funerary offerings, and this formula is often expanded in an interesting way, with adjurations to passers-by to recite the requisite words, or with enumerations of the benefits hoped for in the life after death. Scraps of autobiography or self-laudatory phrases are not infrequently appended.[3] Sometimes, as already noted, hymns to the gods take the place of the more usual texts.

The **magical papyri** in Turin, Leyden, and other collections are mostly later than the Eighteenth Dynasty,[4] though many of them doubtless represent much older archetypes. One collection of magical spells falls, however, well within our period;

[12] A. MARIETTE, *Les Papyrus égyptiens du Musée de Boulaq*, Cairo, 1871–2, II, 11–13.

[13] *Zeitschrift für ägyptische Sprache*, 42, 12–42.

[1] N. DE G. DAVIES, *The Rock Tombs of El Amarna*, especially vols. 4 and 6, in *Archaeological Survey of Egypt* published by the Egypt Exploration Society, London, 1903–8. Mainly excerpted thence in a convenient single volume, M. SANDMAN, *Texts from the Time of Akhenaten* (*Bibliotheca Aegyptiaca, VIII*), Brussels, 1938.

[2] The principal publications are as follows. Cairo: H. O. LANGE and H. SCHÄFER, *Grab- und Denksteine des Mittleren Reichs*, in *Catalogue général.... du musée du Caire*, 4 vols., Cairo, 1902–25. London: *Hieroglyphic Texts from Egyptian Stelae, &c., in the British Museum*, 8 parts, London, 1911–39. Paris: P. PIERRET, *Recueil d'inscriptions inédites du musée égyptien du Louvre*, 2 parts, Paris, 1874–8; A. GAYET, *Musée du Louvre: Stèles de la XIIe Dynastie*, in *Bibliothèque de l'École des Hautes Études*, Paris, 1886; A. MORET, *Catalogue du Musée Guimet, Galerie égyptienne*, 2 vols., Paris, 1909. Brussels: L. SPELEERS, *Recueil des inscriptions égyptiennes des Musées Royaux du Cinquantenaire à Bruxelles*, Brussels, 1923. Berlin: *Ägyptische Inschriften aus den königlichen Museen zu Berlin*, 2 vols., Leipzig, 1913–14. Vienna: W. WRESZINSKI, *Ägyptische Inschriften aus dem k. k. Hofmuseum in Wien*, Leipzig, 1906. Various German and Swiss Museums: *Ägyptische Grabsteine und Denksteine*, vol. i. *Karlsruhe, Mülhausen, Strassburg, Stuttgart*, by W. SPIEGELBERG and B. PÖRTNER; vol. ii. *München*, by K. DYROFF and B. PÖRTNER; vol. iii. *Bonn, Darmstadt, Frankfurt a. M., Genf, Neuchâtel*, by A. WIEDEMANN and B. PÖRTNER; Strassburg, 1902–6. Leyden: P. A. A. BOESER, *Beschreibung der ägyptischen Sammlung in Leiden: Die Denkmäler der Zeit zwischen dem alten und mittleren Reich und des mittleren Reiches: erste Abteilung, Stelen*, The Hague, 1909. Copenhagen: M. MOGENSEN, *Inscriptions hiéroglyphiques du musée national de Copenhague*, Copenhagen, 1918; O. KOEFOED-PETERSEN, *Les Stèles égyptiennes*, being *Publications de la Glyptothèque Ny Carlsberg*, No. 1, Copenhagen, 1948. Stockholm: M. MOGENSEN, *Stèles égyptiennes au musée national de Stockholm*, Copenhagen, 1919. Berkeley (Univ. of California): H. F. LUTZ, *Egyptian Tomb Steles and Offering Stones*, Leipzig, 1927. The stelae of many other museums, in Italy, Russia, &c., have likewise been published, but it has been necessary to confine this note to publications of primary importance. Two valuable works not restricted to any single collection are D. DUNHAM, *Naga-ed-Dêr stelae of the First Intermediate Period*, Boston (Museum of Fine Arts), 1937; J. J. CLÈRE and J. VANDIER, *Textes de la première période intermédiaire et de la XIème Dynastie* (*Bibliotheca Aegyptiaca, X*) Brussels, 1948.

[3] J. JANSSEN, *De traditioneele Egyptische autobiografie vóór het nieuwe rijk*, 2 vols., Leyden, 1946.

[4] Magical fragments of the late Middle Kingdom exist in the still unpublished Ramesseum papyri. Others written in Dyn. XIX belong to the Chester Beatty papyri referred to above, p. 20, n. 11.

it contains spells for the protection of mothers and their children.[1] It was the common belief that the dead could exercise a potent influence upon the fortunes of the living for good or evil; hence the letters addressed to deceased parents and other relatives which have been found upon earthenware vessels deposited in the tombs.[2] Likewise inscribed upon pots are denunciations of various foreign chieftains and others deemed hostile to Egypt;[3] and a fresh series of similar character has been discovered written upon actual images of the enemies in question.[4]

§ 14. Secular non-literary documents. Out of the practice of magic arose the science of medicine; some important **medical papyri** have survived.[5] The oldest pages, dating from the end of Dyn. XII, were found at Illahûn (wrongly known as Kahûn) and deal with gynaecological cases;[6] from the same place came fragments of a veterinary papyrus.[7] Far surpassing these in both size and interest are two magnificent manuscripts written at the beginning of Dyn. XVIII: the Ebers papyrus[8] gives instruction in the treatment of many maladies, besides describing the heart's action and explaining various medical terms; the Edwin Smith papyrus[9] is mainly concerned with wounds, but adds on the *verso* a number of magical and medical prescriptions of sundry kinds. Later than these is a well-preserved papyrus[10] showing marked affinity to the Ebers. To be assigned to the Nineteenth or Twentieth Dynasty are several other manuscripts[11] of which the archetypes were certainly many centuries earlier. This class of composition presents serious difficulties owing to the technical nature of its subject-matter; further obstacles to comprehension are the many unidentifiable names of drugs and diseases, not to speak of the probability of textual corruptions.

[1] A. Erman, *Zaubersprüche für Mutter und Kind*, in *Abhandlungen der königl. Preuss. Akademie der Wissenschaften*, Berlin, 1901.

[2] A. H. Gardiner and K. Sethe, *Egyptian Letters to the Dead*, London (Egypt Exploration Society), 1928. Other examples found later, *JEA.* 16, 19–22; 20, 157–69.

[3] K. Sethe, *Die Ächtung feindlicher Fürsten, Völker und Dinge auf altägyptischen Tongefässscherben des Mittleren Reiches*, in *Abhandlungen der Preuss. Akademie der Wissenschaften*, Berlin, 1926.

[4] G. Posener, *Princes et pays d'Asie et de Nubie*, Brussels, 1940.

[5] Convenient editions of the main texts by W. Wreszinski. General characterization, see H. Grapow, *Untersuchungen über die altägyptischen medizinischen Papyri*, Leipzig, 1935. Many details have been discussed by such scholars as V. Loret, F. von Oefele, B. Ebbell, and W. R. Dawson.

[6] F. Ll. Griffith, *Hieratic Papyri from Kahun and Gurob*, London, 1898, Pls. 5–6.

[7] *Op. cit.*, Pl. 7. The unpublished Ramesseum papyri (Dyn. XIII) contain fragments of three more medical texts, only one of which, however, shows any degree of completeness.

[8] G. Ebers, *Papyros Ebers*, 2 vols., Leipzig, 1875. Transcription of the whole into hieroglyphic, W Wreszinski, *Der Papyrus Ebers*, Leipzig, 1913.

[9] J. H. Breasted, *The Edwin Smith Surgical Papyrus*, 2 vols., Chicago, 1930.

[10] G. A. Reisner, *The Hearst Medical Papyrus*, Leipzig, 1905; transcribed in W. Wreszinski, *Der Londoner medizinische Papyrus und der Papyrus Hearst*, Leipzig, 1912.

[11] The largest are the London text published by Wreszinski (*op. cit.*) and one in Berlin edited in his work *Der grosse medizinische Papyrus des Berliner Museums*, Leipzig, 1909. Other more fragmentary examples in A. H. Gardiner, *Hieratic Papyri in the British Museum*, Third Series, London, 1935.

Several works on **mathematics** have been found; the two most important are the Rhind papyrus in the British Museum[1] and another in the Moscow collection.[2] The problems dealt with are all of a purely practical order, but in some cases involve a considerable degree of knowledge.

A **lexicographical** book emanating from the already-mentioned Ramesseum find contained lists of birds, animals, cereals, parts of an ox, geographical names, and the like, but the earlier portions are very fragmentary.[3]

The **legal** documents which have been preserved are less numerous than one might have expected. Some wills were discovered among the Illahûn papyri, as well as deeds of sale, census-lists, &c.[4] From the neighbouring site of Medînet Ghurâb come several agreements concerning the work of certain female slaves, together with the *procès-verbal* of a lawsuit connected with the same subject.[5] A more obscure document in which a female slave plays a prominent part[6] is interesting for its legal form and terminology, agreeing with those of a highly important stela discovered at Karnak more than twenty years ago, but unfortunately still unpublished;[7] this records the sale of the office of mayor at El-Kâb under an obscure king of Dyn. XVII. The only other *procès-verbal* of a lawsuit falling within our period dates from the reign of Tuthmosis IV and is very fragmentary.[8] A long inscription in a tomb at Asyûṭ (early Dyn. XII) records the arrangements made with the local priesthood for periodic funerary offerings to be made on behalf of the tomb-owner after his death, the text being set forth in a number of paragraphs well illustrating the character given to written contracts at this period.[9]

Of high importance for our knowledge of the **administration** of Egypt are a long inscription of Dyn. XVIII setting forth the duties of the vizier and a complementary text recording the advice given to the vizier[10] on the occasion of his appointment by the Pharaoh.[11] Earlier than the phase of the language covered by this book are the royal decrees, dating from the Old Kingdom, conferring upon the staffs of

[1] T. E. PEET, *The Rhind Mathematical Papyrus*, London, 1923; A. B. CHACE, *The Rhind Mathematical Papyrus*, 2 vols., Oberlin, Ohio, 1927.

[2] W. W. STRUVE, *Mathematischer Papyrus des staatlichen Museums der schönen Künste in Moskau*, Berlin, 1930; see too *Ancient Egypt*, 1917, 100–2; *JEA*. 15, 167–85. Fragments of similar treatises, GRIFFITH, *op. cit.*, Pl. 8; *Zeitschrift für ägyptische Sprache*, 38, 135–40; 40, 65–6.

[3] A. H. GARDINER, *Ancient Egyptian Onomastica*, 3 vols., Oxford, 1947; the Ramesseum Onomasticon, vol. i, pp. 6–23; vol. iii, Pls. 1–6.

[4] GRIFFITH, *op. cit.*

[5] *Zeitschrift für ägyptische Sprache*, 43, 27–45.

[6] P. C. SMITHER, *The Report concerning the Slave-girl Senbet*, in *JEA*. 34, 31–4.

[7] Cairo 52453, see *Bulletin de l'Institut Français d'Archéologie Orientale*, 30, 891.

[8] P. Mook, see *Zeitschrift für ägyptische Sprache*, 63, 105–15.

[9] F. LL. GRIFFITH, *The Inscriptions of Siûṭ and Dêr Rîfeh*, London, 1889, Pls. 6–8; translation and discussion by G. Reisner, *JEA*. 5, 79–98.

[10] N. DE G. DAVIES, *The Tomb of Rekh-mi-Rēʿ at Thebes*, two vols., New York (Metropolitan Museum of Art), 1943; the texts, vol. ii, Pls. 26–8, 119–22; translation, vol. i, pp. 88–94.

[11] *Op. cit.*, the texts, vol. ii, Pls. 14–15, 116–18; translation, vol. i, pp. 84–8.

various temples[1] immunity from external interference. Dispatches passing between the Capital and certain officials stationed in the fortresses of the Second Cataract throw light upon sides of Egyptian official life not illustrated elsewhere.[2] Many fragments of account-books and the like have been found, the most interesting being a journal detailing the distributions of food made at the court of a king Sebkḥotpe of Dyn. XIII,[3] the records of a royal dockyard of the time of Tuthmosis III,[4] and some apparently related accounts on two papyri at Leningrad[5] and on two others in the Louvre.[6]

A large number of **private letters** exist, some dating back as far as Dyn. VI. The finest of all, still unpublished, were discovered by H. Winlock in a Dyn. XI tomb at Thebes and deal with the agricultural and domestic interests of one Ḥeḳanakhte and various associates and relatives of his.[7] Many more come from Illahûn and belong to the second half of Dyn. XII.[8] Curiously few letters of Dyn. XVIII have come to hand, but a series of six, all centring round the person of a scribe named ʿAhmosĕ, well illustrate the epistolary style of the period.[9]

Turning now to **historical records**[10] of one kind and another, the earliest of these are the private autobiographies from the tombs and the royal decrees just mentioned; of great interest also are the inscriptions left by the leaders of expeditions to distant mines or quarries such as those of Sinai[11] and the Wâdy Ḥammâmât.[12] It is not until the end of Dyn. XII that official monuments with historical texts really

[1] R. WEILL, *Les Décrets royaux de l'ancien empire égyptien*, Paris, 1912. Additional examples, edited by W. C. HAYES, see *JEA.* 32, 3–23.

[2] P. C. SMITHER, *The Semnah Dispatches, loc. cit.*, 31, 3–10.

[3] A. MARIETTE, *Les Papyrus égyptiens du Musée de Boulaq*, 2 vols., Paris, 1871–2: No. 18, completely transcribed with commentary by A. SCHARFF in *Zeitschrift für ägyptische Sprache*, 57, 51–72, and autographed pages 1–24**.

[4] Edited by S. R. K. GLANVILLE in *op. cit.*, 66, 105–21; 68, 7–41.

[5] On the (so-called) *verso* of *Pap. Leningrad 1116 A* and *B* in the publication cited below p. 24*a*, n. 4.

[6] *Pap. Louvre 3226*, published in H. BRUGSCH, *Thesaurus Inscriptionum aegyptiacarum*, Leipzig, 1883–91 (vol. v), 1079–1118.

[7] Sole consecutive account as yet, *Bulletin of the Metropolitan Museum of Art: The Egyptian Expedition, 1921–1922*, pp. 36–49.

[8] GRIFFITH, *Hieratic Papyri from Kahun and Gurob*, Pls. 27–37. From later finds, A. SCHARFF, *Briefe aus Illahun*, in *Zeitschrift für ägyptische Sprache*, 59, 20–51, and autographed pages 1–12.

[9] Those in the Louvre edited by T. E. Peet in *JEA.* 12, 70–4, those in the British Museum by S. R. K. Glanville, *JEA.* 14, 294–312.

[10] A convenient but incomplete collection of the texts, *Urkunden des ägyptischen Altertums herausgegeben von Georg Steindorff*; the historical texts edited by K. SETHE: *Abt. I, Urkunden des alten Reiches*, 2nd ed., Leipzig, 1932–3; *Abt. IV, Urkunden der 18. Dynastie* (4 vols. to end Tuthmosis III), Leipzig, 1906–9 (vol. i, 2nd ed., 1930); *Abt. VII, Urkunden des mittleren Reiches*, one part only, 1933. For Dyn. XI, see above, p. 21, n. 2, end. Many pieces are given also in the reading-books of K. Sethe and A. de Buck (p. 18, top). For translations see J. H. BREASTED, *Ancient Records of Egypt*, 5 vols., Chicago, 1906–7.

[11] A. H. GARDINER and T. E. PEET, *The Inscriptions of Sinai, Part I*, London (Egypt Exploration Fund), 1917; a revised and enlarged edition is being prepared by J. Černý.

[12] J. COUYAT and P. MONTET, *Inscriptions hiéroglyphiques et hiératiques du Ouadi Hammâmât*, in *Mémoires . . . . de l'Institut Français d'Archéologie Orientale du Caire*, 2 vols., Cairo, 1912–13.

begin; among the oldest are some boundary-stones erected by Sesostris III at Semnah in the Second Cataract. In Dyn. XVIII such monuments become frequent; they record either warlike campaigns or the dedication of great buildings to the gods; particularly valuable are the many texts of the kind which Tuthmosis III caused to be placed in the temple of Karnak.

§ 15. **The literature of the early periods.**[1] Several **stories** have been preserved to us from the Middle Kingdom. The masterpiece is the tale of Sinūhe,[2] an official at the court of Ammenemes I, who, overhearing the news of the murder of that king, fled away in panic to Palestine; there he rose to a position of great influence, but in old age was overcome by longing for his Egyptian home; his pardon and return to the royal palace are recounted with great vivacity and humour. Another book tells how a peasant of the Wâdy Naṭrûn, the oasis nearest to Egypt, is robbed of his asses whilst on his way to that land; he complains to the high steward of the king, and with such eloquence, that the high steward is ordered to detain him and to make him talk; in the end the peasant's petitions are reported to the king and the wrong inflicted is made good.[3] The romance of travel finds expression for the first time in the story of a shipwrecked sailor who is cast upon a wonderful island where a kindly serpent holds sway.[4] Of more popular character is an unfortunately mutilated book of tales relating wonderful events which happened in the reigns of the Pharaohs Djoser, Nebka, Snofru, and Cheops; the last tale of the four contains a legend of the origin of the Fifth Dynasty.[5] A fragment seems to deal with the fortunes of a cowherd who was tempted in the marshes by a goddess in human shape.[6]

Didactic treatises containing wise maxims and proverbial truths were greatly to the taste of the Egyptians. The earliest complete example of such a *sbōyet* or 'instruction' is ascribed to the vizier Ptaḥḥotpe who lived under Asosi of the Fifth

[1] See A. Erman, *The Literature of the Ancient Egyptians*, translated by A. M. Blackman, London, 1927; G. Lefebvre, *Romans et Contes égyptiens*, Paris, 1949; most of the texts mentioned below are translated in one or both of these important books, so that no further references to them will be given. Three stories have been translated also by B. Gunn in B. Lewis, *Land of Enchanters*, London, 1948.

[2] A. H. Gardiner, *Die Erzählung des Sinuhe und die Hirtengeschichte*, Leipzig, 1909, in *Literarische Texte des mittleren Reiches, herausgegeben von A. Erman*; also Id., *Notes on the Story of Sinuhe*, Paris, 1916. The text also in A. M. Blackman, *Middle-Egyptian Stories*, Part I (*Bibliotheca Aegyptiaca, II*), Brussels, 1932.

[3] F. Vogelsang and A. H. Gardiner, *Die Klagen des Bauern*, Leipzig, 1908, in *Literarische Texte des mittleren Reiches, herausgegeben von A. Erman*; also F. Vogelsang, *Kommentar zu den Klagen des Bauern*, Leipzig, 1913, in K. Sethe, *Untersuchungen zur Geschichte und Altertumskunde Ägyptens*, vol. 6. Translation by A. H. Gardiner in *JEA*. 9, 5–25.

[4] [W. Golénischeff], *Les Papyrus hiératiques, Nos. 1115, 1116 A et 1116 B de l'Ermitage Impérial à St.-Pétersbourg*, 1913, Pls. 1–8. Transcription, translation, and notes by A. Erman in *Zeitschrift für ägyptische Sprache*, 43, 1–26; the text also W. Golénischeff, *Le Conte du Naufragé*, Cairo, 1912, in *Bibliothèque d'étude de l'Institut Français d'Archéologie Orientale*; A. M. Blackman, *op. cit.*, pp. 41–8.

[5] See A. Erman, *Die Märchen des Papyrus Westcar*, Berlin, 1890, being *Mittheilungen aus den Orientalischen Sammlungen*, part 5.

[6] Published in the book mentioned above in note 2.

Dynasty, and contains advice, much of it unfortunately obscure, which might serve his son in his administrative career.[1] The same papyrus preserves the remains of similar counsels addressed by a vizier of the Third Dynasty to his children, of whom one, named Kagemni, followed him in his high office.[2] A book that enjoyed immense popularity in the schools, but which has come down to us only in a late and impossibly corrupt version, is the 'Instruction of Akhtoy, the son of Duauf'; here the various trades and professions are reviewed, and the conclusion is drawn that the occupation of scribe alone confers dignity and staves off misery.[3] Two kings left 'instructions' as a legacy to their successors; no book was more admired than the 'Instruction of Ammenemes I', the literary testament of a Pharaoh of great achievements who appears in a dream to his successor Sesostris I and recounts the story of his assassination and of the ingratitude with which his favours had been rewarded.[4] Of no less interest is the advice given to his son and heir Merikarēʿ by a Ninth Dynasty king whose name is lost; here much stress is laid on piety and reference is made to various historical events.[5] The actual authorship of the various works above mentioned is of course open to doubt, the more so since the Egyptians' love of ancient attributions is amply attested in the medical writings and the Book of the Dead.

A related group of texts is best described under the name of **pessimistic literature.** This kind of literature seems to have sprung up under the influence of the catastrophes which overwhelmed Egypt at the close of the Sixth Dynasty, bringing in their train centuries of social upheaval and political disruption. The key-note is one sounded by the conservatives and aristocrats of all ages: wickedness and misery are everywhere rife, and the poor have usurped the place of the rich. Such a book of laments is that of the prophet Ipuwēr, who none the less seems able to descry the dawning of a happier day.[6] Another prophetic book predicts the coming of king Ameny (i.e. Ammenemes I, the founder of Dyn. XII); the supposed speaker is a sage of the time of Snofru (Dyn. IV) named Neferroḥu.[7] One Khakheperraʿsonb, a priest of Heliopolis, is yet another critic of his own age, who naïvely voices his desire for original phraseology and new expressions wherewith to unburden

[1] G. JÉQUIER, *Le Papyrus Prisse et ses variantes*, Paris, 1911; E. DÉVAUD, *Les Maximes de Ptahhotep*, Fribourg, 1916.

[2] Transcription and translation by A. H. Gardiner in *JEA.* 31, 71–4.

[3] H. BRUNNER, *Die Lehre des Cheti, Sohnes des Duauf*, in *Ägyptologische Forschungen herausgegeben von Alexander Scharff*, Heft 13, Glückstadt–Hamburg, 1944.

[4] G. MASPERO, *Les Enseignements d'Amenemhaît Ier à son fils Sanouasrît Ier*, Cairo, 1914, in *Bibliothèque d'étude de l'Institut Français d'Archéologie Orientale*; A. VOLTEN, *Zwei altägyptische politische Schriften*, in *Analecta Aegyptiaca*, vol. iv, Copenhagen, 1945, pp. 82–128. See too the article by B. Gunn in *JEA.* 27, 2–6.

[5] *Pap. Leningrad 1116 A*, recto, [W. GOLÉNISCHEFF], *op. cit.*, Pls. 9–14, Suppl. A–C; A. VOLTEN, *op. cit.*, pp. 3–81. Also translated by A. H. Gardiner in *JEA.* 1, 20–36.

[6] A. H. GARDINER, *The Admonitions of an Egyptian Sage*, Leipzig, 1909.

[7] *Pap. Leningrad 1116 B*, recto, see [W. GOLÉNISCHEFF], *op. cit.*, Pls. 23–5, Suppl. C–D. Translated by A. H. Gardiner in *JEA.* 1, 100–6.

his troubled heart.[1] A composition of a very unusual type is the dialogue between a man weary of life and his own soul;[2] in stanzas of considerable beauty the man describes his disgust at the world he lives in and his longing for death, but he is haunted by the fear lest in seeking a voluntary death he may be deserted by his soul; the arguments on both sides are full of obscurity, but the soul appears to give way in the end, won over by the man's plea that the dead have power, like gods, to chastise the evil of the world they have left.

Of **secular poetry** little remains. Some hymns to Sesostris III[3] well illustrate the use of the refrain and the penchant felt by the Egyptian writers for a rhythmical parallelism of members. Music and song were the regular accompaniment of every banquet, but the legends written beside the figures sculptured on the tomb-walls seldom give more than the opening words. In the tomb of Neferḥotpe at Thebes a harper urges his listeners to eat, drink, and be merry, for death is the common lot and none may tell what lies beyond.[4] On the opposite wall such cynicism is sternly rebuked:[5] is not the West the universal home, where all may find rest and where wrangling is no more? The Nineteenth Dynasty has bequeathed to us some tender little love-songs;[6] of these a few may well belong to the Middle Kingdom.

To sum up, what has survived to us from the literature of Early Egypt is but a small selection of fortuitous samples. We are fortunate enough to possess a few of those writings by which the Egyptians themselves laid most store; but the study of other books of which we have but single copies, and which may therefore be conjectured to have enjoyed less celebrity, shows that the ancient taste differed considerably from our own, and that possibly many works in which we could find real poetic beauty have been lost through lack of appreciation at the time they were written. The best characteristics of Egyptian literary art are its directness, its love of the picturesque, and its sense of humour; the worst defects are a leaning towards bombast, a monotony in the metaphors used, and a very limited range of sentiment. The impression with which we are left is that of a pleasure-loving people, gay, artistic, and sharp-witted, but lacking in depth of feeling and in idealism.

[1] British Museum 5645, published as an appendix in A. H. GARDINER, *Admonitions*, see above, n. 6.

[2] A. ERMAN, *Gespräch eines Lebensmüden mit seiner Seele*, in *Abhandlungen der königl. preuss. Akademie der Wissenschaften*, Berlin, 1896; A. SCHARFF, *Der Bericht über das Streitgespräch eines Lebensmüden mit seiner Seele*, in *Sitzungsberichte der Bayerischen Akademie der Wissenschaften*, Munich, 1937. For the conclusion see the article by H. Junker in *Anzeiger der phil.-hist. Klasse der Österreichischen Akademie der Wissenschaften*, 1948, Nr. 17.

[3] F. LL. GRIFFITH, *Hieratic Papyri from Kahun and Gurob*, London, 1898, Pls. 1–3.

[4] For this and other such poems see now M. LICHTHEIM, *The Songs of the Harpers*, in *Journal of Near Eastern Studies*, iv. 178–212.

[5] A. H. GARDINER, *In Praise of Death*, in *Proceedings of the Society of Biblical Archaeology*, 35, 165–9.

[6] W. MAX MÜLLER, *op. cit.* Important new examples in A. H. GARDINER, *The Chester Beatty Papyri, No. 1*, London, 1931, ch. 3.

EXTRACTS ADAPTED FROM ORIGINAL EGYPTIAN TEXTS AND USED AS READING-LESSONS

LESSON I

§ 16. **Direction of writing.**—Hieroglyphic inscriptions consist of rows of miniature pictures arranged in vertical columns or horizontal lines. These columns or lines, as well as the individual signs within them, read usually from right to left, but more seldom, and then only for special reasons, from left to right. In spite of the preference shown by the Egyptians for the direction from right to left, that from left to right has been adopted in modern printed books on grounds of practical convenience.

The signs that represent persons, animals, and birds, as well as other signs that have fronts and backs, almost always face the beginning of the inscription in which they occur, so that the direction in which this is to be read is but rarely in doubt.[1] For example, the words [hieroglyphs] must be read from left to right because the birds, men, kid, and basket with handle all face toward the left.

Upper has precedence over lower, both as regards lines of hieroglyphs and as regards the signs within the lines. Thus in the word [hieroglyphs] the order of the signs is [hieroglyph] + [hieroglyph] + [hieroglyph] + [hieroglyph] + [hieroglyph] + [hieroglyph] + [hieroglyph].

[1] Exceptions occur in vertical columns, but affect only the order of these, not the signs within them; exx. *P. Kah.* 7; MAR. *Karn.* 16; *Rekh.* 2. 9.

Here is a short inscription written in all four possible ways. The arrows show the direction in which the writing is to be read in each case; the letters give the order of the lines; the numbers indicate the sequence of the individual signs.

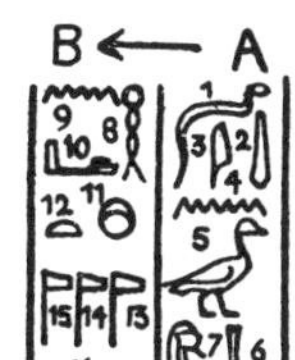

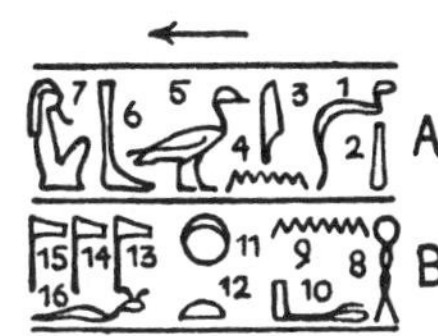

Note the effort that is made to arrange the hieroglyphs symmetrically and without leaving unsightly gaps. Observe, further, that no divisions are marked between the individual words.

§ 17. **Phonograms** or **sound-signs** (§ 6, 2) are of three kinds:

1. **Uniliteral** or **alphabetic** signs, representing single consonants. Exx. [hieroglyph] *f*; [hieroglyph] *r*.

2. **Biliteral** signs, or combinations of two consonants. Exx. [hieroglyph] *m*+*n* (or more briefly *mn*); [hieroglyph] *p*+*r* (*pr*). See below, § 31.

3. **Triliteral** signs, or combinations of three consonants. Exx. [hieroglyph] *n*+*f*+*r* (*nfr*); [hieroglyph] *ḥ*+*t*+*p* (*ḥtp*). See below, § 42.

These three kinds of phonograms will receive detailed consideration in turn. The most important, as being the most frequent of occurrence, are the uniliteral or alphabetic signs (§ 18).

[1] See SETHE, *Alphabet* and the Sign-list at the end of this book.

§ **18**. The **alphabet**[1] is shown in the adjoining table (p. 27). How the Egyptians named their letters is unknown; the student will find it convenient to refer to them in terms, partly of the sounds which they approximately represent (column 4 of the table), partly of the objects which they depict (column 3); thus 𓊃 is called 'bolt *s*'; 𓈖 is '*n*'; 𓄿 is 'the vulture'.

For transliteration into English writing, the symbols given in the second column should be used; these are our own letters differentiated by diacritical points or marks wherever the sounds to be indicated are unknown to English or would there have to be represented by more than one letter.

The remarks in column 5 should be carefully read, though the comparisons with Hebrew and Arabic letters will be of interest only to students acquainted with Semitic languages.

[2] See *ÄZ.* 34, 51–62.

§ **19**. **On transliteration.**[2]—As in other languages, words in Egyptian were made up of sounds partly consonantal and partly vocalic; but, as explained in the Introduction (§ 7), hieroglyphic writing consistently ignored and omitted the vowels. Thus the two signs 𓅱𓋴 might in effect represent *was, wes, ews, awsa* or any other combinations of vowels with *w*+*s* which the language permitted. Since we are thus as a rule ignorant of the actual pronunciation of early Egyptian words, the only mode of transliteration that can be regarded as strictly scientific is a mode which renders the consonants alone; therefore in most recent books on hieroglyphs 𓅱𓋴 will be found transliterated simply *ws*, without reference to the particular vocalization attaching to those consonants in each individual word.

A little practice will accustom the serious student even to such uncouth transliterations as *ḥnꜥ*, *ꜥḏꜣ*, *wiꜣ*, or *ꜥꜣ*; but since he will need sometimes to refer orally to the words thus rendered into modern written characters, a convenient method of pronunciation must also be devised. The course usually adopted is to use the English vowel *e* in every case except where the consonants *ꜣ* and *ꜥ* occur; in those two cases *a* (pronounced as in French) is substituted for *e*. Thus the following pronunciations are obtained: *men* for *mn*, *djed* for *ḏd*, *sedjem* for *sḏm*, *nefret* for *nfrt*; but *ḥena* for *ḥnꜥ*, *adja* for *ꜥḏꜣ*, *weya* for *wiꜣ* and *aa* for *ꜥꜣ*. Individual teachers have their own methods of pronunciation, but the method just described is probably as good as any, and is recommended here. In order to help the beginner, vocalized transliterations of the kind just indicated have been added to the purely consonantal transliterations in the vocabularies accompanying the first two lessons. Thus '𓐍𓏏 *ḫt* ("chet") thing' must be understood as meaning that the Egyptian word 𓐍𓏏, having the signification 'thing', is to be transliterated in writing as *ḫt*, but may be pronounced conventionally 'chet', with 'ch' as in Scotch 'loch', see the alphabet, column 4. *But it must never be*

THE ALPHABET

SIGN	TRANS-LITERATION	OBJECT DEPICTED	APPROXIMATE SOUND-VALUE	REMARKS
	ꜣ	Egyptian vulture	the glottal stop heard at the commencement of German words beginning with a vowel, ex. *der Adler*.	corresponds to Hebrew א *'āleph* and to Arabic أ *'alif hamzatum*.
	ỉ	flowering reed	usually consonantal *y*; at the beginning of words sometimes identical with ꜣ.	corresponds to Hebrew י *yōdh*, Arabic ي *yā*.
(1) (2) \\	*y*	(1) two reed-flowers (2) oblique strokes	*y*	used under specific conditions in the last syllable of words, see § 20.
	ꜥ	forearm	a guttural sound unknown to English	corresponds to Hebrew ע *ꜥayin*, Arabic ع *ꜥain*.
	w	quail chick	*w*	
	b	foot	*b*	
□	*p*	stool	*p*	
	f	horned viper	*f*	
	m	owl	*m*	
	n	water	*n*	corresponds to Hebrew נ *nūn*, but also to Hebrew ל *lāmedh*.
	r	mouth	*r*	corresponds to Hebrew ר *rēsh*, more rarely to Hebrew ל *lāmedh*.
	h	reed shelter in fields	*h* as in English	corresponds to Hebrew ה *hē*, Arabic ه *hā*.
	ḥ	wick of twisted flax	emphatic *h*	corresponds to Arabic ح *ḥā*.
	ḫ	placenta (?)	like *ch* in Scotch *loch*	corresponds to Arabic خ *ḫā*.
	ẖ	animal's belly with teats	perhaps like *ch* in German *ich*	interchanging early with *š*, later with *ḫ*, in certain words.
(1) (2)	*s*	(1) bolt (2) folded cloth	*s*	originally two separate sounds: (1) *z*, much like our *z*; (2) *ś*, unvoiced *s*.
[1]	*š*	pool	*sh*	early hardly different from *ẖ*.
	ḳ	hill-slope	backward *k*; rather like our *q* in *queen*	corresponds to Hebrew ק *qōph*, Arabic ق *ḳāf*.
	k	basket with handle	*k*	corresponds to Hebrew כ *kaph*, Arabic ك *kāf*. Written in hieratic.
	g	stand for jar	hard *g*	
	t	loaf	*t*	
	ṯ	tethering rope	originally *tsh* (*č* or *tj*)	during Middle Kingdom persists in some words, in others is replaced by *t*.
	d	hand	*d*	
	ḏ	snake	originally *dj* and also a dull emphatic *s* (Hebrew צ)	during Middle Kingdom persists in some words, in others is replaced by *d*.

OBS. Later alternative forms are for *w*, for *m*, for *n*, and for *t*. Of these, arose from an abbreviated form of in Middle Kingdom hieratic, so that it appears in our transcriptions of hieratic texts belonging to a time when was not yet written in hieroglyphic;[2] and originate in the biliteral signs for *ỉm*[3] and *tỉ* respectively, while is taken from the word *nt* 'crown of Lower Egypt'.[4] Note also that is used for *g* in a few old words.

[1] The form usually employed in printed books is not found on the monuments until a quite late period; early detailed forms are and . [2] *ÄZ.* 29, 47. [3] As *m* not before Tuthmosis I, *ÄZ.* 35, 170. [4] Already sporadically as *n* from early XII Dyn., ex. PETRIE, *Gizeh and Rifeh* 13*g*.

forgotten that the vocalizations thus provided are purely artificial makeshifts and bear little or no relation, so far as the vowels are concerned, to the unknown original pronunciations as heard and spoken by the Egyptians themselves.

OBS. By an elaborate process of inference scholars have succeeded in determining from the Coptic the position and the quantity of the original vowels in a large number of words; but the quality is far less easily ascertainable.[1]

[1] See particularly *Verbum*, vol. I; also below, Appendix A.

In this book 𓋴, originally unvoiced *s* (*ś*), and 𓊃, originally more like *z* than the *s* by which it is usually transliterated, will both be consistently transliterated as *s*, since the two sounds had undoubtedly become fused by the time of the Middle Kingdom; only when it is required to indicate the original sounds, will *ś* be used for 𓋴 and *z* for 𓊃.

In many Middle Egyptian words 𓆓 *ḏ* had already obtained the value of 𓂧 *d*, and 𓍿 *ṯ* the value of 𓏏 *t*, as is proved by the occasional substitution of 𓂧 for original 𓆓, and of 𓏏 for original 𓍿. These changes of sound were, however, confined to certain words, and it is advisable always to transliterate written 𓆓 as *ḏ* and written 𓍿 as *ṯ*, even where we chance to know that these signs were sounded as *d* and *t* respectively. For 𓍿 *ṯ* with a tick see Sign-list, under V 14.

The hieroglyphs 𓐍 *ḫ* and 𓄡 *ẖ* interchange, but much more rarely than the consonants mentioned in the last two paragraphs. They must be distinguished carefully in transliteration.

𓉔 *h* and 𓎛 *ḥ*, like 𓎡 *k* and 𓈎 *ḳ*, represent quite distinct sounds, and must never be confused.

OBS. 1. It follows from what has been said that biliteral and triliteral signs containing an original *ḏ* and *ṯ* should be transliterated with these letters unless accompanied by alphabetic *d* or *t*. Thus 𓇅 is read *wḏ* except in such a form as 𓇅𓅱𓂧𓂧𓏏 *wddt* and 𓊹 is read *nṯr* except in such a writing as 𓊹𓏏𓂋𓏏𓁐 *ntrt*.

OBS. 2. In Dyn. XVIII and even earlier, 𓆓 and 𓍿 are sometimes found for original 𓂧 *d* and 𓏏 *t* by a kind of false archaism. Exx. 𓇅𓅱𓆓𓎛𓅱 *wḏḥw* for *wdḥw* 'table of offerings';[2] 𓍿𓈖 *ṯn* for *tn* 'this' (f.).[3]

OBS. 3. Suffixes which are, or once have been, independent words are in this book preceded by a dot, ex. 𓋴𓐙𓅓𓏏𓅱𓆑 *sḏm·tw·f* 'he is heard', originally 'one (*tw*) hears (*sḏm*) him (*f*)'. A hyphen is used only in compound words, exx. 𓂋𓉐 *r-pr* 'temple'; 𓇋𓏠𓈖𓊵𓏏𓊪 *'Imn-ḥtp* 'Amenḥotpe', a man's name. Grammatical endings like the *t* of the feminine are not marked as such in transliteration, ex. 𓅭𓏏𓁐 *s3t* 'daughter'.[4]

[2] *Bersh.* i. 12, right; 34. Sim. *ḏrp* for *drp*, *Siut* 4, 27.

[3] *Urk.* iv. 648, 12. So *nṯ* for *nt* 'of' (f.), *Kopt.* 8, 4. 7. 12; *ṯw* for *tw* 'one', *Amrah* 29, 5.

[4] See GUNN, *Stud.* p. x.

§ 20. Semi-vowels and weak consonants.

—The hieroglyphs 𓇋 *ỉ* and 𓅱 *w* are consonant-signs, but the consonants represented by them being closely related to the vowels *i* and *u* respectively, they exhibit peculiarities in their employment which entitle them to the appellation of **semi-vowels.** Indeed, the Egyptians seem to have regarded them, except at the beginning of words, as but little more essential than the unwritten vowels, and they are therefore frequently omitted in hieroglyphic writing. This is particularly true of grammatical endings, though full writings might there have appeared indispensable for the avoidance of ambiguity. For example: *ḏdw* means 'speaking', a masculine participle, but this is very often written summarily as *ḏd*; the same writing *ḏd* is also, however, the proper form of the infinitive *ḏd* 'to say'.

Here we touch upon one of the principal sources of difficulty in the interpretation of Egyptian texts. Summary writings are so much commoner than full ones, that grammatical distinctions are obliterated and become a mere matter of inference. When, in a given context, the beginner is told that a form written *ḏd* is to be understood as *ḏdw*, he should take this assertion on trust until such time as he is able to appreciate or criticize the reasons which prompted it.

is transliterated *ỉ* because it seems, from the start, to have possessed two sound-values in Egyptian: 1, *y* or *ị* like י *yōdh* in Hebrew, ex. *ỉꜥḥ* 'moon', Hebrew יָרֵחַ, Coptic ⲓⲟϩ; 2, *ꜣ*, ex. *ink*, 'I', Hebrew אָנֹכִי, sometimes written in the Pyramid Texts.

y is barely found as initial letter in Middle Egyptian except in the interjection *yḥ* 'hey' (§ 258).[1] Elsewhere it is employed only in grammatical endings corresponding to *ỉỉ* or simply *ỉ* in Old Egyptian. Whereas can occur either as last letter or as last but one, exx. masc. *mry* 'beloved', fem. *mryt*, (less often) can occupy only the last place;[2] there it has the value *y* of *ỉ*, which it sometimes replaces, ex. *Ḏrty* 'Djerty' (a town), Dyn. XVIII for *Ḏrtỉ*,[3] Dyn. XI. For the origin of see § 73, 4.

ꜣ and *r* may be termed **weak consonants,** since they are very susceptible of change or omission; both tend to be replaced in writing by *ỉ*.

[1] In *ym* 'sea', *Onom.* i. 162*, *y* is 'group-writing', § 60.

[2] An obscure exception, § 177.

[3] *Tôd*, pl. 22. Sim. *ʾIwny* for earlier *ʾIwnỉ*, Cairo 20001.

21. Absence of the article.—Old and Middle Egyptian dispense, as a rule, with any equivalent of the English article, whether definite or indefinite. Thus *rn* may be rendered, according to the demands of the context, by 'the name', 'a name', or simply 'name'.

OBS. For Egyptian equivalents of both articles, appearing first in Middle Egyptian and becoming regular only in Late Egyptian, see below, §§ 112 end; 262, 1.

EXERCISE I

(*a*) *Learn and write out from memory, both in hieroglyphs and in transliteration, the following words*:

m ('em') 1, in; 2, by means of, with (of instrument); 3, from, out of.

n ('en') 1, to, for (in sense of dative); 2, to (of direction, only to *persons*).

r ('er') 1, to, into, towards (of direction towards *things*); 2, in respect of.

pn ('pen') this m(asculine) } follows its noun.

tn ('ten') this, f(eminine) } follows its noun.

ḳy ('key') other, another, m. } precedes its noun.
ḳt ('ket') other, another, f. }

ỉm ('yem') there, therein, therewith, therefrom.

bw ('bew') place, m., singular only.

ḫt ('chet') thing, f.

Ptḥ ('Pteḥ') Ptah, name of the god of Memphis.

ỉw ('yew') is, are.

rn ('ren') name, m.

ḏd ('djed') say, speak.

ḥnʿ ('ḥena') together with.

(*b*) *Write in hieroglyphs the following combinations of letters*:

(N.B. Here and elsewhere the student should conform to Egyptian usage with its preference for a symmetrical arrangement of the signs (§ 16). The individual words will, however, best be kept separate, contrary to the practice of the monuments.)

hn, ʿrḳ, grḥ, sfṯ, ptr, my, snb, ẖrd, ỉꜣḫ, wỉꜣ, ḏsf, ḳnd, ptpt, wšb, ṯsm.

(*c*) *Translate into Egyptian, adding transliterations to the hieroglyphs*:

(N.B. The words are to be translated in the order of the English, unless a different order is indicated by small numerals before the words, or unless instructions to the contrary have been given in the Lessons or Vocabularies.)

(1) To another place. (2) To Ptah. (3) [2]Another [3]thing [1]is there. (4) In this name. (5) [2]Ptah [1]is there in this place. (6) Together with another name. (7) A [2]thing [1]is in this place. (8) [2]Ptah [1]speak(s) in respect of this thing.

LESSON II

§ 22. **Ideograms** or **sense-signs,** as we have seen § 6, 1, are signs that convey their meaning pictorially. More often than not they are accompanied by sound-signs (§§ 6, 2; 17; 18) indicating the precise word to be understood.

Thus ⊙, a picture of the sun, immediately suggests to the mind, besides the notion of the sun itself, also the notions of light and time; the addition of sound-signs is indispensable to define the exact meaning and the exact word intended in a particular context. Hence ⊙ enters into the words *rʿ* 'sun', 'day' (also written); *hrw* 'day', 'daytime' (also written); *rk* 'time', 'period'; *wbn* 'rise', 'shine' (also written).

Obs. Note that one and the same word may often be written in several different ways; such different writings are called *variants* of each other.

Similarly, [hieroglyph], depicting a boat, appears in the words [hieroglyphs] *wi3* 'solar bark'; [hieroglyphs] *ḫd* 'fare downstream'; [hieroglyphs] *dpt* 'boat'.

[hieroglyph] (also, but less frequently, [hieroglyph]) represents a combined palette, water-bowl, and reed-holder. Hence it is used in the words [hieroglyphs] *sš* 'write' (the spelling [hieroglyphs] is almost confined to the Old Kingdom; [hieroglyphs] *sš* 'scribe'; [hieroglyphs] *nʿʿ* 'smooth', 'finely ground', originally of pigments.

[hieroglyph], an animal's ear, is found in [hieroglyphs] *sḏm* 'hear', more rarely written [hieroglyphs] with all the component consonants; also in [hieroglyphs] *id*, [hieroglyphs] *sẖ* 'be deaf', and various other words.

As the example of [hieroglyphs] shows, it is by no means necessary that an ideogram, when accompanied by phonograms, should be accompanied by *all* the signs needful to express its complete sound-value. It is only from full writings that the sound-value of ideograms can be ascertained; these are, however, on the whole rarer than short and summary writings.

§ **23.** In several of the examples quoted in § 22 the ideogram follows one or more phonograms and ends the word. In cases such as these it is called a **determinative,** because it appears to determine the meaning of the foregoing sound-signs and to define that meaning in a general way. Words written ideographically may also have determinatives, ex. [hieroglyphs] *sš* 'scribe'.

Only some of the commonest words, like [hieroglyph] *ḏd* 'speak', [hieroglyphs] *ḥnʿ* 'together with', lack determinatives; and many, like [hieroglyphs] *ḥḳr* 'hungry man', [hieroglyphs] *wʿr* 'flee', have more than one.

Obs. The name 'determinative' is in many cases historically inaccurate, the ideogram having been the original sign with which the word was first written, and the phonograms having been prefixed to it subsequently for the sake of clearness. In such cases it might be more truly said that the phonograms determine the *sound* of the ideogram, than that the ideogram determines the *sense* of the phonograms.

§ **24. Generic determinatives.**—Ideograms that serve to determine a considerable number of different words can naturally only express the *kind* of sense borne by these, and not their specific meaning; they are therefore called **generic determinatives.**

The following is a list of the more important generic determinatives; they may be learnt gradually. For fuller details the Sign-list at the end of the book must be consulted.

[hieroglyph] man, person.

[hieroglyph] woman.

[hieroglyphs] people.

[hieroglyph] child, young.

[hieroglyph] old man, old, lean upon.

[hieroglyph] official, man in authority.

[hieroglyph] (Dyn. XVIII [hieroglyph] or [hieroglyph]), exalted person, the dead.

god, king.

or king.

god, king.[1]

or goddess, queen.[1]

high, rejoice, support.

praise, supplicate.

force, effort.

[2] eat, drink, speak, think, feel.

lift, carry.

weary, weak.

enemy, foreigner.

enemy, death.

or lie down, death, bury.

mummy, likeness, shape.

head, nod, throttle.

hair, mourn, forlorn.

eye, see, actions of eye.

actions or conditions of eye.

(less accurately) nose, smell, joy, contempt.

ear, states or activities of ear.

tooth, actions of teeth.

force, effort (interchangeable with).

substitute for in hieratic, less often in hieroglyphic.

offer, present.

arm, bend arm, cease.

envelop, embrace.

phallus, beget, urinate.

leg, foot, actions of foot.

walk, run.

move backwards.

limb, flesh.

tumours, odours, disease.

bodily discharges.

and cattle.

savage, Typhonian.[3]

skin, mammal.

bird, insect.

small, bad, weak.

fish.

snake, worm.

tree.

plant, flower.

or vine, fruit, garden.

wood, tree.

corn.

or grain.

sky, above.

sun, light, time.

[1] The king was often thought of as the incarnation of the falcon-god Horus, and the queen as the incarnation of the cobra-goddess Edjō, commonly known as Buto; moreover, both deities were typical of their class, whence the employment of falcon and cobra as determinatives of royalty and of divinity; but the former alone was so used at an early date.

[2] Note the difference from in the position of *both* arms.

[3] This animal represents the god Seth, identified by the Greeks with Typhon, the brother and murderer of the good god Osiris, and the enemy of Horus, son of Osiris.

night, darkness.

star.

fire, heat, cook.

air, wind, sail.

stone.

copper, bronze.

∘ ∘ ∘ sand, minerals, pellets.

water, liquid, actions connected with water.

(less often) sheet of water.

irrigated land.

land (later often replaces).

road, travel, position.

desert, foreign country.

foreign (country or person).

town, village, Egypt.

house, building.

door, open.

box, coffin.

shrine, palanquin, mat.

boat, ship, navigation.

sacred bark.

clothe, linen.

bind, document.

rope, actions with cord or rope.

knife, cut.

hoe, cultivate, hack up.

× break, divide, cross.

cup.

vessel, anoint.

(less accurately) pot, vessel, beverages.

bread, cake.

or loaf, cake, offering.

festival.

(also vertically , older form) book, writing, abstract.

[1] royal name, king.

| one; the object depicted (§ 25).

| | | (also , , ∘ ∘ ∘) several, plural.

\ substitute for signs difficult to draw (mostly hieratic).

[1] The hieroglyphs spelling the royal name are written inside this; see below, p. 74.

This occasion may be taken to urge upon the student the desirability of acquiring a good hieroglyphic handwriting. In writing, the printed forms of the hieroglyphs may be abbreviated where needful, but care must be taken not to ignore any essential or characteristic feature. The transcriptions from the hieratic and demotic shown in Plate II (facing p. 10) are examples of the author's own hieroglyphic handwriting; though not to be regarded as models to be copied, they will serve to show the kind of way in which modern Egyptologists represent the old hieroglyphic script. Note that these transcriptions are written from right to left, i.e. with the signs pointing to the right (§ 16). It is important for the student to be able to write with equal ease in both directions, so that, when copying a text, he can retain the direction of his original.

§ 25. **Purely ideographic writings.**—When ideograms stand for the actual objects which they depict, the phonetic signs that would indicate the names of those objects are often dispensed with. Ideograms so employed are usually followed by the stroke-determinative ı; if the noun is feminine, the stroke is preceded by ⌓ *t*, the feminine ending (§ 26).[1]

[1] *ÄZ.* 45, 44.

Masculine exx.: *rꜥ* sun; *ḥr* face.

Feminine exx.: *niwt* town, city; *ꜣḫt* horizon.

Obs. 1. The stroke ı was early extended to other uses as well; not only was it retained when such words as *rꜥ* 'sun', *ḥr* 'face' were employed in their derivative meanings of 'day' and 'sight' respectively, but it is sometimes found also with ideograms that have become purely phonetic, the whole ideographic word being transferred to a phonetic usage; so *sꜣ* 'son', which is written with an ideogram belonging to the old word *zt* (*zꜣt*) 'pintail duck'.

Obs. 2. Ideograms meaning what they depict, and therefore accompanied by the stroke ı, were in the Old Kingdom often accompanied by phonetic signs; a few cases have survived in M.E., ex. *s* 'man' (varr. and).

§ 26. Egyptian distinguishes two genders, **masculine** and **feminine.** Most feminine words ended in ⌓ *t* (probably vocalized *-at*),[1a] exx. *st* 'woman', *niwt* 'town'. Most other nouns are masculine, as *rꜥ* 'sun', *ḥr* 'face'.

[1a] In *status absolutus* (§ 78) the *t* had probably fallen as early as O.K., cf. Hebr. Arab. and see *ÄZ.* 44, 80, n. 2.

§ 27. **Verbal sentences** are those in which the predicate is a verb-form having the sense of a simple finite verb in English or Latin ('loves', 'loved', *amat*, *amavit*).

In such sentences the normal **word-order** is: 1. verb, 2. subject, 3. object, 4. adverb or adverbial phrase (preposition with noun).

Exx. *wbn rꜥ m pt* the sun rises in the sky.

rḫ sš sḫr m hrw pn the scribe knows a counsel on this day.

Obs. Sentences having in the Egyptian a verb-form serving merely as copula are in this book grouped for convenience sake with the non-verbal sentences, see § 28.

§ 28. **Non-verbal sentences.**[2]—This is a convenient class-name for all those sentences which either have in the predicate no proper verb at all, or else have one with the attenuated meaning of the **copula** ('is', 'are', 'was', etc.).

[2] K. Sethe, *Der Nominalsatz im ägyptischen und koptischen*; see in Abbreviations under *Nominals.*

The copula (i. e. that 'link' between subject and predicate expressed in English by some part of the verb 'to be') is often left unexpressed in Egyptian, as happens regularly in Semitic and less frequently in Greek and Latin.

Ex. *rꜥ m pt* the sun is in the sky.

Non-verbal sentences are classified according to the nature of their **predicate.** There may be distinguished:

1. Sentences with **adverbial predicate,** such as 'the scribe is there', 'the scribe is in the city'. Note that a preposition together with its noun constitutes

an adverbial phrase, so that predicates like 'in the city' come under this head. See in detail Lesson X.

2. Sentences with **nominal** or **pronominal predicate,** such as 'the scribe is a knave', 'he is a knave', 'I am he', 'who are you?' The term 'nominal' here means 'consisting of a noun' (Latin *nomen*) and the reference is to nouns substantive only. See Lesson XI.

3. Sentences with **adjectival predicate,** such as 'the scribe is good'. See Lesson XII.

No small part of the first twelve lessons will be devoted to mastering the different ways in which Egyptian expresses sentences of these three kinds.

OBS. 1. Hitherto it has been usual to group together the sentences described by us as 'non-verbal' under the heading of the 'nominal sentence'. This is a term borrowed from Arabic grammar and has a signification rather different from 'non-verbal sentence' as here employed.

OBS. 2. The sentences expressing existence or non-existence described below §§ 107–9 are partly verbal, partly non-verbal. Another type of sentences to be dealt with in Lesson XXIII is non-verbal in form, though its predicate has verbal meaning; we shall refer to it as the 'pseudo-verbal construction'.

§ 29. Sentences with adverbial predicate.—The word-order is the same as in verbal sentences (§ 27); since there is no object, and since the copula is in many cases omitted, this means that the order is 1. subject, 2. adverb or adverbial phrase.

Exx. [hieroglyphs] *Rʿ im* (the sun-god) Rēʿ (is) there.

[hieroglyphs] *rʿ m pt* the sun (is) in the sky.

To introduce such sentences the word [hieroglyphs] *iw* is frequently used. This is an old verb (perhaps a specialized variation of the verb [hieroglyphs] *iw* 'come') which has only this one form, and is employed in certain cases to be specified below with the meaning of the copula ('is', 'are', etc.).

Ex. [hieroglyphs] *iw rʿ m pt* the sun is in the sky.

When the subject is a *noun*, the word *iw* occurs only in *independent statements* or assertions made with a certain detachment, and in these the presence of *iw* is much more common than its absence. Thus the difference between *iw rʿ m pt* and *rʿ m pt* is that, whereas the former type of sentence gives considerable prominence and importance to the affirmation which it contains, the latter is the form of words chosen for simple, unobtrusive *description*, particularly when there has to be expressed the equivalent of an English *adverb clause*, i.e. clause of time, circumstance, condition, etc.; see the next section.

When the subject is a *pronoun*, the sentence with *iw* has a wider use, see below, §§ 37. 117.

§ 30. **Dependence, tense and mood in Egyptian.**—The student must realize from the start that Egyptian is very sparing in its use of words meaning 'when', 'if', 'though', 'for', 'and', and the like; consequently, it often devolves upon the translator to supply the implicit logical nexus between sentences, as also between words.

Similarly, distinctions of *tense* and *mood* are not marked in the same clear way as in English.

What is said here applies both to verbal and to non-verbal sentences, though in verbal sentences the ambiguity of meaning may sometimes result from the fact that the omission of vowels in the writing has obliterated differences between verb-forms which were really distinct and possessed distinct significations. In their particular contexts any of the following renderings may be legitimate:

wbn rʿ m pt
- the sun rises in the sky
- the sun rose in the sky
- the sun will rise in the sky
- when the sun rises in the sky
- when the sun rose in the sky
- if the sun rise in the sky
- let the sun rise in the sky
- that the sun may (might) rise in the sky, etc.

rʿ m pt
- the sun is in the sky
- the sun was in the sky
- let the sun be in the sky
- when the sun is (was, will be) in the sky
- the sun being in the sky (circumstantial), etc.

When, however, a sentence with adverbial predicate like the last is introduced by *ỉw*, the range of possible meanings is narrower, and almost confined to main clauses embodying an assertion (see above § 29, below § 117); thus we obtain:

ỉw rʿ m pt
- the sun is in the sky
- the sun was in the sky
- but also to express an emphatic contrast:
- whereas the sun is (was) in the sky.

At the present stage of his knowledge, the beginner will do well to translate all these sentences as referring to present time. On the other hand, if the sense appear to demand it and the rules already given permit, he may insert in his renderings such an English word as 'when'.

Ex. *wbn rʿ, ỉw tꜣ m ršwt*, (when) the sun rises, the earth is in joy.

LESSON II

VOCABULARY

rḫ ('rech') become acquainted with, know.

ḫm ('chem') not know, be ignorant of.

gr ('ger') be silent, cease.

ḫd ('ched') fare downstream, northwards.

hꜣ ('ha') go down, descend.

sḏm ('sedjem') hear; with *n* 'to', hearken to, obey (a person).

wbn ('weben') rise, shine forth.

var. *rꜥ* ('ra') sun, day; with det. , Rēꜥ, sun-god.

ỉꜥḥ ('yaeh') moon.

tꜣ ('ta') earth, land.

pt ('pet') sky, heaven.

sḫr ('secher') plan, counsel.

hrw ('herew') day, day-time.

grḥ ('gereḥ') night.

ršwt ('reshwet') joy, gladness.

dpt ('depet') boat.

wỉꜣ ('weya') ship, bark, particularly divine ship.

nḏs ('nedjes') poor man, commoner.

varr. , *s* ('se') a man.

st ('set') woman.

sš ('sesh') scribe.

ꜣḫt ('achet') horizon.

pr ('per') house.

nỉwt ('neywet') town, city.

var. *š* ('she') lake, pool.

EXERCISE II

(*a*) *Transliterate and translate*:

(*b*) *Write in hieroglyphs and in transliteration*:

(N.B. Words in brackets are not to be translated.)

(1) The scribe goes down into another boat. (2) Ptah knows this counsel.

(3) (When) this poor man fares downstream to the city, the house is in joy. (4) The moon rises in the sky. (5) The scribe is silent by day and by night (render: in day, in night). (6) This land is in joy, (when) Rēꜥ goes down into the bark. (7) A pool is in this city. (8) This woman hearkens to the scribe. (9) A man is there in the house.

LESSON III

§ **31**. The **biliteral signs** (§ 17, 2), or combinations of two consonants, are of great importance, and a few must be learnt in each of the next lessons.

i. Signs with *ꜣ* as the second consonant:

ꜥꜣ	*pꜣ*	*ḫꜣ*	, old , *sꜣ* (*šꜣ*)	*tꜣ*
wꜣ	*mꜣ*	*ẖꜣ*	*šꜣ*	*ṯꜣ*
bꜣ	*ḥꜣ*	*sꜣ*	*kꜣ*	*ḏꜣ*

§ **32**. **Phonetic complements.**—The biliteral signs (and similarly the triliteral signs, see below § 42) are almost always accompanied by alphabetic signs expressing part or the whole of their sound-value. Thus is to be read *šꜣ*, never *šꜣꜣ*, which would be written ; similarly is to be read, not *bbꜣꜣ*, but simply *bꜣ*. Alphabetic signs used in this way are called **phonetic complements.**

The exact mode of combination varies with the individual signs. In the list of § 31, , , , , , and follow the pattern of , the remainder (except) vacillating between this arrangement and that exemplified by , where the first consonant precedes the biliteral sign and the second follows it; with the exceptional arrangements and are found. What is customary in each case must be learnt by use.

The complete absence of phonetic complements is uncommon, but is seen in such words as *ḫꜣ* 'thousand', *sꜣ* 'son', *bꜣk* 'servant', *kꜣt* 'work', 'construction'.

§ **33**. The **personal pronouns** appear in Egyptian under several different forms, each of which has its own restricted field of employment. There must be distinguished:

1. Suffix-pronouns, see below § 34.
2. Dependent pronouns, see below § 43.
3. Independent pronouns, see below § 64.

§ **34.** The **suffix-pronouns** (more briefly **suffixes**) are so called because they must follow, and be suffixed to, some preceding word. They are as follows:

Sing. 1, c.	*·i*	I, me, my.	Also fem.,[1] not occurring before Dyn. XIX.[2] Kings sometimes (§ 24);[3] , rarely for kings in Dyn. XII,[4] is replaced by [5] or [6] in Dyn. XVIII, when occurs for gods.[7] Other writings of the suffix: [8] or [9] on early M.K. coffins; in inscriptions sometimes ,[10] seldom .[11] The suffix was regularly omitted in O.K.; so too sometimes later.[12]
Sing. 2, m.	*·k*	Thou, thee, thy.	Reversed in hieratic, viz. .
„ 2, f.	*·ṯ*	Thou, thee, thy.	Later also *·t*.
„ 3, m.	*·f*	He, him, his, it, its.	
„ 3, f.	*·s*	She, her, it, its.	Old only *·ś*, later also
Plur. 1, c.	*·n*	We, us, our.	Rarely
„ 2, c.	*·ṯn*	You, your.	Or *·ṯn*, later also or *·tn*.
„ 3, c.	*·sn*	They, them, their.	Or *·sn* (old *·śn*), later also written or ; exceptionally , , .[12a]
„ 3, c.	*·w*	They, them, their.	Also written , a later suffix, a few examples of which are found as early as Dyn. XVIII.[13]
Dual 1, c.	*·ny*	We two, us two, our.	Obsolete in M.E. except in archaistic texts;[14] usually replaced by the plural suffixes.[15]
„ 2, c.	*·ṯny*	You two, your.	
„ 3, c.	*·sny*	They two, them two, their.	

OBS. 1. For , *st* 'them', 'it' (§ 46) as object of the infinitive, i.e. used like the suffixes, see § 300.

OBS. 2. For the forms assumed by the singular suffixes after dual nouns, see below § 75, 2.

OBS. 3. In *imytw·ny* 'between them' (§ 177) *·ny* might be a very rare suffix 3rd pers. dual; or after verbs is best explained differently, see § 486, OBS. 2.

OBS. 4. The exceptional writings of *·sn* without *n* are paralleled by even rarer ones with *·ṯn*; reasons have been given[16] for thinking that the final *n* fell away at an early date, though revived for *·ṯn* in Coptic.

§ **35.** Among the chief uses of the suffix-pronouns are the following:

1. as *genitive* after nouns, with the sense of our possessive adjectives. Exx. *pr·f* 'his house', lit. 'house of him'; *niwt·sn* 'their city', lit. 'city of them'.

[1] LAC. *TR.* 17, 9; *Westc.* 6, 7.
[2] MAR. *Abyd.* i. 25.
[3] Berl. *Äl.* i. p. 258; *Urk.* iv. 163.
[4] *Ikhern.* 6. 8.
[5] *Urk.* iv. 366; 840, 7.
[6] *Urk.* ix. 808, 14; 813, 14.
[7] *D. el B.* 47; *Urk.* iv. 612.
[8] LAC. *TR.* 22, 3; 24, 1.
[9] LAC. *TR.* 13, 16. 25; 14, 1. 7.
[10] *Bersh.* i. 14, 9. 11. 12; *Urk.* iv. 119.
[11] Cairo 20057, *q*.
[12] Dyn. XI, *Hamm.* 114, 13–16; Dyn. XVIII, *Urk.* iv. 572, 2. 6; 1031, 2–10.
[12a] *Ann.* 29, 6; *JEA* 16, 64 (5); 24, 6, n. 15.
[13] First of all in *iw·w* 'they are', exx. *Urk.* iv. 54, 10; 1021, 4.
[14] ERM. *Hymn.* 12, 3; 13, 5; MAR. *Abyd.* i. 29.
[15] *Urk.* iv. 362, 12; 425, 17.
[16] CLÈRE in *Groupe ling. d'ét. Chamito-Sémitiques*, ii. 66.

2. *after prepositions*, as *n·i* 'to me'; *ḥnꜥ·s* 'together with her'.

3. as *nominative* with the simple tenses of the verb. Exx. *dd·k* 'thou sayest' (§ 39); *sdm·n·t* 'thou (f.) hast heard' (§ 67).

Obs. Note that *pr·f* in Egyptian may mean, not merely 'his house', i.e. 'the house of him', but equally well 'a house of his', contrary to the use of the English possessive adjectives; exx. below in § 115.[1]

[1] Cf. also *P. Pet.* 1116 B, 6, qu. § 96, 2.

§ 36. **'Myself', 'thyself', etc.**—Egyptian distinguishes no special reflexive pronouns. Hence *dd·f n·f* could quite well mean 'he says to himself'.[2]

For emphatic 'myself', 'thyself', etc. use may be made of *ds·*, later also written, with appended suffix.[3] This is found

1. after nouns, as in *Rꜥ ds·f* Rēꜥ himself, i.e. in person.[4]

2. to strengthen a suffix when used as genitive; ex. *rn·i ds·i* my own name.[5]

3. adverbially, with the meaning 'by one's own effort'; ex. *sn n·k ḳrwt ds·sn* the bolts open to thee of themselves.[6]

In later times 'myself', 'thyself' are regularly paraphrased by *ḥꜥw·i* (§ 73, 3), *ḥꜥw·k*, lit. 'my (thy) members'; early examples also occur, some preposition always preceding.[7]

[2] Exx. *Sebekkhu* 8; *Peas.* B 1, 22; Cairo 20497, 1; *Westc.* 11, 8.

[3] Without suffix, *Pt.* 181.

[4] Louvre C 3, 16. Sim. *T. Carn.* 2; *Urk.* iv. 364, 10; after *ink*, Louvre C 3, 7; *sw ds·f* 'himself', Brit. Mus. 552, 2.

[5] *BH.* i. 26, 197. Sim. *Siut* 1, 278–9; Cairo 20003, 7; *Westc.* 6, 24. Anticipating a suffix serving as subject, *Westc.* 7, 8.

[6] *Urk.* iv. 116. Sim. *Pt.* 181. *Ds iry, Adm.* 2, 12.

[7] *M ḥꜥw·f*, *Peas.* B 1, 83, sim. *Bersh.* ii. 22, 9, 16. *R ḥꜥw* 'than itself', *Sin.* B 66. *Wpw-ḥr ḥꜥw·k ds·k* 'except thyself', Budge, p. 291, 10; 366, 10. *N ḥꜥw·i* 'by myself', 'alone', *Mill.* 2, 2.

§ 37. **The suffixes as subject of *iw*.**—Like other verbs, *iw* 'is', 'are' (§ 29) may have a suffix for its nominative. The student must remember that the sentence with *iw*, though here for reasons of convenience classed as non-verbal (§ 28), is verbal in actual form.

Ex. *iw·n m pr·f* we are in his house.

We have seen above (§ 29) that, if the subject of a sentence with adverbial predicate is a noun, the effect of placing *iw* before it is to give it the importance of a more or less independent assertion. This rule does not necessarily hold when the subject is a suffix-pronoun; the suffixes must lean on some preceding word, and *iw* is the word most commonly used to support the suffixes in the case before us.

Hence such a sentence as *iw·n m pr·f* may have two meanings: (1) either it is a main clause, the assertion 'we are in his house', as above; (2) or else it may be a subordinate clause of some kind.

Ex. *rš sš, iw·n m pr·f* the scribe rejoices, (when) we are in his house.

§ 38. **Sentences with the *m* of predication.**—Egyptian cannot say *iw·k sš* for 'thou art a scribe', but only

iw·k m sš, lit. thou art (as) a scribe.

Here the preposition *m* has the signification 'in the position of', 'as'; hence it may be termed the ***m* of predication.** By its aid the pattern of the sentence with adverbial predicate may be adopted in order to express sentences which in English have a nominal predicate. An example with nominal subject would be:

iw nḏs pn m sš this commoner is a scribe.

Obs. The predicate here usually, if not always, expresses what in logic is termed an 'accident', an acquired attribute rather than a permanent 'property'.

§ 39. The *śḏm·f* form of the verb.—We have incidentally become acquainted with a form or tense of the verb in which the subject, sometimes a noun (§ 27) and sometimes a suffix (§ 35, 3), is added directly to the signs expressing the verbal notion; exx. *sḏm·f* 'he hears', *sḏm sš* 'the scribe hears'. In describing the various parts of the Egyptian verb it is usual to take the verb *sḏm* 'hear' as paradigm or model; and since, following the example of Semitic grammar, precedence over the 1st pers. sing. is given to the 3rd pers. sing., the verb-form to which reference has just been made is known as the ***śḏm·f***[1] **form** (pronounce *sedjemef*).

We shall see later (§ 411, 1) that the *śḏm·f* form appears to have originated in a passive participle followed by a genitival suffix-pronoun; an original 'heard of him' came to mean 'he hears' or 'he heard'.

To create the *passive* of the *śḏm·f* form, an element *·tw*, sometimes more briefly written *·t(w)*, is inserted immediately after the verb-stem, as in *sḏm·tw r pn* 'this utterance is heard', or *sḏm·tw·f* 'it (i. e. this utterance) is heard'. The element *·tw* is really an **indefinite pronoun** like our 'one', French *on*, and is sometimes still so used independently, ex. *ḏd·tw* 'one says', 'it is said' (see too below § 47); from this use *sḏm·tw·f* 'he is heard' was doubtless derived on the analogy of the active *sḏm·f*.

Obs. The suffix-pronoun after *·tw* was undoubtedly felt as the subject of a passive, not as the object of an active; otherwise the dependent pronouns (§ 44, 1), not the suffixes, would have been used.[2] However, such constructions as *ḫr·tw śḏm·tw·f* (§ 239), *iw·tw śḏm·tw·f* (§ 463) show that the origin was not altogether lost from sight.

The full form follows any determinative that the verb-stem may have, as *rḫ·tw·f* 'he is known'. The shorter writing may either precede or follow the determinative, but is more correct than . The passive ending *·tw* is in all cases inseparable from the verb-stem.

The full paradigm of the *śḏm·f* form is as follows:

	Active	Passive
1st sing. c.	*sḏm·i* I hear	or *sḏm·tw·i* I am heard
2nd „ m.	*sḏm·k* thou hearest	or *sḏm·tw·k* thou art heard
„ „ f.	*sḏm·ṯ* thou hearest	or *sḏm·tw·ṯ* thou art heard
3rd „ m.	*sḏm·f* he (*or* it) hears	or *sḏm·tw·f* he is heard
„ „ f.	*sḏm·s* she (*or* it) hears	or *sḏm·tw·s* she is heard

[1] The transliteration with *ś* is here adopted since the term has to apply to Old Egyptian no less than to Middle Egyptian. The paradigm and exx. below are written with *s*, as being solely Middle Egyptian.

[2] *'Itḥ·tw st* in *Urk.* iv. 658, 4 is 'that one might pull them' rather than 'that they might be pulled'.

	Active	Passive
1st plur. c.	*sḏm·n* we hear	or *sḏm·tw·n* we are heard
2nd „ „	*sḏm·ṯn* you hear	*sḏm·tw·ṯn* you are heard
3rd „ „	*sḏm·sn* they hear	or *sḏm·tw·sn* they are heard
Before nouns	*sḏm* hears *or* hear	or *sḏm·tw* is *or* are heard
Indefinite	*sḏm·tw* one hears.	

The duals are omitted, since they are ordinarily replaced by the plurals; nor has it been considered necessary to encumber the paradigm with the variant writings of the suffix-pronouns, for which see § 34.

When the subject of the *śḏm·f* form is a *suffix*, this is inseparable from the verb-stem or, in the passive, from the verb-stem accompanied by *·tw*; *·tw* is itself inseparable from the verb-stem.

When, on the other hand, the subject is a *noun*, this, under given conditions (§ 66), may be separated from the verb.

Exx. *ḏd·s n·f* she says to him.

ḏd n·f sš the scribe says to him.

ḏd·tw n·f r pn this utterance is said to him.

iw grt rꜥ m pt now the sun was in the sky.

When the *agent* has to be expressed after the passive of *sḏm·f*, or indeed after any other passive form of the verb,[1] it is introduced by the preposition *in* 'by'.

Ex. *ḏd·tw r pn in s* this utterance is (to be) said by a man.[2]

Much more rarely, the preposition *ḫr*, properly 'with' or 'near', is used for the same purpose.[3]

[1] Old perfective, ex. *Sh. S.* 40; participle, exx. *Eb.* 1, 13; *Urk.* iv. 331, 12; infinitive, see § 300.

[2] Exx. *Sin.* B 205–6; Louvre C 3, 12.

[3] *Pt.* 634; *Eb.* 47, 19; *Urk.* iv. 137, 10; 490, 17.

§ 40. **Meaning of the *śḏm·f* form.**—This difficult topic is reserved for detailed discussion in Lessons XXX, XXXI. Provisionally, it may be said that the *śḏm·f* form excludes the meaning of hardly any English tense or mood; see too above § 30. As a past tense, it is to no small extent replaced by another form, the *śḏm·n·f* (pronounce *sedjemnef*) form, to be described in Lesson V. In most cases the student will do well, at this stage of his knowledge, to render *śḏm·f* as an English present. But to serve as indications of the wider meaning, three common uses are here specified, and may be utilized at once; the employment in clauses of *time* has been previously mentioned (§ 30 end).

1. The *śḏm·f* form is often used without any introductory particle in rendering the equivalent of an English *clause of purpose*; see below §§ 219. 454, 3.

Ex. *hꜣb·k sš, ḏd·f sḫr·k* thou sendest the scribe that he may say thy plan.

2. Or else it may express a *wish* or *exhortation*; see §§ 440, 5; 450, 4.

Ex. *hꜣb·k sš* mayst thou send (*or* send thou) the scribe.

3. Preceded by the particle *iḫ*, the fundamental meaning of which appears to be 'then' or 'therefore' (§ 228), the *śḏm·f* form serves to express a *consequence* destined to take place in the future, or else an *exhortation* based on previously stated facts.

Exx. *iḫ ḏd sr* then the official will say.

iḫ ḏd·k n sꜣ·k then shalt thou say to thy son.

VOCABULARY

mꜣꜣ see.

ḏꜣ cross; ferry across.

rš rejoice, be glad.

hꜣb send.

sꜣ son.

sꜣt daughter.

var. *it* (not *itf* or *tf*)[1] father.

bꜣk man-servant.

bꜣkt maid-servant.

var. *wꜣt* road, way, side.

ḫꜣ office, hall, diwân.

kꜣt construction, work, device.

ṯꜣty[2] vizier.

ꜥꜣ donkey, ass.

sštꜣ secret.

itrw river.

msḥ crocodile.

r mouth, utterance.

ḥr face, sight.

ḥr upon, concerning, because of; before suffixes written

m in, with (of instrument), from, as; before suffixes *im*.

[1] The apparent *f* written in this word has been shown to be a determinative with some unascertained symbolic meaning, see *Ann.* 43, 311. Until recently *it* and *tf* were held to be distinct words, see *ÄZ.* 48, 18.

[2] For the reading with final *-y* see Cairo 20184, *k*; Brit. Mus. 572.

EXERCISE III

(*a*) *Transliterate and translate*:

(1) (2) (3) (4)

(*b*) *Write in hieroglyphs and transliteration* :

(1) The crocodile is in the river. (2) The moon rejoices, when the sun is in his horizon. (3) Then (*ỉḫ*) shall thy name be heard by the vizier. (4) This scribe is in his office by day (and) by night. (5) The donkey goes down to the city upon another road. (6) The scribe sends this boat, that we may cross in it. (7) He rejoices because of thy utterance. (8) This land is in joy, when thou art in the sky. (9) He fares down to this city, his daughter with him.

LESSON IV

§ **41**. **Biliteral signs** (continued from § 31) :—

ii. with *ỉ* as second consonant :

mỉ   , less accurately , *mỉ*[1]   *tỉ*

iii. with *ꜥ* as second consonant :

wꜥ   *ḫꜥ*

iv. with *w* as second consonant :

ꜣw   *nw* (rarely also for *ỉn*)   *ḥw* (rare)   *šw*

ỉw   *nw*   *ḫw*   *ḏw* (later *dw*)

mw   *rw*   *sw* (old *św*)

v. with *b* as second consonant :

ꜣb   *nb*

[1] Sometimes used to accompany, or even to replace, a simple *m* when used as a grammatical afformative.

§ **42**. The **triliteral signs** (§ 17, 3) represent combinations of three consonants, and have naturally a far more restricted use than the biliteral signs. They need be learnt only as occasion arises.

Like the biliteral signs, they are usually accompanied by phonetic complements (§ 32). Two arrangements are particularly frequent : the one consists in adding the third consonant only, exx. *ꜥḥꜥ* stand up, arise ; *ḫpr* become ; *sḏm* hear.

The other consists in appending both the second and third consonants, exx. *nfr* good, happy, beautiful; *ˁnḫ* live; *ḥtp* rest, become at peace.

OBS. The student may be puzzled at finding in *sḏm* here treated as a triliteral sign, while in § 22 it was described as an ideogram. This contradiction must be explained. In the case of the triliterals the distinction between phonograms and ideograms becomes particularly precarious. Thus probably all words containing the consonants *ḥ+t+p* are etymologically connected with the verb-stem *ḥtp* 'rest', 'be propitiated'; they are, moreover, all written with the sign representing a loaf placed on a reed-mat—a sign taken over from a word *ḥtp* 'altar', perhaps literally 'place of propitiation'. The sign in any given word may be described as *ideographic* in so far as any connexion of meaning is discernible between that word and the word for 'altar', 'place of propitiation'; it may be described as *phonetic*, on the other hand, in so far as the sound-value outweighs, or throws into the shade, such similarity of meaning.

§ 43. **Personal pronouns** (continued from §§ 33-5):—

2. The **dependent pronouns**[1] are less closely attached to a preceding word than the suffix-pronouns (§ 34), but can never stand as first word of a sentence.

Sing. 1, c.	*wi*	I, me.	Or . Varr. as in the corresponding suffix (§ 34), [2] [3] [4] [5] etc.	
,, 2, m.	*ṯw*	Thou, thee.	Later also *tw*.	
,, 2, f.	*ṯn*	,, ,,	Later also *tn*.	
,, 3, m.	*sw*	He, him, it.	Originally *św*.	
,, 3, f.	*sy*	She, her, it.	Early ; later also written or . Originally *śy*.	
,, 3, f.	*st*	(see § 46).	Later writings , [5a]. Originally *śt*.	
Plur. 1, c.	*n*	We, us.	Rarely *n*.	
,, 2, c.	*ṯn*	You.	Or *ṯn*, later also or *tn*.	also used as suffixes (§ 34).[5b]
,, 3, c.	*sn*	They, them.	Or *sn*, later also written or . Originally *śn*.	

OBS. 1. For the *sw*, *sy*, and *st* which, from Dyn. XVIII onwards, are occasionally found as subject to an adverbial predicate or to the old perfective, and which may stand at the beginning of the sentence, see below § 124. See too Add., § 148, 1, OBS.

OBS. 2. A form is very rarely found as object in place of *ṯn* 'you'.[6] In one text 'thou' (f.) is used strangely as a suffix-pronoun.[7] Both are probably explicable by § 34, OBS. 4.

§ 44. Among the chief uses of the dependent pronouns are the following:

1. as *object* of any form of the verb[8] except, as a rule, the infinitive. Exx. *hꜣb·k wi* 'thou sendest me'; *ḏꜣ·n·f sw* 'he ferried him over'.

OBS. *Sn* as object is uncommon, usually being replaced by *st* of § 46; some exx. may, however, be quoted.[9]

[1] See *ÄZ.* 30, 16.

[2] *Urk.* iv. 158, 16.

[3] *Urk.* iv. 385, 4.

[4] *Urk.* iv. 158, 17.

[5] *Hamm.* 199, 6.

[5a] SPIEG.-PORTN. I. 4, 16.

[5b] So too an archaistic dual, *sny*, ERM. *Hymn.* 12, 2.

[6] ERM. *Gramm.*[3] p. 83, n. 2.

[7] ERM. *Hymn.* p. 40.

[8] After active old perfective, ex. LAC. *TR.* 1, 54; after imperative, *Sh. S.* 179; after participles and *śḏmty·fy* form, see § 375.

[9] *Dend.* 9. 11 A; *Urk.* v. 162, 6; *Urk.* iv. 346, 12; 618, 5.

2. after a number of particles like *isṯ* 'lo', *mk*[1] 'behold', *nn* 'not', *ntt* 'that', as well as the relative adjective *nty* 'which' (§ 199); in these cases the pronoun frequently serves as *subject* when an adverbial predicate follows.

Exx. *mk*[1] *wỉ m-bꜣḥ·k* behold, I am before thee.[2]

mk ṯw m bꜣk·i behold thou art my servant, lit. as my servant. Note that the *m* of predication (§ 38) is employed also in this case.[3]

nn s(y) m ib·i it was not in my heart.[4]

sšm pn nty wi ẖr·f this state in which I was, lit. this state which I (was) under it.[5]

3. as *subject* after adjectival predicate.

Ex. *nfr tw ḥnꜥ·i* thou art happy with me;[6] *tw* here is for *ṯw*, and is to be carefully distinguished from the indefinite pronoun of § 47.

§ 45. **Reflexive use of the dependent pronouns.**—Like the suffixes (§ 36), the dependent pronouns are used reflexively.

Ex. *rdi·n·(i) wi ḥr ẖt·i* I placed myself on my belly.[7]

§ 46. The pronoun *st* appears to be an old form of the dependent pronoun 3rd sing. f.,[8] which has been specialized for certain particular uses, mainly in place of the 3rd plur. 'they', 'them', or of the neuter 'it'.

1. as *object* of the verb.

Exx. *ꜥnn·sn st* they turned themselves about.[9] Note the reflexive meaning.

di·k sḏm st sꜣ·k thou shalt cause (that) thy son hear it.[10]

2. after the particles, etc., named in § 44, 2.

Exx. *mk st ḫft ḥr·k* behold, they (my gifts to thee) are before thee.[11]

bw nty st im the place where it is, lit. which it (is) therein.[12]

3. as *subject* after adjectival predicate.

Ex. *nfr st r ḫt nbt* it is more beautiful than anything.[13]

Obs. For *st* as object of the infinitive, like a suffix, see § 300.[13a]

§ 47. The **indefinite pronoun** *tw* 'one', French *on*, which we have found used like a suffix in the *śḏm·f* form, ex. *ḏd·tw* 'one says' (§ 39), may also be employed after the particles mentioned in § 44, 2 and others like *ḫr*, § 239; *kꜣ*, § 242.

Ex. *mk tw ḏd·tw* behold, one says, lit. behold one, one says.[14]

Obs. For an independent use of *tw* at the beginning of a sentence, see below § 333; a unique ex. before *sḏm·tw*, see Add. § 148, 1, Obs. For its employment as

[1] See above p. 44, n. 1.

[2] *Sin.* B. 263. Sim. *Sh. S.* 108.

[3] Exx. below § 119, 1.

[4] *Sin.* B 223–4.

[5] *Sin.* B 173–4.

[6] *Sin.* B 31.

[7] *Sh. S.* 161; *tw*, *ib.* 13, 72; *sw*, *Eb.* 52, 1; *sy*, *Westc.* 10, 7; *ṯn*, *Urk.* iv. 656, 1.

[8] Inferred from the old extended form *śtt*, *ÄZ.* 30, 20.

[9] *Westc.* 11, 15.

[10] *Siut* 1, 270. Sim. *Sh. S.* 86–7.

[11] *Siut* 1, 272.

[12] *Westc.* 9, 3–4. Sim. *Sh. S.* 115, after *nn*.

[13] *Sh. S.* 134. Sim. *Urk.* iv. 693, 8.

[13a] Unusual or problematic uses, see p. 41, n. 2; M.u.K.vs. 6, 5.

[14] *Urk.* iv. 1090. *Mk tw* followed by *ḥr* + infinitive, see § 324, second ex.

indicating the passive voice in the *śḏm·f* and other forms of the suffix conjugation see §§ 39. 410; in the pseudo-verbal construction *ỉw·tw* occurs (an ex. in § 332), as well as *wn·ỉn·tw* (§ 470); cf. also *ḫr·tw* (*kꜣ·tw*, *ỉw·tw*) *śḏm·tw·f*, §§ 239. 242. 463. A very exceptional example after the infinitive used absolutely, § 306 (last ex. but one). Syntactically, *tw* is treated as of masculine gender, see § 511, 5.

§ **48. Adjectives** may be used as *epithets*, as *predicates*, or as *nouns*.

1. when used as *epithets* they follow their nouns, *agreeing with them in number and gender*. The ending sing. f. is *t*, as with the noun; for the plural, see below §§ 72. 74.

Exx. *sḫr pn bỉn* this evil counsel.

ḫt nbt nfrt every good thing.

These examples illustrate the fact that *nb* 'every', 'any', 'all', and demonstrative adjectives which, like *pn*, follow their noun, have precedence of position over other adjectives. So too the suffixes when used possessively.

Ex. *sꜣt·f šrỉt* his little daughter.

The word for 'other', m. *ky*, f. *kt*, precedes its noun, see Exercise I (*a*); so too the demonstratives *pꜣ* 'this' and *pf*(*y*) 'that', see below § 111.

With the adjective *nb* the plural ending (§ 72) is usually, the fem. ending often, omitted in writing, exx. *nṯrw nb*(*w*) 'all gods'; *ḫt nb*(*t*) 'everything'.

OBS. The masc. plur. ending is, however, sometimes shown;[0] Copt. *nim* is invariable.

[0] Dyn. XII, *Ann.* 39, 189, 8; *Ächt.* p. 25; Dyn. XVIII, *Urk.* iv. 384, 1.

2. when used as *predicate*, the adjective precedes its subject, and *is invariable both in gender and in number*.

Exx. *nfr ỉb·ỉ* my heart is happy.

bỉn sy she is bad.

Note that a dependent pronoun, not a suffix, is here used as subject (§ 44, 3).

3. when used as a *noun*, the adjective is generally followed by some appropriate determinative. Exx. *šrỉ* 'small boy', 'lad'; *nfrt* 'beautiful woman'; *nfrt* 'beautiful cow'.

§ **49.** The ending *·wy*, much more rarely[1] written, as regularly in Old Egyptian, is sometimes added to adjectival predicates in order to give them an exclamatory force.

[1] *Siut* 3, 12; 4, 31; *Urk.* iv. 817, 9.

Ex. *nfr·wy pr pn* how beautiful is this house![2]

[2] Exx. *P. Kah.* 2, 11; *Pt.*627.629; ERM. *Hymn.* 6, 1; Cairo 20089, *d* 6.

OBS. It is probable that this *·wy* is merely the masc. dual ending (below § 72) with a special signification; in this case *nfr·wy* would mean 'twice beautiful', compare modern Arabic *marḥabatên* 'twice welcome'.

§ **50.** The Egyptian adjective has no special forms to indicate the degrees of comparison. **Comparison** is effected by means of the preposition *r*, which here signifies 'more than', literally perhaps 'relatively to'.

Ex. *ꜥšꜣ st r ḫt nbt* they were more numerous than anything.[3]

[3] *Urk.* iv. 693, 8.

§ **51.** The sense of the English **neuter** ('it', 'thing') is expressed in Egyptian by the feminine. Exx. *dwt* 'an evil (thing)', 'evil';[1] *ḥr·s* 'on account of it'.[2] Compare too the use of *st*, see above § 46.

[1] *Pt.* 299. Sim. *nfrt*, *bint*, *Peas.* B 1, 152.
[2] *Peas.* B 1, 39.

§ **52.** The meaning of the **dative** is rendered by means of the preposition *n* 'to', 'for'.

Exx. *hꜣb·k sš n nb·k* thou sendest the scribe to thy lord.
dd·n n·ṯn we speak to you.

VOCABULARY

var. *di* give, place.[1]
var. *rdi* give, place.[1]
ꜥnḫ live; life.
ḥtp rest, go to rest, become at peace; set (of sun); peace (noun).
ꜥḥꜥ stand up, arise.
ḫꜥ appear, shine (of sun, gods or king).
sḫꜣ remember.
nfr good, beautiful, happy.
bin bad, miserable.
dw evil, sad.
ꜥšꜣ plentiful, rich, many.
var. *ꜥꜣ* great, large.
iḳr excellent.
šw empty, free (with *m* of, from).
ib heart, wish.
var. *nb* lord, master.
nb every, any, all.
mw water.
ẖrd child.
ity sovereign, monarch.
mi like.
mitt likeness; *m mitt* likewise.

[1] In this verb appearing in two variant forms (§ 289, 1) is probably an ideogram depicting some gift, perhaps a loaf; , increasingly common as Dyn. XVIII is approached, represents a hand holding such a gift. For is sometimes substituted , the two usually not being distinguished in hieratic; *di* is not identical with *mi*.

EXERCISE IV

(N.B. In analysing complex examples like (1) and (2), the student should first transliterate the whole, and then divide it into its component sentences and clauses.)

(*a*) *Transliterate and translate*:

(1)

(2)

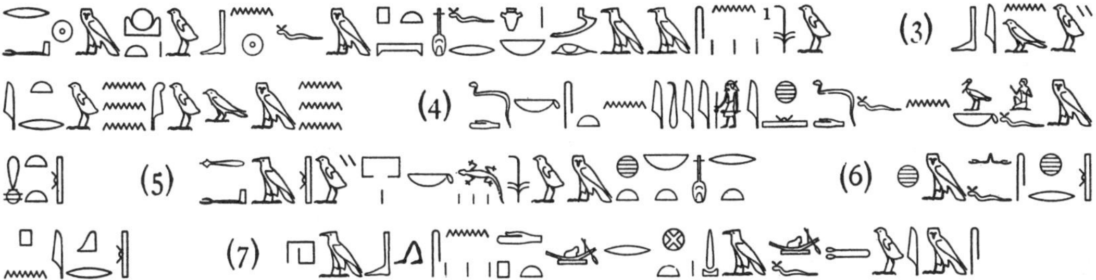

(*b*) *Write in hieroglyphs and transliteration*:

(1) How beautiful is this thy house! Behold, it is in my sight (lit. face) like heaven. (2) The sun sets in life[2] every day. (3) Behold, thou art with me as a maid-servant. (4) She is more beautiful than her daughter. (5) Evil is on every side (lit. road). (6) Then we will stand up (and) speak to our good lord. (7) Every man is in joy, when he hears (lit. they hear) it. (8) Mayest thou go down in peace to thy city. (9) How excellent is this thy counsel in (lit. upon) my heart, (O) sovereign, my lord!

[1] For the plural suffix see § 510, 2. [2] A common Egyptian phrase meaning perhaps 'to set in full vigour'.

LESSON V

§ 53. **Biliteral signs** (continued from § 41):—

vi. with *p* as second consonant:

wp *kp*

vii. with *m* as second consonant:

ỉm *nm* or *ḥm* *km* *gm* *tm*

viii. with *n* as second consonant:

ỉn *wn* (rare) *nn* *ḫn* *sn* (*śn*), later

wn *mn* *ḥn* *ẖn* *šn*

PECULIARITIES OF HIEROGLYPHIC WRITING.[1]

§ 54. The classification of the hieroglyphs into (1) ideograms or sense-signs and (2) phonograms or sound-signs (§ 6) covers the entire ground, but, as shown in § 42, Obs., the line of demarcation between the two classes is often difficult to draw. Nor must it be imagined that all the signs contained in the sub-divisions of these main groups stand on an equal footing and conform to identical rules; on the contrary, custom plays a very important part in deciding what writings are possible and what are not, though variant spellings are very numerous. A few examples will make this statement clearer.

[1] See Erm. *Gramm.*[4] §§ 16–89, where this subject is dealt with in greater detail; also Lef. *Gr.* §§ 9–66.

'House' (*pr*) is written , much more rarely ; such a writing as is never found.

'To be firm', 'remain' (*mn*) is always or the like, never .

The club-sign is used with phonetic (or semi-phonetic) value in a few words like *ḥm* 'slave', *ḥmt* 'female slave', as well as in the common expression *ḥm·f* 'His Majesty' (see further below, Excursus A, p. 74); but it has not otherwise obtained currency as a biliteral for *ḥm*, the sign being used for that purpose.

Yet again, some signs used phonetically must be preceded by letters representing the whole of their sound-value: so in *ỉb* 'thirst', which is phonetic inasmuch as the entire word *ỉb* 'kid' enters bodily into the writing of the etymologically unrelated verb for 'thirst'; here alone is not phonetic, since such a writing as without would be quite abnormal in early times. It is useful to describe such signs as *phonetic determinatives*; other examples are in *ḫn* 'sentence', 'saying'; (*tr*) in *ḥtrỉ* 'pair of horses'; (*ꜣr*) in *mꜣỉr* 'miserable'.

Enough has been said to indicate that a correct theoretical account of all hieroglyphic spellings would be a very long and tedious undertaking. *The method of this book is largely based upon the view that beginners, having once mastered the main principles of the writing, should not inquire too curiously into the nature of individual spellings, but should learn both the hieroglyphic groups and their transliterations mechanically.* It is as unnecessary—to take an extreme instance—for the beginner to know why 'king', strictly 'king of Upper Egypt', variant , is to be read *nsw* and not *swtn*[1] as it would be for a learner of English to know why the word pronounced *plow* is now written 'plough'.

The student must, accordingly, expect to find in the Vocabularies a number of spellings which he will not at once understand. In order, however, to elucidate a few simple problems that may perplex him at an early stage, some paragraphs will be devoted to certain types of peculiar writing.

§ 55. **Abbreviations.**—These are commonest in monumental inscriptions, stereotyped phrases, formulae, titles, and the like.

Exx. *ꜥnḫ wḏꜣ snb*, in full 'may he live, be prosperous, be healthy' (below § 313, end), attributes bestowed on the king and on honoured persons by the gods, and prayed for by men on their behalf; often appended as a token of respect to words for 'king', 'lord', etc.

 or *mꜣꜥ-ḫrw*, fuller writing 'true of voice', an epithet added to the names of dead persons and hence often practically equivalent to our 'deceased'. Originally applied to Osiris with reference to the occasion when his regal rights, being disputed by Seth, were vindicated before the divine

[1] See *ÄZ.* 49, 15; *Rec.* 38, 69–70. Etymologically the word appears to mean 'belonging to (*nỉ*) the sedge (*swt*)', the plant-emblem of Upper Egypt, as the papyrus *wꜣḏ* was of Lower Egypt. The etymological feminine *t* of *swt* remains in the writing of 'king', although variants show *nsw* to have been the consonantal value as early as the Pyramids. Some scholars prefer to transliterate *nỉśwt* or *n-śwt*, but serious difficulties then arise in the case of the derivatives *nsyt* 'kingship', *nsyw* 'kings', etc. A recent alternative view regards *nsw* and *nỉśwt* as entirely different words, see *JNES.* 6, 8.

tribunal in Heliopolis. The same epithet is also used in connexion with Horus as the 'triumphant' avenger of the wrongs done to Osiris.

wḥm ʿnḫ 'repeating life', another epithet given to deceased persons in Dyn. XVIII and thereabouts.

kꜣ nḫt, in full, 'victorious bull', an attribute ascribed to the Pharaoh.

n-sw-bit[1] 'king of Upper and Lower Egypt', literally 'he who belongs to the sedge of Upper Egypt and the bee of Lower Egypt'; compare *bity* 'king of Lower Egypt', a derivative in *-y* from *bit*.[2]

ḥꜣty-ʿ, literally 'foremost in position', a common term for local princes or mayors.

imy-r ḥmw-nṯr 'overseer of the priests', more fully (§ 73).

[1] Vocalized as *in-sibya* in a cuneiform tablet from Boghaz Keui; see *ÄZ.* 49, 17.

[2] *ÄZ.* 28, 125; 49, 19.

§ 56. **Graphic transpositions.**[3]—Signs are sometimes transposed, either in order to give a more pleasing appearance or for some less assignable reason.

A small sign may be placed under the breast of a bird even when the latter has to be read first; thus, according to the word in which it occurs, may be read either *tw* or *wt*; similarly either *tꜣ* or *ꜣt*.

Thin vertical signs show a peculiar tendency to precede a bird which they ought properly to follow. Exx. *wḏ* instead of ; *wḏꜣ* in place of ; *ꜣḥt* 'field' as variant of ; *mr* 'pyramid' always for .

Economy of space is one reason for such writings as for *sbꜣ* 'star'; for *ḥry-ḥb(t)*[4] 'lector-priest'. So too in vertical columns is of frequent occurrence for *-yt* and for *ḫr rdwy* 'under the feet (of)'.

[3] See *Rec.* 25, 139; *Pyr.* iv. § 17.

[4] Probable meaning 'holder of the ritual book', hence *ḥb(t)*, not *ḥb*; see *JEA.* 41, 11, n. 3. Sim. *ẖr(t)-nṯr* 'necropolis' omits the fem. ending, *JEA.* 24, 244; so too *nb(t)*, § 48, 1.

§ 57. **Transpositions with honorific intent.**—There is a common tendency to write words like *nsw* 'king' and *nṯr* 'god', as well as the names of specific kings and gods, before closely connected words which in actual speech were pronounced first. Exx. *sš nsw* 'scribe of the king'; *ḥm-nṯr* 'servant of god', i.e. 'priest'; *mi Rʿ* 'like Rēʿ'; *mry Imn* 'beloved of Amūn'.[5] Note that abbreviated writings are here frequent.

[5] Cf. also 'beloved of his lord' written *nb·f mry*, e.g. *Sinai* 87; 'praise god' written *nṯr dwꜣ*, e.g. p. 173, last ex.

§ 58. **Monograms.**—(1) In certain verbs involving the notion of movement the ideogram is combined with a phonogram.

So with *i*: *ii* come.

" *s*: *is* go (imperative); *ms* bring, offer; *sb* bring, conduct, pass.

" *š*: *šm* go.

" *ṯ*: *iṯ* take, carry off.

" *nw*, *in*: *in* bring, fetch.

" *sšm*: *sšm* guide, lead.

(2) Some other common monograms are:

or in *tr* season — *mm* — *ḥrt-hrw* daytime
in *rnp* be young — *rs(w)* southern — *ꜥḥ* palace
mi, m — *Šmꜥw* Upper Egypt — *wḏꜥ* judge

§ **59. Defective and superfluous writings.**—Such writings as for *rmṯ* 'men', 'people', and for *ḥnḳt*[1] 'beer' are in no way at variance with the rules already given, but are apt to puzzle beginners. The omission of *m* and *n* here is probably due to calligraphic reasons; but the Egyptian was under no obligation to prefix to an ideogram more phonetic signs than were needed to remove obscurity. Conversely, a superfluous *w* is inserted in *i(w)f* 'flesh', 'meat', Coptic showing that *if* is to be read.[1a]

§ **60. Group-writing.**[2]—A peculiar method of writing with biliteral instead of alphabetical signs, e.g. *ꜥꜣ* for *ꜥ*, *ḥꜣ* for *ḥ*, and with some other groups, e.g. *hꜣ* for *h*, for *t*; especially often in foreign words or etymologically obscure names, e.g. , a foreign land, to be transliterated *'Ihi*, not *'Iꜣhwiw*[3]; *ꜥmṯ*, not *ꜥꜣmiṯw*,[4] a man's name. Traces already in the Pyramid Texts, and partial exx. even in some M.E. words, e.g. *ḏdti·f* for *ḏdt·f*, § 409.

§ **61. Determination of compounds.**—Compounds and other closely connected groups of words may show one common determinative or group of determinatives; exx. *bw-nb* 'every one', lit. 'every place'; *rḫ-ḫt* 'a wise man', lit. 'a knower of things'.[5] Doubtless for this reason titles preceding the name of their owner are usually left without a determinative of their own, ex. *sš Nḫt* 'the scribe Nakht'.

§ **62. Avoidance of the repetition of like consonantal signs in contiguity.**[6]—When, for inflexional or other reasons, two like consonants either fell together or else came into close contact so as not to be separated by a full vowel, there was a strong tendency to write them but once. Thus, within the limits of a single word, *m(w)t*[7] is written for *m(w)t·ti* (§ 309), *inf* for *in·n·f* (§ 413). In the kind of verbs known as geminating (see below § 269) this rule is still stricter, the alternative writing with repetition being practically excluded.

The same tendency not seldom manifests itself when a word ending with a certain consonant is immediately followed by another word beginning with the same consonant, ex. *ir·n·i ist* for *ir·n·i is st* 'lo, I did it'.[8] This case occurs particularly often with uniconsonantal words or the like, so that they then find no expression at all in the writing; exx. *ḏꜣ·tw irf m* for *ḏꜣ·tw irf m m* 'by what means (lit. with what) shall one ferry across?';[9] *smi·sn·f* for *smi·sn n·f* 'they report to him'[10] beside .[11]

1 Reading from late variants (BRUGSCH, *Wörterbuch* 976) and from Coptic *henkĕ*. Cf. also the play on words *Pyr.* 37, 39.

1a See *Onom.* II, 237*.

2 See M. BURCHARDT, *Die altkanaanäischen Fremdworte und Eigennamen im Aegyptischen*, Leipzig, 1909–10. Also particularly W. F. EDGERTON, 'Eg. Phonetic Writing' in *JAOS* 60, 473, mainly an answer to W. F. ALBRIGHT, *The Vocalization of the Eg. Syllabic Orthography*, New Haven, 1934.

3 *JEA*. iv, Pl. IX, 10. Sim. *Urk.* iv. 648, 5; 650, 6.

4 *Urk.* iv. 1119, 2. Sim. in Dyn. XII, *BH.* ii. p. 30.

5 *Leb.* 145–6.

6 See *ÄZ.* 56, 61.

7 *Sh. S.* 38, contrasted with 106. Sim. *nḫt(·ti)*, *Peas.* B 1, 116.

8 *Urk.* iv. 363.

9 *Peas.* B 1, 199.

10 *Urk.* iv. 1111.

11 *Urk.* iv. 1112.

Conversely, a consonant is sometimes abnormally repeated, doubtless to mark the retention of a sound that in other combinations had fallen away; exx. *sb·sn͡n wi* for *sb·sn wi* 'they shall convey me';[1] *mṯn͡n wi* for *mṯn wi* 'behold ye me';[2] *wꜣt͡t·n* for *wꜣt·n* 'our road'.[3]

See Add. for § 62A.

§ **63. Doubtful readings.**—A consequence of the complex and often defective nature of hieroglyphic writing is that scholars are still often in doubt as to the correct transliteration of words. Thus *ḥnḳt* 'beer' (§ 59) is in other books on Egyptian almost universally read *ḥḳt*; in old-fashioned works *nsw* 'king' is regularly rendered as *swtn*; and so forth. Among readings which are not yet fully established we incline to *gnwty* for 'sculptor', *sḏꜣwty* for 'treasurer'. Where there is a choice, shorter readings are preferable to long ones; thus we read *mni* for 'moor', though the stem is probably *mini*.

See Add. for § 63A.

§ **64. Personal pronouns** (continued from §§ 43–6):

3. The **independent pronouns**[4] almost always stand at the beginning of the sentence (exceptions § 300), and are more or less emphatic in meaning.

Sing. 1, c.	*ink*	I.	Also written ,[5] or ; early also [6]; king sometimes ,[7] [8]
„ 2, m.	*ntk*	Thou.	
„ 2, f.	*ntṯ*	Thou.	Later also *ntt*.[9]
„ 3, m.	*ntf*	He, it.	
„ 3, f.	*nts*	She, it.	From Dyn. XVIII also
Plur. 1, c.	, *inn*	We.	Hitherto noted only in very late texts.[10]
„ 2, c.	*ntṯn*	You.	Later also *nttn*.
„ 3, c.	*ntsn*	They.	Later also

These pronouns often stand in parallelism to the particle (§ 227) or preposition (§ 168) *in* followed by a noun, and are clearly related to that word etymologically.

OBS. This series is closely connected with the personal pronouns in Hebrew and Arabic. The element *in* is probably demonstrative in origin,[11] the *t* may be that of the feminine, and the variable endings are mainly those of the suffix-pronouns.

In the Pyramid Texts and the Old Kingdom the place of the forms above given for the 2nd and 3rd pers. sing. is occupied by an earlier type of independent pronoun formed from the dependent pronouns by the addition of *t*.[12] The two masculines have survived into Middle Egyptian as archaisms.

Sing. 2, c.	*ṯwt*	Thou.	Later *twt*.[13]
„ 3, c.	*swt*	He, she, it.	Originally *śwt*.

OBS. *Ṯwt* and *św t* were originally masculines only; in Middle Egyptian they are found for both genders.[14] *Swt* as a particle meaning 'but', see below § 254.

[1] *Sin.* B 171. Sim. LAC. *TR.* 47, 21. 23. For the loss of *n* in *·sn*, *ṯn* see § 34, OBS. 4.
[2] LAC. *TR.* 78, 3; MAR. *Abyd.* ii. 30, 33.
[3] *Peas.* B 1, 7–8. Sim. *Sh. S.* 7; *Kopt.* 8, 6. 9. So already in Pyr., see *ÄZ.* 44, 80, n. 2 and above p. 34, n. 1a.
[4] *ÄZ.* 29, 121; 30, 15; GUNN, *Studies*, p. 46.
[5] Cairo 20007.
[6] *ÄZ.* 23, 8.
[7] *Urk.* iv. 813, 9.
[8] *Urk.* iv. 835, 15.
[9] *M. u. K.* 2, 8. 9.
[10] *JEA.* 27, 106.
[11] *PSBA.* 22, 325.
[12] *ÄZ.* 30, 17. For *śtt* see above p. 46, n. 8.
[13] Already in ERM. *Hymn.* 1, 5.
[14] *Ṯwt*, see ERM. *Hymn.* 1, 5; *Urk.* iv. 222, 10; 229, 12; 343. 10. *Swt*, see *ib.* 221, 14; 257, 9. 11; 258, 2.

§ 65. The uses of the independent pronouns to be noted at this point are:

1. as *subject* of sentences with directly juxtaposed *nominal* predicate.

Exx. *ỉnk ỉt·k* I am thy father.

ntf sꜣ·s he is her son.

ṯwt nb·ỉ thou art my lord.

2. as *subject* of sentences with *adjectival* predicate. This use is almost confined to the 1st pers. sing.

Ex. *ỉnk nfr* I am good.

In both uses a certain degree of emphasis rests upon the pronouns, and in some contexts it would be desirable to translate, 'it is I (who am) thy father', 'it is I (who am) good', etc.

Observe carefully that it is against Egyptian usage to employ the independent pronoun when the predicate is adverbial; 'thou art in the house' may be rendered by … or by …, but not by …

§ 66. Word-order.—It is now necessary to supplement what was said on this score in §§ 27. 29.

The dative (§ 52) differs from other adverbial phrases (i.e. preposition accompanied by a noun) in its tendency to follow as closely as possible the word that governs it. The following sentence exemplifies the usual word-order.

smỉ sš sštꜣ pn n nb·f m nỉwt tn the scribe reports this secret to his lord in this city.

This word-order is, however, modified when the *subject* or *object* is a pronoun; also when the preposition *n* governs a suffix-pronoun so as to form a *dative* case. In these conditions the rule is *that a noun must not precede a pronoun and that the dependent pronoun must not precede a suffix.*

Exx. *hꜣb·f ṯw* he sends thee.

hꜣb ṯw sš the scribe sends thee.

ḏꜣ ṯn sꜣ·f his son ferries you across; *or* 'you ferry his son across', since *ṯn* may be the suffix just as well as the dependent pronoun.

wšb·n·ỉ n·f st I answered (*śḏm·n·f* form § 67) it to him.[1]

ỉn n·k st sš the scribe brings it to thee.

hꜣb·n n·n nb·n nfr šꜥt ḥr·s our good lord has sent to us a despatch about it.

twt·wy n·s st how like (to) her it is![2]

nn n·k st it does not belong to thee, lit. it is not to thee.[3]

ỉw n·k hrw nfr holiday is thine, lit. a good day is to thee.[4]

ỉw·f n·ỉ he is mine, lit. he is to me.[5]

Certain particles, termed **enclitics** (§ 226), which cannot stand at the beginning of a sentence, may take precedence of the subject (when a noun) or

[1] *Sh. S.* 86–7. Sim. *Peas.* B 2, 38–9.

[2] *Urk.* iv. 368.

[3] *Peas.* B 2, 26.

[4] *Urk.* iv. 1166.

[5] Common as a m. proper name.

the object or the dative. Such are *grt* 'now' (often best left untranslated), *rf* (with wishes, commands, questions, etc.), and *ḥm* 'assuredly' in the following examples.

ir·n·(i) grt mꜥḥꜥt·(i) r rd n nṯr ꜥꜣ now I made my tomb at the staircase of the great god.[1]

sḏd·i rf n·k mitt iry let me relate to thee the like thereof.[2]

Similarly in more complex constructions, as *ti sw ḥm iy·f* 'and now indeed he was returning'.[3] See § 148, 1.

Such non-enclitic particles as *mk* 'behold', *nn* 'not' (§ 44, 2) stand at the beginning of the sentence, preceding even the verb. Examples below § 119, and often.

Obs. Exceptional word-order is more often than not due to motives of emphasis, see below §§ 146 foll.; but compare also § 507.

§ 67. **The *śḏm·n·f* form.**—This second common form of the verb is constructed, as regards its pronominal or nominal subjects, as well as in its mode of expressing the passive, exactly like the *śḏm·f* form (§ 39). From that form it differs only in the insertion of an *inseparable* element *n* immediately after the verb-stem or after any determinative which the verb-stem may have.

Exx. *sḏm·n·i ḫrw·f* I heard his voice.

sḏm·n nṯr ḫrw the god heard the voice.

sḏm·n st nṯr the god heard it.

sḏm·n·tw ḫrw the voice was heard.

pr·n·f he went out.

hꜣb·n n·k nb·k thy lord has sent to thee.

ms·n·tw·i I was born.

Observe that the rules of word-order given in § 66 apply also here. A full paradigm is unnecessary; the one point to remember is that the formative *n* is inseparable from the verb-stem.

In its origin the *śḏm·n·f* form appears to have resulted from the combination of a passive participle with a dative of possession or agential interest. Thus *pr·n·f* would mean 'gone out to him', *sḏm·n·f* 'heard to him'.

Since the *śḏm·n·f* form expresses essentially what *occurs* or *happens* to someone or by his agency, it was at the start no less indeterminate, as regards time-position, than the *śḏm·f* form. We shall later on become acquainted with one affirmative use (§ 414, 5) in which the *śḏm·n·f* must be translated as an English present; and so too very frequently when it is preceded by the negative word *n* 'not' (§ 105, 3). These are, however, exceptional cases; almost

[1] Cairo 20099, 2. Sim. *ib.* 20538, ii. *c* 1; 20539 ii. *b* 6.

[2] *Sh. S.* 21. Sim. *ib.* 12; before dep. pron. *ib.* 10.

[3] *Sin.* R 15.

everywhere else the *śḏm·n·f* form is restricted to *past* time. It is thus employed of past time in affirmative sentences, where it may have the meaning of the English *past* tense ('he heard'), of the English *present perfect* ('he has heard'), or of the English *past perfect* ('he had heard'); the latter two uses are particularly common in *clauses of time* (see below § 212).

Exx. . . . as a man longs to see his home *ir·n·f rnpwt ꜥšꜣt m nḏrt* (when) he has passed many years in imprisonment.[1]

His Majesty proceeded in peace, *sḫr·n·f ḫftyw·f* (when) he had overthrown his enemies.[2]

[1] *Leb.* 141. Sim. *P. Kah.* 28, 21; 29, 12; *Urk.* iv. 1090, 14.

[2] *BH.* i. 8, 10. Sim. *Peas.* R 7. 59.

§ 68. **The compound verb-form *iw śḏm·n·f*.**—We have seen (§ 29) that *iw*, properly the copula 'is' or 'are', confers upon sentences with adverbial predicates the value of a detached or independent statement. It is also frequently employed before the *śḏm·n·f* form in main clauses to mark some more or less important event in a narration.

Exx. The prince came to the king and said: *iw in·n·i Ḏdi* I have brought Djedi.[3] English present perfect.

iw wp·n·f r·f r·i he opened his mouth to me.[4] English past tense.

The student should make use of this form at the beginning of narrative sentences in the Exercises, reserving the simple *śḏm·n·f* for subsidiary sentences. The form *iw śḏm·n·f*, to which we shall return later (§ 464), gives a certain smoothness and elegance to recitals of past events.

[3] *Westc.* 8, 8. Sim. *Sin.* B 189–90; *P. Kah.* 30, 31; *Peas.* B1, 74–5; *Urk.* iv. 17, 7.

[4] *Sh. S.* 67. Sim. *BH.* i. 25, 13; Brit. Mus. 614, 3; *Hamm.* 113, 9; 199, 6; Cairo 20538, ii. *b* 3. 4; 20543, *a* 13; *Urk.* iv. 34, 5. 11. 16; 55, 16; 131, 14; 748, 2. 6. 10.

§ 69. **Verbal sentences as noun clauses.**—A striking characteristic of Egyptian is the ease with which it can treat an entire sentence as a noun. We often find words having the form of verbal sentences, without any equivalent of English 'that' by way of introduction, as *object* of verbs of saying, thinking, wishing, etc., or as *subject* of their passives; and a similar use occurs after prepositions. Sentence-like groups of words thus used we call **noun clauses.**

We shall be much concerned with such constructions in the later parts of this book. For the moment all that is needful is to state the principle and to illustrate it in one particular case, namely after the verb (*r*)*di* 'give', 'place', 'cause' (§ 70).

§ 70. **The *śḏm·f* form after (*r*)*di*.**—The verb (*r*)*di* 'give', 'place' often takes as *object* another verb in the *śḏm·f* form, and then means 'cause' or 'allow'.

Ex. *di·i sdm·tn* I cause you to hear, lit. I give (that) you hear.[5]

Similarly as *subject* of the passive of (*r*)*di*.

Ex. *rdi·t(w) iry·i hrw m Iꜣꜣ* I was allowed to pass (lit. one gave I passed) a day in Yaa.[6]

[5] Cairo 20538, ii. *b* 9. Other exx. see § 452, 1 *a*.

[6] *Sin.* B 238.

LESSON V

VOCABULARY

in bring, fetch, remove.

wp open.

šm go, walk.

gm find.

wꜥb be pure, clean; det. (ordinary) priest.

wšb answer (*n* 'to' persons).

ḥkr hunger (vb. and n.); hungry.

ib thirst (vb.); thirsty.

mnḫ efficient, beneficent, excellent.

ḥꜣy naked.

Kmt the Black Land, i.e. Egypt.

Dšrt the Red Land, i.e. the Desert.

ẖnw interior; det. , the (royal) Residence.

sn brother; *snt* sister.

ḥmt woman, wife.

ḥm (male) slave; *ḥmt* female slave.

varr. *nsw* king of Upper Egypt, king.

var. *nṯr* god.

t bread.

ḥnḳt beer.

ḥbs clothes, clothing.

ṯsm hound, dog.

(early also) *sꜣ* back; *m-sꜣ* at the back of, following after.

ꜥ hand, arm.

EXERCISE V

(*a*) *Transliterate and translate:*

(1)

(2)

(3)

(4)

(5)

(6)

(7)

(8)

(9)

(*b*) *Write in hieroglyphs and transliteration*:

(1) The scribe opened his mouth that he might answer the king: (O) sovereign, my lord! Thou art greater than any god. Thou art my lord, I am thy slave. This thy humble servant[1] is like a hound following after thee. The Black Land (and) the Red Land rejoice (because) thou art (*ỉw·k*) beneficent king. (2) He caused them to go down to the boat. (3) How evil is thy utterance; thou art not (§ 44, 2) my brother. (4) She is my sister; she is in thy hand as a slave.

[1] 'This thy humble servant' is to be rendered simply *bꜣk ỉm* 'the servant there', a respectful circumlocution for the 1st pers. sing. in Middle Egyptian. See *ÄZ*. 27, 122; 30, 126.

LESSON VI

§ **71. Biliteral signs** (continued from § 53):—

ix. with *r* as second consonant:

ỉr *pr* *mr*[1] *ẖr* (not to be confused with *g*).

wr or *mr* *ḥr* *ḏr*

x. with *ḥ* as second consonant:

bḥ[2] *pḥ* *mḥ* *nḥ*

[1] Also with value *ꜣb*, § 41.

[2] Also with value *ḥw*, § 41.

§ **72. Number of nouns and adjectives.**[3]—There are three numbers in Egyptian, *singular*, *plural*, and *dual*. The *dual* is used only for pairs of things or persons.

Sing. m. has no special ending. Ex. *sn* brother.

" f. ends in *-t*. Ex. *snt* sister.

Plur. m. " " *-w*. Ex. *snw* brothers.

" f. " " *-wt*. Ex. *snwt* sisters.

Dual m. " " *-wy*. Ex. *snwy* pair of brothers.

" f. " " *-ty*. Ex. *snty* pair of sisters.

Note that the plural of *nsw* 'king' is written or *nsyw* (?)[4]

[3] See FAULKNER, The *Plural and Dual in Old Egyptian*, Brussels, 1929; ERMAN, *Die Pluralbildung des Aegyptischen*, Leipzig, 1878; also *Rec*. 35, 75. For the dual, see *ÄZ*. 47, 42.

[4] Cf. *ỉtyw* 'fathers', but here *-yw* is written out only rarely before Dyn. XIX, see *ÄZ*. 48, 25.

§ **73. Writing of the plural and dual.**—1. The oldest method consisted in the repetition of the ideogram with which the singular was written, thrice for the plural, twice for the dual.

Exx. Sing.	Plur.	Dual
( ) *pr* house.	*prw* houses.	*prwy* the two houses.
( ) *ỉrt* eye.	—	*ỉrty* the (two) eyes.

This method of writing is archaistically retained in many monumental inscriptions of the Middle and New Kingdoms. The phonetic spelling of the words often precedes the ideograms, which thus appear as determinatives (§ 23).

Exx. Plur. *srw* officials. Dual *tḫnwy* pair of obelisks.
" *nhwt* trees. " *ˁty* pair of limbs.

2. On the same principle, words that are written purely phonetically may have their component sound-signs, or some of them, repeated. This again, so far as Middle Egyptian is concerned, is for the most part a consciously archaistic practice.

Exx. Sing.	Plur.	Dual
nṯr god.	*nṯrw* gods.	*nṯrwy* pair of gods.
rn name.	*rnw* names.	———
ḥkꜣ magic.	*ḥkꜣw* magical spells.	———

3. Towards the end of the Old Kingdom a **determinative of plurality,** consisting of three strokes ׀׀׀, , or , more rarely of three dots ∘∘∘, , came into general use.[1] As a rule it accompanies some sign or signs which in earlier times would have been written thrice, and serves as substitute for the repetition.

Exx. *snw* 'brothers' for old
nṯrw 'gods' " "
prw 'houses' " "

Sometimes, however, the 'plural strokes' stand independently as the mark of plurality, as in *nfrw* 'beautiful' (m. plur.); they may even accompany words that are plural only in meaning, not in grammatical form.

Exx. *sn* they. *rḫyt* people, subjects. *ˁšꜣ* many.

4. The sign \\, less frequently ׀׀, which is seen in the dual endings *-wy* and *-ty* (§ 72), was originally a mark of duality employed, like the plural strokes ׀׀׀, to obviate the repetition of ideograms; thus the archaic writing *snty* 'pair of sisters' was at first no more than an abbreviation of . Since, however, Old Egyptian orthography habitually omitted the *-y* of the dual endings *-wy* and *-ty*, the substitute \\ of the original pair of ideograms soon came to be interpreted as that semi-vowel. By the beginning of the Middle Kingdom, accordingly, \\ had ceased to be a special mark of duality and had become a sound-sign for *-y*, with a use restricted to the terminations of words. Henceforth 'pair of sisters' is written *snty*, where \\ is *y* and where the determinatives have to be added.

Obs. The sign originally represented consonantal (semi-vocalic) *y*, but at the beginning of some words it seems to have possessed a value indistinguishable from *ꜣ*; hence it is transliterated *ỉ*. At the end of words *y* is written or \\, but not as a rule interchangeably; may occur as last letter but one, see above § 20.[2]

[1] Superstition, as well as motives of abbreviation, helped in the development; see *Rec.* 35, 73; *ÄZ.* 51, 18.

[2] On this question see *Verbum*, i. §§ 109 foll.

§ 74. Omission of the plural and dual endings.—As seen in the last section, the plural and dual numbers of nouns were usually indicated by repetitions of signs or by the use of special determinatives. All the more readily, therefore, could the actual phonetic terminations *-w* and *-wt*, *-wy* and *-ty*, be omitted in the writing. Hence we find in place of *srw* 'officials', in place of *nbty* 'pair of ladies'; indeed, the abbreviated spellings are the commoner, the full feminine plural being especially rare. For example, usually, nay possibly always, replaces the theoretically correct full writing * *ḥmwt* 'women', 'wives'.

In the case of adjectives, the plurals and duals of which were formed in the same way as with nouns, such abbreviated spellings are yet more common. The ending of the feminine plural is here *never* fully written out, and even the plural strokes may be omitted; and are equally legitimate writings of *nfrwt*. In the masculine plural of the adjective the plural strokes are often dispensed with, exx. *ꜣpdw ḏdꜣ(w)* 'fat birds';[1] *kꜣw wꜣḏw* 'sturdy oxen'.[2]

OBS. As we have seen (§ 48), *nb* 'all', 'any', 'every' was early often written as though invariable, but occasional variants show that this was not the case.

[1] *Peas.* R 105 = B 1, 62. Sim. *Sin.* B 196; *Sh. S.* 165; *Urk.* iv. 1105, 4.
[2] *Th. T. S.* ii. 22.

§ **75.** After nouns in the dual

1. the sign for the suffix 1st pers. sing. is occasionally preceded by *y*, exx *ꜥwy·ỉ* 'my hands';[3] *rdwy·ỉ* 'my feet'.[4]

2. the suffixes 2nd and 3rd m. sing. and 3rd f. sing. sometimes show an ending *-y*,[5] exx. *ꜥwy·fy* 'his two hands'[6] (also written [7]); *spty·ky* 'thy two lips';[8] *mnty·sy* 'her two thighs'.[9] In this case the dual ending is occasionally omitted after the noun, ex. *gs(wy)·fy* 'its two sides'.[10]

[3] *Sh. S.* 87.
[4] *Sin.* B 16.
[5] *ÄZ.* 13, 76.
[6] *Sin.* B 63.
[7] *P. Kah.* 1, 3.
[8] *Peas.* B 1, 167.
[9] *P. Kah.* 6, 9.
[10] *Sh. S.* 85; see *Rec.* 38, 197. A convincing ex. *Arm.* 103, 8.

§ **76.** The use of *·fy* just mentioned (§ 75, 2) is extended, strictly speaking inaccurately, to certain words

1. having dual form but singular meaning, ex. *pḥ(wy)·fy* 'its end'.[11]

2. having singular form but a meaning with some implication of duality, ex. *sn-nw·fy* 'his fellow', lit. 'his second'.[12]

[11] *Leb.* 65.
[12] *Leb.* 106. See too below § 263, *ḥr sn-nw ·sy*.

§ 77. Apparent duals and plurals.—1. Certain words ending in *-w*, mostly **abstracts**, are by a false analogy written like plurals (§ 73, 2. 3); exx. *nfrw* 'beauty'; *mnw* 'memorial', 'monument'; *hꜣw* 'neighbourhood', 'time'. Similarly, certain words ending in *-wy* and *-ty*, though not really duals, are apt to be written as such; exx. *ḫꜣwy* 'night'; (var.) *nỉwty* 'belonging to a town'. However, (var.) *pḥty* 'strength' was early a true dual;[13] whether *ḥnty* 'period', 'end' was so or not is doubtful.

2. Other words sometimes written like plurals, such as *ỉrp* 'wine',

[13] Coffins, B 4 C, 84.

nbw 'gold', are treated grammatically as singulars; *mw* 'water' is sometimes a plural,[1] sometimes a singular.[2]

3. Many **collectives**[3] in *-t* are written with the plural strokes, though they are really feminine singulars and are so treated syntactically; exx. *mnmnt* 'herd'; *ḥnyt* 'sailors'.

4. The plural of *rmṯ* 'man' (Latin *homo*) is written or , but appears from such phrases as 'all men'[4] to be properly a feminine collective *rmṯ(t)*; very rarely the writing *rmṯt nbt* is found.[5]

§ **78. Status pronominalis.**—When a suffix-pronoun is added to certain feminine nouns, an apparently intrusive *-w* occasionally appears before the feminine ending *-t*. Exx. *dpt* 'boat',[6] but *dpwt·f* 'his boat';[7] *wꜥbt* 'meat',[8] but *wꜥbwt·f* 'his meat'.[9]

OBS. This phenomenon is due to a displacement of the accent when the suffix is added; some such pronunciation as *dắpĕ* (from original *dắpwat*) may be assumed for the *status absolutus*, becoming *depwắtef*, with the original *w* retained under the protection of the accent, in the *status pronominalis*. The Latin terms here used are borrowed from the grammarians of Coptic, where such modification of the noun before the suffix is regular.

§ **79. Adjectives in -*y*.**[10]—The ending *-y* is employed to form adjectives from nouns and prepositions. Exactly the same formation exists in the Semitic languages, and the Arabic grammarians have invented for it the term *nisbe*-adjectives, or 'adjectives of relationship'; this name is sometimes applied to the Egyptian counterparts. Examples are:

	From *rsw* 'south wind', m.[11]	From *mḥyt* 'north wind', f.[11]
sing. m.	or *rsy* 'southern'.	, or *mḥyty* (*mḥty*) 'northern'.
,, f.	or *rsyt* (*rst*).	or *mḥytyt* (*mḥtt*).
plur. m.	or *rsyw* (*rsw*).	or *mḥytyw* (*mḥtyw*).
,, f.	or *rsywt* (*rswt*, *rst*).	or *mḥytywt* (*mḥtwt*, *mḥtt*).

From the preposition *r* (*ir*) 'to'.

sing. m. , or *iry* 'relating to', 'connected with'.

,, f. or *iryt* (*irt*).

plur. m. *iryw*, *irw*.

,, f. or *irywt* (*irwt*, *irt*).

As the above writings indicate, the formative *-y* is never written out in the feminines, and the semi-vowels *y* and *w* are also elsewhere usually suppressed; for reasons of practical convenience, the less correct transliterations given in brackets are to be preferred as a rule. The *-y* of the m. sing. is often, but by no means always, written out, and as regards the m. plur. the latent

[1] Leyden V 3, 4; *Westc.* 9, 18.
[2] *Sin.* B 233.
[3] See *Rec.* 31, 83.
[4] *Peas.* R 52.
[5] *Siut* 1, 225. See too *Rec.* 35, 77.
[6] *Peas.* B 1, 126.
[7] *Peas.* B 2, 103.
[8] *Siut* 1, 276.
[9] *Siut* 1, 275. Other exx., see *JEA.* iv. 35, n. 8; also *sḏꜣwt·i*, Brit. Mus. 574, 12–13 and with *y* for *w*, *sḏꜣyt·(i)*, *Siut* 5, 7.
[10] See *ÄZ.* 19, 44; 44, 93.
[11] See *ÄZ.* 44, 1.

presence of that semi-vowel is betrayed by the use of the sound-sign *tiw* (*tyw*)[1] in derivatives from f. nouns (so *mḥytyw* above) or from m. words ending in *t*, ex. *ḫftyw* 'opponents', 'enemies', an adjective used as a noun and derived from the preposition *ḫft* 'before', 'opposite'.

OBS. In Old Egyptian the formative was either omitted or else written with -*i*. An alternative ending -*w* survives in some nouns like *ẖrw* 'lower part' and *mitw* 'peer'.[2]

Prepositions that have a special form before the suffixes exhibit the same or a similar form in their derivative adjectives in -*y*.

Exx. *iry* 'relating to' from *r* 'to' (form with suffixes *r·* but occasionally also *ir·*)

ḥry 'above' „ *ḥr* 'upon' („ „ „ *ḥr·*)

imy '(who is) in' „ *m* 'in' („ „ „ *im·*)

In titles and the like these adjectives are sometimes abbreviated in such a way as to be indistinguishable from the prepositions from which they are derived. Exx. *imy-r* 'overseer', variants ,[3] lit. 'one-who-is-in-the-mouth' (of his subordinates); *ḥry-tp ꜥꜣ* 'great chief' of a province, lit. 'great one-who-is-over-the-head'.

Owing to their resemblance in sound to duals, some adjectives in -*y* from feminine nouns are written with a twofold ideogram (see above § 77, 1).

Exx. *niwty* from *niwt* 'town' in the expression *nṯr niwty* 'local god'.

ꜣḫty „ *ꜣḫt* 'horizon' „ „ *Ḥr ꜣḫty* 'Horus of the horizon'.

§ **80.** Adjectives derived from prepositions may, like the latter, govern a noun or pronoun.

Exx. *ḥry sštꜣ* 'he who is over the secret', a common title.

imyt·f 'what is in it', lit. that-being-in it.

The adjective *mity* (also *mitw*, § 79 OBS.), which is derived from a f. noun *mit* 'copy', may similarly take a suffix, ex. *mity·f* 'his equal'.[4]

From the noun *tp* 'head' and its derivative preposition *tp* 'upon' (§ 173) comes the adjective , varr. , , *tpy*, also written , with the two meanings (1) 'foremost', 'chief', 'first' and (2) 'being upon', ex. *ꜣInpw tpy ḏw·f* 'Anubis (who is) upon his mountain'. There is also a secondary adjective *tpty* 'first', but this hardly occurs until Late Egyptian.

The beginner must bear in mind that such adjectives in -*y*, in their most summary writings, are easily mistaken for their originating prepositions; the example *ꜣInpw tpy ḏw·f* just quoted is a case in point, doubt here being the more justifiable, since a prepositional phrase may sometimes be closely linked to a noun, ex. *nb-r-ḏr* 'lord of the universe', lit. 'lord to the end' (§ 100, 1); see further § 158.

[1] Differing from *ꜣ*, with which it is often confused, only in the rounded back of the head and the rather plumper breast. But in painted inscriptions the colour is brown.

[2] *Pt.* 69. 75. 435.

[3] This hieroglyph represents the tongue, which is 'what-is-in-the-mouth'; hence its value *imy-r* is due to a kind of graphic pun, see *ÄZ.* 40, 142; 42, 142.

[4] *Siut* I, 350. The suffix in *mḥty·f*, 'his northern one', scil. 'boundary', *B.H.* i. 25, 50, has its ordinary possessive sense; sim. the first ex. on p. 63.

On occasion some word may intervene between an adjective in *-y* and the word it governs.

Exx. *imt·sn ḥ3t* 'their originals', lit. their that-being-in-front.[1]

iry nb sšm every functionary, lit. every one-relating-to a business.[2]

ny wỉ Rʿ I belong to Rēʿ, lit. I am (§ 44, 3) belonging to Rēʿ.[3]

[1] *Urk.* iv. 99; cf. *Peas.* B 1, 193.

[2] *Urk.* iv. 1106.

[3] *Eb.* 1, 7.

§ **81**. Like other adjectives, those ending in *-y* are often employed as nouns.

Exx. *sḫty* 'peasant', 'fowler', properly 'one-belonging-to-the-country *sḫt*'.

imntt 'the west', from *imnty* 'western'.

ẖr(t)-nṯr 'the necropolis', lit. 'that under-(i.e. possessing-)-the-god'.[4]

ḥryw-šʿ 'those-upon-the-sand', i.e. the Bedâwîn.

[4] See above p. 51, n. 4.

VOCABULARY

ir make, do.

pr go forth, go up.

pḥ reach, attack.

mr love, wish.

mḥ fill (*m* with).

ḥ3ḳ capture, take as plunder.

dbḥ ask for, beg.

imnty western.

i3bty eastern.

wr great, important, much.

K3š Ethiopia, the Cush of the Bible (f.)

irtt (earlier *irṯt*) milk.

mnw monument.

mnmnt cattle.

rmṯ man; *rmṯ(t)* people.

rd foot.

nḥḥ eternity.

t3š boundary.

mr pyramid.

it barley, corn.

ḫt body.

ḫ3st hill-country, (foreign) country.

ẖr under, carrying, holding (preposition).

EXERCISE VI

(*a*) *Transliterate and translate*:

(1) [hieroglyphs] (2) [hieroglyphs]

(3) (4)

(5) (6) (7)

(8)

(9)

(10)

(*b*) *Write in hieroglyphs and transliteration*:

(1) They went forth to Cush, they reached its southern boundary, they captured its towns, they brought away all its inhabitants (lit. those-under it) (and) all its cattle. (2) He loved his brothers (more) than his own wife. (3) I have made for thee many great monuments (and) have placed them in the Southern City.[1] (4) Thou fillest thy hands with (*ḫr*) all good things. (5) Rēʿ placed him as king in this land, all southern (and) northern countries (being) under his feet. He is our beneficent lord; all his plans are like (those of) Rēʿ himself. (6) He is the god who-is-in my body.

[1] 'Southern City' was a name commonly given to Thebes.

LESSON VII

§ **82. Biliteral signs** (continued from § 71):—

xi. with *s* as second consonant:

ỉs *ms* (*mś*) *ns* (*nś*) *ḥs* *šs* (*šś*) *gs* (*gś*)

xii. with *ḳ* as second consonant: *ʿḳ*

xiii. with *k* as second consonant: *sk* (*śk*)

xiv. with *t* as second consonant:

mt *mt* (also *mwt*) *ḫt* *st* (*śt*)

SYNTAX OF NOUNS AND PRONOUNS

§ **83. Subject and object.**—Egyptian shows no trace of case-endings, and the syntactic relations of nouns were indicated either by the word-order (§§ 27. 66) or by the use of prepositions and the like, e.g. the use of *n* 'to', 'for' to express the dative (§ 52).

With the personal pronouns, the subject of narrative verbs, i.e. the nominative, is expressed by the suffixes (§ 35, 3), and the object, i.e. the accusative, by the dependent pronouns (§ 44, 1).

Obs. The use of the Latin case-names vocative, dative, etc., in reference to Egyptian is more convenient than strictly scientific. In the case of the genitive, at all events, it could hardly have been avoided.

§ **84.** Verbs taking two direct objects hardly exist in Egyptian.[0] To express the **predicative adjunct** found in English after verbs of 'making', 'becoming', and the like, Egyptian uses the *m* of predication (§ 38).

Exx. *ir·n wi ˁry·i m rḫḫy* my pen made me celebrated, lit. as a known one.[1]

rdi·n·f wi m ḥry niwt·f he placed me as chief (*or*, he made me chief) over his town.[2]

ḫpr·f m 19 it becomes 19.[3]

The same construction is found with verbs of 'seeing' and 'knowing', as *mꜣꜣ* 'see', 'regard (as)',[4] *siꜣ* 'recognize (as)',[5] and *gm* 'find (as)'.[6]

After the verbs of 'appointing', 'making' *r* 'to' is apt to be used in place of *m*, with little, if any, difference of meaning.

Ex. *rdi·n·f sw r r-pˁt ḥꜣty-ˁ* he placed him as (lit. into, i.e. so as to be) prince and chieftain.[7]

The verb *sbꜣ* 'teach' takes a direct object of the person and introduces the thing taught by *r* 'concerning'.[8]

See Add. for § 84A.

§ **85.** The **genitive** is of two kinds, *direct* and *indirect*.[8a]

A. The **direct genitive** follows the noun that governs it, immediately and without connecting link.

Exx. *imy-r pr* overseer of the house, i.e. steward.

nb imꜣḫ possessor of veneration, venerable.

rḫ ḫrt-ib nb·f knowing the desire of his lord.[9]

This form of genitive is usual wherever the connexion between governing and governed noun is particularly close, as in titles, set phrases, etc. Hence an epithet belonging to the governing word will normally follow the genitive.

Ex. *imy-r sḫtyw mnḫ* an efficient overseer of fowlers.[10]

Examples where the direct genitive is separated from its noun are of extreme rarity.[11]

In expressions like *ḥm-nṯr* 'priest', lit. 'servant of god', *ḥwt-nṯr* 'temple', lit. 'house of god', *pr-nsw* 'palace', lit. 'house of the king', *sꜣ-nsw* 'prince', lit. 'son of the king', the priority given to 'god' and 'king' is purely graphic, and due to honorific reasons; see § 57.

[0] See, however, n. 8 below.

[1] *Urk.* iv. 119. Sim. *PSBA.* 18, 201, l. 5.

[2] *Bersh.* i. 33. Sim. *BH.* i. 44, 7.

[3] *Rhind* 24. Sim. *Peas.* B 1, 237; *Urk.* iv. 113, 11.

[4] *Adm.* 1, 5; *Ikhern.* 8. Rather differently, Budge, p. 46, 14.

[5] *Urk.* iv. 1095, 1.

[6] *Urk.* iv. 1208, 6.

[7] *BH.* i. 25, 46–7. Sim. *Sebekkhu* 14. 17; *Peas.* B 1, 237; *Urk.* iv. 31, 9; after *ir* 'make', *Pt.* 486.

[8] *Pt.* 37. 399. Very rarely with two objects, Brit. Mus. 581; *Lit. Fr.* 6, 3, 11.

[8a] Combined e.g. in the frequent *st Ḥr nt ˁnḫw* 'Horus-throne of the living', *Urk.* iv. 137, 12 and *passim.*

[9] Brit. Mus. 614, 1.

[10] *Sin.* B 244. Sim. *Peas.* B 1, 16.

[11] Exx. *Siut* 1, 288. 301.

After Dyn. XII filiation is sometimes expressed by the help of the direct genitive, ex. [hieroglyphs] *ꜥIꜥḥ-ms sꜣ ꜣIbn* ʿAḥmose, son of Yeben'.[1] In Dyn. XII and earlier a peculiar inversion is frequent; [hieroglyphs] *Nḥry sꜣ Ḫnm-ḥtp sꜣ Ḫnm-ḥtp*[2] means 'Khnemḥotpe, son of Khnemḥotpe, son of Neḥri', not 'N., son of Kh., son of Kh.' as it would have done later; and here, as often, the determinative is absent after the two fathers' names. This mode of writing shows much variation, the word for 'son' being sometimes omitted.

The use of the suffixes after nouns with the meaning of English possessive adjectives ('my', 'thy', etc. § 35, 1) also exemplifies the direct genitive.

OBS. Coptic shows that the direct genitival relation led to loss of accent and consequent reduction of the vowel in the first of the two words, cf. Copt. *nĕb-ēi* 'lord of a house' beside *nēb* 'lord'; *yĕh-eloole* 'vineyard' beside *yōhe* 'field', Eg. *ꜣḥt.*[2a] The *status constructus* so formed has left no trace in hieroglyphic writing.

§ 86. B. In the **indirect genitive** the noun is preceded by the **genitival adjective** [hieroglyph] *ny* 'belonging to', a derivative in *-y* (§ 79) from the preposition [hieroglyph] *n* 'to' 'for'.[2b] The genitival adjective agrees in number and gender with the governing word as follows:

sing. m. [hieroglyph] *ny*	plur. m [hieroglyph] *nyw*	rare and archaistic	dual m. [hieroglyph] *nywy*[3]
„ f. [hieroglyph] *nyt*	„ f. [hieroglyph] *nywt*		„ f. [hieroglyph] *nyty*[4]

The transliterations given are those demanded by strict etymology, but since these words were probably already much reduced by the M.K., there is some ground for the handier renderings m. sing. *n*, m. plur. *nw*, f. sing. and plur. *nt*.

At an early period the genitival adjective shows a tendency to become invariable in the form [hieroglyph]. The dual is very rare; from M.K. on [hieroglyph] is often replaced by [hieroglyph], which may also, though far less frequently, stand for [hieroglyph].

Exx. [hieroglyphs] *nsw n Kmt*, the king of Egypt.[5]

[hieroglyphs] *niwt nt nḥḥ*, the city of eternity.[6]

[hieroglyphs] *wrw nw ꜣbḏw*, the great ones of Abydus.[7]

[hieroglyphs] *ꜥꜣw n sḫty pn*, the asses of this peasant.[8]

[hieroglyphs] *ḥmwt nt wrw*, the wives of the chiefs.[9]

When an adjective or other word intervenes between a noun and its genitive, it is the indirect genitive which is used.

Exx. [hieroglyphs] *inw nb nfr n sḫt* all good produce of the country.[10]

[hieroglyphs] *imyw-r·k nw rwyt* thy overseers of the portal.[11]

[hieroglyphs] *sḏꜣwt im·f nt pr-ḥḏ* valuables were in it belonging to the treasury.[12]

See Add.

OBS. For the genitival adjective as predicate, see § 114, 2; before *śḏm·f* and *śḏm·n·f*, see §§ 191–2; before the infinitive, see § 305; before prep. + noun, see § 158; after adjectives, see § 95; after passive participles, see § 379, 3.

[1] *Urk.* iv. 1. Sim. *ib.* 2, 11; 30, 6; 1119, 2.

[2] *BH.* i. 26, 159. See *ÄZ.* 12, 8; 49, 95; 71, 69; much material ANTHES, *passim.*

[2a] Note the suppression of the fem. ending *-t*; see *JEA.* 27, 44, n. 1.

[2b] Perhaps a demonstrative in origin, see *PSBA.* 22, 322.

[3] *Eb.* 74, 12.

[4] LAC. *TR.* 2, 61; 22, 92; 23, 19.

[5] *Sin.* B 165.

[6] *Th. T. S.* i. 30 F.

[7] Louvre C 3.

[8] *Peas.* R 42.

[9] *Urk.* iv. 185.

[10] *Peas.* R 35.

[11] *Pt.* 442.

[12] *Sin.* B 287–8. Sim. *ib.* B 30–1; *Kopt.* 8, 2.

§ **87.** The **vocative** may stand at the beginning or at the end of a sentence; more rarely it stands in the middle, but it must not interrupt a sequence of words belonging very closely together.

Exx. *ḥsw, ḥs tw Ḥry-š·f* O praised one, may Arsaphes (the god of Herakleopolis Magna) praise thee.[1]

sḏm rk n·i, ḥꜣty-ꜥ hearken thou to me, O prince.[2]

mk wi r nḥm ꜥꜣ·k, sḫty, ḥr wnm·f šmꜥ·i I will take away thy ass, peasant, because it is eating my corn.[3]

In ordinary parlance no introductory interjection was used; but in religious and semi-religious texts *i*, var. [4] is frequent for 'O', the synonym *hꜣ*,[5] var. , being much rarer. Exx. *i nb snḏ* 'O lord of fear';[6] *i ꜥnḫw* 'O living ones';[7] *hꜣ sš Nbsny* 'O scribe Nebseny'.[8]

§ **88. Adverbial uses of nouns.**—1. Indications of *time* are often expressed by a noun used absolutely, i. e. without preposition. The normal position of such a noun is towards the end of the sentence, in the position regularly occupied by adverbs.

Exx. *šms ib·k tr n wnn·k* follow thy desire so long as thou livest, lit. time of thou-art.[9]

iw sꜥnḫ·n·(i) 'Iwmitrw rnpwt ḳsnt I nourished (the town of) Imiotru in troubled years.[10]

Very common as adverbs are *ḏt* 'eternally', lit. 'eternity', and *rꜥ nb* 'every day'. Note the mathematical use of *sp 10* 'ten times'.[11]

If the adverbial phrase is a *date*, it may begin the sentence:

Ex. ... *ḥꜣt-sp 12 ... wḏꜣ ḥm·f* year 12 ... His Majesty proceeded.[12]

2. Nouns may further be employed to qualify adjectives or adjective verbs, like the accusative of respect in Latin or the genitive in Arabic; a very common use.

Exx. *spd ḥr* sharp of face, i. e. clever.[13]

nṯr·ṯn bnr mrwt your lovable god, lit. your god sweet of love.[14]

rḫ·n·f ꜣḫ·i n·f ib he knew I was serviceably minded towards him, lit. that I was beneficial to him in heart.[15]

§ **89. The noun with the function of a sentence.**—1. This use is frequent in *headings, lists* and the like.

Exx. *kt pẖrt* another remedy. Title introducing a prescription.[16]

wrs 1 head-rest, 1. Item in a list of goods.[17]

ꜥfty Nḫt the brewer Nakht. Written over the picture of a brewer.[18]

2. Not infrequently, however, such self-sufficient phrases *convey comments* or even *narrate a fact.*

Exx. *sšr mꜣꜥ* a real remedy. Comment accompanying a spell.[19]

[1] *Peas.* B 1, 196. Sim. *ib.* R 90; *Sin.* B 156; *Leb.* 17; *P. Pet.* 1116 B, 6.

[2] *Sh. S.* 12. Sim. *Peas.* B 1, 26; B 2, 133; *P. Kah.* 1, 2.

[3] *Peas.* B 1, 11-2. Sim. *P. Pet.* 1116 B, 12-3.

[4] *Siut* 3, 1; Louvre C 166; C 177; Cairo 20538 i. c 12.

[5] *Wb.* ii. 471; these particles always at the beginning of the sentence.

[6] Cairo 20089, 7. Sim. LAC. *T.R.* 7, 1; 8, 1.

[7] Cairo 20014. Sim. *ib.* 20003, 1.

[8] BUDGE, p. 467, 12.

[9] *Pt.* 186. Sim. *Peas.* B 1, 139; *PSBA.* 18, 202, 8; *Hamm.* 114, 4.

[10] Cairo 20001. Sim. *Sin.* B 45.

[11] *Rhind* 1. Sim. *ib.* 6.

[12] *Seas.* no. 340. Sim. *Sin.* R 5-6; *Peas.* B 1, 224.

[13] *BH.* i. 8, 10. Many exx. *Sin.* B 48 foll.

[14] Cairo 20119, c 4; Sim. 20040, 17-8.

[15] Berlin *ÄI.* ii. p. 26.

[16] *Eb.* 44, 19. Sim. headings of accounts, etc. *P. Boul.* xviii. 2. 10. 16. 19. 23. 36.

[17] *P. Kah.* 18, 15.

[18] *BH.* i. 29.

[19] *Eb.* 2, 6. Rather differently, *Westc.* 10, 21.

kt ḥswt ỉryt n·ỉ another favour that was done to me. In the midst of a narrative; the favour is then recounted as a kind of apposition.[1]

If the eleven workmen are waiting here for their remuneration (?), *bw nb nfr* all well and good, lit. everything good.[2]

OBS. These uses will be found recurring in the case of the nominal parts of the verb: with the infinitive § 306, and with the participles and relative forms § 390.

§ 90. **Apposition.**—Words in apposition may be separated from one another by other words.

Ex. *ꜥr nṯr r ꜣḫt·f, n-sw-bỉt Sḥtp-ỉb-Rꜥ* the god mounted up to his horizon (i. e. his tomb), the king of Upper and Lower Egypt Seḥetepibrēꜥ.[3]

A suffix-pronoun may be used to anticipate a noun placed in apposition after it.

Ex. How shall this land fare *m ḫmt·f, nṯr pf mnḫ* without him, that beneficent god?[4]

A style of apposition common to Egyptian and the Semitic languages[4a] is found in three special cases:[5]

1. to indicate the *material* of which a thing is made.

Ex. *ḥnꜥ ꜥš ḫꜣy(t) wrt* together with the great altar of cedar, lit. together with cedar, the great altar.[6]

2. with *measures* and *numbers.*

Ex. *ḥnḳt, ds 2* beer, two jugs, i. e. two jugs of beer.[7]

3. with indications of *locality.*

Ex. *Tꜣ-wr ꜣbḏw* Abydus in the Thinite nome (province), lit. Thinite nome, Abydus.[8]

OBS. For the nominal subject in apposition to a dependent pronoun, see §§ 132. 139; to the demonstrative *pw*, see § 130. For the *m* of predication emphasizing a noun in apposition, see § 96, 2. For *n ỉs* negativing a noun in apposition, see § 247, 2.

§ 91. **Co-ordination and disjunction.**—1. Egyptian has no special word for 'and'. The co-ordination of nouns or adjectives is often effected by direct juxtaposition.

Exx. *gm·n·ỉ dꜣbw ỉꜣrrt ỉm* I found figs and grapes there.[9]

tꜣš·f rsy mḥty its southern and northern boundary.[10]

The repetition of a preposition, a suffix or an adjective may help out the sense.

Exx. *ỉꜣwt·ṯn prw·ṯn* your offices and your houses.[11]

ḫt·ỉ nbt m šꜣ m nỉwt all my property in country and in town.[12]

[1] *BH.* i. 26, 121. Sim. *Hamm.* 110, 2; *Urk.* iv. 940, 4; *ÄZ.* 69, 30, 16.

[2] *P. Kah.* 31, 5.

[3] *Sin.* R 6. Sim. *ib.* B 240; Brit. Mus. 614, 12. 13.

[4] *Sin.* R 67–8. Sim. *Westc.* 9, 15; LAC. *TR.* 6, 1; 21, 41; 23, 29.

[4a] In Arabic known as *badal* 'substitution', *ÄZ.* 71, 56.

[5] See *ÄZ.* 28, 15.

[6] Louvre C 11, 7. Sim. *P. Kah.* 19, 16; *Urk.* iv. 206. 635. 636.

[7] *Peas.* B 1, 84. Sim. *ib.* R 5; *Rhind* 41, 4; 42, 4; *Urk.* iv. 6, 7–8.

[8] Leyd. V 3, 4. 8. Sim. *ib.* 7; Cairo 20105; *Urk.* iv. 80, 15. See *ÄZ.* 29, 120.

[9] *Sh. S.* 47–8. Sim. *Peas.* B 1, 84; *Westc.* 9, 23.

[10] *BH.* i. 8, 20.

[11] Cairo 20093, 3.

[12] *P. Kah.* 12, 4. Sim. Cairo 20001, 6; *Siut* 1, 286.

Closely connected words may be coupled by means of *ḥr*, lit. 'upon'.

Ex. *ḏꜥ ḥr ḥyt* wind and rain.[1]

Or else *ḥnꜥ* 'together with' is employed, especially when the co-ordination is less close.

Ex. *msw·i ḥnꜥ snw·i* my children and my brothers.[2]

2. 'Or', like 'and', may be left unexpressed.

Ex. *ṯsw nb ḥ3ty-ꜥ nb* any commander or any prince.[3]

Here the repetition of *nb* assists the meaning; a repeated preposition or suffix may have the same effect, as was seen in the case of 'and' above.

A special word for 'or' is *r-pw*, which is placed after the last of the alternatives.

Ex. *m nb, m sn, m ḫnms r-pw* as lord, as brother, or as friend.[4]

§ 92. Gender of nouns.—A few remarks must be added to what has been already said on this topic (§ 26).

1. The names of foreign countries are treated syntactically as feminines, ex. *K3š ḫst* 'the vile Ethiopia (Cush)'.[5] The same holds good of names of towns[6] and, in part at least, of those of the nomes or provinces.[7]

2. *ḫt* (orig. *iḫt*) is fem. when it means 'things' or 'property', but is apt to be treated as a masc. when it means 'something', 'anything', ex. *ḫt mr* 'something painful'.[8] With the plur. the use is variable.[8a]

3. *ḫt* 'wood', 'tree' is not really a fem., the *t* being radical; cf. *ḫt nḏm* 'sweet(-smelling) wood',[9] *ḫt ḳ3* 'a high tree'.[10]

4. *ẖt* 'body', 'belly' is usually fem.,[11] but instances occur where it is treated as masc.[12]

[1] *Westc.* 11, 14. Sim. *Siut* 4, 17; *Urk.* iv. 659, 16.

[2] *Sh. S.* 128. Sim. *Peas.* B 1, 94; *Sin.* B 84; *Siut* 1, 304.

[3] *Kopt.* 8, 9. Sim. Cairo 20040, 9–15; *Eb.* 99, 2–3.

[4] *Pt.* 279. Sim. *Eb.* 6, 14; 24, 3; 93, 6–7. After each of two alternatives, *Eb.* 39, 17.

[5] *BH.* i. 8, 10. Sim. *Sin.* R 55; *Urk.* iv. 697, 9.

[6] Cairo 20025, 12–13; *Siut* 4, 13–4; *Urk.* iv. 689, 10. 15.

[7] *Siut* 1, 151; Brit. Mus. 1203; but m. see *BH.* i. 8, 20.

[8] *Sh. S.* 124; *P. Turin* 132, 9. Sim. *ḫt ꜥ3, Sin.* B 215. See too *Eb.* 42, 18; 107, 20.

[8a] *P. Ram. IV*, C 22; *Hearst* 6, 2, contrasted with *Eb.* 1, 20; 47, 9.

[9] *Urk.* iv. 719, 3.

[10] *Sh. S.* 156.

[11] *Eb.* 36, 6. 15.

[12] *Eb.* 36, 8; 41, 14. See too *Verbum* ii. § 14, 3. 4.

VOCABULARY

ꜥḳ enter.

wsṯn var. *wstn* stride.

nḫt be mighty, victorious; mighty (adj.).

sns worship.

var. *šsp* receive, take.

st (earlier *šṭ*) shoot, throw, pour.

dw3 adore (in the morning).

mwt mother.

var. *ms* child.

ḏw mountain.

st place.[1]

varr. , *ḫrw* voice, sound.

ꜣwt oblations, offerings.

var. *wdḥw* (for *wdḥw*, § 19, Obs. 2) table of offerings.

var. *isft* evil, wrong-doing.

šbw food.

ḥst praise, favour (noun).

var. *sḫꜣw* remembrance, memory.

varr. , *mꜣꜥ* true, real, just.

(det. also ; abbrev.) *sbꜣ* door.

imnt (also *imntt* § 81) the West.

dwꜣt netherworld.

ḏt eternity, everlasting.

ḫr with, before, (speak) to.

[1] For the reading see *ÄZ.* 46, 107.

EXERCISE VII

(*a*) *Study the following funerary wishes from a Theban noble's tomb* (*Dyn. XVIII*)[1]:

imy-r (§ 79)	*pr*	*sš*	*'Imn-m-ḥꜣt*	*mꜣꜥ-ḫrw*	*ꜥḳ·k*
O overseer	of the house,	scribe	Amenemḥēt,	true of voice *or* justified } see § 55.	Mayst thou enter (and)

pr·k	*m*	*'Imnt*	*wstn·k*	*ḥr*	*sbꜣ*	*n*	*dwꜣt*	*dwꜣ·k*
go forth	from	the West,	mayst thou stride	through	the door	of	the netherworld,	mayst thou adore

Rꜥ	*wbn·f*	*m*	*ḏw*	*sns·k*	*sw*	*ḥtp·f*	*m*	*ꜣḫt*
Rēꜥ	(when) he rises	in	the mountain,	mayst thou worship	him	(when) he sets	in	the horizon,

šsp·k	*ꜣwt*	*ḥtp·k*	*ḥr*	*šbw*	*ḥr*	*wdḥw*	*n*	*nb*	*ḏt*
mayst thou receive	oblations	(and) be satisfied	because of	food	(from) upon	the altar	of	the lord	(of) eternity.[2]

[1] Adapted from *Th. T. S.* i. 27.

[2] The 'lord of eternity' is Osiris, the god of the dead. A large part of the temple offerings was passed on for use in private tomb-chapels 'after', as the texts say, 'the god had been satisfied therewith'.

(*b*) *Transliterate and translate*:

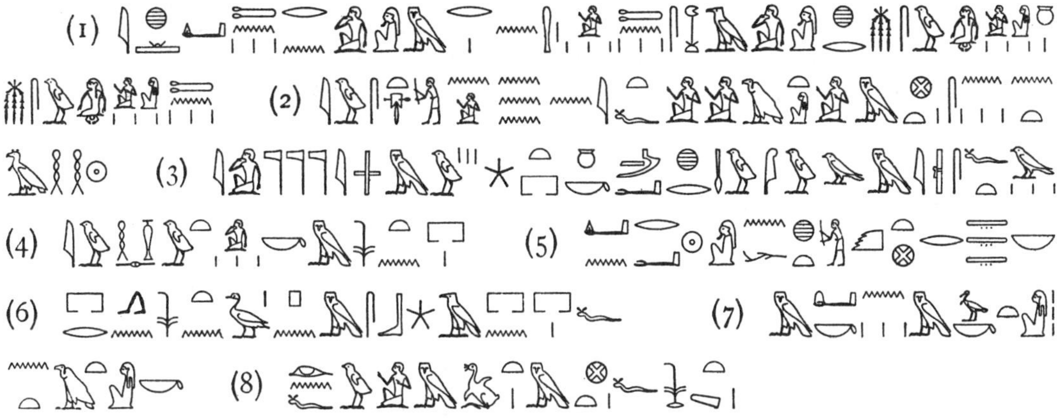

(*c*) *Write in hieroglyphs and transliteration*:

(1) I am (one) good of counsels in the house of his lord. (2) Mayst thou hearken, O sovereign my lord, to this (the) daughter of thy handmaid. (3) The overseer of the city found his brothers and sisters at (*ḥr*) the door of the palace. (4) My praises reached heaven. (5) The wife of the priest went down into the boat. (6) Thy hands are mightier than (those of) all the gods of Egypt. (7) The gods are satisfied when they receive oblations upon their altars. (8) May I hear thy counsels every day. (9) He sees the gods in their beautiful places of the West.

EXCURSUS A

The Titulary and other Designations of the King.[1]

The student now possesses the knowledge of Egyptian writing and grammar requisite to decipher the royal names and titles occurring on innumerable monuments of stone. The 'titulary' (*nḫbt*)[2] consisted of five 'great names' (*rn wr*),[3] which were assumed by the Pharaoh on the day of his accession. We have not here to study the gradual development of the titulary; it will answer our purpose to illustrate it in the forms in which it occurs in Middle Egyptian. The following is the full titulary of Sesostris I (Dyn. XII):

Ḥr ꜥnḫ mswt, nbty ꜥnḫ mswt, Ḥr nbw ꜥnḫ mswt, n-sw-bit Ḫpr-kꜣ-Rꜥ, sꜣ Rꜥ S-n-Wsrt, di ꜥnḫ ḏdt wꜣs mi Rꜥ ḏt Horus 'Life-of-births', Two Ladies 'Life-of-Births', Horus of gold 'Life-of-Births', King of Upper and Lower Egypt 'Kheperkerēꜥ' ['the *ka* of Rēꜥ comes into being'], Son of Rēꜥ 'Sesostris' ['man of (the goddess) Wosret'],[4] (may he be) granted life, stability and wealth like Rēꜥ eternally.[5]

[1] See H. MÜLLER, *Die formale Entwicklung der Titulatur der ägyptischen Könige*, Glückstadt, 1938; A. MORET, *Du caractère religieux de la royauté pharaonique*, Paris, 1902, ch. I.

[2] *Urk.* iv. 80, 11; 160, 11; BR. *Thes.* 1077, 19.

[3] *Urk.* iv. 261, 3. 14–17; BR. *Thes.* 1077, 19.

[4] The name *S-n-Wsrt* belonging to three kings of Dyn. XII was formerly read *Wsrtsn* (Usertesen), whereby its identity with the Sesostris of Manetho (see p. 76, n. 1) was obscured. See *Unt.* 2, 1–24; *ÄZ.* 41, 43.

[5] *BH.* i. 25, 59–62.

A titulary of Tuthmosis III (Dyn. XVIII) from Sinai is similar in form: *Ḥr kꜣ nḫt ḫꜥ m Wꜣst, nbty wꜣḥ nsyt mỉ Rꜥ m pt, Ḥr nbw sḫm pḥty ḏsr ḫꜥw, n-sw-bỉt Mn-ḫpr-Rꜥ, sꜣ Rꜥ Ḏḥwty-ms-nfr-ḫpr*(*w*), *mry Ḥtḥr nbt mfkꜣt* Horus 'Strong-bull-arising-in-Thebes', Two Ladies 'Enduring-of-kingship-like-Rēꜥ-in-heaven', Horus of gold 'Powerful-of-strength, holy-of-diadems', King of Upper and Lower Egypt 'Menkheperrēꜥ' ['the form of Rēꜥ remains (?)'], Son of Rēꜥ, 'Tuthmosis ['Thoth is born'] beautiful-of-forms', beloved of Hathor, lady of the turquoise.[1]

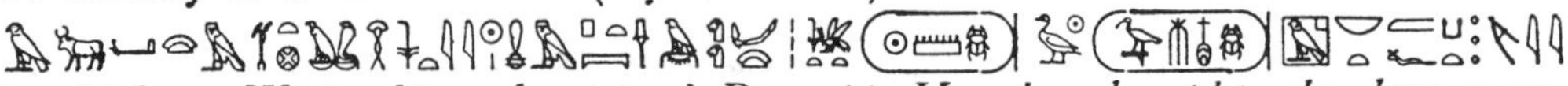

The comparison of these two titularies discloses five elements common to both; these common elements are followed by names that are variable in the case of every king. The underlying idea is that the king, while being the re-incarnation of Horus, or protected by the goddesses called the Two Ladies, or appearing as the golden Horus, reveals his individuality by exhibiting the divine nature under some aspect peculiar to himself; thus Sesostris I is the Horus who infuses life into all who are born, Tuthmosis III is the golden Horus who is powerful of strength and whose diadems are holy. Similarly, the names in the two 'cartouches' or 'royal rings' describe the nature of the king in his capacity of 'King of Upper and Lower Egypt' and of 'Son of Rēꜥ' respectively. Whereas an Englishman distinguishes two different kinds of name, Christian and family name, the Egyptian kings distinguished five, which we term the Horus name, the *nebty* name, the golden Horus name, the *prenomen* and the *nomen*. These we shall now consider in turn.

1. The **Horus name**, less suitably called banner-name or *ka*-name, represents the king as the earthly embodiment of the old falcon-god Horus, who early became the dynastic god of Egypt, and as such was identified with the sun-god Rēꜥ, himself also at some very early period the dynastic god. This name is frequently written within a rectangular frame, at the bottom of which is seen a design of recessed panelling such as we find in the façades of early brick tombs and in the false doors of Old Kingdom maṣṭabas;[2] on the top of the rectangular frame is perched the falcon of Horus, in more elaborate Dyn. XVIII examples crowned and accompanied by sun and uraeus;[2a] see the annexed figure. It is not quite certain whether the building symbolized by the rectangle and façade (together termed the *srḫ*)[3] was the king's palace or his tomb. The former alternative is the more probable, since in the oldest times the Horus name was the commonest designation of the king, and it is unlikely that a purely sepulchral name should have been chosen for the purpose. Still, its associations with the *ka* or 'spirit' came to be very close. On the whole, we may conclude that the Horus name denotes the aspect of Horus worn by the king whilst dwelling in the palace.

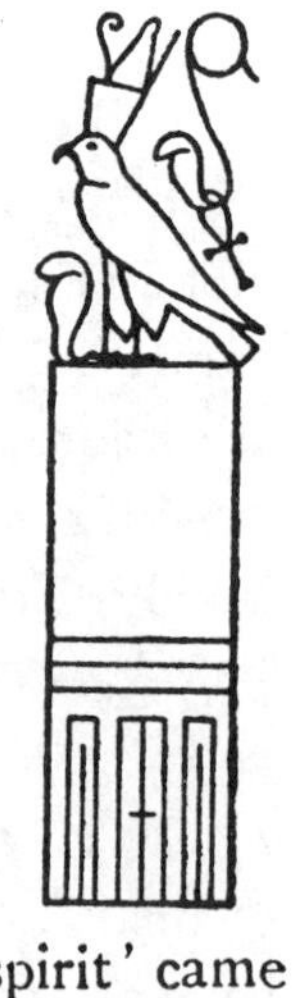

[1] *Sinai* 196; after the first cartouche is a long string of epithets not belonging to the name. Both the titularies quoted conclude with epithets not belonging to the names ('may he be granted life', etc. and 'beloved of Hathor', etc.). These are so typical that it seemed advisable to retain them.

[2] *Seas.* pp. 21–2;

[2a] On these symbols see *JEA.* 30, 50–1.

[3] *ÄZ.* 34, 167.

2. The ***nebty* name**, so called because the probable reading of the group [hieroglyphs] is *nbty* 'the two ladies',[1] displays the king as standing in a special relation to the two principal goddesses of the period immediately preceding Dyn. I, when Egypt was still divided into two kingdoms; these were the vulture-goddess [hieroglyphs] *Nḫbt* Nekhbet of the Upper Egyptian city of El-Kâb and the cobra-goddess [hieroglyphs] *Wꜣḏt* Edjō[1a] of the Lower Egyptian city of [hieroglyphs] *Dp*; these cities were in the close vicinity of the early capitals of [hieroglyphs] *Nḫn* Hieraconpolis and [hieroglyphs] *P* Pe respectively, and it is to this reason that the two goddesses owed their prominence. Probably Menes, the founder of Dyn. I, was the first to assume the *nebty* title, symbolizing thereby the fact that he had united the two kingdoms.[2] The Greek interpretation κύριος βασιλειῶν 'lord of crowns' is probably secondary; doubtless protection by the goddesses was in the mind of the Egyptians, not merely ownership of the crowns with which the goddesses were identified.

3. The **golden Horus name** is more disputed. Some high authorities[3] have supposed, on the strength of the Greek equivalent ἀντιπάλων ὑπέρτερος 'superior to (his) foes' on the Rosetta stone, that the monogram [hieroglyph] symbolized Horus as victorious over [hieroglyphs] *Nbt(y)* 'the Ombite', i.e. the god Seth who was worshipped at Ombos near the modern Ḳûs.[4] This was, no doubt, the interpretation of Greek times, but the evidence of the earlier periods points in another direction. In a context dealing with the titulary of Tuthmosis III that king says 'he (Amūn) modelled me as a falcon of gold' ([hieroglyphs] *bἰk n nbw*),[5] and Ḥashepsowe calls herself 'the female Horus of fine gold' ([hieroglyphs] *Ḥrt nt ḏꜥm*);[6] the concept of the golden falcon can be definitely traced back to Dyn. XI,[7] and an inscription of Dyn. XII describes the golden Horus name as the 'name of gold' ([hieroglyphs] *rn n nbw*).[8] King Cheops (Dyn. IV) and king Merenrēꜥ (Dyn. VI) have the title [hieroglyph] with two falcons over the 'gold' sign; but the two falcons are normally a circumlocution for the reconciled enemy-gods Horus and Seth, so that, on the hypothesis here combated, Horus and Seth would both seem to be indicated as vanquishers of Seth. Lastly, the names following the group [hieroglyph] are far from being always of a bellicose character. There seems but little doubt that this group meant 'Horus of gold' except perhaps in the very latest periods;[9] but exactly what god was intended is a problem still unsolved.

4. The **prenomen** is the name which follows the title [hieroglyph] *n-sw-bἰt* 'he who belongs to the sedge and the bee'; the plant [hieroglyphs] *swt* symbolizing Upper Egypt is supposed to be identical with the flowering *scirpus*-reed or sedge, Egyptian [hieroglyph] *šmꜥ*, a common emblem of Upper Egypt;[10] the exact connexion of the bee with Lower Egypt is still obscure. In effect the title means 'king of Upper and Lower Egypt', and the Rosetta stone translates it by βασιλεὺς τῶν τε ἄνω καὶ τῶν κάτω χωρῶν. The *prenomen* itself is almost always compounded with the

[1] *Rec.* 17, 113; *PSBA.* 20, 200.

[1a] Commonly called Buto, see above p. 32, n. 1; also *JEA.* 30, 55.

[2] See *Unt.* 3, 13; also *Ann.* 44, 279 ff.

[3] H. BRUGSCH, *Die Aegyptologie* (Leipzig 1897), 202; SETHE, in J. GARSTANG, *Maḥâsna and Bêt Khallâf* (London, 1902), 19.

[4] We must carefully distinguish between this Ombos, which is that mentioned by Juvenal in his fifteenth Satire, and the other, the present Kôm Ombo, some 25 miles north of Aswân, where there is a much visited temple dating from Graeco-Roman times.

[5] *Urk.* iv. 161.

[6] *Urk.* iv. 237.

[7] LAC. *TR.* 55, 5.

[8] Berl. *ÄI*, i. p. 138.

[9] So MORET, *op. cit.* p. 22, quoting his earlier work *Rec.* 23, 23; THIERRY, *op. cit.* 66–83. Further discussion, *Mitt. Kairo*, 4, 9 ff.

[10] GRIFFITH, *Hieroglyphs*, p. 29. Keimer agrees, however, that the sign is too schematically shown to be identifiable with any particular species.

name of the god Rēʿ; typical examples are (hieroglyphs) *Sḥtp-ib-Rʿ* 'propitiating the heart of Rēʿ' (Ammenemes I), (hieroglyphs) *Nb-mꜣʿt-Rʿ* 'lord of truth is Rēʿ (Amenophis III); one of the first cases of Rēʿ as an element in a king's name is with (hieroglyphs) *Rʿ-ḫʿ·f*[0] Chephren of Dyn. IV, and the instances without Rēʿ all date before Dyn. IX. The *prenomen* and *nomen* are invariably written within 'cartouches' (this French word means an ornamented tablet of stone, wood, or metal destined to receive an inscription) or 'royal rings'. The cartouche depicts a loop formed by a double thickness of rope, the ends tied together so as to offer to the spectator the appearance of a straight line;[1] strictly speaking the loop should be round, as it is in one or two very early examples,[2] but becomes elongated and oval because of the length of most hieroglyphic names enclosed in it. The Egyptians called the cartouche (hieroglyphs) *šnw*[3] from a verb-stem *šni* 'encircle', and it seems not unlikely that the idea was to represent the king as ruler of all 'that which is encircled by the sun', a frequently expressed notion.[4] Another name of the cartouche, not found before Dyn. XIX, is (hieroglyphs) *mnš*.[5]

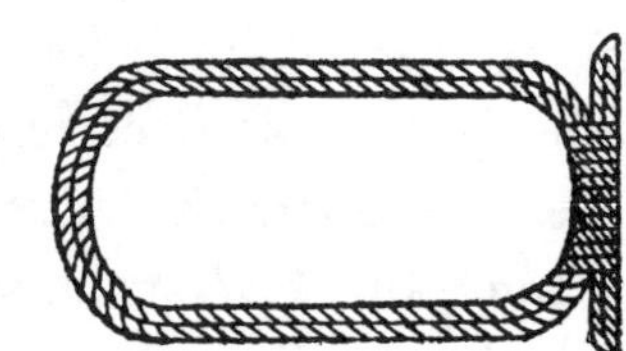

[0] Ranke (*JAOS* 70, 65) has made it probable that the divine name Rēʿ was originally read before *-ḫʿ·f*, in which case the Herodotean Chephren would be due to later misinterpretation.

[1] Examples showing the rope as such are rare, even in quite early times. That here illustrated is from Cairo 1558, a relief dating from the reign of Sahureʿ (Dyn. V).

[2] *ÄZ.* 35, 4; QUIBELL, *Hierakonpolis* (London, 1900), i. 38.

[3] *ÄZ.* 34, 167.

[4] *Sin.* B 213; *Urk.* iv. 82, 13; 102, 11; 283, 16. A less plausible explanation *Bull.* 11, 141.

[5] *ÄZ.* 43, 158.

5. The **nomen** is introduced by the epithet (hieroglyphs) *sꜣ Rʿ* 'son of (the sun-god) Rēʿ'. The name in the cartouche was, as a rule, that borne by the king before his accession to the throne; it is almost the equivalent of our family name, for Dyn. XI affects the *nomina* (hieroglyphs) *ʾIn-t·f* Antef and (hieroglyphs) *Mnṯw-ḥtp* Menthḥotpe, Dyn. XII the *nomina* (hieroglyphs) *ʾImn-m-ḥꜣt* Ammenemes and (hieroglyphs) *S-n-Wsrt* Sesostris; Dyn. XIII shows several kings of the name (hieroglyphs) *Sbk-ḥtp* Sebkḥotpe and Dyn. XVIII consists almost entirely of rulers named (hieroglyphs) *ʾImn-ḥtp* Amenophis and (hieroglyphs) *Ḏḥwty-ms* Tuthmosis. The first Egyptian kings to distinguish a *nomen* and a *prenomen* were those of Dyn. V.

In the period covered by this book the five names of the titulary have a rigidly fixed order. The principal name is the *prenomen*, and this is often found alone or accompanied only by the *nomen*. Only very rarely does the Horus name serve for identification purposes, ex. (hieroglyphs) *Ḥr Ḫʿ-m-mꜣʿt* 'Horus Appearing-in-truth', i. e. Amenophis III.[6]

[6] *Tarkhan* i. 79, 11; MAR., *Karn.* 34, 29.

To introduce the king's name the phrase (hieroglyphs) *ḥm n* is often found; this we translate 'the Majesty of', but the origin of the expression is obscure. One example will suffice:

(hieroglyphs) *ḥꜣt-sp 19 ḫr ḥm n nṯr nfr nb tꜣwy N-mꜣʿt-Rʿ, sꜣ Rʿ, ʾImn-m-ḥꜣt* year 19 under the Majesty of the good god, lord of the two lands Nemaʿrēʿ, son of Rēʿ, Ammenemes (III).[7]

As speaker the king often refers to himself as (hieroglyphs) *ḥm·i* 'My Majesty',[8] var. (hieroglyphs) *ḥm·i*;[9] he is addressed as (hieroglyphs) *ḥm·k*[10] 'Thy Majesty', var. (hieroglyphs);[11] the 3rd

[7] *Hamm:* 17, 1.

[8] *Urk.* iv. 158, 10.

[9] *Urk.* iv. 101, 1.

[10] *Sin.* B 236.

[11] *Westc.* 5, 2. 3.

pers. *ḥm·f* 'His Majesty',[1] var. [2] is also exceedingly common. The word *ḥm* also occurs in the stilted phrase *m ḥm n stp-sꜣ* 'in the Majesty of the palace'.[3] The plural *ḥmw·ṯn* is found addressed to gods or even to honoured men ('your worships');[4] Ḥashepsowe, who styled herself king, though a woman, employs the feminine form *ḥmt·i*.[5] The translation of *ḥm* as 'Majesty' is a mere makeshift; the precise meaning of the Egyptian word thus used is unknown, though a word of similar appearance means 'slave'.[5a]

The ordinary word for king is , *nsw* (§ 54); far less common is *ity*, var. ,[6] which we conventionally translate 'sovereign'; another fairly common appellation is *nb* 'the Lord'.[7] We cannot here discuss other epithets of the king, such as *nṯr nfr* 'the good god' (perhaps rather 'the beautiful god'), *nb tꜣwy* 'the lord of the two lands', *Ḥr nb ꜥḥ* 'Horus, lord of the castle'; for *nb-r-ḏr* see § 100, 1. As regards the term Pharaoh (Hebrew פַּרְעֹה, Greek Φαραώ, Coptic ⲡⲣ̄ⲣⲟ : ⲡⲟⲩⲣⲟ),[8] the facts are as follows.[9] The Egyptian original *Pr-ꜥꜣ* 'Great House' was used in the Old Kingdom as part of many phrases like *smr Pr-ꜥꜣ* 'courtier of the Great House', and clearly there referred to the palace itself or to the court, and not to the person of the king. From the end of Dyn. XII onwards the term is written *Pr-ꜥꜣ ꜥnḫ wḏꜣ snb* 'Great House, may it live, prosper, be in health' with the auspicious wish-formula discussed §§ 55. 313; but still it seems to mean only the palace. The earliest certain instance where *Pr-ꜥꜣ* refers actually to the king is in a letter to Amenophis IV (Akhenaten), which is addressed to *Pr-ꜥꜣ ꜥnḫ wḏꜣ snb nb* 'Pharaoh, l. p. h., the Master'.[10] From Dyn. XIX onward it is used occasionally just as *ḥm·f* 'His Majesty' might be used; we read 'Pharaoh went forth', 'Pharaoh said', etc. In other words the term has become a respectful designation for the king, just as the head of the Ottoman government was termed the Sublime Porte. The final development was when a proper name was added to the title, as in the 'Pharaoh Hophra' of the Old Testament; the earliest Egyptian example of this use is under one of the Shoshenḳs of Dyn. XXII.

In conclusion, a few words must be said concerning the way in which the royal names may be best represented in English. The Horus name, *nebty* name, and golden Horus names ought perhaps to be translated; so far as that is possible, at least, for the epithets employed as names are often very obscure in their meaning. The *prenomen* and *nomen*, on the contrary, must be left in their Egyptian forms, for to replace (*e.g.*) 'king Tuthmosis' by 'king Thoth-is-born' would be obviously absurd. The question now arises as to how such names as *Ḏḥwty-ms* should be vocalized, for only in the rarest cases do we know how an old Egyptian name was really pronounced. The practice followed by a number of writers, to whom the author of the present work belongs, is to utilize the names

[1] *Hamm.* 192, 3.
[2] *Westc.* 6, 1. 2. 13.
[3] See GARD. *Sin.* p. 83.
[4] *ÄZ.* 47, 89; *Tarkhan* i. 79, 5.
[5] *Urk.* iv. 363, 6.
[5a] Recent discussions: *ÄZ.* 75, 112; *JEA.* 29, 79.
[6] *Pt.* 7; *Sh. S.* 173; *Urk.* iv. 15, 9.
[7] *P. Boul.* xviii, 2. 12; *Urk.* iv. 1092, 14; 1112, 13.
[8] *ÄZ.* 53, 130.
[9] *PSBA.* 23, 72.
[10] *P. Kah.* 38, 17. However, *Arm.* pl. 93, 5 probably dates from Tuthmosis III, see *ib.* p. 160; cf. also Brit. Mus. 148 (*Hier. Texts* vii, pl. 43), Tuthmosis IV.

given by the historian of Egypt Manetho (first half of the 3rd cent. B.C.),[1] so far as the forms handed down by the excerptors of Manetho are fairly recognizable as transcriptions of the hieroglyphic writing; so, for example, Tuthmosis for *Ḏḥwty-ms*, Sesostris for *S-n-Wsrt*, and so on. When, however, the Manethonian form is either absent or barely recognizable as an equivalent of the hieroglyphs, a guessed transcription will be found preferable, for example Ḥaremḥab for *Ḥr-m-ḥb*, where Manetho gives Harmais. We shall deal further with such guessed transcriptions in Appendix B at the end of this book. Here we need only warn the student against one specially barbarous transcription of a royal name; Thothmes is still used for the Manethonian Tuthmosis by many Egyptologists who ought to know better.

For the various names of the Egyptian kings see H. GAUTHIER, *Le Livre des rois d'Égypte*, 5 vols., Cairo 1907–17, in *Mémoires . . . de l'institut français d'archéologie orientale.* In English there is the smaller work, E. A. W. BUDGE, *The Book of the Kings of Egypt*, 2 vols., London, 1908.

[1] Manetho was an Egyptian priest contemporary with the first two Ptolemies, who wrote an Egyptian history in three books. Only excerpts remain, which are preserved in the works of Josephus, Africanus and Eusebius. See WADDELL, *Manetho* (Loeb Classical Library), London, 1940.

LESSON VIII

§ **93. Biliteral signs** (continued from § 82):—

xv. with *d* as second consonant:

šd *ḳd* *ḏd* (later *dd*).

xvi. with *ḏ* as second consonant:

ʿḏ (later *ʿd*) *wḏ* (later *wd*,) *nḏ* *ḥḏ*

SYNTAX OF ADJECTIVES

§ **94.** The sentence with *adjectival predicate* will be treated fully below in Lesson XII.

For the adjective as *epithet*, see above § 48, 1, where it was seen to follow its noun and agree with it in number and gender. It remains to be noted that such an adjective may on occasion be separated from its noun by a genitive or by an adverb.

Exx. *swt·f nt R-ḳrrt ḏsrt ỉmt Sỉwt* his holy places of Roḳereret which are in Siûṭ.[2]

wʿ ỉm nb each one thereof.[3]

Occasionally, however, epithet and noun adhere so closely together that they are treated as a compound. Exx. *t-ḥḏ·sn* 'their white bread';[4] *gs-ḥry·sn* 'their upper side'.[5]

[2] *Siut* I, 237.

[3] *Siut* I, 277. Sim. *wʿ ỉm·ṯn nb*, *ib.* I, 288.

[4] *Siut* I, 225.

[5] *Eb.* 70, 4. Cf. *smr-wʿty nb*, *BH.* i. 25, 101, qu. § 137.

Two much rarer methods of expressing the adjective as epithet now call for description:

1. The adjective is used as a noun and the qualified noun follows as an indirect genitive.

Ex. *ḥwrw n rḫty* a wretched washerman, lit. a wretch of a washerman.[1]

OBS. See below § 262, 1 for *wꜥ n* 'one', 'a'; the construction of *nn n*, *nꜣ n* 'these' (§ 111) is also comparable, as well as *nhy n* 'a few', 'a little', and *ḥḥ n* 'many' (§ 99).

2. The adjective follows its noun as an indirect genitive.

Ex. *ꜥ n ṯbwt n ḥḏ* a pair of white sandals, lit. of sandals of white.[2]

OBS. Here again the adjective is used as a noun. For a similar construction with noun clauses, see below § 191.

§ 95. It has been seen (§ 88, 2) that nouns may be used, like the accusative of respect in Latin, to qualify adjectives. The *indirect genitive* is sometimes employed similarly, when a suffix-pronoun follows the noun in question.

Exx. *sš iḳr n ḏbꜥw·f* a scribe excellent with (lit. of) his fingers.[3]

Twenty women *m nfrwt nt ḥꜥw·sn* who are beautiful of body, lit. as beautiful ones of their members.[4]

In the masculine instances it is not quite certain that *n* is the genitival adjective. It might be the preposition *n*; for a similar ambiguity see § 379, 3 below.

§ 96. The emphatic and the emphasized adjective. 1. It happens not seldom that an adjective bears an emphasis such as to make the meaning of the whole sentence dependent upon it.

Exx. *ir ib ḳn m st ḳsnt, sn-nw pw n nb·f* as for a heart (which is) brave in evil case, it is the equal of its lord.[5]

wr twꜣ n sfw r nḫt greater is the claim of the *mild* man than (that of) the *strong*.[6]

ḏd·i wrt I speak a (thing that is) important.[7]

2. As the above renderings show, the emphasis of the adjective often requires to be brought out in English by a relative clause ('which is', 'that is'). Egyptian occasionally utilizes the *m* of predication (§ 38) with the same intention; the adjective then ceases to be a mere epithet, and is employed as a noun.

Exx. Seek out for me *sꜣ·tn m sꜣꜣ, sn·tn m iḳr* a son of yours who is (lit. as) wise, a brother of yours who is (lit. as) excellent.[8]

iry·i m wrt I will do (something) which is (lit. as) great.[9]

[1] *Peas.* B 1, 169. Sim. *ib.* 175; Berl. *ÄI.* i. p. 261, 3.

[2] LAC. *Sarc.* i. p. 46. Sim. *Bersh.* i. 14, 4. 7; *Urk.* iv. 497, 8; 654, 14.

[3] *Sh.S.* 188. Other exx. *Rec.* 38, 210.

[4] *Westc.* 5, 10.

[5] *Adm.* p. 104. Sim. below § 144, 4.

[6] *Pt.* 319. Sim. *Peas.* B 1, 284, qu. § 148, 3.

[7] Cairo 20538, ii. *c* 9.

[8] *P.Pet.* 1116 B, 6. Sim. *Westc.* 5, 10 qu. § 95; *JEA.* iv. Pl. 8, 7–8; *Urk.* iv. 814, 17.

[9] *Urk.* iv. 350.

It is not possible to distinguish between *m* + adj. used as noun and the case where *m* + a real noun is employed as a kind of emphasized apposition.

Ex. ..... *ỉ ꜥnḫw tpyw tꜣ, m ḥmw-nṯr ḥmwt-nṯr ..... nw r-pr pn* O ye who live upon earth, such as are (lit. as) priests and priestesses ..... of this temple.[1]

OBS. We shall find similar uses in connexion with the relative adjective (§ 199, end) and the participles (§ 393).

§ **97. Comparative and superlative.**—The Egyptian adjective has no special forms for the degrees of comparison. The preposition *r* is used, as we have seen (§ 50), to render the meaning of the *comparative.*

The meaning of the *superlative* may be conveyed by a genitive.

Exx. *wr n wrw* greatest of the great.[2]

ink wr wrw m tꜣ r ḏr·f I was greatest of the great in the entire land.[3]

Or else by means of *ỉmy* (§ 80).

Ex. *wr ỉmy sꜥḥw* greatest of (lit. being in) the nobles.[4]

The repetition of a suffix may help to indicate superlative meaning.

Ex. *sꜣ·f smsw·f* his eldest son, lit. his son his eldest.[5]

For 'very' *wrt* 'greatly' (§ 205, 4) is of common occurrence.

Ex. *štꜣ wrt* very difficult.[6]

The common phrase *r ḫt nbt* 'more than anything'[7] conveys much the same sense. So too *wꜥ* 'one', 'alone':

Ex. *wꜥ ỉḳr* alone excellent, i.e. uniquely excellent.[8]

EQUIVALENTS OF ENGLISH ADJECTIVES, ETC.

§ **98.** The word for **'other'** has an ending *ỉ*, doubtless dual in origin:

sing. m. *ky* (*kỉỉ*) plur. m. *kywy* (*kỉwy*),[9] varr. [10] [11] [12]

„ f. *kt* (*kỉtỉ*) „ f. *kt* (*kỉtỉ*), only known from Old Eg.[13]

The transliterations in brackets give the correct etymological values.[14] *Ky* is no true adjective, but a noun to which another may be added in apposition.

Exx. *ky sp* another time, lit. another, a time.[15]

kt pḫrt another remedy.[16]

kywy nsyw other kings.[17]

A suffix may be attached to the word for 'other':

Ex. *kty·f wꜣt* its other side.[18]

ky and *kt* are frequently used as nouns; for the plural 'others' the phrase *kt-ḫt*,[19] var. *kt-ḫy*,[20] lit. 'other things', is common.

1. Cairo 20026. Sim. *Bersh.* i. 14, 2.
2. *Peas.* B 1, 53. 88. Sim. *Westc.* 9, 7. See too *ÄZ.* 55, 65.
3. *Urk.* iv. 410.
4. *BH.* i. 32. Sim. *ib.* 26, 152 (*ỉmy n*); LAC. *TR.* 80, 28; also *Siut* 1, 224 (*spd wn ỉmy nṯrw*); cf. further *Urk.* iv. 893, 16 (*nty m* instead of *ỉmy*).
5. Cairo 20750; *BH.* i. 25, 54.
6. *Bersh.* i. 14, 1.
7. Ex. *Peas.* B 2, 132.
8. *Urk.* iv. 68. Sim. *ib.* 495, 14; 557, 3.
9. *Adm.* p. 100; *Urk.* iv. 85. 102.
10. *ÄZ.* 34, 35.
11. *Urk.* iv. 320, 17; 322, 14; 331, 12.
12. *PSBA.* 18, 201, l. 6.
13. *Urk.* i. 78, 5.
14. See *ÄZ.* 40, 92.
15. *Urk.* iv. 1109.
16. *Eb.* 31, 17.
17. *Urk.* iv. 102.
18. *Peas.* Bt. 30.
19. *Peas.* B 1, 46.
20. *Urk.* iv. 20, 11; 1089, 11. Without det., *ib.* 736, 13.

'One' ..... 'other' is expressed by *wʿ* ..... *ky*:

Ex. *iw wȝt·f wʿt ẖr mw, kt ẖr it* its one side was under water, the other under corn.[1]

Or else by *ky* ..... *ky*:

Ex. *ḥpt·n ky ky* one embraced the other.[2]

Or else by *wʿ* 'one' ..... *sn-nw·f* 'his second':

Ex. *wʿ ḏd·f ḫft sn-nw·f* one said to (lit. before) the other.[3]

Or else is merely implied:

Ex. *rdi·n wi ḫȝst n ḫȝst* land gave me to land.[4]

§ **99**. **'Many', 'few', 'a little'.**—For these notions *ḥḥ* 'million' (§ 259) and *nhy* 'a little' are often used with the indirect genitive.

Exx. *ḥḥ n sp* many times, *or* often.[5]

nhy n rmṯ a few men.[6]

nhy n ḥmȝt a little salt.[7]

§ **100**. For **'entire', 'complete', 'whole'** several phrases are used.

1. *r ḏr·f*, lit. 'to its end'. Exx. *tȝ pn r ḏr·f* 'this entire land';[8] *mšʿ r ḏr·f* 'the entire army';[9] *dr·n·f s(y) r ḏr·s* 'he had subdued the whole of it';[10] also without suffix, *nn n ḫt r ḏr* 'all these things'.[11] Note too the phrase *nb-r-ḏr* lord of the universe', lit. 'lord to the end', a title given to the sun-god[12] or the king;[13] so too *nbt-r-ḏr* is an epithet of the queen.[14]

2. *mi ḳd·f*, lit. 'like its form'. Ex. *wnwt ḥwt-nṯr mi ḳd·s* 'the entire priesthood of the temple'.[15] A rarer synonym is *mi ḳi·f*.[15a]

3. *r ȝw·f* 'according to its length'. Exx. *hrw r ȝw·f* 'the entire day';[16] *tȝ ḫnyt r ȝw·s* 'the entire navy';[17] without suffix *nn r ȝw n rnpwt* 'all these years'.[18]

§ **101**. **'Each', 'every',** of time, is rendered by the noun *ṯnw* 'number', later *ṯnw*, followed by a direct genitive in the singular.

Exx. *r ṯnw rnpt* every year, lit. at every year.[19]

ṯnw dwȝw every morning.[20]

§ **102**. *s* 'man' is common for **'someone', 'anyone'**; also, combined with a negative word, for **'no one'.**

Exx. *ir ḫr·k s* if thou examine someone.[21]

nn wn ib n s no one has a heart, lit. not is a heart to a man.[22]

§ **103**. For **'everyone', 'everybody'** *s nb* 'every man'[23] is the most usual expression; but *bw nb*, lit. 'every place',[24] and *ḥr nb*, lit. 'every face',[25] are also frequent.

1 *Peas.* R 46. Sim. *Urk.* iv. 744, 4–6.
2 *Urk.* v. 48. Sim. *BH.* i. 26, 165; *Peas.* B 1, 152.
3 *Urk.* iv. 26. Also exceptionally *wʿ* ... *wʿ*, *Westc.* 8, 22.
4 *Sin.* B 28–9. Sim. *BH.* i. 25, 40–1; *Semnah Disp.* 2, 8; *Urk.* iv. 652, 10.
5 *Eb.* 30, 17; *Urk.* iv. 1091, 8.
6 *Adm.* 7, 3. Sim. *P. P.* 1116 B, 7.
7 *Peas.* B 1, 48. Sim. *Pr.* 1, 6.
8 *Westc.* 9, 11; *P. Pet.* 1116 B, 1.
9 *Kopt.* 8, 2; *Urk.* iv. 655, 16.
10 *Sin.* B 111.
11 *Siut* 1, 269.
12 *Urk.* v. 51. 64. 73; *Hearst* 6, 7.
13 *Mill.* 2; *Adm.* 15, 13.
14 *Sin.* B 172. 274.
15 *Kopt.* 8, 2. Sim. *Siut* 1, 151.
15a *Peas.* B 1, 41; *Westc.* 6, 14.
16 *Pt.* 380. 382.
17 *Urk.* iv. 6.
18 *Adm.* 13, 2.
19 *BH.* i. 8, 17; *Urk.* iv. 55. 70. 719.
20 *Urk.* iv. 117.
21 *Eb.* 38, 3.
22 *Leb.* 121.
23 *Sh. S.* 6; *Leb.* 112. 119.
24 *Siut* 3, 3. 6; *Pr.* 1, 12; *Leb.* 107. 111.
25 *Adm.* 6, 3; *Urk.* iv. 17, 10.

'Each one', 'each' is also represented by *s nb*;[1] but [hieroglyphs] *wꜥ nb* 'every one'[2] is equally common.

'Everything', 'anything' is [hieroglyphs] *ḫt nbt*, lit. 'all things';[3] [hieroglyphs] *ḫt* alone is also used for 'something',[4] 'anything',[5] see above § 92, 2.

NEGATION

§ **104.** Egyptian is rich in **negative words,** each of which possesses its own peculiar syntactic uses. For the moment we are concerned only with the commonest of these, which appears in two forms, [hieroglyphs] *nn* and [hieroglyphs] *n*. Old Egyptian did not make the distinction and Dyn. XI still often uses [hieroglyphs] for [hieroglyphs].[5a] For [hieroglyphs] religious texts show the variants [hieroglyphs] and [hieroglyphs], seeming to point to the reading *nn*.[6] In a few texts [hieroglyphs] interchanges with the particle [hieroglyphs], so that their phonetic values must have been very similar; [hieroglyphs] is also sometimes written as [hieroglyphs], and the preposition [hieroglyphs] *n* 'to' has [hieroglyphs] as a common variant (§ 164). Late Egyptian writes [hieroglyphs] *bn* for [hieroglyphs] *nn*, and an instance occurs already in Dyn. XVIII.[7]

The distinction between [hieroglyphs] *nn* and [hieroglyphs] *n* is rather obscure; possibly [hieroglyphs] is always a predicate 'not is.....', 'it is not (the case that).....', while [hieroglyphs] is more closely linked to the word which it precedes and qualifies; cf. οὐ and μή in Greek.[8] In carelessly written texts the two are apt to be confused, especially after the middle of Dyn. XVIII. See further below § 235.

Obs. The replacement of the sign of negation by [hieroglyphs] in some MSS. of the Book of the Dead is clearly due to superstitious reasons.

§ **105. Negation of the narrative verb.**—The negative word precedes the verb, and specializes its meaning in a strange way.[9]

1. [hieroglyphs] *n sḏm·f* has *past* meaning for the most part, and as such provides the ordinary method of negating the narrative *sḏm·n·f* form.

Exx. [hieroglyphs] *n ir·(i) ḫt n šrr nb, ir·n·(i) ḫt n ḥꜣty-ꜥ* I did not do things for any small man, I did things for the prince.[10]

[hieroglyphs] *ii·n·i .... n ḫpr nhw m mšꜥ·i* I returned .... there had not occurred loss in my army.[11]

We shall see in § 455 that *n sḏm·f* may occasionally refer to events in the present or the future, but such cases are not common enough to delay us here.

2. [hieroglyphs] *nn sḏm·f* has *future* meaning; see further below § 457.

Ex. [hieroglyphs] *nn wṯs·f dšrt* he shall not (*or* never) wear the red crown.[12]

3. [hieroglyphs] *n sḏm·n·f* has often *present* meaning.

Exx. The mouth is silent [hieroglyphs] *n mdw·n·f* and does not speak.[13]

[hieroglyphs] *ꜥnw pw, n rdi·n·f sꜣ·f* he is one who comes again, he does not turn (lit. give) his back.[14]

[1] Parenthetically like *quisque* after a plural, *Urk.* iv. 752, 14; *ÄZ.* 69, 31, 19.
[2] *Siut* 1, 277. 288; *Urk.* iv. 747, 17.
[3] After negative, *P. Kah.* 5, 58; *Eb.* 109, 2.
[4] *Eb.* 42, 18; 104, 2; 107, 12. 20.
[5] After negative, *Eb.* 27, 13; 110, 3.
[5a] See Gunn, *Studies*, ch. 25.
[6] See Gunn, *Studies*, ch. 10.
[7] *Urk.* iv. 650, 3, qu. § 491, 2.
[8] A different formulation of the same standpoint in Gunn, *Studies*, ch. 26.
[9] See Gunn, *Studies*, chs. 11–13.
[10] Brit. Mus. 1372.
[11] *BH.* i. 8, 10–11.
[12] *Kopt.* 8, 8.
[13] *Pt.* 13.
[14] *Sin.* B 58.

The three rules given above are sufficiently accurate for the purposes of the beginner, but will require considerable elaboration in the sequel, where it will appear that the Egyptians themselves approached the matter from a quite different angle from that of tense or time-distinction. To avoid giving a wrong impression from the start, we will enter somewhat more deeply into the discussion of *n śḏm·n·f* (see further § 418). It has been seen (§ 67) that *śḏm·n·f*, though in use mainly a past tense, etymologically expresses no more than that something happens to someone or through his agency. Hence *n śḏm·n·f* means in effect 'it does not happen that he hears', a certain space of time being envisaged during which his hearing might have taken place. We may define the function of *n śḏm·n·f* as *to deny the occurrence of an action throughout the course of a more or less prolonged period.* Hence it is common in generalizations, proverbs, and statements of custom, for all of which English usually employs the present tense. But *n śḏm·n·f* may also be employed where the context is *past* or *future.*

Exx. He found the canal stopped up *n sḳd·n dpt ḥr·f* and no boat sailed upon it.[1]

Such and such things must be done to prevent a snake from coming out of its hole, *n pr·n·f* and it will not (*or* never) come out.[2]

It is not quite easy to explain the reason why *n śḏm·f* and *nn śḏm·f* are not used in these two instances; nor is it possible to affirm that they might not have been used. Nevertheless two things are clear: first, *n śḏm·n·f* occurs only in contexts where, in the widest sense of the word, a generalization is being made; and second, a position of affairs is implied which *n śḏm·n·f* declares not to be interrupted by a negative instance.

The student must realize clearly that the affirmative and negative uses of the Egyptian verb-forms are separate things, not to be confounded with one another. For instance, it cannot be taken for granted, because *śḏm·n·f* may be rendered 'he had heard', that *n śḏm·n·f*, the same form with the negative word *n* in front of it, may be rendered 'he had not heard'. In point of fact, *n śḏm·n·f* appears never to have this meaning.

§ 106. 'Never'.—All three forms of negation described in the last section can, if the context requires it, be translated with 'never' instead of 'not', as is shown by several of the examples there quoted. If, however, it be desired to state more explicitly and emphatically that something has never happened, *n sp* followed by the *śḏm·f* form may be employed.

Exx. *n sp iry·i ḫt nbt ḏwt r rmṯ nb* never did I do anything evil against any people.[3]

n sp ir·t(w) mitt ḏr pꜣt tꜣ never had the like been done since the primal age of the earth.[4]

[1] *Urk.* iv. 814.

[2] *Eb.* 97, 19.

[3] Cairo 20729, *a* 3.

[4] *Urk.* iv. 374.

See further below § 456, where grounds are given for thinking that *sp* is here a verb meaning 'occur', so that *n sp iry·i* would mean literally 'it did not occur that I should do'.

EXISTENTIAL SENTENCES

§ 107. To express **existence,** whether absolute or as relative to some situation, i.e. presence, the verb [hieroglyphs] *wnn* 'exist', 'be' (perhaps originally 'move', 'run') is used.

1. The *sḏm·f* form of this verb varies according to the time and the duration which are envisaged. The longer form [hieroglyphs] *wnn·f* is commonly employed for the *future*, but may refer to any time-position where the notion of *duration* is stressed; the shorter form [hieroglyphs] *wn·f* lays no stress on duration, and tends rather to have *past* reference.

Exx. [hieroglyphs] *wnn pt, wnn·ṯ ḥr·i* so long as heaven shall exist, thou shalt exist with me; lit. sky shall exist, thou (fem.) shalt exist.[1]

[hieroglyphs] *ḥḏ·n·i, wn hrw* I set out early, (when) it was day, lit. (when) day was.[2]

Of the two forms, *wnn·f* alone is common in main clauses.

2. The phrase [hieroglyphs] *iw wn* (in which *wn* is *sḏm·f* form, § 462) means 'there is', 'there was'.

Ex. [hieroglyphs] *iw wn nḏs, Ḏdi rn·f* there was a commoner, whose name was Djedi.[3]

Since *iw* is avoided after words like [hieroglyphs] *isṯ* 'lo', [hieroglyphs] *nn* 'not', [hieroglyphs] *nty* 'who' (§ 44, 2), here *wn* occurs alone with the meaning of *iw wn*.

Exx. [hieroglyphs] *ist wn ḥmt·f* and he had a wife, lit. lo, there was a wife of him.[4]

[hieroglyphs] *nty wn wr n wrw·f* whose great ones have one greater, lit. who there existed a great one for his great ones.[5]

Note that absolute existence is but rarely asserted; usually there is some qualification in the form of a genitive, an adverbial phrase or an adjective, as is indeed the case with several of the examples above quoted. When such a qualification occurs, there is a tendency for it, rather than the notion of existence, to become the real predicate, the verb *wnn* then degenerating into a mere copula (§ 28). Hence we shall find the model of the existential sentence much employed in sentences expressing possession (§§ 114–15), sentences with adverbial predicate (§§ 118. 120) and sentences with adjectival predicate (§ 142).

OBS. For a case where the *iw* of *iw wn* is changed into *wnn* according to the rules enunciated in §§ 118, 2; 150, see below § 150. And for a case where *iw* in *iw wn* is omitted after *n wnt* 'there does not exist' (§ 108), see § 394. So too *ir wn* 'if there be' occurs for a theoretic *ir iw wn*.[6]

[1] *Urk.* iv. 348, 9. Sim. *ib.* 305, 8; 306, 11; 1151, 3; *D. el B.* 155; CAULFIELD, 4.

[2] *Sin.* R 34. Sim. *T. Carn.* 14. 15 after *mi* 'as though', qu. § 157, 3.

[3] *Westc.* 6, 26. Sim. *ib.* 2, 5; FRASER, *Scarabs* 263. Interrogative exx. with *in*, see *Sin.* B 120. 133. Before an adjectival predicate, see § 467, end.

[4] *Peas.* R 2. Sim. *Urk.* iv. 139, 2.

[5] *Peas.* B 1, 89. Sim. *ib.* 304.

[6] *L. to D.* Berlin bowl. A further development, see *JEA.* 27, 112.

§ **108. Non-existence** or **absence** is expressed (1) by means of [hieroglyphs] *nn wn* 'there exists not', 'there existed not'.[1] Since *wn* here represents *iw wn* with *iw* suppressed (see § 107, 2), this phrase escapes from the rule (§ 105, 2) that *nn* + *śdm·f* always has reference to future time.

Exx. [hieroglyphs] *nn wn pḥwy·fy* there is no end to it, lit. there does not exist its end.[2]

[hieroglyphs] *nn wn mꜣr n ḥꜣw·i* there was none wretched in (lit. of) my time.[3]

People say: [hieroglyphs] *nn wn* there is nothing, lit. there does not exist.[4]

2. More rarely [hieroglyphs] *n wnt*[5] occurs with identical meaning; *wnt* is possibly the *śdmt·f* form of the verb, see below § 402, end.

Ex. [hieroglyphs] *n wnt šsꜣw·sn* there is no remedy for them.[6]

3. Frequently [hieroglyphs] *nn* '(there is) not' stands alone for 'there does (did) not exist'.[7]

Exx. [hieroglyphs] *nn mꜣꜥtyw* there are no righteous.[8]

[hieroglyphs] *nn is-ib dns sḫr-ḫt* there is none light-hearted who is heavy (i.e. slow to move) as regards his appetites (lit. the counsel of the body).[9]

As in the sentences expressing existence, so too in those expressing non-existence, some qualification is as a rule added, and this is apt to become the real predicate; exx. below §§ 114; 120; 144, 4; 394.

OBS. In a sequence of parallel denials of existence, if the first begins with *nn wn*, the second is likely to omit *wn* as superfluous; *nn* may then be rendered 'nor'.[10]

§ **109. 'Without'.**—We have seen (§§ 29. 30) that sentences of various kinds may be used, without the help of conjunctions, to express the equivalents of English adverb clauses. Sentences having as predicate [hieroglyphs] *nn* 'there is not' (§ 108) are frequently so used, and in this case *nn* may often best be translated 'without'.

Ex. [hieroglyphs] *di·sn n·k nḥḥ nn ḏrw·f, ḏt nn ḥnty·s* may they give to thee everlasting without an (lit. there is not its) end, and eternity without a (lit. there is not its) term.[11]

[hieroglyphs] *nn wn* and [hieroglyphs] *n wnt* (§ 108) are less often employed in this way.

Exx. [hieroglyphs] *hꜥw rd, nn wn mnt·f* a healthy body without malady, lit. its malady does not exist.[12]

[hieroglyphs] *wꜣḥ ḫt, n wnt ꜣbw* making offerings unceasingly, lit. offering things, there was not cessation.[13]

OBS. *Nn* is very commonly used in this manner with the infinitive as its subject, and there occurs a similar use with the lighter negative word *n* (§ 307). For *nn* + noun + suffix employed as a relative clause see § 196, 1.

[1] See GUNN, *Studies*, pp. 122 foll.; 160–1.

[2] *Leb.* 130. Another ex. below § 115.

[3] *BH.* i. 8, 19. Sim. *Hat-Nub* 11, 9, qu. § 394, end.

[4] *Adm.* 6, 4.

[5] See GUNN, *Studies*, ch. 19.

[6] *Eb.* 100, 15. Sim. Turin 156, 4.

[7] See GUNN, *Studies*, ch. 17. Rarely written *n*, *ib.* p. 195.

[8] *Leb.* 122. Sim. *Adm.* 2, 2; *Sin.* B 84.

[9] *Peas.* B 1, 209. See too below §§ 144, 4; 394.

[10] Exx. *BH.* i. 8, 19; *Sin.* B 62–3.

[11] *Sin.* B 212. Sim. *ib.* 299; *Adm.* 6, 1; *Urk.* iv. 163, 15.

[12] Turin 159, 5.

[13] *Urk.* iv. 519. Sim. *Bersh.* ii. 21, top 14.

VOCABULARY

mḥy be neglectful, careless.

nḏnḏ converse, take counsel.

ḥḏ be white, bright; white (adj.)

ḳd build.

var. *ḥm* Majesty (with suffixes or genitival adj.)

sr official, noble.

ḥꜣty-ʿ chieftain, local prince, mayor (plur. *ḥꜣtyw-ʿ*).

bỉty king of Lower Egypt.

bꜣw might (plur.)

var. *šnwt* granary.

rnpt year.

rk time, period.

hꜣw environment, neighbourhood, time.

sp occasion, time, deed, fault.

bỉt qualities, talent.

ḳd form, character; good character, virtue.

ḏr end, limit.

mꜣr wretched.

ḏr since (prep.).

tp head; upon (prep.).

EXERCISE VIII

(*a*) *Transliterate and translate*:

(1) (2) (3) (4) (5)[1] (6) (7) (8) (9)

[1] I.e. the time when the sun-god reigned upon earth, the oldest period of Egyptian legendary history.

(*b*) *Write in hieroglyphs and transliteration*:

(1) Thy praises are in the mouth of everyone. They say: how great is the might of Thy Majesty! (2) He shall not receive bread (from) upon the altar of any god. (3) There was none wretched of my environment, there was none hungry of my period. (4) He does not say (either) good or evil. (5) Thou art greatest of the officials of the palace. (6) His Majesty answered the vizier, he did not answer this woman (*ḥmt*). (7) There was a god in this (foreign) country, whom (lit. him) the people of Egypt did not know. (8) They gave him praises on account of his very excellent qualities. One said (*śḏm·f* form) to another: 'there is no fault in (lit. of) him'.

LESSON IX

DEMONSTRATIVE ADJECTIVES AND PRONOUNS

§ **110.** The **demonstratives**[1] conform to a common pattern, as will be seen from the following list.

	Sing. m.	Sing. f.	Plur. c.
This (obsolescent)	*pw*	*tw*	*nw*
„ (later as adj.)	*pwy*	*twy*	——
This (near me)	*pn*	*tn*	*nn*, var.
That	*pf*, var. *pfy*	*tf*	*nf*[2]
„ (later form)	*pfꜣ*	*tfꜣ*, var.	*nfꜣ*,[3] var.[4]
This, the	*pꜣ*,[5] rarely ,[5a] hieratic [5b]	*tꜣ*	*nꜣ*

In this series three demonstrative stems, characterized by the consonants *p*, *t* and *n*, are utilized for the sing. m., sing. f., and plur. c. respectively; and with these stems are combined other demonstrative elements such as *n*, *f* and *ꜣ*. The resultant compounds may be compared with *celui-ci*, *celui-là* in French.

The forms beginning with *n*, though called plurals for convenience, are really singulars with the meaning of Latin *hoc*, *illud*. In earlier use was a set of real plurals: m. *ipn*, *ipw*, etc.; f. *iptn*, *iptw*, etc. *'Ipn* and *iptn* are still occasionally employed in Middle Egyptian, but mainly[6] after a noun accompanied by a suffix, ex. *ˁwt·i iptn* 'these my members'.[7] Some corresponding duals, occurring only in religious texts, are too rare to be specified here.[8]

[1] See *Rec.* 35, 70; *ÄZ.* 47, 59; 50, 101.

[2] *P. Kah.* 7, 61; *Siut* 4, 24.

[3] *Eb.* 108, 20.

[4] *Leb.* 34. 37.

[5] *Urk.* iv. 3, 3; 125, 3; 654, 8; written *pꜣy* as emphatic 'this', *ib.* 654, 16.

[5a] Louvre C 11, 5. 6; *Pr.* 2, 5.

[5b] Rarely too in hierogl. influenced by hieratic, *Kopt.* 8, 4.

[6] Exception, *Urk.* iv. 257, 2 in an archaic text.

[7] *Eb.* 1, 5.

[8] See *ÄZ.* 45, 57.

§ **111. Construction of the demonstratives.**—As *epithets* the singulars (together with the plurals *ipn*, *ipw*) all follow their noun, excepting *pꜣ*, *tꜣ*, which invariably precede it. Exx. *st tn* 'this place'; *hrw pfy* 'that day'; but *pꜣ šfdw* 'this papyrus-roll'.[1] Exceptionally, *pf*, *tf* and *pfꜣ*, *tfꜣ* may precede their noun, as in *pf gs* 'that side';[2] *tfꜣ pẖrt* 'that remedy'.[3]

The plurals in *n* all precede their noun, and are connected with it by the genitival adjective (§ 86). Exx. *nn n srw* 'these officials';[4] *nꜣ n ꜥwt* 'these dwellings'.[5] Occasionally the noun is in the singular, ex. *nn n sḫty* 'these peasants', lit. 'this of peasant'.[6] Before Dyn. XVIII the vernacular began to drop the genitival *n*, ex. *nn ḥmwt* 'these women';[7] but this practice, which later became regular, is very rare in Middle Egyptian, and is not found in good monumental texts.

The demonstratives beginning with *n* are thus really singular *pronouns*, not plural adjectives, and often occur with the neuter sense of 'this' and 'that'. Exx. *ḏd·n·f nn* 'he said this';[8] *pty nꜣ* 'what is this?'[9] Participles agreeing with these apparent neuters are in the sing. m. form, but the suffix 3rd sing. f. (*·s* 'it') is used in referring back to them (§ 511, 3).

For the same demonstratives as subject of sentences with nominal predicate, see below § 127, 2. The singular *pw* is very widely used in a similar way as an equivalent, invariable in gender, of the pronouns of the 3rd pers. 'he', 'she', 'it', 'they', ex. *Rꜥ pw* 'he is Rēꜥ'; for this construction and its extensions, see §§ 128–31. 140.

Otherwise, the singular demonstratives are seldom used except as epithets. *Pꜣ* rarely occurs as a predicate, when it may be translated 'such', referring to something that precedes or follows; ex. *pꜣ pw Wsir* 'such is Osiris', lit. 'this is he, (namely) Osiris'.[10] *Pn* and *pfꜣ* are found still more rarely as virtual neuters meaning 'this' and 'that', ex. *rḫ·i pfꜣ r pn* 'I knew that from this'.[11]

Obs. From *pꜣ* and *tꜣ* as demonstrative pronouns are derived the prefixes *p-n-* 'he of' and *t-nt-* 'she of', which, however, occur in our period only as components of proper names.[12] The genitival adjective seems to have fallen away early, since *pꜣy* and *tꜣ* are found as variants of *p-n-* and *t-nt-* at the beginning of Dyn. XVIII or even earlier.

§ 112. Meaning of the demonstratives.—*Pn*, *tn*, *nn* are the commonest words for 'this', i.e. near me, at hand, both of time and of place. They are apt to be used in a manner rather redundant to our way of thinking.

Ex. *ḏd·in sḫty pn n ḥmt·f tn* then said this peasant to this his wife.[13]

Pw, as an epithet, is confined to high-flown diction and religious texts, where the preference for archaic words is very marked; ex. *fnd·k pw špss* 'this thy noble nose' in a speech to the Pharaoh.[14] Even in religious texts *pw*, *tw* tend to give place to *pwy*, *twy*, forms employed only as

1 *Pr.* 2, 5.
2 *Leb.* 16.
3 *P. Kah.* 5, 27. Sim. *Leb.* 77.
4 *Peas.* B 1, 51. Sim. *Sin.* B 256.
5 *P. Kah.* 12, 13. Sim. *Urk.* iv. 172, 12; 186, 4. *Nw*, e.g. *Eb.* 2, 5.
6 *Peas.* B 1, 75. Sim. *ib.* 9. 81–2; *Meir* iii. 13; in all these cases preceded by *wꜥ m* 'one of'.
7 *Westc.* 5, 12. Sim. *ib.* 9, 21. 27.
8 *Sin.* R 56. Sim. *Pt.* 507.
9 *Westc.* 11, 10. *Nw*, e.g. *Urk.* iv. 175, 7.
10 *Rec.* 39, 121. Sim. *Peas.* B 1, 19; *Rhind* 57.
11 *Urk.* iv. 119.
12 See *ÄZ.* 54, 104.
13 *Peas.* R 5.
14 *Sin.* B 237. *Tw*, sing. f., Cairo 20153. 20497. 20691.

epithets; ex. *nṯr pwy ꜥꜣ* 'this great god', where the M.K. texts have *pw*, and those of Dyn. XVIII *pwy*.[1] Note the curious use in vocatives, ex. *ḥkꜣy pw* 'thou (lit. this) magician'.[2] For the other uses of *pw* see above § 111.

Pf, pfy, pfꜣ, with their feminines and plurals, are employed where some opposition between 'that yonder' and 'this here' is intended; but also, like Latin *iste*, to express some emotional stress, whether of disgust or of admiration; exx. *ḫr pf* 'that (vile) enemy',[3] *ẖnw pf špsy* 'that noble Residence (of long ago)'.[4] Note that such a nuance of admiration is particularly often applied to things and persons belonging to the past.

Pꜣ, tꜣ, nꜣ are both the most recent and the weakest of the demonstratives. Frequently they mean 'this', like *pn, tn, nn*;[4a] exx. *tꜣ ḏꜣtt* (?) 'this province';[5] *nꜣ n gmḥwt* 'these candles'.[6] So particularly with designations of time, exx. *m tꜣ ꜣt* 'at this moment';[7] *m pꜣ hrw* 'on this day', 'to-day'.[8] Elsewhere, however, they have merely the force of the **definite article**, their regular use in Late Egyptian and onwards. So already before Dyn. XVIII: *nꜣ n ỉt nty m pꜣ mẖr* 'the corn which is in the storehouse'.[9]

[1] *Urk.* v. 15. *Pwy, twy* also *Westc.* 9, 11; 10, 9.

[2] *Urk.* v. 177, 7. 11. 14; *Westc.* 7, 20; 8, 1.

[3] *Urk.* iv. 8. Sim. *ib.* 648, 14; 661, 15.

[4] *Adm.* 10, 8–11. Sim. *Sin.* B 44.

[4a] In this sense written *pꜣy* in L. E.; the same distinction already *Urk.* iv. 654, 16, see p. 85, n. 5.

[5] *Peas.* R 66 (B 16 *ḏꜣtt* (?) *tn*); sim. *nꜣ*, *ib.* R 120 (B 75, *nn*).

[6] *Siut.* 1, 297.

[7] *Leb.* 116; *P. Kah.* 11, 19; *Urk.* iv. 27, 16; 658, 10.

[8] *Th. T. S.* iii. 26; *Paheri* 3.

[9] *Peas.* R 4. Many exx. *Paheri* 3.

EQUIVALENTS OF THE ENGLISH POSSESSIVE ADJECTIVES

§ 113. The sense of English 'my', 'thy', etc. is usually conveyed, as we have seen (§ 35, 1), by means of the suffix-pronouns, which are appended to their nouns as direct genitives. Some less frequent alternatives have now to be considered.

1. From the demonstratives *pꜣ, tꜣ, nꜣ* (§§ 110–112) are derived the **possessive adjectives**; it will suffice to quote the forms of the 1st and 2nd pers. sing.

	With sing. m. noun	With sing. f. noun	With plur. noun
Sing. 1, c. 'my'	*pꜣy·ỉ*[10]	*tꜣy·ỉ*	*nꜣy·ỉ n*
„ 2, m. 'thy'	*pꜣy·k*	*tꜣy·k*	*nꜣy·k n*

Similarly for the other persons and numbers. Forms without *y* are sometimes found, ex. *pꜣ·s* 'her'.[11] Hieratic almost always etc.[11a]

The possessive adjective is not uncommon in the more popular writing of Dyn. XII and after, but does not become usual until Late Egyptian. Its construction is identical with that of the demonstratives from which it is derived.

Exx. *tꜣy·ỉ ḥmt* my wife.[12]

nꜣy·s n ẖrdw her children.[13]

2. *ỉry*, more rarely written *ỉrw* (?), is sometimes used as an unchangeable substitute for the suffixes of the 3rd pers. sing. or plur. It seems to

[10] *Urk.* iv. 894, 9; *Paheri* 3; in hierogl. usually without *ꜣ*.

[11] *Urk.* iv. 1067. Sim. *ib.* 1069. 1070. *Tꜣ·n*, *T. Carn.* 5.

[11a] Without *y*: *P. Kah.* 36, 41; *T. Carn.* 7.

[12] *P. Kah.* 12, 12.

[13] *P. Kah.* 12, 10. Sim. *Pr.* 2, 3.

be nothing more than the adjective *ỉry* 'relating to' become invariable in this particular use,[1] and is often best rendered by the English 'thereof', 'thereto'.

Exx. His Majesty had sent an army, *sꜣ·f smsw m ḥry ỉry* and his eldest son was the chief thereof.[2]

hp ỉrw (?) the law appertaining thereto.[3]

So too after prepositions, exx. *ḫft ỉry* 'according thereto';[4] *ḥr-sꜣ ỉry* 'thereafter';[5] *m-m ỉry* 'among them'.[6]

3. A more emphatic equivalent of the English possessive adjective, corresponding roughly to our 'of *mine*', 'of *thine*' is provided by the series *n·ỉ-ỉmy*, *n·k-ỉmy*, etc., for which the variants , etc. are found. These phrases follow their noun.

Exx. *m-ḫt ỉꜣw n·k-ỉmy* after thy own old age.[7]

hdmw n·sn-ỉm(y) footstools belonging to them.[8]

OBS. In origin this *-ỉmy* was probably the adverb elsewhere written without *y*, § 205, 1, cf. Copt. *ᵉmmau* 'there' after *wentai* 'I have', lit. 'there is with me'.

SENTENCES EXPRESSING POSSESSION

§ 114. Egyptian has no verb meaning 'to possess', 'to have', nor yet any verb meaning 'to belong to'. In order to express these notions, use is made of the preposition *n* 'to', together with its derivatives.

1. When *n* itself is employed, the rules governing the sentence with adverbial predicate (§§ 29; 37; 44, 2; Lesson X) come into play. Note, however, that when *n* is followed by a suffix, it acquires that precedence in word-order which we have noted in § 66 as peculiar to the dative. Compare for this construction the Latin *est mihi, sunt mihi.*

Exx. *ḫt·ỉ nbt m šꜣ m nỉwt n sn·ỉ 'Iḥy-snb* all my property in country and in town (shall belong) to my brother 'Iḥysonb.[9]

wnn·s n ... Sbk-nḫt it (my office) shall (belong) to Sebknakhte.[9a]

ỉw n·k ꜥnḫ thou shalt have life, lit. life is to thee.[10]

nn wn ỉb n s no man has a heart.[11]

nn ỉs n sbỉ ḥr ḥm·f there is no tomb for him-who-rebels against his Majesty, i. e. the rebel shall have no tomb.[12]

nn n·k st it does not belong to thee.[13]

2. When the subject is a pronoun, the genitival adjective *n(y)* may be employed as predicate. According to § 48, 2 this will be invariable in number and gender, and according to § 44, 3 the dependent pronoun must be used. The association between adjectival predicate and pronominal subject is here so close, that in the case of the 3rd person m. *sw*, f. *sy*, the biliteral sign *ns* is regularly found linking the two together as , .

---

[1] Variable still in *mitt irt* 'the like thereof', *Hamm.* 114, 15; *JEA.* 16, 19. Sim. Cairo 20539, i. *b* 3; *ÄZ.* 58, 24*.

[2] *Sin.* R. 12. Sim. *Sh. S.* 22; *Leb.* 63; *Adm.* 7, 12.

[3] *Urk.* iv. 1092. Sim. *BH.* i. 25, 83; *Urk.* iv. 53. 659. 743.

[4] *P. Kah.* 29, 43.

[5] *Eb.* 55, 1.

[6] *Urk.* iv. 114, 5.

[7] *Urk.* iv. 1021. Sim. *ib.* 650, 5; 1068, 10; *Rhind* 56–9; *Westc.* 9, 11. On one coffin *n·k-ỉmyt* after a fem. noun, S 1 C 239. 243.

[8] *Urk.* iv. 666.

[9] *P. Kah.* 12, 4. Sim. *Eb.* 99, 4.

[9a] LAC. *Stèle jur.* 6.

[10] *Urk.* iv. 561. Sim. *ib.* 244, 10; *P. Kah.* 11, 21.

[11] *Leb.* 121. Sim. *Pt.* 315 (in L 2 with *n wnt*).

[12] Cairo 20538, ii. *c* 19. Sim. *Peas.* B 2, 110–1.

[13] *Peas.* B 1, 292; B 2, 26.

Exx. *n(y)-wi Rꜥ* I belong to Rēꜥ, lit. I am belonging-to Rēꜥ.[1]

n(y)-s(y) imy-r pr it (this province, f.) belongs to the steward.[2]

So too in indications of measurement.

Ex. *n(y)-sw mḥ 30* it (the snake) was of 30 cubits.[3]

3. For 'belongs to me', 'belongs to thee', or alternatively 'I am (thou art) owner of', the independent pronouns of § 64, or at all events forms evidently very closely akin, are employed;[4] some emphasis is here laid on the possessor. If the subject be pronominal, it is represented by the dependent pronouns.

Exx. *ntk nbw* to thee belongs gold.[5]

ink sy she belongs to me.[6] A personal name.

In certain religious texts of the M.K. *nnk* is written for 1st pers. sing. in this employment.[7] For another possible use of *nnk*, see § 300, near end.

Obs. For the same purpose Late Egyptian uses forms[7a] clearly descended from the older *ṯwt*, *św̓t*, definitely proving the kinship with the independent pronouns.

4. *N·i-im(y)*, *n·k-im(y)* (§ 113, 3) occur with the same meaning and with a like construction.

Exx. *n·k-imy ḥḏ* to thee belongs silver.[8]

ꜥntyw, *n·i-im sw* the incense, it belongs to me.[9]

Obs. *Ntf* is found as a noun meaning 'its content',[10] and *n·k-imy* similarly as a noun meaning 'thy possessions'.[11]

§ **115**. To convey the meaning 'I have (had) a.....', 'thou hast (hadst) no.......' the existential sentences of §§ 107–8 may be employed, the subject being qualified by a suffix-pronoun (see § 35, Obs.).

Exx. *ist wn ḥmt·f* and he has a wife, lit. lo, there was a wife of him.[12]

nn wn tp·f he has no head, lit. not exists a head of him.[13]

n wnt swwt·s it has no reeds.[14]

So too in cases where *nn* is best rendered as 'without' (§ 109).

Ex. *mk tw m niwt, nn ḥkꜣ-ḥwt·s* behold, thou art a city without a ruler, lit. as a city, not is a ruler of it.[15]

See Add. for § **115a**.

[1] *Eb.* 1, 7. Sim. *ÄZ.* 57, 7*; Nav. 1, 7; *Nebesh.* 11.
[2] *Peas.* B 1, 16.
[3] *Sh. S.* 62. Sim. *Rhind* 45. 46; Budge p. 219, 3.
[4] See *ÄZ.* 34, 50; 41, 135.
[5] *Urk.* iv. 96. Sim. *Adm.* 10, 4.
[6] Berl. *Hi. Pap.* iii. 42 *a.* Sim. Brit. Mus. 1203; *ÄZ.* 54, 49.
[7] See *ÄZ.* 54, 40; 58, 53.
[7a] See *ÄZ.* 50, 114; *JEA.* 20, 13.
[8] *Urk.* iv. 96. Sim. *ib.* 244, 11–12; *Ann.* 39, 189, 9.
[9] *Sh. S.* 151. Sim. *Sin.* B 222.
[10] *Rhind* 49.
[11] *Peas.* B 1, 103–4.
[12] *Peas.* R 2.
[13] *P. Ram.* unpubl.
[14] *Urk.* v. 151. Sim. *Bersh.* ii. 21, 14.
[15] *Peas.* B 1, 190. Sim. *Sin.* B 13. 47. 212.

VOCABULARY

biꜣ var. *by* marvel (*n* at).

ḫpr become, happen.

ḫnm join, endue (*m* with).

smn make firm, establish.

snḏ (later *snd*) fear; *snḏw* (*sndw*) fear (noun).

nḏm be sweet, agreeable; adj. sweet, agreeable; n. sweetness.

iwnn sanctuary.

ỉs tomb, tomb-chamber.

sḫnt supporting pole, support.

nbw gold.

ḥḏ silver.

ḥḳꜣ ruler, chieftain.

ṯꜣw brea.h, wind.

ḥryt apprehension, dread.

mrwt love (noun).

ỉꜣmt charm, favour.

šnbt breast.

ḥꜥ piece of flesh; plur. flesh, body.

fnd nose (earlier *fnḏ*).

var. *sꜣ* magic knot, amulet, protection.

ꜣt moment.

nḏty helper, avenger.

EXERCISE IX

(*a*) *Study the following text;*[1] *Amen-Rēꜥ, the god of Thebes, addresses the Pharaoh Tuthmosis III (Dyn. XVIII, 1501–1447* B.C.)

sꜣ·ỉ	*nḏty·ỉ*	*Mn-ḫpr-Rꜥ*	*ꜥnḫ·*	*ḏt*	*wbn·ỉ*	*n*	*mr(w)t·k*
My son,	my avenger,[2]	Menkheperrēꜥ,[3]	{may he live}	eternally:	I shine forth	through	love of thee.[4]

ḫnm	*ꜥwy·ỉ*	*ḥꜥw·k*	*m*	*sꜣ*	*ꜥnḫ*	*nḏm·wy*	*ỉꜣmt·k*
Endue	my hands	thy body	with	the protection	of life.[5]	How sweet is	thy charm

r	*šnbt·ỉ*	*smn·ỉ*	*tw*	*m*	*ỉwnn·ỉ*
against	my breast!	I establish	thee	in	my sanctuary.

by·ỉ	*n·k*	*dỉ·ỉ*	*bꜣw·k*	*snḏw·k*	*m*	*ṯꜣw*	*nbw*
I marvel	at thee.	I place	thy might (and)	the fear of thee	in	lands	all,

ḥryt·k	*r*	*ḏrw*	*sḫnwt*	*nt*	*pt*
the dread of thee	to	the limits	of the (four) supports	of	heaven.

[1] Extracts from the so-called 'Poetical Stela', found in two examples at Karnak; see *Urk.* iv. 611. 620.

[2] Throughout Egyptian temple-ritual runs the conception of the king as 'the living Horus', and consequently any god who is worshipped and regarded by him as his father, becomes thereby identified with the god Osiris, whom Horus vindicated and avenged after his murder by the wicked god Seth.

[3] Prenomen of Tuthmosis III, see Excursus A, p. 73.

[4] Note here and in *snḏw·k, ḥryt·k* below the counterparts of the Latin 'objective' genitive.

[5] Amen-Rēꜥ is here the sun-god, bestowing life by means of his rays.

(*b*) *Transliterate and translate*:

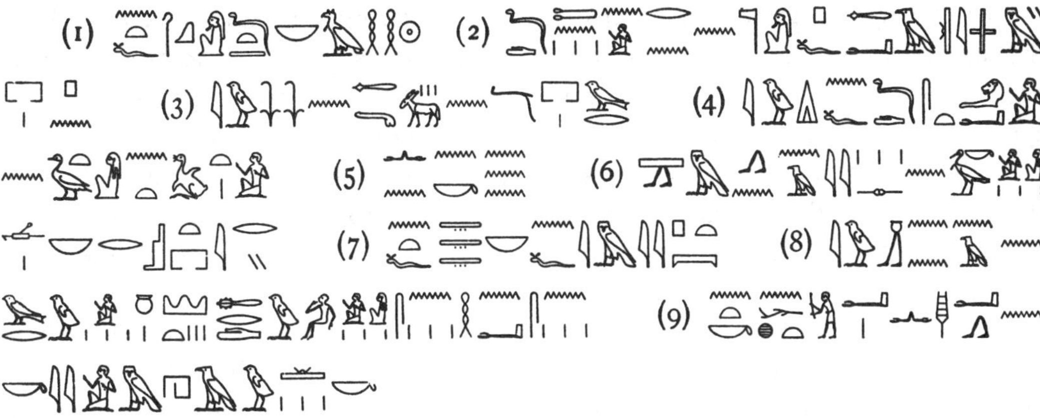

(*c*) *Write in hieroglyphs and transliteration*:

(1) To thee belongs the sky and (lit. with) all that-is-in it. (2) Never had the like happened in the time of any king. (3) How pleasant is the voice of these women in (*ḥr*) my heart! (4) (May) the gods of Egypt give the breath of life to thy nose,[1] that thou mayst adore Rēʿ every day. (5) The overseer of works built for me a tomb on the west of my city. (6) Others shall not hear this. (7) Rēʿ caused him to arise as ruler of this entire land. (8) Then shalt thou say the like thereof to thy children. (9) Silver and gold are in thy house, there are no limits to (lit. of) them. (10) Life is thine in this thy city of eternity (i.e. the tomb).

[1] For the Egyptians the concrete symbol of life was the breath, which the gods 'gave into the nose' of the king, the king doing likewise for his subjects.

LESSON X

SENTENCES WITH ADVERBIAL PREDICATE[1]

[1] See SETHE, *Nominalsatz*, §§ 3–21; LEF. *Gr.* §§ 637 foll.

§ 116. This topic has been touched upon in many previous sections; we must now gather together what has been already learnt and supplement it with further details.

First let it be noted that the term predicate ought, in grammar, strictly to include the copula ('is', 'are', etc.). It is, however, extremely convenient to use the term in a looser sense, and we shall not hesitate to speak of an adjective, an adverb, or a noun as of itself constituting a predicate.

The *adverbial predicate* may consist either of an actual adverb, like *im* 'there', or else of an adverbial phrase composed of a preposition + a noun, ex. *m pr·f* 'in his house'. In the latter event two special cases call for remark: (1) the preposition used may be the datival 𓈖 *n* 'to', 'for', which serves to convey the notion of possession and involves certain deviations from the usual word-order (see § 114, 1); (2) the preposition may be the 𓅓 *m* of predication (§ 38) or the 𓂋 *r* of futurity (§ 122), and then the predicate corresponds to an English nominal predicate, i.e. a predicate consisting of a noun.

Neither of these special cases affects the expression of the copula or of the subject; in other words, the same rules as to subject and copula which hold of the adverbial predicate generally hold of it also in the case of the *n* of possession, the *m* of predication, and the *r* of futurity.

The *copula* is often left unexpressed. When it is expressed, one of the two verb-stems *iw* 'be' (§ 29) or *wnn* 'exist' (§ 107) is employed. The different shades of meaning resulting from the insertion of the copula in its various forms will be studied in the following sections.

When the *subject* is a *noun* or *demonstrative pronoun* nothing prevents it from standing at the beginning of the sentence; but it may be preceded, either by *iw* or by a *sḏm·f* form from *wnn* (in these cases conforming strictly to the type of the verbal sentence, § 27), or else by a particle like *mk* 'behold' or *nn* 'not', which modifies the meaning of the sentence as a whole. When the subject is a *personal pronoun*, some supporting word must necessarily precede it, since the independent pronouns are normally not used with adverbial predicate (§ 65, end), and the suffixes and dependent pronouns must always be attached to some preceding word. The suffix-pronouns are employed after the copula in its various forms (thus *iw·f*, *wn·f*, *wnn·f*), but when the supporting word is a particle of the kind above alluded to, it is as a rule the dependent pronouns which are used (exx. *mk sw*, *nn sw*).

As just stated, the employment of the independent pronouns as subject of the sentence with adverbial predicate is exceedingly rare, and may be archaistic, since a few instances occur in the Pyramid texts.[1] In Middle Egyptian only the following have been noted:

[hieroglyphs] *ink ḏs·(i) m ḥꜥwt* I myself was in joy.[2]

[hieroglyphs] *ḥꜣty·i n ntf m ẖt·i* my heart, it was not in my body.[3]

OBS. For important ramifications of the sentence with adverbial predicate see below Lesson XXIII on the pseudo-verbal construction. For cases where the grammatical subject is the logical predicate, see § 126.

§ 117. **The presence or absence of** 𓇋𓅱 ***iw* in sentences with adverbial predicate.**—The verb *iw* states facts as such, declares this or that to be the case. 1. With *nominal* subject it serves to introduce some statement, often a description, of outstanding interest, and the clause containing it must be translated as a main clause.

[1] *Pyr.* 1093. 1114.

[2] Louvre C 3, 7.

[3] *Sin.* B 255 (corrupt in B 39). Sim. *ib.* B 185.

Exx. *iw šdw·k m sḫt* thy field-plots are in the country.[1] Statement of fact.

iw dꜣbw im·f ḥnꜥ iꜣrrt figs were in it, and also grapes.[2] Description of the land Yaa.

iw ms itrw m snf forsooth, the river is blood, lit. as blood.[3] In a pessimistic description of Egypt. Note the *m* of predication. (§ 38).

iw nꜣ m sbꜣyt this is an (lit. as an) instruction.[4] The subject is here a demonstrative pronoun.

Only rarely does it happen that such sentences have the value of English subordinate clauses; they have such a value, for example, when a strong contrast is expressed or a medical symptom emphasized.

Exx. It was he who subdued the foreign lands, *iw it·f m ẖnw ꜥḥ·f* (while) his father was within his castle.[5]

iw ḥt·s mi ntt ẖr sḏt and her body is like what is on (lit. under) fire.[6]

When *iw* is omitted, the statement or description becomes less obtrusive.

Exx. *ḫrt·k m pr·k* thy rations are in thy house.[7] In the midst of an argumentative passage.

dḳrw nb ḥr ḫtw·f all kinds of fruit (lit. all fruits) were on its trees.[8] Part of a description.

psšw m ꜥwnw the apportioner is (now) a spoiler, lit. as a spoiler.[9] From a descriptive passage; note the *m* of predication.

This too is the ordinary way of expressing an attendant circumstance; it is impossible to draw a hard and fast line between descriptive sentences and clauses of circumstance.

Exx. Every man was caused to know his order of march, *ḥtr m-sꜣ ḥtr* horse (following) after horse.[10]

I passed three days alone, *ib·i m sn-nw·i* my heart being (lit. as) my (sole) companion.[11] Note the *m* of predication.

2. When the subject is a *suffix-pronoun*, the sentence with *iw* has a wider range of meaning, see above § 37. On the one hand, it may express an independent statement or description.

Exx. *iw·i ẖr ḥswt nt ẖr nsw* I was in receipt of (lit. under) favours from (lit. of under) the king.[12]

iw·f m imy-ḥꜣt n irr he is (lit. as) a pattern for the criminal (lit. the doer).[13] Note the *m* of predication.

On the other hand, sentences introduced by *iw* + suffix may be quite subordinate in meaning, i.e. may serve as *clauses of time or circumstance* (§ 214).

[1] *Peas.* B 2, 65. Sim. *Sin.* B 217; *Westc.* 7, 17; *Urk.* iv. 244, 10.

[2] *Sin.* B 81. Sim. *ib.* R 8; *Peas.* R 46–7; *Leb.* 134; *Adm.* 2, 8.

[3] *Adm.* 2, 10.

[4] *Urk.* iv. 1090. Sim. *Leb.* 34.

[5] *Sin.* B 50. Sim. *Urk.* iv. 2, 10. See too below § 323. Rather differently *Urk.* iv. 657, 13.

[6] *Eb.* 97, 3. Sim. *P. Kah.* 7, 38.

[7] *Peas.* B 1, 93. Sim. *ib.* 7.

[8] *Sin.* B 83. Sim. *ib.* B 186–7. 239–40; *Sh. S.* 48–51; *Urk.* iv. 657, 10. 12. 14.

[9] *Peas.* B 1, 248.

[10] *Urk.* iv. 652, 10. Sim. *Sin.* B 244. 290; *Sh. S.* 16; *Westc.* 7, 15; 10, 1; Cairo 20001, 5; *Urk.* iv. 1104, 1–11.

[11] *Sh. S.* 42. Sim. *Urk.* iv. 139, 7.

[12] *Sin.* B 309–10. Sim. *P. Kah.* 11, 21; *Urk.* iv. 59, 5; 405, 7. 9.

[13] *Peas.* B 1, 218. With *r* of futurity, see § 122 below.

Exx. A storm went forth, *ỉw·n m Wꜣḏ-wr* (while) we were in the Great-green (the name given to the open sea).[1]

Men and women are in jubilation, *ỉw·f m nsw* (now that) he is king.[2] Note the *m* of predication.

OBS. A certain contradiction may seem to be involved in the use of *ỉw* to introduce (1) detached independent sentences and (2) clauses subordinate in meaning, even though the latter use is confined, or nearly confined, to examples where a suffix-pronoun is the subject. The difficulty disappears if we assume that what we take to be a clause of circumstance was originally felt as *parenthetic*, i.e. as an independent remark thrown into the midst of, and interrupting, a sequence of main sentences. The use of parentheses to express temporal and circumstantial qualifications is frequent in all languages. In Late Egyptian and Coptic *ỉw* becomes increasingly common as the mark of a clause of time or circumstance.

§ 118. Tense and mood in the sentence with adverbial predicate.—1. The types of sentence studied in § 117 are strictly regardless of time, and there is nothing about the form of the examples translated there with 'is' to prevent them, in a different context, from being translated with 'was' or even with 'will be'; the example *ỉw n·k ꜥnḫ* in 114, 1 contains a promise for the future, and may, accordingly, be freely translated 'thou shalt have life'.

So too the simple unintroduced sentence with adverbial predicate may express a *wish* or *command*.

Ex. *ḏd·ṯn: ṯꜣw n ꜥnḫ r fnḏ n wꜣḥy Sbk-ḥtp* ye shall say: The breath of life (be) to the nose of the ..... Sebkḥotpe.[3]

Similarly, when the negative word *nn* precedes (§ 120).

Ex. *nn rn·f m-m ꜥnḫw* his name shall not be among the living.[4]

2. When, however, it was desired to convey *more explicitly* some temporal or modal distinction of meaning, this could be contrived by the use of the verb *wnn* or of the particles to be enumerated in § 119.

The *future* is frequently expressed by means of *wnn·f*, a *śḏm·f* form from *wnn* 'exist', 'be' already familiar from the existential sentences (§ 107), of which we have here a development.

Exx. *wnn tꜣy·ỉ ḥmt ỉm* my wife shall be there.[5]

wnn·f m ḫbd n Rꜥ he shall be in the disfavour of Rēꜥ.[6]

The other *śḏm·f* form of *wnn*, namely *wn·f* (§ 107), is probably never used in simple affirmative statements with adverbial predicate; it is, however, common in a number of usages.[7] So, for example, in order to express *purpose* (§ 40, 1).

Ex. *ỉỉ·n·(ỉ) wn·(ỉ) m sꜣ·ṯ* I have come that I may be thy protection.[8]

[1] *Sh. S.* 33. 102. Sim. *ib.* 67; *Sin.* B 2; *Leb.* 83; *Mill.* 2, 2; *Urk.* iv. 974, 16.

[2] *Sin.* B 68. Sim. *Ikhern.* 7; *Urk.* iv. 2, 14.

[3] Cairo 20164. Sim. *ib.* 20003, 4; *Sin.* B 269. 274; *P. Kah.* 11, 20.

[4] MAR. *Abyd.* ii. 30, 37.

[5] *P. Kah.* 12, 13. Sim. *Sin.* B 43; *Siut* 1, 281; *Leb.* 142. 145; *Urk.* iv. 651, 17.

[6] *JEA.* ii. 6. Sim. *Sin.* B 77; *Siut* 4, 25; *Urk.* iv. 573, 10.

[7] *Wn·f* in clauses of time see below § 454, 1, end.

[8] *Urk.* iv. 239, 17. Sim. *ib.* 1024, 12.

So too after *iḫ* (§ 40, 3).

Ex. *iḫ wn·i m šms n nṯr* therefore let me be in the following of the god.[1]

And again after *rdi* 'cause' (§ 70).

Ex. *rdi·n·s wn·k m nṯr* she has caused thee to be (lit. that thou be) a god.[2]

In none of these last cases could *iw* have been employed. The verb *wnn* thus supplies various parts of the Egyptian verb for 'to be', *iw* itself occurring almost only in main clauses,[2a] and having a very restricted range of employment. The same phenomenon is to be observed in many other languages, where the different parts of the verb 'to be' are taken from various stems; so English 'be', 'are', 'were', Latin *sum, erat, fuit,* German *bin, wäre, ist.* We shall frequently have occasion to refer to this important rule.

> OBS. In theory *wnn* could supply any missing parts of *iw*, when followed by an adverbial predicate.[3] In practice it is not possible to illustrate all the different cases, though what will be called the pseudo-verbal construction (Lesson XXIII) supplies examples of some (e.g. *wn·in·f* § 470) which would otherwise be missing.

§ 119. Particles used in the sentence with adverbial predicate.— Some of these have been mentioned already in § 44, 2, where it was seen that they are followed by a dependent pronoun, when the subject of the sentence is pronominal. For fuller details see below §§ 230 foll.

1. *mk* (for the variant writings see § 234) is a compound of which the first element appears to be an imperative, 'behold', and the second element is a pronoun 2nd sing. m.[4] When a woman or several persons are addressed, a different pronoun is apt to be used. Thus we have the series:

mk behold thou, sing. m. or general.

mṯ, later *mt*, behold thou, sing. f.

mṯn, later *mtn*, behold ye.

This particle appears to depict the sense of the sentence which it accompanies as *present* and *visible to the mind*; more often than not the time referred to is the present.

Exx. *mtn špswt ḥr šdw* behold, noble ladies are (now) on rafts, i.e. have been deprived of their luxurious boats.[5]

mk wi r-gs·k behold I am in thy company, lit. at thy side.[6]

mk tw m minw behold thou art a herdsman.[7] Note the *m* of predication (§ 38), which is indispensable here and in all similar cases.

2. *isṯ*, later *ist*, archaistically *sṯ*, the form used in Old Egyptian before pronouns, is clearly related to the enclitic particle *is* 'lo', 'indeed' (§ 247).[8] It describes a *situation* or *concomitant fact*, and sentences introduced

[1] Cairo 20538, ii. c 7; 20539, ii. b 12.

[2] *Mitt.* viii. 10. Sim. MAR. *Abyd.* ii. 30, 29; *P. Kah.* 36, 34; *Urk.* iv. 776, 14 *Arm.* 103, 11.

[2a] Partial exceptions, p. 93, n. 5.

[3] Old perfective (§ 309) *wn·k(i)*, Brit. Mus. 574, 4; *sḏm·ḫr·f* form (§ 471) *wn·ḫr·i*, *Urk.* iv. 1080, 11 (collated); the participles *wnn* and *wn*, see § 396.

[4] See *Rec.* 28, 186; 35, 217.

[5] *Adm.* 7, 10. Sim. *ib.* p. 108; *Siut* 1, 269.

[6] *Sh. S.* 108. Sim. *Sin.* B 77; *Peas.* B 1, 231; *Siut* 1, 272.

[7] *Peas.* B 1, 177. Sim. *ib.* 168. 171. 174; *Bersh.* ii. 21, left, 7.

[8] See *Rec.* 19, 187; 28, 186.

by it may often, though by no means always, be rendered as clauses of time or circumstance.

Exx. I spent many years under king Antef, *ỉsṯ tꜣ pn ẖr st-ḥr·f* (while) this land was under his charge..... *sṯ wỉ m bꜣk·f* I being his servant.[1]

Year 30, *ỉsṯ ḥm·f ḥr ḫꜣst Rṯnw* lo, His Majesty was in the land of Retjnu.[2]

Followed by the enclitic particle *rf* (below § 252), *ỉsṯ* announces a situation with a view to some further narrative. The meaning is very much that of the French *or*, and may best be rendered in English by 'now'.

Ex. *ỉsṯ rf pr Ḏḥwty-nḫt pn ḥr smꜣ-tꜣ* now the house of this Djeḥutnakht was on the river-bank.[3]

3. *ỉsk*, *sk* (below § 230) are archaic variants of *ỉsṯ*, *sṯ*, and have the same meaning.

Exx. *ỉsk ḥmt·s m ỉnpw* when Her Majesty was a child.[4] Note the *m* of predication.

sk wỉ m šmsw·f when I was in his following.[5]

4. *tỉ*[6] has similar meaning to *ỉsṯ*, from which it may possibly be derived. Examples do not occur until after Dyn. XII, and then at first only with *sw* 'he';[7] later it may be followed also by *wỉ* 'I', or, more rarely, by a noun.

Exx. I was his companion *tỉ sw ḥr prỉ* when he was upon the battle-field.[8]

I knew thy qualities *tỉ wỉ m sšy* when I was in the nest.[9]

tỉ ḥm·f ḏs·f ḥr ḫtm ỉꜣbty lo, His Majesty was himself in the eastern fortress.[10]

5. *ḫr*, earlier or *ỉḫr*, indicates what comes next in order, and may be translated 'and', 'further', or even sometimes 'accordingly', 'so'. Examples with adverbial predicate are rare, and no instance with pronominal subject has been found.

Ex. *ḫr r-5 r-15 m wꜣḥ ḥr·f* so $\frac{1}{5}+\frac{1}{15}$ is what-is-to-be-added to it.[11]

6. The rare *nḥmn* means 'assuredly' or the like.

Ex. *nḥmn wỉ mỉ kꜣ* assuredly I am like a bull.[12]

7. *ḥꜣ*, variant , expresses a wish.

Ex. *ḥꜣ n·ỉ šsp nb mnḫ* would I had (lit. that there were to me) any efficacious idol.[13]

8. *ḥwy-ꜣ*, a compound with the enclitic particle *ꜣ*, also expresses a wish.

Ex. *ḥw-ꜣ wỉ ỉm* would that I were there.[14]

[1] Brit. Mus. 614. Sim. Cairo 20543, 9. 17; BUDGE, p. 284, 9; *Urk.* iv. 1020, 8.

[2] *Urk.* iv. 689. Sim. *ib.* 137, 16; BUDGE, p. 280, 8.

[3] *Peas.* R 44. Sim. *Westc.* 6, 10–11.

[4] *Urk.* iv. 260. Sim. *ib.* 219, 4.

[5] Louvre C 15. Sim. *Urk.* iv. 157, 3 (*ỉsk wỉ*).

[6] See *Proc. SBA.* 15, 471.

[7] *Sin.* R 13. 15.

[8] *Urk.* iv. 890. Sim. *ib.* 898, 11; 926, 17.

[9] *Urk.* iv. 897. Sim. *ib.* 209, 7; 271, 12; 613, 7.

[10] *Urk.* iv. 661. Sim. *ib.* 86, 7.

[11] *Rhind* 21. Sim. *ib.* 22. 23; *Urk.* iv. 1104, 8. 9 (varr.).

[12] *Sin.* B 118. See *Rec.* 24, 34; *ÄZ.* 43, 159.

[13] *Peas.* Bt. 25. Sim. *Adm.* p. 97.

[14] LAC. *TR.* 31, 5. Cf. p. 249. n. 2a.

§ 120. Negation of the sentence with adverbial predicate.—The word *nn* is placed before the subject, which may be either a noun or a dependent pronoun (§ 44, 2).

Exx. *nn mwt·k ḥnꜥ·k* thy mother is not with thee.[1]

nn wỉ m-ḥr-ỉb·sn I was not in the midst of them.[2]

Sentences of this type may on occasion be equivalent to English clauses of time or circumstance.

Ex. *wỉn·sn tp-tꜣ nn tw ỉm·f* they decline (existence) on earth (§ 158, 2), thou not being in it.[3]

The model of the sentence expressing non-existence (§ 108) is used when universals are denied; the subject is then an undefined noun and the negation may be expressed by *nn* alone, or by *nn wn*, or more rarely by *n wnt*.

Exx. *nn wḫꜣ m-ḥr-ỉb·sn* there was none ignorant in their midst.[4]

nn wn ḫnt m ẖt·f there was no greed in his body.[5]

n wnt ỉw-ms ỉm there is no misstatement therein.[6]

Very rarely *n ỉs* 'not indeed' is used; for *ỉs* see below § 247.

Ex. *n ỉs ꜥbꜥ ỉm* there is indeed no boasting therein.[7]

Before *ỉw* and *wnn* the negative word is extremely rare. Certain examples can, however, be quoted:

n ỉw·k m pt thou art not in heaven.[8]

n wnn sꜣ·f ḥr nst·f his son shall not remain (lit. be) upon his seat.[9]

According to § 105, 2 negation of the future is expressed by *nn sḏm·f*; the last example is, therefore, an exception to the rule, if be a *sḏm·f* form; hence a doubt arises whether it may not be the *sḏm·n·f* form, see § 413.

§ 121. Position of the adverbial predicate.—The normal position is after the subject (§ 29); a pronominal dative may, however, sometimes precede it (§ 66).

Sometimes a short adverbial predicate may intervene between the subject and some words which are joined to it or qualify it.

Exx. *rmw ỉm ḥnꜥ ꜣpdw* fish and birds were therein, lit. fishes were there together with birds.[10]

ḥꜣty·k n·k n ỉmy-ḥꜣt thou shalt have thy former heart, lit. thy heart is to thee of being-in-front.[11]

§ 122. Use of the preposition *r* to indicate a future condition.—Closely parallel to the *m* of predication is what may be termed the ***r* of futurity.**

Exx. *ỉw·f r smr* he shall be (lit. is towards) a Companion.[12]

[1] *M.u.K.* verso 2, 3; sim. *Siut* 3, 69. Demonst. pron. as subject, *Urk.* iv. 415, 12.

[2] *Sh. S.* 131. Sim. *Sin.* B 223–4, qu. § 44, 2; *Pt.* 435; *Eb.* 101, 15; 108, 20.

[3] Cairo 583, 3. With nom. subj. *ÄZ.* 69, 27, 4.

[4] *Sh. S.* 100. Sim. *Eb.* 69, 3; *Urk.* iv. 122, 13; 123, 3; *Arm.* 103, 5.

[5] *BH.* i. 7. Sim. *Adm.* 3, 2; *Buhen*, p. 91.

[6] *Urk.* iv. 973. Sim. Cairo 20765, 3–4.

[7] *Urk.* iv. 973.

[8] *Ḥarḥ.* 68; sim. *ib.* 69. Also some doubtful cases written with GUNN, *Studies*, ch. xxi.

[9] *BH.* i. 25, 98–9.

[10] *Sh. S.* 50–1. Sim. *Sin.* B 81–2, qu. § 117.

[11] *Urk.* iv. 115. Sim. between noun and gen., *ỉm·(f) Sin.* B 287–8; *Sh. S.* 35–6; Berl. *ÄI.* i. p. 258, 16–7; *ḥnꜥ·(ỉ)*, *Hamm.* 114, 11.

[12] *Sin.* B 280. Sim. *Siut* 1, 227; *Meir* iii. 8; *Peas.* B 1, 95. 215; Cairo 20538, ii. *c* 18.

mt sw r wnmw behold, it is for food.[1]

OBS. For the use of this *r* after verbs of 'appointing', 'making', see § 84; and for its development with the infinitive see § 332.

§ 123. Omission of the subject before adverbial predicate.—Instances are occasionally found:

Exx. *iw mi sḫr nṯr* it was like the counsel of god.[2]

nn m iw-ms ḫft-ḥr·ṯn (this) is not falsehood before you.[3]

nn wn ḥr-ḫw·f there was none beside him.[4]

n ḏd·i ḥꜣ n·i r ḫt nbt I did not say 'Would that I had' (lit. would that to me) about anything.[5]

See further below § 153 for the omission of the subject in wishes, greetings and the like.

§ 124. The pronominal compound *tw·i*.—In Dyn. XVII are found the earliest traces of a new method of expressing the pronominal subject when the predicate is adverbial. The full paradigm, some forms of which do not occur until the Late Egyptian stage of the language, is as follows:

	Sing.	Plur.
1st pers. c.	*tw·i* I.	*tw·n* we.
2nd pers. m.	*tw·k* thou.	*tw·tn* you.
" " f.	*tw·t* thou.	
3rd pers. m.	*sw* he, it.	*st* they.
" " f.	*sy* (later *sw*) she, it.	
Impersonal	*tw·tw* one.[6]	

Exx. *sw ḫr tꜣ n ʿꜣmw, tw·n ḫr Kmt* he is in possession of (lit. under) the land of the Asiatics, we are in possession of Egypt.[7]

sy m ḥr·f mi tꜣ pt it seemed to him like heaven, lit. it (the temple) was in his face like the sky.[8]

OBS. These new pronominal forms are conjectured[9] to have arisen from *ntt wi* 'that I', etc., see § 223. At all events the parallelism of *sw*, *sy* and *st* (perhaps from **t·sw*, **t·sy*, **t·st* by assimilation of *t* to *s*) with *tw·i* warrants the distinction of them from the dependent pronouns of § 43. See § 330 for an extension of this construction.

1 *Th. T. S.* ii. 11.

2 *Sin.* B 43. Sim. *ib.* 215. 224; *Leb.* 81.

3 *Urk* iv. 101. Sim. *Adm.* p. 101.

4 *BH.* i. 26, 155. So too after *nn* 'there is nothing', *Peas.* B 1, 120; after *n wnt*, with same meaning, *Pt.* 212.

5 *Urk.* iv. 61. Sim. *ib.* iv. 506, 8.

6 *Urk.* iv. 656, 5.

7 *T. Carn.* 7. Sim. *Urk.* iv. 649, 15.

8 Graffito in the temple of Saḥurēʿ (Möller.)

9 See ERM. *Spr. d. Westc.* p. 119, n. 2.

VOCABULARY

var. *bṯ* abandon, forsake.

sb send; pass (time).

km complete; completion.

skꜣ plough, cultivate.

šms follow, accompany, serve; *šmsw* or *šmswt* following, suite (noun).

iꜣw old; *iꜣwt* old age.

- *ḥmw* rudder.
- (abbrev.) *ꜣpd* bird.
- *rm* fish.
- *ꜣḥt* field.
- *ꜣbd* month.
- var. *iꜣt* office, rank.
- varr. , *nst* seat.
- var. *ḥb* festival, holiday.
- *ḥnw* jubilation, praise.
- *r-pr* temple, chapel, shrine.
- *ḥwt* house, large edifice; *ḥwt-nṯr* temple.
- *ḥꜣty* heart, breast.
- *iw* wrong, crime.
- *kꜣ* high, tall; *kꜣw* height.

EXERCISE X

(*a*) *Transliterate and translate*:

(1) (2)

(3) (4)

(5) [1] (6)

(7) [2]

(8) (9) (10)

[1] See p. 423, Add. to § 86. [2] The ordinary priests (*wꜥb*) served in the temples in rotation, one month at a time.

(*b*) *Write in hieroglyphs and transliteration*:

(1) I crossed in a boat without a rudder (lit. not was its rudder). (2) Thou shalt be an old man of thy city. (3) All my property shall belong to my brothers and sisters. (4) There were old men there and (lit. with) children. (5) He caused me to be in the following of His Majesty, when he was at (lit. upon) his southern boundary. (6) He entered into the temple, the entire town being in festival. (7) I say to the birds which-are-in the heaven and to the fishes which-are-in the water: How great is the might of this god! (8) I ploughed my fields with my own asses. (9) My office was (that of) he-who-is-over the secrets. (10) God sends it to thee in the completion of a moment.

LESSON XI

SENTENCES WITH NOMINAL OR PRONOMINAL PREDICATE[1]

§ **125.** We have seen that, with the help of the prepositions which have been termed the *m* of predication (§ 38) and the *r* of futurity (§ 122), the model of the sentence with adverbial predicate could be utilized by the Egyptians to express the meaning of English sentences with nominal or pronominal predicate; examples have been quoted in §§ 117. 118. 119. 122. In the present lesson we have to learn that apart from the method just alluded to, Egyptian possessed a specific and well-characterized model for constructing sentences with a noun or pronoun as predicate. The principal divergences from the sentence with adverbial predicate are that here the independent pronouns of § 64 are freely used, that *iw* and *wnn* are not employed, and that the demonstrative word *pw* (§ 110) makes its appearance as an important syntactical element.

The principle underlying the Egyptian sentence with nominal or pronominal predicate is the principle of *direct juxtaposition*, the *subject preceding the predicate* as in the sentence with adverbial predicate. This construction is still very common in Middle Egyptian when the subject is a *personal pronoun*, and a previous lesson has taught us that in this case the independent pronouns are used (§§ 65, 1); the copula is not expressed.

Exx. *ink šmsw* I was a follower.[2]

ntk it n nmḥ thou art the father of the orphan.[3]

swt nb·n he is our lord.[4]

When the subject is a *noun*, direct juxtaposition is practically obsolete, though it was still common in the Pyramid Texts. A few Middle Egyptian examples may be quoted, notwithstanding.

Exx. *mkt·t mkt Rꜥ* thy (f.) protection is the protection of Rēꜥ.[5]

rn n mwt·s Ṯwiꜣ the name of her mother is Tjuia.[6]

Other examples will be found below § 127, 1. 2. 3.

OBS. The old construction nom. subj. + nom. pred. survives also in the important construction *in* + noun + participle, see below §§ 227, 3; 372; 373; to this the counterpart with pronominal subject is of the form indep. pron. + participle, quite in accordance with the examples quoted above.

§ **126. Subject and predicate.**—In sentences having an adverbial predicate there is no risk of confusing subject and predicate, since an adverb or adverbial phrase is by its very form precluded from being a subject in the grammatical sense. The necessity of defining the terms 'subject' and 'predicate' becomes urgent, however, when we proceed to consider the sentence with

[1] See SETHE, *Nominalsatz*, §§ 22 foll.; LEF. *Gr.* §§ 603, foll.

[2] *Sin.* R 2. Sim. *Urk.* iv. 61, 14; 118, 3; 1069, 6–7.

[3] *Peas.* B 1, 62. Sim. *ib.* 140. 161; *ntt*, *M. u. K.* 2, 3–9; *ntf*, BUDGE, p. 38, 7. 9.

[4] *Rifeh* 7, 35. *Twt*, LAC. *TR.* 11, 9; ERM. *Hymn.* 1, 5, qu. Exerc. 31 (*a*); *Urk.* iv. 228, 15.

[5] *M. u. K.*, verso 4, 7.

[6] FRASER, *Scarabs*, no. 262. See also *Peas.* B 1, 158–9; *Westc.* 7, 17–8; *Hamm.* 43, 12. More complex exx. *Urk.* iv. 271, 9; 558, 15.

a noun or pronoun as predicate; for we are evidently not justified in speaking of sentences with nominal or pronominal predicate unless we are able to distinguish the subject from the predicate in any given sentence, and here the criterion of form fails us. In English such a criterion is often afforded by the agreement of the copula with the subject in person and number, as in 'I am your friend', 'they are a united family'; in Egyptian no such help is forthcoming, and we are consequently thrown back upon the logical definitions of subject and predicate as respectively 'the thing spoken of' and 'that which is affirmed or denied of the subject'. A good test for the **logical predicate** is to cast the sentence into the shape of a question; then the elements which correspond to the interrogative word constitute the logical predicate. Thus in 'I am your friend' the logical predicate is 'your friend' whenever the sentence answers the question '*what* am I?'

Returning now to the Egyptian sentence with adverbial predicate, we find that more often than not the adverbial predicate does state exactly *what* is affirmed or denied of the subject. In *ỉw nꜣ m sbꜣyt* 'this is (as) an instruction' (§ 117) the corresponding question would be '*what* is this?' and consequently *m sbꜣyt* is the logical predicate, besides being the grammatical predicate. Such is the natural or normal state of affairs, and we may define the **grammatical predicate** as that element in a sentence (or even in a subordinate clause, § 182) which either by position or by form would normally express the meaning of the logical predicate; and the **grammatical subject** as that element which in like manner would normally express the meaning of the logical subject. A distinction between the two kinds of predicate would, of course, be unnecessary in practice, if both always coincided; but we have now to see that such is not the case. In the sentence *ỉw dꜣbw ỉm·f ḥnꜥ ỉꜣrrt* 'figs were in it and grapes' (§ 117) we are indeed informed *where* figs and grapes were, so that *ỉm·f*, the grammatical predicate, is in a secondary sort of way also *a* logical predicate; but this is not the real point of the sentence, which is to tell us *what* was there, and accordingly *dꜣbw ḥnꜥ ỉꜣrrt* 'figs and grapes', although they are grammatically subject, must undeniably be considered as the real logical predicate. Such cases are frequent,[1] not only in Egyptian, but also in English, where a stress is laid in pronunciation upon the logical predicate whenever this does not coincide with the grammatical predicate; thus 'he is in the house', with even intonation, answers the question '*where* is he?' and 'in the house' is simultaneously grammatical and logical predicate; but if we say '*he* is in the house', the question answered is '*who* is in the house?' and the stressed word '*he*' is logical predicate, although it is grammatically subject. So in the English translation of the above-quoted Egyptian sentence, a slight stress is laid on the two words '*figs*' and '*grapes*'.

[1] Sim. *Sin.* B 68. 83; *Sh. S.* 42, all quoted in § 117.

In the Egyptian sentence with nominal predicate it is certain, both from general considerations and from examples like those of § 125, that the normal word-order was 1. logical subject, 2. logical predicate, as in English and as in the Egyptian sentence with adverbial predicate; hence the formulation adopted in § 125. When, therefore, as we shall find to be the case in many instances, the logical predicate precedes the logical subject, we are justified in regarding this as a departure from the normal word-order, i. e. as an *inversion* quite analogous to the use of stressed '*he*' in the English sentence, '*he* (and no one else) is my brother'.

OBS. The definitions of grammatical subject and predicate have been framed to accord with the fact that in some sentences with adjectival predicate, as well as in verbal sentences with *sḏm·f* and similar forms, the word-order is 1. gramm. pred., 2. gramm. subj.; for the reasons of this see below §§ 137, OBS.; 411, 1. Later on, the term 'grammatical subject' will sometimes be used in antithesis to 'grammatical object' or again to another kind of subject for which we have coined the name 'semantic subject', see below § 297, 1. When 'subject' is written without qualification, either there has seemed but little likelihood of confusion, or else the word so described is subject in more senses than one, as in § 125.

§ 127. The *logical predicate comes first* in the following cases, exemplifying the kind of inversion explained at the end of § 126:

1. When the logical subject is *rn·f* 'his name', *rn·s* 'her name'.

Ex. *nḏs Ḏdì rn·f* a commoner whose name is Djedi, lit. a commoner, Djedi is his name.[1]

Note that in this case, as well as in others quoted below under 2 and 3, direct juxtaposition is used in spite of the fact that the grammatical subject is not a personal pronoun.

2. When the logical subject is a *demonstrative pronoun.*

Exx. *dpt mwt nn* this is the taste of death.[2]

wꜣt Ḏḥwty nw r pr Mꜣꜥt this is the road of Thoth to the house of Māʿet.[3]

3. When the logical predicate is an *interrogative pronoun*; in this case the logical subject, if a pronoun, is a dependent pronoun, since it occupies the second place.[4]

Exx. *ìšst tr ìḫt ìrt·n·k n·s* what is, pray, the thing which thou hast done to it?[5]

ptr rf sw who is he?[6]

4. When the logical predicate is an *independent pronoun.* The greater emphasis of the independent pronouns always tends to give them the force of the logical predicate. Possibly the second and third examples of § 125 would

[1] *Westc.* 7, 1. Sim. *Sin.* B 81; *Peas.* R 1. 2; *Eb.* 51, 15–6. *Rn* + indirect genitive *Urk.* iv. 744, 4–6. The last ex. of § 125 is exceptional.

[2] *Sin.* B 23.

[3] LAC. *Sarc.* i, p. 212; Sim. *JEA.* 16, 19, 1. Exx. with *nꜣ*, *P. Kah.* 29, 21; *P. Pet.* 1116 A, 58; *P. math. Mosc.* 13, 4; with *nfꜣ*, *Leb.* 37.

[4] For alternative ways of expressing 'who art thou?' see § 495, end.

[5] *Urk.* v. 160, 11.

[6] *Urk.* v. 10. Sim. *m ty tw* 'who art thou?' *Lisht* 20, 33.

have been better translated 'it is *thou* (who art) the father of the orphan' and 'it is *he* (who is) our lord' respectively. When the pronoun is stressed in this manner, it is not seldom accompanied by the enclitic particle [hieroglyphs] *is* 'indeed' (§ 247).

Ex. [hieroglyphs] *ink is ḥḳ3 Pwnt* it is I (who am) the ruler of Pwēnet.[1]

It is no absolute rule, however, that the pronoun, when accompanied by *is*, is to be understood as logical predicate. Nor yet is such the case with [hieroglyphs] *wnnt* and [hieroglyphs] *wnt*, which are similarly used;[2] these are probably fem. participles from the verb *wnn* 'be' which have come to be employed as particles meaning 'indeed', 'really', see below § 249.

Exx. [hieroglyphs] *ink wnnt imy ib n nb·f m3ʿ* I was indeed one truly in the heart of his lord.[3]

[hieroglyphs] *ink wnt mry rmṯ* I was indeed one beloved of people.[4]

§ 128. Use of [hieroglyphs] *pw* for the pronoun 3rd pers.—The use of the demonstratives exemplified in § 127, 2 gave rise to an idiom of the highest importance; the demonstrative pronoun [hieroglyphs] *pw* (§§ 110. 111) came to be employed as logical subject after logical predicates consisting of a noun, not however with its own proper meaning of 'this' or 'that', but as an equivalent for 'he', 'she', 'it' or 'they' invariable in number and gender. Compare French *ce* in *c'est, ce sont.*

Exx. [hieroglyphs] *Rʿ pw* it is Rēʿ *or* he is Rēʿ.[5] Answer to the question *ptr rf sw* 'who is he?' quoted above § 127, 3.

[hieroglyphs] *ḥmt wʿb pw n Rʿ* she is the wife of a priest of Rēʿ.[6] Answer to the question 'who is this Reddjedet?' quoted below § 132.

[hieroglyphs] *ḥwrw pw* they are wretches.[7]

The logical predicate may be an independent pronoun:

Ex. [hieroglyphs] *ntf pw m m3ʿt* it is he in truth.[8]

Or else, rather rarely, it may be a demonstrative pronoun:

Ex. [hieroglyphs] *p3 pw* this is it.[9]

Sometimes *pw* is absent in places where we might expect it; it is then impossible to be sure whether there is a deliberate omission of *pw*, for sake of brevity or some other reason, or whether we have the construction of § 89, 2.

Ex. [hieroglyphs] *ṯ3w n r* (it is mere) breath of the mouth.[10]

Obs. For 'he is Rēʿ', as we have seen § 125, *ntf Rʿ* can also be said; but in that case the pronoun is more emphatic and tends to obtain the value of the logical predicate '*he* is Rēʿ.'

§ 129. Position of [hieroglyphs] *pw*.—If the logical predicate consists of several words, *pw* may be intercalated before some of them.[11]

Exx. [hieroglyphs] *sḫty pw n Sḫt-ḥm3t* he was a peasant of the Wâdy Natrûn.[12]

[1] *Sh. S.* 151. Sim. Lac. *TR.* 19, 45; *Sin.* B 232; Nav. Ib, 17.

[2] See *Verbum*, ii, § 978.

[3] Brit. Mus. 614, 7. Sim. Cairo 20543, 16; *Mitt.* ix. 18.

[4] Turin 1447. Sim. Leyden V 4, 12; Louvre C 1, 10; *ÄZ.* 34, 27.

[5] *Urk.* v. 10. Sim. *Sin.* B 47. 57. 58. 60; *Urk.* iv. 17, 11. 16.

[6] *Westc.* 9, 9.

[7] Berl. *ÄI.* i. p. 258.

[8] *Sin.* B 268.

[9] *Rhind* 60.

[10] *Urk.* iv. 123. Sim. *ib.* 122, 16.

[11] Rules in H. Abel, *Zur Tonverschmelzung im Altaegyptischen*, Leipzig, 1910, ch. 1.

[12] *Peas.* R 1. Sim. *Sin.* B 30–1; *Eb.* 103, 9; *Westc.* 9, 9, qu. n. 6 above; *Urk.* iv. 249, 4.

[hieroglyphs] *tꜣ pw nfr, ꜣIꜣꜣ rn·f* it was a good land, whose name was Yaa.[1]

[hieroglyphs] *Ḥw pw ḥnꜥ Sꜣ* they are Ḥu and Sia.[2] Answer to the question 'who are these gods?'

OBS. Compare the similar intercalation of short adverbial predicates, above § 121.

§ 130. [hieroglyph] *pw* in sentences where both subject and predicate are nouns.—As we have seen (§ 125), the original method of expressing sentences where both subject and predicate were nouns was by direct juxtaposition; but long before the Middle Kingdom that method had become obsolete and had given place to another based on the use of *pw* described in § 128. The *logical predicate* (or part of it, § 129) *comes first* and is followed by *pw* as a purely formal logical subject; the real logical subject is added in apposition to *pw*.

Exx. [hieroglyphs] *dmỉ pw ꜣImnt* the West is an abode, lit. an abode (is) it, namely the West.[3]

[hieroglyphs] *mnw pw n s nfrw·f* a man's goodness is his monument, lit. the monument it (is) of a man, (namely) his goodness.[4]

Rarely either the subject or predicate may be a demonstrative.

Exx. [hieroglyphs] *bỉt·ỉ pw nꜣ m wn mꜣꜥ* this is my character in reality.[5]

[hieroglyphs] *pꜣ pw Wsỉr* such is Osiris, lit. this (is) he, Osiris.[6]

The substitution of this construction for the method of direct juxtaposition was evidently due to the desire to indicate the logical predicate more clearly than could be done by that method, in connection with which inversions were frequent. Now a demonstrative word like 'this' is far more often logical subject than logical predicate; we are more prone to say that 'this' is so-and-so than that so-and-so is 'this'. Hence the intercalation of a demonstrative in a sentence in which both subject and predicate are nouns (in Egyptian it must occupy the second place, inversion here being the rule, § 127, 2) is apt to mark the preceding noun as the real logical predicate. The effect of such an intercalation will be felt by comparing French *c'est lui le roi* with *il est le roi*, where the use of *ce*, just like that of *pw* in Egyptian, points unmistakably to *lui* as the logical predicate.

Thus whereas in the old method of direct juxtaposition the first word (the grammatical subject §§ 125–6) could be almost as easily logical predicate as logical subject (though the latter was of course its proper function), in the sentence with intercalated [hieroglyph] *the first word is, in the vast majority of cases, not the logical subject, but the logical predicate.*

The tragedy of language is, however, that it is constantly perverting the constructions which it creates to purposes for which they were not primarily intended; by a *second* inversion (the first being that of § 127, 2) the sentence

[1] *Sin.* B 81. Sim. *Pt.* 330; *Urk.* v. 11, 1.
[2] *Urk.* v. 30, 9
[3] *Leb.* 38. Sim. *ib.* 20–1; *BH.* i. 25, 76; *Westc.* 8, 13; *Urk.* iv. 369, 1; 519, 9.
[4] *PSBA.* 18, 203, 16. Sim. *Peas.* B 1, 232–3.
[5] *Urk.* iv. 973, 10. Sim. *ib.* 973, 8.
[6] *Rec.* 39, 121. Sim. *Rhind* 57. 58; *Peas.* B 1, 19. *Nꜣ pw* + rel. form 'these it is which ....' *ÄZ.* 69, 32, 23. Similar in appearance, but different in reality, are cases like *tꜣ pw kꜣt* 'it is that girl', *Westc.* 12, 22; sim. *Eb.* 103, 6–7, cf. *ib.* 103, 9, qu. § 190, 1.

with *pw* could sometimes have the logical subject in the first place, thus returning to the original word-order (§ 125).

Exx. *pẖrt pw nt ḥꜥw·s mrḥt* oil is the remedy of her body.[1] The sentence raises the question what is the best preservative for a woman's body, and the answer is 'oil'.

bwt·i pw ḥs my abomination is excrement.[2]

§ 131. Owing to the frequent intercalation of *pw* between a noun and some words that qualify it (§ 129), an ambiguity is apt to arise which requires careful attention. In a sentence like *Nwn pw it nṯrw*,[3] nothing but the context can decide whether the intended meaning was 'it (or 'he') is Nun, the father of the gods' (*it* in apposition to *Nwn*, § 90) or 'the father of the gods is Nun' (*it* in apposition to *pw*, § 130).

§ 132. The dependent pronoun in place of *pw*.—This construction is a development of that of *ptr sw*, above § 127, 3, and occurs only with interrogatives.

Ex. *pty sy tꜣ Rd-ḏdt* who is this Reddjedet?[4] Lit. who is she, this Reddjedet?

§ 133. Tense and mood in the sentence with nominal predicate.—As in the sentence with adverbial predicate, so too here it is usually the context which provides the key to the intended tense and mood. The verbs *iw* and *wnn* (§§ 117. 118) are not, as a rule,[5] found in company with any of the constructions described in §§ 125–130, so that if it was desired to utilize those verbs, the Egyptians had recourse to the *m* of predication; examples above §§ 117. 118.

On the other hand, *mk* 'behold' and various particles like it[6] may occur at the beginning of the sentence with *pw*.

Exx. *mk ẖrt·i pw im·k* behold, that is my due from thee.[7]

isṯ sꜣ pw mnḫ lo, he was a beneficent son.[8]

smwn sḫty·f pw probably he is a peasant of his.[9] For *smwn* 'probably' see § 241.

So too with the particle of wishing *ḥꜣ* (§ 119, 7).

Ex. *ḥꜣ rf grḥ pw m rmṯ* would that it were the end of men.[10]

OBS. Clauses of time and circumstance utilize the *m* of predication and conform to the rules for adverbial predicate; see above §§ 117; 119, 2. So too the construction *wnn·f (wn·f) m* is employed after prepositions (§ 157, 2) and *ir* 'if' (§ 150). For exceptional cases where a clause with real nominal predicate follows a preposition, see § 154 end.

[1] *Pt.* 328. Sim. *P. Kah.* 8, 25. 26. 27; *Pr.* 1, 12; *Eb.* 1, 8; BUDGE, p. 209, 6.

[2] LAC. *TR.* 23, 3.

[3] *Urk.* v. 8.

[4] *Westc.* 9, 8. With *m* 'who?' *Urk.* v. 30, 8; *pw* 'who?' § 498. Sim. with *tn* 'whence?' § 503, 4; *tn* is, however, an adverbial predicate.

[5] *'Iw* exceptionally before the indep. pron., see § 468, 3.

[6] *Ḫr* before the construction with direct juxtaposition (§ 125), see *Westc.* 7, 17–8.

[7] *Sh. S.* 159–60. Sim. *Pt.* 414; *Rhind* 57; *Urk.* iv. 20, 14.

[8] *BH.* i. 26, 166–7.

[9] *Peas.* B 1, 44.

[10] *Adm.* 5, 14.

§ 134. Negation of sentences with nominal or pronominal predicate.—Examples are uncommon. Before a noun followed by *pw* *nn* is used.

Ex. *nn ꜥḥꜣ pw ḥnꜥ ky* it means (lit. is) no fighting with another.[1]

Note, however, that *n* is employed if *pw* is preceded by the enclitic particle *ỉs* 'indeed'.

Ex. *stỉ* (for *ỉsṯ*) *n tr ỉs pw n ỉwt r bỉꜣ pn* lo, it was indeed not the season for coming to this mining region.[2]

With *n* . . . . *ỉs* occasionally *pw* is omitted as superfluous.

Ex. *n sꜣ·ỉ ỉs* he is not my son.[3]

In one case the pronoun *st* 'they' appears to be substituted for *pw*:

n rmṯ ỉs nt šft st they are not people of worth.[4]

Before the independent pronouns the negative word used is *n*.

Exx. *n ỉnk tr smꜣ·f* I am not, forsooth, a confederate of his.[5]

n ntf pw m mꜣꜥt it is not he in truth.[6]

Later, however, instances with *nn* can be found.[7]

[1] *Urk.* iv. 122. Sim. Cairo 20530, 7. With *pw* omitted, *Urk.* iv. 122, 15.

[2] *Sinai* 90. Sim. *Siut* I, 288; *Peas.* B 1, 95–6.

[3] Berl. *ÄI.* i. p. 258, 20. Sim. LAC. *TR.* 47, 34.

[4] Berl. *ÄI.* i. p. 258, 13.

[5] *Sin.* B 114. Sim. with *ỉs*, LAC. *TR.* 72, 41.

[6] *Sin.* B 267.

[7] *Westc.* 9, 6. See also GUNN, *Studies*, p. 170.

VOCABULARY

wsḫ be broad, wide; broad, wide (adj.); breadth (noun).

var. *pḫr* go round; *spḫr* cause to circulate.

ḥms sit down, sit, dwell.

spr draw nigh, approach; petition (*n*).

ṯs raise up.

nfw rêis, skipper.

var. *smr* courtier, friend (of the king).

ṯsw commander (of a fortress or army).

mšꜥ army, expedition.

var. *ḏt* serf (fem.).

ḥꜣtt rope in front of a ship.

pḥwyt rope at back of a ship.

mꜣꜥt truth, right, justice.

nfrw beauty.

ꜥꜥwy sleep.

mryt river-bank.

ỉtn sun's disk, sun.

ỉrt eye.

ꜥnḫ ear.

ptr, var. *pty*, who?

ꜥꜣ here.

'Iwnw, Heliopolis, On of the Bible, a town near Cairo.

('I)tm Atum, the solar god of Heliopolis.

EXERCISE XI

(*a*) *Study the following extract from a self-laudatory inscription*:[1]

ỉnk	*grt*	*ḥꜣty*	*n*	*nb*	*ꜥnḫ, wḏꜣ, snb* (§ 313)
I	(am), moreover,	the heart	of	the Lord	(may he live, be prosperous and healthy),

ꜥnḫwy	*ỉrty*	*ỉty*	*mk*	*wỉ*	*m*	*nfw*
the ears and	eyes	of the Sovereign.	Behold,	I	(am as)	a skipper

n·f-ỉmy	*ḫm·n·(ỉ)*	*ꜥꜥwy*	*grḥ*	*mỉ*	*hrw*
belonging to him.	I am ignorant of	sleep	night	as well as	day.

ꜥḥꜥ·ỉ	*ḥms·ỉ*	*ḥꜣty·ỉ*	*ḫr*	*ḥꜣtt*	*pḥwyt*
I stand up	and sit down[2]	my heart	under (i.e. attentive to)	the prow-rope	and the stern-rope.

[1] NEWBERRY, *Life of Rekhmara*, 7, 16, collated and slightly restored; see *ÄZ*. 60, 69. [2] I.e. pass all my time.

(*b*) *Transliterate and translate*:

[1] The four personal names mentioned in this passage are to be rendered Amenemḥēt (*ʾImn-m-ḥꜣt* 'Amūn at the front'), Senbsumaꜥi (*Snb-sw-mꜥ·ỉ* 'he is healthy with me'), Ptaḥḥotpe (*Ptḥ-ḥtpw* 'Ptah is content') and ꜥAnkhu (*ꜥnḫw*, shortening for some such name as *Ḥr-ꜥnḫw* 'Horus lives').

(*c*) *Write in hieroglyphs and transliteration*:

(1) O great (*wr*) overseer of the house, thou art the rudder of the entire land. (2) Behold, thou art here, thou art happy (*nfr*) with me, thou hearest the speech (*r*) of Egypt; thou shalt be the commander of my army. (3) Thou shalt have a tomb on the west of Heliopolis. (4) I was indeed greatest of the courtiers. (5) This is the way to the Residence. (6) (King) Amenemḥēt is Atum himself, he gives the breath of life to (*r*) the nose(s) of everyone.

LESSON XII

SENTENCES WITH ADJECTIVAL PREDICATE

§ 135. Sentences with adjectival predicate[1] follow, in principle, the pattern of the sentences with nominal predicate, but there are many important differences. Some of the relevant facts have been stated already in previous sections (§§ 44, 3; 46, 3; 48, 2; 49; 65, 2).

To most[1a] Egyptian adjectives there corresponded an adjective-verb, and indeed it is highly probable that the adjective was simply a participle from such a verb. Thus *nfr* is a verb 'be beautiful, good' and the adjective *nfr* may well mean properly 'being good'. We shall frequently have occasion to note that some form of the adjective-verb is substituted for the adjective itself in constructions where the latter cannot be used, just as we found (§ 118) the verb *wn* substituted for *iw* where the latter cannot be used; in fact, the two cases will be shown to be remarkably analogous and parallel.

[1] See SETHE, *Nominalsatz*, §§ 32–37; 63–67; 85–86, etc.; LEF. *Gr.* §§ 623 foll.

[1a] Not, however, to the *nisbe*-adjectives of § 79.

§ 136. Independent pronoun + adjective.—This is the construction usual with the 1st pers. sing.

Exx. *ink ꜥšꜣ mrt* I am one rich in serfs.[2]

ink bnr n pr nb·f I was one pleasant to the house of his lord.[3]

The characteristic and regular use of the suffix 3rd pers. sing. (*nb·f* 'his lord') in this last example indicates that *bnr* means 'one pleasant' rather than simply 'pleasant', in other words that it is here a noun rather than an adjective. Thus the construction is merely a special case of that described in § 125.

As in the corresponding construction with nominal predicate just alluded to, so too here the pronoun is apt to have emphatic force and tends to become the logical predicate. Here again (see above § 127, 4), the particle *is* 'indeed' often serves to give emphasis to the pronoun, though without always giving it the importance of the logical predicate.

Exx. *ink is mꜣꜥ-ḫrw tp tꜣ* I was indeed one justified upon earth.[4]

n ink is ḳꜣ sꜣ I am not one high of back, i. e. overweening.[5]

Here *ink* is logical predicate: *I* am not overweening, whatever others may be.

Examples with any independent pronoun other than that of the first person are very rare, if the predicate be an adjective pure and simple.[6]

OBS. For the closely related construction with independent pronoun and participle see below § 373.

[2] *Sin.* B 154–5. Sim. *ib.* 153; *Siut* I, 228.

[3] Brit. Mus. 581. Sim. Cairo 20531, *c* 2.

[4] *Urk.* iv. 67. Sim. *ib.* 1078, 17.

[5] *Sin.* B 230.

[6] But *ntf mnḫ*, *Urk.* iv. 861, 8.

§ 137. Adjective + noun or dependent pronoun.—Except in the case of the 1st pers. this is the usual construction. The adjective precedes the subject and is invariable in number and gender; it may be accompanied by the exclamatory ending *·wy*, see above § 49.

Examples with a *noun* as subject:

nfr mtn·i my path is good.[1]

wr ḥst·i m stp-sꜣ r smr wꜥty nb greater was my praise in the palace than (that of) any Unique Friend.[2]

Examples with a *dependent pronoun* as subject:

nfr tw ḥnꜥ·i thou art happy with me.[3]

ꜥšꜣ st r ḫt nbt it was more plentiful than anything.[4]

twt·wy n·s st how like (to) her it is![5]

With the 1st pers. sing. the construction independent pronoun + adjective (§ 136) is preferred,[6] except in the case of the adjective *ny* 'belonging to'; the construction both of *ny* and of the expressions for 'belonging to me, thee', etc. (*ink, ntk*; *n·i-imy, n·k-imy*) has been seen to conform to that of the adjectival predicate; see above § 114, 2. 3. 4.

Attention must here be drawn to two very important points:

1. In the construction here discussed the adjectival predicate *precedes* its subject; we have good reason for thinking that, whenever an apparent adjectival predicate *follows* its subject, this predicate is not really an adjective at all, but *the old perfective tense of the adjective-verb*; see below § 320, end.

2. With nominal subject it is impossible to distinguish between the construction adj. + subj. and the *śḏm·f* form of the adjective-verb; with a singular pronoun as subject, on the other hand, the distinction is clearly marked, since *the adjectival predicate demands the dependent pronouns*, whereas the *śḏm·f* form employs the suffixes. For the uses of the *śḏm·f* form of the adjective-verb see below §§ 143. 144.

OBS. The construction dealt with in this section is obviously closely related to those cases with nominal predicate where the secondary and inverted word-order 1. log. pred., 2. log. subj. has become stabilized and customary; see § 127, particularly under 3.

§ 138. The same construction with a following dative serves to combine the notion of an adjectival predicate with that of possession; see above § 114, 1.

Ex. The land of Yaa .... *wr n·f irp r mw* it is more abundant in wine than in water; *or* it has more wine than water; lit., great to it is wine more than water.[7]

§ 139. Adjective + dependent pronoun + noun.—An example of an uncommon kind is

rd·wy sw ib·i how strong is my heart! Lit. how firm is it (namely) my heart.[8]

Here *sw* exercises much the same function as *pw* in its developed use with nominal predicate, above § 130; a still closer parallel above § 132.

[1] *Peas.* B1, 3. Sim. *ib.* B1, 108–9; *Sin.* B155; ERM. *Hymn.* 4, 2; 14, 2.

[2] *BH.* i. 25, 101. Sim. *Bersh.* i. 14, 10; *Sh.S.* 29–30; 99–100; Cairo 20543, 13.

[3] *Sin.* R55. Sim. *P. Kah.* 3, 33.

[4] *Urk.* iv. 693. Sim. *ib.* 687, 16; 879, 4; *Sh. S.* 63. 134.

[5] *Urk.* iv. 368.

[6] But see *Adm.* p. 104, an ex. with a genuine adj.; also the exx. with a participle, Add. to § 374.

[7] *Sin.* B82. Sim. *Sh. S.* 150, qu. § 144, 1; *P. Pet.* 1116 B, 10.

[8] *Paheri* 3; Sim. *Urk.* iv. 1166, 10. See too *Nominalsatz*, §§ 85. 86.

§ 140. Adjective + *pw*.—Examples similar to those with nominal predicate (§§ 128. 130) are found when the predicate is adjectival, only much more rarely.

Exx. *ḥns pw, n wsḫ ỉs pw* it (the path) was narrow, it was not broad.[1]

n wr ỉs pw wr ỉm such a great one is not really great, lit. not great indeed is he, the great one there.[2]

OBS. For *nfr pw* as a means of expressing negation, see below § 351, 2.

§ 141. The adjective as impersonal predicate with following dative.—In the constructions already studied the adjective predicated is an inherent quality. We are here to become acquainted with a construction in which the adjectival predicate is followed by the dative; this is used when a *contingent*, *accidental* or merely *temporary* qualification has to be expressed. The difference is best illustrated by German, where *er ist kalt* means 'he is cold' in temperament, while *ihm ist kalt* signifies 'he is cold', meaning 'he *feels* cold'; so too in the French *il a froid* as contrasted with *il est froid*.

Exx. *nfr n·tn* it will go well with you.[3]

ꜥꜣ n·ỉ mm wrw I am become great among the princes.[4]

wsḫ n·(ỉ) m ꜥḥꜥw·ỉ, ꜥšꜣ n·(ỉ) m mnmnt·ỉ I became extensive in my wealth, I became rich in my flocks. Lit. it was broad to me in my wealth, it was plentiful to me in my flocks.[5]

bỉn·wy n·ỉ how ill it is with (lit. to) me.[6]

nfr·wy n tꜣ ḥwt-nṯr how well it goes with the temple (when a certain thing happens).[7]

The same construction occurs with *pw*, but extremely rarely.

Ex. *ḳsn pw n bw ntf ỉm* it goes wretchedly with (lit. it is wretched to) the place where he is.[8]

OBS. 1. The word with adjectival meaning in this construction is doubtless a true adjective with omitted subject, see below § 145. That it cannot be an impersonal *sḏm·f* form seems clear from the occasional presence of the exclamatory ending *·wy*; another reason is given below § 467. The occasional presence of *·wy* also proves that the adjectival word + *n* cannot be identified with the *sḏm·n·f* form; we may also point to the absence of any examples where the *n* is separated from its noun, as may happen with the *sḏm·n·f* form. None the less, the *sḏm·n·f* form originated in a very similar way, see §§ 386; 389, 3, end; 411, 2. For an undoubted *sḏm·n·f* form from the adjective-verb, see below § 144, 3.

OBS. 2. For *nfr n* as a means of expressing negation, see § 351, 1.

§ 142. Tense and mood in the sentence with adjectival predicate.—As in the sentences with adverbial and nominal predicate the tense must, as a rule, be inferred from the context. Examples with both present and past

[1] *Peas.* R 45. Sim. *Urk.* iv. 1087, 8, where *nn* for *n* is in accord with later custom, see GUNN, *Studies*, p. 169.

[2] *Peas.* B 1, 165.

[3] *Urk.* iv. 123; sim. *Sinai* 90, 20–1. Present time, see *Urk.* iv. 366, 5; v. 170, 17.

[4] *ÄZ.* 57, 1*. Sim. *Mitt.* ix. 18.

[5] *Sin.* B 146–7. Sim. *ib.* 106; Cairo 20512, *b* 4.

[6] *Adm.* 6, 8.

[7] *Th. T. S.* i. pp. 40. 64. Pl. 15. Sim. *Bersh.* i. 15.

[8] *P. Pet.* 1116A, 91.

meaning have been quoted in the foregoing sections, and *nfr n·tn* in § 141 is an example with future meaning.

The verbs *iw* and *wnn* (§§ 117. 118) have a certain limited use before the adjectival predicate when its subject is a dependent pronoun.

Exx. He has reached old age serving the Pharaoh, *iw nfr sw m pꜣ hrw r sf* while he is better to-day than yesterday.[1]

mk wnn nḏm sy ḥr ib·f behold, it will be pleasant in his heart.[2]

wn·in nfr st ḥr ib·sn thereupon it was agreeable in their hearts.[3] For the *śḏm·in·f* form of *wnn* here used see below §§ 429, 1; 470.

For *iw* + adj. + *n* see below § 467. Much more commonly, however, it is the old perfective tense of the adjective-verb, preceded by its subject, which is used after *iw* and *wnn*, see §§ 320. 323. 326.

The particles *mk* 'behold', *isṯ* 'lo', and *ḫr* 'further'[4] are found before adjectival, as before nominal, predicate.

Exx. *mk nfr sḏm n rmṯ* behold, it is good for men to hearken, lit. good is a hearkening to men.[5]

mk dḥr pw behold it (the office of vizier) is bitter.[6]

isṯ štꜣ wrt wꜣt lo, very difficult was the road.[7]

In wishes and in various dependent constructions the adjective itself cannot be used at all, and recourse was had to the *śḏm·f* form of the adjective-verb; see the next section.

OBS. Clauses of time and circumstance are expressed by the help of the old perfective; see below §§ 314. 322. 323.

§ 143. The *śḏm·f* form of the adjective-verb.—Just as *iw* can be used only in a restricted number of cases and is elsewhere replaced by the *śḏm·f* form of *wnn* (see above § 118), so too the adjective must often be replaced by the *śḏm·f* form of the adjective-verb.

So, for example, in clauses of *purpose* (§ 40, 1).

Ex. *di·n·k sy m tp·k, wr·k im·s, kꜣ·k im·s, ꜥꜣ šfšft·k im·s* thou hast placed it (the eye of Horus) in thy head, that thou mayst be eminent by means of it, that thou mayst be exalted by means of it, that thy estimation may be great by means of it.[8]

So too, again, after the verb *rdi* 'cause' (§ 70).

Exx. *di·i wsḫ swt ir wi* I will cause to be spacious the places of him who made me.[9]

di·i sꜥꜣ·f m ꜥꜣ·k I will cause him to become acquainted with thy greatness.[10] Lit. (that) he become acquainted.

[1] *Th. T. S.* iii. 26.
[2] *P. Kah.* 3, 36.
[3] *Pr.* 2, 6. Sim. *Peas.* B 2, 131.
[4] *Sin.* B 202–3.
[5] *Leb.* 67. Sim. *ib.* 86–7; *Sh. S.* 182.
[6] *Urk.* iv. 1087.
[7] *Bersh.* i. 14, 1.
[8] ERM. *Hymn.* 16, 1–2. Sim. probably Cairo 20538, ii. *c* 18 (2nd pers. plur.).
[9] *Urk.* iv. 163. Sim. *ib.* 102, 12; 505, 13.
[10] *Sh. S.* 139. Sim. *Eb.* 59, 9; *Urk.* iv. 198, 7; 766, 5.

A similar use of the adjective-verb is found, as we shall see later, after other verbs (§ 186, 1) and after prepositions (§ 157, 4). The cases are exactly the same as those in which *wn·f* is found in place of *iw·f*. We have already pointed out (§ 137 end) that the *śḏm·f* form of the adjective-verb can be clearly distinguished from the adjective itself only when the subject is a singular pronoun, in which case a suffix-pronoun is used.

§ 144. Negation of sentences with adjectival predicate.[1]—Examples quoted in §§ 136. 140 show how the sentence with adjectival predicate was negated when the subject was either an independent pronoun or else *pw*. In most other cases the adjective-verb, not the actual adjective, appears to be used, and the rules followed are those already stated in § 105.

1. *N śḏm·f* has often *past* reference.

Exx. *n ḫs·i ḥr ib* I was not weak in the heart, i.e. I was not deemed weak.[2]

n ꜥꜣ r·i m šnyt my mouth has not been great (i.e. I have not been self-assertive) among the courtiers.[3]

But it may also have *present* reference.

Exx. *n is·k* thou art not light.[4]

n wr n·k ꜥntyw thou hast not much incense, lit. not great is incense to thee.[5]

2. *Nn śḏm·f* has *future* meaning.

Ex. *nn šw·k im·f ḏt* thou shalt not be bereft of it eternally.[6]

3. *N śḏm·n·f* denies a *continuous* or *repeated* action, irrespectively of the time at which the negative instance may occur.

Exx. *n nḏm·n n·f ḫtḫt im* reversal thereof (lit. receding therefrom) is not pleasant to him.[7]

n šw·n drpw·f his offerings will not (ever) be lacking.[8]

OBS. Most examples of *n śḏm·n·f* are ambiguous, since it might be possible to view them as negative cases of adjectival predicate with following dative (§ 141). However, the first of the two examples quoted above is placed beyond all doubt by the separation of *nḏm·n* from its nominal subject.

4. Negative universals follow the model of the sentences expressing non-existence (§ 108). The best examples contain participles or other adjectival parts of the verb; see below § 394. Here only one type will be quoted:

nn ꜥt im·i šwt m nṯr no member of me is void of god, lit. there is not a member in me void of god.[9]

OBS. The negation of wishes, commands, and clauses of purpose with adjectival predicate is contrived by means of the negative verb *tm*. Not all these cases can be illustrated; an example of a negatived clause of purpose in § 347, 4.

[1] See GUNN, *Studies*, ch. 27.

[2] *Puy.* 35; Sim. *Urk.* iv. 1082, 15; *Nu* 102, 7; BUDGE, 256, 1.

[3] Louvre C 55. Sim. *Sinai* 90, 15; *Nu* 125 *b*, 25. 32. 36. 40.

[4] *Peas.* B 2, 103. Sim. *ib.* B 1, 177; LAC. *TR.* 1, 55.

[5] *Sh. S.* 150.

[6] *Urk.* iv. 500. Sim. *Sin.* B 258; *Siut* 1, 295; *Five Th. T.* 25. 26.

[7] *Siut* 1, 280–1. 310. Sim. *Sm.* 3, 17–18.

[8] *Urk.* iv. 519. Sim. *ib.* 1077, 3; ERM. *Hymn.* 13, 5; *Pt.* 282–3; *Peas.* B 1, 316–7.

[9] BUDGE, p. 113, 4. Sim. *ib.* p. 115, 10; 262, 10; *Pt.* 56; *Peas.* B 1, 208–9.

§ 145. Omission of the subject.—When the nature of the subject is clear from the context, it is occasionally omitted.

Ex. Inspecting the netting of the desert-animals, *isṯ ꜥšꜣ wrt r ḫt nbt* and lo, (they were) much more numerous than anything.[1]

Or again, the subject may be omitted if it is perfectly vague. Thus in the construction *nfr n·i* 'it goes well with me' (§ 141) the implicit subject is the vague 'it' or 'things'.

This subjectless use of the adjectival predicate occurs also after *iw*, cf. § 142. The cases thus arising are discussed at length in § 467.

[1] *Bersh.* i. 7.

VOCABULARY

iw come.

mdw speak, talk. *mdt* speech, word.

nḥm take away, rescue.

ꜣḫ be beneficial, advantageous.

wsr be powerful, wealthy.

ꜥḳꜣ be precise, accurate.

mty be exact, precise.

ḳsn be difficult, disagreeable.

dns be heavy, irksome.

Ḏḥwty Thoth, the ibis-headed god of writing and mathematics.

iwsw balance.

rḫyt common people, subjects.

var. *sꜥḥ* dignitary; rank, dignity.

ḫrt share, portion.

mꜣꜥty righteous.

iwyt wrongdoing.

snf last year.

ḥꜣt front; *m ḥꜣt*, *r ḥꜣt* formerly, before.

mꜣi(r)w (§ 279) misery.

m-ꜥ in the hand of; from; owing to; together with.

EXERCISE XII

(*a*) *Transliterate and translate*:

(1)

(2) (3) (4) (5) (6) (7)

[1] Read *mtꜥ*.

(*b*) *Write in hieroglyphs and transliteration*:

(1) My portion was not (too) great (*wr*). (2) I rescued the poor man from him (who was) more powerful than he. (3) (When) the mistress of the house speaks, it (*pw*) is irksome in (*ḥr*) the heart of the maid-servants. (4) I was one important (*wr*) in his office, great in his rank, a noble in front of the common people. (5) I cause thee to be greater than any courtier. (6) Her clothes were white. (7) Behold, thou art beneficial to thy lord; it goes well with thee because of it. (8) The river will not be empty of crocodiles. (9) No man (*rmṯ*) is powerful like Rēꜥ.

LESSON XIII

EMPHASIS BY ANTICIPATION

§ 146. A noun, adverb, or adverbial phrase which has been removed from its regular place and put outside and in front of the sentence is said to stand in **anticipatory emphasis.** The word or phrase thus given prominence becomes, as it were, the pivot upon which the whole sentence turns; the effect is, however, sometimes different from what might be expected; thus in the two first exx. of § 147 the stress is upon the *predicate*, not upon the *subject*.

Except in the case of a mere adverbial expression, a **resumptive pronoun** must be substituted within the sentence itself for the word thus emphasized. Such a pronoun appears also in the parallels from modern languages, e.g. *cette confiance, il l'avait exprimée*; 'every man that dies ill, the ill is upon *his own* head'.

§ 147. Anticipatory emphasis in non-verbal sentences. 1. The *subject* is put at the head of the sentence.

Exx. *ḫbswt·f, wr sy r mḥ 2* his beard, it was greater than two cubits.[1]

ꜥntyw n·i-im sw the incense, it belongs to me.[2]

[1] *Sh. S.* 63.

[2] *Sh. S.* 151. Sim. *Sin.* B 222. 255.

ḥknw pf dd·n·k int·f bw pw wr n iw pn that spice which thou didst speak of bringing, it is the main thing of this island.[1]

2. A *genitive* is emphasized.

Ex. *wˁ im nb, mkꜣ ib·f, nḫt ˁ·f, r sn-nw·f* each one of them, his heart was stouter, his arm stronger, than his fellow('s).[2]

3. *Adverbs* or *adverbial phrases.* See the examples with *ir*, below § 149.

§ 148. Anticipatory emphasis in verbal sentences.—1. The *subject* is put at the beginning:

Exx. *mw m itrw swri·tw·f, mr·k* the water in the rivers, it is drunk if thou desirest.[3]

mk ntr rdi·n·f ˁnḫ·k behold, god has caused thee to live.[4]

mk tw dd·tw behold, one says.[5]

An independent pronoun may be used before the *śdm·f* and *śdm·n·f* forms.

Ex. *ink pr·n·i* it is I (who) have come forth.[6]

This example shows the *śdm·n·f* form; the construction *ntf śdm·f* has always future meaning, see below § 227, 2. See Add. for the construction *sw śdm·f*, etc.

2. The *object* is put at the beginning:

Ex. *snty·k di·n·i sn m sꜣ ḥꜣ·k* thy sisters, I have placed them as a protection behind thee.[7]

3. A *genitive* is put at the beginning:

Ex. *in iw wsfw spry r ˁḥˁ r r n pr·f* a sluggard, shall a petitioner stand at the door of his house?[8] For the construction see § 332.

4. A noun which virtually follows a preposition:

Ex. *ntyw im·s, n sp wˁ im* those that were in it, not one of (them) was left.[9] The adverb *im* 'therefrom' is equivalent to *im·sn* 'of them'.

5. An *adverb* or *adverbial phrase.*

m-ḫt nn wdꜣ ḥm·f r šnˁ n wdn after this His Majesty proceeded to the workshop of offerings.[11]

mk in-gꜣw-n ipwty ˁꜣ ḥnˁ·i, iw ꜣ rdi·n·i iwt·f behold, through lack of a messenger here with me I have caused him to come.[12] *'In* is the initial form of the preposition.

Such examples as ..... *ḥꜣt-sp 12 .... wdꜣ ḥm·f* 'year 12 .... His Majesty proceeded',[10] are more probably to be explained by § 89, 1.

§ 149. Anticipatory emphasis by means of *ir*.—The preposition *r* may have the meaning 'as to', 'concerning', and when occurring at the beginning of a sentence exhibits the original full form *ir*. This *ir* is often

[1] *Sh. S.* 152.

[2] *Sh. S.* 100.

[3] *Sin.* B 233. With past meaning, see § 450, 1.

[4] *Sh. S.* 113-4. Sim. *Sin.* B 142-3; *Bersh.* i. 14, 5.

[5] *Urk.* iv. 1090. Sim. *Sin.* R 15, qu. § 66.

[6] LAC. *TR.* 72, 21. Sim. *ÄZ.* 57, 8*.

[7] *Urk.* iv. 618. Sim. *ib.* 1075, 11; *Sh. S.* 11; *Sin.* B 223.

[8] *Peas.* B 1, 284. Sim. *Adm.* 7, 7; *Th. T. S.* ii. 8.

[9] *Sh. S.* 107.

[10] *Seas.* 340.

[11] *Urk.* iv. 685. Sim. *ib.* 836, 6.

[12] *P. Kah.* 31, 8-10; translation dubious.

placed before a word which is to be emphasized, the resulting expression then being an adverbial phrase in anticipatory emphasis, as described in § 148, 5.

1. In reference to the *subject* of the sentence.

Exx. *ỉr sf, Wsỉr pw* as for yesterday, it is Osiris.[1]

mk ỉr ṯꜣty, mk nn (read *n*) *bnrỉ ỉs pw* behold, as to the (office of) vizier, behold it is not pleasant.[2]

ỉr ḥm nb r pn, n ꜥḳ·n·f as to anyone who does not know this spell, he shall never enter.[3]

2. In reference to some other member of the sentence.

Exx. *ỉr ntt nbt m sš ḥr pꜣ šfdw sḏm st* as to all which is in writing on the papyrus-roll, hear it.[4]

ỉr nsw nb sḫm-ỉr·f nb nty r ḥtp n·f . . . . . . nn ḥtp n·f nbty as to every king and every potentate who shall forgive him . . . . . the Two Ladies shall not forgive him.[5]

ỉr m-ḫt ỉꜣwt n·k-ỉmy, ỉw·w m sꜣ n sꜣ but (lit. as to) after thy own old age, they are (heritable) from son to son.[6]

As several of the above examples indicate, a frequent motive for the use of *ỉr* was the desire to lighten the sentence by placing outside it some lengthy and cumbrous member; so particularly when this member consisted of several co-ordinated nouns.[7]

§ 150. *ỉr* 'if' before the *śḏm·f* form.—A variety of the construction described in the last section is the use of *ỉr* with the meaning 'if' before the *śḏm·f* form; the verb with its adjuncts is here used as a noun clause, i.e. in place of a noun (above § 69), and the strict translation would be 'as to he-hears'. When *ỉr* is thus employed, the *if*-clause precedes the *then*-clause.

Ex. *ỉr sḏm·k nn ḏd·n·ỉ n·k, wnn sḫr·k nb r ḥꜣt* if thou hearkenest to this that I have said to thee, every plan of thine will go forward, lit. will be to the front.[8]

When the predicate of the *if*-clause is *adverbial*, the verb 'to be' is used in its *śḏm·f* form *wnn·f*; see above § 118, 2.

Ex. *ỉr wnn·k ḥnꜥ rmṯ* if thou art together with people.[9]

When the predicate is *nominal*, *wnn·f* is likewise used, together with the *m* of predication; see above §§ 116; 133 Obs.

Ex. *ỉr wnn·f m ẖrd wr, ꜥm·f st m ꜥm* if he be a big child, he shall swallow it down, lit. swallow it with a swallowing.[10]

In both these cases we may think of the construction as the conditional form of sentences with adverbial predicate introduced by *ỉw* (§ 117); thus *ỉr wnn·k ḥnꜥ rmṯ* is the conditional form of *ỉw·k ḥnꜥ rmṯ*. Similarly the existential clause with *ỉw wn* (§ 107, 2) appears conditionally as *ỉr wnn wn*.

1 *Urk.* v. 11. Sim. *Siut* 1, 300; Berl. *Äl.* i. p. 257, 9.

2 *Urk.* iv. 1087.

3 *Urk.* v. 95.

4 *Pr.* 2, 4–5.

5 *Kopt.* 8, 7–8. Sim. *Urk.* iv. 1021, 8–9.

6 *Urk.* iv. 1021. Sim. Munich 3, 22, qu. Exerc. 29, (*b*) 3; *ỉst ỉr m wn·f* (§ 157, 1) *Ann.* 37, pl. 2, 19.

7 Exx. *Siut* 3, 62; Cairo 20458, *b* 1.

8 *Pt.* 507–8. Sim. *ib.* 463. 564; *Leb.* 39. 56; *Sh. S.* 70; *Peas.* B 1, 162. 167.

9 *Pt.* 232. Sim. *Eb.* 49, 22; *Sin.* B 125.

10 *Eb.* 49, 22. Sim. *Pt.* 84. 119. 145. 197.

Ex. *ỉr wnn wn sprw* if there shall be a petitioner.[1]

When the predicate is *adjectival*, the *śḏm·f* form of the adjective-verb is employed; see above § 143.

Ex. *ỉr ỉḳr·k, grg·k pr·k* if thou art well-to-do, thou shalt found thy house.[2]

Obs. This kind of clause is negatived with the help of *tm·f*, the *śḏm·f* form of the negative verb; see below § 347, 6. For other modes of negation, see §§ 351. 352.

§ 151. *ỉr* 'if' before the *śḏm·n·f* form.—Doubtless this was the construction regularly employed to express an *unfulfilled condition*. Examples are, however, of extreme rarity.

Ex. *ỉr šsp·n·ỉ ꜣs, ḫꜥw m ḏrt·ỉ, ỉw dỉ·n·ỉ ḫt ḥmw* if I had made (lit. taken) haste, (with) weapons in my hand, I should have caused the cowards to retreat.[3]

§ 152. Emphasis of sentences by means of *rf*.—The enclitic particle *rf*, among other uses (§ 252, 3), serves to emphasize whole sentences, which then depict a situation and point forward to some further occurrence; *rf* is hence usually to be translated by English 'now' (French *or*), but sometimes may be better rendered 'now when'.

Exx. *ỉw·ỉn rf sḫty pn* now this peasant came, etc. . . . . . ; and said, etc.[4]

pḥ·n·f rf ḏd mdt tn now when he had reached the saying of this word, one of his asses filled his mouth, etc.[5]

This use is particularly common after *ỉsṯ* 'lo'.

Ex. *ỉst rf ỉn·n·sn mnỉwt·sn* now they had brought their bead-necklets, etc. . . . . . . and they presented them to His Majesty.[6]

An example of *ỉsṯ rf* with adverbial predicate following has been quoted above § 119, 2.

Thus *rf* may do for whole sentences what *ỉr* does for parts of sentences. The two are etymologically related, for, as we shall see later (§ 252), *rf* is derived from the preposition *r* combined with the suffix 3rd sing. m.

§ 153. Emphatic use of adverbial predicates.—In *wishes* or *exhortations* an adverbial predicate is sometimes found at the beginning of a sentence; the subject may follow, or, if clear from the context, may be omitted altogether.

Exx. *n kꜣ·k ỉnw n sḫt* to thy *ka* (spirit) the tribute of the field![7] Words spoken by a bringer of offerings.

ḥꜣ·k, ỉpwty n nṯr nb turn thee back (lit. behind thee), thou messenger of any god.[8]

m ḥtp nfr wrt in very good peace! Greeting at the beginning of a letter acknowledging a despatch from the king.[9]

[1] *Urk.* iv. 1090, 11. Sim. *ib.* 1093, 5, qu. § 395.

[2] *Pt.* 325. Sim. *ib.* 175. 370. 428.

[3] *Mill.* 2, 3. Sim. *Adm.* 12, 6, obscure.

[4] *Peas.* B 1, 52. Sim. *ib.* 88. 139.

[5] *Peas.* R 59. Sim. *Sin.* B 248; *Ann.* 37, pl. 2, 16.

[6] *Sin.* B 268. Sim. *ib.* 173; *Peas.* B 1, 71.

[7] *Bersh.* i. 20. Sim *Meir* i. 2. 3; *Th.T.S.* i. 16.

[8] Budge, p. 93, 4. Sim. *ib.* 97, 10; 98, 13. 15; Lac. *TR.* 73, 2.

[9] *Sin.* B 205. Sim *Westc.* 7, 23.

PREPOSITIONS

§ 154. Use of the prepositions.—The employment of prepositions before *nouns* and *suffix-pronouns* is by this time very familiar to the student. Another common and important use is that before the *infinitive* and other nominally used parts of the verb. Since, however, these verb-forms have not yet been treated, only one or two instances will be given by way of illustration.

Exx. I went *r smỉt st* to report it.[1] *Smỉt* is infinitive (§ 299).

smỉ nfr n h3b sw reporting well to him who sent him,[2] lit. to him having-sent (perfective active participle, § 359) him.

sḫmḫ ỉb Ḥr m mrt·n·f diverting the heart of Horus (i.e. the king) with what he wishes.[3] *Mrt·n·f* is perfective relative form, § 387, 3.

More remarkable is the use of the prepositions to introduce noun clauses of the kind already described (§ 69); compare English '*since* I came', '*after* he went', '*for* he was young'. In Middle Egyptian the noun clauses thus employed have nearly always a verbal predicate, and as a rule it is the *śḏm·f* form that introduces them (§ 155). After a few prepositions the *śḏm·n·f* form is also found (§ 156), as well as the *śḏm·f* passive (§ 423, 3), and in one case the construction noun + old perfective (§ 327) occurs. Further, a verb-form called the *śḏmt·f* form is rather frequently found after prepositions (§§ 407–9). At the present stage we can deal only with the uses of the prepositions before the two common verb-forms (*śḏm·f* and *śḏm·n·f*) thus far discussed.

In early religious texts the preposition is occasionally found before a clause with an independent pronoun as subject and with nominal or adjectival predicate; this *n* is to be rendered 'because', 'for'.

Ex. *n ṯwt ỉs twt pw n nbw* for thou art that image of gold.[4]

Similar examples with *mỉ* 'according as' may be quoted from the end of Dyn. XVIII and later.

Ex. *mỉ ntk m3ꜥ m ḥwt Ptḥ* according as thou art one true in the house of Ptah.[5]

§ 155. The *śḏm·f* form after prepositions.[6]—The *śḏm·f* form introducing a noun clause (§ 154) is found after a number of different prepositions, see below § 222. The time which it indicates is, more often than not, identical with that of the main clause; such time we may fitly describe as the *relative present*.

Exx. *mdw·k ḫft wšd·f tw* thou shalt speak when (lit. corresponding to) he addresses thee.[7]

sbn dpt r mrr·s the ship drifts as (lit. according to) it likes.[8]

[1] *Sh. S.* 157.

[2] Louvre C 174.

[3] Brit. Mus. 614, 2.

[4] *B. of D.* ch. 133 in Cairo coffin 28085, 301. Sim. *Urk.* iv. 258, 2.

[5] DÜM. *H. I.* ii. 40 *a*, 28. Sim. *Inscr. dédic.* 66; *Kuban* 18. With *pw* after the pronoun (cf. § 128, end; § 130) DÜM. *H. I.* ii. 40 *a*, 22. 25.

[6] See SETHE, *Verbum*, ii. § 151.

[7] *Pt.* 129.

[8] *Peas.* B 1, 126–7.

šms·i nb·i ḫft ḫnt·f r sḫrt ḫftyw·f I followed my lord when (lit. corresponding to) he sailed upstream to overthrow his enemies.[1]

If, however, the context and the meaning of the preposition demand it, the *śḏm·f* form thus employed may refer to *relatively future* time, i. e. to time which is future as compared with that of the main clause.

Ex. .... *smnḫ·n·(i) ṯw ... n-mrwt ir·k n·i ḫt* I have equipped thee .... in order that (lit. through love of) thou mayst perform rites (lit. things) for me.[2]

With *ḏr* 'since' and *r-sꜣ* 'after' the time of the *śḏm·f* form is relatively past.

Exx. .... (a god) for whom the kings work *ḏr grg·tw tꜣ pn* since this land was founded.[3]

They shall give a candle to his *ka*-priest *r-sꜣ sꜣḫ·sn sw* after they have done religious service to him.[4]

Strictly, therefore, we must regard the *śḏm·f* form after prepositions as timeless, as dependent for its time on the context, and still more on the nature of the preposition. It must be noted, however, that when relatively past time has to be indicated explicitly, the *śḏm·n·f* form is used (below § 156); and further that, as we shall see later (§§ 444, 3; 454, 4), and as will soon be illustrated in the case of the verb *wnn* (§ 157, 1), the *śḏm·f* form was liable to assume different forms according to the sense to be expressed.

Note that the prepositional character of the Egyptian preposition can be retained in translation by employing the English gerund; so in the examples quoted above, 'through love of thy performing rites for me', 'since the founding of this land'. Otherwise, English must often substitute a conjunction or conjunctional phrase (ex. 'in order that'). Renderings with the English gerund have the advantage of marking the temporal indeterminateness of the *śḏm·f* form.

Lastly, observe that the construction with *ir* 'if' (§ 150) strictly belongs under this head, *ir* being simply the preposition *r* 'to', 'as to' in the form which it must assume at the beginning of a sentence. So too we have one example of *in-mrwt* for *n-mrwt* 'through the love of', 'in order that' (§ 181) at the head of a sentence;[5] *in* is here initial form of *n*, as in *in-gꜣw-n* 'through lack of' quoted in § 148, 5.

§ 156. The *śḏm·n·f* form after prepositions.[6]—This construction is found only with *m-ḫt* 'after', *r* 'until', *mi* 'like', and *ḫft* 'according as'. The time is in every case antecedent to that of the main clause; such time we may call *relative past.*

Exx. *ḫr m-ḫt grg·n·i pr* now when I had founded (or, after my having founded) a house.[7]

[1] *BH.* i. 8, 6.

[2] *Siut* I, 271. Sim. Berl. *ÄI.* i. p. 258, 21.

[3] *Urk.* iv. 95. Sim. *Sin.* B 69.

[4] *Siut* I, 313. Sim. *ib.* 298.

[5] *Peas.* B 1, 79.

[6] See SETHE, *Verbum*, ii. § 366.

[7] *Urk.* iv. 3, 2. Sim. *ib.* 5, 4; *Eb.* 91, 16–17; 96, 21.

The daughter of the nomarch reigned *r ḫpr·n s3·s m nḫt-ꜥ* until her son had become a strong man.[1]

Thou shalt traverse the sea in sandals *mi ir·n·k tp t3* as (lit. like) thou didst upon earth.[2]

Horus . . . who smites the chieftains who have attacked him *ḫft wḏ·n n·f it·(·f) Rꜥ nḫtw r t3 nb* according as his father Rēꜥ has decreed for him victories over every land.[3]

See too the example after *ir* 'if', above § 151.

§ 157. Prepositions before noun clauses with adverbial, nominal, or adjectival predicate.—Here again the usual expedient of employing the *śḏm·f* form of *wnn* 'be' (§ 118) or of the adjective-verb (§ 143) is adopted.

1. With *adverbial* predicate the form *wn·f* (§ 107) is used where no stress is laid on the duration of the act, or unless specifically future time is referred to.

Ex. I was a priest . . . . . together with my father *m wn·f tp t3* when (lit. in) he was upon earth.[4]

The other form of the *śḏm·f* of *wnn*, namely *wnn·f*, is employed when the sense is *future* or else markedly continuous.

Exx. *ḥnꜥ wnn·ṯn m-s3 ḫnty·(i)* and (lit. together with) ye shall be after my statue.[5]

m-ḫt wnn Ḥr m nḫn·f while Horus was in his youth.[6]

2. When the predicate is *nominal*, the *śḏm·f* form of *wnn* is likewise employed, together with the *m* of predication.

Ex. *ḏr wn ḥm·i m inp* since My Majesty was a child.[7]

3. Here we must call attention to the peculiar use of *wnn* after *mi* 'like' and *r* 'than'.

Exx. *iw·i ḥr·f mi wn bik* I was upon him as though it were a falcon, lit. as though a falcon were (upon him).[8]

sꜥ3·n·f wi r wn·i r ḥ3t he made me greater than I was before.[9]

4. With *adjectival* predicate, the *śḏm·f* form of the adjective-verb is used.

Exx. Bandage all wounds . . . . *r nḏm·f ḥr ꜥwy* so that (lit. to) he may become well immediately.[10]

The god put it in my heart . . . . to make his house flourish *mi ꜥ3·f r nṯr nb* inasmuch as (lit. like) he is greater than any god.[11]

The princes came . . . . to do obeisance to the might of His Majesty . . . . . *n ꜥ3 ḫpš·f* because his power was (so) great.[12]

[1] *Siut* 5, 29.

[2] LAC. *TR.* 22, 33. Sim. *Amrah* 29, 2; *Urk.* iv. 624, 5.

[3] *Urk.* iv. 593.

[4] *ÄZ.* 47, Pl. 1 (p. 88), 3; sim. *Urk.* iv. 897, 13; after *mi*, *Arm.* 103, 11; after *ist ir* (§ 149, 2), *Ann.* 37, pl. 2, 19; after *ḏr*, *ib.* 390, 7.

[5] *Siut* 1, 317.

[6] BUDGE, p. 232, 6.

[7] *Urk.* iv. 157.

[8] *T. Carn.* 14. Sim. *ib.* 15; *Urk.* iv. 547, 10.

[9] *Urk.* iv. 150. Sim. *ib.* 879, 4.

[10] *Eb.* 46, 21–2. Sim. LAC. *TR.* 72, 34.

[11] *Urk.* iv. 198. Sim. *ib.* 3, 3; Leyden V 4, 2; Louvre C 172 qu. Exerc. xiii. (*a*).

[12] *Urk.* iv. 662. Sim. *ib.* 654, 5; 736, 11.

Further examples of cases 1, 2, and 4 above have already been quoted in connection with *ir* 'if'; see § 150.

OBS. To negate clauses of this kind, the *sdm·f* form of the negative verb *tm* may be used; see below § 347, 5. 6.

§ 158. Prepositions serving to form epithets and nouns.—1. Since adjectives in *-y* (§ 79) can be formed from most simple prepositions, it is these which are usually employed when a noun has to be qualified by a phrase consisting of preposition + noun.

Ex. [hieroglyphs] *wꜥbw imyw hꜣw·sn* the priests who-are-in their times, i.e. the priests of any given time.[1] *Imyw* is m. plur. of the adjective from *m*.

Certain fixed phrases consisting of preposition + noun have, however, come to be regularly used as epithets; so, for example, *r ḏr·f, r ḏr* 'complete', lit. 'to (its) end' and *mi ḳd·f* 'entire', lit. 'like its form', both quoted above § 100. Along similar lines has been created the common phrase [hieroglyphs] *bꜣk im* 'this thy humble servant', lit. 'the servant there',[2] in which *im* is the adverbial form of the preposition *m* 'in'. Similarly [hieroglyphs] *wꜥ im nb* 'every one thereof', 'every one of them'.[3]

Certain idiomatic phrases consisting of preposition + noun are made into epithets by the help of the genitival adjective.

Exx. [hieroglyphs] *hswt·i nt ḫr nsw* my favours from (lit. of with) the king.[4] A curious parallel is afforded by the French *mes faveurs de par le roi.*

[hieroglyphs] *imꜣḫy n ḫr nsw* one honoured by (lit. of with) the king.[5]

[hieroglyphs] *ḫnt·s n tp itrw* her procession on (lit. of upon) the river.[5a]

2. Another way of analysing the last-named expressions would be to say that *ḫr-nsw* 'with-the-king' serves as a noun. Sentences can be quoted where preposition + noun together function as a noun.

Exx. [hieroglyphs] *r-sꜣ msyt pw* it was after supper.[6]

[hieroglyphs] *ḥr m pw irt m mitt* wherefore is it that the like is done? Lit. on account of what is it, the doing accordingly?[7]

[hieroglyphs] *st šꜣꜥ-m Yrḏ nfryt-r pḥw tꜣ wꜣ r bšt ḥr ḥm·f* lo, from Yeraza to the ends of the earth had fallen into rebellion against His Majesty.[8]

[hieroglyphs] *m sꜥꜣ tp tꜣ* in extolling (life) upon earth.[9]

§ 159. Position of the prepositions.—The prepositions always precede the word which they govern, whether it be a noun or some verb-form. The governed word thus seems to be a direct genitive, as in the Semitic languages. This view is confirmed by the fact that some, at least, of the simple prepositions are derived from nouns, exx. [hieroglyph] *tp* 'upon', lit. 'head'; [hieroglyphs] *ḥꜣ* 'behind',

[1] *Siut* 1, 311. Sim. BUDGE, p. 260, 6.

[2] See above p. 58, n. 1; and for some analogous phrases GRIFFITH, *Kahun Papyri*, pp. 78. 105; *ÄZ.* 59, 22.

[3] *Sh. S.* 99; *Sin.* B 246. *Wꜥ im* alone, *Eb.* 54, 20; *Adm.* 7, 14.

[4] *Bersh.* i. 14, 8. Sim. *Sin.* B 310; *BH.* i. 25, 57–8.

[5] *BH.* i. 25, 115–6.

[5a] *Eleph.* 25. Sim. *Urk.* iv. 186, 13.

[6] *Mill.* 1, 11.

[7] *PSBA.* 35, 166.

[8] *Urk.* iv. 648. Sim. *ḫnt šꜣꜥ-r Nhrn, ib.* 649, 9; *r-mn-m Šꜣt*, subj., ib. 618, 1.

[9] *PSBA.* 35, 166. Sim. Cairo 583, 3, qu. § 120; possibly also *Leb.* 78.

lit. 'back of the head'; cf. American 'back of......', French *faute de.* Moreover, in the compound prepositions the second element is often a noun (§ 178), and in some cases the genitival adjective here appears between the preposition and a governed noun, ex. *m-ẖnw-n iw pn* 'within (lit. in the interior of) this isle';[1] contrast with suffix *m-ẖnw·f* 'within it'.[2]

Egyptian shows a repugnance to placing so weak a word as a preposition at the beginning of a sentence, but *m-ḫt* is sometimes so used, see § 148, 5. Apart from this, and excepting the exclamatory sentences of § 153, the only prepositions ever placed at the beginning appear to be *r* and *n* in their initial forms *ir* and *in*; for *in* see § 155, end, and for the very common *ir* see §§ 149–51. The cases where preposition + noun together function as a noun (§ 158, 2) can hardly be quoted as exceptions to this rule.

Note that what is here said of the position of the prepositions holds good both when they are followed by a mere noun and when they are followed by a noun clause.[3]

[1] *Sh. S.* 175.
[2] *Sh. S.* 115.
[3] However, *m* introducing subordinate clauses at beginning of the sentence, § 444, 2: also independently, p. 374, n. 7.

§ 160. Negation of the prepositions.—The uses of *nn* and *n is* to negative a group consisting of preposition + noun will be dealt with in connection with the adverbs (§ 209).

VOCABULARY

ꜥr ascend, approach.

ḫrp undertake, make offering of.

rd grow.

mꜣ(w) be new, fresh; *m mꜣwt* anew, lit. in newness.

inr stone.

ꜥš cedar (properly 'pine').

ꜥꜣ door.

ꜥt house, department; *iry-ꜥt* official, one belonging to a department.

ꜥt limb, member.

Wsir Osiris, the god of the dead.

kꜣ spirit, soul, double, see below p. 172.

ḫtyw staircase, terrace, hill-side.

rwdt hard stone, sandstone.

pꜣt antiquity, old time.

var. *ẖrt-hrw* daytime.

var. *Šmꜥ(w)* Upper Egypt.

var. *Tꜣ-mḥw* Lower Egypt.

var. *tpy* (who is) upon, chief, first.

nty who, which.

iwty who not, which not.

EXERCISE XIII

(*a*) *Study the following sentences from a funerary stela:*[1]

rdi·n	*wi*	*ỉmy-r*	*kꜣt*	*m*	*ḫrp*	*ntt*
Placed	me	the overseer	of works[2]	as	officer in charge of that which (is)	and

iwtt	*n*	*mnḫ·i*		*n*	*ỉḳr·i*	*ḥr ib·f*
that which (is) not,[3]	because	I was efficient	and	because	I was excellent	in his heart

r	*ỉry-ꜥt* (§ 61)	*nb*	*nty*		*ḥr·f*	*iw*	*ḫrp·n·(i)*
more than	official	any	who	(was)	with him.	I undertook	

kꜣt	*m*	*rw-prw*	*nw*	*nṯrw*	*Šmꜥ(w)*	*Tꜣ-mḥw*[4]	*ink*
works	in	the temples	of	the gods	of Upper and Lower Egypt.		I was

nb	*ỉꜣmt*	*bnr*	*mrwt*
a possessor	of favour,	sweet	of love.

[1] Louvre C 172, published SHARPE, *Eg. Inscriptions*, i. 82.
[2] I.e. chief builder or architect.
[3] 'That which is and that which is not', i.e. everything.
[4] The sign for *Tꜣ-mḥw* is here identical with that for *ḥꜣ*, from which it is usually distinguished. *Šmꜥ* must not be confused with *rsw* 'south', see below in the Sign-list, under M 24–6.

(*b*) *Transliterate and translate:*

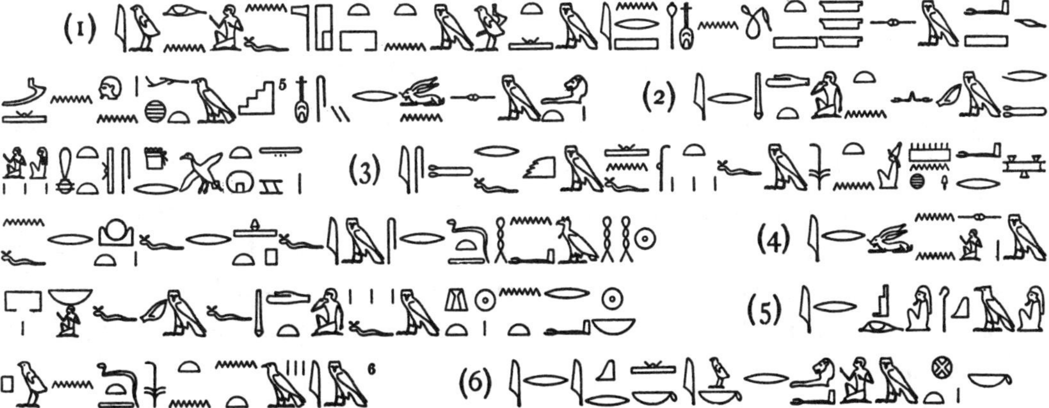

[5] The hill-slope in question is presumably that of the Lebanon.
[6] *Ntyw ỉm* 'those who are there', a common periphrasis for 'the dead'.

(*c*) *Write in hieroglyphs and transliteration*:

(1) To thy *ka*, my good lord![1] (2) As for Heliopolis, it is the principal city of Egypt. (3) There is no man void of wrong-doing. (4) This ruler, he placed me in front of his children, he made me commander of his army, because my hands prospered more than (those of) any servant of his. (5) If thou goest up to heaven, behold he is there; if thou goest down to the netherworld, behold he is there likewise. (6) He followed his lord when (*m*) he was in (lit. upon) this (foreign) land. (7) If I had heard it, I would have given him gold (*ỉw śḏm·n·f* form).

[1] Words spoken by an attendant offering wine.

LESSON XIV

PREPOSITIONS (*continued*)

N.B.—*The details of this lesson are intended for reference only. For this reason the uses with the infinitive, the* śḏmt·f *form, etc., have been enumerated, although those verb-forms belong to a later part of the book.*

§ 161. Egyptian prepositions are either *simple* or *compound*. The simple prepositions consist of one word only; those which consist of more than one word are called compound.

The simple prepositions (§§ 162–177) are enumerated in the approximate order of their importance; the compound prepositions (§§ 178–181) are classified according to their mode of formation. Only the more important and typical meanings are given. Note that before verb-forms like *śḏm·f* and *śḏm·n·f* the Egyptian prepositions must frequently be rendered by an English conjunction, exx. *m* 'when', *ỉr* 'if', see above § 155. For further remarks see Add.

THE SIMPLE PREPOSITIONS

§ 162. 𓅓 *m*, before suffixes 𓇋𓅓 *ỉm*., indicates *position* generally, the main lines of development being 'in', 'from', and the instrumental 'with'.

1. of *place*. 'In' a place, house, boat, etc. *M ỉb* 'in the heart', *m r* 'in the mouth'. Not as a rule meaning 'into' after verbs of motion, *r* having superseded *m* in this sense; but *ʿḳ m*, *tkn m*, *ẖn m* 'approach', 'draw near to'. So too *dỉ m ỉb* 'place (a plan) in the heart'; *dỉ m ḥr* 'command', 'charge', lit. 'place in the face'.

2. of *time*. 'In' this year, day, time. *M šmw* 'in the summer'; *m dwꜣw* 'to-morrow', *m sf* 'yesterday'; *m grḥ* 'in the night'; *m rnpt ꜣ* 'for three years'.[1]

[1] *Urk.* iv. 4, 14.

3. of *states.* *M ršwt, imw* 'in joy', 'grief'; *m snb* 'in health'; *m ḥst nt* 'in the favour of'.

4. of *manner.* *M mꜣꜥt* 'in truth', 'truly'; *m mꜣwt* 'anew'; *m mitt* 'likewise'.

5. of *kind,* where 'consisting of' is often the best rendering. *M inr, ḏbt* 'of stone', 'brick'; *ꜥḥꜥw m rnpwt* 'period of years'. Here may be included the *partitive* use, exx. *wꜥ im·sn* 'one of them' (§ 262, 1); *in im·f* 'bring (some) of it'.[1]

6. of *equivalence* or *predication,* see above §§ 38. 84. 96. 'As', ex. 'I sailed down *m sꜣ ḥꜣty-ꜥ* as the son of a prince';[2] rarely with suffix, ex. *it·ṯn im·i* 'your father, namely myself'.[3] Also sometimes to define a suffix subject.[3a]

7. of *instrument.* *M ḫpš·i* 'by my strong arm'; *m sḫrw·i* 'by my counsels'. *Mḥ m* 'fill with'; *ꜥpr m* 'equip with'.

7a. of *concomitance,* almost like *ḥnꜥ* 'together with', § 171.[3b]

8. of *separation.* *Pr m* 'go out from'; *ii m* 'return from'; *šꜣꜥ m* 'begin from'; *šw m* 'free from'.

9. idiomatically with verbs. *'In m* 'have recourse to';[4] *irt m* 'act according to';[5] *mḥ m* 'seize upon';[6] *mdw m* 'speak against';[7] *rḫ m* 'know (something) of (someone)';[8] *ẖnm m* 'join with'; *sḫm m* 'gain control over'; *sbṯ m* 'laugh at'.

10. with infinitive. In various uses as above, ex. *m wḥm* 'again', lit. 'in repeating'. Particularly with verbs of movement (below §§ 304, 2; 331), ex. *m prt* '(engaged) in going forth'.

11. with *sḏm·f.* (*a*) 'when', ex. *m wn·f tp tꜣ* 'when he was upon earth' (§ 157, 1). (*b*) 'as', 'as truly as' (almost equivalent to 'if'), ex. *m mrr·ṯn ꜥnḫ* 'as truly as ye love life' (§ 444, 2). (*c*) 'though' (rare): ex. [hieroglyphs] *m msdd ib·f* 'though his heart hates (it)'.[9] (*d*) curiously, with the *m* of predication, almost like a relative clause: 'a *hotp-di-nesu* formula [hieroglyphs] *m ir n·f sꜣ·f* being what (lit. as) his son made for him';[10] see below §§ 444, 3; 454, 4.

12. with *sḏmt·f* (doubtful). 'When', see below § 407, 2.

§ 163. [hieroglyph] *r*[11] originally [hieroglyph] *ir*,[12] form with suffixes [hieroglyph] *r·*, seldom [hieroglyph] *ir·*;[13] at the beginning of sentences [hieroglyph] *ir* occurs with the meanings 'as to' and 'if', see §§ 149–51. Original signification apparently 'to', 'towards'.

1. of *place.* 'To' heaven, the West, Thebes, his abode, etc., with verbs of motion. To place an amulet 'upon' the neck;[14] 'at' the feet of; make a tomb 'at' the stairway of the great god;[15] *spr r* 'arrive at' even of reaching persons,[16] though *n* is here usual with other verbs of motion.

2. of *persons.* *Wp r* 'open the mouth' *r* 'to' a person, to address him.[17] After verbs of speaking *n* is far commoner than *r*.[18]

[1] *Westc.* 11, 25. Sim. *Peas.* B 1, 93; *P. Kah.* 31, 12. 15.

[2] *BH.* i. 8, 7. Sim. Munich 4, 6.

[3] Cairo 28083 (*Sp*), 141.

[3a] *Urk.* iv. 651, 10, *kꜣ·sn* (§ 436) *m nꜣ n ḫrw.* Sim. *Th.T.S.* iv, p. 10, n. 4.

[3b] *BH.* i, 8, 12; *Hamm.* 114, 12. See *JEA.* 25, 166.

[4] See *Rec.* 39, 105.

[5] See *Unt.* 4, 107.

[6] *Urk.* iv. 660, 8.

[7] See *ÄZ.* 29, 49.

[8] *Pt.* 179; *Urk.* iv. 368, 7.

[9] *Urk.* iv. 969, 3. Sim. *P. Kah.* 36, 42; *Eb.* 70, 24.

[10] Cairo 20027. Sim. *ib.* 20048. 20117. 20225. 20235. 20372. Rather differently 'such as', *Urk.* iv. 46, 7; 198, 2.

[11] See G. Roeder, *Die Praeposition R,* Berlin 1904.

[12] So before noun, *Ḥarḥ.* 763.

[13] *Siut* I, 275; Petr. *Court.* 22, 2; *Menthuw.* 18.

[14] *M.u.K.* 9, 3.

[15] *Sebekkhu* 8.

[16] *Westc.* 7, 13; Lac. *TR.* 11, 1.

[17] *Sh. S.* 81.

[18] *R* after *in·sn*, see Lac. *TR.* 23, 15. 29, qu. § 436.

3. of *time.* *R tr n* 'at time of';[1] *r tnw rnpt* 'every year' (§ 101); *r nw,* 'at the (right) time';[2] *r hrw 4* 'for (extending over) four days'.[3]

4. of *purpose* or *futurity.* *R m* 'to what purpose?' (§ 496); *r ḥ3ty-ꜥ* 'to be prince', see §§ 84. 122. 332. Also with verbs, *ii r* 'come for', *h3b r* 'send for'.[3a]

5. of *measurement.* *10 r 10 r 10* 'ten by ten by ten (cubits)'.[4]

6. of *respect.* Speak, report, 'concerning'; *sb3 r* 'teach about' (§ 84); *r hp* 'according to law'. *'Ir* 'as to', see § 149.

7. of *comparison.* 'More than' after adjectives, adverbs, and verbs, see §§ 50. 207. Also in *ꜥš3 r smnt* 'too many to record';[5] stomach too heavy *r wnm* 'to eat'.[6] For the abbreviation characteristic of Egyptian comparisons see § 506, 4.

8. of *separation.* *Ḫrw-r* 'apart from' (§ 179); *ḥ3p r* 'conceal from'; *stn r* 'distinguish from'; *rḫ, si3 r* 'know', 'discern' one 'from another'.[7]

9. of *opposition.* *'Irt r* 'act against'.[8] Of debts, *ip r* 'charge against'.[9]

10. with infinitive. Besides other uses (e.g. above 7) very common of *futurity,* ex. *iw·f r sdm* 'he shall hear', see below § 332. Also of purpose, ex. *r sḫrt ḫftyw·f* 'in order to overthrow his enemies'.[10] Further, after particular verbs: *ib* 'wish', ex. *ib·i r nḥm Kmt* 'I wish to save Egypt';[11] *dw3,* ex. *dw3·k r sin·st* 'thou shalt rub it early in the morning', lit. 'thou shalt use the morning to rub it';[12] *snd r* 'fear to';[13] *sb3 r* 'teach to'.[14]

11. with *śdm·f.* (*a*) 'so that', ex. *sḫm·k m mw r ḥtp ib·k* 'mayst thou have access to water so that thy heart may be satisfied'.[15] (*b*) 'until', ex. 'the king loved me .... *r sdr·f m ḥtp r 3ḫt·f* until he went in peace to his horizon'.[16] (*c*) 'more than', see above § 157, 3.[17] (*d*) 'according as' ex. *r mrr·f* 'according as he desires'.[18] (*e*) 'if', in the form *ir,* see § 150.

12. with *śdm·n·f.* (*a*) 'until', see above § 156. (*b*) 'if', in the form *ir,* see § 151.

13. with *śdmt·f.* 'Until', see below § 407, 1.

§ 164. *n,* before nouns not infrequently written and consistently so in certain papyri of early Dyn. XVIII, often wrongly transcribed as by modern scholars;[19] before suffixes always ; in some rare instances written at the beginning of the sentence, see §§ 148, 5; 155 end. Indicates the person or thing *affected.*

1. of *dative.* 'To' a person, so with *rdi* 'give', *swd* 'hand over'. *Ḏd, smi n* 'speak', 'report to'. Also with other verbs: *wd n* 'command'; *sdm n* 'hearken to', 'obey' a person; *h3b, in n* 'send', 'bring to'. Hence of motion:

[1] *Sin.* R 20.
[2] *Urk.* iv. 1106, 9.
[3] *Peas.* B 1, 31.
[3a] *Griff. Stud.* 57.
[4] *Rhind* 45. Sim. *Hamm.* 191, 4.
[5] *Urk.* iv. 1211, 15.
[6] *Eb.* 36, 5.
[7] *Sin.* B 256; *P. Kah.* 6, 12; *Urk.* iv. 970, 1; *Ann.* 37, pl. 2, 15.
[8] See VOG. *Bauer,* p. 101–2.
[9] *Urk.* iv. 1120, 1. Sim. *ḥrt-ꜥ r* 'arrears against', *BH.* i. 8, 17.
[10] *BH.* i. 8, 7. Sim. *Sin.* B 17. 243; *Peas.* R 3; B 1, 33; *Sh. S.* 157, qu. § 154.
[11] *T. Carn.* 4.
[12] *Eb.* 18, 14. Sim. *ib.* 19, 21; 21, 11; 60, 15.
[13] *Urk.* iv. 974, 4.
[14] *Siut* 5, 22.
[15] *Paheri* 5. Sim. *Siut* 1, 266; *Eb.* 46, 21, qu. § 157, 4; *P. Kah.* 29, 43, qu. § 326.
[16] Brit. Mus. 614, 12. Sim. *Hamm.* 110, 4; *Th. T. S.* iii. 26, 12.
[17] Rather differently, *Peas.* B 1, 104.
[18] *Hamm.* 114, 8; *Urk.* iv. 617, 9.
[19] See GUNN, *Studies,* ch. 9.

h3 'go down', *šm* 'go', *iw* 'come' *n* 'to' a person, whereas *r* is used of movement 'to' or 'towards' a *thing.*

2. of *advantage.* *'Ir* 'to make' (something) *n* 'for' a person; absolutely, *ir n* 'act on behalf of', 'help';[1] *nfr, 3ḫ n* 'good', 'useful for'.

3. of the person *interested.* For example after imperatives, see § 337, 2.

4. of *possession*: 'belonging to'. See above § 114, 1.

5. of *cause.* *Rm n* 'weep at' a thing;[2] *n ḥḳr* 'through hunger';[3] a judge deaf *n ḏb3w* 'for the sake of rewards'.[4] So *n-mrwt, n-ʿ3t-n,* below § 181.

6. with certain verbs. *Dg n* 'look at'.[5] *Ḫsf n* 'punish', lit. 'ward off for'.

7. in certain expressions. *N šw, i3dt* 'in the sun', 'the dew'.[6]

8. of *time.* *N 3bd 2* 'within two months';[7] *n wnwt* 'in an hour';[8] *n ḏt* 'for ever'.[9]

9. with *sḏm·f.* 'Because'; ex. above §§ 157, 4 end.

10. with non-verbal clause introduced by an independent pronoun, 'because', 'for'. See above § 154.

OBS. For *n* after adjectives, see above § 141, and as component of the *sḏm·n·f* form, see § 411, 2.

§ 165. *ḥr,* more rarely alone,[10] with suffixes *ḥr·* or occasionally ,[11] signified originally 'upon'.

1. of *place.* Strictly 'upon': the ground, a road, a chariot, a bed. *Ḥr mw ḥr t3* 'on water and on land'. I followed *ḥr rdwy·i* 'on my feet', i.e. 'on foot'. But often much more indefinitely: *ḥr rs, mḥt* 'to the south', 'north'; *ḥr ḫt ḳ3* 'up a high tree'; *ḥr sb3* 'at (or 'through'?) the gate'; *ḥr Kmt* 'in Egypt'.[12] So with various verbs: *sn, sw3 ḥr* 'pass by'; *ḥms ḥr dmi* 'besiege a town', lit. 'sit down at'.[13] Also figuratively: *ḥr ib·k* 'in thy heart'.[14]

2. of *provenience.* *Nbw ḥr ḫ3st* 'gold from the desert-land'. Honey *ḥr pr-ḥḏ* 'from the Treasury'.[14a] *'Ii ḥr* 'come from'.[15]

3. of *privation.* Despoil (*ʿwn*) the poor man 'of' (*ḥr*) his property;[16] *wpw-ḥr* 'excepted from' (§ 179).

4. of *time* (rare). *Ḥr 3bd 2* 'in two months'.[17] He makes a delay *ḥr hrw 3* 'for three days'.[18]

5. of *occasion.* *Pr ḥr ḫrw* 'come forth at the voice'.

6. *distributively,* Latin *per.* They give a loaf *ḥr wʿ im nb* 'each of them'.[19]

7. of *cause* (very common). *Ḥtp, hr ḥr* 'pleased', 'content on account of' something. *'Ib ḏw ḥr* 'heart sad concerning', *rs tp ḥr* 'vigilant concerning', *mhy ḥr* 'neglectful about' something. *Ḥs ḥr* 'praise for' something. *H3b, ii ḥr* 'send (a letter)', 'come concerning' something. Also of barter, *rdi* 'give'

[1] VOG. *Bauer,* p. 101.
[2] *Peas.* B 1, 25; NAV. 64, 16.
[3] *Sin.* B 151; *Urk.* iv. 665, 11.
[4] *Urk.* iv. 118, 16.
[5] *Sin.* B 279; *Peas.* B 2, 106.
[6] See *ÄZ.* 31, 51.
[7] *Sh. S.* 168.
[8] *Urk.* iv. 751, 16; *Arm.* 103, 7.
[9] *BH.* i. 25, 6.
[10] *Siut* 1, 273 foll. *passim.*
[11] *Sin.* B 95. 173. 193; *Leb.* 121. Once only, *iḥr·*, see p. 209, n. 6.
[12] *Sin.* B 26.
[13] *Urk.* iv. 3.
[14] *Peas.* B 1, 104.
[14a] MAR. *Karn.* 33.
[15] *Semnah Disp.* 2, 8; 4, 8; *Urk.* iv. 767, 3.
[16] *Peas.* B 1, 232.
[17] *Sh. S.* 174.
[18] *Urk.* iv. 1110, 16.
[19] *Siut* 1, 290. 294. Sim. *P. Kah.* 12, 9.

this *ḥr* 'for' that.[1] Again *ꜥḥꜣ ḥr* 'fight on behalf of';[2] *ḫsf ḥr* 'protect', lit. 'ward off on account of'.[3] Note further *sbỉ ḥr* 'rebel against' the king.

8. of *addition*. *Gs·f ḥr·f* 'its half is (added) to it'.[4] So too for purposes of co-ordination, ex. *ḏꜥ ḥr ḥyt* 'wind upon (i.e. and) rain'; see above § 91, 1. *Šbn ḥr* 'mixed with'. *Ps, wrḥ, wt ḥr* 'cook', 'anoint', 'bandage with' something.

9. of *marks*. *Ḥr rn* 'having upon it the name';[5] *ḥr ḫtm* 'having upon it the seal'.[6] A very curious use, cf. Engl. 'all over snow', 'cow in calf'.

10. with infinitive, properly 'on' or 'while' of a *concomitant* act, ex. *ỉỉ·n·ỉ ḥr šms·f* 'I returned (on) accompanying him'.[7] This use leads to extensive developments, see below § 319. Also referring to past events, probably as an extension of use 2 above, ex. His Majesty returned *ḥr sḫrt Rṯnw* 'from (or 'after') overthrowing (or 'having overthrown') Retjnu'.[8]

11. with *śḏm·f*, 'because', ex. *ḥr mꜣꜣ·f wỉ* 'because he sees me'.[9]

§ **166**. *ẖr*, less often, with suffixes *ẖr·*, 'under'.

1. 'under' the sky, the feet, etc. Rarely, however, simply 'at'.[9a]

2. 'under', 'carrying' a load. *H̱r ỉnw, ꜣwt-ꜥ* 'bringing tribute', 'presents'; the crocodile departed *ẖr·f* 'carrying him off';[10] fields *ẖr ỉt* 'under corn'.[11] With verbs *ꜣṯp, mḥ ẖr* 'loaded', 'filled with'.

3. metaphorically, in various uses. Loaded *ẖr mꜣrw* 'with sorrows'; lands *ẖr ršwt* 'in joy'. *H̱r ḏbꜥwt·ỉ* 'under my seal'; *ẖr st-ḥr·f* 'under his charge'. *H̱r sḫ*,[12] *sḫr* 'under (i.e. influenced by) the counsel', 'will' of someone. This state (*sšm*) which I was 'in', *ẖr·f*, lit. 'under it'.[13] Also of *cause*: tired *ẖr šmt ꜣwt* 'through long journeying'.[14]

§ **167**. *ḫr*, 'with' or 'near' someone. Restricted to a limited set of uses.

1. 'Under' a king. *Ḫr ḥm n* '(Year....) under the Majesty of', very frequent. So too *ḥswt nt ḫr nsw* 'favours (of) under the king' (§ 158, 1); *ỉmꜣḫy ḫr* 'honoured with' a god, etc.

2. 'To' a person. *Ḏd ḫr* 'speak to' a person, his children, etc. *Ḫprt ḫr·ỉ* 'what happened to me'.[15] Gods give health, etc. *ḫr·ỉ* 'to me'.

3. 'By' of the agent (rare). See above § 39, end.

OBS. For the related particle *ḫr* see § 239; and for the perhaps different *ḫr* as component of the *śḏm·ḫr·f* form see below § 427.

§ **168**. *ỉn*, less frequently, has as sole function to express the agent ('by' someone) after verbs, chiefly the infinitive (§ 300) and the various passive forms (§ 39, end). It cannot be clearly distinguished from the particle *ỉn* (§ 227), in connection with which it will be dealt with further. Very much more doubtful

1 *Siut* I, 274. 292. 296; *Rhind* 62.
2 Berl. *ÄI.* i. p. 258, 21.
3 *Leb.* 24.
4 *Rhind* 25. Sim. *ib.* 24. 26.
5 *Urk.* iv. 766, 2. But also 'mention *ḥr rn·f* 'by its name', *Arm.* 103, 3.
6 *Westc.* 11, 24.
7 *BH.* i. 8, 10, qu. § 300.
8 *Urk.* iv. 740. Sim. *ib.* 745, 12; *Siut* I, 308; *Ann.* 37, pl. 2, 15.
9 *Sin.* B 117. Sim. *Peas.* B 1, 11–2; *Urk.* iv. 3, 3; 654, 5; *Eb.* 37, 10. 17.
9a In *ẖr tp·k* 'at thy head', *ẖr rdwy·k* 'at (or 'by') thy feet', *JEA.* 27, 144.
10 *Westc.* 4, 7. Sim. *Urk.* iv. 4, 7.
11 *Peas.* R 47, qu. p. 79, top.
12 *Sin.* B 113. 182.
13 *Sin.* B 174, qu. § 44, 2.
14 *Eb.* 102, 13. Sim. *ib.* 102, 5.
15 *ÄZ.* 47, Pl. 1 (p. 88), 2.

is the question whether it is at all connected with the preposition *n*, of which, as we have seen (§ 164), the rare initial form is *in*.

OBS. For the possibly different *in* which serves to form the *śḏm·in·f* form, see § 427.

§ 169. *ḫft*, so written apparently for reasons of symmetry in place of the much rarer, means properly 'face to face with'.

1. 'in front of'. Him who is *ḫft·k* 'opposite thee', i.e. with whom thou art talking.[1] *Ḏd ḫft* 'speak with', 'say to', not uncommon.[2] Especially also *ḫft-ḥr* 'before the face of' (§ 178).

2. 'in accordance with'. Act *ḫft sš pn* 'according to this writing';[3] *ḫft ḫꜣy* 'according to measure';[4] respect him *ḫft ḫprt n·f* 'in proportion to what has accrued to him'.[5]

3. 'as well as' (very rare). Male and female slaves *ḫft ẖrdw·sn* 'as well as their children'.[6]

4. of *time*. Year 43 .... *ḫft ḥꜣt-sp 25* 'corresponding to year 25' in the Oryx nome.[7]

5. with infinitive, 'at the time of', 'when'. Words to be recited *ḫft wꜣḥ pẖrt* 'when applying remedies'.[8]

6. with *śḏm·f*. (*a*) 'when' (common). Exx. *ḫft ḫss·f* 'when he is humble';[9] *ḫft wn·f mr* 'when he was ill'.[10] (*b*) 'according as', 'in proportion as' (seldom), exx. not high-tempered *ḫft wsr·(i)* 'in proportion as I was powerful';[11] I built it *ḫft mrr·f* 'according as he desired'.[12]

7. with *śḏm·n·f*. 'According as'; an ex. above § 156.

8. with *śḏmt·f* (doubtful). 'When'; see below § 407, 2.

§ 170. *mi*,[12a] sometimes, hardly ever with suffixes,[12b] expresses *likeness*.

1. of *resemblance*. 'Like' a dream, the will of god, etc.; *mi m* 'like what?', 'how?' (§ 496). So often in similes, ex. *iw·i mi s itw m ꜥḫḫw* 'I was like a man caught in the dusk'.[13] For the abbreviation sometimes found in comparisons, see below § 506, 4.

2. of *conformity*. He went down *mi nt-ꜥ·f* 'according to his habit';[14] act *mi wḏt* 'according to commands'; *mi ntt r hp* 'according to what is lawful'.[15]

3. 'as well as' (seldom). Exx. *hy n·k mi nbt-r-ḏr* 'hail to thee as well as (to) the lady of the universe';[16] *hrw mi grḥ* 'day as well as night'.[17]

4. with infinitive in the meaning 'like'.[18]

5. with *śḏm·f*. (*a*) 'as when', ex. his rays illuminate the two lands

[1] *Pt.* 79. Sim. *Urk.* iv. 26, 15.
[2] *Sin.* R 67; B 267; *Urk.* iv. 26, 16; 649, 14.
[3] *Meir* ii. 6.
[4] *Pt.* 228.
[5] *Pt.* 180.
[6] *Urk.* iv. 665.
[7] *BH.* i. 8, 3.
[8] *Eb.* 1, 10. Sim. *ib.* 97, 4; *Urk.* iv. 734, 15; 742, 4; 757, 15.
[9] *Pt.* 76. Sim. *Leb.* 147; *Siut* 1, 297; *Urk.* iv. 742, 2.
[10] *P. Kah.* 13, 34.
[11] Brit. Mus. 614, 9; cf. *Peas.* B 1, 214.
[12] *Rifeh* 7, 31. Sim. *Urk.* iv. 116, 17.
[12a] *Mr* in early O.K., see Sign-list, W 19.
[12b] Examples, *Wb.* ii. 36, 9.
[13] *Sin.* B 254. Sim. *ib.* 118.
[14] *Westc.* 3, 2. 11.
[15] *Urk.* iv. 1088.
[16] *Sin.* B 274. Sim. *Urk.* iv. 368, 1.
[17] MAR. *Abyd.* ii. 29, 22. Sim. *ib.* 13.
[18] Exx. *Leb.* 131. 133. 138; *Eb.* 53, 22; 108, 2.

[hieroglyphs] *mi wbn Rꜥ* 'as when Rēꜥ shines'.[1] (*b*) 'according as', ex. [hieroglyphs] *mi dd·k* 'according as thou sayest';[2] especially in the phrase [hieroglyphs] *mi mrr bꜣk im* 'according as this thy humble servant desires'.[3]

6. with *sdm·n·f* (rare). See above, § 156.

7. with the passive *sdm·f*. See below, § 423, 3.

8. with the *sdmt·f* form (doubtful). See below, § 407, 2.

9. with non-verbal clause introduced by an independent pronoun. See above, § 154.

§ 171. [hieroglyphs] *ḥnꜥ* 'together with', in Dyn. XVIII rarely written [hieroglyphs] *ḥn*.[4]

1. 'together with' someone, less commonly something. So too with verbs, *mdw ḥnꜥ* 'talk with', *ꜥḥꜣ ḥnꜥ* 'fight with'. Never 'with' of instrument, which is *m*.

2. of *co-ordination*, where English has 'and'; see above § 91, 1.

3. with infinitive. Sometimes found curiously to continue an injunction, where English uses a finite form, ex. [hieroglyphs] . . . . . . [hieroglyphs] *ir·ḫr·k* . . . . *ḥnꜥ rdit n·f pḫrt* 'thou shalt make . . . . . and shalt give (lit. with giving) to him remedies'.[5] So frequently in letters, contracts, etc., where however *ḥnꜥ* may co-ordinate an infinitive with a preceding infinitive;[6] for a further development of this construction see § 300, Obs. Also continuing construction with *ḥr* + inf., ex. *iw·f ḥr wnm* . . . . *ḥnꜥ swri* 'he eats . . . . and drinks', lit. 'with drinking'.[7]

4. with *sdm·f* (rare), ex. on that day on which the enemies . . . . were destroyed [hieroglyphs] *ḥnꜥ sḥkꜣ·tw sꜣ·f Ḥr* 'and (lit. with) his son Horus was caused to rule'.[8]

§ 172. [hieroglyphs] *ḥꜣ* 'behind', derived from a noun *ḥꜣ* 'back of head'.

1. 'behind' a person.[9] *Nw ḥꜣ* 'look behind' oneself;[10] *ꜥn ḥꜣ* 'turn behind' oneself, i.e. turn back;[11] *iwt ḥꜣ* 'come behind', 'take unawares', of evils;[12] *ḥꜣ tꜣ* 'behind bread', i.e. 'at meals'.[13]

2. 'around'. *Pḫr ḥꜣ inb* 'move around a wall'.[14] So too frequently *sꜣ ḥꜣ* 'a protection around' a person, where however there may be a sense of enveloping from behind, as with wings, etc.

§ 173. [hieroglyphs] *tp*, an old word for 'head', is used as a preposition meaning 'upon' in certain phrases; [hieroglyphs] *tpw·k* 'upon thee'[15] is a quite exceptional writing with the suffix. Most commonly *tp tꜣ* 'upon earth', i.e. living. Also *wršyw tp inb* 'watchers upon the wall';[16] the child came forth *tp ꜥwy·sy* 'upon her hands', i.e. upon the hands of the midwife;[17] and others.[18]

§ 174. [hieroglyphs] *ḫnt*, rarely written [hieroglyphs], once [hieroglyphs],[19] seems akin to a word for 'face' and signifies properly 'in front'.

1. 'in front of', mainly in a tag applied to the Pharaoh [hieroglyphs] *ḫnt kꜣw ꜥnḫw nb* 'in front of the souls of all living'.[20]

1 *Urk.* iv. 806. Sim. *ib.* 687, 13; *Sin.* B 225; *Peas.* B 1, 242. 244; *Leb.* 137. 141.
2 *Leb.* 150. Sim. *Urk.* iv. 753, 7. 9.
3 *P. Kah.* 28, 2; 35, 9; 36, 52.
4 *Urk.* iv. 839, 16; 842, 4. 15; 862, 14.
5 *Eb.* 40, 8. Sim. *Peas.* R 128.
6 Exx. *P. Kah.* 28, 43; 29, 22; 31, 1; 35, 15; *Siut* 1, 293. 294. 307.
7 *Westc.* 7, 3.
8 *Urk.* v. 12. Sim. *Siut* 1, 317, qu. § 157, 1; Lac. *TR.* 5, 6.
9 *Westc.* 10, 8. 15. 22.
10 *Urk.* iv. 697.
11 *Hamm.* 110, 3.
12 *Urk.* 1077, 9; cf. *Sin.* B 59.
13 *Pt.* 135.
14 See *PSBA.* 25, 334.
15 Erm. *Hymn.* 12, 3. 4; 14, 1.
16 *Sin.* R 45.
17 *Westc.* 10, 10. 17. 24.
18 *Urk.* iv. 160, 12.
19 *BH.* i. 25, 101–2.
20 Exx. *D. el B.* 11. 18. 48.

2. 'among', with the notion of 'foremost among'.[1] So with *ṯn*,[2] *sṯn* 'distinguish', *stp* 'choose'[3] 'among' a number. *Rdi* 'give' something 'out of' one's possessions.[4] Also as a mathematical term.[5]

3. in certain expressions. *Pr ḫnt* 'issue from' of a child as engendered by father;[6] *rdi ib·(f) ḫnt* 'pay attention to', lit. 'place the heart in front of'.[7]

§ 175. *ḫt* means 'through', 'pervading'. The fear of Pharaoh is *ḫt ḫ3swt* 'throughout the foreign lands';[8] the influence of the god is *ḫt ꜥwt* 'pervading the members' of his spouse.[9]

§ 176. *ḏr*, derived from a stem meaning 'end', signifies 'since'.

1. mainly of *time*. *Ḏr rk* 'since the time of'; *ḏr nṯr* 'since (the time of) the god'.[10]

2. of *cause*. Scarcely except in the phrase *ḏr-ntt* 'since', 'because' (§ 223).

3. with *śḏm·f*. 'Since' of time, exx. *ḏr ms·tw·f* 'since he was born';[11] *ḏr wn ꜥ3mw m-ḳ3b-n T3-mḥw Ḥt-wꜥrt* 'since the Asiatics were in Avaris of Lower Egypt'.[12]

4. with *śḏmt·f*. 'Since', but also strangely 'before', 'until', § 407, 1.

§ 177. *imytw*,[13] old *imywti*,[14] varr. ,[15] ,[16] means 'between', and possibly had its origin in the fem. dual of the adjective *imy* 'being in' (§ 79). In Dyn. XVIII it is sometimes preceded by the preposition *r*, for which rare earlier instances substitute *m*; exx. ,[17] ,[18] *r-imytw*, *m-imywti*,[19] *m-imytw*.[20]

1. 'between' two things, ex. *imytw b3ty* 'between two bushes'.[21] Also followed by *r*, ex. *imytw ḫ3st tn r Nhrn* 'between this country and Nahrin'.[21a]

2. 'in the midst of', ex. *r-imytw srw* 'in the midst of the nobles';[22] even with a sing., *imytw ḏ3ḏ3·f* 'in the midst of its head'.[23]

This preposition occurs also with the ending *·ny*, which may be a very rare suffix-pronoun, see § 34, Obs. 3.[23a] Exx. *imytw·ny* 'between them', i.e. the obelisks;[24] *imytw·ny ḫpdw·k* 'between thy buttocks', lit. 'between them, thy buttocks'.[25] The construction may also be *r-imytw·ny* . . . . *r* . . . . 'between . . . . . and . . . . .'[26]

[1] Exx. *Siut* I, 272; *Sinai* 181; *Urk.* iv. 298, 9.
[2] *BH.* i. 25, 10. 101.
[3] *Urk.* iv. 888, 7.
[4] *Siut* I, 276.
[5] *PSBA.* 16, 204; *Siut* I, 286.
[6] *Bersh.* i. 33; *Urk.* iv. 161. 228; cf. *Pt.* 630.
[7] *P. Kah.* 29, 37; 35, 11. 15; Louvre C 55; *Urk.* iv. 1093, 2.
[8] *Sin.* B 44. Sim. *Siut* I, 268; *Adm.* 3, 1. 3; 7, 9; *Urk.* iv. 138, 1.
[9] *Urk.* iv. 221.
[10] *Urk.* iv. 1092, 3. Sim. *ib.* 86, 4; Leyd. V 4, 13.
[11] *Sin.* R 93 = B 69. Sim. *Urk.* iv. 95, 16, qu. § 155; 162, 6; 994, 3.
[12] *Urk.* iv. 390, 7. Sim. *ib.* 157, 7, qu. § 157, 2.
[13] *Eb.* 30, 1.
[14] *ÄZ.* 57, 7*.
[15] *Sin.* B 5. 249.
[16] *Sin.* R 28; *Urk.* iv. 894, 2.
[17] *Urk.* iv. 131. 365.
[18] *Urk.* iv. 287, 7.
[19] *ÄZ.* 57, 7*.
[20] *Eb.* 108, 14.
[21] *Sin.* R 28. Sim. *Urk.* iv. 365, 4; 894, 2.
[21a] *ÄZ.* 69, 29, 12.
[22] *Urk.* iv. 131, 8. Sim. *ib.* 12; *Sin.* B 249.
[23] *Eb.* 30, 1.
[23a] Allen prefers to regard this *ny* as the adverb of § 205, 1, see *AJSL* 44, 123.
[24] *Urk.* iv. 362, 15.
[25] *P. Kah.* 3, 35. Sim. *Eb.* 108, 14.
[26] *Urk.* v. 68, 5. Sim. *m-imywti·n*, *ÄZ.* 57, 7*.

COMPOUND PREPOSITIONS

§ 178. For definition see § 161. The present list lays no claim to completeness.

A. **Prepositions formed by the addition of a noun to one of the simple prepositions.**—In a few cases the genitival adjective *n(y)* is added when the governed word is a noun, but is absent when a suffix follows.

n ib (n) 'for the sake (lit. 'heart') of'.[27] With *śḏm·f*, 'in order that' (rare).[28]

[27] With noun, *L. to D.*, Berlin bowl; with suffix, *BH.* ii. 7; *Urk.* iv. 1164, 11; Ledr. 22, 5.
[28] *Eb.* 91, 16.

m-ỉsw 'in return for', 'as payment for',[1] varr. ,[2] [3]

r-ỉsw, with the same meaning as *m-ỉsw*.[4]

m-ꜥ, lit. 'in the hand of' is common in various meanings.

1. 'together with' a person (like *ḥnꜥ*). X came *m-ꜥ Y* 'with Y';[5] thy heart is *m-ꜥ·k* 'with thee'.[6] *Ḫtm m-ꜥ* 'contract with' someone.[7]

2. 'in the possession, charge of': my portion of everything being *m-ꜥ·ỉ* 'in my hand'.[8]

3. 'from': a letter 'from' a person;[9] bring something 'from' someone;[10] *nḥm, nḏ m-ꜥ* 'rescue', 'save from';[11] *nḏnḏ m-ꜥ* 'inquire from'.[12]

4. 'through', 'because of' someone or something: *ḫpr m-ꜥ* 'happen through' i.e. 'be done by';[13] *m-ꜥ sḫrw tꜣ* 'because of the state of the land'.[14] Especially also in the phrase *m-ꜥ ntt* 'seeing that' (below § 223).

r-ꜥ 'beside', 'near', var. *r-r-ꜥ*,[15] is uncommon. His soul shall live *r-ꜥ nb-r-ḏr* 'beside the lord of the universe'.[16]

ḫr-ꜥ (n) 'under the hand of', 'in the charge of'.[17]

m-ꜥb 'in the company of', 'together with'.[18]

r-ꜥḳꜣ 'on an equality with',[19] 'at the level of'.[20]

m-bꜣḥ,[21] usually written or , lit. 'in the foreskin (?) of', a very common preposition for 'in the presence of', mainly in the presence of respected personages. An extended form is *m-bꜣḥ-ꜥ*.[22]

m-m 'among' people, very common;[23] varr. ,[24] [25] and even .[26] Perhaps a simple reduplication of *m* (§ 162), cf. *ḫtḫt* below, p. 134.

tp-mꜣꜥ (n) 'accompanying', 'escorting', lit. 'on the temple of'.[27]

r-mꜣw (n) 'in the sight of',[28] var. .[29]

r-rḫt 'to the knowledge of',[30] varr. ,[31] ;[32] the literal sense may be 'so that . . . . may know', see p. 304, n. 1.

m-ḥꜣw 1. 'in the neighbourhood of' a person or place;[33] 2. 'at the time of' someone.[34]

m-ḥꜣt 'in front of': he placed me *m-ḥꜣt ẖrdw·f* 'in front of his children';[35] to shrink 'at the prospect of' work.[36]

r-ḥꜣt 'in front of', 'before', temporally;[37] but also locally 'in front of' a person.[38]

ḫr-ḥꜣt 'before': *bḥꜣ ḫr-ḥꜣt* 'flee before';[39] 'in front of' i.e. superior in rank to;[40] 'in front of' in a procession.[41] Also temporally 'before'.[42]

1 *Siut* I, 270; *D. el B.* 16. 24.
2 *P. Kah.* 13, 25.
3 *Siut* I, 294, cf. 306.
4 *ÄZ.* 58, 16*.
5 *Th. T. S.* ii. 36, 17; 37, 31. 34.
6 *Sh. S.* 16; *Urk.* iv. 117, 13.
7 *Siut* I, 295.
8 *Urk.* iv. 123, 10. Sim. *Siut* I, 299; Brit. Mus. 614, 5; *Sin.* B 240. 269.
9 *P. Kah.* 28, 12; 29, 26. 30.
10 Brit. Mus. 614, 6.
11 *Sin.* B 203. Sim. *Eb.* 1, 8. 14; *Pt.* 299.
12 R. *IH.* 26, 12.
13 *Sh. S.* 22; *Leb.* 10; *Eb.* 20, 23; 69, 17.
14 *Adm.* 2, 4. Sim. *ib.* 3, 4; *Bersh.* i. 14, 2; with inf. *Pt.* 644.
15 *Menthuw.* 13.
16 *Urk.* iv. 62, 6. Sim. *ib.* 1104, 6. 15.
17 *Siut* I, 272. 277. 304.
18 *Bersh.* i. 14, 5; BUDGE, p. 292, 16; *Urk.* iv. 877, 15; 931, 8; 1094, 10.
19 *Peas.* R 122; cf. *Urk.* iv. 1104, 12.
20 L. *D.* iii. 228 *bis*.
21 *Sin.* B 253. 263.
22 Cairo 20542, *a* 7; *P. Pet.* 1116 B, 8; *Urk.* iv. 776, 14.
23 Brit. Mus. 614, 7; Cairo 20011, 4.
24 *Urk.* iv. 116, 2.
25 *Urk.* iv. 66, 16.
26 *Sin.* B 280. Cf. *Urk.* iv. 1024, 12.
27 See *JEA.* 27, 146.
28 CART.-NEWB. *Th. IV*, Pl. 11; Cairo 34019, 14.
29 *Urk.* iv. 367, 17.
30 CART.-NEWB. *Th. IV*, Pl. 11.
31 *Urk.* iv. 835, 12.
32 Cairo 34019, 14.
33 *Sin.* R 32. 80.
34 *Westc.* 6, 24; *Rhind*, title.
35 *Sin.* B 108. Sim. *Siut* I, 151; Cairo 20531, *d*.
36 *Sinai* 90, 16.
37 *Urk.* iv. 1104, 14.
38 Cairo 20318; *Urk.* iv. 808, 16.
39 *Sin.* R 87; *Urk.* iv. 711, 2.
40 *Sin.* B 48; *BH.* i. 25, 103–4; *Urk.* iv. 1092, 8.
41 *Sin.* B 194; *Urk.* iv. 1095, 5.
42 *Urk.* iv. 766, 3.

m-ḥ3w 'in excess of': offerings 'in excess of' what existed before.[1] So also *m-ḥ3w-ḥr*: (*a*) 'in addition to';[2] (*b*) 'over and above' i.e. 'except', less common.[3]

ḫft-ḥr, lit. 'before the face of'. 'In front of' someone, opposed to *ḥ3* 'behind';[4] 'before' someone, i.e. before someone's eyes.[5] *Ḫft-ḥr-n* 'in presence of' the entire land.[6]

m-ḥr(y)-ib 'in the midst of', varr. [7] (common), ;[7a] 'in the midst of' a number of people.[8]

ḥr-ḫw, lit. 'in exclusion of': (1) in the phrase *wꜥ ḥr-ḫw·f*, which appears to mean 'exclusively unique';[9] (2) in phrases like *nn wn ḥr-ḫw·f* 'there is none beside him';[10] (3) also elsewhere as 'beside' or 'except', ex. none survived *ḥr-ḫw·i* 'except me'.[11]

r-ḫft 'in front of' (rare).[12] With the same sense .[12a]

m-ḫmt 'in the absence of', 'without'; *m-ḫmt·f* 'without him';[13] the palace is *m-ḫmt b3kw·f* 'without its tribute'.[14]

m-ḫnt lit. 'in the face of' (rare); 'within' the palace;[15] also 'out of', ex. gold brought *m-ḫnt T3-sty* 'out of Nubia'.[16]

m-ḫsfw 'at the approach of', 'in meeting' someone,[17] var. .

r-ḫt 'under the authority of', lit. 'at the staff of',[18] less correctly written .[19]

m-ḫt 'after', 'accompanying', var. (very common).

1. of *place*: the princes *nty m-ḫt·f* 'who were with (or 'accompanying') him';[20] *m-ḫt swtwt·f* 'accompanying his promenades' in his chariot.[21]

2. of *time* (frequent); 'after' death, old age, etc.; *m-ḫt nn* 'after this'.

3. with infinitive, always 'after'.[22]

4. with *sḏm·f*. Really always 'after', but often equally well translated as 'when'. Exx. His Majesty raged *m-ḫt sḏm·f st* 'when he heard it';[23] *ḫr m-ḫt spr·f r Ḏdì* 'now when he approached Djedi', the palanquin was set down.[24] So too when the main verb refers to the future, exx. the priest shall give offerings *m-ḫt pr·f* 'after he has gone forth' having performed ceremonies in the temples;[25] *ìr m-ḫt ḥtp ḥm n nṯr pn* 'now after the Majesty of this god is satisfied' with his offerings, one shall cause to go forth, etc.[26] Note that when the clause with *m-ḫt* precedes the main clause, the preposition is usually, though not universally,[27] introduced by *ìr* (§ 149) or by the particle *ḫr* (§ 239); *ḫr* is used when the main verb is past, and *ìr* when the main verb is future.[27a]

[1] *D. el B. (XI)* i. 24; *Urk.* iv. 188, 2. Sim. *P. Kah.* 17, 14.
[2] *Urk.* iv. 843, 11.
[3] *Urk.* iv. 1108, 14.
[4] *Westc.* 10, 7. 14. 22. Sim. *Bersh.* i. 18, 3.
[5] *Siut* 1, 272; *P. Pet.* 1116B, 21; *Sh. S.* 176; *Peas.* B 1, 280.
[6] *Urk.* iv. 2, 2.
[7] *Sin.* B 200; *Sh. S.* 101. 131; *Pr.* 2, 2.
[7a] *Renni* 1, 1.
[8] *Bersh.* i. 15; ii. 13, 16; *Urk.* iv. 18, 10.
[9] *Urk.* iv. 942. Cf. *Siut* i. 214–15.
[10] *BH.* i. 26, 155. See too *JEA.* iii. 241–3.
[11] *Sh. S.* 108. Sim. *Ikhern.* 9.
[12] *Urk.* iv. 893, 17.
[12a] *ÄZ.* 61, 92.
[13] *Sin.* R 68. Sim. *Mill.* 2, 4; *Urk.* iv. 390, 9.
[14] *Adm.* 10, 4.
[15] *Urk.* iv. 603, 8. Sim. *ib.* 357, 13.
[16] *Ikhern.* 4.
[17] LAC. *TR.* 43, 1; BUDGE, p. 12, 2; 46, 12; 137, 12.
[18] *Urk.* iv. 54, 10; 55, 15; 453, 9; 1044, 13.
[19] *Urk.* iv. 1021, 4.
[20] *T. Carn.* 3. Sim. *Sin.* R 23; B 244; *Kopt.* 12, 3, 2.
[21] *Urk.* iv. 3, 6.
[22] *Siut* 1, 278; *Eb.* 41, 1. 9; 59, 11; 63, 14; *Urk.* iv. 916, 2.
[23] *Urk.* iv. 139, 10. Sim. *Pr.* 2, 3.
[24] *Westc.* 7, 13. Sim. *ib.* 8, 22.
[25] *Siut* 1, 308. Sim. *ib.* 298; *P. Kah.* 3, 32; *Westc.* 3, 2; 11, 26; *Eb.* 56, 21; 76, 13; 97, 3.
[26] *Urk.* iv. 768. Sim. *P. Kah.* 22, 8; 29, 18; *Eb.* 87, 9; 88, 14.
[27] *P. Kah.* 3, 32; *Urk.* iv. 836, 6; *Ann.* 37, pl. 2, 26.
[27a] Exception, *Ann.* 42, 19, 25.

5. with *śḏm·n·f*, for examples see above § 156. The past meaning of the verb following *m-ḫt* is here doubtless strongly emphasized. Again in this case *ḥr m-ḫt* is used when the main verb is past,[1] and *ỉr m-ḫt* when it is future.[2]

6. with the passive *śḏm·f* form (rare). 'After'; see below § 423, 3.

7. with *śḏmt·f* (doubtful). 'After'; see below § 407, 2.

8. with noun + old perfective; see below § 327.

ḫt-ḫt 'through',[3] like the simple preposition *ḫt* (§ 175). Rare.

m-ẖnw (*n*),[4] lit. 'in the interior of', common; sometimes strangely written ,[5] later and less frequently .[6]

1. 'within' a place: the city, island, boat, temple, body.

1a. 'in' before abstracts, ex. *m-ẖnw hrt* 'in contentment'.[6a]

2. 'out of': go out 'from' a room;[7] bring tribute 'out of' this island.[8]

m-sꜣ, lit. 'in the back of' (common). Almost always *spatially* 'after', 'following after'. Come, go, be 'after' someone, i. e. follow him or accompany him.[9] *Sḥs m-sꜣ* 'run after' i. e. persecute.[10] 'After' in the sense of looking after, being in charge of.[11] Metaphorically *pẖr m-sꜣ* 'go round after', i. e. 'seek for';[12] *rdỉ ỉb m-sꜣ* 'be anxious about', lit. 'give the heart after'.[13]

r-sꜣ, lit. 'towards the back of' (common). Almost always *temporally*.

1. 'after' supper, a storm, illness.[14] *R-sꜣ nn* 'after this'.[15]

2. with infinitive 'after' doing something.[16]

3. with *śḏm·f* 'after': exx. *r-sꜣ sꜣḥ·ỉ tꜣ* 'after I have reached land';[16] *r-sꜣ swỉ·f st* 'after he has drunk it'.[17]

ḥr-sꜣ, lit. 'on the back of'; except in one or two special meanings less common than *m-sꜣ* and *r-sꜣ*.

1. of *place*, 'upon' the earth, the desert.[18] *Šm ḥr-sꜣ·f* 'walk behind him'.[19]

2. 'outside' a fortress or wall.[20]

3. of *time*: one is heard *ḥr-sꜣ sn-nw·f* 'after the other';[21] men who shall come *ḥr-sꜣ nn* 'after this'.[22]

m-sꜣḥt, var. , 'in the neighbourhood of'.[23]

r-swnt 'as the price of', 'in exchange for'.[24]

m-ḳꜣb (*n*)[25] 'in the midst of', lit. 'in the folds of' (not uncommon): people,[26] pyramids,[27] a place.[28]

n-gꜣw 'through lack of',[29] once written at the beginning of a clause *ỉn-gꜣw* (§ 148, 5).

r-gs 'at the side of', 'beside' (common). For 'beside' people in various senses: 'in the presence of' witnesses;[30] 'in the company of' someone;[31] practically equivalent to 'except' in *ky r-gs·f* 'another beside him'.[32]

[1] *P. Kah.* 4, 3; Cairo 20541, *a* 10; *Urk.* iv. 3, 2; 5, 4.
[2] *P. Kah.* 3, 34; *Eb.* 91, 16–7; 96, 21.
[3] Brit. Mus. 614, 5. 6; Cairo 20512, *b* 4.
[4] With *n* before noun, *Sh. S.* 43. 175. Without *n*, *Sin.* B 50. 283.
[5] See *ÄZ.* 59, 61.
[6] See *ÄZ.* 25, 33–4.
[6a] *Pt.* 117. Sim. LAC. *TR.* 17, 31; *ÄZ.* 57, 107.
[7] *Sin.* B 283.
[8] *Sh. S.* 175.
[9] *Siut* 1, 278. 317; *Sin.* B 245; *Urk.* iv. 651, 17; 652, 10.
[10] *Sin.* B 227.
[11] *Sin.* B 239. 242.
[12] *Urk.* iv. 971, 11.
[13] *P. Kah.* 27, 9.
[14] *Mill.* 1, 11; *Sin.* B 7; *Peas.* B 1, 244; *Leb.* 131.
[15] *Sin.* R 31; *Eb.* 60, 15.
[16] *Sh. S.* 180.
[17] *Eb.* 21, 13. Sim. *ib.* 41, 16; *Siut* 1. 298. 313; *P. Kah.* 35, 22; *Urk.* v. 95, 4.
[18] *Urk.* iv. 112, 2; 146, 14; 383, 15; 975, 2.
[19] *Westc.* 7, 5.
[20] *Urk.* iv. 138, 16; 661, 12.
[21] *Urk.* iv. 1104, 13.
[22] Louvre C 52.
[23] *Urk.* iv. 28, 2; 912, 13; *D. el B.* 134, left; Berl. leather, 1, 16.
[24] *Westc.* 11, 8; *ÄZ.* 43, 33.
[25] With *n* before noun, *Sh.S.* 136; *Urk.* iv. 390, 7. Without *n*, *Sin.* B 196. 281. 300.
[26] *Sin.* B 196. 281; *Sh. S.* 127. 136; *Urk.* iv. 390, 8.
[27] *Sin.* B 300.
[28] *Urk.* iv. 390, 7; cf. *Mill.* 2, 11.
[29] *Sin.* B 154; *Leb.* 64. 128.
[30] *P. Kah.* 13, 1. 30; *Urk.* iv. 1088, 14.
[31] *Sh.S.* 108; BUDGE, p. 103, 14; 286, 3.
[32] *Peas.* B 1, 44. 46.

ḥr-gs 'beside', much rarer than *r-gs* in the same sense.[1]

r-tp (*n*),[2] var. *r-tp-ꜥ* (*n*)[3] 'into the presence of', very rare.

ḥr-tp, lit. 'on the head (of)', mainly in the phrase *ḥr-tp ꜥnḫ wḏꜣ snb* 'on behalf of the life, prosperity and health' of the king.[4]

m-ṯnt-r 'apart from' what was done before, lit. 'in distinction from'.[4a]

§ 179. B. **Compound prepositions consisting of adverb + preposition.**—In this much smaller class an adverbially used noun (§ 88, 1) or some part of a verb is prefixed to one of the simple prepositions.

tp-m, with suffixes *tp-im·*, 'before', lit. 'head in'. To come 'in front of' a person;[5] also 'in the direction of' a place.[6] Of time, 'before' old age.[7]

nfryt-r 'down to', lit. 'end to'; of *time*, 'down to' My Majesty, year 16, etc.;[8] of *place*, 'down to' the ends of the earth,[9] etc.; also metaphorically, 'down to' the lowest official,[10] alone 'down to', i.e. 'with the sole exception of', someone.[11]

ḏr-ꜥ-r 'right down to' (lit. 'end to') death.[12]

Here belong such phrases as *ḫntt-r* . . . . *pḥt-r* . . . ., 'southward to . . . . . ., ending at . . . . . .' (a place);[13] *ḫnt-r* . . . . *mḥt-r* . . . ., 'southward to . . . . . ., northward to . . . . .';[14] all precious stones *ḥꜣt-r* 'starting with' silver and gold, *pḥwy-r* 'down to' ivory and ebony.[15]

Some part of the verb, perhaps the old perfective (§ 309), adverbially used, enters into the composition of the following:

wpw-ḥr, with suffix *wp-ḥr·*, lit. 'separated from'.

1. 'except' a person or thing.[16] Very strangely, *wpw-y* 'except me'.[16a]

2. with infinitive, like *ḥnꜥ* (see § 171, 3), where English uses 'but' and translates with a finite verb, ex. not one looked behind *wpw-ḥr ifd* 'but they fled'.[17]

3. before *sḏm·f*, with the meaning 'but', ex. *wpw-ḥr nfnḏdf* (sic) *ḥꜥw·i* 'but my limbs . . . . . . -ed'.[18]

ḥrw-r, var. ,[19] lit. 'apart from', is used for 'besides', 'as well as' something.[20] Later, the *r* is omitted (rare).[21]

šꜣꜥ-m 'beginning from', used either of *place*[22] or of *time*.[23]

šꜣꜥ-r, apparently 'beginning to', strangely comes to mean 'as far as' of *place*.[24] Cf. *r-šꜣꜥ-r*, § 180.

§ 180. C. **Compound prepositions containing an infinitive.**

r iwd . . . . . *r* 'between' one thing 'and' another, lit. 'to separate . . . . . . from'.[25] Not before end of Dyn. XVIII.

[1] BUDGE, p. 7, 11; 86, 15; 287, 10.
[2] *ÄZ.* 43, 28.
[3] *Urk.* iv. 1074, 1.
[4] *Urk.* iv. 334, 11; 335, 16; 336, 11; 768, 10. Sim. Cairo 20543, 14; *Hamm.* 47, 5.
[4a] *Urk.* iv. 584, 17; *Ann.* 42, 4.
[5] *Peas.* B 1, 40. 74; *Westc.* 10, 6; 12, 16.
[6] *Urk.* v. 26, 3.
[7] *Westc.* 7, 17.
[8] *Urk.* iv. 34, 10; 367, 4; 390, 11.
[9] *Urk.* iv. 648, 6; 125, 12.
[10] *Urk.* iv. 1107, 12.
[11] *P. Kah.* 33, 14.
[12] CHAB. *Oeuvr. Div.* 5, Pl. 6; *Five Th. T.* 19.
[13] Brit. Mus. 614, 4; cf. *Urk.* iv. 1129, 3.
[14] *Abyd.* iii. 29. Sim. PETR. *Qurneh*, 3, 2, 4; Cairo 20543, 10.
[15] Louvre C 14.
[16] Louvre C 14; *P. Kah.* 27, 10; *Eb.* 39, 9; Berl. *ÄI.* i. p. 256; BUDGE, p. 308, 12; 408, 1; 497, 8.
[16a] *Ann.* 36, 137 (pl. II, 1).
[17] *Urk.* iv. 697. Sim. *ib.* 363, 17; 439, 2; 661, 13.
[18] *Sin.* B 228.
[19] *Urk.* iv. 665, 13.
[20] *Sin.* B 89. 90. 299; *Urk.* iv. 702, 15; 703, 12; 823, 12.
[21] *Urk.* iv. 8, 1.
[22] *Urk.* iv. 125, 12; 648, 6; 1120, 4.
[23] *Urk.* iv. 743, 6; 776, 4; 895, 16.
[24] *T. Carn.* 4. 5. 6; *Urk.* iv. 649, 9.
[25] *Ann.* 37, pl. 2, 16; *Amarn.* 5, 28, 18; NAV. 15 A, iii. 17.

r-mn-m, lit. 'to remain in' with the meaning 'as far as', alike of *place*[1] and of *time*; [2] 'as far as' her buttocks.[3]

r-šꜣꜥ-r 'down to' this day.[3a] Cf. *šꜣꜥ-r*, § 179.

r-ḏbꜣ, lit. 'in order to replace'. 'Instead of' someone;[4] not until Late Egyptian does this become the equivalent of English 'in exchange for', in Middle Egyptian *m-ỉsw*, *r-swnt* or *r-ḏꜣt*.

r-ḏꜣt, var. *r-ḏꜣwt*, lit. 'so as to cancel', i.e. 'in return for' a monument, act, wrong, or like.[5] Common in Dyn. XVIII.

m-snt-r 'in the likeness of',[6] 'in accordance with',[7] lit. 'in being-like to'.

Obs. *r-mn* 'together with', 'as well as', possibly a development of *r-mn-m* and perhaps the original of Late Egyptian *ỉrm*, Copt. *nem* 'with';[8] in one text only.[8a]

§ 181. D. Compound prepositions used mainly as conjunctions.—

The following phrases are followed either by the infinitive or by *śḏm·f*.

n-ỉḳr (n), lit. 'through the excellence of'; with *śḏm·f*, ex. he gave it to me as commander of soldiers *n-ỉḳr mnḫ·(ỉ) ḥr ỉb* 'by virtue of my being efficient in (his) heart', i.e. 'because he thought me so efficient'.[9]

n-ꜥꜣt-n, var. *n-ꜥꜣt-nt*,[10] much more rarely *m-ꜥꜣt-n*,[11] lit. 'through (in) the greatness of'. Equivalent to English 'inasmuch as', with *śḏm·f*, exx. *n-ꜥꜣt-n mrr·f mꜣꜥt* 'inasmuch as he loved truth';[12] *n-ꜥꜣt-n mnḫ·f ḥr ỉb* 'inasmuch as he was efficient in (his lord's) heart'.[13]

n-wr-n, lit. 'through the greatness of'. 'Inasmuch as', with *śḏm·f*;[14] much less common than *n-ꜥꜣt-n*.

n-mrwt, varr. ,[15] once at the beginning of a sentence *ỉn-mrwt*,[16] lit. 'through love of'. (1) 'In order that', commonly with *śḏm·f*, exx. I have equipped thee *n-mrwt ỉr·k n·ỉ ḫt* 'in order that thou mayst perform ceremonies for me';[17] *n-mrwt mnḫ pꜣ t-ḥḏ* 'in order that the white bread may be established'.[18] (2) More rarely with the infinitive, ex. *n-mrwt srwd pꜣt·ỉ* 'in order to make flourish my offering-bread'.[19] So too rarely *m-mrwt* (or *-mryt*) with the infinitive.[20]

sb-tw (?) or possibly *sỉ-tw* (?), 'in quest of', var. , a phrase of obscure origin,[21] employed with the infinitive: ex. the foreigners come *sb-tw*(?) *rdỉt n·sn ṯꜣw n ꜥnḫ* 'seeking that might be given (more literally perhaps 'in quest of the giving') to them the breath of life'.[22]

m-snḏ 'through fear' (very rare): with *śḏm·f*, ex. *m-snḏ mꜣꜣ wršyw* 'through fear that the watchers should see'.[23] Sim. *n-snḏ-n*,[24] *n-snḏ*.[25]

[1] *BH.* i. 25, 35. 53; 26, 145; *Urk.* iv. 808, 2.
[2] *Westc.* 7, 3.
[3] *P. Kah.* 5, 19.
[3a] *P. Mook* 2, 1 = *ÄZ.* 63, 106.
[4] *Urk.* iv. 2, 12.
[5] *Urk.* iv. 66, 15; 439, 8; 752, 17; 1107, 6; 1109, 8.
[6] *Urk.* iv. 168, 10; 1150, 14.
[7] *Rhind*, title; *Urk.* iv. 121, 9.
[8] Against *ÄZ.* 64, 9.
[8a] *Ann.* 42, 6, 6. 7; 16, 16. 17, etc.
[9] Munich 4. *N-ỉḳr-n*, see Leyd. V 4, 2.
[10] Brit. Mus. 614, 11.
[11] Munich 3, 21.
[12] *BH.* i. 25, 45. 75. Sim. *Hamm.* 113, 15; *Urk.* iv. 100, 3.
[13] *Urk.* iv. 409, 17.
[14] Cairo 20086; Turin 1584; *Urk.* iv. 749, 16. With noun, Coffins, B1P, 114.
[15] Berl. *ÄI.* i. p. 258, 21.
[16] *Peas.* B 1, 79.
[17] *Siut* 1, 271. Sim. *Urk.* iv. 100, 4.
[18] *Siut* 1, 275. With *wn(n)*, see Turin 1447; *Peas.* B 1, 79; *Meir* iii. 11, qu. § 326; *Urk.* iv. 366, 15.
[19] *Urk.* iv. 415, 16. Sim. *ib.* 776, 14; 835, 7; 840, 5.
[20] *Siut* 3, 12; Cairo 20539, ii. *b* 13; *Urk.* iv. 1099, 2.
[21] See *ÄZ.* 48, 45.
[22] *Urk.* iv. 1099, 1. Sim. *ib.* 342, 3; 809, 11.
[23] *Sin.* B 18.
[24] Budge, p. 353, 6.
[25] *L. to D.* Cairo linen, 3; Lac. *TR.* 80, 17–8.

tp-ʿ, lit. 'upon the hand'. 'Before', (1) with the infinitive, ex. *wnm tp-ʿ sḏr* 'to be eaten before going to bed';[1] (2) with *sḏm·f*, ex. the storm broke as we were on the sea *tp-ʿ sȝḥ·n tȝ* 'before we reached land'.[2]

r-tnw-sp 'every time that' (very rare). With *sḏm·f*, ex. this is what I shall say *r-tnw-sp gmm sw bȝk im* 'every time that this (thy) servant finds him';[3] *tnw* alone in the same sense, 'shooting (to hit the mark) every time he tries'.[4]

[1] *Eb.* 13, 1. Sim. *ib.* 34, 13; *Peas.* B 1, 110.

[2] *Sh. S.* 33. 103. Sim. *Adm.* 16, 1.

[3] *P. Kah.* 36, 26.

[4] *ÄZ.* 69, 30, 16.

VOCABULARY

ʿḥȝ var. fight.

wȝḥ (1) trans. place, put down; (2) intrans. endure; adj. enduring, durable.

rwd (orig. *rwḏ*) be hard, flourish; adj. flourishing.

stp choose; noun, *stpw* the choicest, best.

ḏd be stable; *ḏd(t)* durability, stability.

sʿȝ make great, magnify.

sḫnt make prominent, promote.

sḫmḫ-ib amusement, lit. distraction of heart.

ȝwt-ib joy, lit. expansion of heart.

ḫrt-ib desire, wish; lit. what belongs to the heart.

wȝs dominion, lordship: an old word, occurring only in formulae.

st-ḥr charge, care; lit. place of the face.

wʿʿw privacy.

(properly) *ssr* thing, concern.

inw tribute, gifts.

ʿḥ palace.

ʿḥʿw period, space.

twt (masc.) statue, image.

wn being: in the phrase *n wn mȝʿ* in true being, truly.

ḏbʿt signet-ring.

sḏȝt (reading not quite certain) precious thing, treasure.

ḏt estate, domain; *bȝk n pr ḏt* or *bȝk n ḏt* servant of the estate, liegeman.[1]

Ḥr the god Horus.

[1] See GARD. *Sin.* p. 77, n. 2.

EXERCISE XIV

(*a*) *Reading lesson : extract from a biographical inscription of Dyn. XI :*[1]

(N.B. The interlinear transliteration and translation are henceforth replaced by a division into sentences designed to show the structure of the passage studied. Students should, at least in the early stages of their reading, always write out the original texts which they study, paying special attention to good writing; an arrangement such as is here offered will be found conducive to a clear understanding of the Egyptian.)

ỉw ỉr·n·(ỉ) ꜥḥꜥw ꜥꜣ m rnpwt
ḫr ḥm n nb·(ỉ) Ḥr Wꜣḥ-ꜥnḫ n-sw-bỉt Sꜣ-Rꜥ-ꞽIntf,
ỉsṯ tꜣ pn ẖr st-ḥr·f,
ḫntt-r ꜣbw,
pḥt-r Tꜣ-wr[2] *Ṯn(ỉ)*
sṯ wỉ m bꜣk·f n ḏt·f,
ẖr tp·f n wn mꜣꜥ.
ỉw sꜥꜣ·n·f wỉ,
sḫnt·n·f st·(ỉ),
dỉ·n·f wỉ m st ḫrt-ỉb·f
m ꜥḥ·f n wꜥꜥw,
sḏꜣt m-ꜥ·(ỉ) ẖr ḏbꜥt·(ỉ)
m stpw n nfrt nbt
ỉnnt[3] *n ḥm n nb·(ỉ) m Šmꜥw m Tꜣ mḥw,*
m sšr nb n sḫmḫ-ỉb,
m ỉnw n tꜣ pn mỉ ḳd·f,
n snḏw·f ḫt-ḫt tꜣ pn;
ỉnnt[3] *n ḥm n nb·(ỉ) m-ꜥ ḥḳꜣw ḥryw-*
n snḏw·f ḫt-ḫt ḫꜣswt. [*tp dšrt,*

[1] Brit. Mus. 614, ll. 3–6 = *JEA* 17, 55.
[2] See § 90, 3. *Tꜣ-wr* was the Egyptian name of the 'nome' or province of Abydus.
[3] See § 369, 2.

'I passed a long space of years under the Majesty of my lord, Horus Enduring-of-Life, the King of Upper and Lower Egypt Son-of-Rēꜥ-Inyōtef, while this land was under his charge southwards to Elephantine and ending at This of the Abydus nome, and while I was his liegeman under his command (lit. head) in very truth. He exalted me, and promoted my place, and put me in a position of his desire, in his palace of privacy, treasures being in my care under my seal of the best of every good (thing) which-used-to-be-brought to the Majesty of my lord from Upper and Lower Egypt, consisting of every thing of enjoyment and of the tribute of this entire land, owing to the fear of him throughout this land; (also) which-used-to-be-brought to the Majesty of my lord by the hand of the chieftains who are over the desert, owing to the fear of him throughout the foreign lands.'

(*b*) *Write in hieroglyphs and in transliteration*:

(1) My lord gave to me my city as prince, he gave it to me as commander of the army, by virtue of my being efficient in the heart of His Majesty. (2) I give (use *sḏm·n·f*) to thee all life, stability and dominion, all health and all joy with (*ḫr*) me in exchange for this beautiful, flourishing, efficient monument. (3) I caused my image to be made at this my southern boundary in order that (lit. through love) ye might flourish on account of it and in order that ye might fight on behalf of it. (4) I have paid attention to (*rdi·n·i ib·i ḫnt*) the house of my lord; I have not been neglectful concerning his children, his cattle or anything of his. (5) My office is more beautiful to-day than it was yesterday. (6) Thy pyramid shall be in the midst of the pyramids of the Royal Children (*msw nsw*).

LESSON XV

SUBORDINATE CLAUSES

§ **182.** A part of a sentence which is equivalent to a noun, adjective or adverb, while having a grammatical subject and predicate of its own, is called a **subordinate clause**, or more specifically a **noun clause, adjective clause,** or **adverb clause.**

1. Noun clauses. See below §§ 183–193.
2. Adjective clauses, better known as relative clauses. See below §§ 195–204.
3. Adverb clauses. See below §§ 210–223.

When a subordinate clause has nothing to distinguish it from a complete sentence except its meaning and its syntactic function (e.g. the replacing of a nominal object, § 69) it is called a **virtual subordinate clause.** Clauses of this kind are more common in Egyptian than in English, though in English they are by no means rare, exx. 'I know he does', 'the day he met us'.

Other subordinate clauses are marked off as such by means of connecting links like the relative adjective *nty* 'who, which, that' and the conjunctive particle *ntt* 'that'.

NOUN CLAUSES

§ 183. **Noun clauses**, or subordinate clauses which exercise the function of nouns, remain as a rule without introduction (*virtual noun clauses*), but sometimes are ushered in by a word for 'that' (*ntt, wnt*, § 187).

Verbal noun clauses, i. e. those which have a narrative verb-form as grammatical predicate (§ 27), are commoner than non-verbal, for we shall see (§ 186) that noun clauses with adverbial, nominal, or adjectival predicates were conformed to the type of the verbal sentence by use of the *śḏm·f* form of *wnn* 'be' or of the adjective-verb; see already above §§ 118. 143. 150. 157.

We shall treat noun clauses from the standpoint of their function as syntactic elements in the main clause, beginning with their use as *object*, already familiar in the employment of *śḏm·f* after *rdỉ* 'cause' (§ 70).

§ 184. ***Śḏm·f* as object after certain verbs.**—1. After some verbs like *rdỉ* 'cause' (§ 70) the *śḏm·f* form has *prospective* meaning, i. e. points to an act that may or will occur in the future. Such verbs are *wȝḥ* 'permit',[1] *wḏ* 'command',[2] *mr* 'wish',[3] *rḫ* 'know',[4] *ḥmt* 'think',[5] *snḏ* 'fear',[6] *sḫȝ* 'remember', 'recollect', *gm* 'find a means', 'be able', *ḏd* 'say', 'think', besides the compound *dỉ m ỉb* 'determine', lit. 'place in the heart',[7] and the supposed imperative *sȝw* 'beware lest' (§ 338, 3).

Exx. *rḫ·n·f ḫrp·ỉ n·f st* he knew I should administer it for him.[7a]

ḏd·n·f ꜥḥȝ·f ḥnꜥ·ỉ he said he would fight with me.[8]

iw·ỉ sḫȝ·ỉ spr·ỉ r nṯr I used to remember that I should draw nigh to the god.[9]

n gm·n·f dgȝ·f n kꜥḥwy·fy he is unable to look (lit. he does not find he may look) at his shoulders.[10]

After the passives of the same verbs the *śḏm·f* form naturally becomes *subject*; see § 70 for an example with *rdỉ*.

Ex. *mk wḏ* (§ 422, 1) *swꜥb·k pȝ r-pr n ȝbḏw* behold, it has been commanded that thou shouldst cleanse the temple of Abydus.[11]

The above examples show that this use of *śḏm·f* was common even when its subject was identical with that of the main verb. Not infrequently, however, it seemed unnecessary to repeat the subject, and in such cases the *śḏm·f* was regularly replaced by the infinitive. See below § 303, and compare English 'I wished to go' with 'I wished he would go' and 'I wished I could go'.

2. After some verbs like *rḫ* 'know',[13] *mȝȝ* 'see', *gm* 'find', the objective *śḏm·f* has not necessarily prospective meaning, but may refer to the same time as the main verb (*relative present* time, § 155).

[1] *Peas.* B 1, 269.
[2] Brit. Mus. 101, horiz. 4, qu. p. 169.
[3] Turin 1447; Cairo 20100, 4; Brit. Mus. 223. 233; Louvre C 181.
[4] *Urk.* iv. 368, 14; 807, 3.
[5] *Sin.* B 7.
[6] *Sin.* B 18.
[7] *Urk.* iv. 198, 5–9.
[7a] *Urk* iv. 368, 14.
[8] *Sin.* B 111. Sim. LAC. *TR.* 35, 10; *Ächt.* p. 43.
[9] *Siut* 1, 267.
[10] *Sm.* 1, 25; 2, 14.
[11] Louvre C 12, 6.
[13] *Urk.* iv. 363, 6.

Exx. *gm·n·s ir·tw m ḫnw·f* she found it (the noise) was being made in it.[1] *'Ir·tw* is elliptic for *ir·tw·f.*

The heart of His Majesty was refreshed *n mȝȝ ḫnn·sn* at seeing them row.[2]

Obs. To negate the *śḏm·f* form thus used as object the negative verb *tm* is employed, see § 347, 1.

§ 185. **Śḏm·n·f as object of verbs.**—This use is of rare occurrence; the *śḏm·n·f* form then refers to time anterior to that of the main verb (*relative past time*, § 156).

Ex. *ir gm·k ṯs·n·f* if thou findest it (the stomach) has become constricted, lit. has tied.[3]

§ 186. **Virtual noun clauses with adjectival, adverbial or nominal predicate as object of verbs.**—After the verbs quoted in § 184 the construction is the same as after *rdi* 'cause'. 1. Thus in noun clauses with *adjectival* predicate the *śḏm·f* form of the adjective-verb replaces the adjective itself (§ 143).

Exx. *mȝ·n ḥm·f ḳnn·i* His Majesty saw that I was brave.[4]

ist gm·n ḥm·i nfr wrt skȝ šrt lo, My Majesty had found that the cultivation of barley was very good.[5]

2. Similarly, in noun clauses with *adverbial* predicate the *śḏm·f* form of *wnn* 'exist', 'be' is employed, since *iw* cannot stand in this position (§ 118, end).

Ex. *mr·n·f wn·i m Mȝdw* he desired me to be in Medâmûd.[6]

3. Noun clauses with *nominal* predicate could doubtless also be expressed in the same way, use being made of the *m* of predication (§§ 38. 125); but instances also occur where the object consists of the construction with *pw.*

Ex. *gm·n·i ḥfȝw pw* I found it was a snake.[7]

So too the type of sentence introduced by the independent pronoun (§ 125) is found as the object of *rḫ.*

Ex. *rḫ·nn·sn* (read *rḫ·n·sn*) *ink nb·sn* they know I am their lord.[8]

§ 187. **Use of ntt and wnt for 'that'.**—The particle *ntt* (§ 237) and the much rarer *wnt* (§ 233) are occasionally used for 'that' after verbs of *seeing* and *knowing.*

Exx. *rḫ·kwi ntt ḥtp·f ḥr·s* I knew that he would be pleased on account of it.[9]

rḫ·n·ṯn ntt ir sr nb ..... n nḏm·n n·f ḫtḫt im ye know that as to every prince ..... reversal thereof is not pleasant to him.[10]

[1] *Westc.* 12, 4. Sim. *Urk.* iv. 751, 2.

[2] *Westc.* 5, 15; 6, 2.

[3] *Eb.* 40, 19. Sim. *ib.* 39, 13.

[4] *Urk.* iv. 9, 16; sim. *ib.* iv. 892, 6. After *rḫ*, *Sin.* B 76. 107; *Urk.* iv. 363, 6; Berl. *Äl.* ii. p. 26, qu. § 88, 2; after *ptr*, *Siut* 1, 220; after *sįȝ*, *P. Kah.* 7, 31.

[5] *Urk.* iv. 747, 9. Sim. after *mȝȝ*, *Sin.* B 108; after *mr*, *Pt.* 298.

[6] Cairo 20712, *a* 10. Sim. *Urk.* iv. 341, 8.

[7] *Sh. S.* 61. Sim. after *ib* 'suppose', *ib.* 58.

[8] *Urk.* iv. 346, 3–6.

[9] *Urk.* iv. 835; sim. *ib.* 593, 5, qu. § 452, 2; with *śḏm·n·f*, *Sin.* B 181; *JEA* 16, 19, 1.

[10] *Siut* 1, 310. Sim. *ib.* 280–1.

He brought the book .... [hieroglyphs] *ḫft mꜣꜣ·f ntt štꜣw pw ꜥꜣ* when he saw that it was a great secret.[1]

[hieroglyphs] *siꜣ·n ḥm·i wnt nn irty·fy st nb ḥr-ḫw·k* My Majesty perceived that there was none who would do it except thee.[2]

The examples show that *ntt* and *wnt* may introduce both verbal and non-verbal clauses. As stated in § 44, 2, a dependent pronoun may on occasion be attached directly to *ntt*, and the same is true of *wnt*.

Exx. [hieroglyphs] *ḫr mꜣ·tw ntt st ḥr ḫtm n sr iry* one shall see that it is provided with the seal of the proper official.[3]

[hieroglyphs] *r rḫt Stḫ wnt sn ḥnꜥ·k* until Seth knows that they are with thee.[3a]

Obs. For a different type of construction (the pseudo-verbal construction) after *ntt* and *wnt*, see below § 329. Note that after verbs of saying 'that' is not *ntt* but *r-ntt*; on this and other phrases introducing the content of a speech see §§ 224–5. Noun clauses introduced by *ntt* may be preceded by a preposition, see § 223.

§ 188. Virtual noun clauses as subject.—The use of noun clauses as *subject* is very much rarer than their use as object. 1. We have already noted (§§ 70. 184) that noun clauses may be employed as subject after the passives of *rdi* 'cause' and similar verbs; other cases occur less frequently.

Ex. [hieroglyphs] *ḫpr is, iwd·k tw r st tn, n sp mꜣ·k iw pn* it shall happen, when thou sunderest thyself from this place, never shalt thou see this island more.[4]

So too in the expression [hieroglyphs] *n sp* 'never' *sp* appears to be the *śdm·f* form and takes another *śdm·f* form as its subject; see above § 106, below § 456. Similarly a *śdm·f* form may serve as subject after *ir wdf* 'if (so and so) fails (to take place)', lit. 'if it delay that ....'; see § 352.

2. On rare occasions the *śdm·f* form is found after the phrases expressing non-existence (§ 108).

Exx. [hieroglyphs] *nn wn mwt·k ḥr ḫꜣst* thou shalt never die (lit. it does not exist that thou diest) in a foreign land.[5]

[hieroglyphs] *n wnt ḳd·i ḥr r-pr·f* I never slept because of his temple, i.e. perhaps, I was constantly vigilant concerning it.[6] The time referred to appears to be the past.

Obs. It seems not improbable that *nn śdm·f* 'he will not hear' (§ 105, 2) is to be explained in this way.

3. An adjective or adjective-verb may be predicate to a virtual noun clause introduced by the *śdm·f* form.

Exx. [hieroglyphs] *nfr·wy sdm sꜣ n it·f* how good (it is) that a son should hearken to his father.[7]

[1] Nav. 148, 22. After *rḫ*, *Urk.* iv. 364, 2.

[2] *Ikhern.* 9. Sim. *Sin.* B 215.

[3] *Urk.* iv. 1111, 11. Sim. *Destr.* 85, *nty twi* for *ntt wi*.

[3a] *ÄZ.* 58, 29*. For a further development of this construction see p. 253, n. 11a.

[4] *Sh. S.* 153. So too *ḫpr·n*, *ib.* 130. 166; *P. Pet.* 1116B, 1. Sim. after *ḫpr m-ꜥ·f*, *Leb.* 10. Some regard *ḫpr* and *ḫpr·n* in such cases as impersonal.

[5] *Sin.* B 197.

[6] *Urk.* iv. 363. Sim. Piehl, *IH.* iii. 75, past time.

[7] *Pt.* 556. Sim. *ib.* 543; *P. Kah.* 32, 12; *Adm.* 3, 9. Without *·wy*, *Leb.* 29; *Westc.* 9, 22; *JEA* 16, 19, 3–4.

ỉr wr ḏd·f snf if it bleeds much, lit. if it-gives-blood is much.[1]

To be explained in the same way are the formulae of valediction in letters *nfr sḏm nb* (*ꜥnḫ wḏꜣ snb*) 'may the hearing of (my) lord (lit. that the lord hears) be good'[2] and *nfr sḏm·k* 'may thy hearing be good'.[3]

So too after *nfr pw* with the meaning 'there is (are) not', and possibly after the nearly synonymous *nfr n*; see below § 351.

§ 189. Virtual noun clauses as predicate with *pw* as subject.—Under this head we have to deal with extensions of the constructions discussed in §§ 128. 130.[4]

1. ***Śḏm·f pw.*** This construction is not rare in glosses, where *pw* can best be translated 'this means'; compare in French *c'est que.*

Exx. I am Rēꜥ in his first appearances; *wbn·f pw dwꜣw m ꜣḫt·f* this means (lit. it is) that he arises of mornings in his horizon.[5]

ỉr rwt nt ḥꜣty rww·f sw pw ḥr mnḏ·f ỉꜣby as to 'movement of the heart' this (phrase) means that it moves itself in his left breast.[6]

ỉr ḏd·f ny, ꜥnḫ·f pw if he says *ny*, this means he will live.[7]

Elsewhere *pw* must be rendered 'that is how....'

Ex. *ḫpr ḥnnk pw n 'Iwnw* that is how the *ḥnnk*-priest of Heliopolis came into being.[8]

Literary manuscripts often end with a colophon of the type *ỉw·f pw, ḥꜣt·f r pḥwy·fy, mỉ gmyt m sš.*[9] This doubtless means: Here ends the book, and it has been copied, start to finish, from some other old manuscript. Literally perhaps: this is it arrives, its front to its end, like what was found in writing.

2. In rare cases *pw* after the *śḏm·f* form simply serves to introduce the logical subject, the construction being that of § 130.

Ex. *rš·f pw rḫs* to slaughter is his joy, lit. is he rejoices.[10] *Rḫs* is the infinitive (§ 298).

§ 190. Other noun clauses where *pw* serves as subject.—1. *ỉnk pw*, etc. *Pw* is here inserted in a whole sentence beginning with the independent pronoun 'I', and has the meaning of French *c'est que.*

Ex. *ỉnk pw sḫꜣ·n·ỉ mwt mwt·ỉ* I have been thinking about (lit. it is I have recollected) the mother of my mother.[11] Answer to the question 'what has come to thy heart?'

With a noun in the place of *ỉnk.*

Exx. *Rꜥ pw ḏd·n·f n Ḥr* it so happened that Rēꜥ (lit. it is Rēꜥ he) spoke to Horus.[12]

[1] *Eb.* 109, 15.

[2] *P. Kah.* 27, 2; 29, 24. 45.

[3] *P. Kah.* 28, 3. 6. 10. Sim. *ib.* 32, 16.

[4] For *śḏm·f* as directly juxtaposed predicate (§ 125 end) without *pw* see the example *BH.* i. 25, 63.

[5] *Urk.* v. 6, 8. Sim. *ib.* 6, 15; 10, 5; 23, 15.

[6] *Eb.* 101, 12. Sim. *ib.* 100, 14, qu. § 347, 2; 102, 15.

[7] *Eb.* 97, 13. Sim. *ib.* 97, 14. 15.

[8] *ÄZ.* 57, 5*. Sim. *ib.* 4*.

[9] *Sh.S.* 186–7. Sim. *Sin.* B 311; *Leb.* 154–5; *Pt.* 645–6. Shortened, *P. Kah.* 4, 27.

[10] *Peas.* B 1, 176. Sim. *Sin.* B 60.

[11] *Urk.* iv. 27, 14. Sim. *ib.* 364, 16.

[12] *ÄZ.* 58, 16*. Sim. *ib.* 57, 4*; 58, 18*.

If he has pain in his neck ..... thou shalt say concerning it: *nꜣ pw n mtw n nḥbt·f šsp·n·sn mrt* it is (because) the vessels of his neck have caught an illness.[1]

Similarly with other forms of verbal predicate not yet discussed, see below §§ 325. 332 end. This construction is specially appropriate to *the beginnings of narratives and the answers to questions.*

2. *nt pw* is possibly equivalent to *ntt pw* 'it is the fact that' and seems to correspond roughly to our use of *i. e.* = *id est* = 'that is to say'.

Exx. *nt pw mdw·f ḫnt mtw nw ꜥt nbt* that is, it (the heart) speaks out of the vessels of every member.[2]

nt pw mtw·f m ḥꜣ m st ỉb that is, its (the heart's) vessels are in the back of the head and in the place of the heart.[3]

The view of this construction here taken is the more probable since *ỉn nt pw* once occurs with a fairly clear interrogative sense 'Is it the case that?' See below § 494, 3.

§ 191. The *sḏm·f* form serving as a genitive. Note that here, as after prepositions (§ 155, towards end) the *sḏm·f* form may often be best translated by the English gerund ('his hearing').

1. Appended as a direct genitive (§ 85. A) to a noun expressing *time.*[4]

Exx. *mỉ Mnw rnpt ỉy·f* like Min (in the) year of his coming'.[5]

ỉnk grt ḫnrt·s hrw ꜥḥꜣ·s I was its (my town's) stronghold (on the) day (that) it fought.[6]

ky sỉꜣ ẖrd hrw mss·tw·f Another (way to) know about a child (on the) day it is born.[7]

OBS. That the verb-form was felt as a genitive is indicated by the analogy of the construction under 2 below, and by similarities in the Semitic languages.

2. After the genitival adjective (§ 85. B). See further below, §§ 442, 5; 452, 5. Often best translated by an English adjective (relative) clause.

Exx. *ḫt nbt nfrt nt šsp ḥm·f* all good things which His Majesty received. *Or*, all good things of His Majesty's receiving.[8]

m ḥwn·k n wn·k ỉm·f in thy youthful vigour in which thou wast.[9] Lit. in thy youth of thou-wast-in-it.

Or else it may correspond to an English clause of *time* or *place.*

Exx. *tr n wnn·k* so long as thou livest, lit. the time of thou-shalt-be.[10]

r bw n wnn·k ỉm·f to the place where thou shalt dwell, lit. of thou-shalt-be-in-it.[11]

Elsewhere the relation to the antecedent noun is less easily defined.

[1] *Eb.* 103, 9. Sim. *ib.* 103, 6 (*pt pw mt*).

[2] *Eb.* 99, 5.

[3] *Sm.* 1, 7, where *Eb.* 99, 4 has *ḥr-ntt* 'because'. *Sin.* B 126 is obscure. In *Rhind* 4. 6 *nt pw* replaces *ntt pw* of *ib.* 1. 5; these formulae may be rendered respectively 'that is it' (*scil.* the answer) and 'that is the number in question', lit. 'the equivalent'.

[4] See GUNN in *JEA.* 35, 21 ff.

[5] *Urk.* iv. 18. Sim. *ib.* 280, 13; *Buhen* 52.

[6] ANTHES, 24, 8. Sim. *ib.* 24, 3 (*wḏꜣ·sn*); DE BUCK, iii. 262, *k* (*ḥꜥ·f*).

[7] *Eb.* 97, 13. Sim. *P. Ram. IV*, C 17.

[8] *Urk.* iv. 707. Sim. *ib.* 518, 5; 758, 16.

[9] *Urk.* iv. 497, 10.

[10] *Pt.* 186. Sim. *ib.* 481. 624; *P. Kah.* 2, 19; *JEA.* 39, Pl. 2, 5.

[11] *Paheri* 5.

Exx. *sp pw n ḥsf·tw n Ḏḥwty-nḫt pn* is it a case for (lit. of) one's punishing this Dḥutnakhte?[12]

m ḥr(yt) nt mḫꜣ·f sw through dread of his equalling him.[13]

The virtual noun clauses thus introduced are mostly short[14] and attached to words like *hrw*, *tr*, *sp* with which a genitive is usual.

When expression of the subject of the subordinate verb is superfluous, the infinitive may take the place of the *śḏm·f* form, see § 305 and compare § 184, 1, end.

[12] *Peas.* B 1, 46–7.

[13] *Sin.* B 124.

[14] Longer examples, BUDGE, 52, 4–6; 71, 9.

§ 192. **The *śḏm·n·f* form after the genitival adjective.**—The *śḏm·n·f* form is similarly used when the reference is to relative past time, but this construction is of very rare occurrence.

Ex. *ink nsw n sḫpr·n·f, sꜣ-mr·f n ir·n·f n·f* I am a king whom (lit. of) he bred up, a son-who-loves[2a] whom (lit. of) he made for himself.[3]

[2a] For the active meaning see *Pyr.* 1130.

[3] *Urk.* iv. 812, 8–9 completed by *ib.* 807, 7–8. Sim. *ib.* 671, 3.

§ 193. **Noun clauses in other positions.**—Other uses of noun clauses are more conveniently classified elsewhere. Thus the employment of *śḏm·f*, *śḏm·n·f*, etc. to introduce virtual noun clauses after prepositions (above §§ 154–7) will be treated under the head of adverb clauses, the preposition being regarded as inside the subordinate clause, instead of, as hitherto, outside it (§§ 210, 2; 222); and similarly when the preposition is followed by *ntt* (§ 223). Again, virtual adverb clauses (§§ 210. 212–221) might be taken as noun clauses used adverbially, since the noun itself has a corresponding adverbial use (§ 88, 1). Lastly, virtual relative clauses (§ 195, 1) might, if it had suited our general scheme of classification, have been regarded as virtual noun clauses in apposition.

§ 194. **Idiomatic phrases used as nouns.**—A peculiarity of Egyptian is its fondness for semi-proverbial sentences or phrases which are used as nouns; cf. English 'a ne'er-do-well'.

Ex. *ꜥnḫt n Kmt m hꜣy·i-in·tw-n·i* the corn of Egypt is common property.[4]

The *m* here employed seems to be the *m* of predication, and the phrase translated 'common property' means literally 'I go down and there is brought to me'. So too *pr-hꜣ·f* 'he goes and comes'[5] means a 'popular resort'; *iw·f-ꜥꜣ·f* 'he comes and grows' means a man who rises in rank, as one might say 'a *crescit eundo*';[6] *iw-ms* 'but there is',[7] var. ,[8] means a statement to which exception can be taken, an 'untruth' or 'misstatement'. So too proper names, ex. *Ỉw·f-n·i* 'He-is-mine', name

[4] *Adm.* 6, 9. Sim. *ib.* 10, 3.

[5] *Adm.* 6, 12; *Urk.* iv. 387, 13.

[6] Brit. Mus. 574; Leyd. V 4, 5; cf. also *sꜣꜣ·f-ir·f* 'a he-knows-and-does', *ib.* 6; *ḫpr·f-iṯ·f* 'a he-grows-and-seizes', *JEA* 32, 55, n. *v*.

[7] *Sin.* B 37; *Urk.* iv. 776, 10; 808, 13; 973, 11.

[8] Berl. *Äl.* i. p. 258, 14.

of a man, *Mrr·f-ỉrr·f* 'Whenever-he-wills-he-does', name of the great god of primordial times.[1]

Non-verbal expressions of a similar character are also to be found:

Exx. *šnyt m tp-ḥr-mꜣst* the courtiers were head-on-lap, i.e. in mourning.[2]

s nb m ḥr-m-ẖrw every man is face-downcast, i.e. abashed.[3]

In both these examples the subject is followed by the *m* of predication (§ 38).

[1] CHASS. *Ass.* p. 100; LAC. *TR.* 78, 15. See too *Pyr.* 412, qu. § 442, 4.

[2] *Sin.* R 10 (restored).

[3] *Leb.* 119. Similar phrases *Siut* 3, 24; *ÄZ.* 34, 39, n. 6.

VOCABULARY

ỉnḥ surround, enclose.

var. *ḥsb* count, reckon.

ḫntš take pleasure, have enjoyment.

swtwt walk about.

sḳbb refresh oneself.

var. *gꜣ(w)* be narrow, deprived of (*m*).

ḏdḥ shut in, confine.

ʿbꜥ boasting, exaggeration.

mꜣʿ edge, brink.

mrḥt oil.

ḫnt (for *ḫnrt*) prison.

ẖnmt well, cistern.

nw water (a rather select word).

nht sycamore, tree.

tr time, season, period.

dmỉ town, habitation.

ḏd mdw to be recited, lit. to say words, as heading (§ 306, 1).

Šrḥn Sharuhen, a place in Palestine.

Kftỉw a Mediterranean land, probably Crete, and its people.

ʾIpt-swt Most-select-of-Places, name of the temple of Karnak at Thebes.

EXERCISE XV

(*a*) *Reading lesson: funerary wishes from a Theban noble's tomb* (*Dyn. XVIII*):[1]

Ḏd mdw: [*ẖrw*;

ỉmy-r pr ḥsb (§ 353) *ꜣḥt, sš ʾImn-m-ḥꜣt, mꜣʿ-*

swtwt·k r mrr·k (§ 444, 3)

ḥr mꜣʿ nfr n š·k,

[1] *Th. T.S.* i. 27.

ḫntš ib·k m mnw·k,
sḳbb·k ḫr nhwt·k,
ḥtp ib·k m nw
m-ḫnw ḫnmt irt·n·k (§ 382),
r nḥḥ ḥnʿ dt.

[1] Orig. wrongly through misinterpretation of in the hieratic draft as . [2] A common abbreviation.

'Recitation. O steward who-keeps-count-of the fields, scribe Amenemḥēt, true of voice. Mayst thou walk according as thou desirest on the beautiful edge of thy pool. May thy heart take delight in thy monument. Mayst thou refresh thyself beneath thy trees, and thy heart be appeased with water from the cistern which-thou-hast made—for ever and ever.'

(*b*) *Transliterate and translate*:

[1] A feminine equivalent of *snḏ*. [2] 'How often'.

LESSON XVI

RELATIVE CLAUSES

§ **195. Relative clause,** or **Adjective clause,** is the name given to that kind of subordinate clause (§ 182) which is equivalent to an adjective. A relative clause can, like an adjective, be used either as *epithet* or as *noun*; when used as an epithet, the noun or pronoun to which it is attached is called the **antecedent**; when used as a noun, the antecedent is inherent latently in the relative clause itself.

Egyptian relative clauses fall into two groups: 1. **virtual relative clauses,** i.e. groups of words resembling main clauses simply juxtaposed to their antecedents (if any), a construction comparable to the apposition of one noun to another (see § 193, end); 2. clauses introduced by a word which is adjectival in form and agrees with the antecedent in number and gender. The latter class subdivides into: 2 *a.* clauses introduced by the **relative adjective *nty*** (§ 199) or by the **negative relative adjective *ỉwty*** (§ 202); and 2 *b.* clauses introduced by the **relative forms** (§ 380), these last being extensions of the passive participles which cannot be discussed until a later stage.

Egyptian shows close kinship with the Semitic languages in the fact that its relative words, though able to indicate the gender and number of the antecedent, are incapable of expressing their case or the manner of their dependence upon the other members of the relative clause. Thus while English can say 'the man *whom* I saw', '*whose* son I saw', '*in whom* I trusted', Egyptian must substitute 'who I saw *him*', 'who I saw *his* son', 'who I trusted *in him*'. The pronoun thus inserted in Egyptian relative clauses is called a **resumptive pronoun,** a term which we have employed already in another connection (§ 146). Occasionally an English relative adverb is represented by an adverb in Egyptian, as in *bw nty ḥm·f ỉm* 'the place *where* His Majesty is', lit. 'the place *which* His Majesty is *there*'; in this case *ỉm* 'there' is called a **resumptive adverb.**

In any clause which the beginner suspects of being relative, he should make a practice of looking first of all for the resumptive word. This found, he will know whether to translate 'who' or 'whose' or 'to whom' or 'where', etc., and with this knowledge he will find that the other members of the clause quickly fall into place.

Obs. English is apt to employ a relative clause to make some additional statement, ex. 'I saw John to-day, who (=and he) sent you his greetings'. This spurious kind of relative clause is unknown to Egyptian.

§ 196. **Virtual relative clauses.**—When the antecedent is *undefined* in meaning (exx. '*a* man', 'men'), almost any kind of sentence may be joined to it without introduction with the sense of an English relative clause. Examples of different types follow.

1. Non-verbal:

Exx. *s stwt m nḥbt·f* a man on whose neck are swellings, lit. a man, swellings are on his neck.[1]

s ḫry šnʿ m gs·f ỉꜣby, ỉw·f ḫr ḏrw·f a man having a hardness in his left side, which is under his ribs, lit. it is under his flank.[2]

[1] *Eb.* 51, 19. Sim. *Sh. S.* 120–1; *Sin.* B 286; *Rhind* 62, 2. With ellipse of the resumptive suffix *Westc.* 7, 12–3.

[2] *Eb.* 41, 5.

dꜣ·n·ỉ m wsḫt, nn ḥmw·s I crossed in a barge which had no rudder, lit. not (was) a rudder of it.[1]

ỉw wn nḏs, Ḏdỉ rn·f there is a commoner whose name is Djedi, lit. Djedi is his name.[2]

msḏr nḏs sḏm·f an ear whose hearing is poor, lit. poor is its hearing.[3]

špss pw ꜥꜣ n·f ḫt he was a wealthy man who had great possessions, lit. great to him were possessions.[4]

2. Verbal:

Exx. *msḏr dỉ·f mw ḥwꜣ* an ear which emits an offensive discharge, lit. it gives a foul water.[5]

mỉ s wnm·n·f kꜣw nw nht like a man who has eaten fruit of the sycamore.[6]

kꜣt pw, n ỉr·tw·s ḏr bꜣḥ it is a work which (lit. it) had not been made since antiquity.[7]

gm·n·ỉ ḥfꜣw pw, ỉw·f m ỉỉt I found it was a snake that (lit. it) was coming.[8] Here the rel. clause is only partly verbal, see § 331.

For the old perfective in virtual relative clauses see below § 317.

§ 197. It but rarely happens that virtual relative clauses of this kind are used as nouns, i. e. lack an expressed antecedent.

Ex. *ỉn·n·ỉ mḥ 60 m ꜣw·sn* I brought some (trunks) 60 cubits in length, lit. I brought, sixty cubits (are) in their length.[9]

In the following examples, the relative clause is used as nominal predicate.

ink mr·f nfrt, msḏ·f ḏwt I am one who (lit. he) loves good and hates evil.[10]

sḫpr·f pw wnnty·fy he is one who (lit. he) brings into existence him who is to be.[11]

The construction of the example last quoted must be carefully distinguished from the *sḏm·f pw* of § 189.

§ 198. Occasionally an unintroduced relative clause is found after an antecedent which is *defined* in meaning, ex. *the* man.

1. Non-verbal, perhaps always in connexion with personal names:

Ex. *Ḥrỉ sꜣ Snfrw, ỉt·f ḥr sn-nwt nt ḏꜣmw* Hori's son Snofru, whose (lit. his) father is on the second (register?) of the troops.[12]

[1] *Sin.* B 13. Sim. *ib.* B 47; *Peas.* B 1, 190–1.

[2] *Westc.* 7, 1. Sim. *ib.* 9, 5; *Peas.* R 39–40.

[3] *Eb.* 91, 2. Sim. *Hearst* 4, 14.

[4] *P. Pet.* 1116 B, 10.

[5] *Eb.* 91, 3. Sim. *ib.* 30, 1 (*gm·tw·f*); 49, 7. 8; 51, 16; *Leb.* 121; *Westc.* 7, 1.

[6] *Eb.* 102, 2. Sim. *ib.* 105, 16.

[7] *Urk.* iv. 57. Sim. *Sin.* B 58; *Peas.* B 1, 174; *Urk.* v. 178, 10.

[8] *Sh. S.* 61–2. Sim., with *ḥr* + inf. see below § 323.

[9] *Urk.* iv. 535, with the numeral and suffix restored.

[10] Brit. Mus. 159; 614, 8. Sim. *ib.* 1059. See GUNN, *Studies*, p. 60, no. 11; and cf. also the expression *ỉw·f-ꜥꜣ·f* qu. § 194.

[11] Cairo 20538, ii. *c* 15.

[12] *P. Kah.* 9, 2. Sim. *Hamm.* 43, 12; *Sebekkhu*, top, 4; *Urk.* iv, 6, 11.

2. Verbal (very rare):

Ex. *hrw pwy sḥtm·tw ḫftyw nw nb-r-ḏr ỉm·f* that day on which (lit. in it) the enemies of the lord of the universe were destroyed.[1]

§ 199. The relative adjective *nty*.—Of greater importance are the relative clauses introduced by the relative adjective *nty*, which is normally used when the antecedent is *defined* in meaning, though sporadic instances also occur of its employment when the antecedent is *undefined*, ex. *s nty ẖr st* 'a man who has a lump (?)'.[2]

We have seen (§ 191) that the equivalent of an English relative clause is sometimes produced by placing the *śḏm·f* form after the genitival adjective *n* (*ny*). The **relative adjective** *nty* is nothing more than an extension of the genitival adjective formed by the addition of *-y* (§ 79) to its feminine *nt*, cf. late *tpty* 'chief' beside *tpy* from *tp* 'head', 'upon'.[3]

The relative adjective agrees in number and gender with the antecedent, whether implied or expressed, in the following forms: m. sing. *nty*, f. sing. and plur. *ntt*, m. plur. *ntyw*, var. .[4] When the antecedent is expressed, however, *nty* is often found in place of *ntyw*, ex. *srw nty r-gs·f* 'the officials who were at his side'.[5] Later, *nty* appears to become invariable, ex. *nty* (for *ntt*) *n wꜥ nb m nꜣ n tḫnw* 'what belongs to each one of these obelisks'.[6] An archaic writing of m. sing. *nty* occasionally found in Middle Egyptian is *nt(y)*.[7]

Nty may be used either as *epithet* or as *noun*, i.e. without separately expressed antecedent. In the latter case it may be followed by the adjective *nb* 'all', 'every', so as to yield the meaning 'everyone who', 'anyone who', 'whoever', or 'everything which', 'whatever'.

Exx. *nty nb rn·f ḥr wḏ pn* everyone whose name is on this stela.[8]

.... *pꜣy·ỉ pr ... ḥnꜥ ntt nbt ỉm·f* my house ... together with whatever is in it.[9]

If special emphasis is to be laid on the relative clause, the *m* of predication may be placed before the relative adjective on the principle explained and illustrated in § 96, 2.

Ex. .... *ỉr sš nb h(ꜣ)bw ṯꜣty ..... m nty nn st ḥbs* as for any writings which the vizier sends ..... being writings (lit. as) which are not covered (i.e. signed and sealed).[10]

§ 200. *Nty* in relative clauses with adverbial predicate.—1. When the subject of the relative clause is *identical with* the antecedent, it is not specially expressed, being implicit in the relative adjective itself.

[1] *Urk.* v. 12, 5–6. Sim. *Th. T. S.* i. p 56 (*hrw ms·n·tw·k ỉm·f*); It seems unlikely that these passive verbs are relative forms, see § 388.

[2] *Eb.* 93, 1. Sim. *ib.* 89, 20; 102, 16; *Sin.* B 34, qu. § 200, 1; *Sh. S.* 51. 115, qu. § 200, 1, end.

[3] See *PSBA.* 22, 37.

[4] *Hamm.* 191, 8.

[5] *Peas.* B 1, 43. Sim. *T. Carn.* 2.

[6] *Urk.* iv. 747.

[7] Brit. Mus. 614, vert. 5; *Th. T. S.* ii. 22; LAC. *TR.* 6, 3; 10, 9.

[8] Leyd. V 103. Sim. Cairo 20057; *Dend.* 11 B. Cf. also *pꜣ nty nb* as in L. E., *Urk.* iv. 690, 4.

[9] *P. Kah.* 11, 23. Sim. *Pr.* 2, 4.

[10] *Urk.* iv. 1109. Sim. *ib.* 1090, 12 as read in *Unt.* v. 115.

Exx. *ḫnty·f nty m ḥwt-nṯr* his statue which is in the temple.[1]

mỉ ntt r hp conformably with what is according to law.[2]

rmṯ Kmt ntyw ỉm ḥnꜥ·f people of Egypt who were there with him.[3]

nsw ntyw ỉm king of those who are there (yonder), i.e. the dead; epithet of Osiris.[4]

When, however, the negative word follows the relative adjective, a pronoun is inserted.

Ex. *nn ntt nn st m-ḫnw·f* there was nothing which was not within it.[5]

2. When the subject of the relative clause is *different from* the antecedent, it must of course be expressed. The resumptive pronoun or adverb (§ 195) then gives the clue as to how the relative adjective is to be translated.

Exx. *bw nty nṯrw ỉm* the place where the gods are, lit. the place which the gods are there.[6]

To be drunk *ỉn nty mrt m ẖt·f* by him in whose body the pains are, lit. by him who the pains are in his body.[7]

ỉr nṯr pn nty ḥr·f m ṯsm as to this god whose face is (that of) a dog.[8] Note the *m* of predication.

If the subject of the relative clause be pronominal, usually a dependent pronoun is employed.[8a]

Exx. It had been told to the king *ḥr sšm pn nty wỉ ẖr·f* concerning this state in which I was, lit. which I (was) under it.[9]

I know *bw nty st ỉm* the place where it is.[10]

With the 2nd and 3rd pers. sing., however, the suffixes are generally used, and combine with the relative adjective in the forms *ntk*,[11] *ntf*,[12] variants ,[13] (rare)[14] and ;[15] these forms seem, however, only to occur in the phrase *bw ntf* (or *ntk*) *ỉm* 'the place where he is' or 'thou art'.

OBS. There could be no objection in theory to relative clauses with *nty* having a nominal or adjectival predicate, but no examples are forthcoming. An example with the *m* of predication is quoted above.

See Add. for § 200 A.

§ 201. *Nty* in relative clauses with *śḏm·f* and *śḏm·n·f*.—The relative adjective is comparatively seldom followed by these verb-forms.

Exx. *ỉrwy·k(y) ỉpn nty mꜣꜣ·k ỉm·sn* these eyes of thine with which thou seest, lit. which thou seest with them.[16]

pꜣ t ḥnkt. . . . . nty rdỉ·n·ỉ n·ṯn sw the bread and beer . . . . which I have given (lit. which I have given it) to you.[17]

1 *Siut* 1, 290.
2 *Urk.* iv. 1088. Sim. *ib.* 121, 14.
3 *Sin.* B 33–4.
4 BUDGE, p. 478, 3.
5 *Sh. S.* 51. 115. Sim. *Urk.* iv. 1109, 12, qu. § 199, end.
6 Cairo 20485. Sim. Brit. Mus. 614, vert. 5; *Westc.* 8, 5; *Paheri* 5, top register.
7 *Eb.* 14, 6.
8 *Urk.* v. 67, 1.
8a However, the plurals are ambiguous (§ 43). *Ṯn*, see BUDGE, p. 260, 2–3; *sn*, *ib.* p. 174, 10.
9 *Sin.* B 173–4.
10 *Westc.* 9, 3–4.
11 NAV. 99, Einl. 16.
12 *Bersh.* ii. 19, 1, 14.
13 *Urk.* v. 156, 1.
14 *Rec.* 35, 223.
15 BUDGE, p. 491, 12.
16 BUDGE, p. 191, 10 (*Nu*).
17 *Siut* 1, 295. Sim. *P. Leyd.* 345, recto, G 3, 14.

Negative examples are rather more common.

Exx. [hieroglyphs] *in·n·sn ntt n in·tw mitw·sn* they brought (things) the likes of which had not been brought (before), lit. that which their likes had not been brought.[1]

[hieroglyphs] *mi nty n mr·f* like one who has not been ill.[2]

The last example shows that the subject of the relative clause is in this case expressed, although identical with the antecedent; but it may happen that the suffix of the *sdm·f* form is omitted as obvious.

Ex. [hieroglyphs] *mi ntyw n ḫpr* (for *ḫpr·sn*) as though they had never existed, lit. like ones who have not come into being.[3]

The rarity of *nty* with a following verb-form is due to the fact that the natural method of expressing the same meaning is provided by the participles (§ 353), the *sdmty·fy* form (§ 363), and the relative forms derived from the passive participles (§ 380). Nevertheless, we shall later have occasion to quote examples in which *nty* is followed by the construction with the old perfective or with *ḥr* (or *r*, § 332) + infinitive (rather common, see § 328), or again by the negatived verb-form *n sdmt·f* (§ 402).

OBS. Since *iw* cannot be used after *nty* in Middle Egyptian, the phrase *iw wn* 'there is' must be reduced simply to *wn*; for an example of *nty wn*, see above § 107, 2.[3a] For the Late Egyptian use of *iw* after *nty*, see below § 468, 4.

§ 202. The negative relative adjective [hieroglyphs] *iwty*.[4]—

A common word for 'which not . . . .', doubtless a *nisbe* adjective (§ 79) from the feminine of an obsolete equivalent **iw* surviving only in the O.E. negative particle [hieroglyphs] 'that not . . . .', cf. [hieroglyphs] 'that' from [hieroglyphs] 'which' (§ 237).[5] Besides the archaic writing [hieroglyphs],[6] the Book of the Dead offers the variants [hieroglyphs] *ity*[6a] and, very rarely, [hieroglyphs] *i(w)ty*.[7] A form [hieroglyphs] *iwtw*[8] also occurs, chiefly when there is no antecedent. The fem. and plur. forms follow the model of *nty* and the other adjectives in *-y*.

The rare form [hieroglyphs][9] is a puzzle; it is more probably a writing of *iwty* influenced by [hieroglyphs] *nn* than a separate negative adjective *nnty*.

§ 203. Uses of [hieroglyphs] *iwty*.—

The negative relative adjective is used like *nty*, only more rarely, and with a few additional employments. The corresponding main clauses may be seen by substituting [hieroglyphs] *nn* (or [hieroglyphs] *n*) for *iwty*.

1. with *adverbial predicate*, not common.

Ex. [hieroglyphs] *iꜣt ṯwy* (for *twy*) *nt ꜣḫw iwtt sḳdw ḥr·s* that mound of the blessed on which are none sailing, lit. which-not sailing ones are on it.[10]

Here belongs also the phrase [hieroglyphs] *iwty n·f* 'he who has nothing',[11] lit. 'who-not (things are) to him', the implied subject *ḫt* 'things' being left unexpressed.

[1] *Urk.* iv. 330. Sim. *Eb.* 48, 1; *Westc.* 5, 11. With *n sdm·n·f* (§ 417), *Peas.* B 1, 316.

[2] *Eb.* 47, 18. Sim. *ib.* 65, 14; *Sh. S.* 73; Brit. Mus. 581, vert. 11; *Urk.* iv. 751, 14.

[3] *Urk.* iv. 7; *Ann.* 42, 10. Sim. ANTHES, 22, 18.

[3a] *Nty wn* for *nty wn n·f* 'who possesses' *Rev. d'Ég.* V. 254. An ex. of the negative *nty nn wn*, see *ÄZ.* 69, 28, 11.

[4] See *ÄZ.* 31, 82. For the reading see the Sign-list under D 35.

[5] See *ÄZ.* 50, 113.

[6] *Ann.* 5, 235, 17.

[6a] NAV. *Einleitung*, 56. 62. 77. 84.

[7] *Rec.* 35, 223.

[8] *Peas.* B 1, 64. 122; *Pt.* 169; *Dend.* 11 A.

[9] *Siut* 1, 249. 349. See too *ÄZ.* 31, 83, n. 2.

[10] BUDGE, p. 369, 8. Sim. *ib.* p. 340, 9; 371, 3.

[11] *Adm.* 8, 2. Sim. Brit. Mus. 581, vert. 9; *Urk.* iv. 1078, 10. Note in *Mill.* 1, 6 *iwty·fy* as var. of *iwty n·f* of the Brooklyn tablet, *Mél. Masp.* I 481; sim. *iwty·f*, *Urk.* iv. 919, 5.

2. The phrase *ỉwty sw* has much the same sense as *ỉwty n·f* just mentioned, but is perhaps to be explained as meaning properly 'a no one' on the basis of a possible *nn sw* 'he does not exist' (§§ 44, 2; 108, 3).

Ex. *dỉ·n·ỉ ḫt n ỉwty sw* I gave things to the nonentity, i. e. the pauper.[1]

3. *'Iwty* followed by noun + suffix denies *possession*, like the similar sentences with *nn* exemplified in § 115.

Exx. *mḏꜣt ỉwtt sš·s* a book without writing, lit. which not is writing of it.[2]

m twꜣw n ỉwty ḫt·f do not beg from (lit. to) him who has no property.[3]

For a further development of this construction with the infinitive, see § 307, 2.

4. *ỉwtt* 'that which does not exist' in the common phrase *ntt ỉwtt* 'that which exists and that which does not exist', i. e. everything.[4]

5. with following *śḏm·f*, fairly frequent:

Exx. *ỉwty sḏm·f n ḏd ḫt·f* who does not listen to his belly's prompting.[5]

A lake *ỉwtt sḫm·tw m mw ỉmy·s* of the water whereof one cannot gain control, lit. which one does not gain control of the water that is in it.[6]

6. with following *śḏm·n·f*, not very common.

Ex. *ỉwt(y) sḏr·n rmṯ špt r·f* one on account of whom no one spent the night disappointed.[7]

7. Whether *ỉwty* can be used with the passive *śḏm·f* is very doubtful; see below § 424, 3 end.

§ 204. Other equivalents of English relative clauses.—It will be useful here to summarize various modes of expression which, while not constituting relative clauses from the Egyptian point of view, are often best rendered as such in English.

1. the adjectives in *-y*, especially when derived from prepositions, ex. *ỉmyw-ḥꜣt* 'those who were aforetime', lit. 'those-being-in-front'. Note particularly *bw ḫry·f*, lit. 'the place being-under him',[8] which is identical in meaning with *bw ntf ỉm* 'the place where he is'. So also other adjectives, ex. *nfrt* 'what is good', lit. 'a good (thing)'; see § 96, 1.

2. the emphatic epithet introduced by the *m* of predication (§ 96, 2), ex. *sꜣ·ṯn m sꜣꜣ* 'a son of yours who is wise', lit. 'as a wise one'.

3. the original meaning of all participles (§§ 353 foll.) and of the *śḏmty·fy* form (§ 363) was that of relative clauses in which the subject is identical with

[1] *Cat. d. Mon.* i. 177; Cairo 20537; *ib.* 20539, i. *b* 4; *Urk.* iv. 48, 17.

[2] *Eb.* 30, 7. Sim. *Siut* 1, 265; Louvre C 1, 11; *Urk.* iv. 1077, 8.

[3] *Pt.* 164. Sim. *Peas.* B 1, 64; *Adm.* 8, 4. 5; 9, 4. 5.

[4] *Hamm.* 113, 8; 114, 3; *Siut* 1, 234; cf. *Peas.* R 97–8.

[5] *Pt.* 235. Sim. *Urk.* iv. 97, 8; 410, 6; 959, 15; 971, 14; BUDGE, p. 313, 14.

[6] BUDGE, p. 373, 6. Sim. *Ann.* 5, 235, 17–8.

[7] Brit. Mus. 159, 11. Sim. *Ḥarh.* 418; Louvre C 168, 3.

[8] *Urk.* iv. 116, 1; 892, 9. Sim. *bw ḫry ḥm·f*, 567, 3; *bw ḫry·k*, 621, 1.

the antecedent. Exx. *sḏmyw* 'those who hear', lit. 'hearing ones', *mry nb·f* 'one who is beloved of his lord', *sḏmty·fy* 'one who will hear'. This rule applies also ultimately to the relative forms, on which see §§ 380 foll.

Under this head fall also the participles of *wnn* 'exist', which closely correspond in their uses to the relative adjective *nty*; see below § 396.

4. As we have seen (§§ 191. 192), the genitival adjective *n* (*ny*), when followed by *sḏm·f* or *sḏm·n·f*, may sometimes be translated as a relative clause, ex. *ḫt nbt nfrt nt šsp ḥm·f* 'all good things which His Majesty received', lit. 'of His-Majesty-receives'. So too with the infinitive (§ 305), ex. *sꜥḥ n sḏm n·f* 'a noble who is to be listened to', lit. 'a noble of listening to him'.

VOCABULARY

ii come.

iṯ, var., take away, seize.

wmt be thick; adj. thick, stout.

wn open.

mn remain, be established.

var. *mwt* die; death.

mr be ill; adj. ill, painful.

rhn lean, *ḥr* upon.

swi (old *swr*, § 279) drink.

sbꜣ teach, *r* concerning.

snb be healthy; n. health.

šps be noble; adj. noble; *špssw* riches.

ḳꜣꜥ, var. *ḳꜥ*, spew out.

dr drive out, crush.

ꜥ-ẖnwty audience-chamber.

pẖrt remedy, medicament.

mnw fortress.

ḥmsw sloth, lit. sitting.

sḳr-ꜥnḫ prisoner, lit. one smitten living.

šfdw papyrus-roll, book.

šmꜣ nomad, foreigner.

Gb Geb, the earth-god.

ḥr ꜥ immediately, lit. on the hand.

EXERCISE XVI

(*a*) *Transliterate and translate*:

(1)

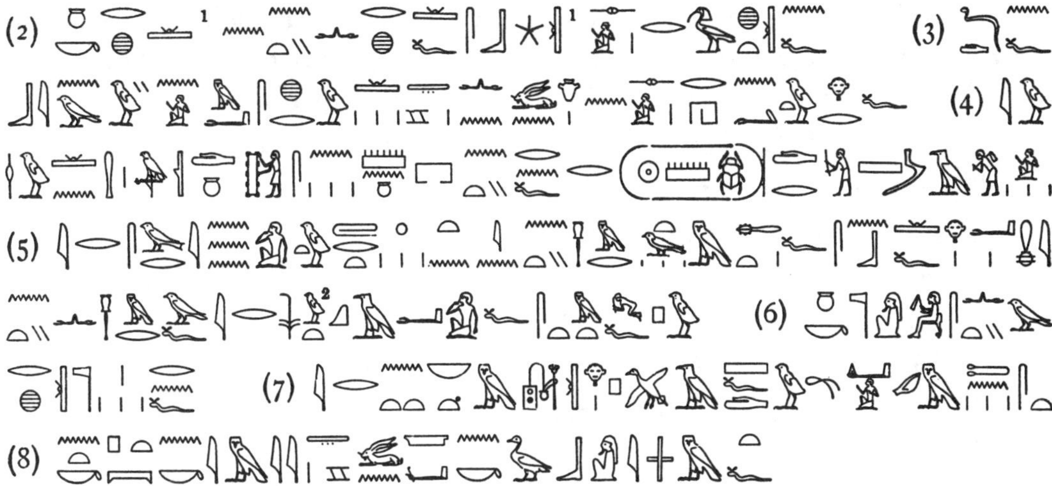

(*b*) *Write in hieroglyphs and transliteration*:

(1) I brought away the chief of this country as a prisoner, I seized all that was in his town. (2) Those who were in the ship died. (3) The king's son gave to me a house in which were riches without end; there was nothing which was not therein. (4) He is, moreover, a god who has no equal; he is stout of heart, one who does not allow sloth to assail his heart (lit. he does not place sloth behind his heart). (5) I gave to him who had as to (lit. like) him who had not. (6) The overseer of all that exists, Nakht, whose father is Sonb. (7) There is none who knows[3] the place where he is. (8) He in whose heart is iniquity, his name shall not remain upon earth. (9) The gods who are in Heliopolis are in festival, when they see this great god in his bark.

[1] Participles, 'one who knows', 'one who teaches', see § 204, 3. [2] 'But', § 254. [3] *rḫ* (participle).

LESSON XVII

ADVERBS

§ 205. There are but few words in Egyptian which can be classified specifically as **adverbs**. 1. Such are, however, the following:

ꜥꜣ,[1] rare var. *ꜥꜣy*[1a] 'here'.

mín 'to-day'; the reading *smn* has been proposed.[2]

r-sy, more rarely written *rs-sy*[3] 'entirely', 'quite',[4] after negatives 'at all'.[5]

gr,[6] *grw*,[7] rare var. [7a] 'also'; after negatives 'further', 'any more';[7b] once at least,[7c] as in O.E.,[8] used enclitically like M.E. *grt* (§ 255).

ṯn 'where?', 'whence?' (§ 503).

[1] *ÄZ.* 31, 107; 50, 99.
[1a] *P. Kah.* 32, 5; without det., *L. to D.*, Cairo linen, 10.
[2] *ÄZ.* 58, 11.
[3] GARD. *Sin.* p. 153.
[4] *Adm.* 6, 5; *Urk.* iv. 519, 8; 945, 4.
[5] *Sin.* R 21; *Eb.* 37, 17; 75, 14; 91, 16; *Urk.* iv. 115, 2; 1074, 3.
[6] *P. Kah.* 29, 42; *Eb.* 97, 15; *P. Pet.* 1116 A, 91. 93.
[7] *P. Pet.* 1116 A, 27; *Paheri* 3; *Tarkhan* i. 79, 44; *Haremhab* 23.
[7a] *P. Kah.* 31, 16; *Pt.* 412.
[7b] *Sin.* B 230, 259; *Ḥaremḥab* 23. See too *JEA.* 31, 35, n. ee.
[7c] *P. Pet.* 1116 A, 93.
[8] Exx. *Urk.* i. 125, 13; WEILL, *Decr.* 9.

There is also a series of adverbs connected with the simple prepositions, but derived from the adjectives of § 79; probably all originally ended in *-w* or *-ỉ*:

ỉm (from *m*) 'there', 'therein', 'thence', 'therewith'.

mm,[1] var. [2] 'therein', apparently a mere Dyn. XVIII variant of *ỉm*.

my, var. *mỉ*,[3] 'likewise', 'accordingly'.[4]

ny, 'therefor', 'for (it)'.[5]

ḥnꜥ,[6] var. [7] 'therewith', 'together with (them)'.

ḫftw,[8] var. *ḫft*,[9] 'accordingly'.

ḫntw,[10] var. *ḫnt*,[11] 'before', 'earlier'.

ḫry 'having (it)', lit. 'under'.[11a]

ḏr 'at an end'.[12]

Obs. Here doubtless belong *ỉry*, *ỉrw*, and *-ỉmy* found in special uses, § 113, 2, 3.

2. Other adverbs correspond to the compound prepositions, many originating, like the latter, in the combination of a preposition with a noun. Only a few examples need be quoted: *m bꜣḥ* 'formerly',[13] 'in front';[14] *ḫr ḥꜣt* 'formerly';[15] *m ḫt* 'afterwards';[16] *ḥr sꜣ* 'subsequently', 'later';[17] *tp ỉm* 'previously'.[18]

3. Any combination of preposition + noun constitutes an adverbial phrase, and has been so treated in dealing with the sentences with adverbial predicate (Lesson X). Some fixed and frequent expressions deserve special notice: *m mỉn* 'to-day'[19] (beside simple *mỉn*, above under 1); *m sf* 'yesterday';[20] *m dwꜣ(w)* 'to-morrow';[21] *m mỉtt* 'likewise';[22] *n wn mꜣꜥ* 'in reality';[23] *n sp* 'at once', 'together';[24] *r ḥrw* 'up', lit. 'to above';[25] *r ḫntw* 'out', lit. 'to outside';[26] *ḥr ꜥwy* 'immediately', lit. 'upon the hands',[27] var. *ḥr ꜥ*;[28] *ḏr ꜥ* 'long ago'.[29] This is a mere arbitrary selection, which might perhaps have been bettered.

4. Adverbs derived from adjectival or verbal stems exhibit various forms. Rarely they show the ending *-w*, exx. *ꜥꜣw* 'greatly',[30] *mrw* 'painfully'.[30a] *ḫnmw* 'in friendly fashion'.[31] Much more frequently there is no special ending, exx. *nfr* 'happily',[32] 'well',[32a] *ꜣs* 'quickly',[33] *wdf* 'tardily',[34] *ꜥšꜣ* 'often',[35] *wr* 'much'.[36] For 'very' the feminine *wrt* is common.

5. Adjectival adverbs are also formed with the help of the preposition *r*: *r mnḫ* 'thoroughly',[37] *r ỉḳr* 'exceedingly';[38] *r wꜣḏ* 'vigorously';[39] *r ꜥꜣt* 'greatly'.[40]

6. Reference was made in § 88 to the adverbial use of nouns. Some particularly common examples, besides the dates, are *ḏt* 'eternally'; *rꜥ nb* 'every day'. So too whole phrases such as *ḥꜣt·f r pḥwy·fy* '(from) its beginning to its end'.[41]

1 *Urk.* iv. 501, 3; 776, 10.
2 *Urk.* iv. 835, 14; *Arm.* 103, 5.
3 *Eb.* 100, 10.
4 Lac. *TR.* 57, 11. 13.
5 *Sm.* 2, 22; 3, 13; see *PSBA.* 40, 5; a rare use, p. 258, n. 14.
6 *Sh. S.* 130; *Eb.* 105, 12; *Sm.* 2, 6.
7 *Bersh.* i. 14, 3; *ÄZ.* 69, 32, 22.
8 *BH.* i. 25, 106-7.
9 *Pr.* 2, 7.
10 *Pt.* 177. 179. 432.
11 *Sh. S.* 155; *Eb.* 37, 1.
11a *Mill.* 1, 9.
12 *Adm.* 6, 4.
13 *D. el B.* (*XI*), i. 24; *Urk.* iv. 607, 12.
14 *Urk.* iv. 768, 14; 966, 14.
15 Louvre C 3, 16.
16 *Eb.* 37, 9; 56, 3. 16; 78, 4.
17 *Pt.* 260; *Eb.* 40, 8; *Urk.* iv. 664, 17.
18 *Pt.* 431.
19 Lac. *TR.* 19, 4; *Sin.* B 186.
20 *Adm.* 4, 5.
21 *Urk.* iv. 656, 4.
22 *Pt.* 591; *Westc.* 8, 24.
23 *Peas.* B 1, 75-6; Brit. Mus. 614, 4.
24 *Leb.* 154.
25 *Leb.* 59; *Peas.* B 1, 4.
26 *Leb.* 82. 131.
27 *P. Kah.* 5, 36; *Eb.* 22, 3.
28 *Peas.* R 48; *Hearst* 2, 6.
29 *Pt.* 177; *Adm.* p. 98.
30 *Peas.* B 1, 25.
30a Coffins, G 1 T 316.
31 *Sin.* B 254.
32 Brit. Mus. 614, vert. 4; *Urk.* v. 63, 7.
32a Louvre C 174, qu. § 375; Pol. § 65*a*.
33 *P. Kah.* 22, 8.
34 *P. Kah.* 6, 14.
35 *Eb.* 37, 17; 56, 9.
36 Louvre C 12, 17.
37 *Eb.* 20, 13; 66, 18; 97, 17.
38 *Ḥarmḥab* 20; *Kuban* 9.
39 *Meir* ii. 4.
40 *Eb.* 37, 20; Brit. Mus. 828.
41 *Sin.* B 311.

§ 206. **Syntax of adverbs.**—Like adjectives, adverbs can be used either *attributively* or as *predicates*. Their use as predicates formed the theme of Lesson X. As attributes (or epithets) they may qualify a *verb* or an *entire sentence*:

Exx. *ỉw ḥs·n·f wỉ ḥr·f r ꜥꜣt wrt* he praised me for it very greatly.[1]

ỉỉ·n·ỉ mỉn m Ḫr-ꜥḥꜣ I have come to-day from Kherꜥaḥa.[2]

Alternatively, an adverb may qualify an *adjective*:

Exx. *nfr wrt mꜣꜣ r ḫt nbt* it was very good to see (lit. very good was to see) more than anything.[3]

ỉnk sš ỉḳr wrt I am a very excellent scribe.[4]

Or else it may qualify *another adverb*; this applies mainly to *wrt* 'very' as used in the first example of this section.

More remarkable is the employment of adverbs to qualify *nouns*, an employment found in a restricted number of common phrases and modes of expression; the phrases *bꜣk ỉm* 'this thy humble servant', lit. 'the servant there', *nb-r-ḏr* 'lord of the universe', lit. 'lord to the end' (§ 100, 1), and *wꜥ ỉm nb* 'every one thereof', have already been discussed in connection with the prepositions (§ 158).

We reserve for the next Lesson such sentence-adverbs as *smwn* 'probably', *kꜣ* 'then', which are usually classified as conjunctions.

[1] Brit. Mus. 828. Sim. *Peas.* B 1, 25; Louvre C 12, 13. 17.

[2] BUDGE, p. 483, 14.

[3] *Bersh.* i. 14, 4. Sim. *ib.* 14, 1. 10.

[4] Louvre C 167. Sim. *Sin.* B 265-6; *Urk.* iv. 227, 12; 355, 12.

§ 207. **Comparative and superlative.**—The adverb, like the adjective (§ 97), shows no distinct forms for the degrees of comparison. The meaning of the English adverb 'more' is, as we have seen (§§ 50; 163, 7), conveyed by the preposition *r*. So too after a verb:

Ex. *sꜥꜣ·n·ỉ sw r ỉmt-ḥꜣt* I made it greater than it was formerly, lit. I made it great more than what-was-in-front.[5]

The tag *r ḫt nbt* 'more than anything' is common after adverbs, as after adjectives.[6] Several examples of *wrt* 'very' were quoted in the last section. The same meaning could be produced by a repetition of the adverb, indicated in the writing by the signs *sp sn* 'two times', 'twice'; exx. *mꜣꜥ mꜣꜥ* 'very truly';[7] *ꜥšꜣ ꜥšꜣ* 'very often'.[8]

[5] *Urk.* iv. 766, 6. Sim. 767, 15.

[6] *Bersh.* i. 14, 4. 10; Louvre C 12, 13. 17.

[7] *ÄZ.* 45, Pl. vi. 16. 17.

[8] *Eb.* 40, 18; 48, 11; 57, 4; with twofold *sp sn*, *ib.* 67, 7.

§ 208. **Position of the adverb.**—For the position of *adverbial predicates* in the sentence see above § 121.

The *attributive* adverb follows the particular word which it qualifies, see the examples in § 206. If, however, it qualifies a whole sentence it may precede this; for adverbs and adverbial phrases at the beginning of the sentence, either introduced by *ỉr* or without introductory word, see §§ 148, 5; 149, 2.

We shall see that, of the sentence-adverbs to be studied in the next Lesson, some are regularly placed at the head of the sentence, while others cannot occupy this place, but come as near to the beginning as possible; the latter are called **enclitics**, see §§ 245–256. The adverb *mỉn* 'to-day' shows a marked tendency to be used as an enclitic, though sometimes it is found farther on in the sentence.

Exx. *ỉw mỉn ỉb·f ỉr* to-day is his heart appeased.[1]

ḏd·ỉ n m mỉn to whom shall I speak to-day?[2]

§ 209. Negation of the adverb. *n ỉs* (§ 247, 2) occurs sometimes with the meaning 'but not' before an adverb or adverbial phrase.

Ex. *rwd ỉnm·f, n ỉs wrt* his skin is hard, but not very.[3]

After another negative word, *n ỉs* must be translated 'except' or 'unless'.[3a]

Ex. *m ḥnt, n ỉs r ḫrt·k* do not be greedy except as regards thy own due.[4]

It seems likely that *nn* 'not' could be similarly employed, but no certain instances are forthcoming.

[1] *Sin.* B 149. Sim. *ib.* 189; *Peas.* B 1, 180; *Adm.* 5, 2; after *in*, *Sin.* B 162.

[2] *Leb.* 104–5. Sim. *Adm.* 3, 7; 12, 5.

[3] *Eb.* 104, 8. Sim. *ib.* 107, 7; *Peas.* B 1, 261; *Westc.* 8, 16.

[3a] A different view, SÄVE-SÖDERBERGH, *Äg. Denkm.* 12.

[4] *Pt.* 317. Sim. *ib.* 372; *Pr.* 1, 3.

ADVERB CLAUSES

§ 210. An **adverb clause** (§ 182) is any part of a sentence which, while having a subject and predicate of its own, functions as an adverb. In Egyptian, adverb clauses fall into two classes, of which the second subdivides into two.

1. **Virtual adverb clauses.** These have either no introductory particle or only such a one as might occur, like *isṯ*, in a main clause; they have thus the appearance of complete sentences simply juxtaposed, without link, to the real main clause. There is a similar absolute use of nouns (§ 88, 1), so that those who wish may regard the virtual adverb clauses as noun clauses used absolutely as adverbs; see above § 193.

2. **Prepositional adverb clauses.** Just as an adverbial phrase may consist of preposition + noun (§ 28, 1), so too an adverb clause may consist of preposition + noun clause. But noun clauses, as we have seen (§ 183), are either virtual, i. e. dispense with any special introductory particle, or else are introduced by a word for 'that'. Accordingly we obtain:

2 *a.* **Prepositional adverb clauses without *ntt*.** These consist of preposition + virtual noun clause, ex. *ḥr sḏm·f* 'because he hears'.

2 *b.* **Prepositional adverb clauses with *ntt*** (or *ỉwtt*). Ex. *ḥr-ntt sḏm·f* 'because he hears', lit. 'because of that he hears'.

The three varieties of Egyptian adverb clause thus resulting from our two main classes will be discussed in turn.

§ 211. Difficulties in connection with virtual adverb clauses in Egyptian.—This topic was touched upon as far back as Lesson II (§ 30), where it was learnt that the verbal sentence *wbn rˁ m pt* might, in certain contexts, correspond to English 'when (*or* if) the sun rises in the sky' or 'that the sun may (*or* might) rise in the sky', and that the non-verbal sentence *rˁ m pt* might correspond to English 'when the sun is (*or* was) in the sky' or 'the sun being in the sky', etc. Such virtual adverb clauses play an important part in Egyptian, and our task in the next few sections will be to illustrate the range of English meanings covered by them. By way of preface, we must caution the student that there is here a serious risk of imputing to the Egyptian writers distinctions which are, in fact, due only to the analysis of our English translations. It must be remembered that in *form* the virtual adverb clauses are complete sentences, and that what they *say* is simply (e.g.) 'sun rises in sky' and 'sun in sky'. But we must take care not to run into the opposite error of maintaining that, because the Egyptians used one and the same form of words for (e.g.) 'the sun rises in the sky' and 'when the sun rises in the sky', therefore they did not *feel* that the first was a statement and the second a clause of time. Such a contention would be absurd; broadly speaking, the Egyptian must have known as well as we do the difference between an assertion and a temporal qualification; often, however, he was content with leaving the matter to the discrimination of the listener, where we should be at pains to convey our precise intention. This being so, we are reduced to guessing at the meaning, and since we guess from the English standpoint and not (except to a very limited extent) from the Egyptian, we are apt to be mistaken, the more so, because an Egyptian virtual adverb clause may often be translated in several different ways without materially altering the sense of the passage as a whole.

Thus a difficulty in connection with virtual adverb clauses is that we frequently cannot be sure that they were not felt as independent sentences. We have only the precarious guidance of our English translations to help us to a decision, and the additional difficulty now presents itself that formally independent sentences in English are often virtually subordinate in meaning; exx. 'you enter the house (= if you enter), I leave it'; 'he had pinned his hopes on the meeting (= since he had), therefore he was bitterly disappointed'. As a general rule, when Egyptian statements which are ultimately subordinate in meaning are very long, they may be presumed to have been felt as separate sentences; examples will be found among the statements with *rf* and *ist rf* quoted in §§ 119, 2; 152. We cannot, however, be confident that the Egyptian feeling in such cases was identical with our own. To sum up, the boundary line between independent sentences and virtual adverb clauses is, both in English and Egyptian, a shifting and uncertain one.

§ 212. Virtual clauses of time, with verbal predicate.—In this common variety of adverb clause, the *śḏm·f* form refers to time identical with, and the *śḏm·n·f* form to time anterior to, that of the main clause: a state of affairs more briefly expressed by saying that *śḏm·f* has here relative present time, and *śḏm·n·f* relative past time.

Like the adverbs of which they are the equivalent, such virtual clauses of time may either *follow* or *precede* the main clause (§ 208). For the much rarer case when the clause of time occurs parenthetically between elements of the main clause, cf. the first example above in § 188, and see further below in § 507, 6.

The following examples with *śḏm·f* illustrate the cases where the main verb is past, present, and future and where the adverb clause precedes or follows the main clause.

ḏd·in Ḏḥwty-nḫt pn, mꜣꜣ·f ꜥꜣw n sḫty pn then said this Djeḥutnakht, when he saw the asses of this peasant.[1]

ii wḫ, sḏr ḥr mṯn ḥr rdit n·(i) iꜣw when night came, he who spent the night upon the road gave me praise.[2]

pḥw pḥ·tw·f, grw gr·tw attacking when he is attacked, desisting when the enemy (lit. one) desists.[3]

ḫnt·k, dd·tw n·k iꜣw when thou farest upstream, praise is given to thee.[4]

iḫ wšb·k, wšd·tw·k so that thou mayst answer, when thou art addressed.[5]

sḏr·k, sꜣw n·k ib·k ḏs·k when thou liest down, guard for thyself thine own heart.[6]

Examples with *śḏm·n·f* have been quoted earlier (§ 67, end), but two will be added here by way of contrast to the above, and in order to illustrate the position either before or after the main clause.

ḥd·k sw, rdi·n·k sḏm·f nꜣ ḥd(w)·k sw ḥr·s thou shalt punish him after thou hast caused him to hear that on account of which thou punishest him.[7]

ḥḏ·n tꜣ, iw·i ḥr·f mi wn bik when day had dawned, I was upon him as though it were a falcon.[8]

The adverb clause may be reinforced, and its meaning made more apparent, by some particle or, to be more precise, sentence-adverb. Thus the enclitic *rf* may serve, as we have seen (§ 152), to point forward to a main clause, so that the clause which it accompanies is best translated with 'now when'.

[1] Peas. R 41–2. Sim. *Urk.* iv. 837, 13.

[2] *Siut* 3, 10. Sim. Brit. Mus. 828, 4; *Sebekkhu* 12–13.

[3] Berl. *ÄI.* i. p. 257, 8. Sim. *Sin.* B 52–3; *Urk.* iv. 19, 6; 520, 3.

[4] *D. el B.* 114. Sim. Berl. *ÄI.* i. p. 258, 12, qu. Exerc. XXX (1).

[5] *Sh. S.* 14–5.

[6] *Mill.* 1, 5. Sim. *Hamm.* 191, 8; *Sh. S.* 153, qu. § 188.

[7] *Urk.* iv. 1090.

[8] *T. Carn.* 14.

So too *isṯ* 'lo' (§§ 119, 2; 231) may accompany a clause of time.[1]

Exx. They were plundering Megiddo at this moment, *ist itḥ·tw pꜣ ḫrw ḫsy n Ḳdš* while the vile chief of Kadesh was being drawn (up into the city).[2]

isṯ wỉ ḫd·ỉ ...... sḏꜣwtyw(?) ...... *ḥr mꜣꜣ stꜣ·ỉ* when I sailed down (to do homage) ..... the treasurers .... witnessed my introduction.[3]

Tuthmosis III made as his monument to Amūn .... the erecting of his sacred place .... and it was adorned with eternal work *ist gm·n ḥm·f wꜣ r wꜣs* after His Majesty (lit. lo, His Majesty) had found (it) gone to ruin.[4]

.... *ist nsw km·n·f ꜥḥꜥw·f ..... sḥr·f r pt* now when the king had completed his period .... he flew to heaven.[5]

So too *ti* (§§ 119, 4; 243) occasionally in Dyn. XVIII.

Exx. Happy is the temple of Amūn .... *ti sw šsp·f nfrw·s* when he receives its good things.[6]

ti ḥm·f iṯ·n·f iwꜥt·f, ḥtp·n·f ṯntt Ḥr when His Majesty had taken his heritage, he reposed upon the throne of Horus.[7]

Obs. Virtual clauses of time may be negatived by *tm·f*, the *śḏm·f* form of the negative verb, see below § 347, 3.

§ 213. Virtual clauses of circumstance with verbal predicate.— Sometimes a *śḏm·f*, or more rarely a *śḏm·n·f* form, similar to those dealt with in the last section cannot be translated as a clause of time, but serves rather to express an *attendant circumstance*. In such a case English often uses a participle, particularly after verbs of *seeing*, *finding* and the like.

Exx. *iw ir·n·i tꜣš·i, ḫnt·i ityw·i* I made my boundary, going further south than (lit. I out-fronted) my fathers.[8]

There is none like him *mꜣꜣ·t(w)·f hꜣ·f R-pḏtyw* when he is seen charging (lit. he charges) the Ropedjetiu.[9]

gmm·k sw šm·f iw·f ḫr ḏbꜥw·k if thou find it (the hardness) going and coming under thy fingers.[10]

m-ḫt gmt ḥm·f tḫn pn km·n·f 35 n rnpt wꜣḥ ḥr gs·f after His Majesty found this obelisk having (lit. it had) completed thirty-five years lying on its side.[11]

Sometimes a *śḏm·f* form alternates with the *śḏm·n·f* of narrative to express concomitant facts of a descriptive nature; these, though strictly subordinate, may have to be translated as English main sentences.

[1] See *Rec.* 19, 187, where many examples are quoted.

[2] *Urk.* iv. 658.

[3] Munich 3, 15–6.

[4] *Urk.* iv. 882. Sim. *ib.* 197, 17; 818, 3; 834, 14.

[5] *Urk.* iv. 895–6.

[6] *Th. T. S.* i. p. 40. Sim. *Urk.* iv. 836, 9; 1163, 3. To be translated as an independent sentence, *Sin.* R 15, qu. § 66, end; *Urk.* iv. 270, 12.

[7] *Urk.* iv. 83.

[8] Berl. *ÄI.* i. p. 257, 4. Sim. *Sin.* B 45–6; *Peas.* B 2, 117; *Herdsman* 24; Cairo 20712, *a* 8; *T. Carn.* 14–5; *Urk.* iv. 863, 8; *Arm.* 103, 4.

[9] *Sin.* B 52–3.

[10] *Eb.* 40, 1. Sim. *Urk.* iv. 9, 11–2; *Urk.* v. 161, 14–6; 162, 6–9.

[11] Marucchi, *Gli Obelischi* I, left. Sim. *Eb.* 107, 17; *Sm.* 10, 13.

Ex. I heard (*sḏm·n·i*) his voice as he was speaking, being near at hand; [hieroglyphs] *psḫ ib·i, sn ꜥwy·i* my heart was distraught, my arms opened wide.[1]

Later on (§ 314), we shall find that the verb-form known as the old perfective is very commonly employed in virtual clauses of circumstance, particularly (§ 315) after the verbs of *seeing* and *finding* above mentioned. In that case, however, the circumstance is more of the nature of a state or condition, whereas with the *sḏm·f* or *sḏm·n·f* form it involves an action.

OBS. Virtual clauses of **concession** are so rare as not to require separate treatment here; in any case they would not differ in appearance from virtual clauses of circumstance; see the first ex. in § 507, 6.

[1] *Sin.* B 2-3. Sim. *Urk.* iv. 102, 3-7; 835, 1-5; 1078, 12-3 (collated).

§ 214. Virtual clauses of time and circumstance with non-verbal predicate.—Clauses of time and circumstance are so closely akin, that it would be neither easy nor desirable to distinguish between them again here. The topic has been dealt with incidentally in Lessons X, XI and XII, where references will be found.

To sum up what has been previously stated, when the predicate is *adverbial*, the subject may be introduced in various ways. The following table will recall the details.

NOMINAL SUBJECT	PRONOMINAL SUBJECT
noun alone, frequent (§ 117, 1)	[pronoun cannot stand alone, § 117, 2]
iw + noun, only in marked contrasts (§ 117, 1)	*iw* + suffix, very common (§ 117, 2)
[*wn* + noun]	*wn* + suffix, past time, rare[2]
isṯ, *ist*, *sṯ*, or *sk* + noun (§ 119, 2. 3)	*sṯ*, *isṯ*, *ist*, or *sk* + dep. pron. (§ 119, 2. 3)
ti + noun, seldom, and only after Dyn. XVIII (§ 119, 4)	*ti* + dep. pron., not common until Dyn. XVIII (§ 119, 4)
nn 'not' + noun (§ 120)	*nn* 'not' + dep. pron. (§ 120)

[2] See § 118, 2, p. 94, n. 7; also § 454, 1.

OBS. For an important development of these constructions, in which their form is employed to introduce the equivalent of English verbal predicates, see below Lesson XXIII.

When the predicate of a virtual clause of time or circumstance is *nominal*, it is not usual to employ any of the specifically nominal constructions of Lesson XI. Recourse is had to the *m* of predication, and the model of the sentence with adverbial predicate is followed. Examples in §§ 117, 2; 119, 2.

When the predicate is *adjectival*, the adjective itself is but rarely used; see however an example after *iw*, § 142. As a rule, the adjective-verb (§ 135) is substituted, the construction subject + old perfective being employed. Examples below in § 322.

Theoretically, there is nothing to prevent any of these clauses from preceding the main clause in anticipatory emphasis (§§ 146 foll.). In general, however, they will be found to follow; only when the subject is introduced by *ist* is the position before the main clause at all common.

§ 215. Virtual clauses of circumstance used as predicate.—We must here mention some rare but interesting examples where a virtual clause of circumstance is used as an adverbial predicate after *iw* or *wnn* (cf. §§ 117. 118).

Exx. Seek out for thyself all beneficent deeds *r wnt sḫr·k nn iw im·f* until thy conduct is void of wrongdoing, lit. there is no wrongdoing in it.[1]

If I see a bull *wnn·f irty·f stp* which has streaming eyes, lit. which is its-eyes-streaming.[2]

The last quotation exemplifies the construction noun + old perfective to be discussed in Lesson XXIII. In certain other examples, it is also possible to interpret the noun as a virtual genitive in anticipatory emphasis according to § 148, 3.

Exx. *iw it·k 'Imn-Rꜥ ib·f ḥtp ḥr irt·n·k n·f* thy father Amen-Rēꜥ is content of heart (lit. is his-heart-being-content) at what thou hast done for him.[3] Or else: thy father Amen-Rēꜥ, his heart is content.

wn·in ḥm·f ib·f wꜣ r ḏwt ḥr·s thereupon His Majesty was downcast concerning it.[4] Lit. either 'His Majesty was his-heart-being-fallen-into-evil', or else 'His Majesty, his heart was fallen, etc.'

OBS. Not improbably such compound tenses as *iw sḏm·f*, *iw sḏm·n·f* should be explained under this head; see below § 461.

§ 216. Virtual clauses of condition.—These are closely allied in meaning to clauses of time, and it often happens that a subordinate *sḏm·f* form may be translated indifferently 'if', 'when', or 'whenever'.

Ex. *ṯꜣw m pt ḫnm·tw·f, ḏd·k* the air in heaven, it is breathed if (*or* when *or* whenever) thou sayest.[5]

Cases occur, however, where 'if' is more appropriate in the English rendering.

Exx. *mr·ṯn ꜥnḫ msḏ·ṯn ḫpt, iw·ṯn r drp n·i* if ye love life and hate death, ye shall offer to me.[6] However, for 'if' we might substitute 'as', see below § 218.

ḫr ḥꜣt nt N pn r tꜣ, ḫr Nwt r tꜣ if the face of this N (= an Eg. personal name) fall to the ground, Nut will fall to the ground.[7]

The Egyptians showed great liking for the form of sentence exemplified in the last quotation, where the repetition of the same verb-form suggests the

[1] *Pt.* 87. Sim. *Rec.* 4, 131, 4; *Urk.* iv. 501, 10, qu. § 396, 1.

[2] *P. Kah.* 7, 36. Sim. *Urk.* iv. 1166, 12.

[3] *Urk.* iv. 580, 3. Sim. LAC. *TR.* 15, 16.

[4] *Westc.* 9, 12.

[5] *Sin.* B 234. Sim. *Pt.* 349 (*wn*), qu. § 454, 1; *Urk.* iv. 123, 4 (*ir.tn*). With *if*-clause first, *Peas.* B 1, 257.

[6] Cairo 20003. Sim. *ib.* 20043, *h* 2; 20141, *a* 3.

[7] QUIB. *Saqq.* 1906–7, p. 32. Sim. LAC. *TR.* 4, 33–40; 5, 3–5; *Urk.* iv. 479, 6–17; 1057, 3.

correspondence and interdependence of the two clauses. Compare in § 107 a common type of example with *wnn*, where the most suitable rendering is 'so long as heaven shall exist, so long shalt thou exist'.

Lastly, note the use of *n is* (§§ 209; 247, 2) to express the meaning 'if not . . .', 'unless'.

Ex. *nn di·n ˁḳ·k ḥr·n, in bnšw n sbꜣ pn, n is ḏd·n·k rn·n* we will not allow thee to pass by us, say the posts of this door, unless thou hast told us our name.[1]

OBS. With adverbial predicate, virtual clauses of condition are extremely rare;[2] the prepositional type with *ir* is here preferred, as also when the clause of condition has to contain a nominal or adjectival predicate, see above § 150. Virtual clauses of condition were possibly negated by *tm*, see § 347, 3.

§ 217. 'Whether . . . . . or whether' clauses.—A repetition of words was also the regular Egyptian method of expressing alternative conditions; compare French *soit . . . . . soit* and the repetition of words usual in Egyptian co-ordination and disjunction (§ 91).

Ex. *mꜣ·sn pt, mꜣ·sn tꜣ, mkꜣ ib·sn r mꜣiw* looked they at sky or looked they at earth, their hearts were stouter than (those of) lions.[3]

We may note two examples where the repeated element is not a *śḏm·f* form.

iw šms·n·(i) nb ˁꜣ, šms·n·(i) nb nḏs, n iw ḫt im (whether) I served a great lord (or whether) I served a little lord, no cause of complaint arose, lit. nothing came therein.[4]

m wi m ḫnw, m wi m st tn, ntk is ḥbs ꜣḫt tn whether (lit. behold, § 234) I am at the Residence, or whether (lit. behold) I am in this place, it is thou who canst hide this horizon.[5]

OBS. The alternatives suggested by repetition are not necessarily subordinate clauses; in one passage, at least, they seem to express the meaning of main clauses presenting alternatives, cf. *iw·f mwt·f ḫr·s, iw·f ˁnḫ·f ḫr·s* 'he either dies or lives from it', lit. 'he dies under it, he lives under it'.[6]

§ 218. Virtual clauses of asseveration.[7]—Under this separate head must be placed certain formulae used in oaths and adjurations.

Exx. *ˁnḫ n·(i) S·(n)-Wsrt, ḏd·n·(i) m mꜣˁt* as (king) Sesostris lives for me, I have spoken in truth.[8]

wꜣḥ 'Imn, wꜣḥ pꜣ ḥḳꜣ as Amūn endures and as the Prince endures.[9] This is the usual legal oath from Dyn. XVIII on.

Clauses of this kind contain implications both of comparison and of condition.

Such clauses as *mr·tn ˁnḫ, msḏ·tn ḫpt* quoted in § 216 are perhaps to be understood in the same way.

[1] BUDGE, p. 264, 3–4.

[2] See, however, *Rhind* 28, beginning; and with the repetition just noted, *Peas.* B 1, 120.

[3] *Sh.S.* 28–30. Sim. LAC. *TR.* 2, 3–6.

[4] Cairo 20001.

[5] *Sin.* B 232–3. Sim. with *mk*, *Peas.* B 1, 313–4; with *sk*, *Eb.* 39, 18–9.

[6] *P. Kah.* 7, 51–3.

[7] See in general J. A. WILSON in *JNES.* 7, 129. The oaths with *ˁnḫ*, see *ib.* 132; *Wb.* i. 202.

[8] *Sebekkhu* 4–5. Sim. ANTHES, no. 49, 4; somewhat differently, *ib.* no. 22, 19; Berl. *ÄI.* i. p. 258; 16; with *n·tn* (2nd pers. plur.), *Siut* 3, 1.

[9] *ÄZ.* 43, 30. 35. 37. 39. Sim. in simple asseveration, *Urk.* iv. 38, 10; 488, 17.

The usual oath sworn by the king in Dyns. XVIII–XIX was as follows: *ꜥnḫ n·i mry w(i) Rꜥ, ḥs w(i) it·i 'Imn* as Rēꜥ lives for me and loves me, and as my father Amūn praises me.[1]

That it is a mistake to render 'as [I] live for myself'[1a] is indicated by the absence of any such variant as *. Grammatically, there is no objection to *Rꜥ* as subject of two *śḏm·f* forms, see § 488, and the sense thus obtained is confirmed by Hathor's once addressing the sun-god with the words 'as thou livest for me';[1b] if Rēꜥ, in the same text, swears 'as I live for myself'[1c] it is clearly for lack of a superior being to invoke. However, one badly written ex. of the royal oath shows 'as I live',[2] and an official of Dyn. XII once uses similarly.[3] In Dyn. XVIII *ꜥnḫ* appears as a noun for 'oath',[4] and even as a verb 'to swear'.[5]

§ 219. Virtual clauses of purpose.—The use of *śḏm·f* to express purpose (above § 40, 1) seems to be an extension of its use to express an attendant circumstance; quite unambiguous cases are rare.

Exx. It is a case for letting thy attendant come to me ..... *hꜣb·i n·k sw ḥr·s* that I may send him to thee concerning it.[6]

m it ḥm·f dr·f isft when His Majesty came that he might repress wrongdoing.[7]

I opened my mouth to my soul, *wšb·i ḏdt·n·f* that I might answer (*or*, answering) what he had said.[8]

It is often difficult or impossible to distinguish clauses of purpose from the *śḏm·f* in wishes and exhortations, for which see above § 40, 2; on this difficulty see § 337.

When the predicate in clauses of purpose is adverbial, *wn·f* is employed, see § 118, 2; so too with the *m* of predication, when the predicate is nominal. With adjectival predicate, the *śḏm·f* form of the adjective-verb is used; an example was given in § 143.[9]

Obs. The verb in a virtual clause of purpose may be negatived by the help of the negative verb *tm*, see below § 347, 4.

§ 220. Virtual clauses of result.—It is sometimes necessary to translate *śḏm·f* with a clause introduced by 'so that', 'that'.

Ex. *n ink tr smꜣ·f, wstn·i m ꜥfꜣ·f* I am not, forsooth, a confederate of his, that I should strut in his enclosure.[10]

Obs. We shall see that *iḫ* + *śḏm·f* may often be well rendered in English by 'so that he may hear' (§ 228); moreover, the *śḏm·in·f* form was used to express results (§ 429). From the Egyptian point of view, however, both these methods of expressing consequences were undoubtedly main, not subordinate, clauses.

[1] *Urk.* iv. 751, 17 foll.; 365, 14; 651, 2; 843, 6; 846, 17. Dyn. XIX, Kuentz, *Qadech* 360; *ÄZ.* 44, 37; *ib.* Pl. 1, 8.

[1a] So wrongly *Suppl.* 8; *Wb.* i. 202. 6.

[1b] *Destr.* 14. Sim. said to a dead father, *JEA.* 16, 19, 7.

[1c] *Destr.* 27.

[2] *Urk.* iv. 139, 12.

[3] *Sinai* 53, 16.

[4] *Urk* iv. 80, 17. Sim. Cairo 583, 9.

[5] *Urk.* iv. 86, 1.

[6] *Peas.* B 1, 38–9.

[7] *BH.* i. 25, 36. Sim. *ib.* 25, 5; Cairo 20056, *c*; *Mill.* 1, 2–3; *Urk.* iv. 807, 5–6.

[8] *Leb.* 4.

[9] Old examples, *Pyr.* 618 *a*. 1558 *c*.

[10] *Sin.* B 114–5. Sim. *ib.* 183–4; 255–6; *Peas.* B 1, 49; *Urk.* iv. 1091, 5.

§ 221. Virtual clauses of cause.—In these clauses the *sḏm·n·f* form is apt to be used, since the act assigned as cause is as a rule anterior to the action expressed in the main clause. Examples are uncommon.

Ex. [hieroglyphs] *ḏd·n·f nn, rḫ·n·f ḳd·i* he said this, because he had discerned (*or*, because he knew) my character.[1]

[1] *Sin.* B 32. Sim. *ib.* B 107; *Ikhern.* 9.

§ 222. Prepositional adverb clauses without *ntt*.—Turning now to this second class of Egyptian adverb clauses (see § 210, 2 *a*), we find that little remains to be said about them, since they have been discussed in detail in connection with the prepositions (§§ 154–7; 162–181). We may, however, classify them according to the various meanings which they express.

1. clauses of *time*. With *m* 'when'; *r* 'until'; *ḫft* 'when'; *ḏr* 'since'; *m-ḫt* 'after'; *r-sꜣ* 'after'; *tp-ꜥ* 'before'; *r-tnw-sp* 'every time that'.

2. clauses of *condition*. With *ir* 'if'. Cf. too with *m* or *mi* 'according as'.

3. clauses of *asseveration*. With *m* or *mi* 'according as'.

4. clauses of *concession*. With *m* 'though'.

5. clauses of *purpose*. With *n-mrwt* (rarely *n-ib-n*) 'in order that'.

6. clauses of *result*. With *r* 'so that'.

7. clauses of *cause*. With *n* 'because'; *ḥr* 'because'; *n-iḳr-(n)* 'by virtue of the fact that'; *n-*(or *m-*)*ꜥꜣt-n(t)* 'inasmuch as'; *n-wr-n* 'inasmuch as'.

8. clauses of *comparison*. With *r* 'than'; *r* 'according as'; *ḫft* 'according as'; *mi* 'as when'; *mi* 'according as'.

9. clauses of *co-ordination*. With *ḥnꜥ* 'and'.

10. clauses of *exception*. With *wpw-ḥr* 'but'.

For the position of such prepositional adverb clauses see above § 159. To negate the verb in them use is made of the negative verb *tm*, see below §§ 347, 5; 408.

§ 223. Prepositional adverb clauses with [hieroglyphs] *ntt* 'that'.—In this third type of adverb clause (§ 210, 2 *b*), which always follows the main clause, a preposition is again used as introductory word, but the noun clause governed by the preposition is ushered in by [hieroglyphs] *ntt* 'that' (see § 187). Whereas the prepositional adverb clause without *ntt* is essentially verbal (except in the instances quoted at the end of § 154), that with *ntt* uses various types of sentences, verbal no less than non-verbal.

The prepositional phrases thus employed are [hieroglyphs] *ḥr-ntt* 'forasmuch as', 'because', [hieroglyphs] *ḏr-ntt* 'since', more rarely [hieroglyphs] *mꜥ-ntt* 'seeing that',[2] [hieroglyphs] *ḫft-ntt* 'in view of the fact that',[3] and [hieroglyphs] *n-ntt*[4] 'because', perhaps also written

[2] *Meir* i. 5; *Siut* 1, 289; *P. Kah.* 28, 41.
[3] *P. Kah.* 11, 19.
[4] LAC. *TR.* 33, 3; 72, 16.

defectively *ntt.*[1] The clauses introduced by these all come under the head of clauses of *cause.* The common *r-ntt* seems likewise often to usher in a reason, when it may be translated 'inasmuch as', 'seeing that';[2] but it has also another use to be discussed later (§ 225).

Non-verbal examples:

The Osiris N has not suffered shipwreck ..... N *ḏr-ntt rn n Rꜥ m ẖt nt Wsir N* since the name of Rēꜥ is in the body of the Osiris N.[3]

ḏr-ntt ir gr m-ḫt pḥ ssḫm ib pw n ḫrwy since he who desists after attack is a strengthener of the enemy's heart.[4]

ḥr-ntt ink sꜣ wꜥb mi wꜥ im·tn nb forasmuch as I am the son of a priest like any one of you.[5]

ḥr-ntt dns tw r·i because thou art too heavy for me, lit. heavier than I.[6]

Verbal (and pseudo-verbal, § 329) examples:

ḏr-ntt hꜣb ṯw ḥm·i since My Majesty sends thee.[7]

ḫft-ntt wi tn·kwi in view of the fact that I am old.[8] For the old perfective here, see below § 329.

Sharpen your weapons *r-ntt iw·tw r ṯḥn r ꜥḥꜣ ḥnꜥ ḫr pf ḫsy m dwꜣ* seeing that it is intended to engage issue (lit. one is going to join to fight) with that vile enemy to-morrow.[9]

ḥr-ntt ntf ir·f n·i pꜣ t ḥnḳt for it is he who will make for me the bread and beer.[10]

The last example but two shows that, if the construction requires it, the dependent pronoun 1st sing. may be placed after *ntt.* So too 2nd sing. m. *tw,*[10a] 3rd sing. m. *sw,*[11] f. *s(y).*[12] In MSS. of Dyn. XVIII onward, particularly of the Book of the Dead, such writings as *ntt-twi*, *nty-sw* are not rare,[13] and lend colour to the view that the pronominal compound *tw·i* (§ 124) originated in this construction; *twtw* is, indeed, found after *ḥr-ntt.*[14]

However, just as *ntk* and *ntf* have been seen to occur in the phrase *bw ntk (ntf) im*, in place of *nty tw, nty sw* (§ 200, end), so too after *ntt* the suffixes 2nd and 3rd sing. m. are preferred to the dependent pronouns.

Exx. *ḏr-ntt·f m wꜥ mm nw* since he is one among these.[15]

ḏr-ntt·k i·t(i) m ḥtp since thou art come in peace.[16] *'I·t(i)* is the old perfective, see below § 329, end.

An obscure instance of *ḥr-iwtt* 'because ..... not' may also be quoted,[17] where *iwtt* (from *iwty* § 202) seems to be the negative counterpart of *ntt.*[18]

[1] *Sin.* B 76.

[2] *Urk.* iv. 656, 3, qu. below; 660, 7. 8; 751, 15; BUDGE, p. 244, 3; 308, 13.

[3] BUDGE, p. 281, 7. Sim. with *ḥr-ntt*, LAC. *TR.* 23, 21.

[4] Berl. *ÄI.* i. p. 257, 9.

[5] *Siut* I, 288. Sim. *Peas.* B 1, 62; Leyd. V 3, 6; BUDGE, p. 31, 12.

[6] *P. Kah.* 3, 33. Sim. *ib.* 28, 21; 29, 12.

[7] *Ikhern* 5. Sim. *ib.* 6; BUDGE, p. 308, 14. With *ḥr-ntt*, LAC. *TR.* 23, 13 (negatived). 25; *Siut* 1, 282. 296. 301.

[8] *P. Kah.* 11, 19. With *ḥr-ntt*, LAC. *TR.* 23, 17; BUDGE, p. 24, 3.

[9] *Urk.* iv. 656.

[10] *Siut* I, 323; sim. *ib.* 316. *'In* + noun + participle (§ 227, 3) see *P. Kah.* 35, 17; indep. pron. + participle (§ 227, 3), see *P. Kah.* 29, 39.

[10a] *Pt.* 53. 54.

[11] NAV. 17, 71 (*La*); after *r-ntt*, *Urk.* iv. 649, 11; 751, 15.

[12] *Sin.* B 76.

[13] *ÄZ.* 30, 17.

[14] *Urk.* iv. 656, 5.

[15] BUDGE, p. 286, 8 = LAC. *Sarc.* i. p. 213; sim. *ib.* ii. p. 114.

[16] *ÄZ.* 19, 18.

[17] *Siut* 3, 11.

[18] So too earlier *iwt* in *n-iwt* 'because not', see *ÄZ.* 50, 110.

VOCABULARY

ʿwꜣ rob, steal.

wḏ command.

ḥwn be young, rejuvenated.

swḏ, var. , hand over, bequeath.

šnʿ repel, turn back (someone).

iḥ ox.

ʿꜣ door; *iry-ʿꜣ* door-keeper.

wnwt priesthood, priests (collective).

Pr-ʿꜣ the Great House or palace; Pharaoh (see above p. 75).

nfr-ḥꜣt diadem, or like; *iry nfr-ḥꜣt* keeper of the diadem (?)

hy, var. *hꜣy*, husband.

ḫnw chattels, belongings, lit. vessels.

ḫꜣrt, var. *ḫꜣrt*, widow.

nmḥ orphan, waif, poor man.

sf yesterday; *m sf* yesterday, adverb.

sḫty peasant, fowler.

ššp image, idol.

šmsw follower, attendant.

ꜣs quickly.

tn where? whence?

ḫrw down, lower part; *m ḫrw* downcast.

EXERCISE XVII

(*a*) *Reading lesson; from a funerary stela of Dyn. XII*:[1]

iry nfr-ḥꜣt šmsw Pr-ʿꜣ Nb·(i)-pw-Snwsrt,[2]

ḏd·f n wnwt ḥwt-nṯr nt ꜣbḏw,

ḥwwt·f[3] *nt n-sw-bit*:

ḥwn nsw m ʿnḫ·ṯn,[4]

mn n·ṯn mnw n nṯrw·ṯn niwtyw,

[1] Brit. Mus. 101, see *JEA*. 21, 1. The position of the signs and not very regular orthography are here retained.

[2] A compound name 'Senwosret-is-(my)-lord'; on its last element *S-n-Wsrt*, see above, p. 71, n. 4.

[3] Town names being fem. (§ 92, 1), *f* can refer only to the *nṯr* of *ḥwt-nṯr* or to the name of Osiris implicitly present, see *JEA*. 23, 261; hence our translation 'its' is not strictly accurate.

[4] This formula (cf. *Urk*. iv. 365; old writing *ḥn*) elsewhere has no suffix after *ʿnḫ*; here perhaps a mistake.

wnn·ṯn ḥr ḥswt nt ỉty·ṯn,
swḏ·ṯn ỉꜣwt·ṯn n ẖrdw·ṯn,
wnn msw·ṯn mn (§ 326) *ḥr nswt·ṯn*
m ỉꜣwt·ṯn nt ḏt;
nn ḥḳr·ṯn,
nn ỉbỉ·ṯn,
ỉw wḏ·n nṯr ꜥꜣ wnn·ṯn tp tꜣ ḥr ḥswt·f;
nn šnꜥ·tw·ṯn m st ḳsnt,
ḥr ḥswt nt nṯrw·ṯn nỉwtyw,
ḏd·ṯn:[1] *ḥtp dỉ nsw*[2] *Wsỉr nb ꜣbḏw,*
nṯr ꜥꜣ Wnn-nfr,[3]
ḫꜣ m t ḥnḳt kꜣw ꜣpdw, prt-ḫrw[4] *m ḥb nb,*[5]
n kꜣ n ỉry nfr-ḥꜣt šmsw Pr-ꜥꜣ
Nb(·ỉ)-pw-Snwsrt, ỉr n (§ 361) *'Itꜣ.*

[1] The promises are clearly all dependent on the condition that the priests shall recite the funerary formula.
[2] See below pp. 170–2.
[3] A name of Osiris, in Greek Onnophris, probably meaning 'he who is happy'.
[4] See below p. 172.
[5] The sign serves also as det. (=) of *ḥb* preceding, see § 62A (Add.)

'The keeper of the diadem (?) and attendant of the Great House Nebipusenwosret. He says to the priesthood of the temple of Abydus, and (of) its chapels of the king of Upper and Lower Egypt:—The king shall be rejuvenated in your (?) life, the monuments of your city gods shall stand firm for you, ye shall be in (lit. under) the favour of your sovereign, ye shall hand on your offices to your children, and your offspring shall be established upon your seats in your offices of eternity; ye shall not hunger, ye shall not thirst, nay the great god has commanded that ye be on earth in his favour; ye shall not be repelled in (any) difficult place, (being) in the favour of your city gods; (according as) ye shall say: An offering which the king gives (to) Osiris, lord of Abydus, (even) the great god Onnophris; a thousand of bread, beer, oxen and fowl, invocation-offerings at every feast, to the spirit of the keeper of the diadem (?) and attendant of the Great House, Nebipusenwosret, son of Ita.'

(*b*) *Write in hieroglyphs and transliteration*:

(1) Now when he had heard this, he went forth very quickly to the door (*sbꜣ*) of the temple, and sat down beside the door-keepers who were there. And one of (lit. in) them said to him: ²Whence ¹hast-thou-come? And he was silent, his face downcast, and he answered them not. (2) It shall be well with you, (if) ye do the like. (3) As my father lives for me, I speak in truth. (4) Would I had (some) potent (*mnḫ*) idol, that I might steal the belongings of

this peasant by means of it. (5) He loved me, (because) he knew my arms were vigorous. (6) She is more beautiful than she was yesterday. (7) I was a possessor of favour upon the earth, forasmuch as I was a father of the orphan and a husband of the widow.

(*c*) *Translate into hieroglyphs in several different ways*:

(1) His Majesty honoured him *when he was* a child. (2) I knew *that* she was a goddess *because* she had said these words. (3) *When* he had arrived at the city, he found no one.

EXCURSUS B

The Formula of Offering employed in the Funerary Cult.

Throughout the period covered by this book, the presentation of food-offerings, whether real or fictitious, and alike in temple and in tomb, was called *ỉrt ḥtp-dỉ-nsw* 'performing (the rite named) *ḥotp-di-nesu*', or 'a-boon-which-the-king-gives'. The offerer, who is in theory Horus, the son and heir of the dead Osiris, stands with arm upraised in the attitude of invocation (his gesture is that of *nỉs* 'calling' or 'invoking') before the shrine, statue, or stela of the god or deceased parent, and pronounces the *ḥotp-di-nesu* formula; there was deemed to be little difference in the efficacy of this, whether actual offerings were present or whether they were only imagined or desired.

We will here quote one short, but typical, example of the *ḥotp-di-nesu* formula, as inscribed on innumerable stelae and other funerary monuments:

Ḥtp dỉ nsw Wsỉr nb Ḏdw, nṯr ꜥꜣ, nb ꜣbḏw,
dỉ·f prt-ḫrw (m) t ḥnḳt, kꜣw ꜣpdw, šs mnḫt,
ḫt nbt nfrt wꜥbt ꜥnḫt (§ 384) nṯr ỉm,
n kꜣ n ỉmꜣḫy S-n-Wsrt, mꜣꜥ-ḫrw.

'A boon which the king gives (to) Osiris, lord of Busiris,[1] the great god, lord of Abydus, that he may give invocation-offerings consisting of bread and beer, oxen and fowl, alabaster and clothing, all things good and pure on which a god lives, to the spirit of the revered Senwosret, justified.'[2]

The phrase *ḥtp dỉ nsw* is one of very ancient date;[3] in spite of a slight doubt as to whether *dỉ* is the verb-form which we shall come to know as the relative form (§ 382), as well as some uncertainty as to the precise meaning of *ḥtp*, the phrase may with approximate accuracy be rendered 'a boon which the king gives'. In the Old Kingdom this phrase is frequently employed in reference to favours of various kinds bestowed upon his subjects by the king;

[1] A town in the centre of the Delta.

[2] Brit. Mus. 198 (Dyn. XII).

[3] For a full discussion see *Th. T. S.* i. 79–93; critically reviewed by G. FARINA in *Rivista degli studi orientali* 7, 467.

among such boons we find clothing, coffins, a sacrificial ox, or again even the rank and title of prince. The food-offerings made by the living Pharaoh in the pyramid-temple of his deceased father or predecessor were likewise known as *ḥtp nsw* 'a boon of the king'. In fact, it would seem as though all funerary gifts and privileges were in a certain sense boons given by the king, though certain deities like Anubis, the god of embalmment, Osiris, at once the dead king and king of the dead, or Geb, the earth-god, were also desired or recognized as givers of like benefits. Hence in the Old Kingdom we find on almost every funerary false door or lintel some such formula as the following:[1]

Ḥtp dỉ nsw, ḥtp (dỉ) ʾInpw, ḫnty sḥ nṯr, tpy ḏw·f,
pr n·f ḫrw[2] *m ḥb nb*[3] *rʿ nb,*
Ptḥ-špss.

'A boon which the king gives, and a boon (which) Anubis, in front of the divine booth, he who is upon his mountain, (gives): (namely) that there may be (made) invocation-offerings for him at every festival and every day; Ptaḥshepses.'

There are many variants, and in place of the food-offerings here aspired to we frequently find reference to such benefits as a goodly burial in the West, or power to walk 'on the roads upon which the revered ones walk'. The point to be observed, however, is that in the Old Kingdom the king and whatever god is named are mentioned *in parallelism* with one another as givers of the boon or boons bestowed; the phrase *ḥtp dỉ nsw* is followed by the co-ordinated phrase *ḥtp dỉ ʾInpw* (*Wsỉr*, *Gb*) 'a boon which Anubis (*or* Osiris, *or* Geb) gives', though for the complete writing *ḥtp dỉ ʾInpw* is frequently substituted, as in the example quoted, or even alone.

That the *ḥotp-di-nesu* formula found in Middle Egyptian is the direct outcome of the Old Kingdom formula discussed above is quite apparent; but it is equally apparent that in the later period it had undergone re-interpretation. A series of variants shows that the divine name which follows the phrase *ḥtp dỉ nsw* was now understood as a dative, though it is only at a far later period that the preposition *n* was inserted. The best proof of this re-interpretation is the fact that, if one god is named after the phrase *ḥtp dỉ nsw*, the following clause of purpose has *dỉ·f* 'that he may give' (see the example which served as our starting-point) with a singular suffix-pronoun, whereas if several gods are named we find *dỉ·sn* 'that they may give'; had the king and the god (or gods) been still regarded as collateral givers of the funerary benefits, the verb *dỉ·sn* with plural suffix would have been found in all cases.

Thus, in the Middle Kingdom and later, the idea underlying the *ḥotp-di-nesu* formula is that the king gives, or has given, or is to give, an offering to some god in his temple, in order that the latter in turn may give offerings to a private

[1] *Saqq. Mast.* 28.

[2] The signs following *n·f* are here determinatives, see p. 172.

[3] *Cf.* p. 169, n. 5.

individual in his tomb or wherever a memorial of that individual has been dedicated. The view thus indicated of the source of private funerary offerings corresponds to the actual practice of the Twelfth Dynasty and later, since of the vast quantities of food accruing to the temples only a small portion was consumed by the priests, the rest being distributed by contract or otherwise to the persons in charge of private funerary cults;[1] such persons, if not the sons or immediate relatives of the priests, were known as *ḥmw-kꜣ* 'soul-priests', lit. 'servants of the *ka*' (see below). In Middle Egyptian may be rendered 'an offering which the king gives', since the boon therein contemplated was always food-offerings. Many more divine names are used than in the Old Kingdom, when only a few funerary and chthonic deities were regarded as givers of boons in company with the king.

The difficult expression obviously had *pr ḫrw* 'the voice goes forth' as its starting-point, these words referring to the *ḥotp-di-nesu* formula accompanying the presentation. The actual offerings were, however, so closely associated with the expression that this often received the determinative and practically acquired the meaning 'make an offering'. Throughout the Old Kingdom *pr* was treated grammatically as a transitive verb with *ḫrw* as object, whether or not the whole was consciously felt to mean 'send forth the voice' with evocative magical intent.[2] Side by side with this verbal use was the compound noun *prt-ḫrw* of which the first element was the infinitive *prt* 'a going' or 'sending' forth (§ 298).[2a] Both verbal and nominal uses are perhaps best paraphrased with the help of the term 'invocation-offerings', as in our translations above. After O. K. the writing is shown by the variant[3] to be equivalent to *di·f prt-ḫrw m t m ḥnḳt* 'that he may give an invocation-offering consisting of bread and of beer'. Various other species of offering then follow in abbreviated spellings; is for *kꜣw* 'oxen' and for *ꜣpdw* 'fowl';[4] *šs*, often written or , has the early variants [5] and [6] and so must mean 'alabaster', doubtless in allusion to the seven alabaster oil-jars[7] deemed indispensable to the dead; is *mnḫt* 'clothing'.[8] In Dyn. XVIII was, however, sometimes interpreted as *prt-r-ḫrw* 'coming-forth-at-the-voice offerings',[9] but it is not clear whether this referred to the emergence of the offerings themselves or to the coming forth of the deceased from his burial chamber at the call of the offerer.[10]

In Middle Egyptian the funerary oblation is said to be made *n kꜣ n* 'to the *ka* of' the deceased. In this context the word *kꜣ*, if translated at all, is best translated 'spirit'.[11] The term appears to embrace the entire 'self' of a person regarded as an entity to some extent separable from that person. Modern concepts to which that of the *ka* occasionally corresponds are 'personality', 'soul', 'individuality', 'temperament'; the word may even mean a man's 'fortune' or 'position'.[12] The Egyptians conceived of such notions in a more personal

[1] See above, p. 70, n. 2. The technical term in O. K. for this 'diversion' of offerings was *wdb* 'change', see *JEA.* 24, 86; 25, 215.

[2] Clère in *Mél. Masp.* i, pp. 753 ff.

[2a] No other transitive use of *prt* occurs in Egyptian, though it does in Coptic.

[3] Brit. Mus. 162.

[4] See *Bull. Metr. Mus. New York* 9, 239; Nav. ch. 125, *Nachschrift* 4. In very late times 'oxen' was read *iḥ*, see Brit. Mus. 330; Florence 1660. 1661.

[5] *Pyr.* 745; Saḳḳârah, tomb of Mereruka.

[6] *Pyr.* 1332; sim. without ꜣ and *š*, *Saqq. Mast.* i. 23; Berl. *AI.* i. p. 99.

[7] Ex. *Saqq. Mast.* i. 28.

[8] *Šs* and *mnḫt* phonetically, Turin 1447.

[9] Exx. Budge, p. 150, 16; 261, 4; 366, 7. The last two signs determine the entire phrase, see § 61.

[10] Elsewhere 'at the voice' is *ḥr ḫrw*, exx. *Pyr.* 796; Louvre C. 74. However, late exx. show *r ḫrw* with the same meaning, see *Wb.* I, 528, 11; *Rec.* 7, 119.

[11] Bibliography for the *ka*, see *Th. T. S.* i. 99; add *ÄZ.* 49, 126.

[12] Cf. *ir·n nb tꜣwy kꜣ·f* 'one whose fortune the lord of the two lands made', *Urk.* iv. 486, 3; sim. *Bersh.* ii. 21, 15.

and tangible way than we do; hence the *bai* ('soul', see below), the 'shadow' (*šwt*), and the 'corpse' (*ẖꜣt*) were all apt to be viewed as beings distinct from, and as it were the doubles of, the person to whom they belonged. The student must beware of the attempts which have been made to give a harmonious and self-consistent account of the nature of the *ka*; this always remained a shadowy and ill-defined concept, variously regarded in different contexts. A second word for 'soul' is *bꜣ*, in Dyn. XVIII often written , for which a longer, but more precise, rendering would be 'external manifestation'. Both in life and in death an individual man might assume different forms; the form taken by him was called his *bai* (*bꜣ*), and one of the typical shapes was that of a bird, as is seen in the hieroglyphic writing of the word.[0]

[0] For a recent discussion of the *bai* see *ÄZ.* 77, 78 ff.

LESSON XVIII

DIRECT AND INDIRECT SPEECH

§ **224**. By way of conclusion to the lessons on subordinate clauses, some notice may be accorded to the Egyptian methods of introducing the *content of a speech.* It must be observed that the highly developed indirect speech found in Latin, where all the pronouns after 'he said' or the like are reduced to 3rd pers., hardly exists in Egyptian. The nearest approach to it is found in such examples as the second in § 184, where 'he said he would fight with me' presupposes as its original 'he said, I will fight with him (*or* thee)'.[1]

[1] Sim. *P. Kah.* 29, 17–8. See too ERM. *Gramm.*[4] § 533.

Contrary to expectation, *ntt* 'that' is not found after verbs of saying. The speech is usually introduced directly, without any introductory phrase. So very frequently after *ḏd·f* 'he says', 'he said', and its equivalent *ḏd* (§ 450, 1).

Exx. . . . . *r-pꜥt ḥꜣty-ꜥ . . . . Sꜣ-nht, ḏd·f: ink šmsw* the prince . . . . . . Sinuhe said: I was a henchman.[2]

 ḥry-tp nsw imꜣḫw Ṯti, ḏd: ink mry nb·f he who is at the head of the king, the revered Tjetji, says: I was one beloved of his lord.[3]

[2] *Sin.* R 1–2. Sim. *Peas.* B 1, 53. 74. 88; *Sh. S.* 69.

[3] Brit. Mus. 614, 3.

So also after other forms of, and substitutes for, the verb 'to say'.[4] When the main verb either has nothing to do with speaking, or else only hints at it, the phrase *r ḏd* (§ 304, 3) 'saying', lit. 'in order to say', is often used.

[4] *Sin.* B 23; *Peas.* R 2. 5. 41; *Leb.* 4. 56. 86; *Westc.* 8, 13. After *sḏm*, *Mill.* 2, 5.

Exx. I went round my enclosure rejoicing *r ḏd: ir·tw nn mi m* and saying: How (comes it that) this is done?[5]

 ꜥḥꜥ·n dwꜣ·n·f n·i nṯr ꜥꜣ r ḫt nbt r ḏd: wꜣḏ·wy ir nꜣ n nṯr·f thereupon he praised god for me more than anything, saying: How happy is he who has done this for his god![6]

[5] *Sin.* B 202. Sim. *Westc.* 3, 6; 12, 23. 24; *Urk.* iv. 649, 4; 751, 8.

[6] Louvre C 12, 12–14. Sim. *P. Kah.* 13, 23–4; *Urk.* iv. 1106, 1. 3; 1108, 6.

In Dyn. XII *r ḏd* is already found quite tautologically after verbs of saying.

Ex. *ꜥḥꜥ·n ḏd·n·f n·sn r ḏd: mṯn rdỉ·n·ỉ n·ṯn* then he said to them, saying: Behold, I have given to you, etc.[1]

Here *r ḏd* cannot well be translated 'that'; but by Dyn. XVIII it had acquired this value, since it is now, though very rarely, used even after *rḫ*.

Ex. *ỉw·ỉ rḫ·kwỉ r ḏd ẖnw·f pw* I know that it is his resting-place.[2]

When insistence is laid on the fact that the words given are the exact words of the speaker, *m ḏd* is apt to take the place of *r ḏd*.

Ex. *ꜥḥꜥ·n rdỉ·n sr pn wḏt m ḥr·ỉ m ḏd* thereupon this official placed the command before me as follows, lit. in saying.[3]

In dialogue the speeches occasionally follow one upon the other without any indication of the speaker, in accordance with the practice adopted in modern novels.[4]

§ 225. *r·ntt* introducing statements.—In addition to its meaning 'inasmuch as' (§ 223) *r-ntt* is used, especially in official writing, to express the content of some communication; it is perhaps best translated 'to the effect that'.

Ex. *swḏꜣ ỉb pw n nb*[4a] *r-ntt hrw nb n nb ꜥḏ wḏꜣ* it is a communication to (lit. a making easy the heart of) (my) lord to the effect that all the affairs of (my) lord are safe and prosperous.[5]

Occasionally this *r-ntt* is found without any preceding verb, and is then practically untranslatable.[6]

PARTICLES

§ 226. The name **particle** is given by grammarians to any minor invariable part of speech like a preposition or a conjunction. Here, however, it will be used as a class-name for those relatively unimportant words (like *mk*, *ỉsṯ*, *grt*, *ỉs*) of which the characteristic is that they usually stand either at or very near the beginning of the sentence. The words in question are as a rule classed as 'conjunctions', though this term is often clearly inappropriate. The name 'sentence-adverb' is much nearer the mark, since they frequently serve to modify, or to present in a certain light, the substance of an entire sentence. But since some, like *swt* and *ỉs*, may be used also to qualify mere phrases or even single words, the vaguer term 'particle' will be retained.

The Egyptian particles may be **enclitic** or **non-enclitic**. Only the latter can stand as the first word of a sentence. The others, which owe their name to the Gk. *enklitikos* 'leaning upon', need the support of a preceding word, presumably because they possess no accent or tone-vowel of their own.[7]

Many of the words here to be enumerated have been discussed already; in such cases it will suffice to supplement the statements made previously.

[1] *Siut* I, 275.

[2] *Urk.* iv. 736, 16, *ỉw* and *·f* restored.

[3] Louvre C 12, 5. Sim. *ib.* C 11, 1; *P. Kah.* 13. 27; Munich 3, 18; *Th. T. S.* iii. 26, 5.

[4] Exx. *Sin.* B 36. 43, contrasting the same passages in R; *Sh. S.* 73; *Westc.* 5, 7; *Eb.* 69, 3-4; *Urk.* v. 155-6; LAC. *TR.* 23, 19-22, qu. § 506, 1.

[4a] See § 313 for this word and its adjuncts not here transliterated.

[5] *P. Kah.* 27, 8. Sim. *Kopt.* 8, 3. 4; *Urk.* iv. 2, 9 (after *ḏd·f*); 138, 13; 649, 5.

[6] *Urk.* iv. 649, 11; 650, 8.

[7] HANS ABEL, *Zur Tonverschmelzung im Altaegyptischen*. Leipzig, 1910. But see also ERMAN, *Unterschiede zwischen d. koptischen Dialekten bei d. Wortverbindung* in *Sitzungsber. d kön. . . . Preuss. Akad. d. Wiss.*, 1915, x.

Non-enclitic particles (§§ 227–244):—

§ 227. ***ỉn* 'indeed'.**—This particle, with which the preposition *ỉn* 'by' introducing the agent (§ 168) is clearly identical, serves to lay a stress of one kind or another on sentences or parts of sentences. It enters into the composition of those independent pronouns which begin with *n* or *ỉn* (§ 64), so that these are found in several uses parallel to, i.e. forming paradigm with, *ỉn* + noun.[1]

1. When employed to qualify whole sentences, *ỉn* gives to them *interrogative* force. See in detail below §§ 492–4.

Exx. *ỉn ꜥwꜣ·tw·ỉ rf m ḏꜣtt·f* shall I be robbed in his province?[2]

ỉn ỉw·k r s n nḥḥ wilt thou be a man of eternity?[3]

2. In its other uses *ỉn* emphasizes some particular noun. So in the construction *ỉn* + noun + *sḏm·f* (or independent pronoun + *sḏm·f*), which has always *future* sense.[4] See further below § 450, 5 *e*.

Exx. As to everyone who shall lift up his hand to this image, *ỉn Ḏḥwty ḥs·f sw* Thoth shall praise him.[5]

ỉn wr n pꜣ ẖrdw 3 .... ỉn·f n·k sy the eldest of the three children .... shall bring it to thee. Or better: it is the eldest of, etc. .... who shall bring, etc.[6]

As the second of these examples shows, the effect of *ỉn* thus placed before a grammatical subject in anticipatory emphasis (§ 148, 1) may be to give it the value of the logical predicate (§ 126). Only when this occurs can we render in English 'it is X who will'. In other instances, as in the first, *ỉn* merely marks the presence of this stereotyped future construction.

3. A related construction consisting of

{ *ỉn* + noun / *or* independent pronoun } + { perfective / *or* imperfective } active participle

yields the counterpart, for *past* or *present* time, of the future construction just described. Some attention must here be given to the use of *ỉn*, although the participles belong to a later stage in our studies; see below § 373.

Exx. *ỉn sš Ỉꜥḥ-msw spẖr snn pn* it was the scribe ꜥAḥmosĕ who copied this writing. Lit. verily the scribe ꜥAḥmosĕ was the-one-who-copied this writing.[7]

ỉst ỉn ḥm·ỉ sdf(ꜣ) ḥbw tp-trw lo, My Majesty provided for the festivals of the seasons. Lit. lo verily My Majesty was the-one-who-provisioned the festivals of the beginning of seasons.[8]

In this construction has survived the otherwise almost obsolete mode of expressing a nominal predicate after nominal subject by direct juxtaposition (see above § 125); for the participle is merely an adjective of a special sort, here used

[1] See *ÄZ.* 29, 121; *JEA.* 20, 13.
[2] *Peas.* B 1, 18.
[3] *Peas.* B 1, 95.
[4] See Gunn, *Stud.* ch. v.
[5] *Hat-Nub* 10, 12.
[6] *Westc.* 9, 7–8.
[7] *Rhind*, title.
[8] *Urk.* iv. 750.

as a noun. *In* merely reinforces the first word; in the Pyramid Texts may still be found rare examples of *in* + nom. subj. + a noun, not a participle, as predicate.[1] The parallel construction consisting of indep. pronoun + participle (ex. *ntf dd st* 'he it is who says it'; see further below § 373), falls into line with indep. pron. + nom. pred., which, as we saw in § 125, is common at all periods.

Here again *in* is apt to give to the grammatical subject the value of the logical predicate, and in this case the English equivalent is of the form 'it is X who did' or 'does'. Examples occur, however, where we must render simply 'X does' or 'X did', *in* having hardly any force at all.[2]

When, in either of these constructions (2) and (3), the subject is the interrogative pronoun *m* 'who?', 'what?', the combination *in* + *m* is sometimes shortened and welded together in the form or much more rarely [3] *n-m*.

Exx. *in m dd sw* who says it?[4]

n-m in tw who is it that has brought thee?[5]

n-m irf hsf·f bw hwrw who then will repel evil?[6]

4. When introducing the agent after a passive form of the verb (§ 39, end) or the infinitive (§ 300), *in* has clearly the function of a preposition, and has therefore been classified under that head (§ 168). Nevertheless, the alternation of *in* + noun with the independent pronouns to express the agent after the infinitive proves that *in* here is the same word as in the uses (2) and (3) above. For examples see below § 300, towards end.

5. A very rare extension of the prepositional use of *in* is to introduce a noun defining a pronoun which either precedes or follows.

Exx. *smn·s wi in 3st hr 3kr* she establishes me, does (lit. by) Isis, on Earth.[7]

in iwꜥ·(i) pw .... swt rdi n·i s(y) it is this (my) heir, ... he has given it to me.[8]

Obs. For *in* as formative in the *sdm·in·f* form of the verb, see below § 427; and as a means of indicating the speaker, below § 436.

§ 228. *ih* may ultimately be a noun related to *ht*, *iht* 'thing', and the interrogative pronoun *ih* 'what?' (§ 501) is doubtless derived from it. As a particle *ih* means 'then' or 'therefore', often best rendered 'so that', and is always followed by the *sdm·f* form of the verb (§§ 40, 3; 118, 2).

In its commonest signification *ih* expresses a *desired future consequence*.

Exx. *wn n·i, ih dd·i m3t·n·i* open to me, so that I may say what I have seen.[9] Literally: open to me; then I will say, etc.

Pour water on thy hands, *ih wšb·k wšd·t(w)·k* so that thou mayst answer when thou art addressed.[10]

[1] *Pyr.* 1370a; 1988a. See *Nominalsatz*, § 24.

[2] For a detailed analysis of the meanings of *in* see GUNN, *Studies*, pp. 61 foll.

[3] *Harhotpe* 431.

[4] *P. Kah.* 8, 24; *Rhind* 35.

[5] *Sh. S.* 69. 84. Sim. *Urk.* v. 148, 3.

[6] *Peas.* B 106. Sim., but with *in m*, *Urk.* v. 168, 15; *Westc.* 9, 6.

[7] LAC. *TR.* 43, 5.

[8] LAC. *TR.* 47, 35–6.

[9] BUDGE, p. 186, 10. Sim. 1st pers. *Pt.* 30; *Peas.* B1, 30; Cairo 20040, *a* 2; Leyd. V3, 5.

[10] *Sh. S.* 14–5. Sim. 2nd pers. *Pt.* 619; *Peas.* B1, 178; BUDGE, p. 165, 13.

Would that it were the end of men ...... [hieroglyphs] *iḫ gr tꜣ m ḫrw* then would the earth cease from noise.[1]

From this meaning subtle gradations lead to the use in *exhortations* and even *commands*.[2] Note, however, that in every shade of meaning the sentence with *iḫ* 'then', 'therefore' refers to some still future result of precedent actions.

Exx. Is Thoth mild? [hieroglyphs] *iḫ ir·k iyt* in that case thou shalt do mischief.[3] The question is a rhetorical substitute for an *if*-clause assuming an absurdity.

[hieroglyphs] *iḫ ir·n dmi n sp* then let us make a habitation together.[4]

For the use of *wn·f* after *iḫ*, when the predicate is adverbial, see § 118, 2; and of *tm·f*, when the construction is negatived, see § 346, 4; for the forms of *sḏm·f* which are employed, see §§ 440, 4; 450, 5, *a*.

[1] *Adm.* 6, 1. Sim. 3rd pers. *Sin.* B 168; *Pt.* 33. 39. 600. 626; *Leb.* 45–6; *Urk.* iv. 492, 7; 945, 2.

[2] Best ex. *Urk.* iv. 80, qu. § 440, 4.

[3] *Peas.* B 1, 150. Sim. *Urk.* iv. 1088, 5; 3rd pers. *ib.* 650, 13; *Peas.* B 1, 80.

[4] *Leb.* 154. Rather similarly Cairo 20538, ii. *c* 7, qu. § 118, 2.

§ 229. [hieroglyphs] *iḫr*. See below § 239.

§ 230. [hieroglyphs] *isk*[5] or [hieroglyphs] *sk*,[6] the latter form being preferred when a dependent pronoun follows, may be regarded merely as archaic writings of [hieroglyphs] *isṯ* and [hieroglyphs] *sṯ* (§ 231); in the Old Kingdom certain words normally written with *ṯ* (*č*) are found to have variant writings with *k*, whether as different pronunciations or as attempts to render an obscure consonant.[7]

[5] *Eb.* 1, 19; *Urk.* iv. 219, 4; 228, 4; 260, 17 (*isṯ*, 14), qu. § 119, 3; 261, 12; BUDGE, p. 291, 4. 6. With dep. pron. *Urk.* iv. 157, 3.

[6] Louvre C 15, qu. § 119, 3; Cairo 20453; *Eb.* 39, 18.

[7] ERM. *Gramm.*[3] § 120; SETHE, *Verbum*, i. § 285, 2; EMBER, in *Johns Hopkins University Circular*, New Series, 1919, no. 6, pp. 29–31.

§ 231. [hieroglyphs] *isṯ*,[8] in Dyn. XVIII often [hieroglyphs] *ist*, with the alternative rarer forms [hieroglyphs] *sṯ* and [hieroglyphs] *st*, exceptional writings [hieroglyphs] *isti*[9] and [hieroglyphs] *sti*;[10] [hieroglyphs] is properly the form to be employed when a dependent pronoun follows (§§ 44, 2; 119, 2), but this distinction is no longer consistently observed in Middle Egyptian.[11] *'Isṯ* is clearly derived from the enclitic particle [hieroglyphs] *is* 'lo', 'verily' (§ 247) by the addition of an abbreviated form of the dependent pronoun 2nd m. sing.; this origin was, however, no longer felt, since forms varying according to the gender and number of the persons addressed, such as are found in the case of *mk* (§§ 119, 1; 234), are here wanting. The translation 'lo' is purely conventional; the function of the particle is to describe situations or concomitant facts. It is used both in verbal (§§ 152; 212; 402; 414, 1; 422, 1) and in non-verbal (§§ 119, 2; 133; 142; 214) sentences, as well as in the type of sentence which we shall call pseudo-verbal (§ 324). Sentences introduced by *isṯ* are sometimes to be rendered as independent sentences and sometimes as clauses of time or circumstance. Common combinations of particles are [hieroglyphs] *isṯ rf* (see above §§ 119, 2; 152) and [hieroglyphs] *isṯ grt* 'but lo'.[12] For [hieroglyphs] *isṯ* used as an enclitic see § 248.

[8] For the forms see *Rec.* 28, 186; and for the use, *Rec.* 19, 187.

[9] *Hamm.* 47, 3.

[10] *Sinai* 90, 2, qu. § 134.

[11] See, however, Brit. Mus. 614, 4, qu. § 119, 2.

[12] Berl. *ÄI.* i. p. 258, 20; *Siut* 1, 279; BUDGE, p. 280, 8.

§ 232. [hieroglyphs] *isw* is rare and may have the same meaning as *isṯ*; it appears to introduce main clauses only.

Ex. [hieroglyphs] *isw Sḫmt pw* lo, he is (like) Sachmis.[13]

[13] *P. Kah.* 2, 20. Sim. *ib.* 2, 12–19. Before a verb, *Mill.* 2, 1 (doubtful).

§ 233. *wnt* 'that'[1] is probably the feminine singular of the perfective participle from *wnn* 'be', 'exist'. It serves to introduce noun clauses as object of certain verbs (§ 187), and is much rarer and more restricted in use than its synonym *ntt* (§ 237).

§ 234. ***m* and its derivatives.**[2]— *m*, older, is possibly an obsolete imperative meaning 'behold'. Instances of its occurrence in this simple form are very rare; one has been quoted in § 217, and another, likewise followed by the dependent pronoun 1st sing., may now be added:

m wỉ m ꜣḫ pn behold, I am this spirit.[3]

Everywhere else, *m* is welded together with a pronoun of 2nd pers. which resembles a suffix-pronoun, but which is probably always an abbreviated form of an old dependent pronoun. In Middle Egyptian, the element *m* is usually supplemented, and occasionally replaced, by a sign borrowed from the imperative *ỉmỉ* 'give' (§ 336); this sign is in Dyn. XII identical with the ideogram in *rdỉ* 'give', but in Dyn. XVIII is usually differentiated from it as; hieratic does not distinguish it from, and is also not infrequently found in hieroglyphic. Hence we obtain:

mk,[4] in Dyn. XII,[5] in hieratic regularly and also elsewhere[6], in Dyn. XVIII sometimes,[7] besides an archaistic spelling.[8] *Mk* is used when a single male person, or else no one in particular, is addressed.[9]

mṯ,[10] later writing,[11] when a woman is addressed.

or *mṯn*, later, *mtn*, when several persons are addressed.[12]

All these forms may serve as supports to the dependent pronouns; for examples see §§ 44, 2; 119, 1; § 324. For the indefinite pronoun *tw* 'one' after *mk* see §§ 47. 324.

Mk and its congeners are essentially *pictorial* in meaning, serving to depict some fact as vividly present in the mind. With non-verbal sentences the time referred to is usually the *present*, and in English one must practically always render as an independent sentence, not as a subordinate clause; examples with adverbial (§ 119, 1), nominal (§ 133), and adjectival (§ 142) predicate have already been quoted.

With the *sḏm·f* form, curiously enough, the event which *mk* serves to picture is nearly always, not present,[13] but *future*.

Exx. *mk šsp·n wnwt bỉnt* behold, we shall have a bad time, lit. receive an evil hour.[14]

mk ỉb·k sšm·f n·k tw behold, thy heart shall guide thee for thyself.[15]

mk wnn rn·k r nḥḥ behold, thy name shall exist for ever.[16]

[1] *Rev. Eg.*, nouv. sér. 2, 53.
[2] *Rec.* 28, 186; 35, 217.
[3] *Urk.* iv. 547.
[4] *Rekh.* 10; *Urk.* iv. 509, 17.
[5] *BH.* ii. 7; *Meir* i. 2; Louvre C 18.
[6] *Bersh.* i. 22; ii. 21; *Paheri* 7.
[7] *Rec.* 26, 3; *D. el B.* 69.
[8] *Siut* 1, 271. 272.
[9] *Rhind* 61 *a*, 6.
[10] *Th. T. S.* ii. 11.
[11] *Paheri* 7.
[12] Mar. *Abyd.* ii. 30, 33; *Adm.* 7, 1.
[13] Present perhaps *Urk.* iv. 1092, 2; *Paheri* 7.
[14] *P. Kah.* 32, 18. Sim. *Siut* 1, 323.
[15] *Urk.* iv. 519.
[16] *Siut* 4, 23. Sim. *ib.* 1, 315; *Th. T. S.* ii. 8. Cf. also *P. Kah.* 3, 36, qu. § 142.

With the *śdm·n·f* form, *mk* has the effect of giving to this the meaning of the English *present perfect*.

Ex. [hieroglyphs] *mk pḥ·n·n ḫnw* behold, we have reached home.[1]

The usual negation of the *śdm·n·f* form being *n śdm·f* (§ 105, 1), we find *mk n śdm·f* meaning 'behold, he has not heard' (§ 455, 1). The passive *śdm·f* form often serves as the passive of *śdm·n·f*; hence, when preceded by *mk*, it has *present perfect* sense (§ 422, 1).

For *mk* where the predicate is the old perfective, or else *ḥr* + infinitive, see below § 324.

Lastly, *mk* may be used simply with a following noun or dependent pronoun to indicate what is present; cf. French *voici*.

Exx. [hieroglyphs] *mk bi3yt ḫprt m rk it·k* here is (lit. behold) a wonder which happened in the time of thy father.[2]

[hieroglyphs] *mk wi* here am I.[3] Cf. French *me voici*.

Obs. In a biographical inscription of Dyn. XVIII *mk* is strangely used before the infinitive where we should expect the preposition *ḥr*; the constructions in question are *wn·in·f ḥr śdm* (§ 470)[4] and *ˁḥˁ·n·f ḥr śdm* (§ 482, 1).[5]

§ **235.** [hieroglyph] *nn*, with shortened form [hieroglyph] *n*, is the common word for 'not'; see above § 104. For the various uses of the two forms see §§ 105. 108. 120. 134. 144. 200. 201. 209. 258. 307. 334. 346. 394. 402. 418. 424. 445. 455. 456. 491. As we have seen §§ 44, 2; 120, [hieroglyph] may be followed by a dependent pronoun.

Obs. In certain cases *nn* and *n* cannot be used, and are replaced by the negative verb from the stems *imi* and *tm*, see below §§ 342–50.

§ **236.** [hieroglyphs] *nḥmn*[6] 'assuredly' or the like, may likewise be followed by a dependent pronoun. The particle is rare, but examples with adverbial (§ 119, 6) and verbal predicates are both found. An example of the latter is [hieroglyphs] *nḥmn wi pr·n·i m S3w* of a truth, I have come forth from Sais.[7]

See below § 324 for an example of *nḥmn* + noun + old perfective.

Obs. *Nḥmn* is doubtless connected with the enclitic *ḥm* (§ 253), which has the same meaning. In the earlier hieratic exx. [hieroglyph] is written for [hieroglyph], see §§ 24; 119, 6.

§ **237.** [hieroglyphs] *ntt* 'that' is properly the f. sing. of the relative adjective *nty* used as a neuter (§ 199); cf. French *qui* 'who', *que* 'that'. It introduces noun clauses when these are objects of certain verbs (§ 187). Such noun clauses with *ntt* may also follow certain prepositions and, in conjunction with them, form adverb clauses (§ 223). For [hieroglyphs] *r-ntt* ushering in statements see § 225, and for the problematical construction [hieroglyphs] *in ntt* see § 494. The dependent pronouns may follow *ntt*, see § 44, 2, but in their place are sometimes found the suffixes of 2nd and 3rd pers. sing., see § 223, end.

[1] *Sh. S.* 2. Sim. *Siut* I, 270. 271. 275; *P. Kah.* 29, 41; 30, 40; *Eb.* 90, 18.

[2] *Westc.* 6, 15. Sim. *Sin.* B 264.

[3] Budge, p. 29, 2; Lac. *TR.* 33, 4.

[4] *Urk.* iv. 5, 2. 11; perhaps also *ib.* 1069, 16.

[5] *Urk.* iv. 4, 9, cf. *ib.* 7, 16. Perhaps mere mistakes of the scribe in transcribing his hieratic original.

[6] See *Rec.* 24, 34; *ÄZ.* 43, 159.

[7] *Hearst* 6, 6; without *wi*, *Eb.* 1, 2.

§ **238.** (1) [hieroglyphs] *ḥ3*, var. [hieroglyphs], and (2) [hieroglyphs] *ḥwy*, more rarely [hieroglyphs] *ḥw*, are synonymous particles serving to introduce *wishes* or *requests*; the enclitic particle [hieroglyph] *3* (§ 245) is often used to strengthen them and is particularly common with *ḥwy*.

Examples in the sentence with adverbial (§ 119, 7. 8) and nominal (§ 133) predicate have already been quoted.

These particles are still more frequent with a verbal predicate; so with the *śdm·f* form (see further below § 450, 5, *b*).

Exx. [hieroglyphs] *ḥ3 di·tn p3 it n p3y·tn ḥry-ḳni* pray give ye the corn to your palanquin-bearer.[1]

[hieroglyphs] *ḥwy 3 wd3 ḥm·k r š n Pr-ˁ3* O that Thy Majesty would proceed to the lake of the Great House![2]

Similarly with the subject placed by anticipatory emphasis immediately after *ḥ3*.

Ex. [hieroglyphs] *ḥ3 3 3t sḥtm·s* would that a moment would destroy![3]

To express an unfulfilled wish the *śdm·n·f* form was used:

Ex. [hieroglyphs] *ḥ3 rf ir·n·i ḫrw·i m t3y 3t* would that I had made my voice (heard) at that moment![4]

We have seen that *n śdm·f* is the usual negation of the *śdm·n·f* form (§ 105, 1); hence *ḥ3 n śdm·f* is employed for 'would that he had not heard!'[5]

For *ḥ3* + noun (or *ḥw 3* + dep. pron.) + old perfective see below § 324.

Lastly, note that *ḥ3* may be used as a noun meaning 'wish', 'would-that!'.

Ex. [hieroglyphs] *nn ḥ3 3 m-ḫt·k* there is no 'would that!' with thee.[6]

For an example of *ḥ3 n·i* 'would that I had!' as object of *dd* 'say' see § 123.

§ **239.** [hieroglyphs] *ḫr*, also written [hieroglyph] (regularly so in Dyn. XVIII), old form [hieroglyphs] *iḫr*,[7] indicates what comes next in order, and may be translated 'and', 'further', or even 'accordingly', 'so', 'then'. This particle is probably derived from the verb *ḫr* 'fall', and the preposition *ḫr* (§ 167) is obviously closely related.

Examples in the sentence with adverbial (§ 119, 5), nominal (§ 133), and adjectival (§ 142) predicate have been already quoted, as well as cases where a clause or phrase of time with *m-ḫt* is in anticipatory emphasis and is introduced by *ḫr* (§ 178, under *m-ḫt*, 4. 5).[8]

The construction *ḫr śdm·f* expresses what will be found to happen, what may be anticipated, or the like, and is often best rendered by the English *future*. See below § 450, 5, *c* for the *śdm·f* forms used in this construction.

Exx. The official who acts like this, [hieroglyphs] *ḫr rwd·f ˁ3 m t3 st* he will flourish here in this place.[9]

[hieroglyphs] *ḫr km* $\frac{2}{3}$ *r-5 r-10 r-30 r 1* now $\frac{2}{3}+\frac{1}{5}+\frac{1}{10}+\frac{1}{30}$ amounts (*or* will be found to amount) to 1.[10]

[1] *Westc.* 11, 7. Sim. *ib.* 15; *Peas.* B 1, 36 (*rdi·tw*); *Adm.* 12, 2; 13, 5; *Th. T. S.* ii. 11.
[2] *Westc.* 5, 2. Sim. *ib.* 9, 23; *ÄZ.* 38, 136. 140; BUDGE, p. 399, 9.
[3] *Peas.* B 1, 111–2.
[4] *Adm.* 6, 5.
[5] *Urk.* iv. 658, 8, qu. § 455, 1.
[6] *Urk.* iv. 96. Sim. PIEHL, *IH.* iii. 75.
[7] Cairo 20543, *a* 11; Brit. Mus. 614, 12; Lutz, 34, 66, 3.
[8] Sim. with *m*, Brit. Mus. 614, 12.
[9] *Urk.* iv. 1090. Sim. *ib.* 690, 5 (*di*); 1105, 16; 1109, 3; 1110, 3; 1111, 11, qu. § 187.
[10] *Rhind* 22.

The same construction occurs also with the subject placed after *ḫr* in anticipatory emphasis (§ 148, 1), when it may conveniently be called the *ḫr·f sḏm·f* construction. This has always future reference, and hence is closely parallel in meaning to the verb-form *sḏm·ḫr·f* to be considered later (§§ 427. 430–1).

Exx. *ḫr ṯ3ty h(3)b·f* then the vizier shall send.[1]

ḫr·f di·f in·t(w)·f r ʿryt he shall cause him to be brought to the court.[2]

ḫr·tw nḏ·tw·s it shall be ground, lit. one shall grind it.[3]

Note that the emphasized subject, when a pronoun, is a suffix, not a dep. pron., and that in the passive only *tw* (not *tw* + subject) follows *ḫr*. For *ḫr·tw* 'one says', see § 436.

As used before other verb-forms, *ḫr* calls for no special remark.[4]

§ 240. *sw* 'then', only in archaic or archaistic religious texts and where inexplicable as the obscure pronoun treated in the Add. to § 148, 1.[5]

Exx. *sw ḫr ḳsw·sn* then fell their bones.[6]

sw di (§ 422) *irt n Ḥr* then was given the eye to Horus.[7]

§ 241. *smwn*[8] 'probably', 'surely' is perhaps a compound from *sy* + *m* + *wn* 'it is as though it were', and is found with sentences of various kinds. An example with nominal predicate has been quoted (§ 133); other examples are:

smwn rf ḥtp·f ḥr snsw·s surely he will be content with her worship.[9]

smwn·k r rdit m3·i bw wršw ib·i im surely thou wilt grant me to see the place where my heart dwells.[10]

For the construction of this last example see § 332, and note the use of the suffix as subject.

§ 242. *k3* 'so', 'then', var. , is doubtless akin to the similarly written verb 'to plan', 'devise'. Combined with *sḏm·f* it serves to express either a simple *future* event arising out of what has previously been said, or else an *injunction* or *determination*.

Exx. O that (*ḫw*) thou mayst do as I say; *k3 ḥtp M3ʿt r st·s* then Right will rest in her place.[11]

k3 ir·tw ḫft iry then one shall act accordingly.[12]

For the forms of *sḏm·f* found after *k3* see § 450, 5, *d*. The construction *k3 sḏm·f* is negated by the help of the negative verb *tm*, see § 346, 5.

When the predicate in this construction is adverbial, the copula assumes the form *wn·f*, as after *iḫ* (§ 118).

Ex. *k3 wn·k ḥnʿ·f m s wʿ* then thou shalt be with him as one man.[13]

[1] *Urk.* iv. 1106. Sim. *Siut* 1, 297.

[2] *Urk.* iv. 1107. Sim. *ib.* 1111, 12; *P. Kah.* 22, 1–2; *Peas.* B 1, 151. 162; *Eb.* 48, 3–4; 87, 9–10.

[3] *Eb.* 59, 9. Sim. *ib.* 44, 3; *Urk.* iv. 1109, 6.

[4] Before *sḏm·n·f*, *Sin.* B 147; *n sḏm·n·f*, *Urk.* iv. 1089, 2; *sḏm·ḫr·f*, *Rhind* 55; noun + old perfective, *Sin.* B 75–6; *Paheri* 3; passive *sḏm·f*, *Urk.* iv. 46, 6, qu. § 422, 2.

[5] *ÄZ.* 71, 50.

[6] *Cen.* 84, 8. Sim. *ib.* 85, 40.

[7] *Cen.* 85, 19.

[8] GARD. *Sin.* p. 59.

[9] *ÄZ.* 35, 16.

[10] *Sin.* B 158.

[11] *Urk.* iv. 1074. Sim. *Adm.* 12, 2; 13, 6; *ib.* p. 105.

[12] *P. Kah.* 29, 43. Sim. *ib.* 13, 36; 31, 1. 13; 36, 16. 23; *Westc.* 9, 17; *Urk.* iv. 655, 3.

[13] *P. Kah.* 31, 20–1.

With the subject in anticipatory emphasis (§ 148, 1) there is hardly any perceptible difference in the sense.

Exx. [hieroglyphs] *kꜣ bꜣk im in·f sw* then this thy humble servant shall fetch it.[1]

[hieroglyphs] *kꜣ·k ir·k mitt* thou shalt do the like.[2]

[hieroglyphs] *kꜣ·tw psš·tw ḫt·f* his property shall be divided.[3]

This construction is conveniently described as the *kꜣ·f sḏm·f* construction, and is closely related to the *sḏm·kꜣ·f* form to be described below (§§ 427. 433–4). For *kꜣ·f* 'he will say' see § 436.

OBS. Other uses of *kꜣ* are unimportant.[4] Once *kꜣ* . . . . *kꜣ* seems to mean 'whether . . . or'.[5]

§ **243.** [hieroglyph] *ti*, rarely written [hieroglyphs] *ti*,[6] is always followed by a noun or dependent pronoun, and serves to introduce clauses, usually short clauses, of a descriptive or circumstantial nature. These may have either adverbial (§ 119, 4) or verbal (§ 212, end) predicate. [hieroglyph] may be ultimately a shortening of [hieroglyphs] *isṯ*, the two particles being identical in meaning and use.[7] See further § 119, 4.

§ **244. Retrospect.**—Reviewing the contents of §§ 227–243, the student will find that the name 'sentence-adverb' is, on the whole, a fair description of the non-enclitic particles. It is strange how many of them help to give future meaning to a following *sḏm·f* form—so *in*, *ḥꜣ*, *ḫr*, and *kꜣ* when the subject follows in anticipatory emphasis, and *iḫ*, *ḥꜣ*, *ḫr*, *kꜣ*, and in part *mk* when such is not the case. The two particles *in* and *ḫr* bear a close relationship to prepositions, and in these and one other case (*kꜣ*) there is an obvious kinship to three similarly built narrative verb-forms to be studied later (*sḏm·in·f*, *sḏm·ḫr·f*, *sḏm·kꜣ·f*, see below, §§ 427 foll.). The non-enclitic particles vary as regards the pronouns which follow them before adverbial or verbal predicate;[8] whereas most (*isk*, *isṯ*, *mk*, *nn*, *nḥmn*, *ntt*, *ḥꜣ* and *ti*) require the dependent pronouns, the three which may be suspected of verbal origin (*ḫr*, *smwn*, and *kꜣ*) demand the suffixes; in this matter *in* and *ntt* present peculiarities for which the student is referred to the relevant sections.

[1] *P. Kah.* 36, 15. Sim. *ib.* 22, 7.
[2] *Urk.* iv. 1090. Sim. *Westc.* 3, 3.
[3] *Urk.* iv. 1068. Sim. *ib.* 768, 12; *P. Kah.* 22, 9.
[4] *Westc.* 9, 14 (elliptical); 11, 25 (*kꜣ* + *in* + noun + *sḏm·f* (§ 227, 2).
[5] *Pt.* 78–9.
[6] *Urk.* iv. 83.
[7] *Rec.* 28, 186; GARD. *Sin.* p. 153.
[8] With nominal pred. we find *isṯ ink*, see *ÄZ.* 60, 84; *ntt ink*, see § 223.

VOCABULARY

[hieroglyphs] var. [hieroglyphs][1] *wnm* eat;

[hieroglyphs] *wnmt* food.

[hieroglyphs] *wrḥ* anoint.

[hieroglyphs] var. [hieroglyphs] *rm* weep.

[hieroglyphs] *ḫꜣꜥ* throw, let go.

[hieroglyphs] var. [hieroglyphs] *swꜣ* pass.

[hieroglyphs] *smnḫ* furnish, adorn.

[hieroglyphs] *dp* taste.

[1] Due to an early confusion in hieratic between the signs [hieroglyph] and [hieroglyph].

ip(w)ty messenger, envoy.

irtyw mourning.

pnw mouse.

mnḥ wax.

nt-ꜥ custom, habit (f.).

hn box.

ḥnwt mistress.

ḥry-pr servant (or like).

ḫprt what has happened, occurrence.

sšm condition; procedure.

štꜣ mysterious, difficult.

Mn-nfr[1] Memphis.

Mḏꜣyw Medjay, a Nubian people.[2]

[1] Originally the name of the pyramid and pyramid-city of Phiops I at Ṣaḳḳârah. The name means '(Phiops is) established and beautiful'.

[2] The name has been equated with that of the modern Bedja-peoples of the Eastern Desert and the Sudan. In Dyn. XVIII men of this stock were employed as police, and the word practically comes to mean 'policeman'. See now *AEO.*, under No. 188 of On. Am.

EXERCISE XVIII

(*a*) *Transliterate and translate*:

(1) [hieroglyphs] (2) [hieroglyphs] (3) [hieroglyphs] (4) [hieroglyphs] (5) [hieroglyphs] (6) [hieroglyphs]

(7) [hieroglyphs]

(*b*) *Write in hieroglyphs and transliteration*:

(1) He wept saying: How evil is this condition in (*ḥr*) which I am! Would that I had never (lit. not) seen this city! (2) If he is ill, thou shalt send to his wife concerning it. (3) Now when the messenger of the chief (*wr*) of the Medjay arrives at the Residence, thou shalt be with him like a brother. If he say to

thee, 'Who shall give me food?' thou shalt answer him saying, 'I will give it to thee'. Thou shalt not allow him to express a want (lit. say 'would that to me!') about anything. Behold, I have furnished thee with fields and (lit. with) cattle and serving-men in order that (lit. through love of) thou mayest act accordingly. (4) May I serve (*śdm·f* form only) the Lady of the Universe (§ 100, 1), so that she may tell me (of) the beauty of her children.

LESSON XIX

PARTICLES (*continued*)

Enclitic particles (§§ 245–257):—

§ **245.** [hieroglyphs] *ꜣ*[1] appears to have a vague exclamatory or interjectional force, as may be concluded from its use, already illustrated, after the particles of wishing *ḫꜣ* and *ḫwy* (§§ 119, 8; 238).[1a] In a few Middle Egyptian passages, for the most part rather obscure, it seems to have some such meaning as 'indeed'.

Ex. [hieroglyphs] *sḏmw, n ꜣ sḏm·n·k* thou hearer, indeed thou hearest not.[2]

§ **246.** [hieroglyphs] *irf*, see below § 252.

§ **247.** [hieroglyphs] *is* seems to be ultimately interjectional in character and to have some such meaning as 'lo'; the non-enclitic particles *isk* and *ist* (§§ 230. 231) are evidently derivatives; perhaps also *isw* (§ 232).

1. One of the main functions of *is* is to give a certain impressiveness or emphasis to the statements in which it occurs:

Exx. [hieroglyphs] *iw ḫpr·n·k is m sḏty ḥm·i* thou hast indeed grown up as a foster-son of My Majesty.[3]

[hieroglyphs] *rḫ·n·i is nḥḥ pw Wꜣst* I know indeed that Thebes is eternal.[4]

[hieroglyphs] *n ii·n is ḫt ḏs·s* wealth does not indeed come of itself.[5]

2. A common use of *is* is to emphasize the negative word,[6] which here appears as [hieroglyph] *n* even in cases where [hieroglyph] *nn* would be expected; later, however, *n* in this use is occasionally replaced by *nn*.[7] An example of [hieroglyphs] *n is* in the sentence with adverbial predicate was quoted in § 120; with nominal (§ 134) and adjectival (§ 140) predicate the combination [hieroglyph] .. [hieroglyphs] *n is . . . pw* is not uncommon, and it was seen in § 134 that here *pw* is apt to be omitted as superfluous. The use of *n is* to negative an adverb or adverbial phrase has been illustrated in § 209; it is then translatable as 'but not' or, after another negation, as 'except'.

[1] See *JEA* 34, 12.

[1a] Cf. too *nfr·w(i)ꜣ* 'how beautiful', Pyr., *Bull.* 32, 60.

[2] *Peas.* B 1, 180. Sim. *ib.* 181. 224. 293; B 2, 125; *Sin.* B 217. 260; *P. Kah.* 30, 39; 31, 10; 32, 6; 33, 10; *Urk.* iv. 158, 9.

[3] *Ikhern.* 6. Somewhat similarly *Sh. S.* 153, qu. § 188, 1; *Peas.* B 1, 276; *Adm.* 12, 1.

[4] *Urk.* iv. 164. Sim. *ib.* 363, 7; 367, 9.

[5] *Pt.* 181. Sim. Turin 276, *Rec.* 3, 119.

[6] See GUNN, *Studies*, pp. 170–1 and ch. 23.

[7] *Pt.* 213; *Westc.* 9, 6, qu. § 368; *Urk.* iv. 1087, 8.

So too *n is* may be employed to negative a noun in apposition.

Ex. .... *ir gm·k dꜣisw .... m ḥwrw, n is mitw·k* if thou find a disputant .... who is a poor fellow, one not thy equal.[1]

For *n is* meaning 'if not', 'unless' before the *sdm·n·f* form see § 216, end.

3. *Is* may also emphasize single words; so *iw min is* 'to-day indeed',[2] *mtn is* 'behold ye indeed'.[3] Similarly, it is used after the independent pronoun in both affirmative and negative sentences with nominal (§ 127, 4) and adjectival (§ 136) predicate, tending to confer upon the pronoun, as we have seen, the value of a logical predicate.

4. Further, *is* may help to characterize a sentence as a question; see § 491, 2.

5. When placed after a noun, *is* has sometimes the meaning of the preposition 'like': a construction common in the oldest Egyptian,[4] but of which only a few instances have survived in later times.

Ex. *ir·n·i n·f m mtt nt ib, nsw is n nṯr nb* I acted for him in loyalty of heart, as a king (does) for every god.[5]

OBS. In Late Egyptian *is* is often employed like *ist* at the beginning of sentences; however, in the sporadic examples of this found as early as Dyn. XVIII *is* is possibly an interrogative particle, see (4) above and § 491, 2 below.

§ 248. *isṯ* 'lo' (§ 231) appears to be used enclitically in a few examples.

Ex. *ir ist ḫꜣ sdm(w)·k im·f, iw wsḫt im·f* lo, as for the office in which thou judgest, there is a broad hall in it.[6]

§ 249. *wnt* and *wnnt*[7] are used after the independent pronoun *ink* 'I' in the sense of 'indeed', 'really'; for examples see above § 127, end. Though *wnt* and *wnnt* are probably the f. sing. of the perfective and imperfective participles respectively, no difference of meaning is discernible between them.

Only very rarely are these particles found in sentences with verbal predicate.

Ex. *wnn·i wnnt sdr·ki* I was indeed sleeping.[8] For the construction see § 326.

The particles here treated are, at least for practical purposes, to be distinguished from the *wnt* which means 'that' (§ 233) and from the *wnt* which occurs in *n wnt* 'there does not exist' (§ 108, 2).

§ 250. *m(y)*,[8a] also written ,[9] is occasionally found after imperatives or, quite exceptionally, after the *sdm·f* form when used to express a wish.

Exx. *mi m(y), ib·i* pray come, O my heart.[10]

wdꜣ m(y) ib·k may thy heart prosper.[11]

In a few religious texts this *my* is found non-enclitically.

Ex. *m(y) ṯs ṯw, nb sꜣwt* pray raise thyself up, thou lord of walls.[12]

[1] *Pt.* 75.

[2] *Sin.* B 189.

[3] *Adm.* 7, 1. 2. 3. 9.

[4] Exx. *Pyr.* 4 b. 5 b. 57 d. 63 b. 220 c. and very often.

[5] *Urk.* iv. 367. Perhaps sim. *ib.* 324, 12; *Sin.* B 223.

[6] *Urk.* iv. 1092. Sim. *ib.* 561, 8; 563, 8; *Rhind*, title.

[7] In Old Eg., see *Verbum* ii. § 978.

[8] *Urk.* v. 171, 2.

[8a] Full writing, *Pyr.* 264, 520; so, too, in L. E. and later, *Wb.* II, 36, 6.

[9] *ÄZ.* 57, 104; 58, 17*; MAR. *Abyd.* ii. 30, 33.

[10] *Adm.* p. 105. Sim. *Destr.* 3. 16; *P. Pet.* 1116 B, 12; *Hearst* 11, 4, qu. § 252, 2.

[11] *Meir* iii. 3; *w* is restored.

[12] LAC. *TR.* 36, 2. Sim. DE BUCK, i. 7, b; *P. Ch. Beatty X*, rt. i, 4; *XIII*, 11.

§ 251. *ms*[1] hints that some thought, statement, or the like has been overlooked by the person addressed, and conveys some tinge of surprise or reproof at this omission. It may sometimes be translated by 'surely'.

Exx. *ỉw ms špsw m nḫwt* surely, nobles are in mourning.[2]

wnn ms nty ỉm m rḫ-ḫt nay, but he who is yonder (i. e. dead) shall be a wise man (lit. one knowing things).[3]

Obs. For the compound noun *ỉw-ms* 'untruth', lit. 'but-there-is', see above § 194. In one instance *ms* is found after *mk* 'behold' and followed by a dependent pronoun.[4]

§ 252. *rf* and the related particles.—The preposition *r*, combined with a suffix, is used enclitically as a particle; the suffix-pronoun originally employed was that demanded by the context in each case,[5] but later the particle thus formed manifested a tendency to become stereotyped and invariable in the form *rf*, var. *ỉrf*. The literal meaning is 'as to him' ('me', 'thee'), but the function of these particles is to express emphasis of one kind or another.

1. *r·ỉ* is occasionally found in conjunction with a verb in 1st sing.

Ex. *ḏd·kỉ r·ỉ n·f* then spoke I to him.[6]

2. *r·k*, later often written *ỉr·k*, with the feminine *r·ṯ*, var. *ỉr·t*, is not uncommon with the imperative.

Exx. *sḏm r·k n·ỉ* hearken thou to me.[7]

ḏd ỉr·k n·ỉ st tell it to me.[8]

m(ỉ) r·ṯ come thou (fem.).[9]

ḥm ỉr·t m(y) retreat thou (fem.).[10]

With the plural imperative is found *ỉr·ṯn*[11] or *r·ṯn*,[12] but only rarely, the invariable *ỉrf* (below 3) usually taking its place.

After the 2nd pers. of the *sḏm·f* form used in wishes and exhortations, *r·k* is but rarely found.

Ex. *nb sgr, dỉ·k r·k n·ỉ ḫt·ỉ* thou Lord of Quiet, give thou me my property.[13]

3. The invariable *rf*, later writing *ỉrf*, has several different uses.

(*a*) First, it is found after plural imperatives.

Ex. *sḏmw ỉrf tn* hearken ye.[14]

Similarly after *ḥꜣ* 'would that' (§ 238)[15] and after *sḏm·f* used in wishes.[16]

(*b*) Second, *rf* and *ỉrf* are common in questions.

Exx. *ỉn nn rf dỉ·k swꜣ·ỉ* wilt thou not let me pass?[17]

wnn ỉrf tꜣ pf mỉ m m-ḫmt·f what will that land be like without him?[18]

1 See *Adm.* pp. 21–2.
2 *Adm.* 2, 7. Sim. *Westc.* 2, 5; 11, 22; 12, 22; *Sinai* 90, 12.
3 *Leb.* 145. Sim. *ib.* 142. 143.
4 *Westc.* 12, 22.
5 See especially *Pyr.* 1102.
6 *Sin.* B 45. Other exx. *Sinai* 90, 5; Lac. *TR.* 23, 99; 28, 9.
7 *Leb.* 67. Sim. *ib.* 148; *Sh.S.* 12; *Ikhern.* 9; *P. Kah.* 3, 30.
8 Budge, p. 266, 1. Sim. *Hearst* 14, 12.
9 *Urk.* iv. 255.
10 *Hearst* 11, 4. Sim. *Urk.* iv. 480, 7.
11 Lac. *TR.* 18, 17.
12 Lac. *TR.* 19, 31; 60, 5.
13 *Peas.* B 1, 29–30.
14 *Urk.* iv. 120. Sim. *ib.* 367, 13; 390, 2; 508, 12.
15 *Adm.* 5, 14, qu. § 133; 6, 5, qu. § 238.
16 *Peas.* R 79. Sim. 1st pers. *Sh. S.* 21.
17 *Peas.* R 59. Sim. *ib.* B 1, 18. 124. 149; *Adm.* 12, 5. 14.
18 *Sin.* B 43. Sim. *Peas.* B 1, 106; *Westc.* 9, 4. 15; *M. u. K.* 1, 6; *Adm.* 14, 14.

(*c*) Occasionally in sentences with a certain exclamatory and emphatic force. So for example after *smwn* 'probably',[1] *mk* 'behold',[2] and *ḥr-ntt* 'because'.[3] Here we must recall the anticipatory use of *ist rf* and *rf* alone which was explained above in § 152; so again after an emphasized word, ex. .... *ḏs·k irf .... int·k* 'thyself .... thou shalt bring'.[4]

4. *rs*, with the 3rd f. suffix used as a neuter, is very rare.

Ex. *ḫpr·n rs, nn wi ḥnꜥ* it happened, indeed, I was not with (them).[5]

§ 253. *ḥm*,[6] also written [7] or ,[8] occurs almost only in main clauses, where it has the meaning 'assuredly', 'indeed'. Being a particle of asseveration, it is frequent in statements, promises, or predictions referring to the future.

Exx. *iw·i ḥm r irt ẖnt·i* assuredly I will make my rowing.[9]

wnn·(i) ḥm ḥr stp sꜣ·i ḥꜣ sꜣt·(i) assuredly I will spread my protection about my daughter.[10]

Ḥm is sometimes found, however, also in statements of present fact, to which it lends a certain emphasis.[11]

Ex. *ḫr ḥm nfr wꜣḥ-ib nḥm wi m-ꜥ mwt* nay, good indeed is the clemency which has saved me from death.[12]

So too *ḥm* may occur in an *if*-clause with which some alternative condition is contrasted.

Ex. .... *ir ḥm gm·k .... ir swt gm·k* if, on the one hand, thou findest .....; if, on the other hand, thou findest ......[13]

Obs. Hence, doubtless, is derived the non-enclitic particle *nḥmn* (§ 236), which has much the same meaning.

§ 254. *swt* is used in statements in order to mark a contrast, and corresponds to English 'but'.

Exx. I do not know the number thereof .... *iw·i swt rḫ·kwi bw nty st im* but I know the place where it is.[14]

If thou do not let me go forth vindicated (certain evil results will follow); *ir swt di·k pr·i* but if thou cause me to go forth.[15]

Occasionally the adversative *swt* occurs in a mere clause or phrase, not qualifying an entire sentence; in this case 'however' is the closest translation.

Exx. Greet our entire household, *m msdd·i swt* though I may dislike (it).[16] Lit. while I am disliking, however.

Let all that is good be done with them, *nn swt rdit swꜣ kꜣi* but without letting a boat pass.[17] For the construction see § 307, 1.

[1] Ex. *ÄZ.* 35, 16, qu. § 241.
[2] *Sh. S.* 10.
[3] *Adm.* p. 97.
[4] *Westc.* 7, 8; for *int·k* see § 450, 4.
[5] *Sh. S.* 130.
[6] *Urk.* iv. 225, 13; 285, 15.
[7] *Westc.* 5, 7; *Eb.* 110, 1.
[8] *Sin.* B 76. 203.
[9] *Westc.* 5, 7. Sim. *Urk.* iv. 344, 17.
[10] *Urk.* iv. 225. Sim. *ib.* 285, 15; *Th. T. S.* i. 10.
[11] In past narrative, *Sin.* R 15, qu. § 66, end.
[12] *Sin.* B 203. Sim. *ib.* 76; *Peas.* R 61 (*mk ḥm*); *Leb.* 151; *Adm.* 13, 9; *Urk.* iv. 221, 7.
[13] *Eb.* 110, 1–3. Sim. Lac. *TR.* 2, 25; Budge, p. 147, 11.
[14] *Westc.* 9, 3. Sim. *Sin.* B 37; *Peas.* B 1, 124.
[15] Nav. 65, 13. Sim. Lac. *TR.* 2, 48; *Siut* 1, 225; 4, 79; *Eb.* 30, 13; *Urk.* iv. 1110, 15.
[16] *P. Kah.* 36, 42.
[17] Berl. *ÄI.* i. p. 256, 5. Sim. *Peas.* R 128, with *ḥnꜥ* + infinitive.

In a number of examples *swt* has little or no force, merely introducing a main clause or indeed an entire narrative.

Ex. *ḏd·ỉ swt, dỉ·ỉ sḏm·tn* I speak, I cause you to hear.[1]

OBS. *Swt* is doubtless ultimately identical with the indep. pron. of the 3rd m. sing., for in Late Egyptian and Coptic *ntf* acquires a like adversative meaning.

§ 255. *grt*, early also *ỉgrt*,[2] rare variant ,[2a] in inscriptions of Dyn. XVIII sometimes written ,[3] takes the place, in Middle Egyptian, of Old Eg. *gr* (rarely *ỉgr*), which hardly survives later except as an adverb meaning 'also', '(not) any more' (§ 205, 1). Hence the proper meaning of *grt* was doubtless likewise 'also', 'moreover'. In use, however, *grt* has a much weakened signification; the nearest English equivalent is the 'now' which claims the listener's attention, but frequently it is best left untranslated.

It stands at the beginning of new paragraphs.

Exx. *ỉr·n·ỉ grt rnpwt m ḥḳꜣ m Mꜣ-ḥḏ* now I spent years as prince in the Oryx-nome.[4]

ỉw grt ḫrp·n n·f ḥm·ỉ mnw ꜥšꜣ wrt My Majesty undertook for him very many monuments.[5]

Also at the beginning of descriptions or explanatory comments.

Exx. *nṯr pw grt, nn sn-nw·f* he is a god who has no equal (lit. second).[6]

n grt ḥḏ·n ḥꜣty-ꜥ nb ỉmy hꜣw·f ḫtmt ky ḥꜣty-ꜥ no prince in his time destroys what another prince contracts for.[7]

Grt is found even at the very beginning of narratives.[8] It occurs frequently in the phrase *ỉr grt* 'now as to .....' with some emphasized word (§ 149).[9]

An example may be quoted where *grt* is used exactly like the adverb *gr* 'also' (§ 205, 1); this example confirms the relationship of the two words.

n ỉꜥ·n n mw grt they do not wash off through water either (*or* also).[10]

OBS. *'Iw grt* is a common combination; a case may even be quoted where it introduces indep. pron. + participle, the construction of § 227, 3.[11] *'Isṯ grt*, see § 231.

§ 256. *tr*, sometimes shortened to , *ty*, seems to express surprise or indignation, and may be translated 'forsooth', 'I wonder', or the like.

Ex. *n ỉnk tr smꜣ·f* I am not, forsooth, a confederate of his.[12]

Such examples are, however, exceedingly rare. *Tr* is common, on the other hand, in questions.

Exx. *tm·k tr sḏm ḥr m* wherefore, pray, dost thou not hearken?[13]

m t(y) sn nn n nṯrw ỉmyw-bꜣḥ who are they, these gods who are in the presence?[14]

[1] *ÄZ.* 47, Pl. I, 2, opp. p. 88. Sim. *Peas.* B 1, 283. 307; *Urk.* iv. 26, 12; 1074, 10. After imperatives, *Peas.* R 3; B 1, 81.

[2] Cairo 20503, 1; Brit. Mus. 1164, 9. 12.

[2a] *Rec.* 37, 139, l. 36.

[3] *Urk.* iv. 344, 11; 1110, 7.

[4] *BH.* i. 8, 15. Sim. Berl. *ÄI.* i. p. 258, 20; *Sin.* B 219; *Hamm.* 110, 7; *Urk.* iv. 1105, 12.

[5] *Urk.* iv. 173, 6. Sim. *ib.* 168, 12; 171, 11; 172, 1; 174, 9; *Hamm.* 113, 10.

[6] *Sin.* B 47. Sim. *ib.* 51; *Peas.* B 1, 17.

[7] *Siut* 1, 281. Sim. *ib.* 279.

[8] Ex. Cairo 20099, 2, qu. p. 55, top.

[9] Berl. *ÄI.* i. p. 258, 19; Cairo 20539, i. *b* 21; *Urk.* iv. 1105, 7; *Urk.* v. 24, 9; 26, 12; 28, 10.

[10] Louvre C 14, 12.

[11] Munich 4, 6–7, qu. § 468, 3.

[12] *Sin.* B 114, with note. Sim. GAYET, *Temple de Louxor* 63; *ÄZ.* 57, 6*.

[13] *Peas.* B 1, 180. Sim. *ib.* 201; *Eb.* 2, 3; *Pt.* 274, qu. § 495.

[14] *Urk.* v. 30.

sy ty pw wȝt šmt·k ḥr·s which, pray, is the road upon which thou wilt walk?[1]

The interrogative pronoun *ptr*,[2] 'who?' 'what?' (§ 497), also written *pt*,[3] *pty*,[4] and more fully *pw-tr*,[5] *pw-ti*,[6] is evidently a compound of *pw* and *tr*; for *pw* alone as an interrogative 'who?' see below § 498.[7]

A strange employment is also found in which a suffix is appended to *tr*, apparently in apposition to a preceding *m* 'who?'

Ex. *n-m tr·k i* who art thou that hast come? Perhaps lit., who, pray, (namely) thou, has come?[8] For the construction see above § 227, 3.

[1] *Urk.* v. 168, 12. Sim. *ib.* 172, 2. 4; 173, 13; 177, 13.
[2] *Sin.* B 122. 183. 261.
[3] *P. Kah.* 5, 6.
[4] *Rhind* 36. 39. 51.
[5] *Mission*, i. p. 219.
[6] *Adm.* 3, 7. 13; 4, 6.
[7] *Urk.* iv. 1078, 13; 1079, 1; 1081, 16 (collated).
[8] *Urk.* v. 148, 3. Sim. *ib.* 165, 6; 171, 11.

§ **257. Accumulation of particles.**—Finally, it must be pointed out that Egyptian is by no means averse from accumulations of particles. Examples will be found in many of the above paragraphs; compare, for instance, *ist rf* § 231; *mtn is* § 247, 3; *ḫr ḥm* § 253; so also *mk ḫr*,[9] *mk grt*[9a] and many others.

[9] *Urk.* iv. 1088, 10; 1092, 13.
[9a] *JEA.* 16, 19, 3. 5; *P. Kah.* 30, 40; *Siut* I, 269.

INTERJECTIONS

§ **258.** The number of Egyptian words which can definitely be classed as **interjections** is very small. Here belong, in the first place, the words , *i* and *hȝ*, which occasionally accompany the vocative, see above § 87. Closely related to the latter is probably *hy*, which may best be translated 'hail', ex. *hy n·k* 'hail to thee'.[10] *yḥ* 'hey' is a still rarer interjection exhorting to movement or the like.[11] We have discussed *isṯ* 'lo', *mk* 'behold', and *ḥȝ*, *ḥwy* 'would that' under the head of non-enclitic particles or sentence-adverbs (§§ 231. 234. 238). Here, for want of a better rubric, we may place *tiw* 'yes'[12] and the rare use of *nn* for 'no'.[13]

For interjectional sentences beginning with an adverbial phrase, see above § 153. Sentences consisting only of a noun or of a nominal phrase (§ 89, 2) may also be regarded in this way. On the interjectional *ḫy* 'what a ....!' see § 258 A, below, p. 427.

[10] *Sin.* B 274.
[11] *D. el B.* 89; *Paheri* 5.
[12] *Westc.* 8, 14; *Adm.* 6, 13; *ÄZ.* 43, 42.
[13] *Peas.* B 1, 200.

VOCABULARY

ms bear, give birth; form, fashion (statue).
nḏ protect, rescue, *m-ꜥ* from.
rs wake (intrans.).
var. *ḫsf* oppose, repress, repel; with *n*, punish.
ḫsr drive away, dispel.
sꜥr cause to mount up, bring.
smȝꜥ make true.
smḫ forget.
šn conjure, exorcize.

ḏm be sharp, sharpen; det. pronounce, *rn* a name.

ʿꜣm an Asiatic.

pḏty a bowman, foreigner.

psḏt ennead of gods, company of nine gods.

mʿḥʿt, var. *miḥʿt* tomb.[1]

mtwt poison.

rḳ-ib disaffected, envious, lit. downward inclined of heart.

ḥkꜣ magic; also plur. *ḥkꜣw*.

ḫfty enemy, opponent.

kkw darkness.

snṯr incense.

var. *sḏt* fire, flame.

var. *m* who? what?

[1] The use of the sign for *mi* here indicates that the initial *ʿ* of the stem *ʿḥʿ* has changed into *i*. See *Sphinx* 13, 157.

EXERCISE XIX

(*a*) *Transliterate and translate*:

(1) [2]

(2)

(3)

(4)

(5)

(*b*) *Write in hieroglyphs and transliteration*:

(1) The overseer of priests Ḥarḥotpe says: I adorned this tomb for my father anew, in order that (*n-mrwt*) his name might be firm and flourishing therein for eternity. (2) O Isis, if thou allow this child to live, I will give to thee incense upon the flame; but if thou take him from me, I will not allow thee to receive offerings upon the altar, I will not allow thy name to be pronounced in thy temple. (3) Would that he would give me my clothing! (4) If thou awake in peace, Great-of-Magic[3] awakes in peace. (5) They fashioned a statue, the like of which had not been seen since the time of the god. (6) Shall this peasant be punished for this evil word?

[2] See above, p. 65, n. 8a.

[3] *Wrt-ḥkꜣw*, name of a female divinity, identified with the crown of the Pharaoh.

LESSON XX

NUMBERS[1]

§ 259. The writing of the numerals.—A vertical stroke ı is used for the units, and special signs for the various powers of ten. The seven signs employed are as follows:—

1		10,000	
10		100,000	
100		1,000,000	
1,000			

The higher values are written in front of the lower, and to indicate the numbers between 1 and 10, and between any power of ten and the next higher power, the signs in question are repeated as many times as is necessary. Hence we find for 152,123,[2] for 966.[3]

The word for 'million' *ḥḥ*, which was also used for 'many' (§ 99), early fell into disuse; probably as a consequence of this loss, a new method of expressing the higher values was occasionally employed.

Exx. 100,000 × 101 = 10,100,000.[4] (100,000 × 4) + (10,000 × 7) = 470,000.[5]

In hieratic the tens and units, when referring to the days of the month, are invariably laid on their side, ex. *sw 18* 'day 18'.[6] Traces of a similar use, though as regards the units only, are sometimes found in Middle Kingdom hieroglyphic, exx. *tpy (n) ꜣḫt sw 18* 'first (month of) inundation, day 18';[7] *5 ḥryw rnpt, sw 5* 'the 5 (days) upon the year, day 5' i.e. the fifth epagomenal day,[8] beside .[9] The horizontal position becomes thus associated more with ordinal than with cardinal meaning; in hieratic texts this position is apt to be found in the words for 'third', 'fourth', etc., ex. *3-nw sp* 'the third time'.[10]

§ 260. The names of the numbers.[11]—Very few of these are written out in Middle Egyptian, though an example of *snw* 'two'[12] and another of *ḫmt* 'three'[13] may be cited. Since, however, derivatives involving the names of the numbers sometimes occur, e.g. *ỉfdt* 'a four', 'a quartet', *Ḫmnw* 'Eight-town', i.e. El-Ashmûnên in Upper Egypt, it is desirable for the student to become acquainted with them. The transcriptions given below are based on phonetic writings in the Pyramid Texts and elsewhere, or else on inferences from Coptic; a few details remain uncertain.

[1] See K. SETHE, *Von Zahlen und Zahlworten bei den alten Ägyptern*, in *Schriften d. Wiss. Ges. Strassburg*, 25. Heft, 1916.

[2] *Urk.* iv. 630.

[3] *Urk.* iv. 666.

[4] *Harris* 73, 5.

[5] *P. Kah.* 8, 19.

[6] *P. Kah.* 12, 6.

[7] *Siut* 1, 283. Sim. *ib.* 277. 299.

[8] *Siut* 1, 305. 312.

[9] *Siut* 1, 297.

[10] *Peas.* B 1, 139. Sim. *ib.* 194. 240. 266. 290; *Eb.* 86, 20.

[11] See *ÄZ.* 47, 1.

[12] *ÄZ.* 45, Pl. VI, 12. See, too, *JEA.* 16, 19, l. 8.

[13] *ÄZ.* 45, Pl. VI, 13.

1 *wꜥ(yw)*	10 *mḏ(w)*	100 *št* orig. perhaps *šnt*
2 *snw(y)*	20 [*ḏbꜥty*??]	1,000 *ḫꜣ*
3 *ḫmt(w)*	30 *mꜥbꜣ*	10,000 *ḏbꜥ*
4 *fdw*	40 *ḥm*	100,000 *ḥfn*
5 *dỉw*[1]	50 *dỉyw*	1,000,000 *ḥḥ*
6 *sršw* or *sỉšw*	60 *sr(syw)* or *sỉ(syw)*	
7 *sfḫ(w)*	70 *sfḫ(yw)*	
8 *ḫmn(w)*	80 *ḫmn(yw)*	
9 *psḏ(w)*	90 *psḏyw*	

[1] See SETHE, *Pyr.* iii. p. 9, 121 *c.*

The bracketed consonants fell away at different times, mostly early. All the units, except *snwy*, which is a dual, have a masculine ending *w*; from 3 upwards they were plurals, but in Middle Egyptian, having mostly lost the *w*, they are already treated as singulars (see below § 261). The tens, from 50 upwards, are plurals of the units. The word for 100 is fem. sing., but the higher numbers are masc. sing.

We know from various sources that the units had fem. forms as well as masculine. There existed also a set of collectives corresponding to the English 'triad', 'trio', 'quartet', etc.; an example from Middle Egyptian is [hieroglyphs] *dỉwt* 'a set of five'.[2]

[2] *Urk.* iv. 139.

The way in which combinations of tens and units (e.g. 'twenty-five'), etc., were expressed in spoken Middle Egyptian is largely a matter of conjecture, and cannot be discussed here.

Unlike the other numbers, 'one' is often written out, m. [hieroglyphs] *wꜥ*,[3] f. [hieroglyphs] *wꜥt*.[4] Derivatives are: [hieroglyphs] *wꜥ(w)* 'be alone', [hieroglyphs] *wꜥty* 'sole', 'unique', [hieroglyphs] *wꜥꜥw* 'privacy', 'solitude'.

[3] *Peas.* B 1, 161; *Urk.* iv. 18, 1. 3; 19, 13.

[4] *Sin.* B 266; *Eb.* 4, 8; 11, 1.

§ 261. **Construction of the cardinals.**—The numeral follows the noun, which, as a general rule, exhibits the singular form.

Exx. [hieroglyphs] *mḥ 1* one cubit.[5] [hieroglyphs] *s 2* two men.[6]

[hieroglyphs] *msḏr·f 2* his two ears.[7] [hieroglyphs] *rnpt 20* twenty years.[8]

[hieroglyphs] *ḥfꜣw 75* seventy-five snakes.[9]

[hieroglyphs] *ḥnḳt ds 100* one hundred jugs of beer.[10]

[hieroglyphs] *dmỉ ḫꜣ* a thousand towns.[11]

[hieroglyphs] *s ḏbꜥ* ten thousand men.[12]

Frequently, however, the noun shows the plural form; not, however, (*a*) with the numbers 1 and 2, (*b*) nor yet, as a rule,[13] in indications of *time* or of *measure*.

Exx. [hieroglyphs] *spw 4* four times.[14] [hieroglyphs] *st-ḥmwt 20* twenty women.[15]

[hieroglyphs] *ỉḥw 618* six hundred and eighteen (head of) cattle.[16]

[5] *Siut* 3, 13; *Westc.* 10, 10.

[6] *Adm.* 12, 14.

[7] *Eb.* 100, 2.

[8] *P. Pet.* 1116 A, 58.

[9] *Sh. S.* 127.

[10] *Westc.* 4, 13.

[11] *Urk.* iv. 660.

[12] *P. Pet.* 1116 A, 101.

[13] Exceptions: *rnpwt 54*, *ÄZ.* 47, Pl. I, 6: *hrww 4*, *Hearst* 10, 4. 13.

[14] *Hearst* 11, 14. Sim. *Rhind* 41.

[15] *Westc.* 5, 9.

[16] *Urk.* iv. 688. Sim. *ib.* 698, 7; 699, 5. 6.

When the noun and numeral are accompanied by a demonstrative or possessive adjective, this adjective is made to agree with the noun in gender, though it always shows singular number, even when the noun has the plural form.

Exx. *pꜣ s 2* the two men.[1]

hrw 3 pn these three days.[2]

tꜣ ỉt ḥkꜣt 6 the six *ḥeḳat* of corn.[3] For ⁰⁰⁰ see below § 266, 1.

pꜣ·ỉ ẖrdw 4 my four children.[4]

When no noun is present, the adjective is singular and masculine.

Exx. *3 pn* these three.[5] *pꜣ 21* the twenty-one.[6]

Only in the case of the numbers 100 and 1,000 does the demonstrative follow the gender of the numeral, without reference to the gender of the thing that is numbered.

Exx. *tꜣ t 100* the hundred loaves.[7] *Št* is feminine.

pꜣ t 1,000 the thousand loaves.[8] *Ḫꜣ* is masculine.

What has been said above of the demonstrative applies equally to the word for 'other'.

Exx. *ky nḥsy 6* another six Nubians.[9]

kt št r-sꜣ kt št one hundred (years) after another hundred.[10]

The explanation of the puzzling facts set forth above is given by Old Egyptian and Coptic. It thence becomes clear that the method of writing the numeral after the word denoting the thing numbered was purely graphic; doubtless it was borrowed from book-keeping, just as £6 is the regular symbol in English account-books for 'six pounds'. It is just possible that Egyptian measurements like *mḥ 4* were sometimes read as *mḥ fdw*, lit. 'cubit, four'; but if so, this manner of reading was merely derivative and a reflection of the manner of writing.

From the evidence which we possess it is plain that in actual speech the number always preceded the noun numbered. The only exception is *snw* 'two', which was pronounced after its noun, cf. Coptic *p-son snau* 'the two brothers'. In all other cases the noun indicating the thing numbered came at the end. When the number is relatively small, the noun is in the plural and in apposition to the word denoting the number; with the highest numbers (see below § 262, 2) the noun numbered is in the singular and introduced by *m* or *n*. The word denoting the number is in all cases a singular noun (the units were originally plural, but early became singular, § 260), and hence the accompanying demonstrative and possessive adjectives and the word for 'other' are always singular. The variability in gender which they exhibit when the number is a low one is due to the fact that the units had masc. forms when the following noun in apposition

[1] *P. Kah.* 13, 28. Sim. *Urk.* iv. 1106, 12.

[2] *Siut* 1, 296.

[3] *Peas.* R 6. Sim. *Rhind* 77 (*pꜣ*).

[4] *Urk.* iv. 1070. *Pꜣ* and plur. noun, *Westc.* 3, 17; 9, 7; *M. u. K.* vs. 4, 8.

[5] *Peas.* B 1, 151.

[6] *Rhind* 62.

[7] *Rhind* 65.

[8] *Rhind* 76.

[9] Semnah Disp. 1, 12.

[10] *Siut* 4, 25.

was masc., and fem. forms when that noun was fem. The rules for the demonstrative, etc., become intelligible when we realize that what is written *pꜣ·i ẖrdw 4* was read *pꜣ·i fdw, ẖrdw* 'my masculine four, (namely) children'; 'my four cows' would have been *tꜣy·i fdt, iḥwt* 'my feminine four, namely cows', though written *tꜣy·i iḥwt* (or *iḥt*) *4*. On the other hand, with the hundreds the demonstrative is always fem., since *št* 'hundred' is an unchangeable fem. noun; *ḫꜣ* 'thousand' is, on the contrary, masculine, and consequently any adjective agreeing with it would have to be masculine likewise.

§ 262. The construction of the lowest and highest numbers.—1. The word for 'one', when written phonetically, as a rule follows its noun.

Exx. *dmi wꜥ* one city.[1]

wꜣt·f wꜥt its one side.[2]

Or else it precedes it and is connected with it by the genitival adjective.

Ex. *wꜥ n mṯn* one road.[3]

At a later stage of the language, the last-named construction gives rise to the **indefinite article**; an early example is *wꜥw n ḳꜣḳꜣw* 'a ship'.[4]

'One of (several)' is expressed by *wꜥ m*.

Exx. *wꜥ m nꜣ n ꜥꜣ* one of these asses.[5]

wꜥ im·ṯn nb every one of you.[6]

For the use of *wꜥ* to convey superlative meaning see above, § 97, end; and for its meaning 'one' as contrasted with 'other' see § 98.

2. The words for 1,000 and 1,000,000 are sometimes written before their noun, which is usually in the singular, and are connected with it either by the *m* of predication or by the genitival adjective. The same doubtless held good of the words for 10,000 and 100,000, but here we have no evidence.

Exx. *ḫꜣ m t ḥnḳt* a thousand of bread and beer.[7] Abbreviated writing.[8]

ḫꜣ·k pn n rnpt this thy thousand years, lit. of year.[9]

m ḥḥ pn n rnpwt in this million of years.[10]

Similar writings occur where the word for 100 is involved.

Exx. *120 nt ḫꜣ-tꜣ* one hundred and twenty thousands-of-land (a land-measure).[11]

tꜣ 365 n nṯr the 365 gods.[12]

In late Egyptian the construction with *n(y)* has been extended also to the tens. Sporadic examples may be found from Dyn. XII onwards.

Ex. *35 n rnpt* 35 years.[13]

§ 263. The ordinal numbers.—1. For 'first' *tpy*, varr., the adjective from *tp* 'head', is used and follows its noun.

Exx. *sp tpy* the first time.[14] *wdyt tpt* the first campaign.[15]

[1] *Urk.* iv. 1069.
[2] *Peas.* R 46.
[3] *Urk.* iv. 650.
[4] *Westc.* 8, 3. Sim. *ib.* 6, 3.
[5] *Peas.* B 1, 9. Sim. *ib.* 81–2; *Siut* 1, 287.
[6] *Siut* 1, 288. Sim. *ib.* 285.
[7] Cairo 20003. Sim. *ib.* 20006. 20009, *k.* 20011. 20012. 20053.
[8] Cairo 20004. Sim. *ib.* 20007. 20012, 2. 20046.
[9] *Urk.* iv. 539; 1058, 15. Sim. *ḥḥ·f n kꜣ* (sing.) LAC. *TR.* 78, 9.
[10] *Urk.* iv. 306.
[11] *Sebekn.* 7. Sim. *Urk.* iv. 893, 15 with *n* for *nt*.
[12] *P. Turin* 137, 3.
[13] MARUCCHI, *Gli Obelischi*, 1. Sim. *Ann.* 29, 7, 8, *13 n hrw*; *B. of D.* ed. NAV., ch. 125, Intr. 3, some MSS. *pꜣ 42 n nṯr*.
[14] *Urk.* iv. 175.
[15] *Urk.* iv. 740.

2. The ordinals from 2 to 9 are formed by the addition of an ending m. [hieroglyphs] *-nw*, f. [hieroglyphs] *-nwt* to the stem of the cardinals. As a rule this ending is appended to the numerals, exx. [hieroglyphs] *2-nw* '2nd' (m.), [hieroglyphs] *6-nwt* '6th' (f.), but a few phonetic writings are found, ex. [hieroglyphs] *ḫmt-nw* 'third';[1] [hieroglyphs] *sn-nw* 'second' is not uncommon.[2]

When used as epithets these ordinals may precede their noun.

Ex. [hieroglyphs] *4-nw sp* the fourth time.[3]

[hieroglyphs] *m sn-nwt·f ỉ3t* in his second office.[4]

This is the older use; the second example shows that a suffix may be attached to the ordinal; so too in the adverbial phrase [hieroglyphs] *ḥr sn-nw·sy* 'again', lit. 'for its second (time *sp*)',[5] and compare *kty·f* in § 98.

Later, the ordinal follows like a true adjective.

Exx. [hieroglyphs] *sp·f 3-nw ḥb-sd* his third time of Jubilee.[6]

[hieroglyphs] *wḏyt 6-nwt* the sixth expedition.[7]

Less commonly, the ordinal precedes its noun and is connected with it by means of the genitival adjective.

Ex. [hieroglyphs] *5-nw n ḥb* the fifth festival.[8]

3. From 10 upwards, the ordinals are formed with the aid of the participle m. [hieroglyphs] *mḥ*, f. [hieroglyphs] *mḥt* 'filling', 'completing'; the compound thus created follows its noun.

Exx. [hieroglyphs] *wḏyt mḥt-10* the tenth campaign, lit. the campaign completing ten (campaigns).[9]

§ 264. Use of the cardinals as ordinals.—In dates like [hieroglyphs] *ḥ3t-sp 2, (3bd) 2(-nw n) 3ḫt, sw 18*[10] it seems certain that the numbers after the words for 'year' and 'day' are cardinals, though in sense they are ordinals.[11] Similarly we might write in English 'year two', 'day eighteen' whilst meaning 'second year', 'eighteenth day'. The month-number in Egyptian was, on the contrary, almost certainly an ordinal, and it is probable also that the word for 'month' (*3bd*) was omitted in speech and [hieroglyphs] *n* inserted before the name of the season. This emerges from the following facts. Though [hieroglyphs], i.e. 'first month' is invariable in hieratic[12] and occasional in hieroglyphic,[13] in the latter it is often replaced by [hieroglyphs] *tpy* 'first', very rare var. [hieroglyphs].[14] exx. [hieroglyphs] *tpy (n) šmw* 'first (month of) summer';[15] [hieroglyphs] *tpy n 3ḫt* 'first (month) of inundation'.[16] A very late hieratic text has correspondingly [hieroglyphs] *4-nw n šm* 'fourth (month) of summer';[16a] the Dyn. XII writing [hieroglyphs][17] at least shows the *n*. The thirtieth day of the month was described as [hieroglyphs] *ʿrḳy*[18] (also [hieroglyphs][19] and [hieroglyphs],[20] the full phonetic writings [hieroglyphs].[21] [hieroglyphs][22] being rare in Middle Egyptian); this word again points to an ordinal meaning for the cardinal numbers of the days. For the general system of dating, see Excursus C at the end of this lesson.

[1] *ÄZ.* 45, Pl. 6, l. 12.
[2] *ÄZ.* 45, Pl. 6, l. 12. Sim. *Sin.* B 47; *Sh. S.* 42.
[3] *Peas.* B 1, 194. Sim. *ib.* 224. 226; *Eb.* 86, 20.
[4] *Siut* 3, 20; the sign for *ỉ3t* is uncertain.
[5] *Urk.* iv. 4, 9; 5, 10; 10, 3.
[6] *Urk.* iv. 590.
[7] *Urk.* iv. 689. Sim. BUDGE, p. 327, 14; 328, 1. 5. 9. 13.
[8] *Urk.* iv. 741. Sim. *ib.* 740, 17; *Hearst* 2, 3 = *Eb.* 86, 19.
[9] *Urk.* iv. 709. Sim. *ib.* 716, 13; 721, 10; BUDGE, p. 377, 5; 378, 2.
[10] *P. Kah.* 12, 6.
[11] See *Unt.* iii. 92. 96.
[12] *P. Kah.* 14, 9; 22, 11; 24, 27; *Urk.* iv. 44, 8. 12. 16.
[13] *Urk.* iv. 45.
[14] L. *D.* ii. 150 *f.*
[15] *Urk.* iv. 648, 9; 649, 3. Sim. Cairo 20026.
[16] Louvre C 166. Sim. *Hamm.* 114, 2; L. *D.* ii. 150 *f.*
[16a] P. Leyd. I 32, 4, 2 (unpubl.) qu. MÖLL. *Rhind*, p. 73. Sim. BR. *Thes.* 271. 447.
[17] Louvre C 1. Sim. *Hamm.* 113, 3.
[18] *P. Kah.* 15, 13; 23, 1; *Urk.* iv. 771, 7.
[19] Cairo 20541; *Urk.* iv. 823, 16; 836, 2.
[20] Cairo 20026.
[21] Brit. Mus. 155.
[22] BUDGE, p. 252, 5.

We shall see below (§ 265), in dealing with the fractions, that there too the cardinal numbers have ordinal meaning.[1] Much more doubtful is the following: [hieroglyphs] *ꜥḥꜥ·n·i ḫd·kwi ḥr šms m 6 n ẖnw* I sailed downstream in the escort (lit. in following) with five others of the Residence.[2] Lit. perhaps 'as six', the text seeming to say he *was* six or represented them; hardly 'with six (others)' as has recently been suggested.[2a]

[1] *Cf.* perhaps *sp 2* 'a second time', *Peas.* B 1, 88.

[2] *Sebekkhu* 17. Sim. *ib.* 13; the sense seems guaranteed by the late *Abbott* 4, 15.

[2a] *JEA.* 25, 167; for *m* 'together with' see § 162, 7A.

[2b] *Zahlworte*, p. 60.

§ 265. **Fractions.**[2b]—The commonest method of expressing fractions in Egyptian was by the use of the word [hieroglyph] *r* 'part', below which (or partly below it in the case of the higher numbers) was written the number described in English as the denominator. Thus [hieroglyph] *r-5* 'part 5' is equivalent to our $\frac{1}{5}$, [hieroglyph] *r-276* 'part 276' to our $\frac{1}{276}$.

For the Egyptian the number following the word *r* had ordinal meaning; [hieroglyph] *r-5* means 'part 5', i.e. 'the fifth part' which concludes a row of equal parts together constituting a single set of five. As being the part which completed the row into one series of the number indicated, the Egyptian *r*-fraction was necessarily a fraction with, as we should say, unity as the numerator. To the Egyptian mind it would have seemed nonsense and self-contradictory to write *r-7 4* or the like for $\frac{4}{7}$; in any series of seven, only one part could be the seventh, namely that which occupied the seventh place in the row of seven equal parts laid out for inspection. Nor would it have helped matters from the Egyptian point of view to have written *[hieroglyphs] *r-7(+)r-7(+)r-7(+)r-7*, a writing which would likewise have assumed that there could be more than one actual 'seventh'. Consequently, the Egyptian was reduced to expressing (e.g.) $\frac{4}{7}$ by $\frac{1}{2}$ (+) $\frac{1}{14}$. For more complex fractions even as many as five terms, all representing fractions with 1 as the numerator and with increasing denominators, might be needed; thus the Rhind mathematical papyrus, dating from the Hyksos period, gives as equivalent of our $\frac{2}{61}$ the following complex writing: [hieroglyphs] *r-40 r-244 r-488 r-610* '$\frac{1}{40}+\frac{1}{244}+\frac{1}{488}+\frac{1}{610}$'. It is not generally known that the same cumbrous methods of expression were in common use with the Greeks and Romans. It would seem also that a relic of them survives in the use of English ordinals in the names of our fractions, though we speak of 'one-third' and 'three-fifths' without any qualms.

For $\frac{1}{2}$ the Egyptians used the word [hieroglyph] *gs*, lit. 'side'. In place of hieroglyphic [hieroglyph], hieratic employs ×, which was originally read *ḥsb* 'fraction' (*par excellence*), but later understood as *r-fdw* 'part 4'; rarely × or + occurs in hieroglyphic, ex. [hieroglyphs] *ḥnḳt, stꜣ 1 n ds* $\frac{1}{4}$ 'beer, 1 *stꜣ*-vessel of $\frac{1}{4}$ of a pint'.[3] Similarly, where the hieroglyphs have [hieroglyph] *r-3* '$\frac{1}{3}$', hieratic has a sign [hieratic sign], which may presuppose a hieroglyphic *[hieroglyph], probably to be understood as 'one part' (out of three).

[3] *Siut* 1, 302. Sim. *Sinai* 139, 8.

Though the Egyptians were unable to say 'three-sevenths' or 'nine-sixteenths', yet they made a restricted use of certain fractions which appear, at first sight, to stand on the same footing: a great rôle is played in Egyptian arithmetic by the fraction *rwy*[1] 'the two parts' (out of three) i.e. $\frac{2}{3}$, and a very rare sign *r-3* (perhaps to be read *ḫmt rw*) can be quoted for 'the three parts' (out of four), i.e. $\frac{3}{4}$.[2] These 'complementary fractions' represent the parts remaining over when 'the third' or 'the fourth' is taken away from a set of three or four, and indeed their existence is practically postulated by the terms *r-3*, *r-4*. But we must be careful to note that in *r-3* = $\frac{3}{4}$ the numeral is a cardinal, not an ordinal, and that the expression means 'the three parts' and was not construed, as with ourselves, as meaning 'three *fourths*'. In ordinary arithmetic the only complementary fraction used was $\frac{2}{3}$. Compare in English 'two parts full', i.e. two-thirds full, doubtless a survival of the old Egyptian way of regarding the same fraction.

Some examples of the symbols above explained may now be quoted from the Rhind papyrus and elsewhere:

$5+\frac{1}{2}+\frac{1}{7}+\frac{1}{14}=5\frac{5}{7}$.[3]

$2+\frac{1}{2}+\frac{1}{4}+\frac{1}{14}+\frac{1}{28}=2\frac{6}{7}$ (half of $5\frac{5}{7}$ just quoted).[4]

$2+\frac{2}{3}+\frac{1}{6}+\frac{1}{12}+\frac{1}{36}+\frac{1}{54}=2\frac{26}{27}$.[5]

ir hrw n ḥwt-nṯr r-360 pw ḫnt rnpt as for a temple day, it is the three hundred and sixtieth part of (lit. out of) the year.[6]

r-9 n 9 m 1 the ninth of nine, namely one.[7]

$\frac{2}{3}$ *n r-10 n r-10·f* $\frac{2}{3}$ of $\frac{1}{10}$ of $\frac{1}{10}$ of it.[8]

§ 266. Other kinds of fractions; weights and measures.

—In their measures for corn and for land, the Egyptians appear to have preserved a more primitive kind of fractions obtained by halving. In discussing these, we shall deal also with the terms for weights and linear measurements.

1. **The corn-measure.**[9]—The symbols employed in this, as shown in the accompanying cut, are derived from the ancient myth according to which the eye of the falcon-god Horus, often depicted on the monuments in the form 𓂀, was torn into fragments by the wicked god Seth.[10] Later, the ibis-god Thoth miraculously 'filled' or 'completed' (*mḥ*) the eye, joining together the parts, whereby the eye regained its title to be called the *wḏꜣt*, 'the sound eye'. In accordance with this myth the sign ◁ was used for $\frac{1}{2}$, ○ for $\frac{1}{4}$, ⁀ for $\frac{1}{8}$, ▷ for $\frac{1}{16}$, ◡ for $\frac{1}{32}$ and ❘ for $\frac{1}{64}$. These fractions together add up to $\frac{63}{64}$; presumably the missing $\frac{1}{64}$ was supplied magically by Thoth.

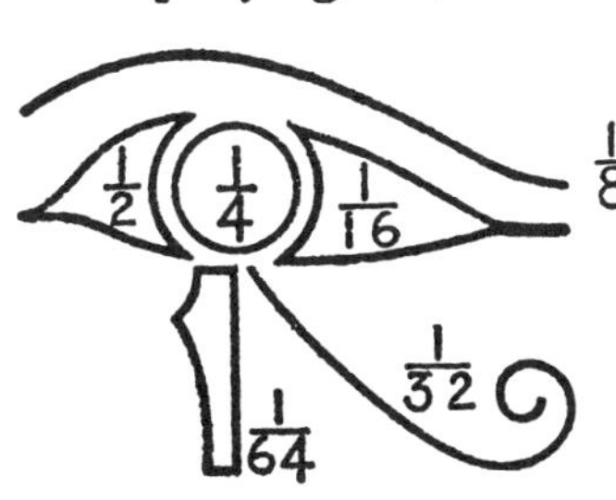

[1] In hieroglyphic, *Urk.* iv, 630. 637; MAR. *Karn.* 34, 22. For the reading see the Sign-list under D 22.

[2] VARILLE, *Karnak I*, Pls. 27. 28. See further *Zahlworte*, p. 98.

[3] *Rhind* 34.

[4] *Rhind* 34.

[5] *Rhind* 42.

[6] *Siut* 1, 285.

[7] *Rhind* 41.

[8] *Rhind* 46.

[9] See in general *PSBA.* 14, 421–35; SETHE, *Zahlworte* 80; MÖLLER, *Hieratische Paläographie*, i. pp. 66–7; ii. p. 62. Later discussions, *ÄZ.* 65, 42; 66, 33.

[10] See *ÄZ.* 48, 99.

With the exception of $\frac{1}{2}$,[1] no hieroglyphic examples of this notation have been found before Dyn. XX, but the hieratic equivalents are of frequent occurrence. These are regularly employed in connection with the *ḥeḳat*-measure (*ḥḳꜣt*), written ,[2] ,[3] ,[4] ,[5] ,[6] or ,[7] rather more, as emerges from recent measurements of the *hin* (see below) than a gallon = 4·54 litres; but they also serve as fractions of the 'double *ḥeḳat*', written ,[8] ,[9] ,[10] as well as of the 'quadruple *ḥeḳat*' written once in hieroglyphic ,[11] in hieratic regularly [12] and later, less correctly, ;[13] the quadruple *ḥḳꜣt* makes its first appearance in the Rhind mathematical papyrus (Hyksos period) and was much used at a later date, then becoming known as the *ỉpt* '*oipĕ*', Greek οἰφι.

Fractions below $\frac{1}{64}$ of the *ḥeḳat*, whether single, double, or quadruple, were indicated in terms of the *ro*-measure (*r*) of $\frac{1}{10}$ $= \frac{1}{10} \times \frac{1}{32} = \frac{1}{320}$ *ḥeḳat*; to avoid confusion with the ordinary fractions like $\frac{1}{3}$, $\frac{1}{4}$ (§ 265), the multiples of the *ro*-measure were written as , , and ;[14] for 5 *ro*, being $\frac{1}{64}$ *ḥeḳat*, is written. For quantities smaller than the *ro*-measure itself the ordinary fractions were used.

We must next describe the curious way in which multiples of the *ḥeḳat*-measure were indicated in hieratic; , stand respectively for 100 and 200 single, double, or quadruple *ḥeḳat*, and with as a basis $100 \times \frac{1}{2} = 50$ *ḥeḳat* is written ; similarly stands for $100 \times \frac{1}{4} = 25$ *ḥeḳat*,[15] while and represent 10 *ḥeḳat* and 20 *ḥeḳat* and the units are denoted by mere dots, e. g. = 2 *ḥeḳat*, = 7 *ḥeḳat*.

Exx. *ḥḳꜣt* $\frac{1}{2}$ *1* $\frac{1}{4}$ *8* $\frac{1}{4}$ $\frac{1}{16}$ $\frac{1}{64}$ (*1 r*) ($\frac{2}{3}$ *r*) $= 50 + 10 + 25 + 8 + \frac{1}{4}$ *ḥeḳat* (= 80 *ro*) + $\frac{1}{16}$ *ḥeḳat* (= 20 *ro*) + $\frac{1}{64}$ *ḥeḳat* (= 5 *ro*) + 1 *ro* + $\frac{2}{3}$ *r* = 93 *ḥeḳat* 106$\frac{2}{3}$ *r* = 93$\frac{106\frac{2}{3}}{320}$ *ḥeḳat* = 93$\frac{1}{3}$ *ḥeḳat*.[16]

bdt ḥḳꜣt : 1 ḥḳꜣt $\frac{1}{2}$ *1 6* $\frac{1}{2}$ $\frac{1}{8}$ $\frac{1}{32}$ (*3 r*) $\frac{1}{3}$ = spelt, *ḥeḳat* 100 + 50 + 10 + 6 + $\frac{1}{2}$ *ḥeḳat* (= 160 *ro*) + $\frac{1}{8}$ *ḥeḳat* (= 40 *ro*) + $\frac{1}{32}$ *ḥeḳat* (= 10 *ro*) + 3$\frac{1}{3}$ *ro* = 166$\frac{213\frac{1}{3}}{320}$ = 166$\frac{2}{3}$ *ḥeḳat*.[17]

48 ḥḳꜣt = 4800 *ḥeḳat*.[18]

Only very rarely are the fractions for $\frac{1}{3}$ and $\frac{2}{3}$ substituted for the signs of the Horus-eye notation.

Ex. *ḥḳꜣt* $\frac{1}{2}$ *2* $\frac{2}{3}$ = 50 + 2 + $\frac{2}{3}$ = 52$\frac{2}{3}$ *ḥeḳat*.[19]

In hieroglyphic, on the other hand, multiples of the *ḥeḳat* seem to have been expressed with the ordinary notation.

Exx. *ỉt šmꜥ ḥḳꜣt 645* corn of Upper Egypt, 645 *ḥeḳat*.[20]

ḏꜥm ḥḳꜣt 88$\frac{1}{2}$ fine gold, 88$\frac{1}{2}$ *ḥeḳat*.[21]

In Dyn. XVIII the 'sack' *ḫꜣr* (rare variant)[22] comes into vogue as the multiple 4 of the quadruple *ḥeḳat* = 16 single *ḥeḳat*. One, two, or three quadruple *ḥeḳat* (the *oipĕ* of Dyn. XX) are expressed, as previously, by dots, and fractions of the quadruple *ḥeḳat* by means of the Horus-eye notation.

1 *Urk.* iv. 756, 8; *Puy.* 36, reversed; hieratic also seems to reverse this sign.
2 *Siut* 1, 279; *Rhind* 44; *Urk.* iv. 429, 12.
3 *Puy.* 35; *Urk.* iv. 720, 7.
4 *Puy.* 36.
5 *Peas.* R 5; *P. Boul.* xviii. 47; *Rhind* 82, 6. 7.
6 *Rhind* 35. 37.
7 *P. Kah.* 18, 26. 30; *Rhind* 64.
8 *Rhind* 82, 11.
9 *P. Kah.* 15, 65–7; *Urk.* iv. 763, 9.
10 *PSBA.* 15, 306.
11 *Urk.* iv. 667, 14.
12 *Rhind* 41–6; *P. Louvre* 3226, 4, 9.
13 Möller, *Hieratische Paläographie*, ii. p. 62.
14 In hieratic only; the transcriptions are conjectural, see *PSBA.* 13, 533.
15 In hieroglyphic *Sinai* 139, 8. An isolated case where $\frac{1}{3}$ is employed for 33$\frac{1}{3}$ *ḥḳꜣt*, see *Rhind* 82, 7.
16 *Rhind* 82, 10. Sim. *Rec.* 28, 69, down to $\frac{1}{104}$ *r*, see *JEA.* ix, 91.
17 *Rhind* 82, 6. Sim. *P. Boul.* xviii. 47.
18 *Rhind* 41. Sim. *ib.* 43.
19 *P. Kah.* 15, 50. Sim. *ib.* 15, 52; *P. Pet.* 1116 A, vs. 101. 179.
20 *Urk.* iv. 195. Sim. *ib.* 762, 3. 6; *Mar. Karn.* 33.
21 *Urk.* iv. 429. Sim. *Puy.* 36.
22 *P. Kah.* 22, 14; *Sm.* 21, 10; see further *Wilb.* Comm., 61, n. 2. The word *ḫꜣr* also *Siut* 1, 292; *Westc.* 12, 4.

Exx. *bn(r)i ḥḳꜣt ḫꜣr 20 2* dates, quadruple *ḥeḳat*, 20 sacks and 2.[1] A somewhat strange way of expressing (4 × 20) + 2 = 82 quadruple *ḥeḳat*.

štbt 226, mnt ḥḳꜣt 1 + ½ + ¼ + ⅛, ir n ḫꜣr 105 3 ½+¼ crates (?), 226, content 1⅞ *ḥeḳat*, making (§ 422, 3) 105 sacks and 3¾ *ḥeḳat*.[2]

It seems evident that the 'sack' (*ḫꜣr*) of Dyn. XVIII was a modification of the *ḫꜣr* 'sack' of 5 quadruple, or 20 single, *ḥeḳat* mentioned in the Rhind mathematical papyrus.[3]

A jar *hnw* '*hin*' used for liquids (beer, milk, honey, etc.),[4] but apparently also for grain,[5] is shown by the Rhind papyrus to have contained $\frac{1}{10}$ *ḥeḳat*;[6] actual inscribed examples average about ·503 litre.[6a] Other vessels employed as liquid measures were named *ds* (especially for beer),[7] *hbnt* (wine, incense),[8] *stꜣ* (a very small measure for beer),[9] *mn*,[10] var. *mni*[11] (oil, incense); the size of these has not been determined.

2. **Measures of length.**[12]—Measurements of small objects are given in terms of the cubit of about 20·6 inches = 523 millimetres[13] and its subdivisions, 1 cubit being equal to 7 palms or 28 digits. 'Cubit' is ,[14] [15] *mḥ*, abbrev. ,[16] ,[17] or ;[18] 'palm', i.e. palm-breadth, is *šsp*,[19] abbrev. ,[20] ;[20a] 'digit', i.e. finger-breadth, is *ḏbꜥ*. A much less often mentioned linear measure is the *nbiw* '*nebiu*', lit. 'pole', perhaps equal to 1¼ or 1⅓ cubit.[20b]

Exx. *sḫb·ḥr·f mḥ 1 šsp 3 m mw ꜥꜣw* then it (the serpent) swallows 1 cubit and 3 palms of the great waters.[21]

You are to make ½ + ¼ of a cubit . . . . . *gs·f 3½, r 4·f 1½ ¼; dmḏ, šsp 5, ḏbꜥ* half of it is 3½ (palms), one-fourth of it is 1½ ¼ (palms); total, 5 palms and a digit.[22] Here the digit is represented in hieratic by ∖.

mḥ 4, šsp 4, ḏbꜥ 2 four cubits, 4 palms and 2 digits.[23]

The chief multiple of the cubit was the *ḫt* 'rod' of 100 cubits, also called *ḫt n nwḥ* 'rod of cord'.

Exx. *swsḫ·n·i wꜣt n wdḥw·i m ḫt n nwḥ 21* I made a wide road (lit. made wide a road) for my offerings consisting of 21 rods of cord, i.e. 2,100 cubits.[24]

ꜣḥt n ḫt 10 r ḫt 2 a field of 10 rods by 2 rods.[25]

A much larger linear measure was the *itrw* 'river-measure',[26] the Greek 'schoenus', now estimated on good grounds at 20,000 cubits = 10·5 km.[26a] However, in one place a smaller *itrw* occurs in conjunction with the *ḫt* 'rod', and with two fractions of this which we shall find below as measures of area:—

The distance between stela and stela on the hill east of Akhetaten *irw n itrw 6 ḫt rmn ḥsb mḥ 4* makes 6 *itrw*, 1¾ rods and 4 cubits.[27] For *irw n* 'makes' see § 422, 3.

[1] *P. Louvre* 3226, 4, 9. Sim. *P. Pet.* 1116 A, vs. *passim*. In hieroglyphic *Urk.* iv. 667, 14.

[2] *P. Louvre* 3226, 29, 2.

[3] *Rhind* 41. 43.

[4] *Peas.* B 1, 94; *P. Kah.* 5, 11. 32. 33; *Eb.* 53. 10.

[5] *Rhind* 83.

[6] *Rhind* 80, 81.

[6a] *Ann.* 40, 80, a recent computation.

[7] *Siut* 1, 302; *Peas.* B 1, 84; *P. Kah.* 26, 3. 13; *Rhind* 71.

[8] *ÄZ.* 45, Pl. 8; *Rekh.* 6; *Urk.* iv. 718, 6.

[9] *Siut* 1, 302; *P. Kah.* 26, 4. 14.

[10] *Urk.* iv. 699, 15; 718, 7.

[11] *Urk.* iv. 712, 15.

[12] *PSBA.* 14, 403; MÖLLER, *Hieratische Paläographie*, i. p. 65.

[13] See *JEA.* iv. 136.

[14] *Hamm.* 114, 14.

[15] *Urk.* iv. 425, 17; 459, 9.

[16] *Bersh.* i. 14, 1.

[17] *Urk.* iv, 640.

[18] *BH.* i. 26, 200; *Urk.* iv. 373, 9.

[19] *ÄZ.* 59, 44*; *Rhind* 56. 58.

[20] *P. Kah.* 23, 30.

[20a] See the Sign-list, under D 48.

[20b] *Cen.* p. 93; *Wb.* II, 243, 9; 244, 2; HAYES, p. 36.

[21] *ÄZ.* 59, 47*. Sim. *P. Boul.* xviii. 4.

[22] *Rhind* 58.

[23] *ÄZ.* 59, 44*. Sim. *Arm.* 93.

[24] *Urk.* iv. 133.

[25] *Rhind* 49. Sim. *ÄZ.* 59, 44*.

[26] See *ÄZ.* 41, 58.

[26a] BORCHARDT in *Festschrift . . . . Lehmann-Haupt* (*Janus*, 1921), 119; see also *JEA.* 30, 33.

[27] *Amarna* v. 26, 18–19, see *ib.* p. 33, n. 8. According to BORCHARDT, here perhaps an *itrw* of 5,000 cubits.

3. **Measures of area.**[1]—A set of fractions obtained by halving, like the fractions of the corn-measure, was used in connection with the *sṯ3t*, the Greek 'aroura', varr. [2] [3]; this was a measure of 1 square *khet* (see above, 2), or 100 cubits squared, i.e. 2735 square metres, or roughly $\frac{2}{3}$ acre. The fractions of the *sṯ3t* are *rmn* = $\frac{1}{2}$ *sṯ3t*, × *ḥsb* = $\frac{1}{4}$ *sṯ3t* and *s3* = $\frac{1}{8}$ *sṯ3t*; in Middle Egyptian they have been found only in hieratic, but of the three hieroglyphic forms derived from Ptolemaic texts two, namely and ×, certainly were used in Middle Egyptian, since they occur as measures of length (see above, 2). Smaller parts of the aroura are expressed in terms of the *mḥ* 'cubit', i.e. a strip of land 100 cubits in length with a depth of 1 cubit = $\frac{1}{100}$ *sṯ3t*. A measure of ten arouras is written *ḫ3*, lit. 'thousand', more fully (*ḫ3-t3*); [4] an abbreviated writing is |.

Exx. *3ḥt ḫ3 2, sṯ3t 2* twenty-two arouras of field.[5]

|||| (*ḫ3?*) *4 sṯ3t 2 rmn* forty-two and a half arouras.[6]

× *sṯ3t 8* $\frac{1}{2}$ $\frac{1}{4}$ $\frac{1}{8}$ *mḥ 10* $\frac{1}{2}$ $\frac{1}{4}$ $8\frac{7}{8}$ arouras, $10\frac{3}{4}$ cubits; or 89,825 square cubits.[7]

4. **Weights.**[8]—From Dyn. XVIII onwards the weight employed for metals of all sorts was the [9] *dbn* '*deben*', (originally ,[9a] less correctly , phonetically [10]) of 10 *ḳdt* '*kitě*'; actual weighing shows it to have amounted to about 91 grammes, or a little more than 1,400 grains.

Ex. *ḥḏ dbn 761, ḳdt 2* silver, 761 *deben* and 2 *kitě*.[11]

For weights smaller than the *kitě* the ordinary fractions were used.[12]

The values of different articles were in Ramesside times expressed in terms of *deben* and *kitě* of gold, silver or copper.[13] For Dyn. XVIII there is not much evidence of the kind, but in one or two documents we find articles valued in terms of the *deben* and the 'seal' (once written phonetically *šʿty* [14]); the latter was equivalent to $\frac{1}{12}$ *deben*.[15]

Ex. *iḥ 1, irw n šʿty 8* 1 ox, making 8 seals.[16]

[1] See *PSBA.* 14, 410; SETHE, *Zahlworte* 74; MÖLLER, *Hieratische Paläographie*, i. p. 65.
[2] *Urk.* iv. 6, 8. 15.
[3] *Siut* 1, 313.
[4] *Sebekn.* 7, qu. § 262, 2.
[5] *Siut* 1, 313. Sim. *ib.* 325.
[6] *P. Kah.* 21, 3. Sim. *Rhind* 48. 53.
[7] *P. Kah.* 21, 19. Sim. *Rhind* 54. 55.
[8] See *PSBA.* 14, 435.
[9] MAR. *Karn.* 34, 30-1: the same sign reversed, *D. el B.* 81
[9a] Berl. *ÄI.* i. 72, O. K.
[10] *Peas.* B 1, 166. Sim. Cairo 31, 652, see WEIGALL, *Weights*, pl. 6.
[11] *Urk.* iv. 692. Sim. *ib.* 630. 637. 638.
[12] *Urk.* iv. 630. 637.
[13] See SPIEGELBERG, *Rechnungen aus der Zeit Setis I* (Strassburg, 1896), Text, p. 87.
[14] *Rhind* 62.
[15] *ÄZ.* 43, 45. Confirmed by a papyrus in author's possession.
[16] *ÄZ.* 43, 35. Sim. *ib.* 43, 39; *P. Boul.* 11.

VOCABULARY

psš divide.

ḫ3 measure (vb.)

sbḥ cry out.

kf uncover.

3w length.

Imn Amūn, the god of Thebes.

W3ḏ-wr the sea, lit. the great green.

ʿḳw provisions, revenue.

ʿḳyw members of household.

wdpw butler.

ꜥnḫw victuals.

dꜣt (or *wḏꜣt*) remainder, balance.

mnt quantum, fixed ration.

mnꜥt nurse.

rḫt amount, number (m.).

ḥfꜣw snake.

ẖnt (for *ẖnrt* [1]) harîm.

sḫw breadth (from stem *wsḫ*).

var. *stp-sꜣ* palace.

šnꜥ ergastulum, magazine.

tḫn obelisk.

dmd (old *dmḏ*) total.

ds jug, beer-jug.

ḏꜥm fine gold.

šbn various (adj.).

[1] In this and the perhaps identical word for 'prison' (above, p. 146) the spellings vacillate between *ẖnt* and *ẖnrt*, partly owing to the similarity of hieratic and . Both words are probably derived from *ẖnr* 'restrain'.

EXERCISE XX

(*a*) *Study the following excerpt from a papyrus of accounts relating to the Royal Court (Dyn. XIII)*: [2]

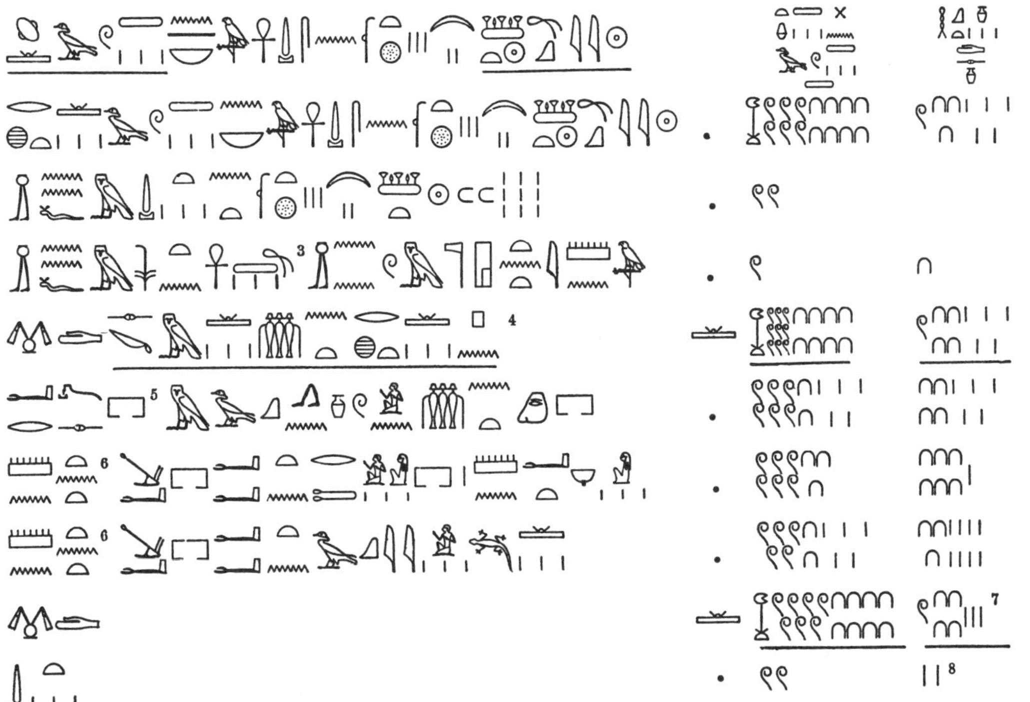

[2] *P. Boul. XVIII*, 31, printed exactly as in the original. Words there written in red are here underlined. Several readings are disputed, the hieratic containing difficult ligatures. [3] Rather uncertain on account of the unexpected . [4] This rubric is the heading to what follows and was inserted after the word for 'total' in order to economize space. [5] Others read . [6] Others read . [7] An error for 144. [8] An error for 1.

	t šbn ꜥḳw	*ḥnḳt ds*
ḥsb ꜥḳw n nb (*ꜥ. w. s.* § 313, end) *n ḥꜣt-sp 3* (*ꜣbd*) 2(*-nw n*) *ꜣḫt*, *ꜥrḳy*.		
rḫt ꜥḳw n nb (*ꜥ. w. s.*) *n ḥꜣt-sp 3* (*ꜣbd*) 2(*-nw n*) *ꜣḫt*, *ꜥrḳy*	1680	135
ỉn (§ 422, 1) *n·f m ḏꜣt nt ḥꜣt-sp 3* (*ꜣbd*) 2(*-nw n*) *ꜣḫt*, *sw* 29	200	
ỉn (§ 422, 1) *n·f m ꜥnḫw* (?) *nsw ỉnnw* (§ 369, 4) *m ḥwt-nṯr nt 'Imn*	100	10
dmd. *Sšm ḫnt rḫt pn.*	1980	145
dỉw (§ 422, 1) *r stp-s*(*ꜣ*) *m ꜥḳ n wdpw n ḫnt*	625	45
mnt(?) *nt šnꜥ ddt* (§ 369, 4) *n rmṯ pr mnꜥwt*	630	61
mnt(?) *nt šnꜥ ddt* (§ 369, 4) *n ꜥḳyw ꜥšꜣw*	525	38
dmd	1780	143 (*sic*)
ḏꜣt t	200	2 (*sic*)

ACCOUNT OF THE REVENUE OF THE LORD (l. p. h.) of yr. 3, second month of inundation, last day.	various kinds of bread, loaves	beer, *des*-jugs
Amount of the revenue of the Lord (l. p. h.) of yr. 3, second month of inundation, last day	1680	135
Was brought to him as balance of yr. 3, second month of inundation, day 29	200	
Was brought to him as king's victuals (?) which are brought from the temple of Amūn	100	10
Total.	1980	145
EXPENDITURE OUT OF THIS AMOUNT.		
Was given into the palace at the entry of the butler of the harîm	625	45
Ration of the ergastulum which is given to the people of the house of the nurses	630	61
Ration of the ergastulum which is given to the ordinary members of the household	525	38
Total	1780	143 (*sic*)
Balance	200	2 (*sic*)

(*b*) *Write in hieroglyphs and in transliteration*:

(1) It happened (on) one of these days I heard a noise and uncovered my face and found it was (*pw*) a snake of (*ny-sw*, lit. it was of) 10 cubits in its length. (2) Thou (*ntk*) shalt divide for them $1\frac{31}{32}$ *ḥeḳat*[1] of corn. (3) Year 7, first month of summer, day 1 under the Majesty of the Horus 'Great of Might' (*ꜥꜣ bꜣw*), King of Upper and Lower Egypt, Nemaꜥrēꜥ, Son of Rēꜥ, Ammenemes,[2] tribute of the prince (*wr*) of the Medjay, 265 *deben* of gold (lit. gold, 265 *deben*).

[1] *ḥḳꜣt* $1 + \frac{1}{2} + \frac{1}{4} + \frac{1}{8} + \frac{1}{16} + \frac{1}{32}$.

[2] For these royal names see above, p. 74, bottom.

(4) He went to the door a fourth time, and found no one there. (5) He gave her three-fifths of all his possessions (*ḫt*). (6) The twelfth hour of the night. (7) They cried out with one voice (lit. mouth). (8) He was the third of these three (write 'third' and 'three' phonetically).

EXCURSUS C

The Divisions of Time and Method of Dating.[1]

The Egyptian year (*rnpt*) was divided into 12 months (*ꜣbd*) of 30 days (*hrw*), completed to 365 days by the addition of the five so-called epagomenal or 'added' days (*5 ḥryw rnpt*, § 259). Though for dating and calendrical purposes generally the year of 365 days perforce served as the basis, there was clearly a tendency to regard the year as of only 360 days; thus for purposes of calculation the daily income of a temple is stated as $\frac{1}{360}$ of the yearly revenue.[2] In dating, the year was further divided into three 'seasons' (*tr*) of four months each: 1. *ꜣḫt*, var. , 'inundation'; 2. *prt* 'winter', presumably the season of the 'emergence' (*pr*) of the fields from the water; 3. *šmw* 'summer', daringly guessed to mean 'deficiency (*wšr*) of water'. The word for 'day' used in dates seems from Coptic to have been *sw*, not *hrw*;[3] the plural *sww* (?) is not infrequently found written out in Middle Egyptian with the meaning 'dates'.[4] Similarly the word for 'year' used in dates is not *rnpt*, which never has ☉ as a determinative, but , which we now know to read *ḥꜣt-sp*; in *ḥꜣt-sp* the round sign is the ideogram of *sp* 'occasion'; only at a late period is the ordinary determinative of time ☉ substituted in this word for . We shall have more to say about the meaning of *ḥꜣt-sp* below.

The way in which the numerals are indicated in dates has been studied above in §§ 259. 264. We may now give one or two examples:—

ḥꜣt-sp 2 (ꜣbd) 3(-nw n) ꜣḫt sw 1, ḫr ḥm n n-sw-bit N-mꜣꜥt-Rꜥ year 2, third month of inundation, day one under the Majesty of king Nemaꜥrēꜥ (i. e. Ammenemes III).[5]

m ḥꜣt-sp 24 (ꜣbd) 2(-nw n) prt, ꜥrḳy, hrw-ḥb mḥ-10 n 'Imn m 'Ipt-swt in year 24, second month of winter, last day, tenth festival-day of Amūn in Ipet-sut (i. e. Karnak).[6] Note that, as often, the king (Tuthmosis III) is not mentioned. This date occurs in the midst of a sentence; at the beginning of a text the preposition *m* is never used.

tpy (n) ꜣḫt, wpt-rnpt, ḥb Ḫnmw first month of inundation, opening of the year (= day 1), feast of Chnum.[7]

Very rare writings of the regnal year are seen in *ḥꜣt-sp 30* 'year 30';[8] *ḥꜣt-sp 44* 'year 44';[9] *ḥꜣt-sp 33* 'year 33'.[10]

[1] See in general K. SETHE, *Die Zeitrechnung der alten Aegypter im Verhältnis zu der der andern Völker*, in *Nachrichten d. k. Gesellschaft d. Wissenschaften zu Göttingen, Phil.-hist. Klasse*, 1919–20.

[2] See *Siut* 1, 285, qu. § 265.

[3] Not *ssw* as formerly read; see the writings *Wb.* iv, 57.

[4] *Adm.* 11, 4; *Urk.* iv. 112, 12.

[5] *Hamm.* 43.

[6] *Urk.* iv. 836.

[7] *Urk.* iv. 823.

[8] Cairo 20516.

[9] Leyd. V 4; sim. *Urk.* iv. 606, 6.

[10] *Rhind*, title.

On the strength of the testimony already quoted the student will have concluded that the Egyptians dated their inscriptions by the years of their kings' reigns; throughout the whole of the Pharaonic history no use was ever made of a continuous era. Even the numbering of the regnal years was, however, a secondary development.[1] In the earliest Dynasties each separate year was named after some conspicuous event that happened in it, e. g. 'the year of fighting and of smiting Lower Egypt'. In the Fifth and Sixth Dynasties this ancient method of dating survived in a modified form; an event which occurred biennially was the census of the cattle, and this became the standard event by which the years were dated. Examples are [hieroglyphs] *ḥ3t sp 14 ṯnwt iḥ ꜥwt nb* 'beginning of time 14 of the numbering of the oxen and of all small cattle' (like sheep and goats);[2] [hieroglyphs] *ḥ3t m-ḫt sp 18* 'the beginning after time 18'.[3] Note that in this last date, which appears to refer to the 37th year of Phiops I (Dyn. VI), the words *ṯnwt iḥ ꜥwt nb* are omitted as obvious and unessential. Still more would this be true when the census of the cattle came to be taken every year, as may possibly have happened towards the end of the reign of Phiops II. There is no definite evidence that a census of cattle ever occurred annually, nor do we know precisely when the 'times' (*sp*) in question ceased to be biennial; but certain it is that henceforth *ḥ3t-sp* meant 'year' in dates—the reading *ḥ3t* instead of *rnpt* is proved by the variants [hieroglyphs] and [hieroglyphs] for [hieroglyphs] in texts of the Ptolemaic temple at Edfu.[4]

There is testimony to show that in the Middle Kingdom and earlier the Pharaohs dated their second regnal year from the New Year's Day (*wpt-rnpt* = 1st day of 1st month of inundation) following the actual day of their accession, and that their first year consisted merely of the odd months and days after the demise of their predecessor.[5] In Dyn. XVIII, however, a new system came into vogue and continued until at least the end of Dyn. XX: year 1 was dated from the actual day of accession and year 2, accordingly, from its anniversary in the following civil year, so that the civil year now always contained parts of two regnal years.

Grave consequences resulted from the fact that the Egyptians used a civil year of 365 days, whereas the astronomical year has approximately $365\frac{1}{4}$ days.[6] Since they never resorted to intercalation of a day such as we carry out in leap-year, it followed that four years after the coincidence of the beginning of the astronomical year with the beginning of the civil year New Year's Day of the civil calendar would already occur one day earlier than the event which marked the beginning of the astronomical year. In about 120 years the civil year would be a whole month in advance of the astronomical year, and in about 1460 years, when the civil and astronomical years would again coincide, any given annual astronomical event would have fallen in turn on every different day

[1] For all that follows see now *JEA*. 31, 11; fundamental is *Unt.* 3, 60–100.

[2] *Unt.* 3, 79.

[3] *Sinai* 16.

[4] Disputed by EDEL in *JNES*. 8, 35; a reply to appear *ib.* later.

[5] In Dyn. XII, however, coregencies were common.

[6] The following paragraph has been re-modelled to meet the objections raised by O. NEUGEBAUER in *Acta Orientalia*, vol. 17, to ED. MEYER'S thitherto generally accepted views in his *Ägyptische Chronologie*, Berlin, 1904.

of the civil calendar. It must have been early recognized that the Nile began to rise afresh about the same time (near July 19th of the Julian calendar) that the brilliant star Sirius (the dog-star), after having been invisible for a prolonged period, was first again observed in the sky shortly before sunrise. Consequently this latter event, described by modern astronomers as the heliacal rising of Sirius and by the Egyptians as *prt Spdt* 'the going up of (the goddess) Sothis', came to be regarded as the true New Year's Day (*wpt-rnpt* 'the opening of the year'), i.e. *tpy* (*n*) *ꜣḫt sw 1* 'first month of inundation, day 1'. Had this event always formed the beginning of the Egyptian civil year, the Inundation season (*ꜣḫt*) would have corresponded roughly to middle July—middle November, Winter (*prt*) to middle November—middle March, Summer (*šmw*) to middle March—middle July. Owing to the above-mentioned defect in the civil year, it sometimes happened that the real summer fell in the winter of the civil calendar, and *vice versa*. We know on the authority of Censorinus that a coincidence of the civil New Year's Day and the heliacal rising of Sirius took place in A.D. 139, and thence it is calculated[1] that a similar coincidence must have occurred in B.C. 1317 and 2773. In the period covered by this book three records of Sothic risings have come down to us, namely from an unspecified year of Tuthmosis III (11th month, day 28),[2] from year 9 of Amenophis I (11th month, day 9),[3] and from year 7 of Sesostris III (8th month, day 16).[4] Combination of these dates with those previously mentioned yields as the approximate corresponding years B.C. 1469, 1545, and 1877; the two first dates fit in admirably with other considerations, but the third has been thought by some to allow too small an interval between the Twelfth and the Eighteenth Dynasty.

In the Aramaic papyri of the Persian period and in the subsequent Greek and Coptic documents from Egypt the twelve months are no longer numbered and allotted to one or other of the three seasons, but receive names derived from certain feasts. The month-names in their Greek forms are Thōuth, Phaōphi, Athyr, Khoiak, Tybi, Mekhir, Phamenōth, Pharmouthi, Pakhōn, Payni, Epiph, and Mesorē. To translate as 'the 5th of Pharmouthi', as many scholars still do, is a gross anachronism, the more reprehensible since some of the originating feasts were in Dyns. XVIII–XX celebrated not in the month to which they gave their name, but on the first day of the following month.[5] Thus Dyn. XVIII inscriptions inform us that the feast of Ernūtet, who gave her name to Pharmouthi, took place on the 1st day of the 1st month of summer,[6] not in the 4th month of winter. A calendar from year 9 of Amenophis I gives the entire series of month-names in similarly advanced positions,[7] whereas another calendar of Ramesside date[8] shows the names in the places accorded to them in Greek times. Unsolved problems present themselves in connexion with these facts.[9] Clearly the only scientific course is to render as 'fourth month of winter'.[10]

[1] The figures here given are taken from Winlock's article in *Proc. Amer. Philosoph. Soc.*, 83, 447, where most of the recent literature is quoted.

[2] *Urk.* iv. 827.

[3] *Eb.*, calendar at beginning.

[4] *ÄZ.* 37, 99.

[5] See *ÄZ.* 43, 136.

[6] DÜM. *Kalenderinschr.* 38; cf. L. *D.* Text, iii. 283.

[7] Above, n. 3.

[8] *Ann.* 43, 179.

[9] See my discussion in *Rev. d'Ég.* 10, 9–31, a reply to R. PARKER in *The Calendars of Ancient Egypt*, Chicago, 1950. An additional piece of evidence *JEA.* 41, 123.

[10] It may sometimes be convenient to abbreviate as '8th month' or simply 'viii'.

The Egyptians were the first to divide the day into 24 hours (*wnwt*, var.); there were twelve hours of the day and twelve hours of the night.

Exx. *wnwt mḥt-10 nt hrw* tenth hour of the day.[1]

wnwt 4-nwt nt grḥ fourth hour of the night.[2]

These hours, which had their own religious names, were used mainly for religious and astronomical purposes.[3] Ordinary parlance made shift with such phrases as *m dwꜣ* 'in the morning',[4] *nw n sty-r* 'the time of perfume of the mouth', i. e. time for the mid-day meal;[5] *msyt* 'supper'[5a] *r tr n ḫꜣwy* 'at time of night'.[6] The Egyptians seem to have had no very precise instruments for measuring the hours, and the hours of the day were longer in the summer than in the winter.[7] Still less was it possible to fix the length of a short space of time to which the name *ꜣt* 'minute', 'moment' was given.

In conclusion, reference must be made to the 'decans', the 36 constellations, or parts of such, which rise at particular hours of the night during the 36 different periods of ten days constituting the year. These periods or 'decades' are named according to the calendar months in which they occur, with the addition 'first decade', 'middle decade , and last decade', exx. (*ꜣbd*) *3(-nw n) ꜣḫt*, *hrw* (?) *10 tpy*, *hrw* (?) *10 ḥry-ib*, *hrw* (?) *10 ḥr-pḥwy*.[8] The various decans have their own names, which have survived in Greek;[9] examples are Gk. Σμάτ, Gk. Χώου, Gk. Ἐρῶ.

[1] *D.elB.* 114.
[2] *D.elB.* 116.
[3] Exception, *Urk.* iv. 655, 14.
[4] *Eb.* 18, 2.
[5] *Eb.* 50, 20; *T. Carn.* 14. See, too, *ÄZ.* 71, 86.
[5a] STRICKER in *Oudh. Med.* 1948, 57, n. 2.
[6] *Sin.* R 20.
[7] L. BORCHARDT, *Altägyptische Zeitmessung*, Berlin 1920, in E. VON BASSERMANN-JORDAN, *Die Geschichte der Zeitmessung und der Uhren*; a brief account, R. W. SLOLEY in *JEA.* 17, 166.
[8] CHASS. *Ass.* p. 146.
[9] S. SCHOTT, *Die altäg. Dekane*, in *Stud. d. Bibliothek Warburg*, pt. 19; see, too, SETHE, *op. cit.* p. 98.

LESSON XXI

THE VERB (INTRODUCTORY)[10]

§ 267. Verbs of different classes.—In dealing with the *śḏm·f* (§ 39) and *śḏm·n·f* (§ 67) forms it served our purpose to regard these as built up from unchangeable verb-stems, to which the necessary inflexions were appended as suffixes. Only in the case of the verb *wnn* 'be' were we compelled to admit (§ 118) the existence of different forms of the *śḏm·f*, namely *wnn·f* and *wn·f*, each with its own particular range of meaning. It has now to be learnt that, while unchangeable stems are in the majority, they are by no means universal; in other words, that *wnn* is no isolated case.

A classification of Egyptian verbs is therefore required, and the basis of this must be the *mutability* or *immutability* of the stem. A second mark serving to distinguish the different verbal classes is the gender of the infinitives, some classes having masculine infinitives like *ꜥnḫ* 'to live', while others have infinitives showing the feminine ending *-t*, ex. *mst* 'to bear', 'to give birth'.

[10] See SETHE, *Das ägyptische Verbum*, Leipzig, 1899–1902, and for the present lesson especially vol. i. §§ 314–482. General theory, see *Some Aspects*, 4 ff.

§ 268. Verbs with mutable stems.—It must be remembered that in hieroglyphic writing the vowels are ignored and only the consonantal skeletons of words are exhibited to the reader (§ 19). Hence it is quite possible *a priori* that one and the same hieroglyphic writing *sḏm·f* might conceal several differently vocalized verb-forms such as **seḏmaf* and *^{e}*sḏāmef*, or even a form with doubled medial consonant like **seḏḏāmef*.[1] That such was actually the case cannot be directly proved for verbs like *sḏm* 'hear', in which the component consonants *s*, *ḏ* and *m* are strong and different from one another; but it may be inferred with great probability from the fact that variations of writing explicable only if due to differences of vocalization analogous to our postulated **seḏmaf* and *^{e}*sḏāmef* occur in the case of two classes of verbs, namely (1) those in which the final radical consonant is identical with the preceding consonant (geminating verbs like *wnn*), and (2) those in which the final consonant is one of the semi-vowels *ỉ* or *w* (*ultimae infirmae* verbs like *pr(ỉ)* 'go forth', *rš(w)* 'rejoice'). These classes of verbs we shall proceed to discuss in turn.

§ 269. Geminating verbs.—These verbs have the peculiarity that the last two radical consonants of their stem are identical, ex. *wnn* 'exist'. Now we have seen (§ 62) that when two identical consonants fell together in pronunciation, or at least were not separated by an accented vowel, there was a strong tendency to write them but once, and this tendency would naturally become the rule where there was the additional inducement that a vital difference of meaning could thereby be emphasized. Hence, when we find a regularly occurring spelling *wnn·f*, we may conjecture that a vowel of some importance fell between the two consonants *n* of the verb-stem; in cases where, on the contrary, *wn·f* is consistently found we may suppose that the two like consonants had fallen together, yielding some such pronunciation as **wennaf*, corresponding to **seḏmaf* assumed in § 268 as one of the possible values of *sḏm·f*.

In the case of *wnn·f* a plausible pronunciation would be *^{e}*wnānef*, pointing to a similar pronunciation *^{e}*sḏāmef* in the corresponding form of the immutable verb *sḏm*. There is, however, another possibility (it is no more than such) to which but little attention has been paid hitherto, and which may turn out to be applicable in certain cases, though it evidently cannot hold in all, e. g. the infinitive. This possibility is that the first of the two like radicals has been doubled, as in the Hebrew *piʿēl* or the Arabic second form; the effect of such doubling is necessarily to hold the last radical apart from the doubled middle radical, whether the vowel following the latter be accented or unaccented.[2] Hence *wnn·f* might represent a pronunciation **wennānef* (instead of *^{e}*wnānef*), pointing to **seḏḏāmef* from the immutable *sḏm*.

[1] The asterisk denotes hypothetical vocalizations. The small ^{e} indicates the initial helping-vowel discussed in § 272.

[2] This follows from the fact that, alike in Semitic and in Egyptian, a doubled consonant must both close a syllable and begin a second one, in other words must always be followed by a vowel. See Appendix A at the end of the book.

OBS. The existence of geminating verbs in Egyptian is established beyond a doubt, but the reasons for the appearance or absence of the gemination in the hieroglyphic writing are largely a matter of conjecture.[1] For the infinitive we have the evidence of Coptic, ex. *χbob* 'to be cool' from Eg. *ḳbb*; since the vocalization here corresponds to that of immutable intransitive verbs like Coptic *ᵉnšot* 'be hard', from Eg. *nḫt*, it would appear that the presence of the gemination in the writing is due in this case solely to the existence of an accented vowel between the two like consonants. Conversely, after *dì* 'cause' the *śḏm·f* form of the verb *ḳbb* 'be cool' would show the hieroglyphic form *ḳb·f* (§ 452, 1); but Coptic has *tkbof* for 'to make him cool' (Eg. **dìt ḳb·f* 'to cause that he be cool'), and there is reason to think that this was pronounced *tkebbof*, a form analogous to Coptic *tsᵉnkof* 'to suckle him' from the immutable triliteral stem *snḳ* 'suck';[2] here, then, the single writing of *b* in hieroglyphic *ḳb·f* would seem due to the last two radical consonants of *ḳbb* falling together without an intervening vowel. For the geminating *śḏm·f* forms and participles in hieroglyphic, however, no explanation is forthcoming from the Coptic. Our enquiry will tend to show that the geminating *śḏm·f* is entirely dependent, for the writing of the gemination, on its origin in the geminating passive participle (the imperfective passive participle), see §§ 356, OBS.; 411, 1; 438, OBS. But since gemination in the participles is associated with notions of *repetition* or *continuity* such as might well find formal expression in the doubling of the medial radical consonant, the hypothesis that the geminating *śḏm·f* forms are comparable to Hebrew *piʿēl* forms appears at least worth examination.

[1] See *Rec.* 40, 73.

[2] See *Verbum* ii. § 216.

§ 270. **Weak verbs.**—In the case of the weak verbs ending in 𓇋 *ì* or 𓅱 *w* matters are complicated by the fact that these consonants (or semi-vowels, § 20) were often omitted in the writing. Accordingly, a hypothetical form like **merwāt·* from the stem *mrw* (or *mrì* § 281) 'love' might in one place be written out as 𓌻𓂋𓅱𓏏𓀀 *mrwt·*, while in another place it might, no less correctly, be rendered 𓌻𓂋𓏏𓀀 *mrt·*. Scholars have shown, however, that under certain conditions, e. g. after another consonant and before a short unaccented vowel, the original *ì* and *w* of stems were apt to disappear, not only from the written, but also from the spoken language.[3] For this reason, when we encounter a form like 𓉐𓂋𓅱𓂻 with a flexional element *-w* added to the verb-stem *prì*, we cannot be certain whether some such pronunciation as **pariew* or **periaw* is to be assumed, or whether *ì* had here fallen away so that only **parew* or **peraw* was spoken; nothing but an undoubted full variant writing 𓉐𓂋𓇋𓅱𓂻 *prìw* (or 𓉐𓂋𓇋𓇋𓅱𓂻 *pryw*, as Middle Egyptian would write it, see OBS. below) could settle the question in favour of the former pair of alternatives. Thus the presence or absence of *ì* and *w* in the hieroglyphic writing of weak verbs is but a precarious criterion of differences of form.

[3] *Verbum* i. §§ 94. 170.

Fortunately, however, the weak verbs display in certain forms a more trustworthy criterion, namely a gemination similar to that which was described in the last section. It is supposed that in some circumstances the final *ì* or *w* became assimilated to the preceding radical, so that forms like 𓌻𓂋𓂋𓀀𓆑 *mrr·f* from original *mrw·f* came into existence. Probably such gemination or repetition of the penultimate radical would only occur where the repeated consonants were separated by a vowel of some importance; and it is even possible that a doubling of the radical penultimate consonant has to be assumed, in addition to the assimilation just mentioned. Thus, on the same lines as were discussed in connection with the geminating verbs (§ 269), so too [hieroglyphs] might theoretically represent either **ᵉmrāref* from **ᵉmrāief* or **merrāref* from **merrāief*; the latter possibility is one not hitherto taken into account.

OBS. In most Middle Egyptian verbs and verb-forms *i* near the end is written [hieroglyphs] *y*, see above § 20. A few verbs, however, seem to show [hieroglyph] as a strong, i.e. immutable, consonant. In [hieroglyphs] *smi* 'report' and [hieroglyphs] *dmi* 'touch' this might be due to the change in value of [hieroglyph] from *mr* to *mi* (see W 19 in the Sign-list); both *r* and *i* are kept in the spelling [hieroglyphs] *swri* 'drink', for *swi* from old *zwr*; but no similar explanations seem possible for [hieroglyphs] *šri* 'block', [hieroglyphs] *tni* 'grow decrepit'.

§ 271. **The geminating and non-geminating *śḏm·f* forms.**—To the writing out or omission of the gemination in forms from the mutable verbs there regularly corresponds a difference of meaning. Hence the *śḏm·f* form, which, as we have seen, sometimes geminates and sometimes does not, really comprises at least two separate forms. The distinction of these is, however, a matter of considerable difficulty, the discussion of which is best deferred until Lessons XXX, XXXI. Henceforth use will be made of both forms in the Exercises, but the exact nuance of meaning which they imply may for the moment be ignored.

§ 272. **The prothetic [hieroglyph] *i*.**[1]—In both Old and Late Egyptian a valuable clue to the vocalization of verb-forms is provided by the sporadic appearance of the sign for *i* (old [hieroglyph], late [hieroglyphs])[1a] at their beginning. This 'prothetic *i*' undoubtedly indicates a short helping-vowel *ᵉ* before two initial consonants not separated by a vowel. Middle Egyptian examples are very rare, but a few may be collected from our texts: [hieroglyphs] *iḏdw* (i.e. perhaps **ᵉḏdaw*) 'one whom .... speaks (of)',[2] imperfective relative form (§ 387, 1); [hieroglyphs] *iḫm-sk* 'an Indestructible' (name given to the circumpolar stars), lit. 'one not knowing destruction',[3] perfective active participle (§ 359); [hieroglyphs] *ind ḥr·t* 'hail to thee',[4] a formula which perhaps originally meant 'I salute thy face', but which appears very early in this subjectless form.[5] The imperatives of *2-lit.* verbs (§ 336) also occasionally show the prothetic *i*, which also is once found in [hieroglyphs] *iḫr·k* 'upon thee'[6] (**ᵉḫrak*) for the normal [hieroglyphs]. In Dyn. XVIII [hieroglyphs] is found a few times in place of *i*, ex. [hieroglyphs] *iwrḫw* 'knowing ones',[7] perfective active participle (§ 359).

OBS. In Semitic the consonant *'alif* has sometimes a similar function, and is there called 'prosthetic'; 'prothetic' is, however, a more suitable term.

[1] See SETHE, *De Aleph Prosthetico*, Berlin, 1892.

[1a] Exceptionally in Dyn. XIII in *śḏm·f* form of *ḏd* 'say': Louvre C 10; *JEA.* 33, Pl. II, 5.

[2] *Sebekn.* 3. Sim. active participle *iḏdt* 'who says' *JEA.* 32, Pl. VI, 32.

[3] Brit. Mus. 101, horiz. 7.

[4] ERM. *Hymn.* 1, 1. Sim. Cairo, 20517, *e* 3; 20520, *d* 1.

[5] Instructive passages are *Pyr.* 1989. 2019. 2035. 2042.

[6] *Rec.* 35, 219.

[7] *Urk.* iv. 481, 17; 972, 11. Sim. *iwḫmw*, *ib.* 480, 9. Also in the noun *iwgrt* 'the silent one', a designation of the necropolis.

§ 273. General characteristics of verb-stems.—As in the Semitic languages, the typical verb-stem consists of three radical consonants, ex. *sḏm* 'hear'. There existed, however, a considerable class of biliteral stems, ex. *mn* 'remain', 'endure', though it may be shown that many of these originally belonged to one or other of the classes with three consonants, such as *wḏ* 'command', Arabic وصى (*waṣa*); *tm* 'be closed', Arabic تمّ (*tamma*). Whereas the verbs just quoted had, owing to some inherent weakness, passed in prehistoric times from the triconsonantal to the biconsonantal class, there are other apparently biliteral stems, such as *m(w)t* 'die', which prove on closer inspection to be really triliterals. Similarly, there are but few stems of four and five consonants which cannot be accounted for as due to expansion from originals of three consonants. The most important methods of expansion are (1) reduplication, (2) afformative additions. These are dealt with in the next three sections.

§ 274. Reduplication.[1]—Verbs signifying continuous or repeated human actions, habitual occupations, sounds, colours, and violent movements are apt to be created from biliteral or triliteral stems by the repetition of two of the radical consonants. Thus are formed quadriliteral verbs like *nḏnḏ* 'take counsel' from *nḏ* 'ask', *snsn* 'fraternize' from *sn* 'brother', *ptpt* 'crush' (simplex unknown), and quinquiliterals like *ḥꜣgꜣg* 'exult' from *ḥꜣg* 'be pleasant, glad'; *swtwt* 'walk', 'promenade' (simplex unknown). After Dyn. XII the graphic abbreviation *sp sn* 'two times', 'twice' (see above § 207) is sometimes used as a substitute for the consonants to be repeated, exx. *ršrš* 'rejoice'[2] from *rš(w)* 'rejoice', *sksk* 'destroy'[3] from *sk* 'perish'.

A half-reduplication also occurs, giving rise to a number of verbs of the type *sḫs* 'run', *nḫn* 'be young', *grg* 'furnish', 'equip'; in none of these cases do we possess a well-attested simplex.

Much rarer is a reduplication of the final consonant only. Verbs comparable to the Hebrew *piʿlēl* may perhaps occur in the case of *snbb* 'converse',[4] *spdd* 'supply',[5] and *špss* 'be rich',[6] 'enrich';[7] these appear to be immutable quadriliterals derived from the triliteral adjectives *snb* 'healthy', *spd* 'ready', and *šps* 'noble' respectively. Some verb-forms of passive meaning which may be compared to the Hebrew *puʿlal* will be dealt with in §§ 360. 425.

More problematic is the kind of reduplication exhibited in the Hebrew *piʿēl*. This consists in the doubling of the second radical consonant of a triliteral stem, and would in no case be apparent in the Egyptian writing, though its effects might, as explained above (§§ 269. 270), sometimes be visible in the gemination found in geminating and weak verbs. That *piʿēl* verbs did exist in Egyptian is probable *a priori*, and seems further likely from the transitive

[1] See *Verbum* i. §§ 327–40.

[2] MAR. *Abyd.* ii. 30, 29.

[3] *Urk.* iv. 729, 16; cf. *ib.* 8.

[4] *Urk.* iv. 559. Sim. in O.K., *Ti* 111. Lit. perhaps 'mutually inquire health'.

[5] *ÄZ.* 45. Pl. VI, 7; *Inscr. dédic.* 87.

[6] Brit. Mus. 614, 11; Cairo 20543, 20.

[7] *Inscr. dédic.* 83.

meaning occasionally found with some usually intransitive verbs, exx. [hieroglyphs] *Ḏḥwty ḥtp nṯrw* 'Thoth who pacifies the gods';[1] [hieroglyphs] *sinw snb irt* 'the physician who heals the eye',[2] where *ḥtp* (= **ḥttp*?) and *snb* (= **snnb*?) are active participles from stems usually meaning 'be at peace', 'be healthy'. Whether Coptic offers any cogent evidence has been both asserted[3] and denied.[3a]

This debatable question is discussed at some length because such *piʿēl* verb-forms may turn out to be commoner in Egyptian than has been suspected, see above § 269, end. In any case, the student should realize the difference between a geminating verb and a reduplicated verb. Gemination, as understood in the term 'geminating verb' (§ 269), is a constitutional peculiarity of the stem that leads to the single writing, in certain forms, of two identical radicals, ex. [hieroglyphs] from [hieroglyphs]; geminating verbs are therefore mutable. Reduplication, on the other hand, is a secondary expansion of verb-stems by repetition of part of their constituent radicals, ex. [hieroglyphs] from [hieroglyphs]; reduplicated verbs are immutable.

OBS. 1. As applied to particular verb-forms, 'geminating' has a less technical meaning; it signifies no more than that two identical radicals follow one another in the writing. Thus both [hieroglyphs] and [hieroglyphs] are 'geminating' *śḏm·f* forms, though of the two stems involved *wnn* alone is a 'geminating verb'. Similarly, [hieroglyphs] and [hieroglyphs] are called 'non-geminating' *śḏm·f* forms.

OBS. 2. Hebrew can parallel all the above-mentioned kinds of reduplication. With the Egyptian verb-forms corresponding to the Hebrew *piʿlēl* (see above) compare the names of small animals, ex. [hieroglyphs] *ḫprr* 'beetle',[4] besides nouns like [hieroglyphs] *ḥnmmt* 'sun-folk', 'mankind', [hieroglyphs] *wḥmmyt* 'repetitions'.[5]

§ 275. Afformative prefixes: (1) the causatives in [hieroglyph] *ś*.[6]—The consonant [hieroglyph] *ś*, later also [hieroglyph] *s*, when prefixed to a verb-stem, gives to it causative meaning. The new verbs thus formed are derived not only from transitive and intransitive verbs, but also occasionally from nouns and prepositions.

Exx. [hieroglyphs] *smn* 'make to remain', 'establish' from [hieroglyphs] *mn* 'remain'.
[hieroglyphs] *sʿnḫ* 'make to live', 'nourish' „ [hieroglyphs] *ʿnḫ* 'live'.
[hieroglyphs] *smsi* 'make to give birth', 'deliver' „ [hieroglyphs] *msi* 'bear'.
[hieroglyphs] *sḥb* 'make festal' „ [hieroglyphs] *ḥb* 'festival'.
[hieroglyphs] *smi* 'report', 'announce' „ [hieroglyphs] *mi* 'like'.

Some causatives, particularly those derived from transitive stems, do not possess full causative force, but have meanings different from that of the simplex.

Exx. [hieroglyphs] *sip* 'revise', 'test', 'account for' from [hieroglyphs] *ip* 'count'.
[hieroglyphs] *swḏ* 'hand over', 'bequeath' „ [hieroglyphs] *wḏ* 'command'.
[hieroglyphs] *sḏd* 'relate' „ [hieroglyphs] *ḏd* 'say'.
[hieroglyphs] *snḏm* 'sit', 'make oneself comfortable' „ [hieroglyphs] *nḏm* 'be sweet', 'be agreeable'.

[1] *Leb.* 23.
[2] *ÄZ.* 53, 111; sim. *ib.* 95. Further exx. VOG. *Bauer*, index, p. 234, 1st. col., end.
[3] See *Verbum* i. § 344.
[3a] *ÄZ.* 73, 131.
[4] See *Rec.* 35, 228.
[5] *Adm.* p. 97.
[6] See *Verbum* i. §§ 350–6.

Except in one case, the causatives fall into the verb-classes to which they would belong if the afformative *ś* were a radical letter; thus *sʿnḫ* 'make to live', from a triliteral stem, has a masculine infinitive like the quadriliteral *wsṯn* 'stride'; *smsỉ* 'to deliver', from a triconsonantal stem with weak final *ỉ* (a *tertiae infirmae* verb, § 281), has an infinitive *smsy* with masculine gender resembling *ḫrty* 'to travel by land', the infinitive of a *quartae infirmae* verb (§ 285). The exception alluded to is the case of the causatives of the biliterals; these, unlike the triliterals to which they might be expected to conform, have feminine infinitives, ex. *smnt* 'to establish'.

OBS. The causatives in *ś* are evidently related to those with *š* or *s* in Semitic (Assyrian, Aramaic, and Minaean).

§ 276. Afformative prefixes: (2) the prefix *n*.[1]—The verbs beginning with this afformative are intransitive and in almost every case derived from quadriliteral reduplicated stems, exx. *ngsgs* 'overflow', synonymous with *gsgs*, and *nftft*,[2] doubtless with much the same meaning as *ftft* 'leap'.

[1] See *Sphinx* 14, 201.

[2] *Sin.* R 27.

THE VERB-CLASSES

§ 277. Classification according to number and nature of the radical consonants.—We shall now proceed to classify the different kinds of Egyptian verb-stems, premising that only such distinctions will be noted as may prove useful in the study of Egyptian texts. Coptic shows that adjective-verbs like *sbŏk* 'to be small' were vocalized otherwise than transitive verbs like *sōtᵉm* 'to hear', but such facts as these must be ignored in this grammar, since they cannot be followed up in the hieroglyphs. It should be observed, further, that weak verbs written shortly like , hitherto rendered *pr*, will in the following paragraphs be transliterated with all the radicals of the stem, ex. *prỉ*. Consistency in this matter is neither possible nor desirable. As a general rule it is safest to supply as few unwritten consonants as possible; it is simpler, and for that reason better, to transliterate as *pr·f* even where we may be reasonably sure that *pry·f* would represent the spoken consonants. On the other hand, in grammatical discussions it is often desirable to write *pry·f* or better *pr*(*y*)·*f*.

The basis of our classification will be the number of radical consonants, whether weak or strong, single or reduplicated. The designations of the classes are those usually adopted, though they are not altogether satisfactory. By *biliteral*, *triliteral*, *quadriliteral*, and *quinquiliteral* verbs are meant those having two, three, four, or five immutable (strong) consonants respectively, though there is really no reason (e.g.) for refusing the name 'triliteral' to triconsonantal stems with identical second and third radicals (the *secundae geminatae* class, § 280) or to those having a weak third radical (the *tertiae infirmae*, § 281). The notion of gemination inherent in the names *secundae* and *tertiae* (*litterae*) *geminatae* is also misleading, since both here and in the *tertiae* and *quartae infirmae*, so far from gemination or doubling being employed for making twofold a consonant that was originally single, its presence actually warns us that the verb-stem in question possessed from the beginning a final radical letter which was specially prone, either from inherent weakness or from its identity with the penultimate, to disappear from the writing. See above §§ 269. 270. 274.

1. Verbs with two consonants only.

§ **278. Biliteral verbs**, abbreviated *2-lit.*, exx. *wn* 'open', *mn* 'be firm'. The infinitives are masculine, and of the form quoted. For the originally triliteral character of these verbs see above § 273; and that many of them may be derived from *tertiae infirmae* (below § 281) is perhaps hinted by the feminine infinitives of their causatives (above § 275 and below § 282). Some biliteral verbs show a repetition of the last radical letter in the perfective passive participle (§ 360); but such forms are due to reduplication (§ 274), and are not to be explained, as hitherto, as survivals from the time when the verb-stems in question belonged to the *2ae gem.* or *3ae inf.* class. The verb *šm* 'go' has a fem. infinitive, but is classed with the biliterals because it does not, as a rule, show gemination[1] in verb-forms where this would be expected if the verb belonged to the *tertiae infirmae.*

2. Verbs with three radical consonants.

§ **279. Triliteral verbs**, abbreviated *3-lit.*, exx. *sḏm* 'hear', *wḏꜣ* 'prosper'. The infinitives are masculine and show the forms just quoted. A few verbs ending in *ỉ* and *w* belong to this class, like *dmỉ* 'touch'[2] (above § 270, Obs.) and *ꜣbw* 'brand'.[3] Likewise *sw(r)ỉ*, a spelling intended to convey that the verb-stem now to be read as *swỉ* originated in *swr* (*zwr*); so, too, *dꜣỉ(r)* = *dꜣỉ* from original *dꜣr* 'suppress', and one or two more. The originally *3-lit.* verb *ḳmꜣ* 'create' is often spelt , and the writing of *m* after *mꜣ* may indicate that it had lost *ꜣ* and so fallen into the *2-lit.* class as *ḳm*; so, too, *ỉm(ꜣ)*[4] 'be gracious', *sm(ꜣ)* 'slay'. Triliteral is *m(w)t* 'die', the medial *w* being omitted in the writing; the same view is perhaps also to be taken of some other verbs usually classed as *2-lit.*

§ **280. *Secundae geminatae* verbs,** abbreviated *2ae gem.* These are triconsonantal verbs in which the second and third radicals are identical and hence, under certain vocalic conditions (§ 269), are written once only. The infinitives are masculine and show the gemination, ex. *ḳbb* 'to be cool'.

[1] Exception, *šmm·t* (imperf. *sḏm·f*), Erm. *Hymn.* 3, 4–5.

[2] For a possible fem. infinitive see below, p. 224, n.0

[3] *Sinai* 90, 7.

[4] *Pyr.* writings vacillate between *ỉmꜣ* and *ỉꜣm*.

The *2ae gem.* verbs *mꜣꜣ* 'see' and *wnn* 'exist' display certain peculiarities. This class of verbs is a small one—between twenty and thirty are known—but most of its members are important. The following is a list of the chief among them :—

ꜣmm seize, grip.
wnn be, exist.
wrr be great.
mꜣꜣ see.
rnn nurse.
hnn bow, assent to.
ḫnn destroy.
šmm be hot.
šrr be small (later *šri*).
ḳbb be cool.
gnn be soft.
tkk attack, violate (frontier).

§ 281. ***Tertiae infirmae* verbs,** abbreviated *3ae inf.* These are verbs in which the third and last radical consonant is a weak *i* or *w*—the latter distinguishable from the former only in a few cases (*ršw* 'rejoice', *šfw* 'swell', *gꜣw* 'be narrow'), since forms with *w* are apt to be replaced by others with *i*. The weak final radical is but rarely written out, in the case of *i* mainly when it is followed by the flexional ending (§§ 270. 296) *i* or *w*, in which case the two combine as *y*, ex. *pry* for *pri·i* 'I go forth'. (For sake of convenience this form is transliterated *pry·i*.) As explained in § 270, gemination is a characteristic feature of the *3ae inf.* class, ex. *mrrw* 'who is loved'. The infinitives are feminine and without gemination, ex. *mrt* 'to love'. Three verbs of this class call for particular comment :—

iri 'make', 'do' is usually written without the expected phonetic complement ; writings with as a rule correspond to the geminating forms of other verbs. No doubt some abnormality of pronunciation is responsible for this peculiarity of writing, but since we are unable to define the nature of that abnormality it seems desirable, for practical reasons, to transliterate the forms of ***iri*** as though they conformed to the ordinary spelling ; the infinitive (§ 299) we shall transliterate, accordingly, as ***irt***, and the imperf. act. participle (§ 357) as ***irr***. This is the more necessary because variants with as a phonetic complement sometimes occur. Thus is a rarer writing of the infinitive, and is fairly common for the imperf. act. part. To sum up, while forms like clearly lack, and forms like clearly possess, the gemination, forms like are ambiguous ; the probability is in favour of the gemination, but exceptionally must be read simply ***ir*** without gemination.[1]

iṯi 'take', 'seize' often shows a variant writing , and since there are also geminating forms with ,[2] clearly *ṯ* here had already passed into *t*.[3] The said spellings should, accordingly, be read as ***it*** and ***itt***.

[1] See *ÄZ.* 58, 45 (also 59, 71) for the facts ; a rather different practical attitude is taken here.

[2] Imperf. act. part., *Pt.* 92 ; imperf. *sḏm·f*, *Pt.* 168.

[3] For further evidence see the Sign-list under V 14. 15.

The doubly weak verb for 'strike' appears to have existed in two forms, namely *ḥii* and *ḥwi*; no geminating forms are found, but in Middle Egyptian the infinitive is feminine, see below § 299.

More than one hundred verb-stems can be assigned to the *3ae inf.* class; the following is a selection of the most important:—

ꜣwi extend.
ꜣbi wish.
ibi thirst.
iri make, do.
iṯi, var. *iti*, take, seize
wpi divide, open, judge.
pri go forth, go up.
fꜣi carry, lift.
mri love, wish.
msi bear, give birth.
mki protect.
rmi weep, beweep.
ršw rejoice.
hꜣi go down, fall.
hri be content.
ḥꜥi rejoice.
ḥwy, *ḥii* strike.
ḥsi praise, favour.
ḥḏi destroy, damage.
ḫꜥi appear in glory.
ḫni alight, stop.
ḫdi fare downstream, north.
ẖni row.
ẖsi be feeble, vile.
sꜣw guard, prevent.
sti shoot, pour, kindle.
šni encircle, surround.
šdi take, withdraw.
ḳni be brave.
kꜣi devise, think out.
ksi bow down.
gꜣw be narrow.
gmi find.
tḥi disobey, violate.
dgi see, look.
ḏꜣi cross (the river), ferry across.

An interesting spelling is *psi* 'cook' from earlier *fs(i)*, the older and later initial radicals being retained side by side.

§ 282. **Causatives of biliteral verbs,** abbreviated *caus. 2-lit.*, ex. *smn* 'make to remain', 'establish'. As pointed out above (§ 275), the infinitives are feminine, ex. *smnt*. Geminating forms do not occur. These verbs show relationship with the *quartae infirmae*, among which are some verbs with similar characteristics (ex. *ḥmsi* 'sit').

3. Verbs with four radical consonants.

§ 283. **Quadriliteral verbs,** abbreviated *4-lit.*, with masculine infinitives. Many of these are due to reduplication, ex. *ḫtḫt* 'be reversed', but others, like *wsṯn* 'stride', consist of four different strong radicals. Here must be classed also the **causatives of triliterals,** abbreviated *caus. 3-lit.*, ex. *sꜥnḫ* 'make live'; see above § 275.

§ **284.** ***Tertiae geminatae*** **verbs,** abbreviated *3ae gem.*, are mutable verbs with identical third and fourth radicals. The very existence of the class is problematic, since stems like *spdd* 'supply', *snbb* 'converse' are, as we have seen (§ 274), immutable quadriliteral verbs. Under this head would fall **causatives of the *secundae geminatae,*** abbreviated *caus. 2ae gem.*, ex. *sḳbb* 'make cool', but these also may possibly have to be classed with the quadriliterals, non-geminating forms being of great rarity.

§ **285.** ***Quartae infirmae*** **verbs,** abbreviated *4ae inf.*, in which the fourth radical is *i* or *w*. From the analogy of the *3ae inf.* one would expect this class to show geminating forms and feminine infinitives, but no single example of the class has both characteristics. Gemination occurs with some, like *msḏi* 'hate' and *nṯry* 'be divine', and a fem. infinitive with others, like *wꜣsi* 'be ruined', *ḥmsi* 'sit'. A few having masc. infinitive and no gemination, like *ḫrty* 'travel overland', *mꜣwy* 'be renewed', might well be classed with the *4-lit.* (§ 283); so too, for example, *ḥḥy*, properly doubtless *ḥ(y)ḥy*, though the second radical is never written. In *mini* 'moor' (m. infinitive) the written *i* is not improbably the second radical; such is apparently not the case with the *w* of 'speak' (f. infinitive), though the full reading appears to be *m(w)dw*. Under this head must be placed the **causatives of *tertiae infirmae,*** abbreviated *caus. 3ae inf.*, partly with masculine and partly with feminine infinitives, exx. *smsy* 'to make to give birth', *sḫpt* 'to bring nigh'; no geminating forms appear to occur.

4. Verbs with five radical consonants.

§ **286. Quinquiliteral verbs**, abbreviated *5-lit.*, with masculine infinitives. This class seems in all cases to have arisen through reduplication, exx. *nftft* 'spring away', *ḥbꜣbꜣ* 'waddle'. Whether *swtwt* 'walk', 'promenade' is the **causative of a quadriliteral** (abbreviation *caus. 4-lit.*) is uncertain; no other example of the last-named class has been noted in Middle Egyptian.[0]

[0] A few *6-lit.* verbs have been quoted, but only from O. E.; see Lef. *Gr.* § 225, end.

§ **287.** ***Quintae infirmae*** **verbs**, abbreviated *5ae inf.*, constitute another rather dubious class of verbs. It is very doubtful whether the three feminine words *ḥꜥꜥwt*, *ṯḫḫwt*, and *rnnwt*, with the almost synonymous meanings 'joy', 'gladness', 'exultation' are really infinitives of this class; more probably they are mere nouns. The masc. infinitive *ḫbb* 'dance',[1] if really a writing of *ḫb(i)bi*, as the *3ae inf.* simplex *ḫbi* might suggest, possibly belongs here. The rare **causatives of *quartae infirmae*,** abbreviated *caus. 4ae inf.*, have masculine infinitives, ex. *smꜣwy* 'renew'.

[1] Gard. *Sin.* p. 70.

§ 288. **Compound Verbs** have little to distinguish them except the place of the determinative at the end, not after each component part. Exx. [hieroglyphs] *ʿšꜣ-r* 'chatter', lit. 'be manifold of utterance', [hieroglyphs] *ḥm-ḫt* 'retreat'.

§ 289. **Anomalous Verbs**, abbreviated *anom.* This class comprises some very common verbs which, but for certain peculiarities, would have to be assigned to the *3ae inf.* class.

1. **'Give'.**[1] *Rdi* (originally perhaps *rḏi*) has a feminine infinitive *rdit*, written [hieroglyphs] or [hieroglyphs]. The sign [hieroglyph] characteristic of the verb is probably an ideogram representing a loaf brought as a gift;[2] for this, from the early Middle Kingdom onwards, is often substituted as a purely graphical variant [hieroglyph], [hieroglyph], or even [hieroglyph], the latter two being due to a confusion of the signs in hieratic. In a few parts of the verb (e.g. the old perfective, § 310) writings with initial *r* ([hieroglyphs], [hieroglyphs], [hieroglyphs]) exist side by side with others ([hieroglyph], [hieroglyph], [hieroglyph]) in which *r* is omitted; since, however, in certain forms (infinitive, § 299; *sḏmty·fy* form, § 364) the writing with *r* is as regular (rare exceptions may be found) as it is irregular in other forms (*sḏm·f* after *ir* 'if', § 454, 5, as well as after *rdi* itself, § 452, 1),[3] the evidence points to real loss of *r* having occurred in the latter; Coptic nowhere shows any trace of *r*. In any case it seems wise to omit *r* in transliteration wherever it is not written, though the signs [hieroglyph] and [hieroglyph], if ideographic, would not originally point in either direction. The geminating forms [hieroglyphs] and [hieroglyphs] are never accompanied by *r*, and are probably to be read *dd*, though doubtless they arose from *rdd*; [hieroglyphs] is in fact substituted for them in some archaizing texts,[4] and the name of the town [hieroglyphs] *Ddw* (originally *Ḏdw*) is occasionally spelt [hieroglyphs][5] or [hieroglyphs].[6] So too [hieroglyph] is substituted for [hieroglyph] in the early or archaic writing of certain non-geminating parts of the verb.[7] The final radical of the stem, the semi-vowel *i*, is only written out when fused with a flexional *-w* or *-i* (ex. the perf. pass. participle [hieroglyphs] *rdy*, for *rdi-w* ?), and certainly disappeared early in particular forms. The view that *rdi*, *di* is a single verb which early suffered the loss of both its first and its third consonant in certain forms seems preferable to the view that *rdi* and *di* are two distinct verbs obscurely related in their origin. The imperative is almost entirely replaced by [hieroglyphs] *imi*, from a quite different stem (§ 336).

2. **'Come'.**[8] [hieroglyphs] *iw* and [hieroglyphs] *ii* are clearly two distinct verbs, though they are equally clearly related. The infinitives are fem., namely [hieroglyphs] *iwt* and [hieroglyphs] *it* (also [hieroglyphs] *iit*). No geminating forms occur. While some parts of the verb, like the infinitive (§ 299) and the *sḏm·n·f* form (§ 413), display forms from both stems, in others only *iw* is employed (*iwty·fy*, § 364; *iw·in·f*, § 428); forms from *ii* tend to oust forms from *iw*. From *iw* comes a peculiar *sḏm·f* form [hieroglyphs] *iwt·f* analogous to *int·f* (below under 3). Here again the imperative is from a different stem, [hieroglyphs] *mi* being as a rule employed (§ 336).

[1] See *Verbum* i. § 453–462; *ÄZ.* 39, 75. 130; 50, 92 n., 95; ERMAN, *Gr.*[3], § 265.

[2] Doubts as to the nature of the sign, GRIFF. *Hier.* p. 64.

[3] For the Coptic see *Nachr. d. kön. Ges. d. Wiss. z Göttingen*, 1919, 139.

[4] *Urk.* iv. 260, 13; v. 76, 2.

[5] *Rifeh* 5, 8.

[6] Leyd. V 3; Brit. Mus. 572.

[7] Imperative, § 336; *sḏm·n·f*, § 413; *sḏm·f*, § 448.

[8] See *Verbum* i. §§ 463–479.

3. **'Bring'.** The verb *ỉnỉ* or *ỉnw* shows in most respects the characteristics of the *3ae inf.* class, and has a fem. infinitive *ỉnt*. It is, however, of great interest as possessing three distinct *śḏm·f* forms, a geminating form *ỉnn·f* (§ 439) and two non-geminating forms *ỉn·f* and *ỉnt·f* (§ 448), the latter comparable to *ỉwt·f* from the verb for 'come' (above 2). In the *śḏm·n·f* form we find a less common writing beside *ỉn·n·f* (§ 413).

§ 290. Verbs with initial *ỉ* and *w* often omit these weak consonants in derivatives, exx. *ꜣḫt* 'season of inundation' from *ỉꜣḫ* 'be inundated', *ꜥbw* 'purification' from *wꜥb* 'be pure'. So too in the nouns formed by a prefixed *m*,[1] exx. *mnḫt* 'clothing' from *wnḫ* 'clothe oneself', *mrḥt* 'fat' from *wrḥ* 'anoint'. Certain verb-forms written simply with have been shown to belong to *wdỉ* 'push', 'thrust', but it will possibly turn out that all the Middle Egyptian examples are from the verb *rdỉ*, *dỉ* 'give'.[2]

§ 291. Classification of verbs according to meaning.—The meaning of verbs not only affected their stem-form, as we have seen (§§ 274. 276), but is also of importance for syntactic reasons. The following distinctions may be made:—

1. **Transitive verbs** are those which take a direct object, exx. *sḏm* 'hear' (a thing), *rdỉ* 'give'. Verbs with two objects do not exist, the remoter object found after some English verbs being expressed in Egyptian by the help of prepositions.[2a] For *m* and *r* after verbs of 'making', see § 84. 'Teach somebody something' is .... *sbꜣ* ... *r* 'teach ... concerning'.[3] Some words expressing psychic activities tend to have different meanings in different forms; thus *rḫ* 'perceive', 'learn' has a preference for past forms (like *śḏm·n·f*) whenever 'knowing', i.e. the result of the activity, is intended; cf. Latin *novi*. So too *mrỉ* 'love', 'wish' seems to prefer the *śḏm·n·f* form when it means 'wish', and *sḫꜣ* 'recall', 'recollect' when it means 'remember'.

2. **Intransitive verbs** are those which have no direct object. Here we may distinguish

a. **Verbs of motion**, exx. *šm* 'go', *ꜥḥꜥ* 'arise', 'stand'.

b. **Adjective-verbs**, exx. *nfr* 'be good', *ꜥꜣ* 'be great'.

c. Other intransitives, exx. *wrš* 'pass the day', *ḥꜥỉ* 'rejoice', *mꜣḫ* 'burn'.

OBS. The verbs *mn* 'be ill (of)', *wnḫ* 'be clad (in)', *wrḥ* 'be anointed (with)', *ḥtp* 'rest (upon)' can take an object and are, therefore, not real intransitives. See Add., § 84 A.

§ 292. Denominative verbs are verbs derived from nouns.

Exx. *ỉb* 'wish'[4]	from *ỉb* 'heart', 'desire'.
nswy (?) 'be king'[5]	,, *nsw* 'king'.
ḫmt 'do for third time'[6]	,, *ḫmt* 'three'.

[1] See H. GRAPOW, *Über die Wortbildungen mit einem Präfix* m- *im ägyptischen*, in *Abh. d. kön. Preuss. Akad. d. Wiss.* 1914, no. 5.

[2] See *Sitzb. d. kön. Preuss. Akad. d. Wiss.* 1912, 914 foll.; *ÄZ.* 50, 95 n.

[2a] The exceptions after *srwḫ* in *Sm.* (Index, p. 561) are doubtless merely apparent, *m* being sometimes inserted.

[3] *Pt.* 37; Leyd. V 6.

[4] *Urk.* iv. 651; *Th. T. S.* iii. 21; *T. Carn.* 4.

[5] *Mill.* 1, 2; *Urk.* iv. 58, 16.

[6] PIEHL, *IH.* iii. 77.

VOICE, MOOD, AND TENSE

§ **293. Voice.**—Egyptian distinguishes an **active** and a **passive** voice. The passive participles have a wider range of employment in Egyptian than they have in English; see below § 376.

§ **294. Mood.**—With the means at our disposal it is not possible to distinguish different moods in Egyptian, if such existed.[1] A rough classification of Egyptian verb-forms will be found in § 297, 3.

[1] For an attempt see C. E. SANDER-HANSEN, *Über die Bildung der Modi im Altägyptischen*, in *Kongl. Danske Vidensk. Selskab*, Copenhagen, 1941.

§ **295. Tense.**—It is clear that Middle Egyptian had not yet developed, as Coptic later did, a precise set of tenses relating the time of the verbal action to the time-standpoint of the speaker. The tenses which we discover in the earlier period are concerned, like the Semitic tenses, rather with the singleness or repetition, the momentariness or continuity, of the notion expressed by the verb; though particular forms have already become specialized for use in connection with past or future time, and so approximate to our English tenses. In the participles we shall distinguish (1) an **imperfective** tense ultimately implying repetition or continuity, and (2) a **perfective** tense without any such implications. From these will be shown to spring the later tenses (including *sḏm·f* and *sḏm·n·f*) known as the 'suffix conjugation'. Besides the tenses of the suffix conjugation, there is an earlier tense to which we shall give the name **old perfective**, owing to its relationship to the Semitic perfect; this tends to have static meaning and to refer to the past, but its original signification cannot be precisely fixed. The great wealth of compound verb-forms (see Lesson XXXII) evidently owes its origin in part, but only in part, to an effort to acquire definite tense-distinctions.

OBS. 1. The terms 'perfective' and 'imperfective' have been substituted for the usual 'perfect' and 'imperfect', because we require the name 'perfect' for the more precise English tenses. In connection with our English translations we shall often speak of 'he has heard' as the *present perfect*, and of 'he had heard' as the *past perfect*, while 'he heard' is described as the *past* tense.

OBS. 2. The first edition of this work distinguished in the relative forms (§ 380) also a 'prospective' tense. Here this distinction has been abandoned.

§ **296. Inflexion.**—Differences of verb-form were marked, partly by variations in the position and quality of the vowels—variations only to a small extent deducible from the writing, see above §§ 268–272—and partly by the use of **flexional endings.** The latter consist of the suffix-pronouns (§ 34), the indefinite pronoun *tw* (§ 47), a few prepositions and sentence adverbs (*n*, *in*, *ḥr*, *kꜣ*),[2] the gender-endings m. 𓅱 *-w*, f. 𓏏 *-t*, besides a few less easily analysable elements, e.g. 𓏏𓇌 *-ti*, 𓇌 *-y* (for old *ỉ*), and 𓅱 *-w*. In the case of *w* and *y* it is often impossible to be sure whether they are flexional elements, or whether they are the final weak

[2] An alternative theory views *in*, *ḥr*, *kꜣ* differently, see below, § 427.

radicals from *3ae inf.* and *4ae inf.* stems. Still greater trouble is caused by the fact that *i* (*y*) and *w* are apt to be omitted in the writing of the flexional endings, just as much as in the writing of the verb-stems (above § 270). Hence one and the same summary writing may represent a large selection of different verb-forms. For example,

śḏm may be:

1. infinitive (§ 299).
2. imperative sing. or plur. (§ 335).
3. *śḏm·f* form before nominal subject (§ 39).
4. = *śḏmw*, 3rd pers. m. sing. or plur. old perfective (§ 309).
5. = *śḏmw*, passive *śḏm·f* form before nominal subject (§ 420).
6. m. sing. of perf. or imperf. participle, active or passive (§ 362).
7. = *śḏmw*, masc. sing. imperf. or perf. relative form before nominal subject (§ 380).
8. = *śḏmw*, negatival complement (§ 341).

śḏmt may be:

1. f. sing. or plur. perf. or imperf. participle, active or passive (§ 362).
2. 2nd pers. f. sing. of the *śḏm·f* form (§§ 34. 39).
3. f. sing. imperf. or perf. relative form before nominal subject (§ 380).
4. = *śḏm·ti*, 2nd pers. c. sing. or 3rd pers. f. sing. old perfective (§ 309).
5. *śḏm·tw* passive of the *śḏm·f* form before nominal subject (§ 39).
6. *śḏmt·f* form before nominal subject (§ 409).

The student must not allow himself to be discouraged, and still less to be rendered sceptical, by the great ambiguity displayed in the writing of the various verb-forms. Their separate existence has been elicited with certainty in almost every case, partly through the alternation of fuller and more summary writings, partly through syntactic observations, and partly through differences of meaning. Only by scrupulous study of both syntax and morphology does accurate interpretation of the hieroglyphic texts become possible. Attention to the rules laid down in this grammar will enable the learner quickly to pass in review the various possibilities and to choose that which is appropriate in the particular context.

TERMINOLOGY

§ 297. It is desirable here to discuss the meaning of several terms which will be constantly used in connection with the verb.

1. **Semantic subject and object**,[1] abbreviated 'subject^{s}' and 'object^{s}'. While the terms 'subject' and 'object' will be used normally in the sense of 'nominative' and 'accusative', they will often be needed to express the relations

[1] See *Rev. ég.* n.s. ii. 42–4; also *Philologica*, i. 3 (London, 1922).

of meaning familiar to classical students in the terms 'subjective genitive' (ex. *amor matris* 'a mother's love') and 'objective genitive' (ex. *amor patriae* 'love of country'). It lies in the nature of our conception of verbal meaning to regard this as springing from a certain source and proceeding in a certain direction. We shall adopt the term **semantic subject** to denote *that noun or pronoun from which the verbal action, actively conceived, appears to start or spring*, and the term **semantic object** to denote *any noun or pronoun which the verbal action, actively conceived, affects in the course of its progress.* Thus in '*he* is', '*he* flourishes', '*he* strikes', '*John*'s wooing of Mary', 'the Rubicon was crossed by *Caesar*' the italicized words are semantic subjects. In the following sentences the italicized words or phrases are semantic objects: he is *my friend*, he struck *him*, he gave the *book* to *him*, John's wooing of *Mary*, the boy who was found *fault* with, the *Rubicon* was crossed by Caesar.

In 'he filled the jug with water', 'jug' will be called the **direct semantic object**, because we may say, passively, 'the jug was filled'; 'water' is only an **indirect semantic object.** Every noun preceded by a preposition may be regarded as an indirect semantic object of the active notion in the verb.

OBS. What is here called 'semantic subject' is often called 'logical subject'; the latter is, however, a far less suitable term, and is, moreover, required for another purpose; see above § 126.

2. **Agent.**—We reserve, however, the name of **agent** for that particular subject[s] which is expressed in the external form of an indirect object[s] (see under 1), i. e. there where it is introduced by a preposition. The agent is found after passives of all kinds, as well as after that neutral part of the verb, the infinitive. The prepositions which introduce it in Egyptian are *in* and much more rarely *ḫr*; see above § 39, end. After the infinitive a pronominal agent is sometimes expressed by the independent pronouns, into which, as we have seen (§ 227), *in* enters as a component element; see below § 300, end.

3. **Verbal and other kinds of verb-forms.**—A broad distinction may be drawn between parts of the Egyptian verb which are fundamentally *verbal*, i. e. function primarily as the predicates of verbal sentences (§ 27), and those which function primarily as other parts of speech. To the former class belong the old perfective (Lesson XXII), the imperative (§ 335), and the various forms of the suffix-conjugation (§ 410), of which the *śḏm·f* and *śḏm·n·f* forms are the principal representatives. The forms here described as 'verbal' would in Latin be called 'finite', as being limited, unlike the 'infinitive', in respect of person and number; but the term 'finite' is inappropriate to Egyptian, since the *śḏmty·fy* form (§ 363) and the relative forms (§ 380) are limited in person and gender, and yet are not essentially verbal in function. It will be found useful to describe

verb-forms which are normally used in main clauses to embody affirmations as 'narrative' verb-forms; the *sḏm·f* and *sḏm·n·f* forms are good examples, and the only 'verbal' verb-form which cannot be described as 'narrative' is the imperative, which does not narrate but commands. The infinitive is a *nominal* part of the verb, i.e. functions as a noun. Other grammarians use the term 'nominal' to describe also the participles, *sḏmty·fy* form and relative forms, but for many reasons we shall prefer to regard these as *adjectival*; not the least important of these reasons is that the participles are best regarded as the equivalents of English adjective, or relative, clauses (§ 353). The so-called *sḏmt·f* form (§ 401) is 'nominal' at least in origin. We shall find grounds for thinking that the so-called negatival complement (§ 341) is ultimately *adverbial* in function, and it will be shown (§ 311) that the old perfective, though originally 'verbal' and 'narrative' in character, had become mainly 'adverbial' in its Middle Egyptian uses.

LESSON XXI A

THE INFINITIVE

[1] See *Verbum* ii. §§ 544 foll.

§ 298. The **infinitive**[1] is a noun denoting the action or state expressed by a verb-stem. It corresponds, therefore, to English infinitives like 'to make', 'to flourish', 'to be', or else to English gerunds like 'making', 'flourishing', 'being'. It differs from other nouns, first of all, in the facility with which it can replace narrative verb-forms, ex. [hieroglyphs] *wḏ·n·i n·f irt st* 'I commanded him to make it' in place of [hieroglyphs] *wḏ·n·i ir·f st* 'I commanded that he should make it' (*sḏm·f*, § 184); second, it differs from other nouns in the close resemblance of its construction to that of the narrative verb-forms; thus it may be followed by an 'agent' (see § 297, 2), and may even, on occasion, have a grammatical subject or a direct grammatical object of its own (§ 301).

Though strictly neutral in voice, as also in tense, the Egyptian infinitive has usually an active implication; for example, [hieroglyphs] *irt* tends to signify 'to make' more often than 'to be made'. Cases are found, however, where translation as a passive is necessary in English.[2]

[2] See GUNN, *Stud.* ch. vi.

Exx. [hieroglyphs] *iw sȝ·k r ḥbs ḥr·s* thy back shall be covered by it, lit. thy back is towards covering through it.[3]

[3] *Pt.* 407. Sim. *P. Pet.* 1116 A, 49.

[hieroglyphs] *rḫt ḳrḥwt nty r irt r inw* number of vessels which are to be made for tribute.[4] Here French could render literally *qui sont à faire.*

[4] *P. Kah.* 26, 2. Sim. *Siut* 3, 1; *Rhind* 82.

A rather precarious distinction is made between infinitives that are nominal and infinitives that are verbal, the former name being given to those which, from the point of view of syntax, have nothing to distinguish them from nouns, while the latter, for one or other of the reasons given above, are more like narrative verbs. The nominal infinitive may be qualified by an adjectival epithet, may take an indirect genitive after it, may be put into the plural, may serve as predicate in the sentence with *pw*, and so forth.

Exx. *šmt nbt* every proceeding, lit. going.[1]

m ḥst nt Skry in the favour of Sokar![2] Epistolary greetings frequently take this form.

ꜥḥꜥw nw ꜣ 11 the positions (lit. standings) of the eleven birds.[3]

swḏꜣ ib pw n nb (ꜥnḫ, wḏꜣ, snb) it is a communication to (lit. a making easy the heart of my) lord, may he live, be prosperous and hale.[4] The commonest formula of letters.

Employments like these need no further discussion. The Egyptians themselves appear to have felt a distinction between the verbal and nominal uses of the infinitive, since in the latter the *3ae inf.* verbs sometimes substitute fuller writings for the short verbal writing, e. g. *mrwt*, *mryt* 'love' for the usual *mrt* 'loving', '(to) love'. But it must be remembered that, owing to the absence of written vowels, nouns regarded by us as infinitives may often conceal forms not really infinitival at all; doubt is legitimate, for instance, in the case of *ꜥḥꜥw* 'positions' quoted as the third example above.

Obs. The name 'complementary infinitive'[5] has been given to certain forms from verb-stems which serve as cognate accusatives to various parts of the same verb, exx. *wbn·k wbnt* 'thou risest a rising',[6] *ḫnn·sn ḫnt* 'they row a rowing'.[7] Such complementary infinitives sometimes agree with the ordinary infinitive in respect of gender, and sometimes differ from it in that respect; being to all intents and purposes mere nouns they do not concern us further. Note that a form *msyt* resembling the fem. perf. pass. part. occurs as 'complementary infinitive' with the passive: *n ms·n·t(w)·i is msyt* 'I was not born a being-born'.[8] See further below § 405.

§ 299. Forms of the infinitive.—See above §§ 278–289. The various verb-classes differ as regards the gender of their infinitives, the immutable verbs having masc. infinitives without special ending, while some mutable verbs have fem. infinitives ending in *-t*. Possibly in the older stages of Egyptian the infinitives ending in *-t* were treated syntactically as feminines, though in an example like *ḥst·i pḥ·s pt* 'the praise of me reached heaven'[9] it is far from certain that *ḥst* is an infinitive.

In Late Egyptian all verbally used infinitives were treated syntactically as masculines, and could be preceded under certain circumstances by the masculine definite article *pꜣ*.[10] One or two instances of this occur already in Dyn. XVIII.

Ex. *mḥ pw m dmi ḫꜣ pꜣ mḥ m Mkti* the capture of Megiddo is the capture of a thousand towns.[11]

[1] Brit. Mus. 614, 10.
[2] *P. Kah.* 27, 4.
[3] Louvre C 14.
[4] *P. Kah.* 27, 1. Different examples with *pw*, e.g. *Eb.* 8, 9; 98, 8; for *sḏm pw ir(w)·n·f* see below § 392.
[5] See *Verbum*, ii. §§ 720 foll.
[6] Lac. *TR.* 47, 24.
[7] *Westc.* 5, 4.
[8] *Rec.* 16, 130.
[9] *BH.* i. 8, 9.
[10] See *Verbum* ii. §§ 556–61.
[11] *Urk.* iv. 660. Sim. *ÄZ.* 55, 85, 2.

Our evidence does not, however, include any Middle Egyptian instance of *pꜣ* before an infinitive which is feminine in form. In the Middle Egyptian construction exemplified in *prt pw ir(w)·n·f*, 'thereupon he went forth', lit. 'it is a going forth which he made' (see below § 392), the masc. gender of the relative form *ir(w)·n·f* does not prove that the infinitive was treated syntactically as a masculine, since *ir(w)·n·f* agrees with *pw*, not with the infinitive.

2-lit. Masc.; exx. *wn* 'open', *mn* 'be firm'. *Šm* 'go' has a fem. infinitive *šmt*, an indication that this verb-stem once belonged to the *3ae inf.*

3-lit. Masc.; exx. *sḏm* 'hear', *wḏꜣ* 'prosper'.[0]

2ae gem. Masc. and geminating; exx. *ḳbb* 'be cool'; *wnn* 'exist'. 'See' presents the peculiarity of showing several forms or writings: *mꜣꜣ*, *mꜣn*[1] and *mꜣ*;[2] the two latter are rarer than the first and occur only when an object follows.

3ae inf. Fem.; exx. *mrt* 'love', *prt* 'go forth'. For fuller forms like *mrwt* see above § 298; they are mainly nominal, but *rmyt* 'weep' is found verbally.[3] The masc. is found in place of the fem. in the phrase *m ḫd* 'in sailing northward'; also *ḥsy* 'sing'[4] is from a *3ae inf.* stem. 'Make' has *irt*, much more rarely *irt*.[5] 'Take away' has *itt*.[6] 'Strike' has *ḥ(y)t*,[7] but the related word for 'rain', which is perhaps infinitival, appears both as[8] and as *ḥyt*.[9]

caus. 2-lit. Fem.; exx. *smnt* 'establish'; *smit* 'report'.[9a]

4-lit. Masc.; exx. *ptpt* 'crush', *wsṯn* 'stride'.

caus. 3-lit. Masc.; exx. *sꜥnḫ* 'make live'; *sḥtp* 'propitiate'.

caus. 2ae gem. Masc.; exx. *sḳbb* 'make cool'; *sgnn* 'soften'.

4ae inf. Partly masc., exx. *ḥrty* 'travel overland';[10] *mꜣw*, var. *mꜣwy*, 'be renewed';[11] and partly fem., exx. *ḥmst* 'sit', *m(w)dt* 'speak'. In the masc. forms the last weak radical is frequently written, but in the fem. forms seldom, except in *ḫsfyt* 'travel upstream' and *ḫntyt* 'sail southwards', for which the writings *ḫsft* and *ḫnt*[12] (the latter in the phrase *m ḫnt* 'in faring southward') also occur.

caus. 3ae inf. Either masc., ex. *smsy* 'bring to birth',[13] or fem., exx. *sḫpt* 'bring as offering';[14] *sḳdwt* 'sail'.[15]

5-lit. Masc.; ex. *nftft* 'spring away'.

caus. 4ae inf. Masc.; ex. *smꜣwy* 'renew'.

anom. 'Give' has almost always *rdit*; *dit* is uncommon.[16] With 'come' both *iit* (*iit*)[17] and *iwt*[18] are found. 'Bring' has *int*;[19] abnormal writing with suffix *int·f*, this having by now acquired the same sound as the passive of the *sḏm·f* form.[20]

[0] If *dmit* in *Sh.S.* 79 is infinitive (*ÄZ.* 52, 109), it is the sole ex. of fem. inf. in this class.

[1] With suffix, *Peas.* R 123; *Mill.* 1, 8; *Eb.* 36, 15. With noun, *Th. T. S.* ii. 35, 6.

[2] With suffix, *Peas.* B 1, 78. With noun, *Rec.* 1, 133; *Urk.* iv. 611, 16; 620, 6.

[3] *Peas.* B 1, 25.

[4] *Westc.* 12, 1.

[5] *Sin.* B 5. 117. 282.

[6] *Peas.* B 1, 93.

[7] *Westc.* 12, 10; *Sin.* R 14; *Eb.* 69, 18. Without *ḥ*, *Sin.* B 72.

[8] *Westc.* 11, 14; *Urk.* iv. 84, 9.

[9] *Rhind* 87, 8.

[9a] *Sh. S.* 157; *Westc.* 8, 7.

[10] *Westc.* 7, 12; Berl. *ÄI.* i. p. 255, 3.

[11] *Pt.* 9.

[12] *Urk.* iv. 83, 9.

[13] *Westc.* 10, 5.

[14] *D. el B.* 110, bottom.

[15] *Urk.* iv. 322, 6.

[16] Cairo 20057; *Ikhern.* 3; *ÄZ.* 45, Pl. VIII A.

[17] *Sh. S.* 62; *BH.* i. 29.

[18] *Sin.* B 248; *Westc.* 8, 4; 12, 6.

[19] *BH.* i. 29.

[20] *Urk.* iv. 6, 3.

§ 300. Subject and object of the infinitive.—The terms 'subject' and 'object' are here used in their semantic sense (see above § 297), i. e. refer to the meaning of the verb as *actively*, not passively, conceived.

The following statement incorporates a general rule of considerable importance, although, as we shall see, it will require subsequent qualification:—*The subject*[s] *of the infinitive is expressed as an agent with the help of the preposition* in *'by', while the object*[s] *is represented by the direct genitive, i. e., in the case of the pronouns, by the suffixes.*

Exx. *šdt sꜣḫw in ḫryw-ḥbt ˁšꜣw* reciting of glorifications on the part of the ordinary lector-priests.[1]

gmt·f in ḥm·f finding him by His Majesty, i. e. His Majesty found him.[2] See below § 306, 2.

ii·n·i ḥr šms·f I returned accompanying him, lit. on accompanying him.[3]

The point to be noticed is that, whereas after other parts of the verb (the *sḏm·f* form, participles, etc.) the direct object[s] is expressed by the dependent pronouns, these being felt as accusatives, after the infinitive it is expressed by the suffixes, a fact pointing to their being felt as genitives. The only common exception to this rule is the pronoun *st*, var. (§ 46), which is employed for (*a*) the 3rd pers. neuter, (*b*) the 3rd pers. plur., (*c*) the 3rd pers. dual, and (*d*) more rarely the 3rd pers. fem. sing.

Exx. (*a*) *ˁḥˁ·n šm·kwi r smit st* I went to report it.[4]

(*b*) *wn·in ḥm·f ḥr rdit st n·i r ḥmw* His Majesty gave them to me as slaves.[5] The word-order *st n·i* shows that *st* was felt as a suffix (§ 66).

(*c*) ..... *kt nt ...... srwḫ pḥwy, skbb st* another (remedy) for ..... giving relief to the hinder parts and cooling them.[6]

(*d*) *wḥm-ˁ m rdit st ḥr mrḥt sꜣt* the second thing (lit. repetition) consists in adding it (viz. *msdmt* eye-paint) to fat of goose.[7]

When the agent is pronominal, use may be made of the independent pronouns; for the correspondence of the independent pronouns and *in*+noun, see above § 227. Examples are not common.

Exx. *ḥnˁ prt ntsn m-sꜣ ḥm-kꜣ·f* together with the going forth on their part after his *ka*-priest.[8]

m ḏd st ntf r-gs iry-sšm through the saying of it on his part in the presence of the (proper) functionary.[9]

ḏd ntsn then said they, lit. saying on their part.[10] See below § 306, 2.

In the one instance where an independent pronoun of the 1st pers. sing. is found after the infinitive it is written *nnk*;[11] for the writing *nnk* see § 114, 3.

[1] *Siut* 1, 68. Sim. *ib.* 126; *Bersh.* i. 18, top; *BH.* i. 13, vert.

[2] *Urk.* iv. 6.

[3] *BH.* i. 8, 10.

[4] *Sh. S.* 157. Sim. *Sin.* B 215.

[5] *Urk.* iv. 4. Sim. *BH.* i. 25, 113; *Peas.* B 1, 49. Reflexive, *Pr.* 2, 6.

[6] *Eb.* 31, 7.

[7] *Eb.* 59, 7.

[8] *Siut* 1, 307. Sim. *ib.* 278. 291. 312. 313.

[9] *Urk.* iv. 1088, 14.

[10] *Rec.* 8, 128, 18.

[11] Leyd. 88, 10, qu. Exerc. XXVI (*a*).

The rarity of this construction is due partly to the existence of the alternative to be discussed in the next section, partly to the fact that the expression of the semantic subject is by no means common, a frequent motive for the use of the infinitive being the lack of any need to name the subject. See below § 302.

Obs. Towards the end of Dyn. XVIII the independent pronoun changes places with the infinitive in a particular construction, the outcome of § 171, 3. A theoretical ***ḥnˁ irt ntk*'... with doing on thy part' becomes *ḥnˁ ntk irt* '... with on thy part doing',[0] and out of this idiom develops the conjunctive tense of Late Egyptian and Coptic.[0a]

§ 301. Subject[s] and object[s] of the infinitive conformed to the construction of the suffix-conjugation.

—Some special cases call for study.

With *intransitive* infinitives the subject[s] can always be added as a direct genitive, whether noun or suffix. Exx. *m prt s(t)m* 'at the going forth of the *setem*-priest';[1] *m prt·f tpt* 'at his first going forth'.[2]

With *transitive* verbs the same construction is possible, but only where subjects[s] and object[s] are both expressed.

Exx. *ḫpr·n tp-wꜣt nfrt m rdit Mntw tꜣwy n iti Nb-ḫrw-Rˁ* a good beginning came about in Mont's giving the two lands to king Nebkherurēˁ.[3]

sp tpy irt·n·k ḫr ḥm·i rdit·k n·i nsyt·k on the first occasion what thou didst do unto My Majesty was (§ 125, end) that thou gavest (lit. thy giving) to me thy kingship.[4]

grḥ pf n irt ꜣst iꜣkb m-sꜣ sn·s Wsir on that night of Isis' making mourning for (lit. after) her brother Osiris.[5]

rdit·f sw r r-pˁt ḥꜣty-ˁ his appointing (lit. giving) him to be prince.[6]

The last example, which is of a very rare kind, shows that the pronominal object[s], if not immediately following the infinitive, becomes the dependent pronoun as after the *sḏm·f* form; and this suggests that, whenever the object[s] of an infinitive is separated from it by an extraneous element, as in

m rdit n·f t-ḥḏ in giving to him white bread,[7]

this object[s] is to be regarded, not as a direct genitive, but as an accusative. It has been seen, in dealing with the syntax of nouns (§ 85), that a direct genitive cannot easily be separated from its antecedent.

Externally, at least, the construction illustrated above is that customary after all other parts of the verb, and analogy seems to have been at work.

Obs. 1. When, in constructions like the above, the verb-form is masc., we cannot always be sure that it is really the infinitive, and not a *sḏm·f* form (see above §§ 155. 191).[8] Again, when it is fem., the doubt arises whether the supposed infinitive is not the *sḏmt·f* form, an obscure category of the verb to be discussed later (§§ 401 foll.).

[0] Early exx., *L. to D.*, Moscow bowl, 2; *JEA.* 14, Pl. XXXV, 14–5.
[0a] *JEA.* 14, 86.

[1] *BH.* i. 24, 3.
[2] *Cairo* 20057, *d.* Sim. *ḳnt·i*, 'my bravery', *Urk.* iv. 7, 9.
[3] Turin 1447.
[4] *Urk.* iv. 271. Sim. *ib.* 558, 15.
[5] *Urk.* v. 104, 6. 10.
[6] *BH.* i. 25, 30, with error *fdit·f* for *rdit·f*.
[7] *Siut* 1, 290.
[8] A case in point is p. 145, 1st ex.

OBS. 2. For the change of the pronominal object[s] from the suffix (genitive) into the dependent pronoun (accusative) a comparison with Arabic is instructive: 'if only the objective complement of the act (and not likewise its subject) be expressed, it is put after the *nomen actionis* in the genitive; unless it be separated from the *nomen actionis* by one or more words, in which case it is put in the accusative because the genitive can never be divided from the word that governs it'. WRIGHT, *Arabic Grammar*,[3] ii. p. 57, B.

§ 302. The infinitive as substitute for a noun clause with the *śdm·f* form.—In Lesson XV it was seen that the *śdm·f* form, with whatever other words accompany it, is constantly employed as a noun clause, i.e. as equivalent to a noun in the various syntactic positions which can be occupied by a noun. In the following sections it will be shown that a parallel set of uses existed for the infinitive, this being used in preference to the *śdm·f* form whenever the mention of subject[s] seemed superfluous.

§ 303. The infinitive as object of certain verbs.—The infinitive is commonly used as object of such verbs as [hieroglyphs] *ꜣb* 'cease',[1] [hieroglyphs] *ꜣbi* 'desire',[2] [hieroglyphs] *wḥm* 'repeat',[3] [hieroglyphs] *wḏ* 'command', [hieroglyphs] *mꜣꜣ* 'see', 'see to', [hieroglyphs] *mri* 'love', 'desire',[4] [hieroglyphs] *rḫ* 'know how to',[5] [hieroglyphs] *snḏ* 'fear',[6] [hieroglyphs] *sḫꜣ* 'remember',[7] [hieroglyphs] *šꜣ* 'order',[8] [hieroglyphs] *šꜣꜥ* 'begin', [hieroglyphs] *kꜣi* 'devise', 'plan',[9] [hieroglyphs] *rdi* 'give', 'grant', [hieroglyphs] *di m ib·f* 'place in one's heart', 'determine',[10] [hieroglyphs] *ḏd* 'think',[11] as well as after the verbs *iri* 'make', *pw* 'do in the past', which will be treated as auxiliaries (§§ 484–5); also occasionally after the imperative [hieroglyphs] *sꜣw* 'beware of' (§ 338, 3) and after the negative verb *tm*, see below § 344.

Exx. [hieroglyphs] *wḏ ḥm·f sꜥḥꜥ wḏ pn* His Majesty commanded to set up this inscription.[12]

[hieroglyphs] *iw mꜣ·n·i šꜣd ḥrt nt ḥm·f* I saw to the excavation of the tomb of His Majesty.[13]

[hieroglyphs] *šꜣꜥ·n ḥꜣty·i šms ḳd·i* my heart began to follow my sleep.[14]

[hieroglyphs] *di·n·(i) n·k irt ḥḥw m ḥbw-sd* I give to thee to celebrate millions of *sed*-festivals.[15]

The infinitive was used only when the expression of the subject[s] of the subordinate action appeared unnecessary; when it was preferred to insert this the *śdm·f* form was used, as was seen in § 184 after many of the same verbs.

§ 304. The infinitive after prepositions.—In the enumeration of the meanings of the prepositions (§§ 162–181) due attention was paid to their very common use with a following infinitive, and this was seen to run parallel, in almost every case, to an employment with the *śdm·f* form; the latter employment was dealt with in § 155.

[1] *Eb.* 93, 6.
[2] *Urk.* iv. 834, 1; 837, 3.
[3] *Eb.* 70, 14; *Urk.* iv. 893, 5.
[4] *Louvre* C 14, 5; *Peas.* B 1, 78, qu. § 315.
[5] *Westc.* 7, 4; 10, 5.
[6] *Sin.* B 215.
[7] *Adm.* 11, 2-6.
[8] *Sin.* B 51.
[9] *Sin.* B 112; 144, qu. § 385.
[10] Brit. Mus. 213.
[11] *Sin.* B 7.
[12] *Hamm.* 192. Sim. Brit. Mus. 202; *Urk.* iv. 618, 16; 647, 5.
[13] *Urk.* iv. 57, 3. Sim. *ib.* 521, 10; 524, 7; 1088, 5.
[14] *Mill.* 1, 12–2, 1. Sim. *Urk.* v. 6, 14. 15.
[15] *Urk.* iv. 292. Sim. *ib.* 223, 14. 16; 481, 1. 7–9; 570, 12; *Th. T. S.* i. 30, B. D.

Three particular cases lead to important developments to be discussed in Lesson XXIII.

1. *ḥr*. The infinitive after *ḥr* expresses a *concomitant circumstance*,[1] often best translated in English by a participle. There seems hardly any difference of meaning between this use and the use of the *śḏm·f* form described in § 213.

Exx. *ỉst ḫd·n ḥm·f ḥr ḥꜣḳ dmỉw* lo, His Majesty went northwards plundering (lit. on plundering) towns.[2]

dbn·n·ỉ ꜥfꜣy·ỉ ḥr nhm I went round about my encampment rejoicing.[3]

ỉst wrš ḥm n n-sw-bỉt Ḫwfw mꜣꜥ-ḫrw ḥr ḥhy n·f nꜣ n ỉpwt lo, the Majesty of king Cheops, justified, spent all his time seeking for himself the secret chambers.[4]

So too sometimes qualifying the object after *gmỉ* 'find' and *mꜣꜣ* 'see'.

Exx. *gm·n·f sw ḥr prt m sbꜣ n pr·f* he found him going forth from the door of his house.[5]

rḳt-ỉb pw ḥr mꜣꜣ·f wỉ ḥr ỉrt ỉpwt·f it is envy because he sees me performing his business.[6]

It will be seen below that the verb-form known as the old perfective (§ 315) has a corresponding use, but while the old perfective indicates *states*, *ḥr* + infinitive applies essentially to *action* as in progress; thus with transitive verbs it is active, with verbs of motion it stresses the movement itself rather than its result, and with adjective-verbs it emphasizes the becoming and not the being.

2. *m* occasionally takes the place of *ḥr* with verbs of motion. Thus in the last example but one *ḥr prt* in one manuscript is replaced by *m prt* in another.[7]

3. *r*. The infinitive after *r* often expresses *purpose* or *result*.

Ex. *wḏꜣ ḥm·f m ḫd r sḫrt Mnṯw Sṯt* His Majesty proceeded north to overthrow the Beduins of Asia.[8]

Beyond the three important uses above described, the chief construction of interest is that after *ḥnꜥ* to be described just below. We may mention once again, as of special interest, the comparative use of *r* after adjectives, ex. *ꜥšꜣ r smnt* 'too many to record', lit. 'many as compared with recording' (§ 163, 7), the use of *r* as 'to' after *ỉb* 'wish', *dwꜣ* 'rise early', *snḏ* 'fear', *sbꜣ* 'teach' (§ 163, 10), and the employment of *ḥnꜥ* 'together with' (§ 171, 3; § 300, Obs.) and *wpw-ḥr* 'except' (§ 179, 2) as equivalent to English 'and' and 'but' with a following finite tense.

Obs. When subject[s] closely follows the verb-form, it is to be presumed that the verb-form is not the infinitive, but the *śḏm·f* form (§ 155), or alternatively, if there is an ending *-t*, the *śḏmt·f* form (§§ 407–9).

[1] For the use with the meaning 'after' see § 165, 10.

[2] *Urk.* iv. 697. Sim. *ib.* 699, 1; *BH.* i. 8, 10; *Sin.* B 239. 249; *Siut* 1, 278. 297; *Westc.* 8, 2.

[3] *Sin.* B 201. Sim. *Peas.* B 1, 31; *Westc.* 8, 21. 23.

[4] *Westc.* 7, 6–7. Sim. after *wrš*, *P. Kah.* 30, 18; *Paheri* 3, qu. § 492, 5; see *Rec.* 39, 108.

[5] *Peas.* B 1, 34–5. Sim. *Westc.* 12, 13; *Urk.* iv. 1073, 5–6.

[6] *Sin.* B 116–7. Sim. *Urk.* iv. 657, 17.

[7] *Peas.* R 84.

[8] *Sebekkhu* 1. Sim. *Peas.* B 1, 33; *Sh. S.* 157; *BH.* i. 8, 11. 14; *Urk.* iv. 648, 14. 15; 693, 13. 14.

§ 305. The infinitive after the genitival adjective.—We saw in § 191 that the *sḏm·f* form may be employed after the genitival adjective *n* (*ny*) with a variety of meanings. The infinitive occurs in exactly the same way whenever the expression of the subject[s] was felt to be unnecessary. Only in very rare cases is the infinitive substituted for *sḏm·f* when the subject[s] is added; an example (*grḥ pf*, etc.) has been quoted in § 301, and a doubt might possibly be felt about the last example but one (*mḥȝ·f*) in § 191, where the form (*sḏm·f* or inf. + suffix) is ambiguous.

Among the notions expressed by *n* + infinitive are *time, place, means, purpose* and the like, and the kinship of the phrase thus formed with a relative clause may often be realized by means of a paraphrase.

Exx. *grḥ pf n irt hȝkr* on that night of celebrating the *Hȝkr*-festival, i. e. when the *Hȝkr*-festival is celebrated.[1]

r n wnm t m ẖrt-nṯr an incantation for eating bread in the necropolis.[2]

ʿḥ n stȝ a brazier which can be moved about, lit. of dragging.[3]

pẖrt nt smȝ ḥfȝt a prescription for killing a snake.[4]

wȝt nt prt a way of going out.[5]

Specially noteworthy is the use of such infinitival genitives to describe how a man can be, or deserves to be, treated.

Exx. *s iḳr n wbȝ n·f ib* an excellent man to be confided in, lit. of opening to him the heart.[6]

nsw swt n swhȝ n·f a king, indeed, to be boasted of, lit. of boasting for him.[7]

Note that in several cases the infinitive is best translated by an English passive.

§ 306. Absolute uses of the infinitive.—Like other nouns (§ 89), the infinitive may be used as the equivalent of a sentence, i. e. as significant and complete in itself.

1. Thus it often occurs absolutely in *headings* to scenes, *titles* to parts of books and the like; compare above § 89, 1. The subject[s], or agent, is introduced by *in*.

Exx. .... *ḥmst r sḏm sprw m ḫȝ n ṯȝty in r-pʿt ḥȝty-ʿ ..... Rḫ-mi-Rʿ* sitting to hear the petitioner in the office of the vizier by the prince ..... Rekhmerēʿ. Description above a painted scene.[8]

ḫsf ʿȝpp m wiȝ Rʿ to repel Apopis from the bark of Rēʿ. Title of an incantation.[9]

dr sty ḫnš m šmw to remove a foul odour in the summertime.[10] Heading of a recipe in a medical papyrus.

[1] *Urk.* v. 104, 17. Sim. *ib.* 103, 10; 105, 13; 107, 9; *Siut* 1, 308; *Urk.* iv. 1072, 16.

[2] Lac. *TR.* 45, 1. Sim. *ib.* 29, 1, 48, 1.

[3] *Urk.* iv. 639, 21.

[4] *Eb.* 21, 8. Sim. *ib.* 31, 17; 46, 2; 79, 2. 5.

[5] *Eb.* 52, 3.

[6] *Bersh.* ii. 21. 4. Sim. Leyd. V 4, 12; *Urk.* iv. 415, 13.

[7] *Amada* 6. Sim. *ib.* 7; *Hamm* 12, 3.

[8] *Urk.* iv. 1117. Sim. *ib.* 1159, 10; 1161, 3; 1175, 17; 1187, 9; *BH.* i. 30. 32.

[9] Lac. *TR.* 35, 1; Sim. *ib.* 36, 1; 39. 1; 53, 1; 63, 1; *P. Kah.* 6, 8. 12.

[10] *Hearst* 2, 17 = *Eb.* 86, 8 (*pẖrt nt dr*, etc.).

Here belongs the very common phrase *ḏd mdw*, lit. 'the speaking of words', which has a double employment in Middle Egyptian. Written fully it is found in magico-medical papyri at the beginning of rubrics with prescriptive meaning.

Ex. *ḏd mdw ḫft wꜣḥ pẖrt* to be spoken when applying remedies.[1]

Secondly, it occurs in the abbreviated writing at the beginning of all divine speeches on temple and tomb walls, e.g. *ḏd mdw in Ḥtḥr* 'words spoken by Hathor'.[2] On many Middle Kingdom coffins stands at the top of every column of text, serving much the same purpose as our inverted commas.

2. Again like other nouns (§ 89, 2), the infinitive is used in *narrative* to announce incidents of outstanding importance. The subject^{s} may be presented as an agent with the help of *in*, or else may be appended directly to the infinitive in accordance with § 301.

Exx. *rdit in ḥm·f pr ḳn nb n mšʿ·f* then His Majesty caused (lit. causing by His Majesty) every brave of his army to go forth.[3]

ḥꜣt-sp 16, (ꜣbd) 3(-nw n) prt, irt ḥm·f tꜣš rsy r Ḥḥ year 16, month 3 of winter: His Majesty made (lit. His Majesty's making) the southern boundary at Ḥeḥ.[4]

wdꜣ ḥm·f ...... spr ḥm·f ..... rdit ḥm·f tp-nfr His Majesty proceeded ...... His Majesty arrived ..... His Majesty made (lit. gave) a good beginning.[5]

rs m ʿnḫ ..... iit·tw r ḏd n ḥm·f waking in life (in the royal tent); one came to tell His Majesty.[6] Note the indefinite pronoun *tw* (§ 47), a very rare use.

rdit·f wi m-ḥꜣt ẖrdw·f he placed me in front of his children.[7]

Obs. Various doubts and difficulties present themselves at this point. When the infinitive is closely followed by *in* + noun it is indistinguishable, if of masc. gender, from the *śḏm·in·f* form (below § 429, 1). When subject^{s} immediately follows the verb, a choice arises between the infinitive and the *śḏm·f* form, the latter being unquestionably excluded only with verbs whose infinitive ends in *-t*, while with the verb *iwt* 'come' this ambiguity is always present, as one of its *śḏm·f* forms is *iwt·f* (§ 447). When the hypothetical infinitive ends in *-t*, the question arises whether it may not be the *śḏmt·f* form, see below § 406; so, for instance, in the last example above, where the doubt is intensified by the fact that no parallel forms without *t* from immutable verbs are there to suggest the infinitive. Reasonably certain examples of the narrative infinitive are those in which forms ending in *-t* alternate with forms not ending in *-t*, and where both are parallel to real narrative tenses like *śḏm·n·f*. These criteria place our third and fourth examples beyond doubt. A different kind of question arises in connection with examples like the second above; here the infinitive (if it be such and not the *śḏmt·f* form) may be, not a narrative infinitive, but one in apposition to the preceding date.

[1] *Eb.* 1. 10; 2, 6; *Hearst* 6, 10; 11, 5.

[2] *Urk.* iv. 236. Sim. *ib.* 239, 3; 242, 6. 9. 10. 13.

[3] *Urk.* iv. 894. Sim. *ib.* 9, 3; 653, 8; 655, 5; *Ann.* 37, Pl. II, 27; also the exx. *gmt·f in ḥm·f* and *ḏd ntsn* in § 300.

[4] Berl. *Äl.* i. p. 257, l. 3. Sim. *Hamm.* 48, 3; 191, 1.

[5] *Sebekkhu* 1–2. Sim. *ib.* 12–14; *Urk.* iv. 9, 11; 54, 14; 61, 7.

[6] *Urk.* iv. 656, 13–14. Sim. *ib.* 695, 5–6. Without subject^{s}, *ib.* 656, 6–7; 685, 10–11; 729, 15–16; 730, 8–10; *Hamm.* 123, 3.

[7] *Sin.* B 107. Sim. *ib.* B 4–5. 5. 15. 23. 86. See below § 406 for these doubtful cases.

§ 307. The infinitive after *nn* and *n*, and after the negative relative adjective.—1. Just as *nn* is used with a nominal subject to predicate non-existence (§ 108), so too it is used with the infinitive as its subject to express the non-performance or non-occurrence of some verbal action.[1] This construction is hardly employed, however, except to qualify some preceding statement, and in this case, as with nominal subject (§ 109), it is often best to translate *nn* as 'without'.

Exx. I caused his weapons to be carried off ..... *nn tšt ḥr ꜥḥꜣ* without desisting from the fight. Lit. not was desisting.[2]

These things shall belong to thy son ...... *nn rdỉt psš·f st n ẖrdw·f* without his being allowed to divide it among his children.[3] Lit. not is the allowing that he divide it for his children.

pr·k ꜥḳ·k, nn ḫnḫn·k, nn šnꜥ·k ḥr sbꜣ n dwꜣt mayst thou go out and in, without being driven back, and without being turned away from the door of the netherworld. Lit. there is not the driving back of thee, etc.[4]

As the last example shows, when object[s] is added to the infinitive, it is often more idiomatic in English to render this as a passive, e. g. 'without (thy) being driven back' instead of actively 'without driving thee back'.

A very uncommon case is where, in agreement with § 301, the noun following the infinitive is subject[s], not object[s].

Ex. *sm(ꜣ) pdtyw, nn sḫt ḫt* slaying the bowmen, without blow of a stick, lit. there is not striking of a stick.[5]

Rarely an agential dative is inserted after *nn* when the infinitive is intransitive.

Ex. *nn n·s prt m Ỉmnt* she cannot go forth from the west, lit. not to her is going forth.[6] Note that this example is a main clause.

n ỉs (§ 209) can be used when the negatived infinitive definitely restricts the scope of a preceding clause.

Ex. *n grt sḏm·n ỉmy-r šnt ỉṯꜣ, n ỉs nḏrt m-ꜥ·f* an overseer of lawsuits cannot judge a thief, except he be (?) imprisoned with him, lit. not indeed is there imprisoning with him.[7]

Very rarely *n wnt* (§ 108, 2) is used in place of the usual *nn*.

Ex. My Majesty has commanded to consecrate the holy ground south of Abydus, *n wnt rdỉt ḫnd rmṯ nbt ḥr pꜣ tꜣ ḏsr* without allowing any people to tread upon this holy ground.[8] Lit. there is not the allowing that any people tread, etc.

Exceptionally and, so far as our evidence goes, only when two parallel infinitives are negated and these have no object[s], *n* is found in place of *nn*.

[1] See GUNN, *Stud.* pp. 155 foll.

[2] *Sebekkhu* 4. Sim. *Peas.* B 1, 79; *Hamm.* 113, 7; *Sh. S.* 17; *Westc.* 5, 17; 11, 11.

[3] *Siut* 1, 272. Sim. *Sin.* R 22; *P. Kah.* 12, 12; 35, 13; Berl. *ÄI.* i. p. 256, 5, qu. § 254.

[4] *Urk.* iv. 498. Sim. *ib.* 65, 9; 520, 8; *Siut* 1, 293; 4, 33; *Bersh.* ii. 21, top, 1.

[5] *P. Kah.* 1. 4.

[6] *Leb.* 77. Sim. *Adm.* 8, 6.

[7] *P. Kah.* 30, 11-3.

[8] *Amrah* 29, 2. Sim. *Dend.* 37 *b*, 387.

Ex. Would that it were the end of men (§ 133), [hieroglyphs] *n iwr, n mst* without conception, without birth.[1]

This use is, up to the present, unexplained.

2. Just as sentences of the type [hieroglyphs] *nn sšw·s* may be made adjectival by the mere substitution of the negative relative adjective *iwty* for *nn* (§ 203, 3), so too with the construction *nn* + infinitive discussed above under 1.

Exx. [hieroglyphs] *iwtw ḫsf·f m nṯrw* who is not repelled among the gods.[2] Some variants omit the suffix as unessential.

[hieroglyphs] *iwt(y) rḫ rn·f* whose name is not known.[3]

One might, in explaining these instances, hesitate between the infinitive and the form which we shall term the passive *śḏm·f*, but there is no definite evidence in favour of the latter, and the infinitive seems indicated by Coptic equivalents like *at-sontᵉf* 'uncreated', lit. 'who-not (there is) creating of him'. See below § 424, 3.

[1] *Adm.* 5, 14; *Urk.* iv. 57, 4–5. Sim. *ib.* 97, 15–6; 546, 6–7.

[2] *Urk.* v. 10, 13. Sim. BUDGE, p. 107, 13; 497, 14.

[3] *Rec.* 35, 223.

§ 308. Negation of the infinitive.—To express such notions as 'not-hearing', 'not-to-hear' use must be made of the negative verb [hieroglyphs] *tm*, the discussion of which belongs to a later stage in our studies; see below § 348.

OBS. It must be carefully noted that the constructions of § 307 do not constitute negations of the infinitive in the sense here meant, since there the negative word *nn* or *n* is the existential predicate 'is not', while the infinitive is subject.

VOCABULARY

[hieroglyphs] *wḏꜥ* divide, sever; judge, judge between.

[hieroglyphs] var. [hieroglyphs] *mki* protect.

[hieroglyphs] var. [hieroglyphs] *sn* smell, kiss.

[hieroglyphs] *ḳb* (*ḳꜣb*) double (vb.).

[hieroglyphs] *iw* island.

[hieroglyphs] *ꜥwꜣ-ir(y)·f* brigand.

[hieroglyphs] var. [hieroglyphs] *wr* chieftain.

[hieroglyphs] *wḏyt* (military) expedition.

[hieroglyphs] *psd* back.

[hieroglyphs] var. [hieroglyphs] *mfkꜣt* turquoise.

[hieroglyphs] *nḫtw* victory.

[hieroglyphs] *ḥtpw* peace.

[hieroglyphs] *ḥtpw-nṯr* offerings (to the gods).

[hieroglyphs] *ḫsbd* lapis lazuli.

[hieroglyphs] *šsr* arrow.

[hieroglyphs] *Rṯnw* Retjnu, name of Palestine and Syria.

[hieroglyphs] *Wp-wꜣwt* Wepwawet 'Opener-of-the-ways', the wolf-god of Abydus and Asyûṭ.

EXERCISE XXI

(*a*) *Reading lesson: words accompanying a scene of foreigners, who bring tribute to the vizier Rekhmereʿ (reign of Tuthmosis III, Dyn. XVIII).*[1]

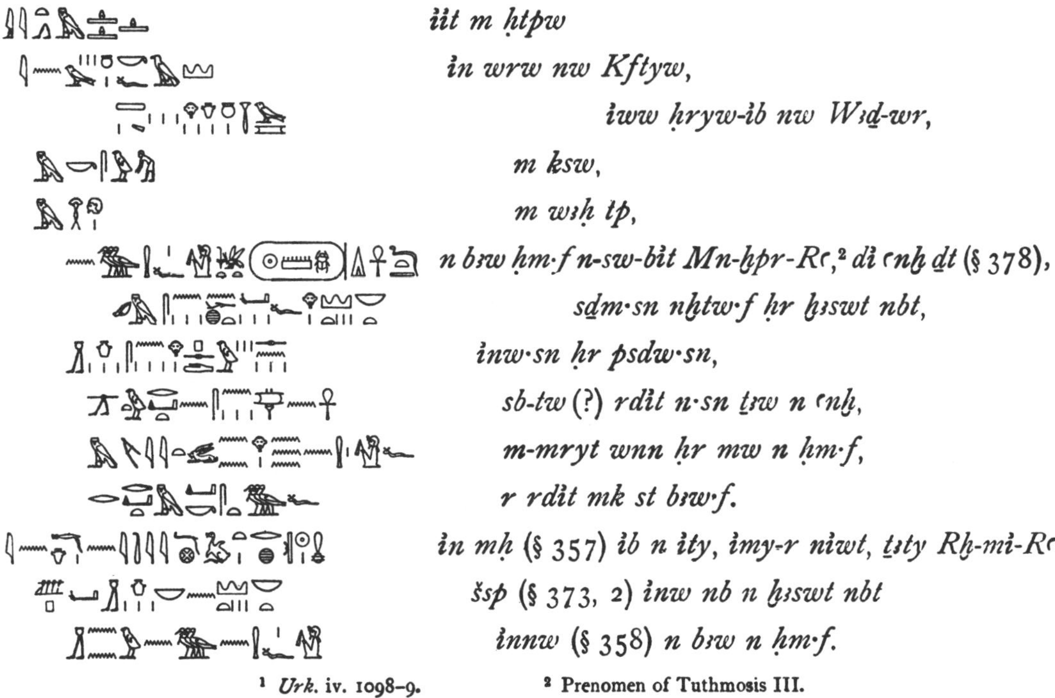

ỉỉt m ḥtpw
ỉn wrw nw Kftyw,
ỉww ḥryw-ỉb nw Wȝḏ-wr,
m ksw,
m wȝḥ tp,
n bȝw ḥm·f n-sw-bỉt Mn-ḫpr-Rʿ,[2] *dỉ ʿnḫ ḏt* (§ 378),
sḏm·sn nḫtw·f ḥr ḫȝswt nbt,
ỉnw·sn ḥr psdw·sn,
sb-tw (?) *rdỉt n·sn ṯȝw n ʿnḫ,*
m-mryt wnn ḥr mw n ḥm·f,
r rdỉt mk st bȝw·f.
ỉn mḥ (§ 357) *ỉb n ỉty, ỉmy-r nỉwt, ṯȝty Rḫ-mỉ-Rʿ*
šsp (§ 373, 2) *ỉnw nb n ḫȝswt nbt*
ỉnnw (§ 358) *n bȝw n ḥm·f.*

[1] *Urk.* iv. 1098–9.
[2] Prenomen of Tuthmosis III.

'Coming in peace by the chieftains of Keftiu (Crete) and of the islands in the midst belonging to the sea, in bowing down, in bending (lit. putting down) the head, through the might of His Majesty, the King of Upper and Lower Egypt, Menkheperrēʿ, granted life eternally, when they hear of his victories over all countries; their tribute on their backs, seeking that may be given to them (lit. in quest of the giving to them) the breath of life, through desire of being loyal subjects (lit. being upon the water) of His Majesty, so that (lit. to cause that) his might may protect them. It is the trusty servant (lit. heart-filler) of the sovereign, the overseer of the city, the vizier Rekhmerēʿ, who receives all the tribute of all lands, which is (wont to be) brought through the might of His Majesty.'

(*b*) *Write in hieroglyphs*:

(1) To do justice is the breath of the nose. (2) Thou wast placed in order to hear disputes (*mdt*), to judge between disputants (lit. two), and to repress the brigand. (3) My Majesty dedicated (*ḫrp*) to him gold, silver, lapis lazuli and turquoise in order to make all the monuments of my father Amūn. (4) Thou didst seize thy city without fighting, without an arrow being shot (lit. shooting an arrow). (5) My Majesty commanded to double these offerings, (making them)

into (literally 'as') a thousand various (kinds of) bread, when (*m-ḫt*) My Majesty came (infinitive) from having (*ḥr*) crushed Retjnu in the first campaign of victory. (6) It is better to give than to receive (lit. receive from another). (7) Giving praise to Osiris, smelling (i.e. kissing) the earth for Wepwawet, by the prince Nebseny.[1] (8) A book for driving out all snakes.[2] (9) Send thou to me (news) about his health, without letting him know it.

[1] Legend beside the picture of a man with arms raised in adoration. [2] Title of a book.

LESSON XXII

THE OLD PERFECTIVE

§ 309. The **old perfective**,[1] often known under the less suitable name of 'pseudo-participle', is the sole surviving relic in Egyptian of the Semitic finite verb (§ 3). It differs from the various forms of the suffix conjugation, i.e. verb-forms like *sḏm·f* (§ 410), in the possession, for the persons, of special endings of its own not identifiable with any of the Egyptian pronouns. This will be best made clear by the following paradigm from the immutable verb *sḏm* 'hear'.

Sing.	1, c.	*sḏm·kwi.*	So often in hierogl. and regularly in hieratic. Rarer writings of the ending are ,[2] ,[3] ,[4] ,[5] or, as always in O.K., simply .[6]
,,	2, c.	*sḏm·ti*	Also , more rarely .
,,	3, m.	*sḏm(w).*	The fuller writing is rather less common.
,,	3, f.	*sḏm·ti.*	Also , more rarely .
Plur.	1, c.	*sḏm·wyn.*	Rarely .[7]
,,	2, c.	*sḏm·tiwny.*	Also rarely .[8]
,,	3, m.	*sḏm(w).*	Much less commonly ;[9] but also sometimes *sḏmy.*[10]
,,	3, f.	*sḏm·ti.*[11]	Hardly except in very ancient texts; in Middle Egyptian regularly replaced by 3rd masc. form.[16]
Dual.	3, m.	*sḏm·wy.*[12]	
,,	3, f.	*sḏm·ty,*[13] varr. ,[14] .[15]	

Thus, only the endings of 1st sing., 1st plur., and 2nd plur. have a very distinctive character. The 2nd sing. and 3rd f. sing. are identical, as also 3rd m. sing. and plur. Moreover, the summary writings for *sḏmw* and for *sḏm·ti*, which are exceedingly common, are easily confused with other parts of the verb (§ 296). In order to recognize the old perfective easily, close attention to its syntactic uses is required.

[1] See *Verbum* ii. §§ 1 foll. Also *ÄZ.* 27, 65; 29, 85.

[2] *Urk.* iv. 3, 3. 9; Louvre C 174.

[3] Brit. Mus. 614, 11. 14; *Urk.* iv. 749, 17; *ÄZ.* 47, Pl. I, 7. 8. 13.

[4] Louvre C 1, 14; *Sinai* 139, 12.

[5] *Bersh.* i. 14, 2; *Th. T. S.* ii. 9. 11.

[6] *Hamm.* 1, 7; Leyd. V 88, 10. 11.

[7] *Urk.* iv. 244, 4.

[8] *Five Th. T.* 27. 28.

[9] *Leb.* 63; *Urk.* iv. 758, 16; *Ann.* 37, Pl. II, 13–14.

[10] *Wny*, Cairo 20003; *dwny*, *Sm.* 3, 10; *ḥry*, Budge, 304, 13; 305, 6. 9. Sim. in O.K., Weill, *Décr.* Pl. 9, vert. 1.

[11] *Eb.* 36, 18; 41, 1; 109, 1; 110, 5.

[12] *Sm.* 11, 18.

[13] Erm. *Hymn.* 11, 4.

[14] *Eb.* 37, 18; 38, 18.

[15] *Eb.* 109, 20; but see *Rec.* 35, 216.

[16] 3rd plur. f., *Siut* 1, 235; *Hamm.* 114, 11. 12; *Urk.* iv. 707, 10. 3rd dual m., *Sin.* B 169; *Pt.* 11. 14; *Eb.* 73, 6. 3rd dual f., *Sin.* R 9. B 272; *Urk.* iv. 365, 2.

Turning now to details, for 1st sing. some hieratic texts which otherwise write the ending *·kwỉ* in full display the abnormal writings *ḏd·kỉ* 'I said'[1] and *wn·k* 'I was';[2] in several instances the enclitic particle *rf* follows,[3] so that these writings may indicate some special form.

In 2nd sing. and 3rd f. sing. the ending or *·tỉ* follows the determinative, if any; the shorter writing, which is usual in the older hieratic texts, has the ending *·t(ỉ)* before the determinative. Exx. *ḥr·tỉ* 'thou art content',[4] *šm·tỉ* 'she is gone',[5] but *pr·t(ỉ)* 'thou art come',[6] *mḥ·t(ỉ)* 'it is full'.[7] With verb-stems ending in *t* the ending may disappear entirely, in accordance with § 62, ex. *nḫt(·tỉ)*.[8]

The endings *·kwỉ*, *·wyn*, *·tỉwny* follow any determinative that there may be; but the *w* of the 3rd m. sing. and plur., if written out, regularly precedes it.

In certain *3ae inf.* and *4ae inf.* verbs the ending of the 3rd m. sing. and 3rd plur. is apt to be written as *y*, exx. *hꜣy* 'has fallen',[9] 'have fallen'[10] (beside *hꜣw*[11]); *wꜥy* '(he) being alone'[12] (beside *wꜥw*[13]); *ḫnty* '(it) being prominent';[14] *ḫsy* '(they) being faint';[14a] isolated ex. 1st plur., 'we having fared down'.[14b] This *y* is apparently due to the fusion of the ending, which in the oldest Egyptian was *ỉ* more commonly than *w*, with the final *ỉ* or *w* of the stem.

Any separately expressed subject, whether noun or pronoun, must be placed *before* the old perfective; see Lesson XXIII for further details.

Exx. *mk tw ỉw·t(ỉ)* behold, thou art come.[15] Lit. behold thee, thou art come.

ỉst mnỉwt nbt sspdw m ḫt nbt nfrt lo, all ports were supplied with everything good.[16]

OBS. 1. The old perfective was discovered and compared with the Semitic perfect by Erman, who gave to it the name 'pseudo-participle' here abandoned. In particular, a close resemblance has been noticed between the Egyptian old perfective and the Akkadian (Semitic Babylonian) 'permansive', an important similarity being that both can be used with passive, as well as with active, meaning;[17] a difference is that the old perfective shows an additional *ỉ* not present in any Semitic parallel, cf. Eg. *sḏm·kwỉ* with Akkad. *kašdāku*. Contradictory views have been taken, however, with regard to the age of the Akkadian permansive. Brockelmann held it to be a secondary formation,[18] but the consensus of recent opinion attributes to it an antiquity not much less than that of any other Semitic tense.[18a] One scholar[19] sought to discover in Akkadian two tenses, a 'durative perfect' and a 'durative imperfect', which might have been compared to the traces of an apparently similar distinction in Egyptian, see below, § 310, end; however, the hypothesis in question has not found favour with other Semitists. There are also Hamitic analogies to be taken into consideration,[20] but here the external resemblances are much less striking, the facts different in the different tongues, and the meanings less conspicuously comparable.

[1] *Sin.* B 45. 114. Sim. *wn·kỉ*, *Sin.* B 252, qu. § 326.
[2] *Sh. S.* 136. So too hierogl., Brit. Mus. 574, 4.
[3] *Sh. S.* 136; *Sin.* B 252; Brit. Mus. 574, 4. With *r·ỉ*, *Sin.* B 45.
[4] *P. Kah.* 13, 24.
[5] *Westc.* 12, 23.
[6] *Sin.* B 182.
[7] *Hamm.* 191, 4.
[8] *Peas.* B 1, 116. Sim. *mwt(·tỉ)*, *Sh. S.* 38.
[9] *Eb.* 37, 16; 42, 16. Sim. *ỉry*, *Rifeh* 1, 16; *dy* 'being placed', *Ann.* 39, 189.
[10] *Eb.* 37, 4.
[11] *Sh.S.* 130; *Pt.* 8.
[12] *P.Kah.* 28, 24.
[13] *P.Kah.* 33, 14.
[14] *Eb.* 37, 18; 38, 18.
[14a] *Ann.* 37, Pl. II, 13.
[14b] LUTZ, 66, 2.
[15] *Sin.* B 257.
[16] *Urk.* iv. 719.
[17] FR. DELITZSCH, *Assyrian Grammar*, § 87, *b*.
[18] *Grundriss d. vergleich. Grammatik d. sem. Sprachen*, i. p. 583, f. *a*.
[18a] G. R. DRIVER, *Problems of the Hebrew Verbal System*, pp. 9–31, 80–4.
[19] A. UNGNAD, *Das Wesen des Ursemitischen*, Leipzig, 1925.
[20] M. COHEN, in *Mém. de la Société de Linguistique de Paris*, 22 (1921), p. 242; E. ZYHLARZ, *Ursprung und Sprachcharakter des Altägyptischen*, esp. pp. 7. 72.

To sum up, the relationship of the Egyptian old perfective to a Semitic counterpart seems indisputable, and the Akkadian permansive illustrates that relationship at its closest; but the exact nature of the connexion has still to be determined.

OBS. 2. In transliterating the old perfective it seems advisable to place a dot before those endings which are written *after* the determinative and were, accordingly, regarded as suffixes (exx. *sḏm·kwi*, *sḏm·ti*), but to omit the dot elsewhere (exx. *sḏmw*, *sḏmt*); *sḏmt* may, however, be conveniently represented by *sḏm·t(i)*.

§ 310. Forms of the old perfective in mutable verbs.—In the normal forms no gemination is seen.

2ae gem. *ḳb·ti* '(it) is cool';[1] *wn* '(he) is existing'.[2] On the rare geminating forms see at the end of this section.

3ae inf. *h3·kwi* 'I went down';[3] *h3·ti* 'is (f.) fallen'.[4] The third weak radical is not written, and in 3rd m. forms like *hrw* 'were content'[5] the *w* is the personal ending; however, in the rarer alternative *y* (§ 309), the semi-vowel of the stem is probably combined with the ending. On the rare geminating forms see at the end of this section.

'Make' is written normally without *r*, exx. *ir·kwi* 'I acted'[6] (active, § 312, 1); *irw* '(they) being made'[7] (passive, § 312, 2). The exceptional writing is probably to be viewed as a geminating form *irr·kwi*, see below.

4ae inf. *ḫnt·ki* 'I sailed upstream';[8] *nḏr·ti* '(it) being held fast'.[9] In the 3rd masc. the ending is sometimes omitted, ex. *mini* 'had landed',[10] sometimes written as *y*, ex. *w3sy* '(it) was ruined'[11] (see above § 309). The form *špss·kw* 'I was wealthy'[12] probably belongs to the *4-lit.* verbs, see § 274.

anom. 'Give' shows forms both with and without *r*: 1st sing. *rdi·kwi*;[13] 3rd f. sing. [14] and [15] *rdi·ti*; but also 1st sing. *di·kw*;[16] 2nd m. sing. *di·t(i)*;[17] 3rd m. sing. (agreeing with f. plur. noun) *di(w)*;[18] 3rd m. plur. *diw*,[19] etc. An example of the geminating form, namely *dd·kwi* 'I am placed',[20] can be quoted from Dyn. XVIII; in Late Egyptian, curiously enough, the old perfective is always written with .

'Come' shows forms from both stems. From *iw*: 2nd m. sing. *iw·t(i)*;[21] 3rd m. sing. *iw*.[22] From *ii*: *iy·kwi*;[23] 3rd m. sing. *iw*,[24] *i(w)*;[25] 2nd plur. *i·tiwn(y)*.[26]

'Bring' shows no peculiarities, ex. *in·kwi*.[27]

The above enumeration of forms contains only two examples with gemination. Nevertheless, a few more geminating old perfectives may be quoted:—

2ae gem. 3rd f. sing. *gnn·ti* 'it is soft';[28] 3rd f. plur. *wnn·ti* 'they being'.[29]

[1] *Eb.* 36, 15; 37, 3. Sim. *T. Carn.* 5 (*ḳb·wyn*).
[2] *Leb.* 127; Brit. Mus. 574, 16. Sim. *Urk.* iv. 385, 3; *Puy.* 35 (*wn·kwi*).
[3] *Sh. S.* 24. 169.
[4] *Eb.* 51, 18.
[5] *Siut* I, 276. 282. 289.
[6] *Mill.* 2, 1.
[7] *Urk.* iv. 1159, 17. Sim. *ir*, Cairo 20543, 14.
[8] *BH.* i. 8, 11. 14.
[9] *Eb.* 109, 6.
[10] *Westc.* 7, 11.
[11] *Bersh.* ii. p. 25.
[12] Brit. Mus. 614, 11, qu. § 312, 4.
[13] *Sin.* B 286; *Sh. S.* 39. 177.
[14] *Eb.* 43, 17.
[15] *Sh. S.* 4, qu. § 322.
[16] *Urk.* iv. 472, 15.
[17] *Sin.* B 193.
[18] *Hamm.* 114, 12.
[19] *Hamm.* 114, 12. Sim. m. sing. *BH.* i. 26, 126.
[20] *Urk.* iv. 119, 10.
[21] *Sin.* B 257.
[22] *Sin.* B 265; *Pt.* 9; *Paheri* 3, reg. 1.
[23] *Westc.* 8, 12.
[24] Brit. Mus. 614, vert. 4.
[25] *Hamm.* 114, 11.
[26] *Five Th. T.* 27. 28.
[27] *Urk.* iv. 55, 13; 530, 12.
[28] *Eb.* 105, 2; 107, 15. 18.
[29] *Eb.* 110, 5, qu. § 326.

3ae inf. 1st sing. *h3j·kwi* 'I go down';[1] so, too, *irr·kwi* 'I acted' (see below) and *s33·ti* 'beware' (below § 338, 3). Exx. of 3rd m. formerly quoted (*h33*,[2] *prr*[3]) are really imperf. act. participles (§ 357).

anom. 1st sing. *dd·kwi*, see above.

The evidence is too slight to admit of certain conclusions, but it is remarkable that these geminating forms occur only (with the exception of *dd·kwi* just mentioned) in *generalizing*, *characterizing* passages, i. e. in passages of the kind where, as we shall see later, the participles (§ 355) and the *sḏm·f* form (§ 440) also display the gemination.

Exx. *irr·kwi m ˁḳ, nn ḏd·f* I used to act as one who entered without being announced, lit. without saying of him.[4] In the next line we read *prr·i ḥs·kwi* I used to go forth having been praised.

iw·i h33·kwi spw 3 r ḥḳ3t I go down (lit. am gone down) three times into the *ḥeḳat*-measure.[5]

There is thus a distinct possibility that the geminating old perfective may possess implications of *repetition* or *continuity*.

§ 311. **Meaning and use.**—There can be no doubt but that, in an early lost stage of the Egyptian language, the old perfective was a freely used narrative tense with both active and passive meanings. In historic times, however, and particularly in Middle Egyptian, this tense has become much restricted and specialized in its use.

First, it has been restricted and specialized in respect of *person*. The 1st person[6] alone is used independently in main clauses (§ 312); the 2nd and 3rd persons, except in some idiomatic phrases (§ 313), require a noun or pronoun, this usually preceding,[7] upon which to depend. It will be seen, as we proceed (§ 314), that the effect of the dependence just mentioned was to give to the old perfective more and more the status of an *adverb* (virtual adverb clause). Often it is added as a qualification to a noun or pronoun exercising some syntactic function in a main clause (§§ 314 foll.). When, on the other hand, the preceding noun or pronoun has no other function than to serve as subject of the old perfective, then that verb-form resembles an adverbial predicate, and all the rules for the sentence with adverbial predicate come into play. The resulting construction will in this book be termed 'the pseudo-verbal construction', and will be described in detail in the next Lesson.

Second, the old perfective has undergone restriction as regards *meaning*. Here we reach some very important rules. The old active-transitive employment as a past tense survives only in a few patently archaistic examples, though it is still common, both for past and for present reference, with the verb *rḫ* 'know'. *The old perfective from other transitive verbs has passive meaning*, ex. *h3b·kwi*

[1] *Rhind* 35. 37. 38.
[2] *Eb.* 42, 18, qu. § 323.
[3] *Eb.* 105, 11.
[4] Munich 3, 16; hardly to be rendered as LEF. *Gr.* § 346.
[5] *Rhind* 35.
[6] Exx. of plural are very rare; see *Urk.* iv. 244, 4.
[7] Rare exceptions, § 314, end.

'I have been sent'. With verbs of motion it describes, not so much the movement itself as *the position reached as the result of the movement*, ex. *hꜣ·kwi* 'I went down' to the mines. Lastly, it is frequent with *adjective-verbs* (ex. *wsr·kwi* 'I was powerful') and with some other intransitives (ex. *mꜣḫ* 'burned'). In all these cases the old perfective expresses a *state* or *condition* of things; as contrasted with the essentially dynamic suffix conjugation it is *static* or at least relatively so. The time-position indicated by the old perfective depends upon the context; but in its narrative uses it must be translated with the English past ('burned', 'was rewarded') or the English present perfect ('has perished', 'has been sent').[0]

OBS. The negative construction *n sḏm·n·f*, which serves to negate various verb-forms envisaging a protracted span of time, is often used in close association with the old perfective; see § 418. This is exactly what would be expected, seeing that the old perfective refers to a static, enduring condition of things.

§ 312. Independent use of the 1st person.

—1. The few surviving examples of the active-transitive use (already rare in Old Egyptian) are narrative in the 1st person.

Exx. *wd·ki rn·i r bw ḫry nṯr* I set my name at the place where the god was.[1]

ir·kwi mi sꜣ-tꜣ n smt I acted as the snake of the desert.[2]

ḏd·ki I said.[3]

Alone among verbs *rḫ* 'know' has a more frequent use in the old perfective, see below § 320.

Ex. *rḫ·kwi ꜣḫ·s n irr sy tp tꜣ* I knew that it (i.e. right) was profitable to him who performed it upon earth.[4]

2. With *passive* meaning from *transitive* verbs, in narrative. The *sḏm·n·f* form supplies the corresponding active.

Exx. *fḳꜣ·kwi m ꜥ-ḫnwti* I was rewarded in the audience-chamber.[5]

h(ꜣ)b·kw m ipt n sr mn I have been sent on a mission to the official so-and-so.[6]

3. With *verbs of motion*, in narrative.

Exx. *ḫnt·ki r int biꜣw n nbw* I sailed upstream to bring marvels of gold.[7]

ḫn·kwi r iw n Km-wr I stopped at an island of the Great-Black.[8]

4. With *adjective-verbs* and other intransitives.

Exx. *špss·kw ꜥꜣ·kw* I was wealthy and I was great.[9]

rs·kwi ḥr·s grḥ mi hrw I was watchful concerning it night and day alike.[10]

[0] Very rarely with Engl. present; with an adj. verb, *ḥtp·kwi* 'I am content', Brit. Mus. 101, qu. p. 348, top.

[1] Brit. Mus. 574. Sim. *rdi·ki* 'I caused', *Bersh.* i. 14, 2; *ib·kwi* 'I supposed', *Sh. S.* 58; *in·k(i)* 'I brought', *Ann.* 39, 189.

[2] *Mill.* 2, 1. Sim. Munich 3, 16, qu. § 310, end; *M. u. K.* 5, 10.

[3] *Sin.* B 45. 114.

[4] Turin 156, 3. Sim. *Urk.* iv. 835, 16, qu. § 187.

[5] Louvre C 174. Sim. *BH.* i. 8, 13; *Sin.* B 286. 291. 292. 293; *Urk.* iv. 2, 2. 4; 55, 13; 160, 6; 504, 13.

[6] *Urk.* iv. 1108.

[7] *BH.* i. 8, 11. Sim. *ib.* 15; *Sh. S.* 23-5; *Hamm.* 1, 7; *Urk.* iv. 363, 15; 390, 14.

[8] *Sin.* B 21.

[9] Brit. Mus. 614, 11. Sim. *ib.* 14; Louvre C 1, 14; *Urk.* iv. 505, 17; 749, 17.

[10] *Urk.* iv. 185 (*mi hrw* restored). Sim. *sḏr·kwi*, *Sin.* B 294.

Thus the independent use of the 1st person in main clauses illustrates the variety of meanings which the old perfective may convey, according as the verb in question is transitive or intransitive, a verb of motion or an adjective-verb (§ 311, end). The same variation of meaning runs through all uses of the old perfective, and cannot be specifically mentioned in each section.

§ 313. Exclamatory use of the 2nd and 3rd persons.—The 2nd and 3rd persons of the old perfective are used independently only in certain *greetings*, *exhortations* and the like. Note that it is just in these cases that Egyptian is wont to employ an adverbial phrase; see above § 153.

So in two phrases for 'beware', 'keep away'.

Exx. *ḥr·tỉwny r wnm ꜥdw* beware of (lit. be ye far from) eating the *ꜥadu*-fish.[1]

sꜣꜣ·tỉ ḥr sp n mḥt-ỉb beware of any occasion of neglectfulness.[2] Compare the use of *sꜣw*, below § 338, 2.

Similarly in certain greetings.

Exx. *ỉỉ·tỉ n·ỉ* welcome to me! Lit. thou art come to me.[3]

ḏd·tw n·f ỉw m ḥtp ỉn wrw nw ꜣbḏw there is said to him 'welcome!' by the great ones of Abydus.[4]

A greeting of similar appearance *ỉỉ·wy* 'welcome!'[5] is probably a participle followed by the admirative ending *-wy*; see below § 374.

Further examples of a similar kind:

snb·t(ỉ) (*sp* 2), *nḏs*, *r pr·k* farewell, farewell (lit. be thou healthy, twice), good fellow, to thy home![6]

ḥs·tỉ, *n rḫ·ỉ tnw ỉry* so please thee (lit. thou being praised), I do not know the number thereof.[7]

Here belongs the exceedingly common expression (above § 55) *ꜥnḫ(w)*, *wḏꜣ(w)*, *snb(w)* 'may he live, be prosperous, be healthy!' (conveniently abbreviated in translation as 'l. p. h.') found after the word *nb* '(my) lord'[8] and the names of honoured persons,[9] particularly in letters.[10] This formula is found also, but only sparsely before Dyn. XVII, following various terms connected with royalty, as *ỉty* 'sovereign',[11] *ḥm·f* 'His Majesty',[12] *pr-ꜥꜣ* 'the Great House', i.e. the royal palace,[13] *pr-nsw* 'the king's house',[14] *stp-sꜣ* 'the palace'.[15] Similar phrases are *ꜥnḫ(w) ḏt* 'may he live eternally!' placed after kings' names,[16] and *ꜥnḫ·tỉ* 'may she live!' after names of queens[17] and princesses.[18] For the use of *ꜥnḫ(w) ḏt*, etc. as object of *ỉr* 'make' see below § 378.

OBS. It is not impossible that some of these exclamatory old perfectives may be relics of fuller formulae. In all languages greetings and the like are apt to be cut down to the briefest form, ex. 'morning!' for 'I wish you a good morning!'

[1] *M. u. K.* 8, 6. Sim. *ib.* 8, 7. 8. 9. 'Keep away from (*r*)' *Destr.* 88; *Ḥarḥ.* 421; *Sm.* 18, 18. The sing. *ḥr·tỉ*, *Peas.* B 1, 306, *Sm.* 19, 2; BUDGE, p. 101, 7; *Destr.* 37.

[2] *Pt.* 154. Sim. *ib.* 260. 281. 300; *P. Pet.* 1116 A, 48. 122.

[3] *Urk.* iv. 611; 620, 5. Sim. *Ḥarḥ.* 195; Brit. Mus. 155, 20. Plural *ỉ·tỉwny*, *Five Th. T.* 27. 28.

[4] Brit. Mus. 614, vert. 4; Louvre C 3, 12.

[5] See further *ÄZ.* 29, 99.

[6] *Sh. S.* 158; sim. *P. Kah.* 4, 23. *Wn·tỉ* (*sp sn*), *Puy.* 54, lower half, centre.

[7] *Westc.* 9, 2–3.

[8] *P. Kah.* 27, 1. 11; 28, 2. 9, etc. It has now been proved (*JEA.* 31, 107) that in M.E. *nb* 'lord', without *·ỉ* 'my', is to be read, though L. E. has *pꜣy·ỉ nb* in similar contexts.

[9] *Sh. S.* 189; *BH.* i. 8, 12.

[10] *P. Kah.* 27, 13; 29, 31; 30, 25; 31, 48; 35, 24, etc. Fem. with *t* added, *ib.* 30, 1. 24.

[11] *Westc.* 8, 8; 9, 6; *Urk.* iv. 3, 5; 15, 9.

[12] *Urk.* iv. 8, 11; 9, 11; 80, 9. 17.

[13] *Westc.* 5, 2; 8, 10; an ex. in Dyn. XII, *P. Kah.* 16, 30.

[14] *Westc.* 4, 22; 6, 14.

[15] *Urk.* iv. 194, 1; 651, 1; 1021, 3.

[16] GAUTHIER, *Livre des Rois*, i. 223, 266; ii. 198. The 2nd pers. in addresses, *Urk.* iv. 564, 10; 580, 14.

[17] GAUTHIER, *op. cit.* i. 250; ii. 163. 193.

[18] GAUTHIER, *op. cit.* i. 337; ii. 341.

§ 314. Use of the old perfective as a clause of circumstance.—A common adverbial use of the old perfective is as a *virtual clause of circumstance* (see above § 213). In this employment, which is frequent with all persons, the old perfective links up with some preceding noun or pronoun of the main clause, and serves to describe or qualify it in some way.

Exx. *spr·n wḏ pn r·i ꜥḥꜥ·kwi m-ḥr-ib whwt·i* this command reached me (as) I stood in the midst of my tribe.[1]

ir·n·i hrw 3 wꜥ·kwi I spent three days alone, lit. I being alone.[2]

rdi·i rḫ·k tw, iw·k m ss, ḫpr·t(i) m nty n mꜣ·t(w)·f I will cause thee to know thyself, thou being as ashes, having become as one who is not seen.[3]

wꜣḥ ꜥnḫ·ṯn tp tꜣ wḏꜣ·tiwny your life shall be long upon earth, you being prosperous.[4]

wḏꜣ ḥm·f ḥr wrryt nt ḏꜥm, sꜥbw m ḫkrw·f nw rꜥ-ḫt His Majesty set out on a chariot of gold, adorned (lit. he being adorned) in his panoply of war.[5]

iswt·n ii·t(i) ꜥḏ·t(i) our crew returned safely, lit. it being safe.[6]

n sp mꜣ·k iw pn, ḫpr(w) m nwy never shalt thou see this island (again), it having become sea.[7]

As our translations show, the old perfective may be rendered in English in many ways: by a predicatival adjective ('alone') or a participial construction ('you being prosperous', 'it having become'), by a clause of circumstance ('as I stood'), or by an adverb ('safely').[7a] It may even be opportune at times to render it by a main clause.

Ex. *pt ḥr·k, di·t(i) m mstpt, iḥw ḥr itḥ·k* heaven is over thee, thou art placed in the hearse, oxen drag thee.[8]

Without a pronoun to lean upon the old perf. *di·t(i)* could not here have been used. Rare cases occur, however, where the pronoun does not precede, but *follows.*[8a] In *ḫnt(y) pḥ·n·f Wꜣwꜣt* 'sailing upstream he reached Wawat'[8b] *ḫnt(y)* is shown to be old perf. by the parallel elsewhere ...;[8c] conversely, *ḫnt·kwi* here is shown by *ḫnt(y)* to be circumstantial, though as a 1st pers. it might well have been a main verb (§ 312, 3).[8d]

§ 315. The old perfective qualifying the object of certain verbs.—A special case of the construction described in the last section is the use with such verbs as *gmi* 'find', *mꜣꜣ* 'see', and more rarely *rdi* 'cause', with its imperative *imi* (§ 336).

Exx. *gm·n·i sw rḫ(w) st* I found that he knew it, lit. I found him he knowing it.[9]

[1] *Sin.* B 199–200.

[2] *Sh. S.* 41. Sim. *T. Carn.* 3; 3rd m., *wꜥy*, *P. Kah.* 28, 24.

[3] *Sh. S.* 72–3.

[4] *Urk.* iv. 66. Sim. *P. Kah.* 31, 7.

[5] *Urk.* iv. 657. Sim. *ib.* 758, 16; 765, 15; 766, 1; 879, 8; *Sin.* B 272; *BH.* i. 25, 8; *Kopt.* 8, 11.

[6] *Sh. S.* 7. For *ii·ti* see § 322.

[7] *Sh. S.* 154. Sim. *BH.* i. 25, 37.

[7a] Occasionally best rendered as a clause of *result*, ex. *smnw* 'so that it was established', MAR. *Karn.* 37, 41. See further *Verbum* ii. § 3; *JEA.* 22, 36.

[8] *Sin.* B 193–4.

[8a] LEF. in *Misc. Greg.* 129.

[8b] Tomb in Moꜥalla, ed. VANDIER. Sim. *pr(y)*, *Urk.* iv, 54, 15; 59, 13.

[8c] ANTHES, 14, 6. Prob. sim. 1st plur., LUTZ, 66, 2.

[8d] In most cases the choice between main and circumstantial use is disputable. ALLEN in *AJSL.* 44, 130: 49, 160 unduly favours the latter.

[9] *Sh. S.* 157. Sim. *P. Kah.* 6, 13. 14; 30, 30; *BH.* i. 25, 39; 26, 133; *Westc.* 12, 20.

m mrr·k mꜣ·i snb·kwi so truly as thou wishest to see me in health.[1]

di·n·i sw sš(w) ḥr šnwy·i I caused it (the dust) to be strewn on my hair.[2]

imi rn·i nfr(w) m niwt·k cause my name to be fair in thy city.[3]

With the passives of these verbs, it is of course the subject, not the object, which is qualified.

Ex. *gm·n·tw nꜣy·sn irp wꜣḥw m nꜣy·sn nmw* their wine was found lying (lit. placed) in their presses.[4]

The verbs *gmi* and *mꜣꜣ* are those whose object, as we have seen, is not seldom qualified by *ḥr* + infinitive (§ 304, 1), or alternatively by the *śḏm·f* form (§ 213). In both these constructions, however, the qualification consists of an *action*; with the old perfective it consists rather of a *state* or *condition*.

§ 316. The old perfective qualifying the subject of certain verbs.—A second special case of the construction described in § 314 is the use of the old perfective to qualify the subject of verbs like *wrš* 'spend all day', *sḏr* 'spend all night', 'lie',[5] and more rarely *ḏr* 'end', *pri* 'come forth'.

Exx. *wrš·s sḏr·t(i) ḥḳr·t(i)* she spends all day lying hungry.[6]

ḏr·in·f ḥms(w) at last he sat down, lit. he ended being seated.[7]

prr ib th(w) ḥr·s the heart becomes (lit. comes forth) confused through it.[8]

For a corresponding use with *ḥr* + infinitive see above § 304, 1.

§ 317. The old perfective in virtual relative clauses.—Like the *śḏm·f* and other narrative verbal forms (§ 196), the old perfective is often appended to a noun with the meaning of an epithet, i.e. as a virtual relative clause. The noun, as we should expect, is usually *undefined*.

Exx. *šʿt ist snwḫ·ti ḥr mrḥt* an old book boiled with oil.[9]

wrrt bꜣk·ti m nbw a chariot wrought in gold.[10]

Instances in which the antecedent is *defined* are much rarer. This is, however, regularly the case with *dmḏ* 'entire' and *tm* 'complete'; here again the old perfective may be adverbial, the phrases *r ḏr·f, mi ḳd·f* (§ 100) suggesting that the Egyptians conceived of such notions as 'entire' adverbially.

Exx. *psḏt dmḏ·ti* the entire ennead (cycle of nine) of the gods.[11]

irt tm·ti the complete eye.[12]

[1] *Peas.* B 1, 78. Sim. *Th. T. S.* ii. 11.

[2] *Sin.* B 201; *šnwy·i* is emended. Sim. *Pt.* 162; *Rec.* 2, 115, 176.

[3] *Sh. S.* 159. Sim. Vienna 142, qu. Erm. *Gramm.*[3] § 335.

[4] *Urk.* iv. 687.

[5] Exx. *Adm.* 7, 11. 14; Brit. Mus. 159, 11, qu. § 203, 6; *Menthuw.* 11; *M.u.K.* 7, 5.

[6] *P. Kah.* 5, 33.

[7] *Leb.* 75. Sim. *Urk.* v. 128, 9 = 130, 7.

[8] *Eb.* 102, 5. Sim. *ib.* 99, 20–1; 100, 21; 101, 6; *Peas.* B 1, 113.

[9] *Eb.* 49, 1. Sim. *ib.* 52, 21; 73, 6; 76, 15; 97, 18. 19.

[10] *Urk.* iv. 663. Sim. *ib.* 174, 14; 667, 2; 669, 6. 15; *Westc.* 9, 10; 11, 17–18.

[11] *Rec.* 39, 120. Sim. *Hamm.* 114, 11 (*dmd*); *Bersh.* i. 14, 4. 10 (*dmdt*).

[12] *Eb.* 99, 20. Sim. *ib.* 99, 14. 18 (*tm*); Brit. Mus. 580 (*tmw*). See *Verbum* ii. § 1004.

An unexpected example with a defined antecedent might be: *ptr wrt r ꜥbt ḫꜣt·i m tꜣ ms·kwi im·f* what is a greater thing than that my corpse should be interred (lit. the uniting of my corpse) in the land in which I was born.[1]

However, a recent conjecture[2] regards *tꜣ* here as equivalent to 'Egypt' and renders '. . . . . in Egypt, seeing that I was born in it.'

[1] *Sin.* B 159–60.

[2] *JEA.* 22, 37.

§ 318. **Other uses of the old perfective.**—In all other uses of the old perfective it is preceded by a nominal or pronominal subject of its own. Most of these uses will be dealt with in the next Lesson, but a few will remain over to be discussed under the heading 'compound narrative forms' (Lesson XXXII).

VOCABULARY

wꜣi be far; with *r*, fall into (bad condition, etc.)

wꜥi be alone.

wrš spend all day, pass time.

bꜣk work (trans. and intr.).

pḏ, var. *pd*, stretch; adj. wide.

nḥb unite, link together; equip with (*m*).

ḥꜥi rejoice.

ḥr be far from (*r*).

sꜣḥ endow with (*m*).

sꜥḥꜥ erect.

grg furnish with (*m*).

dhn promote, appoint.

ꜥꜣt precious stone.

wꜣw wave.

var. *wꜣs* ruin.

wrrt chariot.

mꜣst lap.

šs cord.

nb nswt tꜣwy lord of the Thrones of the Two Lands, a common epithet of the god Amen-Rēꜥ.

EXERCISE XXII

(*a*) *Translate into English*:

[1] An attitude of mourning.

[1] The reference is to a foundation ceremony.

(*b*) *Write in hieroglyphs*:

(1) I have given to thee all lands and all foreign countries under thy feet, thou living and enduring like Rēʿ for ever. (2) His Majesty endowed him with a tomb in front of (*m-ḫft-ḥr n*) his city, it being equipped with fields, and furnished with slaves, male and female. (3) Thou arisest in the sky new and young every day. (4) Welcome ye to the temple of your city god. (5) They brought their tribute on their back(s), a chariot wrought in gold and precious stones without end. (6) They found this temple fallen into ruin. (7) I was precious (*iḳr*) in his sight (lit. on his heart). (8) He was found spending the day eating and drinking.

LESSON XXIII

THE PSEUDO-VERBAL CONSTRUCTION

§ 319. The name **pseudo-verbal construction** has been chosen, for want of a better, to bring under one common head those sentences or clauses in which either the old perfective or *ḥr* (or *m* or *r*) + infinitive serves as predicate to a preceding noun or pronoun. The following are some of the commoner models:—

mšʿ ḥr prt the army {goes / went / going} forth, lit. {(is) / (was) / (being)} on going forth.

mšʿ pr(w) the army {is gone / went / being gone} forth.

iw·f ḥr prt he {goes / went / going} forth.

mk sw pr(w) behold, he is gone forth.

wnn·f ḥr prt he will go forth, lit. be on going forth.

These examples have the common characteristic that, while expressing the meaning of ordinary verbal sentences (§ 27), they conform to the pattern of the sentence with adverbial predicate (Lesson X). The name pseudo-verbal here given to them is strictly accurate in the case of *ḥr*+infinitive, since this, while conveying the signification of a narrative verb-form, is in fact an adverbial phrase (§ 28). With the old perfective the designation pseudo-verbal is more open to criticism. It is true, however, that in Middle Egyptian the old perfective was no longer a narrative verb-form in the full sense, but was mainly reserved for employments of an adverbial kind (§ 311). Nor can it be denied that, in all the above examples, the subject is introduced in exactly the way it would be if the predicate were adverbial. Thus there can be little doubt that the old perfective here is a virtual clause of circumstance used as predicate; cf. § 215.

Under the same heading we shall include the sentences having *m*+infinitive (§ 304, 2) or *r*+infinitive (§ 304, 3) as predicate; these will be treated at the end of the Lesson. We shall postpone, on the other hand, certain constructions which agree with those here considered in having as predicate the old perfective or *ḥr*+infinitive, but in which auxiliary verbs other than *ỉw* or *wnn* are used or in which *wnn* appears in verb-forms not yet described; see §§ 396, 2; 470–1; 482.

§ 320. The respective meanings of *ḥr*+infinitive and of the old perfective.—In discussing the sentence with adverbial predicate we saw that variations of tense and mood, if indicated at all, were indicated by the various particles which might be used (*mk*, *ỉsṯ*, etc.), or by the various forms of the verb 'to be' which might be chosen (*ỉw*, *wn*, *wnn*, §§ 118–9). The same holds good of the pseudo-verbal construction, this being, in fact, no more than an elaboration of the ordinary sentence with adverbial predicate. The pseudo-verbal construction possesses, however, a further means of indicating varieties of temporal *nuance* in the choice between *ḥr*+infinitive and the old perfective. These two forms of predicate must be discussed together, and apart from *m* or *r*+infinitive, because they often occur in parallelism with one another, and are indeed to a large extent mutually complementary. This complementary character of *ḥr*+infinitive and the old perfective has been observed already in the employment of both to express a concomitant circumstance appended, as an adverbial qualification, to the subject or object of a preceding main clause (§§ 304, 1; 314–5).

The difference between *ḥr*+infinitive, on the one hand, and the old perfective, on the other, may best be summed up by saying that the former is dynamic, active, and expressive of *action*, while the latter is static, passive, and expressive of *condition*. The meanings conveyed in each case vary according to the nature of the particular verb in question; the following table will serve to illustrate the point in detail.

Nature of verb	*ḥr* + infinitive	Old perfective
TRANSITIVES	*actively* and stressing the action itself. Exx. *wnm* 'eats';[1] *gmḥ* 'beholds';[2] *šms* 'accompanied';[3] *snḫt* 'made victorious'.[4] Note especially: *rḫ* 'sought to know'.[9] *ḏd* 'says'.[12] *mn* 'suffers from', trans. not adj. verb.[13]	*passively* and stating the result of the action. Exx. *ḏbꜣw* 'is stopped up';[5] *rdỉ·t(ỉ)* 'is placed', 'has been placed';[6] *ꜣtp·kwỉ* 'am loaded';[7] *dỉw* 'were placed'.[8] Exceptionally, active: *rḫ* 'knows';[10] *rḫ·tỉ* 'knew' (f.)[11] [*cf.* *ḏd·kỉ* 'I said' above § 312]
INTRANSITIVES	expressing action as in occurrence, *dynamically*.	expressing action as achieved, *statically*.
1. vbs. of motion.	emphasize the movement itself. Exx. *sḫs* 'flee';[14] *sḫsḫ* 'ran';[15] *mnmn* shook'.[16] Note especially: *ꜥḥꜥ* 'rise up'.[21]	emphasize the result of the movement. *hꜣw* 'is come';[17] *ỉỉ* 'is come';[18] *pr* 'went forth';[19] *hꜣꜣ·kwỉ* 'I go down'.[20] *ꜥḥꜥ* 'standing';[22] *ꜥḥꜥ·kwỉ* 'I stood'.[23]
2. adjective-vbs.	rare, expressing the process of becoming. Ex. *mꜣwy* 'renews itself'.[24]	very common, expressing the state of being. Exx. *nfr·t(ỉ)* 'is happy';[25] *tꜣ·t(ỉ)* 'is hot';[26] *ḥḳr·kỉ* 'am hungry';[27] *ḫmw* 'was hot'.[28]
3. others.	when the *active* aspect predominates. Exx. *ꜣḳ* 'is perishing';[29] *spr* 'make supplication';[30] *mdt* 'was speaking';[31] *ḫpr* 'come into being',[32] 'came about'.[33] So too with verbs expressing emotion and the gestures connected therewith. Exx. *nhm* 'jubilate';[38] *nmỉ* 'shouted';[39] *ỉmt* 'mourn';[40] *snḏ* 'fears'.[41]	when the *statical* aspect predominates. Exx. *ꜣḳ* 'is perished';[34] *mn* 'remained';[35] *gr* 'is silent';[36] *ḫpr* 'is become'.[37] So too with verbs expressing emotion and the gestures connected therewith. Exx. *ḥꜥw* 'is in joy';[42] *snm* 'are sad';[43] *rmw* 'are in tears';[44] *snḏw* 'was afraid';[45] *hr·tỉ* 'art content'.[46]

As the translations given in the table show, the tense to be assigned to these two kinds of predicate is largely dependent on extraneous causes—the time of the context generally, or else the particle or auxiliary used to introduce the subject. Nevertheless it is clear that the old perfective tends to have past meaning, while *ḥr*+infinitive is more appropriate to the present or relatively present. The reason is that a condition, such as is expressed by the old perfective, usually implies an antecedent action conducing to that condition. 'Being come' is the result of 'having come', and it is legitimate to translate in either way. Similarly when a man says 'I am sent' he means that he 'has been sent'.

The variation in meaning between *ḥr rḫ* 'sought to know' (very rare) and *rḫ(w)* 'knows', 'knew' (old perfective) is interesting; we shall see (§ 414, 4) that the *sḏm·n·f* form of this verb is employed in the meaning 'knows' or 'knew', cf. *novi* in Latin, ἔγνωκα in Greek, while the *sḏm·f* form tends to mean 'to obtain knowledge of', 'learn'.[47] See too §§ 367, end; 389, 3; 455, 1.

Some comment is needed in regard to the adjective-verbs. *Whenever a seemingly adjectival predicate follows its subject, it is not the adjective itself, but the old perfective of the adjective-verb.* This is proved by examples like the following, where the endings are written out in full.

ṯꜣw·k n ꜥnḫ nḏmw m šrt·ỉ thy breath of life is sweet in my nostril.[48]

ỉw ḥnksyt·k nfr·tỉ m-bꜣḥ Ptḥ-Skr thy hair is beautiful in the presence of Ptah-Sokar.[49]

It seems impossible to detect any difference of meaning between real adjectival predicates (§ 137) and adjective-verbs in the old perfective; see § 374.

[1] *Westc.* 7, 2.
[2] *Adm.* 7, 12.
[3] Louvre C 12, 12.
[4] *Urk.* iv. 657, 9.
[5] *Pt.* 22.
[6] *Sh. S.* 4.
[7] *Peas.* B 1, 70.
[8] *Hamm.* 114, 12.
[9] *Mett.* 190.
[10] *Westc.* 7, 4; *Urk.* iv. 751, 15.
[11] *Urk.* iv. 363, 6.
[12] *Leb.* 35; *Adm.* 2, 1.
[13] *Eb.* 25, 4; 32, 21.
[14] *Adm.* 8, 13.
[15] *Urk.* iv. 894, 8.
[16] *Sh. S.* 60, qu. § 322.
[17] *Sin.* B 168.
[18] *Th. T. S.* ii. 12. 23.
[19] *Sh. S.* 32; *Urk.* iv. 654, 8.
[20] *Rhind* 35, qu. § 310, end.
[21] Cf. *m ꜥḥꜥ*, *ÄZ.* 37, 97.
[22] *Leb.* 144.
[23] *Sin.* B 1.
[24] *Pt.* 9.
[25] *Sin.* B 76.
[26] *Leb.* 90.
[27] *Th. T. S.* ii. 11.
[28] *Sin.* B 22.
[29] *Pt.* 12, qu. § 322.
[30] *Peas.* B 2, 113.
[31] *Sin.* B 2.
[32] *Adm.* p. 101.
[33] *BH.* i. 8, 16.
[34] *Pt.* 12.
[35] *Sin.* B 138.
[36] *Pt.* 13.
[37] *Pt.* 24; *Adm.* 8, 4.
[38] *Bersh.* i. 15, top.
[39] *Sin.* B 141.
[40] *Adm.* 5, 5. 6.
[41] *Adm.* 7, 6.
[42] *Bersh.* i. 15, bottom.
[43] *Adm.* 2, 5.
[44] *Adm.* 5, 5.
[45] *Sin.* B 215. Sim. *sdꜣ* 'trembling', *Urk.* iv. 616, 8.
[46] *P. Kah.* 13, 24.
[47] E.g. *Peas.* B 1, 287. Sim. infinitive, *BH.* i. 29.
[48] *Urk.* iv. 944. Sim. LAC. *TR.* 88, 5.
[49] BUDGE, p. 386. Sim. *Urk.* iv. 1153, 5.

§ 321. *ḥr* with omitted infinitive for 'says', 'said'.—*Dd* is often idiomatically omitted after *ḥr*.

Ex. *s nb ḥr : n rḫ·n ḫprt ḫt t3* every man says: We do not know what may happen throughout the land.[1]

§ 322. The pseudo-verbal construction without introductory word.—The subject can stand without introduction only when it is a noun, a pronoun needing the support of a particle or of an auxiliary verb. This use is common in descriptive and narrative passages.

Exx. .... *mk pḥ·n·n ḫnw .... ḥ3tt rdì·t(ì) ḥr t3 .... s nb ḥr ḥpt sn-nw·f* behold, we have reached home ...... the prow-rope has been placed on land ...... every man is embracing his fellow.[2]

ìrty nḏsw, ʿnḫwy ìmrw, pḥty ḥr 3ḳ n wrd-ìb the eyes are dim, the ears dull, the strength is perishing through weariness of heart.[3]

ḥ3ty nb m3ḫ(w) n·ì, ḥmwt ṯ3yw ḥr ʿʿì every heart burned for me, women and men murmured.[4]

ḫtw ḥr gmgm, t3 ḥr mnmn the trees cracked and the earth shook.[5]

In three of the four examples the old perfective and *ḥr*+infinitive are seen in parallelism;[6] the first two are drawn from descriptions or characterizations relating to present time, the last two from narratives of past events.

The pseudo-verbal construction without introductory word is rather rare in main clauses, since here *ìw*, or some particle like *mk*, is usually employed to lend importance to the statement. Nevertheless, instances may be quoted even at the beginning of speeches.

Exx. Thereupon I said to him: *n-sw-bìt Sḥtp-ìb-Rʿ wḏ3w r 3ḫt* King Seḥetepibrēʿ has gone to the horizon, i.e. has died.[7]

This peasant said: *ḫ3w n ʿḥʿw ḥr s3t n·f* the measurer of the corn-heaps pilfers for himself.[8]

On the other hand, just as in the sentence with adverbial predicate, the normal way of expressing a *virtual clause of circumstance* (§§ 117. 214) is to leave the nominal subject without introduction.

Exx. *nʿt m ḫd ìn ḥm·f, ìb·f 3w* then His Majesty fared downstream, his heart rejoicing, lit. being extended.[9]

.... *wḏ3 ḥm·f ḥr wrryt nt ḏʿm ...... ìt·f ʾImn ḥr snḫt ʿwy·f* His Majesty went forth on a chariot of gold .... his father Amūn making victorious his arms.[10]

Sometimes a virtual clause of *time* (§ 214) assumes the same form.

[1] *Adm.* 2, 3. Sim. *ib.* 2, 7; 6, 4. 13; *Urk.* iv. 17, 10. 12.

[2] *Sh. S.* 1–5. Sim. old perf., *ib.* 32. 101–2; *Leb.* 63. 117. 118. 120; *Peas.* B 1, 188. 193.

[3] *Pt.* 11–2. Sim. *ḥr*+inf., *Sin.* B 194; *Leb.* 105. 112; *Peas.* B 1, 98 foll.; *Hamm.* 114, 8.

[4] *Sin.* B 131–2. Sim. old perf., *ib.* 93. 133. 138. 250; *BH.* i. 8, 15; *Hamm.* 114, 12; *Urk.* iv. 59, 16.

[5] *Sh. S.* 59–60. Sim. *Hamm.* 114, 11; *Sin.* B 141. 176. 228–30. 253–4. 301–4; *Urk.* iv. 60, 1; 659, 5.

[6] So too in narrative *Bersh.* i. 14, 5–6.

[7] *Sin.* B 36 = R 59–60. Sim. *Westc.* 5, 19; *Urk.* iv. 656, 15.

[8] *Peas.* B 1, 104–5.

[9] *Urk.* iv. 5. Sim. *ib.* 28, 10; 113, 6. 8; 134, 15; 365, 2; *Sin.* B 162; *BH.* i. 26, 177–8; *Siut* 1, 271; *Hamm.* 47, 13.

[10] *Urk.* iv. 657, 5–9. Sim. *ib.* 1160, 8; *Westc.* 7, 16.

Ex. *m hrww šmw, pt tꜣ·t(i)* on days of summer, when the sky is hot.[1]

§ 323. The pseudo-verbal construction introduced by *iw*.—As in the sentence with adverbial predicate (§ 117), a difference of usage occurs according as the subject is nominal or pronominal.

In *main clauses* this construction is common alike with nominal and with pronominal subject. The following examples illustrate its use with *ḥr* + infinitive and with old perfective, with suffix subject and with noun subject, for present time and for past time.

iw·i ḥr rdit pꜣy·i mty n sꜣ n sꜣ·i I am (herewith) giving my (office of) regulator of a (priestly) order to my son.[2]

iw srw ḥr rdit n·k the nobles give to thee.[3]

iw·sn ḥr ifd m gbgbyt they fled headlong, lit. in precipitation.[4]

iw mšꜥ pn n nsw ḥr mꜣꜣ this army of the king looked on.[5]

iw·k swt sꜣ·t(i) m t·k nay, but thou art sated with thy bread.[6]

iw niwt rḫ(w) st im·i the city knows it of me.[7]

iw·i bs·kw r sḏm sḏmt I was admitted to hear what is heard.[8]

iw nṯr pn wḏꜣ(w) m ḥtp this god proceeded in peace.[9]

In virtual clauses of *circumstance* or *time* the pseudo-verbal construction with *iw* is common when the subject is a suffix-pronoun, but not when the subject is a noun (§§ 117. 214).

Exx. *sḏm·n·i ḫrw·f, iw·f ḥr mdt* I heard his voice as he was speaking.[10]

Has His Majesty gone on another road, *iw·f wꜣ(w) r snḏ n·n* having fallen (lit. he is gone) into fear of us?[11]

So too in *virtual relative* clauses (§ 196).

Ex. .... *iw wn nḏs .... iw·f ḥr wnm t 500 ..... iw·f rḫ(w) ṯs tp ḥsḳ* there is a commoner ..... who eats 500 loaves ..... and who knows how to join together a head that has been cut off.[12]

Whereas with pronominal subject, as explained in § 116, a supporting word like *iw* is indispensable, such is not the case when the subject is a noun, so that *iw* is then, as a rule, dispensed with (§ 322). Nevertheless, *iw* is found before a nominal subject in certain sentences which approximate to clauses of *circumstance* or *time*, while standing forth with a certain independence of their own.

[1] *Leb.* 88. Sim. *ib.* 90.

[2] *P. Kah.* 11, 17–8. Sim. *ib.* 5, 6–7; 12, 7–10; *Meir* iii. 23.

[3] *Peas.* B 1, 301.

[4] *Urk.* iv. 658. Sim. *Sebekkhu* 3; Louvre C 11, 5. 8; *Urk.* iv. 894, 7. 8. 10.

[5] *Hamm.* 110, 5–6. Sim. *ib.* 4; *ÄZ.* 45, Pl. VIII, A.

[6] *Peas.* B 1, 124–5. Sim. *ib.* B 1, 159. 260; 1st pers., *Leb.* 127; *P. Kah.* 13, 26. 27; *Peas.* B 1, 15–6; 3rd pers., *P. Kah.* 29, 17; *Urk.* iv. 693, 11; *Arm.* 103, 3.

[7] *Urk.* iv. 437. Sim. *ib.* 58, 7; 339, 16; 773, 14; *Eb.* 36, 16; 37, 16.

[8] *ÄZ.* 47, Pl. 1, 8. Sim. *Urk.* iv. 894, 2.

[9] Mar. *Abyd.* ii. 29, 16. Sim. *Sin.* B 307.

[10] *Sin.* B 2. Sim. *Th. T. S.* iii. 26, 7; *Pt.* 71; *Westc.* 5, 5.

[11] *Urk.* 651. Sim. Leyd. V 88, 11, qu. Exerc. XXVI, (*a*).

[12] *Westc.* 6, 26–7, 4. Sim. *Herdsm.* 2.

So, for example, when a strong *contrast* is marked:

Exx. Shall our vanguard fight, *iw nꜣ n pḥwy ꜥḥꜥ ꜥꜣ m ꜥrn, n ꜥḥꜣ·n·sn* while the rearguard stops here in Aruna and does not fight?[1]

I was a Ḥeḳayeb (personal name) of danger abroad, *iw s nb ḥr ḫtm ꜥꜣ·f* while every man was shutting his door.[2]

Or again, when characters of importance, such as medical symptoms, are being described.

Ex. *ir ḫꜣ·k s ḥr mn r-ib·f, iw ꜥt·f nbt dns·ti r·f* if thou examine a man suffering from his stomach, while every limb of his is too heavy for him.[3]

The following example is perhaps best translated as a clause of *result*:[3a]

If thou drinkest with a drunkard, *šsp·k iw ib·f ḥtpw* take thou (so that) his heart is content.[4]

Obs. For the participial form of this construction, employing participles from the stem *wnn*, see below § 396, 2. For *iw* followed by an adjective verb see § 467.

§ 324. The pseudo-verbal construction introduced by non-enclitic particles.—It is hardly necessary to discuss the exact nuances of meaning in the sentences thus obtained; reference must be made to the corresponding section of the Lesson on the sentences with adverbial predicate (§ 119), as well as to Lesson XVIII on the particles.

Exx. *mk wi ḥr spr n·k, n sḏm·n·k st* behold, I make supplication to thee, and thou dost not hear it.[5]

mk tw ḥr ḏd behold, one is saying.[6]

mtn bꜣ·i ḥr tht·i behold, my soul wrongs me.[7]

mk tw nḫt·(ti) wsr·t(i) behold, thou art strong and influential.[8]

mtn nb ḫt sḏr(w) ib(w) behold, the (former) possessor of wealth passes the night thirsty.[9]

isk wi ḥr irt n·ṯ nyny lo, I do thee obeisance.[10]

ist ḥm·f ḥr dhn wrw m mꜣwt lo, His Majesty appointed chieftains anew.[11]

ist wi ꜥḥꜥ·kwi sḏm·n·i lo, I was standing and I heard; *or*, as I was standing, I heard.[12]

ist ib·k ḥꜥ(w) ḫft irr·i lo, (*or* while) thy heart rejoiced in accordance with my doing.[13]

ti sw hꜣb(w) r ḥwt ḫꜣswt now he had been sent to smite the foreign countries.[14]

nḥmn sꜣ·f ꜥḳ(w) r ꜥḥ assuredly his son has entered into the palace.[15]

[1] *Urk.* iv. 650, 5–7.
[2] *JEA* 16, 195, 9.
[3] *Eb.* 42, 18. Sim. *ib.* 37, 18.
[3a] See above, p. 240, n. 7a.
[4] *Pr.* 1, 9.
[5] *Peas.* B 2, 113–4. Sim. *Urk.* iv. 509, 17.
[6] *P. Kah.* 28, 36. Sim. *Meir* i. 3, bottom.
[7] *Leb.* 11. Sim. *Peas.* R 61; *Adm.* 7, 6; 8, 10. 12. 13.
[8] *Peas.* B 1, 116. Sim. *ib.* 219–20; 1st pers. sing., *Herdsm.* 1; *Urk.* v. 40, 1; 3rd pers., *Westc.* 12, 22–3; *Peas.* B 1, 76–7; 1st pers. plur., *Westc.* 10, 5.
[9] *Adm.* 7, 10. Sim. *ib.* 7, 1. 4. 8; *Peas.* B 1, 130; *Urk.* iv. 654, 14.
[10] *Urk.* iv. 347, 11.
[11] *Urk.* iv. 663. Sim. *ib.* 365, 6; 716, 14.
[12] *Sin.* R 24–5. Sim. present time, Budge, p. 168, 7.
[13] *Urk.* iv. 272, 10. Sim. *ib.* 662, 8; 692, 15. Present time, *ib.* 502, 16.
[14] *Sin.* R 13.
[15] *Sin.* R 70.

Note, too, with *ḥꜣ* and *ḥw ꜣ* 'would that' (§ 238):

ḥꜣ tꜣ mḥ(w) m mityw·f would that the earth were full of his equals![1]

ḥw ꜣ ṯw ip·t(i) would that thou wert found perfect![2]

§ 325. The pseudo-verbal construction with *ink pw*, etc.—The phrase *ink pw*, which we found (§ 190, 1) before the *śḏm·n·f* form at the *beginning of narratives* or in *answers to questions*, occurs also in the pseudo-verbal construction. Examples are, however, rare.

Exx. *ink pw ḥr nkꜣy m ḫprt* I am meditating upon what has happened, lit. it is I-am-on-meditating, etc.[3]

I said to him: *ink pw hꜣ·kwi r biꜣ* I went down (lit. it is I-went-down) to the mine-country.[4]

In these examples *pw* is subject, and the remaining words constitute a noun clause serving as predicate; one may compare the French *c'est que*.

Sometimes a noun takes the place of *ink*.

Exx. *Rꜥ pw ḥr mdt ḥnꜥ 'Imy-wḏ* it happened (lit. was) that Rēꜥ was at variance (lit. speaking) with the Imy-wedj serpent.[5]

s pw wn(w), Ḫw-n-'Inpw·rn·f there was a man whose name was Khunanūp; lit. it is a-man-existed.[6] Beginning of a story.

See too an example with *r*+infinitive § 332, end.

Rather similarly also in glosses; compare § 189, 1.

Ex. *ir ḫnws-ib, tꜣw pw ḫns(w) ḥr ḥꜣty·f* as for *ḫnws* of heart, this means (lit. is) that heat has spread (*ḫns*) over his heart.[7]

§ 326. The pseudo-verbal construction with *wnn*.—As in the sentence with adverbial predicate (§ 118), so too in the pseudo-verbal construction *wnn·f* is used to indicate *future* time.

Exx. *wnn·k ḥr rdit di·tw n·f ꜥḳw* thou shalt cause (lit. shalt be on causing) provisions to be given to him.[8]

wnn·i wḏꜥ·kw ḥnꜥ·f I will be judged together with him.[9]

wnn ms nty im ꜥḥꜥ(w) m wiꜣ nay, but he who is yonder shall stand in the bark (of the sun-god).[10]

In similar examples with *past* meaning it is to be presumed that the *śḏm·f* form of *wnn* (if such it be, rather than *śḏm·n·f*, § 413) possesses an implication of *continuity*.

Exx. *mt wnn·f wꜥr(w)* behold, he was fled.[11]

nnk tm, wnn·i wꜥ·kwi to me belonged the universe (when) I was alone.[12] *Wnn·i* here introduces a virtual clause of time (§ 212).

[1] Brit. Mus. 562.

[2] LAC. *TR.* 86, 110.

[3] *Adm.* p. 105.

[4] *Sh. S.* 89.

[5] *ÄZ.* 57, 3*.

[6] *Peas.* R 1. Sim. *Westc.* 6, 5 in the answer to a question.

[7] *Eb.* 101, 21. Sim. *Urk.* v. 53, 1–2, qu. § 326.

[8] *Peas.* B 1, 83. Sim. *Urk.* iv. 225, 13, qu. § 253; 650, 5, qu. § 492, 6; 1111, 15; BUDGE, p. 152, 11.

[9] Cairo 20458, *b* 4.

[10] *Leb.* 143–4. Sim. *Urk.* iv. 62, 6, qu. § 365, 2; 66, 15. 17; 518, 14; BUDGE, p. 285, 1. 14.

[11] *P. Kah.* 34, 20. Sim. *Urk.* v. 171, 2, qu. § 249; *Urk.* iv. 688, 15 (with *ist*).

[12] *ÄZ.* 54, 47. Sim. LAC. *TR.* 30, 2, in a main clause.

wnn Šw pw ḥr irt imt-pr n Gb it means that Shu was (engaged) in making a testament for Geb.[1] For the construction see above § 325.

The pseudo-verbal construction may also, in rare cases, be employed where *wnn* itself is in the old perfective.

Exx. *wn·ki rf dwn·kwi ḥr ẖt·i* now (while) I was stretched on my belly.[2]

If you find it.......... *wnn·ti ḥr šmt iwt* and it keeps on moving, lit. it being on going and coming.[3]

Or else it may be employed where *wnn* is in the infinitive.

Ex. *r n tmt* (read *tm*) *skt, wnn ꜥnḫw* a spell for not perishing, but for keeping alive.[4]

So too after the participles of *wnn* (below § 396, 2) and after several forms of that verb to be discussed later (§§ 470–1).

These combinations with different forms of *wnn* 'be' find their explanation in the last paragraph of § 118, where the very restricted employment of *iw* was remarked upon, and where *wnn* was regarded as supplying its missing parts. From this point of view *wnn·f ḥr sḏm* is simply the future tense of *iw·f ḥr sḏm*, and *wn·ki rf dwn·kwi* simply the old perfective form of *iw·i dwn·kwi*. On the same lines we might expect to find *wn·f ḥr sḏm* after the particle *iḫ*, as object of *rdi*, and so forth. The comparative rarity of such developments of the pseudo-verbal construction makes it impossible to illustrate all the varieties that doubtless occurred in the Middle Egyptian literature; but we may at least quote some examples with the *sḏm·f* form of *wnn* after prepositions. In agreement with the rules already laid down (§§ 107; 157, 1), the form *wnn·f* either marks *simple futurity* or else lays stress on the *duration* of the act in question, whereas *wn·f* is without reference to any particular time and lays no stress on duration.

Exx. *ir·n·i nw, n-mrwt wnn rnw·sn mn n ḏt* I made this, in order that their names might be enduring eternally.[5]

ḫft wnn sḏꜣwty bity imy-r mšꜥ Rn-snb ḥr ṯs m mnnw Ḫrp-ḪꜥkꜣwRꜥ-mꜣꜥḫrw when the royal chancellor and general of the army Rensonbu was commanding in the fortress 'Khaꜥkaurēꜥ-the-deceased-is-leader'.[6]

ḏd·n n·i pꜣy·i it, ḫft wn·f mr(w) my father said to me, when he was ill.[7]

kꜣ ir·tw ḫft iry, r wn kꜣ n ḥkꜣ ḥr ḥst·k one shall do accordingly, so that the soul of the Prince may praise thee.[8]

[1] *Urk.* v. 53, 1–2. Sim. *ib.* 4, but with *wn*.

[2] *Sin.* B 252–3. Sim. *Sh. S.* 136–7.

[3] *Eb.* 110, 5.

[4] BUDGE, p. 120, 11.

[5] *Meir* iii. 11. Sim. *Urk.* iv. 853, 12.

[6] L. *D.* ii. 151, *c.* Sim. after *ir* 'if', *ir wnn ꜣḫw ḥr ꜣḫ* 'if the blessed dead become blessed', Cairo 34057, see *JEA.* 32, 104.

[7] *P. Kah.* 13, 34, restored. Sim. with old perf., *r wn·f mꜣꜥ* 'that he may be vindicated', *PSBA.* 18, 203, 12; *n-mrwt wn rn·i mn*, *Urk.* iv. 366, 15.

[8] *P. Kah.* 29, 43–4. Sim. after *m*, *Urk.* v. 35, 11; after *n-mrwt*, *Peas.* B 1, 79–80.

§ 327. *m-ḫt* 'after' with noun + old perfective.—The sentence with simple adverbial predicate does not appear to admit of government by prepositions (§ 154), but examples may be quoted where *m-ḫt* 'after' is followed by noun + old perfective:

ỉw dỉ·n·(ỉ) ỉt šmꜥ n 'Iwnỉ n Ḥfꜣt m-ḫt 'Iw-m-ỉtrw sꜥnḫ·t(ỉ) I gave corn of Upper Egypt to Yuni and Ḥefat (names of towns), after Imiotru (another town) had been fed.[1]

ḫr m-ḫt hrw swꜣ ḥr nn now after (some) days had passed over these things.[2]

§ 328. The pseudo-verbal construction after the relative adjective *nty*.—Two cases must here be considered, namely, that in which the subject of the relative clause is identical with the antecedent and that in which it differs from it.

1. When the subject of the relative clause is identical with the antecedent, it is latent in the relative adjective itself and requires no further expression.

Exx. *mỉ nty ḥr sḫꜣt kt mdt* like one who is thinking of something else, lit. who is on recalling another saying.[3]

ỉmy-r ꜥ-ḫnwty n kꜣp Kkỉ nty sb(w) r Mꜣdw the chamberlain of the secret apartments Keki who had been sent to Medâmûd.[4]

ꜣḥt·f nty tkn(w) n nỉwt rst the fields of his which are near to the Southern City.[5]

2. Examples are rare in which the subject is different from the antecedent and in which, accordingly, a noun or pronoun has to be inserted after *nty*, though, from the analogy of § 200, 2, we might have expected their frequent occurrence.

Exx. *ỉr ḏw pf Bꜣḫw nty pt tn rhn·tỉ ḥr·f* as for that mountain of Bakhu on which this heaven rests.[5a]

Ex. *pty nꜣ ntt n ỉy·wyn r·s, nn ỉrt bỉꜣyt n nꜣ n ẖrdw* what is this purpose for which (lit. this which .... as regards it) we have come, without doing wonders for the children?[6]

See also the examples below § 333, and one which is negatived in § 334.

OBS. Late Egyptian can use the pseudo-verbal construction with *ỉw* after the relative adjective; see below § 468, 4.

§ 329. Subject + old perfective after *ntt* and *wnt*.—This construction is common after *ntt*, both as 'that' and also when it is preceded by a preposition; see §§ 187. 223.

Exx. This despatch is brought *r rdỉt rḫ·k ntt ḥm·ỉ (ꜥnḫ, wḏꜣ, snb) ḫꜥw m n-sw-bỉt* to let thee know that My Majesty (l. p. h.) is arisen as king of Upper and Lower Egypt.[7]

[1] Cairo 20001. Sim. *JEA*. 16, 195, 6–7; SETHE, *Sprüche*, 24*, 6 (J 6).

[2] *Westc.* 12, 9. Sim. *ib.* 3, 10. 17; 7, 11. Once with *ỉr m-ḫt*, *Ann.* 42, 19, 25.

[3] *Eb.* 102, 16. Sim. *ib.* 32, 21; *Westc.* 10, 4; *P. Kah.* 22, 13; *Urk.* iv. 690, 4; 1023, 12.

[4] *P. Boul.* xviii, 6. Sim. *Pt.* 389.

[5] *Urk.* iv. 1110. Sim. *ib.* 649, 16; *Leb.* 47. 49; *P. Kah.* 16, 32; *Hearst* 6, 5–6; Cairo 20003, 1; 20537, 4.

[5a] SETHE, *Sprüche*, 44*, 8 (Aa).

[6] *Westc.* 11, 10–12. Sim. *Urk.* iv. 1092, 12, doubtful.

[7] *Urk.* iv. 80 = 81, 6. Sim. *ib.* 81, 3.

It is a communication to (my) lord [hieroglyphs] *r-ntt ḥ3w nb n nb* (*ʿnḫ, wḏ3, snb*) *ʿḏ wḏ3* to the effect that all the affairs of (my) lord (l. p. h.) are safe and prosperous.[1]

It is a communication [hieroglyphs] *r-ntt wi spr·kwi r dmi n Ḥwt-Pds* to the effect that I have arrived at the town of Ḥa-pedes.[2]

[hieroglyphs] *ḥr-ntt wi rḫ·kwi rnw·ṯn* because I know your names.[3]

Similarly, but much more rarely, after *wnt*.

Ex. [hieroglyphs] *iḏd·k n Ḥr wnt wi ḥʿ·kwi m m3ʿ ḫrw·f* thou shalt say to Horus that I was rejoiced at his triumph, lit. at his-voice-becomes-true.[4]

Note in the above examples the characteristic use of the dependent pronouns. Instead of these the suffix-pronouns are apt to appear for the 2nd and 3rd sing. masc.; see above § 223, end.

[1] *P. Kah.* 37, 15–16. Sim. *ib.* 27, 8. Sim. with *mʿ-ntt*, *ib.* 28, 41.

[2] *P. Kah.* 30, 28. Sim. with *sw*, 3rd pers. m. sing. *Urk.* iv. 751, 15.

[3] *Urk.* v. 60, 9. Sim. Lac. *TR.* 23, 17; with *ḫft-ntt*, *P. Kah.* 11, 19, qu. § 223. Sim. *s(y)*, 3rd pers. f. sing., after *ntt* for *n-ntt*, *Sin.* B 76.

[4] Louvre C 10.

§ 330. The pseudo-verbal construction after the pronominal compounds [hieroglyphs] *tw·i* etc.—Evidence has been quoted in § 223 suggesting that the pronominal compounds of § 124 originated in the fusion of the final *t* of *ntt* with the dependent pronouns or suffix-like pronouns found following that word. Hence it is not surprising to encounter, from Dyn. XVII onwards, examples of the pseudo-verbal construction after the pronominal compounds.

Exx. [hieroglyphs] *twtw ḥr 3s·n m šmt* one is hurrying us in (our) going.[5]

[hieroglyphs] *tw·n ḳb·wyn ḫr t3·n Kmt* we are undisturbed in possession of (lit. cool under) our (part of) Egypt.[6]

[hieroglyphs] *p3 nḥ·k sw ḫpr(w)* that which thou wouldst pray for, it has happened.[7]

[hieroglyphs] *sy nfr·ti wrt* it (the field) is very good.[8]

[hieroglyphs] *hrw nfr(w), twtw ḳbw, n3 n iḥw ḥr itḥ* the day is fine, one is cool, the oxen are drawing (the plough).[9]

[5] *Paheri* 3.

[6] *T. Carn.* 5. Sim. *ÄZ.* 43, 28, 4; 37, 19; Dav. *Ken.* 42.

[7] *D. el B.* 155. Sim. *ÄZ.* 69, 28, 10.

[8] *Paheri* 3.

[9] *Paheri* 3.

§ 331. The pseudo-verbal construction with *m*+infinitive.—As noted already in § 304, 2, [hieroglyph] *m*+infinitive is used with verbs of motion as an occasional substitute for *ḥr*+infinitive; possibly the former lays more emphasis than the latter on the gradual, drawn out, character of the movement.

The constructions employed with this form of predicate differ in no way from those employed with *ḥr*+infinitive. It suffices, therefore, to give examples.

Exx. [hieroglyphs] *s 10 m iwt, s 10 m šmt ḥr st3·i r ʿḥ* ten men came and ten men went (lit. were in coming .... in going), conducting me to the palace.[10] See § 322 for the absence of an introductory word before the subject.

[10] *Sin.* B 248–9. Sim. *Pr.* 2, 4.

gm·n·ỉ ḥfꜣw pw ỉw·f m ỉỉt I found it was a serpent which was coming, lit. it was in coming.[1] Cf. § 323 for *ỉw*.

mt wỉ m hꜣt r Kmt, behold, I am going down to Egypt.[2] For *mt* cf. § 324.

sꜣ tpy n wnwt ḥwt-nṯr tn nty m ꜥḥꜥ m ꜣbd the first phylē of the priesthood of this temple which is entering upon its monthly duties, lit. is in rising in the month.[3] For the relative adj. cf. § 328.

It is a communication *r-ntt nb* (*ꜥnḫ, wḏꜣ, snb*) *m ḫntyt* to the effect that (my) lord (l. p. h.) is sailing south.[4] For *r-ntt* cf. § 329.

Possibly in all the three last examples, and certainly in the first of them, the action referred to lay in the future, not in the present. So too in English we say 'he is going down' for 'he is about to go down'.

§ 332. The pseudo-verbal construction with *r*+infinitive.—This construction is often used to express *future* action, whether simply or as conditioned by the speaker's will; in other words, it corresponds alike to English 'will' and to English 'shall'. One may compare the construction with the *r* of futurity discussed above in § 122.

Exx. *ỉb n ḥm·k r ḳbb n mꜣꜣ* the heart of Thy Majesty will be refreshed at seeing.[5]

ỉw dpt r ỉỉt m ḫnw a ship will come from home.[6]

ỉw·s r mst wḏf she will give birth late.[7]

ỉw·tw r šnt st r pr-ḥḏ it shall be inquired about (lit. one shall inquire about it) at the Treasury.[8] Note that the use of *ỉw·tw* provides the passive of this construction.

mk wỉ r nḥm ꜥꜣ·k, sḫty behold, I will take away thy ass, peasant.[9] For *mk* see § 324.

The above examples show that the various modes of introducing the subject found with *ḥr*+infinitive here repeat themselves. For an example after the particle *smwn*+suffix see § 241. The construction *ỉw·f r sḏm* is particularly common, and has survived into Coptic as a specific future tense. One even finds *wnn·f r sḏm*, though this involves a tautologous insistence on the notion of futurity.

Ex. *wnn nb* (*ꜥnḫ, wḏꜣ, snb*) *r ỉrt hrw ꜥꜣ* (my) lord (l. p. h.) shall spend a day here.[10]

The construction *wnn·f r sḏm* occurs also after *ỉr* 'if',[10a] but in this case it is simply a substitute for *ỉw·f r sḏm*, according to the rule given in § 150.

Ex. *ỉr wnn·f r rdỉt st* if he will give it.[11]

In one example *wnt* may similarly be taken as the equivalent of *ntt ỉw*:

ỉw ḏd·n·sn wnt sn r ḥḏt tpw they said they would destroy heads.[11a] For the dependent pronoun after *wnt* see § 187.

[1] *Sh. S.* 61–2. Sim. *P. Kah.* 33, 33–4; *Urk.* iv. 7, 1.

[2] *Peas.* R 2–3. Sim. *P. Boul.* xviii. 22.

[3] *ÄZ.* 37, 97. Sim. *ntyw m ḫpr*, *Urk.* iv. 120, 13; 1083, 5. 14.

[4] *P. Kah.* 35, 26, *ḫntyt* completed.

[5] *Westc.* 5, 4. Sim. *P. Pet.* 1116 B, 35. 61–2. After *r-ntt*, *ÄZ.* 59, 24 (1, 1).

[6] *Sh. S.* 119–20. Sim. *P. Pet.* 1116 B, 63. 68; *Pt.* 407; *Sin.* B 203. 234; *Peas.* B 1, 281; *Westc.* 9, 10–11.

[7] *P. Kah.* 6, 14. Sim. *Sin.* B 71.

[8] *Urk.* iv. 694. Sim. 'shall'; *ib.* 1023, 15; *P. Kah.* 13, 27; Cairo 20003, 4.

[9] *Peas.* B 1, 11. Sim. *ib.* 12; 313–4; *Sh. S.* 117. 167; *Th. T. S.* ii. 11.

[10] *P. Kah.* 32, 8.

[10a] Cf. too with *ḥr* p. 250, n. 6.

[11] *P. Kah.* 36, 13.

[11a] *Nofru* 33.

Note the use with the relative adjective *nty*; cf. § 328.

Ex. [hieroglyphs] *ir nsw nb sḫm-ỉr·f nb nty r ḥtp n·f* as to every king and every potentate who shall forgive him.[1]

An isolated example shows the pronominal compound *tw·ỉ* (§§ 124. 330) as subject:

[hieroglyphs] *tw·ỉ r ṯḥn ḥnʿ·f sd·ỉ ẖt·f* I will engage with him that I may cleave open his belly.[2]

Another example illustrates the use of *pw* described in § 325:

[hieroglyphs] *nsw pw r ỉỉt n rsy* it is (the case that) a king will come belonging to the south.[3]

§ 333. **The construction** [hieroglyphs] ***tw r śdm.***—In a few passages the indefinite pronoun *tw* (§ 47) is unexpectedly found as subject without support from a preceding particle or auxiliary verb.

Ex. [hieroglyphs] *tw r šsp ḫʿw nw ʿḥꜣ* one shall take weapons of warfare.[4]

This construction is found also after the relative adjective *nty*.

Exx. [hieroglyphs] *ir·tw m ntt tw r wḏ n·f* one shall do according as one shall command him.[5]

[hieroglyphs] *ir rf nty ṯw* (for *tw*) *nb r gmt·f m-ẖn nꜣ n wḏw* as for everyone whom one shall find within the stelae.[6]

In the last example the position of *ṯw* before *nb* is noteworthy; compare § 375, Obs.

§ 334. **Negation of the pseudo-verbal construction.**—Lastly, we have to consider how the pseudo-verbal construction could be negated. Examples are rare; a few cases occur where [hieroglyphs] *nn* is followed by a dependent pronoun, once in a relative clause with *nty*.

Exx. [hieroglyphs] *nn wỉ ḥr sḏm st* I do not hear it.[7]

[hieroglyphs] *nn st ꜣḫ n·k* it is not profitable to thee.[8]

Writings [hieroglyphs] *m nty nn st ḥbs* such as (lit. as which they) are not clothed, i. e. provided with official seals or dockets.[9]

Compare with the second of the above examples the following:

[hieroglyphs] *nn ꜣḫ n·k* it is not profitable to thee.[10]

Here we have possibly an ellipse of the pronoun *st*, but it is also conceivable that this is an instance of *nn* with future meaning before the *śḏm·f* followed by a dative (cf. § 144, 2), in imitation of the construction of adjective + dative (§ 141); the meaning would then be 'it will not profit thee'.

As a rule, the meaning conveyed by the pseudo-verbal construction is negated in a quite different form. We have seen (§ 105, 3) that [hieroglyphs] *n śḏm·n·f*

[1] *Kopt.* 8, 7–8. Sim. *P. Kah.* 6, 12. 16; 26, 2, qu. § 298; *Westc.* 9, 24.

[2] *T. Carn.* 4.

[3] *P. Pet.* 1116 B, 57–8. Cf. *Rhind* 73, qu. § 502.

[4] *P. Pet.* 1116 B, 39. Sim. *ib.* 66; *Pt.* 82; *Sall.* ii. 4, 6, var. in ostracon formerly belonging to M. Naville.

[5] *P. Kah.* 22, 5. Sim. *Adm.* 4, 7.

[6] *Amrah* 29, 5.

[7] *Sh. S.* 74–5, with a faulty sign omitted.

[8] *P. Pet.* 1116 A, 48. Sim. *Leb.* 126.

[9] *Urk.* iv. 1109.

[10] *Peas.* B 1, 293.

is the natural medium employed for denying the occurrence of an action throughout the course of a more or less prolonged period; as such, it is clearly the most appropriate negative counterpart of the old perfective with its implications of permanence and stability;[1] *n śḏm·n·f* also serves to negate *ḥr*+infinitive when this chances to describe a continued or repeated action.[2] The negation of the construction with *r*+infinitive is, of course, *nn śḏm·f* (§ 105, 2).[3] It is only in Late Egyptian that *nn* can stand before *ỉw·f r śḏm*; one instance falling within our period is quoted below, § 468, 4.

[1] Exx. in § 418.
[2] See the first ex. in § 324; also *Adm.* p. 107.
[3] Exx. *P. Pet.* 1116 B, 41. 42; *Kopt.* 8, 8.

VOCABULARY

ꜥwn be rapacious.

ꜥḏ, var. *ꜥḏ*, be in good condition, safe.

wḏꜣ be whole, sound, prosperous. Caus. *swḏꜣ* make prosperous; *swḏꜣ ỉb* see § 225.

mꜥr be fortunate, happy.

nḏś be poor; of eyes, dim.

hrw be satisfied, quiet.

ḥtp pardon, *n* someone.

smỉ report, announce.

smn (caus.) retire; rest.

ḏbꜣ stop up, block.

bw place; also forms abstracts, as *bw nfr* good; *bw bỉn*, evil.

nḫtw hostages, securities.

ḫnt-š garden.

sꜣ body (of men); corps; regiment.

dwꜣt morning; also *dwꜣ* (m.).

dpt taste (noun).

Gbtyw Coptus, a town in Upper Egypt.

EXERCISE XXIII

(*a*) *Reading lesson: extract from the archives of the temple of Illahûn, dating from the ninth year of Sesostris III.*[1] *The headings here underlined are written in red in the original.*

smỉ sꜣ tpy n wnwt ḥwt-nṯr tn,

nty m ꜥḥꜥ m ꜣbd.

ḏdt·n·sn (§ 382) *pw:*

[1] *P. Berl.* 10003 A ii. 16–19, published MÖLLER, *Hieratische Lesestücke*, i. p. 18.

hꜣw·k nb ꜥḏ wḏꜣ,[1]
šsp·n·n ḥnw nb n ḥwt-nṯr,
ḫt nbt nt ḥwt-nṯr ꜥḏ wḏꜣ,
m-ꜥ sꜣ 4-nw n wnwt ḥwt-nṯr tn,
nty m smnt m ꜣbd.
iw ḥwt-nṯr mꜥrt m bw nb nfr.[2]

[1] The formula generally used by officials in reporting to their superiors. It is doubtless the 'overseer of the temple' (*imy-r ḥwt-nṯr*) who is here addressed. [2] Partly destroyed.

'Report of the first phylē (i.e. company) of the priesthood of this temple which is entering upon (lit. rising up in) the month(ly duties). What they said was: All thy business is safe and sound. We have received all the property of the temple—everything belonging to the temple being safe and sound—from the fourth phylē of the priesthood of this temple which is retiring from the month(ly duties). The temple is fortunate in all prosperity.'

(*b*) *Translate into English*:

(1)[1] (2) (3) (4) (5) (6) (7) (8)

[1] From the Annals of Tuthmosis III; *pꜣ nty nb* is Late Egyptian for *nty nb*.

(*c*) *Write in hieroglyphs*:

(1) Now after three days had passed over this, His Majesty sailed southward, his heart rejoicing (*ꜣw*, lit. expanded). (2) A remedy for (lit. of) every limb which is ill. (3) Behold, I am come to you. (4) She was silent at that moment, for (*ḥr-ntt*) she knew that the slave was there. (5) As to every prince (*ḥꜣty-ꜥ*) who shall petition (lit. approach) the lord (l. p. h.) to pardon him, his property shall be taken from him. (6) Thou shalt be seated beneath the trees of thy garden. (7) How unhappy (*ḳsn*) is old age! All taste is gone. The mouth is silent and does not speak. (8) Whoever comes to us, he shall be listened to.

LESSON XXIV

THE IMPERATIVE

§ 335. As in other languages, the **imperative**[1] expresses a command or exhortation addressed directly to one or more persons. It is thus implicitly in the 2nd person. In M. E. no difference of form is visible for masc. and fem.[1a]

The *singular* has no flexional ending, exx. *sḏm* 'hear', *in* 'bring'.

The *plural* had originally the ending *i*, and some rare Middle Egyptian instances may be quoted where this *i* has coalesced with a preceding radical *i* to form *y*, as in *my* (from *mi-i*), 'come',[2] *rmy* (from *rmi-i*) 'weep ye'.[3] The same ending *y* is found once, at least, with a strong verb, ex. *itḥy* 'drag ye'.[4] The later ending seems to be *w*, but examples where this is written out are so rare as to be not beyond suspicion; so *ḏdw* 'say',[5] *šmw* 'go'.[6] As a rule the plural imperative presents the same appearance as the singular, exx. *ssnb* 'preserve',[7] *ir* 'make',[8] but it is by no means unusual to find the plural determinative, exx. *wḏꜣ(w)* 'proceed',[9] *sḫꜣ(w)* 'remember';[10] *imi(w)* 'give'.[10a]

§ 336. Forms from the mutable verbs.—A final semi-vowel is never shown and gemination is also unusual. The forms quoted below are singulars, unless otherwise stated.

2ae gem. *mꜣ* 'see';[11] but also *mꜣꜣ*,[12] as regularly in O.K.

3ae inf. *iꜥ* 'wash';[13] *ḫn* 'row'.[14] 'Make', 'do' has *ir*.[15] In *is* 'go', 'hie thee',[16] the *i* is the prothetic *i* discussed in § 272; the verb-stem is uncertain, but doubtless began with *s*. (Note that in Old Egyptian the prothetic *i* is often found with imperatives of the *2-lit.* class;[17] Middle Egyptian examples are *irḫ* 'inquire'[18] and *ims* 'bring'.[19]) For the rather rare plurals in *y* see § 335.

4ae inf. *msd* 'spurn'.[20]

anom. Imperatives from the stems *(r)di* 'give' and *ii, iw* 'come' are uncommon, exx. *di*,[21] plur. *dy*,[22] *rd(y)*,[22a] 'place'; *ii* 'come'.[23] Ordinarily they are replaced by imperatives from other stems, as follows:—

imi[24] 'give', 'place' is written with a determinative,[25] sometimes differing from, but often identical with the latter. In early hieratic no distinction is made between and, and scholars conventionally use in transcribing from hieratic, thus[26] or.[27] Also in hieroglyphic texts for is not rare, exx.,[28].[29] The hieroglyphic variant (Dyn. XVIII)[30] is due to an ancient misinterpretation of hieratic as.

[1] See *Verbum* ii. §§ 492 foll. Also *ÄZ.* 31, 42.
[1a] But Copt. has m. *amou*, f. *amē* 'come'; f. see too *Orb.* 5, 1.
[2] LAC. *TR.* 19, 36; *Th. T. S.* ii. 7. 22.
[3] *Adm.* 10, 3. Sim. *ršy*, *P. Pet.* 1116 B, 61; *ḥry*, Stockholm 55, 13; *dgy*, *Siut* 3, 43; *dy*, *ÄZ.* 58, 18*.
[4] *Urk.* iv. 1023, 16.
[5] *BH.* i. 8, 5.
[6] *Adm.* 10, 3.
[7] *Th. T. S.* ii. 11. Sim. *Pr.* 2, 5; *Sinai* 90, 19; LAC. *TR.* 78, 5. 19; *Urk.* iv. 656, 2.
[8] *Siut* 5, 46.
[9] *Sin.* B 282. Sim. *Urk.* iv. 100, 16—101, 6; 656, 1; 752, 9–12.
[10] *Adm.* 11, 3. 4. 6.
[10a] Stockholm 55, 13.
[11] *Sh. S.* 179; LAC. *TR.* 18, 17; 19, 36; *Urk.* iv. 1087, 4.
[12] *Peas.* B 1, 247.
[13] *Sh. S.* 13.
[14] *Westc.* 6, 6.
[15] *Peas.* R 52; B 1, 68. 81; *Sin.* B 188.
[16] See *ÄZ.* 48, 41–2.
[17] A different view, ERM. *Gramm.*[3] § 381, n. 2.
[18] *ÄZ.* 57, 104.
[19] *Meir* i. 10.
[20] *Pr.* 1, 4.
[21] *Rhind*, no. 41; *Pt.* 250.
[22] *ÄZ.* 58, 18*.
[22a] Coffins, L 1, 185. 188.
[23] *Peas.* B 1, 67; *Eb.* 2, 2; 60, 17–19.
[24] *Urk.* iv. 651, 7. 9.
[25] An early example of the sign, *Ptah.* (E. R.A.), 32 (Dyn. V).
[26] *Sin.* B 73. 125. 257; *Sh. S.* 13.
[27] *Sin.* R. 103; *Peas.* R 111; *Leb.* 148.
[28] *Meir* iii. 23.
[29] *Kopt.* 8, 5; *Urk.* iv. 654, 16. 17.
[30] BUDGE, p. 126, 4. Sim. *Urk.* iv. 20, 11. 15; 101, 4. 6.

It is from *imi* 'give' that has been borrowed as a biliteral sign for *mi* (also for initial *m*, § 41), chiefly introduced by *m* as , with the variants , ; so in the imperative *mi* 'come' next to be treated.

mi[1] 'come' is more often written , both in hieratic[2] and in hieroglyphic.[3] For a writing *my* of the plural see above § 335.

A similarly written word *m* (Coptic ⲙⲟ) means 'take', and occurs rarely in ancient religious texts; ex. *m n·k irty·k* 'take to thyself thy eyes'.[4] Since this *m* is always accompanied by a dative, use is occasionally made of the sign *mn*, ex. *mn n·k* for *m n·k*;[5] this graphic peculiarity is similar to the writing of *n(y)-sw* 'he belongs to' with , see above § 114, 2.

The negative verb *imi* forms an imperative , which is dealt with below in § 340.

For 'bring' *in*[6] is common.

§ 337. Use of the imperative.—The independent use is quite common.

Exx. *is in n·i ifd m pr·i* go fetch me a cloth from my house.[7]

dwꜣ(w) nsw N-mꜣꜥt-Rꜥ praise ye king Nemaꜥrēꜥ.[8]

An imperative is often followed by a *śḏm·f* form continuing and elaborating the command.

Ex. *my, nṯrw, ir·ṯn mkt·f* come, ye gods, and give him protection, lit. make his protection.[9]

In such cases it is impossible to decide whether the *śḏm·f* form should be classified as expressing an exhortation (§ 40, 2) or as introducing a clause of purpose (§§ 40, 1; 219).

Often some adjunct is added to reinforce the meaning of the imperative.

1. This adjunct may be a *dependent pronoun*.

Exx. *wḏꜥ tw ḏs·k* give judgment thou thyself.[10]

wḏꜣ(w) tn r ꜥ-ẖnwti proceed ye to the hall of audience.[11]

For other examples see below under 3 and § 338, 3. In the common *ꜣs tw* 'haste thee',[12] *ꜣs* is probably transitive[13] and *tw*, accordingly, direct object.

2. Or again liveliness may be imparted to the imperative by adding a *reflexive dative*.

Ex. *ꜥpr n·k bꜣw m nfrwt nbt nt ẖnw* equip for thyself a bark with all the fair ones of the Residence.[14]

3. Commoner than either of these modes of reinforcement is the use of *r* + suffix explained in § 252, 2, or else the employment of the related particle *irf* (§ 252, 3). A few typical examples are quoted again here.

[1] *Meir* i. 10. Sim. *Th. T. S.* ii. 22.
[2] *Sin.* B 160; *P. Kah.* 32, 17; *M. u. K.* 2, 9.
[3] *Urk.* iv. 1075, 10. Sim. *Th. T. S.* ii. 7.
[4] ERM. *Hymn.* 13, 4. Sim. *ib.* 12, 2. 3. 4.
[5] *Puy.* 57; MAR. *Abyd.* i. 26, g; 33; 39, a.
[6] *Peas.* R 48; *Westc.* 4, 6. 23; 8, 9.
[7] *Peas.* R 47–8. Sim. *Sin.* B 73–4; 274–5; *Sh. S.* 13; *Peas.* B 1, 67–9.
[8] Cairo 20538, ii. c 10. Sim. *Urk.* iv. 20, 9–16; 100, 16–7.
[9] LAC. *TR.* 17, 15. Sim. *Meir* i. 10, reg. 3 (*iry·k*); *Sin.* B 199 (*iwt·k*).
[10] *Peas.* B 2, 133. Sim. *ib.* B 1, 213.
[11] *Sin.* B 282. Sim. *Urk.* iv. 660, 9.
[12] *Paheri* 3; *Rekh.* 13; plur. *ꜣs(w) tn*, *Paheri* 3.
[13] Cf. *ḥr ꜣs·n* 'is hurrying us', *Paheri* 3, qu. § 330.
[14] *Westc.* 5, 2–3. Sim. *Sin.* B 188. 190; *Pt.* 233; see GUNN, *Stud.* p. 74. For the employment in this use of the adverb *ny* (§ 205, 1) instead of *n·tn* see *JEA.* 38, 18, n. 6; sim. probably *n(y)*, *P. Ḥeḳ.* II. 32.

Exx. *sꜣ r·k* tarry thou.[1]

mꜣ ir·ṯn Ḥr, nṯrw behold ye Horus, ye gods.[2]

sḏm(w) irf ṯn hearken ye.[3]

In the last instance the particle *irf* is accompanied by the dependent pronoun *ṯn*, this being used in the manner described above under 1.

4. The rather rare particle *m(y)* 'pray' is similarly used with imperatives; examples have been quoted in § 250.

§ **338. Special uses of the imperative.**—1. The imperative *ir* 'make' is occasionally used with an infinitive as a periphrasis for the simple imperative. So with a verb of motion.

Ex. *ir n·k iwt r Kmt* return thou (lit. make for thyself coming) to Egypt.[4]

A technical term in Egyptian mathematics was X, *wꜣḥ-tp m X* 'multiply *x*' (*n* times), doubtless literally 'bow the head at' (or 'over'); instead of this imperative[5] is rarely found X *ir wꜣḥ-tp m X* with the same meaning.[6]

The negation of this form of periphrasis is *m ir*, for the use of which see § 340, 2.

2. To express the equivalent of an imperative for the 3rd person, *imi* 'give', 'cause' is employed, with following *sḏm·f* form as after *(r)di*. Compare in English 'let him hear'.

Exx. *hꜣ n·f, imi rḫ·f rn·k* go to him, let him learn thy name, lit. cause that he learn thy name.[7]

imi sḏm n·n nb·n nḫt let our mighty lord hearken to us.[8]

imi dhn·t(w)·f m tꜣ ꜣt let him be appointed at this moment, i. e. at once.[9]

To negative this construction use is made of *m rdi* 'let not', see below § 340, 3.

3. It is appropriate here to discuss some phrases for 'beware lest'. The commonest is *sꜣw*, var. , 'beware', lit. 'guard', followed by the *sḏm·f* form.

Exx. *sꜣw ḏd·f sḫr·f* beware lest he say his plan.[10]

sꜣw ḏd·ṯn beware lest ye say.[11]

Sꜣw is always regarded as an imperative, probably rightly, although the presence of the final radical *-w* does not altogether favour this view.[12] The imperative from this verb is perhaps also to be seen in *sꜣt*,[13] of which one variant is *ꜥḥꜣt* 'fight',[14] in case these writings are to be analysed as *sꜣ tw* and *ꜥḥꜣ tw*, i.e. imperative + dependent pronoun (§ 337, 1), respectively; such writings

[1] *P. Kah.* 3, 30.
[2] LAC. *TR.* 18, 17.
[3] *Urk.* iv. 367, 13.
[4] *Sin.* B 188.
[5] *Rhind*, nos. 21. 26. 43. 57.
[6] *Rhind*, no. 43. More often *ir·ḫr·k* (§ 431, 1) *wꜣḥ-tp*, *ib.* 45. 46. 50. 59.
[7] *Sin.* B 73-4. Sim. *ib.* B 125.
[8] *Urk.* iv. 654. Sim. *ib.* 651, 7. 9.
[9] *P. Kah.* 11, 19. Sim. *Kopt.* 8, 5-6; *Westc.* 8, 3.
[10] *Pt.* 419. Sim. *ib.* 438; *Pr.* 2, 2; *Peas.* B 1, 145; *P. Kah.* 29, 17; *Siut* 1, 270.
[11] *Urk.* iv. 365. Sim. *Pt.* 223; *Eb.* 95, 12.
[12] For *sꜣw* as an imperative meaning 'guard' see *Mill.* 1, 5, qu. § 212.
[13] *Pt.* 300.
[14] *Pt.* 300. Sim. *ib.* 149. 281.

would, of course, be very abnormal, but the explanation is supported by the fact that *sꜣw ṯn* (plur.)[1] and *ꜥḥꜣ tw* are actually found.[2] On the other hand, *sꜣt* might be interpreted as *sꜣ·t(i)*, 2nd sing. of the old perfective, the construction being that of § 313. In Dyn. XVIII *sꜣꜣ·ti* occurs for 'beware' in a number of places,[3] and can be nothing but the old perfective; for the unusual gemination see above § 310, end.

As to the construction of these various phrases, *sꜣw* alone seems to be followed by *śḏm·f*, which is sometimes replaced by a noun[4] or an infinitive.[5] After *sꜣt*, *ꜥḥꜣt* and *sꜣꜣ·ti* we find either *ḫr* + a noun[6] (or infinitive[7]) or else the vetitive *m* 'do not' (§ 340).[8] After *ꜥḥꜣ tw* the vetitive *m* is found.[9]

§ 339. Object of the imperative.—Like all other parts of the verb except the infinitive (§ 300), the imperative takes the dependent pronoun as its object, when the object is pronominal.

Exx. *mꜣ wi* see (thou) me.[10] *ṯs sw* raise him.[11]

§ 340. Negation of the imperative.—1. In order to effect the negation of the imperative use is made of *m*, the imperative of the verb *imi* (§ 342). This is followed by a special verb-form to be discussed hereafter (§ 341), to which the name *negatival complement* will be given.

Exx. *m snḏ* do not fear.[12]

m rdi kt m st kt do not put one thing in the place of another.[13]

m ir sw r tkn im·k do not make him an intimate, lit. into one-who-draws-nigh to thee.[14]

When the verb thus negated is an *adjective-verb*, a noun followed by the suffix of the 2nd pers. is apt to be added with the meaning of the Latin accusative of respect. See above § 88, 2, and further below §§ 343 Obs.; 345.

Exx. *m ꜣd ib·k r·f* let not thy heart be angry against him, lit. be not angry as to thy heart.[15]

m ꜥꜣ ib·k ḫr rḫ·k do not be puffed up (lit. great as to thy heart) on account of thy knowledge.[16]

2. From Dyn. XVIII onward the vernacular replaced the simple vetitive *m* by *m ir* 'do not make', to which the infinitive was added as object. A few examples may be found already in texts of the Tuthmoside period.

Ex. *m ir snḏ* do not fear.[17]

3. The negation of the construction *imi śḏm·f* 'let him hear' (§ 338, 2) is *m rdi śḏm·f* 'do not cause (*or* allow) that he hear'.

Exx. *m rdi šm·n ḫr mṯn pf štꜣ* let us not go upon that difficult road.[18]

m rdi sḏm·tw n·sn let them not be listened to.[19]

[1] *Urk.* iv. 752, 12.
[2] *Pt.* 157 (= *ꜥḥꜣt* 149); 611.
[3] *Pt.* 154. 260. 281. 300; *P. Pet.* 1116 A, 122; without gemination, *ib.* 48.
[4] *M. u. K.* 3, 7 foll.
[5] *M. u. K.* 8, 6–9.
[6] *Pt.* 154. 260. 300.
[7] *P. Pet.* 1116 A, 48.
[8] *Pt.* 149. 281. 475.
[9] *Pt* 157. 611. Sim. *P. Kah.* 3, 32. Allen (*AJSL.* 44, 132) regards *m* in both cases as prep. A possible ex. of *r* + *śḏm·f* after *sꜣw tw*, *Pt.* 612–3.
[10] *Sh. S.* 179. Sim. 2nd pers., *ib.* 13; *Pt.* 299.
[11] *Sin.* B 256–7. Sim. *Pr.* 2, 5.
[12] *Sh. S.* 111. Sim. *Pt.* 169. 476.
[13] *Peas.* B 1, 152. Sim. *Pt.* 389; *Urk.* iv. 1090, 9; 1091, 2.
[14] *Pt.* 486. Sim. *ib.* 477.
[15] *Pt.* 76. Sim. *ib.* 489–90. A very exceptional instance *Peas.* B 1, 222.
[16] *Pt.* 52. Sim. *ib.* 374; *Pr.* 2, 1; plural, *Urk.* iv. 752, 9.
[17] *Paheri* 3. Sim. *ib.* 7; *Th. T. S.* iii. 33.
[18] *Urk.* iv. 650 (slightly restored). Sim. *ib.* 1107, 3. 7. 14; *Peas.* B 1, 222. 224.
[19] *Urk.* iv. 1070, 4. Sim. *ib.* 1070, 7; 1107, 13; 1110, 6.

THE NEGATIVAL COMPLEMENT

§ 341. The special verb-form[1] used after the vetitive *m* 'do not' (§ 340, 1) will be called the **negatival complement**, since it is only employed after this and the other parts of what we shall term 'the negative verb' (below §§ 342–350). Hitherto it has been known, less suitably, as the 'predicative' form.

The principal characteristic of the negatival complement is the ending *w*, which, however, more often than not is left unwritten. Gemination appears in the case of the *2ae gem.* verbs, but not elsewhere; the *4ae inf.* display some curious full writings retaining the final radical. The details are as follows:

2-lit. Exx. *ꜣd* 'be angry';[2] *mḥ* 'fill', 'be full'.[3] With *w*, ex. *ꜣdw* 'be eager'.[4]

3-lit. Exx. *wšb* 'answer';[5] *snb* 'be in health'.[6] With *w*, exx. *mꜣꜥw* 'be right';[7] *twꜣw* 'importune'.[8]

2ae gem. With gemination, exx. *ḥnn* 'destroy';[9] *šmm* be hot'.[10] From *wnn* is found *wnn* 'be'.[11] 'See' has *mꜣꜣ*.[12]

3ae inf. Without gemination and without final radical, exx. *fꜣ* 'lift up';[13] *ḫs* 'be humble'.[14] Showing *w*, exx. *hꜣw* 'fall';[15] *stw* 'pierce'.[16] 'Make' yields the form *ir*,[17] and 'seize' both *itw*[18] and *it*.[19]

caus. 2-lit. Exx. *sꜥrw* 'cause to go up';[20] *swḫw* 'make dark.[21]

caus. 3-lit. Exx. *sḫpr* 'create';[22] *sḏnw* 'make wrathful'.[23]

4ae inf. With final *w* or *i* (*y*), as well as the ending *w*, exx. *m(w)dww* 'speak',[24] *m(w)dyw*,[25] as well as *m(w)dw*;[26] *bꜣgyw* 'be weary'.[27] Other verbs seeming to belong to this class are *ṯꜣwyw* 'rob'[28] and *sꜣwyw*[29] 'proclaim', var. *sꜣw*.[30]

anom. 'Give' shows *rdi*.[31] 'Come' has only *iw*.[32] 'Bring' has *in*.[33]

The negatival complement is a verb inasmuch as it may take an object of its own—the dependent pronoun if the object is pronominal.[34] It appears always to have active meaning, since when such notions as 'untrodden' have to be expressed, it is the negative verb which is put into the passive voice, and not the negatival complement (§ 397, 1). The syntactical relation of the negatival complement to the negative verb which it follows is not very clear. It will be seen later (§ 344) that from Dyn. XVIII onwards the infinitive is apt to be substituted for the negatival complement, and must have been felt as the object of the negative verb; hence one might argue that the negatival complement is likewise the direct object. There is reason to think, however, that both stems of the negative verb (i. e. *imi* and *tm* § 342) were originally intransitive, and if so,

[1] See *Verbum* ii. §§ 1016 foll.
[2] *Pt.* 76.
[3] *Pt.* 53.
[4] *Pr.* 1, 9.
[5] *Pt.* 476.
[6] *P. Kah.* 7, 53.
[7] *Eb.* 49, 8.
[8] *Pt.* 164.
[9] *Siut* 1, 268.
[10] *Eb.* 91, 6.
[11] *Eb.* 75, 14.
[12] *Adm.* 8, 1.
[13] *Pt.* 178.
[14] *Pt.* 490 (489).
[15] *P. Kah.* 5, 56. 58.
[16] *Pt.* 124.
[17] Louvre C 15, 3; *Sin.* B 74; *Pt.* 99. 486.
[18] *Pt.* 474.
[19] *Pt.* 608.
[20] Mar. *Abyd.* ii. 30, 38.
[21] *Pt.* 460.
[22] *B. of D.* Nu, ch. 27, 3.
[23] *Pt.* 389.
[24] *Pr.* 1, 2.
[25] *Pt.* 159.
[26] *Pt.* 126; *Siut* 1, 229.
[27] *Eb.* 86, 13.
[28] *Pt.* 450.
[29] *Pt.* 453.
[30] *Pt.* 453.
[31] *Peas.* B 1, 152; *P. Kah.* 22, 6; *Pt.* 596. 609; *Eb.* 26, 14; 27, 2.
[32] *Pt.* 479.
[33] *Pt.* 608; *Westc.* 11, 22.
[34] *Pt.* 65, qu. § 349; 477; 486, qu. § 340, 1; 503.

the negatival complement must be adverbial, not objective; for instance, *m śḏm(w)* 'do not hear' may, at the start, have signified 'do not be (in) hearing', *śḏm(w)* being analogous to an adverbial predicate. It is possible, therefore, in spite of certain difficulties of form, that the negatival complement is a survival of the 3rd pers. m. of the active old perfective (§ 311), become stereotyped and invariable for all persons and numbers in this particular use.

THE NEGATIVE VERB

§ 342. The negative words *nn* and *n*, discussed in §§ 104–6 and again in § 235, have a very wide range of employment, which will, however, be found on examination to be almost confined to statements and to certain virtual subordinate clauses derived from these. In order to negate other kinds of clauses, as well as the nominal and adjectival parts of the verb (§ 297, 3), the Egyptians had recourse to what we shall term the **negative verb.** In English 'not' is a sentence-adverb, and so are the Egyptian negatives *nn* and *n*; the peculiarity of the Egyptian negative verb lies in the fact that here it is the negation which is conjugated, and not the verb which is to be negated; it is as though in English we were to replace 'if he does not heed (*or* heeds not) thy words' by 'if he *nots heed* thy words'.

The negative verb comprises forms from two stems, namely *ỉmỉ* and *tm*. The verb-stem *ỉmỉ*,[1] var., is employed only in the *śḏm·f* form with hortative or optative meaning, and in the imperative, where, as we have seen, it is shortened to *m* (§ 336, end). The original meaning of the stem is unknown, but it may be conjectured from its analogy to *tm* and from its construction to have signified 'not be'.

The *2-lit.* verb *tm*,[2] varr., very rarely,[3] has a much wider use (§§ 346–350). It is an interesting fact that the cases where *tm* is employed are, in the main, those in which *wnn* is substituted for *ỉw* 'is', 'are', and those in which the adjective-verb replaces the adjective itself, as explained on many previous occasions (§§ 118. 143. 150. 157. 186. 326). The meaning of *tm* seems to have been 'be complete' (cf. § 317) in the sense of being 'finished'; *tm·f śḏm(w)* would thus mean 'he is finished (with) hearing', i.e. 'he does not hear'.

Obs. In a few difficult passages *tm* appears to mean 'not exist' or 'cease'.[4]

§ 343. The subject of the negative verb.—The negative verb has a subject of its own, either explicit or implicit. The subject is naturally explicit in the 'narrative' forms of the negative verb, like *ỉmỉ·k śḏm(w)* 'thou shalt not hear', perhaps literally 'thou shalt not be (in) hearing', and like *tm·f śḏm(w)* 'he does not hear', lit. 'he is finished (with) hearing'. It

[1] See *Verbum* ii. §§ 1009 *bis*—1015.

[2] See *Verbum* ii. §§ 994 *bis*—1009. Reasons for its use, Pol. Ét. § 31.

[3] Cairo 20512, *b*.

[4] *Eb.* 92, 13; 93, 14; 96, 21.

is implicit in the imperative *m sdm(w)* 'do not (thou) hear' and in such adjectival forms as the participle *tm sdm(w)* '(he who is) not hearing' (below § 397). The infinitive *tm sdm(w)* 'not to hear' ('to be finished with hearing') is, of course, subjectless as a rule.

Now while the subject of the negative verb, if expressed and *pronominal*, differs in no respect from that of any other verb, a curious transposition is seen in the cases, which are relatively rare, where the subject is a *noun*. There seems to have been a reluctance to separate the negatival complement from the negative verb by any element more important than a mere suffix-pronoun. Consequently, *when the subject is a noun, this is placed, not before, but after, the negatival complement.*

Exx. *ir tm hзw n·s ht nbt* if nothing descends for her, i.e. if she does not menstruate.[1] With pronom. subj. we should have *ir tm·f hзw.*

tm spr bw dw r·k lest (lit. in order that not, *sdm·f*, § 40, 1) evil come to thee.[2]

tm hwз s m hr-ntr for a man not to rot in the necropolis.[3] Title of an incantation; *tm* is infinitive and *s* subject to it according to the unusual construction explained in § 301.

im(i) mзз rmt let not men see.[4]

Very rarely a similar transposition seems to occur even when the subject is a suffix.

Ex. *imi dn·tn Wrt* ye shall not sting the Great one.[5] *'Imi·tn dn* is the usual construction, see the third example in § 345.

OBS. This postponement of the nominal subject must not be confused with the absolute use of the noun in the same position (§ 340, 1); in *m ᶜз ib·k* 'be not puffed up', *m* is imperative and has the implicit subject 'thou', lit. 'be not great as to thy heart'. The postponement occurs also when the infinitive takes the place of the negatival complement (§ 344), see an example § 347, 2. That the word following the negative verb is the negatival complement and not the *sdm·f* form, to which it usually bears a close resemblance, is indicated by the ending *-w* of *hзw* in the first example above. For the difference in word-order of noun and pronoun compare in Egyptian *dd n·k ntr* beside *dd·f n·k*, and in French *il voit cet homme* beside *il le voit.*

§ 344. Use of the infinitive after *tm*.—In Late Egyptian the infinitive is regularly used after *tm* in place of the earlier negatival complement. Examples are found already in Dyn. XVIII and even earlier.[5a]

Exx. *ir ..... tm·f irt sbзyt·k* if ..... he does not carry out thy instructions.[6]

tз-ntr tmm hnd·f the god's land which has never been trodden, lit. having-been-finished the treading of it.[7] The suffix as object shows that *hnd* must be infinitive (§ 300); *tmm* is perf. pass. participle, § 397, 1.

[1] *P. Kah.* 5, 56. 58, *ir* restored. Sim. *Coffins*, B 2 L, 250.

[2] *Peas.* B 1, 214. Contrast, with suffix, *Pt.* 374, qu. § 347, 4.

[3] LAC. *TR.* 25, 1.

[4] *Destr.* 5. Sim. *Harh.* 350; LAC. *TR.* 73, 6. 17; *ÄZ.* 57, 104; *B. of D.* Nu, 27, 3; 64, short 11 = long 22; other exx., *ÄZ.* 60, 85.

[5] LAC. *TR.* 33, 5. Sim., with *·i* 1st sing., *ib.* 73, 18.

[5a] *Kopt.* 8, 10.

[6] *Pt.* 208 (L 2). Sim. *Urk.* iv. 32, 10; 655, 4; 693, 12, qu. § 346, 2.

[7] *Urk.* iv. 344.

§ 345. Use of *imi*.—Apart from its employment in the imperative form *m*, already illustrated in § 340, *imi* occurs only in the *śḏm·f* form to express a negative *wish* or *command* (prohibition); for the use of *śḏm·f* see § 40, 2.

Exx. *im(i)·k ir ḫt r·s* thou shalt do nothing concerning it.[1]

im(i)·f ḥwꜣ rsy let it not putrify at all.[2]

imi·ṯn bdš ḥrw·ṯn ḥr·s do not be downcast because of it. Lit. ye shall not be faint as to your faces because of it.[3]

The last example shows that the same absolute use of the noun as was illustrated above (§ 340, 1) in connection with the vetitive *m*, may occur also when the negation is the *śḏm·f* form of *imi*.[4]

When the subject of *imi* is a noun, it is placed after the negatival complement, not before it; examples above § 343, end.

§ 346. *tm* in main clauses.—In Egyptian main clauses the negative word is usually *nn* or *n*, but the *śḏm·f* (or *śḏm·n·f*) form of *tm* occurs in certain cases translatable in English as main clauses.

1. In questions employing an interrogative word, though not after *in*.

Exx. *tm·t ḫn ḥr m* why dost thou (f.) not row?[5]

tm·tw ms in hnw ḥr m why, pray, have not vessels (with grain) been brought?[6]

For Egyptian feeling *tm·t ḫn* in the first example was doubtless a virtual noun clause (§ 188), just as in the English 'why is it that-thou-dost-not-row?'

2. The following example must be similarly explained:

tm·tw rdit rḫt·sn ḥr wḏ pn r tm sꜥšꜣ mdwt the number of them has not been put upon this record in order not to multiply words.[7] *Or*, that the number has not been put ... is in order not, etc.

3. When a double negative is used for emphatic assertion; *tm* is here best translated 'fail'.

Exx. *nn tm·f ir bw nfr n ḫꜣst wnnty·sy ḥr mw·f* he will not fail to do good to the land which will be loyal to him, lit. be on his water.[8] *Nn tm·f* is future according to § 105, 2.

st mw, n tm·n·f ꜥnw the pourer of water (at the tomb), he never fails to return.[9] For *n śḏm·n·f* irrespective of time in generalizations, see § 105, 3.

4. After *iḫ* 'then', 'therefore' (§ 228).

Ex. Give me my property, *iḫ tm·i sbḥ* then will I not (*or* so that I may not) cry out.[10]

5. After *kꜣ* 'so', 'then' (§ 242).

Ex. *kꜣ tm·n rdit ib·n m-sꜣ pḥ n pꜣ·n mšꜥ* then we will not trouble about (lit. place our heart after) the rear of our army.[11]

[1] *Eb.* 110, 3. Sim. *ib.* 56, 6; 79, 3–4; *Peas.* B 1, 131; *Pt.* 99. 205. 331; *Westc.* 10, 9. 16. 23.

[2] *Eb.* 91, 16. Sim. 3rd pers., *Pt.* 453. 460.

[3] *Sinai* 90, 4.

[4] Sim. *Pt.* 178.

[5] *Westc.* 6, 5. Sim. 5, 20; *Peas.* B 1, 180, qu. § 256.

[6] *Westc.* 11, 21–2.

[7] *Urk.* iv. 693. Sim. *JEA.* 12, Pl. XVII, below, 7–8, see POL. *Ét.* 87.

[8] *Sin.* B 74–5. With *n śḏm·f*, see *Urk.* iv. 123, 11.

[9] *Urk.* iv. 519.

[10] *Peas.* B 1, 30. Sim. *Leb.* 46.

[11] *Urk.* iv. 655, *m* restored. Sim. *Hearst* 11, 14.

The similarity of the uses of *tm* to those of *wnn* 'be', mentioned above in § 342, is well illustrated in the last two cases; *tm·f* and *wn·f* are alike found after *iḫ* and *kꜣ*, neither of which could be followed by *nn* or *iw*.

§ 347. The *śḏm·f* form of *tm* in subordinate clauses.—1. The *śḏm·f* form of *tm* is used in virtual noun clauses. In § 346, 1. 2 we have really clauses of the kind serving as *subject*. They may also serve as the *object* of certain verbs (§ 184).

Exx. *iw wḏ·n Gb, it Wsir, tm·i wnm ḥs* Geb, the father of Osiris, has ordered that I should not eat excrement.[1]

rḫ·n·k tm·sn sfn thou knowest they will not be mild.[2]

2. Likewise, in a virtual noun clause serving as *predicate* of *pw* (§ 189, 1).

Exx. *ir r·f mr . . . . tm·f wn r·f pw mdw·f* as for (the expression) 'his mouth is tied . . . . . .' this means (lit. it is) he does not open his mouth that he may speak.[2a] In a series of glosses on medical phraseology, see § 189, 1.

ir ꜥmd ib tm mdt ḥꜣty pw as for (the state) *ꜥmd* of the heart, this means (lit. it is) that the heart does not speak.[3] *Tm* seems likely to be a *śḏm·f* form; for the construction see too §§ 343, Obs.; 344.

3. In a virtual clause of *time* (§ 212) or *condition* (§ 216).

Ex. *kt smꜣꜥ mwyt tm·s mꜣꜥw* another (prescription): to put right the water when it is not in order.[4]

4. In virtual clauses of *purpose* (§ 219).

Ex. *m kꜣ ib·k, tm·f dḥi* exalt not thy heart, lest it (lit. that it may not) be humiliated.[5]

5. After *prepositions* (§ 222).

Ex. *sgr kꜣ ḫrw r tm·f mdw* silencing the loud-voiced so that he does not speak.[6]

6. In *if*-clauses introduced by *ir* (§ 150).

Ex. *ir tm·f wšš st m ḥsbwt ir·ḫr·k n·f spw nw wsšt* if he does not pass it as worms, thou shalt make for him medicaments for passing water.[7]

It will be observed that the cases where *tm·f* is employed are, for the most part, the same as where the *śḏm·f* form of *wnn* or of the adjective-verb is found.

§ 348. *Tm* as negation of the infinitive.—In order to negate the infinitive, the negative verb *tm* is itself put into the infinitive and followed by the negatival complement.

Exx. *tm wnm ḥs* not to eat excrements. Heading of an incantation.[8]

kt nt tm rdi rd šny m irt another (remedy) for

[1] *Ḥarḥ.* 396–7.

[2] *P. Pet.* 1116 A, 53. Sim. after *sꜣw*, Paris, outer coffin of *Sp*, 105.

[2a] *Sm.* 4, 2–3.

[3] *Eb.* 100, 14. Sim. *Sm.* 16, 14–15. Contrast *Eb.* 98, 8 (n. 10 at top of p. 266), where *tm* is infinitive.

[4] *Eb.* 49, 8. Sim. *P. Pet.* 1116 A, 87.

[5] *Pt.* 374. Sim. *Peas.* B 1, 214, qu. § 343; *Urk.* iv. 1088, 12.

[6] *Siut* 1, 229. Sim. after *mi*, *P. med. London*, 17, 2.

[7] *Eb.* 25, 7–8. Sim. *P. Kah.* 5, 56, qu. § 343; 7, 53; 13, 35; *Pt.* 208, qu. § 344; Budge, p. 147, 11.

[8] Lac. *TR.* 23, 2. Sim. *ib.* 63, 1; 75, 2; *P. Kah.* 6, 25; *Eb.* 66, 2.

not letting hair grow in the eye.[9]

tm rdỉ pw wnm·tw ỉt that is the way to prevent the corn being eaten, lit. it is the not causing that the corn be eaten.[10]

tꜣš rs ỉry m ḥꜣt-sp 7 .... *r tm rdỉ sn sw nḥsy nb* the southern boundary made in year 7 ..... so as not to allow any Nubian to pass it.[1]

n pꜣ sp·f tm ỉw his time has never failed to come.[2] *Tm* is here direct object of *pꜣ*, see § 484. As obj. after *wḏ* see Add.

§ 350.[3] *Tm* as negation of other parts of the verb.—We shall see later that *tm* is used to negate the participles, the *śḏmty·fy* form, and the relative forms (§ 397), as well as the *śḏmt·f* form (§ 408). There are also isolated instances of *tm* in the *śḏm·ḫr·f* form (§ 432), and possibly also in the passive *śḏm·f* form (§ 424, 2). In all these cases *tm* itself assumes the verb-form in question, and is followed by the negatival complement or, much more rarely, by the infinitive (§ 344).

(1st ed., p. 265)
[9] *Eb.* 63, 14. Sim. LAC. *TR.* 44, 1.
[10] *Eb.* 98, 8. Sim. *ib.* 98, 5–6.
[1] Berlin *ÄI.* i. p. 255. Sim. *Urk.* iv. 693, 13, qu. § 346, 2. After *m*, *Pt.* 65; after *ḥr*, *P. Kah.* 22, 6; after *n-mrt*, *Bersh.* ii. 21, 15; *Urk.* iv. 840, 5.
[2] *Pt.* 479.
[3] § 349 of 1st ed. is cancelled.

OTHER MODES OF NEGATION

§ 351. *nfr* with the meaning of a negative word.[4]—Besides its senses 'good', 'beautiful', 'happy' the adjective *nfr* has sometimes the signification 'finished', 'at an end';[5] compare the related nouns *nfrw* 'lack',[6] *nfrw* 'end-room',[7] and *nfryt* 'end'[8] in the compound preposition *nfryt-r* 'down to', lit. 'end to' (§ 179); perhaps also as symbol for 'zero'.[8a] This signification gives rise to two idiomatic ways of expressing negative meaning.

1. or *nfr n*;[9] for the writing of the preposition *n* as see above § 164, but here the negative meaning has doubtless helped. The construction of adjectival predicates with datival *n* was seen always to refer to a contingent, accidental qualification (§ 141); so too *nfr n* always denies an *occurrence*.

In the rather rare Middle Kingdom examples there is a doubt whether the following verb is an infinitive or the *śḏm·f* form introducing a noun clause (§ 188).

Exx. *ỉw·ṯn r drp n·ỉ m ntt m-ꜥ·ṯn; ỉr nfr n wnn m-ꜥ·ṯn, ỉw·ṯn r ḏd m r·ṯn* ye shall offer to me with what is in your hands; if there chance to be nothing in your hands, ye shall say with your mouths.[10] Other examples of the same formula write ,[11] ,[12] as invariably in earlier times. To indicate the literal sense we may paraphrase: if at-an-end (be) to there-is (*or* the being) in your hand.

ỉs gm·n ḥm·f nfr n ỉrt·s m ꜥꜣt lo, His Majesty had found that it had not been made in hard stone.[13]

OBS. This idiom was commoner and had a wider use in the Old Kingdom.[14]

[4] See *Rec.* 40, 79.
[5] See below § 389, 3 end.
[6] *Urk.* iv. 1114, 8.
[7] *JEA.* iv. 143, n. 4.
[8] *Urk.* iv. 1107, 12.
[8a] *ÄZ.* 57, 5**, bottom.
[9] See the literature quoted *Sphinx* 7, 211.
[10] Cairo 20003.
[11] Turin 1447.
[12] Brit. Mus. 152.
[13] *Rec.* 22, 20 (Dyn. XXVI, archaistic).
[14] Exx. *Urk.* i. 84, 17; 85, 5; *ÄZ.* 42, 7. 8. 9. 10; WEILL, *Décrets*, pls. 1. 2. After *n-mrwt*, *P.Berl.* 8869, 3-4. After *r* ('so that not'), *Urk.* i. 102, 12. 13. 15. 16; 106, 5.

2. *nfr pw* 'there is (are) not', but with following *śḏm·f* simply 'not'. For *pw* after an adjectival predicate see § 140.

The subject may be a *noun.*

Exx. *nfr pw pẖrwt ỉry* there are no remedies for it.[1] Lit. they are at-an-end the remedies thereof.

ỉr wnn nfr pw ḏddt nbt r·s if it be that there is nothing which has been said about it.[2] Here *nfr pw ḏddt nbt r·s* constitutes a virtual noun clause used as subject of *wnn*, see § 188.

Or else the subject may be an *infinitive.*

Ex. *nfr pw mꜣꜥ tkꜣ ỉm* there was not (even) the offering of a taper there.[3]

Lastly, the *śḏm·f* form may be employed as subject (§ 188), with *past* meaning.

Ex. .... *nꜣ n rmṯ .... nty nfr pw fꜣ·tw n·sn m sf* the people ..... to whom contributions were not made yesterday.[4]

§ 352. *wdf* 'delay', later incorrectly written *wḏf*, is used in the *śḏm·f* form after *ỉr* 'if' with practically the same meaning as a negative word.

The subject of *wdf* may be a *śḏm·f* form used as a noun clause (§ 188).

Ex. *ỉr wḏf rdỉ·k mꜣ·ỉ bꜣ·ỉ šwt·ỉ, gm·k ỉrt Ḥr ꜥḥꜥ·tỉ r·k* if thou failest to let me see my soul and my shadow, thou wilt find the eye of Horus standing up against thee.[5] Lit. if it delay that thou causest, etc.

Or else the subject of *wdf* may be an infinitive.

Ex. *ỉr ḥm wdf ỉn ntỉtỉ dmḏ n N pn ẖrdw·f* but if the joining to this N of his children be delayed, retarded, or waver.[6] In this example two almost synonymous verbs are co-ordinated with *wdf.*

Quite unusual is the construction in

ỉr wdf·k m ḏd n·ỉ ỉn tw r ỉw pn if thou failest to tell me (lit. delayest in saying to me) him who brought thee to this island.[7]

§ 352A. The negative word *w.*[8]—Much more likely to escape notice is this ancient and exceedingly rare word for 'not', which is placed *after* the *śḏm·f* form in *prohibitions.* Only one example has been quoted from Middle Egyptian:

srw·ṯn w mꜥḥꜥt ṯn (for *tn*) *m st·s tn r nḥḥ* ye shall not remove this tombstone from this its place for ever.[9]

[1] *Adm.* 4, 11–12. Sim. BR. *Thes.* 1528, 4 (original *n ỉrr*).

[2] *P. Kah.* 22, 7.

[3] *Urk.* iv. 772, 6. Sim. *Westc.* 11, 23.

[4] *P. Boul.* xviii, 18. See also *ÄZ.* 59, 26.

[5] NAV. 89, 7. Sim. *ib.* 89, 3 (so Ani); *P. Turin* 122, 1. So too already *Pyr.* 1223.

[6] LAC. *TR.* 2, 25. Sim. NAV. 89, 3 (*Aa. Pi*); *Adm.* 10, 5.

[7] *Sh. S.* 70–1.

[8] *ÄZ.* 59, 63; 61, 79. Possibly an enclitic form of the obsolete *ỉw 'not'.

[9] Cairo 20539, i. *b* 20.

VOCABULARY

wḥꜥ interpret, explain.

mḥ drown.

rḳ incline.

spd be keen, ready; caus. *sspd* make ready.

sḏr spend all night, lie.

ḳꜣhs be harsh, tyrannical.

ḏnd be wrathful; wrath (n.).

ỉkb (*ỉꜣkb*) mourning.

btꜣ(w) crime, wrong.

mḫꜣt balance.

mtrw witness.

ḥwrw poor man.

ḫprw forms, stages of growth or development.

var. *ẖr(t)-nṯr* necropolis.

sgr peace, quiet.

ṯs utterance, sentence.

dnỉt dam.

ḏbꜥw accusation, reproach.

ḏꜣḏꜣt magistrates, assessors.

'Iwn-mwt·f Pillar-of-his-Mother, a name of Horus.

H̱nmw Chnum, the ram-headed god of the First Cataract.

EXERCISE XXIV

(*a*) *Reading lesson: beginning of chapter 30* B *of the Book of the Dead, the spell usually inscribed on the heart scarabs, and referring to the weighing of the heart before Osiris*[1]:

R n tm rdỉt sḫsf ỉb n
ỉmy-r pr n ỉmy-r sḏꜣt(?) *Nw, mꜣꜥ-ḫrw,*
ỉr·n (§ 361) *ỉmy-r pr n ỉmy-r sḏꜣt* (?) *'Imn-ḥtp,*[2]
r·f m ẖr(t)-nṯr.

ḏd·f:
ỉb·ỉ n mwt·ỉ (*sp sn*),
ḥꜣty·ỉ n ḫprw·ỉ,

[1] From the papyrus of *Nu*; the heading is an addition borrowed by us from ch. 30 A in the same papyrus.

[2] The name and titles of the deceased and his father are written in black for superstitious reasons. Though they are part of the rubric, they are not written in red, that being the Typhonic colour and unlucky.

m ꜥḥꜥ r·i m mtrw,
m sḫsf r·i m mtrw,
m sḫsf r·i m ḏꜣḏꜣt,
m ir rḳ·k r·i m-bꜣḥ iry mḫꜣt.
ntk kꜣ·i imy ẖt·i,
Ḫnmw[1] *swḏꜣ* (§ 357) *ꜥwt·i.*

[1] The ram-headed god of Elephantine, reputed to have fashioned mankind on a potter's wheel.

'Spell for not allowing the heart of the steward of the treasurer Nu, justified, son of the steward of the treasurer Amenḥotpe, to create opposition against him in the necropolis. He says:—O my heart of my mother! O my heart of my mother! O my heart of my different ages (lit. my forms)! Stand not up against me as witness. Create not opposition against me as a witness. Create not opposition against me among the assessors. Do not weigh heavy (lit. make thy inclination) against me in presence of the keeper of the scales. Thou art my soul which is in my body, the Chnum who makes to prosper my limbs.'

(*b*) *Translate into English*:

(1) [1] [2] (2) (3) (4) (5) (6) (7)

[1] *Iwn-mwt·f* 'Pillar-of-his-Mother', a name of Horus in his aspect of a pious son, clad in a leopard skin and making offerings to his parents.
[2] The person named Any is here identified, as was every dead man of rank, with Osiris.

(*c*) *Write in hieroglyphs*:

(1) If it is not given (lit. one does not give it) to thee, then thou shalt write (lit. send) to me concerning it. (2) Thou wast placed to (be) a dam for the poor man, take heed lest he drown. (3) Mayest thou not be loud (*kꜣ*) of voice in the

house of the lord of quiet. (4) Hearken ye who (*ntyw*) shall come-into-existence (*ḫpr*), I have not done iniquity. (5) Place (lit. give) me in thy presence, so that I may see thy face; then will I not fear (*n* because of) thy wrath. (6) Avaunt from me (p. 239, n. 1), ye evil ones (*ỉsftyw*)! (7) Be not tyrannical in proportion to (*ḫft*) thy power, lest mischief (*bw ḏw*) approach thee. (8) Welcome to thy house, our good lord! (9) I built my tomb near (*m-sꜣḥt*) my lord, in order (*n-mrt*) not to be far from (*r*) him eternally. (10) Do not let these evil things (*mdt*) be said.

LESSON XXV

THE PARTICIPLES

§ 353. The **participle**[1] in Egyptian is an adjective displaying the meaning of a verb as exercised actively by, or passively upon, somebody or something. Like other adjectives, it can be used either as an *epithet* or as a *noun*; exx. *sꜣ sḏmw* 'a hearing son',[2] beside *sḏmw* '(one) hearing', 'a hearer';[3] *ḏwt ỉryt r·f* 'the wrongs done to (lit. against) him',[4] beside *ỉryt r·f* '(that) done to him'.[5]

When used as a noun, the participle may itself be qualified by an adjective. So particularly with *nb* 'every', 'any', exx. *wn nb m st tn* 'everyone who had been (lit. having been) in this place';[6] *wḏdt nbt* 'all that has been (lit. having been) commanded'.[7]

From these examples we perceive that *the Egyptian participle has the meaning of an English relative clause in which the subject is identical with the antecedent;* the first four examples might have been translated equally well 'a son *who* hears', 'one *who* hears', 'the wrongs *which* were done to him', '*what* was done to him'; see above § 204, 3.

It should be noted that the Greek and English use of the participle as equivalent to a clause of time or circumstance (e.g. τὸν δ' ἀπαμειβόμενος προσέφη.... 'then answering him spoke.....') is alien to Egyptian. See, however, § 405 below.

OBS. The equivalence of the participles to English relative clauses explained above is of importance as showing their close relationship to the relative forms (below Lesson XXVI), as well as their distinction from them—a distinction which we may characterize by saying that the participles express 'who'-clauses, while the relative forms express 'whom'- or 'whose'-clauses; see below § 376 for some qualification of this statement as regards the passive participles. The equivalence to English relative clauses may also serve to distinguish the old perfective from the participles; if a form like *sḏmw* or *sḏmt* cannot be translated as a relative clause, there is some likelihood that it may prove to be an old perfective; on the other hand, we have seen that the old perfective has itself an occasional use in virtual relative clauses (§ 317).

1 See *Verbum* ii. §§ 827 foll.

2 *Pt.* 588.

3 *Pt.* 540, 553.

4 *Eb.* 1, 13.

5 *Peas.* B 1, 25.

6 Cairo 20543, 19. Sim. fem., *Urk.* iv. 1105, 5–7.

7 *P. Kah.* 22, 6. Sim. *ib.* 12, 10.

§ 354. Concord, etc.—The participles agree in number and gender with the noun or pronoun to which they are attached, or which is implied in them. The marks of number and gender are the same as in the ordinary adjective.

FEMININE SINGULAR. Exx. *tpt-r prt m r* the utterance which had come forth (lit. having come forth) from the mouth.[1]

mi gmyt m sš like what was found (lit. that having been found) in writing.[2]

MASCULINE PLURAL. Exx. *irw isft* those who do (lit. doing) wrong.[3]

rḫ·kwi rn n nṯr 42 wnnyw ḥnꜥ·k I know the name of the 42 gods who are (lit. being) with thee.[4]

FEMININE PLURAL. Exx. *gmḥwt prrt n·f* the candles which are issued to him, lit. coming forth for him.[5]

rdyt ꜥntyw r šny·sn (women) on whose hair myrrh has been placed, lit. placed myrrh on their hair.[6] For *ꜥntyw* here see § 377.

As with the ordinary adjective (§ 74), the f. plur. ending *-wt* is never written in full. When the participles are used as epithets of a preceding plural noun, they not infrequently dispense with the plural strokes, and the ending *-w* of the m. plur. is often omitted.

Exx. *ityw·i ḫpr ḫr ḥꜣt* my fathers who were (lit. having existed) aforetime.[7]

dmiw ḥꜣḳ m rnpt tn towns sacked in this year.[8]

inbw ḥḳꜣ iry r ḫsf Styw the walls of the Prince which were made to repel the Asiatics.[9]

The plural strokes are frequently added to feminine participles used without antecedent noun to express neuter ideas; exx. *ḫprt* 'that which has happened';[10] *dddt* 'what has been said';[11] *irrt* 'what is done'.[12]

When a participle is used as a noun, a determinative indicating the nature of the person or thing which it serves to describe is sometimes added; exx. *bhꜣw* 'he who flees';[13] *ḥsy* 'one who is praised';[14] *wḏꜥt* 'she who is divorced';[15] *ḥsyw* 'those who are praised'.[16] Occasionally such a determinative occurs even when the participle is used as an epithet, although in that case it is superfluous; ex. *sḫtyw·sn iww n kt-ḫt* 'peasants of theirs who have come to others'.[17] When a participle has one or more adjuncts closely dependent on it, a determinative of the kind here described may conclude the entire phrase (compare above § 61); ex. *dd n·f sꜣ* 'one who turns the back to him'.[18]

It may be noted here, once and for all, that the flexional endings of the participles precede any determinative or determinatives that there may be.

[1] *BH.* i. 25, 25–6.
[2] *Sin.* B 311.
[3] *Leb.* 123. Sim. *ꜥmw*, LAC. *TR.* 30, 9.
[4] NAV. 125, Einl. 3 (*Aa*).
[5] *Siut* 1, 305.
[6] *M.u.K.* 3, 5.
[7] Munich 3, 19. Sim. *P. Boul.* xviii. 44. 46 (*spr*).
[8] *Urk.* iv. 704. Sim. *ib.* 695, 16 (*ṯtp*); 698, 6 (*ḫft*).
[9] *Sin.* B 17. Sim. *P. Kah.* 13, 1. 30.
[10] *Sin.* B 37; *Pt.* 116. 638.
[11] *Pt.* 634.
[12] *Westc.* 12, 2; *Eb.* 53, 14.
[13] *Sin.* B 56.
[14] *Peas.* B 1, 68–9.
[15] *Peas.* B 1, 63.
[16] *Peas.* B 1, 69.
[17] *Peas.* B 1, 45–6. Sim. *Sin.* B 245 (*iw*); 251 (*stꜣw*).
[18] *Sin.* R 81. Sim. *Peas.* B 1, 68; *Adm.* p. 106, qu. § 357.

§ 355. The four kinds of participle.—The Egyptian participle distinguishes an active and a passive voice, as well as two tenses, which we shall describe as imperfective and perfective respectively, see above § 295, Obs. Thus there exist four separate varieties of participle: 1. **imperfective active** (§ 357); 2. **imperfective passive** (§ 358); 3. **perfective active** (§ 359); 4. **perfective passive** (§§ 360–1).

The distinctions of meaning corresponding to the terms perfective and imperfective have been outlined in § 295, and will be discussed in detail in §§ 365–70. They refer to the duration and the frequency of the verbal action rather than to its time-position relatively to that of the speaker. But we discern a tendency for these more primitive aspects of verbal action to become subordinated to the time-standpoint—the standpoint which alone appears important to the modern mind.

The **imperfective** referred originally only to action which was *repeated* or *continuous*, and is regularly used whenever one or other of these aspects is stressed. This tense is better adapted, as we shall see, for the description of *present* and *future* action than for that of past action; but it may be used of past events if their repetition or continuity is to be made very prominent ('who was hearing', 'who used to hear').

The **perfective** seems to have been free of any such implications, presenting the verbal action simply as occurring. Thus it may be used in reference to any time-position, but it is specially useful for reference to the *past* when there is no notion of repetition or continuity ('who heard', 'has heard', 'had heard'). Of the present it is used either when the action is definitely momentary, or when it is in fact habitual, but that aspect is not stressed; see below § 367.

To express the meaning of the future active participle ('who will hear') a particular form known as the *sḏmty·fy* form has been evolved (§ 363). This form is, however, built on too different lines to be included among the participles.

Obs. The existence of a third participial tense, to be known as the 'prospective' tense, is favoured by some, and supposed examples of both active and passive have been quoted.[1] These are not, however, sufficiently differentiated in form from the perfective participles for their separate existence to be admitted. The most striking characteristic would be an ending *-ti* instead of *-t* for the feminine sing.; but see below § 387, 2.

[1] See Gunn, *Stud.* chs. 2. 3.

§ 356. The forms of the various participles.—The four kinds of participle (§ 355) were distinguished formally both by differences of vocalization and by differences of flexional (participial) ending. Since, however, the flexional endings are comparatively seldom written and the differences of vocalization have left no trace in the hieroglyphic writing of the immutable verbs, the determination of voice and tense must often depend solely upon the context. Thus the

m. sing. [hieroglyphs] and the f. sing. [hieroglyphs] may be translated in many different ways, of which the following are the principal: 'who hears', 'who is hearing', 'who was hearing', 'who heard', 'who has heard', 'who had heard', 'who is being heard', 'who was being heard', 'who was heard', 'who has been heard', and 'who had been heard'.

In the *mutable* verbs, tense at least can be discerned. The important general rule is that *the imperfective participles, whether active or passive, show the gemination, while the perfective participles do not.*

To the second half of this rule there is an apparent exception, since certain *2-lit.* verbs show a doubling of the last consonant in the perf. pass. part., ex. [hieroglyphs] *ḏdḏt* 'what was said' (§ 360). But this exception is doubtless really only apparent, the doubling being of the nature of reduplication, a phenomenon different from the gemination seen in the geminating and weak verbs. See §§ 274, end; 278.

Obs. The problem of the gemination, outlined in § 269, here presents itself in crucial form. On the one hand, there seems some connection between the gemination which is the outward characteristic of the imperfective participles and the notion of repetition or continuity which is characteristic of their meaning. On the other hand, it is striking that the gemination persists in the imperfective participles whether they are active or passive, both in masculine and in feminine, alike in singular and in plural, and irrespective of their syntactical function as *status absolutus*, as *status pronominalis* (§ 78) or as *status constructus* (§ 85, Obs.). This persistence of the gemination seems due to some more potent factor than the mere fortuitous position of the vowels, particularly of the accented vowel. The only close analogy in the Semitic languages appears to be the *piʿēl* of double *ʿayin* verbs in Hebrew, corresponding to the second form of geminating verbs in Arabic; there the doubling of the medial consonant serves, not only to indicate intensive or iterative meaning, but also to necessitate the twofold writing of the geminating consonant in all circumstances, see above p. 207, n. 2. Thus the hypothesis suggests itself that the Egyptian imperfective participles may likewise contain a doubled medial consonant. Though based solely on an analogy, this possibility seems well worth consideration.

§ 357. Imperfective active participle.[1]

m. sing. As a broad practical rule, it may be said *that the imperf. act. part. shows no special participial ending, while the imperf. pass. part. ends in* -w.

Exx. [hieroglyphs] *3ḫ n irr r irrw n·f* (it is) more useful for him who does (it) than him for whom (it) is done, lit. than (the one) done for him.[2]

[hieroglyphs] *dd ḥr m ddw n·f ḥr* he who used to give command is (become) one to whom command is given, lit. given to him command.[3]

On closer examination it is found, however, that the imperf. act. part. possessed a participial ending, and that this ending is sometimes written. From the m. plur. *-yw*, older *-iw*, it may be inferred that the original ending was *-i*, which would later appear as *-y*. The original *-i* survives in the noun [hieroglyphs] *sḏmi*

[1] *Verbum* ii. §§ 858 foll. The non-geminating forms there given are here assigned to the perf. act. part.

[2] Berl. *ÄI.* i. p. 180. Sim. Cairo 20609, *a* 6; Florence 1540; *Cat. d. Mon.* i. 89, no. 76. *Cf.* also *Urk.* iv. 1114, 5 (*dhn, dhnw*); 1115, 7 (*irr, irrw*); 1116, 7, qu. § 377, 2 (*šì, šìw*).

[3] *Adm.* p. 106.

'hearer', apparently in the technical sense of 'judge'.[1] The rare *-y* is found in *sḏmy* 'one who listens';[2] *ḫddy* 'which flows downstream';[3] also in *ꜥnḫy* 'living' in the common phrase *bꜣ ꜥnḫy* 'living soul';[4] so too in the nouns *sꜣꜣy* 'loiterer';[5] *wršy* 'watchman',[6] if these are really participial. Less rare, but still uncommon, is the ending *-w*, exx. *sḏmw* 'who hears';[7] *ḥḏdw* 'one who confounds';[8] *wšꜥw* 'which bites'.[9] The more nominal in character a participle is, the greater the tendency to write the participial ending, ex. *in sḏmw sḏm ḏd* 'it is a hearer who hears a saying'[10] (*sḏmw* and *sḏm* both imperf. act. participles), but here again no rule can be made.[11] So too perhaps *wḥmw* 'herald', *šmsw* 'follower'.

m. plur. The fullest writing, which is not rare, is *-yw*, exx. *sḏmyw* 'hearers';[12] *šnꜥyw* 'darting' (fishes);[13] *wnnyw* 'who exist'.[14] Other writings show simply *-w*, exx. *mrrw* 'who love';[15] or more rarely simply *-y*, ex. *mrry* 'who love';[16] or else no ending at all, exx. *wnn* 'which are';[17] *msḏḏ* 'who hate'.[18]

f. sing. and plur. It may be inferred from m. plur. *-yw* (old *-ỉw*) that these forms ended in *-yt* (old *-ỉt*) and *-ywt* (old *-ỉwt*) respectively. Nevertheless only the gender ending *-t* is written.

Exx. *prrt* 'which goes (go) forth';[19] *wnnt* 'which is (are)'.[20] The participial inflexion is exceptionally written in *sdyt* 'which breaks', *wbꜣyt* 'which opens'.[21]

The following imperf. act. participles from mutable verbs are quoted mainly to exhibit the gemination of the verb-stem; see above for all details as to the participial ending and as to the marks of gender and number.

2ae gem. *mꜣꜣ* 'who sees',[22] var. ;[23] *tkkw* 'who attack'.[24] For *wnn* see the examples quoted under the heads of m. plur. and f. sing. and plur.; also below § 396.

3ae inf. *prr* 'which comes forth';[25] *mrr* 'loving';[26] *ḫꜥꜥ* 'who shines forth'.[27] 'Make' shows two forms, both to be read *ỉrr*: is the commoner,[28] but is not infrequent.[29] 'Take' has a geminating form *ỉtt* (from earlier *ỉṯṯ*).[30]

caus. 2ae gem. *sgnn* 'who makes weak'.[31]

4ae inf. With gemination, *msḏḏw* 'who hate'.[32] Without gemination, *ḫnt* 'who used to sail upstream';[33] *mdw* (*mwdw*) 'who speaks',[34] varr. *mdwy*,[35] *mdy*,[36] and *mdww*.[37]

caus. 3ae inf. *sḫrr* 'who makes pleased';[38] *sỉddy* 'making powerless(?)'.[39]

1 *Urk.* iv. 1111, 16–1112, 1 (wrongly divided); *Pt.* 536 (contrasted with *sḏmw* 'one who hearkens').
2 *Pt.* 248 (L 2).
3 *Urk.* iv. 85, 14. So too *mdwy*, *ib.* 1076, 3.
4 *Urk.* iv. 113, 11; 147, 6; BUDGE, p. 1, 13; 51, 3; see also *ib.* 323, 2. Sim. *mdwy* 'who speaks', *Peas.* R 71; *sỉddy*, Cairo 20539 i. *b* 10.
5 *Sin.* B 151.
6 *Sin.* R 44. Sim. *ꜥwꜣy* 'robber', *Peas.* B 1, 302; *spry* 'petitioner', *Peas.* B 1, 284, qu. § 148, 3.
7 *Pt.* 534. 536. 540. 553. 588. Many exx. Berl. *ÄI*, i. p. 257, if not perf.
8 *Pt.* 81. Sim. *ỉww*, *Pt.* 141; *sḫprw*, *ib.* 173.
9 *Eb.* 89, 6.
10 *Pt.* 553.
11 The ending *-w* in the construction with *ỉn*, *Pt.* 141. 173.
12 *Pt.* 30. 72; *Urk.* iv. 1152, 11. Sim. *ỉrryw*, NAV. 68, 12; *msddyw*, Leyd. V 38.
13 *Peas.* B 1, 61. Sim. *ꜥꜣbyw*, *ib.* R 42; *sꜥkyw* *Eb.* 1, 6.
14 BUDGE, p. 159, 14; 249, 10; 252, 9; *D. el B.* 125.
15 *Pt.* 413. Sim. Turin 1447 (*mrrw*, *msḏḏw*); ERM. *Hymn.* 1, 3 (*ḥꜣꜣw*).
16 Cairo 20003.
17 *Eb.* 109, 9.
18 Cairo 20003.
19 Sing., *Siut* 1, 275; plur., *ib.* 305; dubious, e. g. *Urk.* iv. 1105, 5. 7.
20 Sing., *Westc.* 12, 6; plur., *Eb.* 76, 12.
21 *M.u.K.* 1, 4. So too in *ꜥkyt* 'serving maid', *Th. T. S.* ii. 12.
22 *Bersh.* ii. 7 top; 21 top, 3.
23 *Siut* 1, 4. 217.
24 *Urk.* iv. 556, 2; 614, 10.
25 *Siut* 1, 302. 303.
26 *Sh. S.* 147; *P. Kah.* 29, 7; *Urk.* iv. 198, 2.
27 *Urk.* iv. 806, 13.
28 *Siut* 1, 215; 2, 7; Louvre C 14, 2; *Hamm.* 114, 3; *Urk.* iv. 1112, 12. 14; 1113, 6. 7.
29 Louvre C 3, 3; Cairo 20026. 20541; *Urk.* iv. 541, 14.
30 PIEHL, *IH.* iii. 75, 4; ERM. *Hymn.* 11, 5.
31 *Sin.* B 54.
32 *BH.* i. 8, 4; Louvre C 177.
33 *Sin.* B 94.
34 *Peas.* B 1, 21.
35 *Peas.* R 71.
36 *Urk.* iv. 1076, 3.
37 Brit. Mus. 581.
38 *Hamm.* 114, 4; Cairo 20539, i. *b* 2.
39 Cairo 20539, i. *b* 10.

anom. 'Give' has regularly ,[1] *dd*[2] 'who gives', very rarely .[3] From 'come' a few exx. of both *ỉỉ*[3a] and *ỉy*[3b] appear to be indisputable imperf. act. parts. 'Bring' has *ỉnn*.[4]

§ 358. Imperfective passive participle.[5]

m. sing. The ending *-w* (see above § 357, at beginning) is much more frequently written than omitted, exx. *sḫꜣw* 'who is remembered';[6] *sftw* 'which is slaughtered';[7] *ỉrrw* 'which is made'.[8] Examples without *-w*, *wḫꜣ* 'which is sought';[9] *šdd* 'one (over whom is) recited'.[10] Altogether exceptional is a form in *-y*, namely *ḥssy* 'he who is praised';[11] this might possess a special meaning.

m. plur. Only one *-w* is written, and this may well be the participial ending, exx. *ỉpw* 'paid';[12] *ỉnnw* 'which are brought';[13] *ddw* 'which are placed'.[14] Forms without *-w* are occasionally met with, ex. *ỉrr* 'which are made'.[15]

f. sing. and *plur.* Only *-t* is shown. Exx. *ḏdt* 'what is spoken';[16] *ꜣbbt* 'what is desired';[17] *ỉrrt* 'what is done'.[18]

The forms from the mutable verbs display the gemination and are often indistinguishable from the imperf. active forms. Some of the verbs to be quoted are intransitives; see below § 376.

2ae gem. *mꜣꜣw* 'who is seen'.[19]

3ae inf. *nḥḥw* 'being prayed (for)';[20] *prrw* 'being gone forth';[21] *gmmt* 'which is found'.[22] 'Make' has usually forms writing one *r*, ex. *ỉrrw* 'which is done';[23] more rarely the *r* is repeated, ex. *ỉrrw*;[24] a plur. without *r*[25] is certainly a mistake. 'Take' shows a form *ỉṯṯw*.[26]

4ae inf. *msddt* 'she who is hated'.[27]

anom. 'Give' shows forms like *ddw*,[28] *ddt*.[29] 'Bring' shows *ỉnnw*,[30] *ỉnnt*.[31]

Obs. The imperfective relative form, to be treated in Lesson XXVI, will there be seen to be nothing more than the imperfective passive participle in an extended use.

§ 359. Perfective active participle.[32]

m. sing. As a rule no ending is shown, exx. *hꜣb* 'he who sent';[33] *wtt* 'he who begat';[34] *ỉr* 'who made',[35] 'who makes'.[36] Nevertheless sporadic writings point to the existence of a flexional ending *-w* or *-y*, exx. *mꜣw* 'one who saw';[37] *ỉṯw* 'taker';[38] *thw* 'transgressor';[39] *ỉrw* 'one who does', 'makes';[40] *rdỉw* 'giving';[41] *ḳmꜣy* 'which has created';[42] *m(w)ty* 'he who has died'.[43] Such writings are especially

[1] *Siut.* i. 310; Cairo 20539, i. *b* 2.
[2] *Siut.* i. 237; *Adm.* p. 106, qu. p. 273, n. 3.
[3] *Urk.* v. 76, 2.
[3a] *Peas.* B 1, 67; plur. *Pt.* 260 (*Pr.*)
[3b] *Westc.* 8, 11; plur. *Pt.* 260 (L 2).
[4] Cairo 20530, *b* 10.
[5] See *Verbum* ii. §§ 941 foll.
[6] Brit. Mus. 581.
[7] *Siut.* 1, 302.
[8] *Siut* 1, 318. Sim. *M. u. K.* vs. 2, 7 (*šddw*).
[9] *Sinai* 90, 10. Sim. Cairo 20571, *a* 2 (*smỉ*).
[10] *Urk.* v. 96, 7 (*šdd*); *Sinai* 90, 12 (*gꜣ*); *Urk.* iv. 415, 3 (*dd*).
[11] *Pt.* 137. Sim. *mrry*, *Sinai* 30; *Menthuw.* 10; perhaps also *ḥꜣby*, *ib.* 5; *wbꜣy*, *Urk.* iv. 546, 12; *prry·s* *Eb.* 25, 5; 52, 4.
[12] *Rekh.* 5; cf. perhaps *P. Kah.* 13, 25 with plur. strokes.
[13] *Urk.* iv. 344, 11.
[14] *Sin.* B 304.
[15] Leyd. V 4, 12; Louvre C 3, 19. Var. *ỉrrw*, Brit. Mus. 567, 15.
[16] *Eb.* 108, 13.
[17] *Urk.* iv. 975, 6.
[18] *Sin.* B 307; *Eb.* 30, 9; *Kopt.* 8, 7.
[19] Cairo 20538, ii. *c* 12.
[20] *Urk.* iv. 972, 14.
[21] Cairo 20359.
[22] *Eb.* 66, 1.
[23] *Siut* 1, 318; *Pt.* 282; *Eb.* 61, 6.
[24] *M. u. K.* vs. 4, 6; Berl. *ÄI.* i. p. 180, qu. p. 273, n. 2.
[25] Cairo 20024, *b* 7.
[26] *Ann.* v. 239, 33.
[27] *Eb.* 67, 4. 5.
[28] *Siut* 1, 302.
[29] *Rhind*, no. 62; *Eb.* 56, 18.
[30] *P. Boul.* xviii. 12; *Ann.* v. 239, 32.
[31] Brit. Mus. 614, 5. 6.
[32] See *Verbum* ii. §§ 840 foll.
[33] *Siut* 1, 215.
[34] Berl. *ÄI.* i. p. 258, 19.
[35] Budge, p. 213, 16; *Mill.* 1, 7; *Sin.* R 8; *Urk.* iv. 194, 15.
[36] *Bersh.* ii. 13, 15; *Hamm.* 114, 17; *Leb.* 116.
[37] *Menthuw.* 4.
[38] *Peas.* B 1, 164.
[39] *Peas.* B 1, 237.
[40] *Urk.* iv. 429, 2; 533, 8.
[41] *Urk.* iv. 506, 3; 507, 15.
[42] *P. Kah.* 5, 18; *Eb.* 19, 17.
[43] *Menthuw.* 4.

apt to occur when the participle is used as a noun (cf. § 357), ex. *ir r irw* 'doing to the doer (him who does)',[1] or when it is component of a compound, ex. *irw bnrt* 'confectionery-maker',[2] var. ,[3] and it might be thought that here some nominal formation is exemplified, not a participle. But our texts, at least, hardly warrant such a distinction.[4]

m. plur. The ending *-w* is sometimes written, exx. *ḫprw* 'who had existed',[5] *iww* 'who have come',[6] *irw* 'who made',[7] but is sometimes omitted, exx. *ḫpr* 'who had existed',[8] *rdi* 'who had placed',[9] *m(w)t(w)* 'who have died',[10] *iw* 'who had come'.[11] Difficult to explain, and possibly in some cases faulty writings of the imperf. act. part., are some rare examples with *-yw*, ex. *pꜣyw* 'who once did';[12] in this particular instance, however, the *y* may be due merely to the *ꜣ* of the stem, the change of *ꜣ* into *y* being frequent.

f. sing. and *plur.* Only the fem. ending *-t* is shown, exx. *ḫprt* 'which happened', 'has (have) happened';[13] *prt* 'which came forth';[14] *mst* 'who has borne'.[15] In some rare cases where *-yt* is found, this may be due to change of the radical *ꜣ* of the verb-stem into *y*, possibly under the influence of the participial ending; exx. *pꜣyt* 'which once did';[16] *hꜣyt* 'what has fallen'.[17]

To the perfective active participle must be assigned all active participles from the *2ae gem.* and *3ae inf.* class which do not geminate; possible exceptions, see above under m. plur. The gemination is not found in any verbal class.

2-lit. The only point needing remark is the existence of some rare forms with prothetic *i*. On these see § 272.

2ae gem. *mꜣ* 'who sees', 'has seen';[18] *wn* 'which was'.[19]

3ae inf. *pr* 'who went (goes) forth';[20] *šd* 'who fostered';[21] *rmw* 'who bewept'.[22] 'Make' writes *ir*,[23] only very rarely ,[24] which latter is presumably the perfective counterpart of the imperfectives written as and should accordingly be read *ir*, not *irr*. 'Take away' shows a form *iṯ*.[25]

anom. 'Give' has usually the form *rdi*;[26] much rarer are forms without *r*, namely [27] and *di*.[28] 'Come' has forms both in *-w* and in *-i*, namely *iw*[29] and *ii*,[30] var. *iy*.[31] 'Bring' shows *in*.[32]

§ 360. Perfective passive participle: A. forms from *2-lit.* verbs with reduplication.[33]—Contrary to expectation, some biliteral verbs show a repetition of the last radical consonant in the perf. pass. part. The m. sing. is usually written without ending, but occasionally *-y* appears. The forms in question are:—

[1] *Urk.* iv. 910, 13. Contrast without ending, *Leb.* 116.
[2] SPIEG.-PÖRTN. i. no. 9.
[3] Cairo 20418, *b*.
[4] Compare *ir sw* (§ 374) *ḏdt* in *Hamm.* 114, 7 with *irw ḏdt*, *Urk.* iv. 429, 2.
[5] *Hamm.* 191, 5; *Siut* 4, 26. Sim. *wnw*, *BH.* i. 25, 103; *Adm.* 3, 6. 14; *mꜣw*, *Leb.* 79; *ḳdw*, *Leb.* 60.
[6] *Peas.* B 1, 45. Sim. *šmw*, *ib.* R 91.
[7] *Urk.* iv. 665, 11.
[8] Munich 3, 19, qu. § 354. Sim. *spr*, *P. Boul.* xviii. 44. 46.
[9] *Urk.* iv. 665, 3. Sim. *ii*, *P. Boul.* xviii. 42.
[10] *Leb.* 64.
[11] *Sin.* B 245; *Urk.* iv. 691, 13.
[12] *Pt.* 32 (L 2). Sim. *wnyw*, *Urk.* iv. 151, 11; *Adm.* 4, 9; *tmy*, *ib.*; *pryw*, L. *D.* iii. 72, 5; *šdyw*, *M. u. K.* vs. 4. 8.
[13] Sing., *Hamm.* 110, 2; *Eb.* 104, 6. 13. 15; plur., *Eb.* 20, 17. 23; 21, 14.
[14] *BH.* i. 25, 26. 58–9; *Eb.* 1, 18. 19.
[15] *Eb.* 90, 19. 21.
[16] *Urk.* iv. 168, 11; *ÄZ.* 45, 76.
[17] *Eb.* 42, 15.
[18] *Sin.* B 278; f. sing., LAC. *TR.* 47, 5; m. plur., *Leb.* 79.
[19] *Sin.* B 296; *Adm.* 8, 3; f. sing., Brit. Mus. 614, 14; m. plur., *Adm.* 3, 6; 6, 14.
[20] *Urk.* iv. 540, 2; 953, 2; m. plur., *Hamm.* 87, 12.
[21] *Siut* 5, 23; f. sing., *Eb.* 97, 10.
[22] LAC. *TR.* 29, 9.
[23] *Hamm.* 87, 9; *Pt.* 184; Brit. Mus. 159, 12; Cairo 20012, 3; *Siut* 2, 9; f. sing., *Urk.* iv. 21, 6; m. plur., *Leb.* 123; *Urk.* iv. 66, 16.
[24] *Siut* 3, 14; Berl. *ÄI.* i. p. 257, 5 (*irw*); m. plur., perhaps *BH.* i. 26, 212. See too above under m. sing.
[25] *Siut* 1, 233.
[26] *Sin.* B 308; *Hamm.* 110, 8; *P. Kah.* 2, 13; *Westc.* 11, 12; *Urk.* iv. 970, 3.
[27] Leyd. V 4, 7; *Urk.* iv. 358, 8.
[28] *Urk.* iv. 1094, 17.
[29] *Peas.* B 1, 44; m. plur., *ib.* 45; *Sin.* B 245; *Adm.* p. 99.
[30] Cairo 20499, *b* 9; 20530, *b* 17; m. plur., *P. Boul.* xviii. 42.
[31] Cairo 20539, i. *b* 8; *M. u. K.* vs. 2, 8.
[32] *Sh. S.* 69. 71; *ÄZ.* 45, Pl. 8, A.
[33] See *Verbum* ii. § 927.

wḏḏt 'what had been commanded',[1] var. *wḏḏt*,[2] f. sing.

rḫḫy 'one who is known',[3] m. sing.

ḫmmy 'which are unknown',[4] m. plur.; *ḫmm*,[5] m. sing.

šȝȝt 'which had been decreed',[6] f. sing.; *šȝȝt* 'what had been decreed',[7] f. sing. (§ 354).

tmm 'which had not been', lit. perhaps 'which had been completed',[8] m. sing.; *tmmt*,[9] f. sing.

ṯsst 'what was knotted',[10] f. sing.

ḏddy '(to) who(m) has been said',[11] m. sing.; *ḏddt* 'what has been said',[12] f. sing., var. (§ 354).[13]

In several cases forms without the reduplication are also found, exx. *wḏt* 'what has been commanded',[14] var. ;[15] *ḏdt* 'what had been said'.[16] For this and for other reasons, it seems necessary to consider the forms above quoted as a special formation, standing outside the general system of the participles. Hebrew possesses some rare verb-forms which likewise show reduplication of the last radical consonant—the so-called *puʿlal* conjugation, see above § 274.

Obs. These forms have hitherto been supposed to exhibit real gemination, i. e. to be survivals indicating that the *2-lit.* verbs in question once belonged to the *3ae inf.* or *2ae gem.* class, a fact which indeed is demonstrable in the case of *wḏ* (Arab. *waṣa*) and *tm* (Arab. *tamma*). But in the *3ae inf.* and *2ae gem.* gemination is found only associated with imperfective meaning, and no reason has been vouchsafed why it should be found here associated with perfective meaning. As we shall see, the passive *śḏmm·f* form (§ 425) helps to corroborate the view taken above. Moreover, only non-geminating forms are found for the *2-lit.* verbs alike in the perf. relative form (§ 387, 2) and in the passive *śḏm·f* (§ 420); since these forms are derivatives of the perfective passive participle, it seems likely that the original forms of the perfective passive participle in the *2-lit.* class lacked the gemination, cf. *wḏt, ḏdt* quoted above.

[1] *Siut* I, 220. Sim. Brit. Mus. 574, 13.
[2] Louvre C 11, 5. Sim. *P. Kah.* 22, 6; *Urk.* iv. 325, 17.
[3] *Urk.* iv. 119, 3.
[4] *Adm.* p. 97.
[5] *Leb.* 124; Lac. *TR.* 2, 63; *Adm.* 7, 4.
[6] *Sin.* B 262.
[7] *Pr.* 2, 5.
[8] *Urk.* iv. 331, 12; 344, 7; 780, 13.
[9] *Mill.* 1, 3.
[10] Louvre C 168, 1; 170, 5; Cairo 20538, i. *c* 7; *Urk.* iv. 47, 12.
[11] *Pt.* 557.
[12] *Pt.* 568; Louvre C 167, 7. 8; *Urk.* iv. 194, 1.
[13] *Pt.* 632; *Adm.* p. 97.
[14] *Siut* I, 350.
[15] *Westc.* 4, 17; *Urk.* iv. 363, 13.
[16] *BH.* i. 8, 15; *Rhind* 66. Sim. *ḏdw*, *P. Kah.* 13, 24.

§ 361. Perfective passive participle: B. the normal forms.

—The perf. pass. part. agrees with the perf. act. part. in the absence of the gemination.

m. sing. Writings without participial ending are fairly common. So from immutable verbs, exx. *hȝb* 'who had been sent';[17] *ḥsk* 'which has been cut off';[18] 'who has been said (to)';[19] and likewise with *3ae inf.* and *anom.*, exx. *ms* 'born';[20] *pr* 'gone forth (for)';[21] *rdì* 'given (to)'.[22] With the verb-classes just named, however, an ending *-y* is far more frequent, exx. *mry*, *ìry*, *rdy*, *ìny*. It is possible that this *-y* may represent a fusion of the last weak radical with an ending *-w* or *-ì*, but an extremely rare writing is found where a flexion *-w* is written in addition to *-y*, ex. *mryw* 'beloved',[23] and there are grounds for thinking that this may be the original form. Other possible examples with the ending *-y*, like

[17] *Hamm.* 114, 16.
[18] *Westc.* 7, 4. Sim. *sip*, Leyd. V 4, 2.
[19] *Leb.* 100.
[20] *Sin.* B 276. See further below under *3ae inf.*
[21] Louvre C 14, 13.
[22] *BH.* i. 32; *Siut* I, 233.
[23] *Pt.* 2. 43 (L 2).

ḏdy·k 'said by thee', will be quoted below, p. 303, n. 19. A participial ending *-w* is sometimes found with immutable verbs where perfective passive meaning seems required, exx. *ḏdw* 'stated';[1] *nỉsw* 'he who is summoned';[2] and correspondingly *-w* occurs with some non-geminating *3ae inf.* forms, apparently as intentional (archaistic ?) modifications of the usual type in *-y*, exx. *mrw* 'beloved',[3] *ỉtw* 'overtaken'.[4]

Obs. In investigating the participial ending of the perf. pass. part. attention must be paid to its derivatives the passive *śḏm·f* (§ 420, with old endings *-w* and *-y*), the perf. relative form (§ 387, 2) and the relative form *śḏmw·n·f* (§ 387, 3). It will be seen later that the perf. relative form, i.e. that which does not geminate in the mutable verbs, sometimes has past, and sometimes prospective, meaning, and Gunn has assumed the existence of a special prospective pass. part. as origin in the second case.[5] This contention is far from proven, at least in so far as it depends on a supposed fem. ending *·tỉ*, see below. However, the question is legitimate whether what we call the perf. pass. part. does not conceal more than one form.

m. plur. Forms identical with m. sing. are commonest (see above § 354); so for example in the case of forms with no ending at all, participial or otherwise, like *ḥꜣk* 'sacked';[7] *ỉn* 'carried off';[8] the same is true of forms from *3ae inf.* and *anom.* stems showing the characteristic *-y* of m. sing., exx. *ỉry* 'made';[9] *fꜣy* 'carried';[10] *dy* 'placed'.[11] Writings with *-w* also occur, exx. *ꜣtpw* 'laden'[12] (if not 3rd masc. sing. of the old perfective 'being laden'); *ḥsyw* 'praised ones';[13] these are naturally preferred when the participle is used as a noun. A curious *3-lit.* m. plur. is *stꜣy* 'introduced';[14] compare with this another doubtfully plural form *sỉpy* 'entrusted'.[15]

f. sing. and *plur.* The immutable verbs show only *-t*, exx. *hꜣbt* 'sent';[16] *swḏt* 'what was bequeathed'.[17] An ending or *-tỉ* occurs in the Middle Kingdom rarely, but becomes rather frequent in Dyn. XVIII, exx. *ḏdtỉ* 'what is said';[18] *ỉrtỉ* 'what is done';[19] and it has been maintained that this ending marks a special form with prospective meaning;[20] the thesis is far from proven, however, the alternative to it being that *-tỉ* is a mere approximative miswriting of the f. ending *-t*. In forms from *3ae inf.* and *anom.* verbs the characteristic *-y* is usually present, exx. *ỉryt*, *ỉnyt*, *rdyt*; see further below. A genuine f. plur. form is .[21]

We now turn our attention to the various verbal classes.

2-lit. A few forms without reduplication of the second consonant are found, but the reduplication is more usual; see above § 360.

2ae gem. No example appears to have been noted.

3ae inf. The ending *-y* is characteristic of all genders and numbers, see above; exx. m. sing. *mry* 'loved';[22] *f. sing.* *gmyt* 'what was

1 *P. Kah.* 13, 24.
2 *Westc.* 8, 11. Sim. *stpw*, *BH.* i. 8, 12; *snḳw*, *ḳmꜣw*, Lac. *TR.* 5, 1–2.
3 *Sin.* B 206; Cairo 20538 ii. *c* 20; *Urk.* iv. 465, 1. Sim. *ḥsw*, *Sin.* B 206; *Peas.* B 1, 196.
4 *Sin.* B 254.
5 Gunn, *Stud.* ch. 2.
7 *Urk.* iv. 704, 5, qu. § 354.
8 *Urk.* iv. 795, 11.
9 *Sin.* B 17, qu. § 354; *P. Kah.* 13, 1, 30, qu. § 377, 1.
10 *P. Boul.* xviii. 72; sim. *ib.* 18. 38. Other verbs: *ỉty*, *P. Kah.* 19, 1; *ỉny*, *Meir* i. 10; *msy*, *P. Kah.* 11, 22.
11 Louvre C 1, 6.
12 *Sh. S.* 146; cf. *Sin.* B 244.
13 *Peas.* B 1, 69; *Urk.* iv. 119, 2.
14 *P. Boul.* xviii. 60. 74.
15 *Rhind* 67.
16 Leyd. V 88, 10.
17 Berl. *ÄI.* i. p. 257, 5.
18 *Pt.* 153 (L 2); *Urk.* iv. 897, 15.
19 *Urk.* iv. 162, 8.
20 Gunn, *Stud.* chs. 1. 2.
21 *M. u. K.* 3, 5, qu. § 354.
22 *Pt.* 2. 43; *Siut* 1, 234. 246; *P. Kah.* 12, 11; Cairo 20538, ii. *b* 26; 20539 i. *b* 13.

found';[1] m. plur. [hieroglyphs] *ḥsyw* 'praised ones'.[2] There is no gemination. 'Make' has [hieroglyphs] *iry*,[3] much more rarely written with *r*, ex. [hieroglyphs] *iryt*.[4] 'Take away' shows [hieroglyphs] *ity*,[5] besides a form in *-w*, [hieroglyphs] *itw*.[6] Forms showing *-w* instead of *-y* have been discussed in connection with m. sing., together with a very rare form in *-yw*. Examples have also been given of writings without either *-y* or *-w*; often no reason can be assigned for these, but it is noticeable that the omission is more frequent if a closely connected word follows. So, for instance, when a suffix-pronoun follows, exx. [hieroglyphs] *mr·f* 'his beloved'[7] (later variant [hieroglyphs]),[8] f. [hieroglyphs] *mrt·f*,[9] beside [hieroglyphs],[10] f. [hieroglyphs].[11] And again, when the preposition *n* follows, especially in the very common expressions of filiation [hieroglyphs] *ir n*,[12] f. [hieroglyphs] *irt n*[13] 'made by' (lit. 'to') and [hieroglyphs] *ms n*,[14] f. [hieroglyphs] *mst n*[15] 'born to' (lit. 'borne to'). We shall see later (§ 386) that the relative form *śḏmw·n·f* originated in a perf. pass. part. + preposition *n*, and that there the ending, whether radical or inflexional, is usually omitted (rarely *-w* with m. sing.). There is just possibly a slight distinction of meaning between the participles in (e.g.) [hieroglyphs] *mry n it·f* perhaps 'the beloved of his father'[16] (*n* may here be genitival adjective, see below, § 379, 3) and [hieroglyphs] *mr n ḥnwt·f* 'beloved to his mistress',[17] i.e. 'whom his mistress loved', and it might be well to describe all writings like the latter (including *ir n*, *ms n* above) as *śḏmw·n·f* relative forms, rather than as perf. pass. part. + *n*; in this case we should have to transliterate with a dot (*mr·n*, *ir·n*, *ms·n*).

4ae inf. A form in *-y* is [hieroglyphs] *sḫ3yt* 'what has been recalled',[18] though possibly the *-y* may be due in part to the preceding *3*. A form in *-w* is [hieroglyphs] *msdw* 'one who is hated'.[19]

caus. 4ae inf. [hieroglyphs] *sḫnty* 'promoted'.[20]

anom. 'Give' has the form [hieroglyphs] *rdy*,[21] f. [hieroglyphs] *rdyt*,[22] as well as a writing without *-y*, namely [hieroglyphs] *rdi*;[23] also a form [hieroglyphs] *dy*,[24] var. [hieroglyphs].[25] 'Bring' has forms with *-y*, exx. [hieroglyphs] *iny*,[26] f. [hieroglyphs] *inyt*,[27] rarely writings without *-y*, ex. [hieroglyphs] *in*.[28]

§ 362. **Forms of the participles: summary.**—The student cannot be expected to retain in his memory more than a small portion of the details set forth in the last few paragraphs. We shall endeavour, therefore, to provide a concise statement which will serve as a rule of thumb.

Gemination, in the participles, is a sign of the imperfective tense, whether active or passive; a doubt arises only in the case of the *2-lit.* verbs, where a repetition of the second radical consonant indicates the perf. pass. part. 'Give' shows the gemination as [hieroglyphs] *dd-* in both imperfectives, while the verb-stem appears as [hieroglyphs] *rdi-* in both perfectives.

The fem. ending is *-t* and that of the m. plur. is *-w*; but the latter is often not written, and the *-w* of the f. plur. *-wt* is never shown.

[1] *Sin.* B 311; *Sh. S.* 187.

[2] *Peas.* B 1, 69.

[3] *Sin.* B 236. 309; *Rhind*, title 4; fem., *Westc.* 4, 11; 6, 16.

[4] *Peas.* B 1, 25; *BH.* i. 25, 24. Sim. m. *iry*, *Peas.* B 1, 236.

[5] *P. Kah.* 19, 1, m. plur.

[6] *Sin.* B 254.

[7] Cairo 20457, *i*; 20458, *c*; *Siut* 1, 233. 234; often without *r*, *ib.* 20017, *a* 4; 20024, *h*.

[8] *Th. T. S.* i. 3. 18; f., *mrt·f*, *ib.* 1. 3.

[9] Cairo 20004; 20005; often without *r*, 20002; 20029.

[10] *Siut* 1, 234; Cairo 20012, *i*; often without *r*, 20026, *f*.

[11] Cairo 20531, *d*.

[12] Regularly of mother, *Hamm.* 17, 14; 47, 14; Cairo 20020, *d*; 20022, *i*; 20167; but of father, if *ms n* introduces mother, *ib.* 20039, *b*; 20084; 20089, *d* 13.

[13] Of mother, Cairo 20020, *d*; 20023, *aa*; 20028, *h*.

[14] Only of mother, Cairo 20017, *a* 5; 20025, *h*; 20026, *c*.

[15] Only of mother, Cairo 20025, *h*; 20032, *c*.

[16] Cairo 20501. Sim. *ib.* 20008.

[17] Cairo 20506, *b* 3. Sim. *ḥs n*, *Siut* 1, 236, parallel to *mry n*.

[18] *Peas.* B 1, 189. Sim. m. sing., *ib.* B 1, 21.

[19] *Leb.* 101.

[20] *Siut* 1, 339. 351.

[21] *P. Kah.* 29, 15; *Hamm.* 43, 6; *Urk.* v. 72, 6.

[22] Nav. 112, 3; *Urk.* iv. 97, 8.

[23] *Siut* 1, 233; *BH.* i. 32.

[24] Cairo 20089, *d* 5.

[25] m. sing. *Urk.* iv. 7, 6; m. plur. Louvre C 1, 6; *Urk.* iv. 84, 7.

[26] *Urk.* iv. 686, 2; 686, 3; 690, 17.

[27] *Urk.* iv. 664, 17; *Eb.* 95, 10.

[28] *Urk.* iv. 795, 11. *'Int n·f* and *inyt* in close proximity, *JEA.* 31, 7, n. 11.

All four participles possessed a special participial inflexion, which in the case of verbs with final weak radical (*-ỉ* or *-w*) is liable to confusion with this. The ending, whether radical or participial, is frequently omitted, but more often in the active participles than in the passives. Characteristic of the imperf. pass. part. is an ending *-w*, yet the three other participles occasionally present forms with the same ending. A final *-y* is similarly characteristic of the perf. pass. part. from *3ae inf.* and *anom.* stems, but *-y* appears also rarely and exceptionally in both imperf. act. and imperf. passive; particularly noticeable is the m. plur. ending *-yw* in the imperf. act. part. The participial inflexion, like those of gender and of number, precedes the determinative, if any.

THE *ŚḎMTY·FY* FORM

§ 363. But for the peculiar mode of its formation, the *śḏmty·fy* form[1] would have to be regarded as a future active participle. Like the true participles, it is an adjective, and may be used either as an *epithet* or as a *noun*; in the latter case, it may be qualified by *nb* 'every', 'any'. It is best translated as a relative clause in which the subject is identical with the antecedent (a 'who'-clause). The meaning is always *future* and, except in one isolated case, always *active*.

Exx. *ḫꜣst wnnty·sy ḥr mw·f* a country which will be loyal to him, lit. be on his water.[2]

ỉr grt sḫꜣt(y)·fy rn·ỉ nfr but as for him who shall remember my good name.[3]

ꜣḫt n sḏmt(y)·fy what is good for him who shall hear.[4]

swꜣt(y)·fy nb ḥr wḏ pn everyone who shall pass by this stela.[5]

In one single M. E. context the meaning is *passive*:

kꜣ nb sftt(y)·f(y) every bull which shall be slaughtered.[5a]

OBS. For the use of the negative verb *tm* to negate the *śḏmty·fy* form see § 397, 2.

§ 364. Structure and forms from the mutable verbs.—The *śḏmty·fy* form appears to have as its base a noun ending in *-ty* and expressing an activity that may be expected of someone or something. Such nouns are frequently derived from feminine nouns or infinitives, like *ỉpwty* 'messenger', *kꜣwty* 'workman'; but examples also occur which are related to verbs having masculine infinitives, like *sprtỉ* 'petitioner',[6] var. *sprty*;[7] *nḏty* 'helper'.[8] One or two rare examples may be quoted where such a noun seems to take a direct object as a participle would do.

Ex. *m ꜣḫt n sḏmt(y?) st, m wgꜣt nt* (read *n*) *tht(y?) st* being profitable to him who shall obey it and harmful to him who shall disobey it.[9]

[1] See *Verbum* ii. §§ 965 foll.; GUNN, *Stud.* ch. 4.

[2] *Sin.* B 75. Sim. Cairo 20538, i. *d* 1; ii. *c* 23; *Westc.* 10, 13; *Siut* 1, 224–6; 3, 1; *Urk.* iv. 1083, 17.

[3] Cairo 20539, i. *b* 21. Sim. Berl. *ÄI.* i. p. 258, 19.

[4] *Pt.* 49. The form in other syntactic positions, exx. *Pt.* 622; *Urk.* iv. 85, 10; *Adm.* p. 98.

[5] Turin 1547 = *Rec.* iii. 123. Sim. *Urk.* iv. 1110, 11.

[5a] *Siut* 1, 314. 322, strongly supported by the O. K. instance *ỉṯwty·fy* 'who shall be taken', *Urk.* i. 36, 14.

[6] *Siut* 3, 11.

[7] *Urk.* iv. 1110, 7; 1111, 2. 9. 15.

[8] Berlin, *ÄI.* i. p. 258, 18; *Urk.* iv. 611, 17.

[9] *Pt.* 49–50 (L 2). Sim. Cairo 20030, *i* 5.

To some such noun was added a suffix-pronoun[0] of the 3rd person, often accompanied by the *-y* which we noted after duals and nouns affecting the appearance of duals (§§ 75, 2; 76). This pronoun has probably genitival function, *śḏmty·fy* thus meaning 'one (of whom is expected, *-ty*) hearing of him'.

OBS. One theory assumed appositional function, yielding 'a he-hearer'. The objection is that elsewhere the suffix-pronouns always had original genitival function.

The endings exhibit the following writings, apart from the familiar variations of the suffix-pronouns:—

m. sing. , , rarely [1] *-ty·fy*.

f. sing. , or *-ty·sy*. Rare and perhaps faulty, *-t(y)·st.*[1a]

c. plur. or , more rarely [2], [3] or [4] *-ty·sn*.

When the formative *-ty* is written simply *-t*, it occasionally precedes the determinative of the verb-stem, instead of following it, as is more usual, exx. *ỉḳrt(y)·fy* 'who will be excellent';[5] *swȝt(y)·sn* 'who will pass by'.[6] Rare examples occur with *t* in both positions, ex. *swȝt(y)·fy*.[7]

From the mutable verbs the following forms are found:

2ae gem. Shows the gemination; exx. *mȝȝt(y)·sn* 'who shall see';[8] *wnnty·sy* 'which shall be'.[9]

3ae inf. Without gemination, exx. *ḥdt(y)·sn* 'who shall destroy';[10] *šdt(y)·sn* 'who shall recite'.[11] Occasionally the weak radical *-w* appears before the ending, exx. *hȝwt(y)·fy* 'who shall go down';[12] *ḫdwt(y)·sn* 'who shall sail down'.[13] 'Make' shows forms without *r*, ex. *ỉrt(y)·fy* 'who shall make'.[14]

4ae inf. The form *ḫntt(y)·sn* 'who shall sail up'[15] shows no feature of special interest.

anom. 'Give' shows a form *rdỉt(y)·fy*;[16] 'come' a form *ỉwt(y)·sn.*[17]

[0] In defence of this term here see § 411, 1.

[1] Cairo 20043, *h* 2.

[1a] *Eb.* 109, 1; *P. Pet.* 1116 B, rt. 15.

[2] *Pt.* 622. 626.

[3] *Pt.* 600.

[4] *Sinai* 114, W 5.

[5] *Pt.* 567. Sim. Berlin, *Äl.* i. p. 258, 17 (*srwdty·fy*); 19 (*fḳty·fy*); *Siut* 1, 296 (*hȝwty·fy*); LAC. *TR.* 17, 11 (*ḥḳȝty·fy*).

[6] Louvre C 5. Sim. *BH.* i. 41 (*šȝsty·sn*).

[7] *Urk.* iv. 133, 9. Sim. *ib.* 966, 1 (*šdty·fy*).

[8] *Siut* 1, 226. Sim. *Pt.* 600.

[9] *Sin.* B 75. Sim. *Pt.* 563; Turin 1447.

[10] *Siut* 1, 224.

[11] Cairo 20538, i. *d* 2. Sim. *Urk.* iv. 966, 1.

[12] *Siut* 1, 296. 316.

[13] *Siut* 3, 1.

[14] *Siut* 3, 14; *Westc.* 10, 13. 21; 11, 1.

[15] *Siut* 3, 1.

[16] *Siut* 1, 282. 311.

[17] *Siut* 3, 1. Sim. *Sinai* 53, 3; 90, 3; 114, W 5.

LESSON XXVA

USES OF THE PARTICIPLES AND OF THE *ŚḎMTY·FY* FORM

§ 365. **Distinction of the tenses.**—Since, in certain circumstances, both the perfective and the imperfective participles in Egyptian may refer to verbal actions occurring in the past or the present or the future, it seems clear that the distinction between them was not fundamentally one of time-position. As already stated in §§ 295. 355, a careful scrutiny shows that the imperfectives, i. e. the participles showing gemination in the mutable verbs, originally conveyed a notion of *continuity* or *repetition*, while the perfectives expressed the verbal action quite simply and without implication either of such a notion or of its reverse.

The fundamental absence of time-distinction in the participles is drastically shown in an example already quoted for a different purpose:

dd ḥr m ddw n·f ḥr he who used to give command is (become) one to whom command is given, lit. given to him command.[1]

Here the writer is contrasting a past condition of things with the present condition. Nevertheless he uses the imperfective participle in each case, preferring to stress the *habitual* character of the action rather than to bring out the seemingly so vital contrast between past and present. The recognition of that contrast he left to the reader's intelligence.

Every language needs, however, to be able to distinguish between past, present, and future action. It is not difficult to see how the original meanings attributed above to the Egyptian participles might, in practice, amount to time-distinctions. What we call 'present' time is not, as a rule, a mere point of time, namely the precise moment of speaking, but a more or less indefinite span lying partly behind, and partly in front of that moment. An action belonging to the present is not unnaturally regarded as *continued* over the said span, and for this reason the Egyptian imperfective participle was peculiarly adapted to convey present time, the more so, since an action which one 'does' is more often than not of *repeated*, *frequent*, or *habitual* occurrence. When, on the contrary, an action in the past is alluded to, its extension in time is apt to dwindle to a mere point; the stretch of hours or days over which it was continued is forgotten, all that is retained being the mere happening. Hence the Egyptian perfective participle becomes, like the aorist in Greek, the natural instrument for reference to past time. The future active participle, as we have seen, was often expressed by the *śḏmty·fy* form, at the base of which appears to lie a noun conveying a habitual and predictable activity (§ 364). Thus far, therefore, we have the following scheme for the Egyptian active participles:—

PAST TIME. *rdì* 'who gave', perfective active participle.
PRESENT TIME. *dd* 'who gives', imperfective active participle.
FUTURE TIME. *rdìty·fy* 'who will give', *śḏmty·fy* form.

Before we proceed to show how this scheme is complicated by apparently contradictory facts, testimony to its approximate truth must be given.

1. The Egyptian perfective active part. in reference to *past* actions.

Exx. *ìrtt nt mst ṯȝy* the milk of (a woman) who has borne a male (child).[2] 'Has borne', English present perfect tense.

ìn n·f ṯȝbt m dd pr·st he who got himself a corn-loan is one who (now) causes it to go forth.[3] 'Got', English past tense.

Styw ìw m-sȝ·ì the Asiatics who had come in my company.[4] 'Had come', English past perfect.

[1] *Adm.* p. 106. Similar and equally instructive, *Peas.* R 130–8 (= B 1, 84–6).

[2] *Eb.* 26, 1. Sim. *ib.* 42, 15 (*hȝyt*); *Peas.* B 1, 44 (*ìw*); Louvre C 12, 13 (*ìr*).

[3] *Adm.* 9, 5. Sim. *Sh. S.* 71 (*ìn*); *Sin.* B 80 (*wnt*); 156. 229 (*šȝ*); *Th. T. S.* ii. 11 (*mst*); *Sinai* 90, 11 (*ìì*).

[4] *Sin.* B 245. Sim. *ib.* R 8 (*ìr*); *BH.* i. 25, 26, qu. § 354 (*prt*).

2. Imperfective active participle in reference to *present* actions.

Exx. *ỉr skk rnpwt m ḥsy, wnn bꜣ·f ꜥnḫ r-ꜥ nb-r-ḏr* as for him who passes (Engl. present tense) the years as a praised one, his soul shall live beside the lord of the universe.[1]

ỉ mrrw ꜥnḫ, msḏḏw mwt O ye who love life and hate death.[2]

3. *Śḏmty·fy* form in reference to *future* actions.

Ex. *sꜣ·ỉ nb srwdty·fy tꜣš pn* every son of mine who shall strengthen this boundary.[3]

Other examples have been quoted in § 363.

§ 366. Repeated or continued action in the past.—To express these notions use is made of the imperf. act. participle, not the perf. act. part. usual in reference to past events (§ 365, 1).

Ex. *wpwty ḫdd ḫnt r ẖnw ꜣb·f ḫr·ỉ* the messenger who used to go north, or he who used to go southward to the Residence, tarried on my account.[4]

Under this head often fall the characterizing epithets to be described in the next section.

§ 367. The active participles in laudatory epithets.—1. Laudatory epithets are so common in Egyptian inscriptions that it is worth while to devote an entire section to them. The meritorious actions or qualities attributed to the bearers of such epithets are, as a rule, habitual characteristics involving *repetition* or *continuity*. For this reason the imperf. act. part. is very often employed. But almost equally often we find the perf. act. part., and at first sight this alternation seems inexplicable. The cause is, however, a simple one. It is always open to a speaker to describe the same actual fact in different ways. He may be very explicit, and lay stress on the precise way in which an event occurs; or else he may state the fact merely as such, and leave it to his audience to fill in the details. When the imperf. act. part. is used, the former mode of expression is that adopted, and the full English translation would be 'he who is (*or* was) wont to do' something; the perf. act. part. substitutes 'who does (*or* did)' something, stating the fact, but not the custom.

The following examples display pairs of similar or identical epithets, where sometimes the imperfective, and sometimes the perfective, participle is employed.

rdỉ pr s 2 ḥtp who causes (perf. act. part.) two men to go forth contented.[5]

dd pry s 2 ḥtp m prw n r·f who habitually causes (imperf. act. part.) two men to go forth (from the court of justice) contented with the utterance of his mouth.[6]

[1] *Urk.* iv. 62. Sim. *Siut* I, 302 (*prr*); *Sin.* B 54 (*sgnn*); *Eb.* 76, 12 (*wnnt*).

[2] *BH.* i. 8, 4. Sim. *Peas.* B 1, 61 (*šnꜥyw*); *Urk.* iv. 556, 2 (*tkkw*).

[3] Berl. *ÄI.* i. p. 258.

[4] *Sin.* B 94–5. Sim. *Adm.* p. 106 (*dd*), qu. § 365; also *Peas.* B 1, 86, qu. § 373.

[5] *Urk.* iv. 1170, 6.

[6] *Urk.* iv. 49, 1–2. Sim. Cairo 20539, i. *b* 5. A like pair of epithets with *rdỉ* and *dd*, *Urk.* iv. 968, 1 and *ib.* 988, 5.

ỉr ꜣḫt n Ḥr·f who does (perf. act. part.) good to his Horus (i. e. the king).[1]

ỉrr ꜣḫt n nb·f who habitually does (imperf. act. part.) good to his lord.[2]

pr ḥsw going forth (perf. act. part.) praised.[3]

prr ḥsw mrw always going forth (imperf. act. part.) praised and loved.[4]

In many such cases the choice between the perf. and imperf. part. has clearly nothing whatever to do with the time-standpoint, one and the same text employing first the imperfective and then the perfective.[5] There is a doubt whether the Egyptian funerary stelae mean to speak of their possessors as still living or as dead; if the former, English must translate the participles with the present tense ('who does', or 'habitually does'), if the latter, with a past tense ('who did', or 'who used to do'), but the alternative is open to us to employ the participle 'doing' and so, like the Egyptians themselves, to avoid any reference to time-position.

2. It remains to be noted that in the case of particular verbs a preference is naturally given either, on the one hand, to the perfective participle or, on the other, to the imperfective. With, for example, *ỉrỉ* in the meaning 'do', 'make' the imperf. act. part. or *ỉrr*[6] is, in the Middle Kingdom, rather commoner than the perf. act. part. *ỉr*;[7] the latter, on the contrary, is more frequent in Dyn. XVIII.[8] The preference in this case seems to be a mere matter of habit or fashion. In both periods, however, the perf. part. *ỉr* is invariably used when the meaning is 'achieving', 'accomplishing'.

Ex. *nḫt pw grt, ỉr m ḫpš·f* he is a mighty man, achieving with his strong arm.[9]

It is probable that the perf. part. is used in this case because the imperf. *ỉrr*, expressing a prolonged action, would not have conveyed the vigour and immediacy of the verbal notion as here intended. Similarly, since 'finding' is essentially a sudden act, the Egyptian *gmỉ* shows a preference for the perf. part., even though it is implied that the finding in question was a habit of the person to whom it is attributed.

Ex. *gm ḫt gꜣꜣw r·s* finding a thing for which there is a lack, lit. lacked in respect of it.[10] Note the curious combination of perf. act. part. *gm* with the imperf. pass. *gꜣꜣw*.

It seems not impossible, similarly, that the imperf. part. *mꜣꜣ*[11] is preferred when the sense is 'seeing', and the perf. part. *mꜣ*[12] when the act of 'looking' is intended; and a like distinction may sometimes be intended between *mrr* 'loving'[13] and *mr* 'wishing'.[14]

[1] *Urk.* iv. 515, 14. Sim. *ib.* 456, 12; 466, 2; 909, 5.

[2] *Urk.* iv. 960, 3.

[3] *Urk.* iv. 953, 2; 984, 11; 1018, 8.

[4] *Urk.* iv. 453, 12.

[5] Exx. Cairo 20539, i. *b* 5 *dd*; 6 *ỉr*; 7 *gm*; 8 *dd*, *gm*, *rdỉ*. Sim. *Urk.* iv. 967, 9 *rdỉ*, 10 *dd*; 1184, 12 *ỉr*, 13 *dd*.

[6] *Siut* I, 215; 2, 7; Cairo 20026, 5; Louvre C 3, 3; 14, 2; *Hamm.* 114, 3.

[7] *Hamm.* 113, 15; Cairo 20012, 3; *Siut* 2, 9.

[8] *Urk.* iv. 587, 2; 967, 7; 970, 16; 1051, 15; 1055, 1; 1184, 12. 14. But *ỉrr*, *ib.* 960, 3; 1050, 9.

[9] *Sin.* B 52 = R 76. Sim. Cairo 20001, 1; *Urk.* iv. 809, 1. Other like epithets, Cairo 20499, 7; *Bersh.* ii. 13, 15; *Urk.* iv. 427, 12; 456, 11.

[10] Cairo 20539, i. *b* 8. *Gm* also *ib.* ii. *b* 4; *BH.* i. 9; *Dend.* 8; written *gmw*, PETR. *Court.* 22, 2.

[11] *Bersh.* ii. 21, 3. 13; Cairo 20359, 3.

[12] *Sin.* B 278.

[13] *BH.* i. 8, 4; *Sh.S.* 147; *P. Kah.* 29, 7; *Urk.* iv. 198, 2.

[14] *BH.* i. 24 A. B.

OBS. Similarly *rḫ* 'know' affects the perf. tense,[1] as opposed to the imperf. of the same verb in the sense 'learn'; see above § 320, below §§ 389, 3; 414, 4. The distinction of perf. and imperf. is, however, not visible in the active participles of this immutable verb.

[1] Exx. above § 272.

§ 368. The active participles in reference to future events.—While the *śḏmty·fy* form provides the most precise method of referring to future events, a participle may attain approximately the same result.

Ex. ..... *ir rḫ mḏ3t tn .... wnn·f ḥr šmt tp t3* as for him who knows this book, ... he shall walk upon earth.[2]

Here *rḫ* is probably perfective (§ 367, OBS.). Evidently no need was felt of making the tenses agree, and no instance of *rḫty·fy* seems forthcoming.

Elsewhere, however, we find the imperf. part., even occasionally when a single event, neither continuous nor repeated, is in question.

Ex. *mk nn ink is inn n·k sy* behold, it is not I who (will) bring it to thee.[3]

Perhaps the imperfective was felt in such cases to be appropriate through a vague consciousness that the future is a kind of *projection* forwards of the present. Whatever the reason, the imperf. is not seldom used in reference to future events. This use is naturally most frequent when the event in question is to be repeated or is a customary one; in English we may best translate with the present, or the present continuous, tense.

Exx. Thou shalt cause provisions to be given to him, without letting him know *ntt ntk dd n·f st* that thou art giving them to him.[4]

di·f prt-ḫrw (m) t ḥnḳt k3w 3pdw ḫt nbt nfr(t) wˁbt prrt ḥr w(3)ḏḥw n nb-r-ḏr may he give invocation-offerings of bread and beer, oxen and fowl, and all things good and pure which go (i.e. shall from time to time go) up upon the altars of the lord of the universe.[5]

In the first of these examples another MS. has the perf. part. *rdi*;[6] in the common type of formula illustrated in the second example the Middle Kingdom stelae have usually the perf. part. *prt*.[7] Two explanations are possible. Either the perfective participles here express the notions of 'giving' and 'going up' bereft of all implications alike of time and of repetition, or else they are chosen as the participles ordinarily used in reference to the *past*. The actions in question are, in fact, past relatively to the preceding verb, and could be translated in English by the present perfect ('without letting him know that thou hast given', 'all good things which have gone up'). Latin would express both the futurity of the action and its nature as past relatively to another action by using the future perfect, *omnia quae ascenderint*. The second of the two explanations seems the more probable.

[2] BUDGE, p. 152, 10. Sim. *ib.* p. 130, 10; 141, 3.

[3] *Westc.* 9, 6.

[4] *Peas.* R 130; see too § 373.

[5] *Urk.* iv. 48, 8–9. Sim. *ib.* 52, 15; 74, 10.

[6] *Peas.* B 1, 84.

[7] Cairo 20012. 20024. 20534; Brit. Mus. 573. 575. 805.

§ 369. Tense-distinction in the passive participles.—Generally speaking, the same standpoints which hold for the active participles, hold also for the passive; the imperfective expresses *repetition* or *continuity*, the perfective is free from these implications.

1. The perf. pass. part. in reference to *past* occurrences.

Exx. *sš pn ỉny n bꜣk ỉm* this letter that has been brought to this thy servant.[1] Note the Engl. pres. perfect.

ỉmy-rn·f srw fꜣy n·sn m hrw pn list of officials to whom things were brought (Engl. past tense, lit. who were brought-to-them) on this day.[2]

mỉ gmyt m sš according to what had been found (Engl. past perfect) in writing.[3]

2. The imperf. pass. part. in reference to *continued* or *repeated* (*habitual*) actions in the past.

Exx. She went round the room, *n gm·n·s bw ỉrrw st ỉm* but could not find the place where it was being done.[4] For the construction with *st* see § 377, 2.

Finding a well ..... *prt hꜣꜣt hr gs(wy)·sy ỉn mšꜥw n tp-ꜥwy* which had been passed by (lit. come and gone on its two sides) by the expeditions of former times.[5]

In this second example only one of the parallel participles (*hꜣꜣt*) shows the gemination of the imperfective; in the other (*prt*) it is omitted, perhaps by mistake, but perhaps rather because the gemination of *hꜣꜣt* sufficed for both verbs.

3. The perf. pass. part. in reference to *present* states. This use is common in epithets; for the corresponding use of perf. act. part. see § 367. An additional reason why this employment should be common in the passive voice is that an act which 'has been' done '*is* done', and remains done.

Exx. *sꜣ·f mry·f* his son beloved of him, i.e. his beloved son.[6]

ḥsy ḥss ḥsyw thou praised one who art (habitually) praised of those who are praised.[7]

mk fꜣ pw n ỉṯꜣ ỉry·k behold, it is the supporting of the thief which is done by thee.[8]

If the person thus qualified is regarded as dead, or if the context employs past tenses, such epithets are translated in English as pasts, ex. 'my pen made me *m rḫy* one who was known, i.e. celebrated'.[9] See above § 367.

4. The imperf. pass. part. of actions *continued* or *repeated* in the present.

Exx. She heard the sound of singing and jubilation *ỉrrt nbt n nsw* and of all things which are done (*or* are wont to be done) for a king.[10]

[1] *P. Kah.* 35, 38. Sim. *Westc.* 7, 4 (*ḥsk*); 8, 11 (*nỉsw*); *Sin.* B 254 (*ỉtw*); *Pt.* 557 (*ḏddy*).

[2] *P. Boul.* xviii. 11. Sim. *P. Kah.* 13, 1 (*ỉry*); *Eb.* 66, 15 (*ỉryt*); *Urk.* iv. 194, 1 (*ḏddt*); 726, 14 (*ỉny*).

[3] *Sin.* B 311. Sim. *ib.* B 17 (*ỉry*); *BH.* i. 25, 24 (*ỉryt*); *Hamm.* 114, 16 (*hꜣb*); Louvre C 11, 5 (*wddt*).

[4] *Westc.* 12, 3. Sim. Cairo 20543, 19 (*ỉrrw*); Brit. Mus. 614, 5 (above p. 138, *ỉnnt*); *Sin.* B 299 (*ddt*).

[5] *Hamm.* 191, 5.

[6] Louvre C 197; Cairo 20012; *Th. T. S.* i. 3. 18 *et passim*.

[7] *Peas.* B 1, 68–9. Sim. *Urk.* iv. 19, 14; 119, 2.

[8] *Peas.* B 1, 235–6. Sim. *ib.* B 1, 21.

[9] *Urk.* iv. 119, qu. § 84.

[10] *Westc.* 12, 2. Sim. *Kopt.* 8, 7 (*ỉrrt*); *P. Boul.* xviii. 12, 5 (*ỉnnw*); 12, 8 (*ddt*), qu. Exerc. 20, *a*; *Eb.* 66, 1 (*gmmt*).

prrw hꜣꜣw ḫr sḫr·f one who is gone out and come in under his will, i. e. one by whose authority men go out and come in.[1] For the construction see § 376.

mrrw nb·f one who is loved (habitually) of his lord.[2] *Mry* might have been used, see under (3), but then no stress would have been laid on the continuous nature of the king's affection.

5. The perf. pass. part. in reference to *future* events.

Exx. *nts rdi·s n mry·s nb m nꜣy·s n ḫrdw* she shall give (it) to anyone she likes (lit. any who is *or* shall be desired of her) of her children.[3]

ḫr·f šd·f šdt he shall apportion what is to be apportioned.[4] It is the context which here yields the future meaning.

OBS. Probably it is from such uses that the prospective meaning of the perfective relative form is derived. See below §§ 387, 2; 389, 2.

6. The imperf. pass. part. in respect of *continued* or *repeated* events to occur in the future.

Ex. *m tp-tr nb irrw m ḥwt-nṯr tn* in every seasonal feast which is (i. e. is henceforth to be) made in this temple.[5]

§ 370. Tense-distinction in the participles: summary.—This subject is of so much importance that many pages have been devoted to its discussion and illustration. As the net result, the beginner has mainly to remember that the imperfective participle implies *repetition* or *continuity*, while the perfective has no such implications; and, as the inevitable outcome of this position, that the *perfective* participle becomes the natural medium for alluding to events in the *past*, while the *imperfective* is more adapted to the expression of events in the *present* or *future*. Either of the last statements, however, is liable to exception if repetition or continuity is deliberately kept in or out of view; that is to say, the imperfective participles may be used of the past if continued or repeated past action is envisaged, or the perfective participles may be used of present or future action if it is desired to refer to this quite simply as merely occurring. The *sḏmty·fy* form has, on the contrary, no other function than that of a future active participle.

§ 371. Use of the participles to express obligation or the like.—Egyptian lacking equivalents for such notions as 'ought', 'have to', these may be implicit in the meaning of simple participles, whether active or passive.

Exx. …… *mk tw m .... imy-r w ḫsf ḥꜥḏꜣ* behold, thou art ... a district superintendent who has to punish robbery.[6]

ꜣd·k ḥr ꜣdt ḥr·s thou shalt be angry about that which deserves anger, lit. (that) angered upon it.[7]

[1] Cairo 20359, 4–5. Sim. *Urk.* iv. 269, 8 (*ḥꜥꜥw*); 546, 8 (*ḥrrw*); 972, 14 (*nḥḥw*).

[2] *Siut* I, 214. The same phrase also p. 296, n. 4.

[3] *P. Kah.* 12, 10. Sim. *Siut* I, 272; *Sinai* 139, 7 (*iry·t*), qu. § 382.

[4] *Urk.* iv. 1111, 12. Sim. *Pt.* 153 (*ḏdt*).

[5] *Siut* I, 318. Sim. *ib.* 302 (*sftw*).

[6] *Peas.* B I, 192–3. Sim. *ib.* B I, 100–2; *Urk.* iv. 1111, 3. 7. 8 etc.

[7] *Urk.* iv. 1091, 3. Sim. *ib.* 6; *Peas.* B I, 147. 219; *Pt.* 581.

§ 372. The participles as predicate.—Two constructions, in each of which the predicate is a participle, have now to be considered. The more frequent of the two, which will be called the **participial statement** (A), follows the model of the sentence with *nominal* predicate (§ 125); the subject precedes, and is either an independent pronoun or a noun introduced by the particle *ỉn*. In the other construction (B), the participle comes first and is followed either by a noun or by a dependent pronoun as subject; here, accordingly, the model is that of the sentence with *adjectival* predicate (§ 137).

§ 373. A. The participial statement.[1]—This construction was explained in some detail above § 227, 3. The scheme is

{ *ỉn* + noun / *or* independent pron. } + { perf. act. part. for *past* time / *or* imperf. „ „ „ *present* time }

The construction corresponds in meaning to English 'it is he who hears', or to French *c'est lui qui entend.* For a reason that will be explained in § 391 some degree of emphasis rests on the subject, though this emphasis is not always calculated to make the grammatical subject into the logical predicate; see above § 227, 3. Note that the participle, as here used, is *invariable* in number and gender, and hence must be literally translated 'the-one-who-hears (heard)', not 'he (she)-who-hears (heard)'. In very ancient times the participle seems to have taken the number and gender of the subject.[2] No certain examples of this construction with a passive participle are known.[3]

1. With perf. act. part. for English *past* time.

Exx. *ỉn ḥm·f rdỉ ỉr·t(w)·f* it was His Majesty who caused it to be made.[4] Lit. indeed, His Majesty was the-one-who-caused, etc.

ntk rdỉ ỉt·tw ṯ3y·ỉ šrỉt it is thou who hast caused my daughter to be taken.[5] Lit. thou wast the-one-who-caused, etc.

ỉnk šꜥd ḏrt·f it was I who cut off its (the elephant's) trunk.[6]

OBS. For rare examples after the obscure archaistic pronoun *sw* 'he' see Add.

2. With imperf. act. part. for English *present* time.

Exx. *ỉn 2 dd nšwt, ỉn 2 dd snf* two (vessels) give mucus, and two give blood.[7] Lit. indeed, two are the-ones-which-give, etc.

ỉn nṯr ỉrr ỉḳr it is god who makes prosperity.[8]

The liver has four vessels; *ntsn dd n·s mw* it is they which give it water.[9]

For English *future* time the *sḏmty·fy* form is very rarely used.[10] The corresponding idiom for the *future* is *ntf sḏm·f* or *ỉn* + noun + *sḏm·f*, as we saw in § 227, 2; see also § 450, 5, *e*.

[1] See *Verbum* ii. §§ 752–3; GUNN, *Stud.* pp. 59–64.

[2] See *Verbum* ii. § 753.

[3] But see GUNN, *Stud.* p. 59, under 6.

[4] *Sin.* B 308. Sim. *Mill.* 1, 7 (*ỉr*); *Urk.* iv. 194, 15 (*ỉr*); 766, 5 (*rdỉ*). With fem. subj., *Urk.* iv. 12, 12 (*sꜥnḫ*).

[5] *ÄZ.* 55, 85. With the old indep. pron. *swt*, LAC. *TR.* 47, 36.

[6] *Urk.* iv. 894, 1. Sim. *ib.* 895, 1.

[7] *Eb.* 99, 6. Sim. *ib.* 99, 14 (*ỉrr*).

[8] *Pt.* 184. Sim. *Peas.* B 1, 215 (*dp*); *Eb.* 103, 18 (*šꜥ*).

[9] *Eb.* 100, 8–9. Sim. *P. Kah.* 29, 39 (*ntk ỉrr*).

[10] *Urk.* iv. 221, 14.

The above rules as to the tenses are liable to the following exceptions:

(*a*) For *past repeated* action the imperf. act. part. may be employed; see above § 366.

Ex. *ntf dd n·f st* it is he who used to give it to him.[1]

(*b*) When the imperf. part. is used for *present* time, as in the examples quoted above under (2), the sentence normally expresses a statement of custom, a generalization or the like. It may happen, however, that it is important to avoid suggesting that the act described occurs more than once; in this rare case the perf. part. is used.

Ex. *in 5 pr, ḏꜣt m 10* five is subtracted (lit. goes out), the remainder is ten.[2]

(*c*) Occasionally the imperf. act. part. refers to a *future* event; two cases have been quoted above § 368, one in which there is no implication of repetition or continuity,[3] the other of the commoner type where custom is clearly implied.[4]

§ 374. B. The participle as adjectival predicate.—In this construction the participle comes first, according to rule (§ 137), and the following subject, if pronominal, is a dependent pronoun.

Exx. *ḥꜥ sw im r sprw nb* he rejoices (lit. is one-rejoicing) thereat more than any petitioner.[5]

sḥḏw sw tꜣwy r itn he is one who illuminates the two lands more than the sun.[6]

Sometimes the participle thus used is accompanied by the exclamatory ending *·wy* (§ 49).

Exx. *rš·wy sḏd dpt·n·f* how joyful (lit. rejoicing) is he who relates what he has experienced (lit. tasted)![7]

iy·wy tw m-ꜥb sḫwt·k how welcome (lit. come) art thou amidst thy meads![8]

ii·wy occurs also alone as an exclamation 'welcome!',[9] and is probably to be distinguished from a similar use of the old perfective *iw* (§ 313).

The participle employed in this construction is almost invariably the perfective active. No imperfective examples occur, and passive ones only when these are more adjectival than truly participial in meaning. [See, however, Add.]

Ex. *ḥꜣp st r sḫrw dwꜣt* they are more recondite (lit. hidden) than the fashion of the netherworld.[10]

The examples show how often this construction is used in comparisons.

Note that when the subject is a noun or the dep. pron. 3rd sing. f. in its older writing *s*(*y*)[11] the participial predicate is indistinguishable from the *śḏm·f* form.

[1] *Peas.* B 1, 85–6.

[2] *Rhind* 28. *Pr* similarly in another construction *ÄZ.* 57, 6* qu. § 503, 4.

[3] *Westc.* 9, 6.

[4] *Peas.* R 130. Sim. *Urk.* iv. 1111–6, *passim* (cf. Exerc. XXX, iii).

[5] *Pt.* 270; also with *ḥꜥ*, *Sin.* B 66; Mar. *Abyd.* ii. 30, 35; *Urk.* iv. 162, 5. Sim. with other verbs, *Pt.* 314 (*irw*); 410 (*ꜥnḫ*).

[6] Cairo 20538, ii. *c* 12. Sim. with object, *Hamm.* 114, 7 (*ir sw ḏdt*); *Ann.* 37, Pl. 2, 11 (*rḫ sw kꜣt nbt*).

[6] Cairo 20538, ii. *c* 12. Sim. with object, *Hamm.* 114, 7 (*ir sw ḏdt*).

[7] *Sh. S.* 124. Sim. with nom. subject, *Sin.* B 70; *Pt.* 557 (*rš·wy*); *P. Kah.* 2, 1 (*ḥꜥ·wy*); *Peas.* B 1, 117 (*nḫ·wy*); Ledr. 25, 17 (*iy·wy*).

[8] *Urk.* iv. 990; sim. *Amarn.* i. 14. Other verbs, *Cem. of Abyd.* ii. p. 117 (*mn·wy tw*); Brit. Mus. 551, 3 (*ḥꜥ·wy tw*).

[9] *Pt.* 347; *Urk.* iv. 117, 5; 990, 9.

[10] *Urk.* iv. 99. Some late exx. *Nominals.* §§ 80 *a.* 82.

[11] So perhaps *Pt.* 88. 97.

As a rule, the construction participle + subject is found in main clauses. A peculiar use occurs, however, with the pronoun 3rd sing. f. *sy*, the participle + *sy* being substituted for the corresponding form of the old perfective in a number of cases where the latter is habitually used as a virtual adverb clause.[1] The reason for this substitution, which is confined to the 3rd sing. f., is quite obscure.

Exx. *dpt nbt ȝḳ sy* all taste is perished.[2] Cf. § 322.

iw·i rḫ·kwi šwt rd·ti km·t(i) ip sy I know the tuft is flourishing, black and (fully) numbered.[3] Later MSS. *ip·ti*.

gm·f sy nfr sy ḥr sšr r ḥwt-nṯr nbt he found it more perfectly beautiful than any temple.[4] One expects *nfr·ti*, § 315.

ꜥt nbt nty mr sy every member that is ill.[5] Cf. § 328, 1.

VOCABULARY

var. *wȝḏ* be green, fresh; caus. *swȝḏ* make green.

wtt (old *wtṯ*) beget.

bȝgi, var. *bgi*, be remiss, slack.

nṯry (old *nṯri*) be divine.

sḫr overlay.

tḥn (old *ṯḥn*) be dazzling; *stḥn* make dazzling.

ȝbw cessation.

i(ȝ)mw splendour, brilliance.

iwꜥw heir.

var. *inb* wall.

irw form, nature.

irt duty.

abbrev. *pḥty* might, strength.

mꜥnḏt (written *ꜥḏt*) the morning-bark of the sun-god.

old *msktt* the evening-bark of the sun-god.

var. *r-pꜥt* (from *iry-pꜥt*) hereditary prince.

Ḥꜥpy Haꜥpy, the Inundation-god; inundation, high Nile.

ḥḏḏwt brightness.

st-ib pleasure, affection.

var. *Sḫm* Power, personified as deity; a power.

ssmt horse.

sḏȝwty (?) treasurer.

šndyt apron, skirt.

šsp (old *sšp*) light.

[1] In constructions not exemplified below: § 314, *Hirt.* 24; *Urk.* iv. 879, 4; 882, 12; § 316, *Eb.* 25, 6 = 52, 4; § 317, *Urk.* iv. 1160, 7; § 323, *Eb.* 107, 7; § 324, *Urk.* iv. 1163, 3; § 328, 2, SETHE, *Sprüche*, 44*, 8 (S 1); see too § 482, 2. Further exx., *ÄZ.* 71, 52

[2] *Pt.* 25.

[3] *ÄZ.* 57, 10*.

[4] CHAMP. *ND.* ii. 424.

[5] *Hearst* 6, 11, with superfluous plural strokes, see *Eb.* 1, 11. Sim. *Eb.* 60, 10, *tḥn sy* corrected out of *tḥn·ti r·s*.

EXERCISE XXV

(*a*) *Reading lesson. Part of hymn to Rēꜥ from the door-jamb of the tomb of the general, afterwards king, Ḥaremḥab; end of Dyn. XVIII.*[1]

ḏd mdw ỉn r-pꜥt Ḥr-m-ḥb, mꜣꜥ-ḫrw,
dwꜣ·f Rꜥ m wbn·f,
ḏd·f:
ỉ(ꜣ)w n·k ḫpr[1a] *rꜥ nb,*
mss sw tnw dwꜣyt,
pr m ḫt mwt·f, nn ꜣbw.[2]
ỉw n·k ỉtrty[3] *m ksw,*
dỉ·sn n·k ỉ(ꜣ)w n wbn·k,
sṯḥn·n·k[4] *tꜣ m ỉꜣmw ḥꜥw·k,*
ntry·tỉ m Sḫm ỉmy pt,
nṯr mnḫ,
nsw (n)ḥḥ,
nb šsp,
ḥkꜣ ḥḏdwt,
ḥry nst·f m msktt,[5]
ꜥꜣ ḫꜥw m mꜥnḏt,[5]
ḥwn[6] *ntry ỉwꜥw (n)ḥḥ,*
wtt[7] *sw,*
ms sw ḏs·f.
dwꜣ tw psḏt[8] *ꜥꜣ(t),*
hnw n·k psḏt nḏst,
dwꜣ·sn tw m ỉrw·k nfr.

[1] Brit. Mus. 552 (VIII, Pl. 27). [1a] For the 3rd pers. see § 509, 1. [2] [hieroglyph] for [hieroglyph], as often at this period.

[3] Lit. 'the two rows', i.e. the gods of Upper and Lower Egypt; see *ÄZ.* 44, 17 for the expression and *JEA* 30, 27 for explanation; see also the Sign-list under O 19, 20. [4] The sign for *tỉ* is here used simply for *t*.

[5] *Mꜥnḏt* 'the bark of the dawn' and *msktt* 'the bark of the dusk' are the names of the ships in which the sun was supposed to perform his day-journey from east to west and his night-journey from west to east respectively. *Mꜥnḏt* here has borrowed the ending *tt* from *msktt*.

[6] Mixture of two different writings [hieroglyphs] and [hieroglyphs]. [7] The sign for *tyw* seems superfluous.

[8] *Psḏt* 'ennead' or 'cycle of nine gods', see § 260. The Great Ennead consisted of Atum, Shu and Tphēnis, Geb and Nut, Osiris and Isis, Seth and Nephthys.

'Words recited (lit. the saying of words) by the prince Ḥaremḥab, justified, when he adores Rēʿ at his rising; he says:—Praise to thee, who comest into existence every day, who givest birth to thyself every morning, who comest forth from the womb of thy mother without cessation. The two halves (of Egypt) come to thee doing obeisance (lit. in bowing), they give thee praise at thy rising, thou hast made dazzling the land through the splendour of thy body, being divine as the Power which is in heaven, the beneficent god, the king of eternity, the lord of light, the prince of brightness, who is on his seat in the Bark of the Dusk, great in (his) appearances in the Bark of the Dawn, divine stripling, heir of eternity, who begot his (own) self and bare his own self. The Great Ennead adores thee, the Little Ennead makes jubilation to thee; they adore thee in thy beautiful forms.'

(*b*) *Translate into English*:

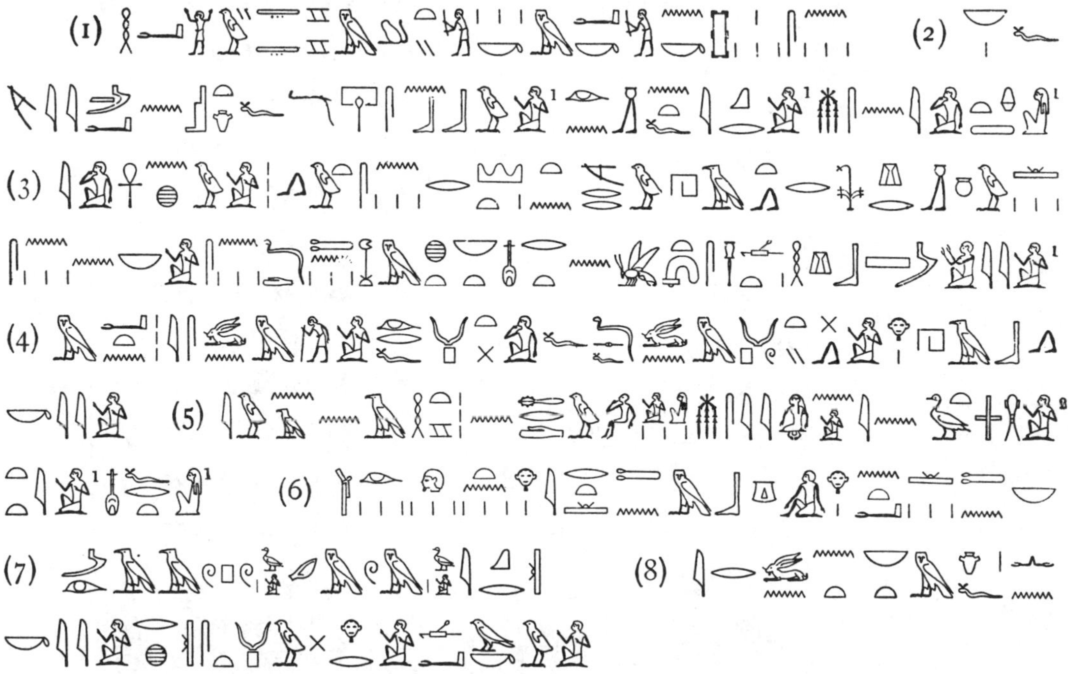

(1) (2) (3) (4) (5) (6) (7) (8)

[1] Names of persons. [2] Title for a subordinate in some official class.

(*c*) *Write in hieroglyphs*:

(1) He maketh green the earth more than a high (*ʿꜣ*) Nile. (2) He did this with loving heart for his father Chnum. (3) It is not I who say it, it is Horus who says it. (4) All that is (use *wnn*) in my house, I have given it to thee. (5) May there be said to thee 'Welcome, welcome' in this thy house of the living! (6) Tribute which was brought to His Majesty in this year: 1056 horses, 183 chariots wrought (§ 317) in gold. (7) Let (*imi*) him who has done it stand up. (8) My statue was overlaid with gold, its apron with fine gold. It was His Majesty who caused it to be made. (9) Who will bring me these books?

LESSON XXVI

SYNTAX OF THE PARTICIPLES AND OF THE *ŚḎMTY·FY* FORM

§ **375. Expression of the object and dative.**—The active participles and the *śḏmty·fy* form may be followed, like the *śḏm·f* form, by such adjuncts as a direct object or a dative.

Exx. *smi nfr n hꜣb sw* who reported well to him who sent him.[1]

ir grt fḫt(y)·fy sw now as for him who shall lose it.[2]

it·f wḏ n·f idbwy his father who allotted to him the two lands.[3]

ntf dd n·f st it is he who used to give it to him.[4]

wꜥb nb rdit(y)·f(y) n·i t-ḥḏ pn every priest who shall give me this white bread.[5]

These examples show that the dependent pronouns are used when the object is pronominal, and that the same rules of word-order apply as in any main clause (§§ 27. 66).

OBS. If a pronominal object or dative follows the participle, and this is also qualified by the adjective *nb* 'every', 'all', that adjective is usually placed after the entire phrase; if, however, both object and dative occur together, *nb* may precede them. See the 2nd and 3rd examples in § 377, 2.

§ **376. Extended use of the passive participles.**—The passive is, by definition, a name given to verb-forms which treat the direct semantic object (i.e. the grammatical object of the active voice)[5a] as a grammatical subject or nominative. It follows that any passive participle ought to be translatable, like any active participle, as a 'who'-clause; and such is, of course, very frequently the case, exx. *mry* 'who is loved', *hꜣb* 'who was sent'. But just as in English a person may be said, not only to be 'sent', but also to be 'sent to', so Egyptian may stretch the meaning of the passive participles in such a way that the antecedent (the word, implied or expressed, with which they agree) is no longer identical with the direct semantic object but with an indirect one, i.e. the case after some preposition.

Exx. *smiw n·sn* those who are reported to, lit. (those) reported to them.[6]

ꜣdt ḥr·s a thing to be angry at, lit. (a thing) angered upon it.[7]

Two points have to be noticed. First, this extended meaning of the passive enables passive participles to be formed from intransitive verbs like *ꜣd* 'be angry', no less than from transitives like *smi* 'report'. Second, Egyptian, unlike English, regularly employs a resumptive pronoun (*n·sn*, *ḥr·s*, § 146).

[1] Louvre C 174. Sim. *Urk.* iv. 767, 13; 781, 4.
[2] Berl. *ÄI.* i. p. 258, 19. Sim. MAR. *Abyd.* ii. 30, 36.
[3] *Urk.* iv. 198.
[4] *Peas.* B 1, 85-6.
[5] *Siut* 1, 282.
[5a] See § 297 for these grammatical terms.
[6] *Bersh.* i. 7. Sim. *irrw n·f*, Berl. *ÄI.* i. 180, qu. § 357.
[7] *Urk.* iv. 1091, 3. Sim. intrans. vbs., *ib.* 1091, 6; 415, 12; 972, 12; *Pt.* 344. 581; *Peas.* B 1, 147.

Had English employed a resumptive pronoun, nothing could have prevented a still further extension of this construction, so that the pronoun would refer, not merely to indirect semantic objects, but even to persons and things still more remotely involved; from 'a person confided in him' (instead of 'a person confided in'), it would have been no far cry to 'a person confided in his judgement', i.e. a person in whose judgement one confides. Egyptian, since it regularly employs a resumptive pronoun, has been able to take this step.

Exx. *prrw hꜣꜣw ẖr sḫr·f* by whose will one comes and goes, lit. (one who is) gone up and come down habitually under his will.[1]

ḥꜥꜥw m irt·n·f nbt over all whose actions one rejoices, lit. one habitually rejoiced at all that he has done.[2] For *irt·n·f* see § 382.

Nothing is more characteristic of Egyptian than such complex constructions with the passive participle. The student will find them easy enough to cope with if he will make a practice of looking for the resumptive pronoun first of all, and then translating the phrase in which it occurs in such a way that the resumptive pronoun appears as an English relative. For example, *ẖr sḫr·f* 'under his will' is transformed into 'under whose will'. Next, the Egyptian passive participle must be turned into an English active verb; and since the Egyptian has not indicated the doer, the English must insert 'one' or 'people' as a quite indefinite subject; *prrw hꜣꜣw* is therefore rendered 'one goes and comes'. Thus is obtained the complete rendering 'under whose will one goes and comes', or more idiomatically, 'by whose will one comes and goes'.

[1] Cairo 20359. Sim. *Hamm.* 47, 10–1; Cairo 20538, ii. *c* 12; *Rifeh* 4, 57.

[2] *Urk.* iv. 269. Sim. *ib.* 546, 8.

§ 377. The retained object after the passive participles.[3]—1. English, because it uses the phrases 'to find fault with', 'to think much of', can also say 'he was found fault with', 'she was thought much of'. This retention of the direct object[s] is exceedingly common with the Egyptian passive participles.

Exx. *ḏd(w) n·f nbw n ḥswt* to whom the gold of favour was repeatedly given, lit. (one) given to him the gold of favour.[4]

imy-rn·f rmṯ iry nn r-gs·sn list of people in whose presence this was done, lit. done this in their presence.[5]

Go to the place where thy fair ones are, *m rdyt ꜥntiw r šny·sn, sntr wꜣḏ r ḥṯṯwt·sn* (women) upon whose hair myrrh, and upon whose shoulders fresh incense has been placed.[6]

nꜣ rdy ḥr im n bꜣk im that concerning which a charge was given (lit. given a charge therein) to this thy servant.[7]

Note that the resumptive pronoun is regularly employed; in the last instance, however, *im* 'therein' serves as a substitute for *m* + suffix.[8] Observe further that in all the above examples, unlike those quoted in § 376, the passive voice can be kept in translation, the retained direct object[s] becoming its subject.

[3] See *Rev. ég.*, n. s. ii. 45. See, however, Add.

[4] *Urk.* iv. 415. Sim. *ib.* 46, 15; *P. Kah.* 35, 28; *Pt.* 557; *Sin.* B 309; Cairo 20498, *a* 5–6; *Adm.* p. 106, qu. § 357.

[5] *P. Kah.* 13, 1. Sim. *ib.* 11, 24; *Sh. S.* 141–2; *Leb.* 100; *Urk.* iv. 795, 9; Budge, p. 231, 4; 268, 6.

[6] *M. u. K.* 3, 5–6.

[7] *P. Kah.* 29, 15.

[8] Sim. *Siut* 1, 296; *Westc.* 12, 3; *Pt.* 282.

Here belongs the formula [hieroglyphs] *ḏdw n·f*, f. [hieroglyphs] *ḏdt n·s* 'called', lit. 'said to him (her)', by which secondary personal names are introduced.

Ex. [hieroglyphs] *'Intf ḏdw n·f 'Iw-snb* Entef who is called Yewsonb.[1]

In introducing such names the *śḏm·f* form *ḏd·tw* is occasionally used in place of the passive participle.[2]

2. When the retained object is a *personal pronoun*, the dependent pronoun is used, as after the active participles (§ 375) and after the *śḏm·f* and *śḏm·n·f* forms.

Exx. [hieroglyphs] *ir·n·i hȝbt wi r·s* I had done what I had been sent for, lit. (that) sent me for it.[3]

[hieroglyphs] *ir grt šdd sw nb ḥr·f rʿ nb* but as to everyone over whom it (this spell) is read every day.[4] Lit. every read-it-over-him.

[hieroglyphs] *ntf šȝ ʿḥʿw r šȝw nb n·f sw* he assigns boats in respect of everyone to whom they have to be assigned.[5] Lit. every assigned-it-to-him.

A weakening of usage is, however, occasionally found in the case of the 2nd and 3rd pers. sing., suffixes being employed instead of the dependent pronouns.

Exx. [hieroglyphs] *m bw pn iny·k im* in this place from which thou wast brought, lit. brought thou thence.[6]

[hieroglyphs] *it·ṯ pw msy·ṯ n·f*, this thy father to whom thou wast born.[7]

One may perhaps compare the substitution of these same suffixes for dependent pronouns after *ntt*; see above § 223, end.

OBS. Compare further the use of the suffixes as subject of the passive *śḏm·f* form, below § 421.

§ **378. Omission of the resumptive pronoun.**—The replacement of *m*+suffix by the adverb *im* was noted in § 377, 1. So too after the relative forms, below § 385.

The name of a reigning Pharaoh is often accompanied by the phrase [hieroglyphs] *di ʿnḫ*, f. [hieroglyphs] *dit ʿnḫ*. This must be considered as a shortening of *rdy n·f ʿnḫ* 'to whom life is given' or perhaps rather of *rdy ʿnḫ·f* 'given that he live'. English can similarly shorten to 'given life' its equivalent of the Egyptian phrase.

The present opportunity must be taken to allude to the use of [hieroglyphs], f. [hieroglyphs], as well as the old perfectives [hieroglyph] *ʿnḫ(w)*, [hieroglyphs] *ʿnḫ·ti* (2nd m. sing.), etc. (§ 313) as object after the verb *iri* 'make'. This use is frequent at the conclusion of dedicatory inscriptions in the temples.

Exx. [hieroglyphs] *ir·f ʿnḫ(w) ḏt*, may he make 'he-lives-eternally'.[8]

[hieroglyphs] *ir·k ʿnḫ·ti ḏt*, mayst thou make 'thou-livest-eternally'.[9]

[hieroglyphs] *ir·f di ʿnḫ*, may he make 'given-life'.[10]

[1] *P. Kah.* 11, 18. Sim. Cairo 20213, 6. 9; Vienna 57; Louvre C 72; fem., *P. Kah.* 12, 8.

[2] Ex. *Urk.* iv. 32, 12 (*ḏd·tw n·f*); Cairo 20141, *a*, 2 (*iw ḏd·tw r·f*).

[3] Leyd. V 88, 10–1. Sim. *Westc.* 12, 3, qu. § 369, 2; *Pt.* 282. 623; *Cat. d. Mon.* i. p. 89, no. 76; *Urk.* iv. 1108, 12; 1109, 7.

[4] *Urk.* v. 96.

[5] *Urk.* iv. 1116.

[6] BUDGE, p. 124, 3–4.

[7] LAC. *TR.* 21, 9. Sim. 3rd pers., *ÄZ.* 47, 122.

[8] *Urk.* iv. 871, 12; 873, 11. Fem. exx., *ib.* 214, 3; 296, 7; 334, 12.

[9] *Urk.* iv. 214, 9; 569, 4; 570, 10; 864, 6. Fem. exx., *ib.* 358, 10; 375, 10.

[10] PETR. *Abyd.* ii. 28; *Urk.* iv. 340, 15; 584, 12; 596, 6. Fem. exx., *ib.* 312, 16; 340, 8; 343, 3. Var: *ir·f n·f di ʿnḫ*, *Kopt.* 10, 1; *Urk.* iv. 881, 13; see also *ib.* 43, 16, where word-order shows that the dative refers to the god, see below § 507, 1.

§ 379. The semantic subject after the passive participles.—1. There are several ways in which the semantic subject, i.e. the performer of the action of the verb as actively conceived, can be expressed after the passive participles. It is sometimes expressed, as after other passives and after the infinitive, in the form of an *agent*, i.e. with the help of the preposition *ỉn* (§ 39, end).

Exx. *ḏwt ỉryt r·f ỉn sn·f Stẖ* the evils done to him by his brother Seth.[1]

nḥḥw n·f snb ʿnḫ ỉn rmṯt nbt one for whom health and life are prayed for by all people.[2]

2. The same meaning can, however, be conveyed by the *direct genitive.*

Exx. *ỉnk mry nbt·f, ḥsy·s m ẖrt-hrw nt rʿ nb* I am one beloved of (*or* by) his mistress and praised of (*or* by) her in the course of each day.[3]

mrrw nb·f one beloved of his lord.[4]

ỉryt ẖry-ḥb(t) that done by (lit. of) the lector-priest.[5]

ḫt nbt nfrt wʿbt ddt pt, ḳmȝt tȝ, ỉnnt Ḥʿpy all things good and pure, given of heaven, created of earth, brought by (lit. of) the inundation.[6] A common formula.

Here belong the examples where the semantic subject after the passive participle is expressed by a *suffix-pronoun.* We have frequently had occasion to point out that the relation of the suffix-pronouns to the words which they follow is that of the direct genitive.

Exx. *sȝ·f mry·f* his son who is beloved of him.[7]

ỉrr ḥsst·sn nbt doing all that is praised of them.[8]

3. An ambiguity arises when the semantic subject is introduced by *n.*

Ex. *mry n ỉt·f, ḥsy n mwt·f* beloved by his father, praised by his mother.[9]

It is not clear whether *n* here is to be regarded as the preposition or as the genitival adjective. Feminine instances like *ḥsyt nt Ḥt-ḥr* 'praised of Hathor'[10] show that the genitival adjective may really be used to introduce the agent. On the other hand, we have seen (§ 361, under *3ae inf.*) that *ỉr n* 'engendered by' and *ms n* 'born to' (lit. 'borne to') make as feminines *ỉrt n* and *mst n* with the preposition *n.*[11] Possibly the use of the preposition *n* to introduce the agent entailed certain changes in the passive participle, producing the *sḏmw·n·f* relative form to be described below. On the other hand, texts exist where *msy n* 'born to' (a father) stand side by side with *ms n* (or *ms·n*) 'borne to', i.e. 'by', (the mother),[12] showing that the full form could be retained if the preposition *n* had a function other than that of introducing the agent.[13]

[1] *Eb.* 1, 13. Sim. *P. Kah.* 11, 22; *Urk.* iv. 689, 17.

[2] *Urk.* iv. 972. Sim. *Hamm.* 191, 5, qu. § 369, 2.

[3] Cairo 20543, *a* 6–7. Sim. *Sinai* 28. 35. 71; *Urk.* iv. 994, 16. See too below, n. 11.

[4] *Urk.* iv. 68. Sim. *Sinai* 27; Louvre C 1, 7 (*ḥssw*).

[5] *Westc.* 4, 11–2.

[6] Cairo 20540. Sim. *ib.* 20430; *BH.* i. 7, 3.

[7] Cairo 20501 and *passim.* Sim. *Peas.* B 1, 21 (*sḫȝy·k*); 118 (*sky·k*); 236 (*ỉry·k*).

[8] Louvre C 1, 4. Sim. *Siut* 1, 267 (*mrrt·f*).

[9] Cairo 20501. Sim. *Urk.* iv. 19, 14; 153, 9; 1011, 10.

[10] Piehl, *IH.* i. 143. Sim. Brit. Mus. 43.

[11] Var. *ms* + direct genitive, Dyn. XI, Pol. § 71.

[12] *Ächt.* p. 32. *N* + suffix, *P. Kah.* 11, 22; *Pt.* 623.

[13] Cf., however, *ỉnt n·f* 'brought to him' qu. p. 279, n. 28.

THE RELATIVE FORMS

§ 380. It was seen in § 353 that the Egyptian participles may nearly always be translated into English by what can be described briefly as 'who'-clauses, i.e. relative clauses in which the subject is *identical with* the antecedent. We have now to consider a class of verb-forms best translated by relative clauses in which there is an expressed subject *different from* the antecedent. Where these verb-forms occur, the relative word in the English rendering appears as 'whom', 'whose', 'where', and so forth, only not as the nominative 'who' or 'which'. Two typical examples may serve as a concrete basis for the discussion to follow:

sḏmw n·f sḏmw one to whom (lit. to him) judges listen.[1]

ḳmꜣt·n bꜣw 'Iwnw nfr·s one whose beauty (lit. her beauty) the souls of Heliopolis created.[2]

The verb-forms here in question are known as the **relative forms**[3] and at first sight seem peculiar to Egyptian. When the antecedent is masculine, they are often outwardly indistinguishable from the narrative *śḏm·f* and *śḏm·n·f* forms, though fuller writings showing a gender-ending *-w* (in one case *-y*) indicate their independent existence as distinct verb-forms. When the antecedent is feminine, the gender-ending *-t* is written after the stem to agree with the antecedent. Thus from the immutable verbs we have the forms

m. *sḏm(w)·f*, very seldom written with *-w* when the subject is a suffix; with nominal subject the writing *sḏmw* is not rare.
f. *sḏmt·f*, much more rarely written or even .

m. *sḏm(w)·n·f*, only rarely written with *-w* *sḏmw·n·f*.
f. *sḏmt·n·f*.

If the verb-stem has a determinative, the gender-ending precedes the determinative, except in the unusual feminine forms with or , ex. , where the analogy of the old perfective has evidently influenced the writing.

Thus, so far as the immutable verbs are concerned, only two varieties of relative form can be detected, one resembling narrative *śḏm·n·f* and the other resembling narrative *śḏm·f*. The mutable verbs show that the latter comprises at least two forms, one with gemination and the other without. Taking now *mrỉ* 'love' as type-verb and quoting only the forms with nominal subject, we obtain:—

Imperfective relative form: m. *mrrw*, also written ; f. *mrrt*.

Perfective relative form: m. *mr*, also written *mry*; f. *mrt*, also written , .

The *śḏmw·n·f* relative form[4]: m. *mr(w)·n*, rarely written ; f. *mrt·n*.

[1] *BH.* i. 26, 155–6.

[2] *Urk.* iv. 361.

[3] See *Verbum* ii. §§ 737 foll.; *Rev. ég.* n. s., ii. 42 foll.; *ÄZ.* 54, 98–103; 59, 65; *Some Aspects*, 7.

[4] In the 1st ed. called 'perfective relative form', a name now transferred to the foregoing form. The name here preferred stresses the close relationship to the 'narrative' *śḏm·n·f* form of §§ 67. 412 ff.

In the first edition of this work the perf. relative form was called the 'prospective relative',[0] since it often looks forward to action lying in the *future*. A recent discovery[0a] shows that in the early M. K. this form, or one not clearly distinguishable from it,[0b] often referred to *past* action, though later superseded in that function by the *śḏmw·n·f* relative form. Thus the non-geminating relative form without *n* is completely parallel in its functions to the 'narrative' perf. *śḏm·f* (§§ 447, 449) and the name 'perfective' is altogether appropriate.

[0] See GUNN, *Stud.* ch. 1.
[0a] By CLÈRE, still unpublished.
[0b] See below, §§ 387, 2; 389, 2.

§ 381. The relative forms as epithets or as nouns.—Like the participles (§ 353), the relative forms can be used either with or without an expressed antecedent, i.e. either as *epithets* or as *nouns*. See below, *passim*.

When the relative form is used as a noun, it may be qualified by the adjective *nb* 'all', 'every', 'any'.

Exx. *kꜣp sy ḥr ssnt·s nbt m ꜣšr* fumigate her over anything which she smells as roast.[1]

ỉr·n·k mỉ wḏt·n nbt ḥm·ỉ thou hast done according to all that My Majesty commanded.[2]

rdỉt·n·f n·ỉ nbt all that he gave to me.[3] For the position of *nbt* after the dative *n·ỉ*, see above § 375, OBS.

[1] *P. Kah.* 5, 8. Sim. *Urk.* iv. 618, 11, qu. § 386, 1.
[2] *Ikhern.* 9. Sim. *Urk.* iv. 353, 12.
[3] *P. Kah.* 12, 9.

§ 382. The relative forms with direct semantic object identical with the antecedent.—In this case (true 'whom'-clauses) *no resumptive pronoun is ever used.*

Exx. *ḫt nbt ddt sr nb nḏs nb r ḥwt-nṯr* anything which any official or any commoner places in the temple.[4]

r rḫ dỉt·ỉ m r·ỉ in order to find out what I could put in my mouth.[5]

ṯn(w)·n·f ḫnt mrt·f whom he distinguished among his servants.[6]

It is extremely significant that Egyptian does not here write *ddt st sr*, *dỉt·ỉ st* and *ṯn(w)·n·f sw*. This absence of the dependent pronoun as object has a remarkable consequence, namely that in the case of the imperf. and perf. relative forms (see the first two examples above) it would be equally possible to regard the verb-form as a passive participle followed by a direct genitive (above, § 379, 2). This becomes still clearer when no adverbial phrase is appended.

Exx. *ỉr·n·(ỉ) mrrt rmṯ, ḥsst nṯrw* I did what men love and what the gods praise.[7] *Or*, I did what is loved of men and what is praised of the gods.

ỉw šꜣ·n·ỉ bꜣkw ỉry·ỉ I determined the work I was going to do; *or*, the work to be done (§ 371) by me.[8]

[4] *Siut* I, 280. Sim. *ib.* 292. 295; *Pt.* 146; *Urk.* iv. 1107, 11.
[5] *Sh. S.* 46. Sim. *Siut* I, 298, qu. § 389, 2.
[6] *BH.* i. 25, 10. Sim. *Sin.* B 148. 162; *Urk.* iv. 684, 14; 734, 14; 743, 5; 780, 5; fem., *ib.* iv. 1071, 8; 1074, 3; Brit. Mus. 614, 10; *P. Kah.* 12, 9, qu. § 381.
[7] *Siut* I, 266. Sim. *Sin.* B 213.
[8] *Sinai* 139, 6–7.

It is obvious that, in particular, the first of these two examples is inseparable, as regards its construction, from *mrrw nb·f* 'one beloved of his lord' quoted in § 379, 2 as an example of the imperf. pass. part. + direct genitive as subject[s]. In other words, we begin to see that the relative forms originated in an extension of the use of the passive participles.

§ 383. The relative forms with direct semantic object different from the antecedent.—In this case the direct object[s] has naturally to be inserted as grammatical object of the relative form, and, if pronominal, is represented by a dependent pronoun. The word-order is the same as after the narrative verb-forms.

Exx. *mḫꜣt tw nt Rꜥ fꜣt·f Mꜣꜥt im·s* that balance of Rēꜥ in which he weighs Right.[1]

nꜣ hd·k sw ḥr·s that for which thou punishest him.[2] For the masculine gender of *hd(w)·k* see above § 111.

ḥssw nb·f šmwt·f whose goings his lord praises.[3] *Or*, whose lord praises his goings.

sḫnt·n mnḫw·f st·f whose efficiency advanced his position.[4]

rdi·n ꜥr·f rḫ·tw·f whom his pen caused to be known.[5] *Or*, whose pen caused him to be known.

ipꜣt nsw nbt .... rdit·n·f iry·(i) n·s ipt every private department of the king ...... for which he caused me to do business.[6]

The article *dd·n nb (ꜥ.w.s.): ink rdi·i ir·tw·f n·k* of which (my) lord (l. p. h.) said: I will cause it to be made for thee.[7]

The important point to be observed here is that the English relative pronoun ('in which', 'for which', 'whose', etc.) is represented in Egyptian by a resumptive pronoun. Save for the presence of the semantic subject and, in the *śdmw·n·f* relative form, of the *·n* which introduces it, these examples show a very close parallelism to the examples of the passive participle quoted above in § 377.

§ 384. The relative forms from intransitive verbs.—Again, with intransitive verbs a resumptive pronoun must be used to represent the English relative pronoun, and may be, for example, a suffix-pronoun after a preposition or a genitive following a noun.

Exx. *ḥꜥꜥw n·f ḥnmmt m 'Iwnw* at whom the sun-people rejoice in Heliopolis.[8]

wꜣt it·n·f ḥr·s the road on which it (the statue) came.[9]

šmw bw nb m šw·f in whose shadow everyone walks.[10]

[1] LAC. *TR.* 37, 3. Sim. QUIB. *Saqq.* 1906–7, p. 32, xii. 3.
[2] *Urk.* iv. 1090, 14.
[3] Louvre C 1, 8–9. Sim. *Siut* 1, 247; *Hamm.* 113, 6.
[4] *Urk.* iv. 957. Sim. *Siut* 1, 221; *Hamm.* 17, 6; *P. Kah.* 1, 6; *Urk.* iv. 361, 9, qu. § 380; 780, 6.
[5] *Urk.* iv. 127.
[6] Brit. Mus. 614, 10.
[7] *P. Kah.* 28, 27. Rather similar after pass. part., *P. Boul.* xviii, 68.
[8] Cairo 20498. Sim. *ib.* 20539, i. *b* 15; *Siut* 1, 234; *Eb.* 99, 15; ERM. *Hymn.* 11, 2–3; *Urk.* iv. 350, 9.
[9] *Bersh.* i. 14, 1. Sim. *Sin.* B 101; *P. Boul.* xviii. 6; *Urk.* iv. 350, 9; 807, 12.
[10] Cairo 20539, i. *b* 11. Sim. *Sin.* B 44–5, qu. § 389, 1; ERM. *Hymn.* 1, 2; *Urk.* iv. § 389, 1. More complex exx. *Suppl.* p. 12 on § 384; *Coffin Texts* iii. 324, *g–h*.

Note that these examples closely resemble the passive participles quoted in § 376; the only difference, indeed, so far as the imperfective relative form is concerned, is that the semantic subject is here expressed.

§ 385. Omission of the resumptive pronoun.—We saw in § 382 that the resumptive pronoun is regularly absent when the direct semantic object is identical with the antecedent ('whom'-clauses). It may, however, happen that the direct object^s of the relative form is a dependent verb (*śḏm·f* or infinitive) and that it is the direct object^s of this dependent verb which is identical with the antecedent. In such cases the resumptive pronoun is sometimes used for the sake of clearness.

Exx. *kꜣt·n·f irt st r·i, ir·n·i st r·f* what he had planned to do (lit. to do it) to me, I did it to him.[1]

ink pw mrrw nṯr sᶜnḫ·f wi it is I whom the god wishes to preserve, lit. that he should preserve me.[2] In this instance the 1st pers. *wi* is illogically and exceptionally substituted for *sw*.

Sometimes, on the other hand, the resumptive pronoun is omitted.

Exx. *dᶜm di·n·f int ḥm·i m-ḫnt Tꜣ-sty* the gold which he had caused My Majesty to bring out of Nubia.[3] *'Int* here is an active *śḏm·f* form (§ 448).

wḏt·n·f irt what he had commanded to be done, lit. to do.[4]

Elsewhere the absence of the resumptive pronoun is common only in association with *im* in its various meanings; so too after the passive participles, § 378.

Exx. *bw wršw ib·i im* the place where my heart dwelleth.[5]

ḥtpt ḏfꜣw mrrt ꜣḫw wnm im the offerings whereof the spirits love to eat.[6]

In this connection we must note an apparent ellipse of the infinitive *wnn* 'to be' after *mr(i)* 'love', 'wish'.

Ex. *r bw nb mry·i im* to any place where I may wish to be.[7]

§ 386. Origin of the relative forms.[8]—1. Throughout our account of the uses of the relative forms (§§ 381–385), the close analogy to similar uses of the passive participles (§§ 353. 376–378) has everywhere been apparent. Indeed, in the case of the imperfective and the perfective relative forms, the distinction is apt to disappear altogether; it does not matter whether we explain *mrrw* in *mrrw nb·f* 'one beloved of his lord', 'one whom his lord loves' (§ 379, 2) as imperfective relative form, or whether we regard it as an imperfective passive participle with the semantic subject *nb·f* in the form of a direct genitive.

[1] *Sin.* B 144–5. Sim. *Pt.* 267.

[2] *Eb.* 1, 10.

[3] *Ikhern.* 4.

[4] *Urk.* iv. 750. Sim. *Adm.* 8, 1 (*tm·n·f mꜣꜣ*).

[5] *Sin.* B 158. Sim. Turin 1447, 8; BUDGE, p. 129, 9–10.

[6] Brit. Mus. 614, vert. 2. With the meaning 'wherewith', QUIB. *Saqq.* 1906–7, p. 32, xii. 3.

[7] BUDGE, p. 150, 12. Sim. *P. Kah.* 6, 21; LAC. *TR.* 83, 25.

[8] See Add. for a partly divergent theory.

So, too, more complex constructions of the imperfective passive participle may be considered as imperfective relative forms from which subject[s] has been omitted as unessential; *ḏd(w) n·f nbw n ḥswt* (§ 377, 1, first example) needs only the insertion of *nb·f* to turn it into a typical example of the imperfective relative form: *ḏd(w) n·f nb·f nbw n ḥswt* 'one to whom his master repeatedly gave the gold of favour'.[0] It thus seems evident that the relative forms are simply an extension of the passive participles. Whereas English can only retain the direct semantic object ('the boy found fault with'), Egyptian feels no difficulty in the simultaneous retention of the semantic subject ('the boy found-of-his-father-fault-with-him'), and thus obtains an exceedingly compact method of producing the equivalent of an English relative clause ('the boy whom his father finds fault with').

[0] *Ann.* V. 248 gives a var. of the ex. qu. p. 299, n. 1 with *fꜣꜣt* in place of *fꜣꜣt·f*. Cf. also the varr. without *nṯr* qu. in GUNN's Appendix on *ꜥnḫt nṯr im*, *Stud.* p. 32.

This explanation of the relative forms is confirmed by the absence of the resumptive pronoun when that pronoun would be the direct object of the relative form (§ 382); the reason why Egyptian does not say **mrrw sw nb·f* 'one whom his lord loves' is because *mrrw* is, in its origin, a passive participle which has inherent in itself the direct semantic object (§ 376, beginning); 'one who is beloved' is not **mrrw sw*, but simply *mrrw*. This point is the corner-stone of the theory of the relative forms here maintained.

There are, however, some good reasons why the relative forms should be classified apart from the passive participles in which they originated. The semantic subject in *mrrw nb·f* had to be explained (§ 379, 2) as a direct genitive. But we saw (§ 85) that it is almost impossible to separate a direct genitive from its noun, whereas the subject of the relative form may be readily separated from it in accordance with the rules of word-order given in §§ 27. 66.

Exx. *mrrt nbt kꜣ·i* all that my soul desires.[1]

ptr ḏdt n·i nb·i what is (it) that my lord says to me?[2]

ḫt nbt nfrt nt Tꜣ-nṯr hꜣbt sn ḥmt·⟨t⟩ r·s every good thing of the Divine Land for which ⟨Thy⟩ Majesty sends them.[3]

[1] *Urk.* iv. 618.

[2] *Sin.* B 261. Sim. *BH.* i. 26, 155–6, qu. § 380.

[3] *Urk.* iv. 346.

It seems clear that these final extensions of the use of the passive participles can only have come about when the semantic subject had ceased to be felt as a direct genitive, and was now, though doubtless not fully consciously, regarded as a nominative, or as on a par with other nominatives. But this is only another way of saying that these involved constructions with the passive participle had come at last to be felt to contain a quasi-narrative *active* form, having a nominative[4] as subject[s] and an accusative as direct object[s]; compare above § 301, OBS. 2. It is at the precise moment when the verb-forms in question were first felt as actives instead of as passives that the relative forms became differentiated as separate grammatical entities from the passive participles.

[4] See § 83, OBS. for this convenient, though not strictly scientific, terminology.

2. This conclusion is borne out by the *śḏmw·n·f* relative form, which we must take to have originated in the perfective passive participle followed by the preposition *n* 'to', 'for' (§ 379, 3); for example, *ḫrw śḏmw n·f* would mean literally 'the voice heard to him', and this would subsequently be felt as active just as the Low Latin *ego habeo factum*, containing a passive participle, becomes the active French tense *j'ai fait*. Note that it is the less common type of perfective passive participle having the ending *-w* even in the *3ae inf.* (§ 361) which lies at the base of the *śḏmw·n·f* relative form, and perhaps this had undergone some shortening, seeing that the ending *-w* is so rarely shown. At all events the preposition has in course of time become detached from its noun and, in cases where the word-order demands, cleaves closely to the verb-form.

Exx. [hieroglyphs] *ỉpt tn rdỉt·n w(ỉ) ḥm·f ỉm·s* this mission wherein His Majesty placed me.[1]

[hieroglyphs] *ḫt nbt rdỉw·n n·ỉ p3y·ỉ sn* all the things which my brother gave to me.[2] For the masc. relative form here see § 511, 2.

It seems hardly likely that the preposition *n* could have become detached from its noun so long as it preserved intact its prepositional value 'to'. Its detachment may, therefore, serve as evidence that the verb-form was by this time no longer felt as a passive participle, but rather was interpreted, in combination with the element *·n*, as the quasi-narrative active form which we call the *śḏmw·n·f* relative form.

The decisive proof of the correctness of this view lies, however, in the quite obvious parallelism of the relative forms to the narrative *śḏm·f* and *śḏm·n·f* forms, the former possessing at least two varieties corresponding respectively to the imperfective and perfective relatives. The active force of the two narrative forms in question is of course undoubted, and this is enough to enable us to ascribe active force also to the corresponding relative forms, although it remains true and certain that these last were derived from passive participles. For further details see below § 387 and, for the relation to the narrative forms, below § 411. This last argument will be better appreciated when the student has mastered the contents of the next two Lessons.

The question now arises as to where the boundary-line between passive participle and relative form is to be set. A necessary condition for every relative form is the presence of the semantic subject. Cases like *mrrw nb·f* are perhaps best classified as passive participle + direct genitive (§ 379, 2); on the other hand, we have inclined to take the *ỉr·n, ms·n* expressing parentage as relative forms (p. 279).[3] But when a clause-like appearance is given to the whole phrase by any addition, whether direct object[s] or an adverbial phrase, then it is doubtless best to treat the verb-form as a relative form. So too when *nb* 'every', 'all' separates the verb-form from its subject[s], as in the examples quoted § 381.

[1] Leyd. V 88, 9.

[2] *P. Kah.* 12, 8. Sim. *ib.* 11; *Urk.* iv. 862, 6. 13.

[3] The matter is not wholly clear, and in this book the transliterations vacillate between *ỉr·n*, *ms·n* and *ỉr n*, *ms n*. See (e.g.) p. 296.

OBS. For the origin of the narrative *śḏm·n·f* form see below § 411, 2, where further considerations bearing upon the origin of the corresponding relative form will be found. For the secondary separation of the agential *n* in Egyptian from the noun governed by it, compare the Greek verbs compounded with prepositions like *κατηγορεῖν*. Another evidence of the origin of the *śḏm(w)·n·f* relative in the perf. pass. part. is afforded by the construction *śmt pw ir(w)·n·f*, the passive of which is *śmt pw iry* (below § 392); from this it seems likely that *ir(w)·n·f* is merely the perf. pass. part. *iry* slightly changed and with the agential phrase *n·f* added to it.

§ 387. **The writing of the relative forms.**—We have just seen that the boundary-line between the relative forms and the passive participles is precarious and shifting. It will be unnecessary, therefore, to do more than supplement the sections already devoted to the originating passive participles.

1. **Imperfective relative form.** Generally speaking, the forms are those of the imperf. pass. part. (§ 358). Note, however, that the m. ending *-w* is very seldom written before the suffixes; exceptions are *ddw·ṯn* 'which you give';[1] *sḫ3w·ṯn* 'which you remember'.[2] As regards the feminine, all writings with or instead of mere *-t* must in mutable verbs[2a] be assigned to the perfective relative form, since these endings are never found in company with the gemination. As in the participles, the plur. strokes sometimes accompany feminines used as neuters, ex. *mrrt* 'what (X) loves';[3] the plurals themselves are indistinguishable from the singulars.

2-lit. Beside usual forms like *ḏdw*,[4] *ḏdt*,[5] occurs, as a great rarity, a form with prothetic *i* (§ 272), ex. *iḏdw*.[6] For 1st pers. sing. we have an example written *ddw·y*.[7]

2ae gem. Forms from 'be' are *wnnw*,[8] *wnn·ṯn*.[9]

3ae inf. Only geminating forms occur, since forms without gemination are to be assigned to the perfective relative form, see below under 2. Exx. *ḥꜥꜥw* '(at) which rejoice';[10] *f33t·f* '(in) which he weighs'.[11]

anom. 'Give' has *ddw·ṯn* (see above) and 'bring' *innt* (fem.),[12] i. e. forms in both cases identical with the imperf. pass. part. 'Come' shows forms from both the *-i* and the *-w* stem, exx. *iyw*,[13] f. *it*[14] and *iww*,[15] var. *iw*.[16]

2. **Perfective relative form.**[17] This form is clearly differentiated from the imperf. rel. form by the absence of gemination in the mutable verbs, and from the *śḏmw·n·f* rel. form by the absence of the formative *-n*. Like the latter it is probably derived from the perf. pass. participle. The outstanding problem with regard to it is whether it should be sub-divided into two distinct relative forms, one with *past* reference,[17] the other with *future* or *prospective* reference.[18] The M. K. examples with *past* reference show no special ending for *m. sing.*, though two isolated instances from outside our period[18a] justify us in assuming

[1] *Siut* 1, 276; *ddw·sn*, *ib.* 289. 292. 298.
[2] Turin 1447. Sim. m. plur., *ḏdw·ṯn*, *Urk.* iv. 651, 8.
[2a] For this qualification see Add.
[3] *Urk.* iv. 750, 4.
[4] *Peas.* B 1, 19.
[5] *Sin.* B 261.
[6] *Sebekn.* 3.
[7] SPIEG.-PÖRTN. i. 4, 17.
[8] *Sin.* B 44.
[9] Turin 1447
[10] Cairo 20498, *a* 3, qu. § 384.
[11] LAC. *TR.* 37, 3, qu. § 383.
[12] *Th. T. S.* i. 30, G.
[13] Cairo 20539, i. *b* 15.
[14] Brit. Mus. 581, horiz. 6.
[15] *Siut* 1, 234.
[16] Louvre C 1, 6; *Hamm.* 113, 5; *Urk.* iv. 17, 1.
[17] See above, p. 298, n. 0a.
[18] See GUNN, *Stud.* ch. 1.
[18a] *Pyr.* 1544 (*wnw·k*); *Ḥaremḥab* 29 (*wnw·tw*).

the unwritten presence of the ending *-w*; the *f. sing.* ending is [hieroglyph] *-t*. It has been maintained that the relative forms with *prospective reference*[0] had a *m. sing.* ending [hieroglyph] *-y* and a *f. sing.* ending [hieroglyph] or [hieroglyph] *-ti*, but the *m. sing.* examples either are from mutable verbs where [hieroglyph] may belong to the stem, or else are doubtfully prospective in meaning,[0a] and although a few indisputable early instances of *f. sing.* [hieroglyph], [hieroglyph] occur, this writing grows much more frequent towards Dyn. XVIII, when there is a far greater chance that it may be a mere graphic variant of [hieroglyph] *-t*, due to the fact that original *-ti* in other verb-forms, i.e. old perfective 2nd masc. and 3rd fem. sing., had already been reduced to *-t* by loss of *-i*. It is certainly strange that such a form as [hieroglyph] *ḏdti*[1] should often have prospective meaning, no less than the *3ae inf.* [hieroglyph] *mrti*;[2] but the great improbability of *-ti* instead of *-t* as fem. ending of a participle or relative form weights the scale heavily against this supposed peculiarity of the prospective meaning; see too a certain case of the writing *-ti* for *-t* below § 409.[2a]

Provisionally, then, the perfective relative is best regarded as a unity, though the possibility remains that if we had full knowledge of the vocalization, we might find it to conceal two sub-forms like the 'narrative' perf. *śḏm·f* to which it is so closely parallel (§§ 447, 449).

If the view taken above be correct, in the immutable verbs the perf. rel. form will be practically indistinguishable from the imperf. rel. Forms from mutable verbs:

2ae gem. [hieroglyph] *wn·k* '(in) which thou wast'.[2b]

3ae inf. Exx. [hieroglyph] *mry·f* 'which he may wish';[3] [hieroglyph] *ms·s* 'which she may bear';[4] [hieroglyph] *ḫnt·k* '(on) which thou mayst alight';[5] [hieroglyph] *ḥs·ti* 'that which . . . . . will praise';[6] [hieroglyph] *gmt·(i)* '(something) that I found'.[6a] 'Make' is without *r*, ex. [hieroglyph] *irt·i* 'what I shall make';[7] [hieroglyph] 'what . . . . had done'.[7a]

4ae inf. [hieroglyph] *ʿwꜣ·(i)* 'whom I plundered'.[7b]

anom. 'Give' shows the stem as *di*, ex. [hieroglyph] *dit·i* 'what I could put'.[8]

3. **The *śḏmw·n·f* relative form.** This relative form, like (on our hypothesis) the perfective relative, is derived from the perf. pass. part. (§ 361); but whereas in the perfective relative the semantic subject appears as a direct genitive, here it is mediated by means of the preposition *n*; see above § 386, 2. In agreement with this origin, the *n* follows any determinative which the verb-stem may have, while the gender endings precede. There is no gemination.

m. sing. The m. ending *-w* is but rarely written; exx. [hieroglyph] *sḥꜣw·n·(i)* 'which I uncovered';[9] [hieroglyph] *irw·n·k* 'which thou hast made';[10] [hieroglyph] *rdiw·n* 'which . . . . gave'.[11]

f. sing. The f. ends in [hieroglyph] *-t*. When the meaning is neuter, the plural strokes may be used, exx. [hieroglyph] *mꜣt·n·i* 'what I have seen';[12] [hieroglyph] *wḏt·n·f* 'what he has commanded'.[13]

[0] Formerly called 'prospective relative form', see above, p. 298, top. LEF. *Gr.* § 483 shares GUNN's view of these endings.

[0a] *Ḏdy·i*, *P. Kah.* 36, 24; *ḏdy·k*, LAC. *TR.* 7, 3; *Westc.* 9, 8; *imy·f*, BUDGE, p. 366, 14; *ḫndy·k*, *ib.* p. 265, 15.

[1] *P. Salt* 834, 1, 2 = GUNN, *Stud.* p. 15, no. 91; *Mill.* 1, 2; *Urk.* iv. 1195, 8. Perhaps *r rḫti* of § 178 is to be taken as 'so that . . . may know', see GUNN, *Stud.* 15; LEF. *Gr.* § 486.

[2] *Urk.* iv. 162, 8. Sim. *ib.* 96, 16 *irti*, *ib.* 162, 8; *Adm.* 3, 7.

[2a] See further Add. to p. 303, n. 2a.

[2b] *Sh. S.* 135–6. Sim. *ib.* 126; *Rec.* 14, 35; before nom. subj. *wnt*, *Sin.* B 215.

[3] *Urk.* v. 4, 10.

[4] *P. Kah.* 12, 10.

[5] *Leb.* 51.

[6] *Urk.* iv. 85, 1.

[6a] VANDIER, Mo'alla, *Ankhtifi*, iv. 23.

[7] *Urk.* iv. 834, 12. Sim. *ib.* 1103, 16; 1108, 15; *Adm.* 3, 7. 13.

[7a] VANDIER, Mo'alla, *Ankhtifi*, ii. c 1.

[7b] *Abyd.* iii. 29.

[8] *Sh. S.* 46, qu. § 382. Sim. *P. Kah.* 27, 9.

[9] *Urk.* iv. 484, 11.

[10] *Urk.* iv. 202, 8.

[11] *P. Kah.* 12, 8, qu. § 386, 2.

[12] *Sh. S.* 143.

[13] *Urk.* iv. 363, 13. Sim. *šꜣt·n·f*, *Sin.* B 51.

2-lit. Exx. [hieroglyphs] *ḫm(w)·n·k* 'whom thou knowest not';[1] [hieroglyphs] *ʿmt·n·f* 'what it has swallowed'.[2] Such writings show that the basic perf. pass. part. is the non-geminating form, not the reduplicating form of § 360.

2ae gem. [hieroglyphs] *m3t·n* 'what .... has seen'.[3] [4]

3ae inf. Exx. [hieroglyphs] *gmt·n·f* 'what he found';[5] [hieroglyphs] *pr(w)·n·f* '(from) whom he has gone forth'.[6] So too *ir·n* and *ms·n* (above § 361) are to be taken as relative forms owing to the invariable absence of the *-y* characteristic of the perf. pass. part. in *3ae inf.* 'Make' is almost always without *r*, exx. [hieroglyphs] *ir(w)·n·i*;[7] [hieroglyphs] *irt·n*;[8] but exceptionally we find [hieroglyphs] *irt·n·sn*.[9] For the writing *irw·n*, see above under m. sing. 'Take away' shows [hieroglyphs] *iṯ(w)·n·i*.[10]

4ae inf. Exx. [hieroglyphs] *mdwt·n·i* '(concerning) which I have spoken';[11] [hieroglyphs] *sntt·n* 'which ..... founded'.[12]

anom. 'Give' shows the stem as *rdi*, exx. [hieroglyphs] *rdi(w)·n·i*;[13] [hieroglyphs] *rdit·n*;[14] only rarely does it appear as *di*, ex. [hieroglyphs] *di(w)·n·f*.[15] 'Come' has only forms from *ii*, exx. [hieroglyphs] *ii(w)·n·sn*;[16] [hieroglyphs] *it·n·f*.[17] 'Bring' yields normally [hieroglyphs] *in(w)·n·i*;[18] [hieroglyphs] *int·n·sn*;[19] but abbreviated writings with one *n* sometimes occur, ex. [hieroglyphs][20] side by side with [hieroglyphs] *in·n*.[21]

§ **388. The supposed passive of the relative forms.**[22]—The certain existence of these could be proved only if well authenticated cases with the m. ending *-w* or the f. ending *-t* were forthcoming. Exx. after *hrw* 'the day on which .....' possibly contain the simple narrative *śḏm·f* or *śḏm·n·f* form, see above p. 150, n. 1.[23] Exx. with the indef. pron. *-tw* are hardly true passives;[23a] in [hieroglyphs] *ḥʿʿt·tw n sḏm ḫrw·s* she at hearing whose voice one rejoices;[24] the three parallel texts give the narrative *śḏm·f* form *ḥʿʿ·tw*; the writing with *t* may well, therefore, be a mistake. Other examples that have been quoted[24a] are late and perhaps illusory, though there is no inherent reason why a passive in *·tw* should not have been constructed for the relative forms when once their origin in passive participles was eclipsed or forgotten.

§ **389. Tense-distinction in the relative forms.**—The various relative forms closely follow in their meanings the distinctions associated with their originating passive participles.

1. **Imperfective relative form.** This is used in reference to *repeated* or *continuous* action, whether in present or past, less certainly in future, time.

Commonest of all are examples which must be translated by the English *present.* Many of these are either aphorisms or statements of custom.

Exx. [hieroglyphs] *irrt i3w n rmṯ bin m ḫt nbt* what old age does to men is evil in every respect (lit. thing).[25]

---

[1] *Urk.* iv. 1090, 5.
[2] Brit. Mus. 566.
[3] MAR. *Abyd.* ii. 29, 8. Sim. *Sh. S.* 143.
[4] No exx. from *wnn* have been found; see now p. 306, n. 5d.
[5] *BH.* i. 25, 38–9.
[6] *Pt.* 630.
[7] *BH.* i. 26, 200.
[8] *Siut* 1, 273.
[9] *Sin.* B 28.
[10] *BH.* i. 8, 19.
[11] LAC. *TR.* 72, 35.
[12] *Siut* 4, 21.
[13] *Siut* 1, 287.
[14] Leyd. V 88, 9.
[15] *Ikhern.* 4.
[16] *Westc.* 11, 10. Sim. *Peas.* B 1, 196.
[17] *Bersh.* i. 14, 1.
[18] *Sh. S.* 175.
[19] *Semnah Disp.* 1, 13; 6, 11.
[20] *Urk.* iv. 780, 11; 781, 1.
[21] *Urk.* iv. 780, 6.
[22] See *Verbum* ii. § 786, with p. 468.
[23] In *Eb.* 97, 13, *hrw mss·tw·f* is suspect on account of the imperf. tense; for the absence of *im* cf. *Pyr.* 606 *c.*
[23a] With m. ending *-w* in obscure context, *Ḥaremḥab* 29 (*wnw·tw*).
[24] *Amarn.* v. 27, 4.
[24a] *ÄZ.* 44, 111.
[25] *Pt.* 20–1. Other exx., *Peas.* B 1, 45. 46, qu. § 391; *Siut* 1, 280; *Urk.* iv. 1154, 6.

s n ꜥḳ hꜣbw wr n wr a serving man (lit. a man of entering) whom (one) great man sends to (another) great man.[1] The *-w* in *hꜣbw*, not *-y*, might show that this is imperfective, not perfective; but see p. 303, n. 18a

Instances expressing repetition or continuity in the *past* are difficult to find.

Ex. How shall this land fare without him, *nṯr pf mnḫ wnnw snḏ·f ḫt ḫꜣswt* that beneficent god fear of whom was throughout the foreign lands?[2]

In honorific epithets, however, there is often a doubt whether one should translate with the English past or present. Egyptian uses the imperfective relative form in either case.

Exx. *hrrw nb tꜣwy ḥr tpt-r·f* on account of whose utterance the lord of the two lands is (*or* was) wont to be pleased.[3]

irr ḥsst·f nbt m ẖrt-hrw nt rꜥ nb who does (*or* did) all that he praises (*or* praised) in the course of every day.[4]

Examples referring to *future* time are uncommon and uncertain.[4a]

Ex. *nfr irrt·i n·k* good is that which I will do for thee.[5] The Syrian prince here promises to treat his guest handsomely; a nuance of custom may be implied. But perhaps is to be interpreted as *irt·i*, see 2 (*b*) below.

2. **Perfective relative form,** see above pp. 298, top; 303. (*a*) With *past* reference.[5a]

Exx. *nn ꜥwꜣ·(i), nn iṯ·(i) išt·f* there is none whom I plundered, none whose property I seized.[5b]

n (for *nn*) *gmt·(i) ir is pw in it(yw·i)* it is not (something) which I found it had been done by my fathers.[5c]

As the marginal notes show, this early M. K. use is in other texts replaced by the *sḏmw·n·f* relative. Only with the two verbs *wnn* 'be' and *ḫpr* 'become' does this use appear to have survived the beginning of Dyn. XII.

Exx. *pḥ·k ẖnw wn·k im·f m-ḳꜣb-n snw·k* thou shalt reach the Residence in which thou wast together with thy brethren.[5d]

ḫprt mrt m spty šd·s (a woman) in the lips of whose vulva disease has come about.[6]

(*b*) With *future* or *prospective* reference, describing events which either will or else might occur in time *future* relatively to the main verb; compare similar future (§ 369, 5) and obligational (§ 371) uses in the perf. pass. part.

Exx. *nn gm·k ḫnt·k hr·s* thou wilt not find (anything) whereon thou mayst rest.[7]

[1] *Pt.* 145–6. Sim. *Sin.* B 158; *Peas.* B 1, 275; *Urk.* iv. 1107, 11.

[2] *Sin.* B 44–5.

[3] *Urk.* iv. 993. Sim. *Siut* 1, 234. 247.

[4] Cairo 20541, 5.

[4a] Certain O. E. exx. expressing futurity or a wish, *Urk.* i. 9, 11; 67, 17 (*irrw*).

[5] *Sin.* B 77. Sim. *Siut* 1, 298. 299.

[5a] CLÈRE's discovery, p. 298, n. 0a.

[5b] *Abyd.* iii. 29; contrast *iṯ·n·(i)*, *Siut* III, 9. Sim. DUNH. No. 84 (*sḫ·(i)*, *ꜣḫꜥ·(i)*); *Bersh.* II, p. 25 (*gmt·f*).

[5c] VAND. *Mo.* iv. 23; contrast *gmt·n·(i)*, CL.-VAND. p. 11, 1. Sim. Leyd. V 4, 6.

[5d] *Sh. S.* 135. Sim. *ib.* 126 (*wn·i*); *Rec.* 14, 35 (*wn·k*); before nom. subj. *Sin.* B 215 (*wnt*); m. exx. with ending *-w*, see p. 303, n. 18a.

[6] *Eb.* 95, 22. Sim. *ib.* 88, 3; 95, 5. 17; 96, 2–3.

[7] *Leb.* 51, restored. Sim. *Sh. S.* 46, qu. § 382; *P. Kah.* 27, 9.

The *šnḏty*-priest shall hand it (the candle) to my *ka*-servant *r-sꜣ ỉr·f ỉrt·f ỉm·s m ḥwt-nṯr* after his doing what he has to do with it in the temple.[8]

ỉrt ḫprw nb mry·f ḫpr ỉm·f the making of all changes into which he may wish to change.[9]

Note that cases with a direct object like the last are very uncommon with the perfective relative. But for them, the very existence of the perf. rel. as distinct from the perf. pass. part. would be doubtful; see p. 302, **bottom.**

3. **The *śḏmw·n·f* relative form.** In the large majority of cases this form refers to action regarded as *past*, i.e. past relatively either to the moment of speaking or to the time of the main verb.

Ex. *nn n ḫt rdỉ(w)·n·ỉ n nn n wꜥbw* these things which I have given to these priests.[1] English present perfect.

wḏ ḥm·f rdỉt smn·tw nḫtw rdỉ(w)·n n·f ỉt·f 'Imn His Majesty commanded to cause to be recorded the victories which his father Amūn had given him[2] English past perfect.

ḫtmt ỉrt·n ḥꜣty-ꜥ, ỉmy-r ḥmw-nṯr Ḥp-ḏf contract which was made by (lit. made to) the prince and overseer of the priests Ḥepdjefi.[3] English past tense.

Note that the *śḏmw·n·f* rel. form is found with such verbs as *rḫ*, *ḫm*, and *mr* whenever they mean, not 'learn', 'ignore', and 'love'—notions implying continuity—but 'know', 'not know', and 'wish', these being regarded from the Egyptian standpoint as definite occurrences resulting from 'having learnt', 'failed to learn', 'conceived a wish'. So even in reference to the present.

Exx. A ship shall come from home *skdw ỉm·s rḫ(w)·n·k* sailors being in it whom thou knowest.[4]

mꜣ·k rḫ(w)·n·k mỉ ḫm(w)·n·k thou shalt regard him that thou knowest like him that thou knowest not.[5]

sḫmḫ ỉb Ḥr m mrt·n·f diverting the heart of Horus with what he wishes.[6]

Naturally the same forms are also employed in contexts referring to the past.

Exx. One whom the god distinguished out of millions *m s mnḫ rḫ(w)·n·f rn·f* as a capable man whose name he knew.[7]

m-ḫt nn ỉr·n ḥm n nṯr pn mrt·n·f nbt ḥnꜥ·s after this the Majesty of this god did all he wished with her.[8]

Obs. For similar uses of *rḫ* and *ḫm* in the old perfective and perf. act. part. see above §§ 320; 367, 2 Obs.

Of considerable interest is an example from the adjectival stem *nfr*:

r ỉw hrw nfr n·ỉ ỉm·f until the day came when it went well with me, i.e. when I died or ended (§ 351).[9]

[8] *Siut* I, 297–8. Sim. *Westc.* 11, 6; *Adm.* 3, 7. 13.

[9] *Urk.* v. 4. Sim. Budge, p. 129, 9; 210, 3.

[1] *Siut* I, 270. Sim. *ib.* 272; *Peas.* B 1, 287; Berl. *ÄI.* i. p. 258, 21; *BH.* i. 8, 18.

[2] *Urk.* iv. 684, *'Imn* restored. Sim. *Sin.* B 144, qu. § 385.

[3] *Siut* I, 296. Sim. *Leb.* 30, qu. § 390; *Sin.* B 202. 205.

[4] *Sh. S.* 121. Sim. *Pt.* 177. 179.

[5] *Urk.* iv. 1090, 5. Sim. *ib.* 971, 3. 10; 1071, 9.

[6] Brit. Mus. 614, 2.

[7] Cairo 20539, i. *b* 9.

[8] *Urk.* iv. 221. Sim. Brit. Mus. 614, 10; Cairo 20024, *c.*

[9] Florence 1774. Rather similarly, Berl. *ÄI.* i. p. 185.

One is tempted to take [hieroglyphs] here as the *śḏmw·n·f* rel. form. But examples from the Pyramid texts show that *n·i* was there still a dative, since to [hieroglyphs] .... [hieroglyphs] 'everything wherewith it goes well with him'[1] (cf. § 141) corresponds [hieroglyphs] (*N*)[2] with *im* before *n* + noun. So too without dative [hieroglyphs] 'the eye of Horus wherewith (one) is powerful'.[3] These constructions are analogous to those of the passive participle studied in § 376, though doubtless no passive participles could be formed from the adjective-verbs.

[1] *Pyr.* 1645.
[2] *Pyr.* 1648.
[3] *Pyr.* 1234.

VOCABULARY

[hieroglyphs] *ʿrf* pack, envelop, enclose.

[hieroglyphs] *wrd* (old *wrḏ*) be weary.

[hieroglyphs] *hꜣp* conceal, hide.

[hieroglyphs] *ḥnk* present, offer.

[hieroglyphs] *šni* (det. also [hieroglyph]) surround, encircle.

[hieroglyphs] *šnṯ* resent, vent anger on.

[hieroglyphs] *šdi* recite, read aloud.

[hieroglyphs] *ḳmꜣ* create.

[hieroglyphs] *ḳni* be brave.

[hieroglyphs] *twt* be like, *n* someone.

[hieroglyphs] *tši* be missing, absent oneself, *r* from.

[hieroglyphs] *dsr* set apart; be set apart, private; adj. holy.

[hieroglyphs] *iwʿt* heritage, inheritance.

[hieroglyphs] *ipt* mission, business.

[hieroglyphs] *imyt-pr* estate, testament.

[hieroglyphs] *imꜣḫy* revered, honoured.

[hieroglyphs] *išt* property, belongings.

[hieroglyphs] *itnw* rebel, adversary.

[hieroglyphs] *wḏ* (dett. also [hieroglyph], [hieroglyph]) stela.

[hieroglyphs] *pꜣt* offering, kind of loaf.

[hieroglyphs] *mꜣʿw* tribute, offerings.

[hieroglyphs] *nsyt* (?) kingship.

[hieroglyphs] *ḥwt-ʿꜣt* temple.

[hieroglyphs] abbrev. [hieroglyphs] *ḥʿw* ships.

[hieroglyphs] *ḥb-sd* jubilee, *sed*-festival.

[hieroglyphs] *ḥry-tp* chief, chieftain.

[hieroglyphs] *sntt* (old *śnṯt*) foundation.

[hieroglyphs] *sḫt* field; countryside.

[hieroglyphs] *stt* ray.

[hieroglyphs] *šnʿw* policing, control, lit. holding in check.

[hieroglyphs] *tit* figure, image.

[hieroglyphs] *ṯbt* sole; sandal.

[hieroglyphs] *Nwt* Nut, the sky-goddess.

EXERCISE XXVI

(*a*) *Reading lesson. Autobiographical text from a stela of Dyn. XII,*[1] *reproduced here without omissions so as to illustrate the difficulties from which few Egyptian texts are wholly free:*

ỉmꜣḫ(y) ỉmy-r šnꜥw[2] *Bb, ḏd* (§ 450, 1):
ỉw ỉr·n(·ỉ) šnꜥw n nsw
m ḫꜣswt ḥrt mỉ ḳd·sn;
n sp gm·t(w) sp n bꜣk ỉm,
m ỉpt tn rdỉt·n w(ỉ) ḥm·f ỉm·s,
n (§ 164) *rwd nnk* (§ 300) *ḥr ỉb·f,*
šnṯ(·ỉ ?) ngyt m Nḥw (?),
m srwd ḫt n nb(·ỉ).
ỉ k (§ 312, 3 or § 314, end) *m ḥtp r Šmꜥ,*
ỉr·n(·ỉ) hꜣbt wỉ r·s.
swd·n(·ỉ) ỉpt(·ỉ) n sꜣ·ỉ,
ỉw(·ỉ) ꜥnḫ·k (§ 323).
ỉr·n·ỉ n·f ỉmt-pr[4] *m-ḫꜣw ỉrt·n ỉt·ỉ,*
pr·ỉ grg (§ 322) *ḥr sntt·f,*
sḫt·ỉ m st·s,
nn tšt·s,[5]
ỉšt(·ỉ) nbt m st ỉr (§ 113, 2).
ỉn sꜣ·ỉ sꜥnḫ (§ 373) *rn(·ỉ) ḥr wḏ pn*;
ỉr·n·f n(·ỉ) ỉwꜥ m sꜣ ḳn,
ỉmy-r mšꜥ n pr-nsw,
ỉmꜣḫy Bbỉ,[6] *mꜣꜥ-ḫrw.*

[1] Leyden V 88, published BOESER, ii. 10.
[2] An abstract from *šnꜥ* 'hold in check'; for the administrative sense see PIEHL, *IH.* iii. 77.
[3] An unknown land; the *nḥ*-bird has here the form of ?.
[4] For two actual *ỉmt-pr* 'testaments' see *P. Kah.* 11. 12.
[5] *Tšt* is more probably perf. pass. part. (§ 394) than infinitive (§ 307).
[6] This appears to be the son, who, accordingly, bore the same name as his father.

'The honoured one, the officer of policings Beb, he said: I made policings for the king in the upper deserts to their full extent. No fault was ever found in (lit. of) this humble servant in this charge wherein His Majesty placed me, through my seeming to him strong (lit. through being strong on my part in his heart) while punishing crime (? lit. I punish what is damaged) in Neḥu, in consolidating the possessions of my lord. I returned in peace to Upper Egypt, (after) I had performed that for which I had been sent. I handed over my charge to my son while I was (yet) alive. I made for him a testament in excess of that which my father had made, my house having been established on its foundation, my field(s) being in their place, there being nothing of it gone astray, all my possessions being in their (proper) place. It is my son who made my name live upon this stela; he acted (as) heir for me, as a stout son, the commander of the army of the palace, the honoured one Bebi, justified.'

(*b*) *Translate into English*:

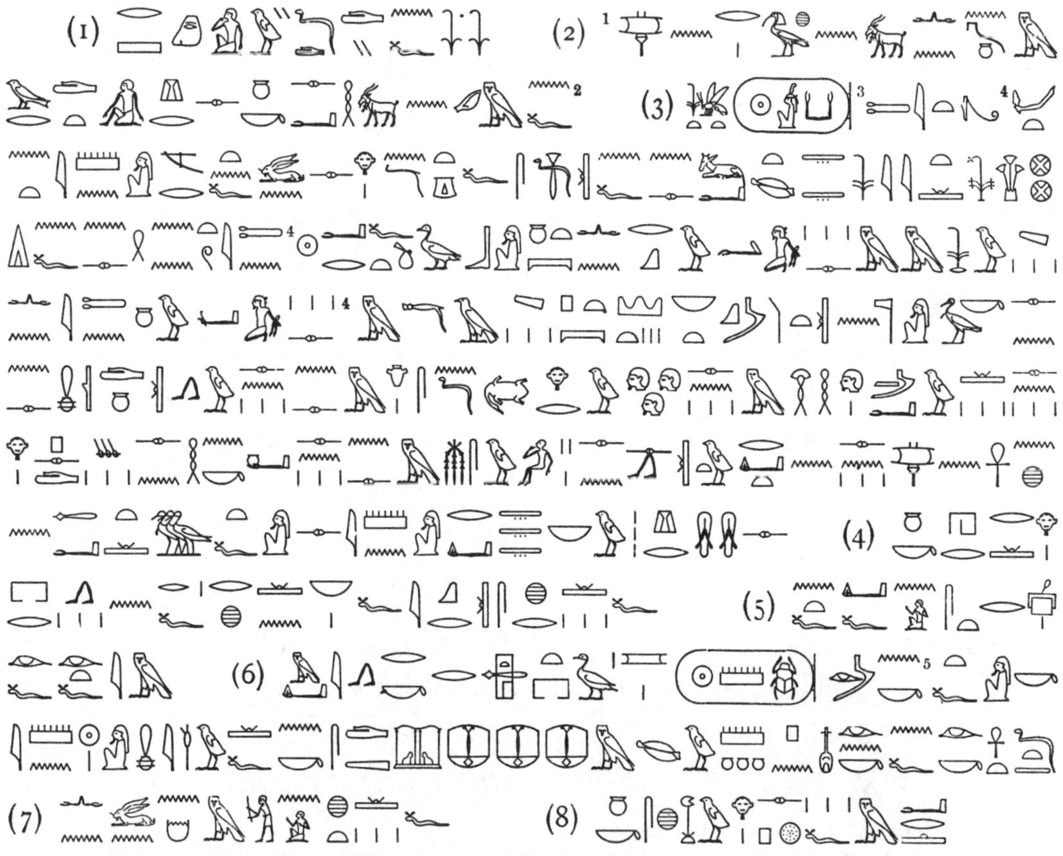

[1] Words addressed by a deceased official to those whom he had asked to pray for him. [2] § 305, end.
[3] Prenomen of queen Ḥashepsowe. [4] § 19, Obs. 2. [5] *mꜣn·k*, an unusual *śḏm·f* form, see § 448.

(*c*) *Write in hieroglyphs*:

(1) I will cause (*di·i*) to be brought to thee ships laden with (*ḫr*) all the riches of Egypt, as is done (lit. like what is done) for a god who loves men in a distant (*wꜣ*) land which men do not know. (2) Behold, I have caused thee to know these things which I gave to these priests in exchange for (*m-isw*, § 178)

that (lit. this) which they had given to me. (3) He who shall hear this shall not say (that) what I have said is exaggeration, but (*wpw-ḥr*, § 179) shall say 'How like her it is!' (4) Adore ye His Majesty; he is Rēʿ by whose rays one sees. (5) I am one to whom hidden matters (*mdt*) are said. (6) He went down to the city, without letting it be known (lit. one know) wherefore he had come. (7) Mayest thou allow mine eyes to see the place where my lord dwells (*ḥmsi*). (8) As for everyone over whom this spell (*r*) is read, his name shall be established in the mouth of the living eternally.

LESSON XXVII

SPECIAL USES OF THE PARTICIPLES AND RELATIVE FORMS

§ **390. Absolute use.**—Just as the noun (§ 89) and the infinitive (§ 306) may stand alone with the self-sufficiency of an independent sentence in *headings*, *titles*, or even in *narrative*, so too the participles and relative forms.

Exx. *ḏddt m ḥm n stp-sꜣ* (*ʿ.w.s.*) what was said in the majesty of the palace (l. p. h.).[1] The words spoken follow.

iy ḥr·s, sš nsw 'Imn-ms he who came concerning it, the royal scribe Amenmosĕ. The whole context is in similar abbreviated style, like the headings in a table of contents; this is not to be taken as a case of nominal predicate with simple juxtaposition (§ 125).[2]

ḏdt·n n·i bꜣ·i what my soul said to me.[3] The words spoken follow.

rdit·n·f n·sn ḥr·s what he gave to them for it.[4] There follows a statement of the things given.

It will be seen later (§ 405) that the so-called *śḏmt·f* form, in two of its usages (§§ 402. 406), is probably a passive participle used absolutely.

§ **391. Use of the participles and relative forms to point to the logical predicate.**—Since, by definition, the participles display the meaning of verbs as exercised actively by, or passively upon, somebody or something (§ 353), their use is apt to attract the listener's interest to that somebody or something, the verbal action itself becoming of merely secondary and derivative importance. Thus, in the examples quoted in the last section, the participles and the relative forms direct the listener's attention to *what* was said, *who* came, *what* was given; in other words, the logical predicate (§ 126) is much more clearly indicated than if these examples had been expressed in the form of ordinary verbal sentences ('this was said in the palace', 'my soul said this', 'Amenmosĕ came', 'he gave to them these things').[5] The same linguistic device lies at the root of the participial statement studied in § 373, where it is

[1] *Urk.* iv. 194. Sim. *ib.* 1021, 3.

[2] *Urk.* iv. 1021, 2. Sim. *Th. T. S.* iii. 26.

[3] *Leb.* 30. 147. Sim. *P. Kah.* 13, 26; Leyd. V 6, 11; *Th. T. S.* iii. 21.

[4] *Siut* I, 274. Sim. *ib.* 284. 292. Also in headings to letters, etc., *P. Boul.* xviii, 6. 26. 27.

[5] See *Nominals.* § 42.

just as much the use of the participles as the employment of the emphatic *ỉn* or of the independent pronouns which gives the status of a logical predicate to the grammatical subject. Herein too lies the secret of English 'it is he who does this' with the meaning of '*he* does this', French *c'est lui qui le fait* with the meaning of *lui le fait.*

So too when *pw* is used (§§ 128–30).

Exx. *mk ỉrrt·sn pw* behold, *that* is what they do.[1]

ỉmy-r pr wr pw sḫꜣy·k it is *the high steward* who is mentioned by thee.[2]

[1] *Peas.* B 1, 46.

[2] *Peas.* B 1, 21. Sim. *ib.* 19. 235–6.

§ 392. The construction *śḏm pw ỉr(w)·n·f* and its passive *śḏm pw ỉry.*[3]—The same principle underlies a mode of narrating events which is much employed in the Middle Kingdom stories. Here it is the action itself which is the centre of interest, and accordingly the action has to appear as a verbal noun, i.e. infinitive, to which are added the words *pw ỉr(w)·n·f* (*śḏmw·n·f* rel. form) 'it is ..... which he did' or passively *pw ỉry* (perf. pass. part.) 'it is .... which was done'. The construction is found almost exclusively with verbs of motion.

Exx. Active. *prt pw ỉr(w)·n·f r ḥrw* thereupon he went up higher.[4] Lit. it was going up higher which he did.

Passive (very rare). *ỉwt pw ỉry r bꜣk ỉm* then they came for this humble servant. Lit. it was a coming which was done.[5]

Other verbs with which this construction occurs exceptionally are *ꜥḥꜥ* 'stand up',[6] *ḥmst* 'sit down',[7] *gr* 'keep silence',[8] *mst* 'give birth'.[9] Note that *ỉr(w)·n·f* and *ỉry* have masculine gender whether the infinitive is of masc. or fem. form. These verb-forms are in apposition with *pw*, according to § 130; *pw* 'it' is treated syntactically as a masculine, just as we saw that the neuter pronouns *nꜣ* and *nn* were treated as masculines (§ 111).

[3] Erm. *Spr. d. Westc.* pp. 99–101.

[4] *Peas.* B 1, 4. With other verbs of motion, *ib.* R 7. 36. 37; B 1, 73; *Sh. S.* 172; *Sin.* B 241; *Westc.* passim (see last note).

[5] *Sin.* B 236. Sim. *Westc.* 12, 19.

[6] *Westc.* 4, 17; 6, 22; 7, 14.

[7] *Westc.* 12, 8.

[8] *Peas.* B 1, 49.

[9] *Hamm.* 110, 5.

§ 393. The emphatic or emphasized participle.—The last two sections have dealt with cases where emphasis rests upon the antecedent of a participle or relative form. It not seldom happens, however, that the stress lies upon the action expressed by these forms, that action constituting a condition or qualification of the meaning of the entire sentence. The same kind of emphasis is found, as we saw in § 96, also with adjectival epithets. As in that case, so too with the participles, the emphasis either is implicit, or else may be made explicit by the use of the *m* of predication.

Exx. *sr pw sr snḏw n·f* the (true) noble is the noble who is *feared.*[10] Implicit emphasis.

ỉr wḏꜥ-rwt m ḫsfw n·f ỉw·f m ỉmy-ḥꜣt n ỉrr as for the judge who *ought to be punished*, he is a pattern for the (wrong)-doer.[11] Here *ḫsfw n·f* (§ 371) is explicitly emphasized by *m*.

[10] *Urk.* iv. 1091. Sim. with active part., *Peas.* B 1, 192–3.

[11] *Peas.* B 1, 217–8. Sim. *M. u. K.* 3, 5, qu. § 377; with active part., *Sin.* B 296; *Adm.* p. 105; with rel. form, *Pt.* 177.

§ 394. The participles and relative forms in negative universal propositions.—In order to express 'there is none (or no.......) who(m).....' the model of the existential sentence with *nn wn* or simply *nn* (§§ 108; 144, 4) is used.

Exx. *nn wn rwi ꜥḥꜣw·f* there is none who can check his arrow.[1]

nn wn ḫmt·n·f r-sy there is nothing at all which he does not know.[2]

nn wn imy-r diwt iṯ·n·i rmṯ·f there was no overseer of five whose people I took away.[3]

I mastered every magical art, *nn swꜣt im ḥr·i* there was nothing thereof which escaped me, lit. passed by me.[4]

My Majesty perceived *wnt nn irt(y)·f(y) st nb ḥr-ḫw·k* that there was not anyone who would do it except thee.[5] Note the *śḏmty·fy* form.

nn gr rdi·n·k mdw·f there is no silent man whom thou hast caused to speak.[6]

Much more rarely *n wnt* is used.

Ex. *n wnt wp st* there being no one who discriminated it.[7]

A strange and interesting case where *n wnt* is combined with (*iw*) *wn*, the *iw* being omitted according to rule (§ 107, 2), is:

All its statues were broken, *n wnt wn sḫꜣ st* there was not existing one who remembered them.[8]

One instance occurs where *iw* is found standing before *nn wn* in order to mark a strong contrast:

I tended it (my city) *iw nn wn rdi n·s* while there was not one who gave to it (the city).[9]

§ 395. The participle after *iw wn*.—We might expect to find instances of *iw wn* + participle corresponding to the examples with *nn wn* quoted in the last section. No actual instance is forthcoming, but there is an indirect one, in which *iw* is changed into *wnn* after *ir* 'if' according to the rule stated in § 150:

ir wnn wn wḫꜥt(y)·f(y) ḫr-ḥꜣt·k if there be one who shall make investigation before thee.[10] Here the *śḏmty·fy* form is used.

§ 396. The participles of *wnn* as equivalents of the relative adjective.—Just as we found *wnt* as an occasional substitute for *ntt* 'that' (§ 187), so too the participles of *wnn* are sometimes used as equivalents of the relative adjective *nty* (§ 199); over *nty* they have the advantage of distinguishing two tenses, so that they can help to define the time and the duration of the facts stated in the equivalents of English relative clauses which they introduce. It

[1] *Sin.* B 62. Sim. *Urk.* iv. 613, 6.

[2] *Urk.* iv. 1074. Sim. *ib.* 971, 3.

[3] *BH.* i. 8, 19.

[4] Louvre C 14, 7. Sim. *Hamm.* 87, 9; *Urk.* iv. 159, 8. With rel. form, *Urk.* iv. 1071, 8.

[5] *Ikhern.* 9. Sim. *Urk.* iv. 1075, 3 (read *ksmty·fy*).

[6] *Peas.* B 1, 285. Sim. *BH.* i. 8, 18. With pass. part., *Sin.* B 309.

[7] *Urk.* iv. 159. Sim. *Amada* 3.

[8] *ÄZ.* 34, 33.

[9] *Hat-Nub*, 11, 9.

[10] *Urk.* iv. 1093.

will be seen that the phrases introduced by the participles of *wnn* may in every case be paralleled by main clauses beginning with *ỉw*, so that, to take a concrete instance, *wnn ꜥnḫw* 'he who is living' may be legitimately considered as the participial counterpart of *ỉw·f ꜥnḫw* 'he is living' (§ 323).

1. Examples with adverbial predicate; corresponding main clauses with *ỉw*, see above § 117.

wn m ỉpwty ḥr hꜣb ky he who was (formerly) a messenger (now) sends another.[1]

sꜣw nw ḳm(ꜣ)w wnnyw m šms Pr-ꜥꜣ companies of pioneers (?) who are (continually) in the following of Pharaoh.[2]

In one example an entire virtual adverb clause is substituted for a simple adverbial predicate; see above § 215:

He planned to restore *mnw wnw nn st ḥr pdw·sn* monuments which were no longer standing, lit. which were they-were-not-on-their-feet.[3]

Akin to the above examples is *wnnw snḏ·f ḫt ḫꜣswt* 'fear of whom was throughout the foreign lands'[4] quoted § 389, 1. There, however, *wnnw* appears to be a relative form rather than a participle, since it is followed by a subject differing from the antecedent; with this view agrees the ending *-w*, which is usual with the imperf. rel. form, but not with the imperf. act. participle.

2. Examples showing the pseudo-verbal construction; so with *ỉw*, § 323.

Exx. *swꜣ·n·ỉ mỉty* (for *mỉtw·ỉ*) *nb wn ḥr ḫrp m pr pn* I surpassed every peer of mine who had been in authority in this temple.[5]

nn n ꜣḫw wnnyw ḥr ꜥḳ prt m R-sṯꜣw these spirits who are wont to go in and out in Rostjaw.[6]

wnt štꜣ m ḥr n rmṯ that which had been difficult in the sight of men.[7] For the masc. *štꜣ* in spite of fem. *wnt* see § 511, 4.

ḥwt-nṯr n nbt Ḳsy wnt wꜣ·tỉ r fḫ the temple of the lady of Cusae which had fallen into ruin.[8]

wnnyw ꜥnḫ r nḥḥ (ye) who are living to eternity.[9]

3. Cases where a participle from *wnn* precedes a narrative verb are of extreme rarity.

Ex. His Majesty has given command . . . . so as to look after the standard-bearer Nebamūn, *wn pḥ·n·f ỉꜣwt ỉw·f ḥr šms Pr-ꜥꜣ* (ꜥ. w. s.) who has reached old age serving Pharaoh (l. p. h.).[10]

Wn pḥ·n·f here evidently serves as the past participle of the compound narrative verb-form *ỉw pḥ·n·f* (§ 68). For this and other analogous developments see below §§ 402. 469–475, especially § 474, 3.

[1] *Adm.* 8, 3. Sim. *ib.* 3, 6. 14; 9, 5; *Sin.* R 23; B 80; Cairo 20543, 19; *Urk.* iv. 389, 2.

[2] *D. el B.* 125. Sim. *Peas.* B 1, 256; *Eb.* 76, 12; 92, 12; 93, 4; *Urk.* iv. 1112, 14.

[3] *Urk.* iv. 501.

[4] *Sin.* B 44–5.

[5] Cairo 20543, 19. Sim. *Urk.* iv. 634.

[6] BUDGE, p. 270, 2–3. Sim. *Eb.* 93, 11–12.

[7] *Siut* 4, 31. Sim. *JEA.* 15, 3, 12.

[8] *Urk.* iv. 386. Sim, *Siut* 1, 235, qu. § 511, 2; *Urk.* iv. 385, 17; 758, 7.

[9] BUDGE, p. 208, 10. Sim. *Eb.* 23, 14. In the constr. of § 394, *nn wnw m(w)t*, *ÄZ.* 72, 85.

[10] *Th. T. S.* iii. 26.

§ 397. Negation of the participles, *śḏmty·fy* form and relative forms.—For this purpose use is made of the negative verb *tm* (§ 342), which itself assumes the required verbal form, being followed by the negatival complement (§ 341) or sometimes, from Dyn. XVIII on, by the infinitive (§ 344).

1. Negation of the *participles.* The imperfective and perfective *active* participles of *tm* are indistinguishable.

Exx. *in ỉb sḫpr nb·f m sḏm m tm sḏm* it is the heart which educates its lord as one who hearkens or as one who does not hearken.[1] *Tm* is probably imperf. act. part., though since the perf. is also used in epithets (§ 367) we cannot be quite sure of the tense.

mdt mꜣt, tmt swꜣ new language which has never (yet) occurred (lit. passed).[2] *Tmt* is perf. act. part.

In the *passive,* the imperfective participle *tm* is distinguished from the perfective *tmm* (§ 360).

Exx. *tm ẖnn wḏt-mdw·f* one whose command is not interfered with.[3] Lit. being finished with the disturbing his command; *wḏt-mdw* is object of the negatival complement, which is always active.

. . . . *tꜣw nb* . . . . . *tmm ḫnd st ỉn kwy bỉtyw* all lands . . . . which had not been trodden (lit. treading them) by other kings.[4]

tmmt bs wr-mꜣw ḥr·s a thing into which the chief of seers (title of the high-priest of Heliopolis) has not been initiated.[5] Lit. (a thing) having been finished with the introducing the chief of seers (object of *bs*(*w*)) upon it. For the construction see too § 377.

2. Negation of the *śḏmty·fy* form.

Ex. *ỉr grt fḫty·fy sw, tmt*(*y*)*·f*(*y*) *ꜥḥꜣ ḥr·f* now as for him who shall lose it (this boundary) and shall not fight on behalf of it.[6]

3. Negation of the *relative forms.*

Ex. *nn st nbt tmt·n·*(*ỉ*) *ỉr mnw ỉm·s* there was not any place in which I did not make monuments.[7]

OBS. The beginner must realize that the constructions of § 394 do not constitute negations of the verbal notion itself. What they negate is the existence of a person or thing described by the help of a participle or a relative form.

§ 398. The participles and relative forms in comparisons.—Egyptian differs from English in its tendency to focus comparison upon some specific *thing,* rather than upon an *action,* so far as this is possible. The participles and relative forms are very useful for this purpose, since they always describe somebody or something, and this may be the thing compared.

[1] *Pt.* 550–1. Sim. *P. Kah.* 1, 9; *Sebekn.* 2; *Urk.* iv. 971, 7. 10.

[2] *Adm.* p. 97. Sim. *ib.* 7, 8. 9. 10. 11; 8, 11; 9, 4.

[3] *Siut* 1, 268.

[4] *Urk.* iv. 780. Sim. *ib.* 344, 7, qu. § 344; 1097, 12; *Sinai* 54; *Adm.* p. 100.

[5] *ÄZ.* 57, 2*. Sim. *Mill.* 1, 3–4; *P. Kah.* 2, 15.

[6] Berlin *ÄI.* i. p. 258, 19. Sim. MAR. *Abyd.* ii. 30, 37; *Urk.* iv. 1109, 4.

[7] Louvre C 15. Sim. *Rifeh* 7, 39; *Adm.* 8, 1; *Urk.* iv. 1074, 5.

Exx. There was made a garden for me .... *mỉ irrt n smr tpy* as is done (lit. like what is done) for a foremost Companion.[1]

It (i. e. this book) has come (to an end) *mỉ gmyt m sš* as it was found (lit. like what was found) in writing.[2]

Then that ship arrived *mỉ srt·n·f ḫnt* as he had (lit. like what he had) foretold beforehand.[3]

m-ḥȝw wnt m-bȝḥ more than there was before, lit. in excess of what was before.[4]

The use above illustrated overlaps with the other in which a *śḏm·f* or *śḏm·n·f* form is employed, see above § 170.

[1] *Sin.* B 307. Sim. with *iry*, *BH.* i. 25, 24; *Kopt.* 8, 7. In relative form, *Siut* I, 278. 291.

[2] *Sin.* B 311. Sim. *Sh. S.* 187.

[3] *Sh. S* 155. Sim. *ib.* 174; *Ikhern.* 9. 10; *Urk.* iv. 780, 9. With pass. part., *Louvre* C 11, 5; *Urk.* iv. 897, 15 (*ḏdt*).

[4] *Urk.* iv. 188. With rel. form, LAC. *TR.* 22, 14.

§ 399. The participles in virtual indirect questions.—The participles may be employed in Egyptian where Latin or Greek would show an indirect question.

Exx. *n rḫ·i in wi r ḫȝst tn* I do not know who (lit. him who) brought me to this country.[5]

Do you know *rdyt P n Ḥr ḥr·s* wherefore (the town) Pe was given to Horus? Lit. that given Pe to Horus on account of it.[6]

[5] *Sin.* B 42. Sim. *Sh. S.* 71. With rel. form, *ib.* 46, quoted above § 382.

[6] *ÄZ.* 58, 15*. Sim. *ib.* 57, 3*.

§ 400. The participles and relative forms as predicate in relative clauses with *ntt*.—The following examples are exceptional:

I cause you to know *m ntt wḏdt ḫr·i* about that which has been commanded to me.[7] Lit. (something) out of that which is what has been commanded to me.

I make eternity clear in your sight *m ntt mrt·n it·i* according as my father wishes.[8] Lit. according to that which is what my father has desired.

Ntt seems entirely superfluous in these examples. As they stand, it appears necessary to take *wḏdt* and *mrt·n i·ti* as directly juxtaposed (§ 125, end) predicates to *ntt*.

[7] *Urk.* iv. 352.

[8] *Urk.* iv. 350.

THE *ŚḎMT·F* FORM

§ 401. Its three uses.—Under the name of the *śḏmt·f* form[9] we shall deal with a verb-form which is partly verbal and partly nominal, and the characteristic feature of which is a formative *t* appended immediately to the verb-stem. The *śḏmt·f* form has three uses: A, after *n* 'not', chiefly with the meaning 'he has (*or* had) not yet heard'; B, as a narrative tense (rather doubtful); C, after prepositions, ex. *r śḏmt·f* 'until he has heard'. These uses will be treated separately, since it is not quite certain that the *śḏmt·f* form has identical origin in all three cases.

[9] See *Verbum* ii. §§ 353-7.

§ 402. A. The construction **n śḏmt·f.**[1]—This construction is particularly common as a virtual adverb clause with the meaning 'before he has (had) . . . . .', lit. 'he has (had) not (yet) . . . . .'

Exx. *m grg dwꜣ n ỉỉt·f* provide not for to-morrow before it has come.[2] English present perfect.

I am sorry for her children . . . . *mꜣw ḥr n Ḫnty n ꜥnḫt·sn* who saw the face of the Crocodile-god before they lived (*or* had lived).[3] English past tense or past perfect tense.

Behold, convulsions (?) occurred *iw·ỉ m-ḫmt·k, n sḏmt šnyt sw(ꜣ)ḏ·ỉ n·k, n ḥmst·ỉ ḥnꜥ·k* when I was without thee, before the courtiers had heard that I was handing over to thee, before I had sat (enthroned) together with thee.[4] English past perfect.

In spite of its common use illustrated above, *n śḏmt·f* is not to be regarded as essentially subordinate in meaning. This seems indicated by sporadic examples after *iw*, after *isṯ*, and after the relative adjective *nty*, all of these being elsewhere regularly prefixed to constructions having the form of main clauses.

Exx. *iw n mrt irt·f* now his eye had not yet been ill.[5]

I was one of those worms which the Unique Lord created *isṯ n ḫprt ꜣst* (when) Isis had not yet come into existence.[6]

m ḥꜥw n ntt n ḫprt do not rejoice over what has not (yet) happened.[7]

The omission of the subject seen in the last example is found elsewhere in cases where the context makes its expression superfluous.

Ex. *sr·sn ḏꜥ n ỉỉt, nšny n ḫprt·f* they could foretell a storm before (it) came, and a tempest before it happened.[8]

After a preposition, *iw n sḏmt·f* becomes *wn n sḏmt·f*; cf. above § 157, 1.

Ex. That is Rēꜥ's beginning to reign as king *m wn n ḫprt stsw Šw* when the supports of Shu had not (yet) come into existence.[9]

Only very rarely is the temporal significance 'not yet', 'before' absent. In one case we must probably translate as a virtual clause of circumstance, not of time.

He sacked the town of Kadesh, *n tšt·ỉ r bw ẖry·f* without my swerving from the place where he was.[10]

Under this head, too, it seems necessary[11] to place the phrase *n wnt* 'there is (was) not', which has been discussed and illustrated in §§ 108; 109; 115; 120; 188, 2; 394. No examples seem to be forthcoming where *n wnt* means 'before there was', 'there was not yet', but this is not the only point in which *wnn* differs from other verbs.

[1] See GUNN, *Stud.* ch. 22.

[2] *Peas.* B 1, 183. Sim. *Leb.* 19 (*ỉỉt·ỉ*); *Urk.* iv. 1090, 10 (*hnnt·k*); *BH.* i. 26, 185 (*fḫt·f*).

[3] *Leb.* 79–80.

[4] *Mill.* 2, 5. Sim. LAC. *TR.* 78, 7 (*ḫprt*); 27 (*ḫprt·tn*); *BH.* i. 41 (*rḫt·f*); *Urk.* iv. 2, 15 (*irt·ỉ*).

[5] *ÄZ.* 58, 20*.

[6] BUDGE, p. 167, 16. Sim. with *sk*, *Eb.* 39, 19.

[7] *Peas.* B 1, 272. Sim. *Westc.* 5, 11.

[8] *Sh. S.* 30–2, but 97–8 has *ỉỉt·f.* Sim. Leyd. V 7; *Urk.* iv. 971, 2.

[9] *Urk.* v. 6.

[10] *Urk.* iv. 892.

[11] Differently, GUNN, *Stud.* ch. 19.

§ 403. Forms of the verb in the construction [hieroglyphs] *n śḏmt·f*.—In the immutable verbs the formative *t* is simply added to the stem; in the text and notes of the preceding section examples have been quoted from the *2-lit.* verbs *fḫ*, *rḫ*, *mr* and from the *3-lit.* verbs *ˁnḫ*, *ḫpr*, *sḏm*.

The following forms are found from the mutable verbs; note that in the *3ae inf.*, *4ae inf.*, and *anom.* verbs the *śḏmt·f* form has the appearance of the infinitive.

2ae gem. Possibly [hieroglyphs] *hnnt·k* 'thou hast heeded'.[1] For [hieroglyphs] *wnt* see § 402.

3ae inf. Exx. [hieroglyphs] *prt·ỉ* 'I had come forth';[2] [hieroglyphs] *tšt·ỉ* 'I swerved'.[3] 'Make' shows [hieroglyphs] *ỉrt·ỉ* 'I had made'.[4]

4ae inf. [hieroglyphs] *ḥmst·ỉ* 'I had sat'.[5]

anom. 'Come' has [hieroglyphs] *ỉỉt·f*,[6] [hieroglyphs] *ỉt*.[7]

§ 404. The passive of [hieroglyphs] *n śḏmt·f*.[8]—When the construction *n śḏmt·f* has passive meaning, the verb-form assumes the appearance of the fem. perf. pass. part.

Exx. [hieroglyphs] *ḫpr·n·ỉ, n myst kȝw, n ỉryt ỉdwt* (?) I came into existence when bulls had not yet been born, and cows had not yet been made.[9]

[hieroglyphs] *ḫpr rn·f, n rd* (read *rdt*) *ˁš, n mst šndt, n ḳm(ȝ)yt ḥmt* (?) *ḥr ḫȝswt·f* his name came into existence before the cedar had grown, before the acacia had been born, before the copper had been created in its mountain-deserts.[10]

Examples with pronominal subject are rare, ex. [hieroglyphs] *mk rk s(y) ḥr wḫrt n šdyt·s* behold, it is (still) in dock, not (yet) having been removed.[10a]

The verb-forms in question are:

3-lit. [hieroglyphs] *wtt* (for *wttt*) 'had been begotten';[11] [hieroglyphs] *spḥ*, doubtless corrupt for *spḥt* 'had been lassoed';[12] [hieroglyphs] *ḳm(ȝ)yt* 'had been created'.[13]

3ae inf. [hieroglyphs] *wpyt* 'had been divided';[14] [hieroglyphs] *msyt*,[15] varr. [hieroglyphs][16] and [hieroglyphs] *mst*[17] 'had been born'; [hieroglyphs] *ỉryt* 'had been made'.[18]

anom. [hieroglyphs] *rdyt* '(it) has been allowed'.[19]

Obs. When the verb is in its abbreviated form, the question arises as to whether the passive of *śḏm·f* is not to be understood.

§ 405. Origin of the verb-form in [hieroglyphs] *n śḏmt·f*.—That the *śḏmt·f* form cannot have originated in the infinitive, as was formerly supposed, seems evident from the number of examples which have been found from *2-lit.* and *3-lit.* verbs, i.e. from strong verbs with masculine infinitives. The discovery of the passive counterpart *n śḏmt* (§ 404) prompts the conjecture that *śḏmt·f* was

1 *Urk.* iv. 1090, 10.
2 *ÄZ.* 12, 87, 11. Sim. *ḥȝt*, *Pap. mag. Ram.*, unpublished.
3 *Urk.* iv. 892, 9.
4 *Urk.* iv. 2, 15.
5 *Mill.* 2, 5.
6 *Sh.S.* 98. Sim. *Peas.* B 1, 183. 271.
7 Leyd. V 7.
8 See *Rev. ég.* n. s. ii. 50–1.
9 Lac. *TR.* 19, 60–1. Sim. *ib.* 80, 15; *Pap. mag. Ram.*, unpubl.
10 *Iouiya* Pl. 22.
10a *Coffins*, M 3 C, 137. Sim. G 1 T, 129, cf. *Pyr.* 779.
11 *Pap. mag. Ram.*, unpublished.
12 *Ann.* 5, 234.
13 *Iouiya*, Pl. 22.
14 Lac. *TR.* 80, 15. Sim. *šdyt*, above, n. 10a.
15 Lac. *TR.* 19, 60.
16 *Pap. mag. Ram.*, unpublished.
17 *Iouiya* Pl. 22. Sim. *Ann.* 5, 234.
18 Lac. *TR.* 19, 61; 80, 15; *D. el B.* 116, 4th hour.
19 *ÄZ.* 59, 5, top, in the autographed pages.

participial in its origin, since both the outward form and the passive meaning of such examples as [hieroglyphs] *n msyt* and [hieroglyphs] *n ỉryt* appear to identify the verbs here as feminine perfective passive participles. The question thus arises: from which participle must the active *śḏmt·f* be derived?

This problem is best approached through a consideration of the *passive* counterpart just mentioned. If *ỉryt* in [hieroglyphs] *n ỉryt* is or originated in the perf. pass. participle which it appears to be, its original meaning will have been 'that having been made' or 'that which has been made'. But there are good grounds for thinking that such meaning could have developed into 'the having been made', '(the fact) that .... has (*or* had) been made', compare the transition from 'that which' into '(the fact) that' in [hieroglyphs] *ntt* and [hieroglyphs] *wnt* (§§ 233. 237), in the Hebrew אֲשֶׁר, the Greek ὅτι, the Latin *quod*, the Italian *che*, and the French *que*. On this basis [hieroglyphs] would signify 'not (is) that .... has (*or* had) been made', the construction resembling that of [hieroglyphs] (more rarely [hieroglyphs]) + infinitive (§ 307); for the use of [hieroglyphs] *n* rather than [hieroglyphs] *nn* the analogy of *n śḏm·f* 'he has not heard' (§§ 105. 455) and of several other forms of the suffix conjugation (§ 410) may have been at work.

In the case of the *active* [hieroglyphs] *n śḏmt·f* there is the difference that the originating *śḏmt·f* must have been a relative form; 'that which he has (*or* had) heard' will have passed into 'the fact that he has (*or* had) heard', the prefixed [hieroglyphs] again signifying 'not (is)'. The objection which might until recently have been raised, namely that the forms in *n śḏmt·f* are those of a relative form[1] having only *prospective* meaning, is now disposed of by the discovery that this form or one very much like it early often had *past* meaning (§ 389, 2: the Perfective Relative form). Now the relative forms have been seen to have evolved out of passive participles (§ 386); it would follow that the same perf. pass. part. gave rise both to the active *n śḏmt·f* and to its passive counterpart, the former having originated in 'not (is) the having been heard of (i.e. by) him'. To this hypothesis there is no serious obstacle, since we shall adduce cogent arguments to prove that both the active *śḏm·f* (§ 411, 1) and the passive *śḏm·f* (§ 421) were derived from passive participles; see especially the last paragraph of § 421.

An alternative theory[2] has, however, been put forward connecting the verb-forms in *n śḏmt·f* and its passive counterpart with the so-called 'complementary infinitive' (§ 298, Obs.), from which various feminine active forms like [hieroglyphs] *wbnt* 'a rising' occur, together with at least one passive form [hieroglyphs] *msyt* 'a being-born'. This theory does not necessarily contradict our own hypothesis; for these feminine 'complementary infinitives' may themselves be derived from fem. pass. participles, as indeed is highly probable in the case of the passive *msyt*.

[1] The Prospective Relative form of § 389, 2 in the 1st ed.

[2] Gunn, *Stud.* pp. 177–9.

§ 406. B. The narrative *śḏmt·f* form.—Whereas the *śḏmt·f* form after the negative *n* is a well-authenticated and clearly differentiated verb-form, such is not the case with that *śḏmt·f* form which occasionally takes the place of *śḏm·n·f* in narrative. Only one example has been quoted from an immutable verb, namely *sꜣḳt* in

[hieroglyphs] *ṯst·i ib·i, sꜣḳt·i ḥꜥw·i, sḏm·n·i ḫrw nmi n mnmnt* (when) I had lifted up my heart and collected my members, I heard the sound of the lowing of herds.[1]

The reading *sꜣḳt* has been doubted on palaeographical grounds,[2] but seems probable. In all other examples that have been quoted, however, the supposed narrative *śḏmt·f* form might well be the infinitive; the verbs in question are [hieroglyphs] *irt·i*,[3] [hieroglyphs] *wpt*,[4] [hieroglyphs] *prt·i*,[5] [hieroglyphs] *rdit·f*[6] and [hieroglyphs] *rdit·i*,[7] var. [hieroglyphs] *rdit(·i)*,[8] [hieroglyphs] *šdt·i*,[9] [hieroglyphs] *ṯst·i*,[10] besides [hieroglyphs] *iwt*,[11] which might be *śḏm·f* form as well as infinitive; see below § 447. That the infinitive can be employed in virtual narrative seems proved by the examples quoted in § 306, 2, in some of which forms in *t* from *3ae inf.* or *anom.* verbs alternate with forms without *t* from *3-lit.* verbs. Nevertheless, when forms in *t* are in close association with *śḏm·n·f* forms, it is legitimate to question whether we have not to do with affirmative examples of *śḏmt·f* in narrative.

Note that even in texts where the suffix 1st sing. [hieroglyph] *·i* is ordinarily written, this is omitted if the reflexive dependent pronoun [hieroglyphs] *wi* follows. Ex. [hieroglyphs] *rdit·(i) wi* 'I placed myself'.[12] Cf. below § 412.

In a few passages besides that quoted above the supposed *śḏmt·f* form either must or may be translated as a virtual clause of time.

Exx. [hieroglyphs] *šdt·i dꜣ, sḫpr·n·i ḫt* (when) I had taken a fire-stick, I created fire.[13]

[hieroglyphs] *ḫpr·n, rdit·(i) wi ḥr ḫt·i r dwꜣ n·f nṯr, ꜥḥꜥ·n ḏd·n·f n·i* it happened, (when) I had placed myself on my belly to thank him, thereupon he said to me.[14]

Occasionally, however, it seems possible or necessary to render as a main clause.

Ex. [hieroglyphs] *irt·i šmt m ḫntyt* I made a departure southward.[15]

§ 407. C. The *śḏmt·f* form after prepositions.—This, at all events, is a genuine use of the *śḏmt·f* form, since examples are found from various immutable verbs where no alternative explanation seems possible. A doubt occurs, however, in the *3ae inf.* and *anom.*, where the verb-form is indistinguishable from the infinitive. Nor is it altogether certain that the *śḏmt·f* as used in this construction is identical with the *śḏmt·f* of the negative *n śḏmt·f*

[1] *Sin.* B 23–5.
[2] MÖLLER, *Hier. Pal.* i. no. 243, followed by ALLEN and GUNN.
[3] *Sin.* B 5; R 45.
[4] *Urk.* iv. 1074, 10.
[5] *Sin.* B 283.
[6] *Sin.* B 86. 107.
[7] *Sin.* R 28; B 15.
[8] *Sh. S.* 166; *Sin.* B 4.
[9] *Sh. S.* 54.
[10] *Sin.* B 23.
[11] *Sin.* B 109; Louvre C 12, 3; *Sinai* 90, 5.
[12] *Sh. S.* 166. Sim. *Sin.* B 4–5, but this MS. often omits the suffix 1st sing.
[13] *Sh. S.* 54–5. Sim. *Sin.* B 15 (=*rdi·n·i* R 41); prob. also, *ib.* B 283.
[14] *Sh. S.* 166–7.
[15] *Sin.* B 5–6. Sim. *ib.* B 4; R 45; B 86. 107.

(§§ 402–5), since here no passive examples like those of § 404 can be quoted to prove the participial origin. There is, however, considerable likelihood that the *śḏmt·f* form is identical in all its uses.

The problem is to discern any difference between the construction prep. + *śḏmt·f* form and the constructions prep. + *śḏm·f* (§ 155) or *śḏm·n·f* (§ 156) form. In all certain examples the time of the action appears to be *relatively past*, i.e. anterior to the time of the main verb, agreeing with the origin proposed for the *śḏmt·f* form in § 405. It seems by no means unlikely that this common employment after prepositions is the reason for the comparative rarity of the *śḏm·n·f* form in this use.

1. Quite certain examples, i. e. examples from immutable verbs, have been found only with the prepositions *r* 'until' and *ḏr* 'since', 'from the moment that', but also 'before', 'until'.[0]

Exx. A torch shall be lighted for thee in the night *r wbnt św ḥr šnbt·k* until the sun has arisen over thy breast.[1] The main verb refers to the future.

m mdw n·f r iꜣšt·f do not speak to him until he has invited.[2] The main verb is a command.

Brewing was done in my presence *r pḥt·i dmi n 'Itw* until I reached (*or* had reached) the town of Itu.[3] In past narrative.

iw·i m tꜣ pn ḥr wḏ·f ḏr ḫprt mini tp ꜥwy·f I have been (lit. am *or* was) in this land under his command until death overtook him, lit. happened upon his hands.[4]

2. The use after *m* 'when', *m-ḫt* 'after', *ḫft* 'when' and *mi* 'like', 'according as' is more doubtful, since instances are forthcoming only from *3ae inf.* and *anom.* verbs. There is nothing to prevent such instances being interpreted as infinitives (see §§ 301. 304), though again there is no positive evidence in favour of this view. The analogy of *r* and *ḏr* favours a provisional classification under the heading of the *śḏmt·f* form.

Exx. . . . . *iḫr m hꜣt sꜣ·f m st·f . . . ., iw šms·n·(i) sw* but when his son (had) gone down into his place . . . . . . I served him.[5]

I filled his temple . . . . when My Majesty came . . . . . on the first occasion of victory . . . . *m rdit·f n·i ḫꜣswt nb nt Ḏꜣhy* when he gave (*or* had given) me all the lands of Djahi.[6]

His Majesty commanded to dig this canal, *m-ḫt gmt·f sw ḏbꜣw m inrw* after he had found it blocked with stones.[7]

My Majesty established a feast . . . . *ḫft it ḥm·i m wḏyt tpt nt nḫt* when My Majesty returned from the first campaign of victory.[8]

[0] See JUNKER, *Gîza III*, 93.

[1] *Urk.* iv. 117, 4; 148, 14; 499, 10. Sim. *Sh. S.* 118 (*kmt·k*); *P. Kah.* 5, 25. 29 (*snbt·s*); *Siut* 1, 278. 308 (*pḥt·sn*). In present time, LAC. *TR.* 21, 33 (*hꜣt·k*); *ÄZ.* 64, 113 (*ḫprt*).

[2] *Pt.* 126. Sim. *ib.* 87 (*wnt*), qu. § 215; 453 (*sdmt·k*). In a wish, possibly *Westc.* 11, 16 (*iwt·n*).

[3] *Sin.* B 247. Sim. *Ann.* 37, Pl. II, 25 (*ḫprt*); also possibly *PSBA.* 18, 202, 9 (*iwt*).

[4] *Urk.* iv. 405. Sim. from *3ae inf.* verbs, 'since', *ÄZ.* 47, 92, 3 (*prt·i*); *Urk.* iv. 386, 2 (*ḥꜥt·i*); 1073, 10 (*prt·i*); 'before', BUDGE, 208, 1 (*ḏꜣt·k*).

[5] Brit. Mus. 614, 12. Sim. *BH.* i. 25, 36 (*it*); *Urk.* iv. 89, 8 (*iwt·f*).

[6] *Urk.* iv. 767. Sim. *ib.* 591, 12 (*rdit·f*).

[7] *Urk.* iv. 814 = 90, 2. Sim. *ib.* 751, 2 (*gmt*); 745, 12 (*it*).

[8] *Urk.* iv. 740. Sim. *ib.* 698, 16; 741, 5; 767, 3 (*it*).

The hands of Isis are over this child *mi rdit·s ʿwy·sy ḥr sȝ·s Ḥr* even as she placed her hands over her son Horus.[1]

iḫ di·tw n·i mȝʿt mi irt·i sy therefore justice shall be given to me, according as I have done it.[2]

§ 408. Negation of the *śḏmt·f* form after prepositions.—An example of the negative verb *tm* in the *śḏmt·f* form can be quoted.

Deal with him privately *r tmt·k mn ḫrt·f* until thou art not troubled about his condition.[3]

§ 409. Forms of the *śḏmt·f* form after prepositions.—In the text or notes of the last two sections examples have been quoted from the following immutable verbs: *pḥ, km, tm* (*2-lit*); *iȝš, wbn, ḫpr, snb, sḏm* (*3-lit*). To these must be added an example of *ḏd* written *r ḏdti·f* 'until he has said';[4] the writing of *ti* for *t* in a MS. of Dyn. XVIII is of importance for the view of the perfective relative form adopted above § 387, 2.

In the case of some mutable verbs there arises the possibility, as we have seen, that the supposed *śḏmt·f* form might be the infinitive. The following exx. will suffice to illustrate the various verbal classes; for further details see the notes of § 407. The preposition is added in brackets after each form quoted.

2ae gem. *wnt* 'has been' (*r*).[5]

3ae inf. *prt·i* 'I went forth' (*ḏr*);[6] *gmt·f* 'he had found' (*m-ḫt*);[7] *irt·i* 'I have done' (*mi*).[8]

caus. 2-lit. *smnt·s* 'she established' (*mi*).[9]

anom. 'Give' has *rdit·f* (*m, mi*)[10] and *dit·f* (*mi*).[11] From 'come' there are both *it* (*m, m-ḫt, ḫft*)[12] and *iwt* (*r, m*);[13] but the latter might be either infinitive or *śḏm·f*, see § 448.

[1] *M. u. K.* 2, 10. Sim. *Urk.* iv. 198, 8 (*dit·f*); 807, 10 (*rdit·f*).

[2] *Urk.* iv. 492. Sim. *ib.* 134, 13–4 (*ḥst·f, rdit·f*); QUIB. *Saqq.* ii. p. 33 (*smnt·s*); *Rekh.* 12 (*wḏȝt*).

[3] *Pt.* 466.

[4] *Pt.* 267, qu. in the Reading lesson opposite.

[5] *Pt.* 87.

[6] *Urk.* iv. 1073, 10.

[7] *Urk.* iv. 814, 12.

[8] *Urk.* iv. 492, 7.

[9] QUIB. *Saqq.* ii. p. 33.

[10] *Urk.* iv. 591, 12; 767, 5; 807, 10.

[11] *Urk.* iv. 198, 8.

[12] *BH.* i. 25, 36; *Urk.* iv. 745, 12; 767, 3.

[13] *PSBA.* 18, 202, 9; *Urk.* iv. 89, 8.

VOCABULARY

ȝmi mix, compound, *ḥr* with.

abbrev. *wt* bandage, bind.

wḏȝ proceed.

ḥnn assent to; attend to.

ḫr fall; caus. *sḫr* overthrow.

ski destroy; empty out.

kn complete, be complete.

gfn rebuff; *gfnw* rebuff (n.)

tkk attack.

ṯni distinguish.

ỉyt mishap, harm.

pr-ḥd treasury (lit. white house).

msyt supper, evening meal.

mstꜣ a liquid of some sort.

sḳd sailor, traveller.

šꜥtt bread or cake of some kind.

šwꜣw poor man.

ḳrsw coffin.

Fnḫw Syrians; hence 'Phoenicians', Gk. Φοίνικες.[1]

[1] *Festschrift für F. Hommel*, Leipzig, 1917–8, i. 305–32.

EXERCISE XXVII

(*a*) *Reading lesson; extract from the book of precepts purporting to have been written by the vizier Ptaḥḥotpe in the reign of Asosi* (*Dyn. V*):[1]

ỉr wnn·k (§ 150) *m sprw n·f*,[2]
ḥr (§ 40, 2) *sḏm·k n ḏd* (§ 511, 4) *sprw.*
m (§ 340) *gfn sw,*
r skt·f ẖt·f,
r ḏdt(ỉ)·f (§ 409) *ỉỉt·n·f ḥr·s.*
mr sprw hnn (§ 303) *ṯsw·f,*
r ḳn·t(w) ỉỉt·n·f ḥr·s.
ḥꜥ sw ỉm r sprw nb.
ỉr ỉrr gfnw m sprw,[3]
ỉw ḏd·tw (§ 462),
ỉw·f tr r m (§ 495) *ỉr·f* (§ 463) *st?*

[1] *Pt.* 264–74, with some omissions.
[2] The manuscript, dating from the Eighteenth Dynasty, divides off connected groups of words by means of red 'verse-points', so called because they are commonest in poetical texts.
[3] This sign is cancelled in red.

'If thou art one to whom petition is made, listen quietly to what the petitioner says (lit. let thy hearing to the speech of the petitioner be quiet). Rebuff him not until he has poured out his heart (lit. body), until he has said that for which he came. A petitioner had rather (lit. likes) that his words should be attended to than that (the thing) for which he came should be accomplished; he rejoices thereat more than any (other) petitioner. As for one who deals (lit. makes) a rebuff to (lit. with) a petitioner, people say, To what purpose, pray, does he do it?'

(*b*) *Translate into English*:

(1)[1] … [2] … (2) … (3) … (4) … [3] … (5) … (6) …

[1] Prescription from a medical papyrus. [2] Passive *śḏm·f*, § 422, 2. [3] § 165, 10.

(*c*) *Write in hieroglyphs*:

(1) She whom he had never seen is (now) possessor (fem.) of his property. He who had not made for himself a coffin is (now) possessor of a treasury. (2) A departure was made from this place at time of supper. (3) All this happened by my hand (ʿ) (even) as he had commanded. (4) There is no poor man for whom the like has been done. (5) Thou art Atum who came into existence by himself, before the plans of the gods had been made. (6) Beware lest thou say, I do not know why this has been done (*give two alternative renderings of this sentence*). (7) (That) happened to (*r*) which no thought (*ỉb*) had been given. (8) They did it before order (*wḏt-mdw*) was given (lit. made) to them.

LESSON XXVIII

THE SUFFIX CONJUGATION

§ **410.** Under the name of **suffix conjugation** are to be understood those really verbal or 'narrative' (§ 297, 3) verb-forms, like the *śḏm·f* and *śḏm·n·f* forms, in which the subject, if pronominal, is denoted by a suffix-pronoun following the verb-stem and whatever flexional elements may be added to the verb-stem. As such, the suffix conjugation is opposed (1) to the 'old perfective' (Lesson XXII), an originally narrative verb-form akin to the perfect of the Semitic languages, (2) to the adjectival verb-forms of the same type as the suffix conjugation, i. e. the 'relative forms' of §§ 380 foll., and (3) to the partly nominal, partly verbal *śḏmt·f* form studied in the last Lesson (§§ 401–9).

The following forms will have to be considered:

1. The *śḏm·f* form, see above §§ 39–40, below § 411, and Lessons XXX–XXXI. Two and probably more varieties existed, which are indistinguishable in the immutable verbs and only with difficulty distinguishable in the mutable verbs. We can, however, definitely discern (*a*) a *perfective* form without gemination, and (*b*) an *imperfective* form showing gemination in certain verb-classes.

2. The passive *śḏm·f* form, see below §§ 419–24.

3. The *śḏmm·f* form, an almost obsolete form with passive meaning; see below §§ 425–6.

4. The *śḏm·n·f* form, see above § 67 and below §§ 412–8.

5. The *śḏm·in·f* form, see below §§ 427–9.

6. The *śḏm·ḫr·f* form, see below §§ 427; 430–2.

7. The *śḏm·kꜣ·f* form, see below §§ 427; 433–5.

Passives of all these forms except 2 and 3, which are passive from the outset, may be made by the insertion of the indefinite pronoun (§ 47) *·tw*, var. *·t(w)*, after the verb-form with its formative element. The formative element (*n*, *in*, *ḫr*, *kꜣ*) and the passive ending are dependent upon the verb-stem to the extent that they are inseparable from it; but they show a certain independence in that they regularly *follow* any determinative which the verb-stem may possess, exx. *m(w)dw·n·f* 'he spoke';[1] *dgg·tw·f* 'he is looked upon';[2] *ms·in·sn* 'they brought';[3] *šd·ḫr·tw·f* 'it shall be removed'.[4] The sole exception to this rule is in the *śḏm·f* form when the passive ending has the abbreviated writing *·t(w)*; in this case it is more often than not written *before* the determinative, ex. *swri·t(w)·f* 'it is drunk',[5] though forms like *ms·t(w)·f* 'he is born'[6] also appear; cf. before the determinative in the ending *·t(i)* of the old perfective (§ 309).

If the subject is a suffix, this is inseparable from the verb-form and follows the determinative.[6a] If, on the contrary, the subject is a noun, this may, under certain conditions already studied (§ 66), be separated from the verb-form.

Exx. *iw·in rf sḫty pn* then came this peasant.[7]

irw n·k ḥb ‘ꜣ there is made for thee a great feast.[8]

We shall see later (§ 486) that impersonal uses, i. e. cases where the subject is omitted, are far from rare, and this applies alike to the active forms of the suffix conjugation and to the passive *śḏm·f* (§ 422). It is perhaps better, however, to describe such examples as *nis·n·tw* 'one called', 'a summons was made',[9] as actives with the indefinite pronoun as subject, than as impersonal passives, though either description is defensible.

The general rules given above must be noted once and for all, as they cannot be repeated in treating of each separate form.

[1] *Pt.* 13.
[2] *Urk* IV. 19, 6.
[3] *Sin.* B 269.
[4] *Eb.* 53, 7–8.
[5] *Sin.* B 233.
[6a] In *śḏm·f* suffix 2nd f. sing. rarely before det. if written, not *ṯ*, but *t*, LEF. *Gr.* § 243, end.
[7] *Peas.* B 1, 52.
[8] LAC. *TR.* 76, 7.
[9] *Sin.* R 24. Sim. *ib.* B 55 (*‘ḥ‘·n·tw*).

§ 411. The origin of the *śḏm·f* and *śḏm·n·f* forms.—It will pave the way for the account to be given of the suffix conjugation if the origin of its two commonest varieties be discussed by way of preface.

1. As regards the *śḏm·f* form, an often held theory[1] supposes this to be ultimately a sentence composed of active participle + pronominal or nominal subject; the whole would thus mean 'he is (*or* was) one hearing'. To this theory there are serious objections. We have already seen that 'he is one hearing' can be expressed in Egyptian either as *ntf śḏm* (§ 373) or else as *śḏm św* (§ 374); it seems gratuitous to postulate a third method. The proposal is to consider *śḏm·f* as a sentence of the same type as *śḏm św*, it being conjectured that the suffix-pronouns are merely worn-down dependent pronouns. This view of the suffix-pronouns may indeed be true in the last resort, but the differentiation of function between dependent pronouns and suffixes probably lies much farther back than the origin of the suffix conjugation, if this, as is supposed with great probability, supplanted an earlier kind of conjugation of which the old perfective is the last survival.

Much more serious, however, is the objection arising from the comparison of the ordinary narrative *śḏm·f* and *śḏm·n·f* forms with the corresponding relative forms. Since the discovery of the perfective, i.e. non-geminating, relative form it has become possible to construct a most striking table of parallelisms.

RELATIVE FORMS	NARRATIVE FORMS
mrr(w)·f, imperfective (§ 387, 1)	*mrr·f*
mr·f and *mry·f*, perfective (§ 387, 2)	*mr·f*, also *mry·f*
mr(w)·n·f[2] (§ 387, 3)	*mr·n·f*.[3]

In face of these parallelisms the interdependence of the narrative and the relative forms seems indisputable; the two series coincide so closely at the end of their development that to assume a distinct origin for each is paradoxical. But the development of the relative forms out of the passive participles can now be traced in some detail; see above § 386. The conclusion seems inevitable: *the narrative* śḏm·f *and* śḏm·n·f *forms must likewise be derived from the passive participles.* Only on this theory can the use of the suffix-pronoun in the *śḏm·f* form be explained; it is a direct genitive such as often serves to express the semantic subject after the passive participles (§ 379, 2); *śḏm·f* thus signifies 'heard of him'.[4] We saw (§ 386) that the passive participles, as extended by the addition of a semantic subject and object and a phrase containing the resumptive pronoun, must at a given moment have been construed *actively*, not passively. If this be granted, no great difficulty should be felt in supposing that at the same moment two separate kinds of verb-form began gradually to be

[1] ERMAN in *ÄZ*. 39, 123; LEXA in *Philologica*, ii. 25–53. So too LEF. *Gr.* § 242; POL. *Ét.* 92 hesitatingly.

[2] In this ed. called the *śḏmw·n·f* relative form.

[3] This form has largely, but not completely, replaced *mr·f* in past narrative, see §§ 414, 1; 450, 1.

[4] See below the Add.

differentiated out of the passive participles, (*a*) the ordinary narrative *śḏm·f* and *śḏm·n·f*, in which the gender-endings were suppressed,[0] and (*b*) the relative *śḏm(w)·f* and *śḏm(w)·n·f* forms, in which the gender-endings were retained.

[0] Cf. the adj. as predicate contrasted with adj. as epithet, above, § 48. So too SETHE, *ÄZ.* 54, 102, though only in reference to *śḏm·n·f*.

The hypothesis here rejected assumes that the narrative *śḏm·f* form, both in its geminating form, ex. *mrr·f*, and in its non-geminating form, ex. *mr(y)·f*, is derived from the *imperfective* active participle, the difference between the two varieties being attributed merely to emphatic or non-emphatic utterance. This view, which reduces the distinction between geminating and non-geminating *śḏm·f* to the level of the distinction between English 'sayeth' and 'saith' or between German *gehest* and *gehst*, seriously underrates the difference in their meanings and syntactic uses. We shall find on closer study that, while the narrative *mrr·f* is definitely imperfective in meaning, the narrative *mr·f* and *mr(y)·f* has partly past and partly prospective signification—the latter, for example, after *ỉḫ* (§ 450, 5, *a*), after *ḥꜣ* (§ 450, 5, *b*), and after verbs like *rdỉ* (§ 452, 1). This agrees well with our view that the perfective relative form originated in the perfective passive participle (§ 387, 2), of which it exemplifies at least two of the three uses (§§ 369, 1. 3; 389, 2).

As a last argument in favour of the origin of the ordinary narrative *śḏm·f* in a passive participle, one may point to its parallelism with the narrative *śḏm·n·f* form. For the latter no other explanation has been advanced than that it originated in a passive participle followed by a dative, since it is no explanation to say that the *n* is a formative element added to an active participle. But if the *śḏm·n·f* originated in a passive participle, why not also the *śḏm·f* form?

2. The *śḏm·n·f* form. We have repeatedly referred to Sethe's view[1] that this had its origin in a passive participle followed by a dative; see above §§ 3; 67; 386, 2; 387, 3. Our own hypothesis that the developed use of the passive participle + dative led to the simultaneous evolution of (*a*) the relative *śḏmw·n·f* and (*b*) the narrative *śḏm·n·f* (see above) is only an elaboration of that view. It is significant that in the relative form *śḏmw·n·f* the participial and gender endings *-w* and *-t* precede the element *n*; hence it seems likely that *n* is no part of the underlying participle. Analogies both in Semitic (§ 3) and in the Indo-European languages speak for the origin of the ending *·n·f* in the dative.[2] If *śḏm·n·f* means properly 'heard (is) to him', then the resemblance to French *il a fait* and German *er hat getan* is obviously very close and illuminating, the more so since English 'he has' (*il a, er hat*) is often expressed in Egyptian by *n·f* 'to him' (§ 114, 1). Compare also *faciendum est mihi* in Latin. But Egyptian also shares with French and German another mode of expression involving the dative of possession; as we have seen (§ 141), *nfr n·f* is opposed to *nfr sw* as *il a froid* to *il est froid* or *ihm ist kalt* to *er ist kalt.* Apparently

[1] *ÄZ.* 47, 140; 54, 98.

[2] See § 307 for rare exx. of a dative designating the semantic subject after the infinitive.

the particular notion which is conveyed by the combination of an adjective or participle with a possessive phrase is *the fortuitous or incidental character of an occurrence.* There is nothing about this combination which definitely demands reference to past time, and the use of the *śḏm·n·f* form after the negative word *n* 'not' (§ 418), as well as the affirmative use to express immediate present time (§ 414, 5), shows that, as with all other Egyptian verb-forms, the tendency to restrict its application to one particular time-position was secondary. The primary function of the *śḏm·n·f* form was thus probably to present the verbal action as an *incident,* as something *happening* or *occurring* to someone, irrespective of time-position.

The origin of the other forms of the suffix conjugation will be discussed as occasion arises. They are obviously all of participial origin, and reason will be found for thinking that the participle in question was in every case a passive one.

THE *ŚḎM·N·F* FORM[1]

§ 412. Endings, etc.—Observe that, even in texts which habitually write the suffix *·i* of the 1st sing., this is apt to be omitted before the reflexive dependent pronoun *wi.* Ex. *rdi·n·(i) wi* 'I placed myself'.[2] For a like omission elsewhere, see § 406.

Impersonal uses of the *śḏm·n·f* form are not rare; note especially *ḫpr·n* 'it happened';[3] also *ꜥḥꜥ·n* 'thereupon', lit. 'there arose', when the passive *śḏm·f* follows (below § 476).

The passive in *·tw* is not very common, since the passive *śḏm·f* form corresponds to active *śḏm·n·f* in various uses; see below § 422. Not infrequently *·tw* serves as impersonal subject: exx. *nis·n·tw* 'one called';[4] *n ꜥḥꜥ·n·tw* 'no one stands'.[5]

Examples where the formative *n* precedes the determinative are rare, and may be considered faulty: exx. *ꜥḥꜥ·n* 'arose';[6] *wḏ·n* 'commanded'.[7]

Obs. For the elliptical omission, in a sequence of *śḏm·n·f* forms, not only of the suffix subject, but also of the formative *n,* see below § 487.

§ 413. Forms from the mutable verbs.

2ae gem. A few geminating forms are known, ex. *kbb·n* 'does (not) grow cool'.[8] 'See' has *mȝ·n·f.*[9] 'Exist' has a form *wn·(i)*[10] 'I was' which might possibly stand for *wn·n·i,* since it is parallel to *mȝ·n·(i)* 'I saw'; cf., however, above § 387, 3 and Add. to the present paragraph; there is often a doubt whether is to be taken as *śḏm·n·f* or as geminating *śḏm·f* (§§ 120, end; 326).

3ae inf. Exx. *ṯȝ·n·f* 'he took';[11] *gm·n* 'found'.[12] 'Make' has *ir·n·f,*[13] only very exceptionally .[14] 'Seize' shows *iṯ·n·f.*[15]

[1] See *Verbum,* ii. §§ 359–89.

[2] *Sh. S.* 156. 161. Sim. *ib.* 53; *Sin.* B 200; Lac. *TR.* 3, 34. 36; *Urk.* iv. 158, 16; 1080, 16; 1083, 2.

[3] *Hamm.* 113, 14. In exx. like *P. Pet.* 1116 B, 1; *Sh. S.* 130; *Urk.* iv. 648, 4 a noun clause serves as subject, see p. 142, n. 4.

[4] *Sin.* R 24.

[5] *Sin.* B 55.

[6] *BH.* i. 8, 9–10.

[7] *Hamm.* 113, 10. Sim. Louvre C1, vert. 4. 5.

[8] *P. Pet.* 1116 A, 68. Sim. *tkk·n, ib.* 33; *ȝmm·n·f, Urk.* iv. 17, 8, *ꜥnn·n·i, ib.* 367, 12.

[9] *Sin.* B 108; *Leb.* 71; passive, *Urk.* v. 61, 17; 62, 2.

[10] *JEA.* 4, Pl. 9, 2, qu. § 414, 1, end. Cf. too *iw wn·sn, Eleph.* 25, qu § 468, 2.

[11] *Peas.* B 1, 22.

[12] *Sin.* R 19.

[13] *BH.* i. 25, 4.

[14] Cairo 20011. 20016.

[15] *Sin.* B 46–7.

4ae inf. Exx. *m(i)ni·n·f* 'he attached';[1] *m(w)dw·n* 'spoke'.[2] *caus. 2ae gem.* *sḳbb·n* 'cooled'.[3]

anom. 'Give' has *rdi·n·f*,[4] *rdi·n·i*[5] and, rather less commonly, ,[6] [7] *di·n·f*. The writing *dy·n·i*[8] is quite abnormal; is found varying with .[9]

'Come' has forms from both stems: ,[10] ,[11] [12] *i·n* are common types; *iw·n·n*[13] and *iw·n·i*[14] are less common.

'Bring' writes normally for *in·n·f*,[15] but is by no means rare.[16]

The absence of gemination in the *3ae inf.* and *anom.* agrees well with the theory (§ 411, 2) that the *śdm·n·f* form originated in the perf. pass. part. Its presence in some forms of the *2ae gem.* is just possibly to be attributed to the former existence in this class of reduplicating perf. pass. participles such as we found for the *2-lit.* verbs, § 360.[16a] The suppression of the participial ending is no more than we should expect to find before the originally prepositional formative *n*, see above §§ 361; 379, 3.

1 *Sin.* B 78.
2 *T. Carn.* 2.
3 LAC. *TR.* 37, 13.
4 *Sin.* B 78.
5 *Siut* 1, 275.
6 *BH.* i. 25, 77.
7 *Siut* 5, 22.
8 LAC. *TR.* 14, 4.
9 LAC. *TR.* 66, 1–3.
10 *Siut* 3, 13.
11 LAC. *TR.* 8, 2.
12 LAC. *TR.* 4, 5.
13 *Urk.* iv. 566, 10. Sim. *Paheri* 1.
14 Leyd. V 3, 5.
15 *Westc.* 6, 10. 12.
16 With one *n*, *Sin.* B 30. 103; *Sh. S.* 114; *BH.* i. 25, 71.
16a For another possibility with regard to *sḳbb* see below p. 343.

§ 414. Affirmative uses of the *śdm·n·f* form.—We have seen that the primitive function of the *śdm·n·f* form was to present the verbal action as an *incident* happening to someone, irrespective of time-position (§ 411, 2, end). Nevertheless, in most affirmative uses it is used solely in reference to events lying in the *past*.

1. It is the usual form in *past narrative*, where it may be rendered, according as the case demands, either (*a*) by the English present perfect, or (*b*) by the English past tense.

Exx. (*a*) *dd·n·i m mꜣꜥt* I have spoken in truth.[17]

pḥ·n·k nn ḥr m how hast thou come to this pass? Lit. on account of what hast thou reached this?[18]

i·n·i ḫr·tn sd·i pꜣsw·tn I have come to you in order that I may break your water-pots.[19]

(*b*) *rdi·n·f n·i mw* he gave me water.[20]

šd·n·t(w)·f n·i it was read aloud to me.[21]

Note carefully that the corresponding negation is *n śdm·f*, not *n śdm·n·f*; see §§ 105, 1; 455, 1.

As already noted, the passive *śdm·n·tw·f* is rather rare (§ 412), the passive *śdm·f* form often taking its place (§ 422, 1). In narrative of the 1st pers. the old perfective is frequently the passive counterpart of the active *śdm·n·f* (§ 312, 2).[22]

The simple *śdm·n·f* form is the staple of most past narrative, but at the beginning of paragraphs it was often felt to need reinforcing. Hence the compound tenses *iw śdm·n·f* (§ 68) and *ꜥḥꜥ·n śdm·n·f* (§ 478), to which we shall return later.

17 *Sinai* 53. Sim. *ib.* 90, 5. 11; *Sin.* B 46–7; *Urk.* iv. 649, 8.
18 *Sin.* B 34. Sim. in a question, *Urk.* v. 160, 8. 9.
19 LAC. *TR.* 10, 7. Sim. with following clause of purpose, *ib.* 32, 2; *Urk.* iv. 614, 15–6.
20 *Sin.* B 27. Sim. *Peas.* B 1, 34; *Sh. S.* 41; *BH.* i. 25, 4; *Hamm.* 113, 14; *Urk.* iv. 38, 14; 151, 1; 649, 14.
21 *Sin.* B 200. Sim. Leyd. V 4, 5; *Eb.* 75, 12.
22 Exx. *Urk.* iv. 55. 160. 530. 1073. 1208.

We pass now to the use after the non-enclitic particles. After *mk*, as already seen (§ 234), the *śḏm·n·f* form corresponds to the English *present perfect*.

Ex. *mk hꜣb·n·i ḥr ḥn·k n imy-r pr* behold, I have written (lit. sent) commending thee to the steward.[1]

After *isṯ* (§ 231) and *isk* (§ 230) the *śḏm·n·f* form describes a situation or circumstance occurring in the past.

Ex. *isṯ gm·n ḥm·f r-pr pn m ḏbt* now His Majesty found (*or* had found) this sanctuary in brick.[2] There follows: His Majesty commanded to make this temple of hard stone.

Examples where such sentences with *isṯ* are best translated as clauses of time have been quoted in § 212. So too after *ti*, ib.

The *śḏm·n·f* form has likewise past meaning after a nominal subject in anticipatory emphasis (§ 148, 1).

Ex. *wgg ꜣs·n·f wi* infirmity has overtaken me.[3]

In conclusion, mention must be made of the rare cases where *wn·i* means 'I was' in past narrative.

Ex. *wn·(i) m biꜣw, mꜣ·n·(i) sw* I have been in the mine-country, I have seen it.[4]

The parallelism of *wn·i* here to an indubitable *śḏm·n·f* form might seem to suggest that it stands for *wn·n·i*, but see Add. to § 413.

2. Not infrequently the *śḏm·n·f* form serves to express *relative past* time, i. e. time which is past relatively to the time of the adjacent context.

Exx. *nhs Wsir ḥr st·f, ip·n·f ḏt·f* Osiris awakes upon his throne, (after) he has recovered his senses, lit. counted his body.[5] Note the English present perfect.

ti sw ḥm iy·f, in·n·f sḳr-ꜥnḫw and now he was returning, and had brought prisoners.[6] Note the English past perfect.

prt pw ir·n nn nṯrw, sms·n·sn Rd-ḏdt these gods went forth, (after) they had delivered Reddjedet.[7] Engl. past perfect.

dd·n·f nn, rḫ·n·f ḳd·i, sḏm·n·f šsꜣ·i he said this, (because) he knew my character, he had heard of my prudence.[8] Engl. past perfect.

In most cases of the kind the *śḏm·n·f* form is best translated as a virtual subordinate clause.[9] It is this same relative past time which the *śḏm·n·f* form expresses in all subordinate clauses where it occurs affirmatively, and there it is contrasted with the *śḏm·f* form, which expresses relative present or future time. The last example shows, however, that *śḏm·n·f* may have relative past time even when the surrounding narrative tenses involve the *śḏm·n·f* form itself. Here again the corresponding negation is *n śḏm·f*, see below § 455, 1.

[1] *P. Kah.* 31, 19. Other exx., p. 179, n. 1.

[2] *Urk.* iv. 879. Sim. *ib.* 28, 11; 834, 14; MAR. *Abyd.* ii. 30, 39; Berl. *ÄI.* i. p. 258, 20. With *isk*, *Eb.* 1, 19; BUDGE, p. 291, 4. 6.

[3] *Sin.* B 168–9. Sim. after *mk*, *Sh. S.* 113–4, qu. § 148, 1. To be rendered as Engl. past, *Sin.* B 142–3. 185; *Bersh.* i. 14, 5. After *ink pw*, etc., see § 190.

[4] *JEA.* 4, Pl. 9, 2. Sim. *Urk.* v. 21, parallel to *i·n·i*; *ÄZ.* 47, Pl. 1, 3.

[5] LAC. *TR.* 12, 7. Sim. *ib.* 12, 1. 4. 13; *Leb.* 141, qu. § 67; *Eb.* 105, 9–10. 17; 106, 18; *Urk.* iv. 613, 9; 1090, 14.

[6] *Sin.* R 15.

[7] *Westc.* 11, 3–4. Sim. *Peas.* R 7. After narrative inf., *Urk.* iv. 5, 14; after *ꜥḥꜥ·n* + noun + old perf., *ib.* 6, 12.

[8] *Sin.* B 32–3; Sim. *ib.* 107. Of time, after *śḏm·n·f*, *Urk.* iv. 814, 16, qu. Exerc. XXVIII, (*a*).

[9] As main clause, after *ist* (*rf*), *Sin.* R 11.

3. After *ḥ3* 'would that!' (§ 238) and after *ir* 'if' (§ 151) the *śḏm·n·f* form is used in reference to unfulfilled action, 'would that' or 'if he had heard'. Examples have already been quoted. The negation after *ḥ3* is *n śḏm·f*, §§ 238. 455, 1; after *ir* it would doubtless be *tm·n·f śḏm(w)*, §§ 151; 347, 6.

4. Some actions necessarily involve resultant states, and languages are apt to differ with regard to the angle from which such verbal notions are viewed. In the case of verbs of motion, English uses 'I have come' and 'I am come' with hardly any perceptible difference. Egyptian, on the contrary, seems to have felt a distinction between the old perfective as in *ii·kwi* 'I returned'[1] (§ 312, 3) or in *mk wi iy·kwi* 'behold, I am come'[2] (§ 324) and the *śḏm·n·f* form as in *i·n·i* (above 1). The latter is certainly preferred when any stress is laid on the movement as an action performed by someone; such a stress occurs, for example, when words indicating the purpose of the movement are added.

Ex. *ii·n·i ꜥ3 r nis r·k* I have come hither to summon thee.[3]

The difference, then, with verbs of motion is that the *śḏm·n·f* form emphasizes the fact of the movement, while the old perfective merely calls attention to the result (§ 320).

Still more conspicuously, Egyptian chooses to look upon 'knowing' as 'having learned', and 'remembering' as 'having recollected'. Hence the verbs *rḫ* 'learn', 'know' and *sḫ3* 'recollect', 'remember' sometimes appear in the *śḏm·n·f* form even where they must be translated by English present tenses.

Exx. *mtn rḫ·n·tn* behold, ye know.[4]

in iw trw sḫ3·n·k dost thou remember?[5]

A similar use of *rḫ* has been noted in connection with the old perfective (§ 320, end) and the *śḏmw·n·f* relative form (§ 389, 3); under the latter head some other like employments have been noticed. It will be seen below (§ 455, 1, end) that here again *n śḏm·f* corresponds as negation to the affirmative *śḏm·n·f*.

5. On a different footing is the common use of the *śḏm·n·f* form in ritual texts and scenes to express an action *simultaneously spoken of and performed.*[6]

Exx. *swꜥb·n·(i) ṯn m mw ipn* I purify thee with this water.[7] A god is depicted sprinkling water over the queen and speaking these words.

di·n·(i) n·k t3w nb I give to thee all lands. Words spoken by the god Dedwen while leading prisoners to the king.[8]

This employment is so invariable as to justify us in regarding writings like ,[9] [10] as short writings for *smn·n·(i) n·ṯ* 'I record for thee', *in·n·(i) n·k* 'I bring to thee' respectively.

[1] *BH.* i. 8, 15.

[2] *Westc.* 8, 12.

[3] *Westc.* 7, 20. Sim. with clause of purpose, above p. 329, n. 19. See, however, *Westc.* 3, 7, where a phrase expressing purpose, follows *mk wi iy·kwi*.

[4] *Siut* 1, 280. 310. Sim. *Ann.* 5, 234, 22; *Urk.* iv. 350, 16; 353, 12.

[5] *Eb.* 2, 3. Sim. *Ḥarh.* 412; *Urk.* iv. 27, 14.

[6] See GUNN, *Stud.* ch. 7.

[7] *D. el B.* 63. Sim. *Urk.* iv. 250, 15 (*sš·n·i*); *Th. T. S.* i. 17 (*wp·n·i*).

[8] MAR. *Karn.* 23. Sim. *D. el B.* 128.

[9] *D. el B.* 60.

[10] MAR. *Karn.* 18; *D. el B.* 128. So too *wn·n·(i) n·k*, *Th. T. S.* i. 17.

In this usage there seems no notion of past time, so that the *śḏm·n·f* form here appears to retain its primitive force of stressing the merely occurrent; such a translation as 'herewith I give to thee' renders the sense closely. Note that this employment is borrowed from Old Kingdom temple scenes, and has not been found in contexts of later origin.

§ **415. The *śḏm·n·f* form in noun clauses.**—In all affirmative subordinate clauses, the *śḏm·n·f* form has *relative past* meaning. This has already often been pointed out, and may be verified, so far as virtual noun clauses are concerned, in the rare cases where *śḏm·n·f* serves as object of a verb (§ 185) or follows the genitival adjective *ny* (§ 192).

§ **416. The *śḏm·n·f* form in relative clauses.**—An example in a virtual relative clause with undefined antecedent is quoted § 196, 2, and another after *nty* in § 201. In both cases the corresponding negation was seen to be *n śḏm·f*. For the *śḏm·n·f* form after *ỉwty* see §§ 203, 6; 418, end.

§ **417. The *śḏm·n·f* form in adverb clauses.**—1. We have observed (§ 414, 2) that where *śḏm·n·f* has relative past meaning it must often be rendered as a virtual clause of *time*; sometimes it may have to be interpreted as a virtual clause of *cause* (§ 221).

2. The *śḏm·n·f* form but rarely follows prepositions; when it does so it has relative past meaning, see above § 156. For *śḏm·n·f* after *ỉr* 'if' see §§ 151; 414, 3.

§ **418. The negative construction *n śḏm·n·f*.**[1]—A broad survey shows that the construction *n śḏm·n·f* is common in *characterizations*, *statements of custom*, and *generalizations* of all kinds. The affirmative verb-forms which it accompanies and continues are, in the main, those usual in such contexts. Thus *n śḏm·n·f* is found in close association with the old perfective,[2] the part of the verb best adapted to the description of more or less permanent conditions (§ 311, end); with the geminating participles[3] (imperfective) or the geminating *śḏm·f* form,[4] parts of the verb often found to imply repetition or continuity (§§ 365 foll.; 440 foll.); or else, finally, with the compound verb-form *ỉw·f śḏm·f*,[5] which we shall see later to be common in proverbs and statements of custom (§ 463).[6]

That the construction *n śḏm·n·f* does not itself explicitly generalize, though it certainly serves to reinforce generalizations, seems evident from the impossibility of linking up any such function with the affirmative uses of the *śḏm·n·f* form. The true *modus operandi* of *n śḏm·n·f* becomes clear when we realize that the best way of confirming a generalization is to assert the absence of any invalidating incident. An example will here be helpful. The sentence

[1] See GUNN, *Stud.* ch. 12, where a different standpoint is adopted.

[2] In its various constructions, viz.:—§ 315, *Urk.* iv. 814, 13, qu. Exerc. XXVIII, (*a*); § 322, *Pt.* 13, qu. below; § 323, *Adm.* 2, 4, qu. below (1); *Urk.* iv. 650, 7, qu. p. 248, top; § 326, *Leb.* 146; *Nu*, ch. 130, 41; *Urk.* iv. 518, 15.

[3] *Peas.* B 2, 101–2; *Nu*, ch. 149, ii. 8, both qu. below; *Urk.* v. 67, 17.

[4] See § 445, 2.

[5] *Peas.* B 2, 98–9; *Eb.* 97, 2; BUDGE, p. 152, 12.

[6] Also with *ḥr* + inf., see § 334.

r gr, n mdw·n·f 'the mouth is silent (old perfective) and does not speak' is found in a description of old age.[1] We have shown reason for thinking that the *śḏm·n·f* form presents the verbal notion as an incident occurring to its doer (§ 411, 2). If so, *n mdw·n·f* may be freely paraphrased as 'an act of speaking does not happen to the mouth', or, in other words, its state of silence is not contradicted by any negative instance.

Naturally, when it is said that such and such an act does not happen to someone, some space of time is envisaged over which it might happen, so that we can now adopt the formulation already proposed in § 105, 3, and define the function of *n śḏm·n·f* as *to deny the occurrence of an action throughout the course of a more or less prolonged period.*

We might also render the sentence above-quoted 'the mouth is silent and *cannot* speak', and it will often be found that a possible, or even the best, rendering for *n śḏm·n·f* is 'he cannot', 'could not', or 'will not be able to hear'.[2] In such renderings, however, an English standpoint is substituted for the Egyptian; English affirms the impossibility of the act, while Egyptian merely states that over a contemplated period it does not occur.

The following examples show that the actions referred to by *n śḏm·n·f* may belong indifferently to present, past, or future time.

1. In reference to *present* actions, the commonest and most typical use. The time-position is often very vague, the statement being of proverbial or generalizing character.

Exx. *ir sḳdd ḫr·f, n sꜣḥ·n·f tꜣ* as for him who sails with falsehood for a cargo (lit. under it (*grg*)), he does not reach land.[3] A proverbial utterance.

iw ms ḥmwt wšr, n iwr·n·tw assuredly women are barren, no one conceives.[4] Description of a prevailing condition.

ink ḫnn, n wrd·n·f I am one who rows and does not tire.[5] Characterization of a person.

2. In reference to *past* actions.

Exx. This peasant spent (*ir·in sḫty pn*) ten days making petition to this Djeḥutnakht, *n rdi·n·f mꜣꜥ·f r·s* and he paid no heed to it, lit. gave not his temple to it.[6] A continued activity is narrated.

n pḥ·n·tw·f m sḫs he was not equalled (lit. reached) in running.[6a] Characterization of the young Amenophis II.

3. In reference to *future* actions.

Ex. *ḥwꜣ·ḫr·s m ẖt·f, n pr·n·s* it shall rot in his belly, without coming out, lit. it does not come out.[7] A medical generalization.

Needless to say, the construction *n śḏm·n·f* is not confined to main clauses.

[1] *Pt.* 13.

[2] Exx. present, *Peas.* B 1, 256; *P. Pet.* 1116 A, 93; past, *Westc.* 12, 3, qu. § 369, 2; *Urk.* iv. 36, 8; 758, 15; future, *Eb.* 97, 19, qu. § 105, 3. TILL (*ÄZ.* 67, 118) exaggerates the frequency of this sense.

[3] *Peas.* B 2, 101–2. Sim. *ib.* 75; B 1, 256. 325; *Adm.* p. 108; *P. Pet.* 1116 A, 43.

[4] *Adm.* 2, 4. Sim. *ib.* 2, 5; 3, 8; 4, 1; *P. Kah.* 33, 8.

[5] *Nu*, ch. 149, ii. 8. Sim. *Sin.* B 58. 59; *Peas.* B 1, 174; *P. Kah.* 30, 11, qu. § 307.

[6] *Peas.* B 1, 31–2. Sim. *Westc.* 5, 1; 12. 3, qu. § 369, 2; Brit. Mus. 614, 7. 9; *Urk.* iv. 77, 7, qu. § 440, 2; 98, 9; 131, 11; 697, 13; 758, 15; 814, 13, qu. Exerc. XXVIII, (*a*); 1195, 9; *Rec.* 29, 164, 9.

[6a] *Ann.* 37, Pl. 2, 12.

[7] *Eb.* 25, 5. Sim. *ib.* 97, 19, qu. § 105. 3; after *wnn*, *Leb.* 146; BUDGE, p. 285, 1.

Besides its use in virtual relative clauses,[8] it occurs also after the relative adjective *nty*.

Ex. *m pḥ nty n pḥ·n·f* do not attack him who does not attack.[1]

After the negative relative adjective *ỉwty* (§ 203, 6) the *śḏm·n·f* form appears to have exactly the same meaning as in *n śḏm·n·f*.

Ex. this noble god who came into being of himself and *ỉwt(y) wḏb·n·f sw ḥr ḏdt·n·f* who does not go back (lit. turn himself) upon what he has said.[2]

[8] Exx. *Urk.* iv. 616, 4. 10.

[1] *Peas.* B 1, 316. Sim. *Eb.* 12, 16.

[2] *Coffins* I, 385, *b*. Sim. *ib.* I, 31, *b*; 404, *c*; Nav. 149 *e*, 30; Brit. Mus. 159, 11, qu. p. 153, n. 7.

§ 418 A. The negative construction *nn śḏm·n·f*.[3]—The examples of this construction are scanty, obscure, and sometimes even possibly corrupt. In a few places *nn śḏm·n·f* denies with emphasis that something *will* (or *can*) occur.

Ex. *nn pr·n·k r ḥrw* never wilt thou go up above.[4]

In two cases it is a *past* event which is denied.

Ex. *nn ỉr·n·ỉ n rmṯ ḏd·tw ꜥbꜥ r·s* I have not acted to(wards) men (so that) people might utter boasts concerning it.[5]

Until better evidence is forthcoming this construction must be regarded with suspicion, the more so since after the middle of Dyn. XVIII tends to take the place of in the writing, see § 104, end.

Obs. The student should examine in every instance of *nn śḏm·n·f* whether *nn* cannot mean 'there is none who(m) ......' in accordance with § 394.

[3] See Gunn, *Stud.* ch. 14. Another difficult case, *L. to D.*, Cairo bowl 7.

[4] *Leb.* 59. Sim. *Pt.* 381. 383. 459. 576; *Urk.* iv. 445, 7.

[5] *Urk.* iv. 751. Sim. *ib.* 847, 3. *Nn* certainly for *n*, *Rec.* 29, 164, 9.

VOCABULARY

ꜣsḫ reap.

wḥm repeat.

fḳꜣ reward.

sꜣỉ be satiated.

sbỉ rebel.

smꜣ, var. (§ 279), slay.

ssn smell, breathe (trans.).

sḳdw travel by water, fare upon (river, sea).

sdꜣ tremble.

šꜣd excavate, dig out.

šdỉ take out, extract, rescue; clear (a canal).

tỉtỉ trample down.

tkn approach, with *m*, more rarely transitive.

wḥꜥ fisherman.

bỉꜣ copper.

bdt, var. *bty*, emmer, a poor kind of cereal.

mr lake, canal.

msḫtyw adze.

nbt basket; island-home (?).

grg falsehood, lie.

dpy crocodile (rare).

Stḫ, varr. *S(w)tḫ*, *Sty* (§ 60), the god Seth.

Ꜣbw Elephantine, an island at the N. end of the First Cataract.

Mṯn Mitanni, a kingdom E. of the Euphrates.

EXERCISE XXVIII

(*a*) *Reading lesson. Inscription cut on a rock in the island of Sehêl, in the First Cataract.*[1]

ḥꜣt-sp 50, tpy (n) šmw, sw 22,

ḫr ḥm n n-sw-bỉt Mn-ḫpr-Rꜥ, dỉ ꜥnḫ.

wḏ (§ 306, Obs.) *ḥm·f šꜣd mr pn,*

m-ḫt gmt·f (§ 407, 2) *sw ḏbꜣw* (§ 315) *m ỉnrw,*

n sḳd·n dpt ḥr·f.

ḫd·n·f ḥr·f,

ỉb·f ꜣw (§ 322),

smꜣ·n·f ḫft(yw)·f.

rn n mr pn:[2]

wn tꜣ wꜣt m nfrt (§ 96) *Mn-ḫpr-Rꜥ, ꜥnḫ ḏt.*

ỉn nꜣ n wḥꜥw-rmw Ꜣbw šd·sn (§ 227, 2) *mr pn*

ṯnw rnpt.

[1] *Urk.* iv. 814.

[2] § 89 or else as p. 100, n. 6.

'Year 50, first month of summer, day 22, under the Majesty of the king of Upper and Lower Egypt, Menkheperrēꜥ, given life. His Majesty commanded to dig this canal, after he had found it blocked with stones, and no boat fared upon it. He travelled down over it, his heart glad, (when) he had slain his enemies. The name of this canal: Menkheperrēꜥ-is-opener-of-the-way-as-(something-) good. The fishermen of Elephantine shall clear this canal every year.'

(*b*) *Translate into English*:

(1)[1] … [2] …

(2) … [3] …

(3) … [4] …

[5] …

(4) …

(5) …

(6) …

(7) …

(8) …

[1] Words spoken by the *ẖry-ḥbt* priest while standing before the mummy on the day of burial, a ceremonial adze in his hand. [2] A personal name.

[3] Perhaps the compound preposition thus spelt p. 132, n. 25. [4] *n-sw-bít.*

[5] Note that nouns denoting persons in a particular position in life are also used in Egyptian to express that position itself, abstractly considered; cf. *ṯꜣty* 'vizier', but also 'the rank of vizier', *Urk.* iv. 1087, 7, qu. § 149, 1; similarly *mty n sꜣ* 'office of regulator of a priestly order', *P. Kah.* 11, 18, qu. § 323.

(*c*) *Write in hieroglyphs*:

(1) I have spoken in truth, I have not spoken lies. (2) Dost thou not remember the name of that great god who is in Heliopolis? (3) I give to thee all things good and pure which are in me. (4) Pleasant words are what thou hast said; the heart cannot have enough (lit. does not become satiated) of (*m*) hearing them. (5) He saw that my arms were strong. (6) I was rewarded with gold three times. (7) The nose is stopped up and cannot smell. (8) I acted as (lit. made) overseer of cattle, and was not neglectful concerning the commands of my lord. (9) Reply, O my heart; a heart that is attacked does not keep silence.

LESSON XXIX

THE PASSIVE *ŚḎM·F* FORM

§ 419. The form of the suffix conjugation (§ 410) next demanding attention is here called the passive *śḏm·f*.[1] Externally, this closely resembles the active *śḏm·f* form long familiar to the student. Confusion with the latter is, however, rendered impossible in practice by the invariable passive meaning; the passive *śḏm·f* signifies 'he was heard' or 'he is heard' despite the absence of the element *·tw* employed to form passives from the other parts of the suffix conjugation. In addition to this distinguishing characteristic, an ending *-w* (with some mutable verbs also *-y*) often helps to identify the form; see the next section.

OBS. The passive *śḏm·f* has been hitherto known as the passive *śḏmw·f*; but since the ending *-w* never appears before a suffix subject in Middle Egyptian and, further, varies occasionally with *-y*, the name here adopted seems more appropriate.

§ 420. Writing of the passive *śḏm·f* and forms from the mutable verbs.—The ending *-w* is fairly common before nominal subject and in impersonal uses, but does not occur in Middle Egyptian before the suffix-pronouns;[2] it is at least as frequent in the verbs with final weak radical, exx. *irw*;[3] *rdiw*,[4] as in the immutable verbs, exx. *šˁw* 'was cut off';[5] *ḳwsw* 'was constructed';[6] but writings without any flexional ending are in all verb-classes of more usual occurrence, exx. *ḥꜣḳ* 'were captured';[7] *ḫfˁ·i* 'I was seized';[8] *rdi* 'was placed', 'caused'.[9]

The much rarer ending *-y* has been thought to be more than a mere alternative to *-w*.[10] But so far as the Middle Egyptian evidence goes, the ending *-y* belongs solely to verbs with a final weak radical, and hence may represent some fusion of that radical with a flexional ending. The ending *-y* occurs mostly before the suffix-pronouns, exx. *msy·i* 'I was born';[11] *iṯy·k* 'thou hast been taken',[12] but instances before nominal subject are also found, as *iry* 'was made';[13] *rdy* 'were placed'.[14]

Note that the passive *śḏm·f* is by no means common with pronominal subject. It is altogether a less frequent verb-form than the narrative tenses hitherto discussed, though it has certain well-marked uses, particularly after *iw* and *ˁḥˁ·n*, see below §§ 465; 481. Apart from the regular use with nominal subject, impersonal employments are often met with, exx. *smiw* 'it was reported';[15] *ir* 'it was done'.[16]

As time went on, Egyptian showed an increasing unwillingness to form parts of the suffix conjugation from stems of more than three radical consonants.

[1] See *Verbum* ii. §§ 443–491.

[2] In old Eg., suffix after *-w*, *Pyr.* 1164. 1509. 1705; after *-y*, *ib.* 1042.

[3] LAC. *TR.* 21, 6; 76, 7.

[4] LAC. *TR.* 2, 72; 3, 45; 4, 45.

[5] *Hamm.* 110, 6.

[6] *Sin.* B 300.

[7] *Urk.* iv. 659, 1.

[8] LAC. *TR.* 59, 3.

[9] *Pr.* 2, 8; *Westc.* 8, 4.

[10] See GUNN, *Stud.* ch. 8.

[11] Cairo 20518, *a* 1; *Sebekkhu* 11.

[12] LAC. *TR.* 86, 95.

[13] LAC. *TR.* 21, 7; *Urk.* iv. 605, 16; 606, 2.

[14] Munich 3, 23.

[15] *Urk.* iv. 4, 8. Sim. *hꜣb*, *Sin.* R 22; *ḏdw*, *Urk.* iv. 661, 8. More often written with *-w* in *Hearst*, without *-w* in *Eb.*; exx. H 2, 5 = E 16, 13; H 3, 1 = E 86, 14. See below p. 340, n. 9.

[16] *P. Boul.* xviii. 6. Sim. *ib. passim*; also *Hearst* 1, 2. 5. 13, written with *-w*.

Hence we find the passive *śḏm·f* of *snfr* 'make beautiful' replaced by a periphrasis in which the passive *śḏm·f* of *iri* has the infinitive of *snfr* as subject:

ist iry snfr twt pn m ḥ3t-sp 22 lo, this statue had been made beautiful in year 22.[1]

Forms of the passive *śḏm·f* from the mutable verbs are as follows:—

2ae gem. *m3* 'have been seen'.[2] The form *3mm·i* 'I have been gripped'[3] probably belongs to § 425.

3ae inf. Without gemination. No ending, *gm* 'was found';[4] *ms* 'have been born';[5] *ms·f* 'he was born'.[6] With *-w*, *wpw* 'are opened'.[7] With *-y*, *ḥsy·i* 'I have been praised';[8] *ḫ3y·s* 'it was measured'.[9]

'Make' shows the forms *ir*,[10] *irw*,[11] *iry*[12] and quite exceptionally *irw*,[13] *ir*[14] (for the reading of these see § 281).

'Take away' is found as *iṯ·k*,[15] *ity·i*.[16]

caus. 3ae inf. *sbšyw* 'it is caused to be vomited'.[17]

caus. 4ae inf. *sḫntw* 'was brought southward'.[18]

anom. 'Give' has forms both with and without *r*, and without gemination: *rdi*,[19] *rdiw*[20] and quite exceptionally *rdy*,[21] beside *di*[22] and *diw*.[23]

'Bring' has *in*.[24]

§ 421. **Origin and relations of the passive *śḏm·f*.**—In several usages, particularly after *iw*, *ʿḥʿ·n*, *mk* and *isṯ*, the passive *śḏm·f* serves definitely as the passive of the *śḏm·n·f* form (see § 422, 1), and the thought thus suggests itself that the former may possibly be nothing more than the latter docked of those elements (*n* + noun, *n* + suffix) which serve to express the semantic subject, the author of the action. To put the matter more concretely, if *śḏm·n·f ḫrw* 'he heard the voice' ultimately means 'heard to him the voice' (§ 411, 2), may not *śḏm ḫrw* 'the voice was heard' ultimately mean 'heard (to *x*) the voice'? There can be no doubt that in final analysis this view is correct, but two reasons prohibit us from identifying the two forms and regarding the passive *śḏm·f* merely as a *śḏm·n·f* form from which the agential element *n·f* has for the nonce been omitted: (1) the passive *śḏm·f* sometimes shows the original participial ending *-w* or *-y* which has completely disappeared from the *śḏm·n·f* form; (2) the passive *śḏm·f* sometimes has a suffix subject of its own, this of course representing the direct semantic object, since the form is passive in meaning.

It is thus clear that the *śḏm·n·f* form and the passive *śḏm·f* have each developed further than the other in certain directions; nevertheless the frequent parallelism of their uses is only explicable if both are regarded as having

[1] *Urk.* iv. 606. Sim. *ib.* 605, 16. Contrast, however, § 423, 3, 1st ex.
[2] Louvre C 11, 2; 12, 16.
[3] LAC. *TR.* 59, 3.
[4] *Urk.* iv. 484, 10.
[5] *Westc.* 11, 5.
[6] LAC. *TR.* 38, 10. Sim. 1st pers., Brit. Mus. 828.
[7] *P. Kah.* 6, 9.
[8] LAC. *TR.* 30, 6.
[9] *Urk.* iv. 669, 13.
[10] *P. Boul.* xviii. 6; *P. Kah.* 9, 11; *Urk.* iv. 667, 10.
[11] *Hearst* 1, 2. 5. 13; LAC. *TR.* 76, 7.
[12] See above p. 337, n. 13.
[13] *Peas.* R 54.
[14] *Hamm.* 19, 10.
[15] LAC. *TR.* 86, 93.
[16] LAC. *TR.* 47, 31. Sim. *ib.* 63, 2.
[17] *Eb.* 85, 16.
[18] *Amada* 18.
[19] *Sh. S.* 5; *P. Kah.* 12, 5; *Westc.* 8, 4. 18.
[20] LAC. *TR.* 2, 72; *Urk.* iv. 897, 7.
[21] Munich 3, 23.
[22] *P. Kah.* 15, 45. 47; *P. Boul.* xviii. 21.
[23] *Hearst* 1, 7; 3, 9; *Urk.* iv. 652, 9.
[24] *Peas.* B 1, 300; *Westc.* 8, 18.

originated in the perfective passive participle. Confirmatory testimony is forthcoming on all hands. The lack of gemination is common to all the forms in question, while the existence of a rare *śḏmm·f* passive closely related to the passive *śḏm·f* (see below § 425) recalls the curious reduplicating perfective pass. participles from *2-lit.* stems which were studied in § 360. The ending *-w* characteristic of the passive *śḏm·f* except with pronominal subject is seen in the relative form *śḏmw·n·f*, which we have shown to be closely akin to the narrative *śḏm·n·f* (§§ 386, 2; 411, 1). The alternative ending *-y* from verbs with final weak consonant (*ultimae infirmae*) is familiar from the perfective passive participle of those same verbs (§ 361).

Further reflection will show the close connection between the passive *śḏm·f* and the construction of the passive participles with retained object (§ 377); indeed it seems not improbable that the passive *śḏm·f* directly originated in that construction, the development being upon lines similar to the development of the narrative *śḏm·n·f* form out of the construction perf. pass. participle + dative (§ 411, 2). To this theory it is not a very grave objection that in the construction of the passive participles with retained object the dependent pronouns were used, whereas with the passive *śḏm·f* the suffix-pronouns are found; for, in the first place, even with the passive participles a certain weakening of usage in favour of the suffixes was observed (§ 377, 2, end), and in the second place, the substitution of the suffixes for the dependent pronouns was bound to occur as soon as the pronoun following the verb-form ceased to be regarded as retained object and was felt as a grammatical subject.

Lastly, the relations of active and passive *śḏm·f* have to be considered. If we are right in supposing that the active *śḏm·f* arose, no less than the passive *śḏm·f*, from a use of the passive participle (§ 411, 1), the sole difference would be that in the active perfective *śḏm·f* the suffix represents the semantic subject, and that in the passive *śḏm·f* the suffix represents the direct semantic object. Hence it is by no means surprising to find uses where the passive *śḏm·f* corresponds closely to the active *śḏm·f*; this is true wherever the passive *śḏm·f* has present or future meaning (§ 422, 2), as well as in its negative uses (§ 424, 1. 2).

§ 422. Affirmative uses of the passive *śḏm·f*.—1. In *past* narrative.

Exx. *rdỉ n·ỉ tp 100 m fḳꜣw* one hundred persons were given to me as reward.[1] English past tense.

msy·ỉ m ḥꜣt-sp 1 n sꜣ Rꜥ 'Imn-m-ḥꜣt I was born in year 1 of the son of the Sun Ammenemes.[2] English past tense.

šsp ḫrpw, ḥw mnỉt the mallet has been taken and the mooring-post driven in.[3] English present perfect.

[1] *Sebekkhu* 17. Sim. Brit. Mus. 574, 3. 5; Munich 3, 23–5; *Urk.* iv. 661, 6. 7; 891, 2. 8; 897, 7.

[2] Cairo 20518, *a* 1. Sim. *Sebekkhu* 11; Brit. Mus. 828.

[3] *Sh. S.* 3–4. Sim. Lac. *TR.* 43, 2; 75, 11; 76, 7.

Impersonal uses are frequent.

Ex. *ir ḫft ipwt tn* it was done in accordance with this commission.[1]

The passive of the construction *iw śḏm·n·f* so much employed in narrative (§ 68) is of the type *iw śḏm·f*. See further below § 465.

Exx. *iw swn int·n·sn* what they had brought was sold.[2] English past tense.

iw rdiw n·k ṯȝw breath has been given to thee.[3] English present perfect tense.

Another favourite construction in narrative, as we shall see later, is *ꜥḥꜥ·n śḏm·n·f*. The passive of this is of the type *ꜥḥꜥ·n śḏm·f*, though examples with suffix-pronoun as subject are of extreme rarity (§ 481), while in the construction *iw śḏm·f* just mentioned none at all has been noted.

It was seen (§ 414, 1) that *mk* placed before the *śḏm·n·f* form gave to that form the signification of the English *present perfect*. So too in the case of *mk* + passive *śḏm·f*.

Ex. *mk ms n·k ẖrdw 3* behold, three children have been born to thee.[4]

After *isṯ* the passive *śḏm·f* describes a situation or concomitant fact belonging to the past, exactly like *isṯ* + *śḏm·n·f* (§ 414, 1). In most cases one can translate with the English *past perfect*.

Exx. *ist ir nȝ n ȝḥt m iḥwt* now these fields had been made into plough-lands.[5]

ist hȝb r msw nsw now the king's children had been sent for.[6] Impersonal; another manuscript (G) has .

The passive *śḏm·f* in reference to past action is negatived by prefixing the word *n* 'not'. See below § 424, 1.

2. In reference to *future* events. The passive *śḏm·f* is frequently used with a vaguely prospective meaning in medical prescriptions and the like.

Exx. His Majesty instituted a festival of victory anew .... *ir sn·nw n ḥb n pȝ ḥb nḫt m hrw n sꜥḳ nṯr* a second festival of the festival of victory is (to be) made on the day of introducing the god.[7]

rdi ḳȝꜥ·s st ḥr-ꜥwy she is (to be) caused to spit it out at once.[8] For *ḳȝꜥ·s* as subject of *rdi(w)* see § 70.

So too impersonally.

Ex. *irw m ḫt wꜥt* it is (to be) mixed together, lit. made as one thing.[9] The Ebers papyrus writes .

Sometimes one may be tempted to interpret what is really a passive *śḏm·f* as an old perfective.

[1] *P. Boul.* xviii. 6. Sim. *Sin.* B 247; *Urk.* iv. 4, 8; 6, 9. *Cf.* too *irw in* (also briefly written *ir·n*) 'made by', i.e. 'written by', *ÄZ.* 43, 33.

[2] *Semnah Disp.* 1, 13; 6, 11. Sim. *Sin.* B 291. 295. 300.

[3] Lac. *TR.* 2, 72. Sim. *ib.* 3, 45; 4, 45; 69, 2.

[4] *Westc.* 11, 5. Sim. Louvre C 11, 1–2; C 12, 6, qu. § 184, 1.

[5] *Urk.* iv. 667. Sim. *ib.* 606, 2, qu. p. 338, n. 1; 659, 6; 690, 2.

[6] *Sin.* R 22. Sim. *ib.* B 173; *Urk.* iv. 657, 4; 686, 13.

[7] *Urk.* iv. 740. Sim. in *then*-clause after 'if', *ÄZ.* 43, 35, 8; 37, 19; 39, 17.

[8] *P. Kah.* 5, 36. Sim., but with noun subject, *ib.* 40, 56; 12, 5.

[9] *Hearst* 2, 7 = *Eb.* 64, 8. Sim. with *-w*, *Eb.* 67, 4 (*diw*); *Hearst* 1, 1 (*ꜥmw*); 1, 2 (*ṯḥbw*); without *-w*, *Eb.* 66, 17 (*ps*); 69, 15 (*gs*).

Ex. [hieroglyphs] *tw* (read *tw r*) *nḥm ḫt s r·f, rdîw n nty m rwty* one shall take a man's property from him, and it shall be given to him who is outside.[1]

Here *rdîw* must be the passive *śḏm·f* with omitted subject, since the old perfective would have had to be *rdî·tî*, *ḫt* being a feminine noun (§ 92, 2).[1a]

After *ḫr*, the passive *śḏm·f* may have future meaning. Compare the corresponding use with active *śḏm·f*, §§ 239; 450, 5, *c*.

Ex. [hieroglyphs] *ḫr ìr n·k ḥtp-dì-nsw* there shall be made for thee a *ḥotp-di-nesu* offering.[2]

3. *Present time.* Several of the examples quoted above may be translated alternatively as presents. So the third example from the end under (1) 'there are born' and the second under (2) 'she is caused'.

Here belong two mathematical expressions [hieroglyphs] *ìr n*, var. [hieroglyphs] *ìrw n*,[3] 'amounting to', lit. 'it is made for', and [hieroglyphs] *ìr m* 'equivalent to', lit. 'it is made as (?)' or 'in (?)'.

Exx. [hieroglyphs] *ḥḏ śwꜣbty m bꜣk n Kftìw ḥnꜥ ḥnw n bìꜣ, ḏrt m ḥḏ, 4, ìr n dbn 56, ḳdt 3* a silver cauldron of Cretan work with four vessels of bronze, (with) the handle of silver, makes 56 *deben* and 3 *kitě*.[4]

List of cakes, [hieroglyphs] *ìr m ḥḳꜣt 12* equivalent to 12 *ḥeḳat*.[5]

The difference between the two expressions remains to be determined.

§ 423. The passive *śḏm·f* in subordinate clauses.—The use of the passive *śḏm·f* in subordinate clauses is very limited, and this limitation constitutes a serious difference between it and the narrative *śḏm·f* and *śḏm·n·f* forms.

1. Nevertheless, when followed by a nominal subject the passive *śḏm·f* sometimes serves as a virtual clause of circumstance.

Exx. [hieroglyphs] *ḥms·s ḥr·s wpw mnty·sy* she shall sit upon it with her legs apart.[6] Lit. her thighs have been opened.

Let him be deprived of his temple-rank, [hieroglyphs] *ptḫ ḥr tꜣ, nḥmw ꜥḳw·f ḏrf⟨·f⟩ wꜥbwt·f* being cast on the ground and his food, title-deed (?) and joints being (lit. have been) taken away.[7]

[hieroglyphs] *ìr·n·ì n·ì mìḥꜥt tw sꜣḫ·tì, smnḫ st·s r rwd nṯr ꜥꜣ* I made for myself this tomb, it being consecrated and its place being embellished at the staircase of the great god.[8]

The last two examples illustrate the close parallelism in use of the passive *śḏm·f* and the old perfective. That in the last example *smnḫ* cannot be old perfective is clear from the facts that its subject *st·s* would in that case have to precede it (§ 322) and that it would then have to be feminine in gender (*smnḫ·tì*).

[1] *P. Pet.* 1116 B, 47. Sim. *Tarkhan* i. 79, 46.

[1a] This argument fails, however, if *ḫ(w)t* is a plur., see § 511, 2. So Gunn.

[2] *Urk.* iv. 46.

[3] *ÄZ.* 43, 35, 6, qu. § 266, 4; *Amarn.* 5, 26, 18, qu. § 266, 2.

[4] *Urk.* iv. 733. Sim. *ib.* 732, 15; *Rhind* 82. 83; Br. *Thes.* 1081. v. 11; vi. 1; 1087, xviii. 10.

[5] *Urk.* iv. 761. Sim. *ib.* 762. 763; *Rhind* 82. 84.

[6] *P. Kah* 6, 9. Sim. *Semnah Disp.* 1, 9; *Westc.* 8, 18. 25; 9, 20; 10, 11–2, see *ÄZ.* 66, 71; Cairo 20512, *b* 2; *Rec.* 36, 215, 39.

[7] *Kopt.* 8, 6. Sim. *BH.* i. 26, 127; *Urk.* iv. 28, 3. 4. 5; *Th. T. S.* iv. 6, top right.

[8] *Sebekkhu* 8. The same formula Cairo 20153. 20497. 20691.

2. In one passage, a statement with passive *śḏm·f* has virtually the sense of a clause of condition:

ḏd n·k: skm m $\frac{2}{3}$ $\frac{1}{15}$ *m 1* it is said to thee: What makes $\frac{2}{3}+\frac{1}{15}$ complete as 1?[1]

Elsewhere the formula introducing the question is *ir ḏd n·k sš* 'if the scribe say to thee'.[2]

3. The use of the passive *śḏm·f* after prepositions is very rare.

Exx. *ḥr m-ḫt snfrw kꜣt tn* now when this construction had been made beautiful.[3]

mi ḏd n·k according as it is said to thee.[4]

§ 424. Negative uses of the passive *śḏm·f* form.[5]

—1. The passive *n śḏm·f* is not common. Perhaps by mere chance, no examples with the ending *-w* have been quoted; a few with *-y* occur.[6]

Sometimes we must translate with the *present perfect* or *past perfect*.

Exx. *n it iḥw·n* our cattle have not been taken away.[7]

iw n·k ib·k, n ity·f thou hast thy heart, it has not been taken away.[8]

n gm wn·i m rw-prw no transgression of mine has (*or* had) been found in the temples.[9]

The last instance shows the similarity of this use to that of *n*+active *śḏm·f* (§ 105, 1); for *n gm·tw* is found in similar contexts.[10]

Sometimes the English *present* affords a more appropriate rendering.

Exx. *n ḫsf ꜥ n ipwty·f ḫt tꜣw Fḫw* (read *Fnḫw*) his envoy is not impeded throughout the lands of the Fenkhu.[11] Lit. the arm of his envoy is not, etc.

n ḫfꜥ·i in Šw I am not seized by Shu.[12]

Examples from religious texts like the last have almost as much application to the past and the future as they have to the present, and might be rendered accordingly. Sometimes we may translate by 'cannot', 'could not'.

Ex. Gold, etc. .... *n ḫꜣy·s* it could not be measured.[13]

Instances with *rḫ* are often best translated with the English present.

Ex. *n rḫ ṯnw* the number is not known.[14]

2. The passive *śḏm·f* in virtual clauses of circumstance (§ 423, 1) appears to have been negatived by the negative verb *tm* (§ 350).

Ex. Let him be deprived of his temple-rank .... *tm sḫꜣt rn·f m r-pr pn* his name not being remembered in this temple.[15]

Apparently *tm* here must be passive *śḏm·f* form; the construction is thus parallel to that of *nḥmw ꜥḳw·f*, the words immediately preceding (see § 423, 1).

[1] *Rhind* 21.
[2] *Rhind* 30. 47. 68.
[3] *Tarkhan* i. 79, 18.
[4] *Rhind* 49. 51. 61.
[5] See GUNN, *Stud.* ch. 15.
[6] LAC. *TR.* 86, 95; 88, 15, qu. below; *Urk.* iv. 669, 13, qu. below.
[7] *T. Carn.* 6.
[8] LAC. *TR.* 88, 15. Sim. *ib.* 63, 2; 86, 95.
[9] *Urk.* iv. 484. Sim. *Th. T. S.* iii. 26, 8.
[10] *Urk.* iv. 133, 3; 151, 3; 1024, 9.
[11] *Urk.* iv. 138. Sim. *ib.* 547, 11–2; *Siut* iv. 33.
[12] LAC. *TR.* 59, 3. Sim. *ib.* 63, 2.
[13] *Urk.* iv. 669. Sim. *Peas.* B 1, 300.
[14] *Urk.* iv. 795.
[15] *Kopt.* 8. 6.

3. There is no sure ground for assigning to the passive *śḏm·f* examples like the following:

[hieroglyphs] *nn bs·k in pḏtyw* thou shalt not be interred by Asiatics.[1]

Here *bs·k* may well be infinitive + suffix, see § 307, 1. To prove the contrary, examples from the *3ae inf.* or *anom.* verb-classes would be necessary. The like holds good of phrases such as [hieroglyphs] *iwtw ḫsf·f* 'not repelled'; see above § 307, 2.

THE *ŚḎMM·F* FORM

§ **425**. This old verb-form, not uncommon in the Pyramids and surviving into the Middle Kingdom practically only in ancient religious texts, is characterized by the doubling of the last radical letter even in the case of the immutable verbs. Its uses and meaning are identical with those of the passive *śḏm·f*, together with which it has hitherto been classified;[2] there seem, however, to be good reasons for regarding it as a separate form, analogous to the Hebrew *puʿlal.*

The subject may be either a suffix-pronoun or a noun. In one or two suspect cases an ending *-w* occurs, exx. [hieroglyphs] *n ḫsffw r·i* 'my mouth is not repelled';[3] [hieroglyphs] *snʿʿw* 'it is to be ground fine'.[4]

Forms from the different verb-classes:

2-lit. [hieroglyphs] *ipp* 'has been examined'.[5]

3-lit. [hieroglyphs] *nḥmm* 'has been taken away';[6] [hieroglyphs] *ḫnrr·i* 'I have been restrained'.[7]

2ae gem. [hieroglyphs] *ꜣmm·i* 'I have been gripped'.[8]

caus. 2ae gem. [hieroglyphs] *sḳbb* 'it is cooled'.[9] This example is classed here, like the preceding *ꜣmm·i*, because the passive *śḏm·f*, consonantly with its origin in the perfective passive participle, does not geminate; but possibly *sḳbb* is to be regarded as a *4-lit.* immutable verb (§ 284), in which case it will belong to the passive *śḏm·f.*

It seems likely that the *śḏmm·f* form was derived from a class of perfective passive participles with doubled last radical, which has survived as such only in the *2-lit.* verbs. See above § 360.

§ **426. Uses of the *śḏmm·f* form.**—The meaning is always passive, and the uses are identical with those of the passive *śḏm·f.*

Exx. [hieroglyphs] *ipp Sp pn ḥr msḫnt* this Sep has been examined in (his) place of origin (?).[10] See above § 422, 1.

[hieroglyphs] *sḳbb* 'it is (to be) cooled'.[11] In a medical prescription, see § 422, 2.

[hieroglyphs] *n nḥmm tp·f m-ʿ·f* his head is not (*or* has not been) taken away from him.[12] See above § 424, 1.

[1] *Sin.* B 259. Sim. *nn šnʿ·k*, *Urk.* iv. 498, 9; 1220, 13; *nn ḫsf·k*, 520, 9.

[2] See *Verbum* ii. §§ 471. 478. 480. 485.

[3] LAC. *TR.* 49, 13; perhaps read *ḫsfw.*

[4] *Hearst* 1, 17.

[5] LAC. *TR.* 38, 11.

[6] *Ann.* v. 241.

[7] LAC. *TR.* 19, 27.

[8] LAC. *TR.* 59, 3.

[9] *P. Kah.* 5, 11. 58. So too *snʿʿw*, above n. 4.

[10] LAC. *TR.* 38, 11.

[11] *P. Kah.* 5, 11. 58. Sim. *Hearst* 1, 17 (*snʿʿw*).

[12] *Ann.* 5, 241. Sim. LAC. *TR.* 19, 18. 27; 49, 13, qu. above n. 3; 59, 3.

THE *ŚḎM·IN·F*, *ŚḎM·ḪR·F* AND *ŚḎM·K3·F* FORMS

§ 427. We now reach three forms of the suffix conjugation which are employed only in main clauses. In structure they agree with the *śḏm·n·f* form in all respects, except that for *n* is substituted one of the three formatives *in*, *ḫr*, or *k3*. These formatives are inseparably appended to the verb-stem (after the determinative, if any), but may under given conditions (§ 66) be separated from their subject, if a noun. See further § 410.

Since the *śḏm·in·f* and *śḏm·ḫr·f* forms appear to contain just those prepositions which regularly serve to introduce the agent after passives (§ 39, end), it has not unreasonably been supposed[1] that the verb-forms in question are derived from passive participles. The analogy to the *śḏm·n·f* form would then be complete, and just as this meant originally 'heard to him', so the *śḏm·in·f* and *śḏm·ḫr·f* forms would have meant originally 'heard by him'. The *śḏm·k3·f* form presents, however, a formidable obstacle to this hypothesis, for not only is *k3* never found as a preposition, but also it reminds us that the prepositional function of *in* and *ḫr* is not their only function. We have found the three words *in* (§ 227), *ḫr* (§ 239), and *k3* (§ 242) alike employed as sentence adverbs, and we have become acquainted with three parallel constructions *in* or *ḫr* or *k3* + noun + *śḏm·f* all expressing, with certain differences of nuance, the equivalent of the English future tense. That in those constructions *in* and *ḫr* cannot be the prepositions seems clear, first from the tautology which would be involved in *ḫr·f śḏm·f* (i. e. the case when the subject inserted after *ḫr* is a pronoun), if this should mean 'by him heard of him', and second from the consideration that Middle Egyptian has the further constructions *ḫr śḏm·f* and *k3 śḏm·f* likewise having future signification; the construction *ḫr* or *k3* + noun + *śḏm·f* would thus seem to differ from *ḫr* or *k3* + *śḏm·f* only by the introduction of a nominal subject in anticipatory emphasis.

How these obviously interrelated facts are to be coordinated is obscure. Meanwhile a startlingly different theory has been mooted[2] and has won considerable support. It will be seen in §§ 436–7 that , and when followed by a noun or suffix-pronoun all express a parenthetic 'says X', 'says he' or the like meaning in some other tense. The generally accepted view assumed an ellipse of the verb *ḏd* 'say'. However, not only is there a verb *k3i* 'plan', but also good evidence has come to light of , var. *i* (from which *in* might be short for *i in*) and , varr. , , *ḫrw* as verbs signifying 'say' and 'cry'. On this basis *śḏm·in·f*, *śḏm·ḫr·f* and *śḏm·k3·f* might have meant originally 'heard —said he', 'heard—cries he' and 'heard—plans he'. That a verb of the kind could serve thus as an auxiliary has been proved or at least made probable for both Chinese and Nubian.[3]

[1] *ÄZ.* 54, 98.

[2] By LEXA in *Philologica* 2, 25–53; *Arch. Or.* 8, 210. Further developed, *Suppl.* 13; FAULKNER in *JEA.* 21, 186; *Some Aspects*, 12. See too LEF. *Gr.* § 285.

[3] WALEY and ARMBRUSTER in *Bull. Sch. Or. Stud.* 7, 573.

§ 428. The *śḏm·in·f* form[1] in the mutable verbs.

2ae gem. *wn·in·f* 'he was'.[2] (The form *wšš·in·f* 'he shall urinate'[3] is not from a *2ae gem.* but from a *3-lit.* stem *wšš*, the doubled *š* being due to assimilation.)

3ae inf. *iʿ·in·sn* 'they washed';[4] *šd·in·k* 'thou shalt remove'.[5] 'Make' shows *ir·in* 'made'.[6]

anom. 'Give' has *rdi·in*,[7] more rarely *di·in·f*.[8] 'Come' has *iw·in*.[9] 'Bring' has *in·in·tw·f*.[10]

The lack of gemination is consistent with the theory that the *śḏm·in·f* form is derived from a perfective passive participle, whether it be analysed as containing the preposition *in* or the sentence-adverb *in*, or whether the theory outlined p. 344, bottom, be adopted.

[1] See *Verbum* ii. §§ 390–405.
[2] *Westc.* 4, 2. Exx. (all *past*) also §§ 470. 472. 473.
[3] *Eb.* 25, 7 = 52, 5.
[4] *Westc.* 10, 11. 19.
[5] *Eb.* 109, 7.
[6] *Peas.* B 1, 31.
[7] *Peas.* B 1, 39.
[8] *Urk.* iv. 158, 17.
[9] *Peas.* B 1, 52.
[10] *Westc.* 4, 24.

§ 429. Uses of the *śḏm·in·f* form.

—Broadly speaking, this verb-form appears to indicate *result* or *sequel*.

1. Thus it is commonly used to introduce any outstanding incident in *past narrative*.

Exx. *ḏd·in sḫty pn* then said this peasant.[11]

stꜣ·in·tw n·f Ḏdi then Djedi was brought in to him.[12]

rdi·in·sn st m pꜣ it then they placed it in the corn.[13]

iw·in rf sḫty pn then came this peasant.[14]

ir·in·tw mi wḏt nbt ḥm·f then it was done according to all that His Majesty commanded.[15]

Beside the impersonal use with *·tw* just illustrated, there is another without it.

Ex. *rdi·in stꜣ·tw msw nsw* then (they) caused the king's children to be brought.[16]

2. Less frequently *śḏm·in·f* is employed to *name* or *describe* a consequence to take place in the *future*; but often a clear *injunction* like *śḏm·ḫr·f* (§ 431, 2).

Exx. If thou examine a man with a pain in his stomach, *rdi·in·k ḏrt·k ḥr·f* then thou shalt lay thy hand upon him.[17] An injunction.

.... praise god, *sdm·in ḫprty·sn* so that those who shall come into being shall hear.[18] A future consequence is described.

No negatived examples have been noted.

OBS. 1. With pronominal subject no confusion with other verb-forms seems possible. With nominal subject, however, confusion may sometimes occur (1) either with the infinitive + the preposition *in*, (2) or with the passive *śḏm·f* impersonally used and followed by the same preposition. The chief criterion of *śḏm·in·f* is the fact that the formative *in* is inseparable from the verb-stem, but this will not serve in all cases.[19]

OBS. 2. For *wn·in* as auxiliary, see below §§ 470. 472. 473.

[11] *Peas.* R 2. 5. 47; *Sin.* B 75; *Pt.* 36. 51; *P. Pet.* 1116 B, 11. Other verbs, *Westc.* 10, 9. 11; 11, 8; *Urk.* iv. 8, 13; 139, 9.
[12] *Westc.* 8, 10.
[13] *Westc.* 11, 13.
[14] *Peas.* B 1, 52.
[15] *Westc.* 4, 17.
[16] *Sin.* B 263.
[17] *Eb.* 40, 19. Sim. *ib.* 25, 7; 51, 22; 65, 17; 91, 21; 109, 7; *P. Kah.* 7, 67–8.
[18] *Siut* 3, 3.
[19] Cf. *Eb.* 34, 9 with *ib.* 35, 14.

§ 430. The *śḏm·ḥr·f* form[1] in the mutable verbs.

2ae gem. *mȝȝ·ḫr·k* 'thou shalt see';[2] *wnn·ḫr·f* 'he shall be'.[2a] But *wn·ḫr·i* 'I was' in *past* narrative;[3] sim. for a *single future* act.[3a]

3ae inf. *šn·ḫr·k* 'thou shalt surround';[4] *šd·ḫr·tw·f* 'it shall be removed'.[5] 'Make' has *ir·ḫr·k* 'thou shalt make'.[6]

caus. 2ae gem. *sšmm·ḫr·k* 'thou shalt heat'.[7]

anom. 'Give' has the form *rdi·ḫr·k*,[8] 'bring' the form *in·ḫr·k*.[9]

Forms without gemination are thus the rule, but perhaps only for *single future* acts. The non-geminating forms from *wnn* are mainly *past*, the geminating always *future*; this suggests derivation from a perfective participle in the former case, from an imperfective in the latter.

§ 431. Uses of the *śḏm·ḫr·f* form.

—Unless the hypothesis set forth p. 344, bottom, be adopted, this verb-form will be akin to the constructions *ḫr·f śḏm·f* and *ḫr śḏm·f* (§ 239), into which the particle *ḫr* enters. If, as we supposed, that particle indicates what comes next in order, *śḏm·ḫr·f* may originally have meant something like 'he proceeds to hear'.

1. In reference to *future* time. The *śdm·ḫr·f* form is common in *injunctions* and statements of *result.*

Exx. *ir·ḫr·k 5 sp 4* thou shalt multiply five by four, lit. make five four times.[10]

st·ḫr·i ḏrt·i I shall have to thrust my hand.[11]

hȝp·ḫr st kkw darkness shall conceal them.[12]

rdi·ḫr·t(w)·f ḥr gs·f wʿ he shall be laid on his one side.[13]

wnn·ḫr·f mi wʿ im·sn then he shall be like one of them.[13a]

An impersonal use is also found.

Ex. *ḫpr·ḫr m 4* it will become 4, i.e. 4 will be the result.[14]

Later (§ 471, 1) we shall find *wnn·ḫr·f* as an auxiliary verb used with future meaning as above.

2. In reference to *present* time, rare and not quite certain; perhaps summing up the result of a situation.

Exx. *sȝ Mrw, tnm·ḫr·f* so then the son of Meru goes on erring.[15] A comment called forth by an act of violence.

That means that his heart is hot, *wrd·ḫr ib·f ḫr·s* and so his heart is weary through it.[16]

3. Occasionally too in reference to *past* events; found only with two verbs.

Exx. *ḏd·ḫr·sn* thereupon they said.[17]

wn·ḫr·i m wfȝ n mdt nbt I was the topic of all talk.[18]

For *wn·ḫr·f* as an auxiliary in *past* narrative see below, § 471, 2.

[1] See *Verbum* ii. §§ 414–432.
[2] *Eb.* 36, 7; 93, 17.
[2a] Exx. below, n. 13a.
[3] DAV. *Rekh.* 12, 29. As auxiliary, § 471, 2.
[3a] As auxiliary, *P. Kah.* 7, 40, qu. p. 390, n. 7.
[4] *P. Kah.* 7, 54.
[5] *Eb.* 53, 7.
[6] *P. Kah.* 8, 27; *Eb.* 36, 9.
[7] *Eb.* 54, 20.
[8] *Eb.* 36, 19; 37, 4.
[9] *Eb.* 54, 19.
[10] *P. Kah.* 8, 27. Sim. *ib.* 5, 2. 5. 14; 7, 54; *Eb.* 48, 4; *Hearst* 2, 9.
[11] *P. Kah.* 7, 23.
[12] LEF. *Sethos* iv. 49.
[13] *P. Kah.* 7, 39. Sim. *ib.* 7, 41; *Eb.* 53, 7–8.
[13a] *Nu* 190, 8. Sim. *ib.* 99, 40; BUDGE, p. xvii, 8.
[14] *Rhind* 62. So too *snb·ḫr*, *Eb.* 75, 13.
[15] *Peas.* B 1, 188.
[16] *Eb.* 101, 7. Sim. *ib.* 101, 10. 13. 19.
[17] *Sinai* 90, 9; *Urk.* iv. 324, 6; 332, 8.
[18] DAV. *Rekh.* 12, 29. Sim. *Griff. Stud.* Pl. 39, 16.

§ 432. Negation of the *śḏm·ḫr·f* form.—In its use with reference to the future the *śḏm·ḫr·f* form is negatived by means of the verb *tm*, see above §§ 342 foll.

Ex. [hieroglyphs] *tm·ḫr·s ḫpr m ḥsbt* it will not result in worms.[1]

§ 433. The *śḏm·kꜢ·f* form[2] in the mutable verbs.

3ae inf. [hieroglyphs] *ḥꜥ·kꜢ·sn* 'they shall rejoice';[3] [hieroglyphs] *pr·kꜢ* 'will go forth'.[4]

These non-geminating forms are consistent with the possible origin of the form in a perf. pass. participle; see above §§ 427. 428. 430.

§ 434. Use of the *śḏm·kꜢ·f* form.—Like the related *kꜢ·f śḏm·f* and *kꜢ śḏm·f* constructions (§ 242), the *śḏm·kꜢ·f* form refers to a future act dependent on something already stated. It is confined to religious texts and temple inscriptions, and certainly did not occur in spoken Middle Egyptian.

It may express a *future consequence* or *determination.*

Exx. If such and such a thing happens, [hieroglyphs] *nḥm·kꜢ·t(w) stp(w)t ḥr ḫꜢwt nṯrw* then the choice joints shall be removed from the altars of the gods.[5]

[hieroglyphs] *ḥꜥ·kꜢ·sn mꜢ·sn tw* they shall surely rejoice when they see thee.[6]

Much more rarely it appears to express an *injunction.*

[hieroglyphs] *srd·kꜢ st ḥmt·t* Thy Majesty shall plant them.[7]

The construction *nn śḏm·f* (§ 105, 2) serves as negation of the *śḏm·kꜢ·f* form.[8]

§ 435. Uses of the *śḏm·in·f*, *śḏm·ḫr·f* and *śḏm·kꜢ·f* forms: summary.—It will have been noted that there is a close correspondence in the uses, no less than in the formation, of these three verb-forms. They are used in main clauses only; and all three may be employed to express *future consequences* of one sort or another, whether enjoined or merely asserted. The *śḏm·in·f* and *śḏm·ḫr·f* forms may serve as rather impressive *narrative* tenses, and the *śḏm·ḫr·f* tense has in addition a not very clear use in reference to the *present.* Observe, finally, that of the three verb-forms the first alone is really common in Middle Egyptian, the other two tending to be replaced in secular texts by such constructions as *ḫr·f* (or *kꜢ·f*) *śḏm·f* and *ḫr* (or *kꜢ*) *śḏm·f.*

PARENTHETIC PHRASES FOR 'SAID HE', ETC.

§ 436. Here we have to consider some parenthetic expressions for 'said he', 'they will say' and the like, which in the past were thought to be merely the three verb-forms just discussed with an ellipse of the initial verb-stem *ḏd* 'say'.[9] Compare the omission of *ḏd* after *ḥr*, above § 321.

[1] *Eb.* 25, 6 = 52, 5.
[2] See *Verbum* ii. §§ 433–442.
[3] *Urk.* iv. 569, 10.
[4] NAV. 65, 12.
[5] LAC. *TR.* 2, 31. Sim. *ib.* 2, 55; 44, 6.
[6] *Urk.* iv. 569, 10. Sim. *ib.* 569, 12.
[7] *Urk.* iv. 346.
[8] LAC. *TR.* 2, 33. 35; NAV. 65, 14.
[9] So still ERM. *Gramm.*[4] § 501.

Exx. *ḥtp·kw ḥr·s, ỉn smt* I am content on account of it, says the desert.[1]

wnm ỉr·k, ỉn·sn r·ỉ eat thou, say they to me.[2]

ỉn·sn, nṯrw ỉpw, r·ỉ say they, namely those gods, to me.[3]

ḫr·s n·ỉ m smỉ says she to me in accusation.[4]

mỉ, ḫr·tw, r srwd mḫrw ỉdbwy come, they say, to make flourish the order of the two lands.[5]

sš Mꜣꜥt, ḫr·t(w) r·f scribe of Truth, he is called. Lit. one says concerning him.[6]

mk wỉ, kꜣ·k here am I (lit. behold me), thou shalt say.[7]

ỉw·f wꜣ r snḏ n·n, kꜣ·sn he has fallen into fear of us, they will say.[8]

In all known M. E. examples the subject of *ỉn* is either a noun or the suffix 3rd pers. plur. or dual, and it is always translatable as a *present*.[8a] *Kꜣ* always refers to the future, and *ḫr* to *present* or *past* indifferently.

§ **437.** Whatever the origin of the *śḏm·ỉn·f*, *śḏm·ḫr·f* and *śḏm·kꜣ·f* forms (§ 427), the derivation of the parenthetic expressions of § 436 from verbs meaning 'say', 'cry' and 'plan' appears certain. The verb *ỉ* 'say'[9] is attested from O. E. onwards and the spelling regular in L. E. 'said he'[9a] occurs as early as the Coffin Texts, ex. *ỉ ỉn Wsỉr* 'said Osiris';[9b] from such writings 'says' seems not to be a *śḏm·n·f* form, but abbreviated from *ỉ ỉn*.[9c] In *kꜣ·k* 'thou wilt say' the determinative of *kꜣỉ* 'plan' is seen. A verb *ḫr(w)* 'cry'[10] connected with *ḫrw* 'voice' is evidenced in the Coffins by, var. , *ḫr·sn* 'say they'.[10a] The strange writings , [10b] and rarely [10c] are found both there and in later M. E. hieratic; the incomprehensible *·fy* is followed by a noun, a dependent pronoun, or both, and seems wholly superfluous.[10d]

Exx. Teti said to me: '. . . . .', *ḫr(y)·fy sw* so said he.[11]

ḫr(y)·fy Rwty r·ỉ says (the god) Ruty to me.[12]

ḫr(y)·fy sw 'Itm says he, namely Atum.[13]

VOCABULARY

nḏ grind.

ḥḳꜣ rule.

ḫbỉ curtail, subtract.

smꜣwy renew, restore.

sdb swallow.

ḳnd be furious, angry.

tꜣ be hot.

ꜥfdt (old *ꜥfḏt*) box.

wꜥbt meat.

bỉt honey.

[1] Brit. Mus. 101. Sim. *Urk.* v. 203, 10; 204, 3.
[2] Lac. *TR.* 23, 15.
[3] Lac. *TR.* 23, 29. Sim. *ib.* 6, 1; 19, 33; 81, 39.
[4] *P. Louvre* 3230, vs. 8. *Ḫr·sn nṯrw*, Budge, p. 179, 16.
[5] *Urk.* iv. 1075. Sim. *ib.* 649, 11.
[6] *Urk.* iv. 1092. Sim. *JEA.* 4, Pl. 9, 5; *Eb.* 9, 20.
[7] Northampton, 20, 21. Sim. *P. Kah.* 3, 34; 31, 16.
[8] *Urk.* iv. 651. Sim. *Peas.* B 1, 129.
[8a] In L. E. of wider range, and perhaps always with *past* meaning.
[9] Faulkner in *JEA.* 21, 177.
[9a] *ib.* 184.
[9b] *Coffins* I, 107 *b.* More exx. *JEA.* 21, 183.
[9c] Fem. exx. (*ib.* 182) show *ỉ* to be old perfective.
[10] Exx. Dyn. XIX, *Griff. Stud.* 85.
[10a] De Buck in this *Gr.* 1st ed., p. xxviii; also *JEA.* 21, 190.
[10b] Griffith *Kahun Papyri*, p. 103.
[10c] *ÄZ.* 59, 28.
[10d] Once even *ḫr(y)·fy·k* 'sayest thou', *Coffins*, B 5 C, 145.
[11] *P. Kah.* 29, 42. Sim. *ib.* 13, 22. 37; 36, 9. *Ḫr(y)·fy st* 'so said they' *Semnah Disp.* 2, 11; 4, 10.
[12] Budge, p. 169, 3. Sim. *ib.* p. 459, 1.
[13] Budge, p. 458, 14. Sim. *ib.* pp. 124, 6; 267, 11; 492, 13. 16.

ḥsmn natron.

ḫꜣwt table of offerings.

ḫꜥw appearance in glory.

sꜣḥ toe.

sipty inspection.

sft (old *šfṯ*) oil for anointing.

abbrev. *smsw* elder, eldest.

sš writing, papyrus, book.

sṯi, var. *sty*, perfume.

ḏbꜥ finger.

ktt little, trifling (adj.).

Wnt the Hare-nome, the 15th nome or province of Upper Egypt.

EXERCISE XXIX

(a) *Reading lesson: extract from a medical book:*[1]

ir gm·k ḏbꜥ sꜣḥ r-pw (§ 91, 2)
mr·sn (§ 196, 2),
pḫr mw ḥꜣ·sn,
ḏw sty·sn,
ḳm(ꜣ)·sn sꜣ,[2]
ḏd·ḫr·k[3] *r·s:*
mr iry·i (§ 371);
ir·ḫr·k[3] *n·f spw nw sm(ꜣ)* (§ 305) *sp:*[4]
siꜣ[5] *Šmꜥ, r-32;*[6]
siꜣ Mḥw, r-32;
sft, r-8.
nḏ(w),
wt(w) ḥr·s (165, 8).

[1] *Eb.* 78, 6–10 = *Hearst* 12, 1–3 with variants.
[2] Var. H. *ḳm(ꜣ)·n sꜣ* 'which a worm has created'.
[3] *Ḏd·ḫr·k, ir·ḫr·k*, the words usually employed to introduce diagnosis and treatment respectively.
[4] Var. H. '*spd*-worm'.
[5] An unknown drug.
[6] The unit to be understood is the *hin* of about ·503 litre (§ 266, 1 end).
[7] Varr. H. *nḏw, wtw*, with *w* written out.

'If thou findest a finger or a toe, which are (*sic*) painful, and around which water circulates, and their smell is evil and they create a *sꜣ*-worm, then thou shalt say concerning it: a disease I must treat. Then thou shalt make for him treatments for killing a *sp*-worm. Upper Egyptian *siꜣ*, $\frac{1}{32}$; Lower Egyptian *siꜣ*, $\frac{1}{32}$; oil, $\frac{1}{8}$. It is (to be) ground up; it is (to be) bandaged with it.'

(*b*) *Translate into English*:

(1) [1] … [2] … [3] … (2) [4] … (3) … (4) … (5) … (6) …

[1] A medical prescription. After *kt* understand *pẖrt*. Parse *sdb in*. [2] Read *prt-šny* 'hair-fruit', a drug. [3] *Ḫpr-ḏs·f* perhaps 'ferment' or like. [4] A short religious spell, with preceding title.

(*c*) *Write in hieroglyphs*:

(1) Another favour which was done to me: my eldest son Nakht was appointed (lit. given) to rule the Hare-nome, having become a Sole Companion, having been placed at the head (*r-ḥ3t*) of Upper Egypt, and a number of dignities having been given to him. (2) Tell me my name, says the keeper of the door. If thou dost not tell me my name, I will not allow thee to pass. (3) Do not be angry for a trifle; people will say thou art hot-tempered (lit. he is one hot of heart, one will say concerning thee). (4) Behold, it has been commanded to thee to make inspection in this temple, to renew its altars and to establish its offerings. (5) This book is to be hidden in a box of silver, without anyone (lit. another) being allowed to see the place thereof except thy own self.

LESSON XXX

THE *ŚḎM·F* FORM

§ 438. Introductory.—We now return to the *śḏm·f* form (§§ 39. 40),[1] by far the most important verb-form in the Egyptian language, and at the same time that which presents the most difficult problems. The writing of such immutable verbs as *śḏm* 'hear' offers no suggestion that more than one kind of *śḏm·f* form is to be distinguished; but in the mutable verbs, and particularly in the *2ae gem.*, *3ae inf.*, and *anom.* classes, a clearly marked distinction is visible

[1] See *Verbum* ii. §§ 136–352.

between *śdm·f* forms which show gemination, like [hieroglyphs] *mɜɜ·f*, [hieroglyphs] *prr·f*, [hieroglyphs] *dd·f*, and *śdm·f* forms which do not geminate, like [hieroglyphs] *mɜ·f*, [hieroglyphs] *pr·f*, [hieroglyphs] *di·f*. Unhappily there are reasons for thinking that the non-geminating *śdm·f* is itself not a unity, but conceals two or more separate forms; see below § 447. However, the ambiguity and inconsistency of Egyptian spelling prevent us from penetrating far into a differentiation of the varieties of the non-geminating *śdm·f*; most of its uses seem consonant with its identification with that non-geminating *śdm·f* form which, in the *3ae inf.*, was vocalized **periaf*, as we may infer from such Coptic survivals as *θmesios* 'cause that she bear', old [hieroglyphs] *dit ms(y)·s*. Broadly speaking, then, we may treat the non-geminating *śdm·f* as a unity, and contrast it with the geminating *śdm·f*. What are the mutual relations of the two?

In § 411, 1 cogent arguments were adduced for deriving the *śdm·f* form from the passive participle + a genitival suffix, the resultant meaning being 'heard of him', i.e. 'he hears', 'heard'. It then became evident that the geminating *śdm·f* must be closely related to the geminating or imperfective passive participle, and the non-geminating *śdm·f* to the non-geminating or perfective passive participle. On grounds of origin, therefore, we appear to be justified in describing the geminating *śdm·f* form as the imperfective *śdm·f*, and the non-geminating *śdm·f* form as the perfective *śdm·f*. In the meanings of the two forms we shall find much that bears out the hypothesis here adopted, the geminating *śdm·f* often conveying notions of repetition or continuity;[1] but it must be frankly admitted that some uses of both exist, where the connection with the perfective or imperfective ground-ideas remains obscure.

[1] First pointed out by GOLÉNISCHEFF, *Le Conte du Naufragé* (*Bibliothèque d'Étude*, vol. 2), Cairo, 1912, pp. 61–4.

OBS. The possibility that the geminating forms may be the counterparts of Hebrew *piʿēl* forms here suggests itself anew; see above §§ 269–70; 356, OBS. On this view *wnn·f* and *mrr·f* might represent some such vocalizations as **wennānef* and **merrāref* respectively. Doubtless the gemination in the imperf. *śdm·f* was due to more fundamental reasons than the gemination seen (e.g.) in the perfect of the Arabic first form from *2ae gem.* verbs, as written without points. There the separate writing of the identical radicals depends wholly on the distribution of the syllables under the influence of the flexional endings; beside *marartu* 'I passed' is found *marra* (for **marara*) 'he passed'. No such variations are found within the Egyptian imperfective *śdm·f*, which maintains its geminating appearance whatever the weight of the flexional endings may be. If the Arabic and Egyptian forms were really analogous one might reasonably expect to find such variations as **ir wn·tn* for 'if ye are', **ir wn nṯr* 'if the god is' beside *ir wnn·f* 'if he is'. In point of fact *ir wnn·* with gemination occurs whatever the following subject may be, or again if no subject immediately follows. Probably the presence and absence of gemination in the two *śdm·f* forms are to be explained by the desire to retain in them the characteristic features of the participles in which they originated. In other words, the gemination of the imperf. *śdm·f* is probably due to its presence in the imperfective passive participle, and the lack of gemination in the perfective *śdm·f* to its absence in the perfective passive participle; see above § 411, 1.

THE IMPERFECTIVE *ŚḎM·F*

§ 439. Forms from the mutable verbs.

2ae gem. [hieroglyphs] *šmm·sn* 'they are hot'.[1] 'See' has [hieroglyphs] *mꜣꜣ·f*,[2] [hieroglyphs] *mꜣꜣ·t(w)·f*;[3] but also exceptionally [hieroglyphs] *mꜣn·k*,[4] which exhibits an unusual change of *ꜣ* into *n* and is elsewhere perfective (§ 448). 'Be' has [hieroglyphs] *wnn·k*.[5]

3ae inf. [hieroglyphs] *hꜣꜣ·s* 'it goes down';[6] [hieroglyphs] *ḫdd* 'flows'.[7]

'Make' has the form [hieroglyphs] *irr·k*,[8] but *r* is occasionally written twice, ex. [hieroglyphs] *irr·f*.[9]

3ae gem. A possible example is [hieroglyphs] *ḫmꜣꜣ·f* 'shrinks'.[10]

4ae inf. Geminating forms are not very common; exx. are [hieroglyphs] *msdd·tn* 'ye hate';[11] [hieroglyphs] *nšnn* 'rages';[12] [hieroglyphs] *nṯrr·f* 'he is divine'.[13]

caus. 2ae gem. [hieroglyphs] *sšrr·f* 'he diminishes';[14] [hieroglyphs] *sḳbb·k* 'mayest thou have refreshment.[15] Possibly, however, both these are *4-lit.* verbs, see § 284.

caus. 3ae inf. [hieroglyphs] *sḳdd* 'fares by water'.[16]

anom. 'Give' shows [hieroglyphs] *dd·f*,[17] also written archaically [hieroglyphs].[18] From 'come' no geminating forms are known, [hieroglyphs] *iw* taking their place; see below § 459. With 'bring' we find [hieroglyphs] *inn·t(w)*.[19]

1 *Eb.* 53, 19. Sim. *ÄZ.* 43, 39, 16.
2 *Peas.* R 41; *Sin.* B 117.
3 *Sin.* B 52.
4 *P. Kah.* 6, 24 (after *ir* 'if').
5 *Pt.* 220. 232; see too §§ 107. 118. 326.
6 *Peas.* B 1, 307. Sim. LAC. *TR.* 4, 35.
7 *Urk.* iv. 687, 13.
8 *Sh. S.* 20; *Peas.* B 1, 163. 164.
9 LAC. *TR.* 78, 17.
10 *Eb.* 39, 8.
11 Louvre C 196. Sim. Cairo 20515; *P. Kah.* 36, 42; *Eb.* 70, 24.
12 *P. Kah.* 2, 19.
13 *Urk.* iv. 363, 6.
14 *Peas.* B 1, 251.
15 *Urk.* iv. 1165, 16.
16 *Peas.* B 1, 267.
17 Berl. *Äl.* i. 258, 12; *Peas.* B 1, 85.
18 *Urk.* iv. 260, 13.
19 *Urk.* iv. 1111, 6.

§ 440. Uses of the imperfective *śḏm·f* in affirmative main clauses.

—Since the imperfective or geminating participles from which the imperfective *śḏm·f* is derived regularly imply the notions of *repetition* or *continuity*, these same notions ought to be perceptible in the imperfective *śḏm·f* itself.

1. Such is apparently always the case in affirmative main clauses referring to *present* or *past* events. With present reference the geminating *śḏm·f* is frequently found in statements of *custom* or *aphoristic truths*.

Exx. [hieroglyphs] *iw swt mꜣꜥt r nḥḥ, hꜣꜣ·s m-ꜥ irr sy r ḫr(t)-nṯr* justice is unto all eternity, it goes down with him who does it to the necropolis.[20] An aphorism.

[hieroglyphs] *inn·tw m ꜥḳ, wn ꜣhw* one has recourse to an intimate, when there is trouble.[21] In this aphorism another MS. has [hieroglyphs], using the *iw śḏm·f* form which regularly has reference to customary acts (§ 462).

To whom shall I speak to-day? There is a lack of intimates; [hieroglyphs] *inn·tw m ḫmm r srḫt n·f* one has recourse to him who is unknown in order to complain to him.[22] Characterization of a period.

Thou art the rudder of the entire land, [hieroglyphs] *sḳdd tꜣ ḫft wḏ·k* the land sails in accordance with thy command.[23] Characterization of a person.

20 *Peas.* B 1, 307. Sim. *Sin.* B 151 (*sꜣꜣ*); 152 (*rww*); Berl. *Äl.* i. p. 258, 12 (*dd·f*), qu. Exerc. XXX. (i); *P. Pet.* 1116 A, 55 (*mꜣꜣ·sn, spp·sn*); *Urk.* iv. 1092, 2 (*ꜣbb·tw*).
21 *Pt.* 349. Cf. *Sin.* B 151, where *iw·i di·i* (§ 463) is parallel to *sꜣꜣ*.
22 *Leb.* 124; sim. *ib.* 117. Sim. too *Adm.* 12, 3 (*ꜣbb·tw*); 12, 4 (*prr*); 12, 14 (*gmm·tw*); p. 102 (*ḫnn·tw, wnn*); *D. el B.* 114 (*dd·tw*), qu. § 444, 1.
23 *Peas.* B 1, 267. Sim. *Sin.* B 61 (*ṯꜣꜣ·f*); Cairo 20538, ii. c 14 (*dd·f*); *P. Pet.* 1116 A, 134 (*irr·f, sḳdd·f*); *Urk.* iv. 18, 10 (*prr·f*); 19, 6 (*dgg·tw·f*); 246, 4 (*irr·s*). Of stars, *Cen.* 84, 1–2 (*sḳdd, prr·sn*).

It is true that in such passages a non-geminating *śḏm·f* is often found either as variant of,[1] or else associated with,[2] the geminating *śḏm·f*; but we have seen (§ 367) that a similar alternation between perfective and imperfective occurs with the participles. It is highly significant for the view here taken that the negative accompanying the geminating *śḏm·f* is usually *n śḏm·n·f* (§ 418).[3]

2. The geminating *śḏm·f* is used, like the imperfective participles (§§ 366; 369, 2), of *past custom*; examples are not common.

Exx. [4] *ḫdd·ỉ ḫr ỉnw·s n nsw ṯnw rnpt nb(t), prr·ỉ ỉm m mȝꜥ-ḫrw, n gm·n·tw dȝt·ỉ* I used to sail down with its tribute to the king every year, and went forth thence vindicated, and no deficiency was found in (lit. of) me.[5] Note the negation *n śḏm·n·f*.[6]

wnn tȝ m sny-mnt the land was topsy-turvy.[7] Here *wnn* might conceivably be *śḏm·n·f*, but several examples of the negation *n śḏm·n·f* are in the neighbouring context.

3. The geminating *śḏm·f* is common in contracts, rules and the like, where the reference is to some *customary* or *prescribed* act destined to occur in the *future*, though we shall see below (under 5) that the gemination occurs also where the act is future, but not customary.

Exx. *dd·f kt hrw n wpt-rnpt* he shall give another on the day of the New Year.[8] In a contract.

dd·tw ḥtp-nṯr pn m-bȝḥ twt pn these offerings shall be placed before this statue.[9] The context narrates the institution of certain festivals.

wnn sš spȝt m ḫȝ·f the writing of the nome shall be in his office.[10] In rules respecting the vizier's administrative duties.

Probably the use of *wnn·f* as a simple future (§§ 107, 1; 118, 2) comes under this head, since 'existence' is a notion which of itself implies some degree of continuity.

4. We shall see hereafter (§ 450, 5, *a*) that the particle *ỉḫ* (§ 228) is always followed by the non-geminating, perfective *śḏm·f*. One single exception to this rule has been found in a coronation decree, where the *custom* to be observed throughout the reign is prescribed.

ỉḫ dd·k dỉ·tw mȝꜥ ḥtp-nṯr n nṯrw Tp-šmꜥ Ꜣbw m ỉrt ḥsswt ḥr-tp ꜥnḫ wḏȝ snb n-sw-bỉt ⸢*ꜥȝ-ḫpr-kȝ-rꜥ dỉ ꜥnḫ*⸣ thou shalt cause offerings to be made (lit. cause that offerings be caused to proceed) to the gods of Elephantine in the Upper Egyptian province in performing what is praiseworthy on behalf of the life, prosperity, and health of the king ⸢Akheperkerēꜥ⸣, given life.[11] The last words contain the point of the sentence: when offerings are made, the name of Tuthmosis I is to be invoked.

[1] *Peas.* B 2, 73 (*hȝ·s*). Sim. LAC. *TR.* 4, 41 (*pr·ỉ*) = *ib.* 5, 3 (*prr·ỉ*).

[2] *Adm.* p. 102 (*rdỉ·tw*); *Urk.* iv. 18, 1 (*dỉ·sn*); 8 (*ỉn·sn*).

[3] *Sin.* B 62; *Adm.* 12, 4. 5. 6; *Cen.* 84, 2.

[4] An abnormal writing of the suffix 1st pers. sing.

[5] *Urk.* iv. 77; sim. Munich 3, 17 (*prr·ỉ*), qu. § 310, end; *Th. T. S.* 3, 12. Other verbs, Brit. Mus. 614, 9 (*ỉrr·ỉ*); *Peas.* B 1, 85 (*dd*), qu. Exerc. XXX, (ii); *Sin.* B 182 (*dd*); *Ann.* 37, Pl. 2, 13 (*ḫnn·f*); *Arm.* 103, 3–4 (*stt·f*).

[6] Sim. Brit. Mus. 614, 9; *Ann.* 37, Pl. 2, 14.

[7] *Rec.* 29, 164, 8.

[8] *Siut* 1, 298. Sim. *ib.* 282. 297; also 304 (*prr·sn*); 315 (*wnn*).

[9] *Urk.* iv. 769, 16, *pn* restored. Sim. *ib.* 4 (*dd·tw*); 17 (*prr*); BUDGE, p. 141, 15 (*šdd·tw*).

[10] *Urk.* iv. 1113, 15. Sim. *ib.* 1111, 15; *ỉnn·tw*, 1111, 6, qu. Exerc. XXX, (iii); 1112, 15.

[11] *Urk.* iv. 80, 15. Again *ib.* 17.

5. The geminating *śḏm·f* is also found in *exhortations* or *wishes*, i. e. in relation to future acts. Since the perfective *śḏm·f* frequently has a similar function (§ 450, 4), the problem is to discover the reason for the choice of the form with gemination.

Sometimes a certain degree of *generality* is discernible.

Exx. *irr ḥm·k m mrr·f* may Thy Majesty do as he wills.[1]

m it(w) irr·k r itw do not rob, (but) act against the robber.[2]

In a few cases, however, it is only a *single* act that is involved.

Ex. Let there be brought an ox-hide or a . . . . -hide, *dd·k sw n ṯbw Ptḥ-wry* do thou give it to the sandal-maker Ptaḥwēre.[3]

It has been conjectured[4] that in such cases the geminating form serves as a noun subject to an adverbial predicate, which would thus acquire a special stress. The above example would then have to be rendered: It is to . . . P that thou shalt give it, lit. (that-)thou-givest-it (be) to . . . . P. Cf. below under 6.

In one case *sḳbb·k*, expressing a wish, is parallel to the *3ae inf.* *ir·k.*

sḳbb·k n šwt nt mnw·f mayst thou have refreshment of the shade of its trees.[5]

Perhaps, however, *sḳbb·k* belongs to the *4-lit.* verbs, see § 284.

6. In *questions* emphasis naturally rests on an interrogative adverbial adjunct, and the geminating *śḏm·f* may then introduce a virtual noun clause as subject, as explained above under 5. The negative examples with *tm·f* (§ 346, 1) favour this explanation.

Ex. *ḥnwt·i, irr·t p3 ib ḥr m* my mistress, wherefore art thou in this mood? Lit. thou-makest-this-heart (is) because of what?[6]

7. A common mode of addressing Middle Kingdom letters calls for remark.

Ex. *dd Ppw n nbt pr Sbk-ḥtp* Pepu gives (this) to the lady of the house Sebkḥotpe.[7]

It is uncertain whether this is the geminating *śḏm·f* or the imperfective relative form ('what P. gives'). The lack of the direct semantic object suggests the latter, and as antecedent the masc. word *sš* 'letter' may be implied.

OBS. The geminating *śḏm·f* is rare after the non-enclitic particles, though exx. with *ist*[8] and *mk*[9] may be quoted. No instance has been found after *ḥ3* 'would that', and the case after *iḫ* quoted above under 4 is quite exceptional. After *ḫr* and *k3*[10] the non-geminating *śḏm·f* is regular, as also in the construction *in* or *ḫr* or *k3* + noun + *śḏm·f* (below § 450, 5). Similarly after *iw* the non-geminating *śḏm·f* is the rule, though there are exceptions (§§ 462–3). Lastly, the gemination is rare after the negative words (§ 445). It would seem that the expressive force of these particles and auxiliaries was felt to be sufficient, without overburdening the phrase with the additional nuance of repetition or continuity.

[1] *Sin.* B 263. Sim. *Peas.* R 6; B 1, 257; *Eb.* 12, 3; 91, 12.

[2] *Peas.* B 1, 164. Sim. *Pt.* 122–3 (L 2).

[3] MÖLL. *HL.* i. 18. Sim. *Urk.* v. 156, 14. In *Eb.* 7, 22; 24, 3 the sense may perhaps be general.

[4] POL. *Ét.* § 28 extends this explanation still further, see below § 446.

[5] *Urk.* iv. 1165. Sim. Stockholm 55, 3; Louvre C 55, 6.

[6] *Westc.* 12, 21. Sim. *Adm.* 5, 9; *L. to D.*, Cairo letter, 4.

[7] *P. Kah.* 30, 1. Sim. *ib.* 32, 1; DAR. *Ostr.* 25375. 25385.

[8] *Th. T. S.* iii. 12 (*prr*, past custom).

[9] *Paheri* 7 (*mrr·i*); *Urk.* iv. 1092, 2 (*3bb·tw*); *Peas.* B 2, 124 (*irr·k*). Frequently also the future *wnn·f*, see p. 178, n. 16.

[10] Exception *Eb.* 23, 12, where, however, *irr·k* may be written for *ir·k*.

§ 441. **The imperfective *śḏm·f* in subordinate clauses** has, as a rule, *relatively present* meaning, i. e. refers to time contemporary with that of the main verb. In this respect it contrasts with the *śḏm·n·f* form, which has relatively past meaning; and resembles the perfective *śḏm·f* form, from which it differs mainly through its inherent notion of repetition or continuity. Sometimes, but much less often than the perfective *śḏm·f*, the geminating *śḏm·f* may refer to *prospective*, i.e. *relatively future*, time; examples below § 442, 1 after *snḏ* 'fear' and *mrỉ* 'wish'.

§ 442. **The imperfective *śḏm·f* in noun clauses.**—1. As *object* of certain verbs or subject of their passives, see above § 184.

After *rdỉ* 'cause' the perfective, non-geminating *śḏm·f* is used in all verb-classes, see below § 452, 1. Now and again geminating forms from *mȝȝ*[1] and *wnn*[2] occur, sometimes even in MSS. which seem trustworthy.

When the *śḏm·f* has *prospective* meaning after other verbs, the gemination is rare. A few examples from the *2ae gem.* class occur, and may be due to the intrinsic meaning of the verb-stems involved (§ 446). So after *snḏ* 'fear' and *mrỉ* 'wish'.

Exx. [hieroglyphs] *m snḏ mȝȝ wršyw* through fear lest the watchmen might see.[3]

[hieroglyphs] *m mrr·ṯn wnn ỉmȝḫ·ṯn ḫr Wsỉr* as ye wish that honour for you should be with Osiris.[4]

So *wnn·ṯn* also after *wḏ* 'command'.[5] After this same verb is once found an example from a *3ae inf.* verb.

[hieroglyphs] *ỉw grt wḏ·n ḥm·f prr·(ỉ) r ḫȝst tn* His Majesty commanded me to go forth to this desert.[6]

Repetition is perhaps not completely excluded by the context here,[6a] but there is nothing beyond the gemination to indicate that a repeated act was meant, and the reference is probably to the single occasion when the royal sarcophagus was fetched.[6b] Nevertheless the scribe may have wished to express himself generally, as could be done in English by the use of the gerund ('commanded my going'); see below under 5.

The *śḏm·f* form which serves as object of certain verbs sometimes has *non-prospective* meaning, for example after *rḫ* 'know' or *mȝȝ* 'see' (§ 184, 2). In this case the imperfective *śḏm·f* is more apt to be found than the perfective (§ 452, 1, *b*), doubtless because what is seen or known is an action in progress or a continuously exerted quality.

Exx. [hieroglyphs] .... [hieroglyphs] *ỉw·(ỉ) rḫ·kw(ỉ) .... dgg ỉrt n snwt·s* I know .... (how one) eye looks at its fellow.[7]

[hieroglyphs] *mȝ·n ḥm·f ḳnn·ỉ* His Majesty saw how valiant I was.[8]

[1] *Eb.* 43, 17 (= *mȝ*, 93, 12); BUDGE, p. 170, 1 (*Nu*); 334, 1 (*Nu*).

[2] *Mitt.* viii. p. 4 (= *wn*, viii. p. 10; ix. p. 3). See further below, p. 379, top.

[3] *Sin.* B 18 = R 44.

[4] Turin 1447. Sim. Brit. Mus. 152.

[5] Brit. Mus. 101, 4, qu. Exerc. XVII, (*a*).

[6] *Hamm.* 113, 10.

[6a] Continuous action after *wḏ* in O. E., *Urk.* i. 301, 3–5 (*srr·f, ỉrr·f*); 305, 17 (*wnn·sn*).

[6b] Single action after *wḏ* in O. E., *Urk.* i. 298, 8 (*dd·k*).

[7] Louvre C 14, 9–10. Sim. *Urk.* iv. 363, 6; after *mȝȝ*, *Westc.* 5, 4 = 5, 15, qu. § 184 end.

[8] *Urk.* iv. 9, 16; sim. *ib.* 892, 6. Qualities after *rḫ*, GARD. *Sin.* p. 178; *Pt.* 76; *Urk.* iv. 363, 6.

2. When the geminating *śḏm·f* is subject of an adjectival predicate (§ 188, 3), a more or less *prolonged process* is doubtless envisaged.

Ex. Reddjedet was in travail *ḳsn mss·s* and her bearing was painful.[1]

3. The geminating *śḏm·f* is found as the predicate of *pw* (§ 189, 1) in the *medical definitions* of the Ebers papyrus. Here the reference is to habit or rule, cases where we have seen the gemination to be usual (§ 440, 1).

Ex. *ỉr ỉb·f mḥ mhh ỉb·f pw* as to (the phrase) 'his heart is drowned' this means that his heart is forgetful.[2]

The negative statement in these definitions is conveyed by *n śḏm·n·f*.[3]

4. The imperfective *śḏm·f* is found in a name (§ 194) given to the supreme god in some religious texts: *Mrr·f ỉrr·f* '(Whenever)-he-likes-he-does'.[4] This complex name is expanded in the Pyramid texts[5] to *Mrr·f ỉrr·f, msḏḏ·f n ỉr·n·f* '(Whenever)-he-likes-he-does,-(whenever)-he-dislikes-he-does-not', where the gemination is again seen to be negatived by *n śḏm·n·f*.

5. The use of the geminating *śḏm·f* in the construction after the genitival adjective (§ 191) well illustrates the notions of repetition or continuity belonging to that form. Whereas (§ 452, 5) the non-geminating *śḏm·f* is employed when the action referred to occurred in the past (*ḥwn·k n wn·k ỉm·f* 'thy youthful vigour in which thou wast') or is a single event (*hrw n ms·s* 'the day when she shall give birth'), the geminating *śḏm·f* is used to describe more *generalized* acts; such as may often best be rendered by an English noun or gerund.

Exx. *wnm·k špssw n dd nsw* thou shalt eat fine things of the king's gift (*or* giving).[6]

ỉt·n·ỉ rnpt 110 m ꜥnḫ n dd n·ỉ nsw I spent 110 years of life which (lit. of) the king gave to me.[7]

I ploughed ..... *m sḫwt nt ỉrr·ỉ ḏs·ỉ* in fields of my own making.[8]

r tr n nšnn pt whenever heaven rages.[9] Lit. at the season of heaven-rages.

§ 443. The geminating *śḏm·f* in relative clauses.—Among the few examples of *śḏm·f* after the relative adjective *nty* the imperfective form *mꜣꜣ·k* is once found (§ 201, first ex.), and that in a MS. of the Book of the Dead which enjoys a good reputation.

On the other hand, in some examples after the negative relative adjective *ỉwty*, the gemination seems due to the *generalizing* or *characterizing* nature of the epithet contained in the relative clause.

Ex. *ỉwty thh·f rdyt m ḥr·f* one who does not transgress the charge laid upon him, lit. what has been placed in his face.[10]

[1] *Westc.* 9, 22 (in 10, 4 *ms·s*). Sim. *Eb.* 109, 15 (*dd·f*), qu. p. 143, n. 1.

[2] *Eb.* 102, 15. Sim. *ib.* 101, 9 (*ktt*); 101, 12 (*rww·f*), qu. p. 143, n. 6; 101, 13; 114, 1 (*wnn*). See too LAC. *TR.* 43, 1.

[3] *N pr·n·f*, *Eb.* 101, 17.

[4] LAC. *TR.* 78, 15–18; CHASS. *Ass.* p. 100; *Mitt.* ix. p. 18.

[5] *Pyr.* 412. See the comments *JEA.* 33, 99.

[6] *Westc.* 7, 21. Sim. *Sin.* B 187. 236; *Paheri* 1; *Urk.* iv. 447, 7. 11.

[7] *Pt.* 642. Sim. *P. Kah.* 3, 9 (*ỉnn*).

[8] *Urk.* iv. 132. Sim. *ib.* 384, 10. For exx. with *wnn·k* see § 191.

[9] *P. Kah.* 2, 19.

[10] *Urk.* iv. 97. Sim. *ib.* 959, 15 (*ḳdd·f*); Brit. Mus. 343 (*bꜣgg·f*); *Urk.* iv. 410, 6 (*bgg·f*); *P. Pet.* 1116 A, 67 (*dd·sn*).

§ 444. The geminating *śḏm·f* form in adverb clauses.—1. The gemination is sometimes found in virtual clauses of *time*, when the notion of repetition is present.

Exx. *ḫdd·k, dd·tw n·k sꜣ-tꜣ* when (*or* whenever) thou sailest northwards, reverence is paid to thee.[1]

prr·ṯn r pt m nrwt, prr·ỉ ḥr tpt ḏnḥw·ṯn when (*or* whenever) ye go up to heaven as vultures, I go up on the tip of your wings.[2]

With the verb *mꜣꜣ* 'see', the gemination occurs irrespective of any notion of repetition; for a possible explanation, see below § 446.

Exx. *wmt ỉb pw, mꜣꜣ·f ꜥšꜣt* he is stout of heart when he sees a multitude.[3] A characterization.

This Djeḥutnakht said, *mꜣꜣ·f ꜥꜣw n sḫty pn* when he saw the asses of this peasant.[4] Statement of a single occurrence.

2. In the *if*-clause of *virtual clauses of condition*, when this precedes the *then*-clause. (But we may also view these examples as clauses of *asseveration*, see § 218.)

Exx. *mrr·k mꜣn·ỉ snb·kwỉ* if (*or* so surely as) thou wishest to see me in health.[5] Variant *m mrr·k.*[6]

mrr·ṯn Wp-wꜣwt . . . . ḏd·ṯn if (*or* so surely as) you love Wepwawet . . . . say ye.[7]

This formula is found with *m mrr·ṯn*[8] and *m mr·ṯn*[9] as variants; there are also various similar formulae beginning in the same way, and these yield the additional variant *mr·ṯn*[10] without *m*. See §§ 454, 1. 4; 458, for further comments on these alternatives.

3. The *śḏm·f* form after *prepositions* (§ 155) may be either the geminating or the non-geminating *śḏm·f*. Which of the two is chosen appears to depend partly on the particular meaning of the preposition and partly on that of the verb in question. In certain cases the choice of the geminating *śḏm·f* seems undoubtedly due to the notion of *repetition* or *continuity* which is involved.

So, for example, after *mỉ* 'as when', 'like' in similes.

Exx. It was like the fashion of a dream *mỉ mꜣꜣ sw ỉdḥy m Ꜣbw* as when a man of the marshes sees himself in Elephantine.[11]

They found their wine lying in their vats *mỉ ḫdd mw* as when water flows.[12] I. e., their wine was as abundant as ever-flowing water.

In the common phrase *mỉ mrr bꜣk ỉm* 'according as this humble servant desires'[13] *mỉ* has a different sense, but the gemination is always present; the phrase occurs in letters, where it follows wishes for the welfare of the person addressed.

1 *D. el B.* 114.

2 Lac. *TR.* 5, 3. Sim. *ib.* 4, 33.

3 *Sin.* B 59. Sim. *ib.* B 52; *Siut* 1, 230; *Ikhern.* 23.

4 *Peas.* R 41–2.

5 *Peas.* R 123.

6 *Peas.* B 1, 78.

7 Cairo 20153; sim. Louvre C 5, 3. In other formulae, Brit. Mus. 223. 233. 239; Berl. *Äl.* i. p. 179. 205.

8 Cairo 20040, *a* 17; 20536, *d* 4. In other formulae, Brit. Mus. 579. 584; Louvre C 177. 196.

9 Cairo 20119, *c* 4; Brit. Mus. 805. In another formula, Cairo 20606, *b* 3.

10 Cairo 20043, *h* 2; 20141, *a* 3; 20164, *a* 2.

11 *Sin.* B 225 = R 65.

12 *Urk.* iv. 687. Sim. *Leb.* 141 (*ṯbb*); *P. Kah.* 1, 7 (*ỉrr*).

13 *P. Kah.* 27, 4. 11. 14. 17; 28, 2. 19; 31, 36; 36, 3. 52.

Examples of *r mrr·f* 'according as he desires' have been quoted § 163, 11, and of *m mrr·k* 'so surely as (or 'if') thou desirest' above under (2) at end. Compare the similar phrase *m msdd ib·f* 'though his heart hates (it)'.[1]

The expression *m dd*, lit. '(being) as gives', i. e. 'by the gift of', seems to occur only where the gift is repeated or generalized.

Ex. *ḫ3 m ḫt nb nfrt m dd Wsir* a thousand of all good things by the gift of Osiris.[2]

Where the non-geminating *m di* is substituted,[3] it seems not unlikely that a single gift is envisaged.

Analogous to *m dd* is *m irr·i* 'by my making';[3a] cf. 'I did not plan works *nn m irr·f* except by his (Amūn's) doing',[3b] but the same phrase in another ex.[3c] is less easily translated.

Another frequent phrase in which generalization seems implied is *r dd ib·f* 'to his heart's content', lit. 'according as his heart gives'.[4]

In the case of the two *śdm·f* forms of *wnn* we found (§§ 157, 1–3; 326, end) the gemination after prepositions either when stress is laid on duration or else when future time is involved; elsewhere the non-geminating form is usual.

The reasons for the gemination or for its absence cannot be followed up in the case of every preposition. The geminating *śdm·f* has been noted, for example, after *n* 'because',[5] *ḥr* 'because',[6] *ḫft* 'according as',[7] *m-ḫt* 'when', 'after',[8] *n-ᶜ3t-n* 'inasmuch as'.[9]

4. In the *if*-clause of *clauses of condition* after *ir* (§ 150). Here a remarkable divergence is observable between verbs of different classes; whereas the *3ae inf.* and *anom.* verbs regularly employ the non-geminating form (§ 454, 5), the *2ae gem.* use the geminating *śdm·f*.

Exx. *ir m33·k ḥr·s w3ḏ* if thou seest her face green.[10]

ir wnn·k ḥnᶜ rmṯ if thou art together with people.[11]

So too with other verbs of the same class.[12] The explanation may lie in the fact that most verbs of the *2ae gem.* class have meanings which inherently imply repetition or continuity (§ 446).

In accordance with the general behaviour of the *3ae inf.* in this case, as noted above, we find *ir gm·k* for 'if thou findest' in the Ebers medical papyrus and elsewhere.[13] If, however, another verb immediately follows *ir* and 'thou findest' occurs only as a second condition, then it is regularly represented by the geminating form *gmm·k*.

Ex. .... *ir ḫ3·k .... gmm·k ḏrw·f šm .... dd·ḫr·k* if thou examinest (him after doing this), ... and thou findest his side warm .... thou shalt say.[14]

In such cases the gemination is doubtless due not, as has been supposed, to the separation of 'thou findest' from *ir* 'if', but to some nuance of repetition or

[1] *Urk.* iv. 969, 3. Sim. *P. Kah.* 36, 42; *Eb.* 70, 24.

[2] Turin 1447. Sim. PIERRET i. 86; *Semnah Disp.* 2, 8.

[3] *Five Th. T.* 25. 26.

[3a] *JEA.* 32, Pl. 6, 31. Sim. *m irr nsw* 'by the king's doing', *Hamm.* 192, 6.

[3b] *Urk.* iv. 363, 10.

[3c] *Urk.* iv. 439, 1.

[4] *Th. T. S.* i. 30, F; *Five Th. T.* 19. Sim. *ḫft dd ib·k*, *Urk.* iv. 116, 17; 499, 6.

[5] L. *D.* iii. 72, 8 (*ḥᶜᶜ.k*).

[6] *Sin.* B 117 (*m33·f*).

[7] *Rifeh* 7, 31 (*mrr·f*).

[8] *Eb.* 56, 21 (*šww·f*); 89, 18 (*irr·tw·f*).

[9] *BH.* i. 25, 46. 75; Brit. Mus. 614, 12; *Hamm.* 113, 15 (*mrr·f*); Munich 3, 22 (*ḥss*).

[10] *P. Kah.* 6, 23. Sim. *ib.* 7, 35. 58; *Eb.* 51, 19; 52, 1. Written *m3n·k* *P. Kah.* 6, 24.

[11] *Pt.* 232. Other exx. with *wnn*, see § 150. See too Add.

[12] *Ḥnn·f*, *Eb.* 104, 8; *šmm·f*; *ÄZ.* 43, 39, 16. But *šmw*, *ib.* 30, 26.

[13] See below p. 375, n. 3.

[14] *Eb.* 37, 2–3. Sim. *ib.* 39, 13; 40, 5. 11; 42, 3. 10; 104, 7. 15.

continuity which it is difficult to catch. In favour of this view it is significant that the corresponding negation is *ir ḫꜣ·k sw, n gm·n·k* 'if thou examinest him and dost not find',[1] for we have seen that the negation *n śḏm·n·f* occurs only in cases where a prolonged period is envisaged (§ 418). Note that the geminating *śḏm·f* form from *wnn* 'exist' may occur after and parallel to *gmm·k* as further continuation of such a complex *if*-clause.[2]

§ 445. Negation of the geminating *śḏm·f*.—1. This form hardly ever follows the negative words.

Exx. *n irr·k st, n irr·⟨s⟩ st* (if) thou dost not do it, she does not do it.[3] But *ir·k, ir·⟨s⟩*, might conceivably be read, see § 281.

nn šrr pꜣ t ḥnḳt this bread and beer will not be trifling.[4] Probably future, in accordance with § 105, 2.[5] For the special leaning of the *2ae gem.* verbs towards geminating *śḏm·f*, see below § 446.

2. In several places we have seen the construction *n śḏm·n·f* serving to negate the geminating *śḏm·f*: in present generalizations, § 440, 1; in past custom, § 440, 2; in medical definitions, § 442, 3; in a divine name, § 442, 4; continuing *if*-clause with *ir*, § 444, 4 end. Since *n śḏm·n·f* denies the occurrence of an action in the course of a more or less prolonged period (§ 105, 3; 418), its employment to negate the geminating *śḏm·f* is important, if indirect, testimony to the notions of continuity or repetition inherent in the latter.

3. After *ir* 'if' the *śḏm·f* form *tm·f* of the negative verb is used, except in the one case mentioned at the end of the last section. Thus the negative form of *ir mꜣꜣ·f* 'if he sees' would be *ir tm·f mꜣꜣ*; see above § 347, 6.

§ 446. Conclusion.—A theory has recently been advanced[6] that the geminating *śḏm·f* was a form specially evolved to serve in the way explained above under § 440, 5. 6, namely as subject to an adverbial predicate. On this view the second ex. in § 440, 1 would have to be rendered '(It is) to an intimate (that-)one-has-recourse when there is trouble'. It is undeniable that both here and elsewhere emphasis often does seem to rest on an adverbial adjunct, but it is equally undeniable that in all the main clauses of § 440, 1. 2. 3 a notion of *repetition* or *continuity* is invariably present; and the frequent appearance of the negation *n śḏm·n·f* in connexion with the geminating *śḏm·f* (§ 445, 2) guarantees that such a notion was the usual motive for the choice of this form. Also there are some main clauses containing the form where no adverbial adjunct exists.[7] Hence the utmost that can be conceded to the new theory is that owing to the *generality* of the geminating *śḏm·f* it was specially prone to be used as a noun, so that in particular cases (e.g. § 440, 5. 6; § 442, 5) this may have provided the motive for its employment.

[1] *Eb.* 39, 8.

[2] *Eb.* 107, 3. 6.

[3] *Peas.* B 1, 121 (var. R 161 *nn ir·s*). Doubtful exx. from *2ae gem.*, see GUNN, *Stud.*, p. 107. For *n wnn·f*, see § 120 end.

[4] *Siut* 1, 295. Sim. *Sin.* B 258.

[5] Contrast, however, *Pt.* 640 (*nn šr*).

[6] POL. *Ét.* § 28. A criticism *JEA.* 33, 95.

[7] Berl. *ÄI.* i. p. 258, 12 (*dd·f*), qu. Exerc. XXX; *Sin.* B 61 (*tꜣꜣ·f*); *Peas.* B 1, 85 (*dd*); *Adm.* p. 102 (*ḥnn·tw*).

There are, however, other directions in which explanations of recalcitrant uses of the imperfective *śḏm·f* may plausibly be sought. Notions of repetition and continuity are perhaps more easily associated with future time than with past; this might possibly account for the future sense of *wnn·f* (§ 118, 2),[1] the single-action wishes of § 440, 5,[2] and the use in clauses of condition (p. 358, bottom). Or again the employment may be due to the inherent meaning of certain verb-stems. This is particularly likely in the case of *2ae gem.* verbs, a class specially rich in adjective-verbs (ex. *wrr*, *šrr*, *ḳbb*, *šmm*) and containing other verbs like *wnn* 'be' and *mꜣꜣ* 'see' that similarly bear an implication of continuity. It is, at all events, a fact that the *2ae gem.* class is found in forms[3] or syntactic employments[4] where the *3ae inf.* and *anom.* verbs do not display the gemination. We are here, however, in a hypothetical region where further speculation appears barely profitable.

[1] So too in *wnn·ḫr·f*, § 430.

[2] Cf. the O. K. exx. of the imperf. rel. form qu. p. 306, n. 4a.

[3] Imperative (§ 336); negatival complement (§ 341); *śḏmty·fy* form (§ 364).

[4] After *ir* 'if' (§ 444, 4) and in *iw·f śḏm·f* (§ 463).

VOCABULARY

ꜣr restrain, hold back.

ꜣd be aggressive, rage, resent.

wḏf (properly *wdf*) lag, delay.

ḥm flee, retire.

ḥm-ḫt retreat (§ 288).

ḫtm shut, close, seal.

ẖsi be timid, weak, feeble.

sḫm be powerful; with *m*, have power over; caus. *ssḫm* strengthen.

sḏ, var. *sḏ*, break, smash.

ꜥḥt (also *iḥt*) field, holding (of land).

w district, region.

ḥm coward, poltroon.

hp law.

ḫnms friend.

ḫrt what belongs to someone or something.

ḫrwy enemy.

sprty petitioner.

šft dignity, worth.

ḳnbt body of officials or magistrates; *ḳnbty* magistrate.

Nḥsy Nubian.

EXERCISE XXX

Reading lesson. The following extracts illustrate the use of the geminating sḏm·f *in reference to present, past, and future time, and exhibit the parallelism of that form with the imperfective participles.*

(i) *Extract from the stela of Sesostris III at Semnah and its duplicate at Uronarti:*[1]

ỉr gr m-ḫt pḥ (§ 298)
ssḫm ỉb pw n ḫrwy.
ḳnt pw ꜣd (§ 298),
ḫst pw ḥm-ḫt.
ḥm pw mꜣꜥ ꜣrw ḥr tꜣš·f,
ḏr-ntt sḏm Nḥs r ḫr (§ 304, 3) *n r;*
ỉn wšb·f dd (§ 373, 2) *ḥm·f.*
ꜣd·t(w) r·f,
dd·f sꜣ·f;
ḥm-ḫt·(tw, § 62),
wꜣ·f r ꜣd.
n rmṯ(t) ỉs nt šft st (§ 134),
ḥwrw pw sdw[4] *ỉbw.*

[1] Berl. *ÄI.* i. p. 257. Variants in the Uronarti stela from a copy by Prof. Steindorff.
[2] So Uronarti; Semnah *m* only, not *sḏm*. For the pregnant sense of *r* cf. [hieroglyphs] *Amada* 5.
[3] The chick *w* is written for *nḥ*.
[4] Uronarti [hieroglyphs]

'He who desists after attack is a strengthener of the enemy's heart. To be aggressive is to be brave, to retreat is timidity. A real coward is he who is debarred from his frontier, for the Nubian hears (only) to fall at a word; the answering of him causes him to retire. If one is aggressive against him, he shows his back; if one retreats he falls into aggression. They are not people of worth; they are caitiffs broken of heart.'

(ii) *From the tale of the Eloquent Peasant.*[1] *The king commands that the peasant be detained, but supplied with the necessary food:*

ỉr grt (§ 255) *ꜥnḫ*[2] *sḫty pn m ḥꜥw·f* (§ 36).
wnn·k ḥr rdỉt (§ 326) *dỉ·tw n·f ꜥḳw,*
nn rdỉt (§ 307) *rḫ·f nt*[3] *ntk rdỉ* (§ 368) *n·f st.*

[1] *Peas.* B 1, 82-6.
[2] Sense clear, but grammar obscure.
[3] For *ntt.*

wn·in·tw (§ 470) *ḥr rdỉt n·f t 10 ḥnḳt ds 2 rꜥ nb.*[1]
dd st ỉmy-r pr wr Rnsy sꜣ (§ 85) *Mrw;*
dd·f st n ḫnms·f,
ntf dd (§ 373, *a*) *n·f st.*

[1] These two signs are inverted in the MS.

'"Further, keep alive this peasant himself. Thou shalt cause him to be given provisions, without letting him know that thou hast given them to him." So they gave him ten loaves and two jugs of beer every day. The chief steward Rensi, son of Meru, used to give them; he used to give them to a companion of his, and his companion used to give them to him (the peasant).'

(iii) *Extract from the rules given to the vizier for the administration of his office:*[1]

ỉr grt sprt(y)·f(y) (§ 365, 3) *nb n ṯꜣty ḥr ꜣḥwt,*
wḏ·f sw n·f (§ 507, 4),
m ḥꜣw sḏm n ỉmy-r ꜥḥwt
ḥnꜥ ḏꜣḏꜣt nt ṯmꜣ.
ỉrr·f wḏf r·f ḥr ꜣbd 2
n ꜣḥwt·f m Šmꜥ Tꜣ-mḥw.
ỉr swt ꜣḥwt·f
nty tkn (§ 328, 1) *n nỉwt rst n ḫnw,*
[2] *ỉrr·f wḏf r·f ḥr hrw 3 m ntt* (§ 200, 1) *r hp.*
[3] *sḏm·f sprty nb ḫft hp pn*
nty m ꜥ·f.
ntf grt ỉnn (§ 373, *c*) *ḳnbtyw nw w.*
ntf h(ꜣ)b sn,
[4] *smỉ·sn n·f ḫrt ww·sn.*
ỉnn·t(w) n·f ỉmt-pr nb;
ntf ḫtm st.

[1] NEWB. *Rekhm.* 2–3, corrected from duplicates in the tombs of User (U) and Amenemopĕ (A).
[2] So U. A; R omits *r*. [3] So A; R *sḏmtf.* [4] So A; R has only one *n* (§ 62).

'Further, everyone who shall make petition to the vizier concerning fields, the vizier shall order him (to come) to him, in addition to listening to the overseer of lands and the officials of the cadaster (?). He shall make a postponement with regard to him for two months for his fields in Upper and Lower

Egypt. But in respect of his fields which are near to the Southern City (i. e. Thebes) or to the Residence, he shall make a postponement with regard to him for three days according to what is in the law. He shall hear every petitioner according to this law which is in his hand. Further, it is he who shall send for (lit. fetch) the district-assessors, and it is he who shall despatch them that they may report to him the state of their districts. There shall be brought to him all wills; it is he who shall seal them.'

LESSON XXXI

THE PERFECTIVE *ŚḎM·F* FORM

§ 447. **The perfective *śḏm·f* not a unity.**[1]—To put the discussion on a sound basis, it must first be admitted that the perfective *śḏm·f* probably embraces two distinct forms, though these are usually indistinguishable even in the mutable verbs. The evidence may be summarized as follows. (1) One verb actually shows three *śḏm·f* forms; this is the anomalous verb *ỉnỉ*, with the geminating (imperfective) form *ỉnn·f* (§ 439) and the two perfective forms *ỉn·f* and *ỉnt·f*, the last a curious form of active meaning with intrusive *t*. (2) The anomalous verb for 'come' has only two *śḏm·f* forms from the stem *ỉw*, but one of these, namely *ỉwt·f*, seems to correspond in usage to *ỉnt·f* from *ỉn(ỉ)* just mentioned, while the other *ỉw·f*, though not showing the gemination, is partly imperfective and partly perfective in its uses; see below § 459. (3) From time to time mysterious forms in *-w* are found from *3ae inf.* and *4ae inf.* stems, exx. *hȝw* 'fall',[2] *mrw* 'love',[3] *ḥmsw* 'sit';[4] such forms it seems natural to distinguish from those of more normal writing. (4) The principal argument, however, is drawn from facts belonging to the two extreme ends of Egyptian linguistic history. The non-geminating *śḏm·f* has survived in Coptic in one use, namely as object after *dỉ* 'cause', and here the *3ae inf.* verbs exhibit the vocalization **perìóf*, older doubtless **periáf*, ex. Boḥairic *θmesios* 'cause that she bear', Eg. *dỉt ms(y)·s*;[5] sporadic variants in Dyn. XVIII, like *dd pry s 2 ḥtp* 'who causes two men to go forth (from the court of justice) contented',[6] confirm the latent presence of the third weak radical *y* in the normal writing after *dỉ*. Professor Sethe has, however, shown from the Pyramid Texts that beside the *śḏm·f* forms from *3ae inf.* verbs used after *dỉ* and *rdỉ*, there are others, never so employed, which have a final *-w* or *-y* corresponding to variant writings with prothetic *ỉ* (§ 272); exx. *ḫꜥw·k*,[7] var. *ỉḫꜥ·k*;[8] *ḥꜥy·f*,[9] var. *ỉḥꜥ·f*;[10] and sometimes these endings and prothetic *ỉ* appear together, exx. *ỉḫnw*;[11] *ỉḫꜥy*.[12] But if,

[1] See *Verbum* ii. §§ 323–352, where, however, different conclusions are reached. Sub-sections (3) and (4) of this paragraph require reconsideration in the light of Edel's researches, for which see above, in the Additions and Corrections, p. xxxiv

[2] *Eb.* 88 19; 91, 16; *Westc.* 3, 2 (all after prepositions); LAC. *TR.* 23, 12 (after negative *n*).

[3] *Siut* 4, 19; Cairo 20538, i. *d* 6–7. For *ršw*, *Siut* 4, 29; *hrw*, *ib.* 31 see p. 47, n. 1.

[4] *P. Kah.* 36, 23 (after *kỉ*). Sim. *caus. 2-lit. sḏdw·tn*, SPIEG.-PÖRTN. i. 4, 11 (after *m*).

[5] See *ÄZ.* 22, 28 foll.

[6] *Urk.* iv. 49.

[7] *Pyr.* 794 *b*.

[8] *Pyr.* 1012 *c*.

[9] *Pyr.* 923 *a*.

[10] *Ib.*

[11] *Pyr.* 1346 *a*.

[12] *Pyr.* 1374 *a*.

as is supposed with much probability, the prothetic *i* represents merely a short helping vowel employed when two initial consonants chance to be juxtaposed without intervening vowel, then we must reconstruct from these writings some such vocalizations as *ᵉ*ḫrʿáwek*, *ᵉ*ẖnáw*; these vocalizations do not square at all with those deducible, as we have just seen, from Coptic, for Coptic points to vocalizations like **ḫaʿrwák*, **ẖenìe*. Thus we are driven to infer for the *3ae inf.* class the existence of at least two types of non-geminating *śḏm·f*, one with the initial consonants juxtaposed without intervening vowel, and the other beginning with an unaccented shut syllable (*per-*, *ḫaʿ-*, *ẖen-*). The Middle Kingdom writings seldom or never permit us to recognize these two types; the rare writings with *-w*, like [hieroglyphs] above quoted, might indeed belong to the *ᵉ*ẖnáw* type, but we could not be certain whether a writing like [hieroglyphs] *gmy·k* should be understood as *ᵉ*gmáyek* or as **gemyák*.

The above argument goes to prove (1) that the non-geminating *śḏm·f* form embraces more than one sub-form, and (2) that these different sub-forms cannot be identified at sight. As a practical measure, therefore, we are forced to treat the non-geminating *śḏm·f* as a unity; does this necessarily render our treatment of it unscientific? Perhaps not, for the following reason. It has been argued (§ 411, 1) that the geminating and non-geminating *śḏm·f* forms are derivatives of the corresponding passive participles, and we have found no reason for thinking that there existed more than one non-geminating (perfective) passive participle. It is quite conceivable that the *śḏm·f* form derived from the perfective passive participle may have developed different vocalizations for different uses, just as the imperfect in Arabic has its subjunctive and jussive moods. These vocalic differences are beyond our purview, and we must necessarily ignore them; but we seem justified in describing the non-geminating *śḏm·f*, on grounds of origin, as the perfective *śḏm·f*, and in seeking to connect its various meanings with those of the originating perfective passive participle.

Obs. In two cases—namely in explaining *n sp śḏm·f* 'he never heard' (§ 456) and *nn śḏm·f* 'he will not hear' (§ 457), as opposed to *n śḏm·f* 'he did not hear' (§ 455)—we shall argue from observed differences in the non-geminating *śḏm·f* forms employed. It may turn out that such forms as *int·f*, *iwt·f* and *gmy·f* are exclusively prospective in meaning.

§ 448. Forms of the perfective *śḏm·f* from the mutable verbs.

2ae gem. Exx. [hieroglyphs] *ḳb·f* 'that it may be cool';[1] [hieroglyphs] 'that they may be'[2] (for probable cases of *śḏm·n·f* similarly written see §§ 413; 414, 1); [hieroglyphs] *m3·k* 'thou wilt see'.[3] The verb 'see' also has the peculiar form [hieroglyphs] *m3n·k*;[4] this we have met with (§ 439) as equivalent of the geminating *śḏm·f*, but it is much commoner as variant of the non-geminating *śḏm·f*.

[1] Lac. *TR.* 37, 11. Sim. *Pt.* 462.
[2] *Urk.* iv. 776, 14. Sim. *P. Kah.* 36, 34.
[3] *Sh. S.* 134. Sim. *Peas.* B 1, 60.
[4] *Peas.* R 103. Sim. *Westc.* 8, 11; 9, 17; *Urk.* iv. 1088, 5.

3ae inf. Exx. *hȝ·k* 'thou goest down';[1] *pr* '(that) should go forth';[2] *ms·t(w)·f* 'is born'.[3] Thus the third weak radical is usually left unwritten; only in the 1st pers. sing. is it apt to combine with the suffix as *-y*, ex. *pry*[4] (for clearness sake to be transcribed *pry·ỉ*), beside shorter writings like *hȝ·ỉ*;[5] it is possible that the difference of spelling may in some cases represent a difference of form, see below § 457. Sporadic writings occur, however, where *-y* appears before other suffixes or before nom. subj., exx. *ỉry·sn* 'that they may make';[6] *ỉry* 'may .... make'.[7] For the rarer writings with *-w*, see § 447.

'Make' as a rule writes but one *r*, see the exx. just quoted, and *ỉr·f*,[8] *ỉr·tw*;[9] but , to be read *ỉr·k*, occurs by way of exception.[10]

'Seize' is occasionally spelt *ỉṯ*,[11] but the writing [12] with the later change of *ṯ* into *t* (§ 281) is commoner.

4ae inf. Exx. *msḏ·ṯn* 'ye hate';[13] *bȝg·f* 'it is weary'.[14] The final weak consonant hardly ever appears, except in 1st pers. sing., ex. *ʿwȝy·ỉ* 'that I might steal';[15] compare, however, *rnpy* 'may flourish';[16] *mdwy·k* 'thou speakest'; also *ḥmsw*, § 447.[17]

caus. 2-lit. Note the strange form *sḏdw·ṯn* 'ye shall relate'.[18]

caus. 2ae gem. For *sḳbb·k* 'mayst thou have refreshment' see § 440, 5.

caus. 3ae inf. Note with final *-y* *smsy·tn* 'that ye may deliver'.[19]

anom. 'Give' has forms with *r*, like *rdỉ·ỉ*,[20] *rdỉ·t(w)*,[21] but also, rather more frequently, forms without *r*, like *dỉ·k*,[22] *dỉ·tw*.[23] In old religious texts spellings like *d(ỉ)·k* are occasionally found.[24] Once we have before nom. subj.;[25] cf. similar forms under *3ae inf.* above.

'Bring' differentiates two forms: one without *t*, ex. *ỉn·ỉ*;[26] another with *t* (see above § 447), ex. *ỉnt·f*;[27] for the latter there appears just before Dyn. XVIII a variant *ỉnt(w)·f*,[28] due to loss of value of *w* and possibly also to confusion with the passive, which[29] thus becomes indistinguishable from the active.

'Come' shows from the stem with *-ỉ* such forms as *ỉy·f*. Far commoner, however, are forms from the *-w* stem, namely a form without *-t*, *ỉw·f*, and second, a form with intrusive *-t* (see § 447), ex. *ỉwt·f*; see below § 459.

Thus the outstanding characteristic of the perfective *śḏm·f* is absence of gemination, just as the presence of gemination is the characteristic of the imperfective *śḏm·f*; no definite obstacle stands in the way of a derivation from the perfective passive participle (§ 411, 1), a derivation which is indeed suggested by the ending *-y* in some *3ae inf.* and *anom.* forms. The forms *ỉwt·f* and *ỉnt·f* may be due to the analogy of the infinitive, or may even be infinitives replacing *śḏm·f* forms that were too much reduced to serve their purpose adequately.

[1] *Peas.* B 1, 54.
[2] *Hamm.* 192, 11.
[3] Berlin *ÄI.* i. p. 258, 18. 20.
[4] *Eb.* 30, 8.
[5] *Eb.* 1, 17.
[6] *Urk.* iv. 485, 1. Sim. *ỉry·k*, *ib.* 1074, 14; *dgy·k*, *ib.* 117, 6; *gmy·k*, *P. Kah.* 6, 18. 23; *ỉry·f*, *Arm.* 103, 5; *mry·f*, *Urk.* iv. 1163, 16; *ỉry·n*, *ib.* 327, 13; *ḫdy·n*, Lutz, 34, 66, 2.
[7] *P. Kah.* 34, 2–3. Sim. *pry*, *Urk.* iv. 49, 1, qu. § 447; *ḥsy*, *ib.* 121, 5; 939, 9; 1207, 7.
[8] *Siut* 1, 323.
[9] *P. Kah.* 29, 43.
[10] *Pt.* 415 (L 2).
[11] Cairo 20001, *b* 4.
[12] *Peas.* B 1, 104. Sim. *ỉṯ·tw*, *Eb.* 2, 3.
[13] Cairo 20003, *a* 2.
[14] *Eb.* 39, 3–4.
[15] *Peas.* Bt. 26.
[16] *Sin.* B 167; sim. *rnpy·k*, *Sh. S.* 168.
[17] *Pt.* 615. 624.
[18] Spieg.-Pörtn. i. 4, 11.
[19] *Westc.* 9, 23–4. Sim. *sḳdy·k*, *Urk.* iv. 113, 17; *sḥry*, Brit. Mus. 580.
[20] *Westc.* 9, 17.
[21] Munich 3, 12.
[22] *Peas.* B 1, 29.
[23] *Westc.* 8, 3.
[24] Lac. *TR.* 44, 6.
[25] Lac. *TR.* 20, 5.
[26] *Eb.* 58, 10. Sim. *Peas.* B 1, 252 (*ỉn·k*).
[27] *P. Kah.* 30, 38; 31, 1; *Ikhern.* 4.
[28] *Westc.* 7, 8; 8, 3.
[29] *Westc.* 5, 11.

§ 449. Meaning of the perfective *śdm·f* form.—In dealing with the perfective passive participle, we found that this could be used to describe events belonging alike to past, to present, or to future time (§ 369, 1. 3. 5); it differed from the imperfective passive participle only in the fact that the latter gives prominence to some notion of repetition or continuity associated with the act described. If, as we have conjectured, the perfective *śḏm·f* originated in the perfective passive participle, it ought to possess substantially the same range of meaning as that participle. Such is, in fact, actually the case, save that the *śḏm·n·f* form has largely superseded the employment of the perfective *śḏm·f* in reference to past events. In past narration, the perfective *śḏm·f* is but little used in affirmative main clauses (§ 450, 1); on the contrary it is quite commonly employed in sentences or clauses negatived by *n* (§ 455). For the description of both present and future actions the perfective *śḏm·f* is of very frequent occurrence, as we shall see. It is important to realize that though this form contains no implication of repetition or continuity, the facts which it describes may nevertheless possess that character; a generalization may be made or a custom affirmed without any explicit avowal that such is its nature; see above § 367 and below § 450, 2.

The perfective *śḏm·f* is distinguishable as such only in the mutable verbs, and it is these which will mainly be considered in the following paragraphs. On occasion, however, we may be compelled to discuss under this head forms from immutable verbs, like *ḏd·f* in § 450, 1. The absence of any hint of repetition or continuity here makes it probable that the form has been rightly classified.

§ 450. The perfective *śḏm·f* in affirmative main clauses.—1. *Past reference*. In Old Egyptian the non-geminating *śḏm·f* is fairly frequent in past narration with verbs showing an object,[1] but towards Dyn. VI the *śḏm·n·f* form can be seen gradually superseding it in this use. Nevertheless, undoubted examples of the earlier custom can still be found in Middle Egyptian.

Ex. *rdi i* (read *wi*) *ḥm·f r sš n ṯm3, ḥs wi ḥm·f ḥr·f r ˁ3t wrt* His Majesty appointed me to be scribe of the cadaster (?); His Majesty praised me for it very much.[2]

This use of *śḏm·f* can be detected with certainty only in the case of verbs with feminine infinitives, since with other verbs the absolute use of the infinitive (§ 306, 2) offers an alternative possibility.

Narrations are often introduced by *ḏd·f* 'he said',[3] once written *iḏd·f*[3a] with prothetic *i* (§ 272). In texts of the early Middle Kingdom *ḏd* is used in the same way,[4] and may be *śḏm·f* with ellipse of the subject.

A similar explanation might be thought to apply to that *ḏd* which occurs at the beginning of Middle Kingdom letters.

[1] See GUNN, *Stud.* p. 72.

[2] Brit. Mus. 828. Sim. *Sin.* B 265 (*wd·s*); 285 (*šm·n*).

[3] *Sin.* R 2. 55; *Peas.* Bt. 24; B 1, 53. 74; *P. Kah.* 4, 5. 23. Sim. *ḏd·i Sh. S.* 88.

[3a] *JEA.* 33, Pl. 2, 5, Dyn. XIII.

[4] Cairo 20001. 20007. 20011. 20012; Brit. Mus. 614, 3; *Hamm.* 1, 3. See now *Arch. äg. Arch.* 1, 81, opposing an argument in POL. § 78.

Ex. [hieroglyphs] *bꜣk n pr dt Nni ḏd n imy-r pr ꞽIi-ib* the servant of the estate Neni speaks to the steward Iyeb.[1]

The *śḏm·f* form is excluded, however, by cases showing the fem. ending [hieroglyph] *-t*. Ex. [hieroglyphs] *snt ḏdt n sn·s* the sister speaks to the brother.[2]

The choice thus lies between an active participle and the old perfective. To the latter the 3rd pers. and active sense are perhaps obstacles. The former view seems preferable, demotic offering an analogous formula.[2a]

In texts where the *śḏm·n·f* form is usual for past narration the *śḏm·f* with a nominal subject in anticipatory emphasis (§ 148, 1) sometimes takes its place. Exx. [hieroglyphs] *ist ḥm·f dꜣ·f ꜥ·f, ḳꜣḫ·f drt·f, ir·f n·s ḥtp-di-nsw* lo, His Majesty stretched forth his arm, and bent his hand, and made for her the funerary oblation.[3]

[hieroglyphs] *wꜥt ḥḏ·t(w)·s* (only) one (wisp) has been damaged.[4]

It will be seen later (§ 462) that *iw* + non-geminating *śḏm·f* served now and then to express past custom. Otherwise, the cases above enumerated appear to exhaust the material for perfective *śḏm·f* in reference to past events, so far as affirmative sentences are concerned. In negative sentences referring to past events perfective *śḏm·f* is, as we have already stated (§ 449), very common; further details below §§ 455, 1; 456.

2. In reference to *present* occurrences; the fact is described simply, without any consideration whether it is a single or a repeated happening, whether it is momentary or prolonged.

Exx. [hieroglyphs] *di·i n·k ꜣpd r pst* I give thee a bird to cook.[5] The act described is a single momentary act.

[hieroglyphs] *rdi·tw mꜣꜥt ⟨r⟩ rwty* truth is cast outside.[6] A prevalent condition is described, but without stress being laid on its continuity.[7]

[hieroglyphs] *ḫꜥ·i m Rꜥ* I arise as Rēꜥ.[8] Descriptions in religious spells are perhaps best classified here, though they might seem to be vaguely prospective or optative.

So too in the compound narrative forms *iw śḏm·f* (below § 462), *ꜥḥꜥ śḏm·f* (below § 477, 1). For a similar use in negative sentences, see below § 455, 2.

3. With *future* reference.

Exx. [hieroglyphs] *ms·s m ꜣbd 1 (n) prt, sw 15* she will give birth on the fifteenth day of the first month of winter.[9]

[hieroglyphs] *mꜣ·k pr·k* thou shalt see thy home.[10]

Other forms employed in this case: [hieroglyphs] *di·i*;[11] [hieroglyphs] *rdi·i*.[12] An isolated writing, [hieroglyphs].[12a] From *wnn* 'exist' the imperf. [hieroglyphs] *wnn·f* is universally employed, provided no particle, or merely *mk* 'behold',[13] precedes; see above §§ 107, 1; 118, 2. The negation of the future is, as we have seen, *nn śḏm·f*; see further § 457.

[1] *P. Kah.* 29, 31. Sim. *ib.* 28, 1; 29, 1; 30, 25; 31, 30.

[2] *L. to D.*, Hu bowl, 1. Sim. *ib.*, Cairo linen, 1.

[2a] *Ib.* p. 13.

[3] *Urk.* iv. 28, 16–29, 1. Sim. *Sin.* R 17. 21; B 113.242–3; *BH.* i. 8, 9; *Urk.* iv. 220, 4.

[4] *Peas.* B 1, 14.

[5] *Meir* iii. 23. Sim. *Peas.* B 1, 14 (*iṯ·k*); 28 (*ḥꜣ·k*, *ꜥwꜣ·k*); *Adm.* 4, 2 (*mr·i*); p. 104 (*di·i*); *P. Pet.* 1116 B, 38 (*di·i*).

[6] *Adm.* p. 102. Sim. *ib.* p. 106 (*dwꜣ·tw*); *Sin.* B 233 (*swri·tw·f*).

[7] Active, ex. *Sin.* B 66 (*mr*); a proverb, *Pt.* 268 (*mr*), qu. Exerc. XXVII, (*a*).

[8] LAC. *TR.* 13, 4. Sim. *ib.* 20, 1 (*ts*); 20, 4 (*di*); 21, 1 (*ḫꜥ*); 21, 45 (*di·f*); *Eb.* 2, 1 (*iy*).

[9] *Westc.* 9, 15. Sim. *Sh. S.* 139 (*sḏd·i*); *Sin.* B 192 (*ir·tw*); Cairo 20303, *k* 8 (*šd·f*); *Eb.* 30, 8 (*pry·i*); *Urk.* iv. 649, 12 (*ꜥḥꜥ·i*).

[10] *Sh. S.* 134. Sim. *ib.* 168 (*rnpy·k*).

[11] *Sh. S.* 139. 140. 146.

[12] *Sh. S.* 72; *Leb.* 41; passive *Sin.* B 281.

[12a] Louvre C 10 (Dyn. XIII) as in L. E.

[13] Exx., § 234 (p. 178, n. 16).

4. The perfective *śḏm·f* is common also in *wishes* and *exhortations*, which are often hard to distinguish from one another and from the simple future use. The addition of the enclitic particles *r·k* or *rf* (§ 252, 2 and 3 *a*) may help to indicate this use.

Exx. *dỉ·k r·k n·ỉ ḫt·ỉ* give thou me my chattels.[1]

ꜣd·k ḥr ꜣdt ḥr·s be thou angry concerning what deserves anger, lit. that angered for it.[2]

ỉry n·k Ḥry-š·f nb Nn-nsw ỉb·k may Arsaphes, lord of Heracleopolis Magna, perform for thee thy desire.[3] *Ỉry* is an exceptional writing (§ 448), *ỉr* being normal.[4]

ỉnt[5] *n·f Ḥp ḥtpt·f, wnm·f m r·f, mꜣ·f*[6] *m ỉrty·f* may the Inundation god bring him his offering, may he eat with his mouth, may he see with his eyes.[7]

ḥsw, ḥs tw Ḥry-š·f thou praised one, may Arsaphes praise thee.[8]

The various verb-classes are sufficiently illustrated in the above examples; one may add *caus. 2ae gem.* *skbb·k* (probably perfective, § 440, 5), *caus. 3ae inf.* *skdy·k*,[9] and *anom.* *ỉwt*.[10] Here probably belongs the use of the perfective *śḏm·f* as continuation of the imperative (§ 337), though this might often be translated as a clause of purpose. For a similar, but nevertheless distinct, use of the imperfective *śḏm·f* in exhortations see § 440, 5.

5. After various *particles*, in reference to *future* events. Whether simple futurity, wishes, commands, exhortations, or consequences are meant depends upon the particle employed. See also Lesson XVIII above.

(*a*) After *ỉḫ* (§ 228) expressing *future consequences* or *exhortations*.

Ex. *ỉḫ ỉr·n dmỉ n sp* then let us make a habitation together.[11]

Forms employed: *2ae gem.* *mꜣ·ỉ*,[12] but also *mꜣn·k*;[13] *wn·ỉ*;[14] *3ae inf.*, see *ỉr·n* above; *4ae inf.* *rnpy*;[15] *anom.* *dỉ·k*.[16] An example with the imperfective *dd·k* has been quoted in § 440, 4, the reason for the gemination being that the command there given is of a general and lasting character.

The negative form of *ỉḫ śḏm·f* is *ỉḫ tm·f śḏm(w)*, see § 346, 4.

(*b*) After *ḥꜣ* or *ḥwy* (§ 238), expressing *wishes*.

Ex. *ḥw ỉry·k ḫft ḏd·ỉ* O that thou mayst act according as I say.[17]

Forms employed: *2ae gem.* *mꜣ·ỉ*;[18] *3ae inf.* *wp·k*;[19] *anom.* *dỉ·tn*,[20] but also *rdỉ·t(w)*.[21]

No negative forms have been found, since *ḥꜣ n śḏm·f*, illustrated below § 455, 1, is the negation of *ḥꜣ śḏm·n·f*.

[1] *Peas.* B 1, 29. Sim. with *dỉ*, *Th. T. S.* ii. 11; Lac. *TR.* 4, 13; *ib.* p. 9, top; *Urk.* iv. 753, 8. Also 1st pers., *śḏd·ỉ rf*, *Sh. S.* 21. 125.

[2] *Urk.* iv. 1091, 3. Sim. *ib.* 1090, 13 (*ḥd·k*); the neg. verb *ỉmy·k*, see § 345.

[3] *P. Kah.* 34, 3. Sim. *ỉry·n*, *Urk.* iv. 327, 13; *dgy·k*, *ib.* 117, 6.

[4] *P. Kah.* 35, 38.

[5] Sim. *Ḥarh.* 618; *Westc.* 7, 8 (*ỉnt·k*).

[6] Sim. *Urk.* iv. 1090, 5 (*mꜣ·k*).

[7] Moscow 1, 6–7. Sim. Brit. Mus. 614, vert. 3 (*dꜣ·f*).

[8] *Peas.* B 1, 196. Sim. *Westc.* 7. 24.

[9] *Urk.* iv. 113, 17; 116, 17.

[10] *Urk.* iv. 116, 15.

[11] *Leb.* 154. Sim. *Urk.* iv. 1092, 18.

[12] Cairo 20040, *a* 2; Leyd. V 3.

[13] *Urk.* iv. 1088, 5.

[14] Cairo 20538, ii. *c* 7.

[15] *Sin.* B 167.

[16] Budge, p. 165, 12; 167, 6. Sim. *Urk.* iv. 492, 7.

[17] *Urk.* iv. 1074.

[18] *Th. T. S.* ii. 11.

[19] *ÄZ.* 38, 140.

[20] *Westc.* 11, 7. 15. Sim. *ÄZ.* 38, 136.

[21] *Peas.* B 1, 36.

(*c*) After [hieroglyphs] *ḫr* (§ 239), expressing *futurity*.

Ex. [hieroglyphs] *ḫr dỉ ḥm·f šm s3·f r ꜥḥꜥ ḥr st·f* His Majesty will cause his son to go to rise up in his place.[1]

The material for the mutable verbs is scanty; *2ae gem.* [hieroglyphs] *m3·t(w)*.[2]

(*d*) After [hieroglyphs] *k3* (§ 242), expressing *future result* or *injunction*.

Ex. [hieroglyphs] *k3 ỉr·tw ḫft ỉry* then one shall act accordingly.[3]

Forms employed: *2ae gem.* [hieroglyphs] *m3n·ỉ*;[4] [hieroglyphs] *wn·k*;[5] *3ae inf.* see *ỉr·tw* above; *4ae inf.* [hieroglyphs] *ḥmsw*;[6] *anom.* [hieroglyphs] *dỉ·ỉ*,[7] but also [hieroglyphs] *rdỉ·ỉ*;[8] from 'come' [hieroglyphs] *ỉw·f*,[9] but also [hieroglyphs] *ỉwt*,[10] see § 459. A form [hieroglyphs][11] looks as though it were imperfective (*ỉrr·k*), but is possibly either a mistake or a writing of the perfective *ỉr·k*.

The negative form of *k3 śḏm·f* is *k3 tm·f śḏm(w)*, see § 346, 5.

The evidence above quoted goes to show that, when a particle precedes, it is the simplest form of *śḏm·f* which usually follows. The particle supplies the special nuance of meaning to be given to the verb, and only in exceptional cases (see under *a* at end, *dd·k*) is that meaning further complicated by the notion of repetition or custom which the imperfective *śḏm·f* would imply. The same holds good in the three already studied constructions to be considered next.

(*e*) The construction *ntf* (or *in X*) *śḏm·f* (§ 227, 2), with *future* meaning.[12]

Exx. [hieroglyphs] *ntf ỉr·f n·ỉ p3 t ḥnḳt* (it is) he (who) shall make for me this bread and beer.[13]

[hieroglyphs] *in ỉdnw Gbw ỉr·f šd nḫn n p3y·ỉ s3* (it is) the deputy Gebu (who) shall act (as) guardian (lit. child-rearer) to my son.[14]

In this construction *in* occurs only when the subject is a noun; when the subject is a pronoun it is the independent pronoun which is employed, usually the later independent pronoun, but more rarely the earlier one. Further exx. are:

[hieroglyphs] *ink rdỉ·ỉ ỉr·tw·f n·k* I will cause it to be made for thee.[15]

[hieroglyphs] *dw3t(y)·f(y) s(y) swt ꜥnḫ·f* he who shall praise her, he shall live.[16] In an archaistic text.

Forms employed: *2ae gem.* no certain instance; *3ae inf.* see *ỉr·f* above; [hieroglyphs] *ḥs·f*;[17] *4ae inf.* [hieroglyphs] *ḥms·s*;[18] *anom.* [hieroglyphs] *rdỉ·s*:[19] [hieroglyphs] *in·f*;[20] [hieroglyphs] *ỉwt·f*.[20a]

OBS. The original meaning of *ntf śḏm·f* may have been 'to him belongs that he should hear', cf. French *il entendra* from *ille intendere habet*.[20b] For the possessive sense of *ntf* see § 114, 3.

(*f*) The construction *ḫr·f śḏm·f* (§ 239), with *future* meaning.

Ex. [hieroglyphs] *ḫr·tw ỉꜥ·tw·s m ỉrtt* it shall be washed in milk.[21]

Forms employed: *3ae inf.* see *ỉꜥ·tw·s* above; [hieroglyphs] *šd·f*;[22] *anom.* [hieroglyphs] *dỉ·f*;[23] [hieroglyphs] *ỉy·f*.[24]

[1] *Urk.* iv. 690, 5.
[2] *Urk.* iv. 1111, 11, qu. § 187.
[3] *P. Kah.* 29, 43; *ỉry·ỉ*, *Adm.* p. 105.
[4] *Westc.* 9, 17.
[5] *P. Kah.* 31, 21.
[6] *P. Kah.* 36, 23.
[7] *P. Kah.* 31, 1. Sim. *ib.* 13, 36.
[8] *Westc.* 9, 17.
[9] *P. Kah.* 29, 20; 36, 16; *Urk.* iv. 836, 16.
[10] PIEHL, *IH.* iii. 76.
[11] *Eb.* 23, 12.
[12] See GUNN, *Stud.* ch. v.
[13] *Siut* 1, 323–4.
[14] *P. Kah.* 12, 14.
[15] *P. Kah.* 28, 27. Sim. *Eb.* 1, 8. With *ntk*, *P. Kah.* 31, 6; *ntf*, *Pt.* 519; *nts*, *P. Kah.* 12, 11.
[16] *Urk.* iv. 257, 14. Sim. *ib.* 251, 8; *Urk.* v. 154, 11.
[17] *Hat-Nub* 10, 12, qu. § 227, 2.
[18] *Urk.* iv. 257, 9.
[19] *P. Kah.* 12, 11.
[20] *Urk.* v. 155, 11; *Westc.* 9, 8, qu. § 227, 2; *Eb.* 58, 10.
[20a] *Urk.* iv. 257, 17.
[20b] *JEA.* 20, 13.
[21] *Eb.* 59, 8.
[22] *Urk.* iv. 1111, 12.
[23] *Urk.* iv. 1107, 5, qu. § 239; *dỉ·tw*, *Eb.* 44, 3.
[24] *P. Kah.* 22, 1–2.

(*g*) The construction *kꜣ·f sḏm·f* (§ 242), *future* meaning, usually *future result*. Ex. [hieroglyphs] *kꜣ·k ir·k mitt* thou shalt do the like.[1]

Forms employed: *3ae inf.* see *ir·k* above; *anom.* [hieroglyphs] *di·tw*;[2] [hieroglyphs] *in·f*.[3]

Obs. *'Isṯ* and *mk* appear to exert less influence over the *sḏm·f* form than the other particles studied above, since they are followed sometimes by the imperfective (above § 440, Obs.) and sometimes by the perfective *sḏm·f*.[4] The more expressive a particle is, the less likely it is to be followed by the imperfective *sḏm·f*, since it would not as a rule be desired further to encumber the meaning with the notions of repetition or continuity which would be implied by that form. This conclusion is confirmed by the use with the negatives *n* (§ 455) and *nn* (§ 457), as well as with the auxiliary verb *iw* (§ 462). In all these cases the perfective *sḏm·f* is usual and the imperfective *sḏm·f* very rare.

1 *Urk.* iv. 1090.

2 *Urk.* iv. 768, 12.

3 *P. Kah.* 36, 15.

4 After *mk*, see *di·i* in *ÄZ.* 59, 24 (1, 5); *in·tw* in *Sin.* B 181 and *Urk.* iv. 80, 8 is more probably *sḏm·n·f*; in *Peas.* B 1, 81 *iw* is ambiguous. After *isṯ*, see an ex. § 212. *'Isṯ wn*, see § 107, 2.

§ 451. The perfective *sḏm·f* in subordinate clauses.—As contrasted with the *sḏm·n·f* form with its relatively past meaning in all affirmative subordinate clauses (§ 414, 2), the *sḏm·f* form has reference to time which is either *relatively present* or else *relatively future* (prospective), i. e. time either contemporary with, or posterior to, that of the main verb; only when preceded by a preposition like *ḏr* 'since' does it refer to relatively past time (§ 454, 4). All this holds good alike of the perfective and of the imperfective *sḏm·f* (§ 441), the sole difference being that the perfective *sḏm·f* is destitute of the additional implication of repetition or continuity usually discernible in the imperfective *sḏm·f*.

§ 452. The perfective *sḏm·f* in noun clauses.—1. As *object* of various verbs, or *subject* of their passives; (*a*) with *prospective*, i. e. *relatively future* meaning (§ 184, 1).

The commonest case is with [hieroglyph] *rdi*, [hieroglyph] *di* 'cause', 'allow' (§ 70) and with the corresponding imperative [hieroglyphs] *imi* (§§ 336; 338, 2). Examples have already been quoted, so that it will be sufficient to detail the forms employed in the case of the mutable verbs: *2ae gem.* [hieroglyphs] *mꜣ·i*,[5] also rarely [hieroglyphs] *mꜣn·i*;[6] [hieroglyphs] *wn·k*[7] (for suspect forms with the gemination see p. 379, top); *3ae inf* [hieroglyphs] *ḥs*;[8] [hieroglyphs] *ir·f*,[9] with 1st pers. sing. [hieroglyphs] *iry·i*;[10] except in 1st pers. sing. *y* is but rarely written, exception [hieroglyphs] *pry*[11] (§ 447); *4ae inf.* [hieroglyphs] *ḥms·s*;[12] [hieroglyphs] *rnpy·k*;[13] *anom.* [hieroglyphs] *di·tw*;[14] [hieroglyphs] *int·f*;[15] [hieroglyphs] *iwt·f*.[16]

After other verbs it is usual to find the perfective *sḏm·f* in the case of the *3ae inf.*; so after *wḏ* 'command' we find [hieroglyphs] *ir·f*,[17] and similar forms occur after *di m ib* 'determine', lit. 'place in (one's) heart',[18] and *ḏd* 'say', 'promise'.[19] So too we have [hieroglyphs] *ḥs* 'that.... should praise' after *mri* 'desire',[20] and [hieroglyphs] *dgꜣ·f* (for *dg·f* from *dgi*) 'that he can look' after *gmi* 'find',[21] The only exception in M. E. is a geminating form *prr·(i)* 'that I go forth' after *wḏ* 'command'.[22]

When the objective *sḏm·f* comes from the *2ae gem.* class, there is some

5 *Sin.* B 158. Sim. *P. Kah.* 3, 37; pass. *mꜣ·tw*, *Eleph.* 22.

6 *Westc.* 8, 11.

7 *P. Kah.* 36, 34. See § 118, 2.

8 *P. Kah.* 28, 26.

9 *Peas.* B 1, 156.

10 *Peas.* B 1, 64; *Sin.* B 100.

11 *Urk.* iv. 49, 1.

12 *P. Kah.* 6, 15.

13 *Urk.* iv. 863, 7. Sim. *P. Kah.* 2, 8.

14 *P. Kah.* 29, 37; 35, 11.

15 *P. Kah.* 30, 38; *Ikhern.* 4.

16 *P. Kah.* 31, 10. Sim. Lac. *TR.* 21, 45; *Westc.* 11, 12; Lutz 34, 66, 11.

17 Louvre C 14, 13.

18 *Urk.* iv. 198, 6 (*ir·i*).

19 Lac. *TR.* 35, 10 (*ir·f*).

20 Brit. Mus. 239; Berl. *ÄI.* i. pp. 179. 205; Cairo 20043, *h* 2.

21 *Sm.* 1, 25, qu. § 184, 1.

22 *Hamm.* 113, 10, qu. § 442, 1.

hesitation between the geminating and non-geminating forms. Geminating *śḏm·f* forms from *m33* 'see' after *snḏ* 'fear', and from *wnn* 'be' after *mrỉ* 'desire' and *wḏ* 'command' have been quoted in § 442, 1. Against these, however, have to be set occasional examples of the non-geminating *śḏm·f* of *wnn* after *mr*.

Ex. [hieroglyphs] *mrt·n·f wn·s ḥr nst·f* who he wished should be (lit. that she should be) on his seat.[1]

(*b*) Objective *śḏm·f* with *relatively present* sense after *gmỉ* 'find'.

Ex. [hieroglyphs] *m-ḫt gmt ḥm·ỉ ỉr·tw ḫt ỉm* after My Majesty had found that ceremonies were being performed there.[2]

2. In the noun clause used as *object* and introduced by *ntt* (§ 187), the perfective *śḏm·f* may have *prospective* meaning.

Ex. Tuthmosis .... whom they created .... [hieroglyphs] *rḫ ntt ỉr·f nsyt* (?) *w3ḥt* knowing that he would have (lit. make) a prolonged kingship.[3]

3. No general statement can be made as to the form of *śḏm·f* when this serves as subject (§ 188), except in the cases of the *śḏm·f* form after [hieroglyphs] *n sp* 'never has', 'never did', lit. 'it has not occurred that ....', 'it did not occur that .....', and after [hieroglyphs] *nfr pw* 'there is (are) not'. In both these cases the perfective *śḏm·f* is used, see below § 456.

4. As *predicate* with *pw* as subject (§ 189) the *śḏm·f* form is imperfective in general definitions (§ 442, 3), but may be perfective even in a general characterization (see § 189, 2). Whether [hieroglyphs] *ỉw·f* in the colophon of literary compositions (§ 189, 1) is perfective or imperfective remains obscure.

5. After the *genitival adjective* (§ 191) the *śḏm·f* form is imperfective or geminating in phrases involving repeated or continued acts (§ 442, 5). In other cases the perfective *śḏm·f* is used.

Exx. [hieroglyphs] *hrw n ms·s* on the day of her giving birth.[4] A single act is envisaged.

[hieroglyphs] *mỉ sḫr·k n wn·k tp t3* according to thy way when (lit. of) thou wast upon earth.[5] For present and future time *wnn·f* would be employed (exx. in § 191).

§ **453. The perfective *śḏm·f* in relative clauses.**—Examples of the perfective *śḏm·f* in virtual relative clauses have been quoted in § 196, 2, and it is doubtless due to mere chance that similar examples have not been found (except negatively as *n śḏm·f*) after the relative adjectives. After the negative relative adjective *ỉwty* there are some instances of the imperfective *śḏm·f*; these have been quoted in § 443. The fact that a clause is relative appears to exert no influence upon the form of the verb occurring therein.

[1] *Urk.* iv. 341, 8. Sim. Cairo 20712, *a* 10, qu. § 186, 2.

[2] *Urk.* iv. 751, 2. Sim. *Westc.* 12, 4, qu. § 184, 2.

[3] *Urk.* iv. 593, 5.

[4] *P. Kah.* 6, 26. Sim. *mdwy·k*, *Pt.* 624.

[5] *Urk.* iv. 520. Sim. *ib.* 497, 10, qu. § 191.

§ 454. The perfective *śdm·f* in adverb clauses.—1. Virtual clauses of *time, circumstance, condition.* A very sketchy treatment is here imposed because of the difficulty of discriminating between main clauses and virtual adverb clauses on the one hand, and on the other hand between the several varieties of virtual adverb clauses, from which, moreover, virtual relative clauses (§ 196) are barely separable.

Differences are here discernible in the different verb-classes, and according as the virtual adverb clause precedes or follows the main clause.

To take the *3ae inf.*, *4ae inf.*, and *anom.* verb-classes first, here the perfective *śdm·f* is usual when the adverb clause *follows* the main clause.

Exx. [hieroglyphs] *nn twt n·f, m33·t(w)·f h3·f R-pdtyw* there is none like him when he is seen charging down upon (lit. he charges) the Asiatics.[1] In the *anom.* class [hieroglyphs] is used to qualify the object of *gmi* 'find'.[2]

[hieroglyphs] *mw m itrw swri·t(w)·f, mr·k* the water in the river is drunk if (*or* when) thou willest.[3] Similarly with other *3ae inf.* verbs;[4] the *anom.* 'come' has [hieroglyph] *iw* in this type of sentence.[5]

Clearly the statement in the main clause is here qualified by subsequent reference to a particular case which narrows its scope; such a particular case could scarcely be expressed by an imperfective *śdm·f* with its generalizing force.

When, on the other hand, the adverb clause *precedes*, the imperfective *śdm·f* is of not uncommon occurrence, probably because the temporal qualification, circumstance, or condition is first presented in a *general* way, the main clause then following to express the consequence resulting therefrom. Examples with *hdd·k* and *prr·tn* were quoted in § 444, 1, and the force of the imperfective was there apparent, since 'when' and 'whenever' were seen to be equally possible translations. There is, however, no reason why the perfective *śdm·f* should not have been employed, and in the case of *mrr·k* 'if (*or* as) thou wishest' (§ 444, 2) we noted that the perfective *śdm·f* occurs as a possible alternative.

Ex. [hieroglyphs] *mr·tn ʿnh, msd·tn hpt* if (*or* as) ye love life and hate death.[6]

Note the *4ae inf.* verb *msd·tn* here; 'come' has [hieroglyph] *ii* in a clause of *time.*[7]

To turn now to the *2ae gem.* class, *m33* 'see' appears usually to show the gemination; see the first example in this section, and others in § 444, 1. Our examples are clauses of *time* following the main clause. But in one instance of this kind *m3·f* is found as a variant of *m33·f.*[8]

With *wnn* 'be', 'exist', so far as our evidence goes, the perfective *śdm·f* is used, whether the adverb clause precedes or follows the main clause.

[1] *Sin.* B 52-3.
[2] *Eb.* 40, 1.
[3] *Sin.* B 233-4. Sim. *Urk.* iv. 890, 10-11.
[4] *Urk.* iv. 123, 4 = 511, 2 (*ir·tn*); *Sin.* R 84 (*h3·f*).
[5] *Adm.* 3, 12.
[6] Cairo 20003, *a* 2. Sim. *ib.* 20043, *h* 2.
[7] *Siut* 3, 10, qu. § 212.
[8] *Sin.* B 60, contrasted with *ib.* 59.

Exx. [hieroglyphs] *inn·tw m ʿḳ, wn ꜣhw* one has recourse to an intimate when there is trouble.[1] Note the English present tense.

[hieroglyphs] *ir·t hrw nfr, wn·ṯ tp tꜣ* mayst thou make holiday, whilst thou art upon earth.[2] English present.

[hieroglyphs] *wn·i m tꜣ pn n ʿnḫw, nn iw n nṯr r·i* when I was in this land of the living, there was no sin toward god (laid) to my charge, lit. against me.[3] English past tense.

Reviewing the evidence, it would appear that the presence or absence of the gemination has but little to do with the fact of use in a virtual adverb clause, but depends, partly on the meaning of the particular verb in question, and partly on the speaker's desire, or lack of desire, to emphasize repetition or continuity. Whichever form of *śdm·f* is employed, the time is always *relative present*; if relative past time has to be expressed, use is made of the *śdm·n·f* form, see §§ 212; 414, 2.

In 'whether ...... or whether' clauses (§ 217) preference is naturally given to the perfective *śdm·f*, one action being here contrasted with another as an alternative condition. Our examples comprise *2ae gem.* [hieroglyphs] *mꜣ·sn*;[4] *3ae inf.* [hieroglyphs] *hꜣ·f*.[5]

2. Virtual clauses of *asseveration*. To the perfective forms [hieroglyphs] *mry* and [hieroglyphs] *ḥs* quoted in § 218 may be added [hieroglyphs] *wn·i*.[6] If the formulae beginning with [hieroglyphs] *mr·ṯn* (§ 454, 1) are translated '*as* ye love', '*as truly as* ye love', rather than as clauses of condition, we shall also have to include under this head the imperfective variant [hieroglyphs] *mrr·ṯn* (§ 444, 2).

3. Virtual clauses of *purpose* (§ 219). Perfective forms are always used, as in the closely related wishes and exhortations of § 450, 4, and as in the *śdm·f* form which serves as continuation of the imperative (§ 337).

Exx. [hieroglyphs] *iw psg·n Sp pn smꜣ pn n 'Itm ḳb·f* this Sep has spat upon this forehead of Atum in order that it may be cool.[7]

Would that I had my son [hieroglyphs] *ḫꜥy·i m ꜥbꜣ·i, swꜥb·f wi, int·f n·i iꜣ m tꜣ wꜥb* that I might arise with my sceptre, that he might purify me, that he might bring me praise from the pure land.[8]

Forms used: *2ae gem.* [hieroglyphs] *ḳb·f*, see above; [hieroglyphs] *mꜣ·k*;[9] [hieroglyphs] *wn·i*;[10] *3ae inf.* [hieroglyphs] *sb·f*;[11] [hieroglyphs] *ir·f*,[12] exceptionally [hieroglyphs] *iry·sn*;[13] *anom.* [hieroglyphs] *di·f*;[14] [hieroglyphs] *int·f*, see above, rarely written [hieroglyphs].[15]

4. Adverb clauses *after prepositions* (§§ 154–7; 162–81; 222). To sum up what has been said previously, four active forms of the type of the suffix conjugation are used after prepositions: the *śdm·n·f* form (§ 156) has always *relative past* meaning, as is true also of the *śdmt·f* form (§§ 407–9); the geminating or

1 *Pt.* 349. Sim. in past context, *Sin.* R 34, qu. § 107, 1.
2 *Urk.* iv. 1163.
3 *Urk.* iv. 123 = 511, 4.
4 *Sh. S.* 28–9, qu. § 217.
5 LAC. *TR.* 2, 3–6.
6 *Urk.* iv. 366, 11.
7 LAC. *TR.* 37, 10.
8 LAC. *TR.* 47, 26–7.
9 *Leb.* 59.
10 *Urk.* iv. 239, 17, qu. § 118, 2; 1024, 12.
11 *Westc.* 7, 22.
12 LAC. *TR.* 14, 7; *Urk.* iv. 807, 6.
13 *Urk.* iv. 485, 1.
14 *Urk.* iv. 807, 5.
15 *Westc.* 8, 3.

imperfective *śḏm·f* appears to differ in no way from the perfective *śḏm·f* as regards time-position, but serves to stress some notions of repetition or continuity which need to be brought to expression (§ 444, 3).

The *time-position* of the perfective (and imperfective) *śḏm·f* after prepositions depends largely on the nature of those prepositions; indeed we had best say, negatively, that the *śḏm·f* form has no specific implications of time-position at all. The illustrative examples quoted in § 155 were mainly from immutable verbs; we quote here a few from mutable verbs.

After *m* 'as' or 'if' the time is *relatively present.*

Ex. *m mr·ṯn nṯrw·ṯn nỉwtyw* as (truly as) ye love your city gods.[1]

After *r* 'until', 'so that' and *n-mrwt* 'in order that'[2] *relative future* time is indicated.

Ex. To be masticated and washed down with beer *r pr ntt nbt m ḫt·f* until all that is in his belly goes forth.[3]

After *r-sꜣ* 'after'[4] and *ḏr* 'since' the time is perforce *relatively past*; so too with *m-ḫt*, when this has the meaning 'after'.[5]

Ex. *ḥsy n nsw ḏr pr·f m ḫt* praised of the king since he came forth from the womb.[6]

To turn now to the *other aspects* which doubtless determined the choice between imperfective and perfective *śḏm·f*. That the imperfective *śḏm·f* implies notions of repetition or continuity absent from the perfective *śḏm·f* seems to be illustrated by the use of the former in similes after *mỉ* 'as when' (§ 444, 3); it is significant too that the imperfective *śḏm·f* is not found after *ḏr* 'since', which is apt to recall a single fact of by-gone times (see above). It appears significant, moreover, that in the dedicatory formula with *m* the non-geminating *śḏm·f* is employed, for here the reference is to a single act.

Ex. A *ḥotp-di-nesu* formula ..... for the steward Djaf ..., *m ỉr n·f sꜣ·f mry·f Mrw* being what (lit. 'as', *m* of predication) his beloved son Meru made for him.[7]

We have seen (§ 444, 2) that *m mrr·ṯn* varies with *m mr·ṯn* in the formula 'as truly as ye love ....' This variation is comprehensible if the imperfective merely stresses the prolonged and general character of the condition, this stress being quite optional and unnecessary to the sense. Similarly, the variation of *wnn·f* and *wn·f* after prepositions (e. g. in the phrase *n-mrwt wnn*[8] or *wn*[9] *rn·f mn* 'in order that his name may be enduring') seems attributable to a like reason; see further above §§ 157, 1–3; 326, end.

5. *If*-clauses with *ỉr* (§ 150). The *2ae gem.* use the imperfective *śḏm·f* (above, § 444, 4),[9a] but all other mutable verbs consistently employ the perfective.

[1] Cairo 20119, *c* 4. Sim. *ib.* 20606, *b* 3; Brit. Mus. 805.

[2] Ex. *Siut* I, 271 (*ỉr·k*), qu. § 155.

[3] *Eb.* 8, 16. Sim. with *r* 'so that', *wn·f*, *PSBA.* 18, 203, 12; *Urk.* iv. 1089, 6.

[4] *Siut* I, 298 (*ỉr·f*), qu. § 389, 2.

[5] *Eb.* 87, 9 (*ỉꜥ·s*); 97, 3 (*bš·s*); *Siut* I, 308 (*pr·f*), qu. § 178, 4.

[6] Louvre C 202. Sim. *Kuban* 14 (*ḫꜥ·k*); *Urk.* v. 42, 12 (*ḥꜣ·k*).

[7] Cairo 20027, *b* 3–4. More exx. § 162, 11. But also *m ỉr* introducing dedicatory formula as label on monuments, exx. Berl. *ÄI.* II, 100; Brit. Mus. 830; *Cat. d. Mon.* I, 24, no. 165.

[8] *Meir* iii. 11.

[9] *Urk.* iv. 366, 15.

[9a] The clauses with *ỉr wn* are not exceptions, see Add. to p. 358, n. 11.

Exx. *ir h3·k r š n m3ʿt* if thou goest down to the sea of Truth.[1]

ir swt di·t(w) it·f pn n·f but if this his father be given to him.[2]

Forms from the various verb-classes: *3ae inf.* *gm·k*;[3] *ḥs·k*;[4] *ir·k*,[5] irregularly also written;[6] but also *iry·f*;[6a] *4ae inf.* *ḥms·k*;[7] *anom.* *di·f*;[8] *in·k*;[9] *iw*,[10] but also *iwt*.[11]

§ 455. **The negative construction *n śḏm·f*.**[12]—It has been seen that the imperfective *śḏm·f* is hardly ever used after the negation *n* (§ 445); the perfective *śḏm·f* is, on the contrary, very frequently so used. Typical forms from the mutable verbs are: *2ae gem.* *m3·i*,[13] but also *m3n*;[14] *3ae inf.* *gm·f*;[15] *ir*;[16] *4ae inf.* *mdw*;[17] *anom.* 'give' shows *r*, as *rdi*;[18] 'come' has *iw*, rarely *i*, and very rarely *iw* (see below § 456); 'bring' has *in*.[19] The abnormal forms *h3w*,[20] *h3y·k*,[21] *iy*,[22] are possibly restricted to present or future reference, but the material is too scanty to allow a safe inference.

As regards meaning, *n śḏm·f* performs no function which cannot also be illustrated in the affirmative *śḏm·f*. Nevertheless, it is clear that there has been unequal development; whereas affirmative *śḏm·f* has been almost entirely superseded in reference to past events by *śḏm·n·f* (above § 450, 1), the negative *n śḏm·f* is the common and normal negation of *śḏm·n·f* in past narrative; see above § 105, 1.

We proceed to illustrate the various uses of *n śḏm·f* in detail. 1. In reference to *past* events. In this very frequent use *n śḏm·f* often stands in conspicuous parallelism to a series of affirmative *śḏm·n·f* forms.

Exx. I nourished (*iw sʿnḫ·n·(i)*) Imiotru . . . . . . *n iṯ·(i) s3t s* I did not take away (any) man's daughter.[23] English past tense.

n rdi·i s3·i n ʿ3m I did not turn my back to (any) Asiatic.[24] English past tense.

n m3·i mity srw pn I have never (lit. not) seen the like of this goose.[25] English present perfect tense.

n sḫs·t(w) m-s3·i no one had run after me.[26] English past perfect.

Similarly, *n śḏm·f* after the particles *mk* (§§ 234; 414, 1) and *ḥ3* (§ 238) is the negation of *śḏm·n·f* after the same particles.

Exx. *mk n wḏ·tw irt mnt iry* behold, one has never (lit. not) commanded to do the like thereof.[27]

ist ḥ3 n ir mšʿ n ḥm·f rdit ib·sn r ḥ3ḳ lo, would that the army of His Majesty had not given over (lit. made the giving) their hearts to plunder.[28]

1 *Peas.* B 1, 54.
2 LAC. *TR.* 2, 37.
3 *P. Kah.* 6, 14; *Eb.* 109, 16.
4 *Pt.* 175.
5 *Pt.* 415. 499.
6 *Pt.* 415 (L 2).
6a *Arm.* 103, 5, of past actions.
7 *Pr.* 1, 3. 8.
8 *Eb.* 97, 15.
9 *Peas.* B 1, 252.
10 *Pt.* 346; *Urk.* iv. 1070, 1.
11 *P. Kah.* 6, 27.
12 See GUNN, *Stud.* ch. xi.
13 *Meir* iii. 23.
14 *Hamm.* 191, 6.
15 *Rifeh* 1, 16.
16 Cairo 20537, *b* 6; for 1st pers. sing. *ir·i*, not *iry·i*, see § 456.
17 *Leb.* 5.
18 *P. Kah.* 28, 30; *Sebekkhu* 4.
19 *Pt.* 231. 348.
20 LAC. *TR.* 23, 12.
21 LAC. *TR.* 85, 129. Sim. *h3y·i*, *ib.* 23, 11.
22 *Pt.* 181. 261.
23 Cairo 20001, *b* 2–4. Sim. *ib.* *b* 8, qu. § 217; *Hamm.* 113, 14; *Sin.* R 30–1; *Peas.* B 1, 50; *Urk.* iv. 118–20; 835, 10; 1031, 7–14.
24 *Sebekkhu* 4.
25 *Meir* iii. 23. Sim. Cairo 20537, *b* 6; BUDGE, pp. 250–1. With adjective-verbs see § 144, 1.
26 *Sin.* B 226–7. Sim. *ib.* 40–1; 184.
27 *Westc.* 8, 17.
28 *Urk.* iv. 658.

We have seen (§§ 320; 414, 4) that Egyptian conceived 'knowing' as 'having learnt'; hence *n rḫ·f* may mean 'he does not know' just as well as 'he did not know'.

Ex. *n rḫ·i in wi r ḫꜣst tn* I do not know who (lit. him who) brought me to this country.[1]

For cases where *iw* is used before *n sḏm·f* see § 468, 1. 2.

2. In reference to *present* occurrences. The commonest way of negating present occurrences is by means of *n sḏm·n·f*, see above §§ 105, 3; 418, 1. Nevertheless cases occur where *n sḏm·f* refers to present events, an employment not rare, as we have seen (§ 450, 2), with affirmative *sḏm·f*.

Exx. *n mdw bꜣ·i ḥnˁ·i* my soul does not speak with me.[2]

n sḫꜣ·t(w) sf, n ir·t(w) n ir m tꜣ ꜣt yesterday is not remembered, the helper is not helped (lit. one does not do to the doer) at this moment.[3]

This use is specially common with adjective-verbs (§ 144, 1), where we are tempted to explain it along the same lines as *n rḫ·i* 'I do not know' considered above under 1.

Ex. *n mwt·i, n šwꜣ·i* I am not dead, I am not poor. Possibly the literal rendering is: I have not died, I have not become poor.[4]

3. In reference to *future* occurrences. In this case the normal negation is *nn sḏm·f* (§§ 105, 2; 457), and the very exceptional examples where *n sḏm·f* refers to future events or aspirations are difficult to explain.

Ex. *n sk rn·f ḏt* his name shall not perish eternally.[5]

One example is found with *n sp*: *n sp mꜣ·k* 'never shalt thou see'.[6] This has been quoted more fully in § 188, 1, and is discussed below in § 456.

4. Rare examples are found where *n sḏm·f* is apparently best rendered 'he cannot hear', a meaning of which *n sḏm·n·f* is the more usual equivalent. It is uncertain whether this meaning was reached along the lines of 1 above ('he has not, *or* never, heard') or whether it came about in some other way; it is also possible that the instances are miswritings or abbreviations of *n sḏm·n·f*.

Ex. *n in·tw ḏrw ḥmt* the limit of art cannot be attained.[7]

5. Lastly, it must be pointed out that *n sḏm·f* may occur in subordinate clauses of various kinds, in so far as the negative verb *tm* is not necessary there. Examples of its use in the virtual relative clause are quoted in § 196, 2, and of its use after *nty* in § 201.

OBS. Towards the end of Dyn. XVIII a confusion between *n* and *nn* begins to manifest itself, and *nn sḏm·f* is sometimes found with the meaning of *n sḏm·f*.[8]

[1] *Sin.* B 42. Sim. *Sh. S.* 148; *Westc.* 9, 3; *Urk.* iv. 365, 11.

[2] *Leb.* 5. Sim. *ib.* 76; *Sin.* B 259; *Sh. S.* 73.

[3] *Leb.* 115–6. Sim. *Adm.* 1, 2; 9, 6.

[4] LAC. *TR.* 1, 55. Sim. *Peas.* B 2, 103, qu. § 144, 1; *Eb.* 47, 18, qu. § 201; 65, 14.

[5] *Urk.* iv. 415. Sim. *ib.* 564, 17; 1032, 14; *Peas.* B 1, 309–10, if not for *sin·n·tw*, B 2, 75.

[6] *Sh. S.* 153–4.

[7] *Pt.* 55, if not for *in·n·tw*. Sim. *P. Pet.* 1116 A, 93, if not for *ḳn·n·tw·f*.

[8] Exx. *Urk.* iv. 511, 8 as contrasted with *ib.* 484, 9; also *ib.* 1195, 2 as contrasted with Lyons 88, 6.

§ 456. The negative construction *n sp śḏm·f*, etc.—1. Formerly the phrase *n sp śḏm·f* for 'he never heard' or 'he has never heard' was explained as consisting of *n śḏm·f* 'he did not hear' or 'he has not heard' (§ 455, 1) with insertion of the adverbially used noun *sp* 'a time', 'once'. It has been observed, however,[1] that the perfective *śḏm·f* form employed after *n sp* sometimes shows a difference from that employed in the simple *n śḏm·f* construction. The best attested case is in the expression *n sp iwt ḫt im·(i)* 'never was there any shortcoming (lit. did anything come) in me'.[2] In the synonymous expression *n iw ḫt im*, lit. 'nothing came therein',[3] *sp* is absent and *iw* is usually substituted for *iwt*—very rare variants are *i*[4] and *iw*.[5]

A similar phenomenon has been observed in connection with the verb *iri* 'do', 'make'. In the first person singular *n ir·i*[6] is regular without *sp*, as against *n sp iry·i*[7] 'I never made', when *sp* is used.

Now it is interesting to note that both *iwt* and *iry·i* are the forms found after *rdi* 'cause' (§ 452, 1), i.e. with prospective meaning. This suggests that *n sp śḏm·f* should be rendered literally 'it did not occur that he should hear', *sp* being taken as the *śḏm·f* form of a verb 'to occur' related to the noun *sp* 'time', 'occurrence'. This hypothesis is the more likely since no good analogy can be quoted for the enclitic insertion of a noun after *n* which was formerly postulated.

The same explanation would apply to *n sp* in its exceedingly rare future sense (§ 455, 3), as also to the equally rare *nn sp* 'never will' (§ 457).

The forms found after *n sp*, *nn sp* are: *2ae gem.* *mꜣ·k*;[8] *wn·i*;[9] *3ae inf.* *iry·i*,[10] passive *ir·tw*;[11] *anom.* *di·(i)* (Old Kingdom);[12] *iwt*;[13] *in·t(w)*, passive.[14]

2. After *nfr pw* 'there is (are) not' (§ 351, 2) the perfective *śḏm·f* is sometimes used. The forms in question are: *3ae inf.* *ir·i*;[15] *fꜣ·tw*;[16] *anom.* *in·t(w)*, impersonal.[17] An isolated imperfective form *inn·t(w)* is uncertain.[18]

§ 457. The negative construction *nn śḏm·f*.[19]—This construction is exclusively limited to events happening in the *future*.

Exx. *nn ms·s r nḥḥ* she will never give birth.[20]

nn di·t(w)·k m inm n sr thou shalt not be placed in the skin of a sheep.[21]

Sometimes *nn śḏm·f* serves to convey the will of the speaker.

Exx. *nn sḫꜣ·i n·k sꜣt ktt int·n·i m sšꜣ* I will not mention to thee a little daughter whom I had obtained by prayer.[22]

nn snḏ·f he shall not fear.[23]

[1] GUNN, *Stud.* p. 95, n. 1.
[2] Cairo 20005, *a* 7; Brit. Mus. 614, 6. 11.
[3] Cairo 20001, *b* 8. Sim. *ib.* 20513, *b* 3; *Urk.* iv. 151, 2; 484, 8.
[4] Cairo 20506, *b* 6.
[5] Cairo 20543, *a* 12, collated.
[6] Brit. Mus. 1372 (suffix omitted), qu. § 105, 1; *Urk.* iv. 505, 1; 1078, 15; 1180, 11; BUDGE, p. 249, 16; 250, 4. 11.
[7] Cairo 20729, *a* 3, qu. § 106. Sim. *Herdsm.* 6, qu. § 457.
[8] *Sh. S.* 153–4.
[9] BUDGE, p. 146, 11.
[10] See above n. 7.
[11] *Hamm.* 114, 15–6; *Urk.* iv. 312, 13; 766, 3; 843, 12.
[12] *Urk.* i. 137, 4.
[13] See n. 2 above. *Sḏm·f* in *Sin.* R 21 is a *crux*; there *n sp* means, not 'never', but 'not a moment'.
[14] *Urk.* iv. 329, 12.
[15] *ÄZ.* 59, autogr. p. 1.
[16] *P. Boul.* xviii. 18, qu. § 351, 2.
[17] *ÄZ.* 59, autogr. pp. 1. 3.
[18] *ÄZ.* 59, autogr. p. 1.
[19] See GUNN, *Stud.* ch. 13.
[20] *P. Kah.* 6, 17. 24. Sim. *Leb.* 50–1; *Peas.* B 1, 56–60; LAC. *TR.* 24, 6; *Siut* 1, 225; *Kopt.* 8, 8; *P. Pet.* 1116 B, 41. 42; *Urk.* iv. 402, 1–2.
[21] *Sin.* B 197–8.
[22] *Sh. S.* 128–9. Sim. *M. u. K.* 2, 3.
[23] *Sin.* B 279.

In these two examples it is hardly possible to translate the verbs as simple futures ('I shall not ....', 'he will not ....'); but often it remains doubtful whether one should render with 'will' or with 'shall'.

Note an example with *nn sp*, lit. 'it shall not occur that .....' (§ 456).

nn sp ỉry·ỉ ḏdt·n·s never will I do what she said.[1]

In one solitary instance *nn śḏm·f* occurs in the course of a narrative of past events and, unless a mere error for *n śḏm·f*, may represent a past future tense.

nn dỉ·ỉ wḥ·f I was not going to let him escape.[2]

The forms from the mutable verbs employed in the construction *nn śḏm·f* are: *2ae gem.* *mꜣ·k*,[3] var. *mꜣn·k*;[4] *3ae inf.* *hꜣ·ỉ*;[5] *mꜣ·s*;[6] *4ae inf.* *ḥms·f*;[7] *anom.* *dỉ·ỉ*;[8] *ỉwt.*[9] Note that in the case of the *anom.* verbs the forms differ from those of *n śḏm·f* and resemble those found after *rdỉ*, *dỉ* 'cause' (above § 452, 1). Hence it seems not impossible that the *śḏm·f* of *nn śḏm·f* is really a noun clause, and subject of the negative word *nn*; the meaning would then be 'it does not exist that he will hear'. Some support for this view may be found in the occurrence of *nn wn m(w)t·k* as an emphatic future 'thou shalt never die' (§ 188, 2); but an example of *śḏm·f* after *n wnt* (§ 188, 2) is probably not future in meaning.

As pointed out in § 108, *nn wn* 'there does not exist', 'there is (was) not' is really only an apparent exception to the rule that *nn śḏm·f* has future meaning, *nn wn* being here a substitute for **nn ỉw wn*.

OBS. See § 455, OBS. for the late writings with *nn śḏm·f* in place of *n śḏm·f*.

§ 458. The perfective *śḏm·f*; conclusion.—Despite the lengthy treatment here accorded to the perfective *śḏm·f* form, the topic is far from exhausted and the results attained are in many respects ambiguous and insecure. Nevertheless, it seems evident from the regularity with which the gemination is avoided in some cases and chosen in others that the distinction between the non-geminating and the geminating *śḏm·f* was of far greater importance than current theory admits; and nothing seems to stand in the way of a derivation of the non-geminating *śḏm·f* from a non-geminating or perfective participle (§ 411, 1). The student must be cautioned, however, against attaching an exaggerated value to the evidence of our texts; it is unfortunately certain that the Egyptians were very careless copyists, and only in original documents written by well-trained scribes can we expect to find a consistently trustworthy distinction between geminating and non-geminating forms. Of the four ways in which the funerary stelae are apt to write 'as truly as (*or* if) ye love' (, , , , § 444, 2) possibly not all are really correct; but our evidence is too scanty to enable us to pick and choose among these variants. In deciding

[1] *Herdsm.* 6.
[2] *T. Carn.* 13.
[3] *Peas.* B 1, 60.
[4] *Peas.* R 103.
[5] *Eb.* 1, 17.
[6] *P. Kah.* 6, 17. 24.
[7] *Kopt.* 8, 8.
[8] *M. u. K.* 2, 3.
[9] *Peas.* B 1, 57.

whether a text should be emended or not we must steer a middle course. When we find *dỉ·k wnn·ỉ* 'thou causest that I be'[1] in a MS. of the Book of the Dead judged on other grounds to be incorrect we may replace it by *dỉ·k wn·ỉ* with some assurance. Similarly we may suspect *wḏ·n ḥm·f prr·(ỉ)* quoted in § 442, 1, but there emendation would be quite illegitimate in view of the O. K. evidence cited p. 355, nn. 6a. 6b.

§ 459. Appendix: the *śḏm·f* forms from *ỉỉ, ỉw* 'come'.[2]—Alone among the mutable verbs, the verb meaning 'come' fails to distinguish clearly-marked geminating and non-geminating *śḏm·f* forms. The *-ỉ* stem writes *ỉỉ*,[3] *ỉỉ*,[4] *ỉy*,[5] and as these forms are found after *n*,[6] they are probably perfective (§ 455), at least in that case. Examples from the *-w* stem are, however, far more frequent, and show two distinct forms, (*a*) *ỉw*, rarely written [7] and (*b*) *ỉwt*. That *ỉw* is sometimes imperfective seems certain, since it occurs in parallelism with many geminating *śḏm·f* forms in a passage prescribing *future custom* (§ 440, 3).

Ex. *ỉw n·f śnw nb m pr-nsw* there shall come to him (the Vizier) all disputes from the palace.[8]

So too *ỉw* is found in *similes* after *mỉ* (§ 444, 3).

Ex. *mỉ ỉw sꜣw, ḏr·f ḥḳr* as when satiety comes and ends hunger.[9]

Lastly, the imperfective relative form provides an analogy, often being written merely; see above § 387, 1.

On the other hand, *n ỉw* 'not came . . . .' (§ 455) provides strong evidence that *ỉw* may occasionally be perfective. In a number of uses and vary with one another, sometimes exciting the suspicion that one of the two is a mistake for the other; so, for example, after *kꜣ* (§ 450, 5, *d*), as a clause of circumstance in the phrase *šm·f ỉw·f* 'he comes and goes'[10] (§ 213), after various prepositions[11] (§ 454, 4), and after *ỉr* 'if' (§ 454, 5). But the consistency with which *ỉwt·f* occurs after *dỉ* 'cause' (§ 452, 1), and *ỉw·f* occurs in the colophon *ỉw·f pw* (§ 189, 1) shows that a real difference existed between the two, although their domains overlap in certain places.

Here only one more problem will be considered, namely the narrative use of.

Exx. *ỉwt nḫt n ⟨R⟩tnw* there came a strong man of Retjnu.[12]

ỉwt·f r ḫꜣst tn he came to this desert.[13]

There is a possibility that *ỉwt* here may be the *śḏm·f* form in accordance with § 450, 1, but it is perhaps more probably the infinitive (§ 306, 2); a third possibility is the *śḏmt·f* form (§ 406).

[1] BUDGE, p. 4, 15.

[2] See SETHE, *Verbum*, ii. §§ 315–9.

[3] Cairo 20506, *b* 6.

[4] LAC. *TR*. 6, 1.

[5] *Sin*. R 15, qu. p. 55, n. 3; *P. Kah*. 32, 12.

[6] *Pt*. 181. 261.

[7] Louvre C 14, 9; Cairo 20543, *a* 12, see p. 377, n. 5.

[8] *Urk*. iv. 1114, 6.

[9] *Peas*. B 1, 242. Sim. *Leb*. 137.

[10] So *Eb*. 40, 1, qu. § 213; 107, 3; 109, 4; *ỉwt·s*, *ib*. 106, 5.

[11] *R* 'until': *ỉw·f*, Louvre C 14, 9; *Hearst* 9, 12; *ỉwt·f* *PSBA*. 18, 202, 9; *Sin*. B 310; *Westc*. 11, 16. *M-ḫt* 'after': *ỉw·f*, *Westc*. 11, 26; *Urk*. iv. 220, 2; *ỉwt·f*, *Hamm*. 114, 15. With *ỉwt·f* the possibility that this is the *śḏmt·f* form (§ 407) has always to be considered.

[12] *Sin*. B 109. Sim. Louvre C 12, 3.

[13] *Hamm*. 17, 15. Sim. *Sinai* 90, 5.

VOCABULARY

ỉp calculate, reckon; caus. *sỉp* pass in review, examine.

fꜣỉ carry, lift.

mkḥꜣ be neglectful.

ḥḏỉ damage, destroy.

stỉ pierce, transfix (with look).

šꜣ appoint, command.

gmḥ look at.

tm be complete, perfect.

thỉ violate, transgress.

var. *ỉt-nṯr* father of the god, god's father, name of a class of elder priests.

wꜥrt leg.

var. *wgg* misery, want.

prw a coming forth; *prw n r* utterance.

mdw staff.

nḏsw poverty.

ḥḏt the white crown of Upper Egypt.

sbꜣyt teaching, instruction.

spꜣt province, nome (*νομός* was the name given by the Greeks to the provinces of Egypt).

sṯsw supports.

ḳmꜣ nature, form.

Sbk the crocodile-god Sobk (Gk. Σοῦχος).

ḏr-ꜥ originally, formerly.

EXERCISE XXXI

(*a*) *Reading lesson: hymn to the white crown of Upper Egypt:*[1]

dwꜣ ḥḏt.

ỉnḏ (§ 272) *ḥr·t, ỉrt twy nt Ḥr,*[2]

ḥḏt ꜥꜣt,

ḥꜥꜥt (§ 384) *psḏt m nfrw·s,*

wbn·s m ꜣḫt ỉꜣbtt.

dwꜣ tn ỉmyw sṯsw Šw,[3]

ḥꜣꜣw (§ 357) *m ꜣḫt ỉmntt.*

[1] Erm. *Hymn.* 1,1—2,1.

[2] For the identification of the crown with the eye of Horus see *Unt.* v. 128.

[3] Shu was the god of the 'void' or atmosphere, and the 'supports of Shu' are the supports with which that god kept heaven apart from earth. By 'those who are within the supports of Shu' the constellations are meant.

sḫꜥ tn ỉmyw dwꜣt.
dỉ·t ỉṯ Sbk Šdty Ḥr ḥry-ỉb Šdt tꜣwy ỉm·t,
sḫm·f ỉm·sn.
dỉ·t ỉwt n·f nṯrw m ksw (§ 77, 1)
Sbk Šdty, Ḥr ḥry-ỉb Šdt.
twt (§ 64, Obs.) *nbt ḫꜥw.*

[1] The original has *t* before the papyrus-roll; the parallelism suggests this emendation. But one might render without emending 'thou being caused to shine for those, etc.', *sḫꜥt* being understood as *sḫꜥ·t(ỉ)*, § 314.
[2] These two oblique strokes (§ 24) here represent two shrines surmounted by bucrania, see *Rec.* 38, 186.
[3] Doubtless named here as god of the capital or royal residence at the close of the Twelfth Dynasty; to that period this hymn must belong. Crocodilopolis, the Greek Arsinoe, is the modern Medînet el-Fayyûm.
[4] MS. inserts another *w* wrongly before *n·f*; *n* is lost in the original and here restored.

'Praise to the White Crown. Hail to thee, thou (lit. that) eye of Horus, the great white one, at whose beauty the Ennead rejoice, when she rises in the eastern horizon. Those who are within the supports of Shu praise thee, (they) who go down in the western horizon. Those who are within the netherworld cause thee to shine forth. Grant thou that Sobk the Crocodilopolite, the Horus who is in the midst of Crocodilopolis, may seize the two lands through thee, that he may have control over them. Grant thou that the gods may come to him doing (lit. in) obeisance, (even) Sobk the Crocodilopolite, the Horus who is in the midst of Crocodilopolis. Thou art the mistress of glorious appearances.'

(*b*) *Translate*:

(1)

(2)

(3)

[1] *Mdw n ỉꜣw* 'staff of old age', an epithet applied to a son who carries on the labours of his aged father. [2] § 393.

(4) (5)

[1] *Wḏ3*, see § 56.

(*c*) *Write in hieroglyphs*:

(1) I will not let thee kiss this child. (2) Would that I might see thy face, then should I know what is in thy heart. (3) Let ten (loaves of) bread and two jugs of beer be given to this thy servant. (4) Never have I seen the like since I was born. (5) I did not let my nome hunger, I gave it corn of Upper Egypt and emmer, I did not let want occur therein until great Niles came. (6) Give to him a pleasant breeze, that he may be among all those who are praised in the land of the living. (7) His Majesty caused the scribe to bring it to him at once.

LESSON XXXII

COMPOUND NARRATIVE VERB-FORMS

§ 460. In the Old Kingdom are seen the beginnings of a process that ended in the complete disappearance of the suffix conjugation, save for some fossilized relics of the *śḏm·f* form (§ 438), and in its replacement by a set of tenses based upon the pseudo-verbal construction (Lesson XXIII). This final result was attained only in Coptic, where the tenses resemble those of French or English in the precision with which they mark distinctions of time. The first step in the process appears to have been the employment of *ỉw* to introduce the pseudo-verbal construction and to produce compound verb-forms, like *ỉw śḏm·n·f* (§ 68), involving the suffix conjugation. Compounds with various parts of *wnn* rapidly followed as a consequence of this development. In Dyn. XI or earlier *ˁḥˁ* 'stand up', 'arise' comes into favour as an auxiliary verb. Various less important auxiliaries of which examples occur in Middle Kingdom texts are passed over in this preliminary survey. In the Hyksos period or thereabouts the pronominal compound *tw·ỉ* began to be used in the vernacular as the subject of adverbial (§ 124) or pseudo-verbal predicates (§ 330), and evidence of its popularity emerges already here and there in the inscriptions of Dyn. XVIII. During the New Kingdom a few more compound verb-forms are invented, but the process becomes mainly one of elimination and specialization; compound verb-forms containing the *śḏm·f* or *śḏm·n·f* forms give place to those containing the old perfective or preposition + infinitive, and each of the survivors obtains its own exclusive range of temporal meaning.

When it is recalled that Middle Egyptian possesses no less than seven forms belonging to the narrative suffix conjugation (§ 410) and that statements could be made, not only by means of these, but also by means of various nominal or nominally used parts of the verb, the wealth of narrative constructions used in main clauses and produced by the development of new compound verb-forms must appear quite extraordinary. Past narration, to take but one example, could be managed in a great variety of different ways, of which the following incomplete enumeration exhibits the main types, though it is not maintained that in the case of the particular verb here chosen every type could be substantiated by documentary evidence.

'His Majesty went forth'

§ 450, 1.	§ 392.
§ 450, 1.	§ 373, 1.
§ 414, 1.	§ 464.
§ 429, 1.	§ 323.
§ 431, 3.	§ 470.
§ 322.	§ 471, 2.
§ 322.	§ 478.
§ 306, 2.	§ 479.
§ 306, 2 and § 406.	§ 482, 2.

These different modes of expression, to which could be added others involving such particles as *ỉsṯ*, *ṯỉ*, *grt*, vary greatly in frequency of occurrence. Each must have possessed its own peculiar rhetorical flavour, its greater or less degree of vivacity, formality, or impressiveness. Some of these shades of meaning may still be indicated by the grammarian, others can only be felt or not even that. From the constructive point of view there was much overlapping; to narrate the same fact one writer might choose the form *prt pw ỉr·n·f*, another *prt ỉn ḥm·f*, a third *ỉw pr·n·f* and a fourth *ʿḥʿ·n pr·n·f*, and our texts reveal the fact that different writers had different preferences.[1] It will be noticed that we view *pr ḥm·f* and *ḥm·f pr·f* as roughly equivalent forms; the reason is that in this and other cases of anticipatory emphasis (§ 148, 1) often no stress on the subject can be detected, and the motive seems to have been mere desire for variety or liveliness. It is doubtful whether in all the pseudo-verbal compounds above exemplified verbs of motion like *prỉ* could employ both the old perfective and *ḥr* (or *m*) + infinitive. If so, the list would have to be augmented accordingly.

[1] E.g., *Sh. S.* uses *ʿḥʿ·n* 26 times, against 4 in *Sin.* B and 5 in *Peas.*

Amid the plethora of verb-forms which Egyptian has thus evolved only a very few seem to have been deliberately created with the intention of marking distinctions of time. Such an intention is, no doubt, apparent in *ỉw·f r śḏm* 'he will hear', and probably the speaker who first prefixed *mk* to *śḏm·n·f* wished to convey the nuance that belongs to the English present perfect. But it appears likely that most of the verb-forms which were developed from time to time aimed at variations of meaning of quite a different kind, and that if in due course they became specialized to past events rather than present, or to future events rather than past, this came about owing to their greater usefulness in the one direction than in the other. We have tried to demonstrate this process in the case of the participles (§ 365), and we have found that the *śḏm·n·f* form had originally no time-restriction at all, but expressed the fortuitous character of an occurrence (§ 411, 2). The like probably holds good of most of the compound verb-forms to be studied below.

A number of narrative compound verb-forms like *ỉw·f ḥr śḏm* (§ 323) have been dealt with already, and the present Lesson must be read in conjunction with Lesson XXIII, where the simpler ramifications of the pseudo-verbal construction were discussed.

THE AUXILIARY *'IW*

§ 461. The origin of *ỉw* is uncertain; some[1] connect it with Hebrew הָוָה or הָיָה 'fall out', 'be', but a more likely view is that it is merely the Egyptian verb *ỉw* 'come' specialized for use as the copula.[2] Be this as it may, *ỉw* as copula exists only in the *śḏm·f* form, and its use is almost entirely restricted to the sentence with adverbial predicate (§ 117). Under the heading of the pseudo-verbal construction we have already dealt with *ỉw·f ḥr śḏm* and *ỉw·f śḏmw* (§ 323); also with *ỉw·f m śḏm* (§ 331) and *ỉw·f r śḏm* (§ 332). In all these cases *ỉw·f* is followed by the equivalent of an adverbial predicate. In the compound verb-forms *ỉw śḏm·f*, *ỉw śḏm·n·f* and the passive *ỉw śḏm·f*, which will now be discussed in turn, the function of *ỉw* is more difficult to determine. A possible view would be that it has become a particle, somewhat like *ḫr* (§ 239). But more probably *ỉw*, as thus employed, should be regarded as an impersonal statement 'it is', i.e. 'the situation is', the following *śḏm·f*, *śḏm·n·f* or passive *śḏm·f* form being a virtual adverb clause (§ 215) serving as predicate of *ỉw*. Compare sentences like *ỉw mỉ sḫr nṯr* quoted in § 123.

OBS. 1. It is hardly possible to regard *śḏm·f* in *ỉw śḏm·f* as a virtual noun clause acting as subject of *ỉw*, for this would yield the meaning 'that he hears is', i.e. exists or comes about; we have no warrant for a use of *ỉw* with existential meaning.

OBS. 2. There are grounds for thinking[3] that, when *ỉw* was followed by a singular suffix-pronoun, the *w* was merely graphic, e.g. was pronounced *ăf*; cf. the occasional use of to represent the prothetic *ỉ* of § 272.[4]

[1] *Wb.* i. 42; *Rec.* 35, 63.

[2] Cf. *Pyr.* 270 *a* with 267 *c*; 2075 *a* with 376 *c*; also passages like 1180 *a* and the varr. 1480 *b*.

[3] *Onom.* 2, p. 237*.

[4] See p. 209, n. 7.

§ 462. The form [hieroglyphs] *ỉw śḏm·f.*—This fairly common compound verb-form is *imperfective*[1] in meaning, i. e. has implications of repetition or continuity. This character it owes rather to the combination with *ỉw* than to the *śḏm·f* form itself, since it is the perfective *śḏm·f* which is here found (see p. 370, Obs.). Forms from the mutable verbs are: *3ae inf.* [hieroglyphs] *pr·ỉ*;[2] [hieroglyphs] *ỉr·sn*;[3] *anom.* [hieroglyphs] *dỉ·tw*;[4] [hieroglyphs] *ỉn·tw*;[5] so too the *2ae gem.* [hieroglyphs] *wn* if, as seems probable, *ỉw wn* 'there is' (§ 107, 2) belongs here. The geminating *3ae inf.* [hieroglyphs] *gmm·tw·s*[6] is an isolated exception.

Passive examples are a good deal commoner than active ones, for a reason that will be mentioned in the next section.

The form *ỉw śḏm·f* is particularly frequent in *generalizations*, where it refers to *vaguely present* or *future* time.

Exx. Eloquence is more hidden than the emerald, [hieroglyphs] *ỉw gm·t(w)·s m-ꜥ ḥmwt ḥr bnwt* (but) it is found with handmaidens at (their) mill-stones.[7]

He who knows this spell goes forth from Field-of-Reeds, [hieroglyphs] *ỉw dỉ·tw n·f šns dsy pr-sn ḥr ḫ3wt nt nṯr ꜥ3* and there are given to him *šns*-bread, beer-jugs and *pr-sn* cakes from the altar of the great god.[8]

Or else a *prevalent* state of affairs is described.

Ex. [hieroglyphs] *ỉw ḥꜥḏ3·tw* men plunder.[9]

Or a person may be *characterized*.

Ex. [hieroglyphs] *ỉw ꜥwn ỉb·k* thy heart is covetous.[10]

The same uses are found also in *past narrative*.

Exx. [hieroglyphs] *ỉw ỉr·ỉ r-ḥry dd tp-rd* I acted (*or* used to act) as a leader who gave instructions.[11] Past habit.

[hieroglyphs] *ỉw grg·t(w) n·ỉ* men used to snare for me.[12] Past custom.

[hieroglyphs] *ỉw ḥms·tw ḥr dmỉ n Ḥwt-wꜥrt* they were besieging the town of Avaris.[13] Prolonged action in the past.

In § 468 examples will be given where *ỉw* appears to be prefixed to the *śḏm·f* form for quite special reasons, and where, accordingly, the compound verb-form *ỉw śḏm·f* is not in question.

§ 463. The form [hieroglyphs] *ỉw·f śḏm·f.*—In this common verb-form the subject, whether nominal or pronominal, is placed after *ỉw* in anticipatory emphasis (§ 148, 1). The effect of this proceeding seems to be very slight, and the meaning and uses of *ỉw·f śḏm·f* are practically identical with those of *ỉw śḏm·f* (§ 462).[14] Here too the perfective *śḏm·f* is employed, except in *2ae gem.* and *caus. 2ae gem.*, exx. *2ae gem.* [hieroglyphs] *nꜥꜥ·s*;[15] [hieroglyphs] *gnn·s*;[16] *3ae inf.* [hieroglyphs] *pr·f*;[17] [hieroglyphs] *ỉr·k*,[18] also exceptionally written [hieroglyphs];[19] *caus. 2ae gem.* [hieroglyphs] *sšrr·f*;[20] *anom.* [hieroglyphs] *dỉ·f*.[21]

[1] In *Pt.* 349 (qu. p. 352, n. 21) *ỉw ỉn·tw* of *Pr.* corresponds to *ỉnn·tw* in L 2.

[2] *ÄZ.* 47, Pl. I (p. 88), 3.

[3] *Eb.* 98, 17.

[4] Budge, p. 209, 12.

[5] *Pt.* 349.

[6] *Pt.* 59 (L 2); *Pr.* has *gm·t(w)·s*, qu. 1st ex. below.

[7] *Pt.* 59. Sim. pass., *ib.* 274, qu. Exerc. XXVII, (*a*); 288; 349; *Peas.* B 1, 291. 308; *Eb.* 47, 19. 21; act., *ib.* 98, 17; *Arm.* 103, 10.

[8] Budge, p. 209, 12. Sim. pass., *ib.* p. 213, 11. 13. 15; 300, 8; act., *ib.* p. 211, 12.

[9] *Leb.* 112.

[10] *Peas.* B 1, 292. Sim. act., *Sh. S.* 73–4; pass., *Peas.* B 1, 236.

[11] *Urk.* iv. 421. Sim. act., *ib.* 489, 2; *ÄZ.* 47, Pl. I (p. 88), 3.

[12] *Sin.* B 89–90. Sim. pass., Munich 3, 18; act., *Sin.* B 95.

[13] *Urk.* iv. 3.

[14] Compare *Pt.* 308 (*Pr.*) with *ib.* (L 2).

[15] *Eb.* 108, 20.

[16] *Eb.* 104, 1.

[17] *Leb.* 82. Cf., however, *Nu* 137 A, 35 (*prr·f*), qu. p. 391, top, after *wnn·ḥr*.

[18] *Peas.* B 2, 15. Sim. *Pt.* 314; *Eb.* 2. 5.

[19] *Peas.* B 1, 261.

[20] *Peas.* B 1, 251.

[21] *Sin.* B 100. 151; *Sh. S.* 19; *Pt.* 140.

The meaning is thus imperfective; the form occurs frequently in *generalizations*, *characterizations*, and *statements of habit* or *custom*, with reference to vaguely present or future time.

Exx. *iw r n s nḥm·f sw* a man's mouth saves him.[1]

As to him for whom this remedy is made .... *iw·f nḏm·f ḥr ꜥwy* he gets well immediately.[2] Here with suffix-pronoun as subject.

Similarly in *past contexts.*

Ex. *iw ḥkꜣ pn n ⟨R⟩tnw di·f iry·i rnpwt ꜥšꜣ⟨t⟩ m ṯsw n mšꜥ·f* this prince of ⟨Re⟩tjnu caused me to spend many years as commander of his army.[3]

We have seen (§§ 117, 2; 323) that virtual subordinate clauses frequently begin with *iw* + suffix; so too *iw* + suffix + *śḏm·f* may be virtually subordinate.

Exx. *sḏm·n·i ḫrw·f iw·f mdw·f* I heard his voice as he was speaking.[4] Virtual clause of time.

If thou seest a man (with) swellings on his neck,[5] *iw·f mr·f ꜥty n nḥbt·f* and he is suffering in the two members of his neck.[6] Virtual relative clause.

Parallel texts in each of these examples have the construction *iw·f ḥr śḏm* (§ 323),[7] which differs in that it lays no stress on the continuous character of the action.

Passive examples of *iw·f śḏm·f* are rare, the *iw śḏm·f* form being regularly substituted for it.

Ex. As to every spirit for whom this is done, ... he eats and drinks (*iw·f wnm·f swri·f*) in the presence of Osiris every day, *iw sṯꜣ·tw·f ḥnꜥ nsyw bityw rꜥ nb* and he is made to enter with the kings of Upper and Lower Egypt every day.[8]

One example of *iw·tw śḏm·tw* can, however, be quoted.

iw·tw sḏm·tw·f m r n r it (this prophecy) used to be heard from mouth to mouth.[9]

Note that, as in the *ḫr·f śḏm·f* construction (§ 239), only the indefinite pronoun *tw* is here placed after the initial formative, not the complex consisting of *tw* + suffix. One example is forthcoming where *tw* is omitted after *iw* and its place taken by the nominal subject of the passive.

iw grt prt·s di·tw·s ḥr t n wḫdy moreover, its seed is placed on the bread of the sufferer.[10]

Obs. For an instance where the suffix subject is omitted after the *śḏm·f* form, see below § 486. For *n śḏm·n·f* as negative counterpart of *iw·f śḏm·f*, see p. 332, n. 5.

[1] *Sh. S.* 17-8. Sim. *Peas.* B 1, 216. 230; *Leb.* 21. 80; *Pr.* 1, 5; *Pt.* 103. 206; Cairo 20538, ii. *c* 11.

[2] *Eb.* 47, 10. Sim. *ib.* 104, 1; 109, 1; *P. Kah.* 7, 52; *Sin.* B 151; *Pt.* 305-8; *Leb.* 69; *Urk.* iv. 20, 1.

[3] *Sin.* B 99-101. Sim. *Siut* 1, 267, qu. § 184, 1.

[4] *Sin.* R 25. Sim. *Herdsm.* 24.

[5] Qu. § 196, 1.

[6] *Eb.* 51, 20.

[7] *Sin.* B 2, qu. § 323; *Eb.* 25, 4.

[8] Budge, p. 300, 7-9. Sim. *ib.* 161, 10-12; 209, 11-12; *Peas.* B 1, 290-1.

[9] *Urk.* iv. 344.

[10] *Eb.* 51, 18.

§ 464. The form [hieroglyphs] *iw sḏm·n·f*.—This very common narrative tense, which is used where English employs either the *present perfect* or the *past* tense, has been amply illustrated in § 68. Sometimes it is given a more impressive turn by the addition of the particle *grt*.

Ex. [hieroglyphs] *iw grt ḫrp·n n·f ḥm·i mnw ꜥšꜣ wrt* My Majesty dedicated to him very many monuments.[1]

Only very rarely is *iw* separated from its *sḏm·n·f* form by a clause of time; see the first example in § 507, 6.

[1] *Urk.* iv. 173. Sim. *ib.* 171, 11. 16; 172, 1; 768, 4; 769, 7; *Hamm.* 114, 13; Cairo 20512, *b* 2; Leyd. V3, 4.

§ 465. The passive [hieroglyphs] *iw sḏm·f*.—In the Old Kingdom *iw* + passive *sḏm·f* is the regular passive of *iw sḏm·n·f* when a nominal subject follows. Middle Egyptian examples have been given in § 422, 1.

Examples with suffix subject do not seem to occur. Here we need add only an impersonal instance:

[hieroglyphs] *iw ir mi ḏd·f* it was done as he said.[2]

[2] *Herdsm.* 23.

§ 466. The auxiliary [hieroglyphs] *iw* followed by an impersonal verb of motion.—Examples are very rare.

[hieroglyphs] *iw ꜥḳ ḫr wpwt nt it·f ḥꜣt-sp 2* the census-list of his father was returned in year 2.[3]

There is no means of deciding whether *iw ꜥḳ* should be regarded as a shortening of *iw ꜥḳ·n·tw* (§ 464), lit. '(one) entered with the census-list', or of *iw ꜥḳw* (§ 465), lit. 'it was entered with the census-list'.

[3] *P. Kah.* 9, 8 restored. Sim. *Sin.* B 248, qu. § 483, 2; *Semnah Disp.* 1, 13 (*iw ḫnt*).

§ 467. The auxiliary [hieroglyphs] *iw* followed by a word of adjectival meaning.

Exx. [hieroglyphs] *iw šw m ꜥḳ-ib* there is a lack (lit. it is lacking) of a confidential friend.[4]

[hieroglyphs] *iw ḳsn r·i ḥr ḳd* it is altogether too irksome for me, lit. irksome more than me.[5]

[hieroglyphs] *sšp n·k, iw wꜥb ḫr nsw* take thou, it is pure before the king.[6] Words spoken while offering.

The construction here is unlikely to be *iw sḏm·f* (§ 462), which is imperfective, since the second and third of our instances refer to particular occasions. In one example [hieroglyphs] *iw nfrw* 'it is good'[6a] the ending *-w* points to the construction *iw* + old perfective (§ 323); this is indirectly confirmed by another example where *iw* is replaced by *wnn* with future meaning (§ 326):

[hieroglyphs] *wnn nfrw ḥr ib·f wrt* it will be very good in his heart.[6b] So too with expressed subject [hieroglyphs] *iw nꜣ wr r·i* 'this is too much for me'.[7] On the other hand, it is difficult to separate cases where a dative follows from the construction of § 141, so that here perhaps a true adjective was used.

[4] *Leb.* 123–4.

[5] *P. Kah.* 3, 33. Sim. *Leb.* 6; *Urk.* iv. 1211, 15.

[6] LAC. *TR.* 88, 46–50.

[6a] *Coffins*, G 1T321.

[6b] *Pt.* 132 (L 2).

[7] *Leb.* 5.

Ex. *iw ꜣḫ n irr st tp tꜣ* it goes favourably with him who does it on earth.[8]

[8] *Urk.* v. 4. Sim. *Hearst* 6, 2.

In a unique and interesting example the phrase *iw wn* affirming existence (§ 107) precedes a sentence with adjectival predicate: *iw wn wr it m ꜣhw, mwt mst ḥtp kt r·s* there is many a father in trouble, and (many) a mother who has borne, and another is happier than she.[1]

[1] *Pt.* 171–2.

OBS. For *in iw* in questions see below §§ 491, 3; 492.

§ 468. Appendix. Exceptional cases of ***iw.***—1. We must note the use of *iw* in statements introduced by *oaths.* The point of departure was probably the normal use of *iw* in instances like

ꜥnḫ n·i mry w(i) Rꜥ ..... iw ir·n·i nn as Rēꜥ lives for me and loves me (§ 218) ....., I have done this.[2]

[2] *Urk.* iv. 752.

Perhaps it is by an extension of such uses that *iw* comes to be employed after oaths to introduce constructions of various other types.

Exx. I swear .... *iw ir pꜣ tḫnwy ..... iw n(y)-st inr wꜥ m mꜣt rwḏt* as for the two obelisks .... they consist of one block of hard red granite.[3]

[3] *Urk.* iv. 366.

As the Prince endures, *iw n tš·i r nsw ḥr pri* I did not swerve from the king on the battlefield.[4]

[4] *Urk.* iv. 38. Sim. *ib.* 847, 3 (*iw nn ir·n*).

As Rēꜥ [lives for] me and loves me ...... *iw wḏꜣ ḥm·i ḥr mtn pn* My Majesty will proceed upon this road.[5]

[5] *Urk.* iv. 651.

In the last of these sentences the construction is not the *iw sḏm·f* form of § 462,[6] since that construction does not serve to express single acts as here.

[6] In *Urk.* iv. 489, 2 *iw* has both functions.

2. Sometimes *iw* is employed to bring out a strong *contrast.* This use has been illustrated in the case of the sentence with adverbial predicate (§ 117, 1), in the pseudo-verbal construction (§ 323, end) and before *nn wn* 'there was not' (§ 394). It is found also with the *sḏm·f* form.

Exx. A herb .... *rd·s ḥr ẖt·s mi ḳꜣdt, iw ir·s ḥrt mi sšn* which grows on its belly like the *ḳꜣdt,* while it flowers (lit. makes flower) like the lotus.[7]

[7] *Eb.* 51, 16. Sim. *Turin* 1447, 5 and possibly *Pr.* 2, 1.

His Majesty caused the garments for the procession ..... to be made large garments, *iw wn·sn m ḥbsw nḏsw* whereas they had (before) been small garments.[8] It is uncertain whether *wn·sn* here is *sḏm·f* or *sḏm·n·f*; see § 413.

[8] *Eleph.* 25. Sim. *Rec.* 29, 165, 13.

I have not boasted .... saying *ir·n·i ḫn, iw n ir sw ḥm·i* I have done a matter, whereas My Majesty had not done it.[9]

[9] *Urk.* iv. 751. Sim. with *st* 'lo' after *iw*, L. *D.* ii. 112, *e*; 113, *b*.

Like the last example under 1 above, the first two quoted here are not to be classified under the heading of the *iw sḏm·f* form.

3. As a rule *ỉw* cannot precede the independent pronouns. There are, however, a few exceptions in statements showing some detachment or emphasis.

Exx. *ỉw grt ỉnk ỉr tp mdḥw rwdt* moreover, it was I who acted as head of the hewers of sandstone.[1]

ỉw ỉnk ḥsy n Ḥtḥr mfk(ꜣ)t, indeed, I was the favourite of Hathor of the turquoise.[2]

4. The rule that *ỉw* must not be employed after *nn* 'not' and *nty* 'who' (§ 107, 2) breaks down in Late Egyptian. A few examples are found within the period covered by this book.

Exx. *mt nn ỉw·ỉ r wꜣḥ·t* behold, I will not leave thee (f.).[3] Dyn. XVIII, in colloquial conversation.

Every steward, scribe or priest *nty ỉw·f r rdỉt pꜣwt·ỉ n ẖry-ḥb(t)* who shall give my offerings to the lector-priest.[4] Reign of Amenophis III.

5. In course of time, as noted § 117, Obs., *ỉw* developed from a colourless verb indicating *independence* into a mere particle expressing *dependence*. The use above under 2 illustrates a stage along this road. Another M. E. example marks a further advance in the same direction.

Ex. *ḥr-ntt nfr ỉb n bꜣk ỉm ỉw sḏm·n·f ꜥ. w. s. nb* (*ꜥ. w. s.*) because the heart of this servant is happy when he has heard that (my) master is living, prospering and in health.[4a] Other exx. of this formula omit *ỉw*.[4b]

6. In conclusion, we must mention the very rare writing of *ỉw* simply as .

Ex. *ỉ(w) dỉ·n ḥm·f ỉn·t(w) n·(ỉ) ỉwꜣ m wꜣḏt* His Majesty caused a bull to be brought to me as raw meat.[5]

Obs. For *ỉw* before an adjectival predicate followed by pronominal subject see above § 142 and the second example above under 1 (*ỉw ny-st*).

[1] Munich 4, 7.

[2] *Sinai* 181, 11.

[3] *Paheri* 7.

[4] *Tarkhan* i, 79, 47.

[4a] *P. Kah.* 36, 54-5.

[4b] *P. Kah.* 28, 21; 29, 12.

[5] *ÄZ.* 45, Pl. 8, A.

THE AUXILIARY *WNN*

§ **469**. In many parts of this book we have insisted that the verb *wnn* 'exist', so far as it is employed as a purely grammatical element, supplies the missing parts of *ỉw* 'is', 'are'; see §§ 118, 2; 142; 150; 157, 1, etc. In dealing with the pseudo-verbal construction it was shown that the forms *wnn·f ḥr sḏm* and *wnn·f sḏmw* find a rational explanation if regarded as expressing the future of *ỉw·f ḥr sḏm* and of *ỉw·f sḏmw* respectively, and cases were quoted where, upon similar lines, compound verb-forms were formed with the old perfective (§ 326), infinitive (§ 326), and participles (§ 396, 2) of *wnn*; a particularly curious compound is *wnn·f r sḏm* 'he will be going to hear', expressing the future of *ỉw·f r sḏm*, itself of future meaning (§ 332). In the next sections we deal with cases which for various reasons could not be dealt with at an earlier stage.

§ 470. ***wn·in·f*** **in the pseudo-verbal construction.**—The *śdm·in·f* form was seen in § 429, 1 to be common in past narrative; *wn·in·f ḥr śdm*[1] and *wn·in·f śdmw* emerge at an early date as explicit *past narrative* forms of *iw·f ḥr śdm* and *iw·f śdmw* respectively.

Exx. *wn·in sḫty pn ḥr rmyt ꜥꜣw wrt* then this peasant proceeded to weep very greatly.[2]

wn·in·i ḥr ḳnt m-bꜣḥ·f then I showed bravery before him.[3] Lit. then I was on being brave.

wn·in·tw ḥr iwꜥ·i m nbw ḥr sn-nw·sy one (i. e. Pharaoh) proceeded to reward me with gold yet again.[4]

wn·in ib n ḥm·f ḳb thereupon the heart of His Majesty was refreshed.[5]

With the 1st pers. sing. of the old perfective the presence of the suffix after *wn·in* is not absolutely essential.

Ex. *wn·in ptḥ·kwi ḥr tꜣ m-bꜣḥ-ꜥ ḥm·f* then I lay prostrate upon the ground before His Majesty.[6]

OBS. Compare with the above the use of *wn·in* before adj. pred. (§ 142); *wn·in·f* before a clause of circumstance, see § 215, end; *mk śdm* for *ḥr śdm*, see § 234, OBS.

§ 471. ***wn·ḫr·f*** **and** ***wnn·ḫr·f*** **in the pseudo-verbal construction.**—For the distinction between the two forms see § 430.

1. In reference to *future* time. In *injunctions* and statements of *result*.

Exx. *wn·ḫr·t(w) ḥr ntš·f m mw ḳb* it (the bull) shall be sprinkled (lit. one shall sprinkle it) with cold water.[7] Single action.

wnn·ḫr·f wꜣḏ mi wnn·f tp tꜣ he shall be flourishing as he was upon earth.[8] Continued state.

2. In *past narrative* (Dyn. XVIII); rare.

Exx. *wn·ḫr·i ḥr šms ity* (ꜥ.w.s.) *ḥr rdwy·i* I accompanied the sovereign (l. p. h.) on my feet.[9]

wn·ḫr ḥswt·i mn·ti m-ḥr-ib ḳꜣw ḥꜥw (read *ḫwꜥw*) my praises were established in the midst of (both) tall and short.[10]

§ 472. ***wn·in śdm·f.***—In agreement with the now familiar principle, this rare form provides a *past* tense of *iw śdm·f* (§ 462). Hence we are not surprised to find a passage where it describes a *past habit*:

The children of the vizier read his advice and found it good, *wn·in ꜥḥꜥ·sn ḥms·sn ḫft*, so they proceeded to live (lit. stand up and sit down) accordingly.[11]

In another passage it refers to a *condition* resulting from a certain action.

wn·in ḫnn sdb·f ḥr mw thereupon its fringe came to be resting on the water.[12] For the unexpected gemination cf. *gmm·tw·s*, p. 385, n. 6.

[1] In O.K., *Urk.* i. 127, 7; 139, 9.

[2] *Peas.* B 1, 24. Sim. *ib.* 42; *Urk.* iv. 4, 13. 15; 5, 7; 659, 9.

[3] *Urk.* iv. 8. Sim. *ib.* 659, 14; *Pr.* 2, 5–6, qu. § 300; *Westc.* 10, 3.

[4] *Urk.* iv. 5. Sim. *ib.* 7, 12; *Peas.* B 1, 84; *Hamm.* 19, 11.

[5] *Westc.* 6, 1. Sim. *ib.* 8, 21; *Peas.* B 2, 117. With suffix subj., *T. Carn.* 7; *Urk.* iv. 685, 12.

[6] *Urk.* iv. 897.

[7] *P. Kah.* 7, 40.

[8] *Nu* 72, 14.

[9] *Urk.* iv. 3. Sim. *ib.* 3, 8.

[10] *Urk.* iv. 1073. Sim. *ib.* 1075, 4; *Eb.* 2, 4–5.

[11] *Pr.* 2, 7.

[12] *Peas.* Bt. 35.

§ 473. ***wn·in·f sḏm·f*** **and** ***wnn·ḫr·f sḏm·f*.**—Two rare developments of *iw·f sḏm·f* (§ 463).

Exx. *wn·in ḥm·f hꜣb·f n·i ḫr ꜣwt-ꜥ* thereupon His Majesty kept sending to me with presents.[1] *Past custom.*

wnn·ḫr irrw n·f nn ꜥḳ·f prr·f he for whom this is done shall come in and go forth.[1a] *Future habit.*

§ 474. Other forms from *wnn* before *sḏm·f*.—1. Strange cases are *ir grt wnn ꜥḥꜥ pꜣ ḥsb 11 ꜥꜣ* if the eleven workmen are waiting here.[2]

ir wnn ḏdy ꜥḥꜥ(w) n ḫpr tp tꜣ if shall be enduring the period of existence upon earth.[2a]

In both exx. *ir wnn* stands for **ir iw* (§ 150). In the second ex. *ḏdy* looks more like an old perfective than a *sḏm·f* form. But if so (cf. § 323 for the basic construction), the nominal subject will have been postponed as is regularly done after the negative verbs *tm* and *imi* (§ 343).

2. Closely analogous to *wn·in·f sḏm·f* (§ 473) is another form *narrating a past continuous action.*

Ex. *wn·i wšd·i ḥmwt ḥr·s* I kept on addressing the workmen concerning it.[3] For *wn·i* possibly *wn·n·i* (§ 413) should be understood.

3. The construction *iw sḏm·f* (§ 462) with the meaning of a relative clause: *iwn·i is pw wnt ir·i* what I used to do was my (real) nature.[4] *Wnt* is perf. participle and *past habit* is expressed.

OBS. The above example seems unique in Middle Egyptian, but analogous constructions are found far earlier; thus *wnt·k ir·k* 'that which thou wast wont to do'[5] must be regarded as relative form of *iw·k ir·k* (§ 463) and *wnw ir·sn* 'who are wont to do'[6] as plural participle of *iw ir·sn* (§ 462).

§ 475. *Wnn* as auxiliary before the *sḏm·n·f* form.—Here we can only quote *wn pḥ·n·f*,[7] the perfect. participle from *iw pḥ·n·f*; see § 396, 3.

THE AUXILIARY *ꜤḤꜤ*

§ 476. The finite verb-forms compounded with *ꜥḥꜥ* 'stand up',[8] 'arise' occur only in main clauses, and always carry the action which is being described one step further on. Originally, no doubt, the subject of *ꜥḥꜥ* was the same as that of the following verb, the form *ꜥḥꜥ·n sḏm·n·f*—to quote only the commonest construction—thus meaning 'he rose up and heard' (see below § 488 for two verbs with one subject). But in further developments this original meaning seems to have become obscured; the passive *ꜥḥꜥ·n sḏm·f*, for example, can barely have been understood as 'he rose up and was heard'. The verb becomes, in fact, less and less literally significant. This may well be the reason that, as auxiliary, it very often lacks its determinative.

[1] *Sin.* B 174-5. Sim. Brit. Mus. 574, 3-4.

[1a] *Nu* 137A, 35.

[2] *P. Kah.* 31, 2.

[2a] *Ḥaremḥab*, left, 7.

[3] *Sinai* 90, 8; sim. *ib.* 90, 13. Also in Old Eg., *Urk.* i. 59, 16.

[4] *Urk.* iv. 973, 14.

[5] *Pyr.* 623, *c.* Sim. *wn(w·i) ḏd·(i)*, *Urk.* i. 57, 15.

[6] *Urk.* i. 50, 3.

[7] *Th. T. S.* iii. 26.

[8] See *ÄZ.* 27, 29.

§ 477. Compounds with in the *sḏm·f* form.—Four very rare constructions fall under this head. The context in each case describes an *event* which will follow as the result of some precedent condition.

1. *ꜥḥꜥ sḏm·f.* Vaguely present time.

Ex. Such and such medicaments are to be taken; *ꜥḥꜥ wšš·f ḏdft nbt* then he passes all worms.[1] Lit. (he) arises and he urinates.

2. *ꜥḥꜥ sḏm·f* with the passive *sḏm·f.* Our example refers to a contingency that may arise in the future.

Ex. As for every commander.... who shall beseech the king to pardon him, *ꜥḥꜥ rdì rmṯt·f ḫt·f ꜣḥt·f r ḥtp-nṯr ìt·ì Mn nb Gbtyw* his people, his property and his fields shall be given for the offerings of my father Min, lord of Coptus.[2]

3. *ꜥḥꜥ sḏm·ḫr·f* with the verb-form of § 430.

Ex. *ꜥḥꜥ ḏd·ḫr·sn n·f* then they shall say to him.[2a]

4. *ꜥḥꜥ* + subject + old perfective. Vaguely present time.

Ex. Such and such treatment is given to remove a swelling, *ꜥḥꜥ·s hꜣ·ty ḥr-ꜥ* then it goes down immediately.[3]

§ 478. *ꜥḥꜥ·n sḏm·n·f.*—A very common narrative tense, used in some texts only to introduce incidents of outstanding interest, but occurring in other texts (e.g. the story of the Shipwrecked Sailor) with almost painful monotony.

Exx. *ꜥḥꜥ·n rdì·n·f n·(ì) nn* thereupon he gave me this.[4] With a transitive verb; lit. (he) arose and he gave.

ꜥḥꜥ·n pḥ·n·(ì) Wꜣḏ-wr then I reached the Red Sea.[5] With a transitive verb.

ꜥḥꜥ·n sbt·n·f ìm·ì then he laughed at me.[6] With an intransitive verb.

ꜥḥꜥ·n spd·n·ì r-gs·f then I showed keenness in his presence.[7] With an adjective-verb.

With verbs of motion *ꜥḥꜥ·n·f* + old perfective (§ 482, 2) is preferred, and that construction is also rather more usual with intransitives. With both transitives and intransitives *ꜥḥꜥ·n·f ḥr sḏm* (§ 482, 1) is a rarer and possibly later equivalent of *ꜥḥꜥ·n sḏm·n·f.* The ordinary passive of *ꜥḥꜥ·n sḏm·n·f* is *ꜥḥꜥ·n* + passive *sḏm·f* (§ 481), but apparently only when the subject is nominal; when it is pronominal *ꜥḥꜥ·n·f* + old perfective (§ 482, 2) seems to have been employed.

§ 479. *ꜥḥꜥ·n·f sḏm·n·f.*—The same construction with the subject in anticipatory emphasis. Very uncommon.

Ex. *ꜥḥꜥ·n ḥm n n-sw-bìt Ḥwny mnì·n·f* then the Majesty of king Ḥuni died.[8]

[1] *Eb.* 20, 7–8.

[2] *Kopt.* 8, 9–10.

[2a] *Coffins*, B 7 C, 3.

[3] *Eb.* 51, 18 = *Hearst* 3, 6.

[4] Br. Mus. 614, 6. Sim. *Sin.* R 51. 58. 59. 67; *Peas.* R 4. 49; B 1, 9. 22; *Sh. S.* 45. 56. 83. 86. 161. 166; *BH.* i. 25, 79; Louvre C 12, *passim*; *Urk.* iv. 140, 3; 185, 10; 654, 13; 894, 3. 5.

[5] *Hamm.* 114, 14. Sim. *ib.* 199, 7. 8.

[6] *Sh. S.* 149.

[7] *Sebekkhu* 14. Sim. *Urk.* iv. 657, 16.

[8] *Pr.* 2, 7–8. Sim. *Westc.* 5, 15–6; 11, 18.

§ 480. **ꜥḥꜥ·n śḏm·f.**—A few instances of this construction may be quoted; the sense differs in no way from that of *ꜥḥꜥ·n śḏm·n·f*.

Ex. *ꜥḥꜥ·n rdi·f wi m r·f* then he placed me in his mouth.[1]

The continuation of this passage shows two more *śḏm·f* forms parallel to *rdi·f* here. These make it difficult to assume a corruption from *rdi·n·f*, as one would otherwise be inclined to do.

§ 481. The passive śḏm·f form after ꜥḥꜥ·n.—The passive *śḏm·f* placed after *ꜥḥꜥ·n* provides the ordinary passive of *ꜥḥꜥ·n śḏm·n·f*. Examples are fairly common, but mostly with *nominal* subject or *impersonally*.

Exx. *ꜥḥꜥ·n mꜣ nꜣ n kꜣt* then these works were inspected.[2]

ꜥḥꜥ·n šꜥw nḥbt·s then its neck was cut.[3]

ꜥḥꜥ·n kd·s in ḥꜣw ḥr snṯt·s thereupon it was (re)built and more added to its ground-plan.[3a] Exceptionally with suffix-pronoun.

ꜥḥꜥ·n rdi ꜥḥꜥ n·f kꜣkꜣw 2 then two boats were caused to wait upon him.[4] Lit. (it) was caused that, etc.

ꜥḥꜥ·n irw mi ḏdt then it was done according to what had been said.[5] Impersonal.

§ 482. The pseudo-verbal construction with ꜥḥꜥ·n·f.—1. The construction with *ḥr*+infinitive is uncommon, since *ꜥḥꜥ·n śḏm·n·f* (§ 478) covers the same ground.

Exx. *ꜥḥꜥ·n·i ḥr iꜣš n mšꜥ nty m dpt tn* then I called to the travellers who were in this ship.[6]

ꜥḥꜥ·n·tw ḥr iwꜥ·i m nbw then I was rewarded (lit. one rewarded me) with gold.[7]

For some curious instances where the particle *mk* appears to be substituted for *ḥr* see § 234, Obs.

2. The form *ꜥḥꜥ·n·f*+old perfective is usual with *verbs of motion.*

Exx. *ꜥḥꜥ·n·i šm·kw ḥnꜥ·f* then I went with him.[8]

ꜥḥꜥ·n ḥm·f wdꜣ m ḥtp then His Majesty proceeded in peace.[9]

It is also fairly common with *intransitives*.

Exx. *ꜥḥꜥ·n·sn hrw ḥr·s* then they were satisfied with it.[10]

ꜥḥꜥ·n Ḥꜥpw wrw ḫpr then great Inundations occurred.[11]

ꜥḥꜥ·n·tw ḥꜥw im wr r ḫt nbt then one rejoiced thereat more than anything.[12]

An example occurs where a participle + dep. pron. 3rd f. sing. is substituted for the old perfective, after the manner described in § 374, end.

[1] *Sh. S.* 76–7; sim. *Westc.* 12, 9. In *Peas.* B 1, 186–7 emend *ꜥḥꜥ·n·sn*, cf. R 72; B 1, 23 is likewise corrupt.

[2] Louvre C 12, 16. Sim. *ib.* C 11, 3. 4; *Pr.* 2, 8–9; *P. Kah.* 13, 23; *Westc.* 7, 9. 14; *Urk.* iv. 655, 15; 659, 1.

[3] *Hamm.* 110, 6. Sim. *ib.* 19, 10.

[3a] *ÄZ.* 34, Pl. 2, 8–9.

[4] *Westc.* 8, 4.

[5] Brussels 250. Sim. *Westc.* 5, 13.

[6] *Sh. S.* 170. Sim. *ÄZ.* 58, 17*; *Urk.* iv. 2, 12.

[7] *Urk.* iv. 7.

[8] Louvre C 12. Sim. *Sh. S.* 155; *BH.* i. 8, 14; *Hamm.* 114, 10; *Westc.* 12, 25–6.

[9] *BH.* i. 8, 10. Sim. *Sh. S.* 129–30; 154–5; Louvre C 12, 15.

[10] *Siut* 1, 276. 282. Sim. *Sh. S.* 131; *Westc.* 6, 3.

[11] *BH.* i. 8, 21. Sim. *Sh. S.* 37–8; *Urk.* v. 53, 7.

[12] Louvre C 12.

ʿḥʿ·n Skmm ḫr s(y) ḥnʿ Rṯnw ḫst then Sekmem fell (i.e. was defeated) together with vile Retjnu.[1]

A few cases of *transitive* verbs also occur, but only with pronominal subject. These have, of course, *passive* meaning; with nominal subject the passive *ʿḥʿ·n sḏm·f* (§ 481) seems to be preferred.

Ex. *ʿḥʿ·n·i rdi·kwi r iw in wɜw n Wɜḏ-wr* then I was cast upon an island by a wave of the sea.[2]

In the second half of the story of the Shipwrecked Sailor the suffix of 1st pers. sing. is omitted after *ʿḥʿ·n*. This seems a quite legitimate construction, a parallel to it occurring after *wn·in* (§ 470, end).

Exx. *ʿḥʿ·n ʿḳ·kwi ḥr ʾIty* then I entered in before the Sovereign.[3]

ʿḥʿ·n in·kwi r iw pn then I was brought to this island.[4]

3. With *r* + infinitive, only in the sentence *ʿḥʿ·n rf Ḏḥwty r psg·s* then Thoth proceeded to (?) spit on it.[4a]

OTHER AUXILIARY VERBS

§ 483. 1. A construction similar to *ʿḥʿ·n sḏm·n·f* (§ 478) is found exceptionally with the verbs *ii* 'come', *pri* 'come forth', *sḏr* 'spend all night', and *ḏr* 'end'.[5]

Exx. *ii·n ḥḏ·n·s pɜy·s rmn* forthwith (lit. came and) she spoilt her side (by ceasing to row).[6]

pr·n fkɜ·n·f ḫry-ḥb(t) ḥry-tp afterwards (lit. went out and) he rewarded the chief lector.[7]

sḏr·n ḳɜs·n·i pḏt·i at night-time (lit. spent the night and) I strung my bow.[8]

ḏr·n ḏd·n·f n·sn in the end (lit. ended and) he said to them.[9]

All these verbs except *ii* show a further analogy with *ʿḥʿ* in that their subject may be qualified by the old perfective; cf. *ḏr·in·f ḥms(w)* 'at last he sat down', lit. 'he ended being seated' (§ 316) with the construction *ʿḥʿ·n·f sḏmw* of § 482, 2.

2. The verb *iw* 'come' appears to be used rather similarly with various parts of the suffix conjugation, particularly in conjunction with the verb *ini* 'bring'.[10] The least obscure examples are:

iw inn·f ḳbḥw ḥr tɜw he shall come and bring coolness upon the heat.[11] *ʾInn·f*, imperfective *sḏm·f*.

iw in rḫt iry m snn the amount thereof shall be brought in copy.[12] *ʾIn* is probably passive *sḏm·f*.

iw iw iɜš n·i one came and called me.[13] See § 466.

In these examples and in others with *ii*[14] the action of 'coming' is probably meant literally, but the close association with a following verb reduces its force almost to that of an auxiliary verb.

1 *Sebekkhu* 2.

2 *Sh. S.* 39–41. Sim. *Urk.* iv. 3, 3. 9; 3rd pers. sing., *P. Mosk* 2, 4 = *ÄZ.* 63, 106; 3rd pers. plur., BUDGE, p. 75, 5–6. See too below, last ex.

3 *Sh. S.* 174. Sim. *ib.* 157. 169.

4 *Sh. S.* 109. Sim. *ib.* 177.

4a *Urk.* v. 35, 12. The best MSS. have *r*, others *ḥr*.

5 See *ÄZ.* 27, 34–6.

6 *Westc.* 6, 4.

7 *Westc.* 6, 14. Sim. *Urk.* iv. 895, 4.

8 *Sin.* B 127.

9 *Pr.* 2, 4.

10 So too *P. Kah.* 36, 13; *Urk.* iv. 247, 7. With *ḫpr*, *Eb.* 106, 5; 108, 19; with *rdi*, *Urk.* v. 174, 5; with *ir*, *Ikhern.* 9.

11 *Adm.* 11, 13.

12 MÖLL. *HL.* i. 20, 8.

13 *Sin.* B 248.

14 *Sin.* R 15; *Peas.* B 171.

§ 484. The auxiliary *p3(w?)* **'have done in the past'.**[1]—Various forms of this not improbably *3ae inf.* verb, which is closely related to the noun *p3t* 'antiquity',[1a] are used with a following infinitive to express past action.

Exx. *n p3 d3yt mnỉ sp·s* never has wrongdoing brought its venture safe to port.[2] Lit. wrong has not done-in-the-past mooring its action.

n sp p3·t(w) ỉrt st dr ḥ3w n-sw-bỉt Snfrw, m3ʿ-ḫrw never had it been done (lit. not occurred that one did the making of it) since the time of king Snofru, the justified.[3]

nfr st r p3yt ḫpr they were more beautiful than that which had existed formerly, lit. that which had-done (perf. act. part.) exist.[4]

sic *n ḫpr mỉtt n b3kw p3·n nb·sn ḥst st* never had the like happened to (any) servants whom their masters had praised.[5] *P3·n* is probably the narrative *śḏm·n·f* form, see § 196, 2.

ỉw p3·n sḏm mỉtt we have been used to hear the like.[6] *'Iw śḏm·f* form, see § 462.

§ 485. The verb *ỉrỉ* as auxiliary.[7]—1. Late Egyptian has a repugnance to verb-forms from stems with more than three radical consonants, as well as from compound and foreign verbs; such verb-forms it therefore paraphrases with *ỉrỉ* followed by the infinitive; compare in old English 'he doth make'. Rare early examples occur already in Middle Egyptian.

ỉw ỉb·f ỉr·f dbdb his heart thumps.[8]

ỉr·s ỉs-ḥ3k m nbdw-ḳd it (the king's uraeus) works devastation among the perverse-of-disposition.[9]

Here belongs the vetitive *m ỉr* 'do not' mentioned in § 340, 2.

2. For some reason unknown, *verbs of motion* sometimes are paraphrased with *ỉrỉ* + infinitive.

Ex. *ỉrt·ỉ šmt m ḫntyt* I made a departure southwards.[10]

ḥtpy(w) ỉrw prt n ḥḳr m-ʿ ḫr pf pardoned ones who had deserted (lit. made a going forth, perf. act. part.) through hunger from that enemy.[11]

An abstract verbal noun (cf. § 77, 1) may be employed instead of the infinitive.

Ex. O ye who live ...... *ỉrt(y)·sn sw3w ḥr wʿrt tn* and who shall pass (lit. make a passing) by this desert tract.[12]

3. The construction *śḏm pw ỉr(w)·n·f* 'it is a hearing which he did' and its passive *śḏm pw ỉry* have been dealt with in § 392.

[1] See *ÄZ.* 45, 73–9.

[1a] The possibly related intrans. vb. *p3* 'fly' is *2-lit.*

[2] *Pt.* 93. Sim. *ib.* 115. 479; *Siut* 4, 15. A question with *śḏm·n·f*, *Mill.* 2, 7.

[3] *Sinai* 139, 10–11. For the *ḫn*-bird in place of *p3* see Sign-list, G 41.

[4] *Unt.* v. 46. Sim. *Urk.* iv. 168, 11; 584, 17; 618, 13.

[5] *BH.* i. 25, 111.

[6] *Sinai* 90, 11. See above, n. 3.

[7] See *Verbum* ii. 553, *a*.

[8] *Eb.* 42, 9–10.

[9] *Urk.* iv. 613. Sim. *Rhind* 43, qu. § 338, 1 (imperative); 46. 50. 51 (*śḏm·ḫr·f*); *Urk.* iv. 606, 2, qu. § 420 (passive *śḏm·f*); *ib.* 658, 8, qu. p. 375, n. 28 (perf. *śḏm·f*).

[10] *Sin.* B 5–6. Sim. *ib.* 19; 188, qu. § 338.

[11] *Urk.* iv. 665.

[12] *Siut* 3, 1.

CONCLUDING REMARKS ON THE SUFFIX CONJUGATION

§ 486. Omission of the subject.[1]—The subject of the verb-forms of the suffix conjugation is sometimes omitted.

Exx. *pr is m ḥt·i n ꜥ iry* it came forth from my body because of the condition thereof.[2] The peasant is referring to his grievance, which he is unable to contain.

dr ṯw, dr mst ṯw damn thee, and damn her that bore thee![3] *Dr ṯw* stands for *dr ṯw nṯr* 'may god destroy thee' or the like.

rdi·in stꜣ·tw msw nsw they caused the king's children to be brought.[4]

ḫpr·ḫr m 4 it will become 4, i. e. the result will be 4.[5]

In these instances the omission is due either to the subject being too clear to need expression, or else to its being vague and a matter of indifference.

The normal way of evading the expression of the semantic subject is, of course, to use the passive voice, which is, indeed, a device serving that very purpose. But the passive may itself be impersonal, and in this case it is the expression of the direct semantic object, if any, which is evaded.

Exx. *smiw n wḥmw nsw* it was reported to the king's herald.[6]

nis·n·tw n wꜥ im a summons was made (lit. one called) to one of them.[7]

Examples with the *sḏm·f* passive are specially common, see § 422. When *·tw* is used we prefer, as a rule, to describe the verb-form as an active having for its subject the indefinite pronoun (§ 410, end).

A similar omission of the subject is found in subordinate clauses.

Exx. *nn rdit hꜣ ḥr ḫt* without letting it fall on the fire.[8] *Hꜣ* is for *hꜣ·s*.

ḫt n rḫ·t(w) a thing which is not known.[9]

rdi·n·i r tꜣ n wr ḥr ꜥwy·i I left (lit. placed) upon the ground because (it) was (too) much upon my hands.[10] This means: because I had too much to carry.

In these cases it is a suffix-pronoun which is omitted, and the noun to which the suffix would have referred has sometimes been expressed in the main clause. We might expect a similar omission of the suffixes in main clauses where the subject is in anticipatory emphasis (§ 148, 1), but in point of fact such a construction is very rare.

Exx. *ns n ḥm·f rtḥ St* the tongue of His Majesty restrains Nubia.[11] *Rtḥ* is possibly for *rtḥ·f*.

iw nh n ktt idn wr a little of a small thing replaces much.[12] *'Idn* is for *idn·f*, see § 463.

[1] See *Verbum*, ii. §§ 183. 373. 396. 418.

[2] *Peas.* B 1, 276.

[3] *Th. T. S.* ii. 11.

[4] *Sin.* B 263–4.

[5] *Rhind* 62. Sim. *Eb.* 75, 13–14.

[6] *Urk.* iv. 4.

[7] *Sin.* R 24.

[8] *Eb.* 61, 7. Sim. *ib.* 39, 15; *Urk.* iv. 1105, 9.

[9] *ÄZ.* 57, 6*; sim. perhaps *Peas.* B 1, 296. So too after *nty*, §§ 201. 402.

[10] *Sh. S.* 54. Sim. after *r*, *Eb.* 92, 13; 97, 17; after *ir* 'if', *Pt.* 482; *P. Kah.* 6, 22. So too with the *sḏmt·f* form, § 402.

[11] *P. Kah.* 1, 8.

[12] *Pr.* 1, 6.

It is perhaps in this way that we ought to explain *ḏd* as a substitute for *ḏd·f* 'he says', 'he said'; see above § 450, 1.

Occasionally the subject which is omitted after a form of the suffix conjugation is subsequently indicated in a round-about way.

Exx. *nn rdỉt ḏꜣ tꜣ r·s ỉn rwdw nb* without allowing it to be interfered with by any controller.[1] Lit. without letting cross-land to it by any controller; *ḏꜣ tꜣ r* is an idiomatic phrase, and the subject is postponed in order not to separate *ḏꜣ* from its object *tꜣ*.

n ỉr·n ꜣbw ỉm none of them (the offerings) suffered delay.[2] Lit. not made delay (any) thereof; *ỉm* is partitive in meaning and equivalent to *wꜥ ỉm·sn*.

Obs. 1. The words *ḫpr*, *ḫpr·n*, 'it happened that ....' are not here taken as impersonal verb-forms, since it seemed preferable to regard the following clause as a noun clause serving as subject; see above § 188, 1.

Obs. 2. In certain cases where *śḏm·n* occurs, particularly after the negative word *n*, it has been explained as a special participial[3] or finite[4] form, the more plausibly since [5] or *ny*[6] is occasionally written instead of simple *n*. An alternative view consists in regarding this *n* or *ny* as a rare suffix-pronoun of 3rd pers. plur. or dual, see § 34, Obs. 3. The probable explanation in most cases, however, is that *śḏm·n* or *śḏm·ny* simply represents the *śḏm·n·f* form with omission of the subject.[7] Ex. *ḫnmsw nw mỉn, n mr·ny* (for *mr·n·sn*) 'the friends of to-day, (they) do not love'.[8] It would almost look as though the origin of *śḏm·n·f* from perf. pass. part. + preposition *n* were here remembered, since for this preposition without noun or suffix the adverb (§ 205, 1) might naturally be substituted, and the rare spellings , correspond closely to , (§ 113, 2).

§ 487. Omission of both subject and formative element.

—Such omissions occur in passages where there is a sequence of parallel verbs, and where consequently subject and formative element are alike superfluous.

Exx. *ꜥḥꜥ·n ꜥꜣg·n·f ꜥt·f nb ỉm·s, nḥm ꜥꜣw·f, sꜥḳ r ḏꜣtt(?)·f* then he belaboured all his limbs with it, took away his asses, and drove (them) into his estate.[9] Understand *nḥm·n·f*, *sꜥḳ·n·f*.

ẖr·tw wrḥ·tw·f m mrḥt rmw 2-nw n hrw, wrḥ m mrḥt db 3-nw hrw, wrḥ m ỉbr 4-nw hrw it shall be anointed with fish-oil on the second day, anointed with hippopotamus-oil on the third day, and anointed with *ỉbr* on the fourth day.[11] *Wrḥ* must twice be understood as *ẖr·tw wrḥ·tw·f*.

So too in a sequence of simple *śḏm·f* forms, the later members are apt to be docked of their suffix subjects.[12] Cases where the first of a series of parallel verbs seems to lack the suffix and formative are better explained otherwise.[13]

[1] *Th. T. S.* iii. 26.

[2] *Urk.* iv. 98, 10.

[3] *ÄZ.* 46, 104.

[4] Gunn, *Stud.* ch. 16. The passive exx. are extremely dubious.

[5] Louvre C 14, 12, qu. § 255, end; *Pt.* 482 (L 1).

[6] *Leb.* 104; *Sh. S.* 131.

[7] With simple *n*, *Pt.* 482. 514; *Eb.* 19, 18. *Mḥ·n* in *Urk.* iv. 426, 2 and *sḥḏ·n*, *ib.* 374, 14 seem from *ib.* 362, 14 to be *śḏm·n·f*, though the reason for the employment of this form is obscure.

[8] *Leb.* 104. Sim. *Cen.* 84, 2.

[9] *Peas.* B 1, 23–4 (*ꜥꜣg·n·f* emended from R 72). Sim. *Westc.* 6, 10; *BH.* i. 8, 20; 25, 32–3; Berl. *ÄI.* i. p. 258, 15; Cairo 20538, ii. *c* 5.

[11] *Eb.* 86, 19–20 = *Hearst* 2, 3.

[12] Exx. *Peas.* B 1, 112–3; *Leb.* 72–3.

[13] For *Urk.* iv. 54, 15; 59, 13 see p. 240, n. 8*b*.

§ 488. Several verb-forms before a single subject.—Examples are not rare.

mrr ḥss sw Ḫnty(w)-ỉmntyw Khont-amentyu (the god of Abydus) shall love and favour him.[1]

ỉr ḥm wdf ỉn ntỉtỉ dmḏ n Sp pn ẖrdw·f but if there delay, lag, or be impeded the joining to this Sep of his children.[2]

n ḥḳs, n wbn mꜣꜥt justice is not scanty nor (yet) in excess.[3]

So too in the construction *ꜥḥꜥ·n sḏm·n·f* (§ 478) and in that of § 483, 1.

[1] Cairo 20046. Sim. *Hamm.* 48, 15.

[2] Lac. *TR.* 2, 25.

[3] *Peas.* B 1, 251–2.

VOCABULARY

ỉꜣš call, *n* a person.

ꜥḏ perceive.

wḥꜣ pull up (corn); hew (stones).

wšd address, question.

wtḫ flee.

nḏ ask, inquire; *nḏ ḫrt* inquire after health of, greet.

ḥỉỉ or *ḥwỉ* strike, smite.

ḫntỉ sail southward, upstream.

ḫnỉ row, trans. and intr.; convey by water.

sḥwy collect.

sḳꜣḥ plaster, caus. of *ḳꜣḥ* clay, mud.

sḳr smite.

gwꜣwꜣ constrict, put rope round neck of.

Ỉwnty-Sty Nubian foreigner (lit. bowman).[1]

ỉst crew.

ꜥrrwt gate.

mty controller; in title *mty n sꜣ* controller of a phyle (*sꜣ*) of priests (see p. 99, n. 1 and Exerc. XXIII, (*a*)).

nhw loss.

nḫnt youth, childhood.

rwd stairway.

var. *ḫrw* enemy.

ḥꜣk-ib rebel.

ḥryw inhabitants, people.

gs side, half; *dỉ ḥr gs* place on one side, dispose of, kill.

[1] The derivation of *Ỉwnty* from *ỉwnt* 'bow' seems probable, although the sign for *ỉwn-* is never accompanied by a bow as determinative. However, this derivation is not accepted *Griff. Stud.* 365.

EXERCISE XXXII

(*a*) *Reading lesson: from the autobiography of the sailor Aḥmosĕ, carved on the wall of his tomb at El-Kâb; early Dyn. XVIII:*[1]

ꜥḥꜥ·n ḥr pf iw,
Tti-ꜥn rn·f,
sḥwy·n·f n·f ẖꜣkw-ib.
wn·in ḥm·f ḥr smꜣ·f,
ist·f m tmt (§ 397) *ḫpr.*
ꜥḥꜥ·n rdi n·i tp 3 ꜣḥt stꜣt 5 m niwt·i.
wn·in·i ḥr ḫnt n-sw-bit Dsr-kꜣ-Rꜥ mꜣꜥ-ḫrw,
iw·f m ḫntyt (§ 331) *r K*(*ꜣ*)*š*
r swsḫ tꜣšw Kmt.
wn·in ḥm·f ḥr sḳr ꜣIwnty-Sty pf
m-ḥr-ib mšꜥ·f,
inw (§ 314 or § 422) *m gwꜣwꜣ* (§ 274).
nn nhw·sn (§ 77, 1),
wtḫw m dy (§ 361) *ḥr gs*
mi ntyw n ḫpr (§ 201).
ist wi m tp n mšꜥ·n.
iw ꜥḥꜣ·n·i r wn mꜣꜥ;
mꜣ·n ḥm·f ḳnt·i.

[1] *Urk.* iv. 6–7.

'Then that enemy, whose name was Tetyꜥan, came and had collected to himself the froward-hearted. His Majesty proceeded to slay him, and his crew were as what has never come into being. Then there were given to me 3 persons, and 5 arouras of field in my city. I proceeded to convey by water king Djeserkarēꜥ (Amenophis I), the justified, as he was sailing upstream to Cush to widen the frontiers of Egypt. His Majesty proceeded to capture that Nubian nomad in the midst of his army. They were brought tightly bound, there was no loss among (lit. of) them; he who fled being dispatched (lit. being one laid on one side) like men that have never come into being. Lo, I was at the head of our army. I fought in very truth and His Majesty saw my valour.'

(*b*) *Translate:*

(1)

(2)

(3)

(4)

(5)

(6)

[1] § 423, 1. [2] § 194. [3] Proper names. [4] Read *ḥwt*. [5] Snofru, first king of Dyn. IV.

LESSON XXXIII

DIFFERENT TYPES OF SENTENCE

§ 489. Sentences are classified in accordance with the different kinds of intention which they embody; for every sentence must embody some intention on the part of the speaker or writer. A roughly adequate classification would comprise: (1) *statements*, arising from the desire to give information; (2) *questions*, by which information is sought; (3) *desires*, a class including commands, exhortations, and wishes; (4) *exclamations*, calling attention to some emotional attitude of the speaker. Three of these types of sentence have been sufficiently, though not consecutively, dealt with in different parts of this book. The remaining type, namely questions, will be treated in the present Lesson.

It must be noted that the form of a sentence does not always reveal the actual intention of the speaker. As everywhere in language, forms originally created for one purpose are apt to be used subsequently for some quite different purpose. Thus a statement introduced by *mr·i* 'I desire' may express a wish no less effectively than *ḥ3* 'would that!' followed by the *śḏm·f* form.[1] Or again a question may be an effective means of making a negative statement or denial; such questions we call *rhetorical questions.*

Ex. [hieroglyphs] *fdḳ·k, n-m ṯs·f* (if) thou sunderest, who shall bind?[2] I. e. none can heal these evils except thee.

In similar fashion a sentence of one type or another may be used as a *subordinate clause,* i. e. may cease to be a complete sentence of itself in order to function as a noun, an adjective, or an adverb in a larger complex sentence. A statement used in place of a clause of condition has been quoted in § 423, 2. Or again, the same sense may be conveyed by a rhetorical question.

Ex. [hieroglyphs] *in iw rf Ḏḥwty sfn·f? iḫ ir·k iyt* does Thoth show leniency? Then mayst thou work ill![3] The sense is: if Thoth is lenient (which he is not), then thou mayst do evil.

In the two examples quoted above the writer was, of course, well aware that he was employing the form of a question, though his intention was to make a strong denial in the first instance, and to convey an *if*-clause in the second. Such *conscious* and deliberate transferences of meaning belong more to the domain of rhetoric than to that of syntax. But there are similar transferences which are effected by quite *unconscious* processes, and it is due to this fact that subordinate clauses exist in Egyptian and elsewhere, these being simply ordinary statements which, through the natural development of language, have come to be employed as noun, adjective, or adverb clauses. The whole subject of subordinate clauses was treated above in Lessons XV, XVI, and XVII.

Just as sentences are thus used to take the place of nouns, adjectives, or adverbs, so too nouns and adverbs (or adverbial phrases) are sometimes employed with the meaning of entire sentences. This topic is dealt with below § 506 under the head of *Ellipses.*

QUESTIONS

§ 490. Various kinds of question.[4]—A question either demands confirmation or denial of its whole content, i. e. requires to be answered with 'yes' or 'no'; or else it may indicate by means of an interrogative word or phrase (e. g. 'who?', 'by what means?') the specific detail concerning which information is desired. We shall call these two kinds of question *questions for corroboration* and *questions for specification* respectively.

Again, questions may be *direct* or *indirect.* Indirect questions are those which depend upon some phrase like 'I ask' or 'tell me'.

Sentences which are questions only in form, but not in meaning, are called *rhetorical questions*; see above § 489.

[1] *Adm.* 4, 2.

[2] *Peas.* B 1, 257. Sim. *ib.* 95. 168; also 284, qu. § 148, 3; *Sin.* B 115. 133; *Leb.* 108. 109; *Sh. S.* 184.

[3] *Peas.* B 1, 149–50. Sim. *M. u. K.* 2, 1. 8.

[4] See Erm. *Gramm.*[3] §§ 504–11.

§ 491. A. Questions for corroboration.—1. It may be conjectured that the earliest interrogation was marked only by the speaker's tone of voice. Middle Egyptian examples of this are rare:

mw ỉm is water there?[1]

sp pw n ḥsf·tw n Ḏḥwty-nḫt pn ḥr nhy n ḥsmn ḥnꜥ nhy n ḥmꜣt is it a case for one's punishing this Djeḥutnakht on account of a little natron and a little salt?[2]

kt ỉḫt ỉrt·n·k n·s what else hast thou done to it? Lit. another thing that thou hast done to it?[3]

In the first two examples the Egyptian seems to say 'water is there', 'it is a case'. English indicates the questions by an inversion of words unknown to the ancient language. Our third example is virtually a question for specification (§ 490), and is quoted here only to illustrate the absence of any mark of interrogation; for the elliptical form see below § 506, 1.

2. Elsewhere *ỉs* (§ 247) appears to mark the interrogative tone; but since this particle means little more than 'indeed', 'verily', the nature of the sentence remains outwardly ambiguous, nor are our examples quite certainly questions.

n ntk ỉs s art thou not a man?[4]

n ỉw ỉs pw ỉwsw gsꜣw is it not wrong, a balance which tilts?[5]

These might conceivably be ironic statements ('thou art not a man, I suppose', 'it is not wrong, I suppose'); but in Late Egyptian initial *ỉs* becomes an interrogative particle,[6] and examples can be quoted even from Dyn. XVIII.

ỉs bn šm ssmt m-sꜣ ssmt will not horse go after horse?[7]

ỉs ḥꜣty·n n ḥmt (?) is our heart of copper?[8]

3. The chief interrogative particle is, however, *ỉn* (§ 227), which stands at the beginning of the question. Particularly common is the combination *ỉn ỉw*; this may be considered as a special interrogative phrase, for it occurs even in constructions which, if they contained statements instead of questions, could not employ *ỉw*. Special sections must be devoted to *ỉn ỉw* and to *ỉn* alone. Both after *ỉn* and after *ỉn ỉw* the interrogative meaning may be reinforced by the enclitic particles *rf*, *ỉrf* (§ 252, 3, *b*), and *tr* (§ 256).

Note that when the answer 'yes' is suggested, the negative word *n* or *nn* is employed, as in English and in the Latin *nonne*? When this is absent either the enquiry is made without prejudice, or else the answer 'no' is expected. Observe, further, that the fact of a sentence being a question exerts no influence upon its syntax; the ordinary forms of verbal, non-verbal and pseudo-verbal construction are all employed after *ỉn* and *ỉn ỉw*.

[1] *Eb.* 69, 3.
[2] *Peas.* B 1, 46–8. See also *ib.* 199–200; after *mk*, Lac. *Stèle jur.* 19.
[3] *Ḥarḥ.* 453.
[4] *Leb.* 31.
[5] *Peas.* B 1, 95–6.
[6] Erm. *Neuäg. Gramm.*² §§ 736–7.
[7] *Urk.* iv. 650 (last word restored).
[8] *Paheri* 3.

§ 492. ***ỉn ỉw.***—1. In sentences with *adverbial predicate.*

Ex. *ỉn ỉw·k m ꜥwꜣy* art thou one robbed?[1] Note the *m* of predication.

2. In *existential* sentences.

Ex. *ỉn ỉw wn ky nḫt ꜥḥꜣ r·f* is there (any) other strong man who could fight against him?[2]

3. In sentences with *nominal predicate* and *independent pronoun* as subject.

Ex. *ỉn ỉw ntt ḥmt* art thou a slave-woman?[3]

Before the independent pronouns *ỉw* is unusual; see, however, § 468, 3.

4. In sentences containing *pw* with *a nominal predicate.*

Ex. *ỉn ỉw mꜣꜥt pw pꜣ ḏd* is the saying true, lit. truth?[4] *'Iw* is not found in the corresponding type of statement.

5. In *verbal sentences* with *śḏm·f* or *śḏm·n·f.*

Exx. *ỉn ỉw sṯꜣ·tw n·k skw* are troops brought to thee?[5]

ỉn ỉw kꜣ mr·f ꜥḥꜣ does a bull love combat?[6]

ỉn ỉw ỉỉ·n·t r sn ẖrd pn hast thou come to kiss this child?[7]

In the instances with *śḏm·f* above it is possible to regard the compound tense *ỉw śḏm·f* or *ỉw·f śḏm·f* as the underlying verb-form, since the meaning is *general,* see §§ 462. 463. An example may be quoted, however, where we should hardly expect the *ỉw śḏm·f* form, a particular occasion being referred to.

ỉn ỉw wrš·n ḥr fꜣt ỉt ḥnꜥ bty shall we spend the whole day carrying barley and emmer?[8]

6. In the *pseudo-verbal* construction.

Exx. *ỉn ỉw pꜣ pr sspd* is the house supplied?[9]

ỉn ỉw·k ḥr·tỉ art thou content?[10]

ỉn ỉw mḫꜣt ḥr rdỉt ḥr gs does the balance behave partially, lit. place on (one) side?[11]

ỉn ỉw wnn tꜣ ḥꜣt n·n-ỉmy ḥr ꜥḥꜣ shall our own vanguard be (engaged) in fighting?[12] In the corresponding statement *ỉw* would not stand before *wnn.*

7. *'In ỉw* has only once been found before the negative word *nn.*[13]

§ 493. ***ỉn* as interrogative particle without *ỉw.***—*'In* alone is less common than *ỉn ỉw,* and naturally does not occur where the corresponding statement would contain *ỉw,* as in the sentence with suffix subject and adverbial predicate (§ 117, 2). Where, however, a choice between *ỉn* and *ỉn ỉw* is possible, the former appears to express some surprise on the part of the questioner, such as English might convey by 'can it be that ....?'

[1] *Peas.* B 1, 302. Sim. *ib.* R 55; B 1, 95; *Adm.* 14, 13; *Urk.* iv. 1163, 8.

[2] *Sin.* B 133-4. Sim. *ib.* 35. 120-1.

[3] *M. u. K.* 2, 8. Sim. with *nn* 'not', *ÄZ.* 55, 85, 2-3.

[4] *Westc.* 8, 12-13. Sim. *Leb.* 20.

[5] *Peas.* B 2, 68 (restored from B 1, 303).

[6] *Sin.* B 123. Sim. *Peas.* B 1, 149, qu. § 489.

[7] *M. u. K.* 2, 1. Sim. *Eb.* 2, 3; *Mill.* 2, 7; *Urk.* iv. 324, 10-11.

[8] *Paheri* 3.

[9] *Westc.* 11, 19-20. Sim. *Sin.* B 126; *Peas.* B 1, 198; *Urk.* iv. 651, 11.

[10] *P. Kah.* 13, 24. Sim. *M. u. K.* vs. 2, 2; *ÄZ.* 58, 15*.

[11] *Peas.* B 1, 148-9; sim. *Meir* i. 5. With *r, Peas.* B 1, 283-4, qu. in part § 148, 3.

[12] *Urk.* iv. 650.

[13] See above n. 3.

1. In questions with *nominal predicate* and *pw*.

Ex. *in pꜣ pw ḫn n mdt ḏdw rmṯ* is this the proverb (lit. utterance of speech) which people tell?[1]

[1] *Peas.* B 1, 19. Sim. *ib.* 103.

2. Before the *śḏm·f* or *śḏm·n·f* form.

Exx. *4-nw sp ꜣ m spr n·k in rf wrš·i r·f* the fourth time of (lit. in) making petition to thee, shall I indeed spend all day at it?[2]

in ḏꜣ·n·k n·i s n rḫ·f ṯnw dbꜥw·f hast thou ferried across to me a man who does not know the number of his fingers?[3]

in nn rf di·k swꜣ·i wilt thou not let me pass?[4]

[2] *Peas.* B 1, 224–5. Sim. *ib.* R 53; B 1, 18. 135. 322; *Westc.* 9, 13.

[3] *Urk.* v. 178. Sim. *Harḥ.* 336; *Peas.* B 1, 115.

[4] *Peas.* R 59. Sim. *Westc.* 5, 19.

§ 494. ***in ntt* 'is it the case that .....?'**—A rare construction; apparently some verb like 'dost thou suppose' is suppressed before *ntt*.

1. Before the passive *śḏm·f*.

Ex. *in ntt itw tꜣ mꜥt in Sḥtp-ib Rꜥ* can it be that the boat was taken by Seḥetepibrēꜥ?[5]

[5] *P. Kah.* 33, 12.

2. With the *pseudo-verbal construction*.

Exx. *in ntt bꜣk im ꜥḳ r ḥwt-nṯr* is it the case that this thy humble servant entered into the temple?[6]

in min rf ntt·f ḥtp(w) is it the case to-day that he is forgiving?[7] Note the suffix after *ntt* in accordance with § 223, end.

[6] *P. Kah.* 32, 6.

[7] *Sin.* B 162–3.

3. In one passage, before the *śḏm·n·f* form, *nt-pw* (§ 190, 2) takes the place of *ntt*.[7a]

in nt-pw wn·n·i sꜣ·f is it the case that I have (ever) opened his door?[8]

[7a] For *nt* perhaps cf. p. 361, bottom, n. 3.

[8] *Sin.* B 115–6.

OBS. The third and fourth exx. here seem to guarantee the literal renderings proposed for the first two. It has, however, been pointed out[8a] that the contexts would yield good sense only if *in ntt* there could be understood to mean 'except that'.

[8a] By GUNN. Full discussion, *Suppl.* 15.

§ 495. B. Questions for specification (§ 490) always contain an interrogative noun or adverb, which occupies just the same place in the sentence as it would occupy in a non-interrogative statement.

Exx. *skm m sꜣwy r-30 m 1* what makes $\frac{7}{10}$ up to 1?[9] Lit. what completes $\frac{2}{3}+\frac{1}{30}$ as 1? *M* 'what?' is *subject*.

iry·i m what shall I do?[10] *M* is *object*.

ii·n·k irf r wnm išst to eat what art thou come?[11] *Išst* is *object* of the infinitive in an adverbial phrase.

wn·k ṯn where hast thou been?[12] *Ṯn* is an *adverb*.

smi·i tw irf n m m nṯr to what god shall I announce thee?[13] *N m* is *dative*.

[9] *Rhind* 22. GUNN and ALLEN regard *m* here as the part. *m(y)* after an imperative, but that seems unsuited to this kind of text.

[10] *Adm.* 2, 9.

[11] LAC. *TR.* 23, 31.

[12] LAC. *TR.* 32, 2.

[13] BUDGE, p. 266, 6. Sim. *Leb.* 116.

ḫpr·n 10 m sȝwy r-10 n m of what is 10 the $\frac{23}{30}$ part?[1] Lit. 10 has become $\frac{2}{3}+\frac{1}{10}$ of what? *N(y) m* is *genitive.*

ỉr·tw nn mỉ m n bȝk th·n ỉb·f how comes this to be done (lit. like what is this done) to a servant whom his heart led astray?[2] *Mỉ m* is an adverbial phrase.

These examples show that Egyptian did not feel the same compelling need as is felt in English to place interrogative words at the beginning of the question. In some examples, a disinclination to separate the interrogative word from an interrogative enclitic particle seems to have dictated a departure from the normal word-order.

Exx. *ỉw·f tr r m ỉr·f st* for what (purpose) does he do it?[3] One might have expected *ỉw·f tr ỉr·f st r m.*

ỉw tr ṯn . . . ·k ꜥšȝ where are thy many cattle?[4]

rdỉ·n·k wnm·k ỉrf ṯn sw where hast thou caused thyself to eat it?[5] An extreme case in which it has doubtless been felt impossible to postpone *ỉrf* beyond the third place.

In other instances where the interrogative word comes early in the sentence, it does so in accordance with rules governing other kinds of words as well.

Exx. *m tr tw* who pray art thou?[6] For the inversion see § 127, 3. However, substantially the same meaning may be expressed by *ṯwt m tr*[7] or by *ntk sy* (§ 499, 3); for *ṯwt* and *ntk* as subject see § 125.

in m ḏd sw what says it? The answer is *in 20 ḏd sw* 20 says it.[8] See § 227, 3 for this and the related constructions.

mỉ m ỉrf s nb ḥr sm(ȝ) sn·f how (is it that) every man slays his fellow?[9] For adverbial phrases in anticipatory emphasis see § 148, 5.

The above examples show that the enclitic particles *ỉrf, rf* (§ 252, 3, *b*) and *tr* (§ 256) are used as freely in questions for specification as in questions for corroboration.

Negative questions for specification are by no means common. In those which we have found, the form is that of the sentence with adverbial predicate, the interrogative phrase serving as predicate and the subject being a virtual noun clause introduced by the *sḏm·f* form of *tm.* Examples have been given in § 346, 1, but one is quoted here to illustrate the type:

tm·k tr sḏm ḥr m wherefore, pray, dost thou not hearken?[10]

The literal rendering would doubtless be: that-thou-dost-not hearken is on account of what? English similarly says: why is it that thou dost not hearken?

[1] *Rhind* 30.

[2] *Sin.* B 202.

[3] *Pt.* 274.

[4] *Rhind* 67.

[5] LAC. *TR.* 23, 39.

[6] *B. of D.* 58, 1 (*Ani*). Sim. *Lisht* 20, 33.

[7] LAC. *TR.* 23, 99. Sim. BUDGE, p. 109, 7–8.

[8] *P. Kah.* 8, 24. 28.

[9] *Adm.* 14, 14. Sim. *ÄZ.* 55, 85, 2.

[10] *Peas.* B 1, 180. Sim. *Westc.* 5, 20; 6, 5, both qu. § 346, 1.

INTERROGATIVE PRONOUNS AND ADVERBS

§ **496.** [1] [hieroglyphs] *m* is the commonest word for 'who?', 'what?' It is used as a noun, not as an adjective. In the rare event of its employment as equivalent of the English interrogative adjective 'what?' it is followed by the genitival *n(y)* or by the *m* of predication, ex. [hieroglyphs] (var. [hieroglyphs]) [hieroglyphs] *n m n* (var. *m*) *nṯr* 'to what god?' lit. 'to whom of (*or* as) god?'[2] Various examples of *m* in reference both to persons and to things have been quoted in the last section; besides its use as genitive, dative, or accusative, it was there seen also as logical predicate in the non-verbal sentence ('who art thou?'). Note particularly the adverbial phrases [hieroglyphs] *m m* 'wherewith?';[3] [hieroglyphs] *mi m* 'how?', lit. 'like what?';[4] [hieroglyphs] *r m* 'to what purpose?';[5] [hieroglyphs] *ḥr m* 'why?', lit. 'on account of what?'[6] As subject of a verbal notion, *m* but seldom follows a form of the suffix conjugation (ex. *skm m* at beginning of § 495); usually it stands at the beginning of the question preceded by the emphasizing (not interrogative) [hieroglyphs] *in*; a participle or the *sḏm·f* form follows *in m*, the constructions thus obtained being [hieroglyphs] *in m ir* 'who made?' for the past, [hieroglyphs] *in m irr* 'who makes?' for the present, and [hieroglyphs] *in m ir·f* 'who will make?' for the future; see above §§ 227, 2. 3; 373; 450, 5, *e*. As already stated in § 227, 3 the writings [hieroglyphs] *n-m*, very rarely [hieroglyphs], are apt to take the place of [hieroglyphs] *in m*, a first step towards the formation of the Coptic word *nim*, which even in Late Egyptian is employed for 'who?', 'whom?' in all kinds of construction.[6a] The extended use of *in m* is perhaps already found in [hieroglyphs] *n-m tr ṯw* 'who art thou?'[7] in an XVIII Dyn. MS. of the Book of the Dead, where older texts have *m* or *ptr*. For *n-m tr·k i* 'who art thou that hast come?' see § 256, end.

§ **497.** [hieroglyphs] *ptr* 'who?', 'what?', also written [hieroglyphs] *pt*, [hieroglyphs] *pty*, as well as more fully [hieroglyphs] *pw-tr*, [hieroglyphs] *pw-ti*[7a] (references § 256). This interrogative pronoun is a combination of the enclitic particle *tr* with the very rare interrogative *pw* (§ 498), the latter being of course derived from the demonstrative *pw* 'this'. *Ptr* stands at the beginning of questions with the function of logical predicate, the subject following it in direct juxtaposition (§ 127, 3).

1. With *noun* or *dependent pronoun* as subject.

Exx. [hieroglyphs] *ptr rn·k* what is thy name?[8]

[hieroglyphs] *ptr rf sw* who is he?[9]

2. With a *relative clause* or its equivalent as subject.

Exx. [hieroglyphs] *pw-ti nty* (read *ntt*) *tw r irt* what shall one do?[10] Lit. what is that which one shall do?

[hieroglyphs] *pty hȝȝt r·f m sšr* what amount of corn goes into it?[11] *Hȝȝt*, imperf. act. part.; lit. what is that which goes into it in corn?

[1] In hieroglyphic, *Urk.* iv. 365, 11.

[2] NAV. 125, *Schlussrede* 43 = BUDGE, p. 266, 6, qu. § 495.

[3] *M. u. K.* 1, 6. 7; written with one *m* only, *Peas.* B 1, 199.

[4] *Sin.* B 43; 202, qu. § 495; *Adm.* 14, 14, qu. § 495.

[5] *Pt.* 274, qu. § 495; *Adm.* 3, 12; BUDGE, p. 267.

[6] *Peas.* B 1, 180, qu. § 495; *Westc.* 6, 5, qu. § 346, 1; 11, 22, qu. § 346, 1; *Urk.* iv. 365, 11, qu. § 504, 1.

[6a] *'In m* 'what?' see the ex. qu. p. 405, n. 8.

[7] BUDGE, p. 241, 14 (Nu, collated).

[7a] For this spelling cf. *swi* § 270, OBS.

[8] BUDGE, p. 263, 1. Sim. *Peas.* B 1, 280; *Rhind* 39. 49. 61. With fem. adj. as neuter, *Sin.* B 159.

[9] *Urk.* v. 10. Sim. BUDGE, p. 262, 16.

[10] *Adm.* 4, 6–7. Rather differently, *Rhind* 62.

[11] *Rhind* 43. Sim. *Urk.* iv. 27, 12, qu. § 511, 4.

ptr ḏdt n·i nb·i what does my lord say to me?[1] *Ḏdt*, imperf. rel. form; lit. what is that which my lord says to me?

In this latter use *ptr* corresponds to English 'who?' or 'whom?' with a finite verb, but Egyptian must use a relative clause, a participle, or a relative form, on the principle explained in § 391.

3. With a *dependent* or *demonstrative pronoun* as actual subject and a *noun* or *noun equivalent* added to this in apposition; see above § 132.

Exx. *pty st, Ḏdi, tm rdi mꜣn·i tw* what is it, Djedi, that thou hast not let me see thee (before)?[2] Lit. what is it, Djedi, the not causing I see thee; *tm* is infinitive.

§ 498. *pw*, familiar as a demonstrative (§ 110), is found rarely as an interrogative 'who?', 'what?' With this meaning it is, however, common as a constituent of *ptr* discussed in the last section.

Ex. *pw sw ʿḳ ḥr bꜣ pn* who is he who enters to this soul?[3]

In one or two cases where *pw* occurs at the beginning of a sentence it may possibly have exclamatory force.

Ex. *pw sp nfr* what a happy occasion![4] Rendering not quite certain.

§ 499. *sy*, also written and even rarely, is a not very frequent word for 'who?', 'what?'; besides this use, *sy* provides the Egyptian equivalent of the English interrogative adjective 'which?', 'what?'

1. With the *adjectival* meaning 'which?', 'what?' *sy* precedes its noun, which is probably in apposition to it; *sy* is invariable in gender.

Exx. *ms·s irf s(y) nw* at what moment will she give birth?[5]

šm·k irf ḥr s(y) wꜣt on what road art thou going?[6]

Note too the phrase *ḥr sy išst* 'wherefore?' below § 500, 4.

2. 'Who?', 'what?' in the sentence with *pw*.

Exx. *s ty ꜣ pw ʿty iptf* what are those two limbs?[7] Another MS. has *s(y) sy ty pw*. For *ty* = *tr* see § 256.

sy pw nṯr msy m min who is the god born to-day?[8]

3. 'Who?' with the *independent pronoun* as subject.

Ex. *ntk sy* who art thou?[9]

§ 500. *išst* 'what?' resembles *m* in its use, but is less common.

1. In the sentence with *pw*.

Exx. *iššy* (read *išst*) *pw iryt* what is to be done?[10] Lit. what is that (to be) done?

Since there is no clear evidence that *išst* ever means 'who?' the sentence *išst pw nty im*,[11] lit. 'what is he who is there?', in the tale of the Eloquent Peasant probably means 'what is (the matter with) him who is yonder?

[1] *Sin.* B 261. Sim. *ib.* 183; *Peas.* B 1, 94; *P. Kah.* 5, 6; *Adm.* 3, 7. 13; BUDGE, p. 263, 11. 13.

[2] *Westc.* 8, 10–11. Sim. with *nꜣ*, *ib.* 11, 10–11, qu. § 328, 2.

[3] *ÄZ.* 57, 6*. Sim. *ib.* 60, 70. 73.

[4] *ÄZ.* 60, 70. Sim. *Sin.* B 161.

[5] *Westc.* 9, 15.

[6] LAC. *TR.* 65, 5. 13. Sim. NAV. 145 B, 7. 8.

[7] *Urk.* v. 172. Sim. *ib.* 168, 12; 177, 13.

[8] LAC. *TR.* 19, 3. Sim. *Urk.* v. 51, 3; BUDGE, p. 267, 8.

[9] BUDGE, p. 129, 14; 241, 15.

[10] *Adm.* 5, 10; sim. BUDGE, p. 457, 10; 458, 8. *Išst pw* alone *Sin.* B 35; *Westc.* 6, 25.

[11] *Peas.* B 1, 129.

2. As *object*.

Ex. *ỉr·k n·sn ỉšst* what art thou doing to them ?[1]

3. After a *preposition*.

Ex. *ꜥnḫ·k ỉrf m ỉšst* on what wilt thou live ?[2]

4. Note the phrase *ḥr sy ỉšst* 'wherefore ?'

Ex. *sḫꜣ·tw nn ḥr sy ỉšst* wherefore is this called to mind ?[3]

5. We can only guess at the meaning of a rare expression *ỉšst ỉry*.

Ex. *swt pw wnn, ỉšst ỉry, dỉ·f r ḥꜣt*. Perhaps : he was one who, whatever was done, advanced (the matter).[4]

§ 501. *ỉḫ* 'what ?' is rare in Middle Egyptian, but becomes common in later stages of the language. It is doubtless related to the interjectional *ḫy* (§ 258 A, below, p. 427), to the particle *ỉḫ* (§ 228), and to *ḫt*, *ỉḫt* 'thing'.[5] Its only certain use in the period here dealt with is the use after prepositions.[6]

Exx. *sdd·tw mdt tn ḥr ỉḫ* why (lit. on account of what) is this matter recounted ?[7]

sw mỉ ỉḫ šmt ḥr mṯn pn what is it like to go on this road ?[8] Lit. it is like what, the going, etc. ?

§ 502. *wr* 'how much ?' Only two examples have been quoted in Middle Egyptian.

n(y)-sw wr r wr how much by how much does it measure ?[9] Lit. it is of how much, by how much ?

wr pw r dbꜣ·s how many will be equivalent to it ?[10] For the construction compare § 332, last example.

§ 503. *ṯn* 'where ?', 'whence ?', also written *tn* and probably less correctly *tny*, *tnw*.

1. With the meaning 'where ?'

Exx. *wd·ỉ sw ỉrf ṯn* where shall I place it ?[11]

ỉw·k tnw where art thou ?[12]

2. In *r tn* 'whither ?'

Ex. *ỉr·t r tn* whither art thou making ?[13] A woman is addressed.

3. With the meaning 'whence ?'

Ex. *ỉ·n·ṯn tn* whence have you come ?[14]

4. *Ṯn* 'whence ?' treated as though it were a nominal predicate ; see § 132.

Ex. *ṯn sw pr* whence is he who has gone forth ?[15]

[1] *Urk.* v. 162, 15. Sim. *ib.* 182, 6 ; LAC. *TR.* 23, 31, qu. § 495.

[2] LAC. *TR.* 23, 35. Sim. *ib.* 23, 18. 25 (*ḥr ỉšst*); 17, 21 (*m ỉšst*).

[3] *Urk.* iv. 27. Sim. *ib.* 324, 8, imitated from *Sin.* R 58.

[4] *Urk.* iv. 503. Sim. *sḫnt ḥꜣty m ỉšst ỉry* 'one advanced of mind in whatever is done (?)', Cairo 583, 3.

[5] Cf. *ḳt ỉḫt*, almost 'what else ?', *Harh.* 453, qu. § 491, 1.

[6] As object (very doubtful), *Herdsm.* 8.

[7] *Urk.* iv. 27. Sim. *L. to D.*, Cairo letter, 4.

[8] *Urk.* iv. 649, restored. Sim. as indirect question *T. Carn.* 3, qu. § 504, 1.

[9] *Rhind* 45.

[10] *Rhind* 73.

[11] *Urk.* v. 156. Sim. LAC. *TR.* 23, 39, qu. § 495 ; BUDGE, p. 495, 9.

[12] BUDGE, p. 109, 3. Sim. LAC. *TR.* 32, 2, qu. § 495 ; *Westc.* 9, 4.

[13] *Westc.* 12, 14.

[14] *Semnah Disp.* 2, 14. Sim. BUDGE, p. 203, 4 ; 241, 15.

[15] *ÄZ.* 57, 6*, parallel to *pw sw ꜥḳ*, qu. § 498.

INDIRECT QUESTIONS

§ **504.** 1. We have seen (§ 224) that indirect speech is of rare occurrence in Egyptian. So too *indirect questions* may show no difference from direct questions.

Exx. *n rḫ·ỉ (sp sn) ỉr·n·ṯw nn ḥr m* I know not, I know not wherefore this has been done.[1]

sꜣꜣ·ỉ sw r ỉḫ pꜣy·ỉ nḫt I should like to know (lit. let me know) to what purpose it is, (namely) my strength.[2] See § 501 for a corresponding direct question with *sw* (§ 124) as subject.

2. Without any interrogative word; cf. the direct questions of § 491, 1.

Exx. *ky mꜣꜣ msy st, nn msy·s* another (way of) seeing (whether) a woman will give birth (or) will not give birth.[2a]

ḥr mꜣ·t(w) ntt st ḥr ḫtm n sr ỉr(y) then one shall see whether (lit. that) it has upon it (§ 165, 9) the seal of (its) proper official.[2b]

3. The meaning of an English indirect question may be rendered in Egyptian by a participle or relative form. See above § 399.

MULTIPLE SENTENCES

§ **505. Multiple sentences and clauses** are those in which some essential member is duplicated, or in which—what amounts to the same thing—some member exerts an identical syntactic function towards more than one part of the same sentence or clause. The sentences quoted in § 488 are multiple because they have two or more verbal predicates, or because one and the same noun serves as subject to several verbs.[2c] It will suffice to quote a few different types.

1. Examples where verb-forms other than those of the suffix conjugation are duplicated:

His Majesty took counsel saying: *r-ntt ḫrw pf ḥs n Ḳdšw ỉw ꜥḳ r Mkti* that vile enemy of Kadesh has come and entered into Megiddo.[3] *Ỉw* and *ꜥḳ* are old perfectives.

prt hꜣt ḫft wḏ·f going forth and coming in (take place) according to his command.[4] *Prt* and *hꜣt* are infinitives, subjects of the adverbial predicate *ḫft wḏ·f*.

ḫnms nb swr(w)·n·ỉ wnm(w)·n·ỉ ḥnꜥ·f every friend with whom I drank and ate.[5] Two *sḏmw·n·f* relative forms.

2. With co-ordinated nouns, each having its own adverbial qualification:

Exx. *ꜥḥꜥ·n rdỉ pꜣ smn r gbꜣ ỉmnty n wꜣḫy, ḏꜣḏꜣ·f r gbꜣ ỉꜣbty n wꜣḫy* the goose was placed at the western side of the hall, and its head at the eastern side of the hall.[6]

[1] *Urk.* iv. 365. Sim. *Sin.* B 126–7.

[2] *T. Carn.* 3.

[2a] *P. med. Berl.* vs. 2, 2.

[2b] *Urk.* iv. 1111, 11. Sim. *ib.* 1109, 6.

[2c] See too the king's oath discussed p. 165, top.

[3] *Urk.* iv. 649 (*ntt* and *ḥs* restored). *Ḥr* + infinitive, *Leb.* 11–13.

[4] *Sin.* R 73–4.

[5] Cairo 20057, *q*.

[6] *Westc.* 8, 18–20; sim. *Peas.* B 1, 201–2; 242–4. Expanded objects, *Sh. S.* 30–2, qu. § 402; *Hamm.* 1, 5–6; *Sin.* B 294–5.

I went down to the sea *m dpt nt mḥ 120 m ꜣw·s, mḥ 40 m sḫw·s* in a ship of 120 cubits in its length and 40 cubits in its breadth.[1]

3. Examples with a particle or auxiliary verb governing two or more parallel verb-forms: *iḫ wšb·k wšd·t(w)·k, mdw·k n nsw* so thou shalt answer when thou art addressed, and speak to the king.[2] *n wšb·f n nn n srw, wšb·f n sḫty pn* he did not reply to these nobles, (nor) did he reply to this peasant.[3] *ꜥḥꜥ·n ssꜣ·n·(i) wi, rdi·n·i r tꜣ* I sated myself and left (lit. placed) on the ground.[4] The auxiliary *ꜥḥꜥ·n* governs both *śdm·n·f* forms.

4. Non-verbal sentences; see also the second example under 1, above.

Exx. *nn ꜥbꜥ, nn grg im* there was no boasting and no falsehood therein.[5] *'Im* is a predicate common to two subjects.

iw ẖnw m sgr, ibw m gmw the Residence was in silence, and hearts were in mourning.[6] *'Iw* is a common member.

ink mry nb·f, ḥsy·f m ẖrt-hrw nt rꜥ nb I was one beloved of his lord, praised of him in the course of every day. *'Ink* is a common subject.[7]

5. Under this head fall cases where 'not' serves to negate a particular member of a sentence.[8]

Exx. *iw mn·f wꜥrty·fy dbbw, nn mnty·fy* he is suffering in his lower legs and the ...... (?), not (in) his thighs.[9]

nn rdit mꜣꜣ ky ḥr, nn ḥm ii m rwty without letting other eyes (lit. face) look on, not (even) a slave who has come from abroad.[10]

In both these instances the negated portion is incomplete without the preceding words. One may compare the use of *n is* 'but not' before an adverb, limiting the scope of a preceding statement (§ 209).

ELLIPSES

§ 506. The term **ellipse** is here taken to mean the omission of any element or elements which might seem desirable, from the grammarian's point of view, for the full and explicit expression of a sentence. In actual parlance any set of words which is capable of conveying a meaning relevant to the hearer, any set of words in which he can discern a reasonable intention on the part of the speaker, is a sentence. As thus defined, a sentence may often consist of a single word, such as 'yes' or 'no' (§ 258); but traditional grammar demands the

[1] *Sh. S.* 25–7.

[2] *Sh. S.* 14–16.

[3] *Peas.* B 1, 50–1. Sim. *Sin.* B 198; Coffins, L 1, 81, compared with BUDGE, p. 185, 13.

[4] *Sh. S.* 52–3. After *iw*, Brit. Mus. 614, 4, qu. Exc. XIV, (*a*).

[5] Louvre C 1. Sim. *Urk.* iv. 122, 13.

[6] *Sin.* R 8–9; *Peas.* R 46–7. In pseudo-verbal constr., *Sin.* B 307–8 (*iw*); *Urk.* iv. 62, 6–7 (*wnn*).

[7] Brit. Mus. 614, 3. Sim. *Peas.* B 1, 62–3.

[8] See GUNN, *Stud.* ch. 18.

[9] *Eb.* 42, 2. Sim. *P. Pet.* 1116 A, 121.

[10] BUDGE, p. 497, 9.

presence of at least subject and predicate. The term 'ellipse' is, for this and for other reasons, a questionable one; but it will serve as a convenient heading under which to group those forms of speech which seem deficient from the standpoint of the grammarian's over-rigid categories.

1. *Questions* and *answers to questions* are often elliptical in the sense just defined; so also are other elements of dialogue.

Ex. *wnm ir·k, in·sn r·i. N wnm·i n·ṯn. Ḥr išst, in·sn r·i. Ḥr-ntt mdw pw m-ᶜ·i ḏsr pt tꜣ* 'Eat', say they to me. 'I do not eat for you.' 'Wherefore?' say they to me. 'Because that staff is in my hand which separates heaven and earth.'[1] Abbreviated for: 'Wherefore dost thou not eat?', 'I do not eat because', etc.

In this passage 'say I' is twice to be understood; see § 224, end. We have, moreover, become acquainted in § 321 with *ḥr* used elliptically for *ḥr ḏd* 'says', 'said'.

2. *Exclamatory wishes, interjectional comments* and the like often have elliptical form.

Exx. *ir tꜣ imt-pr irt·n·i n tꜣy·f mwt ḥr ḥꜣt, sꜣ r·s* as for the testament which I made for his mother previously, let it be cancelled.[2] Lit. back to it!

m ḥst nt Skry in the favour of Sokar![3] A typical epistolary greeting.

in wꜣ n rn·f Tti sꜣ Mn-ḥtp by (accursed be his name) Teti, son of Minḥotpe.[4] *Wꜣ n* may conceivably be for *wꜣ ḏwt n* 'evil befall for'.

Further examples in §§ 153. 313.

3. Egyptian writers are fond of what may be called the *label* mode of statement—the curt substitution of a noun or noun-equivalent in place of an assertion. Examples above in §§ 89 (nouns), 306 (infinitives), 390 (participles or relative forms).

Questions too may assume the form of label words or phrases.

Ex. *pꜣ irf ḏd iw·k rḫ·ti tnw nꜣ n ipwt* (what about) the report (lit. saying) that thou knowest the number of the secret chambers?[5]

4. *Comparison*, from our point of view, is much abbreviated in Egyptian.

Exx. *snd·f ḫt ḫꜣswt mi Sḫmt rnpt idw* the fear of him is throughout the lands like (that of) Sakhmet in a year of pestilence.[6]

sꜥꜣ·n·f nḫtw ḥm·i r nsw nb ḫpr ḏr bꜣḥ he magnified the victories of My Majesty more than (those of) any king who had come into existence before.[7]

[1] LAC. *TR.* 23, 19–23. Sim. *Westc.* 8, 16; 9, 4. 5. 14.

[2] *P. Kah.* 11, 20. Sim. *ib.* 31, 5, qu. § 89, 2; MÖLL. *HL.* i. 19 top, 2 after *iḫ*.

[3] *P. Kah.* 27, 4. Sim. *ib.* 29, 4–5. 34.

[4] *Kopt.* 8, 5. Sim. *Sin.* B 74.

[5] *Westc.* 9, 1–2. Sim. *Ḥarḫ.* 453, qu. § 491, 1.

[6] *Sin.* B 44–5. Sim. *ÄZ.* 58, 18*, 30 *a*; after the *m* of predication, *Urk.* v. 67, 1, qu. § 200, 2.

[7] *Urk.* iv. 767. Sim. *ib.* 59, 3; 618, 15; 862, 16; *Pt.* 319, qu. § 96, 1.

5. *Omission of pronouns.* The omission of pronominal *subjects* was dealt with in §§ 486–7. In such instances as the first one in § 487 a natural result of the abbreviation is that the pronominal *object* should likewise be swept away; but we find elsewhere omissions of the object which we should not have expected.

Exx. *ʿḥʿ·n rdì·n·f r sḫd šmsw* then he made (me) into an instructor of the henchmen.[1]

ìst gm·n ḥm·ì šnw m ḏbt after My Majesty had found (it) surrounded with brick.[2]

In contexts similar to the last the omission of the pronoun seems to be even idiomatic.[3]

OBS. For the omission of the subject (nominal or pronominal) in non-verbal sentences see §§ 123; 128, end; 145.

FINAL REMARKS ON WORD-ORDER

§ **507**. The very strict word-order of Egyptian was described in §§ 27. 29. 66, to which the sections on anticipatory emphasis (§§ 146–9) served as a supplement. The rules there laid down apply not merely to main and subordinate clauses, but also to such parts of the verb as the infinitive, the participles, and the relative forms (see § 375). Exceptions to the rules are of rare occurrence, but under certain conditions were permitted or even obligatory.

1. It is a general rule that a pronoun must not precede the noun to which it refers.[4]

Exx. *dmḏ ꜣbt nt s n·f m ẖr(t)-nṯr* to join a man's family to him in the necropolis.[5] According to the ordinary rules the dative *n·f* should precede the nominal object[8] *ꜣbt.*

ìr swt dmḏ·t(w) n Sp pn ꜣbt·f but if there be joined to this Sep his family.[6] According to rule *n Sp pn* should follow the subject *ꜣbt·f.*

ìw mꜣ·n·ì sʿḥʿ pr-wr m hbny ..... ìn n-sw-bìt Mꜣʿt-kꜣ-Rʿ n mwt·s Mwt nbt 'Išrw I saw to the erecting of a Great-House of ebony ..... by king Makerēʿ for her mother Mut, lady of Ashru.[7] The dative would ordinarily precede *ìn n-sw-bìt Mꜣʿt-kꜣ-Rʿ.*

Apparently a like scruple was not felt when the pronoun in question was a reflexive direct object.

Ex. *rdìt ṯs sw Sp ḥr wnm(y)·f* to cause Sep to raise himself on his right side.[8]

Hardly to be regarded as exceptions are cases where a suffix is followed by a noun in apposition[9] or where the funerary formula precedes the name.[10]

[1] *Sebekkhu* 17. Sim. *Urk.* v. 177, 12; *Harḥ.* 394; *Westc.* 12, 4.
[2] *Urk.* iv. 834.
[3] *Urk.* iv. 197, 17; 818, 3; 882, 13, qu. § 212.
[4] See *ÄZ.* 44, 112.
[5] LAC. *TR.* 2, 1. Sim. *Harḥ.* 344. Cases like LAC. *TR.* 2, 37, qu. p. 375, n. 2, are due to replacement of a proper name by a suffix.
[6] LAC. *TR.* 2, 39–41.
[7] *Urk.* iv. 521.
[8] LAC. *TR.* 39, 1. Sim. BUDGE, p. 287, 16.
[9] *Sin.* R 68, qu. § 90; LAC. *TR.* 23, 29, qu. § 436.
[10] See the text qu. p. 171. Sim. Cairo 20008, 20011.

2. Occasionally *an adverbial phrase precedes the subject or object*, if such a transposition is felt to be convenient. This is felt, for example, when the adverbial phrase belongs very closely to the verb.

Exx. *rdỉ·n·ỉ swꜣ ḥr·ỉ ꜥḥꜣw·f* I caused to pass by me his arrows.[1]

ỉw mỉ ḫt ꜥꜣ wḥm st it is like a big thing to repeat it.[2]

ỉst štꜣ ḥr ỉb n rmṯ ỉtḥ ꜥꜣwt ḥr·s lo, it was difficult in the heart of men to drag great things over it.[3]

dỉ m ỉb·ỉ nṯr ỉr·ỉ mnw·f the god put (it) in my heart that I should make monuments for him (lit. his monuments).[4]

In the last example the context continues 'and that I should cause him to be powerful even as he has caused me to be powerful'. Thus the object is long and complex; this is an additional reason for its postponement. Similar cases are by no means rare.

Ex. The sun is hot; *ḥꜣ dỉ·tw n pꜣ Šw swnt ỉt m rmw* may the sun be given (lit. let one give to the sun) the price of the corn in fish.[5] This is a witticism; the speaker is thinking of the inundation, which will put fish in the place of the crops now being harvested.

Particularly common is the ancient and stereotyped formula of dedication, of which a single example must here suffice.

ỉr·n·f m mnw·f n ỉt·f Ḥr-ꜣḫty sꜥḥꜥ n·f tḫnwy wrwy, bnbnt m ḏꜥm he made as his monument to his father Ḥarakhte the erecting for him of two great obelisks (with) the pyramidion of gold.[6]

The infinitival object usually broadens out into a longish description, after which *m mnw·f* would come in lamely or incomprehensibly.[7]

For the displacement of certain interrogative adverbs or adverbial phrases, in order to avoid separation from the interrogative enclitic particles, see § 495.

3. A strange example, in which subject and object appear to change places for a like reason, is

ỉw grt ỉr·n sš (ꜣ)ḥt m mw nw Tꜣ-wr ꜣbḏw ỉt·ỉ ỉt n ỉt·ỉ ḏr rk Ḥr Wꜣḥ-ꜥnḫ, n-sw-bỉt sꜣ Rꜥ ꞽIntf there served as (lit. made) scribe of the fields in the waters of Abydus of the Thinite nome my father and the father of my father since the time of the Horus 'Enduring-of-life', the king of Upper and Lower Egypt, Son of Rēꜥ, Antef.[8]

Another possible rendering 'I made ..... and my father and the father of my father' is intrinsically rather improbable; its improbability is increased by the fact that this text elsewhere contains no instance of the omission of the suffix of the 1st pers. sing.

[1] *Sin.* B 136. Sim. *ib.* 258.

[2] *Sin.* B 215–6.

[3] *Bersh.* i. 14, 2.

[4] *Urk.* iv. 198. Sim. Cairo 20025, 9–10.

[5] *Paheri* 3. Sim. *Pt.* 28.

[6] *Urk.* iv. 590. Sim. *ib.* 357, 4; 584, 9; 586, 13; 592, 14; 607, 3. Without inf. object, 526, 5.

[7] A good parallel (Old Kingdom) is *Urk.* i. 146, 6–8. Sim. *Pt.* 566–7.

[8] Leyd. V 3.

4. In *wḏ·f sw n·f* lit. 'he shall order him to him',[1] i.e. the vizier shall order him to come to himself, the pregnant and special meaning of the dative is clearly the cause of the inversion.

5. In other cases exceptional word-order is explicable only on grounds of general convenience.

Ex. *ḥnꜥ rdỉt ỉn wꜥb ỉmy ꜣbd·f pꜣḳ nỉw ḥnḳt ḏwỉw n ḫnty·f nty m rwd ḫry n ỉs·f* with the giving by the priest in his month of a bowl of *pꜣḳ*-bread and a jug of beer to his statue which is in the lower stairway of his tomb.[2] Strictly speaking, the object[s] of the infinitive should have preceded the agent.

6. Virtual adverb clauses are sometimes inserted parenthetically for reasons of convenience.

Exx. (*sic*) *ỉw, sk (w)ỉ grt wꜣ·k(w)ỉ r nmḥ, ḫrp·n·ỉ kꜣ* now though I had fallen into (the condition of) an orphan I had oxen at my command.[3] *Ỉw ... ḫrp·n·ỉ* is the form *ỉw sḏm·n·f* of § 464.

nꜥt m ḫd ỉn ḥm·f, ỉb·f ꜣw, m ḳnt nḫt His Majesty fared downstream, his heart rejoicing, in might and victory.[4]

CONCORD

§ 508. Concord, i.e. the assimilation of one element of a sentence or clause to another in some important particular of form, is of three kinds: concord of person (§ 509), concord of number (§ 510), and concord of gender (§ 511).

§ 509. Concord of person.—1. The chief peculiarity of Egyptian here is its strong tendency to treat adjectives and participles as nouns, and hence as of the third person singular, even when they refer to pronouns of the first or second person. See already above § 136.

Exx. *ỉnk mry nb·f* I was one beloved of his lord.[5] English usually says: I was beloved of my lord.

ỉnk rḫ sbꜣ sw r rḫ I am one who knew him who could teach him to know.[6] Contrast English: I knew who could teach me to know.

ỉnḏ ḥr·t ..... ḥḏt ꜥꜣt, ḥꜥꜥt psḏt m nfrw·s hail to thee ..... thou great white one, at whose beauty the Ennead rejoices. Lit. rejoiced the Ennead at *her* beauty.[7]

ỉ ꜥnḫw ...... swꜣty·sn ḥr ỉs pn ...... ỉw·ṯn r drp n·ỉ O ye who live .... and who shall pass by this tomb .... ye shall offer to me[8] The *sḏmty·fy* form is essentially of the third person, yet is here used to qualify a vocative.

[1] *Urk.* iv. 1110, 12, qu. Exerc. XXX, (iii).

[2] *Siut* I, 308.

[3] PETRIE, *Courtiers* 22. Sim. *Sh. S.* 153, qu. § 188, 1; *Urk.* iv. 1020, 7–9.

[4] *Urk.* iv. 5. Sim. *ib.* iv. 894, 1.

[5] Brit. Mus. 614, 3. Sim. *Sin.* R 2–3.

[6] Leyd. V 6.

[7] ERM. *Hymn.* I, 1–2. Sim. *Urk.* iv. 942, 12–13.

[8] Cairo 20003. Sim. *ib.* 20026, *c* 7–10; *Urk.* iv. 1032, 3–4; 1083, 15–17.

2. Pronouns of the 3rd pers. sing. are usually employed in referring back to the phrase *bꜣk im* (§ 158).

Ex. *nfr ib n bꜣk im sḏm·n·f ꜥ.w.s. nb* (*ꜥ.w.s.*) the heart of this thy humble servant is happy now that he has heard of the good health of (my) lord (l. p. h.).[1]

Occasionally, however, *bꜣk im* alternates with the 1st pers. sing.

Ex. *wꜥrt tn irt·n bꜣk* (read *bꜣk im*), *n ḥmt·(i) s(y)* this flight which thy humble servant made, I did not plan it.[2]

With *ḥm·i* 'My Majesty' either the 3rd or the 1st pers. may be used.[3]

Exx. *ḥm·i ḏs·f ir m ꜥwy·f* My Majesty himself acting with his (own) hands.[4] Such use of the 3rd pers. seems to be the rarer case.

ꜣb·n ḥm·i irt mnw n it·i 'Imn-Rꜥ My Majesty wished to make a monument for my father Amen-Rēꜥ.[5]

With *ḥm·k* 'Thy Majesty' pronouns of the 2nd pers. are used.[6]

§ 510. Concord of number in Egyptian is much looser than in English.[7]
1. We have noted (§ 86) the tendency of the genitival adjective *ny* to become invariable in number and gender, but *nb* 'all', 'every' without ending is mere graphic abbreviation (§ 48, 1). The absence of *-w-* from the fem. plur. of adjectives (§ 74) may have had its counterpart in the spoken language.

2. Feminine collectives (§ 77, 3) have fem. adjectives in agreement with them.

Ex. *rmṯ(t) nbt pꜥt nbt rḫyt nbt ḥnmmt nbt* all mankind, all noble people, all commoners, all sun-folk.[8]

When a suffix is involved, usage is variable. Thus we find *tꜣ ḫnyt r ꜣw·s* 'the entire body of marines'[9] beside *ꜥwt nbt ibw·sn rmw* 'all cattle, their hearts weep'.[10]

When *nb* 'every' accompanies a singular noun, either the plural or the singular suffix may be employed. Whereas in the two expressions for 'everybody' *bw nb* and *ḥr nb* (§ 103) the determinative alone would suffice to indicate that they were regarded as plurals,[11] *s nb*, which often has the same meaning, is referred back to with a singular suffix;[12] not infrequently 'each one' is a better translation of *s nb* than 'everyone', see § 103.

3. When a number of persons are described as doing something with some part of their bodies, Egyptian idiom speaks of that part in the singular.

Exx. *iw·ṯn r ḏd m r·ṯn* ye shall speak with your mouths, lit. mouth.[13]

di·i m ḥr n ḥnmmt .... ntyw ib·sn ḫt mnw pn I call to the attention (lit. I put in the face) of mankind ...... whose heart(s) are occupied with this monument.[14]

This rule is, however, liable to exceptions, see *ibw·sn* above under 2.[15]

[1] *P. Kah.* 29, 12. Sim. *ib.* 32, 6; *Sin.* B 178. 205. 213-4.

[2] *Sin.* B 223. Sim. *ib.* 174-7; *P. Kah.* 28, 5-6.

[3] For *ḥm·i* repeated, see Berl. *ÄI.* i. p. 258, 20-1.

[4] *Urk.* iv. 169. Sim. *ib.* 256, 9.

[5] *Urk.* iv. 834. Sim. *ib.* 366, 14; 776, 13-14; *Ikhern.* 5.

[6] *Urk.* iv. 613, 6-7.

[7] Cf. 'a finger *or* a toe which *are* painful', *Eb.* 78, 6, qu. Exerc. XXIX, (*a*).

[8] BUDGE, p. 113, 8-9. Sim. *Urk.* iv. 233, 14.

[9] *Urk.* iv. 6, 9. Sim. *ib.* 390, 2.

[10] *Adm.* 5, 5. Sim. Cairo 20016, *a* 1.

[11] *Ḥr nb* with following plural suffix, *Urk.* iv. 17, 10-11.

[12] *Leb.* 112. 119.

[13] Cairo 20003, *a* 4. Sim. *Adm.* 4, 13; *Urk.* iv. 101, 6.

[14] *Urk.* iv. 364, 11-13. Sim. *ib.* 1083, 13.

[15] Also *Urk.* iv. 613, 13. 14; 614, 11; 615, 2.

§ 511. Concord of gender.—Under this head we have to consider a number of cases where the gender of an adjective, verbal form, or suffix-pronoun differs from what might be expected.

1. When in a sequence of co-ordinated words of both genders the first is masculine, the sequence as a whole is treated as masculine.

Exx. *nṯrw nṯrwt ỉmyw ȝbḏw* the gods and goddesses who are in Abydus.[1]

pȝ t ḥnḳt ỉrrw n·ỉ tȝ ḳnbt nt ḥ(w)t-nṯr nty rdỉ·n·ỉ n·ṯn sw the bread and beer which the staff of the temple make for me and which I have given to you.[2]

1 a. In Middle Egyptian arises a tendency to treat dual nouns, whether masc. or fem., as masc. singulars.[2a]

Exx. *pȝ tḫnwy wrwy* the two great obelisks.[2b]

rdỉw n·ỉ ỉrty·ỉ ȝḫ·ỉ ỉm·f my eyes have been given to me that I may benefit by them.[2c]

2. Old perfectives, participles, etc., referring to feminine plural words take masculine forms, though the suffix-pronoun used in such a case is fem. sing.

Exx. *ỉst mnỉwt nbt spr ḥm·f r·s sspd* all ports to which His Majesty comes were equipped.[3] Note the rel. form *spr*, the old perf. *sspd* and the suffix *s*. That *mnỉwt* is plur. and *sspd* masc. is indicated by the variants *mnỉwt*[4] and *sspdw*[5] in parallel passages.

ỉw ṯs·n·(ỉ) sȝwt wn sky I raised up walls which were destroyed.[6] *Wn* is participle, *sky* old perfective.

ḫt nbt rdỉw·n n·ỉ pȝy·ỉ sn all things which my brother gave to me.[7] Contrast the fem. *nbt* with the masc. rel. form *rdỉw·n*.

The above rule seems almost absolute in the old perf.[8]; the same fact was expressed in § 309 by saying that the ancient form of the 3rd pers. fem. plur. (and dual) is in M.E. regularly replaced by the 3rd pers. masc. form. In the participles and cognate forms, masc. gender referring to fem. plur. nouns is only exceptional; one can quote good instances to the contrary.

Exx. *gmḥwt prrt n·f stt tkȝ ỉm·sn* tapers which go forth unto him and with which lights are kindled.[9]

wp·f wȝwt mrrt·f may he open the ways he desires.[10]

It is noticeable that the preference is given to masc. forms when *nȝ n* or *nn n* 'these' precedes the fem. plur. noun; cf. below under 3.

Exx. *nȝ n gmḥwt rdỉ(w)·n·k n·ỉ* these tapers which thou hast given to me.[11]

nn n ḫt rdỉ(w)·n·sn n·ỉ these things which they have given me.[12]

[1] Cairo 20748, *g* 2. Sim. with adj. *ib.* 20520, *d* 4–5; 20775, *o* 1.

[2] *Siut* 1, 295. Sim. with rel. form, *Urk.* iv. 743, 5; with *sḏmty·fy* form, Turin 1447; *Eb.* 1, 15–16.

[2a] *ÄZ.* 59, 10.

[2b] *Urk.* iv. 366, 13.

[2c] *ÄZ.* 59, 57*, 15–6. Sim. *Urk.* v. 28, 1–2.

[3] *Urk.* iv. 692.

[4] *Urk.* iv. 707, 10.

[5] *Urk.* iv. 719, 7.

[6] *Siut* 1, 235.

[7] *P. Kah.* 12, 8. Sim. *Urk.* iv. 85, 11; 780, 5–6.

[8] More exx. *Verbum* ii. § 50.

[9] *Siut* 1, 305. Sim. *Eb.* 20, 17. 23; 76, 12.

[10] Brit. Mus. 614, vert. 5.

[11] *Siut.* 1, 301. Sim. *P.Kah.* 12, 13; Louvre C 11, 2. Sim. *nty*, *Tarkhan*, 1, 80, 21.

[12] *Siut* 1, 270. Sim. *ib.* 1, 269.

3. When *nꜣ*, *nw*, and *nn* are used as demonstrative pronouns for 'this', 'that', they are referred back to by masc. participles and relative forms; but the resumptive pronoun then used is fem.

Exx. *ỉr nw ỉddw msḏrwy ḥr·s* as for that through which the ears become dulled.[1]

nꜣ ḥd(w)·k sw ḥr·s that for which thou punishest him.[2]

Similarly when the antecedent is an abstract noun:

n wd·n·(ỉ) m-sꜣ bw ḏwy msḏw rmṯ ḥr·s I did not strain after evil on account of which men are hated.[3] For the construction see § 377.

In one instance *nn* is followed by a feminine relative form:

ḏd·n·ỉ nn ḏdt·n·ỉ m mꜣꜥt I have said this that I have said truthfully.[3a]

4. In Late Egyptian the meaning of the *neuter* is expressed by the masculine, whereas in Middle Egyptian it is expressed by the feminine (§ 51). Contrast M.E. *ḏd·f st* 'he says it' with L.E. *ỉw·s(t) ḥr ḏd(tỉ)·f* 'she said it';[4] M.E. *ḏwt* 'evil' with L.E. *pꜣ nfr* 'the good';[5] M.E. *ỉrt·n·k* 'what thou hast done' with L.E. *pꜣ ỉỉr·k nb* 'all that thou hast done'.[6] The transition from the feminine to the masculine seems to have begun with the *old perfective*; here the masculine is usual in Middle Egyptian.

Exx. *smꜣw gmyt wꜣsy* renovating what was found decayed.[7] Contrast the fem. pass. part. *gmyt* with the masc. old perfective *wꜣsy*.

ỉrrt ỉꜣw n rmṯ bỉn m ḫt nbt what old age does to men is evil in all respects.[8]

nn st ꜣḫ n·k it is not profitable to thee.[9]

In the case of the *participles* and *relative forms*, examples of masc. gender for neuter meaning are rare in early times.

Exx. *sḏd·ỉ rf n·k mỉtt ỉry ḫprw m ỉw pn* let me tell thee the like thereof which happened in this island.[10]

wnw m sḏm mk st ḫpr (the things) that were mere hearsay (lit. in hearing), behold they have happened.[11]

n hḏ·ỉ ỉr·n ky I did not destroy what another had made.[13] *'Ir·n* for *ỉrt·n*.

The rare examples where the masc. definite article precedes a relative form of neuter meaning are to be viewed as early cases of Late Egyptian.

Ex. *rdỉt ỉry·ỉ pꜣ wḏ(t)·n pꜣ·ỉ nb* to cause me to do what my lord commanded.[14] The written *t* is probably due to a recollection of the ordinary M.E. form *wḏt·n·f* usual in such contexts.

[1] *Eb.* 99, 15.

[2] *Urk.* iv. 1090, 14. Sim. *ÄZ.* 69, 32 (l. 23).

[3] Brit. Mus. 614, 7–8.

[3a] Lyons 88 = Stockholm 55 = *Urk.* iv. 1196, 8.

[4] *d'Orbiney* 6, 1.

[5] *Anastasi* v. 15, 2.

[6] *Bologna* 1094, 2, 1.

[7] *L. D.* ii. 112, *e*; 113, *b*. Sim. *Bersh.* ii. p. 25; also *wnt šꜣ* 'what had been difficult', *Siut* 4, 31, qu. § 396, 2.

[8] *Pt.* 20–1. Sim. *Eb.* 91, 21–92, 1.

[9] *P. Pet.* 1116 A, 48. Sim. *Pt.* 291.

[10] *Sh. S.* 125. Sim. *ib.* 22.

[11] *Urk.* iv. 500.

[13] Cairo 20741, *c* 2. Sim. *ḏd* for *ḏdt*, *Pt.* 265, qu. Exerc. XXVII, (*a*); *ib.* 543. 553.

[14] *Urk.* iv. 1069. Sim. *D. el B.* 155, qu. § 330.

5. The *indefinite pronoun* [hieroglyphs] *tw* (§ 47) is treated as a masculine.

Ex. [hieroglyphs] *ˁḥˁ·n·tw ḥˁw im* then one rejoiced thereat.[1]

So too the pronoun [hieroglyphs] *st* with the meaning 'them' (§ 46).

Ex. [hieroglyphs] *gm·(i) st ˁḥˁ ḥr mr(y)t* I found them standing on the bank.[1a]

6. The Egyptians were never remarkable for scholarly accuracy, and examples are not infrequent, especially in much-copied texts, where the fem. ending is wrongly omitted.

Exx. [hieroglyphs] *pḫrt 2-nwt ir·n Šw ḥr·f ḏs·f* a second remedy which Shu made on his own behalf.[2] The parallel passages in Ebers[3] have correctly [hieroglyphs] *irt·n*.

[hieroglyphs] *stp·n·f r sɜw Kmt* whom (fem.) he chose to protect Egypt.[4] The epithet immediately preceding contains the correct fem. form [hieroglyphs] *sḫˁt·n*.

OBS. For concord of gender in the case of numbers, see § 261; and for nouns of exceptional gender see § 92.

[1] Louvre C 12. Sim. *Paheri* 3, qu. § 330.

[1a] ROEDER, *Debod*, Pl. 108, iv. *a*. Sim. *ÄZ*. 69, 32 (l. 23).

[2] *Hearst* 5, 7. Sim. *ib*. 5, 9. 11. 12. 15.

[3] *Eb*. 46, 10. 16. 22.

[4] *Urk*. iv. 361. Sim. *ib*. 361, 11; 1082, 3.

VOCABULARY

[hieroglyphs] *iwr* become pregnant.

[hieroglyphs] *ḥsḳ* cut off.

[hieroglyphs] *sšm* lead, guide.

[hieroglyphs] *ipt* private chamber, harîm.

[hieroglyphs] *wr-mɜw* 'Greatest-of-seers', name of the high-priest of Heliopolis.

[hieroglyphs] *wsḫt* hall, court (in temple or palace).

[hieroglyphs] *biɜyt* marvel, wonder.

[hieroglyphs] *mšrw* evening.

[hieroglyphs] *mḥyt* north wind.

[hieroglyphs] *nw* time.

[hieroglyphs] *ḥmt* craft, craftsmanship.

[hieroglyphs] *ḥrt* heaven.

[hieroglyphs] *ḥsw* singer.

[hieroglyphs] *ḥtpt* offerings.

[hieroglyphs] var. [hieroglyphs] *ḫry-ḥb(t)* lector-priest.

[hieroglyphs] *sḫ* counsel.

[hieroglyphs] *šfšft* dignity.

[hieroglyphs] *tp-rd* rules, principles.

[hieroglyphs] *ṯnt* difference.

[hieroglyphs] *ds* flint.

[hieroglyphs] *dfɜ* food.

[hieroglyphs] *imy-ḫt* (adj. from *m-ḫt*) one who goes after *or* accompanies.

EXERCISE XXXIII

(a) *Reading lesson : extract from a book of tales.*[1]

ꜥḥꜥ·n ḏd·n pꜣ . . . w Ḫwfw mꜣꜥ-ḫrw :
pꜣ irf ḏd,
iw·k rḫ·ti tnw nꜣ n
ipwt nt wnt nt Ḏḥwty ?
ḏd·in Ḏdi :
ḥs·ti, n rḫ·i tnw iry,
ity (ꜥ.w.s.) nb·i ;
iw·i swt rḫ·kwi bw nty st im.
ḏd·in ḥm·f :
iw irf tn ?
ḏd·in Ḏdi pn :
iw ꜥfdt im nt ds
m ꜥt sipty rn·s m 'Iwnw ;
m tꜣ ꜥfdt.
ḏd·in Ḏdi :
ity (ꜥ.w.s.) nb·i,
mk nn ink is inn n·k sy.
ḏd·in ḥm·f :
in m irf in·f n·i sy ?
ḏd·in Ḏdi :
in smsw n pꜣ ẖrdw 3
nty m ẖt n Rd-ḏdt
in·f n·k sy.
ḏd·in ḥm·f :
mr·i is st.
nꜣ ḏdy·k,
pty sy tꜣ Rd-ḏdt ?

[1] *Westc.* 9, 1–15 with a few restorations. See too *JEA.* 11, 2.
[2] The traces do not suit 'king', which gives, however, the required sense.
[3] The original has wrongly ; see *ib.* 7, 5. 7.

ḏd·in Ḏdi :
ḥmt wꜥb pw n Rꜥ nb Sꜣḫbw
iwr·ti m ẖrdw 3 n Rꜥ nb Sꜣḫbw,
iw ḏd·n·f r·s :
iw·sn r irt iꜣt twy mnḫt
m tꜣ pn r ḏr·f ;
iw smsw n·sn-imy r irt wr-mꜣw m [*Iwnw.*
wn·in ḥm·f ib·f wꜣ r ḏwt ḥr·s.
ḏd·in Ḏdi :
pty irf pꜣ ib, ity (ꜥ.*w.s.*) *nb·i ?*
in ir·tw ḥr pꜣ ẖrdw 3 ḏd·n·i :
kꜣ sꜣ·k,
kꜣ sꜣ·f,
kꜣ wꜥw im·s ?[1]
ḏd·in ḥm·f :
ms·s irf s(*y*) *nw, Rd-ḏdt ?*
ms·s m ꜣbd 1 (*n*) *prt sw 15.*

[1] Probably the abbreviated form of the suffix 3rd pers. plur. noted p. 39, n. 12a; so too perhaps above, l. 4.

'Then said the [king] Cheops, the deceased: (What about) the saying thou knowest the number of the secret chambers of the sanctuary[1] of Thoth? And Djedi said: So it please thee, I know not the number thereof, O Sovereign, my lord, but I know the place where it is.[2] And His Majesty said: Where is it? And this Djedi said: There is a box of flint in a room called (room of) inspection in Heliopolis; (it is) in that box. ⟨And His Majesty said: Go fetch me that box⟩.[3] And Djedi said: O Sovereign, my lord, behold it is not I who will fetch it for thee. And His Majesty said: Who will fetch it for me? And Djedi said: The eldest of the three children who are in the womb of Reddjedet will fetch it for thee. And His Majesty said: Indeed I should like it! (But as regards) what thou hast said, who is this Reddjedet?[4] And Djedi said: She is the wife of a priest of Rēꜥ, lord of Sakhebu, who is pregnant of three children belonging to Rēꜥ, lord of Sakhebu; and he has said about them (?) that they shall exercise this

[1] A word otherwise unknown, possibly connected with the geographical name *Wnw*, i.e. Shmûn, Hermopolis Magna.
[2] The context seems to demand that *st* should here refer to the number, not to the *ipwt* themselves.
[3] The sense demands the restoration of some such speech on the part of the king. Its omission may have been due to *homoioteleuton*, the recurrence of one and the same word at the end of two consecutive phrases or sentences.
[4] It seems best to take *nꜣ ḏdy·k* as in anticipatory emphasis (§ 148, 5) and as equivalent to *ir nꜣ ḏdy·k*. For the form *ḏdy·k* see p. 303, n. 19. However, GUNN and BLACKMAN attach *nꜣ ḏdy·k* to *st* preceding and render 'I shall be pleased with it, what you are going to say', see *JEA*. 16, 67.

beneficent office throughout the entire land; and the eldest of them shall be high-priest[1] in Heliopolis. Thereupon His Majesty grew sad in his heart because of it. And Djedi said: What is this mood, O Sovereign, my lord?[2] Is it on account of these three children I spoke of? Next your son, next his son, and next one of them![3] And His Majesty said: At what moment will she give birth, Reddjedet? ⟨And Djedi said:⟩[4] She will give birth on the fifteenth day of the first month of winter.'

[1] *Wr mꜣw*, lit. 'greatest of the seers'; this was the particular name of the high-priest of Heliopolis.
[2] Lit. 'heart', i.e. state of heart, mood. *Ỉn ỉr·tw* lit. 'is (it) done?' [3] Rendering doubtful. [4] See § 224, end.

(*b*) *Translate into English, emending if necessary:*

(1) [1] ... (2) ...

[1] Text from a stela showing a minstrel playing the harp before his master.

(*c*) *Translate into Egyptian:*

(1) Then said the courtiers to (*ḫft*) His Majesty: Behold, we will do according to (*m*) all that thou hast commanded, O Sovereign, our lord. (But) wherefore hast thou inquired from us a counsel (*sḫ*)? Does one guide Horus who is in the sky to sail in the heavens? Does one give a rule of knowledge to Ptah, the noble one who-presides-over (*ḥry-tp*) craftsmanship? Does one teach Thoth to speak? There is no difference between (lit. of) these three and (lit. *r* 'from') Thy Majesty. If thou givest instruction (*ḥr* 'face') to him who is ignorant (*ḫm-ḫt*), the morrow dawns (lit. the earth grows light), and he is cleverer than those who know! (2) Hail to thee, thou eye of Horus, who cuttest off the heads of those who accompany Seth! Great is thy dignity (over) against thy enemies, in this thy name of lady of dignity! O Sobk, thou hast placed her in thy head,[1] that thou mayst be great through (*m*) her. (3) It is a greeting to my lord (l. p. h.) to the effect that the two Medjay-people who went to the desert on the fourth day of the first month of summer came to report to me to-day at time of evening, and brought three Nubians, saying that they had found them to the south of the fortress. Thereupon I asked these Nubians, 'Whence have ye come?' Thereupon they said, 'We have come from the Well of Horus.' (4) This book was found by night by the hand of a lector-priest, when this earth was in darkness. The moon shone on this book, on every side of it. It was brought as a wonder to the Majesty of King Cheops, the deceased.

[1] The eye of Horus is here identified with the uraeus (i. e. cobra) in the royal diadem.

NEW PARAGRAPHS AND OTHER ADDITIONS

P. 53. On this page add two new paragraphs:

§ 62 A. Avoidance of the repetition of like hieroglyphic signs.—Analogous to the phenomena illustrated in the early part of § 62 are cases where what is avoided is repetition of signs other than a single consonant, or even of an entire word.

Exx. [hieroglyphs] *ym* 'sea',[1] oldest writing of this Semitic loan-word; [hieroglyph] here serves partly as group-writing for *m* (§ 60 and see Sign-list N 35), but partly also as the determinative of water.

[hieroglyphs] *ḥr ntt* for *ḥr ntt ntt* 'because . . . . what'[2] in a clause quoted below in § 200 A, if the omission of the second *ntt* be not a mere mistake.

§ 63 A. Hieratic and hieroglyphic.—At the outset hieratic writing was no more than a particular summary mode of presenting hieroglyphic (see p. 10), but in course of time the two scripts diverged and developed special orthographic habits of their own. Hieroglyphic, true to its essentially decorative character, remained the more free of the two, exhibiting its signs in greater or less detail as occasion demanded, and disposing them in relatively arbitrary positions. Hieratic, on the other hand, became far more regular and consistent, and invented, in case of need, fashions of spelling suited to itself.[3] Only a few traits of Middle Kingdom hieratic can here be mentioned:

1. Biliteral signs usually have their phonetic complement, exx. [hieroglyphs] *wꜣ* rather than [hieroglyph] alone, [hieroglyphs] *tꜣ* rather than [hieroglyph] or [hieroglyph].

2. Elaborate hieroglyphs are avoided and sometimes replaced by a mere oblique stroke \, ex. [hieroglyphs] *ms* for [hieroglyphs] (see Z 5 in the Sign-list).

3. The repetition of signs in duals and plurals (§ 73, 1) is avoided, exx. [hieroglyphs] *irty* for [hieroglyphs], [hieroglyphs] *srw* for [hieroglyphs], [hieroglyphs] *rnw* for [hieroglyphs], [hieroglyphs] *mnw* for [hieroglyphs] (§ 77, 1).

4. New signs were developed, ex. [hieroglyph] *w* for [hieroglyph], or variant forms retained, exx. [hieroglyph] for [hieroglyph] *pꜣ*, [hieroglyph] for [hieroglyph] *k*, [hieroglyph] for [hieroglyph] as determinative of king or god.

Egyptologists have experienced the practical need of adopting some common standard to which different hieratic hands could be reduced, and instead of selecting one simple style of hieratic for the purpose, have preferred to *transcribe* all hieratic hands into hieroglyphic. In view, however, of the aforementioned divergence of the two scripts, it is necessary to realize that such *transcriptions*, as they are called, are perforce in some degree artificial products, exhibiting the text transcribed in a form more or less different from that which would have been

[1] *ÄZ.* 69, 30, 17, corrected *AEO*, Text, I, p. 162*; also *Amarn.* VI, 25, 18. Sim. p. 169, n. 5.

[2] *Nauri* 8.

[3] Much testimony in E. DÉVAUD, *L'âge des papyrus égyptiens hiératiques d'après les graphies de certains mots*, Paris, 1924.

chosen by a contemporary scribe or sculptor. It belongs to good scientific method not to gloss over such differences, and since the appearance of the first edition of this Grammar most scholars have adopted a more rigid attitude in this matter.[1] In the present edition the transcriptions of most texts have been revised accordingly, and the presence of instead of and of instead of is as a rule a useful indication that the example in question is taken from a hieratic text, not a hieroglyphic one.

Obs. 1. For reasons of economy and spacing it has not proved possible in this edition to revise the transcriptions from hieratic as thoroughly as would have been desirable. In the best modern editions of texts not only is the direction of the originals from right to left retained, but also the positions of the individual signs are scrupulously followed. *The student is urgently counselled to conform to this sound practice*; in particular should not be turned upright as and, if the original writes the plural strokes as , the transcription also should show them thus, not as or .

Obs. 2. The revision of transcriptions in this edition has not as a rule extended to the Book of the Dead and the Coffin Texts, since there it was usually needful to quote certain handy and easily accessible editions where the old style was employed.

P. 65. Add at the place marked the following new paragraph:

§ 84 A. Direct object after verbs of apparently intransitive or passive sense.—Such verbs as *wnḫ* 'be clad (in)', *wrḥ* 'be anointed (with)', *mn* 'be ill (of)' a disease or '(in)' a limb, *ḥtp* 'rest (upon)' sometimes take a direct object.

Exx. *wrḥ(w)·k tpt* mayst thou be anointed with first-quality oil.[2]

ir mn·f mnt·f if he is suffering in his thigh.[3]

iw ḥtp·n nṯr st·f wrt the god rested on his great seat.[4]

P. 66, § 86. At bottom, before the Obs., add:

After *nb* 'lord' the indirect genitive, not the direct, is found when the following noun is qualified by an adjective or demonstrative.

Exx. *nb n ḫ3st nb(t)* the lord of every foreign land.[5]

nb n is pn the lord of this chamber.[6]

P. 89. Before the Vocabulary insert a new paragraph:

§ 115 A. Yet another way of expressing possession is by means of the noun *nb* 'lord', 'possessor', usually followed by a direct genitive.

Exx. *ink nb ꜥ3w nb ḫbsw* I was an owner of donkeys and an owner of ploughlands.[7]

ink nb i3mt I was a possessor of charm.[8]

This use is particularly frequent with abstract words, resulting in the creation

[1] For an exposition of the new principles see *JEA.* 15, 48; cf. also *OLZ.* 1933, 608.

[2] Leyd. K 9. Sim. *Mill.* 1, 8; *Urk.* iv. 1214, 15. *Wnḫ*, *Mill.* 1, 7–8.

[3] *Eb.* 103, 6. Sim. *P. Kah.* 5, 19. Other exx. *Wb.* ii. 66, 19; 67, 21.

[4] *Urk.* iv. 836. Sim. ib. 896, 9.

[5] *ÄZ.* 69, 26, 1. Sim. Cairo 34022, 4.

[6] *Siut* 1, 227. Sim. *Sh. S.* 171; *Peas.* B 1, 16.

[7] Brit. Mus. 1628, 10–1. Sim. plur. 'having' *BH.* i. 8, 21.

[8] *BH.* i. 8, 15. Sim. Cairo 20007, 6.

of an epithet equivalent to an adjective, ex. the very common *nb imꜣḫ* 'lord of reverence',[1] nearly identical with *imꜣḫy* 'revered'.[2]

For cases where the direct genitive following *nb* is replaced by an indirect genitive see above the Add. to § 86.

P. 115. At the end of § 148, 1 add:

Of similar appearance, but of very problematic character, is a construction found in some archaic or merely archaistic texts.[3] Here the 3rd pers. pronouns m. sing. *sw*, f. sing. *s(y)*, plur. *sn* are found before the *śḏm·f* form, but the meaning is not future, but past or present.

Exx. *sw šm·f* he went, lit. he, he went.[4]

sw šnt Gb Geb (lit. he, Geb) quarrelled.[5]

sn sḳdd·sn they (lit. they, they) travel by water.[6]

There is no emphasis on the pronouns in this narrative use, and their employment at the head of the sentence seems to prohibit their identification with the Dependent Pronouns of § 43. Still less is it possible to connect them with the Pronominal Compound of § 124, this being a quite late development. Since a parallel use is found before active participles (Add. to § 373, 1) one might be tempted to regard them as equivalents of the Older Absolute Pronoun (§ 64); however, *śwt śḏm·f*, like *ntf śḏm·f*, has future meaning, see p. 369, n. 16. Out of this employment probably evolved the likewise archaic or archaistic particle *sw* of § 240. Analogous also is a unique example with the Indefinite Pronoun *tw* (§ 47) in a historical text:

tw sḏm·tw m pr-nsw in it·f Ḥr kꜣ nḫt Ḫꜥ-m-Wꜣst it was heard (lit. one, one heard) in the palace by his father the Horus Strong-bull-arising-in-Thebes.[7]

P. 124. At the end of § 161 add:

As in most languages, comparable relations of *time* and *space* are in Egyptian indicated by the same simple prepositions; see (e.g.) the uses of *m*, § 162, 1. 2; of *ḥr*, § 165, 1. 4. A peculiarity of these Egyptian prepositions is that their meaning is strangely vague. Thus *r*, according to the context, may mean either 'to' or 'at' or 'from'. Somewhat similarly with *m*, *ḥr* and *ḏr*.

P. 151. Before § 201 the following new paragraph should be read:

§ 200 A. *Nty* in relative clauses with nominal predicate.—An example of a very rare type is

ḥr-ntt (ntt) pw ꜥnḫ·sn im·s because that is what they live upon, lit. with it.[8] For *ḥr-ntt* see § 223 and for the single writing of *ntt* in place of *ntt ntt*, see § 62 A, above p. 422.

[1] Cairo 20038; 20046, 2.

[2] Cairo 20046, 3.

[3] See *Cen.*, p. 83, n. 5; *ÄZ.* 71, 48.

[4] *Cen.* 85, 23. Sim. *Urk.* iv, 219, 15. 16. With *s(y)*, fem., *Cen.* 84, 3. 16.

[5] *Cen.* 84 3 (*šnt* in semi-enigmatic writing). Sim., but with noun following *sw*, *ib.* 84, 11.

[6] *Cen.* 84, 2. Sim. *ib.* 84, 7.

[7] *Ann.* 37, pl. 2, 19–20.

[8] *Nauri* 8.

P. 266, end of § 349. A unique ex. of the infinitive *tm* as object of *wḏ* 'command':

iw wḏ(·n) n·i ḥm·f tm ḏh(n) t3 n sr nb ꜥ3 r·i His Majesty commanded me not to prostrate myself (lit. touch the earth with my forehead) to any official greater than me.[1]

P. 288. Add at end of § 373, 1:

In some archaic or archaistic texts the independent pronoun is replaced by the obscure 3rd pers. pronoun discussed in the Additions to § 148, 1.

Ex. *sw rdi ib·f r·s* he set his desire towards her.[2]

P. 289, § 374. Add after the fourth line from bottom:

The exclamatory ending *-wy* is found also with passive participles:

ḳd·wy pr·k, 'Itm, snt·wy ḥwt·k, Rwty how (well-)built is thy house, O Atum, how (well-)founded thy mansion, O Ruty.[3]

Not quite certain are the examples alluded to on p. 109, n. 6 with the dependent pronoun of the 1st pers. sing.:

ḥs wi m hrw pn r sf I was one praised more to-day than yesterday.[4] Since this sentence involves a comparison, it is more easily so explained than by taking the three first signs as an exceptional perf. pass. participle with as determinative.[5]

mr wi (?) *m stp-*(for *stp-*)*s3* I was one loved (?) in the Palace.[6] Perhaps emend *mrwt·i* 'my love was' or *mr·kwi* 'I was loved'.

[1] Aswân, stela *temp.* Sesostris I communicated by L. Habachi.

[2] *Urk.* iv. 219, 17. Sim. ib. 220, 1.

[3] Nu, 17, 107.

[4] Brit. Mus. 574, 5.

[5] See above p. 278, n. 3.

[6] Munich 3, 17.

P. 294, n. 3. The first four lines of § 377 require the following qualification:

It seems extremely likely that in M. E. the direct object[s] was felt to be a retained grammatical object, as the comparison with English suggests. Arabic analogies make it possible, however, that at the outset this object[s] was a grammatical subject, such a sentence as 'is given to him gold' having been transformed into 'to whom is given gold' lit. '(he-)given is to him gold', by the addition of a gender ending linking up the passive verb-form with an antecedent implied or expressed; such is the hypothesis favoured by De Buck, in *ÄZ.* 59, 65, followed hesitatingly by me in *Some Aspects*, 23, n. 9. See further the next additional note.

P. 300, n. 8. The divergent theory here alluded to is as follows:

In *ÄZ.* 59, 65 De Buck put forward a theory of the relative forms differing somewhat from that advocated in § 386. He agreed that all the relative forms originated in passive participles, to which was appended, in the case of the imperfective and perfective relatives, a direct genitive (noun or suffix-pronoun) to express the subject[s]. It is in respect of constructions with the passive participle like *dd(w) n·f nbw n ḥswt*, lit. '(one)-given to him the gold of favour', that he disagreed. As already explained in the Add. to p. 294, n. 3, Arabic analogies led him to regard *nbw* here, not as a retained object, but as originally the subject of a sentence with a passive participle as predicate. It is true that, as Sethe had noted before him, Arabic here employs the nominative, not the accusative; De Buck pointed to the construction exemplified in § 374 as evidence that no argument in favour of *nbw* being an implicit accusative could be drawn from the use in similar cases of the dependent pronoun. De Buck is just possibly right in his contention, but if so, the evolution of the relative forms will have been more complex than is set forth in the text of this Grammar.

P. 303, n. 2a. Further note on the fem. ending or in the relative forms:

Except on the ground of meaning a relative form from an immutable verb cannot be proved to be imperfective rather than perfective unless it stands in indisputable parallelism with geminating relative forms from mutable verbs. Such a case is found, however, in the formula *ḏdt pt, ḳmꜣ·t(ỉ) tꜣ, ỉnnt ḥꜥp* 'what heaven gives, earth creates (var. on another stela [1]) and the inundation brings'.[2] Since the fem. ending in the imperfective relative form from mutable verbs is *·t*, not *·tỉ* or *·ty*, the same must be true of the immutable verbs, whence it may be concluded, in agreement with p. 304, top, that or or in such examples is merely a substitute for *·t* and has no significance except as a graphic variant. This conclusion may be extended to a whole series of relative forms from immutable verbs claimed to have prospective meaning,[3] and particularly when or is found in a formula commonly associated with that quoted above, namely *ḫt nbt nfrt wꜥbt ꜥnḫt nṯr ỉm* 'all good and pure things whereon a god lives'. It has been conjectured that when the scribe substituted a writing appearing to read *ꜥnḫ·tỉ* he was varying the tense, and that we ought then to render 'whereon a god would live (*scil.*, if he were in the deceased's place').[4] This has been shown above to be unnecessary, besides being contrary to all likelihood from the standpoint of sense. Such a hypothesis is also contrary to the spirit of the Semitic languages, which are very sparing in the modal distinctions favoured by Greek and Latin. It is true that in certain examples of the perfective relative form (§ 389, 2, *b*) we may find it appropriate to render this as '(whereon) thou mayst rest', '(what) he has to do (with it)' or the like, but the prospective or obligational sense here is probably an importation on the part of the translator, and is not inherent in the Egyptian form itself.

P. 326, n. 4. On the theory here set forth the *sḏm·f* form will have started with transitive verbs followed by an expressed object[5], ex. 'heard of him is (*or* was) this speech'. Such an origin must necessarily be assumed also for the *sḏm·n·f* form. It is idle to speculate exactly when and how the form was extended to intransitive verbs, but it has been seen in §§ 376. 384 that the conception of passives from intransitives was by no means alien to Egyptian feeling.

[1] Cairo 20556. GUNN renders both exx. of *ḳmꜣ·tỉ* prospectively, see below, n. 3.

[2] Cairo 20313.

[3] GUNN, *Stud.*, 14 foll. It is far from easy to decide when such forms should be rendered prospectively, and some of the cases quoted in the notes p. 304, top, are open to serious doubt.

[4] GUNN, *Stud.*, 31.

P. 328, § 413, under *2ae gem.* The problem of a *śḏm·n·f* form from *wnn* requires closer investigation. In Late Egyptian the stem has predominantly past meaning, and there seem to be traces of this specialization of meaning at a far earlier stage. Accordingly it is even plausible that the *śḏm·f* form *wn·i* may have stood in parallelism to the *śḏm·n·f* form *mꜣ·n·i*. On the other hand, the analogy of for *in·n·f* makes it equally possible that may be a writing of *wn·n·(i)*.

P. 358, n. 11. Examples exist, however, where *ir* 'if' is followed, not by *wnn*, but by *wn*. The most easily explicable is *ir wn srḫ m ẖt·ṯ smḫ sw* 'if there be accusation in thy heart (lit. body), forget it'.[1] Here *wn* has probably the sense of *iw wn* 'there is' (§ 107), the element *iw* being ignored altogether, as regularly in Late Egyptian,[2] though a more truly Middle Egyptian procedure in such a case would have been to write *ir wnn wn*, converting *iw* after *ir* into *wnn*, cf. the ex. qu. p. 117, top. In *ir wn ḫpr mi ḏd, wnn rn(·i) nfr mn m niwt(·i)* 'if there be a happening as has been said (i. e. if the proverb just spoken be a true one), (my) good name shall endure in (my) town',[3] the same explanation will hold good if *ḫpr* be infinitive and the equivalent of an undefined common noun.

[1] *L. to D.*, Berlin bowl; also two more less easily explained exx. on the same bowl.

[2] Erm. *Neuäg. Gramm.*[2] §§ 506 foll., where, however, the suppression of *iw* is not pointed out.

[3] *Proc. S.B.A.* Pl. opposite p. 196, l. 16.

ADDITION TO THIRD EDITION

P. 189. After § 258 insert a new paragraph:

§ **258 a.** The interjectional , later *ḫy*[4], is doubtless related to the interrogative *iḫ* 'what?' of § 501. Only one ex. noted before Dyn. XIX.

Ex. *ḫy pꜣ ḫnt nfr n pꜣ ḥḳꜣ* What a good sailing upstream of the Ruler.[5]

[4] Erman, *Neuäg. Gramm.*[2], § 688, Anm.

[5] *Kamose stela*, 30.

APPENDIX A

THE VOCALIZATION OF MIDDLE EGYPTIAN

THE purpose of this book being the practical teaching of hieroglyphics on scientific lines, it has been deemed advisable to avoid the extremely difficult and hypothetical questions connected with the vocalization of the ancient language. From the very outset we have laid stress upon the fact that the vowels are not written in the hieroglyphs; the consequence of this fact is that our consonantal transliterations resemble desiccated skeletons of words far more than the living, vibrating sounds of real speech. From the transliteration *Ỉmn* one fails altogether to realize that the god of Thebes was called *Amāna*, or something like it, by the contemporaries of the Tuthmosids. This Appendix is intended partly to correct the distorted impression which our practical object has forced us to give, and partly to lead up to the discussion as to the most suitable rendering of Egyptian proper names, the subject of Appendix B.

Such knowledge as we have of the pronunciation of the older stages of Egyptian is based on the vocalized forms vouchsafed to us by Coptic, Greek, Assyrian, and Babylonian. Of these Coptic is, of course, by far the most important, being actually the old Egyptian language in its latest stage of development and written in Greek characters (§ 4). The disadvantage of Coptic is, however, its remoteness in time from the stages of the language upon which it is required to shed light; it would be as little legitimate to transfer the Coptic pronunciation of such a word as *ōbᵉt* 'goose' to the old Egyptian equivalent [hieroglyphs] *ꜣpd* as it would be to use modern English pronunciation as our authority for pronouncing Anglo-Saxon. The vowels and consonants of the older language have usually become modified in the lapse of time, so that the more recent equivalents can at best serve only as a basis for inference. A like objection applies to the Greek and Assyrian transcriptions of Egyptian words; these transcriptions are, moreover, comparatively few in number and confined mainly to proper names. Of greater value are the fully vocalized transcriptions of Egyptian names and words which occur, written in Babylonian cuneiform, on the clay tablets known as the El-Amarna letters (14th century, B.C.) and on those constituting the archives of the Hittite capital of Boghaz Keui (13th century).[1] Good examples are *urušša* 'head-rest' for Eg. [hieroglyphs] *wrs*; *kuiḫku* 'Khoiakh vessels', i.e. vessels such as were used at the festival of the month of Khoiakh, for Eg. [hieroglyphs] *kꜣ-ḥr-kꜣ*; *Āna* 'Heliopolis' for Egyptian [hieroglyphs] *Ỉwnw*; *Nibmuarīa* for Egyptian [hieroglyphs] *Nb-mꜣʿt-Rʿ*, prenomen of Amenophis III. Probably these

[1] See H. RANKE, *Keilschriftliches Material zur altäg. Vokalisation* in *Abh. d. kön. Preuss. Akad. d. Wiss.*, Berlin, 1910; also *ÄZ.* 56, 69; 58, 132; by other authors, *OLZ.* 27, 704; *JEA.* 11, 230; *JNES.* 5, 7; 7, 10.

Babylonian transcriptions differ only little from the contemporary Egyptian pronunciations. Hence their great interest; but here again we are handicapped by the extreme rarity of their occurrence and by their restriction to but a few classes of words.

In the main, therefore, we are thrown back upon Coptic for such positive knowledge as we can glean concerning the pronunciation of the earlier stages of the Egyptian language. Now if we examine the word-forms of the Ṣaʿîdic dialect (this seems to have preserved its ancient character better than the other dialects, except in some particulars the Akhmîmic), a definite system of vocalization reveals itself, of which the following are the main principles:—

Rule 1. Every syllable, and consequently every word, begins with a consonant. No syllable can either begin or end with two consonants; where a word appears to begin with two consonants, a short helping vowel ^{e} was pronounced before the first of them, which thus functions as the end of an initial closed syllable.[1] Exx. *ran* 'name', Eg. *rn*; *sō-t^{e}m* 'hear' (infinitive), Eg. *sḏm*; *^{e}n-šot* 'be hard' (infinitive), Eg. *nḫt*.

Rule 2. Open syllables, i. e. those ending in a vowel, have their vowel long. Closed syllables, i. e. those ending in a consonant, have their vowel short. Exx. *nū-t^{e}m* 'sweet', Eg. *nḏm*; *sŏt-m^{e}f* 'hear (inf.) it',[2] Eg. *sḏm·f*.

Rule 3. Each word has only one accented syllable (tone-syllable), which may be open or closed and must be either the last or the last but one (penultimate). The subsidiary unaccented (toneless) syllables are closed and have merely the short helping vowel ^{e}. Exx. *šŏ́r-š^{e}r* 'destroy' (infinitive), Eg. ; *š^{e}r-šṓ-r^{e}f* 'destroy (inf.) him'.

It must be made perfectly clear that Coptic, taken as it stands, shows at least as many exceptions to these rules as exemplifications of them. The following words offend in different ways: *ōš* 'call', 'read'; *nūfĕ* 'good'; *smŏn^{e}t* 'be established' (qualitative); *eŏw* 'praise'; *gĕrăgĕ* 'hunters'; *egŏōš* 'Nubians'. On a close inspection, however, it will usually be found that, even where the rules are ostensibly broken, nevertheless the principles which they embody have been at work. For example, *rŏ* 'mouth' contradicts the second rule by having a short vowel in an open syllable, while *rōf* 'his mouth' contradicts it by having a long vowel in a closed syllable; but it is clear that *rŏ* and *rōf* are related in some such way as *sōt^{e}m* 'hear' and *sŏtm^{e}f* 'hear it' instanced above. Now in *sōt^{e}m* the division of syllables is *sō-t^{e}m*, and the first syllable, being open, demands the long vowel *ō* according to Rule 2 above; in *sŏtm^{e}f* the addition of the suffix alters the syllable-division to *sŏt-m^{e}f*, whence the short vowel *ŏ*. Conversely, *rŏ* 'mouth' is explicable if the original form was *rắꜣ*; when the suffix *·^{e}f* was added,

[1] Such a closed syllable beginning with ^{e} is an exception to the statement with which the rule started, namely that every syllable must begin with a consonant. The Semitic languages exhibit a similar exception. In the hieroglyphs a prothetic *i* is, as we have seen § 272, sometimes used to indicate the presence of the helping vowel.

[2] The direct object of *sḏm* can only be a sound, a word or the like. 'Hear him' is in Egyptian *sḏm n·f*, in Coptic *sōt^{e}m erof*.

the consonant ꜣ would be needed to begin the second syllable; the vowel *ắ* would then fall in an open syllable and accordingly have to be lengthened to *ā*; thus *rōf* would represent an original *rắ-ꜣef*.[1] Proof that ꜣ has fallen away is impossible in this particular case, since 'mouth' is always written ideographically. In countless examples, however, the old hieroglyphic writings at once provide an explanation for the departure of the Coptic equivalents from the rules. Thus *ōš* 'call' begins with a vowel in Coptic because that language has no means of representing the initial ꜥ of ꜥš; *nūfĕ* 'good' owes its short *ĕ* in an open syllable to loss of the final consonant *r*, cf. *nfr* = *nūfe(r)*; *smŏnet* 'be established' has as its prototype the 3rd pers. s. fem. of the old perfective *smn·ti* = *esmắntey* = *esmŏ́nt* (by loss of *ey*)[1a] = *esmŏ́net* (by insertion of *e* before *t* to avoid two consonants at the end of the syllable); *eŏ́w* 'praise' is found to be the Coptic form of *iꜣw* = *eiꜣŏ́w*, a noun of the same form as *snf* 'blood', Coptic *snŏ́f*; *gĕrăgĕ* 'hunters' may be reconstructed as * *grgyw*, m. plur. imperf. act. part. from *grg* 'hunt', the final *-ĕ* being the relic of an unaccented *-yĕw*; it looks as though the entire word must have been vocalized *gerrắgyew*, a form recalling the *piꜥēl*-reduplication which we are tempted to postulate for the imperfective verb-forms (§ 356, Obs.).

We are now in a position to appreciate the arguments proving that ꜣ, *i*, ꜥ and *w* are not vowels, as the earlier Egyptologists supposed, but are consonantal in character. It is true that all these hieroglyphs are used to indicate vowels in the cartouches of the Graeco-Roman period; but an analogy for this perversion of their original function has been found,[2] and there is the serious difficulty that vacillates between the different values *a*, *e*, *ē*, *o* and between the values *a*, *e*, *o*. Again, if we collect the Coptic equivalents of the hieroglyphic words in which these signs occur, we find (1) that , though written *ou*, is employed in a thoroughly consonantal way like *w* or *u̯*; (2) that either is written *ei* or *i* and employed like consonantal *y*, or else disappears altogether; (3) either disappears altogether or else has changed to *ei*, i. e. consonantal *y*; (4) has vanished completely. If it should be argued from 'load', Coptic *ōtep*, that = *ō*, or from 'skin', Coptic *ănŏm*, that = *ă*, or again from 'sun', Coptic *rē*, that = *ē*, we could easily make rejoinder with instances which would show, upon the same lines, that is not only *ō*, but also *ă*, *ĕ*, *ē*, *ī*, *ū*; that is at once *ă*, *ĕ*, *ē*, *ī*, *ŏ*, and *ō*; that may as easily stand for *ă*, *ĕ*, *ŏ*, *ō* as for *ē*. To accept any such conclusions would, of course, be absurd, and it ought to be evident, without further proof, that , and are not equivalent to the vowels in the Coptic words in question, but have here fallen away or become invisible. The matter is, however, settled definitely when examples of the different verbal classes in Egyptian and Coptic are compared with one another.

[1] For the changes *ắ* to *ŏ́*, *ā* to *ō*, see p. 433.

[1a] It is unknown at what stage *ắ* passed into *ŏ́*.

[2] See p. 14, n. 1.

Old writing	Coptic: Infinitive absolute	with nom. obj.	with suffix obj.	Qualitative[1]
2-lit.				
ḳd 'build'	*kōt*	*kĕt-*	*kŏt^{e}f*	*kēt*
ỉp 'count'	*ōp*	*ĕp-*	*ŏp^{e}f*	*ēp*
ỉʿ 'wash'[2]	*yō*	*yă-*[3]	*yăăf*[3]	—
3-lit.				
sḏm 'hear'	*sōt^{e}m*	*sĕt^{e}m-*	*sŏtm^{e}f*	[*sŏt^{e}m*]
ꜣṯp 'load'	*ōt^{e}p*	*ĕt^{e}p-*	*ŏtp^{e}f*	*ŏt^{e}p*
ʿnḫ 'live'	*ōn^{e}h*	—	—	*ŏn^{e}h*
wšb 'answer'	*wōš^{e}b*	—	*wŏšb^{e}f*	—
3ae inf.				
msỉ 'bear'	*mīsĕ*	*mes(t)-*	*mast^{e}f*	*mŏsĕ*
ỉbỉ 'thirst'	*ībĕ*	—	—	*ŏbĕ*
ʿḥỉ 'hang up'	*īšĕ*	*ešt-*	*ašt^{e}f*	*ašĕ*[3]
wnỉ 'pass by'	*wīnĕ*	—	—	—

[1] The Coptic Qualitative is the descendant of the Old Perfective treated in Lesson XXII.

[2] This verb, originally *3ae inf.*, has secondarily attached itself to the *2-lit.* class.

[3] *ă* instead of *ĕ* and *ŏ* under the influence of the guttural *ʿ*, the original presence of which is thus indicated.

Examination of the above table shows that the various Coptic verb-classes have each its own characteristic vowel, which persists unchanged, or nearly so, whatever the neighbouring radical consonants may be. There can be no doubt that the *ō* of *ōp*, of *yō* and of *wōš^{e}b* is the same *ō* as in *kōt* and in *sōt^{e}m*, and similarly that the *ī* in *īše* and *wīne* is the same *ī* as in *mīse*. Hence we may conclude at once that [hieroglyph] in [hieroglyph] is a consonantal *y*, and that the [hieroglyph] seen in [hieroglyph] and implicit in [hieroglyph] is a consonantal *w*. As for the [hieroglyph] of *ꜣṯp*, the [hieroglyph] of *ỉp* and *ỉbỉ*, the [hieroglyph] of *ỉʿ*, *ʿnḫ* and *ʿḥỉ*, they clearly represent consonants which either have fallen away or for some other reason fail to find expression in the corresponding Coptic verbs.

Such considerations as these warrant the conclusion that Coptic displays the ruins of a much earlier phase of Egyptian, in which the division of the syllables and the quantity of the vowels were governed by the strict rules above specified. The question now arises as to what particular phase in the history of the Egyptian language is represented by Coptic in its ruinous condition; is that phase Late Egyptian, Middle Egyptian, or Old Egyptian? The problem must be clearly understood. Coptic is, of course, the ultimate outcome of all preceding stages of Egyptian, including some prehistoric stages of which we have no precise knowledge. What we are now seeking is, however, that particular phase of the language in which the decayed vocalic system of Coptic finds its explanation. An analogy may help to elucidate the problem: many of our great abbey-churches were preceded by Anglo-Saxon, if not by Roman, structures; yet it may be possible in a particular church to ascribe the ruinous portions alone surviving in mass beside other portions not so ruined, to the Perpendicular style of architecture, not to any other style whether earlier or later. Similarly we are able to state with some assurance that the vocalic system found in ruinous condition in Coptic belongs to a phase of the Egyptian language at least as old as Old Egyptian. In order to discover an explanation for *smŏn^{e}t* (see above) we have to go back to the form *smnti* (^{e}*s-măn-t*^{e}*y*); had the Coptic vocalic rules here come into operation only when *smnti* was already reduced to *smnt*, doubtless that later form would have assumed some such vocalization as *s*^{e}*mnŏ́t*, ^{e}*smōn*^{e}*t* or *sŏ́mn*^{e}*t*. The actual form *smŏ́n*^{e}*t* found in Coptic demands that the final syllable -*t*^{e}*y* should have been still intact at the moment when the vocalic rules exerted their influence; now since is sometimes written for simple *t* in the fem. relative form from Dyn. XII onwards (§ 387, 2), ex. , and since this must be copied from the old perfective, it seems necessary to suppose that the *i* of the ending ·*ti* (·*t*^{e}*y*) was lost by then, and possibly even far earlier. Similarly the short vowel in Coptic ^{e}*hkŏ́* 'hunger' must date from a time when the original *r* of *ḥḳr* had not yet fallen away; but this probably occurred as early as the Old Kingdom, since *ḥḳr* 'hunger' and *ḥḳꜣ* 'rule' interchange in the Pyramid texts.[1] Many nouns like *nēb* 'lord' betray the former presence of an ending -^{e}*w* (*nē-b*^{e}*w*), of which hieroglyphic writing subsequent to the Old Kingdom contains no trace. Again, the Coptic *hŏ́* 'face' and the preposition *hi* 'upon' derived from it reveal the loss of the original end-consonant *r* (*hŏ́* = old *ḥắr*; *hi* = old *ḥer*, *ḥey*), whereas the corresponding form with the suffix *hrăf*[2] has preserved the *r*; already in the Old Kingdom *ḥr* 'face' and 'upon' are consistently written without *r*, while the *r* appears consistently in *ḥr·f* 'upon him';[3] that the Coptic pronunciation ^{e}*hraf* holds good of early Middle Egyptian is shown also by the isolated variant (§ 272). Sometimes hieroglyphic writings for which no exact Coptic equivalents can be quoted tell their own tale. We have noted in § 78 that the XIIth Dyn. spelling *dpwt·f* 'his boat', when compared with *dpt* 'a boat', can be explained only as due to the displacement of the accent owing to the addition of the suffix; under the protection of the accent the original *w* of the word (hypothetically *dapwet*) is preserved in *d*^{e}*pwắt*^{e}*f*, while it disappears in *dắp*^{e}*t*. The Coptic laws relating to syllable-division and accentuation here found in full force doubtless originated much earlier than when first observable in our texts, so that we may fairly conclude them to go back to the Old Kingdom or even before.[4]

[1] *Pyr.* 553; see *Verbum* i. p. 143.

[2] In point of fact Ṣaʿîdic has not preserved *hraf* 'upon him'; but the vocalization is guaranteed by the Fayyûmic form ϩⲗⲉϥ, and also indirectly by the Ṣaʿîdic ϩⲣⲁⲓ 'over', see *ÄZ.* 44, 93.

[3] For the tendency of *r* to persist before a suffix-pronoun, though lost in *status absolutus*, cf. O. K. writings of *nṯr·f*, *Wb.* II, 359, 7 in the *Belegstellen.*

[4] Wrongly disputed by EDGERTON, *JNES.* 6, 1 foll. For the early disappearance of final *r* see nn. 2, 3 above, and for the O. K. loss of the fem. ending -*t* see p. 34, n. 1a.

Whereas the division of the syllables and the quantity of the accented vowel can thus often be ascertained, the quality of the vowels is much more doubtful. Nevertheless, a careful comparison of the Coptic, early Greek, and Babylonian word-forms has enabled scholars to form a rough idea of the nature of the Egyptian vowels as early as the Eighteenth Dynasty. It would seem that at this period, and possibly very much earlier, Egyptian had the same vowels as classical Arabic, namely *a*, *i* and *u*, each of which could be either short or long; the *e* and *o* vowels appear to be more recent developments. To summarize very briefly the results attained, starting with Coptic, the following statement may be made:—

Coptic *ō* <[1] old Greek *ū* < Babylonian *ā*. Ex. *Hōr* 'Horus', old Gk. -υρ (in Αθυρ 'Hathor'), Bab. *Ḫāra*. Note that Coptic has kept the *ū* of the old Gk. after *m* and *n*, cf. *Amūn*, Bab. *Amāna*, Gk. (Μι)αμουν; *Anūp*, old Gk. Ανουβις.

Coptic *ē* < old Gk. *ī* < Bab. *ī*. Ex. *rē* 'sun', old Gk. -ρι (in Μεσορι, a month-name), Bab. *rīa* (e.g. in *Nibmuarīa*).

Coptic *ŏ* < old Gk. *ă* < Bab. *ă*. Exx. *hŏtᵉp* 'is pleased' in *Parᵉmhŏtᵉp*, a month-name, Bab. *-ḫatpi* (in the name *Amanḫatpi* = *Ỉmnḥtp*); *mŏse* 'is born', old Gk. μασι (in the king's name Αμασις), Bab. *maššì* (in *Ḫaramaššì* = *Ḥr-ms*). Note that Gk. for the most part represents this old *ă*, late *ŏ*, by ω (ōmega), perhaps because Gk. ο (omikron) had in it a tinge of *u* which was unsuitable.

Coptic *ă* < older *ĕ* < still older *ĭ*. It can be shown that Akhmîmic has often preserved the quality of the vowels better than Ṣaʿîdic; now Ṣaʿîdic *ă* is *ĕ* in Akhmîmic, ex. Ṣaʿîd. *lăs* 'tongue', Akhm. *lĕs*. That *ĭ* was the earlier form of *ĕ* is a matter of inference.[2]

Coptic *ĕ* sometimes at least goes back to Bab. *u*. Ex. *mĕ* 'truth' (Eg. *mꜣʿt*), Bab. *mua* (in *Nibmuarīa*).

The summary account here given must suffice to indicate the kind of means by which the pronunciation of Middle Egyptian can occasionally be elicited. The chief authorities to be consulted are Sethe's great work on the Egyptian verb, and a much later brilliant article entitled *Die Vokalisation des Ägyptischen* in *Zeitschr. d. deutsch. morgenl. Ges.*, 77 (1923), 145–207, reprinted in 1925. See too a review by G. Farina in *Aegyptus*, 1924, 313–25.[3] Research is now beginning to take the further and still more hazardous step of comparing the vocalization of Egyptian with that of the related Semitic languages. Here too Sethe was the pioneer, see the aforementioned article. The conclusions reached by Sethe, though admittedly of a tentative character, coincide, on the whole, with those of W. F. Albright, whose brief independent study, entitled *The principles of Egyptian phonological development*, is printed in *Recueil de Travaux*, 40, 64–70.

[1] This symbol means 'arises from'; the reverse symbol would mean 'gives rise to'.

[2] Curiously paralleled in the case of Ṣaʿîdic *las* 'tongue' by the old Arabic *lisān*. In a number of cases the old Arabic confirms the earliest vocalizations which have been deduced for Egyptian words, hinting that the quality of the Egyptian vowels may have changed very little in the earlier stages of the language.

[3] No adequate attention can be here paid to sceptical voices. Of these the ablest, that of J. Sturm (*Zur Vokalverflüchtigung in der ägyptischen Sprache* in *WZKM* 41, 43 foll., 161 foll.), seeks only to modify, not wholly to reject, the findings of Sethe and others. The above presentation has sought rather to illustrate the method than to assert indisputable results.

APPENDIX B

THE TRANSCRIPTION OF EGYPTIAN PROPER NAMES[1]

[1] See GARDINER-WEIGALL, *A Topographical Catalogue of the Tombs of Thebes*, London, 1913, pp. 14–15. On similar lines also GARDINER, *The Wilbour Papyrus*, III, Translation, Oxford, 1948, p. ix.

THE absence of vocalization in the hieroglyphic writing has the irritating consequence that there can be no fixed norm for the transcription of proper names. Thus [hieroglyphs] *Ḏḥwty-ḥtp*, the owner of a famous tomb at El-Bershah, is called Tehutihetep by one scholar, Thuthotep by a second, Thothotpou by a third, Dḥutḥotpe by a fourth. Other personal names are still less recognizable; a Theban noble of Dyn. XVIII, whose name is written [hieroglyphs] *ỉnnỉ*, appears in Egyptological books variously as Anna, Anena, Ennē, and Ineni. In these circumstances, what line is the learner of Egyptian to adopt? This is the question to be discussed in the present Appendix.

The desirability of a uniform method of dealing with proper names is great and indisputable; yet such uniformity is clearly unattainable. It could scarcely be demanded of the editors of widely read works like Baedeker's Egypt or Breasted's History that they should reconcile the divergent spellings with which their readers have been long familiarized, the more so since the proposed modifications would at best have only the virtue of greater consistency, not really that of greater scientific accuracy. The practice of the present writer conforms more closely to that of Baedeker than to that of Breasted; but since both are founded on sound philological method there is little to choose between them. The following pages suggest certain reasonable principles which the student may adopt, unless he prefer to accept the authority of one or other of the standard works named above.

In a few cases we can actually ascertain the contemporary pronunciation of Eighteenth Dynasty personal, divine or local names; the El-Amarna and Boghaz Keui tablets preserve for us, written in Babylonian cuneiform, such transcriptions as Amanḥatpi for [hieroglyphs], Ḥāra for the god [hieroglyphs] Horus, Ḥikuptaḥ for [hieroglyphs], one of the names of Memphis. But such contemporary evidence is scanty, and the rules of vocalization deducible thence are too incomplete for us to attempt to reconstruct other names on their basis. We are unable to live up to so high a standard. The best we can attain to is the sort of pronunciation which a Greek of the Ptolemaic period might have advocated; upon this we can now and then improve a little by retaining the consonantal values which are known to have obtained in the Eighteenth Dynasty.

In the case of royal names it seems advisable (as already stated in Excursus A, pp. 75–6) to employ the actual Greek forms which have been handed down, so far as they embody the old consonantal skeletons in fairly recognizable form.

Egyptology has from its earliest days been committed to the classical royal names Menes, Cheops, and Mycerinus;[1] and it is, therefore, quite reasonable to add to their number Ammenemes for *ʾImn-m-ḥꜣt*, Sesostris for *S-n-Wsrt*, Amosis for *ʾIꜥḥ-ms*, Amenophis[1a] for *ʾImn-ḥtp*, Tuthmosis for *Ḏḥwty-ms*, Ramesses for *Rꜥ-ms-sw*, etc. In adopting this practice with Baedeker and the German school, we must, however, make sure that we select none but authentic Greek forms, this being the only possible excuse for the employment of the Greek transcriptions with their very un-Egyptian endings. For that reason the German choice of Thutmosis, a hybrid resting on no traditional basis, cannot be defended on the ground that it preserves the sequence of the original consonants (*Ḏḥwt-*) better than the genuine Manethonian forms Tuthmosis or Tethmosis. Where royal names either do not occur in Manetho[2] (exx. 'Aḥḥotpe, Akhenaten), or else occur in that author in much distorted form (exx. Misphres = *Mn-ḫpr-Rꜥ*, Skemiophris = *Sbk-nfrw-Rꜥ*), we must have resort to the same kind of transcriptions (see below) as we should employ if the names in question were not royal but ordinary personal names (exx. Menkheperrēꜥ, Sebknofrurēꜥ).

The same holds in the case of divine names. Long use makes it impossible, even if it were desirable, to abandon the classical forms Osiris, Isis, Horus, Nephthys, as well as a number of others. To these may perhaps be added some of which the Greek transcriptions have been recently discovered from the papyri, exx. Sakhmis for , often called Sekhmet, Thphēnis for , usually known as Tefnut.[3] Amūn is a Coptic rather than a Greek form,[4] but occurs in the royal name Ramesses Miamūn; for various reasons Amūn is preferable to the earlier Greek form Ammon. Sōs, Suchos and Ophois are Greek equivalents of , and , respectively, but are too remote from their Egyptian originals to be really serviceable; in these cases Shu, Sobk and Wepwawet are handier renderings. In cases where no Greek forms have been preserved, we must use such transcriptions as we might employ if the names were mere personal names, exx. Nut for , Māꜥet for .

As regards place-names, the classical forms Abydus, Coptus, Thebes, Elephantine, Heracleopolis Magna, Heliopolis will as a rule serve us best, and where these fail, we may often have recourse to Arabic names, like Assiûṭ, Aṭfîḥ, Denderah, Esna. When the actual site is unknown or doubtful, conventional transcriptions of the old Egyptian names must be used, like Nefrusi for *Nfrwsy*, Menꜥat-Khufu for *Mnꜥt-Ḫwfw*.

We turn now to ordinary personal names.[5] Of these the Greek papyri have preserved a large number complete with their vowels;[6] however the names in question are mainly late ones and as such do not concern us here; also the

[1] Cheops and Mycerinus (see *ÄZ.* 56, 76) are philologically poor forms, but rest on the authority of Herodotus; Manetho gives the less familiar Suphis and Menkheres.

[1a] This is the accepted Manethonian form, but there is another, namely Amenophthis, that comes closer to the original. Amenoth and Amenothes are also genuine forms, though not found in any classical author.

[2] For Manetho see p. 76, n. 1.

[3] Perhaps, however, Tefēnet is preferable to Thphēnis, which has an outlandish appearance.

[4] It is found, however, in Plutarch.

[5] See J. Lieblein, *Dictionnaire de noms hiéroglyphiques*, Leipzig, 1871–92; H. Ranke, *Die ägyptischen Personennamen*, Glückstadt, 1935.

[6] Fr. Preisigke, *Namenbuch*, Heidelberg, 1912. See also W. Spiegelberg, *Aegyptische und griechische Eigennamen, aus Mumienetikettenderrömischen Kaiserzeit*, Leipzig, 1901.

modification or fusion of their component consonants often renders them unrecognizable as equivalents of their hieroglyphic originals. In transcribing Middle Egyptian personal names it is both usual and advisable to reject any actual Greek equivalents there may be in favour of more artificial dressings up of the written consonantal skeletons. In choosing the vowels to clothe these, etymology and grammar must be carefully consulted; thus Ḥarmosĕ as equivalent of hieroglyphic *Ḥr-ms* owes its vocalization to the considerations (1) that the divine name Ḥōr (so Coptic; Bab. Ḫāra) must be in the reduced form Ḥăr- found in such Greek compounds as Ἁρσιησις, Ἁρενδωτης, and (2) that, the meaning being 'Horus is born', *ms* is old perfective (§ 322) and must be given the corresponding Ṣaʿîdic form *mŏsĕ*. One might hesitate as to whether -mosĕ or -mosi, which is the Boḥairic form, is the more suitable English rendering; we prefer -mosĕ, writing -ĕ to avoid its being pronounced monosyllabically; -mosi is less desirable through the danger that -i might be pronounced as in 'bite'. Note further that though Greek parallel names like Ἀμωσις (earlier Ἀμασις) use ōmega, the vowel in question is not really long; on this point see above p. 433. Now it so happens that the name *Ḥr-ms* is recorded in the El-Amarna letters under the form Ḫarramašši; why then do not we borrow from this contemporary transcription at least the vowel *a* of -mašši, and write Ḥarmasi instead of Ḥarmosĕ? The answer is that as a rule we should be unable to maintain so high a standard of vocalization. It is better to content ourselves with artificial graecizing or copticizing forms.

Before pursuing further this question of vocalization, it will be well to consider the values which the Egyptian consonants ought to assume in our transcriptions.[1] Many of them (*w*, *b*, *f*, *m*, *n*, *r*, *h*, *s*, *k*, *g*, *t*, *d*) present no difficulty. In scientific writing it is desirable to differentiate *ḥ* from *h*, *ḳ* from *k*, though these distinctions may be ignored in more popular use. For *ḫ*, *ẖ* and *š* we should use *kh*, *ch* and *sh* respectively. The consonants and are embarrassing. To use *ṯ* and *ḏ* would convey little meaning to the general reader, and such equivalents as *z* and *j* are open to various objections. No suggestions yet made seem really satisfactory; the least unsatisfactory are *tj* for and *dj* for . These transcriptions have at least the advantage of hinting at the relationship of *ṯ* to *t* and of *ḏ* to *d*; and *dj*, at all events, is near enough to the real pronunciation of to pass muster. On the other hand, we must admit that to transcribe *Ḏḥwty-ms* as name of a private individual by Djeḥutmosĕ, while transcribing it as a royal name by Tuthmosis, must seem to the uninitiated a very strange proceeding. The semi-vowel is suitably rendered as *y* except where we have good reason for thinking that it possessed the value of *ꜣ*; and will also be *y*. is best omitted in transcription; its

[1] For recent studies of the consonants see W. CZERMAK, *Die Laute der ägyptischen Sprache*, Vienna, 1931–4: J. VERGOTE, *Phonétique historique de l'Égyptien*, Louvain, 1945.

presence, as in Any,[1] is sufficiently marked by the quality of the vowel employed (*a* instead of *e*, § 19) and by the absence of any supporting initial consonant. On the other hand, has too emphatic a sound to be ignored; its presence should be indicated by the symbol ꜥ, except in the most popular writing, ex. *Rꜥ-ms*, Raꜥmosĕ, more popularly Ramosĕ. In compound women's names with a fem. noun as first element, the fem. ending *-t* should be disregarded in accordance with p. 66, n. 2a, ex. *Nbt-ʾIwnw* Nebōn.[1a]

Where no etymology of a name can be given, scientific reasons for preferring one vocalization to another disappear entirely. In this case it is best to adopt that form which will most clearly recall the hieroglyphic writing. In names like and we shall write Tjenuna and Ita, taking such group-writing (§ 60) to indicate merely the consonants *Ṯnn* and *ʾIt*.[1b] The same course is advisable also in reference to names now known to be abbreviations of others with clear etymologies,[2] exx. *Ḥy* Huy short for Amenḥotpe, *Mḥ* Maḥu short for Amenemḥab. In the latter case the Greek transcription Ἁρμαις of the name of king Ḥaremḥab might embolden us to choose Maḥi rather than Maḥu, but the latter seems preferable, since it reminds us at once that the last syllable is written with the biliteral sign *ḥw*.

A very important class of personal names is that containing the names known as theophorous, i.e. compound names in which one element is the name of a deity.[3] Now in Graeco-Roman transcriptions it is the rule that when such a divine name stands at the *beginning* of a compound, it is less heavily vocalized than when it stands independently or at the end of a compound; compare Ἀμμενεμης with Μιαμουν, Ραμεσσης with Lampares (= *N-mꜣꜥt-Rꜥ* Ammenemes III). To this habit we must closely adhere; to argue from the independent form Θωθ or Θωυθ that must be transcribed Thothmes is to ignore a very characteristic tendency of the Egyptian language. It is probable, indeed, that down to a relatively late period such divine names were not completely bereft, at the beginning of compounds, of their characteristic vowel, but had merely shortened it; thus we find such exceptional Greek forms as Ἀμον- instead of Ἀμεν- (from Ἀμουν) in Ἀμονρασωνθηρ = *ʾImn-Rꜥ-nsw-nṯrw* 'Amen-rēꜥ, king of the gods'; Χνομ- instead of *Χνεμ- (from Χνουμ) in Χνομωνεβιηβ = *Ḫnmw-ꜥꜣ-nb-ꜣbw* 'Chnum the great, lord of Elephantine'.[4] Having, however, decided to adopt a graecizing or copticizing standard for our transcriptions we shall write Amenemḥēt rather than Amonemḥēt. It should be noted, however, that we cannot always go so far in the reduction of divine names as the Greek transcriptions go; thus in Greek compounds *Sbk*, Greek Σουχος, often appears as Σχ- Σεκ- Σοκ-, *Ḫnsw*, Coptic Khōnꜥs, as Χεσ-; by virtue of our principle that the full[5] consonantal skeleton must be maintained we shall write Sebkhotpe for *Sbk-ḥtp*, Khensmosĕ for *Ḫnsw-ms*.

[1] The form Anuy would better remind one of the hieroglyphs, but the well-known designation 'the papyrus of Ani' prompts the adoption of a closely similar form.

[1a] For this reason the queen's name Hatshepsut has been rendered as Hashepsowe in this book. In the names of the goddesses Hathor and Nephthys the fem. ending has survived, but this may be an exception of very early date.

[1b] The issue between Albright and Edgerton (p. 52, n. 2) is still *sub lite*, and our conservative practice is dictated solely by expediency.

[2] See *ÄZ.* 44, 87; 57, 77; 59, 71.

[3] K. HOFFMANN, *Die theophoren Personennamen des älteren Ägyptens* in K. SETHE, *Untersuchungen zur Geschichte und Altertumskunde Aegyptens*, Bd. vii, Heft 1, Leipzig, 1915.

[4] See on this point SETHE, *Vokalisation* (above p. 427), pp. 182–9.

[5] Except in semivocalic endings like *-w*.

LIST OF HIEROGLYPHIC SIGNS

In the following pages an attempt is made to enumerate the commonest hieroglyphs found in Middle Egyptian, to determine the objects depicted by them, and to illustrate their uses. It would be easy enough to augment our list very considerably, though there might be difficulty in finding good forms of the rarer signs which would then have to be included. But such an augmentation might well do more harm than good, by unduly dispersing the student's interest, instead of concentrating it upon the signs most frequently met with. It must never be forgotten that in the eyes of the old Egyptians the hieroglyphic writing always remained a system of pictorial representation as well as a script. Hence the capricious variety exhibited in the more elaborate inscriptions. To take but one example, the sign for 'statue' (A 22) is apt to change sex, head-gear, dress and accoutrements according as the context or the scribe's fancy may dictate. This is the principal reason why the printing of hieroglyphic texts is so unsatisfactory. No fount of type is sufficiently rich or sufficiently adaptable to do justice to the Egyptian originals. Indeed, there is only one wholly satisfactory method of publishing hieroglyphic texts, namely reproduction in facsimile. Two possibilities here present themselves, facsimile by hand and facsimile by photography. The objection to facsimile by hand is, of course, the very laborious nature of the process. Facsimile by photography has the disadvantage that it will serve only for perfectly preserved texts. As a second-best alternative, the employment of autography is to be recommended, as in Sethe's *Urkunden der 18. Dynastie* and in the Brussels *Bibliotheca Aegyptiaca*. The printing of hieroglyphic texts in type is really suitable only for grammatical or lexicographical works, especially where the hieroglyphs are to be combined with European characters. The discussion of this question is not without a practical purpose; it aims at impressing upon the student *the great desirability of a good hieroglyphic handwriting*. Far too lax standards in this respect have been tolerated in the past, and one of our principal aims in creating the new fount of type here employed for the first time was to give a fresh impetus to this side of the hieroglyphic scholar's training. The forms shown in the new fount are those normally used in the tombs of the Eighteenth Dynasty, though in some cases earlier forms had to be added in order to elucidate pictorial meanings which by that time had become either modified or forgotten. The beginner may safely use our types as his models, but he must realize that copying from the actual monuments gives a knowledge of hieroglyphic writing unobtainable in any other way.

The commonest hieroglyphs received their traditional, relatively stereotyped, forms in the very earliest Dynasties. Misinterpretations and confusions may, therefore, be expected at least as far back as the time of the Pyramid-builders. Some of the objects depicted may have been obsolete at a still more remote date, exx. the three-toothed harpoon of bone (T 20) and the form of mast represented by (P 6). In other cases it is the method of depiction, not the object itself, which had become obsolete by the time that inscriptions began to be plentiful.

Who would have guessed that (D 61) represents human toes? This interpretation is, however, supported by the form of that sign in the tomb of Metjen (Dyn. III), where the toe-nails are clearly marked, and is clinched by the fact that the word *s3ḥ* means 'toe'. The investigation of the pictorial meaning of the hieroglyphs is for this reason a very difficult task. But it is a task the interest of which is not confined to archaeology alone, since important lexicographical conclusions depend on the right understanding of the signs. We have a clue to the central meaning of the obscure verb *mḏd* now that the sign (Aa 24) is known to depict the warp being stretched between two uprights. From (A 34) we learn at least something of the quality of the action expressed by the stem *ḫwsi*, 'pound', 'build', 'achieve'. The sign (E 32) which determines *ḳnd* 'to be angry' gives to that verb a colouring definitely distinct from the nearly synonymous *ḏnd*. Without the sign (M 44) we should not realize the idea of 'sharpness' which enters into the Egyptian conception of 'preparedness' *spd*. It is interesting, too, to note that in contexts where an object in contemporary use is intended, the determinative employed to designate it is sometimes brought up to date, while in other employments the corresponding sign retains an archaic appearance, exx. (T 7*) in *3ḳḥw* 'axe' as against (T 7) in *mdḥ* 'hew'; (T 8*) in *bgsw* 'dagger' as against (T 8) in *tpy* 'first'; (T 10) in *pḏt* as against (T 9), earlier, in the verb *pḏ* 'stretch'. However, the full value of the study of the hieroglyphs will not emerge until that study is far more advanced than it is at present. We are still quite ignorant of the origin of many signs, such as (Aa 7), (Aa 20), and (Aa 27).

The modern craving for scientific precision, so contrary to the habit of the Egyptians themselves, has often led in the past to falsification of the actual graphic facts. Thus it has been the habit of scholars to write *ḫrp* 'administrate' with and *sḫm* 'powerful' with . This particular distinction rests, as it happens, on an erroneous assumption, namely that the signs in question were originally different. But in other cases where there really was a difference, as between *šmʿ* and *rsw*, between the rope (*šs*) and the bag (*sšr*), it is astonishing how often even the best scribes are guilty of confusion. Some of these confusions led in course of time to the substitution of one sign for another. Thus (Aa 2) has absorbed quite a number of different signs. Many such confusions arise through hieratic. For instance, hieratic (Aa 8) stands not only for the hieroglyphic sign , as in *ḳn* 'cease' and *ḏ3ḏ3t* 'council', but also for in *ʿḏ* 'district' and for in *sp3t* 'province'. Assimilations of the kind are apt to pass into hieroglyphic as well, where the reason for them is not obvious until their origin in hieratic is pointed out. Thus (M. K. hieratic) constantly takes the place of (M. K. hieratic) in words from the stem *šnʿ*, like *šnʿ* 'magazine' for , a word in which itself is a substitution for an earlier sign . In copying the monuments we must resist the temptation to substitute more correct forms for those actually used. We are not entitled to impose upon the Egyptians our own scholarly preferences.

The first column of our sign-list, showing, as we have said, Eighteenth Dynasty forms, seeks to define the objects depicted in the earlier prototypes of these. Note that our heads of classification are not, nor could they have been conveniently made, mutually exclusive. Thus we might have placed 𓋆 O 44 under F 'Parts of Mammals' because of the horns which are one of its constituent parts, or else under R, the class containing other religious symbols. Classes S, T, U, and V have proved especially troublesome, and signs allotted to one of them might often have been assigned equally appropriately to another or even to more than one other class. Our second column, which deals with the uses of the signs in the writing of words, sometimes necessarily employs the terms 'phonetic', 'ideographic', 'determinative', and 'abbreviation' in ways which are open to criticism. The distinction between phonetic and ideographic uses of signs is not nearly so absolute as might be supposed, see § 42, Obs. It may even happen that a sign is phonetically used in the very name of the object from which it originated. Thus 𓄞𓂧𓅱𓄞 *šdw* 'water-skin' is undoubtedly the word from which 𓄞 (F 30) originated; nevertheless the phonetic complement 𓂧 and the determinative 𓄞 are sufficient evidence that 𓄞 is here the phonetic biliteral sign *šd*; the like is true of 𓂭 in 𓂭𓃀𓅱𓊛 *db3w* 'floats'. Elsewhere, as in 𓊵 when abbreviation for *ḥtp* 'favour' (§ 42, Obs.), or in 𓄔𓅓 *sdm* 'hear' or 𓂻𓅱 *iw* 'come', the terms ideographic and phonetic seem almost equally suitable. Again, within the domain of 'phonetic signs', not all are on the same footing. Save for very rare variants like 𓐍𓂧𓀔 for 𓄡𓂋𓂧𓀔 *ẖrd* 'child' and 𓋴𓄡 for 𓋴𓐍𓂋 *sẖr* 'plan' the sign 𓄡 seems confined to derivatives of the stem *ẖr* (exx. *ẖrt* 'portion', *ẖrt-nṯr* 'necropolis', *ẖryw* 'inhabitants'), whereas 𓃹 is freely used for *wn* even in the words where etymological relationship is out of the question, exx. 𓎛𓃹𓈖𓀔 *ḥwn* 'be young', 𓃹𓈖𓐍 *wnḫ* 'clothe'. Such facts as these go to show the impossibility of a hard and fast classification of the uses of signs. Ideographic uses shade off into phonetic, and there are degrees and varieties within the two main groups of sense-sign (ideogram) and sound-sign (phonogram). We have, on occasion, found it convenient to employ the terms 'semi-ideographic' and 'semi-phonetic', as well as the term 'phonetic determinative' explained in § 54. The objection to the term 'determinative', which is nevertheless too convenient to discard, was stated in § 23, Obs. We shall also make frequent use of the term 'abbreviation' (§ 55), though this is open to the objection that signs so described, ex. 𓋾 *ḥḳ3* 'chief', often represent the original spelling, later amplified by the addition of phonetic and other elements, ex. 𓋾𓈎𓄿𓀙. To sum up, the terminology adopted by us is not intended to bear too technical or too precise an interpretation.

The sign-list which follows is a Middle Egyptian one. With few exceptions it disregards all hieroglyphs that had fallen into disuse by the Eleventh Dynasty, as well as all invented after the reign of Ḥaremḥab. For this reason, the words that are quoted to illustrate the uses of signs are throughout Middle Egyptian words. It has proved impossible, however, to ignore Old Egyptian completely. We have already alluded to the earlier forms of signs which are sometimes added to the later ones in order to illustrate their original meanings. Again, it is often only some passage in the Pyramid Texts which reveals the reading of an ideogram, and we have sought everywhere to indicate the reasons, or at least one sufficient reason, for the accepted reading of each separate hieroglyph. Moreover, Old Egyptian sometimes gives the explanation why one sign rather than another is used in the writing of a particular word. This applies especially to phonetic signs involving an *s*-sound, for Old Egyptian rigorously distinguished 𓋴 *ś* and 𓊃 *z*. The reason why 𓅭𓀀 *sꜣ* 'son', for example, is written with 𓅭 instead of 𓋴 is that the earlier reading of the Middle Egyptian word *sꜣ* 'son' was *zꜣ*, not *śꜣ*. Such facts as these have had to be taken into account.

The transliterations used in the following list call for comment in one particular. The use of brackets ( ) is a double one. Either they imply that a consonant has to be understood which is not written, as in 𓇅𓏏𓆗 *Wꜣḏ(y)t* 'Edjō', or else that a consonant which is written had disappeared from the pronunciation, as in 𓋴𓅱𓇋𓈗𓀁 *sw(r)ỉ* 'drink' (§ 279). When one consonant passed into another in the course of the development of the language the conservative Egyptians sometimes retained in the hieroglyphs both the earlier and the later sound-signs. This is what has happened also in 𓊪𓅱𓏏𓇋𓂋𓀁 'what?', transliterated by us *pw-tỉ* in § 497 and elsewhere; we might well, however, have written *pw-t(r)ỉ*, indicating thereby that the earlier form *pw-tr* had changed into *pw-tỉ*. It is unlikely that ambiguity will arise from this twofold employment of brackets. In some cases, as with *3ae inf.* verbs like 𓉐𓂋𓂻 *prỉ*, the unwritten consonant *ỉ* is added in the transliteration without employing brackets.

The explanations given of individual signs have been confined, as a rule, to normal uses, except where, as with 𓁒 B 3, an abnormal use has been found in a particularly important text. It has not, for example, been thought desirable to record wholly exceptional abbreviations, ex. 𓀜 for *ỉrw*. But even with this abstention the variety of employments must often appear astonishing. Sometimes this variety may be due to the fusion of signs originally distinct, as illustrated above. The diversity of employments as determinative sometimes arises from the fact that a sign may stand, not merely for the object it depicts, but also for actions performed therewith, ex. 𓍁 (U 13) occurs alike in 𓉔𓃀𓍁 *hb* 'plough' (n.) and in 𓋴𓎡𓄿𓍁𓀜 *skꜣ* 'plough' (vb.); so too with 𓌪 (T 30), 𓏛 (Y 1), 𓏞 (Y 3). And, of course, the development of the generic determinatives (§ 24) out of signs of much more specific character greatly increased the range of application of the former, ex. the hieroglyph of the striking man 𓀜 came to be employed where the early O. K. inscriptions particularized by showing a man in the act of sowing 𓀠 or one in the act of reaping 𓀡.

The study of the individual hieroglyphs is still in its infancy, though some admirable pioneering work has been done. The principal authorities are:—W. M. Flinders Petrie, *Medum*, London, 1892; F. Ll. Griffith, *Beni Hasan*, Part III, London, 1896; Id., *A Collection of Hieroglyphs*, London, 1898; N. de G. Davies, *The Mastaba of Ptahhetep and Akhethetep at Saqqareh*, Part I, London, 1900; M. A. Murray, *Saqqara Mastabas*, Part I, London, 1905; A. M. Blackman, *The Rock Tombs of Meir*, Part II, London, 1915; A. Scharff, *Ärchäologische Beiträge zur Frage der Entstehung der Hieroglyphenschrift*, in *Sitz. Bayr. Ak.* 1942, *Heft 3*. An admirable synopsis of the signs employed in the earliest period will be found in Hilda Petrie, *Egyptian Hieroglyphs of the First and Second Dynasties*, London, 1927. Not to increase our references too greatly, we have as a rule preferred to quote less obvious sources.

The letter and number prefixed to the individual hieroglyphs in the following list are those assigned to them in the *Catalogue* (Oxford, 1928) of the new fount of type made for the express purpose of this Grammar. Sometimes, however, the designation will seem to be out of its rightful place, exx. A 59 between A 25, 26, Aa 23, 24 between U 35, 36. This is due either to the sign having been added after the publication of the *Catalogue* or to our desire to present it in a more appropriate position than in the first edition.

Sect. A. Man and his Occupations

1 seated man — Ideo. in *s* (*sỉ*)[0] 'man'. Ideo. or det. 'I', 'me' in *·ỉ*, *wỉ*, *ỉnk*, *·kwỉ*. Det. man's relationships or occupations, exx. *sꜣ* 'son'; *smr* 'courtier'; *ḥwrw* 'wretch'; *ỉrr* 'doer'; also personal names, ex. *ꜥnḫw* 'ꜥAnkhu'. In personal names, is abbrev. for *rḫw* 'men',[1] ex. *Rḫw-ꜥnḫ* 'Reḫuꜥonkh'.

[0] Very rarely written as *sỉ*, exx. *Urk.* v. 179; *Mett.* 18. [1] *Rec.* 9, 57, n. 2.

seated man and woman with plural strokes — Det. people and their occupations, exx. *rmṯ* 'people'; *ꜥꜣmw* 'Asiatics'; *mtrw* 'witnesses'.

2 man with hand to mouth — Det. eat,[1] exx. *wnm* 'eat'; *ḥḳr* 'hungry'; drink, ex. *sw(r)ỉ* 'drink'; speak, exx. *sḏd* 'relate'; *gr* 'be silent'; think, ex. *kꜣỉ* 'devise'; feel, ex. *mrỉ* 'love'.

[1] Old uses, *ÄZ.* 57, 73.

3 [1] man sitting on heel — Det. in *ḥmsỉ* 'sit'. Replaced in hieratic by A 17 or A 17* or even by B 4.

[1] Ex. *Rekh.* 4, 1.

4 man with arms raised (cf. A 30) — Det. supplicate, ex. *dwꜣ* 'adore'; hide, exx. [1] *sdgꜣ* 'be hidden'; [2] *ỉmn* 'hide'.

[1] *Urk.* iv. 385, 13. [2] Leyd. V 4, 2.

5 [1] man hiding behind wall (Dyn. XVIII) — Det. hide, ex. *ỉmn* 'hide'.

[1] *Urk.* iv. 84, 15. Very rare before Dyn. XIX.

6 [1] man receiving purification (in M.E. usually replaced by D 60) — Ideo. in var. Pyr. *wꜥb*[2] 'pure', 'clean'.

[1] Ex. *D. el B.* 56. [2] *Pyr.* 1171.

7 [1] man sinking to ground from fatigue — Det. weary, weak, exx. [2] *wrd* 'tire'; [3] *bdš* 'faint'; [4] *gnn* 'be soft'.

[1] Ex. *D. el B.* 110. [2] Brit. Mus. 101. [3] BUDGE, p. 372, 14. [4] Cf. *Urk.* iv. 943, 4.

A 8 [1] man performing the *ḥnw*-rite — Det. in *ḥnw* 'jubilation'.

[1] Ex. *D. el B.* 89.

9 man steadying basket W 10 on head — Det. in abbrev. [1] *ꜣtp* 'load'; abbrev. [2] *fꜣi* 'carry'; abbrev. [3] *kꜣt* 'work'.

[1] *Sin.* B 244; *Peas.* B 1, 70. [2] *Sin.* B 246. [3] *Urk.* iv. 52, 17.

10 [1] man holding oar — Det. in [1] *sḳdw* 'sail'.

[1] *Th. T. S.* i. 37.

11 [1] man holding the *ꜥbꜣ*-sceptre S 42 and crook S 39 (O.K.) — O.K. ideo. or det. in var. [2] *ḫnms* 'friend'. Later replaced by A 21.

[1] Dav. *Ptah.* i. 4, no. 8. [2] *Saqq. Mast.* i. 23.

12 soldier with bow and quiver — Ideo. or det. in var. [1] *mšꜥ* 'army'. Det. in [2] *mnfyt* 'soldiers'.

[1] Lyons 90. [2] *Urk.* iv. 966, 6.

13 [1] man with arms tied behind his back — Det. enemy, exx. *sbi* 'rebel'; *ḫfty* 'enemy'.

[1] Ex. *Puy.* 30 (*sḳr-ꜥnḫw*).

14 man with blood streaming from his head — Det. die, ex. *mwt* 'die'; enemy, ex. *ḫfty* 'enemy'.

[1] Ex. *D. el B.* 114.

14* as A 14 but blood interpreted as an axe[1] — Use as A 14.

[1] Model taken from temple of Ramesses III at Medînet Habu. Probably in use far earlier.

15 man falling — Ideo. or det. in var. [1] *ḫr* 'fall' and derivatives. Abbrev. [2] for *ḫrw* 'fallen (i.e. conquered) enemy'; also [3] for *sḫrt* 'overthrow' (infinitive).

[1] *Urk.* iv. 653, 15. [2] *Urk.* iv. 658, 11. [3] *Urk.* iv. 140, 5.

16 [1] man bowing down — Det. in *ksi* 'bow down'.

[1] Ex. *D. el B.* 70.

17 child sitting (on lap) with hand to mouth — Det. young, exx. *rnpi* 'be young'; *šri* 'child'; *nmḥ* 'orphan'. Abbrev. , [1] for *ẖrd* 'child'. Phon. *nni* in [2] *Nni-nsw* 'Heracleopolis'.

[1] Especially in the title *ẖrd n kꜣp* 'child of the harîm', written phonetically Thebes, tomb 241, *JEA.* 16, Pl. 17, O.Q. [2] From *nn(i)* 'child', see the reference qu. on W 24.

17* child in sitting posture, arms hanging down — Adapted from hieratic,[1] where it replaces A 3, ex. *ḥmsi* 'sit',[2] or A 17, ex. *msw* 'children'.[3]

[1] Möll. *Pal.* i. no. 31. [2] *P. Kah.* 6, 5. [3] *Hat-Nub* 18, 5.

18 child with crown of Lower Egypt S 3 — Det. child-king, exx. [1] *inp* 'crown-prince', 'royal child'; [2] *wḏḥ* 'weaned princeling'.

[1] Ex. *Urk.* iv. 157, 7. Sim. *rnnt* 'nursling' (fem.), *ib.* 361, 15. [2] *Urk.* iv. 157, 8.

A 19 bent man leaning on stick (clearly distinguishable from A 21 in hieratic,[1] not always so in hieroglyphic)[2]

Ideo. or det. old, in var. *iꜣw* 'old'; var. *smsw* (*śmśw*) 'eldest'; great, in varr. , *wr* 'great one', 'chief'. Det. old, also in *tnỉ* 'old'; lean, exx. *rhn* 'lean'; *twꜣ* 'support oneself'. Phon. or phon. det. *ik* (from a rare *iꜣk* 'be aged'[3]) in [4] var. [5] *iky* 'miner', 'hewer of stone'. In M.K. hieratic is written for *ḥwỉ*, *ḥỉỉ* 'strike'.[6]

[1] Möll. *Pal.* i. nos. 13–14; *ÄZ.* 49, 122. [2] Especially as *wr* 'chief'. [3] *Wb.* i. 34. [4] *Hamm.* 108. [5] *Hamm.* 123, 3. [6] See below A 25.

20 [1] man leaning on forked stick, less senile than A 19[2]

Ideo. or det. in much rarer var. *smsw* (*śmśw*) 'eldest', especially in *sꜣ·f smsw* 'his eldest son', cf. Pyr. [3] *zꜣ·k śmśw*, and in the title var. [4] *smsw hyt* 'elder of the portal'.

[1] O.K., Leyd. *Denkm.* i. 6 in *śmśw h(y)t*. [2] A sign like A 19 is used for *smsw* in hieratic. [3] *Pyr.* 608. [4] *ÄZ.* 60, 64.

21 man holding stick in one hand and handkerchief in the other (always distinct from A 19 in hieratic)[1]

Ideo. or det. in var. *sr* (*śr*) 'official', 'noble'. Det. magnate, exx. *šnyt* 'courtiers'; *smr* 'courtier', 'friend' (of the king). Also det. in [2] *ḫnms* 'friend', here replacing an older sign A 11; in [3] *ẖnti* 'statue' replacing A 22. In hieroglyphic is often hard to distinguish from A 19 (in the word *wr* 'chief') and from A 20.

[1] Möll. *Pal.* i. no. 11; *ÄZ.* 49, 122. [2] Cairo 20245, *l*; 20426, *k*. [3] *Puy.* 20.

22 [1] statue of man with stick and *ꜥbꜣ*-sceptre S 42

Det. in *ẖnt(y)* 'statue' and in *twt* 'statue'. The form of the sign varies according to the nature of the statue to be depicted.[2]

[1] Ex. *Siut* i. 308 (*ẖnty*). [2] Exx. king, *Urk.* iv. 279, 7 (*ẖnty*); 753, 3 (*twtw*).

23 [1] king with stick and club T 3

Det. in *ity* 'sovereign'.

[1] Thebes, tomb 55.

24 man striking with stick

Det. in *ḥwỉ*, *ḥỉỉ* 'strike'. Hence det. force, effort, exx. abbrev. [1] *nḫt* 'strong'; *nḥm* 'take away'; *ḥꜥḏꜣ* 'plunder'; *sbꜣ* 'teach'. In Dyn. XVIII hieroglyphic is mostly replaced by D 40, which either as or as is common also in hieratic.

[1] Exx. *Urk.* iv. 82, 10; 89, 7.

A 25 man striking, with left arm hanging behind back[1] — Rare ideo. used in *ḥwi, ḥii* 'strike'. Serves in this book as a conventional transcription of the hieratic group employed in Dyn. XVII–XVIII papyri and also earlier in Dyn. XI;[2] the explanation of the group is obscure.[3] In papyri of Dyn. XII 'strike' is written with a sign identical with A 19.[3]

[1] Möll. *Pal.* i. no. 16 (Hyksos period). [2] Frequent in the Coffin Texts; see also a hieroglyphic equivalent *Dend.* 11 A. [3] *ÄZ.* 44, 126; 56, 39.

59 man threatening with stick — Det. 'drive away' in *sḥr* 'drive away'.[1]

[1] *Urk.* iv. 618, 7.

26 [1] man with one arm raised in invocation — Det. call, exx. *nis* 'call', 'summon'; [2] *dwi* 'call'. Abbrev. *ꜥš* in [3] *sḏm-ꜥš* 'servant', lit. 'one who hears the call'. Det. in the vocative interjection *i* 'O' (§ 258).

[1] Ex. *Rekh.* 12. [2] *Urk.* iv. 874, 6. [3] *Th. T. S.* iii. 5; reading, *ib.* lowest register.

27 [1] man hastening with one arm raised — Cf. Pyr. [2] *inw* 'messengers'. Hence phon. *in* in *in* 'by' (§ 168).

[1] Ex. *Rekh.* 12. [2] *Pyr.* 1675, the body probably omitted for superstitious reasons.

28 man with both arms raised — Det. high, in varr. , *kꜣ(i)* 'be high'. Det. joy, exx. *ḥꜥi* 'rejoice'; [1] *swꜣš* 'extol'; mourn, in [2] *ḥꜣi* 'mourn'; also, for unknown reasons, in [3] *iꜣs* 'bald'.

[1] *D. el B.* 82. [2] *JEA.* 41, 10–1. [3] *Eb.* 66, 9; cf. too *ꜣst, Wb.* i. 20, 15.

29 [1] man upside-down — Det. in *sḫd* 'be upside down'.

[1] Ex. *Amuda* 17.

30 man with arms outstretched (cf. A 4) — Det. praise, exx. var. *iꜣw* 'praise'; *dwꜣ* 'adore'; [1] *swꜣš* 'extol'; supplicate, ex. [2] *twꜣ* 'claim'; awe, in [3] *tr* 'show respect for'.

[1] *Urk.* iv. 141, 4. [2] *Pt.* 319. [3] *Sin.* R 35.

31 [1] man with his arms stretched out behind him — Det. turn away, ex. [2] *ꜥnw* 'averted' (face).

[1] Möll. *Pal.* ii. no. 5 (Dyn. XVIII.) [2] R. *IH.* 240, 39 (Dyn. XIX).

32 [1] man dancing — Det. dance, ex. [2] *ḫbi* 'dance'; joy, ex. [3] *hy-hnw* 'jubilate'.

[1] Möll. *Pal.* ii. no. 6. [2] *Urk.* iv. 386, 6. Sim. Dyn. XII, *Bersh.* ii. 21, 14. [3] *Urk.* iv. 141, 1.

33 [1] man with stick and bundle or mat on shoulder — Ideo. in var. [2] *m(i)niw* 'herdsman'.[3] Det. wander, exx. [4] *rwi* 'wander'; [5] *šm(ꜣ)w* 'wanderers', 'strangers'.

[1] *Puy.* 50. [2] Berl. *ÄI.* ii. p. 166. [3] *ÄZ.* 42, 119. [4] *Puy.* 50; *D. el B.* 113. [5] *Urk.* iv. 390, 8.

A 34 man pounding in a mortar[1] — Det. in *ḥwsi* 'pound', 'build'.

[1] See the picture *Rekh.* 12. In the accompanying text *ḥwst* is infinitive, hence the verb is *4ae inf.*

35 man building a wall — Ideo. or det. in var. [1] *ḳd* 'build'.

[1] *Urk.* iv. 765, 12; cf. 767, 11.

36 [1] man kneading and straining into a vessel[2] — Ideo. or det. in [3] var. ,[4] *ʿfty* 'brewer'.

[1] From a walking-stick formerly in the possession of N. de G. Davies. See the picture Leyd. V 3 = *Denkm.* ii. 2. [2] *ÄZ.* 35, 128. [3] Cairo 20161, *c* 28. Sim. NORTHAMPT. 4. [4] Cairo 20095; see too *ÄZ.* 37, 84.

37 [1] commoner form of last — Use as last.

[1] Cairo 20018, *n*; Leyd. V 6; see *ÄZ.* 37, 82.

38 man holding necks of two emblematic animals with panther heads (Dyn. XII) — Ideo. in [1] varr. ,[2] [3] *Ḳis*, var. Dyn. XVIII [4] *Ḳsy*, 'Cusae', the modern town of El-Ḳûṣîyah in Upper Egypt.

[1] *Meir* ii. 17, no. 8 = i. 2. [2] *Meir* ii. 17, no. 4 = *ib.* iii. 9. [3] LAC. *TR.* 20, 35; see *Meir* i. p. 1, n. 3. [4] *Urk.* iv. 386, 4.

39 [1] alternative form of last — Use as last.

[1] DAV. *Ḳen.* i. 44.

40 seated god. (Note the slightly curved beard and straight wig) — Det. god (replacing earlier G 7),[1] exx. *Ptḥ* 'Ptah'; *Mnṯw* '(the god) Mont'. Ideo. or det. 'I', 'me' in *·i*, *wi*, *ink* when a god is speaking or, in Dyn. XII, the king.[2]

[1] M. E. hieratic retains G 7, see § 63 A, 4. [2] References for *·i* see § 34.

41 king. (Note uraeus on brow, straight beard, and coif) — Det. king (common Dyn. XVIII), exx. *nsw* 'king'; *ḥm* 'Majesty'; *nb* 'the Lord' (p. 75). Ideo. or det. 'I', 'me' in *·i*, *wi*, *ink* when the king is speaking.[1]

[1] References for *·i* see § 34.

42 [1] the same, but with flagellum S 45 — Use as last (common Dyn. XVIII).

[1] Already Dyn. XII, *Hier.* 8, no. 148 = *Bersh.* i. 15 (*ity*).

43 king wearing crown of Upper Egypt S 1 — Ideo. or det. in var. *nsw* (*nzw*, *ni-śwt*)[1] 'king of Upper Egypt', 'king'. Det. *Wsir* 'Osiris'.

[1] Reading, p. 50, n. 1.

44 [1] the same, but with flagellum S 45 — Use as last.

[1] As abbrev. *nsw*, *Urk.* iv. 332, 10.

45 king wearing crown of Lower Egypt S 3 — Ideo. or det. in var. *bity* 'king of Lower Egypt'.

46 [1] the same, but with flagellum S 45 — Use as last.

[1] *Puy.* 20, 6.

A 47 shepherd seated and wrapped in mantle, holding a stick with appendage[1]

Ideo. in var. Pyr. [2] *m(ỉ)niw*[3] 'herdsman'. Ideo. or det. in var. *s3w* (*z3w*)[4] 'guard', 'protect'. Sometimes inaccurately for A 48 in [5] *ỉry* 'relating to' (§ 79).

[1] MONTET 99. [2] *Pyr.* 1348. [3] Reading, *ÄZ.* 42, 116. [4] Reading with *z*, see *Pyr.* 1163. 1220. [5] *Rekh.* 10; *Urk.* iv. 120, 17.

48 beardless man (or woman?) holding knife (?)[1]

Ideo. (?) or det. *ỉry* in var. *ỉry* 'relating to', 'belonging to' (§ 79).

[1] See DAV. *Ptah.* i. p. 15. Good detailed exx. of the sign are not forthcoming. It may depict the 'door-keeper' (*ỉry ʿrrt*) of some mythical place.

49 Syrian seated holding stick

Det. foreigner, exx. [1] *ʿ3mw* 'Asiatics'; [2] *Iwntyw-Styw* 'Nubian bowmen'.[3]

[1] *Urk.* iv. 614, 1. [2] *D. el B.* 160. [3] See p. 398, n. 1.

50 man of rank seated on chair

Det. revered persons (M.K.; in Dyn. XVIII mainly replaced by A 51 and A 52), exx. *Snbw* 'Sonbu', a personal name; [1] *smr(w)* 'courtiers'. Ideo. or det. 'I', 'me' on M.K. coffins in [2] *·ỉ*, *wỉ*, *ink*. Rarely ideo. like A 51 in [3] *šps* (*špś*) 'noble'.

[1] *BH.* i. 25, 119. [2] References, § 34. [3] *Meir* ii. 11; Leyd. V 4, 12.

51 the same with flagellum S 45

Ideo. in var. [1] *špsỉ* (*špśỉ*) 'be noble' and related words. After M.K., often det. revered persons, ex. [2] *ỉmyw-ḥ3t* 'those of former times'.

[1] *Siut* 1, 231. Sim. *Pyr.* 931. [2] *Urk.* iv. 59, 3. Sim. *ib.* 59, 4 (*ỉm3ḫyw*); 76, 10 (*tpyw-ʿ*); 86, 3 (*ḏrtyw*).

52 noble squatting with flagellum S 45 (common in Dyn. XVIII)

Det. revered persons, especially personal names, ex. [1] *P3-ḥry* 'Paḥeri', a man's name; [2] *sʿḥ* 'deceased noble'. Rarely also for A 51 in [3] *šps* 'noble'.

[1] *Urk.* iv. 122, 5. [2] *Urk.* iv. 123, 12. [3] *Puy.* 20.

53 mummy upright

Det. mummy, ex. [1] *wỉ* 'mummy'; statue, likeness, ex. var. [2] *twt* 'statue'; form, shape, exx. *ḳỉ* 'form'; *ḫprw* 'forms', 'stages of growth'.

[1] Louvre C 15, 8; *Sin.* B 193. [2] *Urk.* iv. 842, 13.

54 recumbent mummy

Det. dead, exx. [1] *m(ỉ)nỉ* 'death'; [2] *nb-ʿnḫ* 'sarcophagus', lit. 'lord-of-life'.

[1] *Urk.* iv. 405, 8. [2] *Urk.* iv. 113, 9.

55 mummy lying on bed (replacing O.K. form with man on bed)[1]

Det. lie, ex. abbrev. [2] *sḏr* 'lie', 'spend all night'; death, exx. [3] *ḫpt* 'decease'; [4] *ḫ3t* 'corpse'.

[1] Ex. *Meir* iv. 4, 1. [2] *Eb.* 6, 9. [3] Cairo 20003, *a* 2. [4] *Th. T. S.* i. 30, B.

For A 59 see above after A 25.

Sect. B. Woman and her Occupations

B 1 seated woman — Det. female, exx. *st* 'woman'; *ḥmt* 'woman', 'wife'; *nṯrt* 'goddess'; woman's relationships, exx. *s3t* 'daughter'; *ḫ3rt* 'widow'; her occupations, exx. *ḥmt* 'female slave'; *šmꜥyt* 'chantress'; her name, ex. *Nfrt* 'Nofret'. As suffix 1st pers. sing. 'I', 'my' (fem.) *·i* has not been noted before Dyn. XIX.[1]

[1] Exx. MAR. *Abyd.* i. 25.

2 pregnant woman — Det. pregnant, exx. [1] *iwr* 'conceive'; [2] *bk3* 'be pregnant'.

[1] *D. el B.* 49. [2] *Urk.* iv. 268, 7.

3 woman giving birth — Ideo. or det. in [1] var. *msi* (*mśi*) 'bear', 'give birth' and the related words.

[1] *Urk.* iv. 13, 16.

4 [1] combination of sign for a squatting woman (cf. B 3) with F 31 [2] — Use as last. In one hieratic MS. substituted for A 3.[3]

[1] Exx. Brit. Mus. 566; Cairo 70040 = ROEDER, *Naos* 42. Also without arms showing, ex. Berl. *ÄI.* i. p. 258, 18. 20. [2] Old exx. show the two signs almost or quite separate from one another, but with the phon. sign *mś* placed as though it were the infant in course of being born, *Urk.* i. 24, 15; 35, 11; 36, 7. [3] *JEA.* 32, Pl. 14, n. 1, 3a.

5 [1] woman suckling child — Det. 'suckle' in *mnꜥt* 'nurse', 'foster-mother'.

[1] Exx. Dyn. XII, *BH.* i. 25, 79; Dyn. XVIII, *D. el B.* 53.

6 [1] woman seated on chair with child on lap — Det. 'nurse' in *rnn* 'nurse', 'rear'.

[1] Exx. L. *D.* iii. 53; *D. el B.* 101.

7 queen wearing diadem and carrying flower — Det. of names of queens.[1]

[1] Ex. *Ann.* 42, 479, from Thebes, tomb 192, *temp.* Amenophis III.

Sect. C. Anthropomorphic Deities

C 1 god with sun and uraeus on head — Ideo. or det. in [1] var. [1] *Rꜥ* '(the sun-god) Rēꜥ'.

[1] *D. el B.* 110.

2 god with head of falcon bearing sun on head G 9 and holding S 34 — Ideo. or det. in var. [1] *Rꜥ* '(the sun-god) Rēꜥ'.

[1] *Urk.* iv. 14, 13.

3 god with head of ibis G 26 — Ideo. or det. in [1] var. *Ḏḥwty*[2] 'Thoth'.

[1] *Bersh.* i. 15. [2] Reading, see on G 26.

4 god with head of ram E 10 — Ideo. or det. in [1] var. *Ḫnmw* 'Chnum'.

[1] *Urk.* iv. 99, 5.

C 5	[hieroglyph]	the same holding [hieroglyph] S 34	Use as last.
6	[hieroglyph]	god with head of dog [hieroglyph] E 15	Ideo. or det. in [hieroglyphs] var. [hieroglyph] *ʾInpw* 'Anubis'; also in [hieroglyphs][1] *Wp-wɜwt* 'Wepwawet'. [1] *Urk.* iv. 99, 10.
7	[hieroglyph]	god with head of Seth-animal [hieroglyph] E 20	Ideo. in [hieroglyph] *Stẖ*[1] (*Śtš*) 'Seth'. [1] Reading, see on E 20.
8	[hieroglyph]	ithyphallic god with feathers, uplifted arm, and flagellum [hieroglyph] S 45	Ideo. or det. in [hieroglyphs][1] var. [hieroglyph] *Mnw*[2] 'Min'. [1] *Urk.* iv. 1031, 4. [2] Reading, see on R 22.
9	[hieroglyph]	goddess with sun and horns	Ideo. or det. in [hieroglyphs][1] var. [hieroglyph][2] *Ḥt-ḥr* 'Hathor'. [1] *Sinai* 141. [2] *Sinai* 95. Also shown seated on chair, *ib.* 105.
10	[hieroglyph]	goddess with feather on head	Ideo. or det. in [hieroglyphs] var. [hieroglyph] *Mɜʿt* 'Māʿet', the goddess of Truth.
11	[hieroglyph]	god with arms supporting (the sky) and [hieroglyph] M 4 on head (often also without [hieroglyph])	Ideo. in [hieroglyph] var. Pyr. [hieroglyphs][1] *Ḥḥ* '(one of the gods) Ḥeḥ'.[2] Hence phon. *ḥḥ* in [hieroglyph] *ḥḥ* 'million', 'many' (§ 259). [1] *Pyr.* 1390. [2] The eight Ḥeḥ-gods were those who held the sky aloft, see Kees, *Götterglaube*, p. 312 and the picture *JEA.* 28, Pl. 4. The sign for 'year' (M 4) was added doubtless on account of the common expression *ḥḥ m* (or *n*) *rnpwt* 'a million years'.

It may prove possible to find images of other deities used as ideo. or det. in M. K. inscriptions, but for lack of positive earlier evidence some models for the hieroglyphic fount have been taken from monuments of Dyn. XIX or later,[1] exx. C 12 [hieroglyph] Amūn, C 17 [hieroglyph] Mont, C 18 [hieroglyph] Tjanen, C 19 [hieroglyph] and C 20 [hieroglyph] Ptaḥ.

[1] *JEA.* 17, 245.

Sect. D. Parts of the Human Body

D 1	[hieroglyph]	head in profile	Ideo. in [hieroglyphs] *tp*[1] 'head' and [hieroglyphs] *tpy* 'chief', 'first'. Det. head, exx. [hieroglyphs] *dɜdɜ* 'head'; [hieroglyphs] *ḥɜ* 'back of head', whence prep. [hieroglyphs] *ḥɜ* 'behind' (§ 172) and [hieroglyphs] *mkḥɜ* 'neglect'; [hieroglyphs] *dhnt* 'forehead', whence [hieroglyphs] *dhn* 'promote', etc.; perhaps with notion throttle, in [hieroglyphs][2] *gwɜwɜ* 'fetter', 'bind fast'. Possibly [hieroglyphs] possessed the value *dɜdɜ* in some cases where there is no evidence to prove it. In one M. E. story the spellings [hieroglyphs] and [hieroglyphs] alternate for the 'head' of a goose, as well as in the common O. K.

D 1 (continued)

personal name .[3] Of the two words for 'head' *ḏꜣḏꜣ* alone has survived in Coptic (*djō*, construct *djĕ-*), also in the prepositions *edjen*, *hidjen*; it is impossible to say how early the latter readings are, and the values *r-tp*, *ḥr-tp* have been provisionally retained above, p. 135, top.

[1] Reading, *PSBA*. 21, 269. [2] *Urk*. iv. 7, 4. [3] *Westc*. Index, p. 30.

2 face

Ideo. in *ḥr*[1] 'face' and derivatives. Hence phon. *ḥr*, exx. *ḥr* 'prepare'; *dḥr* 'bitter', 'sour'.

[1] Reading from Coptic *ho* 'face', derivatives like *hrai* 'upper part', and phonetic use.

3 hair

Det. hair, exx. *šny* 'hair'; *skm* 'grey-haired'; skin, exx. *ỉwn* 'complexion', 'nature'; *ỉnm* 'skin'; mourn, in *ỉꜣkb* 'mourn'; bald, empty, forlorn, exx. *wš* 'fall out (of hair)', whence abbrev. in *gm wš* 'found defective' (of damaged writing or pictures);[1] *ḫꜣrt* 'widow'.

[1] *Eb*. 18, 1; 90, 3; PIEHL, *IH*. iii. 74; reading from *BH*. i. 26, 162. See too *Sitz. Berl. Ak*. 1912, 912.

4 eye

Ideo. in *ỉrt* 'eye', Gk. *ἰρί*.[1] Hence phon. *ỉr*, exx. *ỉrỉ* 'make'; *ỉrtt* 'milk'. Det. see, in varr. ,[2] *mꜣꜣ* 'see', whence as phon. *mꜣ* in [3] *mꜣw* 'lions'. Early det. in other words for see, look, and in connection with other notions involving the eye, exx. [4] *dgỉ* 'look'; [5] *šp* 'blind'; [6] *rmỉ* 'weep'; [7] *rs* 'be wakeful'; later, especially in Dyn. XVIII, mainly replaced as det. by the more specific signs D 5, D 6, D 7, and D 9. From end of Dyn. XVIII a masc. dual . . . *wy* 'eyes' is occasionally found,[8] but whether this points to the existence of a masc. word *ỉr* 'eye' is uncertain.

[1] PLUTARCH, *De Iside* 10. See *Rec*. 17, 93. [2] *Siut* 1, 217, where the doubling indicates gemination, see *Verbum* i. § 390. [3] *Sh. S*. 30. [4] *Sin*. B 279; *Urk*. iv. 19, 6. [5] *Peas*. B 2, 105. [6] *Leb*. 76. [7] *Paheri* 2. [8] *Wb*. i. 108, 1–2.

5 eye touched up with paint

Det. actions or conditions of eye, exx. [1] *dgỉ* 'look'; [2] *šp* 'blind'; [3] *rs* 'be wakeful'.

[1] MAR. *Abyd*. ii. 30, 33. [2] *Urk*. iv. 85, 6. [3] *Urk*. iv. 960, 11.

6 [1] later alternative to last

Use as last.

[1] MÖLL. *Pal*. ii. no. 83, from Dyn. XVIII; very rare, however, as early as this.

D 7 eye with painted lower lid — Det. adorn, exx. [1] *msdmt* 'eye-paint'; [2] *ꜥn* (*ꜥin*)[3] 'beautiful'. From the latter, phon. det. *ꜥn*, ex. [4] *ꜥnw* (*ꜥinw*)[3] 'ꜥAinu', a place-name, see B 8. The use as det. see etc., ex. [5] *ptr* 'behold', is abnormal.

[1] *BH.* i. 38. [2] *Amarn.* iii. 19. Sim. *Urk.* iv. 6, 11, qu. Exerc. XXXII, (*a*). [3] For *ꜥin* as the full reading cf. Semitic *ꜥain* 'eye' and Eg. words qu. below, D 8, n. 1. [4] *BH.* i. 26, 175. [5] *Siut* i. 220.

8 eye enclosed in sign for land ⊂⊃ N 18 — Det. in *ꜥnw*, *ꜥ(i)nw* 'ꜥAinu', the quarry at the modern Ṭurah whence *inr ḥd nfr n ꜥnw* 'fine white (lime)stone of ꜥAinu' was obtained.[1] Hence phon. det. in *ꜥn* 'beautiful'.[2] See too above D 7.

[1] *AEO.* ii. 126*, following *Sitz. Berl. Ak.* 1933, 864. The full value *ꜥin*, corresponding to Semitic *ꜥain* 'eye', is proved by the derivatives *ꜥin* 'coat with limestone (?)', *Urk.* i. 20, 5 (O. K.) and *ꜥyn* 'ꜥAinu-stone' *Wb.* i. 191, 4, 5 (Dyn. XX). [2] *Meir* ii. 12, 3; *Urk.* iv. 52, 16.

9 eye with flowing tears — Ideo. or det. in var. [1] *rmi* 'weep', 'beweep'.

[1] *Rekh.* 4.

10 human eye with the markings of a falcon's head — Ideo. or det. in [1] var. [2] *wḏꜣt* 'the *wḏꜣt*-eye' (or '*wedjat*-eye'), i. e. 'the sound (uninjured) eye' of Horus (§ 266, 1). [1] BUDGE, p. 56, 7. [2] BUDGE, p. 38, 15.

11 part of the white of the *wḏꜣt*-eye — Sign for $\frac{1}{2}$ *ḥeḳat*-measure of corn (§ 266, 1).[1]

[1] Reversed in hieratic, see p. 198, n. 1.

12 o pupil of the eye — Det. in *dfḏ* 'pupil' of eye.[1] As part of the *wḏꜣt*-eye sign for $\frac{1}{4}$ *ḥeḳat*-measure of corn (§ 266, 1). A similar, but smaller, sign appears to have been used for from 1 to 9 *ḥeḳat* (§ 266, 1). To be distinguished from the grain of sand ∘ N 33, and from the circle o, see after Z 8.

[1] BUDGE, 212, 13 (*Nu*).

13 eye-brow (also as part of the *wḏꜣt*-eye — Sign for $\frac{1}{8}$ *ḥeḳat*-measure of corn (§ 266, 1). Also as det. in [1] *inḥ* 'eye-brow(s)'. Det. or phon. det. in some words connected with *smd* (*śmd*) 'eye-brow' itself not found until Greek times.[2]

[1] *M. u. K.* 3, 8. [2] *Wb.* iv. 146.

14 the other (see D 11) part of the white of the *wḏꜣt*-eye — Sign for $\frac{1}{16}$ *ḥeḳat*-measure of corn (§ 266, 1).

15 one of the markings of the *wḏꜣt*-eye — Sign for $\frac{1}{32}$ *ḥeḳat*-measure of corn (§ 266, 1).

D 16 another of the markings of the *wḏ3t*-eye — Sign for $\frac{1}{64}$ *ḥeḳat*-measure of corn (§ 266, 1).

17 markings of the *wḏ3t*-eye (nos. D 15 and 16 together) — Ideo. or det. in [1] var. [2] *tit* 'figure', 'image'.

[1] *Urk.* iv. 887, 2. [2] *Urk.* iv. 53, 17.

18 [1] ear — Ideo. or det. in [2] *msḏr* 'ear', dual [3] *msḏrwy* 'the two ears'.

[1] Thebes, tomb 93. [2] *Amarn.* vi. 15, 6. [3] *D. el B.* 116.

19 [1] nose, eye and cheek — Ideo. or det. in O.K. var. *fnḏ*, later *fnḏ*, 'nose'. Det. nose, ex. 'nose', 'nostril'; smell, exx. *tpi* 'sniff'; *sn* 'smell'; face, in *ḫnt* 'face'; joy, exx. *rš(w)* 'rejoice'; *ḫntš* 'take pleasure'; soft, kind, ex. *sfn* 'be mild'; also in *bṯn* 'be disobedient'; *gfn* 'rebuff'. From *ḫnt* 'face' (see above), phon. det. and (seldom before Dyn. XIX) [2] phon. *ḫnt*, exx. var. *ḫnty* 'in front of' (adj.). Owing to similarity in hieratic sometimes appears in hieroglyphic for Aa 32, ex. for *sty* 'red (?) Nubian (?) pigment'; also for U 31, ex. *ḫni* for *ḫn(r)i* 'restrain'; the hieratic has been often transcribed wrongly in modern books.[3] Confusion of two different stems has contributed to the confusion of signs in words like *ḫnrt*, varr. , *ḫnt* 'prison', 'harîm', 'fortress', which are consequently hard to differentiate.[4]

[1] Exx. *Hier.* 5, no. 59; *Rekh.* 15. [2] *ÄZ.* 55, 86. [3] *Rec.* 39, 20. Sim. in *ḫnrw* 'prisoners', Cairo 20024 = *Musée égyptien* i. 17. [4] *Adm.* 47.

20 semi-cursive variant of last [1] — Use as last, but seldom in careful sculptures or paintings.

[1] Already Dyn. IV, *Medum* 22. Exx. Dyn. XII, Cairo 20538, ii. *c* 13. 14.

21 mouth (Dyn. XII rarely vertically [1]) — Ideo. in *r* (*r3*) [1a] 'mouth', Coptic *rō*. Hence phon. *r*. In group-writing (§ 60) is *r*,[2] ex. *ibr* 'stallion'.

[1] Exx. Louvre C 1, 5; Pol. § 33, *a*. [1a] See above, p. 429, for the original presence of *3*. [2] Burchardt § 77.

(Monograms incorporating D 21.) For see M 6. For see M 24. For see M 25.

22 mouth with two strokes attached — Ideo. in *rwy* [1] 'two-thirds' (§ 265).

[1] Reading, Clère in *Arch. Or.* 20, 629.

23 mouth with three strokes attached — Ideo. in 'three-quarters', probable reading *ḫmt rw* [1] (§ 265).

[1] Clère, *op. cit.* 640.

D 24 [1] upper lip with teeth — Ideo. in *spt*, var. Pyr. [2] *śpt*, 'lip', 'border' (of pool, etc.). Occasionally used by mistake for F 42.[3]

[1] MÖLL. *Pal.* ii. no. 92 *b*. [2] *Pyr.* 1393. [3] *Urk.* iv. 140, 6 (*spr*).

25 two lips with teeth — Ideo. or det. in [1] var. [2] *spty* (*śpty*) 'lips'.

[1] *M.u.K.* 4, 1. [2] *Urk.* iv. 971, 2.

26 [1] liquid issuing from lips — Det. spit, ex. [2] *psg* 'spit'; vomit, exx. *bšỉ* 'vomit'; *ḳꜣꜥ*, var. *ḳꜥ*, 'spew out'; blood, in [3] *snf* 'blood'.

[1] MÖLL. *Pal.* ii. no. 93 (Dyn. XVIII); the same form already *Pyr.* 142 (*pśg*). [2] *Eb.* 30, 17. [3] *P. Kah.* 7, 29.

27 breast [0] — Ideo or det. in var. Pyr. [1] *mnḏ*, later var. [2] *mnḏ*, 'breast'. Det. suckle, exx. [3] *snḳ* 'suckle'; [4] *mnꜥy* 'tutor' (det. transferred from *mnꜥt* 'nurse').

[0] Model from Thebes, tomb 85. So too *Puy.* 59. [1] *Pyr.* 32. [2] *Urk.* iv. 920, 10. [3] *D. el B.* 94. [4] *Paheri* 4.

27* breast (rather commoner shape) [1] — Use as last.

[1] *D. el B.* 94; *Paheri* 4.

28 arms extended so as to embrace? — Ideo. in *kꜣ* 'soul', 'spirit' (p. 172). Phon. *kꜣ*,[1] exx. *kꜣt* 'work'; *ḥkꜣ* 'magic'. In group-writing (§ 60) or is phon. *k*.[2]

[1] Reading, *Pyr.* 300 (*kꜣr* 'chapel'). [2] BURCHARDT § 120.

29 combination of D 28 and R 12 — In *kꜣ* 'soul', regarded as of divine nature.

30 [1] the sign D 28 with an appendage — Det. in [2] *Nḥb-kꜣw* 'Uniter-of-attributes', name of a mythical serpent-deity.[3]

[1] *Pyr.* 229. Sim. *Urk.* iv. 459, 13. [2] MAR. *Karn.* 33, where the appendage takes the form of I 10. [3] *JEA.* 21, 41.

31 [1] combination of D 32 and U 36 — In var. *ḥm-kꜣ* 'servant of the *ka*', '*ka*-priest'.

[1] *Hier.* 9, no. 165 (Bershah).

32 arms enclosing or embracing — Det. envelop, embrace, exx. *ỉnḳ* 'envelop'; *ḥpt* 'embrace'; open arms, in *pgꜣ* 'unfold'.

33 arms engaged in rowing — Ideo. in *ẖnỉ*[1] 'row' and derivatives. Hence phon. *ẖn*, ex. *ẖnnw* 'turmoil'.

[1] Reading, see the varr. of *mẖnt* 'ferry-boat', *Pyr.* 1223 combined with 334.

34 arms holding shield and battle-axe [1] — Ideo. in var. Pyr. [2] *ꜥḥꜣ* 'fight' and derivatives.

[1] Thebes, tomb 93. Elsewhere usually shield and mace, *Hier.* p. 15.
[2] *Pyr.* 574. In M.K. also sometimes *ỉḥꜣ*, see *Sphinx* 12, 108.

34* [1] O.K. form of last — Use as last.

[1] DAV. *Ptah.* i. 5, no. 46.

D 35 [hieroglyph][1] arms in gesture of negation — Ideo. in [hieroglyph] *n*[2] and [hieroglyph] *nn*[2] 'not' (§ 104). Hence phon. *n*,[2] exx. [hieroglyph] *n* 'to', 'for' (§ 164); [hieroglyph] *nnšm* 'spleen'. Ideo. also in [hieroglyph] var. [hieroglyph] *iwty*, var. Pyr. [hieroglyph] *iwti*, 'which not' (§ 202).[3] Det. not know, in [hieroglyph] *ḫm* 'be ignorant'; hence phon. det. *ḫm*, exx. [hieroglyph][4] *ḫm* 'shrine'; also with metathesis *mḫ*, in [hieroglyph][5] *smḫ* 'forget'.

[1] Palms upward, common at all periods, exx. O.K., *Saqq. Mast.* i. 1; M.K., *Meir* i. 5; Dyn. XVIII, *Rekh.* 2. 3. 10; but sometimes palms down, exx. O.K., *Medum* 24; M.K., *BH.* i. 8; Dyn. XVIII, *Rekh.* 4. 15. [2] Readings, Gunn, *Stud.* ch. 9. [3] Reading *JEA.* 34, 27. [4] *Urk.* iv. 96, 4; see on O 34. [5] *Mill.* i, 10.

36 [hieroglyph] forearm — Ideo. in [hieroglyph] *ˁ* 'arm', 'hand'. Hence phon. *ˁ*. Also in hieratic, less often in hieroglyphic, as substitute for [hieroglyph] D 37, [hieroglyph] D 38, [hieroglyph] D 39, [hieroglyph] D 40, [hieroglyph] D 41, [hieroglyph] D 42, [hieroglyph] D 43, [hieroglyph] D 44.

For [hieroglyph] see D 59. For [hieroglyph] see G 20. For [hieroglyph] see G 45. For [hieroglyph] see M 27. For [hieroglyph] see O 12. For [hieroglyph] see P 7. For [hieroglyph] see Aa 22.

37 [hieroglyph] forearm with hand holding [hieroglyph] X 8 — In Pyr. almost exclusively ideo. in [hieroglyph] var. [hieroglyph] *imi* 'give', imperative (§ 336),[1] whereas [hieroglyph] is there common both as (*r*)*di* and as *imi*. In M.K. and later [hieroglyph] is commoner than [hieroglyph] both in *rdi* ([hieroglyph]) and in *di* ([hieroglyph]), but tends in the imperative *imi* to be replaced by [hieroglyph] D 38. In Dyn. XI sometimes replaced by [hieroglyph] D 40[1a] or [hieroglyph] D 44.[1b] Phon. *d* (from *di*) in [hieroglyph] *Ddw* 'Busiris' (§ 289, 1); also *mi* or merely *m* (from *imi*), exx. [hieroglyph][2] var. [hieroglyph][3] *Kmi* 'Kemi', name of a queen; [hieroglyph] *mk* 'behold' (§ 234).

[1] *Verbum* ii. § 537. [1a] *JEA.* 16, 195; Coffin Texts, *passim.* [1b] Cairo 20001, qu. § 327. [2] *Cat. d. Mon.* i. p. 87, no. 44. [3] Mar. *Abyd.* ii. 28, 30.

For [hieroglyph] see G 19.

38 [hieroglyph] forearm with hand holding a rounded loaf — In M.K. and more frequently in Dyn. XVIII det. in [hieroglyph] *imi* 'give' (§ 336). Hence phon. *mi*[1] and more commonly *m*, exx. [hieroglyph][2] *mki* 'protect'; [hieroglyph][3] *Itm* 'Atum'.

[1] Evidence (but mainly with D 36 or D 37) *Verbum* ii. § 538. [2] *Puy.* 20. Sim. *mtn* 'behold', *Siut* i. 275. In O.K., see p. 257, n. 25. [3] *ÄZ.* 46, 140.

39 [hieroglyph] forearm with hand holding bowl [hieroglyph] W 24 — Det. offer, present, exx. [hieroglyph] var. [hieroglyph] *ḥnk* 'present'; [hieroglyph] *drp* 'offer'. In Dyn. IX–XII occasionally as substitute for [hieroglyph] D 37 or [hieroglyph] D 38, ex. [hieroglyph][1] *rdi* 'who causes'; [hieroglyph][2] *Mkt-Rˁ* 'Mektrēˁ', name of a man; also for [hieroglyph] D 36, ex. [hieroglyph][3] *m-ˁ* 'in the hand of'.

[1] *Siut* 5, 5. 8; Brit. Mus. 581, vert. 19. [2] *D. el B.* (XI) ii. 9, D. [3] Cairo 20003, qu. p. 266, n. 10.

D 40 forearm with hand holding stick — From M.K. on tends to replace A 24, exx. var.[1] *nḫt* 'strong'; *itḥ* 'drag'. Also abbrev. for *ḫsỉ* 'examine'.[2] In Dyn. XI sometimes replaces D 37, see there.

[1] *Urk.* iv. 856, 4. [2] *Eb.* 37, 2, qu. § 444, 4, compared with *ib.* 36, 4.

41 forearm with palm of hand downwards — Det. arm, exx. *gbꜣ* 'arm'; varr.[1] [2] *rmn* 'arm', 'shoulder'; *ỉꜣby* 'left'; det. various actions involving movement of arms,[3] exx. *ḥms* 'bend', 'bow'; *rḳỉ* 'incline'; *ḥsỉ* 'sing'; cessation of movement, exx. *grḥ* 'cease'; *nỉ* 'reject'. From this last, phon. or phon. det. *nỉ*, exx. [4] *nỉw* 'ostrich'; [5] var. [6] *nỉw* 'bowl'.

[1] *ÄZ.* 34, 30. [2] Brit. Mus. 572, 12. [3] Reason obscure in *nmỉ* 'traverse'. [4] Reading, see G 34. [5] *Siut* 1, 308. [6] *Eb.* 21, 10.

42 forearm as last, but with upper arm straight — Ideo. or det. in var. *mḥ* 'cubit' (§ 266, 2).

43 forearm with hand holding flagellum S 45 — Ideo. in varr. Pyr.[1] [2] *ḫwỉ* 'protect'. Hence phon. *ḫw*, exx. [3] *ḫww* 'evil'; [4] *sḫwd* 'enrich'.

[1] *Pyr.* 1629. [2] *Pyr.* 1797. [3] *Urk.* iv. 1077, 9. [4] *Urk.* iv. 60, 15.

44 forearm with hand holding the *ꜥbꜣ*-sceptre S 42 — Det. in [1] abbrev. [2] *ḫrp* 'be at the head of', 'control', 'administer' and derivatives.

[1] *Urk.* iv. 31, 7. [2] Cairo 20001, *b* 6, qu. § 327.

45 arm with hand holding the *nḫbt*-wand[1] — Ideo. or det. in var.[2] *ḏsr*, var. Pyr.[3] *ḏśr*, 'clear (a road)', 'be private', 'holy', and derivatives.

[1] See Jéq. 185; used as a brush (?), *JEA.* 32, 51. [2] *Urk.* iv. 864, 15. [3] *Pyr.* 1456.

46 hand — Ideo. in *ḏrt*,[1] occasional varr.[2] *ḏrt*, [3] *ḏꜣt*, 'hand'. Phon. *d*, from the old Semitic word *yad* 'hand',[4] cf. Egypt. *wdỉ* 'put', 'push', 'emit (sound)'.

[1] Reading based mainly on Coptic *tōre*, *tōōt-*, *ÄZ.* 50, 91; formerly read *dt*, the varr. here given being regarded as distinct words. [2] *Pyr.* 440; *Siut* 3, 3. [3] *Pyr.* 1703; Brit. Mus. 574, 18. [4] *ÄZ.* 50, 91.

47[1] hand with curved palm — Det. in *ḏrt* 'hand' when written phonetically; see last.

[1] Chass. *Ass.* Pl. 19, top, l. 6 from left.

46*[1] hand letting fall drops — Ideo. in [2] var. [3] *ỉdt* 'fragrance', O. K. var. [4]

[1] *BH.* i. 17, and so always Pyr. Shown with drops, not curve, *Ikhern.*, col. to left, and so already Petr. *RT.* i. 17, 26. [2] *BH.* i. 17, cf. O.K., *L. D.* ii. 89 c. [3] *Ikhern.*, col. to left, the det. due to confusion with *ỉꜣdt* 'dew'. [4] *Pyr.* 365, *b*.

D 48 hand without thumb — Ideo. in [1] varr. , *šsp* 'palm', more strictly 'a hand-breadth', a linear measure (§ 266, 2).

[1] *Urk.* iv. 190, 10. 12; cf. *ÄZ.* 60, 71 for the reading.

49 fist — Det. grasp, in *ɜmm* 'grasp'; *ḫfʿ* 'seize'.

50 finger [0] — Ideo. or det. in var. Pyr. [1] *ḏbʿ* 'finger' and related words. Hence phon. *ḏbʿ*, ex. *ḏbʿ* '10,000' (§ 259). The two fingers serve as det. accurate, exx. *ʿḳɜ* 'accurate'; *mty* (*mtr*? [2]) 'precise'; also in derivatives of these stems. Apt to be confused in hieroglyphic texts with T 14, though quite distinct in hieratic.[3]

[0] Not a thumb as proposed *ÄZ.* 73, 119; see *Mitt. Kairo* 9, 146. [1] *Pyr.* 118. [2] Possibly two stems *mty* 'precise' and *mtr* 'be present', 'witness' are to be distinguished. [3] MÖLL. *Pal.* i. nos. 117 and 457.

51 finger horizontally — Ideo. or det. in var. [1] *ʿnt* 'nail'. Det. for obscure reasons in *ḥɜi* 'measure'; *ṯɜi* 'take', 'gird on'; *dḳr* 'press'.[2] From the last, phon. det. *dḳr* in abbrev. [3] *dḳr(w)* 'fruit'. As abbrev. appears also to represent *ḳɜw* 'grains (?)' in the medical papyri.[4] In *nḳʿwt* 'notched sycomore figs'[5] either replaces a nail-like notching instrument[6] or more probably expresses the general notion of scratching.

[1] *BH.* ii. 4. [2] GARD. *Sin.* 60. [3] *Urk.* iv. 748, 7 compared with *ib.* 694, 5; see too *PSBA.* 13, 452–3. [4] Compare *Eb.* 87, 5 with *Hearst* 10, 15. [5] KEIMER in *Acta Orientalia*, 6, 288. [6] *Ib.* 293.

52 phallus — Det. male, exx. *ʿɜ* 'ass'; *ṯɜy* 'male', 'man'; abbrev. *kɜ* 'bull'. Phon. *mt* (cf. Hebrew מְתִים 'men'), exx. *mtwt* 'poison'; *ḫmt* 'three'. In O.K. this sign is used of the organ and all that is characterized by it, while D 53 expresses what issues from or is performed by it.[1] In M.K. the use differs somewhat and is less consistent.[2]

[1] *Sphinx* 16, 69. [2] *Sphinx* 16, 186.

53 phallus with liquid issuing from it — For the use of as contrasted with D 52, see the latter. Det. in *ḥnn* 'phallus'; *wsš* 'urinate'; *mtwt* 'poison'; sometimes also (contrary to O.K. usage) in *ṯɜy* 'male', 'man'; *hɜi* 'husband'; regularly (contrary to O.K. usage) in var. *m-bɜḥ* 'in the presence of' (§ 178).

For as substitute for the female organ, see on N 41.

D 54 legs walking — Ideo. in *iw*[1] 'come' (§ 289, 2). Det. movement, exx. *šm* 'go'; *tkn* 'approach'; *h3h* 'hasten'; also lack of movement, exx. *3b* 'stop'; *s3i* 'linger'. The group 'walk', 'step' (plur. ,) reads *nmtt*.[2] For combined with other signs, exx. , , see § 58, 1.

[1] Reading, *Pyr.* 1210 in the divine name *'Iw·š-ʿ3·š*. [2] *ÄZ.* 38, 56; *Sphinx* 6, 53; see the varr. *Pt.* 313 and compare *Ikhern.* 18 with Cairo 20473, *b*.

For see M 18. For see N 40. For see O 35. For see T 32. For see V 15. For see W 25.

55 legs walking backwards — Det. backwards, exx. [1] *ʿnn* 'turn back'; [2] *sbh3* 'cause to retreat'; [3] *ḫtḫt* 'be reversed'.

[1] *Leb.* 83. [2] *P. Kah.* 1, 8. [3] *Siut* 1, 270.

56 leg — Ideo. or det. in var. *rd* 'foot'. Det. leg, foot, exx. [1] *mnt* 'thigh'; *pd* 'knee'; *wʿrt* 'leg', 'shank'. From *pd*, phon. *pds*[2] in varr. , , *pds* 'box'. From *wʿrt*, phon. or phon. det. *wʿr* in abbrev. *wʿrt* 'district' and its derivative title *wʿrtw* 'district official'; also in *wʿr* 'flee'. From [3] *sbḳ* 'leg', phon. det. or phon. *sbḳ* in var. [4] *sbḳ* 'excellent', 'successful'. For some reason unknown, phon. *gḥ* or *gḥs*[5] in [6] var. [6a] *gḥs* 'gazelle'. The group is used to determine various verbs expressing movement, exx. *thi* 'transgress'; [7] *ḫnd* 'tread'.

[1] In Pyr. (ex. *Pyr.* 262) with a very different determinative. [2] *Sphinx* 13, 89. [3] *Wb.* iv. 93, ex. *Pyr.* 1314 (*šbḳ*). [4] *Urk.* iv. 84, 17. [5] *Sphinx* 13, 89. [6] *Urk.* iv. 741, 12. [6a] *Eb.* 98, 7, see *Kêmi* i, 144. [7] Not related to *ḫnd* 'part of foreleg', *Pyr.* 1547; for this word see *Bull.* 30, 866.

57 combination of D 56 and T 30 — Det. mutilate, in [1] *i3ṯ* 'be mutilated' and derivatives. Note abbrev. [2] *i3ṯw* 'place of execution'; [3] var. [4] *si3ty* 'cheat' (n.) appears from the var. to be a causative.[5] Det. also in [6] *nkn* 'damage'.

[1] *Wb.* i. 34. [2] *Wb.* i. 35. [3] *Peas.* B 1, 99. 262–3. [4] *Peas.* B 1, 250. [5] VOG. *Bauer* 94. [6] Brit. Mus. 574, 11; *Westc.* 8, 16.

58 [1] foot — Cf. var. [2] *bw* 'place', 'position'. Hence phon. *b*.[3]

[1] In Dyn. I often very low, exx. DE MORGAN, *Recherches* ii. p. 235, fig. 786; QUIBELL, *Hierakonpolis* i. 38. In M.E. usually lower than other high signs. [2] *Urk.* iv. 512, 15. [3] SETHE, *Alphabet* 152.

D 59 combination of D 58 and D 36 — Phon. *ꜥb*, ex. *ꜥb* 'horn'.

60 combination of D 58 with a vase from which water flows (replaces earlier A 6) — Ideo. in var. Pyr. [1] *wꜥb* 'pure', 'clean'.

[1] *Pyr.* 1171.

For see S 13.

61 toes [1] — Ideo. or det. in var. *sꜣḥ* (*śꜣḥ*) 'toe'. Hence phon. or phon. det. *sꜣḥ* (*śꜣḥ*)[2], exx. *sꜣḥ* 'approach'; *m-sꜣḥt* 'in the neighbourhood of' (§ 178).

[1] L. *D.* ii. 3 (Dyn. III). See *ÄZ.* 34, 77 and above p. 439. [2] For *ś* see *Pyr.* 959.

62 [1] less correct form of last (Dyn. XVIII) — Use as last.

[1] *Rekh.* 3.

63 [1] another form of last (Dyn. XVIII) — Use as last.

[1] Cairo 34002 (Lacau, Pl. 3) = *Urk.* iv. 28, 8.

Sect. E. Mammals

E 1 [1] bull — Ideo. in [2] varr. , *kꜣ* 'bull'. Det. cattle, exx. *ng* 'bull'; *ỉwꜣ* 'ox'; *mnmnt* 'cattle', 'herds'.

[1] The sign is apt to vary in form according to the sex and species demanded in the particular case. [2] Reading, see p. 172, n. 4; but in some contexts the reading may be *ỉḥ* or *ỉwꜣ*.

2 aggressive bull — Ideo. in [1] *kꜣ nḫt* 'victorious bull', epithet of Pharaoh (§ 55). Det. in [2] *smꜣ* 'fighting bull'.

[1] *D. el B.* 120. [2] *Urk.* iv. 2, 13.

3 calf — Det. in *bḥs* (*bḥz*)[1] 'calf'; also in [2] *wndw* 'short-horned cattle'.

[1] *Pyr.* 27. [2] *D. el B.* 140, where the sign differs from the calf only slightly.

4 [1] sacred *ḥsꜣt*-cow — Det. in *ḥsꜣt* (*ḥzꜣt*)[2] 'sacred *ḥsꜣt*-cow'.

[1] Karnak, chapel of Ḥashepsowe. The sign differs considerably elsewhere, exx. *Meir* i. 11; Louvre C 14, 5. [2] For the *z* see *Pyr.* 1029.

5 cow suckling calf — Det. in *ꜣms* 'show solicitude' as towards child or parent.[1]

[1] *Wb.* i. 11.

E 6 horse — Ideo. or det. var. [1] *ssmt* 'horse'. Det. horse, in [2] *ỉbr* (Hebrew אַבִּיר) 'stallion'; [3] *ḥtr* 'team', 'pair' of horses.

[1] *Urk.* iv. 652, 10, qu. § 117. [2] *Urk.* iv. 663, 10. [3] *Urk.* iv. 697, 16.

7 ass — Det. in *ꜥꜣ* 'ass'. In hieratic[1] sometimes replaced by E 20 [2].

[1] The proper form, MÖLL. *Pal.* i. no. 133. [2] References, E 20, n. 5.

8 kid (E 8* kid jumping, form not found before Dyn. XIX)[1] — Cf. *ỉb* 'kid'.[2] Hence phon. det. *ỉb*, exx. *ỉbỉ* 'thirst'; *ỉbw* 'refuge'; only rarely phon. *ỉb*, ex. [3] *ỉbḥ* '*ỉbḥ*-priest'. Det. small cattle, exx. [4] *ꜥwt* 'flocks', 'goats'; [5] *mnmnt* 'herds'.

[1] This later type is wrongly substituted for the earlier in many old publications. See *JEA.* 17, 246. [2] *Wb.* i. 61. [3] *ÄZ.* 37, 91. [4] *Urk.* iv. 664, 13. [5] *Sin.* B 147.

9 newborn bubalis or hartebeest (*Alcelaphus buselaphus*), cf. below F 5, 6.[0] — Phon. *ỉw*, exx. var. Pyr. [1] *ỉwr* 'conceive'; *ỉwꜥ* 'inherit'. In group-writing (§ 60) is used for *ỉ*.[2]

[0] *Ann.* 42, 257. [1] *Pyr.* 820. [2] BURCHARDT § 20.

10 [1] ram (*Ovis longipes palaeoaegypticus*)[2] — Det. in *bꜣ* 'ram'; *Ḫnmw* 'Chnum', a ram-headed god. Det. sheep, exx. [3] *sr* 'sheep'; [4] *ꜥwt ḥḏt* 'white flocks', i. e. 'sheep'.

[1] *BH.* iii. 3, no. 35 (*Ḫnmw*), here represented, as not uncommonly, with the beard characteristic of the male animal. [2] *Rec.* 24, 44; also more fully *Ann.* 38, 297. [3] *Menthuw.* 7. [4] *Urk.* iv. 664, 14.

11 [1] ram (O.K. form of last) — Use as last.

[1] From the picture *Sah.* 1; as hieroglyph, *ib.* 17.

12 pig — Det. pig in *rrỉ* 'pig'; *šꜣỉ* 'pig'.

13 [1] cat — Det. in *mỉw* 'cat'.

[1] Cf. the picture *Musée égyptien* i. 3.

14 [1] greyhound (*slughi*) — Det. dog in *ỉw* 'dog'; *ṯsm* 'hound'.

[1] *D. el B.* 70. Cf. the picture *BH.* iv. 2.

15 recumbent dog[1] — Ideo. or det. in var. *ỉnpw* 'Anubis'. Also [2] as sportive ideo. for the title *ḥry sštꜣ* 'he who is over the secrets'.

[1] So interpreted by the Greeks, rather than as a jackal, *ÄZ.* 41, 97. However, the question is still disputed, see HOPFNER, *Der Tierkult der alten Ägypter* 47. See further below, E 18, n. 2. [2] *BH.* i. 32 (see for reading Cairo 20539, i. *b* 18); Cairo 20457, *i* (see for reading *ib.* 20088, *c* 12); *Urk.* iv. 1118, 14.

16 [1] recumbent dog on shrine — Ideo. or det. in var. *ỉnpw* 'Anubis'. Also [1] like E 15 for *ḥry sštꜣ* 'he who is over the secrets'.

[1] *Urk.* iv. 1120, 7.

E 17 jackal[1] — Ideo. or det. in *s3b*, var. Pyr. [2] *z3b*, 'jackal' and related words, ex. *s3b* 'dignitary', 'worthy'.

[1] The conventional rendering is here retained. The animal is depicted *BH*. ii. 4. The Upper Egyptian *s3b* is, however, the Anubis animal E 15 (*Pyr.* 727); on the other hand, the *s3b* has close connections with Wepwawet, the wolf-god E 18 (*Unt.* iii. 8. 16). [2] *Pyr.* 1257.

18 [1] wolf (?)[2] on the standard R 12 — Ideo. or det. in varr. , *Wp-w3wt* '(the wolf-god) Wepwawet', lit. 'opener of the ways', Gk. 'Οφῶις.

[1] Thebes tomb 100. [2] So interpreted by the Greeks, *ÄZ*. 41, 97, cf. their name Λύκων πόλις for the modern town of Asyûṭ. However, GAILLARD (*Ann*. 27, 33) showed that the skulls found at Asyûṭ were either those of (1) wandering dogs (*canis familiaris*) or (2) crosses of this with the small Eg. jackal (*canis lupaster*) producing the hybrid called *canis lupaster domesticus* by Hilzheimer. Hence, he argues, the description of Wepwawet as a wolf is wrong.

19 [1] O.K. form of last with protuberance (*šdšd*) in front and a mace T 3 passing through the standard — Use as last.

[1] *Pyr.* 126 (W 187). See GARSTANG, *Mahâsna and Bêt Khallâf* p. 19; for *šdšd* also *ÄZ*. 47, 88.

20 animal of Seth, perhaps a kind of pig[1] — Ideo. in var. [2] *Stḫ*,[3] var. Pyr. [4] *Śtš*, '(the god) Seth' Σηθ; later sometimes abbreviated as , . Det. turmoil, exx. *ḫnnw* 'turmoil'; *sḫ3* 'be in confusion'. M. K. hieratic shows a strong tendency to use for E 7[5] and E 27.[6]

[1] *JEA*. 14, 211; see, however, *ÄZ*. 50, 84; 61, 18; the tail is shown as an arrow, *ÄZ*. 46, 90. [2] *Urk*. v. 32, 6. [3] Reading *PSBA*. 28, 123; *ÄZ*. 50, 84. [4] *Pyr*. 17. [5] *Peas*. R 64; *Eb*. 96, 5. [6] Compare *nšny*, *Sh. S.* 32, 98 with *sr*, *ib*. 31, 97.

21 animal of Seth recumbent (var. of last) — Det. turmoil, ex. *nšni* 'storm', 'rage' (vb.).

22 lion — Ideo. or det. in [1] var. [2] *m3i* 'lion'.

[1] *Urk*. iv. 893, 12. [2] *Urk*. iv. 39, 1; 718, 1.

23 recumbent lion — Ideo. in var. Pyr. [1] *rw* 'lion'; *Rwty* 'the Two-lion-god'.[2] Phon. *rw*, exx. var. O.K. [3] *rwyt* 'gate (?)'; *itrw* 'river'. In group-writing (§ 60) or is used for *r*,[4] ex. [5] *Krr* 'Gerār', a Syrian locality; for see on N 35. Through similarity in hieratic[6] is employed in words with U 13 reading *šnʿ*, exx. *šnʿ* 'hold back'; *šnʿ* 'magazine'.

[1] *Pyr*. 1351 with the lion mutilated, see *ÄZ*. 51, 36. [2] *PSBA*. 38, 92. [3] *Gebr*. ii. 12. [4] BURCHARDT § 80. [5] *Urk*. iv. 784, 80. [6] See above p. 439.

24 [1] panther — Ideo. or det. in [1] var. [2] *3by* 'panther', 'leopard'.

[1] *D.el B*. 74. [2] *Urk*. iv. 139, 9.

E 25 [1] hippopotamus — Det. in [2] *db*, var. [3] *dib*, 'hippopotamus'; [4] *ḫ3b* 'hippopotamus'.

[1] From the picture *Bull. Metr. Mus. New York*, Eg. Expedition, 1922–3, 35. [2] *Peas.* B 1, 206. [3] *Th. T. S.* ii. 11. [4] Louvre C 14, 11.

26 [1] elephant — Det. in *3bw* 'elephant'. Semi-phon. in [2] *3bw* 'Elephantine', a town near the First Cataract.

[1] *Cat. d. Mon.* i. 155 (Dyn. XII). [2] *Ib.*

27 giraffe (*mmy*) [1] — For unknown reason, det. *sr* in *sr* (*śr*) [2] 'foretell'.

[1] *Rec.* 38, 205. [2] *Pyr.* 278. The det. of this word is confused with the Seth-animal in M. K. hieratic, see above E 20.

28 [1] oryx — Det. in *m3ḥḏ* 'oryx'.

[1] Ex. *D. el B.* 140.

29 [1] gazelle — Det. in *gḥs* (*gḥś*) [2] 'gazelle'.

[1] Ex. *D. el B.* 140; cf. *ib.* 111. [2] For the reading with *ś* see DAV. *Ptah.* ii. 19.

30 [1] ibex — Det. in *n3w*, var. [2] *nr3w*, var. O.K. [3] *ni3*, 'ibex'.

[1] Ex. *D. el B.* 140; cf. *ib.* 111. [2] *Eb.* 52, 12. [3] DAV. *Ptah.* ii. 19.

31 goat with collar carrying a cylinder seal [1] — Ideo. (?) or det. var. *sʿḥ* (*śʿḥ*) [2] 'rank', 'dignity' and related words. Occasionally replaced by S 20.

[1] Perhaps originated in some attribute *śʿḥ* characteristic of goats, with which was combined the cylinder seal S 20 as det. of sense; if so, the Pyr. form of F 3, a leopard's head with uraeus, might provide a close parallel, see *JEA.* 34, 14; *ÄZ.* 35, 171 connects the word *sʿḥ* 'rank' with Arab. *saraḥa* 'pasture freely'. [2] For the reading with *ś* see *Pyr.* 800.

32 [1] sacred baboon (*Cynocephalus hamadryas*) — Det. in *iʿn* [2] 'sacred baboon'; [3] *ky* 'monkey' Det. in [4] *ḳnd* 'be furious'.

[1] Ex. *D. el B.* 74 (*ʿnʿ*). [2] Varr., see *Rec.* 28, 162; *ÄZ.* 46, 99. 101. [3] *Sh. S.* 165 (*ib.* also *gf*). [4] *Rekh.* 8, 37.

33 [1] monkey — Det. monkey, in *gf*, var. *gif*, 'monkey'.

[1] Ex. *D. el B.* 74 (*gf*).

34 desert hare (*sḫʿt*) [1] — Phon. *wn*,[2] exx. *wnn* 'be'; *swnt* 'sale'.

[1] *BH.* ii. 4. [2] Reading from many Coptic equivalents, exx. *wōn* 'open'; *wōnesh* 'wolf'.

Sect. F. Parts of Mammals

F 1 head of ox — Replaces *k3* E 1 in the formula of offering (p. 172) and like.

2 [1] head of infuriated bull — Det. in *ḏnd* 'rage'.

[1] *Puy.* 20, where the word is written *dnḏ*. Cf. *Pyr.* 63 (*ḏnd*).

3 [1] head of hippopotamus,[1] later form of a sign resembling F 9 — Semi-ideo. in *3t* 'striking power'[2]; phon. *3t* in var. *3t* 'moment', 'attack'.

[1] Thebes, tomb 93, chocolate coloured; see too Cairo 34,002 (LACAU, Pl. 3). [2] See *JEA.* 34, 13, for discussion of the sign and its meanings.

F 4 forepart of lion — Ideo. in *ḥꜣt*[1] 'front' and derivatives, ex. var.[2] *ḥꜣty* 'heart'. Note *ḥꜣty-ꜥ* 'prince'.

[1] Reading, *ÄZ.* 39, 135; *Sphinx* 13, 98. [2] *Cat. d. Mon.* i. 24, no. 165.

5 head of bubalis, cf. above E 9 — Cf.[1] *šsꜣw* (*ššꜣw*)[2] 'bubalis'. Hence phon. or phon. det. *šsꜣ* (*ššꜣ*), exx. var.[3] *šsꜣ* 'be skilled'; [4] *šsꜣw* 'prescription'. Sometimes incorrectly as phon. det. *sšꜣ*, ex.[5] *sšꜣ* 'prayer'.

[1] Depicted *BH.* ii. 4. [2] Written in Dyn. V, DAV. *Ptah.* ii. 19. [3] *Urk.* iv. 134, 8. [4] *P. Kah.* 5, 20. [5] *Sh. S.* 129, qu. § 457.

6 [1] forepart of bubalis — Use as last.

[1] Ex. *Urk.* iv. 97, 7.

7 ram's head — Det. in[1] *šft* 'ram's head', whence also in var.[2] *šfyt* 'worth', 'dignity'; *šfšft* 'dignity'.

[1] *Urk.* iv. 183, 10; 623, 1. [2] *Urk.* iv. 848, 5.

8 [1] forepart of ram — Use as last.

[1] The common form in Dyn. XVIII; but so already Louvre C 30 (M.K.).

9 head of leopard (*bꜣ*)[1] — Det. or abbrev. in var. *pḥty* 'strength'.

[1] See *Rec.* 37, 113; also sculpture from Abu Gurâb in KLEBS, *Reliefs des alten Reichs*, p. 63.

10 head and neck of long-necked animal (Dyn. XVIII) — Det. neck, throat, exx. *ḫḫ* 'throat'; *ḫtyt* 'throat'; also activities connected therewith, exx. *ꜥm* 'swallow'; *nḏꜣ* 'be parched'.

11 [1] O.K. form of last — Use as last.

[1] *Pyr.* 270.

12 head and neck of canine animal — Ideo. in Pyr.[1] var.[1] *wśrt* 'neck'. Hence phon. *wsr* (*wśr*), exx. *wsr*, var. Pyr.[2] *wśr*, 'powerful'; [3] *wsr* 'oar'.

[1] *Pyr.* 286. [2] *Pyr.* 297. [3] *Westc.* 5, 8.

13 horns of ox — Ideo. in *wpt* 'brow', 'top (of forehead)', 'beginning'.[0] Hence phon. *wp*, ex. var. Pyr.[1] *wpi* 'divide', 'open'; in two words reads *ip*, viz. *ipt*[2] 'mission'; *ipwty* 'messenger', var. Pyr.[3]

[0] According to DAWSON, *JEA.* 22, 106, properly the vertex or sagittal line of head; but the rendering 'brow' seems often needed in untechnical contexts.
[1] *Pyr.* 92. [2] Coptic ⲉⲓⲟⲡⲉ; also a L. E. var., ČERNÝ, *Late Ramesside Letters*, 10, 6. [3] *Pyr.* 1440; sim. also later, *Sitz. Berl. Ak.* 1912, 958.

14 combination of F 13 and M 4 — In[1] var.[2] *wpt-rnpt* 'New Year's day'.

[1] *Urk.* iv. 824, 9. [2] *Urk.* iv. 261, 8.

15 [1] combination of the last and N 5 — Use as last.

[1] *D. el B.* 63. Sim. *Siut* 1, 305.

F 16 horn

Ideo. or det. in var.[1] *db* 'horn'; *ḥnt* 'horn'; var.[2] *ꜥb* 'horn'. From this last, phon. or phon. det. *ꜥb*, exx. *ꜥbꜥ* 'boast'; [3] *m-ꜥb* 'together with' (§ 178).

[1] *P. med. Berl.* 11, 12 (Dyn. XIX) = *Eb.* 48, 16. [2] *Rec.* 39, 117. See too *ib.* 38, 61. [3] *D. el B.* 112. Sim. *ꜥbw-r* 'breakfast', *Urk.* iv. 506, 10, cf. *ib.* 59, 7.

17 combination of F 16 and a vase with water, cf. D 60

In [1] var. [2] *ꜥbw* 'purification'.

[1] *D. el B.* 63. [2] *D. el B.* 86, 3.

18 tusk of elephant

Det. tooth, exx. var.[1] *ỉbḥ* 'tooth'; *nḥdt* 'tooth'; also actions connected therewith, exx. *psḥ* 'bite'; *sbt* 'laugh' (influenced by *sbḥ* 'cry'?). From *ỉbḥ*, phon. or phon. det. *bḥ*, exx. *bḥs* 'calf'; *sbḥ* 'cry'. For unknown reason,[1a] phon. det. *ḥw* in *Ḥw* 'Ḥu', the god of authoritative utterance; *ḥw* 'sustenance'; hence in group-writing (§ 60) is *ḥ*[2], ex. *Mḥ* 'Maḥu', a personal name. In words reading *bỉꜣ*, exx. *bỉꜣ* 'firmament', *bỉꜣt* 'wonder', is possibly not a tooth, but a metal spout.[3] Phon. det. *bỉ* in var. *bỉt*[4] 'character'.

[1] *Eb.* 89, 14. [1a] A suggestion, *Ann.* 43, 284. [2] BURCHARDT § 95. [3] *ÄZ.* 38, 151. [4] *Adm.* p. 82.

19 [1] lower jaw-bone of ox [2]

Det. in *ꜥrt* 'jaw'.

[1] Thebes, tomb 100. [2] *Ann.* 44, 313, n. 1.

20 tongue of ox?

Ideo. in *ns* 'tongue'. Hence phon. *ns* (*nś*)[1], exx. *n(y)-sw* 'he belongs to' (§ 114, 2); *nsr* 'flame'. Det. actions connected with tongue, ex. *dp* 'taste'. Sportive ideo. in [2] *ỉmy-r* 'overseer', lit. 'one who is in the mouth' (§ 79). Sometimes confused with the abbreviated det. for death, enemy, Z 6.

[1] For the reading with *ś*, see *nśr* 'flame', *Pyr.* 295. [2] *ÄZ.* 40, 142; 42, 142.

21 ear of ox?

Ideo. or det. ear, exx. var.[1] *msḏr* 'ear'; *ꜥnḫwy* 'the two ears'; also in actions connected with ear, exx. *sḏm*, var. Pyr. [2] *śḏm*, 'hear'; *ỉdỉ* 'be deaf'. Phon. or phon. det. *ỉdn* (cf. Hebr. אֹזֶן 'ear') in var. *ỉdn* 'replace'; *ỉdnw* 'deputy'. In medical papyri 'leaf (of a tree)' is to be read *ḏrḏ*, cf. the late var. [3]; there too [4] *sdm* (Pyr. *śdm*) 'paint' (eyebrows), after *śḏm* 'hear' had become *sḏm*.

[1] *Eb.* 92, 5 compared with 92, 3. [2] *Pyr.* 1461. [3] See *P. med. Berl.* vs. 3, 7 (ed. WRESZINSKI, p. 48) compared with *Eb.* 62, 20. [4] *Eb.* 59, 10.

F 22 hind-quarters of lion or leopard — Ideo. in *pḥwy* 'hind-quarters', 'end'; hence phon. or phon. det. *pḥ*, exx. var. [1] *pḥ* 'reach'; *pḥty* 'strength'. Det. in [2] *kfꜣ* 'bottom' (of vase, etc.); hence phon. or phon. det. *kfꜣ* in [3] var. [4] *kfꜣ-ib* 'trusty'. Also det. in *ꜥrt* 'hind-quarters'.

[1] Berl. *ÄI.* i. p. 257, 8. [2] *Eb.* 54, 22. [3] *Pt.* 433. [4] Cairo 20266, *b* 8; 20399.

23 [1] foreleg of ox (thus always in hieratic) — Ideo. or det. in var. *ḫpš* 'foreleg', 'arm'. Det. in [2] *Msḫtyw* 'the Great Bear', lit. 'the Foreleg'.

[1] Möll. *Pal.* i. 164. Sim. *Five Th. T.* 3. [2] Lac. *TR.* 20, 89, cf. *Griff. Stud.* 373.

24 [1] the same reversed — Use as last.

[1] Common in hieroglyphic at all periods; exx. O.K., Capart, *Rue* 98. 100; M.K., *Meir* ii. 2; iii. 21; Dyn. XVIII, *Five Th. T.* 4.

25 leg and hoof of ox [1] — Ideo. in *wḥmt* 'hoof' of ox.[2] By transference to donkey, semi-ideo. in [3] abbrev. *wḥm(t?)* 'hoof', figuratively for 'asses'.[4] Hence phon. *wḥm* in *wḥm* 'repeat', O. K. var. ,[5] and derivatives.

[1] Keimer, *Ann.* 44, 311. [2] Of ox, *Onom. Ram.* 281 in *AEO* i. 16 (read *wḥmt* for *whmt*). [3] *Dend.* 11, top right. [4] *Rec.* 38, 61. [5] Jéquier, *Les Pyramides des reines Neit et Apouit*, Pl. 13, 382 = *Pyr.* 1622, *b*; pointed out as correction of accepted reading *whm* (see *Rec.* 24, 189) in *Wb.* Belegstellen to i. 340, 11.

26 skin of a goat [1] — Ideo. in [2] var. [3] *ḫnt* 'skin'. Hence phon. *ḫn(w)*,[4] exx. *ḫnw* 'interior'; *ḫn* 'approach'.

[1] Montet p. 316. [2] Petrie, *Deshasheh* 21. [3] *Eb.* 40, 2.
[4] Reading, *Pyr.* 334, variants of *mḫnt* 'ferry-boat'.

27 cow's skin [0] — Det. skin, exx. [1] *dḥr* 'hide', 'leather'; [2] *mskꜣ* 'skin', 'rug'; mammals generally, exx. [3] *wnš* 'wolf'; [4] *pnw* 'mouse'.

[0] See the markings above, Pl. 1, top. [1] *Westc.* 12, 5. [2] Munich 3, 21 [3] *Peas.* R 15. [4] *Eb.* 98, 2.

28 alternative form of last — This form is regular as ideo. dappled in [1] var. [2] *sꜣb šwt* 'variegated of feathers', epithet of the solar Horus, cf. Pyr. [3] *śꜣb* 'variegated'. Sometimes replaces *ꜣb* (U 23), ex. [4] *ꜣbḏw* 'Abydus'.

[1] Exx. with winged disk, *D. el B.* 96; flying falcon, *ib.* 93. [2] Brit. Mus. 826, 9 = *Rec.* 1, 70. [3] *Pyr.* 1211; cf. the common O.K. man's name *Śꜣbw*, exx. Dyn. I, De Morgan, *Recherches*, ii. p. 235, fig. 786; Dyn. V, *Urk.* i. 82, 8. [4] Lac. *Sarc.* i. 184 (collated); Mar. *Abyd.* ii. 22.

29 cow's skin pierced by an arrow — Ideo. or det. in var. *sti* (*śti*)[1] 'pierce' and derivatives. Also phon. *st*, ex. [2] *Stt* '(the goddess) Satis', in spite of the fact that Pyr. write this name [3] *Śṯit* with *ṯ* instead of *t*.

[1] *Pyr.* 1197. [2] Brit. Mus. 852. [3] *Pyr.* 1116; see *ÄZ.* 45, 24.

F 30 water-skin — Cf. *šdw* 'water-skin',[1] 'cushion'.[2] Hence phon. *šd*, exx. var. Pyr. [3] *šdỉ* 'draw forth'; var. [4] *wšd* 'address', 'question'.

[1] *Rec.* 11, 119; cf. PETRIE, *Deshasheh* 19, O.K. ex. with det. waterskin. [2] *Rekh.* 2, 1. [3] *Pyr.* 1030. [4] Brit. Mus. 574, 3.

31 three foxes' skins tied together[1] — Cf. [2] *mst* 'apron of foxes' skins'. Hence phon. *ms* (*mś*), exx. *msỉ*, var. Pyr. [3] *mśỉ*, 'give birth'; [4] *msdmt* 'black eye-paint'.

[1] Bibliography, JÉQ. 93. [2] LAC. *Sarc.* ii. 163. [3] *Pyr.* 1466. [4] *Eb.* 33, 3.

32 animal's belly showing teats and tail[1] — Ideo. in *ẖt* 'belly', 'body'. Hence phon. *ẖ*.[2]

[1] *Medum*, Pl. 12, with p. 30. [2] SETHE, *Alphabet* 155.

33 [1] tail — Det. in *sd* (*śd*) [2] 'tail'. Hence phon. or phon. det. *sd*, ex. var. [3] *sdty*, a title.

[1] Thebes, tomb 93. [2] *Pyr.* 1302. [3] Thebes, tomb 93.

34 heart — Ideo. in var. Pyr. [1] *ỉb* 'heart'. Det. in *ḥꜣty* 'heart'.

[1] *Pyr.* 311.

35 heart and windpipe[1] — For unknown reason, phon. *nfr* in *nfr*, rare var. ,[2] 'good' and related words.

[1] *Hier.* p. 65. Cf. 'Ανθρώπου καρδία φάρυγγος ἠρτημένη, ἀγαθοῦ ἀνθρώπου στόμα σημαίνει, HORAPOLLO, *Hieroglyphica*, 2, 4. [2] Cairo 20011; cf. also Copt. *nūfe* 'good'.

36 lung and windpipe[1] — Cf. [2] *smꜣ* 'lung'. Hence phon. or phon. det. *smꜣ* (*zmꜣ*) in [3] var. *smꜣ* (*zmꜣ*) [4] 'unite' and derivatives.

[1] *ÄZ.* 42, 80. [2] *Eb.* 99, 13. [3] Leyd. V 4, 5. [4] *Pyr.* 2015.

37 backbone and ribs — Ideo. or det. in [1] var. [2] *ỉꜣt* 'back'. Det. in [3] *psd* 'back'. By confusion with M 21, phon. det. *sm* in [4] *sm* 'succour'.

[1] *BH.* i. 25, 34. [2] *Sin.* B 141. [3] *Urk.* iv. 947, 15. [4] Brit. Mus. 581; Leyd. V 4, 9; rather different, *Menthuw.* 11.

38 [1] alternative to last (Dyn. XVIII) — Det. in *psd* 'back'.

[1] Also with four ribs, ex. Cairo 34010, 11 (LACAU, Pl. 7) = *Urk.* iv. 614, 7.

39 backbone with spinal cord[1] issuing from it — Ideo. in var. *ỉmꜣḫ* 'spinal cord',[2] whence also var. *ỉmꜣḫ* 'venerated state'. Rarely det. in [3] *psd* 'back'.

[1] So DAWSON, *JEA.* 22, 107; SCHÄFER had suggested 'marrow', see MÖLL. *Pal.* i. p. 16, n. 1. [2] *ÄZ.* 47, 126. [3] Dyn. XVIII, *Urk.* iv. 373, 9; O.K., *Pyr.* 517.

40 portion of backbone with spinal cord issuing at both ends — Ideo. (?) in *ꜣwỉ* 'stretch out', 'be long'. Possibly hence phon. *ꜣw*,[1] exx. *ꜣwt* 'offerings'; *fꜣw* 'magnificence'.

[1] Reading, see *PSBA.* 18, 187; cf. also *ꜣw* 'announce', *Pyr.* 1141.

F 41 vertebrae conventionally depicted

Rarely det. in [1] *psd* 'back'. As det. of [2] *šꜥt* 'lust for blood' from an old sign [3] depicting stalks of flax tied together and the bolls cut off.[4]

[1] *D. el B.* 116. [2] *Urk.* iv. 18, 5; also *šꜥd* 'cut off', *Urk.* iv. 894, 11. [3] *Pyr.* 763. 1212. [4] See the scene *Paheri* 3.

42 rib

Ideo. or det. in [1] var. [2] *spr* (*špr*) 'rib'.[3] Hence phon. *spr* (*špr*) in *spr* 'approach' and derivatives. Similar signs with which is liable to be confused are D 24, N 11, and N 12.

[1] *P. Boul.* xi. vs. 8. [2] *Siut* 1, 30. [3] *Pyr.* 81.

43 [1] ribs of beef

Det. in [2] *spḥt* 'ribs of beef'.

[1] *Meir* iii. 25; see the picture *ib.* i. 10. [2] *Meir* iii. 21.

44 leg-bone with adjoining meat (two different, seldom distinguishable, signs)

(1) Det. in *iwꜥ*[1] 'thigh (of beef)', 'femur';[2] hence phon. det. or phon. *iwꜥ*, exx. *iwꜥ* 'inherit'; [3] *iwꜥt* 'heritage'. (2) Det. in [4] *swt* (*šwt*) 'leg of beef', 'tibia';[2] hence phon. *isw* (*išw*) in var. *isw*,[5] var. O.K. [6] *išw*, 'exchange'.

[1] *Siut* 1, 276; cf. *Pyr.* 1546. [2] See LORTET-GAILLARD, *La faune momifiée*, p. ix. [3] *BH.* i. 32. [4] *D. el B.* 107. 110; cf. *Pyr.* 64. [5] References, p. 132, top. [6] *Urk.* i. 2, 8.

45 bicornuate uterus of heifer[1]

Ideo. or det. in [2] var. [3] *idt* (?)[4] 'vulva', 'cow'.

[1] *PSBA.* 21, 277; verified together with Griffith in an Oxford laboratory. [2] *P. Kah.* 5, 2. [3] *Eb.* 96, 5. [4] For this reading, not *ḥmt*, see on N 41.

46 [1] intestine

Ideo. in [2] *ḳꜣb* 'intestine'; hence semi-ideo. in *m-ḳꜣb* 'in the midst of' (§ 178); *ḳ(ꜣ)b* 'double'. Ideo. and later phon. also in var. *pḫr* 'turn', 'go round' and derivatives; var. *dbn* 'go round' and derivatives. Det. (from Dyn. XII) in *wḏb*, var. [3] *wḏb*, 'turn' and derivatives.

[1] That this, rather than any of the forms F 47–49, is the correct form is shown by its frequency in good hieroglyphic texts and by the hieratic evidence, see MÖLL. *Pal.* i. no. 183. Hieroglyphic exx.: *m-ḳꜣb*, *Paheri* 9, 11; *pḫr*, O.K., *Gemn.* i. 11; M.K., *Cat. d. Mon.* i. 155; Dyn. XVIII, *D. el B.* 62. 154; *Paheri* 9, 7; *dbn* '*deben*-weight', O.K., Berl. *AI.* i. 72 (no. 8032); *Saqq. Mast.* i. 2; Dyn. XVIII, *Puy.* 36; NORTHAMPT. 1, 21; *wḏb* 'cloth (?)', *D. el B.* 109; *wḏb* 'shore', *Paheri* 9, 24. [2] *Eb.* 42, 12. [3] *Sinai* 139, 10.

47 [1], **(47)** [2], **(46)**, **48** [3], **49** } alternatives to last (N.B. No confusion with [4] M 11 before the Amarna period)

Use as last.

[1] Varies with F 46 for *pḫr* in Pyr.; *Urk.* iv. 270, 7; *D. el B.* 10. 45; *dbn*, *D. el B.* 81. [2] Ex. *pḫr*, *D. el B.* 11. [3] Regularly for *dbn* '*deben*-weight' in the Annals of Tuthmosis III, exx. *Urk.* iv. 699. 718. 733; contrast *pḫr*, *Urk.* iv. 655, 9. 14. Exceptionally also *pḫr*, *Rekh.* 3, 21. [4] In *wḏb*, *Amarn.* iii. 20. Probably never in *ḳꜣb*, *pḫr*, or *dbn*.

F 50 combination of F 46 and S 29 — In [1] *sphr*, var. O.K. [2] *sphr*, 'copy', 'write out'.

[1] *Rhind*, title. [2] WEILL, *Décr.*, Pl. 4, 1.

51 piece of flesh (also sometimes) — Det. limb, flesh, exx. *ˁt* 'limb'; *hˁ* 'flesh'; parts of the body, exx. *nḥbt* 'neck', 'shoulder'; *mist* 'liver'; meat, ex. *iwf* 'meat'. As abbrev. [1] is found for [2] *hˁw* 'members', 'body'; and [3] for *kns* 'vagina'. Possibly a different sign is [4] as phon. *ꜣs* or *ws* in [5] *ꜣst* 'Isis' and [6] *Wsir* 'Osiris', writings found on the M.K. coffins for some superstitious reasons; the former has as rare variant [7] In Dyn. XIX or before changes into the egg H 8 and subsequently becomes a generic det. for goddesses.

[1] *Urk.* iv. 959, 2. [2] *Ib.* 9. [3] *Eb.* 94, 5. 8, cf. 93, 21. [4] Note the position. It has been proposed to derive this phonetic sign from *isw* 'testicle' (*Wb.* i. 131), see NORTHAMPT. p. 9*; another possibility is that it is an adaptation of the hieratic sign for 'son' (*sꜣ*), which is likewise later shown in hieroglyphic as the egg; see on H 8. [5] LAC. *TR.* 2, 81; LAC. *Sarc.* ii. p. 129. [6] *ÄZ.* 46, 94. [7] PETRIE, *Gizeh and Rifeh* 13 F; CAPART, *Recueil de Monuments* i. 20.

52 [1] excrement (Pyr.) — Det. in Pyr. *ḥs* 'excrement'.

[1] *Pyr.* 127. Later replaced, first by N 32 and then by Aa 2.

Sect. G. Birds

G 1 Egyptian vulture (*Neophron percnopterus*)[1] — Ideo. in Pyr. [2] *ꜣ* 'vulture'; hence phon. *ꜣ*. Often indistinguishable from (*tyw*) G 4.

[1] *Hier.* p. 19. [2] *Pyr.* 1303; sim. *ib.* 1729. In the more general sense 'bird', Louvre C 14, 10.

2 two vultures G 1 as monogram — Phon. *ꜣꜣ*, ex. *mꜣꜣ* 'see'.

3 combination of G 1 and U 1 — Phon. *mꜣ*, ex. *smꜣwy* 'renew'.

4 [1] the long-legged buzzard (*Buteo ferox*) — Phon. *tyw*, exx. *ḥrtyw-nṯr* 'necropolis workmen'; *i·tywn(y)* 'welcome ye!' (§ 313). Reading, see § 79. Often indistinguishable from (*ꜣ*) G 1.[2]

[1] A brown bird, with head rounded and breast more prominent than in G 1, see *Hier.* 1, no. 1; cf. SHELLEY, *Birds of Egypt*, Pl. IX. [2] Ex. Cairo 20046, qu. § 488.

5 falcon (exact species not determined[1]) — Ideo. in var. Pyr. [2] *Ḥrw* '(the falcon-god) Horus'.

[1] So KEIMER; taken to be *Falco peregrinus* by LORET, *Bull.* 3, 1; BÉNÉDITE, *Faucon ou épervier*, in *Monuments Piot*, 1909. [2] *Pyr.* 1690.

G 6 falcon with flagellum S 45 — Det. in [1] *bik* 'falcon'.

[1] *Urk.* iv. 159, 13.

7 falcon of Horus on the standard R 12 — Det. in the O.K. writing [1] *Ḥr(w)* 'Horus'. Hence in O.K. and later often archaistically det. of gods, ex. *Imn* 'Amūn', or of the king, ex. *nsw* 'king'. So too regularly in hieratic, while hieroglyphic prefers A 40. Also ideo. in pronouns of 1st pers. sing. when the king is speaking, exx. [2] *·i*, [3] *wi* 'I', 'me'.

[1] *Urk.* i. 132, 3. [2] See p. 39, n. 3. [3] *Urk.* iv. 158, 16.

7* falcon in boat[1]

7** variant form of G 7*[1]

Ideo. for the god of the XIIth nome of Upper Egypt, whose name has been inferred from somewhat complicated data to read *ʿnty* 'ʿAnty', meaning perhaps literally 'he with the claw(s)'. This god occurs also in other parts of Upper Egypt, particularly in the XVIIIth nome, where his name was possibly read differently. Closely connected was also a biune god *ʿntywy* 'ʿAntywey' worshipped in the Xth nome and elsewhere, whom the Greeks equated with their mythical giant Antaeus.[2]

[1] For the sources of these forms see *JEA.* 17, 246. [2] Full discussions in *AEO.* ii., see the Index p. 317 under ʿAnty and ʿAntywey.

For as old symbol of the West, see R 13. For see O 10.

8 falcon of Horus on the sign for gold S 12 — In title of the king *Ḥr* (or *bik*?) *n nbw* 'Horus (or falcon?) of gold'.[1]

[1] See p. 73 above.

9 falcon of Horus bearing the sun N 5 on head — In [1] *Rʿ-Ḥr-ꜣḫty* '(the composite god) Rēʿ-Ḥarakhti.'

[1] In cartouche of the Aten, Sethe, *Göttinger Nachrichten*, 1921, 109, n. 1, cf. *Urk.* iv. 144–5. The sun behind the falcon of Horus in royal titularies was perhaps not read, cf. *Urk.* iv. 211, 15 with *ib.* 4.

10 [1] falcon on a special sacred bark — Det. in [2] *Skr* (*Zkr*) '(the god) Sokar'.[2a] Also det. in [3] *ḥnw* 'the *ḥnw*-bark (of Sokar)'.

[1] Leyd. *Denkm.* i. 17 (*Zkr*). [2] *Dend.* 8; Budge, p. 38, 13. [2a] The often used Sokaris appears to be a spurious classical form; it is doubtful whether Σωχάρης as personal name is derived from that of the god, see *AEO.* ii. 124.* [3] Nav. ch. 1, 21. Sim. *Pyr* 138.

11 archaic image of a falcon — Det. in *ʿšm* (also *ʿẖm*, *ʿḫm*) 'divine image'; also in [1] *šnbt* 'breast'.

[1] *Urk.* iv. 612, 4.

12 archaic image of falcon with flagellum S 45 — Like G 11, det. in *ʿḫm* 'divine image'.[1]

[1] Brugsch, *Thes.* 1078.

G 13 archaic image of falcon with the double plumes S 9 — Ideo. in [1] var. Pyr. [2] *Ḥr Nḫn(y)* '(the god) Horus of Nekhen', i. e. of Hieraconpolis. Det. in [3] *Spdw* (*Śpdw*)[4] '(the god) Sopd'.

[1] *Urk.* iv. 130, 12; 134, 4. [2] *Pyr.* 295. [3] *Sinai* 115. [4] Reading, see *Pyr.* 1534; LAC. *TR.* 20, 14–15.

14 vulture (*Gyps fulvus*; cf. H 4) — Det. in Pyr. [1] *nrt* 'vulture'; hence phon. det. *nr*, ex. *nrw* 'terror'. For obscure reason[1a] in *mwt* 'mother', Copt. *maau*; hence phon. *mt*, exx. [2] *ꜥḫmt* 'river-bank', [3] *mtn* 'road'.

[1] *Pyr.* 1118. [1a] DAV. *Ptah.* i. 19. [2] *Peas.* R 57. [3] *Siut* I, 230.

15 vulture with flagellum S 45 (Dyn. XVIII) — Ideo. in [1] *Mwt* '(the goddess) Mut'.

[1] *Urk.* iv. 413, 16.

16 the vulture-goddess Nekhbet and the cobra-goddess Edjō on baskets V 30 — In *nbty* 'Two-Ladies', title of the king.[1]

[1] See p. 73 for the reading and interpretation.

17 owl[1] — Cf. Coptic ⲙⲟⲩⲗⲁϫ 'owl'.[2] Phon. *m*.

[1] According to KEIMER the hieroglyphs show several members of the family of *Strigidae*. NEWBERRY states that the sign as here printed depicts the Barn owl (*Tyto alba alba*). [2] SETHE, *Alphabet* 153.

18 two owls as monogram — Phon. *mm*, ex. [1] *tmm* 'not having been'. In Dyn. XVIII seems to be used for *im* 'therein' (§ 205).

[1] *D. el B.* 76.

19 combination of G 17 and D 37 (Dyn. XVIII) — Phon. *m* (originally *mi*), ex. *mhy* 'be neglectful'. See D 37 and D 38.

20 combination of G 17 and D 36 (Dyn. XVIII) — Use as last.

21[1] Sennâr guinea-fowl (*Numida m. meleagris*)[1a] — Ideo. in [2] *nḥ* 'the *nḥ*-bird'. Phon. *nḥ*, exx. *nḥi* 'pray'; *nḥḥ* 'eternity'. Some sculptors assimilate this sign to G 1 or G 43.[3]

[1] Exx. O.K., MÖLL. *Pal.* i. no. 229; Dyn. XVIII, *Rekh.* 2, 12. [1a] *JEA.* 26, 79; earlier also *Ann.* 38, 253. 689. [2] BUDGE, p. 397, 12. [3] For the latter see *JEA.* 26, 80, n. 1 and above p. 361, n. 3.

22[1] hoopoe (*Upupa epops*) — Phon. *db* in [1] var. Pyr. [2] *dbt*, var. N.K. *dbt*, 'brick'.

[1] L. *D.* iii. 56, A. [2] *Pyr.* 246.

G 23 [1] lapwing (*Vanellus cristatus*)

Phon. or phon. det. *rḫ(y)t* in var. *rḫyt* 'common folk'.

[1] DAV. *Ptah.* i. 18, no. 410, with p. 20. See too the picture *Th. T. S.* i. frontispiece.

24 lapwing with wings twisted round one another [1]

Use as last.

[1] *Ann.* 26, 186; *AEO.* i. 101*.

25 [1] crested ibis (*Ibis comata*)

Ideo. or semi-ideo. in [2] var. [3] *ꜣḫ* 'spirit', 'spirit-like nature'. Hence semi-phon. *ꜣḫ* in *ꜣḫ* 'be glorious', 'beneficial' and derivatives.

[1] *Hier.* p. 21; *Bull.* 17, 183; *Ann.* 30, 24; 38, 263. [2] *Pyr.* 474. [3] *ÄZ.* 57, 137.

26 sacred ibis (*Ibis religiosa*) on the standard R 12

Det. in [1] *hb* 'ibis'. Det. in varr. [2] *Ḏḥwty* '(the ibis-god) Thoth'.

[1] BRUGSCH, *Thes.* 1075. [2] *ÄZ.* 51, 58.

26* sacred ibis

Use as last, but very rarely without the standard.

27 flamingo (*Phoenicopterus roseus*) [1]

Det. in [2] *dšr* 'flamingo'. Hence semi-phon. *dšr* in var. *dšr* 'red' and derivatives.

[1] Coloured red, *Medum*, frontispiece, no. 6. [2] *B. of D.* ed. LEPS., ch. 31, 9.

28 black ibis (*Plegadis falcinellus*) [0]

Cf. O.K. [1] *gmt* 'the *gmt*-bird'. Hence phon. *gm*,[2] exx. *gmi͗* 'find'; *gmḥ* 'look at'.

[0] GUNN, *Teti*, i. 109, n. 4; *Ann.* 30, 20. [1] Legend to a picture of the bird flying, *ÄZ.* 38, Pl. 5. [2] Reading, compare *gmḥśw* in *Pyr.* 250 with BUDGE, p. 461, 12.

29 jabiru (*Ephippiorhynchus senegalensis*) [1]

Ideo. in *bꜣ* 'soul (in bird form)'. Hence phon. *bꜣ*, exx. *bꜣk* 'servant'; *ḫbꜣ* 'destroy'. In group-writing (§ 60) or or is used for *b* [2].

[1] *Ann.* 30, 1. [2] BURCHARDT § 41.

30 three jabirus as monogram

In *bꜣw* 'spirits', 'might'.

31 heron (*Ardea cinerea* or *Ardea purpurea*) [1]

Det. in *bnw* (*bynw*) [2] 'phoenix'. A very similar bird is det. in [3] *šnty* 'heron'.

[1] *ÄZ.* 16, 104. [2] *ÄZ.* 45, 84. [3] *Urk.* iv. 113, 14. Cf. *ÄZ.* 61, 106.

32 heron on a perch

Ideo. or det. in var. [1] *bꜥḥi͗* 'be inundated'.

[1] *Urk.* iv. 1165, 14.

33 [1] buff-backed egret? (*Ardea ibis*?)

Det. in Pyr. [2] *šdꜣ* 'the *šdꜣ*-bird'. Hence phon. det. in *sdꜣ* 'tremble'; *sdꜣdꜣ* 'tremble'.

[1] Cairo 34010, 12 (LACAU, Pl. 7) = *Urk.* iv. 616, 8. [2] *Pyr.* 2152.

34 [1] ostrich (*Struthio camelus*)

Det. in [1] var. [2] var. Pyr. [3] *ni͗w* 'ostrich'.

[1] Cairo 34001, 18 (LACAU, Pl. 1) = *Urk.* iv. 19, 10. [2] *Eb.* 59, 19. [3] *Pyr.* 469.

G 35 [1] cormorant (*Phalacrocorax*) — Phon. *ꜥḳ*, exx. var. [2] *ꜥḳ* 'enter'; *ꜥḳw* 'revenue', 'provisions'.

[1] See the picture *BH.* iv. 11. [2] *ÄZ.* 57, 6*.

36 swallow or martin[1] (one of the *Hirundidae.* Note the swallow tail) — Phon. *wr* [2], exx. *wr* 'great'; *wrḥ* 'anoint'. A similar sign is det. in [3] *mnt* 'swallow'.[4]

[1] So Carter, confirmed by Keimer, who insists that it is impossible to define the species more closely. Coloured facsimiles, differing much in detail, *Medum*, frontispiece no. 4; *Hier.* Pl. 1, no. 3; contrasted with the 'bad' bird, below G 37, see *Bull. Metr. Mus. New York*, Egyptian Expedition, 1916–7, 18, fig. 17.
[2] Reading, cf. Coptic ⲟⲩⲏⲣ 'how much' = Eg. *wr* (§ 502); but also varr. in *Pyr.* 1183 (*nwrw*) and kindred words. [3] *Urk.* iv. 113, 13. [4] *Hier.* p. 20.

37 sparrow[1] (*Passer domesticus aegyptiacus.* Note the rounded tail) — Det. small, exx. abbrev. [2] *nḏs* (*nḏš*) [3] 'small'; [4] *ḥns* 'narrow'; bad, defective, exx. *bin* 'bad'; *šw* 'empty'; *mr* 'ill', 'diseased'; *ꜣḳ* 'perish'.

[1] So Carter, confirmed by Keimer. Represented with approximative accuracy as a small brown bird, spotted with dark brown on the sides of the throat and crop; see *Bull. Metr. Mus. New York*, Egyptian Expedition, 1916–7, 18, fig. 18; *ib.* 1922–3, 35, fig. 29. [2] *Th. T. S.* i. 11, row 2. [3] *Pyr.* 912. [4] *Peas.* R 45.

38 white-fronted goose (*Anser albifrons*)[1] — Det. in O.K. [2] *gb* 'the *gb*-goose'; hence semi-phon. *gb* in *Gb*, var. *Gbb*, '(the earth-god) Geb', Gk. Κῆβ.[3] Det. in *r*, *ṯrp*, names of kinds of geese[4]; also in *ꜣpd* 'bird', 'goose'. This type may be employed in place of the more exact G 39 in words containing *sꜣ* (*zꜣ*), except when the originals clearly mark the pintail. It may be employed for the indeterminate birds serving as phon. det. in *wfꜣ* 'talk'; *wsf* 'be idle'; *wdf* 'delay' (§ 352); and [5] *ḥtm* 'perish'. Lastly, it may be used for the generalized det. of birds and insects found in hieratic,[6] exx. [7] *ṯnḥr* 'hawk (?)'; [8] *niw* 'ostrich'; [9] *snḥmw* 'locusts'.

[1] *Hier.* p. 22; *Bull. Metr. Mus. New York*, Egyptian Expedition 1916–7, 19. [2] O.K., *L. D.* ii. 61, B; N.K., *P. Harris 500*, recto, 4, 7. 9. [3] Reading, *ÄZ.* 24, 1; 43, 147; 51, 58. 59. [4] Dav. *Ptah.* i. p. 21; cf. *Gemn.* i. 11. 12. [5] A goose according to *Hier.* p. 22. [6] Möll. *Pal.* i. no. 217. [7] *Peas.* B 1, 175. [8] *Eb.* 86, 11. [9] *Hearst* 14, 7.

39 pintail duck (*Dafila acuta*)[1] — Det. in [2] *st* (*zt*, perhaps for *zꜣt*) 'pintail duck'. Hence phon. *sꜣ* (*zꜣ*), exx. (*sꜣ*) [3] 'son'; *sꜣw* 'beam', 'plank'; *ḥsꜣt* 'the divine *ḥsꜣt*-cow'. This type may, if preferred, be employed in place of G 38 in the indefinite uses where the actual nature of the bird in question is unknown.

[1] *Hier.* p. 22; *Bull. Metr. Mus. New York*, Egyptian Expedition 1916–7, 19. [2] *Ptah.* (E. R. A.) 37; *Ti* 25. [3] Reading with *z*, *Pyr.* 1130.

G 40 pintail duck flying — Ideo. in Pyr. [1] later var. [2] *pꜣ* 'fly'. Hence phon. *pꜣ*, exx. *pꜣ* 'the' (§ 110); *spꜣ* 'centipede'. In group-writing (§ 60) (hieratic) is used for *p*.[3] In Dyn. XII is occasionally used for G 41.[4] In hieratic is always replaced by G 41, as also occasionally in hieroglyphic.[5]

[1] *Pyr.* 463. [2] BUDGE, p. 493, 12. [3] BURCHARDT § 46. [4] *ÄZ.* 39, 117, 8 (*ḫn*); *BH.* i. 25, 10 (*tn*). [5] See G 41, n. 10.

41 pintail duck alighting — Det. in *ḫni* 'alight',[1] 'halt'; hence phon. det. *ḫn*, ex. *ḫn* 'speech', 'sentence'. For unknown reasons, phon. or phon. det. *ḳmi* in [2] var. [3] *ḳmyt* 'gum'; phon. det. *sḥw* in [4] *sḥwy* 'collect'. The combination [5] is used to show that is the throw-stick T 14, not the identically shaped warrior's club, serving as det. in [6] var. [7] *ḳmꜣ* 'throw', whence *ḳmꜣ* 'create'; also in [8] *mtn*, O.K. [9] *mṯn*, 'nomad hunter', whence phon. det. *ṯn*, *tn*, exx. *mṯn* 'road'; *ṯni*, var. *tni*, 'distinguish'. Before Dyn. XVIII is sometimes used for G 40 in hieroglyphic,[10] as always in hieratic,[11] where it often serves, like G 38, as an indefinite det. for birds.

[1] Contrasted with *pꜣ* 'fly', *Pyr.* 366. [2] *Eb.* 68, 4. [3] *Eb.* 68, 7; see *ÄZ.* 31, 118. [4] BUDGE, p. 228, 11. Sim. *Urk.* iv. 84, 2. [5] Occasionally in Dyn. XVIII (ex. *tn*, *Paheri* 9, 39) the bird's head hangs as though it had been struck; so often later. [6] *Westc.* 4, 10. [7] LAC. *TR.* 22, 69. [8] *Sin.* R 50. [9] L. *D.* ii. 6, as proper name. [10] Exx. p. 395, nn. 3. 6; Louvre C 11, 3. 6; C 12, 6. [11] MÖLL. *Pal.* i. no. 221 compared with no. 222.

42 fatted duck or widgeon?[1] — Ideo. in [2] var. [3] var. O.K. [4] *wšꜣ* 'fatten'; also in [5] *df(ꜣ)*[6] 'provisions'.

[1] *Hier.* p. 23. Cf. too *wšꜣt* 'widgeon (?)', WRESZINSKI, *Atlas* i. 27. [2] *BH.* i. 27. [3] *Eb.* 89, 3, where the generalized det. G 41 is used. [4] *Gemn.* i. 11. [5] *Urk.* iv. 1165, 13. Sim. *ib.* 1222, 4. [6] For the radical *ꜣ* see *Verbum* i. § 72, 2.

43 quail chick[1] — For unknown reason, phon. *w*.

[1] *Hier.* p. 21; *Ann.* 30, 6.

For , the hieroglyphic adaptation of the hieratic abbreviated form of G 43, see Z 7.

44 two quail chicks G 43 as monogram — Phon. *ww*, ex. *pḥww* 'end'.

45 combination of G 43 and D 36 — Phon. *wꜥ*, ex. *wꜥw* 'soldier'.

46 combination of G 43 and U 1 — Phon. *mꜣw*, ex. *m mꜣwt* 'anew'.

G 47 duckling [0] — Ideo. in [1] *ṯꜣ* 'nestling'. Hence phon. *ṯꜣ*,[2] exx. *ṯꜣy* 'male'; *ṯntꜣt* 'baldachin'. In group-writing (§ 60) is used for *ṯ*.[3]

[0] *JEA.* 27, 133. [1] *Amarn.* vi. 27, 7. Sim. *M. u K.* vs. 2, 2. [2] Reading, *Sphinx* 19, 59. [3] BURCHARDT § 141.

48 [1] three ducklings G 47 in nest — Det. in [2] *sš* (*zš*?) 'nest'. Sometimes [3] takes the place of .

[1] O.K., *Gebr.* i. 5, with the scene. [2] *D. el B.* 131. [3] *Urk.* iv. 897, 12, qu. p. 96, n. 9.

49 ducks' heads protruding from a pool [1] — Ideo. or det. in [2] var. [3] *sš* (*zš*?) 'bird-pool', 'nest'.

[1] See *Ti* 23; *Bersh.* i. 20, where the water of the pool is clearly marked. [2] *Amarn.* vi. 16, 19. Sim. *sšy*, *Urk.* iv. 898, 9. [3] *Bersh.* i. 20.

50 [1] two plovers (?) as monogram — In *rḫty* [2] 'fuller', 'washerman'.

[1] *BH.* i. 29. One bird only, see *BH.* iii. p. 6; *Meir* i. p. 23. In spite of the identity of the consonants *rḫt*, this bird seems to be distinct from the lapwing G 23. [2] Reading, MASPERO, *Études égyptiennes*, i. 91, n. 3; 93, n. 1; *ÄZ.* 20, 189.

51 [1] egret (?) pecking at fish — Det. in *ḥꜣm* 'catch fish'.

[1] *Th. T. S.* ii. 5.

52 [1] goose (?) picking up grain [2] — Det. in *snm* (*śnm*) [3] 'feed' (trans. vb.).

[1] *Puy.* 63; cf. *Th. T. S.* i. 7. [2] See the scenes of 'feeding' (*śnmt*), *Gemn.* i. 11. 12. [3] With fem. infinitive, hence probably *caus. 2-lit.*

53 human-headed bird preceded by R 7 (Dyn. XVIII) — Ideo. in [1] *bꜣ* 'soul'.

[1] Leyd. *Denkm.* iv. 37; see *ÄZ.* 61, 104.

54 trussed goose or duck — Det. in [1] *wšn* 'wring neck of (birds)', 'offer'. For unknown reason, phon. or phon. det. in *snḏ*, var. Pyr. [2] *śnḏ*, later var. *snḏ*, 'fear' and derivatives.

[1] *Siut* 1, 239. [2] *Pyr.* 194.

Sect. H. Parts of Birds

H 1 head of pintail duck G 39 — In formula of offering as abbrev. of *ꜣpdw* 'fowl' (p. 172). Det. in [1] *wšn* 'wring neck of (birds)', 'offer'. This type may be used for H 2 in transcribing hieratic *mꜣꜥ* when the crest is absent.[2]

[1] *Sh. S.* 145; see *Rec.* 38, 200. [2] Exx. *mꜣꜥ* 'temple', *Eb.* 58, 22; *mꜣꜥ* 'real', *Sh. S.* 66; *Peas.* B 1, 76.

H 2 head of a crested bird[1] — Phon. det. *mꜣꜥ*, exx. [2] *mꜣꜥ* 'temple' (of head), cf. [3] *mꜣꜥ* 'real'. Also phon. or phon. det. *wšm*, exx. [4] *wšm* 'ear (of corn)'; [5] *wšmw* 'vessel (for beer)'. From Dyn. XII in place of H 3 as phon. *pḳ* (*pꜣḳ*) in [6] *pḳt* 'fine linen'.

[1] Heron (?); but a duck *mꜣꜥ* occurs MAR. *Mast.* p. 112. [2] *Bersh.* i. 14, 7. [3] See H 1, n. 2. [4] *Urk.* iv. 535, 10. [5] *Urk.* iv. 828, 7. 16. [6] Dyn. XII, *Sinai* 53, 14; Dyn. XVIII, *Rec.* 29, 165 (collated).

3 [1] head of spoonbill (*Platalea leucorodia*; Pyr.) — Phon. det. *pꜣḳ* (*pḳ*), ex. [2] *pꜣḳ* '*pꜣḳ*-cake'.

[1] *Pyr.* 378 = W 486 (*pꜣḳ*-cake). [2] *Siut* 1, 240.

4 head of vulture G 14 (*Gyps fulvus*) — Phon. det. *nr*, ex. [1] *nrw* 'terror'. From Dyn. XVIII sportive writing in [2] late var. [3] *rmṯ* 'people'.

[1] *Urk.* iv. 43, 1. [2] *Urk.* iv. 965, 10. Sim. *ib.* 138, 15. [3] Reading, *ÄZ.* 20, 188.

5 wing — Det. wing, ex. [1] *ḏnḥ*, var. [2] *ḏnḥ*, 'wing'; fly, exx. [3] *ꜥḥi* 'fly'; [4] *pꜣ* 'fly'.

[1] LAC. *TR.* 5, 3. Sim. *Pyr.* 387. [2] *Eb.* 88, 13. [3] *Sin.* R 21. [4] BUDGE, p. 493, 12.

6 feather — Ideo. in var. Pyr. [1] *šwt* 'feather'. Hence phon. *šw*, ex. *Šw* '(the air-god) Shu'. Ideo. as substitute for C 10, in varr. [2] [3] *mꜣꜥt* 'truth'; in the adjective *mꜣꜥ* 'true' and related words is not written, nor has it been found in M.E. hieratic in any words from this stem.

[1] *Pyr.* 1566. Reading, see also *Rec.* 38, 62. [2] *Rekh.* 10, 21. [3] *Urk.* iv. 411, 4, in *ḥm-nṯr Mꜣꜥt*.

6* feather as found in hieratic[1] — With one or two strokes at side in M. E. hieratic for words from the stem *šw*.

[1] Artificial sign to be used in transcribing from hieratic, see MÖLL. *Pal.* i. no. 237. L. E. hieratic uses H 6 for *Mꜣꜥt*, *ib.* ii. no. 236.

7 claw — Phon. *šꜣ* in [1] *Šꜣt*[2] '(the land) Shat'.

[1] *Urk.* iv. 618, 1. [2] Reading, *ÄZ.* 13, 12; *Sphinx* 1, 256. The sign occurs also as det. of *ꜥḏft* 'claw' (*Pyr.* 1779) and as a division of the cubit (*PSBA.* 14, 404), in both cases outside our period.

8 egg — Det. in [1] *swḥt* (*św̌ḥt*)[2] 'egg'. The hieratic contraction[3] of G 39 found in the inverted M.K. method of expressing filiation (p. 66, top) appears in Dyn. XIX hieroglyphic as the egg [4]; that sign may be conventionally used in transcribing the instances in M.K. hieratic. In *pꜥt* 'patricians', 'mankind' is perhaps derived from an earlier sign for a clod of earth.[5]

[1] *Urk.* iv. 361, 14. [2] *Pyr.* 1967. [3] *ÄZ.* 49, 95. [4] GARD. *Sin.* 155. An isolated Dyn. XII instance seems to occur *Sinai* 28. See further F 51, n. 4. [5] *AEO.* i. 12*, 18*, 108*.

Sect. I. Amphibious Animals, Reptiles, etc.

I 1 lizard — Det. in [1] *ḫntꜣsw* 'lizard'; [2] *ꜥš(ꜣ)* 'lizard'. From the latter, phon. *ꜥšꜣ* in var. var. Pyr. [3] *ꜥšꜣ* 'many' and the related words.

[1] *Eb.* 98, 9. [2] Ramesseum medical papyrus, unpublished. [3] *Pyr.* 1146.

2 freshwater turtle — Ideo. or det. in [1] var. [2] *štyw* [3] 'turtle'. '.

[1] *Eb.* 57, 6. [2] *Eb.* 86, 12. [3] Writings with *t* are all late.

3 crocodile — Ideo. or det. crocodile, exx. *msḥ* (*mzḥ*) [1] 'crocodile'; *ḫnty* 'crocodile'; [2] however, for the god Sobk the sign I 5* or I 4 is perhaps invariably used. Det. greedy, in [3] *skn* 'lust after'; [4] *ḫnt* 'be greedy'; perhaps also in [5] *ꜥḫm* 'voracious (?) spirit'; aggression, in [6] *ꜣd* 'be aggressive', 'angry'. For obscure reason,[7] phon. *it* in [8] for *ity* 'sovereign'.

[1] *Rec.* 25, 156. [2] *Wb.* iii. 308. [3] *Pt.* 296. [4] *Peas.* B 1, 291. [5] *Wb.* i. 226. [6] Berl. *ÄI.* i. p. 258, 12. [7] It is just conceivable that by M.K. *ꜣd* had already become *ꜣt*, giving rise to the value *it*. [8] *Sh. S.* 24; *Pt.* 7.

5* archaic stone (?) image of a crocodile [1] — Ideo. or det. in [2] var. [3] *Sbk* (*Śbk*) '(the crocodile-god) Sobk', Gk. Σοῦχος.

[1] DAV. *Ptah.* i. 9, no. 157. Distinguished from I 3 also in hieratic, MÖLL. *Pal.* i. no. 242. [2] *Pyr.* 456; *Sinai* 23, no. 85. [3] *Sinai* 35, no. 106.

4 [1] crocodile on a shrine — Ideo. or det. in var. *Sbk* (*Śbk*) '(the crocodile-god) Sobk'.

[1] Exx. PETR. *Abyd.* iii. 13; *Sinai* 53, 6.

5 [1] crocodile with inward curved tail — Det. in [2] abbrev. [3] *sꜣḳ* (*śꜣḳ*) [4] 'collect', 'gather together'.

[1] PETR. *Abyd.* iii. 29; *Dend.* 8. [2] *Sin.* B 23–4. [3] See n. 1. [4] *Pyr.* 735.

6 piece of crocodile-skin with spines [1] — Cf. [2] var. [3] *ikm* 'shield'. Hence (?) phon. *km*, exx. *Kmt* 'Egypt'; *skm* 'grey-haired'.

[1] *Hier.* p. 23. [2] *Sin.* R 159. [3] LAC. *Sarc.* ii. p. 157.

7 frog (*ḳrr*) [1] — Det. in *Ḥḳt* '(the frog-goddess) Heḳet'. From Dyn. XVIII or XIX sometimes as sportive ideo. for *wḥm ꜥnḫ* 'repeating life' as epithet after personal name.[2]

[1] *Ḳrr* is apparently not known before Dyn. XX. [2] *Sphinx* 7, 215.

8 tadpole — Cf. the O.K. name of a man [1] *Ḥfnr*, i.e. 'Tadpole'. Hence phon. *ḥfn* in *ḥfn* 'one hundred thousand' (§ 259), plur. var. Dyn. XIX [2] *ḥfnw*.

[1] Berl. *ÄI.* i. p. 162. [2] L. *D.* iii. 175, G.

I 9 [sign] horned viper (*Cerastes cornutus*)[0] — Ideo. perhaps in the name of the XIIth nome of Upper Egypt [signs] *Ḏw-ft* 'Mountain-of-the-Horned-Viper', for which a rare var. with [signs] *ft* occurs;[1] cf. also demotic *fy* 'viper'. Hence phon. *f*. For [signs] *it* 'father' see p. 43, n. 1.

[0] KEIMER, *Études d'égyptologie*, VII. [1] SETHE, *Alphabet* 152; cf. the epithet *Ḏw-ftt*, *Pyr.* 1358; see too now *AEO.* ii. 69*, n. 1.

For [sign] see P 9. For [sign] see S 30. For [sign] see U 35.

10 [sign] cobra in repose (*Naja haje*, Gk. ἀσπίς)[0] — Cf. Pyr. [sign][1] var. [signs][2] *ḏt*[3] 'cobra'. Hence phon. *ḏ*. Sometimes also, by a false archaism, for [sign] *d* (§ 19, OBS. 2).

[0] KEIMER, *Études d'égyptologie*, VII, 41; Miss Murray (*JEA.* 34, 117) prefers to identify with *Naja nigricollis.* [1] *Pyr.* 2047. [2] *Pyr.* 697. [3] Doubtless properly *ꜣḏt* from the stem *wꜣḏ*, cf. *Wꜣḏyt* 'Edjō'. See *ÄZ.* 55, 89; SETHE, *Alphabet* 157.

11 [sign] two cobras [sign] I 10 — Phon. *ḏḏ*, ex. [signs][1] *wḏḏt* 'what had been commanded'.

[1] *Siut* I, 220.

For [sign] see M 14. For [sign] see T 5. For [sign] see T 6. For [sign] see V 21.

12 [sign] cobra (erect as on the forehead of the Pharaoh) — Det. in [signs][1] *iꜥrt* 'uraeus'. Det. goddesses, especially those to whom the appearance of a snake was attributed, exx. [signs] *Wꜣḏyt* 'Edjō'[1a]; [signs][2] *Nsrt* (*Nzrt*)[3] 'the goddess Nesret'.

[1] ERM. *Hymn.* 4, 4; see *ÄZ.* 46, 102; the οὐραῖος of HORAPOLLO, *Hieroglyphica*, I. 1. [1a] See above, p. 73, n. 1a. [2] ERM. *Hymn.* 3, 2. [3] *Pyr.* 194.

13 [sign] cobra [sign] I 12 on the basket [sign] V 30 — Det. goddesses, exx. [signs][1] *Wꜣḏ(y)t* 'Edjō'; [signs][2] *nṯrt* 'goddess'. As an element in the royal title [sign] see G 16.

[1] *Urk.* iv. 246, 15. [2] *Urk.* iv. 308, 6.

14 [sign][1] snake — Det. snake, exx. [signs][2] *ḥfꜣw* 'serpent'; [signs][1] *ḏdft* 'snake'; possibly also det. worm, but it is doubtful if *ḏdft* ever had that usually attributed meaning.[3]

[1] *Amarn.* iv. 4, 3. [2] *Sh. S.* 61. [3] *Sphinx* 4, 147; see too *JEA.* 34, 118.

15 [sign] alternative form of last — Use as last.

Sect. K. Fishes and parts of Fishes

K 1 [sign] a fish (*Tilapia nilotica*; Arabic *bulṭi*)[1] — Det. in [signs][2] var. [signs][3] *int* 'the *bulṭi*-fish'. Hence phon. *in*, exx. [signs] *int* 'valley'; [signs] *inb* 'wall'.

[1] GAILLARD 89. [2] Cairo 584, 10 = PIEHL, *IH.* iii. 75. [3] *Eb.* 71, 20.

2 [sign][1] a fish (*Barbus bynni*)[2] — Phon. det. *bw*[3] in [signs] *bwt* 'abomination'.

[1] Thebes, tomb 83. [2] GAILLARD 49. [3] *ÄZ.* 58, 17.

K 3 [1] a fish (*Mugil cephalus*; Arabic *bûri*)[2]

Det. in [3] *ꜥdw* 'the *bûri*-fish'. Hence phon. *ꜥd* (*ꜥḏ*?) in the title [4] *ꜥḏ* (?)-*mr*, var. [5] *ꜥd-mr*, 'administrator (of a province)', probably lit. 'excavator of canal(s)'.

[1] *D. el B.* 109. [2] GAILLARD 93. [3] *Eb.* 82, 9. [4] Dyn. XVIII, *D. el B.* 109; O.K., *Urk.* i. 5, 17; 11, 10. [5] *Urk.* iv. 952, 13. The writing *ꜥḏ* in GARD. *Sin.* 152 is not quite conclusive for the O.K. reading.

4 [1] oxyrhynchus fish (*Mormyrus kannume*)[2]

Ideo. in [3] *ḫꜣt* 'oxyrhynchus'. Hence phon. *ḫꜣ*,[4] exx. var. Pyr. [5] *ḫꜣt* 'corpse'; [6] *ḫꜣrt*, var. [7] *ḫꜣrt*, 'widow'.

[1] *D. el B.* 152. [2] GAILLARD 26. [3] *Ti* 111, fem.; the *t* is written in the tomb of Mereruka, A 13, east wall. [4] Reading, *Verbum* i. p. 156, top. [5] *Pyr.* 474. [6] *BH.* i. 8, 20. [7] *Siut* 3, 5.

5 [1] a fish (*Petrocephalus bane*)[2]

Phon. det. *bs* (*bz*) in *bs*, var. O.K. [3] *ỉbz*, 'introduce', 'enter'. A very similar fish is used as generic det. fish, ex. [4] *rmw* 'fish'; fishy smell, ex. [5] *ḥnš* 'stink'.

[1] Ex. *Rekh.* 10. [2] GAILLARD 17. The characteristics are shown in earlier forms, *Bull.* 11, 41. [3] *Urk.* i. 87, 17. [4] *Urk.* iv. 954, 7. [5] *Hearst* 2, 17.

7 a fish (*Tetrodon fahaka*)[1]

Det. of [2] *špt* 'be discontented'.

[1] GAILLARD 97. [2] Brit. Mus. 159.

6 [1] fish-scale (also written)

Ideo. or det. in [2] var. [3] *nšmt* 'fish-scale'.

[1] Leyd. *Denkm.* ii. 5; not to be confused with L 6. [2] *M. u. K.* 1, 2; see *Rec.* 38, 62. [3] Leyd. *Denkm.* ii. 5.

Sect. L. Invertebrata and Lesser Animals

L 1 dung-beetle (*Scarabaeus sacer*)

Ideo. in [1] var. Pyr. [2] *ḫprr* 'dung-beetle'. Hence phon. *ḫpr* in var. Pyr. [3] *ḫpr* 'become' and derivatives.

[1] *Eb.* 88, 13. [2] *Pyr.* 697. [3] *Pyr.* 212.

2 bee

Ideo. in [1] *bỉt* 'bee'; also in *bỉt*[2] 'honey'. Hence phon. *bỉt*[3] in var. Pyr. [4] *bỉt*(*y*) 'king of Lower Egypt'. For *n-sw-bỉt* 'king of Upper and Lower Egypt' see § 55 and p. 73.

[1] *P. Kah.* 3, 2. [2] Coptic *ebiō*. [3] Reading, *ÄZ.* 30, 113. [4] *Pyr.* 724.

3 [1] fly

Det. in [2] *ꜥff* 'fly'.

[1] From a gold fly given as an honorific decoration, BISSING, *Thebanische Grabfunde* 6; see *PSBA.* 22, 167. [2] *Urk.* iv. 39, 1; 893, 12; see *ÄZ.* 48, 143.

4 [1] common locust (*Acrydium peregrinum*)

Det. in *snḥm* (Pyr. *znḥm*[2]) 'locust'.

[1] SCHIAPARELLI, *Relazione . . . lavori d. Miss. Arch.* ii. p. 171, fig. 156.
[2] *Pyr.* 891.

L 5 centipede — Det. in [1] *spꜣ* (Pyr. *zpꜣ*[2]) 'centipede'.

[1] *ÄZ.* 58, 82. [2] *Pyr.* 669.

6 bivalve shell[1] — For unknown reason, phon. *ḫꜣ*, in M.E. only in [2] *ḫꜣt*, var. [3] *ḫꜣwt* 'table of offerings'.

[1] *BH.* iii. p. 14. Not to be confused with the fish-scale K 6. [2] *Urk.* iv. 163, 7. Reading, see *Sah.* 63; *Pyr.* 58. [3] *Siut* 1, 240.

7 [1] scorpion (modified for superstitious reasons)[2] — Ideo. in *Srḳt* '(the scorpion-goddess) Serḳet', full name in Pyr. [3] *Śrḳt-ḥtw* 'she-who-relieves-the-windpipe'.

[1] Exx. *Sinai* 85. 143; *Five Th. T.* 9. [2] *ÄZ.* 51, 49. 57. [3] *Pyr.* 606; see *PSBA.* 39, 34.

Sect. M. Trees and Plants

M 1 tree — Det. tree, exx. *nḥt* 'sycamore-fig', 'tree', plur. often [1] *nḥwt*; [2] *mnw* 'trees'; *nbs* 'Christ's thorn-tree', '*nebḳ*-tree'; [3] *ỉꜣm*, varr. Pyr. [4] *ỉꜣm*, [5] *ỉmꜣ*, [6] *ỉm(ꜣ)*, unidentified tree. From this last, phon. *ỉꜣm*, *ỉm*—writings with are best transcribed *ỉꜣm* (cf. § 19, Obs. 1)—exx. *ỉꜣmt* 'charm', 'favour'; [7] *ỉꜣm(w)* 'tent'. The rather similar sign which serves as det. in [8] *mꜥr* 'fortunate' may well depict a quite different object.

[1] *Urk.* iv. 1064, 8. [2] *Urk.* iv. 353, 3. [3] *Urk.* iv. 73, 14. [4] *Pyr.* 699. [5] *Ib.* [6] *Ib.* [7] *Urk.* iv. 325, 12. [8] *D.el B.* 57, 4; cf. O.K., *Gebr.* ii. 13; M.K., *Siut* 3, 8; later the det. of *mꜥr* resembles V 29, see on this.

2 herb — Det. plant, flower, exx. *ỉꜣrw* 'reeds'; *ḥrrt* 'flower'. From [1] *ḥnỉ* 'rush', phon. *ḥn*, exx. *ḥnw* 'vessel'; *ḥnskt* 'lock' (of hair). Det. in [2] *ỉsỉ* 'be light' (perhaps like *ỉsw* 'reeds'); hence phon. det. *ỉs*, exx. [3] *ỉsy*, var. O.K. [4] *ỉz*, 'tomb', 'chamber'; [5] *ỉswt* 'old times'. From *ỉ* 'reed' (see on M 17) rarely as sportive writing for *·ỉ* 'I', 'my'[6]; hence also for as det., ex. [7] *s* 'man'. From Dyn. XVIII on sometimes as faulty transcription of hieratic T 24 in [8] *ỉḥwty* 'tenant farmer'.

[1] Lac. *TR.* 22, 63. [2] Vog. *Bauer* 121. [3] *Urk.* iv. 132, 11. [4] *Urk.* i. 16, 4. [5] *BH.* i. 25, 45. [6] *Urk.* iv. 77, 5–6, qu. § 440, 2; sim. *ib.* 401, 16. [7] *Ib.* [8] Petrie, *Tarkhan* i. 80, 19; *Med. Habu* (ed. Chicago), 140, 60.

M 3 [hieroglyph] branch

Ideo. in [hieroglyph] *ḫt* 'wood', 'tree'; hence phon. *ḫt*, exx. [hieroglyph] *ḫtyw* 'terrace'; [hieroglyph] *nḫt* 'strong'. Det. wood, ex. [hieroglyph] *hbny* 'ebony'; wooden objects, exx. [hieroglyph][1] *wḫ3* 'column'; [hieroglyph][2] *ḳniw* 'palanquin'. Vertically [hieroglyph] in [hieroglyph][3] *dʿr*, var. [hieroglyph][4] *dʿ*, 'search out', lit. perhaps 'harpoon' (vb.);[5] here [hieroglyph] is probably corruption of an old sign [hieroglyph] or [hieroglyph].[6]

[1] *Urk.* iv. 765, 13. [2] *Westc.* 7, 12. [3] *Urk.* iv. 384, 12. [4] Thebes, tomb 110. [5] Cf. *dʿ rmw* 'spear fish', *P. Kah.* 33, 16. [6] *Pyr.* 1105 in *dʿbw* 'curly'.

4 [hieroglyph] palm-branch stripped of leaves and notched (rare var. [hieroglyph][1]) to serve as tally[1a]

Det. in [hieroglyph] *rnpi* 'be young', 'vigorous'. Hence *rnp* in [hieroglyph] var. Pyr. [hieroglyph][1b] *rnpt* 'year', with [hieroglyph] ideographically as symbol; with similar sense ideo. in [hieroglyph] *ḥ3t-sp* 'regnal year' (p. 204) and in [hieroglyph][1c] *snf* (from *śn·nw·f* 'its second') 'last year'. Possibly ideo. of time (if not phon. det.) also in [hieroglyph][2] *tr* 'time', 'season', where it usually appears in the form [hieroglyph] M 5 or [hieroglyph] M 6. Elsewhere also [hieroglyph] is an occasional substitute for [hieroglyph] M 5, [hieroglyph] M 6, or [hieroglyph] M 7.[3]

[1] *BH.* i. 8. [1a] *JEA.* 34, 119, cf. HORAPOLLO I, 3 *φοίνικα*; in pictorial representations always with many notches, e.g. *JEA.* 4, Pl. 4; 30, Pl. 4; MORET, *Royauté Pharaonique*, figs. 17. 18. 19. [1b] *Pyr.* 965, as designation of Sothis; Coptic *rompě* 'year'. [1c] *Adm.* p. 102. [2] Written *trw*, *Urk.* iv. 195, 4. [3] In *ptr* 'see', *Siut* 1, 220; Cairo 20538, i. *c* 3; *rnpt* 'vegetables', 'fruit', *ib.* ii. *c* 25.

5 [hieroglyph] combination of [hieroglyph] M 4 and [hieroglyph] X 1

With sportive ideographic intention (palm-branch planted in [hieroglyph]) in Pyr. [hieroglyph] *tr*, var. [hieroglyph] *t(i)*, 'season'.[1] Hence [hieroglyph] (see on M 4 for [hieroglyph]) becomes in M.E. characteristic det. in [hieroglyph][2] abbrev. [hieroglyph][3] *tr* 'season'. However, [hieroglyph] M 6 is a commoner substitute for [hieroglyph], though [hieroglyph] interchanges with [hieroglyph] in some uses really belonging only to the latter, exx. [hieroglyph][4] *pri* 'battlefield'; [hieroglyph][5] *T3-mri* 'Ta-meri', i.e. Egypt.

[1] SETHE, *Pyramidentexte* iv. § 132. [2] *Urk.* iv. 384, 9. Sim. plur. *itr(w)*, *Sinai* 90, 19. [3] *Sinai* 90, 3. 11; *Ikhern.* 14. [4] *Urk.* iv. 32, 10. [5] *Urk.* iv. 102, 11.

6 [hieroglyph] combination of [hieroglyph] M 4 and [hieroglyph] D 21

With sportive ideographic intention in Pyr. [hieroglyph][1] *tr* 'season'. In M.E. det. in [hieroglyph][2] abbrev. [hieroglyph][3] *tr* 'season'. Hence phon. det. *tr*, *ti*, exx. [hieroglyph] *tr* 'pray' (§ 256); [hieroglyph][4] *ḥtr* 'assess' (taxes); also phon. det. *ri*, exx. [hieroglyph][5] *pri* 'battlefield'; [hieroglyph][6] *T3-mri* 'Ta-meri', i.e. Egypt.

[1] SETHE, *Pyramidentexte* iv. § 132, where a word *rr* 'season' is perhaps unnecessarily assumed. [2] *Urk.* iv. 343, 13. [3] *Urk.* iv. 195, 8. [4] *Rekh.* 3, 28. [5] *Urk.* iv. 38, 11. [6] *Urk.* iv. 325, 15. *(Pi)-t3-mri* is Πτίμυρις in a fragm. of Ephorus, there wrongly given as a name of the Delta only, GARD. *Sin.* 81.

M 7 combination of M 4 and Q 3 — With sportive ideographic intention in Pyr. *rnpi* 'be young', 'vigorous'.[1] Hence, in M.E., ideo. or det. in [2] var. [3] *rnpi* 'be young' and derivatives.

[1] SETHE, *Pyramidentexte* iv. § 132. [2] *Amarn.* v. 27, Q 11. [3] *Urk.* iv. 182, 17. More often thus abbreviated in *rnpt* 'vegetables', 'fruit', *Th. T. S.* i. 14; *Urk.* iv. 1167, 10.

8 pool with lotus flowers — Ideo. in [1] var. Pyr. [2] *š3* 'lotus pool', 'meadow'. Hence phon. *š3*, exx. *š3* 'appoint', 'command'; *š3d* 'dig'. In group-writing (§ 60) or is used for *š*.[3] From Pyr. [4] *i3ḫi* 'be inundated', ideo. or semi-ideo. in var. var. O.K. [5] *3ḫt* [6] 'inundation season' (p. 203).

[1] Exx. *Rec.* 24, 180, where the reading *3ḫ* is unnecessarily assumed. [2] *Pyr.* 1223. [3] BURCHARDT § 110. [4] *Wb.* 33. [5] *Urk.* i. 25. [6] Reading, *ÄZ.* 38, 103; 41, 89.

9 lotus flower — Ideo. or det. in [1] *sšn*, var. Pyr. [2] *zššn*, var. M.K. [3] 'lotus'.

[1] *Eb.* 44, 21; *Urk.* iv. 1162, 9. [2] *Pyr.* 266. [3] Cairo 20093, *c*.

10 [1] lotus bud — Det. in [2] *nḫbt* 'lotus bud'.

[1] Thebes, tomb 55. [2] *Urk.* iv. 918, 12.

11 flower on long twisting stalk[1] — Ideo. or det. in [2] var. [3] *wdn* 'offer'. In late Dyn. XVIII also erroneously in place of F 46 as det. in [4] *w(3)ḏbw* 'shores'.

[1] *Hier.* p. 28. The forms in *Pyr.* do not suit this interpretation very well. [2] *Puy.* 52. [3] *Urk.* iv. 452, 3. Sim. *Pyr.* 1127. [4] *Amarn.* iii. 20.

12 leaf, stalk and rhizome of lotus[0] — Ideo. in [1] *ḫ3w nw sšn* 'lotus plants'. Hence phon. *ḫ3*, exx. *ḫ3* 'thousand'; var. [2] *sḫ3* 'remember'. In group-writing (§ 60) or is used for *ḫ*.[3]

[0] *Ann.* 48, 92. [1] *Eb.* 43, 6. [2] *Siut* 1, 267. [3] BURCHARDT, § 100.

13 stem of papyrus — Ideo. in [1] *w3ḏ* 'papyrus column', cf. Pyr. [2] *w3ḏ* 'papyrus'. Hence phon. *w3ḏ* in var. Pyr. [3] *w3ḏ* 'be green' and derivatives. From M.K., phon. *w(3)ḏ* as substitute for V 24, exx. [4] *sw(3)ḏ*, older var. *swḏ*, 'hand over', 'bequeath'; [5] *w(3)ḏḥ*, var. Pyr. [6] *wdḥ*, 'pour out'.

[1] *Urk.* iv. 843, 10. [2] *Pyr.* 1875. [3] *Pyr.* 1530. [4] *Urk.* iv. 55, 10. [5] *Eb.* 94, 13. [6] *Pyr.* 2067.

14 combination of M 13 and I 10 — Phon. *w3ḏ*, *w(3)ḏ*, exx. [1] *W3ḏ-wr* 'the sea', lit. 'the great green'; [2] *sw(3)ḏ* 'hand over', 'bequeath'.

[1] *Sh. S.* 40–1. [2] *Urk.* iv. 121, 8.

M 15 clump of papyrus with buds bent down — Det. papyrus and watery regions, exx. *ỉdḥw* 'swamps' (of the Delta); [1] *dyt* 'papyrus-marsh'. Phon. det. *wꜣḫ* in [2] *wꜣḫ(y)* 'hall of the Inundation' from the Pyr. stem [3] *ỉꜣḫỉ*, whence [3a] *ꜣḫ* 'thicket' (of papyrus). Hence phon. *ꜣḫ* (or ideo. ?) in [3b] var. Pyr. [3c] *Ꜣḫ-bỉt* 'Chemmis' (a Delta place), possibly understood as 'Papyrus-thicket of the King of Lower Egypt'.[3d] Det. in varr. , *Tꜣ-mḥw* 'Lower Egypt', 'the Delta',[4] whence [5] *mḥ-s* 'the crown of Lower Egypt'.

[1] *Bull. Metr. Mus. New York*, 1914, 219. [2] *ÄZ.* 40, 48. [3] *Pyr.* 280. [3a] Coffins, S 2 C 207. [3b] ERM. *Hymn.* 15, 1. [3c] *Pyr.* 2190; without inversion, *JEA.* 24, Pl. II, 3. 6. [3d] See, however, *JEA.* 30, 54, n. 3. [4] *ÄZ.* 44, 10. [5] *Ib.* 20.

16 clump of papyrus — Phon. *ḥꜣ*, exx. var. [1] *ḥꜣ* 'would that!' (§ 238); *ḥꜣḳ* 'capture'. In group-writing (§ 60) or is *ḥ*.[2] As O.K. det. in [3] *Tꜣ-mḥw* 'the Delta' and related words is often replaced in M.E. by M 15, but exx. with are still fairly common,[4] exx. [5] *Tꜣ-mḥw* 'the Delta'; [6] *mḥ-s* 'crown of Lower Egypt'.

[1] Brit. Mus. 562, qu. § 364. [2] BURCHARDT § 94. [3] *Urk.* i. 64, 8; 101, 11. [4] *ÄZ.* 44, 10. [5] Louvre C 172; *Urk.* iv. 583, 7. [6] Brit. Mus. 574, 6.

17 flowering reed — Ideo. in [1] *ỉ* 'reeds'. Hence phon. *ỉ*. For *y* see § 20.[2] In group-writing (§ 60) corresponds to Hebr. י, to א.[3]

[1] *Bersh.* ii. p. 19. Sim. *Eb.* 49, 2. [2] See the full discussion *Verbum* i. §§ 121–4. [3] BURCHARDT, § 16; cf. ALBRIGHT, *Vocalization*, pp. 33–4; 36–7.

18 combination of M 17 and D 54 — In *ỉỉ* 'come' and the related words.

19 heaped conical cakes between reed M 17 and sign like U 36[0] — Det. in ,[1] abbrev. [2] *ꜥꜣbt* 'offering', 'pile of offerings' and the related verb.[3]

[0] DAV. *Rekh.* Pl. 49; p. 44, n. 5. [1] LAC. *TR.* 14, 7. [2] *Urk.* iv. 769, 3. [3] *Wb.* i. 167.

20 reeds growing side by side — Ideo. or det. in varr. , *sḫt* (*šḫt*)[1] 'marshland', 'country' and its derivative *sḫty* 'peasant'. Occasionally phon. *sm* (*šm*) like M 21, ex. [2] *sm* 'occupation', 'pastime'.

[1] *Pyr.* 275. [2] *Urk.* iv. 462, 13. Sim. *sm* 'succour', *Dend.* 15, 15.

M 21 like the last, but with a loop at the side — Ideo. or semi-ideo. in [1] *sm*, var. Pyr. [2] *śm*, 'herb', 'plant'. Hence phon. *sm* (*śm*), ex. [3] *sm* 'succour'.

[1] *Urk.* iv. 775, 15. [2] *Pyr.* 1722. [3] Brit. Mus. 1164, 1, where the form is almost like D 61. But see *Pyr.* 892.

22 rush with shoots [0] — Cf. Pyr. [1] *nḫbt* 'germination', 'shooting up'. Hence phon. *nḫb* in var. Pyr. [2] *Nḫbt* '(the vulture-goddess) Nekhbet'.

[0] According to LORET in *Griff. Stud.* 308 the marsh club-rush (*Heleocharis palustris*). [1] *Pyr.* 4; *Sah.* Text, p. 109. [2] *Pyr.* 1229.

(22) two rushes with shoots — Cf. Pyr. [1] *nnt* 'rushes'. Hence is phon. *nn*, exx. var. *nn* 'this' (§ 110); *nnì* 'be weary'.

[1] *Pyr.* 557.

23 plant regarded as typical of Upper Egypt (probably form of M 26, but without flowers) — Ideo. in *swt* (*śwt*) 'the *śwt*-plant'.[1] Hence phon. *sw* (*św*),[2] ex. *swt* 'but' (§ 254). The word var. [3] 'king of Upper Egypt' probably originally read *nì-śwt* 'he who belongs to the *śwt*-plant', but before M.K. had become *nsw* (*nzw*); 'kingship' is perhaps to be read *nsyt*. For *n-sw-bìt* 'king of Upper and Lower Egypt' see § 55. Sometimes is inaccurately used for M 24 or M 26.[4] In group-writing (§ 60) stands for *s*.[5]

[1] *ÄZ.* 49, 18. [2] Reading from O.K. varr. of *śmśw* 'elder'; also from other words cited *Wb.* iv. 60, 2; 65, 13; 74, 2; cf. too the exceptional writing of *swsḫ* 'make broad', *Ikhern.* 24. [3] *ÄZ.* 49, 15; *Rec.* 38, 69. [4] *ÄZ.* 44, 22. [5] BURCHARDT § 106.

24 combination of M 23 and D 21 — With sportive pictorial intention (plant *śwt* growing from mouth *r*),[1] phon. *rśw* in Pyr. [2] *rśwt* 'South' and the related words.[3] In M.E. 'South' is *rsy*.

[1] SETHE, *Pyramidentexte* iv. § 132. [2] *Pyr.* 470. [3] *ÄZ.* 44, 1.

25 confusion of M 24 and M 26 [1] — Faulty writing either for words connected with *rśwt* 'South', ex. [2] *rsyw* 'southerners', or for words connected with *Šmʿw* 'Upper Egypt', ex. [3] *ìt Šmʿ* 'Upper Egyptian corn'.

[1] *ÄZ.* 44, 22. [2] *Urk.* iv. 909, 3. [3] *PSBA.* 18, 196.

M 26 sedge(?)[0] growing from a sign for land resembling N 17 — Probably as a flowering specimen of M 23, ideo. in [1] var. [2] *Šmʿw* 'Upper Egypt', the reading of which is given by [3] var. O.K. [4] *šmʿ* 'make music'. Hence phon. *šmʿ* in [5] *šmʿyt* 'chantress', 'singer'.

[0] See above, p. 73, n. 10. Depicted as a desert plant, JÉQUIER, *Monument funéraire de Pepi II*, ii, Pl. 43. Identified with M 23, but with flowers, *Mitt. Kairo* 12, 80. [1] *BH.* i. 26, 127; see *ÄZ.* 44, 9. [2] *Urk.* iv. 583, 2; 617, 14. [3] *BH.* ii. 7. [4] *Gebr.* ii. 7. [5] Cairo 20142, *d.*

27 combination of M 26 and D 36 — In [1] *Šmʿ(w)* 'Upper Egypt'. Also phon. *šmʿ* in var. [2] *šmʿyt* 'chantress', 'singer'.

[1] *Urk.* iv. 530, 12. [2] *Th. T. S.* iii. 14.

28 combination of M 26 and V 20 — In the title varr. , *wr mdw Šmʿ(w)* 'greatest of the tens of Upper Egypt'.[1]

[1] *ÄZ.* 44, 18; SETHE, *Zahlworte* 40, n. 7. Some varr. have M 23 instead of M 26.

29 pod from some sweet-smelling tree[1] — Cf. [2] *nḏm* '*nḏm*-tree'. Hence semi-phon. *nḏm* in var. Pyr. [3] *nḏm* 'sweet' and the related words. The tree or wood [4] var. [5] *ssnḏm* is possibly a later deformation of an O.K. word *šśḏ* or *šśḏm.*[6]

[1] *Hier.* p. 26. [2] *Urk.* iv. 73, 14. Formerly taken to be the 'carob-tree', but see *ÄZ.* 64, 51. [3] *Pyr.* 1172. [4] *Westc.* 7, 13. [5] *Ikhern.* 12. [6] *Wb.* iv. 279, 7.

30 a sweet-tasting root? — Ideo. or det. in var. [1] *bnr* 'sweet' and derivatives.

[1] *Urk.* iv. 749, 5.

31 [1] stylised rhizome of a lotus (Dyn. XVIII) — Det. in *rd* 'grow'.

[1] Very variable in shape, exx. *Urk.* iv. 749, 5; CARTER and NEWBERRY, *Tomb of Thoutmosis IV*, 46160. The explanation here substituted for 'plants growing in a pot?' of the 1st ed. is that given by KEIMER, *Ann.* 48, 89.

32 [1] Dyn. XII var. of last — Use as last. A similar sign sometimes in hieratic erroneously borrowed from *rd* 'grow' in *r(w)d* 'be strong'.[2]

[1] *Bersh.* ii. 21. [2] *Sin.* B 76. 108; one would have expected T 12.

33 grains of corn (also written or) — Ideo. in var. Pyr. [1] *it* 'barley', 'corn' and its varieties *it Mḥ* 'Lower Egyptian corn' and *it Šmʿ* 'Upper Egyptian corn'.[2] Det. corn, ex. [3] *Npri* '(the grain-god) Nepri'.

[1] Compare *Pyr.* 1748 with *ib.* 1950. [2] *ÄZ.* 44, 19. [3] *Mill.* 2, 12.

34 bearded ear of emmer — Ideo. or det. in *bdt*, var. [1] *bty*, 'emmer'.

[1] Already Dyn. XI, *PSBA.* 18, 202, 9. Sim. *BH.* i. 8, 21.

35 heap of corn — Det. in [1] *ʿḥʿw* 'heaps'; also in [2] *wbn* 'overflow'.

[1] *D. el B.* 79. Sim. *ib.* 74. [2] *Puy.* 36.

M36 bundle of flax stems showing the bolls[0] (sometimes misinterpreted[1]) — Phon. *ḏr*,[2] exx. *ḏr* 'since' (§ 176); *nḏri* 'hold fast'. Det. in [3] *dmꜣ* 'bind together'.

[0] See the picture *Paheri* 3. [1] Dyn. XII, *Meir* ii. 17, no. 30. [2] Reading, *Pyr.* 582 (*ḏrt* 'hand'). [3] *Urk.* iv. 612, 15, but rather different from *ḏr*, *ib.* 9.

37 [1] bundle of flax stems (O.K. form of M 36) — Phon. *ḏr* like M 36.

[1] Exx. Dyn. V, *Sah.* 28; *Gemn.* i. 13; Dyn. XII, *Meir* ii. 17, no. 28.

38 [1] bundle of flax (O.K.; specialized variant of M 37) — Det. in O.K. *mḥꜥ* (?),[2] var. Dyn. XII [3] *mꜥḥ* (?), *mḥ* (?), 'flax' and in [4] *dmꜣ* 'bind together'.

[1] Montet 194. [2] Reading, *Rec.* 25, 159. [3] *BH.* i. 29. [4] *Sah.* 8; Dyn. XVIII form differs slightly from M 36, see there n. 3.

39 [1] basket of fruit or grain — Det. vegetable offerings, ex. *rnpt* 'vegetables', 'fruit'.

[1] Exx. O.K., *Medum* 16 (*dꜣb* 'figs'); Dyn. XVIII, *D. el B.* 93 (*rnpt*, *ḥnkt*).

40 [1] bundle of reeds — Cf. [2] *isw* 'reeds'. Hence phon. *is* (*iz*), exx. *is* (*iz*)[3] 'tomb'; [4] *iswt* 'crew'.

[1] Elaborate forms, O.K., *Medum* 13; Dyn. XVIII, *Puy.* 20. [2] *Eb.* 19, 13. [3] Ex. O.K., *Urk.* i. 16, 4. [4] *Sh. S.* 7; *Rec.* 28, 113.

41 log of wood stripped of its branches (Dyn. XVIII)[1] — Det. wood, exx. *ꜥš* 'cedar' (properly 'pine' or 'fir'); [2] *wꜥn* 'juniper (?)'; [2] *mr*(*w*) '*meru*-wood'.

[1] See *Ann.* 16, 33. O.K. forms, see *Pyr.* 590. 634; Palermo stone, 6, 2–4. [2] *Urk.* iv. 373, 4.

42 flower? — Phon. *wn*,[1] exx. [2] *wnḏw* 'short-horned cattle'; [3] *ḥwn* 'be young'; [4] var. [5] *wnm* 'eat'. Not distinguished from Z 11 in the earliest hieratic, and replaced by the latter sign in M.K. hieratic,[6] as also regularly in later hieroglyphic.

[1] See *Sitz. Berl. Ak.* 1912, 960. [2] *Urk.* iv. 716, 7. [3] *Urk.* iv. 365, 17. [4] Brit. Mus. 614, vert. 2; see *Rec.* 34, 214. [5] Lac. *TR.* 22, 9; see *ÄZ.* 46, 141. [6] Möll. *Pal.* i. no. 564.

43 [1] vine on props (var.) — Det. vine in [2] *i*(*ꜣ*)*r*(*r*)*t*, var. O.K. [3] *iꜣrrt*, 'vine'; various notions connected with the vine, exx. [4] var. [4] *irp* 'wine'; [5] var. [6] *kꜣny* 'gardener'; fruit generally, exx. [7] *dꜣb* 'figs'; [8] *išd* '*išd*-fruit'.

[1] Thus with a vessel or basket Dyn. XII, *BH.* i. 17 (*irp*); Dyn. XVIII, *D. el B.* 112 (*irp*); *Puy.* 12 (*kꜣm*). In O.K. and often later the vessel or basket is absent, see Dav. *Ptah.* i. 10, nos. 166. 173. [2] *Urk.* iv. 73, 11. [3] *Urk.* i. 103, 14. [4] *BH.* i. 17. [5] Cairo 20167, *b* 2. [6] *BH.* i. 29. [7] *Sin.* B 81. [8] *Eb.* 86, 1.

44 thorn[1] — Det. in [2] *srt* 'thorn'. Possibly it is the same sign, if not a mere triangle, which serves as ideo. or det. in var. [3] *spd* (*śpd*)[4] 'sharp' and the related words.

[1] *Rec.* 28, 167. [2] *Eb.* 88, 4. [3] *Urk.* iv. 535, 10. [4] *Pyr.* 1159.

Sect. N. Sky, Earth, Water

N 1 sky

Ideo. or det. in var. *pt* 'sky'. Det. sky, exx. *Nwt* '(the sky-goddess) Nut'; var. Pyr.[1] *ḥrt* 'heaven', lit. 'the distant one'; high, in[2] *ꜥḥi* 'hang'. In[3] var. O.K.[4] *ỉn-ḥrt* '(the god) Onūris' is a later interpretation, since the name originally meant 'he who fetched the distant one (fem.)'.[5] From *ḥrt* 'heaven', phon. *ḥry, ḥrw* in var. *ḥry* 'above' and the related words. In two words for 'gate' is derived from earlier signs for a gateway like or ,[5a] namely in[6] *rwty* 'the double gate' and in[7] *ht*, var.[8] *hyt*, var. O.K.[9] *ht*, 'portal', whence the title[10] var.[11] *smsw hyt* 'elder of the portal'. There is perhaps a similar contamination in *hꜣt* 'ceiling'.[12]

[1] *Pyr.* 1171. [2] *Amada* 18. [3] Cairo 20057, *a.* 2; 20380. [4] *Gebr.* i. 18. [5] *Unt.* 5, 142. [5a] *Rwt*, see *Wb.* ii. 404, 1. [6] *Sin.* R 9. [7] Cairo 20230, *a.* [8] See n. 11. [9] Leyd. *Denkm.* i. 5. [10] Cairo 20035, *h*; 20086, *h. r.* [11] *ÄZ.* 60, 64. [12] *Urk.* iv. 429, 7.

2 [1] sky with a broken (?) *wꜣs*-sceptre S 40(?) suspended from it (Dyn. XVIII)

Det. night, exx. abbrev.[2] *grḥ* 'night';[3] *wḫ* 'night'; darkness, exx. *kkw* 'darkness';[4] *ꜥḫḫw* 'dusk'.

[1] Thebes, tomb 93. [2] Cairo 20738, *b.* [3] *Siut* 3, 10, qu. § 212. [4] *Sin.* B 254.

3 [1] O.K. form of last

Use as last.

[1] *Pyr.* 265. According to the ingenious theory of Mlle M. CHATELET an oar (or sceptre, N 2) suspended from the sky broken and bound up to symbolize darkness, *Bull.* 18, 21.

4 [1] moisture falling from the sky (Dyn. XVIII)

Ideo. or det. dew, rain, exx.[1] *ỉdt*, var.[2] abbrev.[3] *ỉꜣdt*, 'dew';[4] *šnyt* 'rain-storm'.

[1] *D. el B.* 47. [2] *Eb.* 77, 21. [3] *Eb.* 6, 9. [4] BUDGE, p. 481, 4.

5 sun

Ideo. or det. in var. *rꜥ* 'sun', 'day'; var. *hrw* 'day'; in dates reads *sw* (p. 203). Det. sun or actions of sun, exx. *šw* 'sun'; *wbn* 'rise'; day, exx. *sf* 'yesterday'; *wrš* 'spend all day'; time generally,[1] exx. *wnwt* 'hour'; *ꜥḥꜥw* 'period'; *(n)ḥḥ* 'eternity'. For see N 23.

[1] Development of this use, see SETHE, *Zeitrechnung* (II), 29.

N 6 sun with uraeus (Dyn. XVIII) — Ideo. or det. in [1] var. [2] *rʿ* 'sun'.

[1] *Westc.* 11, 5. [2] Ex. p. 291.

7 combination of N 5 and T 28 — Abbrev.[1] for *ḥrt-hrw* 'day-time', 'course (of day)', lit. 'what belongs to the day'.

[1] Ex. *Urk.* iv. 992, 4.

8 sunshine — Det. (or ideo.) sunshine, exx. [1] var. [2] *ꜣḫw* (Pyr. *iꜣḫw*) 'sunshine'; [3] *psḏ* 'shine'; var. [4] *wbn* 'rise'. From this last, phon. *wbn* in [5] var. [6] *wbnw* 'wound'. Phon. *ḥnmmt* in [7] var. [8] var. Pyr. [9] *ḥnmmt* 'the sun-folk' of Heliopolis.

[1] *Urk.* v. 55, 9. [2] *Urk.* iv. 19, 11. [3] *Urk.* v. 55, 4. [4] *Urk.* iv. 585, 12. [5] *Eb.* 107, 5. [6] *Eb.* 67, 1. [7] *Urk.* iv. 17, 7. [8] Cairo 20498. [9] *Pyr.* 139.

9 moon with its lower half obscured (Dyn. XVIII)[1] — Ideo. or det. in [2] *psḏntyw*, varr. [3] [4] *psdn*, var. Pyr. [5] *pśḏtyw*, 'New-moon festival'. Hence phon. det. *psḏ* in [6] *psḏt* 'divine ennead', 'company of nine gods'. This sign is liable to confusion with the loaf X 6.

[1] Cairo 34002 = LACAU, Pl. 3. Sim. *BH.* i. 24, 1. [2] *Urk.* iv. 177, 9. [3] *Urk.* iv. 27, 4. [4] *Urk.* iv. 836, 1. [5] *Pyr.* 794. [6] Reading, *ÄZ.* 47, 8.

10 alternative form of last (Dyn. XVIII)[1] — Use as last.

[1] MÖLL. *Pal.* ii. no. 573.

11 crescent moon (also vertically)[1] or ([2] when used as det.) — Ideo. or det. in varr. *iʿḥ* 'moon'; hence phon. det. or abbrev. in [3] var. [4] *wʿḥ* 'carob beans'. Combined with N 14, ideo. in var. *ꜣbd* 'month'; for the reading cf. an O.K. personal name [5] *ꜣbdw* and Ṣaʿîdic *eḃŏt* 'month'; in dates abbreviated as , ex. *ꜣbd 3* 'month 3' (§ 264). In abbrev. *šsp* 'palm' (as measure § 266, 1) the sign has doubtless a different pictorial origin.[6] In some inscriptions is written for *spr*, F 42.[7]

[1] *Pyr.* 732. [2] *Pyr.* 1104; *Urk.* iv. 813, 5. [3] *Rec.* 25, 155. [4] *Rekh.* 12; cf. *Eb.* 14, 8. [5] See *Wb.* i. 8; nevertheless the usual reading *ꜣbd* is retained *ib.* i. 65. [6] MÖLL. *Pal.* i. no. 680; ii. no. 680. [7] *Paheri* 5, row 3.

12 alternative form of last (Dyn. XVIII) — In [1] varr. [2] [3] *iʿḥ* 'moon'.

[1] *Urk.* iv. 808, 4. [2] *Urk.* iv. 12, 15; 14, 7. [3] *Urk.* iv. 30, 4. 13.

13 combination of half of N 11 and N 14 — Ideo. in [1] var. [2] . . . *nt* [3] 'half-month festival'.

[1] *Urk.* iv. 112, 8. [2] *BH.* i. 24. [3] Reading unknown, see *Wb.* ii. 198, 2; iv. 147, 1.

N 14 star

Ideo. or det. in var. *sbꜣ*, var. Pyr. [1] *šbꜣ*, 'star'; hence phon. or phon. det. *sbꜣ* (*šbꜣ*), exx. var. *sbꜣ* 'teach' (with derivatives); *sbꜣ* 'door'. Det. star, constellation, exx. [2] *Msḫtyw* 'the Great Bear'; *Spdt* 'Sothis'; time as indicated by stars, exx. *ꜣbd* 'month', see N 11; var. [3] *wnwt* (1) 'hour', (2) 'priesthood'. Also semi-phon. *dwꜣ*, exx. *dwꜣt* 'morning'; var. Pyr. [4] *dwꜣ* 'adore' (in the morning). In the word 'netherworld' (originally the place of the morning twilight,[5] popularly known as 'the Duat' and in this work still transliterated *dwꜣt*) the very common *Pyr.* var. *dꜣt* probably indicates that the *w* had fallen and that the pronunciation already approximated to the Old Coptic *tē*, *tēi*.[6]

[1] *Pyr.* 1038. [2] LAC. *TR.* 20, 89. [3] As 'priesthood', *Kopt.* 8, 4. [4] *Pyr.* 1087. [5] SETHE, *Pyr.*, Commentary, I 49. [6] *ÄZ.* 38, 87.

15 star in circle

Ideo. in [1] var. varr. Pyr. ,[2] ,[3] *d(w)ꜣt* 'netherworld', see N 14, at end.

[1] BUDGE, p. 14, 12. [2] *Pyr.* 5. 8. 802 and after. [3] *Pyr.* 257. 272.

16 [1] flat alluvial land with grains of sand N 33 beneath it

Ideo. in varr. , , *tꜣ* 'earth', 'land'. Hence phon. *tꜣ* (rare), ex. [2] *sštꜣ* 'mystery', 'secret'. In group-writing (§ 60) is phon. *t*.[3] Det. land, in [4] *ḏt* 'estate', whence also in *ḏt* 'eternity'; *ḏt* 'serf'.[5]

[1] O.K. exx. *Pyr.* 75; *Ti* 49. [2] Cairo 20088, *c* 12; 20683, *a* 8. [3] BURCHARDT § 132; an ex. under O 29, n. 5. [4] GARD. *Sin.* 77, n. 2. [5] VOG. *Bauer* 34.

17 [1] alternative form of N 16

Use as last.

[1] Common at all periods. As det. land in Dyn. III, see exx. under N 22.

18 sandy tract[1]

Ideo. in var. *iw*[2] 'island'. In group-writing (§ 60) is phon. *i*,[3] ex. [4] *'Irt* 'Yareth' (Syrian place-name). Det. desert or foreign country, exx. var. *ꜣḫt* 'horizon', more exactly the land of the sun-rise;[5] *Ṯḥnw* 'Libya'; *Stt* 'Asia'; cf. too D 8.[6] Different signs, but with similar outline, are (1) the garment, see after S 26; (2) the cake, see after X 4; (3) the oval, see Z 8.

[1] Exx. showing the sand, *D. el B.* 10 (*tꜣ-ḏsr*); *Puy.* 36 (*Stt*). [2] Reading from old varr. of *iwy* 'deprive of a ship', *Pyr.* 1429. 1742. [3] BURCHARDT § 21. [4] *Urk.* iv. 791, 237. [5] See under N 27. [6] In *Pyr.* 628. 707 also of sea in *Wꜣḏ-wr* 'the great green', as var. of N 37.

19 the last twice repeated (often small)

In [1] *Ḥr-ꜣḫty*, var. Pyr. [2] *Ḥr-ꜣḫti*, 'Horus-of-the-horizon', 'Ḥarakhti'.

[1] *Urk.* iv. 590, 13, qu. § 507, 2. [2] *Pyr.* 337.

N 20 tongue of land — Det. in [1] var. Pyr. [2] *wḏb* 'sand-bank', 'shore'. Hence phon. *wḏb* in [3] var. Pyr. [4] *wḏb* 'turn back' and derivatives. From O.K. onward a sign of like appearance is used in *ḥb-sd* 'jubilee', '*Sed*-festival'.[5]

[1] *D. el B.* 116. [2] *Pyr.* 291. [3] Louvre C 166. [4] *Pyr.* 808.
[5] Exx. Dyn. VI, *Hamm.* 63; Dyn. XII, *Kopt.* 9; Dyn. XVIII, *D. el B.* 37.

21 tongue of land — Det. land, especially in abbrev. , *ỉdb* 'bank', 'region' (dual *ỉdbwy* 'the two banks', i.e. 'Egypt').[1] More widely used in Dyn. XVIII, then often taking the place of earlier N 23, exx. *tꜣ* 'earth'; [2] *ꜣḥt* 'fields'; [3] *dmỉ* 'town'.

[1] *Wb.* i. 153. [2] *Rekh.* 3, 18, qu. Exerc. XXX, (iii). [3] *Urk.* iv. 893, 7.

22 [1] sandy tongue of land (O.K. prototype of both N 20 and N 21) — In *wḏb*, see O.K. varr. under N 20. Det. land, exx. Dyn. III [2] *ꜥḥt* 'field'; [3] *sḫt* 'field'.

[1] Showing the sand, Munich, Inv. 204 (Abu Gurâb, Dyn. V). Sim. but reversed, DAV. *Ptah.* i. 11, no. 219 = *Ptah.* (E.R.A.) 31, in the title *ḫry wḏb*, like last.
[2] Berl. *ÄI.* i. p. 79, 8. 10. [3] Berl. *ÄI.* i. p. 93. Sim. *ꜣḥt*, *Urk.* i. 12, 7.

23 irrigation canal (Dyn. XI–XVIII; early identical with,[1] and clearly a mere differentiation of, N 36) — Det. irrigated land, exx. *tꜣ* 'land'; *tꜣš* 'boundary'; in Dyn. XVIII tends to be replaced by N 21. In Dyn. XI–XII or is found as det. of time, probably corrupted from as used in words for 'to-morrow' and 'yesterday',[2] exx. [3] *tr* 'season'; [4] *rk* 'time'.

[1] Dyn. XI, BISSING-BRUCKMANN, *Denkmäler* 33 A (*ỉdbwy*); *Dend.* 11 A (*tꜣ*).
[2] *ÄZ.* 34, 28; *Rec.* 35, 80. [3] *Th. T. S.* ii. 12; *Meir* iii. 16 (*tr*). Sim. *JEA.* 4, Pl. 8, 10 (*ꜥḥꜥw*). [4] *BH.* i. 8, 19. Sim. Brit. Mus. 614, 3 (*ꜥḥꜥw*).

24 land marked out with irrigation runnels — Ideo. or det. in varr. , *sp(ꜣ)t* (*ṡpꜣt*)[1] 'district', 'nome'; also in *dꜣtt* (?)[2] 'estate'. Det. province, exx. *Tꜣ-wr* 'nome of Abydus'; *Šmꜥw* 'Upper Egypt'; also garden, in [3] *ḥsp* (Pyr. *ḥzp*)[4] 'garden'.

[1] LAC. *Sarc.* ii. 132; the reading *ṡpꜣt* is suggested also by some varr. of the place-name *Ṡpꜣ*, see *ÄZ.* 58, 81, n. 20; 82, n. 4. [2] Reading, see on Aa 8.
[3] *Mission* V 283. [4] *Pyr.* 126.

25 sandy hill-country over edge of green cultivation — Ideo. or det. in var. [1] *ḫꜣst* (*ḫꜣṡt*) 'hill-country', 'foreign land'. Det. desert, exx. varr. [2] ,[3] *smt* (*zmt*) 'desert', 'necropolis'; *ḥrt* 'upland tomb'; *ỉꜣbtt* 'east'; also foreign countries, ex. *Rṯnw* 'Retjnu', 'Syria'. Ideo. in var. Pyr. [4] *Ḥꜣ* '(the desert-god) Ḥa'.

[1] *Urk.* iv. 343, 16; 373, 11; cf. O.K., MAR. *Mast.* p. 188. [2] Cairo 1622, cf. O.K. *Gebr.* ii. 8; *smyt*, Cairo 20011. [3] Proof in title *ỉmy-r smwt ỉꜣbtt*, see *Hier.* p. 31; other exx., *Siut* i. 314. 322. [4] *Pyr.* 1013.

N 26 sand-covered mountain over edge of green cultivation — Ideo. in *dw*[1] 'mountain', plur. [2] *dww*. Hence phon. *dw*[3] (later *dw*), exx. *dwi* 'call'; *3bdw* 'Abydus'; *wndw* 'short-horned cattle'.

[1] Coptic *toou*. The proposal to read *tpy mny·f* in the well-known title of Anubis 'he who is upon his mountain' (*Rec.* 35, 228) needs further investigation. [2] *Th. T. S.* i. 9. [3] Reading, see *pdw*, *Pyr.* 1013; cf. VOG. *Bauer*, p. 70.

27 sun rising over mountain — Ideo. in var. Pyr. [1] *3ḫt* 'horizon' (properly the place in the sky where the sun rises)[2] and its derivatives.

[1] *Pyr.* 154. [2] *Bull.* 17, 189.

28 hill over which are the rays of the rising sun[1] — Ideo. in Pyr. [2] *ḫʿ* 'hill of the sunrise' and in *ḫʿi* 'appear in glory'. Hence phon. *ḫʿ*,[3] ex. *ḫʿm*, var. [4] *ḫʿm*, 'approach'.

[1] DE BUCK, *De egyptische voorstellingen betreffende den oerheuvel*, Leyden, 1922, p. 63. [2] *Pyr.* 542. [3] *Wb.* iii. 243, 2 quotes an O.K. word in which the sign is preceded by the alphabetic signs for *ḫʿ*; Coptic also points to *ḫʿ* rather than *ḫʿ*. [4] GARD. *Sin.* 33.

29 sandy hill-slope[1] — Cf. var. Pyr. [2] *ḳ33* 'hill', 'height'. Hence phon. *ḳ*.

[1] Exx. showing sand, *Meir* ii. 17, nos. 36. 37. [2] *Pyr.* 1652.

30 [1] mound of earth with shrubs[2] — Ideo. or det. in var. *i3t* 'mound'.

[1] Exx. Dyn. IV, *Medum* 11; Dyn. XVIII, *D. el B.* 116. [2] *Bull.* 3, 145.

31 road bordered by shrubs[1] — Ideo. or det. in var. *w3t* 'road' and related words. Det. road, exx. *mtn* 'road'; *ḥrt* 'road' (with related words); travel, in *ʿr* 'mount up' and derivatives; position in general, exx. *ʿ3* 'here' (§ 205); *r-sy* 'entirely' (§ 205); *pf3* 'that' (§ 110); distance, in *ḥnty* 'period'. Abbrev. *ḥr* (see *ḥrt* 'road' above) in [2] var. O.K. [3] *'In-ḥrt* '(the god) Onūris'[4]; in for *ḥrw-r* 'besides' (§ 179); and for superstitious reasons in place of *Ḥr* 'Horus' on M.K. coffins[5]; also abbrev. *w3* in *w3 r* 'fall into' a bad state.[6]

[1] Exx. O.K., *Medum* 9; *Saqq. Mast.* i. 39, no. 47. [2] Leyd. V 3 (in a proper name); Cairo 20446, *a*. [3] *Gebr.* i. 18. [4] Lit. 'he who fetched the distant one'; see *Unt.* 5, 141. [5] *ÄZ.* 51, 58. 59. [6] *Westc.* 9, 12, qu. p. 420.

32 lump of clay or dung (O.K.) — Phon. det. in Pyr. [1] *šinw* 'runners' on account of *sin* 'clay'. Also as alternative for F 52 in O.K. [2] *mḥšḥš* 'filthy one'. In M.E. replaced by Aa 2.

[1] *Pyr.* 1499. [2] *Ti* 112.

N 33 grain of sand, pellet, or like. (For similar signs cf. D 12 and the circle, see after Z 8)

Det. sand, in *šʿy* 'sand'; metal or mineral (often repeated), exx. *nbw* 'gold'; *msdmt* 'black eye-paint', 'koḥl'; medicaments, incense, etc. exx. [1] *tꜣ* 'pellet'; *pẖrt* 'medicine', 'prescription'. A sign of like appearance rarely takes the place of dangerous signs such as A 14 in religious documents, ex. *ḫftyw* 'enemies'; this practice dates from Pyr.[2] Sometimes or is substituted for the plural strokes, exx. [3] *gnwt* 'annals'; [4] *šsrw* 'bags'.

[1] *D. el B.* 10. [2] *ÄZ.* 51, 18. 63. [3] *Urk.* iv. 86, 3. [4] *Urk.* iv. 1143, 13.

34 [1] ingot of metal (Dyn. XVIII; in Dyn. XI the sign resembles W 13;[2] in Dyn. III–V it resembles X 3[3])

Ideo. in 'copper', early perhaps read *biꜣ* and later *ḥmt* (?).[4] Det. objects of copper or bronze, exx. [5] *ʿnḫ* 'mirror'; [6] *ḫʿw* 'weapons'; [7] *mỉnb* 'axe'.

[1] *Puy.* 38. [2] *JEA.* 4, Pl. 9. [3] *Medum* 13; Palermo stone 5, 4; rather different, *Gebr.* i. 13, reg. 3. [4] *ÄZ.* 53, 51, n. 2. The reading *biꜣ* would be confirmed for early times if the compound word written with this sign *JEA.* 4, Pl. 9, l. 10 proved to be really *biꜣ-rwḏ*, the Coptic *barōt* 'copper'. The supposed later reading *ḥmt* (?) is based solely on Coptic *homent, homt.* [5] *Adm.* 8, 5. [6] *Urk.* iv. 656, 2. [7] GARD. *Sin.* 51. 159.

35 ripple of water (rarely vertically)[1]

Cf. *nt* 'water'.[2] Hence (?) phon. *n*. Perhaps phon. *n* too when used as a substitute for D 35 both in *n* 'not' and in *nn* 'not' (§ 104). In group-writing (§ 60), and are all used for *n*,[3] while appears, as does also in Dyn. XIX, to correspond to *l*,[4] ex. [5] *Sḫt ỉnr* 'Field-of-Reeds'. In [6] *ḏt* 'serf' replaces the sign of land N 17, a curious substitution (or error of transcription ?) found also in Pyr.[7]

[1] Louvre C 1. [2] SETHE, *Alphabet* 153. [3] BURCHARDT §§ 67. 69. 71. [4] *Ib.* § 81. [5] *Urk.* iv. 1194, 2. [6] Cairo 20161. [7] *Pyr.* 1217 (*tt*); 1713 (*tkr*).

(35) three ripples

Ideo. in *mw*[1] 'water'. Hence phon. *mw*, exx. *šmw* 'summer'; var. *mww* '*muu*-dancers';[2] *hdmw* 'footstool'; phon. *m* in group-writing (§ 60), ex. [3] *Ynʿm* 'Yenoam', Palestinian place-name. Det. water, liquid, exx. *wꜣw* 'wave'; *fdt* 'sweat'; actions connected with water, exx. *ỉʿỉ* 'wash'; *sw(r)ỉ* 'drink'. The composite det. (in hieroglyphic also) for rivers, lakes, seas comes into vogue in Dyn. XVIII, exx. [4] *ỉtrw* 'river'; [5] *ẖnw* 'brook'.

[1] Coptic *mow*. Cf. *mwt* 'semen', phonetically *Pyr.* 123. [2] GARD. *Sin.* 70. [3] *Urk.* iv. 744, 6. [4] DÉV. *Graphies*, no. 9. [5] *Urk.* iv. 655, 13. Sim. *ib.* 3, 10.

N 36 channel filled with water[1] (later form as det. irrigated land N 23)

Ideo. in [2] var. Pyr. [3] *mr* 'canal', 'channel'. Hence phon. or phon. det. *mr* in var. *mri* 'love';[4] phon. *mi*,[5] exx. var. *mist* 'liver'; [6] *mihꜥt* 'tomb'. Det. rivers, lakes, seas, exx. *Wꜣḏ-wr* 'the sea', lit. 'the great green'; *hꜥpy*, var. M.K. *hp*, 'the inundation', here early interchanging with N 37. For (in hieroglyphic also) as det. of names of rivers, lakes, seas from Dyn. XVIII on, see under N 35. Doubtless an irrigation canal when prototype of the later land-sign N 23, see there. In the fem. collective ,[7] varr. ,[8] [7] *mrt* 'weavers'[9] the sign was probably understood as a weaver's reed,[10] though the occasional presence of or may have indicated the same value *mr* as in the masc. [11] *mr* 'friend(s)', 'partisans'.

[1] Detailed O.K. exx. Berl. *ÄI.* i. p. 80; DAV. *Ptah.* i. 11, no. 218 (*ꜥḏ-mr*). [2] Dyn. XVIII, *Urk.* iv. 815, 1, qu. Exerc. XVIII (*a*). Cf. O.K. *Urk.* i 108, 13; *ÄZ.* 42, 9. [3] *Pyr.* 848. [4] *Verbum* i. § 397, 7. [5] *PSBA.* 16, 142; *Sphinx* 13, 157. [6] *Urk.* iv. 45, 16. [7] *Wb.* ii. 106, 11–20, there confused with *mrt* 'serfs'. [8] *BH.* i. 29. [9] Existence as a separate word doubted *Wb.* ii. 97, 2, but clear proofs DAV. *Seven Private Tombs*, pp. 2–3. 49; *Puy.* 43; *P. Anast.* VI. 20. [10] *ÄZ.* 45, 88. [11] *Wb.* ii. 98, 2.

37 garden pool

Ideo. in var. *š* 'pool'. Hence phon. *š*.[1] Not seldom interchanging in hieroglyphic with [2] N 36, ex. [3] *hꜥpyw* 'inundations'. Appears to be a sign for irrigated land in [4] var. Dyn. III [5] (N 38) *šṯꜣt* 'aroura' (§ 266, 3); cf. the use of N 36 both as a channel of the Nile and, in its use as the early form of N 23, as an irrigation canal. Sometimes replaces the cake (see after X 4) in spellings of *sn* 'open' like , [5a]. Occasionally it serves as a large form of the block of stone O 39, ex. [6] *inr* 'stone'.

[1] SETHE, *Alphabet* 155. [2] Often in *mri* 'love', exx. *Pyr.* 317. 953. 2192. Sim. *Amarn.* i. 22; ii. 23; iii. 6. [3] *PSBA.* 18, 202, 9. Sim. *BH.* i. 8, 21; also *Hamm.* 114, 14, qu. p. 392, n. 5 (*Wꜣḏ-wr*). So too *Pyr.* 435. 564 (*Ḥ(ꜥ)p*); 802 (*Wꜣḏ-wr*). [4] *Urk.* iv. 172, 1. [5] Berl. *ÄI.* i. p. 79, 13. [5a] For this and the possibly homophonous word for 'pass by' see GARD. *Sin.* 72. 160, as well as *Wb.* iii. 454. [6] *Puy.* 38. Sim. *Bersh.* i. 14, 2 (*snt*).

38 garden pool with sloping sides (detailed form of N 37)[1]

Use as last.

[1] Exx. O.K., Berl. *ÄI.* i. p. 75, 11; DAV. *Ptah.* i. 11, no. 213; Dyn. XVIII, *Puy.* 20. 22; *D. el B.* 79. 81.

For see U 18.

39 garden pool full of water (alternative of N 37)[1]

Use as N 37.

[1] Exx. O.K., *Medum* 9. 13; *Ti* 69; M.K., Berl. *ÄI.* i. p. 254.

N 40 combination of N 37 and D 54. — In *šm* 'go'.

41 well full of water[1] — Det. well, ex. [2] *ḫnmt* 'well'; pool, marsh, in ,[3] varr. ,[4] ,[5] O.K. ,[6] *pḥww*[7] 'limits', 'distant marsh-lands'. As substitute for the female organ (cf. O.K. [8]) in *ḥmt* 'woman', 'wife'. Hence phon. *ḥm*, exx. var. [9] *ḥm* 'assuredly' (§ 253); *nḥm* 'rescue'. Also as female organ in var. (here is det.) 'vulva', and derivatively 'cow', where the reading is more probably *idt* than *ḥmt*;[9a] cf. above F 45. For obscure reasons,[10] phon. *biꜣ*, exx. *biꜣ* 'copper'; *biꜣ* 'firmament'; for the reading see [11] var. ,[12] *biꜣw* 'mine'.

[1] With interior zigzag lines for water, *BH.* iii. 6, no. 88; *D. el B.* 16. [2] *Th. T. S.* i. 27. Sim. O.K. *šdwt*, Berl. *ÄI.* i. p. 71, cf. *ÄZ.* 42, 9. [3] *Urk.* iv. 138, 8. [4] *Puy.* 36. [5] *Urk.* iv. 587, 3. [6] MONTET 4. [7] The proposed reading *ḥnw* reposed mainly on *Urk.* iv. 523, 5, but *Puy.* 30 shows the reading there to be false. See also *ÄZ.* 3, 62. [8] From a sculpture at Abu Gurâb; cf. *nk* 'copulate', *Pyr.* 1321. [9] *Urk.* iv. 257, 9. [9a] Full discussion and references, *AEO.* ii. 258*; *Wb.* iii. 76 reads *ḥmt.* [10] *Hier.* p. 34; hardly a copper axe-head as proposed in MÖLL. *Pal.* i. 98, n. 1. [11] *Sh. S.* 23–4. [12] *Sinai* 53, 3.

42 well full of water (a common alternative form of last)[1] — Use as last.

[1] With the zigzag lines, but having a straight line at top, O.K. *Sah.* 48; *Ti* 128 (*ḥmt*).

Sect. O. Buildings, Parts of Buildings, etc.

O 1 house — Ideo. in *pr*[1] 'house', cf. the fem. collective [2] *pryt* 'houses'. Hence phon. *pr* in *pri* 'go forth' and derivatives; only very rarely not initial *pr*, ex. [3] for *ḫpr* 'become'. Det. house, building, exx. *ꜥt* 'room', 'department'; *iwnn* 'sanctuary'; *ḫnw* 'interior'; *mꜥḥꜥt* 'tomb'. Less suitably also in *st* 'seat', 'place'; *nst* 'seat' of office; *ꜣḫt* 'horizon'.

[1] Reading perhaps preserved in Coptic *djeneрōr* 'roof' (p. 8, n. 2), also in Greek transliterations like Φαραώ = Hebrew פַּרְעֹה; Φορώρ = οἶκος Ὥρου; see *ÄZ.* 51, 125. [2] *Ḥaremḥab* 34. 36. 38; also in *pryt Pr-ꜥꜣ* 'courts of Pharaoh', *P. Kah.* 38, 10–11 (Akhenaten), Coptic περπερωι. [3] *ÄZ.* 57, 3*. 5*, very rare.

O 2 combination of O 1 and T 3 — In *pr-ḥḏ* 'treasury', lit. 'white house'.

3 combination of O 1, P 8, X 3, and W 22. — In *prt-ḫrw* 'invocation-offerings'.[1]

[1] See above p. 172.

4 reed shelter in fields[0] — Ideo. in [1] *h* 'room (?)'. Hence phon. *h*.

[0] Probably a reed shelter of the kind still to be seen in Egyptian fields (Iversen). A late sign-papyrus in Copenhagen gives *pr n sḫt* 'field-house' as one of several descriptions of the hieroglyph. [1] *M. u. K.* 1, 7 (with note); *Eb.* 25, 16. The exact meaning is doubtful, but see *Wb.* ii. 470, 2.

5 winding wall (also sometimes) — Det. in [1] *mrrt* 'street'; hence phon. or phon. det. *mr* in [2] var. [3] *Mr-wr* 'Mnevis-bull'. For unknown reason, phon. det. *nm* in [4] var. Pyr. [5] *nmi* 'traverse'; also in [6] *nmi* 'lowing' of cattle.

[1] *BH.* i. 44, 2. [2] *Amarn.* v. 32, 21. [3] Berl. *ÄI.* ii. p. 100. [4] *Sin.* R 32. [5] *Pyr.* 1260. Sim. *ib.* 1370. [6] *Sin.* R 49.

6 rectangular enclosure seen in plan — Ideo. in *ḥwt*[1] 'castle', 'mansion', 'temple', 'tomb'. The full reading *ḥwt*, possibly later *ḥyt*, is suggested by the O.K. personal name *Ḥwti*[2] and by the isolated variant [3] *Nbt-ḥyt*, together with the Coptic equivalent ⲛⲉⲃⲑⲱ[4] of the name of the goddess Nephthys. Hence the transliteration *ḥwt* has been adopted in this Grammar except for the divine name *Ḥt-ḥr*, Gk. Ἀθυρ, 'Hathor' where the element *ḥat-* is clearly in *status constructus*. However, in one passage of Dyn. XII [5] is written for *ḥtt* 'quarry', giving to the mere value *ḥ*.

[1] Perhaps one of the large enclosures of reeds called in Arabic *zarîbah*, the enclosed portion roofed with stalks and reserved for the women and children (Calverley). [2] *ÄZ.* 63, 149. [3] Cairo, unnumbered coffin from Asyûṭ. [4] Preisendanz, *Pap. Graec. mag.* i. 72; cf. also the place-name ϩⲟⲩ, ϩⲱ *AEO.* ii. 33*. [5] *Bersh.* ii. p. 24.

7 alternative form of last (Dyn. XVIII)[1] — Use as last.

[1] Exx. *Puy.* 40; *Rekh.* 16.

8 combination of O 7 and O 29 — In [1] *ḥwt-ꜥꜣt* 'temple', earlier 'castle',[2] lit. 'great castle'.

[1] *Urk.* iv. 575, 8. [2] Berl. *ÄI.* i. p. 78.

9 combination of O 7 and V 30 — In varr. [1], [2] *Nbt-ḥyt* '(the goddess) Nephthys'.

[1] *M. u. K.* vs. 5, 4. [2] See above O 6, n. 3.

O 10 [hieroglyph] combination of [hieroglyph] O 6 and [hieroglyph] G 5 — In [hieroglyph] var. [hieroglyph][1] *Ḥt-ḥr* '(the goddess) Hathor'.

[1] *Sinai* 80.

11 [hieroglyph] palace with battlements[0] — Ideo. in [hieroglyph] var. [hieroglyph][1] var. Pyr. [hieroglyph][2] *ʿḥ*, var. M.K. [hieroglyph][3] *iḥ*, 'palace'.

[0] Earliest depictions, PETR. *RT.* ii. 3, 4 and within an enclosure like O 13, *ib.* ii. 7, 8. 9; later DAV. *Ptah.* i. 12, no. 225; *Hier.* 3, 30. Not two-storeyed, SCHARFF, 22, n. 64. [1] *Urk.* iv. 58, 7. [2] *Pyr.* 141. [3] *Rec.* 14, 167; see *Sphinx* 13, 157.

12 [hieroglyph] combination of [hieroglyph] O 11 and [hieroglyph] D 36 — In var. of *ʿḥ* 'palace', see last.

13 [hieroglyph][1] battlemented enclosure — Det. in [hieroglyph] *sbḫt* 'gateway' and in the related verb *sbḫ* (*šbḫ*) 'wall in',[2] 'enclose'.

[1] Ex. *Urk.* iv. 174, 9. [2] Exx. *Pyr.* 585. 636. Sim. with O 14, *ÄZ.* 60, 63.

14 [hieroglyph] portion and alternative of last[1] — Use as last.

[1] Exx. *Urk.* iv. 422, 2; *ÄZ.* 60, 63.

15 [hieroglyph][1] walled enclosure with buttresses, and with the signs [hieroglyph] W 10 and [hieroglyph] X 1 — Ideo. in [hieroglyph][1] varr. [hieroglyph], [hieroglyph] *wsḫt* (*wšḫt*) 'hall' in palace or temple.

[1] *Rekh.* 10. Varr. with battlements as in O 13, as well as palace O 11, see *Hier.* p. 34.

16 [hieroglyph][1] gateway (?) surmounted by protecting serpents — Ideo. or det. in [hieroglyph][2] *tꜣ* 'curtain (?)' and [hieroglyph][3] var. [hieroglyph][3] *tꜣyt* 'curtain'. Hence semi-ideo. in the title of the vizier [hieroglyph][4] var. [hieroglyph][5] var. O.K. [hieroglyph][6] *tꜣyty* 'he of the curtain'. For [hieroglyph] *tꜣ-wr* 'larboard' see on [hieroglyph] S 22.

[1] *Rekh.* 4. [2] MAR. *Abyd.* i. 19, *a*. [3] LAC. *TR.* 21, 85-6. [4] *Th. T. S.* ii. 14. 17. [5] BUDGE, p. 322, 2, as epithet of Osiris. [6] DAV. *Ptah.* ii. 6. 28; *Saqq. Mast.* i. 17.

17 [hieroglyph][1] O.K. form of last — Use as last.

[1] DAV. *Ptah.* i. 12, no. 232.

18 [hieroglyph] shrine seen from side — Ideo. or det. in [hieroglyph][1] var. [hieroglyph][2] *kꜣ(r)i* (Pyr. *kꜣr*[3]) 'chapel', 'shrine'.

[1] Exx. *D. el B.* 114; *Urk.* iv. 168, 15. [2] *Urk.* iv. 130, 16. [3] *Pyr.* 276.

19 [hieroglyph] primitive shrine — Det. in [hieroglyph][1] *Pr-wr* 'Great House' name of the pre-dynastic national shrine of Upper Egypt at Hieraconpolis (*Nḫn*);[2] also of *itrt* in [hieroglyph] *itrt šmʿ(yt)* 'the row of Upper Egyptian sanctuaries', as seen at the *Sed*-festival;[3] hence also as collective term for 'the gods of Upper Egypt'.[4]

[1] *Pyr.* 648; Brit. Mus. 574, 7. [2] *Unt.* v. 127, n. 2. [3] *JEA.* 30, 27; for references see *ÄZ.* 44, 17. [4] See above p. 291, with n. 3.

O20 [1] shrine — Det. sanctuary, exx. *itrt* 'row of sanctuaries'; [2] *ḥm* 'shrine'; especially of the [3] *Pr-nw* or [4] *Pr-nsr* (*Pr-nzr*), names of the pre-dynastic national sanctuary of Lower Egypt at Buto (*P*). Hence *itrt mḥt* 'the row of Lower Egyptian sanctuaries' and collective term for 'the gods of Lower Egypt'; see on O 19, together with nn. 3, 4 there.

[1] *Lisht*, p. 37. [2] *Urk.* iv. 167, 1. [3] *Pyr.* 1438; Brit. Mus. 574, 8. [4] *Pyr.* 852; BUDGE, p. 88, 20; 319, 11.

21 façade of shrine — Ideo. or det. in var. [1] *sḥ-nṯr* (*zḥ-nṯr*) 'the divine booth'.

[1] *Mitt.* ix. Pl. 7, 1, in the title of Anubis *ḫnty sḥ-nṯr*. Cf. *Hier.* p. 36.

22 open booth supported by a pole — Ideo. or det. in var. *sḥ*, var. Pyr. [1] *zḥ*, 'booth'; hence phon. *sḥ* (*zḥ*) in *sḥ* 'counsel'. In the combination the sign retains a value *ḥb* (*ḥꜣb*) which it formerly possessed when used alone.[2]

[1] *Pyr.* 130. [2] Cf. *Pyr.* 555 (*ḥꜣb* 'catch of wild fowl'); 1672 (*ḥꜣb* 'be festive').

For see W 4.

23 hall used in the *Sed*-festival[1] — Ideo. or det. in [2] varr. [3] [4] *ḥb-sd* (*ḥb-šd*) 'jubilee', '*Sed*-festival'

[1] See *Unt.* 3, 136. [2] *Urk.* iv. 565, 16. [3] *Kopt.* 9. Sim. O.K., *Urk.* i. 97, 6. [4] *Urk.* iv. 569, 8.

24 pyramid with side of surrounding wall — Det. in *mr* 'pyramid', 'tomb' and in names of specific royal pyramids, ex. *Kꜣ-nfr-Imnmḥꜣt* 'the pyramid Amenemḥēt-is-high-and-beautiful'.[1] Hence also in *Mn-nfr* 'Memphis' (p. 183, n. 1).

[1] See *ÄZ.* 32, 88.

25 obelisk — Ideo. or det. in [1] var. [2] *tḫn* 'obelisk'.

[1] *Urk.* iv. 366, 13. [2] *Urk.* iv. 360, 16.

26 stela — Ideo. or det. stela, exx. [1] var. [2] *wḏ* 'stela'; [3] *ꜥḥꜥw* 'station', 'stela'.

[1] *BH.* i. 25, 32. [2] *BH.* i. 26, 141. [3] *Rec.* 20, 40, in the phrase *ꜥḥꜥw n Nb* 'station of the King', see *Unt.* 2, 40.

27 [1] hall of columns — Det. hall of columns, exx. [2] *ḏꜣdw* 'hall of columns'; *ḫꜣ* 'office'. From last, phon. or phon. det. *ḫꜣ* in [3] var. [4] *ḫ(ꜣ)w(y)* 'night'.

[1] *Rekh.* 4. [2] *Urk.* iv. 257, 1. [3] *JEA.* 4, Pl. 8, 3; cf. *Pyr.* 1639. [4] *Puy.* 29, 5 in the name of the feast *ḫt-ḫꜣwy* 'night-ceremonies', cf. *BH.* i. 24; *Urk.* iv. 27, 5.

28 column with tenon at top — Ideo. in *iwn* 'column'; for the reading cf. var. [1] *iwnyt* 'hall of columns'. Hence phon. *iwn*, exx. [2] var. Pyr. [3] *iwnt* 'bow'; *Iwnw* 'Heliopolis'.

[1] *Amada* 14 = *Eleph.* 17. For further evidence see *Sitz. Berl. Akad.* 1912, 961. [2] *Sebekkhu* 5. [3] *Pyr.* 1644.

O 29 wooden column [1] (also found vertically) — Cf. [2] *ꜥꜣ* 'column'. Hence phon. *ꜥꜣ*, exx. *ꜥꜣ* 'great'; [3] var. Pyr. [4] *ḥꜥꜣ* 'infant'. In group-writing (§ 60) or is phon. *ꜥ*,[5] exx. [6] *Tꜥmṯ* 'Taꜥmetj', f. personal name; [7] *Ynꜥm* 'Yenoam', Palestinian place-name.

[1] As support of the booth O 22, *Medum* 10. [2] *P. Kah.* 13, 2. [3] Louvre C 1, 10. [4] *Pyr.* 1105. [5] BURCHARDT, § 26. [6] *Urk.* iv. 11, 9. [7] *Urk.* iv. 744, 5.

30 supporting pole — Ideo. or det. in var. [1] *sḫnt* (*zḫnt*) [2] 'support' of heaven. For a similar sign, but reversed, see after U 12.

[1] Four times repeated, 'the four supports', *Urk.* iv. 843, 2. [2] Reading with *z*, *Pyr.* 1559; *Ḥarh.* 365.

31 [1] door — Ideo. or det. in var. [2] *ꜥꜣ* 'door'; hence very rarely phon. *ꜥꜣ*, ex. [3] *ꜥꜣmt* 'Asiatic woman'. Det. open, exx. *wn* 'open'; *sn* 'open'.

[1] *Puy.* 54; see the picture PETRIE, *Deshasheh* 21. [2] In the title *iry-ꜥꜣ* 'door-keeper', Cairo 20103, *l*; 20184, *k*. [3] *Urk.* iv. 743, 4.

32 [1] gateway — Det. door, gateway, exx. [1] abbrev. [2] *sbꜣ* (*śbꜣ*) 'door'; *sbḫt* 'gateway'.

[1] *D. el B.* 137. [2] *Urk.* iv. 845, 13.

33 [1] façade of palace or tomb — Det. in *srḫ* 'banner' for the Horus name (p. 72).

[1] *Urk.* iv. 160, 12.

34 bolt — Ideo. in [1] *s* (*z*) 'bolt'. Hence phon. *s* (*z*). Also as substitute for R 22 in [2] var. Pyr. [3] *Ḫm* 'Letopolis', the modern Ausîm NW. of Cairo.[4]

[1] *Urk.* iv. 498, 11. [2] Cairo 20498; *Ḥarh.* 535. Det. with the shrine O 20, Cairo 20738. [3] *Pyr.* 1670. [4] From Dyn. XIX onward, however, is often actually written at the beginning of this place-name (GAUTHIER, *Dict. géogr.* V 45), which appears from the Gk. personal name Πετεαρβεσκινιος (gen.) = *Pꜣ-di-Ḥr-nb-Sḫn* really to have read *Sḫm* or *Sḫn* (SPIEGELBERG, *Äg. u. gr. Eigennamen*, 28*, no. 198 a).

35 combination of O 34 and D 54 — In a number of words implying motion and having *s* (*z*) as a characteristic radical, exx. rare var. *sbi* 'go', 'pass', 'send'; *si* 'perish', later replaced by *sbi*; rare var. *ms* 'bring', 'offer'; *is* 'go' (imperative, § 336); var. var. Pyr. [1] *sy* (*zy*) 'who?', 'what?' There is much confusion in the value of , owing to the tendency (1) to write alone for *sb*, and (2) to write for simple *s*.[2]

[1] *Pyr.* 438. [2] *ÄZ.* 48, 31.

36 wall[0] (occasionally horizontally [1]) — Ideo. or det. in var. [2] *inb* 'wall'. Det. wall, exx. [3] *sbty* 'surrounding wall'; [3] *wmtt* 'bulwark', 'fortification'; [4] *snb* 'overleap' a wall.

[0] In the earliest times perhaps plan of a brick enclosure with buttresslike projections, but later certainly interpreted as a wall, cf. A 35 and O 37. See SCHARFF, 18. [1] *Urk.* iv. 764, 9. [2] *Urk.* iv. 765, 7. 16. [3] *Urk.* iv. 661, 5. [4] *Sin.* R 141.

O37 falling wall — Det. overthrow, exx. [1] *wḥn* 'overthrow'; [2] *sẖnn* 'demolish' a wall; slanting, ex. [3] *gsꜣ* 'tilt'.

[1] *Urk.* iv. 780, 7. [2] Cf. *Puy.* 20. [3] *Peas.* B 1, 92.

38 corner of wall — Det. in *ḳnbt* 'corner', 'angle',[0] whence var. *ḳnbt* 'magistrates', lit. perhaps 'those who sit at the corner'. Det. gate, in *ꜥrrt* 'gate'; corner (?), in *mrrt* 'street'. Ideo. or det. in var. *ḥry (n) tm*, an obscure title.[1]

[0] Palermo stone, vs. 5, 2; see too *AEO.* ii. no. 452 of On. Am. [1] *ÄZ.* 40, 96.

39 stone slab or brick (sometimes large like N 37) — Det. stone and similar, exx. *inr* 'stone'; *ꜥꜣt* 'valuable stone' for vessels, etc.; *dbn* '*deben*-weight' (§ 266, 4); *ꜥr* 'pebble'; *ḏbt* 'brick'.

40 stairway — Det. stairway, exx. varr. , [1] *rwd* 'stairway'; var. [2] *ḫtyw* 'terrace', 'terraced hill'.

[1] *Sebekkhu* 8. Reading, see Leyd. V 3, 5. [2] *Urk.* iv. 1031, 6, in connection with Min: for the *ḫtyw* 'platform' of Min see Cairo 20703, *a* 5; also LEGRAIN, *L'aile nord du pylône d'Aménophis III*, 14 A; see too the elaborate study *Kêmi* ii. 41.

41 double stairway — Det. stairway, exx. [1] *ḳꜣy* 'ascent', 'high place'; *iꜥr* [2] 'ascend'.

[1] *Urk.* iv. 364, 3. [2] *ÄZ.* 46, 98.

42 fence outside primitive shrine O 19[1] — Phon. *šsp* (*šzp*) in *šsp*, var. Pyr. [2] *šzp*, 'receive', but early *sšp* ;[3] cf. [4] var. [5] *sšp* 'daylight'.

[1] See the pictures of O 19 *Medum* 9; *Sah.* 22; *Ann.* 25, 126. [2] *Pyr.* 879. [3] *Siut* 1, 225. [4] *P.Kah.* 1, 10; *Peas.* B 1, 201. [5] DE BUCK, ii. 5.

43 [1] O.K. form of last — Use as last.

[1] *Pyr.* 260 (W 387). See too SCHARFF, 13, n. 23.

44 emblem erected outside the temple of Min[1] — Ideo. or det. in [2] var. [3] *iꜣt* 'office', 'rank'.

[1] See *Kopt.* 10, 3; a divergent early form JUNKER, *Gîza I*, 146. [2] Commonest form, exx. *Beni Hasan* I, 25, 11; *Kopt.* 8, 11; *Urk.* iv. 208. [3] BUDGE, 482, 16; *iꜣwt*, given as principal form *Wb.* i. 29, if found at all early, is probably *status pronominalis*, see § 78.

45 domed building — Ideo. or det. in varr. , *ipt* 'harîm'; [1] *ipꜣt* is possibly the fuller form of the same word.

[1] *ÄZ.* 45, 127.

46 older form of last[1] — Use as last.

[1] Exx. O.K., *Urk.* i. 100, 13; M.K., *Bersh.* ii. 21, top 16; Dyn. XVIII, *Urk.* iv. 897, 3.

47 a prehistoric building at Hieraconpolis[1] (Dyn. XVIII form)[2] — Ideo. in varr. , *Nḫn*[3] 'Hieraconpolis', i.e. Kôm el-Aḥmar in Upper Egypt.

[1] *ÄZ.* 53, 57. [2] *Rekh.* 16; but also Dyn. VI, *Gebr.* ii. 6; Dyn. XII, *BH.* ii. 14; Leyd. V 4, 1. [3] Reading, BRUGSCH, *Dict. Géogr.* 353; see too *ÄZ.* 58, 60 and the alternative writing *Mḫn*, *AEO.* ii. no 320 of On. Am.

O 48 (sign) alternative form of last[1] — Use as last.

[1] Dyn. V, *Sah.* 18; Dyn. XII, *Th. T. S.* ii. 6; Dyn. XVIII, *Paheri* 8.

49 (sign) village with cross-roads — Ideo. in (hierogl.) *niwt* 'village'; for the reading cf. Pyr. (hierogl.)[1] *n(iw)tyw*(?) 'those belonging to the lower heaven' and the very late var. (hierogl.)[2] for Ναύκρατις. Det. village, town, ex. (hierogl.) *Wȝst* 'Thebes'; inhabited region, in (hierogl.) *Kmt* 'Egypt', lit. 'the black (land)'; (hierogl.)[3] *dȝtt* (?) 'estate'.

[1] *Pyr.* 1467. The puzzling evidence suggests that the 'lower heaven' had two names, namely *Nỉ(w)t* and *Nnt*, which are much confused in the writing. Crucial passages are *Pyr.* 149. 446. 1691. [2] *ÄZ.* 53, 105. [3] *Peas.* R 68; see Aa 8.

50 (sign) circular threshing-floor covered with grain[1] (printed in older books in the late form (sign)) — Det. in (hierogl.)[2] *spt* (*zpt*) 'threshing-floor'. Hence phon. or phon. det. *sp* (*zp*) in (hierogl.) var. (hierogl.) *sp* 'time', 'occasion' and related words. Note (hierogl.) var. (hierogl.) *sp sn* 'two times' as sign that a word or part of a word is to be repeated in reading (§§ 207. 274), exx. (hierogl.) *ʿšȝ ʿšȝ* 'very often'; (hierogl.) *ršrš* 'rejoice'. For (sign) in (hierogl.) *hȝt-sp* 'regnal year' see p. 204.

[1] *Hier.* pp. 27. 67. [2] MONTET 213–14.

51 (sign) heap of grain on a raised mud floor[0] — Ideo. or det. in (hierogl.) varr. (hierogl.), (hierogl.)[1] *šnwt* 'granary'.

[0] So ERMAN, *Ägypten*, 577, n. 3, probably rightly; for the shape of the heap, cf. *Ti* 124. DAV. *Ptah.* i. 36 thought the sign originally depicted a granary, and was only later interpreted as a heap of corn. However, both early (*ib.* 28; *Ti* 84) and late (ERMAN, *op. cit.* 576) the actual granaries were dome-shaped.
[1] *Urk.* iv. 1050, 13.

Sect. P. Ships and Parts of Ships

P 1 (sign) boat on water — Det. boat, ship, exx. (hierogl.) *dpt* 'ship'; (hierogl.)[1] *ḥʿw* 'ships'; (hierogl.)[2] *ʿḥʿw* 'ships'; sail, travel by water, exx. (hierogl.) *nʿi* 'sail'; (hierogl.) *ḫdi* 'fare downstream'; also det. in (hierogl.)[3] *iw(y)* 'one without a boat'. As abbrev. the sign presents difficulties; (hierogl.)[4] is doubtless *dpt-nṯr*[5] 'the divine bark'; in (hierogl.)[6] 'overseer of ships' there is definite evidence in favour of *ʿḥʿw*,[7] but possibly *ʿḥʿw* is merely a later writing of, or more recent substitute for, *ḥʿw*;[8] the singular (sign) 'boat' doubtless usually stood for (hierogl.)[9] *imw*, but once at least represents the much rarer (hierogl.)[10] *kȝkȝw*.

[1] *Hamm.* 114, 14; *Bersh.* i. 14, 7. [2] *BH.* i. 44, 5; *Rekh.* 3, 34. [3] *Wb.* i. 47. [4] *ÄZ.* 45, Pl. VI, 6. [5] *Adm.* p. 33. [6] *ÄZ.* 45, Pl. VI, 6; Cairo 20023, *s*; *Urk.* iv. 153, 3. [7] Compare Cairo 20143, *c* with *ib. b*; so too without plural strokes and followed by numeral, *Cen.* 90, 1, 5. 6. [8] *ÄZ.* 32, 34. Possibly the relationship is like that of O.K. *šḫw*, Dyn. XVIII *wsḫ* 'breadth'. [9] *ÄZ.* 68, 8. [10] *Westc.* 8, 3–4.

(1) (sign) boat upside down — Det. in (hierogl.) *pnʿ* 'upset', 'overturn'.

P 2 [hieroglyph] ship under sail — Det. in [hieroglyphs] *ḫnti* 'sail upstream'.

3 [hieroglyph] sacred bark (details vary greatly in different cases)[1] — Ideo. or det. in [hieroglyphs] var. [hieroglyph] *wiꜣ* 'sacred bark'. Det. divine boats, exx. [hieroglyphs] *mꜥndt* 'bark of the dawn'; [hieroglyphs] *nšmt* 'the *neshmet*-bark', i.e. the sacred boat of Abydus. Also det. sail, when divine journeys are meant, ex. [hieroglyphs][2] *dꜣi* 'cross' sky, said of Rēꜥ.

[1] For different forms see *Ikhern.* 14. 23 (*nšmt*); Cairo 20024 = *Mus. ég.* i. 17 (*mꜥndt, msktt*); *Urk.* iv. 366, 6. 7 (*mꜥndt, msktt*). [2] *D. el B.* 114.

For [hieroglyph] see G 7*. For [hieroglyph] see G 10.

4 [hieroglyph] fisherman's boat with net — Semi-ideo. in [hieroglyphs] *wḥꜥ* 'fisherman', plur. [hieroglyphs][1] *wḥꜥw*, together with the related words.

[1] *Bersh.* ii. 16 without the plural strokes. Cf. Ṣaꜥidic ⲟⲩⲱϩⲉ 'fisherman'.

5 [hieroglyph] sail — Ideo. or det. in [hieroglyphs] var. [hieroglyphs] *ṯꜣw*[1] 'breath', 'wind'. Det. wind, exx. [hieroglyphs] *mḥyt* 'north wind'; [hieroglyphs] *dꜥw* 'storm'; sail, in [hieroglyphs][2] *ḥtꜣw* 'sail'. Ideo. also in [hieroglyphs] var. [hieroglyphs] *nfw* 'skipper', late var. [hieroglyphs] *nfy*.[3]

[1] Reading, *Pyr.* 309; see *ÄZ.* 24, 86. [2] DÜMICHEN, *Kalenderinschriften* 35, 49. [3] LEPSIUS, *Todtenbuch*, ch. 99, 23. Coptic *neef.*

6 [hieroglyph] mast[0] — Phon. *ꜥḥꜥ*[1] in [hieroglyphs] var. [hieroglyphs] *ꜥḥꜥ* 'stand' and derivatives.

[0] For the problem of the form (also in P 5, 7) see *Sah.* II, p. 161. [1] That *ḥ* forms part of the reading is shown by a late spelling of *ḥꜥw* 'limbs', BRUGSCH, *Wörterbuch*, Suppl. 272.

7 [hieroglyph] combination of [hieroglyph] P 6 and [hieroglyph] D 36 — Use as last, ex. [hieroglyphs][1] *ꜥḥꜥw* 'ships'.

[1] *Urk.* iv. 702, 15.

8 [hieroglyph] oar (also often horizontally in [hieroglyph] § 55) — Det. oar, exx. [hieroglyphs][1] *wsrw* 'oars'; [hieroglyphs][2] *ḥpt* 'oar'. Perhaps from a word [hieroglyph][3] var. [hieroglyphs],[4] 'oar' known only from the king's name [hieroglyphs][5] *Nb-ḫrw(?)-Rꜥ* 'Nebkherurēꜥ' phon. *ḫrw*, exx. [hieroglyphs] var. [hieroglyphs] *ḫrw* 'voice'; [hieroglyphs] *ḫrwy* 'enemy'.

[1] NAV. 99, 23. [2] A secondary word, see *ÄZ.* 62, 4. [3] Value deduced only from phonetic use. [4] *D. el B.* (XI) iii. Pl. 11. [5] Now recognized as distinct from king Nebḥepetrēꜥ, see *Stud. Aeg.* I 38–41; also *ÄZ.* 62, 3.

9 [hieroglyph] combination of [hieroglyph] P 8 and [hieroglyph] I 9 — In [hieroglyphs] var. [hieroglyphs] *ḫr(y)·fy* 'says' (§ 437).

10 [hieroglyph] steering oar — Det. in [hieroglyphs] *ḥmw* 'steering oar'; [hieroglyphs] *ḥmy* 'steersman'.

11 [hieroglyph] mooring post — Det. in [hieroglyphs][1] *mnit* (*minit*) 'mooring post' and the related words. In hieratic often indistinguishable from [hieroglyph] T 14 and consequently so usually transcribed.[2]

[1] Brit. Mus. 574, 14. [2] See MÖLL. *Pal.* i. nos. 457. 472.

Sect. Q. Domestic and Funerary Furniture

Q 1 seat — Ideo. in *st*, var. Pyr.[1] *śt*, 'seat', 'place'. Hence phon. *st* (*śt*),[2] exx. *mꜣst* 'lap'; *nmst* 'jar'; *ws* (*wś*),[3] in *Wsỉr* 'Osiris'; *ꜣs* (*ꜣś*), in rare var. [4] *ꜣst* (*ꜣśt*) 'Isis'. From a word *ḥtmt* 'chair' (Dyn. XIX) phon. *ḥtm*,[2] ex. var. *ḥtm* 'perish'.

[1] *Pyr.* 872. [2] *ÄZ.* 46, 107. [3] *ÄZ.* 46, 92. [4] LAC. *TR.* 43, 4; Coffins, M 4 C, 144.

2 portable seat (sometimes reversed)[1] — Ideo. in [2] *st* 'seat' (rare). Phon. *ws* (*wś*) in rarer var. [3] *Wsỉr* 'Osiris'.

[1] Exx. Cairo 20023. 34049. 34085. [2] *Kopt.* 7, 16, *a.* [3] *ÄZ.* 46, 94.

3 stool of reed matting[1] — Cf. [2] *p* 'base' (for shrine), Ptolemaic [3] *p* 'seat', Coptic *pŏï* 'bench'. Hence phon. *p*.[4]

[1] Depicted *Th. T. S.* i. 15; the earliest forms suggest a stool-covering rather than an actual stool, but exx. of Dyn. II favour the latter, see PETR. *Eg. Hier.* Pl. 38.
[2] *Urk.* iv. 834, 6. [3] DÜMICHEN, *Resultat* 51, 19. [4] SETHE, *Alphabet* 152.

For see M 7.

4 head-rest — Det. in *wrs* (*wrś*)[1] 'head-rest'.

[1] For *ś* see *Saqq. Mast.* i. 1.

5 chest (varies much in form)[1] — Det. box, chest, exx. *hn* 'box'; *ꜥfdt* 'chest'.

[1] Exx. *Bersh.* i. 10. 15; *Urk.* iv. 427, 6; PETR. *Abyd.* ii. 34.

6 coffin (varies much in form)[1] — Ideo. or det. in var. *ḳrsw* (*ḳrśw*) 'coffin'. Det. in *ḳrs* 'bury'.

[1] Exx. *BH.* i. 12; *Puy.* 60. 68.

7 brazier with flame rising from it[1] — Det. fire, exx. *ḫt* 'fire'; *sḏt* 'flame'; heat, exx. *rkḥ* 'heat'; *tꜣ* 'hot'; cook, etc., exx. *psỉ* 'cook' (§ 281); *ꜣbw* 'brand'; torch, in *tkꜣ* 'torch', 'candle'. Also abbrev. [2] for *srf* (*śrf*) 'temperature'; *nsrsr* (*nśrśr*) in [3] *'Iw-nsrsr*, a mythical locality.

[1] *Meir* ii. p. 34. [2] *Eb.* 24, 6 = 46, 10. [3] See the varr. NAV. 110, 17. 19.

Sect. R. Temple Furniture and Sacred Emblems

R 1 [1] table with loaves and jug

Ideo. or det. in [2] *ḫꜣwt*, varr. ,[3] [4] *ḫꜣt*, 'table of offerings'.

[1] *D. el B.* 37. Often the round loaf is on the left, exx. *Paheri* 4; *Urk.* iv. 163, 7. [2] *Siut* I, 240. [3] See on L 6. [4] Cairo 20667.

2 [1] table with conventionalized slices of bread (alternative form of last)

Ideo. or det. in [2] *ḫꜣy(t)*, varr. ,[3] [4] *ḫꜣt*, 'table of offerings'.

[1] Ex. *D. el B.* 140. Sim. O.K., *Sah.* 63. [2] Louvre C 11, 7. [3] *D. el B.* 140. [4] Cairo 20712, *a* 6.

3 four-legged table with loaves and libation vase [1]

Ideo. or det. in [2] *wdḥw* (§ 19, Obs. 2), var. Pyr. [3] *wdḥw*, 'table of offerings'. Also as abbrev., especially in the title [4] *sš wdḥw* 'scribe of the offering-table'.

[1] Forms differ considerably, but in M.E. the four-legged table is characteristic of *wdḥw*, while *ḫꜣwt* has the forms shown under R 1. 2. Dyn. XII, see *Hier.* 8, no. 126; *BH.* iii. 3, no. 21; Dyn. XVIII, *Paheri* 7; Northampt. 3, 7. [2] *Bersh.* i. 12. [3] *Pyr.* 474. [4] Cairo 20023, *n*; 20562, *g*; reading proved by *ib.* 20671, *b*.

4 loaf X 2 on a reed-mat

Ideo. in [1] var. O.K. [2] *ḥtp* 'altar'. Hence semi-phon. *ḥtp* in *ḥtp* 'rest', 'be pleased' and derivatives; the writing is not uncommon in M.K. proper names and occurs also in a hieratic ligature of the same date.[3]

[1] Brit. Mus. 590. [2] *Urk.* i. 107, 17. [3] Ex. *Leb.* 23; see *ÄZ.* 29, 54.

5 [1] censer for fumigation [2] (after O.K. doubtless misunderstood)

Ideo. or det. in var. Pyr. [3] *kꜣp* 'fumigate'. Hence phon. *kꜣp*, ex. var. [4] *kꜣp* 'harîm', 'nursery'; *kp*, ex. [5] *Kpny* 'Byblus', a town in Phoenicia.

[1] Ex. Dyn. XVIII, *D. el B.* 139. The same form, but reversed, already Dyn. V, *Saqq. Mast.* i. 21. Sometimes in Dyn. XVIII somewhat resembles a wrist and hand, exx. *Two Sculptors* 8; *Urk.* iv. 997, 6; later interpreted as a claw. [2] *ÄZ.* 50, 66. [3] *Pyr.* 184. Sim. *ib.* 803. [4] *Urk.* iv. 997, 6. Sim. *kꜣpw* 'crocodile', *Pt.* 262. [5] *Urk.* iv. 535, 6; *Sin.* R 53.

6 [1] O.K. form of last

Use as last.

[1] *Ti* 132, over a scene of fumigation.

7 [1] bowl for incense with smoke rising from it

Ideo. or det. in [2] abbrev. [3] *sntr* 'incense'. Also as equivalent of O.K. W 10* (= Pyr. Aa 4) in [4] var. [5] *bꜣ* 'soul'; also in *bꜣ* 'ram'.[6]

[1] See *Hier.* p. 43. Depicted *Meir* iii. 17. [2] *Urk.* iv. 943, 12. [3] *Paheri* 5; *Urk.* iv. 914, 9. [4] *Urk.* iv. 114, 3. [5] *Urk.* iv. 945, 2. [6] *Wb.* i. 414.

R 8 cloth wound on a pole, emblem of divinity[1] — Ideo. in *nṯr* 'god'. Hence phon. (semi-ideo.) *nṯr*, ex. *nṯry*. var. Pyr. [2] *nṯr(ỉ)*, 'divine'. Very rarely det. for a god, ex. [3] *Gbb* 'Geb', Gk. Κῆβ.

[1] See NEWBERRY, *JEA*. 33, 90; *Meir* ii. p. 35; *Saqq. Mast.* i. p. 45. [2] *Pyr.* 533. [3] *ÄZ.* 43, 148.

9 combination of R 8 and V 33 — Ideo. or det. in var. [1] *bd* '(a kind of) natron'.

[1] *D. el B.* 10. In Pyr. ideo. in *nṯr* 'nitre' (*Pyr.* 1368), det. in *ḥzmn* 'natron' (*ib.*).

10 [1] combination of R 8 and T 28 and N 29 — Ideo. in var. *ẖr(t)-nṯr*[2] 'necropolis'.

[1] Ex. *Paheri* 3. [2] *JEA.* 24, 244.

11 column imitating a bundle of stalks tied together[1] — Ideo. in *ḏd* '*djed*-column'. Hence phon. *ḏd* in var. Pyr. [2] *ḏdỉ* 'be stable', 'enduring' and derivatives. The twofold writing of the sign in the town-name doubtless indicates the change of value from *ḏd* to *dd*, see the varr. § 289, 1.

[1] SCHÄFER, *Griff. Stud.* 424; early exx. as architectural ornament, *Ann.* 25, Pl. 5; 27, Pl. 2. [2] *Pyr.* 1078.

12 standard for carrying religious symbols — Det. in *ỉꜣt* 'standard'. Also accompanying various ideograms for gods, exx. *Mnw* '(the god) Min'; *Ḥꜣ* '(the god) Ḥa'. Cf. also D 29; E 18; G 7; G 26; R 13.

13 [1] falcon G 5 on R 12 with feather (O.K. to Dyn. XII) — As emblem of the West, ideo. in *ỉmnt* 'west' and the related words. For the reading compare Pyr. [2] *ỉmn* 'right', 'right-hand'.

[1] *Sah.* 5. The forms differ greatly, see SETHE, *Rechts* 211. Exx. Dyn. XI, PETR. *Abyd.* ii. 24. 25. [2] *Pyr.* 730.

14 abbrev. of last, omitting falcon and enlarging feather (from Dyn. VI onward)[1] — Ideo. in *ỉmnt* 'west' and related words, including var. *wnmy*, var. Pyr. [2] *wnmỉ*, 'right' hand, side, etc.

[1] SETHE, *Rechts* 215. [2] *Pyr.* 1002. See SETHE, *Rechts* 199.

15 spear decked out as standard[1] — As emblem of the East, ideo. in *ỉꜣbt* 'east' and related words, ex. *ỉꜣby*, varr. Pyr. , [2] *ỉꜣbỉ*, 'left-hand'. From Dyn. XVIII on, by confusion with U 23, phon. *ꜣb*, exx. [3] *Ꜣbḏw* 'Abydus'; *ꜣb·n* 'has desired'.[4]

[1] SETHE, *Rechts* 220. [2] *Pyr.* 730. [3] *Urk.* iv. 11, 49. [4] *Urk.* iv. 28, 1.

16 papyrus-shaped wand with feathers[1] — Ideo. or det. in var. *wḫ* 'the *wḫ*-fetish' of Cusae in Upper Egypt.

[1] With many variant forms, see *Meir* i. p. 2; ii. p. 38.

R 17 [hieroglyph] wig, with fillet and plumes, on pole[1] (Dyn. XVIII) — Fetish of Abydus, ideo. or det. in [hieroglyph] var. [hieroglyphs][2] *Tꜣ-wr* 'the nome of Abydus *or* This'.

[1] See WINLOCK, *Bas-reliefs from the temple of Rameses I at Abydos*, p. 15.
[2] *Urk.* iv. 111, 13.

18 [hieroglyph] variant form of last — Use as last.

19 [hieroglyph] the *uas*-sceptre [hieroglyph] S 40 with fillet and feather — As emblem of the Upper Egyptian nome of Hermonthis and its town, ideo. in [hieroglyphs] *Wꜣst* (*Wꜣśt*),[1] var. Dyn. XX [hieroglyphs][2] *Ws*(*r*), 'Thebes'. For [hieroglyphs] *ỉꜣtt* 'milk' see on S 40.

[1] Reading further proved by demotic, see MÖLLER, *Die beiden Totenpapyrus Rhind*, p. 76*, no. 538. Cf. -*oïs* in the name Χαμοΐς = *Ḫꜥ-m-Wꜣst*, GRIFFITH, *Stories of the High Priests of Memphis*, p. 2, n. 2. [2] Brit. Mus. 303.

20 [hieroglyph][1] conventionalized flower (?) surmounted by horns — As emblem of the goddess of writing ideo. in [hieroglyphs][2] *Sšꜣt*, var. Pyr. [hieroglyphs][3] *Śšꜣt*, late var. [hieroglyphs][4] *Sšt*, '(the goddess) Seshat'.

[1] *D. el B.* 55. [2] *Urk.* iv. 19, 14. [3] *Pyr.* 616. [4] Louvre A 97, qu. *PSBA.* 16, 252.

21 [hieroglyph][1] O.K. form of last — Use as last.

[1] *Saqq. Mast.* i. 1 (Dyn. III–IV).

22 [hieroglyph] two fossil belemnites?[1] — As emblem of the god of Panopolis (Ekhmîm) and of Coptus (Ḳifṭ) ideo. in [hieroglyph] varr. [hieroglyphs], [hieroglyphs] var. Pyr. [hieroglyphs][2] *Mnw* '(the god) Min', Greek Μῖν.[3] The name of Letopolis (Ausîm) in the Delta [hieroglyphs][4] reads *Ḫm*, as the var. Pyr. [hieroglyphs][5] shows; from M.K. onwards [hieroglyph] O 34 is often substituted for [hieroglyph], ex. [hieroglyphs], see on O 34. Hence phon. *ḫm* in [hieroglyphs] var. [hieroglyphs][6] *ḫm* 'shrine'.

[1] *Annals of Archaeology and Anthropology* (Liverpool) 3, 50. The earliest exx. resemble a double-headed arrow. [2] *Pyr.* 424. [3] PLUTARCH, *De Iside* 56. [4] Cairo 20221; sim. *Pyr.* 1270. [5] *Pyr.* 1670. For the localization at Ausîm see *Ann.* 4, 91; *Rec.* 26, 144. [6] *Urk.* iv. 96, 4. This word has no connexion with the Gk. town-name Chemmis and its modern descendant Ekhmîm, the Egyptian original of which was *Ḫnt-Mnw*, see *ÄZ.* 62, 92; *AEO.* ii. 40*.

23 [hieroglyph][1] O.K. form of last — Use as last.

[1] *Saqq. Mast.* i. 8.

24 [hieroglyph][1] two bows tied in a package[2] (sometimes also vertically [hieroglyph]) — As emblem of the goddess of Sais, ideo. or det. in [hieroglyphs][3] varr. [hieroglyphs],[4] [hieroglyph] *Nt* (*Nrt*, *Nìt*)[5] '(the goddess) Neith'.

[1] *D. el B.* 116. [2] *Ancient Egypt* 1921, 35. [3] *Urk.* iv. 414, 5. [4] *D. el B.* 116. [5] Reading, *ÄZ.* 43, 144. The Gk. form Νηῖθ suggests a medial *ì* or *r*.

25 [hieroglyph][1] O.K. form of last — Use as last.

[1] *Ti* 46.

Sect. S. Crowns, Dress, Staves, etc.

S 1 [hieroglyph] white crown of Upper Egypt [0] — Ideo. or det. in [hieroglyphs] [1] var. [hieroglyph] [2] *ḥdt* 'the white crown'. Det. white crown, exx. [hieroglyphs] [3] *šmʿ-s* 'crown of Upper Egypt'; [hieroglyphs] [4] *wrrt* 'great crown'.

[0] ABUBAKR, 25. [1] *Urk.* iv. 16, 8. [2] *Sebekkhu* 12; BRUNTON, *Lahun I* 15. [3] *Urk.* iv. 266, 8. [4] CAPART, *Recueil de Monuments* i. 30.

2 [hieroglyph] the last in basket [hieroglyph] V 30 — Ideo. or det. in [hieroglyphs] [1] var. [hieroglyph] [2] *ḥdt* 'white crown'. Det. white crown, in [hieroglyphs] [3] *wrrt* 'great crown'.

[1] LAC. *TR.* 89, 35. [2] *Kopt.* 8, 8. [3] *Urk.* iv. 16, 11.

3 [hieroglyph] red crown of Lower Egypt [0] — Ideo. or det. in [hieroglyphs] [1] var. [hieroglyph] [2] *dšrt* 'red crown'. Det. red crown, ex. [hieroglyphs] [3] *mḥ-s* 'crown of Lower Egypt'. From Pyr. [hieroglyphs] [4] *nt* 'crown of Lower Egypt' phon. *n*, rare before Dyn. XVIII.[5] Substituted for [hieroglyph] L 2 for superstitious reasons [6] in [hieroglyphs] [7] *sḏꜣwty* (?) *bỉty* 'treasurer of the king of Lower Egypt'; also in [hieroglyphs] [8] *n-sw-bỉt* 'king of Upper and Lower Egypt'.

[0] ABUBAKR, 47. [1] *Urk.* iv. 16, 8. [2] *Sebekkhu* 12. [3] *Urk.* iv. 266, 8. [4] *Pyr.* 724. [5] See p. 27, n. 4. [6] *ÄZ.* 51, 57. [7] *Kopt.* 8, 11. [8] *Urk.* iv. 150, 12.

4 [hieroglyph] the last in basket [hieroglyph] V 30 — Det. red crown, exx. [hieroglyphs] [1] *nt* '*net*-crown'; [hieroglyphs] [2] *mḥ-s* 'crown of Lower Egypt'. Very rarely phon. *n*,[3] like [hieroglyph] S 3.

[1] Brit. Mus. 574, 8. Sim. *Pyr.* 724. [2] Brit. Mus. 574, 6. [3] Dyn. XII, *ÄZ.* 45, 125; Dyn. XVIII, *Urk.* iv. 309, 12.

5 [hieroglyph] combined white and red crowns [0] — Det. double crown in [hieroglyphs] [1] *sḫmty* 'the double crown' of Upper and Lower Egypt, lit. 'the two powerful ones', in Greek ψχέντ [2] (*pꜣ-sḫmty*).

[0] ABUBAKR, 60; *OLZ.* 35, 698. [1] *P. Boul* xvii. 3, 3. [2] Rosetta stone.

6 [hieroglyph] the last in basket [hieroglyph] V 30 — Ideo. or det. double crown, exx. [hieroglyphs] [1] var. [hieroglyph] [2] *sḫmty* 'the double crown'; [hieroglyphs] [3] *wrrt* 'the great crown'.

[1] *Urk.* iv. 565, 14. [2] *Urk.* iv. 278, 6. [3] *Urk.* iv. 255, 7.

7 [hieroglyph] the blue crown [1] — Ideo. or det. in [hieroglyphs] [2] var. [hieroglyph] [3] *ḫprš* 'the blue crown'.

[1] *ÄZ.* 53, 59. [2] *P. Boul.* xvii. 3, 3–4. [3] BR. *Thes.* 1077.

8 [hieroglyph] the *atef*-crown [1] — Ideo. or det. in [hieroglyphs] [2] var. [hieroglyph] [2] *ꜣtf* 'the *atef*-crown'.

[1] ABUBAKR, 7; an early ex. *Sah.* 38, Dyn. V. [2] *Rec.* 39, 117.

9 [hieroglyph] two plumes — Ideo. or det. in [hieroglyphs] [1] var. [hieroglyph] [2] *šwty* 'double plumes'.

[1] *Urk.* iv. 111, 8. [2] *Urk.* iv. 48, 6.

S 10 band of cloth as fillet

Ideo. or det. wreath, exx. [1] *wꜣḥw* 'wreath'; [2] var. var. O.K. [3] *mḏḥ* 'fillet'. From this last, phon. *mḏḥ* (*mdḥ*) in [4] *mḏḥ*, var. [5] *mdḥ*, 'hew' and the related noun [6] varr. [7] [8] *mḏḥ*(*w*) 'carpenter', 'shipwright'.

[1] Brit. Mus. 826. [2] Brit. Mus. 828, in this and the ex. quoted under 3 often wrongly translated 'girdle'. [3] *Urk.* i. 98, 12, in the phrase *ṯs mḏḥ* as above n. 2. [4] *Urk.* iv. 56, 13. [5] *Urk.* iv. 778, 14. Sim. *mḏḥ*, *ib.* 707, 14. [6] Cairo 588. [7] Cairo 20441. [8] Brit. Mus. 223.

11 collar of beads with falcon-headed terminals

Ideo. or det. in [1] var. [2] *wsḫ* (*wśḫ*) 'collar'. Hence occasionally phon. or phon. det. *wsḫ* (*wśḫ*), exx. [3] *wsḫ* 'breadth'; [4] *swsḫ* 'widen'.

[1] Cairo 20539, ii. *b* 8. [2] *Mitt.* 8, 17; *Urk.* iv. 54, 3. [3] *Urk.* iv. 142, 10. [4] *Urk.* iv. 83, 3.

12 collar of beads

Depicted with the name *nbyt* 'collar'.[1] Hence ideo. in var. [2] *nbw* [3] 'gold' and the related words. Det. precious metal, exx. *ḏʿm* 'fine gold'; *ḥḏ* 'silver'.

[1] Jéq. 60; *Rec.* 35, 231. [2] *BH.* i. 8, 13. [3] Reading from Coptic *noub* 'gold', etc. See too *ÄZ.* 8, 20.

13 combination of S 12 and D 58

Ex. [1] *nbi* 'gild', 'fashion'.

[1] Brit. Mus. 826, 3.

14 combination of S 12 and T 3

In *ḥḏ* 'silver', Coptic ϩⲁⲧ.

14* combination of S 12 and S 40

In *ḏʿm* 'fine gold', see under S 40, 41.

15 [1] pectoral of glass or fayence beads (Dyn. XVIII form)

Ideo. or det. in *ṯḥnt*, var. var. O.K. [2] *ṯḥnt*, 'fayence', 'glass', and in other words from the stem *ṯḥn* 'sparkle', 'be dazzling'.

[1] Möll. *Pal.* ii. no. 417. [2] Mar. *Mast.* 113.

16 [1] O.K. form of last

Use as last.

[1] Mar. *Mast.* 113, qu. under S 15.

17 [1] another O.K. form of S 15

Use as last.

[1] *Pyr.* 454 (W 563).

18 [1] bead-necklace with counterpoise

Ideo. or det. in var. *mnỉt* 'bead-necklace', '*menat*'.[2]

[1] *Puy.* 53. 54. [2] Gard. *Sin.* 100.

S19 cylinder-seal attached to bead-necklace[1] — Ideo. in var. *sḏ3wty* (?)[2] 'treasurer', plur. [3] *sḏ3wtyw* (?), and in the related [4] *sḏ3w* (?) 'precious'.

[1] *ÄZ.* 35, 106. [2] Reading doubtful; see *ÄZ.* 32, 66; 36, 146; 37, 86. [3] Munich 3, 15, qu. § 212. [4] GARD. *Sin.* 111.

20 cylinder-seal attached to bead-necklace (as seen from the front)[1] — Ideo. or det. in var. [2] *ḫtm* 'seal' and related words. Det. seal, in [3] *sḏ3yt* 'seal'; *ḏbꜥt* 'signet-ring'. Ideo. or det. in var. *šꜥty* 'seal', a unit of value (§ 266, 4). Also as substitute for S 19, ex. *sḏ3wty* (?) *bity* 'treasurer of the king of Lower Egypt';[4] also as substitute for E 31 (*sꜥḥ*).[5]

[1] *ÄZ.* 35, 106. [2] Cairo 20056, *c*, in the title *sš ḥr ḫtm.* [3] *Siut* 5, 7. [4] Already PETR. *RT.* i. 11, 14; 31, 43; JUNKER, *Gîza I*, 149. [5] *Wb.* iv. 49, exx. *Pyr.* 219; Cairo 20520, *d* 6; BUDGE, 241, 3.

21 ring (possibly a plain finger-ring) — Det. ring, ex. *iwꜥw*, var. *ꜥꜥw*, 'ring'.[1] A similar, if not identical, sign in [2] *sšw* 'ring' (of silver).

[1] *Wb.* i. 51. [2] *Urk.* iv. 701, 12.

22 [1] shoulder-knot[2] — Phon. *sṯ* (*šṯ*), ex. *Sṯt*, var. *Stt*, (1) 'Asia', (2) 'Sehêl', an island in the First Cataract;[3] also *st* in [4] var. *sti* 'pour'. Also, for unknown reason, ideo. or det. in O.K. [5] var. [6] *t3-wr* 'larboard'; here later apparently replaced by O 17.[7]

[1] *Puy.* 36. [2] *Ann.* 29, 33. [3] *ÄZ.* 45, 24 [4] Brit. Mus. 1164, 8. [5] *Ti* 78. 79. See BOREUX, *Études de nautique* 435, n. 8. [6] L. *D.* ii. 96. [7] Already Dyn. VI, *Gebr.* ii. 7.

17*[1] girdle as worn by various gods (Pyr.)[2] — Ideo. in name of the goddess [3] *Šsmtt* (*Šzmtt*) 'Shesmetet'. Phon. *šsm* in [4] *šsmt* 'malachite'; also in [5] *T3-Šsmt* 'To-Shesmet', a region E. of Egypt.

[1] *Pyr.* 1136. In M.E. the form varies greatly (two varr. in above text), sometimes approximating to S 22 or even to S 12. [2] *Griff. Stud.* 316. [3] *Op. cit.* 318; *Rec. trav.* 24, 198. [4] *Urk.* iv. 875. [5] BIRCH, *Alnwick Castle*, Pl. 4.

23 knotted strips of cloth[1] — Ideo. or det. in *dmd*, var. var. Pyr. [2] *dmḏ*, 'unite' and derivatives. Different from Aa 6.

[1] This conventionalized form, *Rekh.* 3; earlier forms, *ÄZ.* 39, 84. [2] *Pyr.* 1036.

24 girdle knot[1] — Ideo. in [2] *ṯst* (1) 'knot', (2) 'vertebra'. Hence semi-ideo. in *ṯs*, var. Pyr. [3] *ṯz*, 'tie', 'bind' and derivatives.

[1] *ÄZ.* 49, 120. [2] *M.u.K.* 8, 3. [3] *Pyr.* 1805.

25 [1] a garment — Cf. O.K. *iꜥ3*, var. *i3ꜥ*, 'skirt (?)'.[2] Hence (?) varr. , , *ꜥ3w* 'dragoman'.

[1] *PSBA.* 37, 117. 246. The sign varies considerably in form. [2] *Wb.* i. 27.

S 26 apron — Ideo. or det. in var. [1] *šndyt*, var. Pyr. [2] *šnḏwt*, 'apron'.

[1] *Rekh.* 4. [2] *Pyr.* 369.

(N 18)[1] a garment — Ideo. or det. in [2] var. [3] *dȝiw* 'loin-cloth'.

[1] *ÄZ.* 49, 106. A form also occurs, *Dend.* 3. [2] *Peas.* Butler 29; *Westc.* 10, 2. [3] *P. Berl.* 10003, 24, in MÖLL. *Pal.* i. Pl. 5.

27 [1] horizontal strip of cloth with two strands of a fringe[2] — Ideo. or det. in [3] var. [4] *mnḫt* 'clothing'.

[1] Sometimes with three (*Urk.* iv. 175, 3) or more strands. [2] JÉQ. 38. That the vertical signs are strands, not single threads, is shown by *Medum* 16. [3] Turin 1447. [4] See p. 172.

28 strip of cloth with fringe, combined with the folded cloth S 29[1] — Det. in *ḥbs* (*ḥbś*) 'clothe', 'clothing'. Det. cloth, ex. *insy* 'red cloth'; *nms* 'head-cloth'; notions connected with clothing, exx. *ḥȝy* 'naked'; *ḥȝp* 'conceal'; *kfi* 'uncover'.

[1] O.K. forms supporting this interpretation are: DAV. *Ptah.* i. 14, no. 288; *Saqq. Mast.* i. 21; L. *D.* ii. 163, *a.* For variant forms appearing to combine V 33 and S 29 see *Ti* 111; PETRIE, *Gizeh and Rifeh* 13 G.

29 folded cloth[1] — Phon. *s* (*ś*); the originating word is unknown. Abbrev. for *snb* in the formula *ʿnḫ wḏȝ snb* 'may he live, be prosperous, be healthy' (§§ 55. 313).

[1] *ÄZ.* 44, 76. This cloth is seen in the hands of many statues and was probably used as a handkerchief, *Rec.* 21, 26. See too *ÄZ.* 58, 151.

30 combination of S 29 and I 9 — Phon. *sf* in *sf* 'yesterday'.

31 combination of S 29 and U 1 — Phon. *smȝ*, ex. [1] *smȝ* 'fighting bull'.

[1] *Urk.* iv. 2, 13.

32 [1] piece of cloth with fringe[2] — Ideo. or det. in [3] *siȝt*, var. Pyr. [4] *šiȝt*, 'piece of cloth'. Hence phon. *siȝ* (*šiȝ*) in *siȝ*, var. O.K. [5] *šiȝ*, 'recognize'.

[1] Thebes, tomb 55. [2] JÉQ. 33. [3] LAC. *Sarc.* i. 111. [4] *Pyr.* 2044. [5] *Urk.* i. 128, 5.

33 sandal — Ideo. or det. in [1] var. Pyr. [2] *ṯbt*, var. Dyn. XVIII [3] *tbt*, 'sandal'. Hence semi-phon. or phon. det. *ṯb*, later *tb*, in [4] *ṯb* 'be shod'; [5] *ṯbw* 'sandal-maker'.

[1] Cairo 20318, *b* 7. [2] *Pyr.* 578. [3] *Urk.* iv. 390, 16. [4] LAC. *TR.* 23, 19; Dyn. XVIII, *tb*, Leyd. V 38. [5] MÖLL. *HL.* i. 18, qu. p. 354, n. 4.

S 34 ☥ tie or strap, especially sandal-strap [1] (as symbol of life known as 'the *ankh*') — Ideo. in ☥ [2] *ˁnḫ* 'sandal-strap'; semi-ideo. (from resemblance) in ☥ [3] *ˁnḫ* 'mirror', etc. Hence phon. *ˁnḫ*, ex. ☥ *ˁnḫ* 'live'; for the initial *ˁ* cf. Ptolemaic var. [4] *ˁnḫy* and demotic.

[1] HASTINGS, *Encyclopedia of Religion and Ethics*, art. Life (Egyptian); *Revue archéologique*, 1925, 101; against this view, SCHÄFER, *Griff. Stud.* 426. [2] LAC. *Sarc.* ii. 158. [3] *Adm.* 8, 5. [4] DÜMICHEN, *Tempelinschriften* i. 37, 2.

(V 39) [1] tie or straps with a different arrangement of the same elements as ☥ S 34 — Ideo. in [2] late var. [3] *tit* 'the *tyet*-amulet'.[4]

[1] *Griff. Stud.* 426; *Mitt. Kairo* iv. 2. From Dyn. III found as decorative symbol in company with ☥ S 34 and R 11† to signify 'life', 'welfare', or like. [2] BUDGE, p. 403, 3. 7. [3] *B. of D.* ed. LEPSIUS, Pl. 75; also as enigmatic sign for *-t(i)* in writing of the name of Sethos I, *Ann.* 40, 310. [4] Of red jasper or glass, in *B. of D.* ch. 156 connected with Isis, see *ÄZ.* 15, 33; 62, 108.

35 sunshade of ostrich feathers — Ideo. in [1] var. Pyr. [2] *šwt* 'shadow', 'shade'. Ideo. or det. in [3] var. [4] *sryt* '(military) standard'.

[1] *Urk.* iv. 1165, 16. Whether this writing has ever to be read *ḫiybt*, another word for 'shadow' found in Dyn. XX and perhaps earlier, is very doubtful; see *ÄZ.* 39, 120. The actual word for 'sunshade' *bht* is not attested before Dyn. XIX; the older *nft* (*Wb.* ii. 250, 10) means 'fan'. [2] *Pyr.* 1487. [3] *Th. T. S.* iii. 21. [4] *Th. T. S.* iii. 23.

36 [1] O.K. form of last (common also in M.E.[2]) — Use as last. In the rare divine name *Ḥp(wy)* 'Hepui', doubtless a personification of the two sunshades accompanying the king;[3] the reading is ascertained from varr. of a very late word showing the signs before that of the fan.[4]

[1] Leyd. *Denkm.* i. 7. [2] Dyn. XII, *ÄZ.* 39, 117, 8; Dyn. XVIII, *Th. T. S.* i. 23. [3] *JEA.* 30, 29, with n. 4; *ÄZ.* 77, 24. [4] *Wb.* iii. 69, 11.

37 short-handled fan [1] — Ideo. or det. in [2] var. [3] *ḫw* 'fan'.

[1] See the pictures *Th. T. S.* iii. 12. 28. [2] *Th. T. S.* iv. 38, G. [3] Commonly so in the title *ṯiy ḫw* 'fan-bearer', ex. *Amarn.* i. 34.

38 crook [0] — Ideo. or det. in varr. [1] [2] *ḥḳ(i)t* 'sceptre'. Hence phon. *ḥḳi*, exx. var. *ḥḳi* 'rule'; *ḥḳit* '*ḥekat*-measure' (§ 266, 1). Also usually replaces the *awet*-sceptre S 39 [3] in hieroglyphic writing, exx. [4] *ˁwt* 'flock(s)'; Pyr. [5] *ˁwt* '*awet*-sceptre'. From the stem *iśḳ* found in two Pyr. words [6] comes the rare divine name var. [7] *iḳs* 'Akes', personification of some part of the royal apparel, later reading *Ḥḳs*.[8]

[0] See NEWBERRY, *JEA.* 15, 84. [1] Cairo 28087, no. 73. [2] On the radical *i* to be understood here see *Rec.* 25, 142. [3] Even in the pictures of the *awet*-sceptre, see Cairo 28083, no. 59; 28087, no. 74, both in LAC. *Sarc.* i. Pl. 45. [4] Exx. O.K., *Gemn.* i. 15; Dyn. XII, *Bersh.* i. 7; Dyn. XVIII, *Th. T. S.* i. 9. [5] *Pyr.* 202. [6] *Wb.* i. 33, 14. 15. [7] DE BUCK, i. 184 f. [8] *JEA.* 30, 29, n. 3; 31, 116; *ÄZ.* 77, 24.

S 39 peasant's crook (N.B. not curved backward like S 38) — Cf. *ˁwt*, name of the sceptre of the shape .[1] Usually replaced in hieroglyphic writing by S 38, but occasionally phon. *ˁwt*, ex. *ˁwt* 'flocks'.[2]

[1] Cairo 28034, no. 69 = LAC. *Sarc.* i. Pl. 45. [2] *Bersh.* i. 27. Sim. O.K., Berl *ÄI.* i. p. 76, 1; DAV. *Ptah.* ii. 18.

40 sceptre with straight shaft and head of Seth (?)-animal[1] (cf. too R 19) — Ideo. or det. in *wꜣs*, var. Pyr. [2] *wꜣś*, '*uas*-sceptre'; hence phon. or phon. det. *wꜣs* (*wꜣś*), ex. varr. , [3] *wꜣsi* 'decay'. In hieroglyphic writing usually represents also the *djam*-sceptre S 41, exx. *dˁm* '*djam*-sceptre',[4] whence phon. *dˁm* in varr. , *dˁm*[5] 'fine gold'. Phon. *wꜣb* (?) in *Wꜣb*(*wy*) (?) 'the Oxyrhynchite nome', on the evidence of a twice found name of a locality [6] *Wꜣbwt*. Phon. *iꜣtt* in [7] varr. [8], [9] *iꜣtt* 'milk', 'cream'.[10]

[1] JÉQ. 176. [2] *Pyr.* 1156. [3] *Urk.* iv. 765, 13 For this curious var. see *ÄZ.* 41, 75. [4] *Pyr.* 1456; LAC. *TR.* 19, 50. [5] Reading, *ÄZ.* 41, 73; 44, 132; see too under S 41. [6] *Hamm.* 114, 11; 192, 13; see KEES, *Gött. Nachr.* 1932, 107. [7] Munich 3, 3. [8] *BH.* i. 17. [9] Turin 1513. [10] *Wb.* i. 27; reading from the name of a goddess *Iꜣt*, see *Pyr.* 131.

For see R 19; for see S 14*.

41 sceptre with spiral shaft and head of Seth (?)-animal[1] — Cf. *dˁm*, name of a sceptre of the form .[2] Hence phon. *dˁm*, occasionally in inscriptions of Dyn. XVIII in [3] *dˁmw* 'fine gold'.

[1] JÉQ. 176; the spiral is well seen in DE MORGAN, *Dahchour 1894*, p. 96, Fig. 224. [2] Ex. Cairo 28034, no. 65 = LAC. *Sarc.* i. Pl. 45. [3] *Urk.* iv. 421, 11. See *ÄZ.* 44, 132.

42 sceptre of authority[1] (it is impossible to distinguish separate forms for the various uses) — Ideo. or det. in var. [2] *ˁbꜣ* '*aba*-sceptre'; hence phon. or phon. det. *ˁbꜣ*, exx. [3] var. [4] *ˁbꜣ* 'stela'; *ˁb*(*ꜣ*) 'shine'. From a sceptre named [5] *sḫm* (*śḫm*), '*sekhem*-sceptre', phon. *sḫm* (*śḫm*), exx. var. [6] *sḫm* 'have power'; very late var. *sḫm* 'sistrum'.[7] Ideo. or det. in var. *ḫrp* 'be at head', 'control' and related words, cf. D 44. In titles is possibly always to be read *ḫrp*; at all events this reading is verifiable in some cases, exx. var. *ḫrp nsty* 'controller of the two seats', a priestly title;[8] *ḫrp kꜣt* 'controller of works', cf. *ḫrp kꜣt* 'to undertake works', 'constructions'.[9]

[1] JÉQ. 181; as hieroglyph, *Hier.* p. 57. [2] *Pyr.* 866. [3] *Leb.* 63. [4] Cairo 20061. Sim. Brit. Mus. 101. [5] LAC. *Sarc.* ii. p. 168. [6] *Rekh.* 2, 9. [7] GARD. *Sin.* 102–3. [8] *ÄZ.* 47, 91. Sim. *ḫrp srḳt* 'controller of the scorpion', *PSBA.* 39, 34; *ḫrp šndwt nbt* 'controller of all aprons', PETRIE, *Gizeh and Rifeh* 27 O, recto 2, compared with *Rekh.* 4. [9] See Louvre C 172, qu. Exerc. XIII, (*a*).

S 43 walking-stick[1] — Ideo. in [2] var. Pyr. [3] *md(w)* 'walking-stick', 'staff'. Hence phon. *md* in var. Pyr. [4] *m(w)dw*[5] 'speak' and derivatives.

[1] JÉQ. 159. Important for the use as a walking-stick is the title *mdw iȝw* 'staff of old age', GRIFFITH, *Kahun Papyri*, p. 30. [2] LAC. *TR.* 23, 21. [3] *Pyr.* 1144. [4] *Pyr.* 1014. [5] Reading, *Verbum* i. § 481.

44 [1] walking-stick with flagellum S 45[2] — Ideo. or det. in var. *ȝms* (*ȝmś*) '*ames*-sceptre'.

[1] Ex. *Medum*, frontispiece. [2] JÉQ. 163; *Wb.* i. 11.

45 flagellum; perhaps originally an instrument used by goatherds for collecting ladanum[1] — Ideo. or det. in [2] *nḫḫw*, varr. [3] [4] *nḫȝḫȝ*, 'flagellum'.

[1] NEWBERRY, *JEA.* 15, 86; see too JÉQ. 187; the conventional name 'flagellum' is here retained. [2] NAV. ch. 182, 14. [3] LAC. *Sarc.* ii. 164. Cf. *nḫȝḫȝ* 'shake', *Pyr.* 2204. [4] Leyd. *Denkm.* iv. 28.

Sect. T. Warfare, Hunting, Butchery

T 1 [1] prehistoric mace with cup- or dish-shaped head[2] — Cf. *mnw* 'mace', name of this type of mace on M.K. coffins.[3] Hence phon. *mnw*, exx. var. Pyr. [3a] *m n·k* 'take to thyself' (§ 336); var. *Swmnw*, var. *Smnw*, 'Sumenu', a town where Sobk was worshipped, possibly Er-Rizeiḳât, 14 km. N. of Gebelên.[4]

[1] *Puy.* 57. [2] WOLF, *Bewaffnung* 4; SCHARFF 25. [3] LAC. *Sarc.* ii. 162; JÉQ. 201. [3a] *Pyr.* 912. [4] *AEO.* ii. 275*.

2 [1] mace with pear-shaped head[2] in act of smiting — Det. in *sḳr* (*śḳr*),[3] var. *sḳ(r)i*, 'smite'.

[1] Ex. O.K., *Sah.* 1. [2] WOLF, *Bewaffnung* 4. [3] *Urk.* iv. 780, 11

3 mace with pear-shaped head[1] (vertical) — Ideo. in [2] var. [3] *ḥḏ* 'mace'. Hence phon. *ḥḏ*, exx. var. [4] *ḥḏi* 'damage'; *ḥḏ* 'be bright', 'white'.

[1] WOLF, *Bewaffnung* 6. [2] LAC. *Sarc.* ii. 18, no. 99. [3] *Mitt.* viii. Pl. 3. [4] *Siut* 1, 224.

4 the same with a strap to pass round hand[1] — Use as last.

[1] WOLF, *Bewaffnung* 6. Exx. LAC. *Sarc.* i. 94, no. 66 (*ḥḏ* 'mace'); *Hier.* 7, no. 85 = *Bersh.* i. 30 (in name *Sȝt-Ḥḏḥtp*); *D. el B.* 110 (*ḥḏw* 'onions').

5 combination of T 3 and I 10 — Use as last.

6 combination of T 3 and two I 10 — Phon. *ḥḏḏ*, ex. [1] *ḥḏḏwt* 'brightness'.

[1] Brit. Mus. 552, qu. Exerc. XXV, (*a*).

For see O 2; for see S 14.

T 7 axe[1] — Det. in O.K. [hier.][2] *mỉbt* 'axe', which is undoubtedly related to M.K. [hier.][3] var. [hier.][4] *mỉnb* 'axe'. Det. in [hier.][5] *mḏḥ*, var. [hier.][6] *mḏḥ*, 'hew', and ideo. in the related word [hier.][7] var. [hier.][8] *mḏḥ(w)* 'carpenter', 'shipwright'.

[1] Ex. O.K., DAV. *Ptah.* i. 13, no. 280. This type was used alike for battle and for hewing wood, WOLF, *Bewaffnung* 8. [2] *Ti* 119. [3] *Sin.* R 160. [4] LAC. *Sarc.* ii. 13, no. 20 (collated), beside picture of an axe. See GARD. *Sin.* 51. 159. [5] *Urk.* iv. 778, 14. [6] See under S 10. [7] Cairo 20268, *a*; 20528, *h*. [8] See under S 10.

7* axe of more recent type[1] — Det. in [hier.][2] *ꜣkḫw* 'axe'.

[1] From Dyn. XII onward, WOLF, *Bewaffnung*, Pl. 3. [2] *Urk.* iv. 39, 1; also without handle, *ib.* 39, 3.

8 dagger of archaic type[1] — Det. of [hier.] *mtpnt* 'dagger'.[2] Phon. in [hier.] var. [hier.] *tpy* 'chief', 'first', 'being upon' (§ 80), value probably derived from an obsolete word *tp* 'dagger' found only once (written [hier.])[3] and obviously related to *mtpnt* mentioned above.

[1] JÉQ. 195; WOLF, *Bewaffnung*, Pl. 13 (= Pl. 4, 1); worn, *Sinai*, Pl. 1. As hieroglyph, PETR. *Eg. Hier.* nos. 757–61; outstanding features the [hier.]-shaped knob and rib-less blade. [2] Legend to picture on M.K. coffins, exx. LAC. *Sarc.* i, Pl. 43, nos. 264, 265, 269; *Wb.* ii. 170, 6 renders 'dagger-sheath' probably on account of the formative *m-*. [3] *Mitt.* viii. Pl. 5.

8* dagger of M. K. and later type[1] — Det. in [hier.] *b(ꜣ)gsw* 'dagger'.[2]

[1] JÉQ. 197; WOLF, *Bewaffnung*, Pl. 4, nos. 6 ff.; often with crescent-shaped or pierced circular top and ribbed blade. [2] *Urk.* iv. 38, 15; also as picture with legend *mꜣgsw* = *b(ꜣ)gsw* on M.K. coffins, LAC. *Sarc.* i. Pl. 43, nos. 255, 257, 259, 261, there often contrasted with the dagger *mtpnt*, see above T 8.

9 bow consisting of oryx horns joined by a wooden centre-piece[1] — Ideo. or det. in [hier.][2] var. [hier.][3] *pḏt* 'bow'. Hence phon. (semi-ideo.) or phon. det. *pḏ*, later *pḏ*, in Pyr. [hier.][4] var. Dyn. XVIII [hier.][5] *pḏ*, later var. [hier.][6] *pḏ*, 'stretch' and the related words.

[1] WOLF, *Bewaffnung* 15, 27; actual specimens in Dyn. I tombs, PETR. *RT.* ii. Pl. 7 A (p. 26); Pl. 36, 35–6 (p. 38). [2] LAC. *Sarc.* ii. 161. Sim. *Pyr.* 673. [3] *Sin.* B 127. This bow regularly in hieratic. [4] *Pyr.* 650. [5] *Urk.* iv. 977, 2. [6] BUDGE, p. 38, 7.

9* better O. K. form of [hier.] T 9[1] — Use as last.

[1] DAV. *Ptah.* i. 15, no. 338 = ii. 23. Also among dets. of *ꜥḥꜣw* 'weapons', *Sah.* 17. The curved ends suggest the horns of a gazelle rather than those of an oryx, but see T 9, n. 1.

10 composite bow with middle tied to bow-string when out of use[1] — Det. in Pyr. [hier.][2] *ỉwnt* 'bow'. From Dyn. XII on preferred to [hier.] T 9 in the hieroglyphic writing of [hier.][3] var. [hier.][4] *pḏt* 'bow', 'foreign people', 'troop'; [hier.][5] *pḏty* 'bowman', while [hier.] is preferred for phon. *pḏ*, *pḏ*.[6]

[1] WOLF, *Bewaffnung*, 14, 26. Of Asiatic origin and at first reserved for the king and high personages. So depicted already BISSING, *Rē-Heiligtum* ii. 13. [2] *Pyr.* 1644. [3] *Amada* 3. [4] *BH.* i. 7 (*pḏt* 9 'Nine Bows'). [5] *Amada* 3. [6] See particularly *Urk.* iv. 977, 2.

(Aa 32) archaic type of bow[1] (sometimes written , from Dyn. XVIII also [2])

Ideo. or det. in [3] *Tꜣ-St(i)*, varr. Pyr. [4] [5] *Tꜣ-Zt(i)*, 'Nubia'; [6] var. [7] *sty*, a Nubian mineral.[8] Also as var. of T 11 with value *sšr* and obscure sense in offering-list.[9]

[1] MONTET, *Kêmi* 6, 43; SCHARFF, 38, 139; depicted QUIBELL, *Hierakonpolis*, I, Pl. 19; II, Pl. 58; CAPART, *Débuts de l'Art*, Pl. 1. Later apparently surviving only in Nubia. [2] *Urk.* iv. 7, 3, qu. Exerc. XXXII, (*a*). [3] *ÄZ.* 45, Pl. 6, 7. [4] *Pyr.* 994. [5] *Pyr.* 1867; see too *ÄZ.* 45, 128. [6] BUDGE, p. 284, 12. [7] *Urk.* iv. 1099, 11. [8] See *Rec.* 39, 22. [9] *Kêmi* 6, 57.

T 11 arrow

Det. in [1] *ꜥḥꜣ* 'arrow'; [2] *šsr* (*sšr*) [3] 'arrow'; from the latter, phon. det. in *sẖr* 'overlay'. Doubtless from an obsolete *zin*, *zwn* 'arrow', phon. or phon. det. *sin*, *swn* (*zin*, *zwn*), exx. [4] *swn*, var. Pyr. [5] *zin*, 'perish'; [6] var. *swnt* 'sale'; 'physician' *swnw*, var. O.K. *zinw*(?), the M.E. reading *swnw* on the evidence of a var. [7] *wr swnw* 'chief of physicians', but Coptic has *saein*.

[1] *Urk.* iv. 190, 12. [2] *P. Kah.* 1, 4. [3] *Pyr.* 1866. [4] *Adm.* 5, 2. [5] *Pyr.* 617. 725; may here read *in*, see *Sitz. Berl. Ak.* 1912, 962. [6] GRIFFITH, *Kahun Papyri*, p. 35. [7] *Wb.* iii. 427, 13.

12 bow-string[1]

Ideo. or det. in [2] *rwd*, varr. Pyr. [3], [4] *rwḏ*, 'string', 'bow-string'. Hence phon. or phon. det. *rwḏ*, *rwd*, exx. *rwd*, var. Pyr. [5] *rwḏ*, 'be hard', 'firm'; *rwdt*, var. [6] *rwḏt*, 'sandstone'. Ideographic det. in *ꜣr* 'restrain'; hence phon. det. *ꜣr*, *ꜣi*, exx. *mꜣi(r)* 'wretched'; *dꜣi(r)*, abbrev. [7] *dꜣr*, 'subdue'.

[1] WOLF, *Bewaffnung* 48. See *ib.* 56–7 against the theory, supported *PSBA.* 22, 65, that the sign as represented depicts a sling. [2] *P. Kah.* 1, 5 certainly meaning 'bow-string'. [3] *Pyr.* 2080. [4] *Pyr.* 684. [5] *Pyr.* 197. [6] *Urk.* iv. 845, 14. [7] *Sin.* B 50, cf. *ib.* R 74; *Sh. S.* 132.

13 [1] pieces of wood joined and lashed at the joint[2]

Semi-ideo. (?) in var. *rs* (*rš*) [3] 'be wakeful', 'vigilant' and derivatives; phon. *rs* in [4] var. [5] *rst* 'foreign hordes'.

[1] *Rekh.* 22. O.K. form *Ti* 80. For a later degraded form due to hieratic see U 40. [2] Associated with the bow in *Pyr.* 921. 1245 and evidently part of the bowman's equipment. On the other hand, from writings like *Pyr.* 502. 597. 1502 several appear to form a shelter. A set of four, with names *pḏ-ꜥḥꜥ*, *nw-n-nṯr*, *ir(y)-nṯr*, *ḏbꜣ-nṯr*, is depicted on M.K. coffins. One may perhaps compare the mantlet or shelter used by the Babylonian archers. Discussed JÉQ. 223. [3] For *š* see *Pyr.* 126. [4] *Amada* 5. Sim. *Ann.* 39, Pl. 25, 2; *Urk.* iv. 200, 17. [5] Louvre C 14, 10.

T 14 (1) throw-stick, (2) club as a foreign weapon of warfare[1]

(1) Det. in [2] *ʿmʿꜣt* 'throw-stick' with the related verb *ʿmʿꜣ* 'throw'; also in [3] *ḳmꜣ* 'throw' and the kindred varr. ,[4] *ḳmꜣ* 'create', 'form' and derivatives. The combination in *ḳmꜣ* above-quoted and in *ṯnỉ* 'distinguish' (from a ἅπαξ λεγόμενον [4a]?) indicates that is here the throw-stick, not the club; see on G 41. (2) As club, is found in [5] var. Pyr. [6] *Ṯḥnw* 'Libya'; varr. , O.K. [7] *ʿꜣm* 'Asiatic'. Extended gradually as det. to all foreign peoples and countries, exx. [8] *Tmḥỉ* '*Temḥi*-land'; [9] var. [10] *Nḥsy* 'Nubian'. (3) takes the place of various other signs, partly due to identity or close similarity in hieratic; thus it takes the place (*a*) of Aa 26 in [11] *sbỉ* 'rebel'; (*b*) of M 3 in [12] *dʿr* 'search for'; (*c*) of P 11 in [13] *m(ỉ)nỉ* 'moor'; (*d*) of T 13, see under that sign; (*e*) probably also of D 50 in [14] *mtr* 'witness' and the like, though examples of such confusions in modern publications may sometimes be due to inexact copying.

[1] WOLF, *Bewaffnung* 7. 57. [2] LAC. *TR.* 22, 69; *Wb.* i. 186. [3] LAC. *TR.* 22, 71. [4] *Urk.* iv. 1044, 5. [4a] *Urk.* i. 127, 2. [5] *D.elB.* 114. An ex. without the vases on a palette of Dyn. I, *ÄZ.* 52, 57. [6] *Pyr.* 455. [7] *Urk.* i. 101, 9. For the various spellings of this word see W. MAX MÜLLER, *Asien und Europa* 121. [8] *Sin.* R 12; det. of this word already in O.K., *Urk.* i. 125, 16. [9] *Urk.* iv. 84, 1. Sim. M.K. as m. personal name, Cairo 20680. In O.K. and as a rule in M.K. the club is absent from *Nḥsy*. [10] Before Dyn. XIX only in the personal name *Pꜣ-Nḥsy*, ex. *Sinai* 221. [11] Exx. *Hamm.* 114, 12; *Kopt.* 8, 7. [12] Cairo 20254, *a*; 20765. [13] *Paheri* 3. [14] Hieratic consistently shows the finger D 50, exx. *Sin.* B 33; *P. Kah.* 13, 30.

15 [1] O.K. form of last

Use as last.

[1] *Sah.* 1 (*Ṯḥnw*).

16 [1] scimetar

Det. in *ḫpš* 'scimetar'.

[1] Exx. DAV. *Ḳen.* i. 20; *Urk.* iv. 726, 17. See WOLF, *Bewaffnung* 66.

17 chariot

Ideo. or det. in [1] var. [2] *wrrt* 'chariot'.

[1] Ex. *Urk.* iv. 704, 15. [2] *Urk.* iv. 712, 10.

18 crook S 39 with a package containing a knife, etc. lashed to it[1]

Ideo. in rare var. [2] *šms*, Pyr. var. [3] *šmś*, 'follow', 'accompany' and derivatives.

[1] The sign probably depicts the equipment of an early chieftain's attendant, *Bull.* 3, 12, n. 2; so too SCHARFF 45; however, SETHE, Commentary on *Pyr.* 230 c, adheres to CAPART'S explanation as an instrument for the execution of criminals *ÄZ.* 36, 125. [2] Cairo 20001, qu. § 217. [3] *Pyr.* 953.

T 19 harpoon-head of bone — Det. in *ḳs* (*ḳś*) 'bone', 'harpoon'.[0] Hence phon. or phon. det. *ḳs* (*ḳś*), in var. Dyn. XVIII *ḳsn* 'be irksome'; *ḳrs* (*ḳrś*), in *ḳrs* 'bury' and derivatives. For reason unknown, phon. or phon. det. *gn* in var. *gnwt* 'annals'; possibly also in var. *gnwty* (?) 'sculptor' (in relief), reading not fully established.[1] Det. bone, ex. *ꜣb* 'ivory'; tubular, exx. [2] *mꜣwt* 'shaft'; [3] *twr* 'reed (?)', whence phon. det. in [4] *tw(r)i* 'be pure'.

[0] In sense 'harpoon', *Pyr.* 1212. [1] See MONTET 291. [2] *Urk.* iv. 666, 15. [3] *Eb.* 55, 16. [4] *Urk.* iv. 752, 11.

20 [1] O.K. form of last — Use as last.

[1] Ex. DAV. *Ptah.* i. 15, no. 339. Of bone or metal, PETRIE, *Tools and Weapons*, Pls. 43, 44.

21 one-barbed harpoon (rarely vertically [1]) — Ideo. in var. Pyr. [2] *wꜥ* 'one' and derivatives.

[1] Ex. *Urk.* iv. 194, 2. [2] *Pyr.* 1226.

22 two-barbed arrow-head[1] — Ideo. in *snw*, O.K. var. ,[2] 'two' and in related words like *sn* (*śn*) 'brother'. Hence phon. *sn* (*śn*),[2a] exx. [3] *sn* (*śn*), var. Pyr. [4] *śin*, 'smell', 'kiss'; *sntr* 'incense'.

[1] Not a spear-head, but an arrow-head, SCHARFF 33; among earliest exx. (PETR. *Eg. Hier.* 753-6) is one with quite short shaft; for later lengthening cf. the sign for 'foot' (D 58); the two barbs yield the notion of duality, contrast the sign for 'one' (T 21), *ÄZ.* 47, 36. [2] *Urk.* i. 147, 3. [2a] For *ś* see *śni* 'loose', *Pyr.* 1100. [3] So already *Pyr.* 1323. [4] *Pyr.* 1027, unless a different word.

23 [1] alternative form of last (Dyn. XVIII) — Use as last.

[1] Ex. *Th. T. S.* iii. 21.

24 [1] fishing-net[2] — Det. in [3] *ꜥḥ*, var. [4] *iḥ*, 'net' animals. Hence phon. *ꜥḥ* or *iḥ*, exx. *ꜥḥt* 'field', 'holding'; *ꜥḥwty*, *iḥwty* 'field-labourer', 'tenant-farmer'.[5]

[1] *Rekh.* 3, 18; reversed, *ib.* 5. [2] *PSBA.* 22, 152; in historic times, however, only used of netting desert animals; see too MONTET 89. [3] *Urk.* iv. 248, 2. [4] *Bersh.* i. 7; see *Sphinx* 12, 107. [5] For the two senses see *JEA.* 27, 21.

25 reed-floats used in fishing and hunting the hippopotamus[1] — Cf. *dbꜣw* 'floats'.[2] Phon. *dbꜣ*, exx. var. Pyr. [3] *dbꜣ* 'clothe', 'adorn'; *dbꜣ*, var. [4] *dbꜣ*, 'replace'.

[1] DAV. *Ptah.* i. p. 37. [2] BUDGE, p. 390, 13. [3] *Pyr.* 272. [4] *Peas.* B 1, 49.

T 26 [1] bird-trap [2] — Ideo. or det. in var. *sḫt* (*šḫt*) 'trap,' 'snare (birds)' and derivatives.

[1] Exx. Dyn. XVIII, *Hier.* 5, no. 52; *Rekh.* 21. [2] See MONTET 53.

27 [1] O.K. form of last — Use as last.

[1] DAV. *Ptah.* i. 15, no. 335, adapted to suit reduction in size.

28 butcher's block [1] (to be distinguished from W 11 and W 12) — Semi-ideo. (?) in var. *ẖr* [2] 'under' (§ 166). Phon. *ẖr*, exx. *mẖr* 'storehouse'; *ẖrt* 'portion', 'due'.

[1] Deduced from T 29. [2] Reading due mainly to the consideration that this preposition never interchanges with *ḫr* (§ 167). The hieroglyphic evidence is conflicting, being substituted for in *ẖrp* = *ḫrp* 'control', *Pyr.* 1143, and in *sẖr* = *sḫr* 'counsel', Cairo 20026, but for in *ẖrd* 'child', BR. *Thes.* 1527; Vienna 64.

29 combination of T 30 and T 28 — Ideo. in [1] var. [2] *nmt* 'place of slaughter'.

[1] *Urk.* iv. 163, 8; see *Pyr.* 214, where the knife is over the block, whereas elsewhere (exx. Pyr. 811. 865) the two signs are written as a monogram. [2] *Urk.* v. 80, 14.

For see R 10; for see W 5; for see N 7.

30 knife (used early [1] also as substitute for the saw) — Det. knife, ex. *ds* 'knife' (semi-ideo. in *ds* 'flint'); sharp, in *dm* 'be sharp', 'pronounce (name)'; cut, exx. *šʿd* 'cut down'; *rḥs* 'slaughter'; *ḫti* 'carve'. Note the abbrev. *dmt* [2] 'knife'.

[1] *Ti* 133, as det. of *wšt* and *tf*. [2] In *ḫry-dmt* 'sufferer (?)', *Eb.* 40, 6; reading from Metternich stela 82, see *Hier.* p. 50. *Wb.* v. 450 takes as referring to the surgeon's knife, but this seems doubtful.

For see D 57

31 knife-sharpener (?) [1] — Phon. *sšm* (*ššm*) in varr. [2] *sšm* (*ššm*) [3] 'guide', 'lead' and derivatives.

[1] This description rests on the supposition that the sign was originally identical with T 33, as would appear from *Pyr.* 70; see below on that hieroglyph. [2] *Siut* I, 247. [3] Reading, *Rec.* 14, 18. For *š* see *Pyr.* 70.

32 combination of T 31 and D 54 — Phon. *sšm* in *sšm* (*ššm*) 'guide', 'lead'.

33 [1] knife-sharpener as carried by butcher (O.K.) [2] — Ideo. in *ššm* (?) [3] 'butcher'.

[1] *Medum* 14. Sim. L. *D.* ii. 4 (tomb of Metjen). [2] MONTET 158.
[3] The reading *ššm* rests on the assumption that T 31 was originally of this form. In the tomb of Metjen (Dyn. III) the sign for *ššm* (L. *D.* ii. 6) is almost identical with the butcher sign (see above n. 1). Possibly we have here to do with a single sign which is becoming differentiated for distinct uses.

34 [1] butcher's knife — Ideo. in [2] *nm* 'knife (?)'. Hence phon. *nm*, exx. *nmḥ* 'orphan'; *ḫnms* 'friend'.

[1] *BH.* iii. 5, nos. 63. 65. Sim. Dyn. XVIII, *D. el B.* 74. [2] Karnak, chamber of Annals, Tuthmosis III, in offering list immediately before *ḫpš* 'foreleg of ox'. Sim. GAYET, *Temple de Louxor* 26.

35 [1] alternative form of last — Use as last.

[1] Exx. O.K., *Gemn.* i. 11; Dyn. XVIII, *Th. T. S.* i. 7.

Sect. U. Agriculture, Crafts, and Professions

U 1 sickle[1] — Ideo. in [2] *mꜣ* 'sickle-shaped end' of the *wiꜣ*-boat P 3. Hence phon. *mꜣ*,[3] exx. *mꜣꜣ* 'see'; *tmꜣ* 'mat'. In group-writing (§ 60) is used for *m*.[4] A sign similar, but not quite identical, in shape is used as det. in [5] *ꜣsḫ* 'reap'; also perhaps in [6] *ḫꜣbb*, var. [7] *ḫꜣbb*, 'crookedness'.

[1] *Medum*, frontispiece, no. 8; DAV. *Ptah.* i. 13, no. 282. [2] LAC. *TR.* 27, 1. 2; BUDGE, p. 212, 7. [3] For the initial *m* cf. Coptic *mě* 'truth', *müi* 'lion', *mūh* 'burn'. [4] BURCHARDT § 56. [5] *Urk.* v. 161, 16. [6] *Peas.* B 1, 107. [7] *Adm.* p. 107; possibly both here and in *Peas.* the lower part of the sickle only. *Ḫꜣb* is a name of the sickle, see *Wb.* iii. 361, 14.

2 alternative form of last — Use as last.

3 combination of U 1 and D 4 — In *mꜣꜣ* 'see'.

4 combination of U 1 and Aa 11 — In *mꜣꜥt* 'truth' and the related words.

5 alternative form of last — Use as last.

For see G 3; for see G 46; for see S 31.

6 hoe — Det. cultivate, hack up, exx. *ꜥd* 'hack up'; *ḫbs* 'cultivate', 'hoe'. For unknown reason,[1] phon. *mr*,[2] exx. *mri* 'love'; *mrḥt* 'unguent'. Sometimes in place of U 8, phon. *ḥn*, ex. *ḥn* 'go', 'depart'.

[1] *Wb.* ii. 98, 11 quotes as gloss in the *Sign Pap.* Pl. 4 the otherwise unknown word *mriw* 'hoe', but only a very uncertain trace of is there. [2] For the initial *m*, cf. Coptic *mě* 'love', *mour* 'bind', *emrō* 'harbour'.

7 alternative form of last — Use as last.

8 [1] hoe, without the rope connecting the two pieces — Det. in Pyr. [2] 'hoe'. Hence phon. *ḥn*, ex. [3] *ḥnw* '*ḥnw*-bark'.

[1] Already Dyn. IV, *Medum* 15. [2] *Pyr.* 1394. [3] NAV. ch. 1, 21.

9 corn-measure with grain pouring out — Det. grain, exx. *bdt* 'emmer'; *sšr* (old *ššr*)[2] 'corn'; measure, exx. [1] *ḥꜣi* 'measure'; abbrev. *ḥḳꜣt* '*ḥeḳat*-measure' (§ 266, 1).

[1] Cairo 20500. Sim. *Urk.* iv. 64, 1. [2] Reading, see *Bull.* 30, 179.

U 10 [hieroglyph] the same beneath [hieroglyph] M 33 — Ideo. in [hieroglyph] var. Pyr. [hieroglyph][1] *it* 'barley', 'corn'. Sometimes in Dyn. XVIII instead of [hieroglyph] U 9 as det. grain, ex. [hieroglyph][2] *bty* (from *bdt*) 'emmer'.

[1] *Pyr.* 1880. [2] *Paheri* 3.

11 [hieroglyph][1] combination of [hieroglyph] S 38 and [hieroglyph] U 9 — In [hieroglyph] *ḥḳꜣt* '*ḥeḳat*-measure' (§ 266, 1).

[1] *Puy.* 35.

12 [hieroglyph][1] combination of [hieroglyph] D 50 and [hieroglyph] U 9 — In [hieroglyph] *ḥḳꜣt* '*ḥeḳat*-measure' (§ 266, 1).

[1] *Puy.* 36.

(O 30) [hieroglyph] pitchfork — Det. in [hieroglyph] *ꜥbt* 'fork'.[1] Possibly not a pitchfork as phon. or phon. det. *sḏb* (*šḏb*), later *sdb*, in [hieroglyph] *sḏb*, var. Pyr. [hieroglyph][2] *šḏb*, later [hieroglyph] *sdb*, 'hindrance', 'obstacle'.

[1] MONTET 227. Sometimes with three prongs, *Wb.* i. 176. [2] *Pyr.* 315.

13 [hieroglyph] plough — Det. plough, in [hieroglyph] *hb* 'plough' (n.); [hieroglyph] *skꜣ* 'plough' (vb.); also in [hieroglyph], var. [hieroglyph] *prt* 'seed'. From *hb* 'plough', phon. *hb*, exx. [hieroglyph] var. O.K. [hieroglyph][1] *hbny* 'ebony'; [hieroglyph] var. [hieroglyph][2] *hbnt*, a liquid measure (§ 266, 1). From Dyn. V onwards replaces [hieroglyph] U 14 as phon. or phon. det. *šnꜥ* in [hieroglyph] *šnꜥ* 'repel'; [hieroglyph][3] *šnꜥw* 'policing'; [hieroglyph] var. [hieroglyph] *šnꜥ*[4] 'magazine' 'ergastulum'.

[1] *Ti* 66. [2] *Urk.* iv. 748, 17. [3] Leyd. V 88, qu. Exerc. XXVI, (*a*).
[4] Reading, *Rec.* 24, 93.

14 [hieroglyph][1] two branches of wood joined at one end[2] (O.K.) — Old sign for *šnꜥ* later replaced by [hieroglyph] U 13.

[1] *Medum* 15 in a place-name *Šnꜥt*; slightly different, *ib.* 12. Elsewhere in O.K. replaced by the plough, exx. *Ti* 86; *Pyr.* 1209. [2] This possibly represents a contrivance for straightening or bending wooden staves, *Ti* 132 = MONTET 311.

15 [hieroglyph] sledge — Cf. [hieroglyph][1] 'sledge'. Hence phon. *tm*, exx. [hieroglyph] *tm* 'be complete' (§ 342); [hieroglyph] *ḥtm* 'perish'.

[1] BUDGE, p. 38, 14. Sim. *ib.* p. 210, 12.

16 [hieroglyph][1] sledge with head of a jackal (Copt. *wōnᵉsh*) bearing a load of metal (?)[2] — Det. in [hieroglyph] *wnš* 'sledge'.[2a] Ideo. (?) in Pyr. [hieroglyph][3] *biꜣi* 'of copper' (adj.). Hence perhaps phon. or phon. det. *biꜣ* in [hieroglyph][4] var. [hieroglyph] *by* (orig. *biꜣ*) 'wonder' and related words; for the reading cf. [hieroglyph][5] *biꜣt* 'wonder' (n.).

[1] *Puy.* 30; a rather different form *Pyr.* 800. [2] *ÄZ.* 53, 51, n. 2. [2a] *Ann.* 39, 189; see too *JEA.* 31, 38. [3] *Pyr.* 800. However, this sign is seldom written in this word, and never in the noun *biꜣ* 'copper', rendering the explanation doubtful. [4] *Urk.* iv. 612, 6. [5] *Hamm.* 110, 2.

17 [hieroglyph] pick excavating a pool [hieroglyph] N 38 — Ideo. in [hieroglyph][1] varr. [hieroglyph], [hieroglyph] *grg* 'found', 'establish', 'snare'. Hence phon. det. *grg* in [hieroglyph][1] varr. [hieroglyph], [hieroglyph][2] *grg* 'falsehood', 'lie'.

[1] Spellings, *Verbum* i. § 338. [2] *Urk.* iv. 1031, 10.

U 18 [1] O.K. form of last — Use as last.

[1] *L. D.* ii. 7 (tomb of Metjen, Dyn. III).

19 adze — Ideo. in Pyr. [1] var. [1] *nwty* 'the two adzes'. Hence phon. *nw* in the group or , exx. *nw* 'this' (§ 110); *nwḥ* 'rope'. In group-writing (§ 60) is used for *n*.[2]

[1] *Pyr.* 311. A ceremonial adze called *nw*, *Th. T. S.* i. 17. [2] BURCHARDT § 69.

20 [1] O.K. form of last — Use as last.

[1] *Gemn.* i. 11. A somewhat similar sign in O.K. as det. of *ʿnt* 'nail', 'claw', *Wb.* i. 188; *Kêmi* iv. 179.

21 adze at work on a block of wood — Det. in O.K. *śtp*[1] 'cut up' ox. Hence semi-ideo. or phon. *stp* (*śtp*), in var. *stp* 'choose' and derivatives; inaccurately also *sṯp*, in [2] *sṯp*, var. Pyr. [3] *śṯp*, 'leap up'.

[1] Ex. *Ti* 127. [2] *Urk.* v. 147, 4. [3] *Pyr.* 947.

22 chisel — Det. in O.K. [1] *mnḫ* 'fashion', 'carve' and [2] *mnḫ* 'chisel'. Hence semi-ideo. in *mnḫ* 'be efficient' and the related words.

[1] Ex. *Ti* 120. [2] Leyd. *Denkm.* iv. 14.

23 chisel (?)[0] — For unknown reason, phon. *mr*,[1] exx. *mr* 'be ill'; *smr* 'friend', 'courtier'. Also for unknown reason, phon. *ꜣb*,[2] exx. *ꜣbi* 'desire'; *ꜣbḫ* 'be united in'.

[0] A similar object is seen used as hair-pin on a Dyn. XI coffin, *Griff. Stud.* 134; Reisner, however, preferred the explanation as a chisel, since no such hair-pins are found early; so too SCHARFF 43; oldest forms, PETR. *Eg. Hier.* 801–8. [1] Reading from varr. of *mr* 'pyramid', *Pyr.* 1649. 1671. [2] Reading from varr. of *ꜣbḏw* 'Abydus', *Pyr.* 794. 798. The view that the original form of the sign, when it has the value *ꜣb*, was a leopard's hide (see *Rec.* 9, 158) is very doubtful, in spite of the word *ꜣby* 'leopard', since from the earliest times the phonetic value of the leopard's (really cow's) hide was *śꜣb*, not *ꜣb*; see on F 28.

For , see Aa 21, 22.

24 [1] stone-worker's drill weighted at the top with stones (Dyn. XVIII)[2] — Ideo. in var. O.K. [3] *ḥmt*[4] 'craft', 'art' and the related words.

[1] Thebes, tomb 93. Sim. *Rekh.* 16. [2] See the pictures *Gebr.* i. 13; *Rekh.* 17. [3] *Urk.* i. 53, 13, in collective sense for 'body of craftsmen'. [4] Reading, *Rec.* 9, 164. For this see too Coptic ϩⲁⲙϣⲉ = *ḥm-ḫt* 'worker in wood'; ϩⲁⲙⲛⲟⲩⲃ = *ḥm-nbw* 'gold-worker'.

U 25 [1] O.K. form of last — Use as last.

[1] *Saqq. Mast.* i. 39, no. 65.

26 [1] drill being used to bore a hole in a bead [2] (Dyn. XVIII) — Ideo. in var. var. Pyr. [3] *wbꜣ* 'open up' and derivatives.

[1] Exx. *Rec.* 22, 107, Plate; *Th. T. S.* iii. 5. [2] See the picture *Gebr.* i. 13. [3] *Pyr.* 1205.

27 [1] O.K. form of last (also used later [2]) — Use as last.

[1] Ex. *Gebr.* i. 13. [2] Dyn. XII, *Bersh.* i. 27; Dyn. XVIII, *Puy.* 54.

28 [1] fire-drill[2] (Dyn. XVIII) — Cf. [3] *ḏꜣ* 'fire-drill'. Hence phon. *ḏꜣ*,[4] exx. *ḏꜣi* 'ferry across'; *ḥꜥḏꜣ* 'pillage'; *ḏꜣt*[5] 'remainder'. Abbrev. for *wḏꜣ* in the formula *ꜥnḫ wḏꜣ snb* 'may he live, be prosperous, be healthy' (§§ 55. 313). In group-writing (§ 60) or is phon. *ḏ*.[6]

[1] Exx. *Puy.* 9; *Th. T. S.* iii. 26, 6. [2] *Hier.* p. 50. [3] *Sh. S.* 54; see *ÄZ.* 43, 161; 45, 85. [4] Reading partly from varr. of *ḏꜣḏꜣt* 'council' (*Pyr.* 309. 1713), partly from Coptic equivalences, ex. ⲟⲩϫⲁⲓ = *wḏꜣ* 'be hale', 'sound'. [5] *Wb.* i. 404, 2 accepts *wḏꜣt* as the N.K. reading on the evidence of L.E. variants, see Spiegelberg, *Rechnungen aus der Zeit Setis I*, p. 40; but the relation of L.E. *wḏꜣt* to older *ḏꜣt* may be like that of L.E. *wsḫ* 'breadth' to O.E. *sḫw*, and *Wb.* v. 517 is probably right in taking *ḏꜣt* as the M.E. reading. [6] Burchardt § 150.

29 [1] O.K. form of last (also common later [2]) — Use as last.

[1] Dav. *Ptah.* i. 13, no. 287. [2] Exx. Dyn. XII, *BH.* i. 8, 10; Dyn. XVIII, *Th. T. S.* i. 1.

30 potter's kiln — Ideo. in O.K. [1] *tꜣ* 'kiln'. Hence phon. *tꜣ*, exx. *tꜣ* 'be hot'; *štꜣ* 'mysterious', 'difficult'. In the geographical name [2] *Ḫt* 'Hittite land' should be read simply *t*, not *tꜣ*, cf. Hebrew חֵת (§ 60).[3]

[1] *Ti* 84; see too the pictures *ib.*; *BH.* i. 11. [2] *Urk.* iv. 701, 11. [3] Burchardt § 131.

31 [1] instrument employed in baking (?) — Ideo. or det. in var. [2] *rtḥty*[3] 'baker'. Hence det. in the related words *rtḥ* 'restrain'; *itḥ* 'prison'. Probably for some reason connected with its use ideo. or det. in *ḫn(r)i* 'restrain'; [4] *ḫnrt*, var. *ḫnt*, 'harîm'. Through similarity in hieratic, sometimes substituted for D 19 or D 20, ex. [5] *ssnt* 'breathe'.

[1] In Dyn. III–IV the ends are curved, not angular, *Saqq. Mast.* i. 1; sim. *Meir* ii. 7. Later the shaft is sometimes shown as double. [2] Unpublished *P. Ram.* [3] Reading, *Rec.* 39, 20. [4] See *Adm.* p. 47 and above, p. 201, n. 1. [5] *Urk.* iv. 76, 8.

U 32 pestle and mortar [1] — Det. of [hieroglyphs] [1a] *sḥm*, O.K. [hieroglyphs] [1b] *zḫm*, 'pound'; also of O.K. [hieroglyphs] [2] *śmn*, [hieroglyphs] *zmn* [2a] 'press down' bread with a stick; from this latter [2b] phon. or phon. det. *smn* (*zmn*) in [hieroglyphs], abbrev. [hieroglyphs] *ḥsmn* 'natron'; [hieroglyphs], abbrev. [hieroglyphs] *ḥsmn* 'bronze'; [3] [hieroglyphs] [4] *smn* (old *śmn*) 'establish'. Det. pound, also in [hieroglyphs] *ḥmꜣt* 'salt'; heavy, in [hieroglyphs] *dns* 'heavy'; [hieroglyphs] *wdn* 'heavy'.

[1] See the hieroglyphs *Medum* 15; *Pyr.* 249; and the picture, Leyd. *Denkm.* i. 10. [1a] *Eb.* 86, 10; cf. *BH* ii. 6. [1b] *Ti* 83. However, *Wb.* iii. 464, 1 interprets this as *zḫ* and reads the preceding word as *śḫm* with *ś*. [2] *Ti* 85. [2a] Leyd. *Denkm.* i. 10; see MONTET 240; *ÄZ.* 61, 13. [2b] Not, as *Wb.* iii. 453, 3, from the homonym *zmn* 'tarry' *Pyr.* 533. 1418. [3] *ÄZ.* 30, 31. [4] *Urk.* iv. 1187, 10, an early instance of a writing that is usual in L.E.

33 pestle — Ideo. in [hieroglyphs] [0] *tit* 'pestle (?)' of red granite (*mꜣt*); hence (?) phon. *ti*, exx. [hieroglyphs] *ḥr·ti* 'thou art content' (§ 309); [hieroglyphs] *ꜥnḫ·ti* 'may she live!' (§ 313); more rarely phon. *t*, especially beside [hieroglyph] *ḥ*, exx. [hieroglyphs] *tḥnt* 'fayence'; [hieroglyphs] [1] *ḥts* 'inaugurate (a feast)'. In group-writing (§ 60) [hieroglyph] or [hieroglyphs] or [hieroglyphs] is phon. *t*,[2] ex. [hieroglyphs] [3] *Ti*, name of a Syrian locality.

[0] MÖLL. *Pal.* i. Pl. 5, left, 16; meaning doubtful. [1] *Siut* 1, 244. [2] BURCHARDT § 134. [3] *Urk.* iv. 784, 74.

34 spindle — Ideo. in [hieroglyphs] [1] *ḥsf* 'spin'. Hence semi-ideo. or phon. *ḥsf* (*ḥśf*) in the related verb [hieroglyphs] var. [hieroglyphs] *ḥsf* (*ḥśf*) [2] 'repel', 'oppose' and its derivatives.

[1] *BH.* ii. 4, in scene of spinning. [2] For *ś* see *Pyr.* 253.

35 combination of [hieroglyph] U 34 and [hieroglyph] I 9 — Use as last.

(Aa 23) [1] warp stretched between two uprights [1a] — Det. in [hieroglyphs] [2] varr. [hieroglyphs] [3] [hieroglyphs] [4] var. Pyr. [hieroglyphs] [5] *mdd* 'hit (a mark)', 'adhere to (a path)' and derivatives.

[1] Thebes, tomb 85. Very various in form; exx. M.K., Brit. Mus. 614, 8; *Siut* 1, 221; Dyn. XVIII, *Puy.* 68; *Th. T. S.* i. 17. [1a] DAVIES, *Seven Private Tombs*, Pl. 35 (p. 50). Perhaps this suggests as the original sense of the stem 'make straight'. [2] *Urk.* iv. 484, 5. Sim. *Peas.* B 1, 212. [3] Brit. Mus. 581. [4] Louvre C 174. [5] *Pyr.* 2048.

(Aa 24) [1] O.K. form of last — Use as last.

[1] *Sinai* 7. See *ÄZ.* 30, 52; 62, 1.

36 club used by fullers in washing [1] — Ideo. in [hieroglyphs] [2] var. [hieroglyphs] [3] *ḥmww* 'fuller (?)'. Hence (?) phon. *ḥm*,[4] in [hieroglyphs] *ḥm* 'slave' and the related words; also in [hieroglyphs], isolated late var. [hieroglyphs],[5] *ḥm* 'Majesty' (p. 74).

[1] *ÄZ.* 37, 82. [2] *BH.* i. 29. [3] *Ib.* [4] Reading from proper names ending in *m* and from the name *Paḫamnâta* = *Pꜣ-ḥm-nṯr* in the El-Amarna letters (see above p. 428), besides late writings in which the sign interchanges with [hieroglyph] N 41; see *ÄZ.* 46, 109; *Sphinx* 14, 143. [5] *Bull.* 28, 103.

For [hieroglyph] see D 31

37 razor [1] — Det. in [hieroglyphs] [2] *ḫꜥḳ* 'shave'.

[1] Razors, see PETRIE, *Tools and Weapons* 61. [2] Ex. *BH.* ii. 4.

U 38 [1] balance — Ideo. or det. in [2] var. [3] *mḫꜣt* 'balance'.

[1] Thebes, tomb 76. [2] Exx. *Paheri* 9, 30; *D. el B.* 81. [3] *ÄZ.* 59, 44*.

39 post of balance — Det. in [1] *wṯst* 'post (of balance)' and in the related verb [2] *wṯs* 'lift', 'carry', 'wear'. Secondarily also det. in [3] *ṯsi* (*ṯzi*) 'raise', 'lift'.

[1] PIEHL, *IH.* iii. 82. [2] *D. el B.* 81. [3] In Pyr. the det. of *ṯzi* is a sack-like receptacle, ex. *Pyr.* 960, but our sign already appears exceptionally, ex. *ib.* 294.

40 semi-hieratic alternative to last (Dyn. XVIII)[1] — Use as last, ex. [2] *wṯsw* 'those who have worn'. Also, owing to similarity in hieratic, used for [3] T 13, ex. [4] *rs-tp* 'vigilant'.

[1] For the hieratic see MÖLL. *Pal.* i. no. 405; ii. no. 405. [2] *Urk.* iv. 85, 12. [3] MÖLL. *Pal.* i. no. 588. [4] Leyd. *Denkm.* iv. 28, 4 *c.* 3. Sim. *srs*, *Urk.* iv. 897, 6.

41 [1] plummet used in connection with the balance[2] — Det. in *tḫ* 'plummet'.

[1] Dyn. XII, Leyd. V 103 = *Denkm.* ii. 13. [2] *JEA.* 9, 10, n. 4.

Sect. V. Rope, Fibre, Baskets, Bags, etc.

V 1 coil of rope — Det. rope, exx. *nwḥ* 'rope'; *ḥꜣtt* 'front-rope' of ship; actions with rope or cord, exx. *itḥ* 'drag'; *ṯs* 'tie'; [1] *mnḫ* 'string' beads; *šni* 'encircle', 'surround'. Probably from *šnw* 'network', phon. or phon. det. *šn* in var. [2] *šnt* 'dispute', the relations of which with *šni* 'exorcise', 'litigate' and with [3] *šnṯ* 'contend' require further study. Another possibly related word is *št* (*šnt*?)[4] 'hundred' (§§ 259. 260). A similar, but doubtless different, sign is det. in [5] *ḫꜣb* 'bent appendage' (of metal?) belonging to the crown.

[1] *M. u. K.* 1, 3. [2] Cairo 20393. 20562, *d*, in the title *imy-r šnt*; cf. too a title *šnt* discussed *JEA.* 9, 15, n. 2. [3] *ÄZ.* 36, 138. [4] *ÄZ.* 36, 135. [5] *Urk.* iv. 200, 15.

For as substitute for G 43, see Z 7.

2 bolt O 34 combined with the cord V 1 used for drawing it[1] — Ideo. in *sṯꜣ* (*šṯꜣ*), later *stꜣ*, 'drag', 'draw'; hence phon. *sṯꜣ* in *sṯꜣt* 'aroura' (§ 266, 3). For an unknown reason det. in *ꜣs* 'hasten'.

[1] *ÄZ.* 35, 105, confirmed by DAV. *Rekh.* ii. 26, 12. The sense of the verb agrees so well with the Dyn. XVIII form just quoted that the suggestion (*Hier.* 44) that this is secondary seems unlikely. An alternative explanation, MONTET 304.

V 3 the same sign with three cords (Dyn. XVIII)

Phon. *stȝw* in [1] *R-stȝw* 'necropolis',[2] particularly that of the Memphitic god Sokar.

[1] Ex. *Th. T. S.* iv. 38, G. [2] *ÄZ.* 59, 159; *Wb.* ii. 398, 9. 10.

4 lasso

Cf. [1] *wȝw* 'lassoes'. Hence phon. *wȝ*,[2] exx. *wȝ* 'far'; *wȝḥ* 'place', 'endure'.

[1] BUDGE, p. 454, 2. Cf. too *wȝt* 'cord' (*Wb.* i. 244) and *wȝwȝt* 'cord' (*Urk.* iv. 166, 12). [2] For the initial *w* see a var. of *wȝr* 'tie up', MONTET 207.

5 looped rope

Det. in [1] *snṯ* (*šnṯ*) 'plan', 'plot out', 'found'.

[1] *Pyr.* 644; *Meir* i. 11; *D. el B.* 37.

6 cord (in early exx. double and looped at top on left)[1]

Ideo. or semi-ideo. or det. in var. [2] *šs*, var. O.K. [3] *šš*, 'cord', 'rope'. Hence phon. *šs* (*šš*), exx. var. (p. 172) *šs* 'alabaster'; *išst* 'what?' (§ 500). There has been much confusion with V 33:[4a] (1) in the words 'linen', 'cloth', 'thing', 'concern', and 'corn', all originally reading *ššr*; however, the fact of the confusion, together with certain writings with metathesis *šsr* (see V 33, nn. 4. 9), make the usually accepted reading *šs* (so in the 1st edition) still just defensible, for final *r* usually falls; (2) as det. in *ꜥrf* 'tie up', 'pack'; (3) as phon. *g* in hieratic, where the two signs are not distinguished in early times;[4] (4) as det. clothes, ex. [5] *isywt* 'rags'; however, this employment to replace S 28 does not appear before Dyn. XIX.

[1] Early forms, *Medum* 13; *Saqq. Mast.* i. 1. 2. [2] *Urk.* iv. 885, 7. [3] DAV. *Ptah.* i. 25. [4] MÖLL. *Pal.* i. nos. 515. 520. [4a] Full discussion, *Bull.* 30, 161. [5] *Adm.* 3, 4; the MS. is probably of Dyn. XIX.

7 loop of cord with the ends downward

Cf. var. Pyr. [1] *šni* 'encircle'. Hence phon. *šn*, exx. *šn* 'tree'; *šnꜥ* 'repel'.

[1] *Pyr.* 213.

8 [1] alternative form of last (Dyn. XVIII)

Use as last.

[1] *Puy.* 57; *Rekh.* 3, 28. So too already *Pyr.* 5.

9 cartouche in original round form[1]

Det. in *šnw* 'cartouche' (p. 74).

[1] See p. 74 for explanation as a double rope encircling (*šni*) the entire region ruled over by the sun or by the king as later embodiment of the sun.

10 cartouche in secondary oval form (p. 74)

Det. in [1] *šnw* 'circuit'; [2] *rn* 'name'; also in names of kings and other royal personages, in which case the component signs are written inside it, ex. *Mn-ḫpr-Rꜥ* 'Menkheperrēꜥ', i. e. Tuthmosis III.

[1] GAYET, *Temple de Louxor*, p. 14. [2] BRUGSCH, *Thes.* 1077, 19.

V 11 sign probably later taken to be a cartouche cut in half and reversed[1]

Det. in [2] *dnỉ* 'dam off', 'restrain'. The hieratic equivalent of the same sign[3] serves also as det. in [4] *pḫꜣ* 'split'. It seems doubtful whether the hieratic word usually transcribed as *dyt* (*dwyt*?) 'shriek' was originally written with this sign.[5]

[1] So at least it appears to be in Dyn. XVIII. Early hieroglyphic exx. are lacking, for the det. of *ḏnỉ* in *Pyr.* 278. 716, namely a kind of hoe, cannot easily be the prototype of our sign. *Ḏnỉ*, later *dnỉ*, may originally have meant 'cut off'; cf. the later word *dnỉt* 'portion', 'fraction', see SETHE, *Zahlworte* 89. [2] *Urk.* iv. 312, 11; 445, 17. [3] MÖLL. *Pal.* i. no. 584; ii. no. 584. [4] *Pt.* 283; *Eb.* 36, 16. [5] In hieroglyphic of Dyn. XIX it has the same det. with which *dnỉ* is written. For the reading see VOG. *Bauer* 69–70; GARD. *Sin.* 99.

12 band of string or linen

Det. bind, exx. *sšd* 'head-band'; *ꜥnḫ* 'garland'; *fḫ*, 'loose', whence [1] *fḫ* 'depart'; from the last, phon. det. in *tꜣw Fnḫw* 'Phoenician lands'. Det. papyrus-books, exx. *šfdw* 'papyrus'; *snn* 'deed'. Phon. or phon. det. *ꜥrḳ* (from *ꜥrḳ* 'bind on') in *ꜥrḳ* 'swear'; var. *ꜥrḳy* 'last day' of the month (§ 264).

[1] *Sinai* 90, 16; see GARD. *Sin.* 20.

13 rope for tethering animals[1]

Cf. Pyr. *ṯṯt* 'fetterer (?)'.[2] Phon. *ṯ*.[3] Sometimes also, by a false archaism, for *t* (§ 19, OBS. 2).

[1] *PSBA.* 22, 65. [2] *Pyr.* 672, epithet of a cat-goddess. [3] SETHE, *Alphabet* 156.

14 the last, with an added diacritical tick

Phon. *ṯ*, both in hieroglyphic and hieratic, but apparently only in a few words, doubtless words in which the value *ṯ* had not changed into *t*, exx. [1] *ṯsỉ* 'lift'; [2] *Ṯṯỉ* 'Tjetji', a man's name.

[1] *Sin.* B 23; *P. Kah.* 2, 7. Sim. *wṯs* 'raise', *Westc.* 12, 23; *sṯsw* 'supports', ERM. *Hymn.* 1, 2. [2] Brit. Mus. 614, 3; *ib.* vert. 2; *ṯsỉ*, *ib.* 13. In other words in this inscription *ṯ* is written without the tick, exx. *sṯ* 'lo', 4; *ỉṯỉ* 'seize', 10.

15 combination of V 13 and D 54

In var. Pyr. [1] *ỉṯỉ*, in M.E. often *ỉṯỉ*,[2] 'seize'.

[1] See *Verbum* i. § 397, 5. [2] Reading, see p. 214, bottom.

16 looped cord serving as hobble for cattle

Ideo. in O.K. [1] *sꜣ* (*zꜣ*) 'hobble'. Hence phon. *sꜣ* (*zꜣ*)[2] in *sꜣ* 'protection'.

[1] L. *D. Ergänzungsband* 40, with the picture. [2] Reading from varr. of *zꜣw* 'guard', *Pyr.* 1203. 1752.

17 [1] rolled up herdsman's shelter of papyrus[2] (Dyn. XVIII)

Ideo. in var. *sꜣ*, var. Pyr. [3] *zꜣ*, 'protection'.

[1] *D. el. B.* 13. [2] *ÄZ.* 44, 77; *Rec.* 30, 39. [3] *Pyr.* 1470.

18 [1] O.K. form of last

Use as last.

[1] DAV. *Ptah.* i. 16, no. 353.

V 19 [hieroglyph] hobble for cattle[1]

Ideo. or det. in [hieroglyph][2] varr. [hieroglyph],[3] [hieroglyph][4] *mḏt* 'stable', '(cattle-)stall'. For unknown reasons, det. in [hieroglyph][5] varr. [hieroglyph],[6] [hieroglyph][7] *tmꜣ* (from *ṯmꜣ*?) 'mat', whence phon. or phon. det. *ṯmꜣ* (*tmꜣ*) in [hieroglyph][8] varr. [hieroglyph],[9] [hieroglyph][10] *ṯmꜣ*, 'cadaster (?)' or kind of land (?); in [hieroglyph] var. [hieroglyph] *ẖꜣr* 'sack' as measure of capacity (§ 266, 1); and in other names of woven or wickerwork objects. By confusion with an older sign for a palanquin or portable shrine,[11] det. in [hieroglyph][12] *ḳni* 'palanquin', whence also in [hieroglyph][13] *ḳni* 'sheaf'; so too in [hieroglyph][14] *kꜣr* 'shrine'; possibly also in [hieroglyph][15] *šṯyt*, name of the sanctuary of Sokar in Memphis.[16] To be distinguished carefully from [hieroglyph] Aa 19.

[1] Made of cord, with a wooden cross-bar to be hidden below the earth, MONTET 95. [2] *Bersh.* i. 18. [3] Cairo 20104, *m* 1; *Rhind* 84. [4] *Meir* iii. 4. Sim. *Pyr.* 2202. [5] *Rec.* 39, 120. [6] *BH.* ii. 13. [7] *Westc.* 7, 15. [8] *Rekh.* 3, 18, qu. Exerc. XXX (iii); *sšw nw ṯmꜣ*, *ib.* p. 25 = *tmꜣ*, *ib.* 3, 26. [9] Brit. Mus. 828, qu. § 450. [10] *Sš n ṯmꜣ*, Cairo 20056; Leyd. V 3. [11] *Pyr.* 300 (*kꜣr*); cf. the picture *Sah.* 65. [12] *Westc.* 11, 7; differently determined, *ib.* 7, 14. [13] *Paheri* 3. [14] LAC. *TR.* 21, 3. [15] *D. el B.* 11. [16] STOLK, *Ptah* (Berlin, 1911), 27.

20 [hieroglyph] the same without the cross-bar (cf. V 21)

Cf. Dyn. XIX [hieroglyph][1] *mḏwt* 'stables'. Hence phon. *mḏ*[2] in [hieroglyph] *mḏw* '10' (§§ 259. 260).

[1] MAR. *Abyd.* i. 53. [2] *ÄZ.* 34, 90.

21 [hieroglyph] combination of [hieroglyph] V 20 and [hieroglyph] I 10 (Dyn. XII onward)

Ideo. in [hieroglyph][1] *mḏt* 'stable', 'cattle-stall'. Hence phon. *mḏ* in [hieroglyph][2] *mḏ* 'be deep' and derivatives.

[1] See V 19, n. 3. [2] BUDGE, p. 458, 9. Sim. *mḏt* 'depth', *Kuban* 32.

For [hieroglyph] see M 28.

22 [hieroglyph][1] whip[2] (Dyn. XVIII)

For unknown reason,[3] phon. *mḥ*, exx. [hieroglyph] var. Pyr. [hieroglyph][4] *mḥ* 'fill'; [hieroglyph] *mḥnyt* 'the coiled one', name of a snake.

[1] Ex. *Hier.* 6, no. 77. [2] *ÄZ.* 35, 106. [3] A derivation from *ḥwi* 'strike' has been suggested, *Hier.* p. 63. [4] *Pyr.* 1682.

23 [hieroglyph][1] O.K. form of last

Use as last.

[1] Exx. DAV. *Ptah.* i. 17, nos. 371. 372. 377; *Sah.* 30; *Ti* 112.

24 [hieroglyph] cord wound on stick (O.K. and M.K. form)[1]

For unknown reason, phon. *wḏ* (later *wd*), exx. [hieroglyph] var. [hieroglyph] *wḏ* 'command'; [hieroglyph][2] *wḏḥ* (for *wdḥ*) 'table of offerings'; [hieroglyph] var. Pyr. [hieroglyph][3] *wḏb* 'turn'.

[1] Exx. O.K., DAV. *Ptah.* i. 14, no. 296; M.K., *BH.* iii. 4, no. 51. [2] *BH.* i. 17. [3] *Pyr.* 1723.

25 [hieroglyph][1] alternative form of last (Dyn. XVIII)

Use as last.

[1] Ex. *Rekh.* 2, 17.

V 26 [1] netting needle filled with twine [2]

Ideo. in [3] var. [4] *ꜥḏ*, also [4] *ꜥd*, 'spool', 'reel'. Hence phon. or phon. det. *ꜥḏ*, later *ꜥd*, ex. [5] *ꜥḏ*, var. [6] *ꜥd*, 'be in good condition'; also *ꜥnḏ* or *ꜥnd*,[7] proved only in the case of *mꜥndt*, var. Pyr. [8] *mꜥnḏt*, 'the morning-bark' of the sun-god.

[1] *Rekh.* 2, 6; *Puy.* 20, 6. [2] See the picture *BH.* ii. 4 = *Bull.* 9, 5. [3] BUDGE, p. 391, 2. [4] NAV. ch. 153, 15. [5] *BH.* i. 8, 15. [6] *Sh. S.* 7. [7] See *Sitz. Berl. Ak.* 1912, 958. [8] *Pyr.* 335. 336; sim. *ib.* 661.

27 [1] O.K. form of last

Use as last.

[1] *Medum* 13. Sim. *Saqq. Mast.* i. 1.

28 [1] wick of twisted flax

Cf. with a similar sign, *ḥꜥt* 'wick';[2] hence[3] phon. *ḥ*. As late det. once in *tkꜣ* 'candle'.[4]

[1] Detailed ex., *Saqq. Mast.* i. 40, no. 68. See too the picture CAPART, *Rue* 37. [2] Dyn. XIX, *Wb.* iii. 39; a hieroglyphic ex. in the Hypostyle Hall, Karnak (Nelson). [3] *ÄZ.* 73, 8, n. 2; *Ann.* 43, 309. [4] MOGENSEN, *Musée nat. Copenhague*, Pl. 24; see SETHE, *Zur Geschichte der Einbalsamierung*, 11*.

29 [1] swab made from a hank of fibre (down to Dyn. XVIII identical for all uses [2])

Det. in O.K. [3] *šk* 'wipe'; hence phon. *sk* (*šk*), ex. *skỉ* 'perish'. For unknown reason, phon. or phon. det. *wꜣḥ*, ex. [4] var. *wꜣḥ* 'place', 'endure'. Also det. in [5] *ḫsr*, var. Pyr. [6] *ḫšr*, 'ward off'. As corruption of a sign resembling M 1, det. in [7] *mꜥr* 'fortunate'.

[1] Detailed ex. *Ti* 132 (*wꜣḥ*). [2] *Wꜣḥ* and *šk* in proximity, see O.K. *Gemn.* i. 22; Dyn. XVIII, *Rekh.* 2. [3] *Rec.* 28, 178; cf. *Sah.* 39. The interpretation as a swab depends on the meaning of *šk* and on its other determinatives in Pyr. [4] *Peas.* B 1, 209. [5] *Urk.* iv. 269, 7. [6] *Pyr.* 908. [7] *Amada* 8.

30 wickerwork basket

Ideo. in [1] var. Pyr. [2] *nbt* 'basket'. Hence phon. in a few words reading *nb*, exx. var. O.K. [3] *nb* 'lord'; *nb* 'every', 'all'.

[1] *Urk.* iv. 896, 10. [2] *Pyr.* 557. [3] *Urk.* i. 126, 9.

For see O 9.

31 wickerwork basket with handle

For unknown reason, phon. *k*.

31* the last, but with handle on opposite side

Regularly in hieratic except in rare O.K. examples.[1]

[1] MÖLL. *Pal.* i. nos. 511, 511 B. Hieroglyphic exx. have not been sought, but must be extremely rare; in Dyn. I–II the few exx. have handle as in V 31, PETR. *Eg. Hier.* nos. 975–9.

V 32 [hieroglyph][1] wickerwork frail[2] (possibly also used as a float by hippopotamus-hunters)[3]

Det. in [hieroglyphs][4] *msnw*, var. Dyn. I [hieroglyphs][5] *mśn*, 'harpooner'; hence (?) phon. *msn* (*mśn*) in [hieroglyphs][6] late var. [hieroglyphs][7] *Msn*, a Lower Egyptian town near Ḳanṭarah.[8] Possibly, but not certainly, the same sign[9] in [hieroglyphs][10] *gꜣwt* 'bundles', 'tribute'; hence phon. det. *gꜣw* in [hieroglyphs] *gꜣw* 'be narrow', and related words.

[1] Exx. O.K., QUIB. *Saqq.* 1911–2, 32 (*Mśn*); *Ti* 115 (*msn*?). [2] See the pictures *Ti* 38. 39; *Gemn.* ii. 1. [3] Guess based partly on the use of the sign to determine *msnw* 'hippopotamus-hunter', partly on the occurrence of a very late word *bb*, with this det., mentioned among the equipment (spears, ropes, etc.) of the *msnw*; see *ÄZ*. 54, 53 and compare the fisherman's reed-floats T 25. But possibly the sign is really the det. of *mśn* 'weave', 'plait', though not so actually found, in which case it would only be phon. det. in *msnw* 'hippopotamus-hunter'. [4] LAC. *TR*. 20, 34. [5] *ÄZ* 57, 138. [6] *Lisht* p. 36. [7] See *ÄZ*. 54, 52. [8] *JEA*. 5, 242. [9] Before Dyn. XVIII it lacks the tie and so resembles [hieroglyph] W 8, see WEILL, *Décrets*, Pls. 2. 3; *Dend.* 8; Cairo 20539, i. *b* 8. [10] *D. el B.* 77.

33 [hieroglyph][1] bag of linen[2]

Ideo. or det. in [hieroglyph] *sšr*, var. O.K. [hieroglyphs][3] *sšr*, var. Dyn. XVIII [hieroglyphs][4] *šsr*, 'linen', 'cloth', cf. especially the compound [hieroglyphs][5] *sšr-nsw*, var. O.K. [hieroglyphs][6] *sšr-nzw*, 'royal linen', 'byssus', Coptic ϣⲉⲛⲥ; the var. [hieroglyphs][7] with [hieroglyph] V 6 makes the hitherto accepted reading *šs-nsw* possible for Dyn. XVIII, as final *r* frequently fell away. Hence phon. *sšr* (read as *šs* in the 1st edition) in [hieroglyphs] var. Dyn. XII [hieroglyphs][8] *sšr*, var. O.K. [hieroglyphs][9] *sšr*, 'thing', 'concern'; also in [hieroglyphs][10] varr. [hieroglyphs],[11] [hieroglyphs][12] *sšr* 'corn'. Perhaps through connection with the stem found in [hieroglyphs] *gꜣwt* 'bundles' (see on V 32) or else with [hieroglyphs] *ggt* 'kidney (?)',[12a] phon. *g* in a few words, exx. [hieroglyphs] var. [hieroglyphs][13] *wgg* 'misery'; [hieroglyphs] *Gbtyw* 'Coptus', a town in Upper Egypt. Det. tie up, in [hieroglyphs] *ꜥrf* 'tie up', 'pack', 'envelop'; also perfume, because kept in bags of linen,[14] ex. [hieroglyphs] var. [hieroglyphs] *sty* 'perfume', cf. [hieroglyph] R 9. As det. clothes not before Dyn. XIX,[15] and then mainly in the form [hieroglyph] V 6 (see on that sign). Note that in M.K. hieratic [hieroglyph] is indistinguishable from [hieroglyph] V 6;[16] in hieroglyphic the two are very often confused.

[1] In O.K. and sometimes later the shape varies greatly. Sometimes like our type, but thinner and inclined at an angle, exx. L. *D.* ii. 22.23; sometimes almost triangular, see below, V 35. Full discussion, *Bull.* 30, 161. [2] Described as *šsrw ꜥrfw* 'tied-up cloths', *Urk.* iv. 1143, 13. [3] *Ti* 115. [4] *Urk.* iv. 1143, 13, *šsrw*, plur. [5] *Urk.* iv. 195, 16. Sim. O.K., *Sah.* 61. [6] L. *D.* ii. 100, *c*. [7] *Urk.* iv. 742, 15. [8] Cairo 20538, ii. *c* 9. [9] *Urk.* i. 149, 9. For writings of possibly the same word with the metathesis *šsr* see *Adm.* p. 101. [10] *Urk.* iv. 743, 1. [11] *Urk.* iv. 372, 14. [12] R. *IH.* 178, 3. [12a] Suggested by Dawson; see *Wb.* v. 208, 7; also *Sign Pap.* 11, 4. [13] *PSBA.* 18, 202, 9. [14] See the picture *D. el B.* 78. [15] See, however, O.K. *ḥnkwt*, *Gebr.* i. 8; also the alternative form of S 28 seen in PETRIE, *Gizeh and Rifeh* 23 G. [16] MÖLL. *Pal.* i. no. 520, without recognizing that V 6 and V 33 are different signs.

V 34 [1] alternative form of last (Dyn. XVIII) — Use as last.

[1] *D. el B.* 94 (*sty* 'perfume').

35 [1] O.K. form of last (rarely also Dyn. XVIII)[2] — Use as last.

[1] DAV. *Ptah.* i. 14, no. 318 = (*E.R.A.*) 37, in *imy-r šsr* 'overseer of linen'. This form of the bag is carried by an attendant, *Ti* 115; cf. too L. *D.* ii. 22, *b*. Other O.K. exx. of the same form of the sign, in *šsr* 'thing', 'concern', *Urk.* i. 136, 5; WEILL, *Décrets*, Pl. 2. [2] In *sšr* 'corn', *Urk.* iv. 372, 14, qu. under V 33, n. 11.

36 receptacle of some kind — Det. in [1] *ḫn* (*ḫnt*?), name of a receptacle given to a temple. Hence (?) phon. or phon. det. *ḫn*, exx. [2] var. [3] *ḫnt* 'occupations'; [4] var. [5] *ḫnty* 'period', 'end' (§ 77, 1).

[1] MAR. *Ab.* i. 10, *b*. [2] *Rekh.* 16. [3] *Paheri* 3. [4] *Urk.* iv. 364, 12. [5] *Urk.* iv. 369, 15.

37 [1] bandage (?) — Det. in [2] *idr* 'bandage', 'bind'. Phon. or phon. det. *idr* in [3] var. [4] *idr* 'herd'; note that [5] appears to read [6] *kꜣ n idr* 'bull of the herd'. For the confusion of and N 41 see *AEO.* ii. 258*.

[1] Karnak, Tuthmosis III unpublished. Rather different, Dyn. XII, *Bersh.* i. 18. [2] *Sm.* 9, 8. 10. 21. [3] *Bersh.* i. 18. [4] Cairo 20001. [5] *Urk.* iv. 699, 13. [6] *Urk.* iv. 195, 10; 196, 1.

38 [1] bandage (O.K.) — Det. in *wt* 'bandage', 'mummy-cloth'. Later replaced by Aa 2.

[1] *Pyr.* 1202 (N 1197).

Sect. W. Vessels of Stone and Earthenware

W 1 sealed oil-jar — Det. oil, unguent, exx. var. [1] *mrḥt* 'unguent'; *mḏt* 'ointment'.

[1] *Urk.* iv. 914, 9; for the reading cf. Cairo 20720, *a* 3.

2 sealed oil-jar, like W 1, but not showing tied ends — Det. in [1] *bꜣs* (*bꜣš*) 'jar'. Phon. *bꜣs* (*bꜣš*) in [2] *Bꜣstt*, var. O.K. [3] *Bꜣštt*, '(the cat-goddess) Bastet'.

[1] LAC. *Sarc.* ii. 13, no. 23. [2] Ex. *Urk.* iv. 432, 9. [3] *Ti* 23.

3 [1] basin of alabaster as used in purifications[2] — Det. in O.K. var. *šs* 'alabaster' (p. 172). Perhaps on account of the purifications characteristic of feasts, det. in var. Dyn. XVIII *ḥb* 'feast'; hence semi-ideo. or phon. *ḥb* in [3] *ḥb* 'mourn'. Abbrev. of *ḥbt* 'ritual book' in W 5. Det. feast, exx. [4] *psḏntyw* 'New-moon festival'; [5] *Wꜣg* '*Wag*-festival'.

[1] Showing the markings of alabaster, *Hier.* 2, no. 9; 9, no. 178; *Kopt.* 9. [2] *Rec.* 39, 54. [3] *Sin.* B 142. [4] *BH.* i. 24. [5] *Siut* i. 299. Sim. *BH.* i. 25, 90–5.

W 4 [sign] combination of [sign] O 22 and [sign] W 3 — Ideo. or det. in [hieroglyphs] var. [sign] *ḥb* 'feast'. Det. feast (much rarer in M.E. than [sign] alone), ex. [hieroglyphs][1] *tp-rnpt* 'feast of the first of the year'.

[1] *BH.* i. 24. Sim. *Wꜣg*, Brit. Mus. 162.

5 [sign] combination of [sign] T 28 and [sign] W 3 — In [hieroglyphs][1] *ḫry-ḥbt*[2] 'lector-priest', lit. 'he who is under (i.e. carries) the ritual book'.

[1] Already M.K., *ÄZ.* 39, 117, 6. [2] Reading, see p. 51, n. 4.

6 [sign][1] O.K. sign for a particular vessel — In [hieroglyphs] *wḥt* 'cauldron'. Later replaced by [sign] Aa 2.

[1] *Saqq. Mast.* i. 2. Rather different, *ib.* 1; *Medum* 13 (here of copper).

7 [sign][1] granite bowl (Dyn. XVIII) — Det. in [hieroglyphs][1] *mꜣt*, var. O.K. [hieroglyphs][2] *mꜣṯ*, 'red granite'; hence phon. det. *mꜣṯ* in [hieroglyphs][3] *mꜣṯ* 'proclaim'. Det. in [hieroglyphs][4] var. [hieroglyphs][5] *Ꜣbw* 'Elephantine', as source of the red granite; hence phon. det. *ꜣb* in [hieroglyphs][6] var. [hieroglyphs][7] *ꜣbt* 'family'.

[1] *D. el B.* 156. [2] *Urk.* i. 107, 2. [3] *Urk.* iv. 261, 3. [4] *Rekh.* 5. Sim. *Urk.* iv. 843, 4. [5] Brit. Mus. 614, 4. [6] LAC. *TR.* 2, 1. [7] Brit. Mus. 159, 11.

8 [sign][1] deformation of the last (Dyn. XI) — In *Ꜣbw* 'Elephantine' and *ꜣbt* 'family', see on W 7. The same sign may serve as the earlier form of [sign] *gꜣw* V 32.[2]

[1] Brit. Mus. 614, 4 (*Ꜣbw* 'Elephantine'). Sim. Cairo 20512, *cc.* [2] See V 32, n. 9.

9 [sign][0] stone jug with handle — Det. in [hieroglyphs][1] *nḫnm*, var. Pyr. [hieroglyphs][2] *nšnm*, 'the *nḫnm*-vase' with its specific oil. Hence (?) phon. *ḫnm*, exx. [hieroglyphs] *Ḫnmw* '(the ram-headed god) Chnum'; [hieroglyphs] *ḫnm* 'join'.

[0] SCHARFF 49. [1] *BH.* i. 17; *Pyr.* 51 (N 311 *a*). [2] *Pyr.* 51 (W 59 *a*). In O.K. [sign] *š* interchanges with later [sign] *ḫ*, see *Verbum* i. § 260.

10 [sign] cup (probably sometimes also a basket, cf. [sign] A 9) — Det. in [hieroglyphs][1] *iꜥb*, var. [hieroglyphs][2] *ꜥꜥb*, 'cup'; hence phon. or phon. det. *iꜥb*, ex. [hieroglyphs] *iꜥb* 'unite'; *ꜥb*, ex. [hieroglyphs] *m-ꜥb* 'in the company of' (§ 178). Det. in [hieroglyphs][3] *wsḫ* (*wšḫ*) 'cup'; hence phon. or phon. det. *wsḫ* (*wšḫ*), exx. [hieroglyphs] *wsḫ* 'be wide'; [hieroglyphs][4] var. [sign] (O 15) *wsḫt* 'hall'; *sḫw*, in [hieroglyphs] *sḫw* 'width'. Det. in [hieroglyphs][5] *ḫnt* 'cup'; hence phon. *ḫnt* in [hieroglyphs][6] var. [hieroglyphs] *ḫnwt* 'mistress'. Det. in [hieroglyphs][7] *ꜥ* 'cup'. In words reading *biꜣ* [sign] sometimes replaces older [sign] N 41, ex. [hieroglyphs][8] *biꜣw* 'rare treasures'.

[1] *Wb.* i. 40; JÉQ. 115; LAC. *Sarc.* ii. 156. [2] *Urk.* iv. 770, 15. [3] JÉQ. 115; evidently very rare, not in *Wb.* i. nor in LAC. *Sarç.* [4] *Urk.* iv. 1220, 16. [5] *BH.* i. 17. [6] *Urk.* iv. 391, 13. [7] *Wb.* i. 158. [8] *BH.* i. 8, 11. Sim. *D. el B.* 81; 84, 6.

10* [sign][1] pot perhaps used also as lamp (O.K.) — Phon. *bꜣ*[2] in conjunction with [sign] G 29, ex. [hieroglyphs][3] *bꜣ* 'soul', or with [sign] E 10, ex. [hieroglyphs] *Bꜣ-pf(i)* 'Bapfi', a god.[1] Later superseded in these uses by [sign] R 7.

[1] *Ann.* 43, 309. [2] Cf. a vessel called *bꜣw* named *Eb.* 4, 9. [3] *Pyr.* 854 (M 386); 1378 (N 1144).

(Aa 4) [sign][1] alternative form of last (Pyr.) — Use as last.

[1] *Pyr.* 854 (N 657); 1098 (N 1252); 1378 (P 616).

W 11 [hieroglyph] [1] (1) ring-stand for jars, (2) red earthenware pot (Dyn. XVIII form, round at bottom) — (1) Ideo. or det. in [hieroglyphs] [2] var. [hieroglyph] [3] *nst* 'seat'. For unknown reason,[3a] phon. *g*. (2) Ideo. or det. in [hieroglyphs] [4] var. [hieroglyphs] [5] *dšrt* 'red pot'. (3) Occasionally substituted for [hieroglyph] O 45 in Dyn. XVIII, ex. [hieroglyphs] [6] *ἰpt nsw* 'king's harîm'.

[1] Ex. *Rekh.* 2, 2 (*g*); *D. el B.* 36 (*nst*). In Dyn. XII still sometimes with bottom straight as *g* (*Bersh.* i. 31), while curved as *nst* (*ib.* 19). [2] *ÄZ.* 47, 91. [3] *D. el B.* 36, in *Nswt-tswy*. [3a] According to Grdseloff (*Ann.* 43, 310) from an O.K. word *gw* (*Ann.* 16, 196); but this is described as an altar. [4] *Rekh.* 11. [5] *D. el B.* 11. [6] *JEA.* 11, 4.

12 [hieroglyph] [1] ring-stand (O.K. form, straight at bottom) — Use as last, in O.K. [hieroglyphs] [2] *nšt* 'seat' and as phon. *g*.[3]

[1] Dav. *Ptah.* i. 13, nos. 255. 258 (*nšt, g*). [2] *Ptah.* (E.R.A.) 32. [3] *Ti* 128 (*gḥšt*).

13 [hieroglyph] red earthenware pot (O.K. form, round at bottom and plain) — Use as W 11, in O.K. [hieroglyphs] [1] *dšrt* 'red pot'. In M.K. a sign of this appearance is used for [hieroglyph] N 34.[2]

[1] *Pyr.* 249. [2] *JEA.* 4, Pl. 9.

14 [hieroglyph] tall water-pot — Ideo. or det. in [hieroglyphs] [1] *ḥst*, var. O.K. [hieroglyphs] [2] *ḥzt*, 'water-pot'; hence phon. *ḥs* (*ḥz*), ex. [hieroglyphs] var. [hieroglyphs] *ḥsἰ* 'praise'. Det. also in [hieroglyphs] [3] *snb(t)*, var. Pyr. [hieroglyphs] [4] *znbt*, 'jar'.

[1] *ÄZ.* 37, 95; Lac. *Sarc.* ii. 166. [2] Montet 393. [3] *Urk.* iv. 874, 3. [4] *Pyr.* 1179.

15 [hieroglyph] water-pot with water pouring from it — Det. in [hieroglyphs] [1] *ḳbb* 'be cool' and derivatives;[2] also in [hieroglyphs] [3] *ḳbḥ* 'libate'.

[1] *Urk.* iv. 970, 15 (*ḳb*). [2] Ex. *sḳbb*, *Urk.* iv. 65, 6. [3] *Amarn.* iv. 3, 8.

16 [hieroglyph] the same in a ring-stand [hieroglyph] W 12 — Ideo. or det. in [hieroglyphs] [1] varr. [hieroglyphs],[1] [hieroglyphs] [2] *ḳbḥw* 'libation' and the related words. Much more rarely det. in [hieroglyphs] [3] *ḳbb* 'be cool'.

[1] *Meir* iii. 17. [2] *BH.* i. 17. [3] Ex. *P. Kah.* 7, 41 (*ḳb*).

17 [hieroglyph] [1] water-pots in a rack (Dyn. XII–XVIII) — Ideo. in [hieroglyphs] [2] *ḫntw* 'racks for water-pots'. Hence phon. *ḫnt*, ex. [hieroglyphs] var. [hieroglyph] *ḫnt* 'in front of' (§ 174) and derivatives.

[1] *Hier.* 2, no. 6. With three pots, not infrequent in M.K., exx. *BH.* i. 8. 15; Leyd. V 2; usual in Dyn. XVIII, exx. *Rekh.* 4; *Paheri* 4. [2] *Urk.* iv. 874, 3.

18 [hieroglyph] [1] O.K. form of last — Use as last.

[1] With four pots, usual in O.K., exx. *Sah.* 1; *Saqq. Mast.* i. 20; more often than not in M.K., exx. Leyd. V 3. 4. 6. 7; only rarely in Dyn. XVIII, ex. *Urk.* iv. 874, 7.

19 [hieroglyph] milk-jug as carried in a net [1] — Det. in [hieroglyphs] [2] *mhr* 'milk-jug'. From a probably obsolete word [hieroglyphs] [3] *mr* 'milk-jug', phon. *mἰ* (old *mr*), exx. [hieroglyphs] *mἰ*, var. Pyr. [hieroglyphs] [4] *mr*, 'like' (§ 170); [hieroglyphs] *dmἰ* 'town'; [hieroglyphs] var. [hieroglyphs] [5] *mἰn* 'to-day' (§ 205).[6]

[1] See the picture *Meir* i. 11 = ii. 18, no. 12. [2] *Meir* ii. 6. [3] *Pyr.* 32; cf. the place-name *Mrt* determined by a sign like W 20, *Medum* 21. [4] *Pyr.* 1665. [5] Chass. *Ass.* 77. [6] The use in Pyr. *zmn* (*Wb.* iii. 453) is un-explained.

W20 milk-jug with a leaf covering the milk[1] — Det. in [2] *irtt*, var. O.K. [3] *irṯt*, 'milk'.

[1] See the pictures *Ti* 114; Dav. *Ptah.* i. 16. [2] *D. el B.* 94. [3] L. *D.* ii. 66.

21 twin wine-jars[1] — Det. in [2] *irp* 'wine'.

[1] For the O.K. form see the picture *Ti* 114; also *Saqq. Mast.* i. 39, no. 55.
[2] *D. el B.* 105.

22 beer-jug — Ideo. or det. in var. *ḥnḳt* 'beer'. Det. pot, measure, exx. [1] *ḳrḥt* 'vessel'; *ds* (O.K. *dś*) '*des*-measure' (§ 266, 1, end); offerings generally, in [2] *inw* 'tribute'; notions connected with fluids, ex. *tḫi* 'be drunken'. As det. in the group 'food and drink', see on X 2. Ideo. in [3] var. Pyr. [4] *wdpw* 'butler'.

[1] *Urk.* iv. 427, 8. [2] *Urk.* iv. 429, 7. [3] See Schäfer-Lange, *Grab- und Denksteine*, iii. 58; *PSBA.* 13, 451. [4] *Pyr.* 120. 124. See too *Sebekn.* 7, 9.

23 jar with handles — Use as last, but not specially in connection with beer. Exx. [1] *ḳrḥt* 'vessel'; [2] *wrḥ* 'anoint'. Also in [3] *wdpw* 'butler', see on W 22.

[1] *Th. T. S.* iii. 12. [2] *Th. T. S.* iii. 4. [3] *Meir* iii. 25.

24 bowl — Phon. *nw*, exx. *nw* (*nyw*) 'of', m. plur. (§ 86); *Nwt* '(the goddess) Nut', probably so to be read in spite of the obscure Pyr. var. ;[1] *ḥnw* 'vessel'. Initial *nw* is preferably written or , see on U 19; final *nw* is sometimes written , exx. *mnw* 'monument'; *Tḥnw* 'Libya'. Great difficulty is caused by 'primeval waters', which may have existed in two distinct forms (1) *niw* or *nww* or *nw*, (2) *nnw* or *nwnw*;[1a] for (1) see Pyr. var. [1b] and a Dyn. XVIII enigmatic equivalent ;[1c] for (2) see Pyr. var. ,[1d] also the female counterpart [2] *nnt* 'the lower heaven', further the personal name presumably to be read *Nnw* on account of [3] *nn(i)* 'child', and lastly Copt. ⲛⲟⲩⲛ 'abyss'. Phon. also *in* (cf. W 25) in var. Pyr. [4] *ink* 'I' (§ 64). Phon. det. in , varr. Pyr. ,[5] [5] *ḏꜣḏꜣt* 'council'; whether the former writing has anything to do with [6] *ḏꜣḏꜣw* 'pot' is doubtful. So too from M.K. replaces O.K. in such words as var. Pyr. [7] *ḳd* 'build'; var. O.K. [8] *ḳd* 'form'; the old phon. det. o here is due to the stem-meaning of *ḳdi* 'go round', while the later may be connected with *ḳd* 'fashion' pots. From M.K. onwards inexplicably accompanies Aa 27, exx. *nḏ* 'protect'; *nḏ* 'ask'; and is found also in [9] *Nḫbt* '(the goddess) Nekhbet'.

W 24 (continued) The writing [hieroglyph] for *m-ḫnw* 'in', lit. 'in the interior (of)' (§ 178) has been explained as a rebus *m(w) ḫ(r) nw* 'water under pot'.[10] Lastly, [hieroglyph] occurs as occasional alternative to [hieroglyph] or [hieroglyph] as det. pot; hieratic often fails to distinguish these signs.[11]

[1] *Pyr.* 1184. 1454. [1a] Fuller collection of relevant writings, SETHE, *Amun und die acht Urgötter* §§ 61, 127. [1b] *Pyr.* 207. 446. [1c] *Rev. d'Ég.* i. 5. [1d] *Pyr.* 1078. 1778. 1780. [2] *Pyr.* 1691. [3] GRIFFITH, *Catalogue of the Demotic Papyri in the Rylands Library* iii. 220, n. 14. [4] *Pyr.* 141. 1098. See *Sitz. d. Berl. Ak.* 1912, 962. [5] *Pyr.* 1713. [6] *Eb.* 66, 17. [7] *Pyr.* 1597. [8] *Urk.* i. 101, 10. [9] *D. el B.* 35. Also in the related place-name *Nḫb* 'El-Kâb', *Paheri* 1. [10] *ÄZ.* 59, 61. [11] MÖLL. *Pal.* i. nos. 495. 497.

25 [hieroglyph] combination of [hieroglyph] W 24 and [hieroglyph] D 54 In [hieroglyph] var. Pyr. [hieroglyph][1] *ini*[2] 'bring', 'fetch'.

[1] *Pyr.* 913. [2] Reading, cf. [hieroglyph] W 24 with the value *in* and see *Sitz. d. Berl. Ak.* 1912, 962; also Coptic ⲉⲓⲛⲉ.

Sect. X. Loaves and Cakes

X 1 [hieroglyph] bread[1] Ideo. (or semi-phon. *t*) in [hieroglyph] varr. [hieroglyph], [hieroglyph][2] rare var. Pyr. [hieroglyph][3] *t* 'bread'; the accepted reading *tꜣ* (so in the 1st edition) has no justification. Hence phon. *t*. Note the spellings [hieroglyph],[4] [hieroglyph][4] for [hieroglyph] *it-nṯr* 'god's father', name of a class of elder priests. In group-writing (§ 60) [hieroglyph] or [hieroglyph] is used for *t*.[5]

[1] SETHE, *Alphabet* 156. Cf. the Pyr. var. of n. 3. and the later writing of *it-nṯr* with the loaf X 2. [2] Common in compounds like *t-rtḥ* 'baked bread', *t-wr* 'large bread', *t-nbs* 'bread of the *nebk*-tree', exx. *BH.* i. 17; cf. the varr. of *t-wr*, *Pyr.* 1946. 2194. [3] *Pyr.* 1723. [4] See *ÄZ.* 47, 94; 48, 21–2. [5] BURCHARDT § 130.

For [hieroglyph] see M 5.

2 [hieroglyph] loaf Det. bread, exx. [hieroglyph] var. [hieroglyph] *t* 'bread'; [hieroglyph] *šns* '*šns*-loaf'. For [hieroglyph] or [hieroglyph] as *t* in group-writing (§ 60) see on X 1. The groups [hieroglyph] or [hieroglyph], representing bread and beer with or without another sign for bread, occur as generic det. food, exx. [hieroglyph] *prt-ḫrw* 'invocation offerings' (p. 172); [hieroglyph][1] *šꜣb* 'meal'; expanded still further in [hieroglyph][2] *ḥtp(w)-nṯr* 'divine offerings'. On M.K. coffins [hieroglyph] is sometimes substituted for [hieroglyph] *Ḏḥwty* 'Thoth' for superstitious reasons,[3] and a similar or identical group serves also rarely for [hieroglyph] *Gb* '(the earth-god) Geb'[4] or for [hieroglyph] *ꞽInpw* 'Anubis'.[5] From the end of Dyn. XVIII [hieroglyph][6] is found as var. of [hieroglyph], [hieroglyph] *it-nṯr* 'god's father', a priestly title, see above under X 1.

[1] Munich 3, 17. Possibly the cursive hieratic ligature seen in *wnmt* 'food', *Sin.* B 104, is to be resolved similarly. [2] *D. el B.* 14. Sim. *Th. T. S.* i. 8. [3] LAC. *TR.* 22, 8; see *ÄZ.* 51, 59. [4] LAC. *TR.* 29, 1. 26. 28. [5] LAC. *TR.* 5, 1. [6] *L. D.*, Text, iii. 15; see *ÄZ.* 48, 22.

X 3 alternative form of last — Use as last. For this as the earliest form of N 34 see on that sign.

4 roll of bread — Det. bread, food, exx. [1] *t* 'bread'; [2] *prt-ḫrw* 'invocation offerings'; [3] (Dyn. XVIII), var. M.K. [4] *snw*[5] 'food-offerings'. From this last, phon. det. *sn* (*zn*), exx. [6] var. *snỉ* 'pass by'; [7] *Snt* 'Senet', a fem. personal name; cf. also Pyr. [8] *ỉznỉỉ* 'are opened'. In *snỉ* 'pass by' and *snt* 'likeness' is subsequently replaced by X 5, while Pyr. in *zn* 'open' later takes the form N 37, see on that sign. Also from *fkꜣ* 'cake', phon. det. *fkꜣ* in *fkꜣ* 'reward'. As det. sometimes takes the place of W 3 (Dyns. XI. XII), ex. *ḥbw* 'festivals'.[9]

[1] *Meir* ii. 8. Sim. *šbt* 'food', *ib.* [2] *BH.* i. 33. [3] BUDGE, p. 159, 7. [4] *D. el B.* (XI) i. 24. [5] This word chances not to have been found before M.K., in which period its spellings are influenced by *šn* 'smell'. Nevertheless, the original value was probably *znw* and this must be regarded as the origin of the phonetic value *sn*; see *Rec.* 35, 61. [6] *BH.* i. 8, 8. [7] *Th. T. S.* ii. 7. [8] *Pyr.* 1408. [9] Brit. Mus. 580. Sim. *ib.* 237 (*Wꜣg* 'Wag-festival'); CL.-VAND. § 33, 10 (*ꜣbd* 'month-festival').

(N 18) alternative form of last — Use as last.

5 semi-hieratic form of X 4 — Det. bread, food (in hieratic only), exx. [1] *t* 'bread'; [2] *ꜥḳw* 'provisions'. From Dyn. XII usually takes the place of as phon. det. *sn*[3] in hieroglyphic [4] *snỉ* 'surpass'; [5] *m-snt-r* 'in the likeness of' (§ 180).

[1] *Pr.* 1, 4. [2] *Pr.* 17, 7. [3] See the intermediate forms in the name *Snt*, Brit. Mus. 461; *Th. T. S.* ii. 38. [4] *Urk.* iv. 102, 4. Sim. 'pass by', *Sh. S.* 9. [5] *Urk.* iv. 168, 10.

6 a round loaf bearing mark of the baker's fingers[1] — Det. in [2] *pꜣt* 'loaf'. Hence phon. det. in [3] *pꜣt* 'antiquity', 'primeval times' and the related words. Apt to be confused with N 9.[4]

[1] DAV. *Ptah.* i. 18, no. 402 and p. 34; *Ann.* 9, 111; also depicted *D. el B.* 135. [2] *Th. T. S.* i. 18. [3] *Urk.* iv. 165, 14. [4] Ex. *pꜣty*, *Urk.* iv. 1168, 6.

7 [1] half-loaf of bread — In O.K. offering-lists described as *gśw* 'half-loaves' or *pḏw* '(pieces) spread out'.[1a] In Pyr. or is ideo. or det. food, exx. [2] *wšb* 'eat'; [3] var. [3] *wnm* 'eat'. After O.K. becomes indistinguishable from N 29 and is practically confined to the word [4] var. [5] *wnm*[6] 'eat'. Exceptionally, however, as det. in [7] *snw* 'food-offerings'.

[1] *Pyr.* 807 (M 113). Often, but not always, taller and narrower than N 29. [1a] GUNN, *Teti*, 207, n. 1. [2] *Pyr.* 805. Sim. *bꜥḥỉ* 'have abundance', *ib.* [3] *Pyr.* 807. [4] *Dend.* 12. Sim. Munich 3, 7. [5] Brit. Mus. 574, 17; *Paheri* 3. [6] For the reading see on M 42 and Z 11. [7] *Urk.* iv. 481, 12.

X 8 [hieroglyph] conical loaf? (in M.E. more often replaced by [hieroglyph] D 37)

Ideo. *give*, in [hieroglyph] *rdi*, [hieroglyph] *di* 'give' (§ 289, 1) and also in Pyr. [hieroglyph] rare varr. [hieroglyph],[1] [hieroglyph][2] for the more usual imperative [hieroglyph] var. M.E. [hieroglyph] *imi* 'give' (§ 336). The use in both stems seems conclusive for the ideographic character of the sign.[3] Possibly the earliest reading of the later stem *rdi* was *rḏi*, cf. the personal name [hieroglyph] var. [hieroglyph][4] and the Pyr. var. [hieroglyph][5] for [hieroglyph] *rḏw* 'efflux'; but verb-forms with repetition of the sign (ex. [hieroglyph]) doubtless indicate the reading *dd*; so in Pyr. already[5a] and see above § 289, 1. From the same stem, phon. *d* (very rare), ex. [hieroglyph][6] *dḳ(r)* 'fruit'. The word [hieroglyph][7] 'provisions' probably reads *di*; in hieratic the inner markings are not shown, so that the sign there resembles [hieroglyph], see before Z 9, and the word has, therefore, often been read *špd*.[8]

[1] *Pyr.* 381. [2] *Pyr.* 392. [3] *Verbum* i. § 454. [4] *ÄZ.* 39, 135. [5] *Pyr.* 788. [5a] *Pyr.* 608. 716. 824. [6] Cairo 20350, *a*. [7] *Sebekn.* 7, 13; *Urk.* iv. 64, 1; *Haremḥab*, right side 9; see GARDINER, *Egyptian Hieratic Texts*, i. 16*, n. 7. [8] So still *Wb.* iv. 112.

Sect. Y. Writings, Games, Music

Y 1 [hieroglyph] papyrus rolled up, tied, and sealed (from Dyn. XII on also vertically [hieroglyph])

Ideo. in [hieroglyph][1] var. Pyr. [hieroglyph][2] *mḏ3t* 'papyrus-roll', 'book'. Hence phon. *mḏ3t*[3] in [hieroglyph][4] varr. [hieroglyph],[5] [hieroglyph][6] *mḏ3t* '(sculptor's) chisel'. Det.[7] *writing and things written*, exx. [hieroglyph] *sš* 'write'; [hieroglyph] *m(w)dt* 'word'; [hieroglyph] *ḥk3* 'magic'; also *abstract notions*, exx. [hieroglyph] *m3ʿt* 'truth'; [hieroglyph] *m3w(y)* 'be new'; [hieroglyph] *rḫ* 'know'; [hieroglyph] *ʿ3* 'great'. In mathematical books and accounts [hieroglyph] is often abbrev. for [hieroglyph] *dmd* 'total'.[8]

[1] *Eb.* 30, 7. [2] *Pyr.* 491. [3] *PSBA.* 21, 269. [4] *Two Sculptors* 8. [5] Leyd. *Denkm.* iv. 14. [6] Common in Dyn. XIX. XX. [7] Old uses, *ÄZ.* 57, 75. [8] Compare *P. Kah.* 8, 13. 14. with *ib.* 8, 62. Sim. *P. Louvre 3226*, 10, 8. This use arises from the habit of separating [hieroglyph] from the phonetic signs for *dmḏ* in M.K. papyri, see Exerc. XX, (*a*), end.

2 [hieroglyph][1] O.K. form of last (also vertically [hieroglyph] from Pyr. on in specific cases)[2]

Use as last.

[1] DAV. *Ptah.* i. 15, no. 341. Sim. in Dyn. XI, exx. Brit. Mus. 614; Louvre C 14. In Dyn. XII, one thread is apt to be shown, not none as here, nor yet on each side as in [hieroglyph] Y 1, exx. Brit. Mus. 581; Louvre C 1. [2] *Pyr.* iv. § 131; Dyn. XI, POL. § 29.

Y 3 [1] scribe's outfit, consisting of palette, bag for the powdered pigments, and reed-holder — Ideo. or det. in [1a] *mnḫd* 'scribe's outfit'; also in var. [2] *sšw* 'writings' and the related words, cf. O.K. [3] *zš* 'write'. Perhaps because pigments were ground fine and smooth, det. in [4] *nʿʿ* 'smooth'; in the Ebers medical papyrus [5] is abbrev. for [6] *snʿʿ* 'made smooth', 'ground fine'. Also det. of the Pyr. word [7] *ṯms* 'red' with its later derivative [8] *tmsw* 'injury', 'harm'.

[1] This form is commonest at all periods, exx. O.K., *Saqq. Mast.* i. 4. 8. 20; M.K., *Bersh.* i. 15. 18. 20; Dyn. XVIII, *Th. T. S.* i. 1; *Rekh.* 5; *Puy.* 20, 7. So too in hieratic, MÖLL. *Pal.* i. no. 537. For the leather bag see SCHARFF 54; QUIB. *Saqq.* 1911–12, Pl. 29; later apparently interpreted as a water-bowl. [1a] *Wb.* ii. 83, 3. [2] *Rekh.* 2, 16, cf. p. 25. [3] *Sah.* 1; *Pyr.* 906. [4] *Herdsm.* 5; *Eb.* 108, 20. Sim. *nʿ*, *Urk.* iv. 717, 12. [5] Exx. *Eb.* 4, 15. 19; 6, 1. [6] *P. Kah.* 5, 50; *Hearst* 1, 17. In O.K. scenes *šnʿʿ* means 'polish', MONTET 290. 306; *snʿʿ ib* 'make calm', lit. 'smooth the heart', *Pt.* 276; BUDGE, p. 262, 14. [7] *Wb.* v. 369. [8] BUDGE, p. 110, 2; 262, 5; cf. *ÄZ.* 60, 74.

4 [1] rarer alternative form of last — Use as last.

[1] Exx. O.K., *Ti* 23. 46; M.K., *BH.* i. 29. 30. 35; Dyn. XVIII, Cairo 34017 = LACAU, Pl. 11. GUNN, *Teti*, 147, n. 1 points out that this alternative form occurs especially often in texts written from left to right, the scribe having omitted to make the customary reversal. So too with certain other signs.

5 draught-board (*znt*) [1] — For unknown reason, phon. *mn*,[2] exx. *mn* 'remain'; *ỉmn* '(the god) Amūn'; *mnḥ* 'wax'.

[1] For this word, see L. *D.* ii. 61, *a*; when it has the draught-board as det., this is much more elaborately made than the sign for *mn*, ex. *Urk.* v. 4, 12. [2] Reading from a large number of Coptic equivalents, exx. *moun* 'remain'; *Amoun* 'Amūn'.

6 [1] draughtsman — Ideo. or det. in [2] var. [2] *ỉb(ꜣ)* 'draughtsman'. Hence phon. *ỉbꜣ* in [3] varr. [3] [4] *ỉbꜣ(w)*, 'dances'.

[1] CAPART, *Rue* 69. [2] *Rec.* 16, 129, Dyn. XX. [3] *BH.* ii. 7. [4] *BH.* ii. 17.

7 [1] harp — Det. in [2] *bnt* (*bỉnt*) [3] 'harp'.

[1] Thebes, tomb 50. [2] *Urk.* iv. 174, 13. [3] Ṣaʿîdic *boinĕ*.

8 [1] sistrum — Ideo. or det. in var. *sššt* 'sistrum'. Between Dyn. XIII–XVIII occasionally phon. *sḫm* (because of *sḫm*, a kind of sistrum [2]), ex. [3] *sḫm-ỉr(y)·f* 'potentate'.

[1] Thebes, tomb 93. [2] GARD. *Sin.* p. 102. [3] *Kopt.* 8, 8. Cf. Cairo 20539, i. *b* 11.

Sect. Z. Strokes, Signs derived from Hieratic, Geometrical Figures

Z 1 stroke (perhaps properly a wooden dowel) [1] — Ideo. or det. one, unity, exx. var. *wʿ* 'one', 7 'seven', lit. 'seven units' (§ 259). Following an ideogram denotes that this means the actual thing that it depicts (§ 25), exx. *r* 'mouth'; *dw* 'mountain'; so too in duals and plurals, exx. [2] *ʿwy* 'the two arms'; [3] *sbꜣw* 'stars'; [4] *ḫꜣswt* 'countries'; in fem. nouns the fem. ending

Z 1 | (continued)

t often intervenes, ex. *ḥst* 'water-jar'. Such writings were often preceded in O.K. by phonetic signs;[5] M.E. survivals of this practice are *s* 'man'; [6] *hrw* 'day'. Ideo. with | is occasionally followed by a det., ex. *Rʿ* 'Rēʿ'. Misunderstanding of the function of | often leads to its displacement, exx. [7] for *s* 'man'; [8] for *š* 'pool'. It is strange that [9] is a later writing of *tꜣ* 'earth', while [10] (also found in Dyn. XVIII)[11] is the usual writing in Dyn. XII; [12] *dmi* 'town' is likewise difficult to explain, as also are many later exx. of the stroke. Already in Pyr. cases occur of ideo. with | being together transferred to a phonetic use;[13] so often in M.E., exx. *ḥr* 'upon' (§ 165); var. *sꜣ* 'son'; so particularly in group-writing (§ 60), exx. *r*; *t*. Along similar lines occurs as det. towns in place of ⊗, ex. [14] *Nn-nsw* 'Heracleopolis'. Occasionally in Dyn. XII | serves merely to fill an empty space, exx. [15] *n* 'for'; [16] *dꜣ·n·i* 'I ferried across'. In Pyr. | was sometimes used (like ⟍ and ◦) to replace human figures, these being regarded as magically dangerous[17]; so in M.K. coffins, exx. [18] for *i* 'O'; [19] for *Ssnb·n·f*, a man's name; extensions of this use appear to be the rare employment of | as suffix 1st pers. sing. *·i* 'I';[20] perhaps also the fairly common writing [21] for , , or *s* 'man'.

[1] *Hier.* p. 37. [2] Cairo 20538, ii. *c* 7. [3] *Sin.* B 271. [4] *Sin.* B 45. [5] *ÄZ.* 45, 46. [6] *Urk.* iv. 81, 4. [7] *BH.* i. 8, 8. [8] *Urk.* iv. 1165, 10. [9] *Urk.* iv. 102, 15; 615, 11. [10] *Sin.* B 43. [11] *Urk.* iv. 96, 3; cf. *ib.* 149, 14. [12] *Sin.* B 306. [13] *ÄZ.* 45, 50. [14] *Peas.* Bt. 17. Sim. *BH.* i. 25, 79. [15] Louvre C 1, 11. [16] Brit. Mus. 562, 7. [17] *ÄZ.* 51, 22. [18] LAC. *TR.* 1, 6; 7, 1; 8, 1. [19] *ÄZ.* 51, 51. [20] Cairo 20057, *q*, qu. § 505, 1; *ib.* 20538, ii. *c* 4. Already in O.K., *Urk.* i. 126, 2. [21] Cairo 20538, i. *c* 4; *Urk.* iv. 1148, 12.

2 ||| stroke | Z 1 thrice repeated (also written , | Z 3; for the vertical writing see below end of text and in Z 3)

Det. plurality (§ 73, 3), common from Dyn. IX onwards, following an ideo. or det. to show that it should be understood three times, exx. [1] *rnpwt* 'years' for O.K. ; [2] *nḏsw* 'poor men' for O.K. . Examples occur already in Pyr., but very rarely, ex. [3] *mrw* 'canals'; these suggest as origin of the use a contraction of plurals like [4] into , but since ◦◦◦, are found as plur. det. from Dyn. VI onward (exx. [5] *wꜣwt* 'roads', [6] *nḏsw* 'poor men') the use of

Z 2 ı ı ı (continued)

ı ı ı as plur. det. cannot be dissociated entirely from the employment of ı, ⸜ or ∘ in Pyr. as substitutes for signs representing human figures which were regarded as magically dangerous;[7] see on ı Z 1; ⸜ Z 5; ∘ N 33. In M.E. ı ı ı is found also with purely phonetic signs, exx. [8] *wrw* 'great ones'; [9] *nfrw* 'beautiful', m. plur.; [10] *nfrt* 'beautiful', f. plur. Sometimes it marks plural meaning in words that are not themselves plural, exx. [11] *sn* 'their'; [12] *ẖnyt* 'sailors', a fem. collective (§ 77, 3); [13] *ꜥšꜣ* 'many'; such plural meaning was probably felt by the Egyptians in words denoting foodstuffs, materials, etc., though singular in form, exx. [14] *t* 'bread'; [15] *ỉwf* 'flesh'; [16] *ḥḏ* 'silver'; so too in fem. participles with neuter meaning, ex. *ḏddt* 'what was said', '(things) said' (§ 354). Lastly, ı ı ı is found with abstracts ending in *w* (§ 77, 1), whether these are really plurals or not, exx. [17] *šmsw* 'following'; [18] *nḏsw* 'poverty'; so too with fem. infinitives, if such they be (§ 298, end), ex. *mswt* 'birth'.[19] For the same sign vertically written in hieratic, see under Z 3; for ≡, and in numbering the days in dates, see § 259; occurs also as phon. det. in *ḥmt* 'think'.

[1] *Siut* 4, 22. [2] *Siut* 3, 12. [3] *Pyr.* 508; sim. *ib.* 396. See *ÄZ.* 51, 18, n. 1. [4] *Pyr.* 292. [5] *Urk.* i. 127, 9. [6] *Urk.* i. 151, 11. [7] *ÄZ.* 51, 18. [8] Leyd. V 4, 12. Sim. *ḏdꜣ(w)*, *Meir* iii. 4; *nḫtw*, *Urk.* iv. 654, 14. [9] Cairo 20086, *b* 12. Sim. *Leb.* 61. [10] Cairo 20086, *b* 14. [11] Dots already in *Pyr.* 287, cf. *Rec.* 35, 67. [12] *Urk.* iv. 1, 16. [13] *Sin.* B 147, as predicate. [14] Cairo 20024, *b* 8. [15] Leyd. V 4, 3. [16] *Urk.* iv. 423, 10. [17] BUDGE, p. 80, 14. [18] *Pt.* 428. [19] *Verbum* ii, § 603.

3 stroke ı Z 1, thrice repeated vertically

Use as last, common in hieroglyphic from Dyn. XII,[1] rarer in hieratic, where the original form was .[2]

[1] Exx. Leyd. V 4. V 88; Brit. Mus. 572. [2] MÖLL. *Pal.* i. nos. 562. 563.

For ∘ ∘ ∘ see on N 33.

4 \\ two diagonal strokes (less often written ıı)

In Pyr. only as det. duality, exx. [1] *ṯn(ỉ)* 'you two' (cf. for the ending [2] *śnỉ* 'they two'); [3] varr. [4] [5] *ꜥw(ỉ)*, also [6] *ꜥw(y)*, 'the two arms'; and in O.K., ex. [7] *pḥw(ỉ)* 'end' (§ 77, 1). In some cases \\ replaced human figures, these being deemed to be magically dangerous, exx. [8] *ꜣḫt(ỉ)* 'the two glorious ones' for ; [9] *sꜣt(ỉ)* 'son and daughter'; [10] *t(w)twỉ* 'the two images'. The last use survives in M.E. [11] *Šdty* 'Crocodilopolite', where, however, the hieratic \\ replaces, not dangerous signs, but signs difficult to

Z 4 \\ (continued)

draw;[12] see below \ Z 5. Elsewhere in M.E. \\ is always phon. *y*, through its constant association earlier with words of dual form, i.e. ending in *ỉ* (*y*); exx. are *·fy*, var. Pyr.[13] *·fỉ*, 'his two' (§ 75, 2); *ỉmnty* 'western'; *sḏmty·fy* 'who will hear' (§ 364). Except in compounds like the last \\ *y* is always final consonant; it has its distinct uses, and 𓇌 is seldom interchangeable with it.[14]

[1] *Pyr.* 2200. Sim. but with dots, *śn*(*ỉ*), *Pyr.* 631. [2] *Pyr.* 1424; see *Rec.* 35, 68. [3] *Pyr.* 1588. [4] *Pyr.* 1533. [5] *Pyr.* 1965. [6] *Pyr.* 1235. [7] *Urk.* i. 126, 14. [8] *Pyr.* 1425. [9] *Pyr.* 1248. Sim. *śnt*(*ỉ*), *Pyr.* 628. [10] *Pyr.* 1329. [11] Erm. *Hymn.* 1, 4, qu. Exerc. XXXI, (*a*). [12] *Rec.* 38, 183; most similar exx. belong to Dyn. XIX or later. [13] *Pyr.* 2048; see *Rec.* 35, 69. [14] *Verbum* i. § 125.

5 \ [1] diagonal stroke as made in hieratic (sometimes also \)

Identical in origin with the stroke \ used in Pyr. as substitute for human figures, these being considered magically dangerous, ex. [2] *śmśw* 'elder' for . In M.E. hieratic used only to replace dets. that were difficult to draw,[3] exx. [4] *ꜣt* 'moment' for ; [5] *sntt* 'base' for . In hieratic texts of Dyn. XVIII sometimes in personal names without preceding phon. signs for B 3, ex. [6] *'Iꜥḥ-ms*(*w*) 'ꜥAḥmosĕ' for .[7] Only very rarely to replace complicated or unusual signs in Dyn. XVIII hieroglyphic, ex. [8] *ỉdt* (?) 'cow', possibly for . Hieratic \\ as substitute for two dets. (see on \\ Z 4) is merely a doubling of \.

[1] See below n. 8. [2] *Pyr.* 608. See *ÄZ.* 51, 20. [3] Möll. *Pal.* i. no. 559. [4] *Pr.* 1, 4; *Leb*, 32. 116. [5] *Rhind* 60, 1. [6] Northampt. 18, 7. [7] Northampt. 22, 33. [8] *Urk.* iv. 1020, 10. Sim. in *ḥfst* 'glory', *ib.* 385, 4. As det. in *smdt* 'staff' (of temple), *Paheri* 9, 39, perhaps by confusion for D 13.

6 [1] hieratic substitute for A 13 or A 14.[2]

Det. death, enemy, exx. [3] *m*(*w*)*t* 'die'; [4] *ḫpt* 'decease'; [5] *ḫft*(*y*) 'enemy'. In hieroglyphic barely distinguishable from F 20.

[1] Möll. *Pal.* i. no. 49, B. For the hieroglyphic form here adopted, see the ex. qu. below n. 4. [2] It is doubtful whether this is abbrev. of A 13 or A 14. Mutilation for superstitious reasons has clearly played a part, see *ÄZ.* 51, 51. [3] Lac. *TR.* p. 9, l. 4. [4] Cairo 20003, 2 = *Musée égyptien* i. 18. [5] *Eb.* 109, 17.

7 𓏲 hieroglyphic adaptation of the hieratic abbreviated form of G 43

The hieratic abbreviation of G 43, best transcribed by 𓏲, occurs with increasing frequency from Dyn. IX onwards.[1] In hieroglyphic 𓏲 *w* does not become really common until the reign of Akhenaten.[2] Not to be confused with V 1.

[1] Möll. *Pal.* i. no. 200, B. Early exx. at Hat-Nub and in the Bershah coffins. [2] Early exx., *Urk.* iv. 2, 12; 148, 8, beginning of Dyn. XVIII.

For as hieroglyphic adaptation of the more cursive hieratic form of G 39, see on H 8.
For as hieroglyphic equivalent of the hieratic forms of T 13 and U 39, see U 40.

Z 8 ⬭ oval

Det. round, in [1] *šnw* 'circuit' and the related words. A different sign from ⊂⊃ N 18.

[1] *D. el B.* 156.

(N 33) ∘ circle

Det. round, from O.K.[1] onwards common in words from the stem *ḳd(ỉ)* 'go round', exx. [2] *ỉḳdw* 'builders'; [3] *ḳd* 'character'. From Dyn. XI increasingly often replaced by ʊ W 24.

[1] Exx. *ḳd* 'form', *Urk.* i. 101, 10. 12; *ḳd* 'mould', *Pyr.* 1597.
[2] Cairo 20609, *a* 6. [3] Brit. Mus. 614, 8.

(M 44) △ triangle?

Ideo. or det. in var. *spd* (*špd*) 'sharp', unless it is there a thorn, as in *srt* 'thorn', see on M 44. In [1] *t-ḥḏ* 'white bread' it signifies a loaf of triangular shape.

[1] *Urk.* iv. 770, 9.

Z 9 × two sticks crossed

Det. break, exx. [1] *ḥḏỉ* 'damage'; ×[2] *gmgm* 'break'; divide, exx. *wpỉ* 'divide'; *psš* 'divide'; × *ḫbỉ* 'lessen', 'subtract'; actions involving something crossed or encountered, exx. [3] *dꜣỉ* 'cross'; ×[4] *wšb* 'answer'; [5] *ꜣbḫ* 'be united'; also in many words where the reason is not apparent,[6] exx. [7] *nkt* 'matter', 'trifle'; *tꜣš* 'boundary'; [8] *wdỉ* 'emit (sound)'. In *ḥsb*, var. O.K. × *ḥšb*, 'reckon', lit. 'break up (numbers)'[9] ⤫ (Z 10), the prototype of ×, has become ⊘ Aa 2; but in × *ḥsb* '$\frac{1}{4}$' (§ 265) the sign has survived as an ideo. Owing to its use as det. in certain stems, × has acquired special phon. or semi-phon. values as follows: (1) *swꜣ*, in [10] varr. ,[11] [12] *swꜣỉ* (*šwꜣỉ*) 'pass by', from ×[13] var. [14] *swꜣ* (*zwꜣ*) 'cut off'; (2) *sḏ*, in [15] var. Pyr. [16] *šḏt* 'flame', from [17] *sḏỉ* 'break'; (3) *ḫbs*, in [18] var. [19] *ḫbsw* 'plough-lands'; (4) *šbn*, in [20] var. [21] *šbn* 'mixed', 'various'; (5) *wp*, in [22] var. Dyn. XX [23] *wp st* 'specify it', a phrase serving to introduce details of accounts; (6) *wr* (reason unknown), exx. [24] *sw(r)ỉ* 'drink'; [25] var. [26] *ḫpr-wr*, a medicament.

[1] *Siut* I, 224. [2] LAC. *TR.* 10, 9. [3] *Sin.* B 13. [4] *Leb.* 4. [5] *Sin.* R 8. [6] See *ÄZ.* 49, 119. [7] *Rekh.* 2, 12. [8] *Sin.* B 140. [9] *ÄZ.* 49, 116; SETHE, *Zahlworte* 77. [10] *Peas.* B 1, 8. [11] *Sin.* B 14. [12] *Sin.* R 39. [13] LAC. *TR.* 7, 4. Sim. in O.K., *Ti* 110. [14] *Rekh.* 2, 13. [15] *Sh. S.* 56; for the reading see DAV. *Ptah.* i. p. 29 and Akhm. ⲥⲛ̄ⲛ̄ⲥⲉⲧⲉ 'holocaust', *ÄZ.* 48, 36. [16] *Pyr.* 124. Sim. *Dend.* 37 F. [17] LAC. *TR.* 10, 7. [18] *Th. T. S.* i. 30. [19] *Th. T. S.* i. 7. [20] *P. Kah.* 15, 68; *Urk.* iv. 769, 9. So usually written in phrases like *t šbn* 'various loaves'. [21] *Hat-Nub* 11, 14. [22] P. Gurob A (unpublished), vs. 2, 18, end of Dyn. XVIII; so often later. [23] *P. Kah.* 40, 3; cf. *wpt* 'specification', GRIFFITH, *Kahun Papyri*, p. 20. [24] *Eb.* 21, 13–14. [25] *Eb.* 96, 3. Sim. *sꜣ-wr*, *ib.* 9, 13. [26] *Eb.* 96, 10.

Z 10 [1] O.K. form of last — Use as last.

[1] Exx. *Medum* 15 (*ḥśb*); *Ti* 110 (*swi*). See *ÄZ.* 49, 116.

11 two planks crossed and joined [0] — Ideo. (?) in varr. , *imy* 'who is in' (§ 79) and derivatives. Hence (?) phon. *imi*, ex. var. *imi* 'not be' (§ 342). Since in hieratic is often identical with M 42, Dyn. XVIII hieroglyphic writes [1] var. O.K. [2] for old var. *wnm* 'eat'; so too [3] for [4] *wnḏwt* 'subjects'.

[0] *Hier.* p. 37. [1] *Urk.* iv. 497, 17; BUDGE, p. 100, 14. [2] *ÄZ.* 42, 10, if not a careless form of . [3] BUDGE, p. 18, 15; 19, 2. [4] MAR. *Abyd.* ii. 30, 28, where is wrongly written for .

Sect. Aa. Unclassified

Aa 1 [1] human placenta ? [2] — Cf. [3] *ḫ* 'placenta (?)'. Hence (?) phon. *ḫ*.

[1] Ex. *Five Th. T.* 3. [2] *Sah.* Text, 77; *JEA.* iii. 235. [3] *JEA.* iii. 243.

2 pustule or gland ? [1] — Det. bodily growths or conditions, especially of a morbid kind, exx. [2] *wbnw* 'wound'; [3] *ḫꜣyt* 'disease'; [4] *wḫd* 'suffer'; [5] *ḫpꜣ* 'navel' (whence phon. *ḫp(ꜣ)* in [6] var. [7] *ḫpw* 'sculptured reliefs'); fat, distended, exx. [8] *ḏdꜣ* 'fat'; [9] *šfw* 'swell'. Replaces a number of O.K. signs that have become obsolete:—(1) = Pyr. V 38, as ideo. or det. in [10] *wt* 'bandage'; [11] *wt* 'embalmer'; [12] *sdwḫ* 'treat', 'embalm'. (2) = O.K. Z 10, as det. in [13] abbrevv. , [14] [15] *ḥsb* 'reckon'; everywhere else has survived as × Z 9. (3) = Pyr. F 52 or O.K. N 32, as det. excrement, in [16] *ḥs* 'excrement'; smell, in [17] *sty* 'odour'; clay, in [18] *sin* 'clay'. (4) = O.K. W 6, as ideo. or det. in [19] var. [20] *wḥꜣt* 'cauldron'; hence phon. *wḥꜣ* in [21] var. O.K. [22] *Wḥꜣt* 'Oasis'. (5) = W 7, as det. in [23] *mꜣt* 'granite'; [24] *ꜣbw* 'Elephantine'. (6) = V 32, det. in [25] *gw*, prob. for [26] *gꜣwt* 'bundles'; hence phon. det. *gꜣ* in [27] *gꜣw* 'be narrow'. (7) = M 41, det. in [28] *ꜥš* 'cedar'.

[1] Conjectured from the very frequent use in the medical papyri and from Aa 3. [2] *Eb.* 70, 2. [3] *Eb.* 36, 14. [4] *Adm.* p. 104. [5] *Eb.* 100, 19. Cf. *JEA.* iii. 203. [6] *Urk.* iv. 422, 11. [7] *Urk.* iv. 425, 2. [8] *Peas.* B 1, 62. [9] *Eb.* 108, 3. [10] *Eb.* 39, 18. [11] *BH.* i. 18. [12] *Eb.* 6, 17. For the reading *sdwḫ*, not *stwḫ*, see *Urk.* iv. 913, 17. [13] *D. el B.* 79. [14] *Th. T. S.* i. 27. [15] Cairo 20296, *i*. [16] BUDGE, p. 123, 7. [17] *Eb.* 71, 17. [18] LAC. *TR.* 72, 42. [19] NAV. ch. 17, 68. [20] *Eb.* 65, 18. [21] *Puy.* 31; reading, see *ÄZ.* 56, 44. [22] *Urk.* i. 125, 14. [23] *Urk.* iv. 623, 5. [24] *D. el B.* 154. [25] *Urk.* iv. 138, 6. [26] *D. el B.* 77. [27] *Eb.* 102, 10. [28] *Urk.* iv. 23, 12; 423, 2.

Aa 3 pustule or gland (?) Aa 2 with liquid issuing from it — Rarer alternative of in its medical or anatomical use, as det. when soft matter or a liquid is meant, exx. [1] *wsšt* 'urine'; [2] *ꜣs* 'soft inner parts (?)'. Also det. in [3] *sṯ* 'odour'.

[1] *D. el B.* 110. Sim. *ḳny* 'bulging', *P. Kah.* 7, 60. [2] *Urk.* iv. 84, 8; cf. *ꜣs*, *Eb.* 97, 8; see now *JEA* 33, 48. [3] *Bersh.* ii. 17.

For Aa 4 (Pyr.) see after W 10*

5 [1] part of the steering gear of ships? — Ideo. or det. in Pyr. [2] var. [3] *ḥpt* in the phrase *iṯi ḥpt* 'take the *ḥpt*', i.e. 'proceed by boat', *r* to a place; cf. M.K. *dsr ḥpwt* 'direct the *ḥpwt*' (plur.), i.e. 'sail'[4]. From M.K. there is a word [5] *ḥpt* 'oar', but the writing in Pyr. makes it impossible to interpret that word as meaning 'oar' from the start.[6] Hence phon. *ḥp*, exx. [7] *Ḥpy* 'Hepy', one of the four sons of Horus; [8] *ḥp* 'Apis-bull'. The full stem may have been *ḥip*, cf. Pyr. [9] *ḥip* 'hasten'.

[1] Apparently made of rushes bound together. See for various forms, KEES, *Opfertanz des äg. Königs* (Leipzig, 1912), Pl. 5; PETRIE, *Royal Tombs* ii. 24, no. 210; L. *D.* ii. 6; *Sah.* 31; *Meir* ii. 17, no. 66. [2] *Pyr.* 873. [3] *Pyr.* 1346. [4] *ÄZ.* 62, 4, n. 3. [5] Brit. Mus. 6655, qu. KEES, *op. cit.* 221. [6] See KEES, *op. cit.* 74 foll. [7] PETRIE, *Gizeh and Rifeh* 13 G. [8] *Meir* i. 11. [9] *Pyr.* 1081.

6 [1] doubtful (different from S 23) — Det. in [2] *tmꜣ* (from *ṯmꜣ*?) 'mat'. Hence (?) phon. det. *ṯmꜣ* in [3] var. [4] *ṯmꜣ* 'cadaster (?)' or kind of land (?).

[1] Brit. Mus. 828. [2] *BH.* ii. 13. [3] Brit. Mus. 828, qu. § 450. [4] *Rekh.* 3, 18, qu. Exerc. XXX (iii).

7 [1] doubtful (in Dyn. XVIII often reversed [2]) — Det. or phon. det. *sḳr* (*śḳr*) in [3] varr. [4] [5] [6] *sḳr* (*śḳr*) [7] 'smite'.

[1] Exx. O.K., *Ti* 60; *Sah.* 1. The sign has been supposed to represent a mat of papyrus, *Rec.* 26, 48. From Dyn. XIX onwards interpreted as a claw or hoof, so already perhaps *D. el B.* 100; in *Gebr.* i. 14 (Dyn. VI) it looks like an arm. The sign is not found in hieratic. [2] Exx. *Urk.* iv. 9, 14; 659, 15. [3] *Urk.* iv. 895, 5. [4] *D. el B.* 100; *Urk.* iv. 780, 11. [5] *Urk.* iv. 36, 7 in *sḳr-ꜥnḫw* 'prisoners of war'. [6] *Sin.* R 14. 15. [7] In O.K. regularly written without *r*, exx. *Ti* 60; CAPART, *Rue* 33; *Pyr.* 1138. 1431.

8 irrigation runnels as in N 24? — Ideo. or det. in [1] var. [2] *ḏꜣtt* 'estate' in the title 'steward of the estate'; the meaning of *ḏꜣtt* and the interpretation of here depend on the not improbable identification of this title with [3] (var.)[4] in another tomb of Dyn. XII; the word [5] var. [6] 'estate' would in this case read *ḏꜣtt*. Hence phon. det. in Dyn. XVIII [7] var. O.K. [8] *ḏꜣḏꜣt* 'magistrates', 'assessors'. For an unknown reason,

Aa 8 (continued)

phon. *ḳn*,[9] exx. [10] *ḳn* 'complete', 'be complete'; [11] *ḳn* 'mat'. In hieratic stands not only for itself but also for certain other signs, whence confusions have resulted both in modern transcriptions and in actual hieroglyphic texts. Thus is found (1) for [12] N 24 in hierogl. [13] *spȝt* 'district'; (2) for V 26 in hieratic [14] var. [15] *ʿḏ* 'desert edge' which hierogl. varr. show should be equated with [16] and [17] respectively. Possibly through some confusion with O 34 [18] is found in Dyn. XVIII hieroglyphic for *smt* 'desert', 'necropolis', as a mediating var. [19] proves; for this reason the name of king [20] var. [21] var. Dyn. I [22] is possibly to be read *Zmty* rather than *Ḫȝśty*,[23] the writing on the Table of Abydus and the Οὐσαφαις of Manetho being probably due to mistaken interpretation of the hieratic.

[1] *BH.* i. 30. 35. [2] *BH.* i. 29. [3] *Bersh.* i. 18. See GRIFFITH, *Kahun Papyri*, p. 31. [4] *Bersh.* i. 27. [5] *Peas.* B 1, 24; *P. Kah.* 11, 21; 15, 63. [6] *Peas.* R 66. [7] *Rekh.* 3, 18. [8] *Ti* 121. [9] Reading from Boh. *kēn* 'finish', 'cease' = Eg. *ḳn* 'complete', see next note; also from varr. of a very late word *ḳn* 'throne', compare CHASSINAT, *Mammisi* 76 with ROCHEMONTEIX, *Edfou* i. 375. [10] *Pt.* 269. Common in L.E., see BRUGSCH, *Wörterbuch*, Suppl. 1251. [11] *Adm.* 10, 5. Sim. *Rekh.* 2, 1. [12] Not in MÖLL. *Pal.* i. ii; perhaps only found *Peas.* R 66, see above n. 6. [13] *Urk.* iv. 484, 2. The reading of *Sebekkhu* 1 is more doubtful. [14] *Sin.* B 9. [15] *Sin.* R 34. [16] Cf. Louvre C 1, vert. 7. [17] Cf. *Hamm.* 48, 9. [18] Especially in the title of Hathor, *ḥrt-tp smt* 'chief over the desert', ex. Cairo 588 compared with *ib.* 593; see too *Urk.* iv. 1003, 5. [19] *Rec.* 28, 169. [20] *Eb.* 103, 2. [21] BUDGE p. 145; cf. the dual *smty* 'the two deserts', *Urk.* iv. 383, 15. [22] *Unt.* iii. 24; GAUTHIER, *Livre des Rois*, i. 6. [23] Sethe and Gunn, however, preferred *Ḫȝśty*, see *Ann.* 28, 155.

9 [1] doubtful

Det. in [1] *ḫwd* 'rich'.

[1] Exx. *D. el B* 110; *Rifeh* 7, 22. Černý conjectures that this may be an abbreviated form of the O.K. sign for *ḫwdt*, 'portable chair', *Wb.* iii. 250, 3.

10 [1] doubtful

Det. in [1] *drf* 'writing'.

[1] Exx. *BH.* i. 7. Rather different forms, *Siut* 1, 263; *Urk.* iv. 776, 10.

11 doubtful[1] (sometimes vertically or)

For an unknown reason, phon. *mȝʿ* in var. *mȝʿt* 'truth' and the related words. Note specially often the writing *mȝʿ-ḫrw* 'true of voice' (§ 55). As a pedestal det. in [2] *tntt* 'raised platform', a unique writing (?).

[1] Neither the form nor the value suits the identification with the flute (*mȝt*) sometimes upheld. According to Kristensen (*Het leven uit den dood* 71) and others (*Griff. Stud.* 45; *Kêmi* i. 127) a platform or pedestal. [2] *Urk.* iv. 200, 9.

12 [1] O.K. form of last

Use as last.

[1] Leyd. *Denkm.* i. 5. Also in Dyn. XII, Leyd. V 6 = *Denkm.* ii. 3. Often tapers from right to left, ex. DAV. *Ptah.* i. 17, no. 393.

For , see U 4. 5.

Aa 13 [1] hardly the two ribs of an oryx as has been suggested [2]

Ideo. or det. in O.K. *ỉm*, plur. *ỉmw*, a part of the body.[2] Hence (?) phon. *ỉm*, exx. *ỉmỉ* 'give', imper. (§ 336); *ỉmw* 'boat'; also, from Dyn. XVIII on, phon. *m*.[3] Ideo. also in var. *gs*, varr. Pyr. ,[4] [5] *gś*, 'side', 'half'. Hence phon. *gs*, exx. [6] var. [7] *gs* 'anoint'; [8] var. [9] *gsti* 'palette'.

[1] Exx. Dyn. XII, *Meir* iii. 23 (*ỉm*); Dyn. XVII, *Kopt.* 8, 5 (*ỉm*); Dyn. XVIII, *Rekh.* 3, 29 (*gs*); *D. el B.* 116 (*ỉm*); there is no difference between *ỉm* and *gs*. [2] *ÄZ.* 64, 10. [3] *ÄZ.* 35, 170. [4] *Pyr.* 925. [5] *Pyr.* 1092. [6] *Hearst* 10, 16. [7] *Sin.* B 293. [8] *Peas.* B 1, 305. [9] MASPERO, *Trois Années de Fouilles*, Pl. 2; see *Sphinx* 12, 117.

14 [1] O.K. form of last

Use as last.

[1] Exx. DAV. *Ptah.* i. 17, nos. 380–2 (*ỉm*).

15 [1] alternative form of Aa 13 (Dyn. XVIII)

Use as last.

[1] Exx. *Paheri* 3; *Amarn.* i. 26 (prep. *m*). This straight form is usual from late Dyn. XVIII on.

16 short form of Aa 13

Used only in [1] var. [2] *gs* 'side', 'half' and as phon. *gs*.

[1] Exx. *Urk.* iv. 429, 12; 630, 17. [2] *Urk.* iv. 367, 9; *D. el B.* 113.

17 [1] back of something [2] (O.K. and M.K. form)

Ideo. in *sꜣ* (*śꜣ*) 'back', Coptic *soi*. Hence phon. *sꜣ* (*śꜣ*),[3] exx. [4] *sꜣwt* 'walls'; *sꜣỉ* 'be satiated'; *šsꜣ* 'be skilled'.

[1] O.K. forms, *Saqq. Mast.* i. 2; *Sah.* 1; MONTET 225; Dyn. XI–XII, Brit. Mus. 614, 9; Leyd. V 4, 5; *Sebekkhu* 4. See also on Aa 18; there is great variety in detail. [2] Inferred from the use of | in *śꜣ* 'back', *ÄZ.* 45, 45; full discussion, MONTET 225–6; Grdseloff adheres to Borchardt's explanation as a razor, *Ann.* 43, 310. [3] For *ś* see *Pyr.* 959 (*śꜣḥ*). [4] *Siut* 1, 235.

18 [1] Dyn. XII–XVIII form of last

Use as last. In group-writing (§ 60) or is used for *s*.[2]

[1] Exx. Dyn. XII, *Bersh.* i. 18; Berl. *ÄI.* i. p. 258, 12; Dyn. XVIII, *Rekh.* 2, 2; *Paheri* 9, 48. This exact form as cover of a quiver, *Medînet Habu* (Chicago) I, 25, B, but this explanation is hard to apply to the earlier counterpart. [2] BURCHARDT § 105.

19 [1] doubtful (different from V 19)

For unknown reason, phon. det. *ḥr*, exx. [1] *ḥr* 'prepare'; *ḥryt* 'dread'. Also det. in *tꜣr* 'preserve (?)' and derivatives.[2]

[1] *D. el B.* 69. [2] *Wb.* v. 355; *Adm.* p. 89; *ÄZ.* 68, 21.

20 [1] doubtful [2]

For unknown reason, phon. *ʿpr* in var. [3] *ʿpr* 'equip' and derivatives.

[1] O.K. forms, *Sah.* 52 (elaborate as in Dyn. III, see WEILL, *IIe. et IIIe. Dynasties*, Pl. 4); *Ti* 25; Dyn. XVIII, *D. el B.* 91; *Puy.* 12. [2] Clearly not identical with the counterpoise *mnḫt*, for which see JÉQ. 65–6. [3] *Pyr.* 1465; Louvre C 14, 7.

21 [1] a carpenter's tool?

Ideo. (?) or det. in varr. , [2], O.K. [3] *wḏʿ* 'sever', 'judge'. In M.K. coffins or is sometimes used as a substitute for the god *Stḫ* 'Seth'.[4]

[1] Exx. O.K., DAV. *Ptah.* i. 17, no. 387; *Ti* 132; Dyn. XVIII, *Rekh.* 10, 14. The lower part looks like a mitre square; see DAV. *Rekh.* ii. 55 for an object of this shape in a scene of carpentering. [2] *Urk.* iv. 1079, 2. [3] *Ti* 132. [4] Exx. *Ann.* 5, 231. 232. 245.

Aa 22 [hieroglyph] combination of [hieroglyph] Aa 21 and [hieroglyph] D 36 — Use as last.

For [hieroglyph] Aa 23 and [hieroglyph] Aa 24 see after [hieroglyph] U 35.

25 [hieroglyph][1] doubtful[1a] — Ideo. (?) in [hieroglyph],[2] var. [hieroglyph][2a] *smꜣ*, var. O.K. [hieroglyph][3] *s(mꜣ ?)*,[4] title of a priest whose function consisted in clothing the god (Min, Horus, etc.), cf. Gk. στολιστής.

[1] Ex. *Sah.* 32. [1a] According to Grdseloff (*Ann.* 43, 357) a phallus sheath conventionalized; but the connexion with the word *smt* (*Urk.* iv. 2, 16) is very far from certain. [2] *Ikhern.* 16. Sim. *Siut* I, 268. [2a] Cairo 20538, ii. *c* 6, confirmed by the writing *smꜣ-tꜣ* of the later form of the word *smꜣty*, GARDINER, *Late-Eg. Miscellanies* 112, 16. [3] *Annals of Archaeology* (Liverpool), iv. 103. [4] On account of *s* apparently not derived from the stem *zmꜣ* 'unite'.

26 [hieroglyph][1] doubtful — Phon. det. *sbi* (*śbi*) in [hieroglyph][2] *sbi* (*śbi*) 'rebel'. Often replaced by [hieroglyph] T 14.

[1] *D. el B.* 115. Sim. *Pyr.* 81. 1722. [2] *D. el B.* 115. Sim. MAR. *Abyd.* ii. 29, 18.

27 [hieroglyph][1] doubtful[2] — For an unknown reason, phon. *nḏ*, exx. [hieroglyph] varr. [hieroglyph],[3] [hieroglyph][4] *nḏ* 'ask', 'inquire'; [hieroglyph] var. [hieroglyph][5] *nḏnḏ* 'take counsel'. Except in [hieroglyph] *inḏ ḥr* 'hail to' (§ 272) [hieroglyph] is usually accompanied in M.E. by [hieroglyph] W 24.

[1] Exx. O.K., *Medum* 11; DAV. *Ptah.* i. 17, no. 376; Dyn. XII, *Th. T. S.* ii. 14; Dyn. XVIII, *Rekh.* 2, 5. [2] The view that the sign depicts a winder for thread (*Hier.* p. 61) is not supported by the earlier forms. It has also been thought to represent a porridge-stirrer, *Man* 1909, no. 96. [3] *Sin.* B 166. [4] *Rekh.* 2, 5. [5] *Sin.* B 113.

28 [hieroglyph] an instrument used by bricklayers ?[1] (different from [hieroglyph] M 40 and [hieroglyph] P 11) — Ideo. (?) in [hieroglyph] var. [hieroglyph][2] *ḳd* 'build', 'fashion (pots)' and related words.

[1] This view is favoured by the fact that the sign sometimes stands alone in the sense of 'builder', ex. *Sah.* 54. Other suggestions are a plasterer's float (*Hier.* p. 49) and a striker used in measuring corn (QUIB. *Saqq.* 1911–12, Pl. 17 and p. 26). [2] *Siut* i. 236. Sim. *Dend.* 11.

29 [hieroglyph][1] O.K. form of last — Use as last.

[1] *Sah.* 54. Sim. DAV. *Ptah.* i. 13, no. 271.

30 [hieroglyph][1] ornamental *chevaux de frise* on tops of walls, cf. [hieroglyph] O 11[2] (sometimes written horizontally [hieroglyph])[3] — Ideo. or det. in [hieroglyph][4] *ḫkr* 'be adorned'; [hieroglyph][5] *ḫkrw* 'ornament', 'adornment' and the related words.

[1] Ex. *Th. T. S.* iii. 12. [2] See the picture BISSING, *Re-Heiligtum* ii. 9; in Dyn. I, PETR. *RT.* ii. 3, 4; 7, 8. Later shown as frieze in tombs. Discussions, *Ancient Egypt* 1920, 111; *Deutsche Literatur Zeitung* 1926, 1879; SCHARFF 22. However, the O.K. form of the hieroglyph (see Aa 31) is quite different. [3] Ex. *D. el B.* 60, 6. [4] *Bersh.* i. 14, 9. Sim. *D. el B.* 60, 6. [5] *Urk.* iv. 657, 6.

31 [hieroglyph][1] O.K. form of last — Use as last.

[1] DAV. *Ptah.* i. 17, no. 392. See *ÄZ.* 34, 162.

For [hieroglyph] Aa 32 see after [hieroglyph] T 10.

INDEX TO THE FOREGOING SIGN-LIST

Sect. A. MAN AND HIS OCCUPATIONS

1 2 3 4 5 6 7 8 9 10 11 12 13
14 14* 15 16 17 17* 18 19 20 21 22 23 24 25 59 26 27 28 29 30 31 32 33 34 35
36 37 38 39 40 41 42 43 44 45 46 47 48 49 50 51 52 53 54 55

Sect. B. WOMAN AND HER OCCUPATIONS

1 2 3 4 5 6 7

Sect. C. ANTHROPOMORPHIC DEITIES

1 2 3 4 5 6 7 8 9 10 11 12 17 18 19 20

Sect. D. PARTS OF THE HUMAN BODY

1 2 3 4 5 6 7 8 9 10 11 12
13 14 15 16 17 18 19 20 21 22 23 24 25 26 27 27* 28 29 30 31 32 33 34 34*
35 36 37 38 39 40 41 42 43 44 45 46 47 46* 48 49 50 51 52 53
54 55 56 57 58 59 60 61 62 63

Sect. E. MAMMALS

1 2 3 4 5 6 7 8 8* 9 10 11 12 13 14
15 16 17 18 19 20 21 22 23 24 25 26 27 28 29 30 31 32 33 34

Sect. F. PARTS OF MAMMALS

1 2 3 4 5 6 7 8 9 10 11 12 13 14 15
16 17 18 19 20 21 22 23 24 25 26 27 28 29 30 31 32 33 34 35 36 37 38
39 40 41 42 43 44 45 46 47 48 49 50 51 52

INDEX TO THE FOREGOING SIGN-LIST

Sect. G. Birds

1 2 3 4 5 6 7 7* 7** 8 9 10 11 12 13 14

15 16 17 18 19 20 21 22 23 24 25 26 26* 27 28 29 30 31 32 33

34 35 36 37 38 39 40 41 42 43 44 45 46 47 48 49 50 51 52 53 54

Sect. H. Parts of Birds

1 2 3 4 5 6 6* 7 8

Sect. I. Amphibious Animals, Reptiles, etc.

1 2 3 5* 4 5 6 7 8 9

10 11 12 13 14 15

Sect. K. Fishes and parts of Fishes

1 2 3 4 5 7 6

Sect. L. Invertebrata and Lesser Animals

1 2 3 4 5 6 7

Sect. M. Trees and Plants

1 2 3 4 5 6 7 8 9 10 11 12 13 14 15 16 17 18

19 20 21 22 23 24 25 26 27 28 29 30 31 32 33 34 35 36 37 38 39 40 41 42 43 44

Sect. N. Sky, Earth, Water

1 2 3 4 5 6 7 8 9 10 11 12 13 14 15

16 17 18 19 20 21 22 23 24 25 26 27 28 29 30 31 32 33 34 35 (35) 36

37 38 39 40 41 42

Sect. O. Buildings, Parts of Buildings, etc.

1 2 3 4 5 6 7 8 9 10 11

12 13 14 15 16 17 18 19 20 21 22 23 24 25 26 27 28 29 30 31 32 33 34

35 36 37 38 39 40 41 42 43 44 45 46 47 48 49 50 51

Sect P. SHIPS AND PARTS OF SHIPS

1 (1) 2 3 4 5 6 7 8 9 10 11

Sect. Q. DOMESTIC AND FUNERARY FURNITURE

1 2 3 4 5 6 7

Sect. R. TEMPLE FURNITURE AND SACRED EMBLEMS

1 2 3 4 5 6 7 8 9

10 11 12 13 14 15 16 17 18 19 20 21 22 23 24 25

Sect. S. CROWNS, DRESS, STAVES, ETC.

1 2 3 4 5 6 7 8 9 10 11 12

13 14 14* 15 16 17 18 19 20 21 22 17* 23 24 25 26 (N 18) 27 28 29 30 31

32 33 34 (V 39) 35 36 37 38 39 40 41 42 43 44 45

Sect. T. WARFARE, HUNTING, BUTCHERY

1 2 3 4 5 6 7 7* 8 8* 9 9* 10

(Aa 32) 11 12 13 14 15 16 17 18 19 20 21 22 23 24 25 26 27 28 29 30 31 32 33 34 35

Sect. U. AGRICULTURE, CRAFTS, AND PROFESSIONS

1 2 3 4 5 6 7 8 9

10 11 12 (O 30) 13 14 15 16 17 18 19 20 21 22 23 24 25 26 27 28 29 30 31 32

33 34 35 (Aa 23) (Aa 24) 36 37 38 39 40 41

Sect. V. ROPE, FIBRE, BASKETS, BAGS, ETC.

1 2 3 4 5 6 7 8 9 10 11 12 13

14 15 16 17 18 19 20 21 22 23 24 25 26 27 28 29 30 31 31* 32 33 34 35

36 37 38

INDEX TO THE FOREGOING SIGN-LIST

For reasons explained p. 442, top, the following signs have been removed from the place to which they were originally assigned and now stand at some distance from the positions indicated by the attached letter and number: A 59, see after A 25; S 17*, see after S 22; V 39, see after S 34; Aa 4, see after W 10*; Aa 23, Aa 24, see after U 35; Aa 32, see after T 10. A few hieroglyphs are treated in more than one place: M 44 also before Z 9; N 18 also after S 26 and X 4; N 33 (smaller than D 12) also after Z 8; O 30 also reversed after U 12. Minor divergences of position like A 46* after A 47, instead of after A 46, need no further notice than is given to them in the Index above.

A SELECTION OF SIGNS GROUPED ACCORDING TO SHAPE

This list aims at facilitating the finding of particular signs in the Sign-list or the Index thereto. Hieroglyphs the subject of which is immediately recognizable, e.g. animals, boats, most buildings and some pots, have been excluded.

Tall narrow signs
M 40 Aa 28 Aa 29 P 11 D 16 T 34 T 35 U 28 U 29 U 32 U 33 S 43 U 36 T 8 T 8* M 13
M 17 H 6 H 6* M 4 M 12 S 29 M 29 M 30 S 37 R 14 R 15 R 16 R 17 P 6 S 40 R 19 S 41 F 10 F 11 F 12
S 38 S 39 T 14 T 15 T 13 Aa 26 O 30 Aa 21 U 39 F 45 O 44 Aa 27 R 8 R 9 T 7* T 3 T 4 V 24 V 25

U 23 S 42 U 34 S 36 F 28 U 26 U 27 U 24 U 25 Y 8 F 35 F 36 U 41 W 19 P 8 T 22 T 23 Z 11 S 44

Aa 25 M 44 V 38 Aa 31 Aa 30 Aa 20 V 36 F 31 M 32 L 7 V 17 V 18 S 34 V 39 Q 7 T 18 T 19 T 20 R 21

R 11 O 28 O 11 O 36 Aa 32 V 28 V 29

Low broad signs

N 1 N 37 N 38 N 39 S 32 N 18 X 4 X 5 N 17 N 16 N 20 Aa 10 Aa 11

Aa 12 Aa 13 Aa 14 Aa 15 N 35 Aa 8 Aa 9 V 26 V 27 R 24 W 8 V 32 Y 1 Y 2 R 4 N 11

N 12 F 42 D 24 D 25 D 13 D 15 F 20 Z 6 F 33 T 2 T 7 F 30 V 22 V 23 R 5 R 6

O 34 V 2 V 3 S 24 R 22 R 23 T 11 O 29 T 1 T 21 U 20 U 19 U 21 D 17 U 31 T 9

T 9* T 10 F 32 V 13 V 14 F 46 F 47 F 48 F 49 M 11 U 17 U 18 U 14 Aa 7 F 18 D 51

U 15 U 16 Aa 24 N 31 O 31 N 36 D 14 D 21 D 22 T 30 T 31 T 33 D 48 V 30 V 31 V 31*

W 3 S 12 N 30 O 42 O 43 V 16

Low narrow signs

Q 3 O 39 Z 8 O 47 N 22 N 21 N 23 N 29 X 7 O 45 O 46 Y 6 M 35 X 3 X 2 X 1 N 28

Aa 17 I 6 W 10 W 10* Aa 4 R 7 M 39 M 36 F 43 F 41 N 34 U 30 W 11 W 12 W 13 T 28 N 41 N 42 V 37 M 31

F 34 W 6 W 7 W 21 W 20 V 6 V 33 V 34 V 7 V 8 S 20 V 20 V 19 Aa 19 Aa 2 Aa 3 N 32 F 52 V 35 H 8 M 41 F 51

D 11 K 6 L 6 F 21 D 26 N 33 D 12 S 21 N 5 N 9 N 10 Aa 1 O 50 O 49 O 48 X 6 V 9 S 10 N 6 N 8 S 11

N 15 M 42 F 38 V 1 Z 7 Aa 16 Z 9 Z 10

EGYPTIAN-ENGLISH VOCABULARY

The main purpose of this much enlarged Vocabulary is indicated in the Preface to the Second Edition, p. vii. Though some rare words have been included, it has proved impracticable to deal completely even with such well-known texts as the Story of Sinuhe and the Shipwrecked Sailor. In order to economize space the words have been subsumed under their stems so far as appeared justifiable and convenient, and hieroglyphic spellings have been dispensed with when deemed unnecessary. Students should realize that the majority of words can be written in several different ways, and that here only typical variants could be shown. As regards the order in which the words are presented, flexional endings like *-y*, *-w*, *-t* have been disregarded; the Old Kingdom distinction between *ś* and *z* is ignored, both being entered under the common head *s*; in choosing between *ẖ* and *ḫ*, *ṯ* and *t*, *ḏ* and *d*, the form more characteristic of, or earlier in, Middle Egyptian has so far as possible dictated the choice. Causatives and reduplicated forms have been entered under the simple stems.

Simultaneously this Vocabulary has to serve as Index to the hieroglyphically written individual words discussed in the Grammar, as well as to the values and uses of the various hieroglyphs enumerated in the Sign-list—these here indicated by letter and number, e.g. W 7. By no means all the words cited in the Sign-list receive references of the kind, the indispensable cases being those where students may desire to know the source of a given writing or the reasons for reading it in the way it has been read. The indexing of the Sign-list has necessitated the inclusion of certain words not belonging to Middle Egyptian, but in all such cases the period to which these belong has been recorded.

ꜣ (G 1)

ꜣ, weak consonant, apt to be replaced by *ꞽ* or *y*, § 20, end; final, lost in some vbs., § 279.

ꜣ encl. part. with exclamatory force, § 245.

var. *ꜣt* (F 3) moment, attack (of cobra), striking power.

ꜣwꞽ (F 40) extend, stretch out; no det. or (be) long; (of heart) old perf., joyful, lit. expanded; *ꜣw* deceased, lit. extended; *ꜣw* det. length; *r ꜣw·f* entire, § 100, 3; *ꜣwt* det. oblations, offerings; *ꜣwt-ꜥ* presents; *ꜣwt-ꞽb* joy; *sꜣwꞽ* lengthen, prolong; *sꜣwꞽ ꞽb* rejoice heart (of).

ꜣꜣ, see under *ꞽꜣt*.

ꜣb (U 23; D 54) stop, cease; *ꜣbw* cessation; *sꜣb* cause to tarry.

ꜣbꞽ desire (vb.), foll. by infin., § 303.

var. *ꜣbt* (W 8) family, kindred.

abbrev. *ꜣby* (E 24) panther, leopard.

ꜣbw (E 26) elephant; det. (T 19) ivory; det. abbrev. *Ꜣbw* (W 7. 8) Elephantine, island in the First Cataract.

ꜣbw (Q 7) brand (vb.), § 279.

ꜣbḫ join together, unite, *m* with.

abbrev. *ꜣbd* (N 11) month, p. 203.

ȝbḏw ʿArabah el-Madfûnah, Abydus, a town in Upper Egypt.

abbrev. (p. 172) *ȝpd* goose, bird; plur. fowl.

ȝfʿ (be) greedy; greed.

ȝm burn; *sȝm* burn up.

ȝmi mix, compound, *ḥr* with.

ȝmm (D 49) seize, grip; *ȝmmt* grasp (n.).

ȝms (S 44), a royal sceptre or staff.

ȝms (E 5) show solicitude.

ȝr (T 12) restrain, hold back, *ḥr* from.

ȝhw pain, trouble.

ȝhd (be) feeble, faint.

var. *ȝḥt* (§ 56) field.

ȝḫ (G 25) be beneficial, advantageous; *ȝḫt* something advantageous, usefulness; *ȝḫ* blessed spirit; var. *ȝḫw* (N 8) sunshine; *ȝḫt* det. the royal uraeus; det. the Beneficent one, i.e. the eye of Rēʿ; *sȝḫ* det. beatify, render blessed; *sȝḫw* det. beatific spells, glorifications.

var. *ȝḫt* (N 27) horizon; *ȝḫt* tomb; var. *ȝḫty* belonging to the horizon, see under *Ḥr*.

ȝḫt, *ȝḫ-bit*, see under *iȝḫ*.

ȝḫʿ scratch (vb.).

ȝs (V 2) hasten, overtake; *ȝs tw* haste thee, § 337, 1; *ȝs* quickly, § 205, 4.

ȝs (Aa 3), soft inner parts (?) of body.

var. *ȝst* (Q 1; F 51) the goddess Isis.

var. det. *ȝsḫ* (U 1) reap.

ȝšr roast (vb.); *ȝšrt* roast meat.

ȝḳ perish.

ȝkhw (T 7*; p. 439) axe.

var. *ȝḳs* (S 38) Aḳes, a divinity personifying some part of the royal apparel.

ȝkr Aker, an earth-god.

ȝtf (S 8) *atef*-crown.

abbrev. *ȝṯp* (A 9), later *ȝtp*, load, *m*, with; *ȝṯpw* det. load (n.).

ȝd (I 3) be aggressive, angry.

i (M 17)

i, semi-vowel with two values *i̯* and *ȝ*, § 20; often omitted in grammatical endings, *ib.*; tends to replace *ȝ* or *r*, *ib.* end; as immutable consonant in some vbs., § 270, Obs.; initial, omitted in some derivatives, § 290; prothetic, § 272. See too under *y*.

·i, suffix-pron. 1st sing. c., I, me, my; varr. , , , , , 1 or omitted, § 34.

var. (A 26) *i* O (in vocative), §§ 87. 258.

var. *i* say, p. 344, bottom; § **437**; see too below under *in*.

i (M 17. 2) reed.

abbrev. *iȝt* (N 30) mound; *iȝȝ* det. , *iȝt* det. , *ȝȝ* det. , ruin(s).

iȝt (R 12) standard, banner, for supporting religious symbols.

abbrev. *iȝt* (F 37) back.

var. *iȝt* (O 44) rank, office.

iȝȝt stick, rod.

var. *iȝw* (A 30) praise (n.).

abbrev. *iȝwi* (A 19) (be) old; *iȝwy*, *iȝwt* old age; *iȝw* old man; *iȝyt* old woman.

iȝby (R 15; D 41) left-hand (adj. and n.); *iȝbt*, later *iȝbtt*, east; *iȝbty* eastern, easterner.

iȝm (M 1), unidentified tree.

ỉꜣm, varr. *ỉmꜣ*, *ỉm(ꜣ)* (§ 279), (be) gracious, charming; *ỉꜣmt* graciousness, charm; *ỉꜣmw* det. splendour, brilliance

ỉꜣm, var. *ỉm(ꜣ)*, tent.

ỉꜣrw reeds.

ỉ(ꜣ)rrt (M 43) vine; *ỉꜣrrt* grapes.

ỉꜣḫi (M 15) be inundated; var. *ꜣḫt* (M 8) inundation season, p. 203; *Ꜣḫ-bỉt* (M 15) Chemmis, town in extreme N. of Delta; cf. too *wꜣḫy* below.

ỉꜣs (A 28) bald.

ỉꜣš, later var. *ꜥš*, call, *n* (someone); call (n.); see too under *sḏm* below.

ỉꜣḳt leeks, leek-like vegetables.

ỉꜣkb (D 3), var. *ỉkb*, mourn.

ỉꜣtt (S 40) milk, cream.

ỉꜣṯ (D 57), var. *ỉꜣt*, be mutilated, missing; *sỉꜣt* purloin, cheat; *sỉꜣty* abbrev. cheat (n.).

abbrev. *ỉꜣdt* (N 4), var. *ỉdt*, dew.

ỉꜣdt net.

ỉi (M 18) come, § 289, 2; welcome!, old perf., § 313; *ỉi·wy* how welcome (is), welcome!, § 374; peculiarities of *sḏm·f* forms, § 459; aux. vb., § 483, 1; *ỉyt* mishap, harm.

ỉꜥꜣ (S 25, O.K.), var. *ỉꜣꜥ*, skirt (?); cf. *ꜥw* below.

ỉꜥi wash; *ỉꜥi ỉb* (?) slake (one's) desire, appetite, wrath.

ỉꜥb (W 10), var. *ꜥꜥb*, cup.

ỉꜥb unite; *ỉꜥbt ẖꜣt*, var. *ꜥbt-ẖꜣt* interment, lit. uniting corpse (with earth); var. *m-ꜥb* (F 16) in the company of, § 178.

ỉꜥn (E 32) sacred baboon.

ỉꜥnw lamentation, sorrow, woe.

var. *ỉꜥr* (O 41; N 31), later *ꜥr*, ascend, mount up, approach; *ꜥrw* det. neighbourhood; *ỉꜥrt* (I 12) cobra, uraeus; *sꜥr* det. make to ascend, offer up.

var. det. abbrev. *ỉꜥḥ* (N 11. 12) moon.

ỉw, rare var. *ỉ*, § 468, 6, is, are; the *w* before sing. suffixes prob. merely graphic, § 461, Obs. 2; perhaps derived from , §§ 29. 461; sometimes has value of copula, § 29; as such replaced by *wnn* in other tenses and moods, § 118, 2; wider use with suffix subj. than with nom. subj., §§ 37. 117, 2; in sents. with adv. pred., §§ 29. 37. 117; presence or absence of, in these, § 117; with nom. subj., § 117, 1; with suffix subj., § 117, 2; do., introducing cl. of time or circumstance, §§ 117, end; 214; here perhaps originally with parenthetic force, § 117, Obs.; not used in sent. with nom. pred., § 125; rare in sent. with adj. pred., §§ 142. 467; introducing pseudo-verbal *ỉw·f ḥr sḏm*, *ỉw·f sḏm(w)*, § 323; *ỉw·f m sḏm*, § 331; *ỉw·f r sḏm*, § 332; with impers. vb. of motion, § 466; with words of adj. meaning, § 467; as aux. vb., **§§ 461–8**; *ỉw sḏm·f*, § 462; *ỉw·f sḏm·f*, § 463; *ỉw sḏm·n·f*, §§ 68. 464; *ỉw* + pass. *sḏm·f*, §§ 422, 1; 465; omitted after *ỉst*, *nn*, *nty*, § 107, 2; however, late exx. after *nn* and *nty*, § 468, 4; very rare after *n*, § 120; use to mark strong contrast, § 117, 1; p. 248, top; §§ 394, end; 468, 2; expressing detachment before indep. pron., § 468, 3; in affirmations preceded by oath, § 468, 1; questions introduced by *in iw*, § 492; *iw wn*, there is, are, § 107, 2; do. foll. by parts., § 395; do. in questions, § 492, 2; *iw-ms*, untruth, misstatement, lit. but there is, § 194.

iw come, § 289, 2; peculiarities of *śḏm·f* forms, § 459; aux. vb., § 483, 2; *iw·f-ꜥꜣ·f* a *crescit eundo*, one who rises in rank, § 194; for see *nmtt*.

iw (N 18) island.

iw (E 9. 14) dog.

iw wrong, crime; *iwyt* wrongdoing.

iw complaint; *siw* bring a complaint, *r* against.

iw(y) one without a boat.

iwyt street.

iwꜣ ox.

iwꜥ (F 44) thigh (of beef), femur.

iwꜥ inherit; *iwꜥt*, *iwꜥꜥt* heritage, inheritance; *iwꜥw* heir.

iwꜥ reward (vb.), *m* with.

iwꜥyt garrison, soldiery; cf. *wꜥw* below.

iwꜥw (S 21), var. *ꜥꜥw*, ring.

iwf (properly *if*, § 59) meat, flesh.

iwn colour, complexion, nature.

iwn (O 28) column; *Iwn-mwt·f* Pillar-of-his-Mother, a name of Horus, p. 269, n. 1; var. *iwnyt* (O 28) hall of columns.

iwnt (O 28) bow (n.); *Iwn(ty)-Sty* (T 10) Nubian foreigner, lit. bowman, p. 398, n. 1.

Iwnw El-Maṭarîyah, Heliopolis, On of the Bible; *Iwnw Šmꜥw* On of Upper Egypt, an epithet given to Thebes.

Iwny Armant, Hermonthis, a town in Upper Egypt.

Iwnt Denderah, Tentyra, a town in Upper Egypt.

Iwnyt Esna, Latopolis, a town in Upper Egypt.

iwr (B 2) conceive, become pregnant.

iwh load (vb.), *m* or *ḥr* with.

iwḥ water (vb.), irrigate.

iwsw balance (n.).

iwty (D 35), varr. *iwtw*, B. of D. *ꜣty*, who . . . not, which . . . not, §§ **202–3**; origin and forms, § 202; with adv. pred., § 203, 1; with noun + suffix, who has not, § 203, 3; with infin. + suffix, § 307, 2; foll. by imperf. *śḏm·f*, § 443; by *śḏm·n·f*, §§ 203, 6; 418, end; *iwty n·f*, *iwty sw*, who has nothing, § 203, 1. 2; *ntt iwtt* what exists and does not exist, i.e. everything, § 203, 4; *ḥr-iwtt* because not, § 223.

iwtn ground, floor.

iwd separate (vb.); *r-iwd* between . . . ., *r* and, § 180.

ib (F 34) heart, wish (n.); as seat of intelligence, etc., second element in many epithets, exx. *wꜣḥ-ib* patient; *wmt-ib* stout-hearted; *st-ib* affection; *ḫrt-ib* wish, desire (n.); *rdi ib m-sꜣ* be anxious about; *di m ib·f* determine, infin. to, § 303; *rdi ib ḫnt* pay attention to; *ib* wish (vb.), § 292.

ib (E 8) kid.

ib suppose, imagine.

ibi (be) thirsty; *ibt* thirst (n.).

ibw refuge.

var. *ib(ꜣ)* (A 32; Y 6) dance (vb.).

ibr (E 6) stallion, Hebr. אַבִּיר.

ibhty, a stone used for beads, etc., from Ibhet, a Nubian region.

ibḥ (F 18) tooth.

ibḥ (E 8), a priest who poured libations or the like.

ip count, calculate, reckon; *ip ḏt·f* take stock of (one's) person, i.e. grow up; *ipt* reckoning; *'Ipt-swt* Ipet-sut, Most-select-of-Places, name of the temple of Karnak; *sip* revise, inspect, assign, *n* to; *sipty* revision.

ipt, *oipĕ*, Gk. οἶφι, a measure of capacity = 4 *ḥekat* or 18 litres, § 266, 1.

ipt (F 13) mission, message, occupation; *ipwty* det. messenger. See *wpi* below.

ipw (m.), *iptw* (f.), archaic plur. of *pw* that; *ipn* (m.), *iptn* (f.), do. of *pn* this, § 110.

varr. (O 45. 46), also (W 11), *ip(ɜ)t* harîm, private apartments.

ifdt a four, quartet, § 260; *ifd* flee; *ifdy*, a cloth, square of cloth.

im·, form of prep. *m* used before suffix-prons., § 162.

im, adv. from prep. *m* (§ 205, 1), there, therein, thence, therewith; apparent varr. (G 18), *mm*, *ib.*; also probably *-imy* in *n·i-imy*, *n·k-imy*, etc., of mine, thine, etc., §§ 113, 3, Obs.; 205, 1, Obs.

imy being in, adj. from prep. *m*, §§ 79. 80; of, following adjs., with superlative meaning, § 97; *imy-wrt* west side; *imyt-pr* estate, property, will, lit. content of house; varr. (F 20) *imy-r* overseer, superintendent, § 79; *imy-rn·f* list of persons; *imy-ḥɜt* prototype, example; *imy-ḫt*, adj. from prep. *m-ḫt* (§ 178), who goes after, accompanies; *imy-sɜ* attendant, bodyguard; *imytw*, also *m-imytw*, *r-imytw*, prep. between, § 177.

var. *imi* (Aa 13) give, place, cause, as imper. of *rdi* give, § 336; foll. by (perf., § 452, 1) *śḏm·f*, § 338. 2; by obj. + old perf., § 315.

var. *imi* negative vb., § **342**; position of subj., § 343; *śḏm·f* form of, in wishes and commands, §§ 342. 345; imper. *m* negating imper., § 340, 1; later replaced by *m ir*, § 340, 2; *m rdi* + *śḏm·f* let him not (hear), § 340, 3.

imi mourn; *imw* mourning.

var. *imw* (P 1) boat.

im(ɜ), etc., see under *iɜm* above.

var. *imɜḫ* (F 39) spinal cord.

var. *imɜḫ* venerated state; *imɜḫw* *imɜḫy* revered, honoured.

var. det. *imn* (A 4. 5) hide (vb.).

'Imn Amūn, the god of Thebes, Gk. Ἄμμων.

var. *imnt* (R 14. 13), later *imntt*, west; *imnty* western; see too *wnmy* below.

imḫt netherworld.

in, rare initial form of prep., §§ 148, 5, end; 155, end; 164.

var. (A 27) *in*, prep., by (of agent), §§ 39, end; **168**; 227, 4; 300.

in, non-encl. part., indeed, § **227**; *in* + noun + (perf. § 450, 5, *e*) *śḏm·f*, § 227, 2; *in* + noun + part., §§ 227, 3; 373; element in indep. prons., §§ 64. 227; relation to prep. *in*, § 227, 4; introducing n. already represented by a pron., § 227, 5; introducing questions, §§ 227, 1; 491, 3; *in iw*, § 492; *in* alone, § 493; *in ntt* is it the case that . . . ?, § 494, 1. 2; *in nt-pw* is it the case that?, § 494, 3; *in m* who?, §§ 227, 3; 496.

in, var. *i in*, says, parenthetic, §§ 436–7; see *i* say, above.

int (K 1) the *bulṭi*-fish.

in delay (vb.); *sin*, same sense.

int valley.

ini (W 25) bring, fetch, remove; var. *inw* gifts, tribute; varr. , *'In-ḥrt* (N 31) Onūris, the god of This, N. of Abydus, Gk. 'Ονοῦρις.

abbrev. *inb* (O 36) wall; also *inbt* det. or .

varr. det. , *'Inpw* (E 15. 16; C 6) the dog-headed god Anubis, Gk. 'Ανοῦβις; (A 18) var. det. *inp* crown-prince, royal child.

inm skin.

, *inn* (late writings) indep. pron. 1st plur. c., we, § 64.

inr (O 39; N 37) stone; *inr ḥḏ* white stone: *n ꜥ(i)nw* of ꜥAinu (D 8), i.e. limestone; *n rwḏt* of hard stone, i.e. sandstone.

inḥ (D 13) eyebrow(s).

inḥ surround, enclose.

inst shank.

inḳ envelop, embrace.

ink (W 24) indep. pron. 1st sing. c., I, § 64; varr. , , , etc.; belonging to me, § 114, 3; *ink pw*, §§ 190, 1; 325.

ind, earlier *inḏ*, (be) ill; illness; *sind* make ill.

inḏ ḥr foll. by suffix, hail to, § 272; see too under *nḏ* below.

ir initial form of prep. *r*, § 163; as to, § 149; if, foll. by *sḏm·f*, § 150 (imperf., *2ae gem.* vbs., § 444, 4; perf., other mutable vbs., § 454, 5; negated by *tm·f*, § 347, 6); if, unfulfilled condition, foll. by *sḏm·n·f*, §§ 151. 414, 3; *ir·*, occasional form of prep. *r* before suffix, § 163, cf. below *irf* encl. part.; *iry*, var. *irw*, adv. from prep. *r*, §§ 113, 2; 205, Obs.; (A 48. 47) relating to, connected with, adj. from prep. *r*, § 79; see too under *ꜥꜣ*, *ꜥt*, *nfr-ḥꜣt*, *sšm*; *irt* duty.

irt (D 4) eye; , reading uncertain (*irwy*?, *brwy*?), eyes.

iri make, do, act, acquire; writings, § 281; as aux. vb., § 485; foll. by infin., *ib.*; § 338, 1; *m ir* do not, § 340, 2; part. *ir* achieving, § 367, 2; *ir n*, f. *irt n*, engendered by, §§ 361. 379, 3; *ir n*, *ir m* amounting to, § 422, 3; *iri n* act on behalf of, help; *iri r* act against, oppose; *irw* form, nature.

var. det. *irp* (W 21; M 43) wine.

irf, var. *rf*, encl. part. used for emphasis, § 252.

irtyw mourning.

irtt (W 20), O.K. *irṯt*, milk.

iḥw (military) camp.

iḥm hold back, detain; det. lag, go slow.

iḥhy jubilation.

iḥ, see *ꜥḥ*.

iḥ, etc., see under *ꜥḥ*.

iḥ ox.

iḥw stable (for horses).

iḥms, see under *ḥmsi* below.

iḫ non-encl. part., then, therefore, introducing desired future consequence, exhortation or command, §§ 40, 3; **228**; foll. by *sḏm·f* (perf., § 450, 5, *a*; rarely imperf., § 440, 4; negated, *tm·f*, § 346, 4; *wn·f*, § 118, 2), *ib.*; interrog., what?, § 501.

[hieroglyphs] *iḫt*, O.K. writing of [hieroglyphs] *ḫt* things, see there.

[hieroglyphs] *iḫm-sk*, see under *ḫm* below.

[hieroglyphs] *iḫmt*, later var. [hieroglyphs] *ʿḫmt*, river-bank.

[hieroglyphs] *iḫr*, non-encl. part., see under *ḫr*.

[hieroglyphs] *iḫḫw*, later var. [hieroglyphs] *ʿḫḫw* (N 2), dusk, twilight.

[hieroglyphs] *is* encl. part., § **247**; after indep. pron., §§ 127, 4; 136; as interrog. part., §§ 247, 4; 491, 2; like, § 247, 5; [hieroglyphs] *n is* see under [hieroglyphs] *n* below; [hieroglyphs] *isw* rare non-encl. part., § 232.

[hieroglyphs] *is* go (imper.) § 336, see too under [hieroglyphs] *s*; [hieroglyphs] *is-ḥꜣḳ* plunder (n.).

[hieroglyphs] later var. [hieroglyphs] *is* chamber, tomb, tomb-chamber.

[hieroglyphs] *isi* (M 2) (be) light (in weight).

[hieroglyphs] *ist* gang, crew.

[hieroglyphs] *isw* (M 40) reeds.

[hieroglyphs] *is* (be) old; [hieroglyphs] var. [hieroglyphs] *iswt* old times, antiquity; *isywt* det. [hieroglyphs] (V 6) rags.

[hieroglyphs] var. [hieroglyphs] *isw* (F 44) exchange, payment; *m-isw*, rarely *r-isw*, in return for, § 178.

[hieroglyphs] *ispt* quiver (n.).

[hieroglyphs] var. [hieroglyphs] *isft* evil, wrongdoing; *isfty* sinner.

[hieroglyphs] *isr* tamarisk.

[hieroglyphs] *isḳ* linger, delay, restrain.

[hieroglyphs] *isk*, var. [hieroglyphs] *sk*, lo, archaic var. of *isṯ*, §§ 119, 3; 230.

[hieroglyphs] *isṯ*, varr. [hieroglyphs] *sṯ*, later [hieroglyphs] *ist*, etc., non-encl. part., lo (or sim.), § **231**; origin, *ib.*; in sent. with adv. pred., § 119, 2; with nom. pred., § 133; with adj. pred., § 142; before pseudo-verbal construction, § 324; introducing virt. cls. of time and circumstance, before *sḏm·f*, § 212; before *sḏm·n·f*, §§ 212. 414, 1; before pass. *sḏm·f*, § 422, 1; before *n sḏmt·f*, § 402; enclitically, § 248.

[hieroglyphs] *išt* property, belongings.

[hieroglyphs] *išst* what?, § **500**; *ḥr sy išst* wherefore?, § 500, 4; *išst iry*, § 500, 5.

[hieroglyphs] *išd*, unidentified tree; det. [hieroglyphs], [hieroglyphs] (M 43), its fruit.

[hieroglyphs] *iḳr* (be) excellent, precious; excellence, virtue, also *bw iḳr*; *n-iḳr* (*n*) by virtue of, § 181; *r iḳr* exceedingly, § 205, 5; *siḳr* advance, promote (a person), adorn (a place).

[hieroglyphs], see under *ḳd* below.

[hieroglyphs] var. [hieroglyphs] *iky* (A 19) miner, hewer of stone.

[hieroglyphs] *ikm* (I 6) shield.

[hieroglyphs] *ikn* draw (water).

[hieroglyphs] *igrt*, early var. of [hieroglyphs] *grt*, encl. part., § 255.

[hieroglyphs] *igrt*, see under *gr* below.

[hieroglyphs] abbrev. [hieroglyphs] *it* (M 33; U 10) barley.

[hieroglyphs] *it*, var. [hieroglyphs] (*i*)*t* (p. 43, n. 1), father; often without [hieroglyphs] in [hieroglyphs] var. [hieroglyphs] *it-nṯr* god's father, name of a class of elder priests.

[hieroglyphs] var. [hieroglyphs] *ity* (I 3) sovereign, p. 75.

[hieroglyphs] rare var. [hieroglyphs] *ʾItm* (D 38) the sun-god Atum.

[hieroglyphs] *itmw* lack of breath.

[hieroglyphs] *itn* sun's disk, sun.

[hieroglyphs] *itn* oppose, thwart, obj. (something), *m* (someone); *itnw* det. [hieroglyphs] opponent, enemy; *itnw* det. [hieroglyphs] difficulties.

later det. *itrw* (N 35) river, Nile; also measure of length = 10·5 km., the Gk. schoenus, § 266, 2.

itrt (O 20) row (of shrines), particularly of those of Upper (det. O 19) and Lower (det. O 20) Egypt as seen at the *Sed*-festival, p. 291, n. 3; collectively, the gods of these shrines; *itrty* det. the two sides, rows, aisles.

itḥ drag, draw, stretch (a bow).

itḥ (U 31) prison.

iṯi (V 15), var. *iṯi* (§ 281), take away, seize; take possession, *m* of; *iṯi ḥpt*, see under *ḥpt* below.

iṯꜣ thief.

idi (F 21) be deaf.

idyt girl, maid.

var. *idt* (F 45; N 41) vulva, cow.

var. *idt* (D 46*) fragrance.

idw pestilence.

abbrev. *idb* (N 21) bank (of river), cultivated area; *idbwy* the two banks, i.e. Egypt.

var. *idn* (F 21) replace; *idnw* deputy, substitute.

idr (V 37) bind; bandage; var. *idr* (V 37) herd, flock.

idḥw (M 15), the marshlands of the Delta; *idḥy* Delta man.

y (M 17; Z 4)

y in grammatical endings representing O.E. *i* or *ii*, §§ 20, end; 270, Obs.; as initial consonant hardly except in group-writing where equivalent of Hebr. י, p. 481, M 17; use of and distinguished, §§ 20, end; 73, 4, Obs.

-y: after duals before suffix 1st sing., § 75, 1; in certain plur. impers., § 335; ending 3rd sing. plur. in certain old perfs., § 309; m. ending in imperf. act. parts., § 357; rare in imperf. pass. parts., § 358; in m. sing. plur. perf. pass. parts., § 361; alleged ending m. sing. in perf. rel. form with prospective meaning, § 387, 2; in pass. *śḏm·f* before suffixes, § 420; in perf. *śḏm·f* of certain vbs., § 448.

-y: origin and nature, §§ 20. 73, 4; after duals added to suffixes 2nd m., 3rd m., f., § 75, 2; do. after ns. dual only in meaning, § 76, 2; ending m. sing. of adjs. derived from preps. and ns., **§§ 79–81**; in *imytw*, § 177; rare ending m. sing. of imperf. act. parts., § 357; in perf. pass. parts. of *2-lit.* vbs., § 360; in *śḏmty·fy* form, § 363; in *ḫr*(*y*)*·fy*, § 437.

ym sea, Hebr. יָם, § 62 A (Add. p. 422).

yḥ, interj., hey!, § 258.

ꜥ (D 36)

ꜥ arm, hand; in compound preps. *m-ꜥ*, *r-ꜥ*, *ḫr-ꜥ*, § 178; advs., *ḥr ꜥ*, *ḥr ꜥwy* immediately; *ḏr ꜥ* long ago, § 205, 3; *ꜥ* piece, pair (*n* of), action, position, state, see too *nt-ꜥ*, *r-ꜥ*, *r-ꜥwy*, *ḥry-ꜥ*; *st-ꜥ* activity, stroke; var. *ꜥ* affairs, business.

ꜥ (W 10) cup.

varr. , *ꜥw* (S 25) dragoman, interpreter; see too *i ꜥꜣ* above.

ꜥt limb, member.

ꜥt room, department, house; *iry ꜥt* official, attached to the department (of).

ꜥꜣ (O 29) column.

ꜥꜣ (N 31) here, § 205, 1.

abbrev. *ꜥꜣ* (O 31) door; *iry ꜥꜣ* doorkeeper.

ʿꜣ (E 7) ass, donkey.

var. *ʿꜣi* (be) great; *ʿꜣw* greatly, § 205, 4; *r ʿꜣt* greatly, § 205, 5; *ʿꜣt* greatness; *n-ʿꜣt-n(t)*, *m-ʿꜣt-n* so greatly (did, etc.), inasmuch as, § 181; *ʿꜣt* (valuable) stone (for vessels, etc.); *sʿꜣ* enlarge, exalt, enrich.

var. *ʿꜣbt* (M 19) offering, pile of offerings; *ʿꜣb* det. (hieratic) be desirable; *ʿꜣbt* self-seeking, selfishness.

abbrev. var. det. *ʿꜣm* (T 14; A 49) Asiatic, f. *ʿꜣmt*.

ʿꜣg flog, beat feet of.

ʿʿw(y) sleep (vb.).

ʿʿny tent.

ʿwt (S 38, Pyr.) *awet*-sceptre.

ʿwt (S 38. 39; E 8) flock, herd (small cattle), goats.

ʿwꜣi rob, steal; robber; one robbed; *Nḥmt-ʿwꜣy*, see under *nḥm* below; *ʿwꜣ-ir(y)·f* brigand.

ʿwn (be) rapacious; defraud, *ḥr*, *m* of; *ʿwn-ib* of rapacious disposition.

ʿwnt stick, club.

abbrev. *ʿb* (F 16) horn; metaphorically, (archer's) bow.

ʿb, see under *iʿb* above.

ʿbt (O 30, p. 517) fork; *ʿʿb* comb (hair).

ʿbw, see under *wʿb* below.

ʿbꜣ (S 42) *aba*-sceptre.

abbrev. *ʿbꜣ* (S 42) stela, table of offerings.

ʿbʿ boasting, exaggeration.

ʿpr (Aa 20) equip, *m* with; learn, master; *ʿprw* equipment.

var. *ʿfty* (A 36. 37) brewer.

ʿfꜣy encampment.

ʿff (L 3) fly (n.).

ʿfnt (royal) head-dress.

ʿfdt, older *ʿfḏt*, box, chest.

ʿm (F 10) swallow (vb.); with *ib* obj., *ʿm ib* lose consciousness, faint; *ʿm ib ḥr* be thoughtless, negligent about; *sʿm* swallow down, wash down (food), *m* with (drink).

ʿmʿ smear; *ʿmʿt* det. mud.

ʿmʿꜣt (T 14. 15) throw-stick.

var. det. *ʿn*, *ʿ(i)n* (D 8. 7) (be) beautiful; det. the good man; *ʿ(i)nw* ʿAinu, the limestone quarries at Ṭurah.

ʿnt (D 51) finger-nail, claw; var. *ʿnty* (G 7*. 7**) ʿAnty, a god, lit. He-with-the-claw(s).

ʿnn (D 55) turn back; *ʿnw* one who (always) returns; det. (A 31) (face) averted.

ʿnḫ (S 34) sandal-strap.

ʿnḫ live; live, *m* on (food, truth); *ʿnḫ n(·i)* as (god, king) lives for me, in oaths, § 218; *ʿnḫ(w) wḏꜣ(w) snb(w)* may he live, be prosperous, be healthy, §§ 55. 313; *ʿnḫ(w) ḏt* may he live eternally, § 313; do. after *iri*, § 378; *di ʿnḫ* given life, § 378; *ʿnḫ* life; det. swear, oath, § 218; *Pr-ʿnḫ*, see under *pr*; *nb ʿnḫ*, see under *nb*; *ʿnḫ n(i)* one living in, attached to, with foll. noun (*niwt* town, *mšʿ* army, *ṯt ḥḳꜣ* the Ruler's table); *ʿnḫw* det. the living; *ʿnḫw* victuals; *ʿnḫtt* means of subsistence; *sʿnḫ* make to live; *sʿnḫ* (portrait-)sculptor.

ʿnḫ garland.

ʿnḫ (S 34) mirror.

ʿnḫt goat.

ʿnḫwy (F 21) the two ears.

ʿnḳt, the goddess Anūkis of Aswân, Gk. Ἀνοῦκις.

ʿntyw myrrh.

ʿnd, older ʿnḏ, (be) few; ʿndt a few (people); sʿnd make few, depreciate.

ʿr, see under iʿr above.

ʿr reed (for writing).

ʿrt sheet (of papyrus or leather).

ʿrt (F 19) jaw.

ʿrt (F 22) hind-quarters.

var. det. ʿrf (V 6. 33) envelop, tie up; bag, bundle.

ʿrrt (O 38), varr. ʿrrwt, ʿrryt, gate, place of judgement.

ʿrḳ (V 12) bind, n on (someone); det. understand; det. , (be) understanding, wise; det. swear, take an oath; var. var. ʿrḳy last day (of the month), § 264; sʿrḳ det. put an end to (enemies).

ʿḥ (O 11. 12), var. iḥ, palace.

ʿḥ (T 24), var. iḥ, net, catch, snare (animals).

ʿḥt field, holding, domain; var. ʿḥwty (M 2), var. iḥwty, tenant farmer, field labourer.

var. ʿḥꜣ (D 34. 34*) fight, r against, ḥnʿ with (against); ʿḥꜣt, ʿḥꜣ tw beware, § 338, 3; ʿḥꜣwty warrior; ʿḥꜣ det. (T 11) arrow.

ʿḥʿ (P 6) stand up, arise, stand fast; attend, ḥr to; ʿḥʿ m ꜣbd start on month's service (as priest); ʿḥʿ ḥmsi pass one's life, lit. stand up and sit down; ʿḥʿ aux. vb., §§ **476–82**; ʿḥʿ śḏm·f, § 477, 1; ʿḥʿ + pass. śḏm·f, § 477, 2; ʿḥʿ + subj. + old perf., § 477, 3; ʿḥʿ·n śḏm·n·f, § 478; ʿḥʿ·n·f śḏm·n·f, § 479; ʿḥʿ·n śḏm·f, § 480; ʿḥʿ·n + pass. śḏm·f, § 481; ʿḥʿ·n + pseudo-verbal construction; sʿḥʿ erect (obelisk, monuments); ʿḥʿw det. position, attendance.

ʿḥʿ (M 35) heap; nb ʿḥʿw wealthy man, lit. lord of heaps.

ʿḥʿw period, space (of time), lifetime.

ʿḥʿw (O 26) stela.

ʿḥʿw (P 6. 1), older ḥʿw, ships.

ʿḫ brazier, fire (for cooking).

ʿḫi (N 1) hang up.

ʿḫm extinguish (fire); det. quench (thirst).

ʿḫmt, see iḫmt above.

ʿḫḫw, see iḫḫw above.

ʿḫi (H 5), var. ʿḫi, fly (vb.).

ʿḫm (G 11), varr. ʿšm, ʿḫm, divine image.

ʿḫmw branches.

ʿ-ḫnwty inner appartments, audience-chamber; see too under ḫn below.

later det. ʿš (M 41; Aa 2) pine, fir, the 'cedar' of the Bible, p. 123, n. 5.

ʿš, see iꜣš above.

ʿš(ꜣ) (I 1) lizard.

ʿšꜣ (I 1) (be) many, abundant, ordinary; ʿšꜣ-r ( ) chatter, § 288; adv., often, § 205, 4; ʿšꜣt multitude; sʿšꜣ multiply; det. curb (vb.) lit. scatter (?).

ʿḳ (G 35) enter, r into (a place,) ḥr, m before, among (persons); ʿḳ(yw) det. intimates; ʿḳyt female servant; ʿḳw provisions, revenue (in food); sʿḳ cause to enter.

ʿḳꜣ (D 50) (be) precise, accurate; det. equality, level; det. adjust, ʿḳꜣw the right rope (in the ferry-boat); r-ʿḳꜣ on a level with, § 178; *sʿḳꜣ* put, set in order.

ʿtḫ strain (vb., in beer-making).

var. *ʿḏ* (V 26. 27) spool, reel.

ʿḏ, later *ʿd*, perceive, recognize.

ʿḏ (V 26), var. *ʿd*, be in good condition.

ʿdw (K 3) the *bûri*-fish.

ʿd (U 6), var. O.K. *ʿḏ*, hack up; *ʿḏ-mr* (K 3) administrator of a province, prob. lit. excavator of canal(s).

var. , hieratic , *ʿḏ* (Aa 8), later *ʿd*, desert-edge.

ʿd (V 26) fat.

, see (*m*)*ʿ*(*n*)*dt* below.

ʿḏꜣ (be) guilty; guilt, crime.

, w (G 43; Z 7)

w, semi-vowel, § 20; often omitted in grammatical endings, *ib.*; immutable in (e.g.) *ꜣbw* 'brand', § 279; initial, omitted in some derivatives, § 290.

-w, ending 3rd sing. or plur. m. of old perf., § 309; of plur. in impers., § 335; of neg. complement, § 341; m. in imperf. act. part., § 357; in imperf. pass. part., § 358; in some perf. act. parts., § 359; in imperf. rel. form, § 387, 1; in *śḏmw·n·f* rel. form, § 387, 3; ending of pass. *śḏm·f* form before nom. subj., § 420.

-w, plur. m. ending of ns. and adjs., § 72; *-wt*, plur. f., *ib.*; *-wy*, dual m., *ib.*; *-ty*, dual f., *ib.*

var. , *·w*, from Dyn. XVIII occasional suffix-pron. 3rd plur. c., they, them, their, § 34.

w, very rare encl. part., not, § 352 A.

w district, region.

wꜣt (V 4), also *wꜣwꜣt*, coil of rope, let loose (*wḥʿ*) in foundation ceremonies.

wꜣi (N 31) (be) far, distant, *r* from; fall, *r* into (decay, etc.); *wꜣw*, adv., afar; *wꜣt*, abbrev. , way, road, side; *r* () *-wꜣt* path, place of passage; *swꜣi* det. var. det. or abbrev. (Z 9) pass, *ḥr* by; pass, of time; *swꜣw* passing (n.).

wꜣw wave.

wꜣwꜣ ponder, deliberate.

Wꜣwꜣt Wawat, region at N. end of Lower Nubia.

Wꜣb(wy)? (S 40), name of the 19th nome (Oxyrhynchite) of Upper Egypt.

var. *wꜣḥ* (V 29) 1. place, put down; permit, foll. by *śḏm·f*, § 184, 1; *wꜣḥ tp* bow the head (in submission); with *m*, multiply, § 338, 1; *wꜣḥ ḫt* () make offerings; 2. endure, (be) enduring, lasting; *wꜣḥ-ib* patient, well-disposed; *swꜣḥ* make to endure.

wꜣḥyt increase, abundance (of corn).

wꜣḥw (S 10) wreath.

wꜣḫy (M 15) hall of the Inundation, reception hall in Palace; cf. too *iꜣḫ* above.

wꜣs (S 40) *was*-sceptre.

wꜣs dominion, lordship, only in fixed expressions like *ʿnḫ, ḏdt, wꜣs* life, stability, dominion.

Wꜣst (R 19) Wise, Thebes.

var. *wꜣsi* (S 40) be ruined, decay; ruin (n.).

wꜣš (A 28) be exalted; *swꜣš* var. det. (A 30) extol.

Wꜣg (W 3) *Wag*-festival, celebrated on the 18th day of the 1st month.

. M 13 incorrectly used for V 24, see under *wḏ* below.

wꜣḏ (M 13) (be) green, fresh; *r wꜣḏ* vigorously, § 205, 5; *wꜣḏ* success, good fortune; *wꜣḏ* (M 13) papyrus column; *wꜣḏyt* colonnade; *wꜣḏ* a pale green stone, felspar (?); *Wꜣḏt* (I 12. 13), the cobra-goddess Edjō, p. 73, n. 1[a]; *Wꜣḏ-wr* the sea, lit. the great green; *ḏyt* (M 15), O.K. *ḏyt* papyrus-marsh; *swꜣḏ* make green, renew.

varr. , *wi* dep. pron. 1st sing. c., I, me, my, § 43; as subj. in *n(y)-wi* I belong to, § 114, 2; with other adj. preds., rare, p. 109, n. 6; with pass. parts., doubtful, p. 425, Add. to § 374.

wi (A 53) mummy, mummy sheath.

-wy, ending added to adj. preds. with exclamatory force, how, § 49; do. added to parts., § 374, with Add. p. 425; prob. originated in dual m. ending, § 49, Obs.

-wy, see under *-w* above.

-wyn, ending 1st plur. c. of old perf., § 309.

var. det. *wiꜣ* (P 3) sacred bark.

win reject, decline.

wꜥ (T 21; Z 1) m., *wꜥt* f., one, alone; §§ 260. 262, 1; *wꜥ n* as indef. art., § 262, 1; foll. by adj., yielding superlative sense, § 97; as numeral, one, usually written I, § 259; *wꜥ* .... *ky*, *wꜥ* ..... *sn-nw·f* one .... other, § 98; *wꜥ nb* everyone, § 103; *wꜥ m* one of (several), § 262, 1; *wꜥi* det. be alone; , *wꜥty* sole, unique; var. det. *wꜥꜥw* privacy, solitude.

wꜥw soldier, cf. *iwꜥyt* above.

wꜥꜣ speak abuse.

var. *wꜥb* (D 60; A 6) (be) pure, clean; *swꜥb* purify, cleanse; *wꜥb* (ordinary) priest; *wꜥbw* det. clean clothes; *wꜥbt* det. place of embalmment, tomb, sanctuary; det. meat; abbrev. *ꜥbw* (F 17) purification; *ꜥbw-r* () breakfast.

wꜥf bend, curb.

wꜥn (M 41) juniper (?).

wꜥrt (D 56) leg, shank.

wꜥr flee; fugitive; *wꜥrt* flight.

abbrev. *wꜥrt* (D 56) administrative district; *wꜥrtw* district official.

abbrev. *wꜥḥ* (N 11) carob-beans.

var. *wbꜣ* (U 26. 27) open up; *wbꜣ-ib*, *wbꜣ-ḥr* intelligent, capable, enlightened; *swbꜣ ḥr* initiate, *r* into (work); *wbꜣ* open court (of temple); var. *wbꜣ* butler.

var. det. ☉ *wbn* (N 8. 5) shine forth, rise (of sun); det. (M 35) overflow; var. *wbnw* (Aa 2; N 8) wound (n.).

wbd burn (vb.).

wpt (F 13) vertex, brow.

wpi divide, open, judge; *wpw-ḥr* except, but, § 179; *wpt* det. × specification; *wp st* (Z 9) lit. specify it, introducing list of items; connected with this stem are *ipt* message, *ipwty* messenger, see above; var. *wpt-rnpt* (F 14. 15) New Year's day, p. 204; var. *Wpt-tꜣ* Earth's Beginning, name given to the extreme south; *Wp-wꜣwt* (E 18) the jackal-god (Gk. wolf) Wepwawet of Asyûṭ, Gk. 'Οφῶις.

wfꜣ talk, talk about, discuss.

wmt (be) thick; *wmt-ib* stout-hearted; *wmt* gateway; *wmtt* det. (O 36) fortification, bulwark.

wn (O 31) open (vb.); *wn-ḥr* instructed, expert; *wn ḥr n* light is given to (someone, that he may see), lit. face (i.e. sight) is given to, etc.

wnỉ (E 34) pass by, disregard; *wn* det. fault, failing.

Wnw El-Ashmûnên, Hermopolis, a town in Upper Egypt.

var. *wnwt* (N 14. 5) hour, p. 206; priestly duties; det. priesthood; *wnwt(y)* hour-watcher, star-watcher.

wnf be glad, gay.

varr. *wnm* (Z 11; M 42; X 7) eat; *wnmt* food; *wnmyt* the consumer, i.e. fire; *snm* (G 52) feed (someone), eat, feed on; det. greed; *snmw* det. food.

wnmy (R 14) right hand (n. and adj.).

wnn exist, be, § **107**; supplies missing parts of *iw*, §§ 118, 2; 142. 150. 157, 1; 326. 395. 396. 469; in sents. with adv. pred., § 118, 2; not in sents. with nom. pred., § 125; in sents. with adj. pred., § 142; in pseudo-verbal construction, § 326; do., itself in old perf. or infin., § 326; *wnn·f r sḏm*, § 332; parts. of, as equivalents of rel. adj., § 396; *wnn·f* with future reference, §§ 118, 2; 326; 440, 3; *wnn·f* after *ỉr*, §§ 150. 395. 444, 4; *wn·f* expressing purpose, § 118, 2; after *iḫ*, *ib.*; as obj. after *rdỉ*, *ib.*; after other vbs., § 186, 2; *wn·f*, *wnn·f* after preps., §§ 157, 1. 2. 3; 326, end; 444, 3; *wn·f*, *wnn·f* in virt. adv. cls., §§ 214. 215. 219; *wnn* as aux. vb., §§ **469–75**; *wn·in·f* in pseudo-verbal construction, § 470; *wn·ḫr·f*, *wnn·ḫr·f* do., § 471; *wn·in sḏm·f*, § 472; *wn·in·f sḏm·f*, *wn·ḫr·f sḏm·f*, § 473; other forms from *wnn* before *sḏm·f*, § 474; before *sḏm·n·f*, § 475; *iw wn* there is, are, § 107, 2; foll. by parts., § 395; in questions, § 492, 2; *nn wn*, *n wnt* there is, are, not, §§ 108, 1. 2; 109; *nn wn*, *n wnt*, before *sḏm·f*, § 188, 2; *ỉr wn* if there be, p. 427, Add. to p. 358, n. 11; var. *wn* being (n.) in phrase *n (m) wn mꜣꜥ* ( ) in reality, lit. of (in) true being, § 205, 3; *wnnt*, *wnt* encl. parts., indeed, really, §§ 127, 4; 249; *wnt* non-encl. part., that, §§ 187. 233; foll. by subj. + old perf., § 329; *wnt* in , see above; *Wnn-nfr(w)* Onnōphris, He-who-is-continually-happy, a name given to the resurrected Osiris, cf. p. 307, bottom.

wnḫ be clad, obj. in, § 84 A, p. 423.

wnš jackal or wolf-like animal; det. (U 16) sledge.

wnḏw (M 42; E 3) short-horned cattle.

var. with (Z 11) *wnḏwt* subjects, people.

wrr (G 36) (be) great, important, much; *wr*, adj.; *wr*, *wrt*, adv., much, very, § 205, 4; *wr* how much?, § 502; *n-wr-n* inasmuch as, § 181; var. *wr* (A 19) prince; *wr mꜣw* greatest of seers, title of the high-priest of Heliopolis; *wr-n-ỉf* haunch (of beef); *wrrt* det. , (S 2. 6) great crown; det. or abbrev. (T 17) chariot; *Wrt* det. the Great one, designation of a goddess; *Wrt-ḥkꜣw*, see under *ḥkꜣ*.

wrḥ (W 23) be anointed with, obj., § 84 A, p. 423; see too *mrḥt* below.

wrs (Q 4) head-rest, pillow.

wrš spend all day, pass time; foll. by subj. + old perf., § 316; *wršy* watchman.

wrd (A 7), O.K. *wrḏ*, be weary.

whi, escape, miss, fail.

whn (O 37) overthrow.

whyt tribe, tribesmen.

wḥ3 pull up (papyrus, flax), hew (stones).

var. *wḥ3t* (Aa 2), var. O.K. *wḥt* (W 6), cauldron; var. *Wḥ3t* Oasis region; *Wḥ3tyw* Oasis dwellers.

wḥꜥ (P 4) loose, break off work; det. unravel, explain; det. fisherman, fowler.

wḥmt (F 25) hoof.

var. det. *wḥm* repeat; foll. by infin., § 303; *wḥm ꜥnḫ* repeating life, living a second time, § 55; *m wḥm*, *m wḥm-ꜥ* a second time, adv.; *wḥmw* det. herald, also a provincial official in charge of judicial matters.

wḫ (R 16), fetish of the Upper Egyptian town Cusae.

wḫ (N 2), also *wḫt*, night; *swḫ* make dark.

wḫ3 (M 3) (wooden) column; det. hall of columns.

wḫ3 require, demand.

wḫ3 (be) ignorant; fool (n.); *swḫ3* make foolish.

wḫd (Aa 2) suffer, bear patiently; pain (n.).

varr. , , earlier *Wsir* (Q 1. 2; F 51) Osiris, local god, king of the dead, the dead king, Gk. Ὄσῖρις.

wsf be idle; idleness.

wsrt (F 12, Pyr.) neck.

var. det. *wsr* (F 12; P 8) oar.

wsr (F 12) (be) powerful, wealthy; power, wealth; *swsr* make powerful.

wsḫ (W 10) cup.

wsḫ (W 10) (be) wide, broad; breadth, with older var. *sḫw*; *swsḫ* det. var. (S 11) widen, enlarge; *wsḫ* det. or abbrev. (S 11) collar; varr. , *wsḫt* (O 15) broad hall, court; *wsḫt* det. , later *wsḫ*, barge.

wsš, var. *wšš*, urinate.

wstn, later *wstn*, stride, move freely.

wš fall out (of hair), be bald; free, unoccupied (of time); *gm wš* (D 3) found defective.

var. *wš3* (G 42) fatten; det. heap (praises).

wšꜥ bite, chew.

wšb (Z 9) answer, *n* (someone); answer (n.).

wšm (H 2) ear (of corn).

wšmw (H 2), a vessel for beer.

var. det. *wšn* (G 54; H 1) wring neck (of bird); make offering of.

wšr dry up, be barren.

wšd (F 30) address, question (vb.).

var. *wgg* (V 33) misery, want.

var. *wt* (Aa 2) wrap (mummy), bandage (vb.); det. embalmer; det. , O.K. (V 38), var. *wt3w*, bandage.

wtḫ flee; *wtḫw* fugitive.

wtt, O.K. *wtṯ*, beget.

wṯst (U 39) post (of balance).

var. det. *wṯs* (U 39. 40) lift up, carry, wear; det. lodge a complaint, denounce; cf. too *ṯsi*.

wdỉ (D 46) put, push, shoot, inflict, emit (sound).

wdpw (W 22) butler.

wdf, later occasionally *wdf*, lag, delay; *ỉr wdf* if (something) delays, i.e. does not happen, § 352; *wdf*, adv., tardily, § 205, 4.

var. *wdn* (M 11) offer, make offerings; offering (n.).

wdn (U 32) (be) heavy.

wdḥ (O.K.), later written *wdḥ*, pour; det. (Q 7) cast (metal objects); abbrev. *wdḥw*, later *wdḥw* (V 25), table of offerings.

wḏ (V 24. 25), later *wd*, e.g. p. 277, n. 2, command (vb.); foll. by *śḏm·f* (imperf. § 442, 1), § 184; by infin., § 303; *wḏ mdw* give command, *n* to; *wḏ*, *wḏt*, *wḏt-mdw* command (n.); abbrev. *wḏ* (O 26) stela; *swḏ*, later *sw(ꜣ)ḏ* (M 14), hand over, bequeath.

wḏỉ send forth, set forth; *wḏyt* (military) expedition; *wḏww* wandering herds.

wḏꜣ (be) whole, sound, prosperous; abbrev. , see under *ꜥnḫ*; *swḏꜣ ỉb* send a communication, write, *n* to, lit. make easy the heart (of), § 225; *swḏꜣ ỉb* communication, letter; abbrev. *wḏꜣt* (D 10) the *wḏꜣt-(wedjat-)* eye, the sound uninjured eye of Horus, § 266, 1; *ḏꜣt* (U 28, n. 5) remainder.

wḏꜣ proceed; cf. too *sḏꜣ* below.

wḏꜣ magazine, storehouse.

wḏꜥ (Aa 21) divide, sever, judge, judge between; *wḏꜥ ryt* () judge (vb.); *wḏꜥt* det. divorced woman.

wḏb (V 25; F 46), var. *wdb*, turn, trans. and intr.

var. *wḏb* (N 20), var. *w(ꜣ)ḏbw* (M 13. 11), sandbank, shore.

wḏnw torrent, flood.

wḏḥ child, weanling; var. det. (A 18) princeling.

wḏḥw, see under *wdḥ* above.

b (D 58)

, see *bw* below.

bꜣ (R 7; E 10) ram; *Bꜣ-pf(ỉ)* (W 10*, Pyr.) Bapfi, a god.

var. *bꜣ* (G 29. 53), old (W 10*, Pyr.), soul, external manifestation, Gk. *βαί*, p. 173; *bꜣw* (G 30) spirits, souls (plur.), might (sing. or plur.).

bꜣw, boat, pleasure-boat.

bꜣt bush.

bꜣbꜣ hole, hiding-place.

bꜣbꜣt, var. *bbt*, flowing stream, swirl.

bꜣḥ foreskin (?); det. or abbrev. or in *m-bꜣḥ*, also *m-bꜣḥ-ꜥ*, in the presence of, § 178; do., adv., formerly, § 205, 2; *ḏr-bꜣḥ* formerly.

bꜣs (W 2) jar.

Bꜣstt (W 2) the cat-goddess Baste(t), Gk. -ουβάστις.

bꜣḳ, an oil-bearing tree (not olive?).

bꜣk work, *n* for, i.e. serve; *bꜣkw* det. work, produce (n.); *bꜣk* det. manservant; *bꜣk ỉm* this (thy) servant, lit. the servant there, p. 58, n. 1; § 509, 2; *bꜣkt* det. maidservant.

bꜣgỉ, var. *bgỉ*, be remiss, slack.

bꜣgsw, varr. *bgsw* (T 8*), *mꜣgsw*, dagger.

bit (L 2) bee; *bit* honey; det. or abbrev. (A 45) *bity* king of Lower Egypt; see too under *nsw* below.

varr. , *bit* (W 10; F 18) character, qualities.

biȝ (N 41) copper; the synonymous (N 34) is provisionally likewise read as *biȝ*; var. *biȝw* (N 41; F 18) mine; *biȝ* firmament.

biȝi (U 16), var. *by*, wonder, *n* at; *biȝt*, var. *biȝyt*, marvel, wonder (n.).

bin (G 37) (be) bad, miserable, act evilly; *bin*, *bint* bad (n.); so too *bw-bin*, see under *bw* below.

bik (G 6) falcon.

abbrev. *bʿḥi* (G 32) be inundated; inundation.

var. *bw* (D 58) place, position; det. *bw nb* everyone, everybody, § 103; *bw ḫry·f* the place where he is, § 204, 1; used to form abstracts, *bw bin* bad (n.), misery; *bw nfr* good (n.), prosperity; sim. with *iḳr*, *mȝʿ*, *ḥwrw*, *ḏw*.

bwt (K 2) abomination.

bwȝw magnates.

bbt, see *bȝbȝt* above.

bnw (G 31) phoenix.

bnt (Y 7) harp.

bnwt millstone.

bnbnt pyramidion.

abbrev. *bnr* (M 30), var. *bn(r)i*, (be) sweet.

bnrw outside (n.).

bhȝ flee; *bhȝw* fugitive; *sbhȝ* det. (D 55) make to flee.

bḥs (F 18; E 3) calf.

varr. det. , *bḥs* hunt (vb.).

Bḥdt Tell el-Balamûn, Beḥdet, the northernmost town of Egypt; secondarily, Edfu in Upper Egypt; *Bḥdt(y)*, the Beḥdetite, epithet of the winged solar Horus.

bḫn tower, fortress; also f., *bḫnt*.

bḫnw greywacke, a hard dark stone found in the Wâdy Ḥammâmât.

bs (K 5) introduce; be initiated, *ḥr* into; det. , mystery, mysterious form.

bsi (K 5) flow, come forth in abundance.

bši (D 26) vomit.

bšt, older *bšṯ*, (be) rebellious.

bkȝ (B 2) be pregnant.

bgi, see *bȝgi* above.

bgȝw one shipwrecked.

bgs (be) bad, fractious.

btȝ run.

btȝ(w) crime, wrong, wrong-doer.

bṯ, var. *bt*, abandon, forsake.

bṯn, var. *btn*, be disobedient, rebel against; *bṯn-ib* rebel, adversary.

abbrev. *bd* (R 9), a kind of natron.

varr. det. , *bdt* (M 34; U 9. 10), var. *bty*, emmer, a kind of coarse wheat.

bdš (A 7) faint, languish.

p (Q 3)

p (Q 3) base, pedestal.

P Pe, Kôm Farâʿîn, Buto, a town in Lower Egypt, p. 73.

abbrev. *pt* (N 1) sky, heaven.

pȝ (G 40), in hieratic always, and in hieroglyphic sometimes, replaced by G 41. 1.

pȝ (G 40; H 5) fly (vb.).

[hieroglyph] varr. [hieroglyphs], hieratic [hieroglyphs], *pꜣ* this, the, sing. m., § 110; construction of, § 111; meanings of, § 112; [hieroglyphs], hieratic [hieroglyphs], *pꜣy·i*, poss. adj. 1st sing. m., my; so too *pꜣy·k*, *pꜣy·f*, etc., § 113, 1; [hieroglyphs] *pꜣy* for [hieroglyphs] *p-n* he of, § 111, Obs.

[hieroglyphs] *pꜣt* (X 6) loaf, bread-offering.

[hieroglyphs] *pꜣ(w?)* have done in the past, aux. vb., § 484; [hieroglyphs] *pꜣt* (X 6) antiquity, primeval times; *pꜣwty* belonging to primeval times.

[hieroglyphs] *pꜣḳ* (H 3), var. [hieroglyphs] *pḳw*, a kind of cake.

[hieroglyphs] *pꜣḳt* (H 2), var. [hieroglyphs] *pḳt*, fine linen.

[hieroglyphs] *pꜣd*, var. [hieroglyphs] *pd* (D 56), knee.

[hieroglyphs] *pis* bring in corn (on back of donkeys).

[hieroglyphs] var. [hieroglyphs] *pꜥt* (H 8) mankind, patricians; see too *r-pꜥt* below.

[hieroglyphs] *pw* this (obsolescent), sing. m., § 110; construction of, § 111; meaning of, § 112; use as pron. 3rd pers., § 128; do. anticipating nom. subj., §§ 130. 189, 2; position of, §§ 129. 130; use in sents. with adj. pred., §§ 140. 141; in questions after *in iw*, § 492, 4; do. after *in* alone, § 493, 1; cl. with *pw* after *gmi* 'find', § 186, 3; in *śḏm·f pw*, § 189; meaning *c'est que*, §§ 190. 325; imperf. *śḏm·f* as pred. of, § 442, 3; perf. *śḏm·f* do., § 452, 4; in *r-pw* 'or', § 91, 2; in *nt-pw*, § 190, 2; in negation *nfr pw*, § 351, 2; [hieroglyphs] *pwy* this, that, sing. m., later substitute for *pw*, § 110; meaning of, § 112; [hieroglyphs] interrog., who?, what?, § 498; see too under *ptr*; whichever, Add. p. xxviii.

[hieroglyphs] *Pwnt* Pwēne(t), popularly known as Punt, the coast-line S. of the Red Sea.

[hieroglyphs] *pf*, var. [hieroglyphs] *pfy*, that (yonder), sing. m., § 110; construction of, § 111; meaning of, § 112; [hieroglyphs] *pfꜣ* (N 31), later form of *pf*, § 110.

[hieroglyphs], see under *psi* below.

[hieroglyphs] *pn*, this, sing. m., § 110; construction of, § 111; meaning of, § 112.

[hieroglyphs] *p-n* he of, § 111, Obs.; see too under *pꜣ* above.

[hieroglyphs] *pnꜥ* (P 1) upset, overturn.

[hieroglyphs] *pnw* mouse.

[hieroglyphs] *pnḳ* bale out.

[hieroglyph] *pr* (O 1) house, f. collective [hieroglyphs] *pryt*; [hieroglyphs] *Pr-ꜥꜣ* Great House, Pharaoh, p. 75; [hieroglyphs] *Pr-ꜥnḫ* House of Life, scriptorium where books were written; [hieroglyphs] *Pr-wr* (O 19), name of the oldest national shrine of Upper Egypt at Hieraconpolis; [hieroglyphs] *Pr-nw* (O 20), [hieroglyphs] *Pr-nsr* (O 20), alternative names of the oldest national shrine of Lower Egypt at Buto; [hieroglyphs] *pr-nsw* palace; [hieroglyphs] var. [hieroglyphs] *pr-ḥḏ* (O 2) treasury, lit. white house; [hieroglyphs] *pr-ḏt* estate; *imy-r pr* overseer of a house, steward; *nbt pr* mistress of a house, married lady; see too *r-pr* under [hieroglyph] *r* below.

[hieroglyphs] *pri* go forth, go up; *pri r ḫꜣ*, *r ḫnt*, go forth abroad, see under *ḫꜣ*, *ḫnt*; as aux. vb., § 483, 1; *pry* det. [hieroglyphs] champion; det. [hieroglyphs] champion bull; *pr-ꜥ* ([hieroglyph]), energetic, valorous; prowess; *prw* det. [hieroglyph] excess; det. [hieroglyph] a coming forth, outcome; *prw n r* ([hieroglyph]) utterance; [hieroglyphs] *prt-ḫrw* (O 3) invocation-offerings, lit. a going or sending forth of the voice, later sometimes interpreted as *prt-r-ḫrw*, p. 172; [hieroglyphs] *prt* winter season, p. 203; [hieroglyphs], abbrev. [hieroglyphs] *prt* (U 13) seed.

[hieroglyphs] *pri* (M 6. 5) battlefield.

[hieroglyphs] *pḥwy* (F 22) hind-quarters, end; *pḥwy-r* down to, § 179; *pḥt-r* northwards to, § 179; [hieroglyphs] *pḥwyt* stern-rope; [hieroglyphs] varr. [hieroglyphs], [hieroglyph] *pḥww* (N 41) distant marshlands.

var. *pḥ* (F 22) reach, attack.

abbrev. *pḥty* (F 9) strength.

pḥrr run.

pḫ3 (V 11) split, break open.

var. *pḫr* (F 46) turn, go round; serve, *n* (someone); *pḫrt* remedy, medicament; det. frontier guards; *spḫr* var. (F 50) cause to circulate, copy, write down; *Pḫr-wr*, Pekher-wēr, Eg. name of the Euphrates.

psi (see § 281) cook, boil.

psḥ bite (vb. and n.).

psḫ be in disorder, distraught.

psš (Z 9) divide; *psšw* divider (of property); *psšt* division, share.

psg (D 26) spit, spit upon.

varr. det. *psd* (F 37. 38. 39. 41), O.K. *pśḏ*, back (n.).

psd, O.K. *pśḏ*, shine.

psḏt (N 9) company of nine gods, ennead, p. 291, n. 8.

psḏntyw (N 9; W 3), varr. *psḏn*, *psdn*, New-moon festival.

, see under *p3ḳt* above.

pg3 spread out, unfold; det. opening (n.).

ptpt tread down, crush.

ptr, var. *pty*, who?, what?, from interrog. *pw*+part. *tr*, §§ 256. 497.

ptr, rare det. (D 7), behold, see.

Ptḥ Ptaḥ, god of Memphis, Gk. Φθᾶ.

ptḫ overthrow.

, see under *p3d* above.

abbrev. *pd* (T 9), earlier *pḏ*, stretch, (be) wide; var. *pḏt* (T 9. 10) bow, foreign people, troop; *pḏt 9* the Nine Bows, traditional name given to the peoples neighbouring Egypt; *pḏty* det. bowman, foreigner, see too *r-pḏt* under *r* below.

pd (vb. showing confusion with *pd* 'knee' and *pd* 'stretch') 1. kneel, 2. run.

varr. , *pds* (D 56) box.

pdswt dunes (of the Delta coast).

pḏ, *pḏt*, see under *pd* above.

f (I 9)

as det. in *it* father, p. 43, n. 1; not to be read in *psi*, see under this above.

·f suffix-pron. 3rd sing. m., he, him, his, it, its, § 34; *·fy* do. after duals, § 75, 2; after words dual in form but sing. in meaning, § 76, 1; after sing. words with dual implication, § 76, 2; in the *śḏmty·fy* form, § 364; not an obsolete dep. pron., § 411, 1.

var. *ft* (I 9, O.K.) viper.

abbrev. *f3i* (A 9) carry, lift, weigh; *f3i ṯ3w* () sail (vb.), lit. carry the wind.

f3w magnificence, splendour.

f3k, var. *fk*, (be) bald, bare.

fn (be) weak, infirm; *sfn* make weak, afflict.

Fnḫw, a term for Syrians, cf. Gk. Φοινίκες.

abbrev. *fnd* (D 19), O.K. *fnḏ*, nose.

abbrev. *fḫ* (V 12) loose, depart; *sfḫ* unloose, take off (garments).

fk3 (X 4), a kind of cake.

fk3 (X 4) reward (vb. and n.).

fk, see under *f3k* above.

ftft leap, see too *nftft* below.

fdi pluck (vb.).

fdt sweat (n.).

fdḳ tear asunder; piece, fraction.

m (G 17)

m- as formative prefixed to some nouns, § 290.

m prep., with suffixes *im·*, in, as, by, with, from; as conj., when, as, though, **§ 162**; *m-ꜥb*, *m-ḫnw*, etc., see under *ꜥb*, *ḫnw*, etc.; *m-ꜥ*, see before *(m)ꜥ(n)dt* below; *m-ḫt*, see under *ḫt*; *m dd* saying, § 224; before infin. of vbs. of motion, in, §§ 304, 2; 331; see too Predication, *m* of, in the Grammatical Index.

varr. , *m* non-encl. part., behold, § 234; foll. by dep. pron., *ib.*; mostly combined with suffix-pron. 2nd pers. (*mk*, *mṯ*, *mṯn*), *ib.*

var. *m* interrog. pron., who?, what?, §§ 227, 3; 496; *in m* as subj., §§ 227, 3; 496; *m m* wherewith?, *mi m* how?, *r m* to what purpose?, *ḥr m* why?, § 496.

m imper. of the negative vb. *imi*, see there.

m imper., take, *n·k* to thyself, also written with *mn* (T 1), § 336.

encl. part., see *m(y)* below.

, *mꜣ* (U 1), sickle-shaped end of a sacred boat (*wiꜣ*).

mꜣꜣ (U 2; D 4) see, see to; foll. by *śdm·f* (imperf. § 442, 1), § 184, 2; by infin., § 303; by obj. + *śdm·f*, § 213; by obj. + *ḥr* + infin., § 304, 1; by obj. + old perf., § 315; rarely in imperf. *śdm·f* after *rdi*, § 442, 1; *wr-mꜣw*, see under *wrr* above; *mꜣw* sight; *r-mꜣw (n)* in the sight of, § 178.

var. det. *mꜣi* (D 4; E 22) lion.

varr. , *mꜣꜥ* (Aa 11; U 4. 5) (be) true, real, just; *n (m) wn mꜣꜥ* in reality, § 205, 3; *bw mꜣꜥ* truth, right; *mꜣꜥ-ḫrw* (§ 55) justified, deceased; *smꜣꜥ-ḫrw* justify, make triumphant, *r* over (enemies); var. *mꜣꜥt* (H 6) truth, right, justice; det. (C 10) Māꜥe(t), the goddess of Truth and Right; *mꜣꜥty* righteous.

mꜣꜥ be offered (of offerings), *n* to; *mꜣꜥw* offerings, tribute; *smꜣꜥ* offer (vb.).

mꜣꜥ send, dispatch; *m mꜣꜥw* (det.) *nfr* with good dispatch, with a good wind.

mꜣꜥ (H 2) temple (of head); *tp-mꜣꜥ* accompanying, escorting, § 178.

mꜣꜥ edge, brink.

mꜣwy, var. *mꜣ(w)*, be new, fresh; *mꜣ* fresh, new; *m mꜣwt* anew, freshly; *smꜣwy* renew.

mꜣwt rays.

mꜣr, var. *mꜣi(r)*, wretched; *mꜣi(r)w* misery; *smꜣr* afflict, harm.

mꜣḥ wreath (of flowers, etc.).

mꜣ-ḥd (E 28) oryx.

mꜣḫ, var. *mꜣḫ*, burn, be consumed.

mꜣst thighs, lap; *tp-ḥr-mꜣst* head-on-lap, i.e. in mourning, § 194.

mꜣgsw, see *bꜣgsw* above.

mꜣṯ (W 7, O.K.), later , *mꜣt* (Aa 2), red granite (from Elephantine).

mꜣṯ proclaim.

var. *mi* imper., come, § 336.

mi (W 19, Pyr. *mr*) prep., like, according to, as well as; conj., as when, according as, **§ 170**; *mi ḳd·f* entire, § 100, 2; *mi m* how?, § 496; *mit(y)* copy (n.); *mity*, var. *mitw* (§ 79, Obs.), like (adj.), equal; *mitt* likeness, the like; *m mitt* likewise, § 205, 3; *my*, var. *mi*, likewise, accordingly, § 205, 1; *smi* report (vb.), § 275; report (n.), acknowledgement (of letter).

miw (E 13) cat, f. *mit*.

very rarely *min* (W 19), to-day, § 205, 1; used enclitically, § 208; *m min* to-day, § 205, 3.

m(i)ni, see under *mni*.

minb (N 34; T 7) axe.

mist (N 36) liver.

var. *m(y)* encl. part. after imper. or *sḏm·f* in wishes, pray, § 250; rarely non-encl., *ib*.

m-ꜥ prep., together with, in the hand of, from, owing to, § 178; *mꜥ-ntt* seeing that, § 223.

(m)ꜥ(n)dt (V 26), O.K. *mꜥnḏt*, the morning bark (ship) of the sun, p. 291, n. 5.

var. det. *mꜥr* (M 1; V 29) (be) fortunate, successful.

mꜥḥꜥt, var. *miḥꜥt* (N 36), tomb.

mw (N 35) water; *ḥr mw n* loyal to, lit. on the water of; *mwy*, also f. *mwyt*, urine, seed, saliva.

mww (N 35) *muu*-dancers, in funerary ceremonies.

mwt (G 14) mother; *Mwt*, var. (G 15), Mut, the chief goddess at Karnak.

mwnf helper, champion.

var. det. *m(w)t* (A 14; Z 6) die, § 279; death; *m(w)t*, *m(w)tt* dead man, woman.

mfkꜣt, var. *mfkt*, turquoise.

var. *m-m* prep., among, § 178.

(G 18) var. *mm*, prob. mere varr. of adv. *im*, see there.

var. *mmy* giraffe.

mnw (T 1), a kind of mace; in writing of *m n·k* take to thyself, see *m* imper., take, above.

mn (Y 5) be firm, remain, be established; *r-mn-m* as far as, § 180; *r-mn* together with, § 180, Obs.; *smn* det. (U 32) establish, make firm; halt, stand down (from office); *mn* det. such a one, f. *mnt* det. ; *mnt* det. such an amount (see pp. 201–2); *mn*, *mnt* example, a similar case; *mnw* monument(s); *Mn-nfr* Memphis, p. 183, n. 1.

mn be ill, obj. of (something), § 84 A, p. 423.

mnt: *m mnt* daily.

mnt (G 36) swallow (n.).

mnt (D 56) thigh.

var. *mni* (appar. originally *m(i)ni*, § 285; P 11; T 14) moor, land; attach, join (someone), *m* to (something, a wife); det. , (A 14. 54) die; death; *mnit* mooring post.

mni, a measure for oil or incense, § 266, 1.

mnit (S 18) necklace with counterpoise, *menat*.

varr. , *mniw* (appar. originally *m(i)niw*; A 47. 33) herdsman.

Mnw (R 22; C 8) Min, the god of Panopolis (Akhmîm) and Coptus (Ḳifṭ), Gk. Μῖν.

mnwt pigeon.

mnw (M 1) trees.

mnꜥ (D 27; B 5) nurse, suckle; *mnꜥt* nurse, foster-mother; *mnꜥy* tutor.

mnfyt (A 12) soldiers.

mnmn move about, be disturbed; *mnmnt* det. , (E 8) herds, cattle; *smnmn* remove.

mnnw, var. *mnw*, fortress.

mnhd (Y 3), O.K. *mnhḏ*, writing outfit.

mnḥ wax.

mnḥ papyrus plant.

mnḫ (U 22) chisel; fashion, carve (O.K.).

abbrev. *mnḫ* (U 22) (be) efficient, beneficent, excellent; *r mnḫ* thoroughly, § 205, 5; *smnḫ* fashion excellently, put in order, honour, advance (someone).

mnḫ string (beads), fasten (amulet on neck).

abbrev. *mnḫt* (S 27) clothing.

mnš (L.E.) cartouche, p. 74.

mn-ḳb bed-chamber.

Mnṯw Mont, the falcon-headed god of Hermonthis (Armant), Thebes, etc.

Mnṯ(y)w: *nw Stt* Beduins of Asia.

mnd (D 27. 27*), var. *bndt*, O.K. *mnḏ*, breast.

mndm basket, crate.

is read *ỉmy-r*, not *mr*, see under *ỉmy* above.

mr (U 23) (be) ill, painful; *mrt* disease; *mrw* painfully, § 205, 4.

mr (U 23; O 24) pyramid, tomb.

mr bind; *mrw* band.

mr (N 36) canal, channel.

mr (N 36) friend(s), partisans; *ḥꜣw-mr* the multitude, the masses.

var. *mrt* (N 36, f.) weavers.

mrt serfs, slaves.

varr. , *mrỉ* (U 7. 6; N 36) love, wish (vb.); foll. by *śḏm·f* (*2ae gem.* imperf., § 442, 1; other vbs. perf., § 452, 1), § 184; by infin., § 303; *Mrr·f ỉrrf* Whenever-he-likes-he-does, a name of the supreme god, § 442, 8; *mrwt* love, wish (n.); *n-mrwt*, *m-mrwt* in order that, § 181; *mrwyty* the beloved.

mrỉ in *Tꜣ-mrỉ* (M 5. 6) Tameri, a name of Egypt.

mryt river-bank, coast, harbour.

mryn Syrian magnate, Babyl. *mariannu*.

mrw desert

mrw (M 41), a red wood from Syria.

var. *Mr-wr* (O 5) Mnevis, the sacred bull of Heliopolis.

var. *mrrt* (O 5. 38) street.

mrh(w) decay (n.).

abbrev. *mrḥt* (W 1) unguent, oil; cf. *wrḥ* above.

mhy be forgetful, negligent, *ḥr* about.

mhwt family, household.

mhr (W 19) milk-jug.

mḥ (V 22) fill, be full, *m* of; as formative in ordinal numbers, § 263, 3; *mḥ ỉb* (be) trusty, trusted; *mḥ* det. seize, *m* (someone or something); *mḥw* a filling.

varr. , , *mḥ* cubit, linear measure of 523 mm., § 266, 2; as measure of area, 27·3 sq. metres, § 266, 3.

later var. *mḥ(y)* be anxious, grieve, *ḥr* about; grief, care (n.).

var. *mḥ* (?), *mꜥḥ* (?) (M 38) flax.

mḥ(ỉ ?) drown.

mḥt dish.

var. *mḥt* north; *mḥt-r* northward to, § 179; *mḥyt* det. north wind; *mḥty* northern, § 79.

mḥw (M 15. 16) papyrus clump, in varr. , *Tꜣ-mḥw* the Delta, Lower Egypt; *mḥ-s* det. , (S 3. 4) crown of Lower Egypt; *mḥ(ỉ?)* det. or Lower Egyptian.

mḥw fish-spearer; *mḥyt* fishes.

mḥnyt the Coiling one, i.e. the uraeus on head of sun-god and king.

mḫ3 balance, equal (vb.); abbrev. *mḫ3t* (U 38) balance (n.); cf. *ḫ3ỉ* below.

m-ḫt, see under *ḫt* below.

mḫnt; *mḫnty*, see under *ḫnỉ* below.

mḫr storehouse.

mḫrw administration, governance.

var. *ms* bring.

mst (F 31) apron of foxes' skins.

msỉ (F 31; B 3. 4) bear, give birth; form, fashion (statue); *ms n*, f. *mst n* born to (mother), §§ 361. 379, 3; *ms* det. child; \ writing of *-msw* in personal names (Z 5); *smsỉ* deliver (in childbirth).

ms encl. part. expressing surprise or reproof, § 251; *ỉw-ms*, see under *ỉw*, at end.

msyt supper, evening meal.

Msn (V 32) Mesen, a town near Ḳanṭarah in Lower Egypt.

msnw (V 32) harpooner, hippopotamus-hunter.

msnḥ turn backwards.

msḥ (I 3) crocodile.

msḫn, also *msḫnt*, resting-place; see too under *ḫnỉ* below.

msḫtyw adze.

Msḫtyw (F 23) the Foreleg, i.e. the constellation of the Great Bear, replacing earlier conception as Adze.

var. det. *mss* corselet.

msk3 hide (of ox).

mskỉ rumour.

(m)sktt the evening bark (ship) of the sun-god, p. 291, n. 5.

mstỉwty descendant (of a god).

mstpt bier (at funeral).

msdmt, see under *sdm*.

msḏỉ, var. *msdỉ*, hate (vb.).

var. det. , abbrev. *msḏr* (F 21; D 18) ear.

var. *mšꜥ* (A 12) army; det. expedition.

mšrw evening.

mšdt ford.

varr. , *mk* non-encl. part. from *m* (see above), behold, § **234**; used in addressing a male person, *ib.*; foll. by dep. pron. as subj., § 44, 2; in sent. with adv. pred., § 119, 1; in sent. with nom. pred., § 133; in sent. with adj. pred., § 142; in pseudo-verbal construction, § 324; *mk śḏm·n·f*, § 414, 1; *mk* + pass. *śḏm·f*, § 422, 1; *mk śḏm·f*, §§ 234; 450, Obs.; with sense of Fr. *voici*, § 234; curiously substituted for *ḥr*, § 234, Obs.

var. *mkỉ* (D 38) protect; *mkt* det. protection; *mkty* protector.

mkt right place.

mkḥ3 neglect, obj. (someone, something).

mg(3?), a class of young recruits.

mt, earlier *mṯ*, non-encl. part. from *m* (see above), behold, in addressing a female, §§ 119, 1; 234.

, see *m(w)t* above.

mt vein, muscle, vessel of body.

mty (D 52. 50) (be) regular, correct, trustworthy, loyal; *mtt n ỉb* rectitude, lit.

regularity (?) of heart; *m mtt nt ỉb·f* following his natural bent (or sim.); *mty* regulator (?) of a phylē (*sꜣ*) of priests.

mtwt seed, poison.

mtwn, O.K. *mṯwn*, place of combat for bulls.

mtn, earlier *mṯn*, non-encl. part. from *m* (see above), behold, in addressing several persons, §§ 119, 1; 234.

mtpnt (T 8) dagger of the form.

mtn reward (vb.); *mtnwt* det. reward (n.).

var. det. *mtr* (D 50; T 14) bear witness to; *mtrw* witness (person); *mtrt* testimony.

mtrt midday.

mṯ non-encl. part., see under *mt* above.

mṯꜣ flout, insult (vb.).

mṯꜣm, see under *ṯꜣm*.

mṯn, non-encl. part., see under *mtn* above.

mṯn, varr. *mtn* (G 14), road; *mtn* nomad.

Mṯn Mitanni, a kingdom E. of the Euphrates.

mdw (S 43) staff; *mdw n ỉꜣw* staff of old age, epithet applied to a son taking over his aged father's work.

mdw (*mwdw*, § 285) speak, talk; *mdw m* speak against; *mdw* dispute, litigate, *ḥnꜥ* with (someone), *ḥr* about (something); *mdw* word, saying; abbrev. *mdw nṯr* the god's words, p. 1; abbrev. *ḏd mdw* (words) to be recited; or placed at top of columns containing spells, etc., § 306, 1; *wḏ mdw*, *wḏt mdw*, see under *wḏ*; *mdt* speech, matter.

mds keen, alert.

mḏw (V 20) ten, §§ 259. 260; construction of, § 261.

mḏ (V 21) (be) deep; *mḏwt* depth.

var. *mḏt* (V 19. 20. 21) stable, cattle-stall.

mḏt (W 1) ointment.

mḏꜣt (Y 1) papyrus-roll, book.

var. *mḏꜣt* (Y 1) sculptor's chisel.

Mḏꜣyw Medjay, a Nubian people, p. 183, n. 2; police.

var. *mḏḥ* (S 10) fillet.

mḏḥ (S 10), var. *mḏḥ* (T 7), hew; *mḏḥ(w)* carpenter.

abbrev. *mḏd* (Aa 23, p. 520) hit (a mark), adhere to (a path).

n (N 35)

n afformative prefix in some reduplicated verb-stems, § 276.

n prep., var., rare initial form *ỉn*, to, for, belonging to (§ 114, 1), through, in (of time); as conj., because, § **164**; in compound preps., §§ 178. 181; in *n·i-ỉmy*, *n·k-ỉmy*, etc., §§ 113, 3; 114, 4; after adjs., indicating possession, §§ 138 141; possibly sometimes to introduce qualifying noun, § 95; in negative *nfr n*, § 351, 1; by, of agent after pass. parts., p. 279, top; § 379, 3; element in *śḏmw·n·f* rel. form, §§ 380. 386, 2; in narrative *śḏm·n·f*, § 411, 2; *.n-ntt* because, § 223.

ny adv., therefor, for (it), § 205, 1; with varr. *n*, *n(w?)* prob. in cases of *n śḏm·n* for *n śḏm·n·f* he does not hear, § 486, Obs. 2.

n(y) genitival adj. § 86; forms, *ib.*; use in indirect genitive, *ib.*; Add. to § 86, p. 423; in genitive between noun and adj. epithet, § 94; mediating adj. epithet, § 94, 1. 2; introducing noun used like Latin accusative of respect, § 95; after demonstratives in *n*-, p. 86, top; as pred., § 114, 2; introducing prep. + noun, § 158, 1; after compound preps. when governing noun, p. 131, bottom; foll. by *śḏm·f*, §§ 191; 442, 5 (imperf.); 452, 5 (perf.); by *śḏm·n·f*, § 192; by infin., § 305; *nîw* (*nw*), pl. m. of *n*(*y*) belonging to, § 86; , see below under *nt-ʿ*.

n suffix- and dep. pron. 1st pl. c., we, us, our; rarely , §§ 34. 43; *·ny* dual of do., early obsolete, § 34.

·ny possibly rare suffix-pron. 3rd dual in *imytw·ny* between them, § 34, Obs. 3.

n not (shortened form of *nn*, see there), varr. discussed, **§ 104**. *N śḏm·f*, with perf. *śḏm·f* form, **§ 455**; negates *śḏm·n·f* in reference to past events, § 105, 1; less commonly negates present (§ 455, 2; adj. vbs. § 144, 1) or future (§ 455, 3) events; with past reference after *mk*, § 455, 1; in unfulfilled wish after *ḥꜣ*, § 455, 1; rarely translatable as 'cannot', § 455, 4; in subordinate cls., § 455, 5; in virt. rel. cls., § 196, 2; after *nty*, § 201; *n sp śḏm·f*, showing a distinctive form of perf. *śḏm·f*, §§ 106; **456**. *N śḏm·n·f*, §§ 105, 3; **418**, common in characterizations, statements of custom, and generalizations: present, § 418, 1; past, § 418, 2; future, § 418, 3; in virt. rel. cls. and after *nty*, *ib.*; with adj. vbs., § 144, 3; negating statements with old perfect., §§ 311, Obs.; 418. *N* + pass. *śḏm·f*, **§ 424**; with past and present reference, § 424, 1. *N śḏmm·f*, § 426. *N śḏmt·f*, **§§ 402–5**; meaning, § 402; forms, active, § 403; forms, pass., § 404; origin, § 405. *N* before *iw* 'is', 'are', very rare, § 120; *n wnn·f* referring to future, § 120; *n* before indep. pron., § 134; rarely negating infin., § 307, 1, end. *n is* in sent. with adv. pred., § 120; in sent. with nom. pred., § 134; negating adv., § 209; before *śḏm·n·f* with meaning 'if not', 'unless', § 216, end; with infin., 'except (?)', § 307, 1; negating a word or phrase, §§ 247, 2, cf. 505, 5, end. *n wnt* there is not, §§ 108, 2; 115; without, § 109; in sent. with adv. pred., § 120; with *śḏm·f* as subj., § 188, 2; with infin. as subj., § 307, 1; with part. or rel. form as subj., § 394; *n wnt wn* there does not exist, *ib.*

n, writing of prep. *n*, see above.

Nt (R 24) Neith, the goddess of Sais, Gk. Νηΐθ.

nt (S 3. 4), the red crown of Lower Egypt.

nt water, see under *nwy* below.

nꜣ this, the, properly with neuter sense, but used as plur. c., § 110; construction of, § 111; meanings of, § 112; concord of, § 511, 3; *nꜣy·i* poss. adj. plur. c., foll. by *n*, my; so too *nꜣy·k* thy, etc., § 113, 1.

nꜣw (E 30), var. *nrꜣw*, ibex.

ni (D 41) reject.

var. *nîw* (D 41) bowl.

var. *nîw* (D 41; G 34) ostrich.

nîwt (O 49) town, village; *Nîwt rst* the Southern City, i.e. Thebes; *imy-r nîwt* overseer of the (pyramid-)city, traditional title of the vizier; *nîwty* (§ 79, end) belonging to (one's own) town, local; townsmen.

ni͗w (*nw*), pl. m. of genitival adj., see under *n*(*y*) above.

perhaps with two distinct readings 1. *ni͗w* or *nww*, 2. *nnw* or *nwnw* (W 24), primeval waters, Copt. *noun*.

ni͗s (A 26) call, obj., *r*, *n* (a person); in funerary cult, invoke, p. 170.

nyny do homage.

nꜥi͗ travel by boat.

nꜥꜥ (Y 3) (be) smooth; *snꜥꜥ* polish, grind fine.

nwti͗ (U 19. 20, Pyr.) the two adzes.

nw (U 19) this, these, properly with neuter sense, but used as plur. c., § 110; construction of, § 111; concord of, § 511, 3.

nw time.

nw (be) weak, limp.

nwi͗ return (also reflex.), *r* to (a place); var. det. collect, tend.

, see under *ni͗w* above.

Nwt Nut, the sky-goddess.

nwy water, flood; also f. *nwyt*, *nwt*, *nt*.

nww hunters.

nwꜣ, later *nw*, look, see.

nwḥ (V 1) rope; *ḫt* ( ) *n nwḥ* rod of cord, a measure of 100 cubits, 52·3 metres, § 266, 2; *nwḥ* bind (vb.).

, see under *i͗nk*.

nwd move crookedly, aslant; *nwdw* crookedness.

nwd ointment, perfume.

nbt (V 30) basket or like; plur., name of distant indeterminate foreign regions; var. *Ḥꜣw-nbwt*, the Hau-Nebwet, inhabitants of those regions, in Graeco-Roman times interpreted to mean the Greeks.

var. *nb* lord, master; use in letters, p. 239, n. 8; owner of (property, attribute), § 115 A, p. 423; *nb* the Lord, i.e. the king, p. 75; *nb tꜣwy* lord of the two lands, do., *ib.*; *nb-r-ḏr* lord (*nbt-* lady) of the universe, § 100, 1; *nbwy* the Two Lords, i.e. Horus and Seth; *nb ꜥnḫ* det. (A 54) sarcophagus; *nbt* mistress, lady; *nbt pr*, see under *pr*; *nbty* (G 16) Two Ladies, title of the king, p. 73; var. *Nbt-ḥwt*, *Nbt-ḥyt* (O 9) the goddess Nephthys, Gk. Νέφθυς.

nb every, all, any, f. *nbt*, pl. m. *nbw* (uncommon), p. 47, n. °; common for both genders and numbers, § 48, 1; use after *nty*, § 199; after parts., § 375, Obs.; after rel. forms, § 381; *s nb* everyone, each one, § 103; *bw nb* everyone, *ib.*; *ḥr nb* everyone, *ib.*; *wꜥ nb* everyone, each, *ib.*; *ḫt nbt* everything, anything, *ib.*

nbyt (S 12), the collar depicted as .

nbw (S 12) gold; det. Gold, name given to the goddess Hathor; *nbi͗* (S 13) gild, fashion; *nby* goldsmith.

Nbt Ombos, near Ṭûkh in Upper Egypt; *Nbt*(*y*) the Ombite, epithet of Seth.

Nbyt Kôm Ombo, Ombi, a town some distance N. of Elephantine.

nbꜣ, var. *nbi͗*, pole; *nbi͗w*, a linear measure larger than 1 cubit, § 266, 2.

nbs Christ's thorn, *nebḳ*-tree.

nbdw-ḳd perverse (O.K. *nbḏ*) of character, epithet given to foreign enemies.

Npri͗, the corn-god Nepri.

nprt edge, brim (of sheet of water).

nf that, § 110; properly with neuter sense, but used as plur., §§ 111–12; construction of, § 111; var. *nf3*, later form of *nf*, § 310.

nf wrong (n.).

nfw (P 5) skipper, rêis; *snf* relieve, release.

nfꜥ remove, drive away.

nfr (F 35) (be) good, beautiful, happy; *nfr n·i* it went well with me, i.e. I died, § 307, bottom; *nfr* adv., happily, well, § 205, 4; *Wnn-nfr(w)*, see under *wnn*; *nfrt* det. beautiful woman; *nfrw* det. recruits; *nfr(w)t* det. cows; *nfrw*, also , *nfr*, beauty, goodness; *bw nfr* goodness; *nfr-ḥ3t* diadem, or like; *iry nfr-ḥ3t* keeper of the diadem; *snfr* embellish. Probably connected are the following words, see § 351:

nfrw shortage; *nfrw* innermost room; *nfr(w)* zero; *nfryt* end; *nfryt r* down to, § 179; *nfryt* rudder-rope; *nfr pw* as negation, § 351, 2; *nfr n* as negation, § 351, 1.

nft, later var. *ntf*, loose, slacken.

nftft leap, cf. *ftft* above.

rare var. *n-m*, for *in m* who?, what?, as subj., §§ 227, 3; 496.

nm (T 34) knife (?); var. *nmt* (T 29) place of slaughter.

nmi (O 5) traverse; *Nmiw-šꜥ* Sand-farers, i.e. Beduins.

nmi (O 5) cry aloud; low (vb., of cattle).

nmꜥ act partially, show partiality, *n* to (someone).

nmḥ poor man, orphan, waif, f. *nmḥyt*; *snmḥ* abase oneself, pray, *n* to.

nms, a royal head-dress.

nmst jug (for water).

nmtt (D 54), plur. var. , walk, steps.

nn non-encl. part., not, § **235**; distinguished from only after Dyn. IX, §§ **104**. 235; negates sents. with adv. pred., §§ 118, 1; 120; with nom. pred. when *pw* is subj., § 134; in questions introduced by *in iw*, with indep. pron. as subj., § 492, 7; as pred. of sents. with infin. as subj., § 307, 1; with part. or rel. form as subj., § 394; negating sent. with pseudo-verbal construction, § 334; *nn sḏm·f* (perf.) with future reference, §§ 105, 2; 144, 2; 457; *nn sḏm·n·f*, obscure, § 418 A; at beginning of sents., § 66, end; foll. by dep. pron. as subj., § 44, 2; *iw* suppressed after, § 107, 2; in questions with sense of *nonne*, § 491, 3; negating single word or phrase, § 505, 5; with meaning 'no', § 258; expressing non-existence, § 108, 3; 'without', § 109; do. with infin., § 307, 1. *nn wn* 'there is (are) not', § 108, 1; 'without', § 109; in sent. with adv. pred., § 120; with *sḏm·f* form as subj., § 188, 2; with part. or rel. form as subj., § 394.

var. *nn* (M 22) this, these, properly with neuter sense, but used as plur., § 110; construction of, § 111; meaning of, § 112; concord of, § 511, 3.

Nni-nsw (A 17; W 24) Ihnâsyah el-Medînah, Heracleopolis, a town in Upper Egypt.

nni be tired, slothful; *nniw* weariness.

nnw, see under *niw* above.

nnm err, go wrong.

var. *nnšm* (D 35) spleen.

nnk belong(s) to me, § 114, 3; after infin., on my part, § 300, end.

, Pyr. , *nrt* (G 14) vulture.

nri be in terror, *n* at; var. *nrw* (G 14; H 4) terror.

nht (M 1) sycomore-fig, tree.

nht shelter (n.).

nhy a little, a few, § 99; *nhw* loss.

nhp rise early; *nhpw* early morning; *snhp* det. spur on.

nhm jubilate.

Nhrn Nahrin, i.e. Mitanni, a kingdom E. of the Euphrates.

nhs wake up (vb.).

nḥ (G 21) guinea-fowl.

var. *nḥi* (G 21) pray for (something); *nḥ*, *nḥt* prayer.

nḥȝ (be) hard, rough, dangerous.

nḥb yoke together, unite; equip, *m* with; *Nḥb-kȝw* det. (D 30) Uniter-of-attributes, name of a mythical serpent; det. Neḥeb-kaw, feast of the month later called Khoiak, see p. 205.

nḥbt neck.

nḥbt (M 10) lotus bud.

nḥp potter's wheel.

nḥm take away, rescue, *m-ʿ* from (someone); *Nḥmt-ʿwȝy* She-who-rescues-the-robbed, consort of the god Thoth at Hermopolis.

nḥmn non-encl. part., surely, assuredly, §§ 119, 6; 236.

var. *nḥḥ* eternity.

var. *Nḥsy* (T 14) Nubian.

nḥdt tooth, molar; see too *ndḥt* below.

nḫ defend, protect; *nḫw* protector.

nḫ·wy how grievous (is)!; *nḫwt* plaint, mourning.

nḫb open up (mine, fields); det. newly opened up field; *nḫbt* det. protocol, titulary, p. 71.

Nḫb El-Kâb, Eileithyias polis, a town in Upper Egypt; *Nḫbt* (M 22; W 24; G 16) the vulture-goddess Nekhbet, p. 73.

var. *Nḫn* (O 47. 48) Kôm el-Aḥmar, Hieraconpolis, a town in Upper Egypt; *r-Nḫn* mouth of (or *iry* attached to) Nekhen; *mi͗nw Nḫn* herdsman (i.e. ruler) of Nekhen, two distinct titles; see too under *Ḥr* below.

nḫn (be) young; child; *nḫnw*, *nḫnt* childhood.

abbrev. *nḫḫw* (S 45), earlier *nḫȝḫȝ*, flagellum (conventional rendering).

abbrev. *nḫt* (D 40) (be) strong, mighty, victorious; strength, victory; *nḫtw* victory, hostages; *nḫtw* det. strongholds; *snḫt* make strong, strengthen.

nẖnm (W 9), one of the seven ritual oils and jug for same.

ns (F 20) tongue.

varr. *nst* (W 11. 12) seat (of office); *nb nswt tȝwy* lord of the Thrones of the Two Lands, epithet of Amen-Rēʿ.

nsw, for *ny sw* he belongs to, § 114, 2.

varr. *nsw* (p. 50, n. 1) king of Upper Egypt, king; plur. var. *nsyw* (§ 72); *nswy* (?), *nsy* (?) be king, § 292; *nsyt* (?) kingship; *n-sw-bi͗t* (§ 55) king of Upper and Lower Egypt, p. 73; *pr-nsw*, see under *pr*; *sȝ-nsw* king's son; sim. with *sȝt*, *mwt*, *sn*, *snt*, *ḥmt* daughter, mother, brother, sister, wife.

nswt flame, fire, cf. *nsrt* below.

nsb lick.

nsr in *Pr-nsr*, see under *pr*; *nsrt* the uraeus-goddess.

nsr burn, blaze (vb.); *nsrt* flame, cf. *nswt* above.

nš supplant, drive away, *ḥr* from.

nšp breathe.

Nšmt, the sacred bark of Osiris at Abydus.

abbrev. *nšmt* (K 6) fish-scale.

nšny rage (vb. and n.).

nḳꜥwt (D 51) notched sycomore figs.

nḳm be in pain, sorrow.

nḳdd, see under *ḳdd* below.

nk copulate.

nkꜣ(y) reflect, *m* upon; cf. *kꜣi* below.

nkn (D 57) damage (n.).

nkt (m.) a little, a trifle.

ng a species of bull.

ngi break open; *ngt* breach.

ngsgs overflow, § 276.

nt-ꜥ custom, observances.

nt-pw it is the fact that, §§ 190, 2; 494, 3.

nty who, which, **§§ 199–201**; antecedent mainly defined, § 199; origin, forms, and writing, *ib.*; foll. by *nb*, *ib.*; foll. by adv. pred., § 200, 1; do. with inserted subj., § 200, 2; in pred. of cl. with *pw* as subj., § 200 A (p. 424); foll. by dep. pron.; § 200, 2; by suffixes, *ib.*; *iw* suppressed after, § 107, 2; foll. by *sḏm·f* (imperf. § 443), § 201; by *sḏm·n·f*, *ib.*; do. negated by *n*, p. 334, top; with construction *n sḏmt·f*, § 402; foll. by pseudo-verbal construction, § 328; *nty wn*, § 201, Obs.; *ntyw im* those who are there, i.e. the dead, p. 123, n. 6; *ntt iwtt* what is and is not, i.e. everything, § 203, 4.

ntb be parched.

ntf indep. pron. 3rd sing. m., he, § 64; belong(s) to him, § 114, 3.

ntf = *nty·f* which he . . . ., § 200, 2.

ntf irrigate, water (vb.).

, see above under *nft*.

nṯry, see under *nṯr* below.

var. *nts* indep. pron. 3rd sing. f., she, § 64.

varr. , , *ntsn*, indep. pron. 3rd pl. c., they, § 64.

ntš besprinkle.

ntk indep. pron. 2nd sing. m., thou, § 64; belong(s) to thee, § 114, 3.

ntk = *nty·k* which thou . . . ., § 200, 2.

ntt conj., that, **§ 237**; foll. by dep. pron. as subj., § 44, 2; introducing noun cls., § 187; after preps., § 223; *r-ntt*, *ḥr-ntt*, etc., see under *r*, *ḥr*, etc.; foll. by subj. + old perf., § 329; foll. by parts. and rel. forms, § 400; in interrog. *in ntt*, § 494, 1. 2.

ntṯ, later *ntt*, indep. pron. 2nd sing. f., thou, § 64.

ntṯn, later *nttn*, indep. pron. 2nd pl. c., you, § 64.

varr. , *nṯr* (R 8) god; *nṯr·f*, O.K. writing with suffix-pron., p. 432, n. 3; *nṯr nfr* the good god, title of the king, p. 75; *it-nṯr*, see under *it*; *ḥwt-nṯr*, see under *ḥwt*; *Tꜣ-nṯr*, see under *tꜣ*; *nṯrt*, var. *nṯrt*, goddess; *nṯry*, O.K. *nṯr(i)*, (be) divine; *snṯr* make divine; *snṯr*, var. *snṯr* (R 7), incense.

ndb cover, overlay, *m* with (metal).

ndbwt area, full extent.

nḏ (Aa 27; W 24) grind; miller.

nḏ ask, inquire, *m-ꜥ* from (someone); *nḏ r* () take counsel, *ḥr* for; *nḏwt-r* counsel (n.); *nḏ ḥr* greet, *n(i)* someone, see too *inḏ ḥr* above; *nḏt-ḥr* homage, gifts; *nḏ ḫrt* inquire the health of; *nḏ* (det.) *i3t* confer rank, *ḥr* on (someone); *nḏnḏ* det. converse, take counsel.

nḏ save, *m-ʿ* from (someone); *nḏty* protector.

nḏ thread (n.).

var. *nḏt* subjects, serfs; cf. *ḏt* below.

nḏyt baseness.

nḏ3 be parched, stifled.

nḏm (M 29) (be) sweet, agreeable; *nḏm-ib* joy, happiness; *nḏm*, a species of tree; *snḏm* sweeten, make pleasant; det. sit, § 275.

nḏnḏ, see under *nḏ* above.

nḏri catch hold of, hold firm; *nḏrt* imprisonment.

nḏḥt, O.K. *nḥḏt*, tusk; see too *nḥḏt* above.

abbrev. *nḏs* (G 37) (be) small, poor, feeble; dim (of eyes); det. poor man, commoner; *nḏsw* poverty.

r (D 21)

r prep., with suffixes rarely *ir·*, to, at, concerning, more than, from; as conj., so that, until, according as, § **163**. Before noun or infin. conveys futurity or purpose, §§ 84. 122. 163, 4. 10; 304, 3; 332. 333; *r m* to what purpose?, § 496; in compound preps., §§ 178–81; to form advs., § 205, 5; *r 3w·f*, *r ḏr·f* entire, § 100, 1. 3; *r-ntt* inasmuch as, § 223; to the effect that, §§ 187, Obs.; 225; *r ḏd* that, saying, § 224. See too *ir*, *irf*, *rf*.

r part, in fractions, § 265; *ro*, smallest measure of capacity = $\frac{1}{320}$ *ḥḳat*, § 266, 1.

r, a species of goose.

r (originally *r3*, p. 429, bottom) mouth, utterance, spell, language, door; *st-r* occasion for speech, authority; *tp-r* utterance; *R-3w* Ṭurah, location of the great limestone quarries, Gk. Τροία; *r-ʿ* place, state; as prep., var. *r-r-ʿ*, beside, near, § 178; *r-ʿ-ḫt* warfare, see under *ḫʿw* below; *r-ʿwy* hands, activity of hands; *r-w3t* path, place of passage; var. *r-pw* or, § 91, 2; *r-pr* temple, chapel, shrine; *r-pḏt* foreign bowmen; *R-st3w* (V 3) necropolis, particularly that under the protection of the god Sokar of Memphis; *r-ḏ3w* fight, battle.

r·i, as encl. part. with 1st sing., § 252, 1.

var. det. abbrev. *rʿ* (N 5. 6) sun; var. *rʿ nb* every day; varr. det. , (C 1. 2) *Rʿ* Rēʿ, the sun-god; *s3 Rʿ* son of Rēʿ, as epithet of king, p. 74; *Rʿ-Ḥr-3ḫty* (G 9) Rēʿ-Ḥarakhti.

rwt (N 1) gateway, outside; *rwty* double doors, outside; later var. *rwyt* (E 23) gateway, place of judgement.

rwi cease, make to cease; depart, *r* from (place, something); var. det. (A 33) wander.

var. *rwd* (O 40) stairway.

rwd (T 12), O.K. *rwḏ*, bow-string.

rwd, O.K. *rwḏ*, (be) hard, vigorous, flourishing; *srwd* (*srwḏ*) make to flourish (varr. with *rd* by confusion with vb. for 'grow'); abbrev. *rwdt* hard stone, sandstone.

rwḏ control, administer; controller, executor.

rpyt statue (of female).

var. *r-pꜥt* (*ỉry-pꜥt*) prince, hereditary prince; *rt-pꜥt* (*ỉrt-pꜥt*) princess.

rf, var. *ỉrf*, encl. part. used for emphasis, also with wishes, commands, questions, etc., §§ 66. 152. **252, 3**; after pl. imper., § 337, 3; after perf. *śḏm·f* in wishes, § 450, 4; *ỉst rf* sentence-adv., now, §§ 119, 2; 152.

rm (K 5) fish (n.).

var. det. and abbrev. *rmỉ* (D 4. 9) weep, beweep; *rmyt* weeping (n.).

r-mn, see under *mn* above.

varr. , *rmn* (D 41) arm, shoulder; side (one of the two sides); *rmn* carry (on shoulder); *rmn*, measure of area, ½ aroura (*stȝt*), § 266, 3.

Rmnn Lebanon, Hebr. לְבָנוֹן.

rare var. *rmṯ* (H 4) men, people; also as collective, var. *rmṯt*, § 77, 4.

rn name; as logical subj., § 127, 1; var. det. (V 10) king's name; *rn wr* great name (of king), p. 71; *rn n nbw* name of gold, i.e. golden Horus name, p. 73; *ỉmy-rn·f*, see under *ỉmy* above.

rn young (of cattle, antilopes, etc.).

rnpỉ (M 7. 4) (be) young, vigorous; *rnpwt* det. and abbrev. (M 39) vegetables and fruit; *rnpt* (M 4) year; , see under *ḥȝt* below; , see under *wpỉ* above.

rnn praise, belaud; *rnnwt* jubilation, § 287.

rnn (B 6) nurse, rear (vb.).

Rnnwtt Ernūte(t), the cobra-goddess of the harvest, Gk. -ρμουθι.

rrỉ (E 12) pig; *rrt* sow.

var. det. *rhn* (A 19) lean, *ḥr* upon.

rhdt jar, cauldron.

abbrev. *rḫw* (A 1) men, fellows.

rḫ learn, become acquainted with, know; foll. by *śḏm·f* (imperf. § 442, 1), § 184; by infin., § 303; by *ntt*, § 452, 2; with active sense in old perf., §§ 312, 1; 320; with pres. meaning 'know' in *śḏm·n·f*, § 414, 4; in rel. *śḏmw·n·f*, § 389, 3; in negation *n rḫ·f*, p. 376, top; *rḫ-ḫt* () learned man; *r-rḫt* to the knowledge of, § 178; var. , old title interpreted in M.E. as 'acquaintance of the king'; *srḫ* det. denounce, accuse; *srḫy* accuser.

var. det. *rḫyt* (G 23. 24) people, common folk.

rḫs (T 30) slaughter (vb.).

rḫt (m.) amount, number.

rḫty (G 50) fuller, washerman.

rs encl. part., § 252, 4.

var. *rs* (T 13, also inaccurately with U 40) (be) wakeful; *rs tp* vigilant; *rswt* dream; *srs* awaken.

var. *rst* (T 13) foreign hordes.

r-sy (N 31), var. *rs-sy*, entirely, quite, at all, § 205, 1.

rsy (M 24) southern; south; *rsw* det. south wind.

ršw (D 19) rejoice; *ršwt* det. joy; *ršrš* (§ 274) rejoice.

rḳỉ (D 41) incline (intrans.); bend; *rḳt-ỉb* envy, hostility; *rḳw*, also *rḳ-ỉb*, det. disaffected one, rebel; *rḳw* det. tilting (n., of scale of balance).

r·k, as encl. part. with 2nd sing. m., § 252, 2.

rk time, period.

rkḥ (Q 7) burning, heat.

rare var. *rtḥty* (U 31) baker.

rtḥ restrain.

r·t, var. *ỉr·t*, as encl. part. with 2nd sing. f., § 252, 2.

, see *rmṯ* above.

r·ṯn, var. *ir·ṯn*, as encl. part. with 2nd plur., § 252, 2.

Rṯnw Retjnu, Eg. name for Palestine and Syria.

rd (D 56) foot; *rdwy* the two feet; *tp-rd* rules, order, principles.

rd, see *rwd* above.

var. det. *rd* (M 31. 32) grow; also inaccurate for *rwd*, see above; *srd* cause to grow, plant.

var. *rdi*, with related forms , *di* (X 8; D 37), give, place, § **289, 1**; cause, foll. by *śḏm·f* (perf. § 452, 1; imperf. only *2ae gem.* rarely, § 442, 1), §§ 70. 184; by *wn·f*, § 118, 2; by *śḏm·f* of adj. vbs., § 143; by obj. + old perf., § 315; give, grant, foll. by infin., § 303; special uses and phrases, see under *ib*, *ḥ3w*, *ḥr*, *ḥtp*, *s3*, *gs*, *t3*; *dy* gift, gratuity; *di(w)* (X 8) provisions, rations.

h (O 4)

h (O 4) room (?).

var. *h3* ha, ho, §§ 87. 258.

h3i go down, descend, fall; attack (vb.); *sh3i* send down, cause to fall.

h3w environment, neighbourhood, time; *m-h3w* in the neighbourhood of, at the time of, § 178; det. neighbours, kindred.

h3t (N 1) ceiling, roof.

var. *h3yt* (N 1), var. *hyt*, portal; *smsw hyt* elder of the portal, usher (in the Palace).

h3b send, *n* to (someone), *ḥr* about (something), i.e. send a message (in writing or otherwise).

h3kr, name of a feast.

hi-ms: *m hi-ms* approaching in humble attitude.

hy interj., hail, § 258; *hy-hnw* (A 32) jubilation, jubilate.

hy (D 53), var. *h3y*, husband.

hb enter, penetrate into; *hbhb* traverse, explore.

hb (G 26. 26*) ibis.

hb (U 13) plough (n.).

var. *hbnt* (U 13), a liquid measure, § 266, 1.

hbny ebony.

hp law.

hmt fare, payment to ferryman.

hmhmt roaring, war-cry.

var. det. *hn* (Q. 5. 6) box, chest.

hnw, a liquid measure of about $\frac{1}{2}$ litre, *hin*, § 266, 1.

hnw (A 8) jubilation.

hnw neighbours, associates.

var. *hnn* nod, bow; attend to; rely, *n*, *ḥr*, *m* on.

hri (*hrw* ?) be content, pleased, quiet; *hrt* contentment, quiet; *shri* make content.

var. *hrw* day, day-time; *irt hrw nfr* make holiday; *ẖrt-hrw*, see under *ẖr* below; *hrwyt* det. journal.

hrp sink, be submerged; *hrp ib* suppress thoughts.

hrmw enclosure for poultry, pen.

hh hot breath.

hḳs be deficient; stint.

hd punish, defeat; (victorious) attack.

hdmw footstool.

ḥ (V 28)

[hieroglyphs], see under *ḥwt* below.

[hieroglyphs] *Ḥ3* (N 25) the desert-god Ḥa.

[hieroglyphs] var. [hieroglyphs] *ḥ3* non-encl. part., would that!, § **238**; in sents. with adv. pred., § 119, 7; with nom. pred., § 133; foll. by perf. *śdm·f*, § 450, 5, *b*; by *śdm·n·f*, § 414, 3; by pseudo-verbal construction, § 324, end; as noun 'wish', 'would that', § 238, end.

[hieroglyphs] *ḥ3* (D 1) back of head; prep., behind, around, § 172; [hieroglyphs] *pr r ḥ3* go forth abroad; [hieroglyphs] *Ḥ3w-nbwt*, see under *nbt* above.

[hieroglyphs] *ḥ3t* tomb.

[hieroglyphs] *ḥ3t-ib* grief, sadness.

[hieroglyphs] *ḥ3t* (F 4) front; *m-ḥ3t*, *r-ḥ3t*, *ḫr-ḥ3t* in front of, before, § 178; *ḫr-ḥ3t* formerly, § 205, 2; *imy-ḥ3t* prototype, example; *imyw-ḥ3t* det. [hieroglyphs] ancestors; [hieroglyphs] *ḥ3t-ˁ* beginning, *m* of (a book, instruction); [hieroglyphs] *ḥ3t-sp* regnal year, p. 204; [hieroglyphs] *ḥ3ty* heart, breast; [hieroglyphs] *ḥ3tt* prow-rope (of a ship); [hieroglyphs] *ḥ3ty-ˁ* (§ 55) local prince, mayor, pl. [hieroglyphs] *ḥ3tyw-ˁ*.

[hieroglyphs] *ḥ3y* (S 28) naked; *ḥ3wt* nakedness; *sḥ3y* lay bare, reveal.

[hieroglyphs] var. [hieroglyphs] *ḥ3w* excess; *rdi ḥ3w ḥr* increase (vb.); *m-ḥ3w* in excess of, 178; *m-ḥ3w-ḥr* in addition to, except, § 178; [hieroglyphs] *ḥ3w-mr*, see under *mr*.

[hieroglyphs] *ḥ3ˁyt* strife, civil war.

[hieroglyphs] *ḥ3p* conceal, hide.

[hieroglyphs] *ḥ3m* (G 51) catch fish, fowl, etc.

[hieroglyphs] *ḥ3k* plunder (vb. and n.); *is-ḥ3k*, see under *is*.

[hieroglyphs] *ḥ3tyw* linen.

[hieroglyphs] varr. [hieroglyphs], hieratic [hieroglyphs] *ḥii*, *ḥwi* (A 25. 19), strike, beat, drive in (mooring post); tread (a road); *ḥii t3* ([hieroglyphs]) go a-wandering; *ḥii* det. [hieroglyphs] flow; [hieroglyphs] *ḥyt* rain; *ḥii sḏb*, see under *sḏb*.

[hieroglyphs] *ḥˁ* piece of flesh, member; pl., abbrev. [hieroglyphs] (F 51) flesh, body; -self, with suffixes, § 36.

[hieroglyphs] *ḥˁt* (V 28, Dyn. XIX) wick.

[hieroglyphs] *ḥˁi* rejoice; *ḥˁˁwt* joy, § 287; *sḥˁi* make to rejoice.

[hieroglyphs] *ḥˁw* (P 1) ships.

[hieroglyphs] *ḥˁ3* (O 29) child, lad.

[hieroglyphs] var. [hieroglyphs] *ḥˁpy* (N 36. 37) inundation (of Nile); Ḥaˁpy, the god of the Inundation.

[hieroglyphs] *ḥˁḏ3* pillage, plunder; plunderer.

[hieroglyphs] *Ḥw* (F 18) Ḥu, deity personifying Authoritative Utterance; [hieroglyphs] *ḥw* food, sustenance.

[hieroglyphs] *ḥwy-3* non-encl. part., would that!, §§ 119, 8; 238.

[hieroglyphs] *ḥwt* (O 6) house, temple, tomb; walled village, in *ḥk3-ḥwt*, see under *ḥk3*; [hieroglyphs] *ḥwt-nṯr* temple; [hieroglyphs] *ḥwt-ˁ3t* (O 8) castle, also of temples; [hieroglyphs] *ḥwt-k3* soul-house, tomb-chapel; [hieroglyphs] var. [hieroglyphs] var. det. [hieroglyphs] *Ḥt-ḥr* (O 10; C 9) the goddess Hathor, Gk. Ἀθῶρ; *Nbt-ḥwt*, see under *nb*.

[hieroglyphs] *ḥw3* rot, decay (vb.).

[hieroglyphs] *ḥwˁ* (be) short; *sḥwˁ* shorten.

[hieroglyphs] var. [hieroglyphs] *ḥwn* (be) youthful; youth; *ḥwnt* maiden.

[hieroglyphs] *ḥwrw* (be) poor, helpless, wretched; wretch; *bw ḥwrw* wretchedness, misery; *sḥwr* abuse, vilify.

[hieroglyphs] *ḥwtf* rob, plunder (vb.).

[hieroglyphs] var. det. [hieroglyphs] *ḥb* (W 3. 4) feast, festival; [hieroglyphs] *ḥb-sd* (O 23) jubilee, *Sed*-festival; [hieroglyphs] *ḥbt* ritual book, see too *ḫry-ḥbt* under *ḫr* below; [hieroglyphs] *ḥb* triumph (vb.);

ḥb mourn, *n* for (someone); *sḥb* make festal.

ḥbꜣbꜣ waddle (of goose).

ḥbs (S 28) clothe, cover; *ḥbsw* clothes, clothing.

Ḥp(wy) (S 36) Ḥepuy, a deity personifying the king's two sunshades.

ḥpt (Aa 5; P 8) oar.

ḥpt (Aa 5), literal meaning obscure; *iṯi ḥpt* proceed by boat; *dsr ḥpt* row (vb.).

ḥp (Aa 5) Apis bull.

ḥpt (D 32) embrace (vb. and n.).

ḥfꜣw (I 14) snake; *ḥfꜣt* female serpent; *ḥfꜣt* det. crawling (n.).

ḥfn (I 8) 100,000, § 259; construction of, § 262, 2.

ḥm (U 36) male slave, f. *ḥmt* det.; var. *ḥm* Majesty, foll. by suffix-prons. or genitival adj., p. 74; abbrev. *ḥm-nṯr* prophet, the highest grade of priests; var. *ḥm-kꜣ* (D 31) soul-priest, *ka*-priest, appointed to tend the funerary cult of private persons.

ḥmww (U 36) washerman, fuller.

varr. *ḥm* (N 41) encl. part., assuredly, indeed, § 253.

ḥmi flee, retire; *ḥm-ḥt* retreat, § 288.

ḥmt woman, wife; *ḥmt nsw* king's wife, queen; *st-ḥmt*, see under *s* (*si*) below.

, see under *idt* above.

ḥm poltroon.

ḥmw (P 10) steering oar; *ḥmy* steersman.

, perhaps later read *ḥmt* (?) (N 34) copper, bronze; see too under *biꜣ* above.

ḥmww (U 24) craftsman; *ḥmt* craft; *ḥmwt* body of craftsmen; *ḥmw-ib* clever, skilful.

ḥmꜣt (U 32) salt.

ḥmꜣgt, a red stone from Nubia.

ḥmsi (A 3. 17*) sit down, sit, dwell; besiege, *ḥr* (a town); *ꜥḥꜥ ḥmsi*, see under *ꜥḥꜥ* above; *ḥmst* session (e.g. of king and courtiers); *ḥmsw* sloth; *iḥms* occupant (in titles).

ḥni (M 2) rush (n.).

ḥn go; see too *ḥnḥn* below.

ḥn (U 8; V 36; Dyn. XIX), a receptacle given to a temple.

ḥn (V 36) command; commend (someone), *n* to (someone); supply, equip, *m* with; *ḥnt* var., abbrev., occupation.

var. *ḥnty* period, end, § 77, 1.

ḥnt (W 10) cup.

var. *ḥnwt* (W 10) mistress.

ḥnt swampy lake.

ḥnw vessel; pl., chattels, belongings.

ḥnt (F 16) horn.

ḥnw (U 8; G 10), name of the sacred bark of the god Sokar.

ḥnꜥ, rare var. *ḥn*, prep., together with, and (§ 91, 1); as conj., and, **§ 171**; foll. by infin., § 300, Obs.; adv., var. *ḥnꜥw* therewith, together with them, § 205, 1.

var. *ḥnmmt* (N 8), the sun-folk of Heliopolis; mankind.

ḥnn (U 8, Pyr.) hoe (n.).

ḥnn (D 53) phallus.

ḥnḥn be detained.

ḥns (G 37) (be) narrow.

ḥnskt lock of hair.

abbrev. *ḥnḳt* (W 22; § 59) beer.

ḥnk (D 39) present, offer; *ḥnkt* offerings (of meat and drink).

ḥnkyt bed, couch.

ḥnt(y) (I 3) be greedy, covetous.

Ḥr (G 5) the falcon-god Horus; *Ḥr-ꜣḫty* (N 19) Horus-of-the-horizon, Ḥarakhti; see too under *Rꜥ*; *Ḥr Nḫny* (G 13) Horus of Nekhen; *Ḥt-ḥr*, see under *ḥwt* above.

ḥr (D 2) face, sight; *m ḥr·f* in his sight; *rdi m ḥr n* charge, command (someone), *r* to (do something); *ḫr st-ḥr·f* under his supervision; *ḥr nb* everyone, § 103.

ḥr prep., with suffixes *ḥr·*, upon, in, at, from, on account of, through, and (§ 91, 1), having on it; as conj., because, **§ 165**; before infin., on, in, §§ 3. 165, 10; 304, 1; 319. 320. 482; do., from, after, § 165, 10; infin. omitted, say(s), said, § 321; *ḥr-ntt* because, § 223; *ḥr m* why?, § 496; compound preps. *ḥr-ḥw*, *ḥr-tp*, etc., see under second word; advs., *ḥr ꜥ*, *ḥr ꜥwy* immediately, § 205, 3; var. *ḥry* adj. (§ 79) who, which, is over, upon; captain; *ḥrt* (N 1) heaven; *ḥrt* (N 31) road, see too *ḥr* 'be far' below; *ḥrty* travel by land; *sḥr* fly aloft; *ḥrt* upland tomb; *5 ḥryw rnpt* the five epagomenal days, p. 203; *ḥry-pr* menial (or like); *Ḥry-š·f* He-who-is-upon-his-lake, Arsaphes, the ram-god of Heracleopolis, Gk. Ἀρσαφής; *Ḥryw-šꜥ* Beduins, lit. those-upon-the-sand; var. *ḥry-tp* chief, chieftain; *ḥry-ꜥ*, also *ḥrt-ꜥ*, arrears; *ḥrw* upper part; *r-ḥrw* adv., up, § 205, 3; varr. *ḥr(y)-ib* middle (n.); *m-ḥry-ib* in the midst of, § 178; var. *ḥry-ib(y)* adj., who is at (a town), localizing deities worshipped away from their own home.

var. det. *ḥr* be far, *r* from; *ḥr·ti*, *ḥr·tiwny r*, keep away from, avoid, § 313; *ḥrw-r* abbrev. apart from, besides, § 179; *ḥryt* dread (n.); *sḥr* (A 59) drive away, banish.

ḥr (Aa 19) prepare.

ḥrrt (M 2) flower.

ḥrst carnelian.

, see *nḥḥ* above.

Ḥḥ (C 11), one of the eight Ḥeḥ-gods who hold aloft the sky.

ḥḥ a great number, million, § 259; construction of, § 262, 2; *ḥḥ n* many, § 99.

ḥhy seek.

ḥs (Aa 2, cf. F 52; N 32) excrement.

ḥst (W 14) water-pot.

ḥs freeze.

ḥs turn back, intrans. or reflexive; turn in homeward direction; *m ḥs* in meeting (someone), in front of (someone).

ḥsi (O.K. *ḥzi*) praise, favour (vb.); *ḥst* praise, favour (n.).

ḥsi (O.K. *ḥsi*) sing; *ḥsw* singer, f. *ḥsyt*.

Ḥsꜣt (E 4) sacred Ḥesa(t)-cow.

abbrev. , *ḥsb* (Aa 2) count, reckon; *tp-ḥsb* right calculation, right order; × *ḥsb* (hieratic) $\frac{1}{4}$, § 265; $\frac{1}{4}$ aroura, § 266, 3.

ḥsp (N 24) garden.

abbrev. , *ḥsmn* (U 32) natron; amethysts; det. or abbrev. bronze.

ḥsḳ cut off, hew off.

, see *ḥnḳt* above.

Ḥḳt (I 7) the frog-goddess Ḥeḳe(t).

var. *ḥḳ(ꜣ)t* (S 38) sceptre.

ḥḳꜣ rule (vb.); abbrev. *ḥḳ(ꜣ)* chieftain; det. Ruler, i.e. the king; *ḥḳꜣ-ḥwt* village headman.

ḥḳꜣt (S 38; U 9. 11. 12) *ḥeḳat*-measure, gallon, § 266, 1.

var. det. *ḥḳr* (be) hungry; *ḥḳrw* hunger.

ḥkꜣ magic; *ḥkꜣy* magician; *Wrt-ḥkꜣw* Great-of-Magic, goddess identified with the royal crown, p. 190, n. 1.

var. det. *ḥkn* exult, *m* at; *ḥknw* exultation, praise (n.).

ḥtt rare var. *ḥtt* (O 6) mine (n.).

ḥtyt (F 10) throat, wind-pipe.

ḥtꜣw (P 5) sail (n.).

var. hieratic *ḥtp* (R 4) rest, go to rest, set (of sun); (be) at peace, pleased, *ḥr* with; forgive, *n* (someone); rest, obj. upon, § 84 A, p. 423; *ḥtp*, *ḥtpw* peace (n.); var. O.K. *ḥtp* (R 4) altar, table of offerings; *ḥtp(w)*, *ḥtpt* det. offerings; *ḥtpw-nṯr* offerings to the gods; *ḥtpt-ḏfꜣ* food-offerings; *dbḥt-ḥtp*, see under *dbḥ*; *ḥtp dỉ nsw* a boon which the king gives, opening words of the formula of funerary offerings, p. 170; *sḥtp* propitiate, pacify.

ḥtmt (Q 1, Dyn. XIX) chair.

var. *ḥtm* (G 38) perish; *sḥtm* destroy; *sḥtmw* destroyer.

ḥtr (M 6) tax (vb.), assess; tax (n.).

ḥtr (E 6) pair of horses; det. pair of oxen (for ploughing).

ḥts (U 33) celebrate (a feast).

ḥdb throw down, be prostrate; det. make a halt, *ḥr* at (a place).

ḥḏ (T 3) mace.

ḥḏ (be) white, bright; *ḥḏ-ḥr* cheerful, bright; *ḥḏḏwt* (T 6) brightness, light; *ḥḏ-tꜣ* () dawn (vb.), lit. the earth becomes light; dawn, morning (n.); *sḥḏ* illumine, make clear; *sḥḏ* in titles, instructor (?); var. *ḥḏ* (S 12. 14) silver; *ḥḏt* (S 1. 2) the white crown (of Upper Egypt); *ḥḏt* white cloth; see too under *t* bread.

var. *ḥḏỉ* (T 3; Z 9) damage, destroy.

ḥḏn (L.E.) be vexed; *sḥḏn* (M.K.) vex.

ḫ (Aa 1)

ḫ, in some words substituted, usually later, for *ḥ*, under which must be sought writings not found here.

ḫt (Q 7) fire.

var. without det. *ḫt* (O.K. *ỉḫt*) things, property, f., § 92, 2; *ḫt nbt* everything, anything, § 103; something, anything, m., § 92, 2.

ḫꜣw (M 12; § 5) lotus-plants; plants (generally).

ḫꜣ 1000, § 259; construction of, § 262, 2; *ḫꜣ-tꜣ*, var. *ḫꜣ*, measure of area of 10 arouras (*sṯꜣt*), § 266, 3.

ḫꜣ (O 27) administrative office, diwân.

ḫꜣỉ (U 9) measure (vb.); *ḫꜣw* measurer; *ḫꜣy* det. measuring cord; see too *mḫꜣ*, *mḫꜣt* above.

abbrev. *ḫꜣỉ* (D 40) examine (a patient).

ḫꜣyt (Aa 2), var. *ḫꜣt*, illness.

ḫꜣyt slaughter, massacre.

ḫꜣwt (R 1), varr. *ḫꜣt* (L 6), *ḫꜣy(t)* (R 2), table of offerings.

ḫꜣwy, var. *ḫ(ꜣ)w(y)* (O 27), night, late evening.

ḫ3ꜥ throw, put, leave, desert; throw down (hippopotamus).

ḫ3b (E 25) hippopotamus.

ḫ3-b3·s the starry sky.

Ḫ3rw Khor, name of Palestine or a part of it (Dyn. XVIII); *Ḫ3r* det. Khorians.

ḫ3ḫ hasten, move quickly; *sḫ3ḫ* hasten (trans.).

var. (N 25) *ḫ3st* hill-country, foreign land; *ḫ3styw* desert-dwellers.

ḫꜥi (N 28) shine, appear (of sun, gods, or king); *ḫꜥw* det. appearance in glory; *nb ḫꜥw* lord of the crowns, epithet of the king; *sḫꜥi* make shine forth.

ḫꜥw (N 34) weapons, *nw r-ꜥ-ḫt* of warfare.

ḫꜥr rage (vb.).

ḫwi (D 43) protect; *ḫw* (S 37) fan (n.); *ḫw* (Aa 1) exclusion, in *wꜥ ḥr ḫw·f* unique; *ḥr-ḫw* except, § 178.

ḫww (D 43) evil (n.).

ḫwsi (A 34) build, accomplish; *sḫws* det. deck out.

ḫwd (Aa 9) (be) rich; *sḫwd* enrich.

ḫbi (A 32) dance (vb.).

ḫbi (Z 9) lessen, subtract.

ḫb3, var. *ḫb*, destroy, overwhelm; *ḫbyt* destruction, slaughter.

ḫbn (be) guilty; *ḫbnt* crime; *ḫbnty* criminal.

ḫbs (U 6. 7) cultivate, hoe (vb.); *ḫbsw* det. , abbrev. (Z 9) ploughlands.

ḫbst tail, beard; *ḫbstyw* det. the bearded ones, i.e. the inhabitants of Pwēne(t).

ḫbd blame, disapprove of.

ḫpi walk, encounter; *ḫpt* det. , (A 55; Z 6) decease, death; *sḫpi* bring (offerings); *ḫpp* strange.

ḫprr (L 1) dung-beetle, scarab.

very rare var. *ḫpr* (O 1) come into existence, become, happen; sometimes used as pass. of *iri* make; *ḫprt* occurrence; *Ḫpri* det. Khepri, the sun-god at his rising; *ḫprw* det. forms, stages of growth; *ḫpr-ḏs·f* lees, dregs; *sḫpr* create, bring to pass, train.

ḫprš (S 7), the blue crown.

var. det. *ḫpš* (F 23. 24) foreleg (of ox), arm, strength; det. (T 16) scimetar.

var. det. *ḫfꜥ* (D 49) seize; grip, grasp (n.).

var. *ḫft* prep, in front of, in accordance with, corresponding to; as conj., when, according as; with infin., at the time of, when, § **169**; *r-ḫft*, *r-ḫft-ḥr* in front of, § 178; *ḫft-ntt* in view of the fact that, § 223; *ḫft-ḥr* presence (n.); in front of, § 178; *ḫftw*, *ḫft*, adv., accordingly, § 205, 1; *ḫfty* det. , (A 14; Z 6) enemy.

ḫm not know, (be) ignorant of; *iḫm-sk* Indestructible, lit. not-knowing-destruction, name given to a circumpolar star, § 272; *m-ḫmt* in the absence of, without, § 178; see too *smḫ* and *sḫmḫ-ib* below.

ḫm be dry; *ḫmw* dust.

varr. , *Ḫm* (R 22. 23) Ausîm, Letopolis, a town in Lower Egypt.

var. *ḫm* (R 22; O 20. 34; D 35) shrine.

ḫmꜥt handle (of oar).

Ḫmnw El-Ashmûnên, Hermopolis, a town in Upper Egypt, § 260.

ḫmntyw, ships of a special kind.

ḫmt three, § 260; do for third time, § 292; *ḫmt-nw* third, § 263; *ḫmt rw* (?) three quarters, § 265.

ḫmt foretell; expect, think, foll. by *sḏm·f*, § 184, 1.

ḫnỉ (G 41) alight, halt; *ḫnw* det. utterance, saying; *ḫnw* det. dwelling-place, chapel; *ḫnt* expense, expenditure; *ḫnyt* det. (strolling female) dancers, musicians; *sḫny* settle down, alight, halt, *ḥr* at; see too *msḫn* above.

ḫnp 1. rob, despoil; 2. offer.

ḫnm 1. smell (vb.); *ḫnmw* smell (n.); 2. give pleasure to (someone), *m* with; *ḫnmw* in friendly, cheerful fashion, § 205,4.

ḫnmt, var. *mḫnt*, red jasper or carnelian.

ḫnms (A 21), O.K. det. (A 11), friend; det. associate with (obj.).

ḫnr (U 31), var. *ḫnỉ* (D 19), restrain; *ḫn(r)ỉ* det. prisoner; *ḫnrt*, varr. , *ḫnt* (p. 201, n. 1), harîm, prison.

var. *ḫnrw* reins.

ḫns fare through (marshes, etc.); *Ḫnsw* Khons, the moon-god at Karnak.

ḫnš stink (vb.).

ḫntw (W 17) racks for water-pots.

ḫnt (W 17. 18; D 19) face; *m-ḫnt* (no det.) within, out of, § 178; var. *imy-ḫnt*, a priestly title; var. *ḫnt* prep., in front of, among, from, **§ 174**; *ḫnty* adj., to the fore in, in front of, § 79; *ḫntt-r* southward to, § 179; *sḫnt* advance (someone, in rank, etc.); *ḫnt* det. front part; *prỉ r ḫnt* go forth abroad; *ḫntw* adv., before (of time), § 205, 1; *ḫntỉ* det. (P 2) sail south, upstream; go farther south than, obj. (earlier kings).

, see under *ḫnr* above.

ḫnty (I 3) crocodile.

ḫnt-š wooded country, garden.

ḫntš take pleasure, *m*, *ḥr* in.

ḫnd (D 56) tread, *ḥr* upon.

ḫr prep., with, near; under (a king); (speak) to, **§ 167**; by (of agent), § 39, end; *n(y) ḫr nsw* from (Fr. *de par*) the king, § 158, 1; *ḫrt* det. what belongs to (someone or something); *ḫrt-ỉb* desire, wish.

ḫr (A 15) fall (vb. and n.); abbrev. *ḫrw* fallen one, i.e. conquered enemy, see too *ḫrwy* below; *sḫr* abbrev. overthrow (vb.).

varr. *ḫr*, O.K. *ỉḫr*, non-encl. part., and, further, § 239; in sent. with adv. pred., § 119, 5; with nom. pred., p. 105, n. 6; with adj. pred., § 142; in *ḫr sḏm·f*, *ḫr·f sḏm·f*, § 239; relation of these to *sḏm·ḫr·f*, § 427.

ḫrw cry (vb.), §§ 427. 437; varr. , *ḫrw* (P 8) voice, sound; *mꜣꜥ-ḫrw*, see under *mꜣꜥ* above; varr. , *ḫr(y)·fy* + dep. pron. and/or noun, parenthetic, says, § 437; *ḫr* + suffix, parenthetic, says, § 436.

ḫrwy enemy; *ḫrwyt* det. war.

var. *ḫrp* (S 42; D 44) be at head of, undertake, make offering of; abbrev. *ḫrp* director, leader; *ḫrp nsty* controller of the two seats (thrones), a priestly title; *ḫrp kꜣt* director of works, builder, architect; *ḫrpw* mallet.

ḫrš bundle (of vegetables).

earlier det. *ḫḫ* (F 10. 11) throat.

ḫsꜣy, var. *ḫsy*, bribe (n.).

ḫsbd lapis lazuli.

ḫsf (U 34) spin.

var. *ḫsf* (U 34. 35) repel, oppose; punish, *n* (someone); *ḫsfw* approach (n.); *m-ḫsfw* at the approach of, § 178; var. det. *ḫsfi* travel upstream.

, , see under *ḫm*, *Ḫm* above.

ḫsr (V 29), var. *ẖsr*, dispel, drive away, ward off.

ḫt fire, *ḫt* things, see at beginning of letter *ḫ* above.

Ḫt (U 30) Khatti, the land of the Hittites.

ḫt (M 3) wood, stick, tree (m., § 92, 3); abbrev. for *ḫt n nwḥ*, see under *nwḥ* above; *r-ꜥ-ḫt*, see under *ḫꜥw* above; *ḫt-ṯꜣw*, also abbrev. *ḫt*, mast; *r-ḫt* under the authority of, § 178.

ḫt prep., through, pervading, § 175; *ḫt-ḫt* prep., throughout, § 178.

ḫt: *m-ḫt* prep., accompanying, after; before infin., when; as conj., before *śḏm·f*, after, when; before *śḏm·n·f*, after, §§ 156. **178**; before pass. *śḏm·f*, after, § 423, 3; before *śḏmt·f*, after, § 407, 2; before noun + old perf., § 327; adv., afterwards, § 205, 2; see too under *imy* above.

ḫti retreat, retire; see too under *ḥmi* above; *ḫtḫt* retreat, be reversed.

ḫti carve, sculpture (vb.).

abbrev. *ḫtyw* (O 40) terrace, terraced hill.

ḫtyw threshing-floor.

ḫtm (S 20) shut, close; seal (vb. and n.); det. fortress; *ḫtmt* det. contract (n.).

ḫdi (P 1) fare downstream, travel north.

ẖ (F 32)

ẖ: see here for various words also written (usually later) with *ḫ*; *ẖ* also often represents earlier *š*.

ẖt (F 32) body, belly, f., rarely m., § 92, 4; det. body of people, generation.

ẖꜣt (K 4, O.K.) oxyrhynchus, a fish.

varr. det. , *ẖꜣt* (A 55. 54; Aa 2) corpse; *iꜥbt ẖꜣt*, *ꜥbt ẖꜣt*, see under *iꜥb* above.

ẖꜣt quarry, mine.

ẖꜣt, var. *ḫꜣt*, swamp, marsh.

ẖꜣbt (V 1), bent appendage of the red crown ; *ẖꜣbb* (V 1. 2), var. *ḫꜣbb*, crookedness.

ẖꜣmi, var. *ḫꜣmi*, bow down, bend (arms, back); *ẖꜣmt-ḫt* () pile of offerings.

abbrev. *ẖꜣr* (V 19) sack, a large measure of capacity, § 266, 1.

ẖꜣrt, var. *ḫꜣrt* (D 3), widow.

ẖꜣẖꜣti tempest.

ẖꜣk-ib disaffected, rebellious; rebel.

ẖꜥm, var. *ẖꜥm*, approach (obj., with hostile intent).

ẖꜥḳ (U 37) shave (vb.); *ẖꜥḳw* barber.

abbrev. *ẖpw* (Aa 2) sculptured reliefs.

ẖpꜣ (Aa 2) navel, navel-string.

ẖpn, var. *ḫpn*, fat (adj.).

ẖms bend, obj. (the back).

ẖnt (F 26) hide, skin (n.).

ẖn tent.

ẖn approach, *m* (someone); *ẖnw* interior, inside; det. (royal) Residence; *m-ẖnw* (det.), rare var. (W 24), in the interior of, inside, § 178; see too *ꜥ-ẖnwty* above.

ẖnw (N 35) stream, brook.

ẖnỉ (D 33) row, convey by boat; *ẖnyt* det. sailors; *mẖnt* ferry-boat; *mẖnty* ferryman; var. det. *ẖnt(y)* (A 22. 21) statue (originally portable?).

ẖnm (W 9) join, become joined, obj. or *m* with; *ẖnmw* house-mates, associates.

var. *Ḫnmw* (W 9; C 4; E 10) Chnum, the ram-god of the First Cataract, Gk. Χνοῦβις.

var. *ẖnmt* (N 41) well (in the desert).

ẖnn destroy, disturb; *ẖnnw* det. turmoil; cf. too *sẖnn*.

ẖr (T 28) prep., under, carrying, at (head or foot), § **166**; *ẖr-ꜥ* in the charge of, § 178; *ẖr-ḥꜣt*, see under *ḥꜣt* above; *ẖr(y)-ꜥ* assistant, subordinate; *bw ẖry·f* the place where he is, § 204, 1; varr. *ẖr(y)-ḥbt* (W 5; p. 51, n. 4) lector-priest, lit. holder of the ritual book; *ẖry tp nsw* he who is at the head of the king, a title; *ẖrt* (a man's) due, duty; *m ẖrt-hrw* (var. N 7) *nt rꜥ nb* in the course of every day; var. *ẖr(t)-nṯr* (R 10; p. 51, n. 4) necropolis; *ẖrty-nṯr* det. necropolis-worker; *ẖryw* kinsfolk, household; *ẖrw* lower part; *ḥr-m-ẖrw* abashed, lit. face downcast, § 194, end.

abbrev. *ẖrd* (A 17) child.

ẖsỉ (be) weak, feeble; of enemies, vile.

ẖkr (Aa 30) be adorned; *ẖkrw* ornament, also *ẖkryt*; *ẖkryt nsw* king's ornament, title of a royal concubine; *sẖkr* adorn.

ẖdb kill.

s (S 29; O 34)

ś, *z*, signs for distinct consonants in O.K., are no longer so distinguished in M.E., and are here treated as a single consonant *s*. Note that the sequences *sš* and *šs* are particularly liable to metathesis. For the causatives in *s-* (§ 275, 1) see under the simple stems.

s (O 34) bolt (n.).

varr. *s* (*sỉ* A 1) man (mostly indefinite, a man); someone, anyone, § 102; *s nb* everyone, each, § 103; *st* (B 1) woman; *st-ḥmt* woman.

rare var. *st* (Q 1. 2) seat, place; in compounds with parts of body forms equivalents of Engl. abstracts, indicating activity of the part, ex. *st-ỉb* affection, lit. place of heart; see also under *ꜥ*, *r*, *ḥr*, *ḏrt*; Isis, see under *ꜣst*; Osiris, see under *Wsỉr*.

st (G 39) pintail duck.

, see *smyt* below.

sꜣ (G 39) son, in filiations written with a hieratic sign giving rise to Dyn. XIX (H 8); *sꜣ mr·f* son-who-loves, epithet of Horus, king, or priest impersonating one of these, p. 145, n. 2 [a]; *sꜣ s* () a man of rank, lit. son of man; *sꜣ-tꜣ* snake, lit. son of earth; see too under *nsw*, *Rꜥ*; *sꜣt* daughter.

(hieratic) *sꜣ*, land-measure of $\frac{1}{8}$ aroura (*sṯꜣt*), § 266, 3.

older var. *sꜣ* (Aa 17. 18) back; in preps., sometimes also as conj., *m-sꜣ*, *r-sꜣ*, *ḥr-sꜣ* after, § 178; do. as advs., § 205, 2; *rdỉ sꜣ* turn the back, i. e. flee; put a stop, *r* to.

var. *sꜣ* cattle-pen, door (?), outside.

sꜣt (Aa 17. 18) outer wall.

sꜣwy (D 22; § 265) two-thirds.

var., see under *sꜣw* below.

sꜣỉ 1. be sated, *m* with; *sꜣw* satiety; *ssꜣỉ* sate, feed; 2. (be) wise, understanding, cf. too *sꜣrt* below.

sꜣỉ linger, lag; *sꜣw ỉwt·f* (var. *ỉt·f*) slow (as regards) his coming, i.e. impatiently awaited.

later var. *sꜣw* (A 47) guard, protect; imper. foll. by *sḏm f* beware lest, §§ 184. **338, 3**, varr. *sꜣt*, perhaps for *sꜣ tw*, and *sꜣꜣ·tỉ* old perf., § 313; foll. by infin. (rare), § 303, or by noun, § 338, 3; *sꜣw* guardian; var. *sꜣ* (V 16. 17) protection, esp. magical; see too under *stp*; *sꜣ* phylē of priests (Lesson XXIII, *a*; p. 247, n. 2), corps, regiment; *sꜣw* magician; *ỉmy-sꜣ*, see under *ỉmy*.

sꜣw beam, plank.

Sꜣw Ṣa el-Ḥagar, Sais, a town in Lower Egypt.

Sꜣwt Asyûṭ, Lycopolis, a town in Upper Egypt.

sꜣb šwt, rare writing for (F 28) variegated of feathers, epithet of the solar Horus.

sꜣb (E 17) jackal; dignitary, worthy.

sꜣmt mourning.

sꜣr need, requirement; *sꜣỉ(r)w* need (n.); *sꜣr* det. needy one.

sꜣrt wisdom, understanding, cf. *sꜣỉ*, 2. above.

var. *sꜣḥ* (D 61) toe.

sꜣḥ approach, touch, reach, obj. or *r*; det. endow, *m* with; det. land given as reward; *sꜣḥw* det. neighbours; *m-sꜣḥt* in the neighbourhood of, § 178; *Sꜣḥ* det. , the constellation Orion.

sꜣsꜣ overthrow.

sꜣḳ (I 5) collect, gather together; with reflex. pron., gird oneself, *r* against.

later var. , *sꜣtw* ground, earth.

sỉ (O 35) in imper. *ỉs* go; det. perish.

var. , *sy* who?, what?, which?, § 499; *ḥr sy ỉšst* wherefore?, § 500, 4.

, see under *sb-tw*.

varr. , , *sy*, dep. pron. 3rd sing. f., she, her, it, § 43; part. + *sy* replacing 3rd f. old perf., § 374, end; use in archaistic texts before *śḏm·f*, p. 424, Add. to § 148, 1.

sy she, it, pron. compound, § 124.

var. Pyr. *sỉꜣt* (S 32) piece of cloth.

sỉꜣ perceive, recognize; *Sỉꜣ* Sia, deity personifying Perception.

sỉn smear (vb.).

sỉn (Aa 2) clay, plaster.

sỉn 1. hasten; 2. delay, see under *ỉn* above.

sꜥb castrate.

var. *sꜥḥ* (E 31; S 20) (be) noble; rank, dignity; nobleman, worthy (n.); det. mummy.

swt (M 23), a plant, perhaps sedge or *scirpus*-reed, p. 73, n. 10.

sw dep. pron. 3rd sing. m., he, him, it, § 43; use in archaistic texts before *śḏm·f*, p. 424, Add. to § 148, 1; do. as non-encl. part., § 240; *swt* old indep. pron. 3rd sing. m., he, very rarely f., she, § 64, with Obs.; as encl. part., but, § 254.

sw pron. compound, he, it, § 124.

swt (F 44) leg of beef, tibia.

, var. , *sww* (?) dates, particular

days; probably plur. of *sw* 'day', as used in dates, p. 203.

swȝi, see under *wȝi* above.

var. *swȝ* (Z 9) cut off (limb); cut down (tree).

swn (T 11) perish, suffer; *sswn* consume, destroy.

swnw (T 11), var. O.K. *zin*, physician.

abbrev. *swn* barter (vb.); *swnt* barter, price; *iri swnt* trade (vb.); *r-swnt* in exchange for, § 178.

sw(r)i (N 35; rarely with Z 9) drink, § 279; *ssw(r)i* make to drink.

var. det. *swh* boast, *n* about.

swḥt (H 8) egg.

swt breeze (m.).

swtwt walk, promenade (vb.).

sbi (O 35) go, pass, send; load (ship); *sbt* det. load, transport (n.).

sb-tw (?), *si-tw* (?) in quest of, seeking for, foll. by infin., § 181.

abbrev. *sbȝ* (N 14) star.

var. *sbȝ* teach, *r* concerning, § 84; *sbȝyt* det. teaching, (book of) instruction; *sbȝt(y)* pupil.

abbrev. *sbȝ* (O 32) door.

later det. *sbi* (Aa 26; T 14) rebel (vb.), *ḥr* against; det. rebel (n.).

var. det. *sbn* slip, go astray.

sbḥ (F 18) cry aloud; cry (n.).

sbḫ (O 14) wall in, enclose; *sbḫt* varr. det. (O 13. 32) gateway.

sbḳ (D 56, Pyr.) leg.

var. *sbḳ* (D 56) (be) excellent, successful; *ssbḳ* honour (vb.).

var. det. *Sbk* (I 4. 5*) the crocodile-god Sobk, Gk. Σοῦχος.

sbty (O 36) surrounding wall.

sbṯ, var. *sbt* (F 18), laugh, *m* at; *ssbt* make laugh.

spt (O 50) threshing-floor.

sp happen, in it did not happen, never, foll. by *sḏm·f*, §§ 106. **456**; time, occasion, blameworthy action; *n sp* together, at once, § 205, 3; *sp 2* after group of signs to be repeated, e.g. after advs., § 207; to indicate reduplication, § 274; see under *ḥȝt* above.

spi remain over; *spyt* remainder.

spt (D 24) lip, edge (of pool, etc.); abbrev. *spty* (D 25) lips.

spȝ (L 5) centipede.

varr. *spȝt* (N 24; Aa 8) district, nome.

var. *spr* (F 42) rib.

spr approach, *r* (place or person); det. petition (vb.), *n* (someone); *sprt* petition (n.); *sprw*, *sprty* petitioner.

spḥ lasso (vb.).

spḥt (F 43) ribs of beef.

var. det. or abbrev. *spd* (M 44, p. 538) (be) sharp, clever, ready; *sspd* make ready; *spdd* supply (vb.), § 274.

Spdw (G 13) the god Sopd.

Spdt the dog-star Sirius; Sothis, the dog-star as a goddess, Gk. Σῶθις, p. 205.

var. *sf* (N 5; S 30) yesterday; *m sf* adv., yesterday, § 205, 3.

sf (be) mild.

sft sword (f.).

sfn (be) gentle, kind.

sft, O.K. *śfṯ*, an oil for anointing.

sft, O.K. *zfṯ*, slaughter (vb.); slaughterer.

, see *stm* below.

var. *sm* (M 21) herb, plant.

var. *sm* (M 21; F 37) 1. succour, tend; 2. occupation, pastime.

varr. , , *smyt* (N 25; Aa 8) desert, necropolis.

var. *smꜣ* (F 36) lung.

var. *smꜣ* unite, (be) united, *m* with; take part, *m* in (holiday); *smꜣy* companion, participant, *n*(*y*) in, lit. of; *smꜣyt* det. , confederates; *smꜣ-tꜣ*() reach land, i.e. be buried; burial; verge (of river).

smꜣ locks, hair-covered part of head.

smꜣ, var. *sm*(*ꜣ*) (§ 279), slay; *smꜣ* (S 31) fighting bull.

smꜣ (Aa 25), a priest of Min, Horus, etc., whose function was to clothe the god.

smỉ, see under *mỉ* above.

smỉ lash (n.).

smwn non-encl. part., probably, surely, § 241.

smn, kind of goose.

varr. , *smr* (U 23) friend (of king), courtier.

smḥ skiff, light boat.

smḫ (D 35) forget (caus. of *ḫm*?).

abbrev. *smsw* (A 19. 20) eldest, elder; see too *ḥyt* above.

smdt subordinates, staff (e.g. of temple).

varr. , later , *sn*, rarely , , *s*, suffix-pron. and dep. pron. 3rd pl. c., they, them, their, §§ 34. 43; as obj. usually replaced by *st*, § 44, 1, Obs.; in archaistic texts foll. by *śḏm·sn*, p. 424, Add. to § 148, 1; *sny*, dual, they two, them two, early obsolete, § 34.

, usually written II, *snw* (T 22) two, § 260; var. *sn-nw* second, § 263, 2; *ḥr sn-nw·sy* adv., a second time; *sn* brother; *snt* sister; *snsn* det. fraternize.

sn smell, kiss (vb.); *sn tꜣ* kiss the ground, *n* before (god or king); *ssn*, later usually *snsn*, sniff, breathe.

snt flagstaff.

snt base-block.

var. *snw* (X 4) food-offerings.

snt feast of the sixth day (of the month).

var. *sn* (N 37; O 31) open (vb.).

var. *snỉ* (X 4. 5) pass by, surpass; *sny-mnt* distress, calamity.

snt (X 5) likeness; *m-snt-r* in the likeness of, in accordance with, § 180; *snty* image, duplicate; *snn* image, portrait; cf. too *snn* document.

snb overleap (wall); *snbt* det. wall.

snb(*t*) (W 14), jar of shape .

snb (be) healthy, rarely trans. heal, § 274: health; abbrev. in , see under *ꜥnḫ*; *snb-ỉb* famine; *snbb* det. converse (vb.); *ssnb* preserve, keep in health.

snf (M 4) last year.

snf (caus.), see under *nfw* above.

snf (D 26) blood.

snm, see under *wnm* above.

snm (be) sad; grief.

snm(*w*) torrential rain.

snn document, deed; see too under *snt* 'likeness' above.

snhy muster (troops, workmen, etc.).

snḥ bind.

var. det. *snḥm* (L 4; G 38) locust, grasshopper.

sns(*y*) praise, adore; *snsw* adoration.

snḳ (D 27) suckle.

snṯ (V 5), var. *snt*, plan, plot out, found; *snṯ*, *sntt* det. ground-plan.

snṯr, see under *nṯr*.

var. *snd* (G 54) fear, *n* (someone); foll. by *sḏm·f* (imperf., § 442, 1), § 184; by infin., § 303; by *r*+infin., § 163, 10; *sndw*, *sndt* fear (n.); *m-snd* through fear (that), § 181; *sndw* the timid man.

sr, kind of goose.

sr (E 10) sheep, ram, f. *srt*.

sr (E 27) foretell.

abbrev. *sr* (A 21) official, noble; *srt* office, magistracy.

srt (M 44) thorn.

abbrev. *sryt* (S 35) military standard.

srwḫ tend (of physician).

srf (be) warm; also abbrev. (Q 7) warmth, temperature, passion.

srf(ỉ) take rest; repose (n.).

srḫ (O 33) banner, to contain Horus-name, p. 72.

srḳ relieve, admit breath to (*ḫtyt* wind-pipe); var. *Srḳt* (L 7), the scorpion-goddess Serḳe(t).

srd glean.

shꜣ disorder, lawlessness.

var. *sḥ* (O 22) booth, arbour, council-chamber; var. *sḥ-nṯr* (O 21) divine booth, shrine of Anubis; *sḥ* counsel.

sḥwy (G 41) collect, assemble; assemblage.

sḥm, O.K. *zḥm* (U 32), pound (vb.).

sḫ beat; *sḫt* blow (n.).

sḫw, see under *wsḫ* above.

var. *sḫt* (M 20) marshland, country; *sḫty* peasant, fowler.

sḫꜣ (probably caus., with f. inf.) remember; foll. by *sḏm·f*, § 184, 1; by infin., § 303; recall, *n* to (someone); *sḫꜣ*, *sḫꜣw* memory.

sḫwn (caus.) dispute (vb. and n.).

var. det. *sḫm* (S 42), sceptre of authority.

var. *sḫm* have power, *m* over; (be) powerful; power (n.); *sḫm* a Power, epithet of deities; *ssḫm* strengthen; *sḫm* (S 42) sistrum; *Sḫmt* the lioness-headed goddess Sakhme(t), Gk. -σαχμις; var. *sḫm-ỉr(y)·f* (Y 8) potentate, magnate; *sḫmty* (S 5. 6) the double crown of Upper and Lower Egypt, Gk. ψχέντ.

sḫmḫ-ỉb recreation, sport, lit. distraction of heart, *sḫmḫ* caus. half-reduplication (§ 274) from *ḫm*, see under this above.

sḫnt (O 30) post, support (of heaven).

sḫr plan, counsel, will, way of acting, state; *sḫry* manager, commander.

sḫs run (vb.).

var. *sḫt* (T 26. 27) trap, snare (birds); weave; make, form (*ḏbt* bricks).

sḫd (A 29) (be) upside down.

sẖ, var. *sẖ*, (be) deaf; *sẖ-ḥr(·f)* turn a deaf ear, *r* to.

sẖꜣk strain, empty to the last drop.

sẖb, var. *sẖp*, swallow (food, drink).

sẖm exert oneself, act violently, cope with, obj.

sẖnn (O 37), var. *sẖnn*, demolish; caus. of *ẖnn* (?), see above.

sẖr cover, coat (a surface), *m* with (gold, etc.).

ssmt (E 6) horse.

ssndm (M 29), a species of tree.

var. det. *ssḫ* smash, destroy.

var. det. var. *sš* (G 48. 49) bird-pool, nest.

, see under *sn*.

sš spread out.

sš (Y 3) write, draw, paint; writing, book, letter, var. pl. ; *sš* scribe.

Sšꜣt (R 20. 21) Sesha(t), the goddess of writing.

sšꜣy pray, *n* to (god); supplication (n.).

sšw (S 21) ring or disc (of metal).

, see *sšp* below.

var. *sšp* (O 42) daylight.

var. *sšm* (T 31. 32) lead, guide; show, *wꜣt* the way; conduct, *ḥb* a festival; det. guidance, scheme, state of affairs; *iry sšm* the proper official; *sšmw*, *sšmy* leader; det. divine shape, form.

sšm (?) (T 33, O.K.) butcher.

abbrev. *sšn* (M 9) lotus.

sšr (V 6. 33) linen; var. *sšr-nsw* royal linen, byssus; *šsrw* (N 33) bags; see too under *šs*.

sšr, var. *sšr* or *šs* (V 6. 33), thing, concern; *mi sšr* (or *šs*) in good condition; *sšr* (or *šs*) *mꜣꜥ* a genuine remedy.

sšr, var. *šsr*, recount, announce.

varr. , *sšr*, later *šs* (V 33. 35), corn.

abbrev. *sššt* (Y 8) sistrum.

sštꜣ, see under *štꜣ* below.

sšd gleam, glitter (like a star).

sšd head-band.

varr. , *sḳr* (Aa 7; T 2) smite; *sḳr-ꜥnḫ* det. living captive.

sḳdi travel by water, fare upon (river, sea); det. (A 10) sailor, traveller.

sk, see under *isk* above.

sk (V 29, O.K.) wipe, sweep; *sk* (M.E.) empty (*ẖt* body, of what one wishes to say).

ski perish, destroy; pass (time); *iḫm-sk*, see under *ḫm* above; *skw* det. var. det. squadrons, companies; battle; *ṯs skw* draw up in line of battle; *sksk* det. destroy.

, see (*m*)*sktt* above.

skꜣ (U 13) plough (vb.).

skm (D 3) grey-haired.

skn (I 3) be greedy, lust, *r* after.

var. det. *Skr* (G 10), the god Sokar of Memphis.

sgr quiet (n.); cf. too *gr* below.

later var. *st*, dep. pron. 3rd sing. f. and pl. c., it, them, § 43; as obj. of vb., § 46, 1; of infin., § 300; as obj. in *itḥ·tw st*, p. 41, n. 2; relation to O.K. indep. pron. 3rd sing. f. *štt*, p. 46, n. 8; after particles, § 46, 2; treated as m., § 511, 5.

, *st*, pron. compound 3rd pl. c., they, § 124.

var. *sti* (F 29; O.K. *šti*) shoot, obj. (arrow); *r* or obj. at (a person, a mark); det. pour (water); det. stare at; later var. , kindle (torch); *stwt* rays.

, see under *sṯi* below.

Styw Asiatics; see too under *Sṯt* below.

Stt (F 29), the goddess Satis worshipped at the First Cataract; see too under *Sṯt* below.

Stỉ (Aa 32, p. 512): *Tꜣ-Stỉ*, Nubia, properly 1st nome of Upper Egypt; *Styw* Nubians; var. *sty* (D 19) red (?) Nubian (?) pigment.

stp (U 21), O.K. *štp*, 1. cut up (ox, O.K.); *stpt* pieces of meat; *stp* det. dismemberment, ruin; 2. var. choose, *ḫnt* out of; *stpw* the choicest, best; *stp sꜣ* extend (magical) protection, *r* over, *ḥꜣ* around; *stp-sꜣ* det. the Palace.

later var. *stm*, a priest who attended to the toilet of a deity or deceased person.

var. *Stẖ* (E 20), later var. *St* (C 7; § 60), the god Seth, Gk. Σήθ.

sṯ, see under *ỉsṯ* above.

sṯỉ, M.K. infin. *sṯt*, later *stỉ* engender, beget; *styt* procreation (n.).

varr. det. *sṯỉ* (V 33; Aa 2. 3), later *sty*, perfume, odour; *sty-r* time for breakfast, p. 206, n. 5.

Sṯt (S 22), later var. *Stt* (N 18), 1. Asia; 2. Sehêl, an island in the First Cataract; hence perhaps 1. *Styw* Asiatics, and certainly 2. *Stt* the goddess Satis, see above.

sṯꜣ, a measure of capacity, § 266, 1.

sṯꜣ (V 2), later *stꜣ*, drag, draw, flow; *stꜣt* (N 37), aroura, a field-measure of about ⅔ acre, § 266, 3; see too *R-sṯꜣw* under *r* above.

sṯsw support, supporting (n.), see too *ṯsỉ* below; *sṯsw Šw* the supports of Shu, p. 380, n. 3.

sṯsy upside down (adj. pl.).

sd be clad, *m* in.

sd (F 33) tail; *sdty*, a title of unknown meaning.

sd (N 20) in *ḥb-sd*, see under *ḥb* above.

sdỉ (Z 9), earlier var. *sḏỉ*, break.

sdꜣ (G 33) egret.

sdꜣ (also *sdꜣdꜣ*) tremble; *sdꜣw* trembling (n.).

sdwḫ (Aa 2) embalm.

sdb swallow (vb.).

var. *sdm* (F 21) paint (eyebrows); *msdmt* (F 31), var. *msḏmt* (D 7), black eye-paint.

var. *sḏt* (Z 9) fire, flame.

sḏty child, foster-child.

sḏꜣ (probably caus.) go, pass by, pass away (die), cf. *wḏꜣ* above.

sḏꜣy-ḥr (caus.), see under *ḏꜣ*.

sḏꜣyt (S 20), var. *sḏꜣwt*, seal (n.); var. *sḏꜣwty* (?) (S 19) treasurer; *sḏꜣw* (?) precious.

var. det. *sḏb* (O 30, p. 517) hindrance, obstacle, harm; *ḥꜣỉ sḏb* impose an obstacle; *dr sḏb* remove an obstacle.

sḏm (F 21) hear; obey, *n* (someone); *sḏmyw* judges; *sḏm-ꜥš* (A 26) servant.

abbrev. *sḏr* (A 55) lie, spend all night; foll. by old perf., § 316; as aux. vb., § 483, 1.

š (N 37)

š, of O.K. later often replaced by *ẖ*; the combinations *sš* and *šs* are particularly liable to metathesis.

var. *š* (N 37. 38. 39) pool, lake; *Tꜣ-š* To-she, Lake-land, i.e. the Fayyûm; see too *Ḥry-š·f* under *ḥr* above.

št (V 1), perhaps originally *šnt*, hundred, § 260.

šꜣ (M 8) lotus pool, meadow, country (as opposed to *nỉwt* town).

šꜣ appoint, command; foll. by infin., § 303; šꜣyt dues, taxes; šꜣw extent, bulk, fate; šꜣty equivalent, equal.

Šꜣt (H 7) Shae(t), a country in the extreme south.

šꜣi (E 12), also šꜣw, pig.

šꜣꜥ begin; foll. by infin., § 303; šꜣꜥ-m beginning from, § 179; šꜣꜥ-r, also r-šꜣꜥ-r, as far as, §§ 179. 180.

šꜣbw food, meal, cf. šbw below.

šꜣmw linen to be washed.

šꜣs go, travel; Šꜣs-ḥtp Shuṭb, Hypselis, a town in Upper Egypt.

Šꜣsw Shasu, the desert region adjoining Egypt to the E.; without det., Beduin of the Shasu-desert,

šꜣd, var. šd, dig, dig out.

šꜥ cut off (heads, etc.); abbrev. šꜥt (F 41) slaughter, ferocity.

šꜥy (N 33) sand; Nmiw-šꜥ, see under nmi; Ḥryw-šꜥ, see under ḥr.

šꜥt dispatch, letter.

var. šꜥty (S 20), measure of weight and value = $\frac{1}{12}$ deben, § 266, 4.

var. šꜥd (T 30; F 41) cut off, cut up, cut down.

šwt (H 6) feather; šwty det. (S 9) double plumes.

šwi (be) empty, free, m of, from; šwt emptiness; Šw, the air-god Shu, Gk. Σῶς.

šwi (be) dry; šw det. ⊙, sun, sun-light.

šwt (S 35. 36) shadow, shade, p. 173.

šww, a herb or gourd.

šwꜣ (be) poor; det. poor man; sšwꜣ impoverish, rob, m of.

šwꜣb persea-tree; šwꜣbt(y), funerary figure later known as wšbty 'answerer', perhaps originally made of persea wood.

šbi change, alter; šbt det. × exchange, price; šbšb det. regulate, transform.

šbw food; from Pyr. wšb eat, cf. too šꜣbw above.

šbb knead (in brewing).

var. šbn (Z 9) (be) mixed, ḥr with; various.

var. det. šp (D 4. 5) (be) blind.

var. špsi (A 50. 51. 52) (be) noble, rich; trans., enrich, Dyn. XIX, § 274; šps(w) nobleman; špst det. noble lady; špsw, špssw det. riches.

špt (K 7) (be) discontented, r with.

šfw (Aa 2) swell (vb.).

šft (F 7. 8) ram's head (?).

šfyt worth, dignity; šfšfyt dignity.

šfdw (V 12) papyrus roll.

šm (N 40) go, depart, § 278.

šm(ꜣ)w (A 33) wanderers, strangers.

varr. Šmꜥw (M 26. 27; N 24) Upper Egypt; see too under 'Iwnw above; Tp -Šmꜥw, the southern end of Upper Egypt from Asyûṭ or Thebes to Elephantine; var. wr mḏw Šmꜥ(w) (M 28) greatest of the tens of Upper Egypt, a title; šmꜥ-s (S 1) the crown of Upper Egypt.

var. O.K. šmꜥ make music; var. šmꜥyt (M 26. 27) chantress, singer.

šmw summer, p. 203; det. harvest (n.).

šmm be hot; šm, var. ḫm, hot; sšmm heat (vb.).

šms (T 18) follow, accompany; *šmsw* det. follower; *šmsw* det. following, suite; *šms-wḏ3* funeral procession.

šn tree.

var. det. *šni* (V 1; Z 8) surround, encircle; varr. det. *šnw* (Z 8; V 9. 10) circuit; cartouche, p. 74; *Šn-wr*, the Ocean supposed to surround the earth; *šnwt* (A 21), var. *šnyt*, courtiers.

šni (V 1) exorcise, conjure; ask about (something); *šnt* enchantment, spell.

šnt (?), see *št* above.

šny (D 3) hair.

šnyt (N 4) rain-storm, cf. *šnʿ* below.

šnw (V 1) network, net.

šnw illness, disease.

var. *šnwt* (O 51) granary.

var. *šnʿ* (U 13. 14; E 23) repel, deter, turn back (trans.); *šnʿw* det. policing, control.

var. *šnʿ* (U 13. 14; E 23) magazine, ergastulum.

šnʿ storm-cloud, cf. *šnyt* above.

var. det. *šnbt* (G 11) breast.

šns, kind of cake or loaf.

šnty (G 31) heron.

šnṯ, later *šnt*, resent, feel hostility towards; *šnt ḫt* vent anger, *r*, *n* on (someone).

abbrev. *šndyt* (S 26) apron.

šnḏt, later *šndt*, the Nile acacia, Arab. *ṣunṭ*.

šrt (D 19) nose, nostril.

šri stop up, close.

šrr, later *šri*, (be) small; *šri* det. boy, son; *šrit* det. girl, daughter; *sšrr* diminish.

abbrev. *šs* (V 6) cord, rope.

šs (V 6) alabaster; abbrev. *šs* (W 3) vessels of alabaster, p. 172.

see under *sšr* above.

šs3w (F 5) bubalis, hartebeest.

abbrev. var. det. *šs3* (F 5. 6) (be) skilled, *m* in; *šs3w* prescription, recipe.

šsp, in M.E. possibly usually *sšp*, later *šp* (O 42. 43), receive, accept.

šsp (N 11) palm, a measure of length = $\frac{1}{7}$ cubit, § 266, 2.

šsp image, statue, sphinx.

see under *sšp* above.

šspt room, chamber.

šspt cucumber.

Šsmtt (S 17*) Shesmete(t), a goddess.

šsmt (S 17*) malachite.

šsr (T 11) arrow.

št3 (be) secret, difficult; *št3w* secret (n.); *sšt3* (be) secret; secret (n.); *ḥry sšt3* varr. (E 15. 16) over the secrets (of), introducing various titles.

štyw (I 2) turtle.

štm (be) insolent; det. abuse (someone), *n* to (someone else).

štyt (V 19), sanctuary of the god Sokar at Memphis.

šdw (F 30) water-skin, cushion.

šdi draw forth, rescue, educate; also in place of *š3d* 'dig out', see above; det. recite, read aloud.

Šdt, Medînet el-Fayyûm, Crocodilopolis;

Šdty, the Shedtite, epithet of the crocodile god Sobk.

šdw plot of ground.

šdyt mound; also *šdy*.

ḳ (N 29)

ḳꜣỉ (A 28) (be) high, tall, loud; long (of time); *ḳꜣw* height (abstract); *ḳꜣꜣ*, *ḳꜣ(y)t* det. (N 29) hill, high ground; *ḳꜣy* det. (O 41) high place; *sḳꜣỉ* raise on high, exalt.

abbrev. *ḳꜣw* (D 51) grains (?).

ḳꜣꜥ (D 26), var. *ḳꜥ*, spew out.

ḳꜣb (F 46) intestine; *m-ḳꜣb* det. in the midst of, § 178; *ḳ(ꜣ)b* double (vb.).

ḳꜣḥ earth, plaster (n.); *sḳꜣḥ* plaster (vb.).

ḳꜣs bind; string (a bow).

ḳꜣḳꜣw, a kind of boat.

ḳỉ (A 53) form, image; *mỉ ḳỉ·f* entire, § 100, 2.

varr. *Ḳỉs* (A 38. 39), later *Ḳsy*, El-Ḳuṣîyah, Cusae, a town in Upper Egypt.

ḳꜥḥ bend the arm; elbow; det. angle, corner; *ḳꜥḥt* det. district.

var. det. *ḳbb* (W 15. 16) (be) cool, calm, secure (as adj. *ḳb*); *sḳbb* cool (vb.), refresh oneself; *sḳbbwy* det. bathroom.

var. det. *ḳbḥ* (W 15. 16) libate; *ḳbḥw* libation; det. Ḳebḥ, the region of the First Cataract; *ḳbḥw* det. birds of the marshes.

ḳfn bake; det. cake, biscuit.

var. *ḳmꜣ* (T 14; G 41) throw (throw-stick); var. *ḳm(ꜣ)* (§ 279) create; nature, form.

var. *ḳmyt* (G 41) gum, resin.

ḳmd devise.

ḳnỉ (be) strong; prevail over; strong man; *ḳnt* valour; *sḳnỉ* strengthen; *ḳnḳn* det. × beat.

ḳn (Aa 8) complete, (be) complete.

ḳn (Aa 8) mat.

ḳnỉ embrace (vb. and n.); *ḳnỉw* det. (M 3) palanquin, carrying-chair.

ḳnỉ (V 19) sheaf.

ḳnbt (O 38, O.K.) corner, angle; det. magistrates; *ḳnbty* magistrate.

ḳnd (E 32) be furious, angry.

ḳrt, earlier *ḳꜣrt*, bolt (of door).

ḳrỉ cloud, storm.

ḳrr (I 7, Dyn. XX) frog.

ḳrrt cavern.

var. det. *ḳrḥt* (W 22. 23) vessel.

ḳrḥt local divinity, ancestral spirit.

ḳrs (T 19; Q 6) bury; *ḳrst* burial; *ḳrsw* coffin, sarcophagus.

ḳs (T 19. 20) bone, harpoon.

ḳsn (T 19) (be) irksome, difficult.

varr. , rarely *ḳd* (Aa 28. 29; W 24; N 33, p. 538; A 35) build, fashion (pots); *ỉḳdw* (N 33, p. 538) builders, § 272; *ḳd* form, character; *nb ḳd* the man of character, virtuous man; *mỉ ḳd·f* entire, § 100, 2; *ḥr ḳd* completely; *ḳdwt* outline (of a drawing).

ḳdd sleep, slumber (vb.); *ḳddw* sleep (n.); *nḳdd* sleep (n.); *sḳdd* cause to sleep, let sleep.

ḳdt, *kitĕ*, a weight of $\frac{1}{10}$ *deben* = 91 grammes, § 266, 4.

k (V 31)

k, in hieratic regularly written (V 31*).

·k suffix-pron. 2nd sing. m., thou, thee, thy, § 34.

·k, ending 1st sing. old perf., see *·kwỉ* below.

var. *kꜣ* non-encl. part., so, then, **§ 242**; in *kꜣ sḏm·f*, *kꜣ·f sḏm·f* (perf., § 450, 5, *d*), § 242; before *tm·f*, § 346, 5; relation to *sḏm·kꜣ·f* form, § 427.

kꜣỉ devise, think out, plan; foll. by infin., § 303; *kꜣ·f* he will say, §§ 436. 437; *kꜣt*, var. *kt*, device, thought; abbrev. *kꜣt* (A 9) work, construction; *kꜣwty* porter, workman. Cf. too *nkꜣy* above.

var. *kꜣ* (D 28. 29) soul, spirit (p. 172), mood, attribute, fortune, person(ality); see too under *ḥwt* house, *ḥm* slave.

varr. *kꜣ* (E 1; F 1) bull, ox, p. 172; *kꜣ nḫt* (E 2) victorious bull, epithet of the king, § 55.

kꜣ, var. *kꜣw*, food.

var. O.K. *kꜣp* (R 5. 6) fumigate.

abbrev. *kꜣp* harîm, nursery.

kꜣp cover (in building), *m* with.

kꜣnw (O.K.) garden; var. *kꜣny* (M 43) gardener, cf. too *kꜣry* below.

var. det. *kꜣ(r)ỉ* (O 18; V 19) chapel, shrine.

kꜣry gardener, cf. too under *kꜣnw* above.

kꜣhs (be) harsh, overbearing.

Kꜣš (f.) Cush (of the Bible), Ethiopia.

kỉ cry aloud, complain, *ḥr* about.

ky sing. m., *kt* sing. f., *kywy* plur. m., other, another, preceding noun, §§ 48, 1; **98**; do. with numeral, § 261; *wꜥ* (or *ky*) . . . . . *ky* one . . . . . other, § 98; *kt-ḫt* others, § 98.

ky monkey.

varr. *·kwỉ*, *·k*, ending 1st sing. old perf., § 309.

Kpny (R 5), older *Kbn*, Jebêl, Byblus, a coast-town in Syria.

kfỉ (S 28) uncover, despoil (someone), *ḥr* of; plunder (a place).

kfꜣ (F 22) bottom (of vase, etc.).

abbrev. *kfꜣ-ỉb* (F 22) trusty, careful.

kfꜥ capture (vb. and n.).

Kftỉw Crete.

km (I 6) black (adj.); *Kmt* the Black Land, Egypt; *Km-wr* the Bitter Lakes E. of Egypt.

km complete (vb.), be complete; completion, success; *skm* make complete.

abbrev. *kns* (F 51) pubic region.

ksỉ (A 16) bow down; *ksw* bowing down, crouching down (n.).

ksm thwart, treat defiantly.

kkw(y) (N 2) darkness.

ktt (be) small, trifling; little one.

g (W 11)

gꜣwt (V 32) bundles.

varr. det. *gꜣw* (V 32; Aa 2) lack, *r* (something), be narrow, short of breath; deprive, *m* of (breath); *gꜣt*, *gꜣw* lack, *n* of; *n-gꜣw* through lack of, § 178; *gwꜣwꜣ* det. (D 1) throttle, choke.

gbb (G 38, O.K.) white-fronted goose.

Gb, older var. *Gbb*, the earth-god Geb, Gk. Κῆβ.

Gbtỉw (V 33) Ḳifṭ, Coptus, a town in Upper Egypt.

gbꜣ (D 41) arm; det. side (of room).

gbgb fall prostrate; *gbgbyt* headlong fall.

gf, varr. *gỉf*, *gwf* (E 33), monkey.

gfn (D 19), var. *gnf*, rebuff (vb.); *gfnw* rebuff (n.).

gmt (G 28, O.K.) black ibis.

gmỉ (G 28) find; foll. by *śḏm·f* (perf., § 452, 1), § 184, 1. 2; by *śḏm·n·f*, § 185; by obj. + *śḏm·f* or *śḏm·n·f*, § 213; by obj. + *ḥr* + infin., § 304, 1; by obj. + old perf., § 315.

gmw mourning.

gmḥ espy, look at; *sgmḥ*, same sense.

gmḥt wick.

gmgm (Z 9) break up, break.

var. *gnwt* (N 33; T 19) annals; var. *gnwty* (?) sculptor.

gnf, see *gfn* above.

gnn (A 7) be soft, weak; *sgnn* soften, weaken.

gr (A 2) be silent; silence; *grw* silent, calm one; *ỉgrt*, var. *ỉwgrt* (p. 209, n. 7), the necropolis, lit. the silent one; *sgr* silence (someone); silence, quiet (n.).

grt, older *gr*, early varr. *ỉgrt*, *ỉgr*, encl. part., moreover, now, §§ 66. **255**; as adv., further, either, §§ 205, 1; 255.

grḥ (D 41) cease, *m* from; finish, *m* (something); *sgrḥ* make to cease, quell.

abbrev. *grḥ* (N 2) night.

varr. *grg* (U 17) 1. snare (vb.); 2. found, establish.

var. *grg* falsehood, lie.

varr. *gḥs* (E 29; D 56) gazelle, f. *gḥst*.

gs (Aa 13–16) side; half, § 265; *r-gs*, rarely *ḥr-gs*, beside, in the presence of, § 178; *gs(wy)·fy* its two sides, § 75, 2; *dỉ ḥr gs* 1. dispose of, kill; 2. show partiality; *gsw* neighbours; *gsw* (X 7, O.K.) half-loaves; *gs-pr* administration (?), in title *ỉmy-r gs-pr*.

var. *gs* (Aa 13) anoint, *m* with.

gsỉ run (vb.).

Gsy Ḳûṣ, Apollonos polis, a town in Upper Egypt.

gsꜣ (O 37) tilt, slant (intrans.).

var. *gstỉ* (Aa 13) palette.

ggt (V 33) kidney (?).

ggwy, var. *ggwt* (V 33), dazzled amazement, *ḥr* at.

t (X 1)

t, often replaces earlier *ṯ*, which is later sometimes written for by a false archaism, § 19, Obs. 2.

-t f. ending in nouns, adjs., and parts., etc., §§ 26. 354; in certain infins., §§ 267. 299; early lost in *status absolutus*, p. 34, n. 1[a]; p. 432, n. 4.

·t suffix-pron. 2nd sing. f., for earlier *·ṯ*, thou, thee, thy, § 34.

t formative in *śḏmty·fy* form, § 363; in *śḏmt·f* form, § 401.

-t summary writing for *·tỉ* in old perf., see *·tỉ* below.

t, see under *ỉt* above.

varr. *t* (X 1. 2. 4) bread; *t-ḥḏ* (M 44, p. 538) white bread.

tꜣ this, the, sing. f., § 110; construction of, § 111; meanings of, § 112; *tꜣy·ỉ* poss. adj. sing. f., my; so too *tꜣy·k*, *tꜣy·f*, etc., § 113, 1; *tꜣ* for *tn-t* she of, § 111, Obs.

varr. , — etc., *tꜣ* (N 16. 17) earth, land; *tꜣwy* the two lands, i.e. Egypt; *tꜣw* lands (as opposed to *ḫꜣswt* deserts), countries; var. *Tꜣ-wr* (R 17. 18), the nome of Abydus and This; *Tꜣ-nṯr* God's Land, generic term for foreign tribute-producing lands, esp. in N.E. and S.E.; *Tꜣ-š* Lake-land, i.e. the Fayyûm; *Tꜣ-mri*, *Tꜣ-mḥw*, *Tꜣ-ḏsr*, see under *mri*, *mḥw*, *ḏsr*; *diw r tꜣ* putting (lit. it was put) to land.

Tꜣ-ṯnn Tatjenen, a Memphite earth-god.

tꜣ (U 30, O.K.) kiln.

tꜣ (Q 7) (be) hot.

tꜣ (O 16. 17, Dyn. XIX), var. *tꜣyt*, curtain; *Tꜣyt* Taye(t), the goddess of weaving; *tꜣty* he of the curtain, epithet of the vizier; var. *Tꜣ-wr* (O 17; S 22) larboard.

tꜣš (Z 9) boundary.

tit (U 33) pestle (?).

varr. *·ti*, *-t*, endings 2nd sing. c., 3rd sing. f. old perf., § 309.

writing for *-t*, f. ending in perf. rel. form, §§ 380. 387, 1. 2; Add., p. 426; in *śḏmt·f* form, § 409.

var. *ti*, non-encl. part. with same sense as *isṯ*, §§ 119, 4; **243**; in sent. with adv. pred., § 119, 4; in virt. cls. of time with vb. pred., § 212; in pseudo-verbal construction, § 324.

tiw interj., yes, § 258.

var. *tit* (V 39, p. 508) the *tyet*-amulet.

abbrev. *tit* (D 17) figure, image.

tisw stick (n.).

ti-šps, a tree and a spice.

var. det. *titi* crush, trample down.

var. *·tiwny* ending 2nd plur. c. old perf., § 309.

tw later form of *ṯw*, dep. pron., see *ṯw* below.

tw indef. pron., one, Fr. *on*, §§ 39. 47; after various particles, § 47; uses, § 47, Obs.; as subj. to *r* + infin., § 333; appended to infin. as subj., p. 230, n. 6; in anticipatory emphasis before *śḏm·tw*, unique ex., Add. to § 148, 1, p. 424; forming pass. of *śḏm·f*, § 39; of *śḏm·n·f*, § 67; of other forms of suffix conjugation, § 410; in supposed pass. of rel. forms, § 388; in *ḫr·tw śḏm·tw·f*, § 239; in *kꜣ·tw śḏm·tw·f*, § 242; in *ḫr·tw* one says, § 436; treated as m., § 511, 5.

tw this (obsolescent), sing. f., § 110; construction of, § 111; meaning of, § 112; *twy*, later form of *tw*, §§ 110–13.

tw·i, *tw·k*, etc., pron. compound, § 124.

twꜣ (A 30) claim, obj. (something), *n* from (someone); det. poor man, inferior.

twꜣ support (vb.), support oneself.

twr (T 19) reed (?).

tw(r)i (T 19) be pure.

twr show respect, obj. or *ḥr* for, cf. too *tr* below.

twt (A 53) 1. (be) like, *n* (someone); statue; *stwt* make resemble, *r* (someone, something); 2. (be) fair, appropriate; 3. be assembled.

tp (D 1) head, chief; beginning (of year, season, morning); *tp nfr* good beginning; *ḥry-tp* chief, chieftain; *tp* det. with numeral, *x* persons; *tp-ḥr-mꜣst*, *tp-r*, *tp-rd*, *tp-ḥsb*, see under *mꜣst*, etc.; *r-tp*, *r-tp-ꜥ* into presence of, § 178; *ḥr-tp* on behalf of, § 178; *tp-m* in front of, in the direction of, § 179; [hieroglyph] *tp* prep., upon, § 173; *tp-mꜣꜥ* accompanying, § 178; [hieroglyph] *tp-ꜥ* conj., before, § 181; [hieroglyph], [hieroglyph] *tpy* (T 8) who, which, is upon, § 80; first, § 263; first (month), § 264; [hieroglyph] *tpyw-ꜥ* those of former times, the ancestors; [hieroglyph] *tpyw-tꜣ* those upon earth, the living; [hieroglyph] *tpt* first quality oil.

[hieroglyph] *tpi* (D 19) sniff, breathe in.

[hieroglyph] *tpḥt*, O.K. *tpḥt*, var. [hieroglyph] *ḥtpt*, cavern, hole (of snake, Nile).

[hieroglyph] *tf*, also [hieroglyph] *tfꜣ*, that (yonder), sing. f., § 110; construction of, § 111; meaning of, § 112.

[hieroglyph], see under [hieroglyph] *it* father.

[hieroglyph] *tfn* orphan.

[hieroglyph] *Tfnt*, the goddess Tefēne(t), Gk. -θφηνις, p. 435.

[hieroglyph] *tmt* (U 15) sledge.

[hieroglyph], see under *'Itm*.

[hieroglyph] *tm* (U 15) be complete, perfect, be closed, § 342; old perf., complete, § 317; *tmw* det. [hieroglyph] the totality (of mankind).

[hieroglyph] *tm* negative vb., §§ **342–4**; **346–50**; nature and origin, § 342; uses analogous to those of *wnn*, § 346, end; position of subj., § 343; foll. by infin. replacing earlier negative complement, § 344; *śḏm·f* or *śḏm·n·f* form of, in main clauses, § 346; in questions for specification, §§ 346, 1; 495, end; in double negatives, § 346, 3; after *iḫ*, § 346, 4; after *kꜣ*, § 346, 5; in subordinate cls., § 347; virt. noun cls., as obj., § 347, 1; as pred. of *pw*, § 347, 2; virt. cls. of time and condition, § 347, 3; of purpose, § 347, 4; after preps., § 347, 5; in *śḏmt·f* form after preps., § 408; after *ir* 'if', § 347, 6; as negation of infin., § 348; in parts., *śḏmty·fy* form and rel. forms, § 397; in pass. *śḏm·f* form, § 424, 2; in *śḏm·ḫr·f* form, § 432; summary, § 350.

[hieroglyph] var. [hieroglyph] *tm* (O 38) in obscure title *ḥry tm*.

[hieroglyph] var. [hieroglyph] *tmꜣ* (from *ṯmꜣ*?, V 19; Aa 6) mat.

[hieroglyph] *tn* this, sing. f., § 110; construction of, § 111; meaning of, § 112; see too *ṯn* below.

[hieroglyph] *tn* dep. pron., later form of [hieroglyph] *ṯn*, see *ṯn* below.

[hieroglyph] *·tn* suffix-pron. and dep. pron., later form of [hieroglyph] *·ṯn*, see *ṯn* below.

[hieroglyph] *t-nt* she of, § 111, Obs.; see too *tꜣ* above.

[hieroglyph] *tn*, [hieroglyph] *tnw*, see *ṯn*, *ṯnw* below.

[hieroglyph] *tni* (A 19) (be) old, decrepit.

[hieroglyph] *tnbḫ* shrink, recoil.

[hieroglyph] *tnm* go astray; *stnm* lead astray.

[hieroglyph] *tnm* beer-jug.

[hieroglyph] varr. det. [hieroglyph], [hieroglyph] *tr* (M 4. 5. 6) season, time.

[hieroglyph] *tr*, varr. [hieroglyph], [hieroglyph] *ty*, encl. part., forsooth, I suppose, § **256**; in questions, pray, § 491, 3; see too *ptr* above.

[hieroglyph] *tr* (A 30), var. [hieroglyph] *t(r)i* (§ 279), show respect for, awe of, cf. *twr* above; *sḏfꜣ tryt*, see under *ḏfꜣ* below.

[hieroglyph] *thi* (D 56) wander, transgress, disobey (command); cause to wander.

[hieroglyph] *tḥnt*, see *ṯḥnt* below.

[hieroglyph] *tḫ* (U 41) plummet.

[hieroglyph] *tḫi* (W 22) be drunken; *tḫw* drunkard.

[hieroglyph] *tḫb* immerse, soak.

[hieroglyph] abbrev. [hieroglyph] *tḫn* (O 25) obelisk.

[hieroglyph] *tši* be missing, stray, *r* from.

[hieroglyph] *tšꜣ*, var. [hieroglyph] *tš*, smash, crush.

[hieroglyph] *tkꜣ* (Q 7) torch.

tkn (be) near, *m* to; approach, obj. (someone); *stkn* bring near.

tks pierce, penetrate.

tkk attack, violate (frontier).

ṯ (V 13)

ṯ, often original of M.E. *t*; sometimes written for the latter as a spurious archaism, § 19, Obs. 2; form with tick (V 14) found sometimes in hieratic and hieroglyphic of Dyn. XI in words where the old value *ṯ* persisted.

·ṯ, later *·t*, suffix-pron. 2nd sing. f., thou, thee, thy, § 34.

var. *ṯt* table (for food).

ṯꜣ (G 47) nestling, child.

ṯꜣ (N 33) pellet.

abbrev. *ṯꜣw* (P 5), wind, air, breath; *ḥt-ṯꜣw*, see under *ḥt*.

ṯꜣy (D 53) man, male.

ṯꜣt(y) vizier, p. 43, n. 2.

ṯꜣỉ 1. take, gird on; 2. rob; *ṯꜣwt* theft.

ṯꜣbt loan (of corn).

ṯꜣm be veiled; *ṯꜣm ḥr n* show indulgence to (someone); *mṯꜣm* det. clinging dress (for girls); det. foreskin.

ṯꜣr (Aa 19) fasten, make fast; *ṯꜣrt* det. cabin.

ṯw, later *tw*, dep. pron. 2nd sing. m., thou, thee, § 43; *ṯwt* old indep. pron. do., used very rarely also for f., § 64, with Obs.

var. Pyr. *ṯbt* (S 33), later *tbt*, sole (of foot), sandal; *ṯb* be shod; *ṯbw* sandal-maker.

ṯmꜣ-ꜥ with powerful arm, epithet of Horus or king.

varr. *ṯmꜣ* (V 19; Aa 6) cadaster (?); kind of land (?).

Ṯmḥ (O.K.), var. *Tmḥw*, Libyan(s).

ṯms (Y 3, Pyr.) red; *tmsw* hurt, injury.

ṯn, spurious archaistic writing for *tn*, sing. f., this, see *tn* above.

ṯn, later *tn*, dep. pron. 2nd sing. f., thou, thee, § 43; very rarely used for suffix-pron. *ṯ*, § 43, Obs. 2.

·ṯn, later *·tn*, suffix-pron. and dep. pron. 2nd pl. c., you, your, §§ 34. 43; rare var. as dep. pron. *twṯn*, § 43, Obs. 2; *·ṯny* dual, early obsolete, you, your, § 34.

Ṯny, This, town near Girga in Upper Egypt.

ṯnỉꜣ (T 14, O.K.) throw-stick (?).

ṯn, var. *tn*, where ?, whence ?, § 503; *r ṯn* whither ?.

ṯnỉ (T 14; G 41), later *tnỉ*, raise up, distinguish, *r* over (others), *ḫnt* out of (a number); *sṯnỉ*, almost synonymously; *ṯnt* distinction, difference.

ṯnw, later *tnw*, number (n.); foll. by noun, each, every, § 101; *r-tnw-sp* every time that, foll. by *śḏm·f*, § 181; *tnw*, do., see Add. p. xxviii; *ṯnwt* number (n.).

Ṯnnt Tjenene(t), goddess worshipped at Hermonthis.

ṯnṯꜣt, rare var. *ṯntt* (Aa 11), baldachin, raised platform for throne.

ṯrp, species of goose.

ṯḥn draw near (to fight), *ḥnꜥ* with.

(S 15. 16. 17, O.K.), later *ṯḥnt*, var. *ṯḥnt*, fayence, glass.

Ṯḥnw (T 14; N 18) Libya; *Ṯḥnw* Libyans.

ṯḥḥ exult; *ṯḥw*, *ṯḥḥwt* exultation, § 287.

ṯst (S 24) knot, vertebra; *ṯs*, var. Pyr. *ṯz*, tie, bind, arrange; *ṯs skw*, see under *skỉ*; *ṯs* saying, utterance; *ṯsw* det. commander; *ṯst* det. hill.

var. det. *ṯsỉ* (V 14; U 39. 40) raise, lift, recruit (vb.); rise, mount (vb.); *ṯsỉ m* feel resentment at, blame; *ṯswt* det. complaints; see too *wṯs*, *sṯsw* above.

ṯsm (E 14) hound.

var. det. *ṯtf* overflow, pour forth.

ṯṯt (V 13, Pyr.) fetterer (?).

d (D 46)

d, often replaces earlier *ḏ*, § 19.

hand, to be read *ḏrt*, see there.

var. *dꜣt* (*dwꜣt*, N 14. 15) netherworld.

var. *dꜣỉw* (N 18, p. 507) loin-cloth.

dꜣb (M 43) figs.

dꜣỉ(r) (T 12; § 279), abbrev. , originally *dꜣr*, subdue, suppress.

, *dỉ*, see under *rdỉ* above.

dyt, see under *wꜣḏ*.

dỉwt a set of five, § 260; *d(ỉw)t* field-labourers.

dỉwt var. *dyt* shriek, cry (n.), cf. *ḏwỉ* below; later is here replaced by (V 11).

dwꜣ morning, to-morrow; rise early, *r* + infin. to do (something), § 163, 10; *dwꜣyt*, var. *dwꜣt* (N 14), morning; var. det. *dwꜣ* (A 30. 4) adore (deity) in the morning; *dwꜣwt* adorations; *dwꜣ nṯr* praise (i.e. thank) god, *n* for (someone).

dwn stretch out.

dws, see *ḏws* below.

db (E 25) hippopotamus.

dbỉ stop up, block (vb.); cf. *ḏbꜣ* below.

var. *dbn* (F 46) go round; *dbnw* circle, circuit; , also with , *dbn* (O 39; F 48) *deben*-weight, of about 91 grammes, § 266, 4.

dbḥ beg for, request (vb.); *dbḥw* request (n.), requirement; *dbḥt-ḥtp* the requisite offerings, full *menu* of offerings.

dp (F 20) taste (vb.); *dpt* taste (n.).

Dp Dep, part of the Delta town of Buto.

dpt ship, boat; *dpt-nṯr* (P 1) god's ship, divine bark.

dpy crocodile.

dm (T 30) (be) sharp; det. *dm* pronounce, *rn* name (of someone); *dmt* abbrev. knife.

dmꜣ (M 36. 38) bind together.

dmỉ (§ 270, Obs.) touch, arrive at; accrue, *r* to; det. abode, town; *sdmỉ* attach, annex (one place), *n* to (another).

dmd (S 23), O.K. *dmḏ*, unite; old perf., entire (§ 317); var. abbrev. (Y 1) total (n.).

dn cut off (heads, etc.).

dnỉ (V 11) dam off, restrain; *dnỉt* det. dam (n.); for see under *dỉwt*.

dnḥ (H 5), O.K. *ḏnḥ*, wing.

dns (U 32) (be) heavy; *dns-ỉb* reticent.

dr remove, quell, drive out.

drp (D 39) offer food, *n* to; feed (someone).

drf (Aa 10) writing (n.).

dhnt (D 1) forehead; *dhn tꜣ* touch

ground with forehead; *dhn* promote (someone), *r* to (a rank).

dḥ (be) low, lowly; *sdḥ* det. bring low.

dḥr (be) bitter; det. (F 27) hide, leather.

ds (W 22) beer-jug, beer-measure, § 266, 1.

ds (T 30) knife; det. flint.

dšr (G 27; Add. p. xxviii) flamingo.

dšr (G 27) (be) red; *dšrt* det. the Red land, the desert; det. and abbrev. (S 3), the red crown of Lower Egypt; det. (W 11. 13) red pot.

dḳr (D 51) press (?), move, expel.

abbrev. *dḳrw* (D 51) fruit.

var. det. *dg* (A 4) hide (trans. and intr.); *sdg*, var. *sdg(ꜣ)*, hide oneself, *r* from; conceal (*r* from); det. hidden place or thing.

var. det. *dgi* (D 4. 5) look, *n* at; see.

, *Ddw*, see *Ḏdw* below.

Ddwn Dedwen, a Nubian god.

ḏ (I 10)

ḏ, often original of M.E. *d*; sometimes written for the latter as a spurious archaism, § 19, Obs. 2.

ḏt body, self; *ip ḏt·f*, see under *ip* above; *n ḏt·f* his own.

ḏt (N 17) estate; det. serf(s), cf. *nḏt* above.

ḏt (N 17) eternity.

ḏꜣ (U 28) fire-drill.

ḏꜣ stretch forth, (arm).

ḏꜣi ferry across (trans. and intr.); *ḏꜣi tꜣ* () *r* interfere with, lit. cross land to; *r-ḏꜣt* in return for, corresponding to, § 180; *ḏꜣt*, var. *ḏꜣyt*, transgression, wrong.

ḏꜣy-ḥr divert onself, amuse oneself; *sḏꜣy-ḥr*, same sense.

ḏꜣt, see under *wḏꜣ* above.

ḏꜣis contend, *ḥnꜥ* with; *ḏꜣisw* disputant.

ḏꜣis, an unidentified plant.

ḏꜣmw youths, troops, generations.

varr. det. , *ḏꜣrw* need, requirement.

Ḏꜣhy Djahy, a name for Phoenicia.

possible varr. , *ḏꜣtt* (?) (Aa 8; O 49) estate.

ḏꜣdw (O 27) hall of audience.

abbrev. *ḏꜣḏꜣ* (D 1) head.

ḏꜣḏꜣw (W 24) pot.

ḏꜣḏꜣt (Aa 8) magistrates, assessors.

ḏꜣḏꜣt harp.

ḏꜥ (M 3, n. 5) spear (vb.), harpoon (fish).

ḏꜥ (P 5) storm.

ḏꜥbt charcoal.

var. det. *ḏꜥm* (S 40. 41) *djam*-sceptre, of spiral shape.

varr. , *ḏꜥm* (S 40. 41. 12. 14*) fine gold.

var. det. *ḏꜥr* (T 14; M 3) seek, search out.

ḏw (N 26) mountain.

ḏw (be) bad, evil; sad (of heart); *ḏwt* evil, sadness.

ḏwi call (someone); cf. too *ḏiwt* above.

ḏws, var. *dws*, malign (someone), *n* to (another).

ḏbt (G 22) brick.

ḏbꜣw (T 25) floats.

db3 (T 25) 1. clothe, adorn; 2. var. *db3* replace; *r-db3* instead of, § 180; *db3w* payment, bribe.

db3 stop up, block (vb.), cf. *dbi* above.

Db3 Edfu, Apollonos polis, a town in Upper Egypt.

db‘ (D 50) finger; finger-breadth, as measure = $\frac{1}{28}$ cubit, § 266, 2; *db‘t* (S 20) signet-ring; *db‘w* reproach, lit. a finger-pointing.

db‘ 10,000, § 259; construction of, § 262.

var. *df(3)* (G 42) provisions; *ḥtpt-df(3)*, see under *ḥtp* above; *sdf3* equip with provisions, provide, *m* with; *sdf3 tryt* ( ) swear.

dfd (D 12) pupil (of eye).

dnd (F 2) rage (vb. and n.).

rare var. *drt* (D 46. 47), also *d3t*, hand; trunk (of elephant); *st-drt* the way to act, how to handle things.

dr (M 36) end, aux. vb. foll. by old perf. § 316; by *śdm·n·f*, § 483, 1; as adv., at an end, § 205, 1; *drw* end, limit (n.); *ini drw* reach boundary (of a country); *r-dr·f* entire, § 100, 1; *nb-r-dr*, see under *nb* above; *dr-‘* end (n.); as adv., originally, long ago, § 205, 3; *dr-‘-r* right down to, § 179; *dr* prep., since; as conj., since, before, until, **§ 176**; *dr-ntt* since, because, § 223; *drtyw* those of yore, the ancestors.

dr, later var. *d(r)i(t)*, wall, enclosure wall (?).

dri (L.E.) (be) hard, firm; adv. (Dyn. XVIII) hard, stoutly.

drw side (of body, chariot, etc.).

drwy colour (n.).

late var. *drd* (F 21) leaf (of tree).

drdri foreigner, foreign.

varr. , , *Dḥwty* (G 26; C 3; X 2) the ibis-god Thoth, Gk. Θωύθ.

ds· with suffix-pron., -self, by (him-)self, § 36.

dsr (D 45) set apart, clear (a road); be private, holy; *dsr ḥpt*, see under *ḥpt*; *T3-dsr* the Sacred Land, i.e. the necropolis; *dsrw* privacy.

dd say, think; foll. by *śdm·f*, § 184; by infin., § 303; abbrev. in , see under *mdw*; *m dd* namely, as follows, § 224; *r dd* (saying) that, § 224; *ddw n·f* called, introducing second name (m.), f. *ddt n·s*; *sdd* det. relate, converse, *ḥn‘* with.

dd (R 11) *djed*-column.

ddi (be) stable, enduring; abbrev. *ddt* stability, duration.

Ddt Tell er-Rub‘a, Mendes, a Delta town.

Ddw, varr. , *Ddw* (§ 289, 1), Abuṣîr Banâ, Busiris, a Delta town.

var. det. *dd3* (Aa 2) (be) fat.

ddb sting, incite.

ddft (I 14) snake.

ddḥ imprison.

Words of Doubtful Reading

(D 4) eyes, see under *irt*.

(D 23) three-quarters, see under *ḫmt*.

(F 45; N 41) vulva, see under *idt*.

(M 23) be king, see under *nsw*.

(N 13) half-month festival.

(N 34) copper, see under *bi3* and *ḥmt*.

(O 35) in quest of, see under *sb-tw*.

(S 19) treasurer, see under *sd3yt*.

(T 19) sculptor, see under *gnwt*.

var. (Aa 8; N 24) estate, see under *d3tt*.

ENGLISH-EGYPTIAN VOCABULARY

For the restricted scope of this Vocabulary see the Preface to the Second Edition, p. vii.

A

A, omitted, § 21; later § 262, 1.
abandon var.
abide ,
able, be foll. by *śdm·f*, § 184, 1.
abomination
about § 165, 7.
above § 79.
absence: in the — of § 178.
absent oneself
abundant
Abydus
accept
accompany
accompanying § 178; § 178; one who accompanies
accordance: in — with § 169, 2; § 170, 2; § 180.
according as § 163, 11 (*d*); § 170, 5 (*b*); § 169, 6 (*b*).
according to § 170, 2; § 169, 2.
accordingly § 205, 1; § 205, 1.
accurate, be
accusation
accuse
acquainted: become — with
act
added to § 165, 8.
addition: in — to § 178.
address
adore
adorn , ; be —ed,
advantageous, be
adversary ,
adze
affair: state of —s
after § 178; , , § 178; § 165, 10.
afterwards § 205, 2.
again ; § 263.
against § 163, 9.
age: old —
aged ,
aggressive, be
agreeable, be
alabaster var.
alight (vb.)
all
allow var. ; var.
alone, be
also var. § 205, 1.
altar
among § 174, 2; § 178.
amount
amulet var.
Amūn
amuse oneself
amusement
an, omitted, § 21; later § 262, 1.
ancestors
and, omitted, §§ 30; 91, 1; §§ 91, 1; 165, 8; §§ 91, 1; 171, 2.
anew
angry, be , ,
annals
announce ,
anoint ,
another m., f., § 98.

answer
antiquity
Anubis
anxious: be — about
any § 48, 1.
anyone, after negation, § 102.
anything §§ 92, 2; 103; § 103.
apart from var. § 179.
appear
appearance in glory
appoint
apprehension
approach
apron
are §§ 29. 117.
arise
arm
army var.
around § 172, 2.
aroura var.
arrow
as § 162, 6. 11; — well — § 170, 3; — when § 170, 5 (*a*).
ascend var.
Asia
Asiatic var. ; —s
ask ; — for
ass
assent (vb.) var.
assessors
assuredly §§ 119, 6; 236; § 253.
Asyûṭ
at, of time § 163, 3; of place § 165, 1.
at all § 205, 1.
attach
attack
attend to
attendant
Atum var.
audience chamber
authority: under the — of § 178.
avaunt (from) § 313.
axe

B

Baboon
back
bad
baker
balance ; (of accounts)
bald
bandage (vb.) var. ; (vb. and n.).
bank (of river)
barge
bark, sacred
barley
basket
Baste(t)
battlefield
be § 107; — not § 342.
beam, wooden
bear (a child) var.
beat
beautiful
beauty var.
because § 164, 9; § 165, 11; § 223.
because of § 165, 7; § 178.
become
Beduins
bee
beer
beer-jug § 266, 1.
beetle
before (prep.) § 178; § 178; § 178; § 179; § 181.
before (adv.) § 205, 1; § 205, 2.

beg

beget

begin

beginning from § 179.

behalf: on — of § 178.

behind § 172, 1.

behold , , § 234.

behold (vb.) , ,

belly

belonging to §§ 86; 114, 1. 2; he belongs to § 114, 2; belongs to me, thee, etc. , § 114, 4; var. ; § 114, 3; what belongs to someone or something

belongings ,

bend ; — the arm

beneath § 166.

beneficent

beneficial, be

bequeath var.

beside (near) , , § 178.

besides § 179; § 178.

besprinkle

best, the

between ; also , § 177; between .... and .... § 180.

beware (lest) §§ 184; 338, 3; , § 313; , § 338, 3.

beweep

bind: — (things) , ; — (person) ; — together

bird

birth ; give —

bite (vb.)

bitter

black, be

Black Land, i.e. Egypt

blind, be

block up ,

blood

boasting

boat ; without a —

body , ; — of men

bolt

bone

book ,

boon: a — which the king gives p. 170.

booth

born to, m. , f. § 361.

bottom ,

boundary

bow (n.) ,

bow down var. ,

bowman

box , , varr. ,

brand (vb.)

brave, be

bread

breadth ,

break var. ;

breast , ,

breath

breathe ,

brewer var.

brick

brigand

bright, be

brightness

brilliance

bring § 289, 3; ; — nigh

brink

broad, be

bronze var.

brother

brow

bud

build var. ;

bull varr. , p. 172; fighting —
bulwark
burden (vb.) var.
burden (n.)
burn
bury
bush
business
but (prep.) § 179.
but (encl. part.) § 254.
butler ,
by (of agent) §§ 39. 168; §§ 39. 167, 3; — (of measurement) § 163, 5; — means of § 162, 7.
Byblus

C

Cake , ; —s
calculate ,
calf
call , ,
called (of names), m. f. § 377, 1.
canal
candle
capture
care: in the — of
careful var.
careless, be
carpenter (vb.)
carry ,
carrying § 166.
carve
case: is it the — that....? , [§ 494.
castle
cat
catch ; — fish
cattle
cauldron var.
cause , § 70.
cavern ,
cease , , , ; make to — [
cedar (properly 'pine')
centipede
cessation
chamber ; audience —
channel
chantress var.
chapel ,
character: good — ,
charge ; in the — of , § 178; [
chariot
charm
chattels
chatter (vb.)
chief (adj.) var. ;
chief (n.), chieftain , , ,
child var. ; ; ;
childhood
chisel var.
Chnum var.
choicest, the
choose
circuit
circulate ,
cistern
city
clay
clean, be
clear: — (a canal) ; — (the road)
clever ,
close
closed, be
cloth ,
clothe , ; — oneself
clothes
clothing var.
cobra
coffin
collar var.

collect
column ; hall of —s var.
come § 289, 2; as imper. var. § 336.
comfortable: make oneself —
coming forth (n.)
command
commander
common people
commoner
Companion, Sole (title)
company: in the — of § 178.
complete, be
complete (adj.) § 100;
completion [§ 317.
complexion
conceal
conceive
concern (n.)
concerning § 165, 7; (speak) — § 163, 6.
condition ; be in good — var.
confine
consisting of § 162, 5.
constrict
construct
construction
content, be
control (vb.) var. ;
controller var.
conversant, be
converse
convey by water
cook
cool: be — ; make —
cool (adj.)
copper
Coptus
copulate
copy (n.)
cord
corn
corps
corpse
corresponding to § 169, 4.
council
counsel ; take —
count
country var. ; ; foreign —
court (in temple or palace)
courtier var. ; —s
cow ; —s
cowardly, be
craft
craftsmanship
create var.
Crete
crew
crime
crocodile
cross
crown: — of Osiris ; blue — ; — of Upper Egypt var. ; ; ; — of Lower Egypt var. ; ; the double — [var.
crush
cry (n.)
cry out
cubit § 266, 2.
cultivate
cultivated lands var.
curb
curse
Cusae varr.
Cush
custom (f.).
cut: — off ; — down (trees) var.

D

Dagger
daily
dam
dam off
damage (vb.)
damage (n.)
dance (vb.)
dance (n.)
dappled var.
darkness
daughter
dawn (vb.)
day var. ; ; (in dates) pl. ; pass the —
day-time , var.
dazzling, be
dead var.
deaf ,
death var. ; ;
deben, a weight of 91 grammes, var. § 266, 4.
decease
deed
deep, be
defeat
defective var.
delay var. § 352.
deliver (in child-birth)
Delta
demolish
Denderah
depart
department
departure
depth
deputy
descend
desert , ,
desire (vb.) , ,
destine
destroy , , , ,
determine §§ 184, 1; 303.
device
devise
dew var.
diadem
die var.
difference
difficult ,
dig
dignitary var. ;
dignity
dim, be
diminish
disaffected
disagreeable, be
discreet
disease ,
disk (of sun)
disobedient, be
disobey
dispatch (n.)
dispel
dispose of (kill)
distinguish ,
district , var.
divide , ,
divine: be —
diwân
do ; — not § 345; — not (imper.) § 340; have —ne in the past § 484.
doctor
dog ,
domain , ,
donkey
door , , ; double —s

door-keeper
double (vb.)
down: — to , , § 179; go —
downstream: fare —
drag , var.
dragoman var.
draw nigh , , ,
dread
dream
drink
drive: — away ; — out
drown
drunken, be
duck
due (n.)
durability var.
duty
dwell

E

Each var. § 101; — one , § 103.
ear var. ; —s
earlier (adv.) § 205, 1.
earth
Earth-god
east
eastern
eat varr. , ,
ebony
edge
educate
efficient
egg
Egypt , ; Upper — var. ; Lower — var.
elder var. ; — of the portal var.
elephant
Elephantine var.
embalm ,
embalmer
embrace ,
emit (sound)
emmer
empty, be
empty out (*ḥt* body)
encircle var.
enclose ,
encounter
end (vb.) §§ 316; 483, 1.
end (n.) ,
endow
endue
endure ,
enduring
enemy , ,
engendered by, m. , f. § 361.
enjoyment, have
ennead
enter
entire , , § 100.
entirely var. § 205, 1.
envelop ,
envious
environment
envoy
equal
equip , ,
erect (vb.)
ergastulum var.
establish , ; be —ed
estate , , ; (property)
eternally ,
eternity ; var.
Ethiopia
evening

evening meal
evening bark of the sun-god
everlasting (n.)
every
everybody , , § 103.
everyone , , § 103.
everything § 103.
evil: be ; — one
evil (n.) , ,
exact, be
exaggeration
examine , ; — (a patient) var.
excavate
exceedingly § 205, 5.
excellent , ,
except § 179; § 178; § 178; § 178.
excess ; in — of § 178.
exchange: in — for § 178.
excrement
exist §§ 107; 118, 2.
exorcise
expect
expedition (military) ,
explain
extend ,
extinguish
extol ,
extract
exultation
eye ; sound — of Horus ; —-paint
eyebrows [

F

Face
failing (n.)
faint
fall ; — into (decay, etc.)
falsehood

family ,
fan
far: be — , ; as — as § 179; § 180.
fare: (upon river) ; northwards
fare upstream, southwards
fashion (vb.) ,
fat (adj.)
father , ; — of the god, a priestly [title, var.
fatten
fault ,
favour (vb.)
favour (n.) , ,
fayence var.
fear (vb.)
fear (n.) , ; through — of [§ 181.
feather
feeble, be
feed (trans.)
femur
ferry across
ferry-boat
festal, make
festival var.
fetch
few § 99.
field , , var.
fight
figs
figure
fill
find
fine linen
finger ; (as measure) § 266, 2.
finger-nail
fire , var. ; —-drill
firm, be ,
firmament
first var. §§ 80; 263, 1.

fish
fisherman
flagellum var.
flagstaff
flame ,
fledgling
flee , ,
flesh ,
flint
flock
flourish ,
flourishing
flower
fly (vb.) ,
fly (n.)
follow ; — upon (road) ; as —s § 224.
follower
following (n.)
following after § 178.
food , , ,
fool
foot
for § 164, 2; § 165, 7.
forasmuch as § 223.
forehead ,
foreign country
foreigner ,
foreleg (of ox)
foremost var. § 80.
foretell
forget
forgetful, be
forgive
form (vb.) ,
form (n.) , , , ; —s
formerly , , , , § 205,2.
forsake var.
forsooth varr. , §§ 256; 491, 3.
fortification
fortress var. ;
fortunate ,
foster
found ,
foundation
fowl var.
fowler
fraction § 265.
fraternize
free
fresh, be , var.
friend ; — (of the king) var.
from § 162, 8; § 178; § 163, 8; § 165, 2. 3; § 174, 3.
front ; in — of , , § 178; § 169, 1; § 174, 1; , § 178; § 178; § 179.
fruit var. ; vegetables and — [var.
full, be
fuller
fumigate
furious, be
furnish ,
further varr. , § 239.

G

Gallon § 266, 1.
garden ,
gardener var.
garland
gate ,
gather together ,
gazelle
Geb
gentle, be
gifts var.

give var. ; var. § 289, 1; as imper. § 336; —n life § 378.
glad, be
gladden ; (with tidings)
gladness ,
glass var.
glorify
glorious, be
go , , ; (imper.) ; — down ; — forth ; — round , ; — to rest ; — up ; — well with § 141; let — ; cause to — up ; one who —es after
goats
god var.
goddess
gold ; fine —
good, be
good (n.)
goose , ,
government
gracious, be varr. ,
granary
granite var.
grapes
grasp (vb.)
grasshopper
great, be ,
greatly § 205, 4; § 205, 5.
green, be
greet
grey-haired
grind
ground (n.)
grow
guard (vb.) var.
guide
gum

H

Ha (interj.) §§ 87. 258.
Ḥa, god of the desert
habit
habitation
hail (interj.) § 258.
hair ,
half § 265.
hall ; ; — of columns
hand var. ; in the — of § 178.
hand over var.
hang up
happen
happily § 205, 4.
happy, be ,
Ḥarakhte
hard stone
harîm varr. , ; ;
harm , var.
harp
harsh, be
haste thee
hasten
hate var.
have, §§ 114–15.
he § 34; § 43; § 64; § 64; § 128.
head , ; back of — ; —-band ; be at the — of
head-rest
health
healthy, be
heaps ,
hear
hearken to
heart ,
heat
heaven ,
heavy ,
heed var.

height ; (hill)
heir
Ḥeḳe(t), goddess
Heliopolis
helper
her , § 34; , § 43; § 113, 1.
Heracleopolis
herb
herd , ,
herdsman varr. ,
here § 205, 1.
heritage
Hermopolis ,
heron
hers, of § 113, 3.
hew: — (stones)
hey (interj.) § 258.
hide (vb.) , ,
hide (n.) ,
high ; —-priest
hill
hill-country
hill-side
him § 34; § 43.
hin, a liquid measure, § 266, 1.
hind-quarters
hippopotamus
his § 34; § 113, 1; § 113, 3.
Hittite land
ho (interj.)
hold fast
holding § 166, 2; — of land
holiday , var.
holy, be
honey
honour (vb.)
honoured
hoof
horizon ; belonging to the — § 79.
horn var. ;
horse ; pair of —s
Horus
hot, be ,
hot breath
hound
hour var.
house ,
how (with adj.) § 49.
how? (interrog.) § 496; — much?
§ 502.
however § 254.
Ḥu
humble: man of — birth ; this thy — servant p. 58, n. 1.
hundred §§ 259. 261; — thousand § 259.
hunger (n.)
hungry, be
hunter: hippopotamus-—
hurt (vb.)
husband var.

I

I § 34; § 43; § 64; § 124.
ibex var.
ibis
idle, be
idol
if, omitted, § 216; §§ 150. 151; — not
§ 216, end.
ignorant, be ,
ill, be ,
image , , ; divine — var.
immediately , § 205, 3.
important
imprison
in § 162; being — § 79.

inasmuch as § 223; , § 181.
incense
incite
incline
indeed § 227; , § 249; § 247; § 253.
indict
inhabitants
inherit
inheritance
iniquity
initiated, be
inquire ; — after the health of
inspection
instead of § 180.
instruction
interior
interpret
introduce , var.
inundated, be , var.
inundation ; — -season var.
irksome, be ,
is §§ 29. 117.
Isis
island
it (m.) § 34; , (f.) § 34; § 46; § 43; , § 64; § 64; § 128.
its (m.) § 34; , (f.) § 34.
ivory

J

Jackal
jar ,
jaw
join
joy , ,
jubilation
jubilee
judge, judge between ,
judges
jug
just
justice
justified var.

K

Karnak
keen, be
Khepri
Khons
kill , ,
kindle var.
king varr. , ; — of Upper Egypt var. ; — of Lower Egypt var. ; — of Upper and Lower Egypt
king, be
kingship
kiss var.
kitě § 266, 4.
knee
knife
knot (vb.)
knot (n.)
know ; — how to ; not —
knowledge: to the — of § 178.
koḥl
Ḳûs

L

Lack: through — of § 178.
lag var.
lake
land (vb.)
land (n.) ; foreign —
languish

lap
lapis lazuli
large ,
lasso (vb.)
last day of the month § 264.
last year
later (adv.) § 205, 2.
laugh
law
lead
lean on
leap
learn
leather
lector-priest var.
left(-hand)
leg , ; — of beef
length
leopard
Letopolis var.
letter ; (official)
libation
Libya
lie down
lie (n.)
liegeman
life
lift , ,
light, be (in weight)
light: (n.) ; grow —
like, be
like: (prep.) § 170; (adj.) § 80; the —
likeness
likewise
limb
limestone
limit
linen ; fine — ,
linger

link together
lion
lip
little ; a — (of something) § 99;
live
liver
lo varr. , §§ 119, 2; 231;
var. § 230; § 232; § 247.
load (vb.)
load (n.)
loaf
local ; — prince
loiter
long ago § 205, 3.
look var. ; — at
loose ,
lord var. ; of the king, p. 75.
loss
lotus
love (vb.) varr. ,
love (n.)
low (of cattle)
Lower Egypt var. ; king of —
var.
lower part
lowly, be
lungs

M

Mace
magazine , var.
magic
magistrates ,
magnificence
magnify
maid-servant ,
Majesty var. , p. 74.
make
male

man varr. ,

man-servant ,

management

mankind ,

many ; § 99.

marshlands (of Delta) , varr. ,

marvel (vb.) var.

marvel (n.) var.

master var.

mat var.

matter (n.)

mayor

me § 34 ; § 43.

meadow

meal

means: by — of § 162, 7.

measure (vb.)

meat ,

medicament

Medjay

member (of body) ; —s of household

memory

Memphis

men , , ,

menat

messenger

midst: in the — of § 177, 2 ; § 178 ; § 178.

might (pl.), ,

mighty, be ,

mild, be

milk var.

million

Min var.

mine (n.) var. ;

mine, of § 113, 3.

miner var.

mirror

miserable ,

misery , var.

mishap

missing, be

mission

mistress varr. , ; — of the house

Mitanni

mix

Mnevis

moment

monarch

monkey ,

Mont

month

monument

moon

moor (vb.) var.

mooring-post

more than § 163, 7.

moreover § 255.

morning ,

morning bark of the sun-god

mother

mound var.

mount up

mountain

mourning , ,

mouse

mouth

much (adj.) ; (adv.) § 205, 4.

multiply

mummy

Mut

my § 34 ; , , § 113, 1.

myrrh

mysterious

N

Naked
name
narrow, be var. ;
natron var. ; var.
nature , ,
navel-string
neck
necklace ,
necropolis var. ; ; var.
neglectful, be ,
neighbourhood ; in the — of , § 178.
Neith
Nephthys var.
Nepri
nest
netherworld var.
network
never , § 106; §§ 106. 456.
new, be var.
New Moon festival
New Year's Day
newly
nigh, draw ,
night , ,
Nile: high — var. ; — -god [var.
no § 258.
no one .... , § 102.
noble var. ; var. ; the —s
noble, be
nomad
nome var.
north
north wind
northern
northwards: fare —
nose var. ;
nostril
not , §§ 104. 235; § 352A; (vb.) , § 342.
nourish
now § 119, 2; § 255.
Nubia ,
Nubian ,
number ,
nurse (vb.)
nurse (n.)
Nut

O

O var. §§ 87. 258.
oar
Oasis
oath
obelisk
obey
oblations
obstacle var.
occasion
occupation var. ;
occur
occurrence
of § 86; consisting — § 162, 5.
offer , , , ,
offerings , , , var. ; — to the gods ; table of — var. ;
office ; (rank) var.
official var. ;
officials, body of
often § 205, 4.
oil (for anointing) ,
ointment
old var. ; ; — age ; — times

O

Ombos
on § 165, 1; § 173.
once, at § 205, 3.
one §§ 260; 262, 1; — of (several) § 262, 1; the — .... the other .... , ... , ... § 98.
one (impersonal) § 47.
Onnōphris
Onūris
open , , var.
oppose var.
opposite § 169, 1.
opponent
or: not expressed, § 91, 2; § 91, 2.
order (vb.) , .
order: in — that , § 181.
Orion
ornament
orphan ,
oryx
Osiris
ostrich var.
other (m.), (f.), § 98; § 98; —s
our § 34; , , § 113, 1.
out (adv.) § 205, 3.
out of § 162, 8; § 174, 2; § 178.
outside (prep.) § 178.
outside (n.) ,
overlay
overleap (wall)
overseer varr. , § 79.
overthrow , , ,
overturn
owing to § 178.
ox , , varr. , (p. 172).

P

Pacify ,
pack up
pain
pair (of horses)
painful, be
palace , ,
palanquin
palette
palm (as measure) varr. , § 266, 2.
panther
papyrus-roll ,
pardon
part § 265.
pass var. ; ; — (time) ; — the day ; — the night ; — in review ; — by
pavement
peace , ; become at —
peasant ; —s
peer § 79, Obs.
pellet
people ; common — ; (as indef. pron.) § 47.
perceive , ,
perfect, be
perfume var.
period , ,
perish , , ,
permit ,
pervading (prep.) § 175.
petition (vb.)
petitioner
phallus
Pharaoh p. 75.
Phoenix
physician
pierce with looks
pig ,

pillage
pillar ,
Pillar-of-his-Mother
pillow
place (vb.) , , ; (imper.)
place (n.) ,
plan (vb.) , ,
plan (vb.) ; (in building)
plank
plant (n.)
plaster (vb.)
pleasant
pleasure, take ,
plentiful
plot out
plough (vb.)
plough (n.)
plummet
plunder ; take as —
poison
poltroon
pool ; bird- —
poor, be var.
poor man , ,
portal var. ;
portion
possess, see § 114.
possessor of
potent
pound (vb.)
pour
poverty
power: divine — var. ; have — over
powerful, be ,
praise (vb.)
praise (n.) , ,
pray (vb.) ,
pray (part.) § 250; § 256.
precious ; — things
precise ,
predilection
pregnant, become ,
prepare ,
prescription
presence: in the — of § 169; , , , § 178.
present (vb.)
preserve
prevent , ,
previously § 205, 2.
priest var. ; ; high- — ; lector- — ; ordinary — ; soul- — var.
priesthood var.
primeval: — times ; — waters
prince ; hereditary — ; local —
princess ; hereditary —
principal § 80.
principles
prison , var.
prisoner
privacy
private, be
probably § 241.
procedure
proceed
prominent, make
promote ,
pronounce (name)
property
prosper
prosperous, be ,
protect , , ,
protection var.
protector
province
prow-rope

prudent, be
Ptah
pull up (corn)
punish ,
pure, be ,
purification
push
put , ; — down
Pwēne(t) ('Punt')
pyramid

Q

Qualities ,
quarter × § 265.
quartet § 260.
quest: in — of § 181.
question (vb.)
quickly § 205, 4.
quiet, be
quiet (n.)
quite var. § 205, 1.

R

Rage (vb.) , ,
rain
raise up
ram ,
rank var. ;
rapacious, be
rays ,
Rēʿ varr. ,
reach
read aloud
ready, be ; make —
real
reality, in § 205, 3.
really , § 249.
reap
rebel (vb.) ; (n.) ,
rebuff (vb.)
rebuff (n.)
recall
receive
recite
recitation § 306, 1.
reckon var. ;
recognize
recollect
red
Red Land
reeds , ,
refresh oneself
refuge (n.) ,
regiment
region
reïs
rejoice , ,
rejuvenated, be
relate
relating to § 79.
remain ; — over
remainder
remedy
remember
remembrance
remiss, be var.
remove ,
renew
renewed, be
repair ,
repeat
repel var. ;
replace var.
report
repress
reproach (n.)
rescue , ,

resent
resentment, show
Residence (of the king)
resin var.
respect: in — of § 163, 6; show — for,
rest (vb.) ,
restore
restrain , ,
retire ,
Retjnu, i.e. Palestine and Syria
retreat
return: in — for , § 178; § 180.
revenue
revered
reversed, be
revise
reward (vb.)
rib var. ; —s of beef
rich, be ,
riches
right, be
right (n.)
right(-hand)
righteous
ring var. ; (as weight) var. § 266, 4; signet- —
rise
river
river-bank , ,
road var. ;
roaring
roast
rob , ,
rod (as measure of length) § 266, 2.
room
rope ,
round, go var.
row
rudder
rug
ruin (n.) var.
ruined, be
rule
ruler
rule(s)
run ,
rush (n.)

S

Sack (as measure) var. § 266, 1.
sad
safe, be var.
sail (vb.) ; — (upon river, sea) ; — downstream, northward ; — upstream, southward
sail (n.)
sailor ; —s,
Sais
sale var.
salt
sanctuary , ,
sand
sandal
sandstone
sarcophagus
satiated, be
satisfied, be
say ; —ing , § 224; (he) —s § 437.
scale (of fish) var.
sceptre , , ,
schoenus § 266, 2.
scimetar
scribe
sculptor var.
sculpture (vb.)

sea
seal (vb.)
seal (n.) , ,
search out
season
seat var. ; var.
second var. § 263.
secret
Sed-festival
see , ,
seed , var. ,
seek ,
seer: 'Greatest of —s', title of high-priest of Heliopolis
Sehêl
seize , ,
self, not expressed § 36; , with suffixes, § 36.
send ,
sensible, be
sentence
serf var. (f.).
Serḳe(t)
servant: man- — , ; maid- — ; this thy humble —
serve
Sesha(t)
set (of sun) ; be — apart
Seth varr. ,
shadow p. 173.
shape ,
share
sharp, be ,
shave
shawabti figure
she , — § 34; § 43; § 64; (pron. compound) § 124; § 128.
sheep
shield
shine ; — forth ,
ship , ; —s, , [abbrev.
shoot ,
shore
short-horned cattle
shriek (n.)
shrine ,
Shu
shut ; — in
Sia
side var. ;
sight ; in the — of § 178.
signet-ring
silent, be
silver
since § 176.
sing var.
singer ; female — var.
sister
sistrum
sit , ; — down
skilled, be
skin ,
skipper
skirt
sky ,
slack, be var.
slaughter (vb.) ,
slaughter (n.) var. ; place of —
slave (male) ; female —
slaves
slay var.
sledge ,
sleep ,
sloth ,
small, be var.
smash var. ,
smell , ,
smite , varr. ,

smooth ; make —
snake
snare (vb.)
so § 242; — that § 163, 11.
Sobk
soft, be
Sokar
soldier ; —s,
sole (of foot)
sole (adj.) § 260.
someone § 102.
something § 103.
son
Sopd
Sothis
soul p. 172; var. p. 173.
soul-priest var.
sound (n.) varr. ,
sound, be
sour
south
south wind
southern
sovereign var.
space (of time)
speak ,
speech , ,
spell (n.)
spend: — all day ; — all night
spew out , var. .
spirit (p. 172),
spit
spleen var.
splendour ,
split
spring (vb.)
stable, be
stability var.
staff
staircase
stairway
stable: (for horses) ; (for cattle)
stall
stand
standard ; (military) —
star var.
statue ,
steal
steering oar
steersman
stela ,
steps varr. ,
stern-rope
sting
stink
stone ; precious —
stop ; — up
storehouse , var. ,
storm
stout, be
street
strength
strengthen
stretch var. ; — out
stride var.
strike var.
strong, be , , ,
subdue var.
subjects
subsequently § 205, 2.
subtract
succour
suck, suckle
suffer ,
suite
summer-season
summon
sun var. ; ;

sun-god
sunder
supper
supply (vb.) , ,
support (n.) ; —s
suppress var.
surely § 241; § 251.
surround ,
survive
sustenance
swallow (vb.) ,
swallow (n.)
swamp
swear ,
sweat
sweet, be
sweetness
sycamore

T

Table of offerings var. ;
tail
take , , , ; (imper.) § 336; — away , , ; — counsel
talk
tall
tardily § 205, 4.
taste (vb.) ; (n.)
Taye(t)
teach
teaching
temperature
temple , ,
ten § 259; — thousand § 259.
tend
tent
terrace
terror var.
test (vb.)
testament
testify to
than § 163, 7.
that (demonstrative) , § 110.
that (conjunction) § 237; § 233; in order —, omitted, § 40.
the, omitted, § 21; § 110.
Thebes
thee (m.) § 34; , § 43.
thee (f.) , § 34; , § 43.
their § 34.
theirs, of § 113, 3.
them §§ 34. 43; § 46; — two § 34.
then § 228; § 242; § 240.
thence § 205, 1.
there , § 205, 1; — is, was, § 107; — is not , , § 108; [§ 351, 2.
therefore § 228.
therefrom § 205, 1.
therein § 205, 1.
thereof var. § 113, 2.
thereupon §§ 478–482.
therewith , § 205, 1.
these , , , § 110.
they , § 34; § 43; § 64; , § 124; § 128.
they two § 34.
thick, be
thigh: — (of beef) ; —s
thine, of § 113, 3.
thing , ; expressed by fem. gender, § 51.
think ; (expect)
third var. § 263, 2.
thirst (vb.)
thirst (n.)
thirsty
this (m.), (f.); (m.), (f.); (m.), (f.) § 110; (neuter) , § 111.

thoroughly § 205, 5.
those , § 110.
Thoth
thou (m.), , (f.) § 34; , (m.); , (f.) § 43; (m.), (f.) § 64; , § 64; (m.), (f.) § 124.
though § 162, 11, *c*.
thousand § 259.
three , var. § 260.
three-quarters § 265.
throat ,
throne , p. 65, n. 8[a].
through § 164, 5; § 166, 3; § 178; § 175; § 178.
throw , ,
throw-stick
thrust
thy (m.), , (f.) § 34; , , etc., § 113, 1.
tibia
tie (vb.) ,
tilt
time , , , ; at the — of § 178; every — that § 181.
tired, be , ,
to § 164; § 163; § 167, 2; § 169, 1.
to-day var. § 205, 1; § 205, 3.
toe
together § 205, 3; — with § 171, 1; § 178.
tomb ; var. ;
to-morrow § 205, 3.
tongue
too § 163, 7.
tooth ,
torch
tortoise
total
touch
town ,
trample down
transgress
transfix (with look)
trap (vb.)
travel ; — downstream ; — upstream ; — overland ; — (by water)
traveller
traverse
treasure
treasurer
treasury
tree , , ; —s
tremble
tribute ,
trifling (adj.)
trouble
true ; — of voice
trusty var.
truth
tumult
turn , var. ; — back ; — back (trans.)
turquoise
two var.
tyrannical, be

U

Uncover
under § 166; § 167, 1.
undertake
unfold
unguent
unique § 260.
unite ; ; ; var. ;
united, be
unless § 216, end.

unloose
untie ,
until § 163, 11. 12. 13.
upon § 165; § 173; § 178; (adj.)
upper var. ; — Egypt var. ; King of — Egypt var. ; King of — and Lower Egypt
upset
upside down, be
uraeus
urinate var.
us §§ 34. 43.
us two § 34.
utterance , , ,

V

Various var.
vegetables var.
vein
verily var. § 231; var. § 230.
vertebra
very § 205, 4.
vessel (of body) ; — (pot) ,
victorious
victory
victuals
view: in — of the fact that § 223.
vigilant
vigorous, be
vile (of enemy)
vine
violate ; — (frontier)
virtue ; by — of § 181.
vizier
voice var.
void
vomit
vulture
vulva var.

W

Waif
wake
wakeful, be var.
walk , ; — about
walk (n.) varr. ,
wall var. ; ;
want (n.) var.
war-cry
warmth
wash
washerman
water , ; primeval —s
water-skin
wave
wax
way var.
we §§ 34. 43; var. § 64; § 124; — two § 34.
weak: be — ; make —
wealthy, be
weapons ,
weary, be , ,
weavers var.
weep var.
welcome § 313; § 374.
welfare
well: it goes — with § 141; as — as § 170, 3.
well (n.)
Wepwawet
west ,
western
what? § 496; var. § 497; § 498; § 499; § 500; § 501; to — purpose? § 496.
when: not expressed, § 30; § 162, 11. 12; § 169, 6. 8.
whence? var. § 503, 3.

where? var. § 503, 1.
wherefore? § 500, 4.
wherewith? § 496.
which §§ 199–201.
which? § 499, 1.
while + infin., § 165, 10.
white ; the — crown of Upper Egypt
whither? § 503, 2.
who §§ 199–201.
who? ; var. § 496; var. § 497; § 498.
whole , , § 100.
whole, be
why? § 496.
wide, be
widow var.
wife
wind
wine
wing var.
winter-season
wise, be
wish (vb.) , , ; (n.)
with (of instrument) § 162, 7; (of persons) § 167, 1; together — § 171, 1; § 178; § 162, 7 *a*.
withdraw
within , § 178.
without , , §§ 109. 307; § 178.
witness (n.)
wolf (or jackal)
woman , ,
wonder var.
wood
work (vb.) ; (n.)
workman
worm
worship ,
worth
would that! , § 238.
wrath
wrathful, be
wreath ,
wretched
wring neck of (bird)
write
writing ,
wrong (n.) , ,
wrongdoing var. ,

Y

Year ; regnal — ; last —
yes § 258
yesterday (n.) ; (adv.) § 205, 3.
you , §§ 34. 43; § 64; —two § 34.
young, be ,
your , § 34; , , § 113, 1.
youth

INDEXES

I. GRAMMATICAL AND ORTHOGRAPHIC

For words written in hieroglyphs see the Egyptian–English Vocabulary

II. GENERAL